COMPUTERS IN EDUCATION

COMPUTERS IN EDUCATION

Proceedings of the IFIP TC 3 Fifth World Conference on
Computers in Education – WCCE 90
Sydney, Australia, July 9–13, 1990

Edited by

ANNE McDOUGALL
Monash University
Melbourne, Australia

CAROLYN DOWLING
Institute of Catholic Education
Melbourne, Australia

NORTH-HOLLAND
AMSTERDAM · NEW YORK · OXFORD · TOKYO

ELSEVIER SCIENCE PUBLISHERS B.V.
Sara Burgerhartstraat 25
P.O. Box 211, 1000 AE Amsterdam, The Netherlands

Distributors for the United States and Canada:
ELSEVIER SCIENCE PUBLISHING COMPANY INC.
655 Avenue of the Americas
New York, N.Y. 10010, U.S.A.

Library of Congress Cataloging-in-Publication Data

World Conference on Computers in Education (5th : 1990 : Sydney, N.S.W.)
Computers in education : proceedings of the IFIP Tc 3 Fifth World Conference on Computers in Education, WCCE 90, Sydney, Australia, July 9-13, 1990 / edited by Anne McDougall, Carolyn Dowling.
p. cm.
Includes bibliographical references and index.
ISBN 0-444-88750-4
1. Computer-assisted instruction--Congresses. 2. Education--Data processing--Congresses. 3. Electronic data processing--Study and teaching--Congresses. 4. Distance education--Congresses. I. McDougall, Anne, 1945- . II. Dowling, Carolyn, 1943- III. IFIP Technical Committee 3, Education. IV. Title.
LB1028.5.W64 1990
371.3'34--dc20
90-37468
CIP

First edition: 1990
Second impression: 1990

ISBN: 0 444 88750 4

Printed in The Netherlands.

FOREWORD

The challenge of editing the Proceedings of an international conference of the dimensions of WCCE 90 is both daunting and exhilarating. In terms of the opportunity to interact with the world-wide community of computer using educators, the role was one to be grasped with enthusiasm. When examined more closely in the light of the sheer number and diversity of papers, and of the standard of editing and production achieved in the past, the task was formidable.

The Proceedings of this conference, as indeed the conference itself, stems from a fine academic and professional tradition. It has been the task of the current organisers, including the Proceedings' editors, to maintain this tradition while modifying it appropriately to give some flavour of the particular time and place.

The papers in this Proceedings were selected by referees in many countries, from more than 550 submitted in response to the initial call for papers for the conference. We are grateful to the many paper referees who assisted us by adding editorial comments as they reviewed the draft papers.

We would like particularly to express our thanks to the authors, who have taken considerable time and trouble to comply with the instructions for the preparation of camera-ready copy of their papers for this publication.

We have appreciated the information and advice offered to us by former editors of World Conference Proceedings, and by Stephanie Smit and John Butterfield of Elsevier Science Publishers B.V. The assistance of Carolyn Sim and Bronwen Dimond with many of the tasks involved in the final preparation of the manuscript has also been invaluable.

Anne McDougall
Carolyn Dowling

PREFACE

IFIP World Conferences on Computers in Education, held only once every five years, provide an opportunity for computer educators around the world to share their ideas and their experiences, their achievements and their frustrations in this rapidly developing field. The fifth World Conference is being held in Sydney, Australia in July 1990 after five years of planning and organisation. We hope that the decision to hold the conference in the southern hemisphere will increase the opportunity for participation by computer educators in developing nations. This concern is reflected in many of the papers and presentations at the conference.

This book contains approximately 190 papers presented at the conference, including keynote and invited papers. Abstracts of more than 350 presentations appear in the *Abstracts Proceedings* published by the Australian Council for Computers in Education. These combined volumes are a permanent record of what happened at WCCE 90.

Papers for the book were selected from the total number of presentations in order to offer a broad cross-section of countries, authors, and themes. All accepted presentations were sent to three independent reviewers: one from the same country as the paper's author, and one from another country, as well as the chairman of the paper's specific stream or mini-conference. The efforts of the hundreds of reviewers, too numerous to be named here, are a vital component of an IFIP world conference. They ensure fair and unbiased treatment of the proposals that we receive. Their contribution is greatly appreciated.

We received over six hundred proposals for papers, presentations, panels, workshops, and meetings, from forty-one countries. In addition, more than fifty proposals arrived during the months following the closing date in October 1989 and were too late to be reviewed for inclusion in the programme. I would like to thank the people, over two hundred of them, who took the trouble to prepare submissions to WCCE 90 but who could not be accepted for presentation. Their efforts, although unrecognised, are nevertheless an important part of the success of a refereed conference. I'm sure they will not be deterred from attending the conference nor from submitting again to the sixth WCCE in 1995.

The overwhelming response to the call for papers indicates the continuing growth and maturing of the computer education community. In order to highlight the diversity and richness of computer education, I structured the fifth World Conference as an 'umbrella' conference. Each sector of computer education has been allocated its own stream or mini-conference under the guidance of its own chairman.

The streams include elementary, secondary, university, vocational education and training, research, and rainbow. 'Rainbow' is a term we coined to describe presentations that cut across these streams, for example presentations on national computer education policies. This stream is like a rainbow because it encompasses all the 'colours' of the computer education spectrum. The mini-conferences include CBT 90, PEG 90, and Teleteaching 90 which respectively address the use of computer based training in industry, new tools in the classroom, and computing in distance education.

In addition, mini-conferences are being held before and after WCCE 90 in Auckland, New Zealand; Cairns, Australia; and Tokyo, Japan. All these mini-conferences are producing separate proceedings or publications, however, some key papers from the New Zealand conference are included in this book. Those papers presented jointly in Sydney and Auckland appear in their Sydney streams.

I am grateful to the stream and mini-conference chairmen, listed elsewhere, who have worked with me to develop the WCCE 90 programme. All have worked towards the goal of producing an internationally representative programme. WCCE 90 is not just a conference open to attendance by delegates from around the world – it has been organised by a *world* committee. International Programme Committee meetings were held at least once a year, sometimes twice, in different parts of the world over the last five years. Twenty to thirty countries were officially represented at these meetings and the costs were borne by each country, many times from the representatives' own pockets. Countries' representatives who were not present at the meetings still had a major role to play in disseminating information within their countries.

It has been hard work for all of us, and all of us have been volunteer organisers over and above our day-to-day paid jobs. Education is one of the few industries that runs non-commerical low budget conferences. WCCE 90 would not have been financially viable without the considerable time and energy provided voluntarily by the members of the international and Australian committees. About eighty people were directly involved in the committees, and these people drew on the resources of their employers and other colleagues to get the job done.

The conference would also not have been financially viable without the monetary support of our sponsors, especially the major sponsors: Microsoft, Commodore, Apple, and IBM. Their contributions, along with that of the Australian Computer Society, the host organisation for the conference, covered the high costs of printing and international communication in the years leading up to the conference. We thank all the sponsors for their support of computer education.

For me it has been an interesting challenge to create and build a large multinational event. However, it has also been an opportunity to forge friendships with colleagues in other countries, to discuss our common problems, and to learn from our differences. I hope readers use the international network that we have built, and that is represented in this book, to add to their experience and knowledge of computer education. I look forward to the next five years of our industry's growth and development.

Sandra Wills
WCCE 90 International Programme Chairman
Melbourne, February, 1990

COMMITTEES AND COUNCILS

WCCE 90 International Programme Committee and National Chairmen

Chairman	Sandra Wills, Australia
Secondary Chairman	Peter Bollerslev, Denmark
University Chairmen	William Atchison, USA & Bernard Levrat, Switzerland
Research Chairman	Robert Lewis, UK
Vocational Chairman	Ben Zion Barta, Israel
Elementary Chairmen	Frank Lovis, UK & Erling Schmidt, Denmark
Distance Chairman	Gyozo Kovacs, Hungary
Teleteaching 90 Chairmen	Gordon Davies, UK & Jan Wibe, Norway
CBT 90 Chariman	Rod Sims, Australia
PEG 90 Chairmen	Jonathan Briggs, UK & Geoff Cumming, Australia
Kids n Classrooms 90 Chairman	Pam Gibbons, Australia
Computer Pals 90 Chairman	Paul Campbell, Australia
Pre Conference Chairman	Ian Mitchell, New Zealand
Post Conference ARCE Chairman	Setsuko Otsuki, Japan
WCCE/85 Liaison	John Hamblen, USA
WCCE/81 Liaison	Bernard Levrat, Switzerland
WCCE/95 Liaison	Brian Samways, UK
TC3 & IFIP Liaison	Wilfried Brauer, Federal Republic of Germany
UNESCO Liaison	Evgeuni Khvilon, UNESCO

Australia	S. Wills
Austria	H. Schauer
Belgium	R. de Caluwe
Bulgaria	Boj. Sendov
Canada	R. McLean
China	H. Chochun
Czechoslovakia	V. Janes
Denmark	P. Bollerslev
Fed. Rep. Germany	U. Bosler
Finland	S. Rautakivi
France	J. Hebenstreit
German Dem. Rep.	D. Schubert
Greece	G. Philokyprou & M. Karavelaki
Hungary	G. Kovacs
Iceland	A. Kristjansdottir
India	B. Nag
Iraq	S. Saloum
Israel	Y. Giveon
Italy	P. Ercoli
Japan	S. Otsuki
Netherlands	H. Wolbers
New Zealand	I. Mitchell
Nigeria	S. Jaiyesimi
Norway	A. Staupe
Poland	S. Waligorski
Portugal	J. Calazans
Singapore	L. Chan
South Africa	G. Wiechers
Spain	A. Vaquero & C. Chamizo
Sweden	L. Gunnarsson & A. Kollerbaur
Switzerland	R. Morel
UK	B. Samways
USA	S. Charp, R. Aiken & H. Jobe
Yugoslavia	A. Mandzic

Australian Programme and Editorial Sub-Committee

Chairman	Sandra Wills, University of Melbourne
Proceedings Editor	Anne McDougall, Monash University, Melbourne
Proceedings Co-Editor	Carolyn Dowling, Institute of Catholic Education, Melbourne
Papers Referee Chairman	Tony Adams, Royal Melbourne Institute of Technology
Panels Chairman	Geoff Cumming, Latrobe University, Melbourne
Abstracts Editor	Jeff Richardson, Monash University, Melbourne
Workshops Co-Chairman	Neville Stern, Royal Melbourne Institute of Technology
UNESCO Liaison	Mike Lally, University of Western Australia

Australian Organising Committee

Chairman	John Hughes, University of Technology, Sydney
Vice Chairman	Toni Downes, University of Western Sydney, Macarthur
Secretariat	Angela Brooks, University of Technology, Sydney
Treasurer	Belinda Robinson, NSW Education Department
Sponsorship	Ken Sinclair, Sydney University
Publicity & Dissemination	Rob McLachlan, Charles Sturt University, Mitchell
Exhibition Manager	Bruce Keepes, Sydney Institute of Education
Logistics Manager	John Harvey, Sydney Institute of Education
Australian Home Hospitality	Marlene Neill, NSW Computer Education Group
Australian Education Visits	Wing Au, University of Newcastle
Education Departments Liaison	Ian Pirie, NSW Education Department
ISTE/USA Liaison	Greg Butler, NSW Education Department
Meetings & Special Events	Paul Jenner, NSW Education Department
Workshops Co-Chairman	Graeme Salter, University of Western Sydney, Macarthur

Australian Council for Computers in Education

Australian Computer Society
New South Wales Computer Education Group
Computers in Education Group of Victoria
Computer Education Group of Queensland
Computer Education Group of Australian Capital Territory
Computer Education Group of Tasmania
Computer Education Group of South Australia
Educational Computing Association of Western Australia
Computer Education Group of Northern Territory

SPONSORS OF WCCE 90

IFIP and ACS are grateful for the support of the sponsors of WCCE 90:

Microsoft

Commodore

Apple

IBM

ASSOCIATE SPONSORS

Epson Australia Pty Ltd
Fujitsu
Toshiba (Australia) Pty Ltd

AFFILIATE SPONSORS

Australian Airlines
Barson Computors Australasia Ltd
Dataflow Computer Services Pty Ltd
Edsoft Australia
Lego Australia Pty Ltd
Qantas Airways Limited
Westpac Training Pty Ltd

TABLE OF CONTENTS

INFORMATICS IN ELEMENTARY EDUCATION

RAINBOW STREAM

WCCE 90 MINI-CONFERENCES

COMPUTERS IN EDUCATION: NATIONAL PERSPECTIVES

CBT 90

Mini-Conference Keynotes

TELETEACHING 90

Mini-Conference Keynote

CONFERENCE KEYNOTE SPEAKERS

Computers in Education
A. McDougall and C. Dowling (Editors)
Elsevier Science Publishers B.V. (North-Holland)

THE PERESTROIKA OF EPISTEMOLOGICAL POLITICS

Seymour PAPERT

Massachusetts Institute of Technology, USA

Recent dramatic political events in the USSR, in Eastern Europe, in Latin America, in South Africa and in China mark a global wave of rejection of hierarchical, authoritarian forms of government. Structures that seemed immutable crumbled with breathtaking swiftness. I use these events to look at change and resistance to change in education, and to present the central question about the uses of computers in education as this: will the new technology become the instrument of fundamental change or will it be the ultimate bastion of resistance to change?

When Mikhael Sergeyevich Gorbachev came to power in 1985 he proposed what in retrospect looks like a minor jiggering of administrative forms...a restructuring that would keep the essential structures of his society intact. We are now witnessing a not untypical behavior of a system which is displaced from a state of equilibrium: it does not stay where you left it but swings precipitately in search of a new equilibrium. Already fundamental ways of thinking are being called into question. Managerial perestroika has given rise to an epistemological perestroika.

Edward Fiske writing in the New York Times, beat me to print in suggesting that the word "perestroika" be adopted for the currently fadish talk of restructuring in our schools. The parallel goes deep. Our large school systems are closer in structure than anything else I know in capitalist America to the bureaucratic, centralized economies that failed so abysmally in the Soviet world. The curriculum is our "Gosplan". In the name of efficiency and accountability a central authority decides what will be done all the way down the hierarchy -- of schools in our case, of factories and farms as well in theirs.

But experiments in decentralization (such as school-based management) are like the first talk of perestroika: here, too, something more is needed than administrative jiggering. We need an epistemological perestroika, a restructuring of our ways of thinking not simply about school but about the nature of knowledge, of thinking itself.

Am I crying in the wilderness? No, I see many manifestations of an epistemological shift, surely part of the global anti-hierarchical wave, directed here not against the hierarchy of politics or economic planning but against the cognitive hierarchy expressed in the value-laden theory of intellectual stages that supports the hegemony of abstract, formal, rule-like thinking. These manifestations crop up in many communities who do not always recognize one another as allies. Feminist writers have spoken with a strong voice against the male-genderized Baconian view of "objective" science. Ethnographers of science have made it clear that thinking in the laboratory does not conform to the canonical form. Ethnographers also show us how many people who "can't do math" in a school sense handle fractions very well in supermarkets and kitchens. These are examples of a broad movement toward a "revaluation of the concrete" -- an affirmation of heterarchy over hierarchy.

From this follows a clearer perspective on the possible roles of the computer: to reinforce the canonical, propositional, rule-based knowledge that lends itself to standardization in curriculum and in software; or to provide a context for the development of pluralistic ways of knowing which will never conform to a standardized curriculum. Science can inform this choice; but it will be made in a new political arena in the battle for epistemological liberty.

Computers in Education
A. McDougall and C. Dowling (Editors)
Elsevier Science Publishers B.V. (North-Holland)

POINT OF VIEW IS WORTH 80 IQ POINTS: THE USER INTERFACE AS AN AMPLIFIER OF HUMAN ENDEAVOUR

Alan KAY

Apple Computer, USA

Historically, humans have extended themselves in two principal ways. First, by creating amplifying tools - physical and abstract structures that can be manipulated - such as the lever, wheel, telescope, language, writing, mathematics. Second, by discovering how to get others to absorb goals - physical and abstract processes that can be managed - such as individuals, clubs, businesses, religions, countries, cultures.

The metaphors of manipulation and management were immediately applied to human-computer communication in the late fifties when researchers first realized that the computer was a medium for extension and not just a calculation engine. The user interface - a simplifying metaphor theatrically portrayed - is the only "computer" most users ever see. Most of the successful designs so far have been of the manipulative amplifying tool type - Xerox PARC windows and pointing interface, spreadsheets, the Macintosh - but now there is an ever increasing need for interfaces that can absorb goals and be managed.

Though not much has yet been discovered about how human mentalities really function, the little that is known is both nonintuitive and crucial to the design process. Though we seem to have the same level of intelligence as thousands of years ago, our much more powerful contexts greatly amplify our ability to think. A user interface matched to human psychology provides a context for thinking and acting whose amplification can be truly remarkable.

As human and technological systems explode with capacity and complexity, the user interface designs of the future will be the principal path to simplicity and control.

Computers in Education
A. McDougall and C. Dowling (Editors)
Elsevier Science Publishers B.V. (North-Holland)

INTERNATIONAL COOPERATION FOR EDUCATIONAL USE OF COMPUTERS IN ASIA AND THE PACIFIC THROUGH UNESCO AND RECENT TRENDS IN JAPAN

NISHINOSONO,Haruo

Kyoto University of Education, 1 Fujinomori Fushimiku Kyoto, 612, Japan

International cooperation in the educational use of computers is being carried out within the Asian and Pacific Programme of Education for Innovation and Development(APEID) of UNESCO. The state of educational computing in the region is changing very quickly, reflecting the rapid progress in computer technology and the prompt reaction of each country to this promising technology. Japan is a very slow comer into the scene of educational computing, but puts great emphasis on information education.

1. COOPERATIVE PROGRAMMES IN THE REGION

APEID(Asian and Pacific Programme of Education for Innovation and Development) organized within UNESCO started in 1971 after the decision of member states to promote international cooperation by means of establishing Associate Centres(ACs) in respective countries and sharing experiences in regional meetings to stimulate educational programmes for innovation and development. A consultation meeting was held every two years to decide programme areas of priority for a regional centre (ACEID) and associated centres in member states. Since the launch of APEID, the mechnism of the regional centre ACEID and Associate Centres in member states has been a very efficient vehicle for sharing experiences concerning innovative educational programmes in the region.

The Japan National Commission for UNESCO has participated actively in the area of educational technology as well as in five other areas; technical and vocational education, special education, curriculum development, primary education and science education, by organizing training courses, workshops and/or seminars and sending experts as mobile teams to conduct workshops in other member states.

The first cycle of the programme lasted from 1973 to 1976, the second cycle from 1979 to 1981, and the third cycle from 1982 to 1986. The fourth cycle started in 1987 and is expected to continue until 1991. The seminars convened in Tokyo and Kyoto every fall are sponsored by the Japan National Commission for UNESCO and are organized by the Japan Council of Educational Technology Centers. The seminar starts with the report presentation of each country introducing its most recent experiences in educational technology, which include trends and issues in the use of computers in education.

In a series of activities for international cooperation in the region, the following occasions have been provided by the APEID programme specifically for the promotion of computer use in schools;

(1)the first one-week seminar on "Computers in Education" in Tokyo, 1984
(2)publication of a book titled "Computers in Education - An outline of country experiences" by PROAP, UNESCO, 1985
(3)Experts Planning Meeting on the Use of Computers in Education in 1985, and publication of a book titled "Developing Computer Use in Education - Guidelines, trends and issues", 1986
(4) a workshop on Software Development in Perth, Australia, 1987 and a one-week seminar on The Evaluation of Uses of Computers in Education at Melbourne, Australia, 1987
(5)an eleven-day seminar on educational technology focusing on Software development in Tokyo, 1988
(6)a book to be published in 1990, "Guidebook on Computer Educational Software"

2. SEMINARS AND PUBLICATION AT THE INITIAL STAGE

ACEID in Bangkok, and the Japan Council of Educational Technology Centers jointly convened the first seminar on "Computers in Education" in Tokyo and Kyoto. The Pacific countries joined the seminar for the first time in 1984. At the preparation stage of this seminar, it was felt to be premature to convene a seminar specifically devoted to the use of computers in education. But at the same time, it was felt necessary to promote the sharing of experiences of specialists facing the difficulties of introducing computers in schools. This first seminar aimed to:

(1) exchange information and experiences, and consider significant examples in the development of computer education and computer (including microcomputer) use in education in different domains;
(2) analyse the main trends in that field, as well as problems encountered in this respect by the national education system and to review instances of effective strategies for coping with the problems;
(3) explore alternative mechanisms for continual updating of information on the application of data processing and use of computers in education; and
(4) produce a survey report on the themes requested from ACEID in the context of 'Background', especially within Asian and the Pacific countries.

As an outcome of this seminar, a book titled 'Computers in Education -An outline of country experiences' came to be published in 1985 as UNESCO reference material which introduced for the first time the current state of computer use in education in Asia and the Pacific region. This book summarized country experiences in Australia, China, India, Japan, the Philippines, Sri Lanka and Thailand. Singapore was the most developed country in Asia, and its policy of introducing computers in schools was described in Part two of the book separately from those of other countries. At that time, many countries including Japan had not made clear their national policies on the use of computers in nonvocational education.

The introduction of computers into schools, however, was being accelerated by the availability of mini- and micro-computers. Personal computers were widely accepted as professional facilities for small business as well as in technical and vocational education. Professor H.N. Mahabala(India) wrote at the end of the book, "In summary, the expectations of a microcomputer in a LDC (less developed country) are different from those in a developed country. They have to serve as workhorses for small businesses. Computer professionals in LDCs have to orient themselves to this challenge, since almost every wisdom about a large system is not applicable in the case of a small system."

The second outcome of the seminar was the publication of another book on the educational use of computers to provide decision makers in the region with reference material giving a quick look at the current state of computer technology and the potential of computers in education. Five specialists from the region (Prof. Jonathan Anderson from Australia, Prof. Hosakere N. Mahabala from India, Prof. Haruo Nishinosono from Japan, Dr. Emma Teodola from the Philippines and Dr. Narong Boonme from Thailand, who attended the seminar in 1984) got together in the Bangkok Office to have an Experts Planning Meeting on the Use of Computers. The participants formulated some suggestions for future regional activities, and also prepared collectively some guidelines for the introduction and/or expansion of computer use in education and for the development of computer literacy, which were compiled, further developed and edited by Prof. Jonathan Anderson.

The following list of contents of the book reflects the most important and urgent issues to be understood by decision makers formulating policy at national and /or local level for the introduction of computers in education.

- Introduction
- Current and Future Developments in Educational Computing
- Policy Issues
- Hardware Considerations
- Computing Across the Curriculum
- Teacher Education and Curriculum Development
- Key Considerations for Educators

3. TOWARD RATIONAL USE OF COMPUTERS IN EDUCATION

The second series of APEID activities for educational computing in the region started in Australia in 1987, coinciding with the start of the Fourth Cycle of APEID in the same year. The workshop on "Software Development" organized by Dr. Mike Lally in Perth, West Australia, was more specifically devoted to the development of a multi-media training package for teacher educators in computer education. After the workshop in Perth, the seminar on "The Evaluation of Uses of Computers in Education" was convened with the co-sponsorship of the Australian Council for Educational Research and the Commonwealth Schools Commission and was organized by Dr. Malcom Rosier. In the seminar, the current situations of each country were introduced and the following themes concerning the evaluation of computer use in education were discussed.

(1) The evaluation of teaching/learning with computers at the classroom and school levels.
(2) The evaluation of teaching/learning with computers at the system level.
(3) The clarification of curriculum needs in relation to computers.
(4) What is actually happening in the use of computers in schools ?
(5) The evaluation of software and hardware for use in schools.
(6) Planning evaluations of the use of computers in the curriculum.
(7) The evaluation of programs for preservice and inservice training of teachers to use computers.
(8) Broader implications of the use of computers and technology, and the future of teaching,learning and the curriculum.

On the other hand, in the First Seminar of the Fourth Cycle APEID(1987-1991) held in Tokyo in 1987, participating countries agreed to launch a programme on the main theme, 'Educational Applications of New Information Technology and Their Implementation'. During the seminar, participants raised the following critical issues on the use of advanced technology in schools.

(1) When discussing media and advanced technologies, the focus is often on the media and technology itself. The content of the media is often forgotten during discussion about the method.
(2) Media is used to improve the spread of learning to overcome the problem of equity; however, discussions of educational uses of media can result in a focus on quantity of education rather than on quality of education. The question was posed as to the relationship between the quantity and quality of education and quality of life. Related to this is the role of media and advanced technologies in improving the quality of education. While audio-visual media and instructionl materials on how to use them exist, the position with computer education is different. The importance of developing an educational authoring package was raised.
(3) Is the aim of education to produce independent learners and should technology serve the learner to achieve this aim? Is a centralized or decentralized system more appropriate in exchanging materials among teachers ? At the same time, the question of resistance to the introduction of new media into educational settings and how to overcome such resistance was raised. The problem of educators taking advantage of new media was seen as critical.
(4) The use of media and advanced technologies in nonformal education was seen as necessary because of the problem of supplying teachers.
(5) The concept of learning centres which can be shared by schools and nonformal education mechanisms needs to be developed further when discussing the use of media and advanced technologies in education.
(6) The question of educational technology being isolated from education during discussions on educational uses of technology was seen as a major problem. The difficulty of discussing issues of technology separately from more general educational issues such as student -centred learning, learning theory and quality of education was highlighted. The role of educational reform in taking appropriate advantage of the media was seen as central.

The second seminar of the fourth programming cycle of APEID Activities was held in 1988, gathering ten participating countries and two staff from UNESCO-PROAP (Principal Regional Office for Asia and the Pacific) in Tokyo. The purpose of the seminar was to exchange experiences and information on the development, evaluation and dissemination of computer educational software for the primary and secondary levels of education and to discuss problems involved in such activities and their implication for teachers. The seminar revealed the unexpectedly rapid introduction of computers in Asian and the Pacific educational settings. Australia, India, Japan and the Republic of Korea took the initiatives in leading the seminar by presenting theme papers prepared by participants as decided in 1987.

4 ISSUES, PROBLEMS AND SOME SOLUTIONS

From the reports of the past regional seminars, we can list issues and problems raised by the participants.

"As all the computers are not compatible and lack of Chinese functions remains, one piece of software cannot be used in different computers, so it affects the dissemination of software."
"As the devices were made in foreign countries and the types are complex, so it brings serious problems of maintenance." (China, 1988)

"Most of the developed educational software is Mathematics software which is developed in the drill and practice mode of content-centered instruction, or English software which is developed in the drill and pracice mode of instruction for vocabulary or grammar. Therefore, some educators may underestimate the educational effect of the computer software, or give the wrong knowledge of the computer."(Rep. of Korea)

"But the Srilankan situation is that one computer is shared by 40 students! Therefore, individualized computer aided learning is not possible. On the other hand, if group learning is allowed, this type of software will end up with one student dominating the process, keeping slow learners always aside."
(Sri Lanka, 1988)

"The transfer and exchange and purchase of software may face problems due to copyright, language and machine compatibility."(Pakistan, 1988)

In spite of numerous problems faced in the educational use of computers in the region, there are, of course, many attempts to solve these problems; educational reform, establishment of new institutes, software development and empirical findings in the region.

"The Information Industry Demand Creating Plan"(1986) and "The School Computer Education Strengthening Plan"(1987) (Republic of Korea)

National educational reform and a policy of coping with the information age and reform of national curriculum .
(Japan, 1985-89)

"Production of a national computer 'Zhonghua Computer'" (China)

National Software Writing Competition (Malaysia)

"With low-cost microcomputers readily available in Thailand, a large number of educational software packages have been developed."(Thailand,1988)

"Many teachers felt that about three computers in the room made the size of the groups involved in computer based activities 'worth planning for'."(New Zealand, 1988)

Discrimination between developed and developing countries in the conventional sense does not reflect the present situation of computer use in education. According to the survey carried out by SEAMEO-RECSAM(South East Asian Ministers of Education Organization, Regional Education Centre for Science And Mathematics), the availabiity of computers in schools is highest in Singaopre (100 percent) and second in Brunei(81 percent). Japan is a very slow comer into this scene with 21.0 percent availability in elementary schools, 44.8 percent in junior secondary schools and 96.3 percent in senior secondary schools in 1989.

The state of the educational use of computers in the region is changing very rapidly. The introduction of new technology in developing countries does not necessarily follow the same process of technological evolution experienced in developed countries. In particular, the microcomputer has very different characteristics in easy operation and maintenace from the main frame computer. The way of developing software by personal computer is also very different from that for the large computer worked out by teams of specialists. The capacity of memory in computers is always increasing, and the price of hardware is decreasing. It is steadily becoming easier to purchase the most sophisticated equipment in less developed countries. The newest software, for example LOTUS 123 or dBASE III, is available and widely used in many Asian countries.

Some countries like China, India and the Republic of Korea are developing their own industries of new information technology, especially computer technology. New Zealand, Sri Lanka and Indonesia do not seem to have such plans at the moment. Meanwhile Japan has no strong intention of pushing the introduction of computers in schools for the encouragement of the computer technology industry. The efforts in some countries to introduce information technology in their schools are explained not only in the context of educational policy, but are closely related to their national policies concerning economic and industrial development.

It is almost impossible to generalize the recent trends of educational computing in the region, due to the rapid changes in technology and the diversity of the cultural, political and economic background in the region. It seems very instructive and fruitful to learn from each other about various case studies by sharing experiences in international gatherings.

5. COMPUTERS IN JAPANESE SCHOOLS

Study of the educational use of computers in Japan started in the middle of the sixties. The first trial adopted a model of CAI applying the theory of programmed instruction for software development. Other types of experiment followed and enlarged the perspectives of computer use in education, but were implemented in limited scale. Heated discussion on the daily use of the personal computer in classroom teaching, however, started around in 1984 after the establishment of various councils and committees in the Ministry of Education, Science and Culture to investigate the potential of computers and other new technological media in education. The discussion was stimulated by the report from CERI(Centre for Educational Research and Innovation) of the OECD which revealed the outstandingly low availability of computers in Japanese schools. Only 0.6 percent of elemetary schools were equipped with computers, in comparison with 43 percent in the U.S.A. and 42 percent in the U.K.. At secondary level, 3.1 percent of junior schools and 56.4 percent of high schools, of which vocational schools were well equipped, were utilizing computers for educational purpose. Meanwhile, it was reported that 100 percent of secondary schools were equipped with computers in the U.K. and 85 percent in the United States in 1983.

The extremely low availability of computers in Japanese schools astonished concerned people in other countries as well as in Japan. This scarcity of microcomputers in Japanese education at that time reflected the existing technological difficulties of dealing with Japanese text with computers. Nowadays, this problem of handling the complicated characters of the written Japanese language has been overcome. Efficient methods of input, processing and output of Japanese characters and sentences have been developed, and sophisticated software for interpreting the language has been implemented in microcomputers.

The delay in introducing computers to Japanese schools has not been caused only by linguistic and technological barriers. It is widely recognized that rigidity of curriculum, excessive uniformity of school education geared to entrance examinations to upper schools and excessive pressure from parents on children concerning the severe entrance examinations are also other reasons for such reluctance. We also cannot forget teachers' confidence in their teaching abilities without relying on the new technology and their preference for direct oral teaching. The surveys conducted since 1983 show the ratio of schools equipped with microcomputers has been increasing drastically at all school levels. The most recent survey shows that 21.0 percent of elementary schools, 44.8 percent of junior schools and 96.3 percent of high schools were equipped with microcomputers in 1989. Computer use in the classroom has a limited and short history in Japan. A recent survey shows that the most common use of the computer at the secondary school level is to manage student records, health care, lesson planning, and other clerical work. In the case of software development, those for instructional use are developped by teachers more in senior secondary schools than in elementary schools. Those for school management use are commercially available.

A great variety of computer hardware is another reason for the delayed diffusion of computers in schools. There is no compatibility in software available in the market and developed voluntarily by teachers and people interested in software development. In 1986, the Center for Educational Computing (CEC) was established with the joint support of the Ministry of International Trade and Industry and the Ministry of Education, Science and Culture. CEC proposed a unified specification for personal computers suitable for school education. In February 1988, computer companies responded to this proposal and submitted their models, which are entirely software compatible, but are not efficient enough to persuade teachers to use them. In Februry 1990, CEC proposed a set of unified specifications of programming language BASIC, LOGO and data format for the exchange of instructional materials. These specifications are expected to be respected by hardware suppliers and software developers.

The Information Center of Software for Learning was established in 1988 and is expected to be a promoting agent for software development, dissemination and quality control through software contests applied by teachers. The National Institute of Educational Research(NIER) is also expected to promote and support the software development through the network of Local Institutes of Educational Training. Teacher trainig courses are also being conducted for the implementation of a new curriculum at central and local training institutes.

6. TOWARD INFORMATION EDUCATION IN JAPAN

Reform of the educational system has been widely discussed since the early eighties. The necessity of carrying out reform in national education and recognition of the delay in introducing computers in schools coincided in terms of urgency and importance with the influence of information technology in the future of society. The gradual shift in perception of the computer from an emphasis on computer potential to information technology and human competency in dealing with information itself emerged through the discussion in the various councils and committees. The emphasis on comprehensive understanding and responsiblity of information technology is an outstanding feature of Japanese national policy for the introduction of computers in schools. In the early reports issued from the councils and committees, the term 'computer' was often used to express the emerging problems in school education. This term changed to 'computer and new media' and finally 'information education'. The term 'information processing education' has been used for the vocational education of information technology at vocational high school, technical college and university levels. The new concept of educating all citizens on information differs from the traditional concept of vocational education. In recent documents and papers, the term 'information education' is often read and widely used. The author proposed the shown chart in the journal 'Education and Information' edited by the Ministry of Education in 1987. The new curriculum at elementary level will be fully implemented in 1992, at lower secondary in 1993, and at upper secondary in 1994. Any specific education on informatics is not to be given at elementary level, 'Basic Informatics' included at lower secondary, and more advanced informatics at upper secondary level.

Area			Relevant subjects
Information education	Informatics education	Information science	Mathematics
			Science
		Information technology	Technical education
			Home science
			Vocational education
	Education on information society	Understanding of information society	Social study
			Physical education
			Language
			Out-of-class activities
		Information culture	Computer graphics
			National language
			Out-of-class activities
			(Music)
		Ethics in information society	Moral education
			Social study

REFERENCES

1)Anderson,Jonathan: "Developing Computer Use in Education - Guidelines, trends and issues", Unesco Regional Office for Education in Asia and the Pacific, 1986.

2)Unesco Regional Office for Education in Asia and the Pacific: "Computers in Education - An outline for country experiences", 1985.

3)Japanese National Commission for UNESCO: "Computers in Education, Final Report of the Third Asian Seminar on Educational Technology in Tokyo, The third programming cycle of APEID Activities", 1984.

4)Japanese National Commission for UNESCO "Final Report of the First Asian and the Pacific Seminar on Educational Technology in Tokyo, The Fourth Programming Cycle of APEID Activities", 1987.

5)Japanese National Commission for UNESCO "Final Report of Asia and the Pacific Seminar on Educational Technology -1988, The Second Seminar of the Fourth Programming Cycle of APEID Activities", 1988 in Tokyo.

6)Nishinosono, Haruo: "The Use of New Information Technology in Education: Evaluating the Experience of Japan and Other Asian Countries", Paper presented in the IIEP Seminar of the 25th Anniversary, 28 Nov.- 2 Dec. 1988, in Paris.

7)Tan Teong Chye: "Audio-visual education and distance education with new information technology in the region" Report submitted in The Asia and the Pacific Seminar on Educational Technology - 1989 in Tokyo.

INFORMATICS EDUCATION AT THE SECONDARY LEVEL

Computers in Education
A. McDougall and C. Dowling (Editors)
Elsevier Science Publishers B.V. (North-Holland)

EDUCATIONAL COMPUTING AT THE SECONDARY LEVEL: NEED FOR RENEWAL WITH VISION

A.K. JALALUDDIN

C-31-C Gangotri Enclave, Alaknanda, New Delhi 110 019, India

After nearly a decade of enthusiasm, induction of the computer into schools has entered a period of reassessment. In the absence of a well-defined conceptual framework of educational computing in schools, computer literacy programmes mostly take the form of computer studies and programming courses at the secondary level. The concept of the computer as an aid to learning within the curriculum is yet to be accepted in the mainstream of secondary education.

The current unqualified stress on the quality of education is unwittingly reinforcing the traditional examination-orientation of secondary education rather than creating a favourable climate for flexible redesigning of methods of instruction. Most initiatives to popularize learning with the computer highlight the importance of Computer-Assisted Learning (CAL) software in qualitatively improving learning of concepts and principles within the curriculum as well as generalized skills like reasoning. The tendency to link CAL packages to specific curricular topics has given currency to the opinion that all that is needed for the secondary grades is a large number of such packages - the more the merrier. While these developments are, no doubt, important landmarks in the recent history of educational computing, they have failed to extend the application of the computer beyond the traditional boundaries of teaching and learning practices. They have also failed to create an awareness of the need to evolve new methodologies for designing instruction and learning strategies in an integrated manner. In the absence of such global thinking, much of the spectacular advances of new information technology may remain underutilized.

A more effective way of promoting educational computing in secondary schools would be to conceptualize information technology inputs as a general resource base for the overall improvement of the quality of learning. This approach has enormous potential in terms of providing both teachers and students with a higher degree of motivation to utilize the resource in their individual ways. Such an initiative, while reducing emphasis on programming, will encourage more creative use of the technology, leading to possible generation of transferable skills across the curriculum and in some cases beyond the curriculum. The cost-effectiveness of this approach may make the induction of technology in a developing country more egalitarian compared with the prevalent elitist trends. Taub's conceptualization of the role of new information technology as an Education Utility is a major contribution in this direction.

1. INTRODUCTION

While traditionally the elementary school happened to be the arena for the introduction of innovative ideas and practices, it is at the secondary level that the educational application of the computer has been most significant in the recent years in most countries. Whether it is in the form of computer literacy or computer studies, the lower secondary level was found to be the most appropriate stage for a meaningful entry of the new technology in schools.

In most cases, the initiative to introduce the computer in schools came from sources outside the system of education. The objectives of these initiatives generally highlight the importance of preparing the younger generation for the challenges posed by the rapidly changing technological environment the world over, and making them active participants in this process of change.

The secondary level of education being preparatory to both specialized and higher education on the one hand and the world of work on the other, these initiatives were reciprocated by the systems of education more as external compulsions for change than out of a genuine realization of their significance in improving their own efficiency.

In the present paper, an effort has been made to conceptualize the possible ways of matching the existing needs for improving the quality of secondary education with the opportunities of evolving new strategies of teaching and learning with the help of new information technology.

2. ADD-ON CHARACTER

In most countries, the curriculum development centres and the agencies traditionally responsible for disseminating educational innovation and providing academic and technical support services to secondary schools had very little active role in the initial stages of induction of the computer in schools. These agencies as well as most educational researchers in the universities, by and large remained sceptical about the actual learning outcome in the curricular areas from computer-based education. Only a small section of educational and curriculum researchers who happened to be interested in learning and instructional theories or were otherwise exposed to interesting educational software, were in a position to see the long-term implications of introducing the computer in schools.

The gap in the perceptions of the role of the computer in the school curriculum among the early enthusiasts of computer literacy and education and those actually associated with the school support system to a great extent hampered the serious and well-planned use of the computer in the context of the curriculum once the initial fanfare was over. In many cases, the enthusiasm was sought to be sustained through widespread introduction of computer studies as an elective course in the secondary grades. These developments have led many countries to seriously reassess their policies regarding computers in schools.

There were some attempts to make use of computer-assisted learning programmes to promote new ways of learning a topic. However, in most cases, no significant improvement in learning in the scholastic areas could be discerned that could be attributed to the use of the computer or CAL software. The failure to establish the advantage of the use of the computer in the curriculum is often explained as a failure of the methodology adopted for testing. It is well known that school tests are hardly designed to assess the general problem-solving skills or other higher-order cognitive abilities of students which are expected to be enhanced through well-designed educational computing programs.

The present task before the systems of education is not just to rationalize the use of the computer as an add-on facility but to evolve a comprehensive strategy of integrating the information technology with the structure of school improvement programmes [1].

An analysis of past experiences of implementing school improvement programmes in different types of schools has made some educational researchers believe that such improvement occurs when the process is established as part of the regular business of educational life [2]. It is only when a school develops the capacity to innovate and become self-renewing, that it can adapt new ideas and inputs from other sources more effectively. In the absence of an environment which encourages innovation, experimentation and improvisation within a school, installing innovative ideas and processing of learning in a 'turn-key' manner would be a fruitless effort. The history of introducing inquiry-learning in science education or educational technology to support classroom teaching in secondary schools is replete with evidence of failure the world over.

The situation was not qualitatively different when pilot projects or prototype national computer-based learning programmes were sought to be widely diffused or institiutionalized in some countries [3]. While in most developing countries, the constraints in widening the scope of such programmes beyond the laboratory stage are invariably masked by economic conditions, the problems of their implementation in the developed world seem to arise out of the inflexibility of the curriculum [4].

3. FEEDBACK FROM SURVEYS

Attempts were made to explore the nature and extent of the use of the computer in the secondary grades in several countries. In his 'Report from the 1989 National Survey of US Schools', Becker has shown that in the secondary grades only a very small portion of instructional activity with school computers was devoted to traditional mathematics or science topics [5]. The situation is not very different in most other countries as the experiences of the Research Coordinators of an International Study on Computer Education (COMPED) sponsored by the International Association for the Evaluation of Educational Achievement (IEA) seem to indicate [6]. The US National Survey also revealed that while only 8 per cent and 6 per cent of the use of the school computer occurred in mathematics and science respectively in the high school grades, about 10 per cent of the science teachers' courses and 50 per cent of the math teachers' courses involved using computers to teach programming or computer literacy and not mathematics or science topics [7].

In the light of his interaction with a large number of computer-user secondary teachers, the present author tends to believe that most of the computer-user teachers get involved in teaching programming rather than exploiting the potential of a CAL package or generic software tools like word processors, databases or spreadsheets in their own area of curricular interest mainly for two reasons. First, the satisfaction and pleasure they derive from the newly acquired skill of programming motivates them more to try their hand in designing small programs however insignificant such a program may prove compared to the commercial products. The technicalities involved in programming also often offered them greater challenges than merely using a given software. Second, in the absence of an intimate familiarity with the mediating role expected of the teacher in providing on-line coaching to the students in an interactive learning mode with the computer, the computer-user teacher does not see any specific pedagogic role in a computer-based learning situation within the curriculum. Many of them fail to see the importance of observing the learners when they are 'reflecting in action' with the computer. The importance of making the learners aware of the principles of general problem-solving while they are actually playing with a simulation package is often undermined by most teachers. The transferability of a learning strategy acquired in a computer environment to a non-computer environment is almost totally neglected in computer-based education programmes.

A CAL package on 'Moving Molecules' provides a very rare opportunity to the learner to manipulate the parameters like pressure, temperature, volume and the number of molecules and to appreciate the causal relationships between these parameters [8]. However, the learners may not take advantage of the package actually to try to measure the mean-free path of the molecules on the screen of the monitor, or to understand the meaning of the pressure of a gas as sum total of the momentum transferred by the molecules on the walls of the container as if in a natural setting, unless the teacher himself sees the potential of the package in that fashion. As Papert frequently points out, we very often fail to associate the new kind of learning with artificially created microworld that occurs very typically in natural settings [9].

4. NEED FOR THEORETICAL CONSTRUCTS

The need for emphasizing the new ideas originating from cognitive psychology and learning theories in understanding the application of the computer within the curriculum is more pronounced when well-known software tools like word processors, databases and spreadsheets are used. Very often we fail to impress on the learner that the important thing in the context of a curriculum is not the tools themselves, but the curriculum material that one is trying to get across. As Bork points out, 'The traditional context of these tools is business application, with little pedagogical context surrounding them' [10]. The pedagogical and curriculum context of a generic software or a tool can only be developed when we see the curriculum in totality, as an instructional design where the content, pedagogy and the methods are aimed at creating most effective learning situations required to achieve a learning objective. It is also important to ask 'What new educational situation can one create using the new information technology that might not otherwise occur in the classroom?' With Collis, we may admit that we have not succeeded yet in demonstrating to the teachers that there are real educational needs that information technology tools can help them address, and more effectively than with other tools [11]. There does not seem to be a straightforward answer to this kind of a question. One might, in turn, have to ask, 'What do we know about the active nature of learning?'

With the rapid development of cognitive science, it is now possible to say that a good instructional design is based on an organization of the conditions of learning in a step-by-step fashion taking due account at each step of the previously acquired capabilities of the learner. The learner also needs specific stimuli to retain these capabilities and to proceed to the next stage of learning. Despite the improved design of the instructional material in print a learner may not be able to control his process of learning without the mediating role of the teacher. There is very little room for prompting text-specific learning strategies and tactics in the design of the printed instructional material. However, it is feasible to transfer a part of such prompting and the mediating role of the teacher to the computer and suitably designed educational computer software [12].

In the realm of educational software, as Thornburg puts it, 'The task of programming boils down to the creation of a metaphorical microworld in which the user can interact with tasks and situations that are designed to aid the acquisition and development of knowledge' [13]. The importance of involving the classroom teacher in creating this metaphorical microworld seems to be the key to effective educational computing in the context of the curriculum.

5. NEED FOR A FLEXIBLE CURRICULUM

Till recently, the involvement of the teacher in designing learning exercises using a software tool or authoring system was seen essentially as an effort to cover some part of a subject matter. It was hardly ever seen as an effective means to analyse the existing school curriculum and to create a database of local ideas, experiences and illustrations which may help the teachers and students to localize the curriculum, as Fothergill lamented [14]. This process of decentralization of not only the implementation of the curricululm but also its design has several important implications in school improvement strategies.

In the first instance, such decentraization removes much of the domination of the content in the existing school curriculum and creates a favourable ground for highlighting the processes involved in learning and planning instruction to promote learning of a retainable nature. Some of the process and planning skills may be acquired by the students by using the computer to literally scan the whole textbook in a given subject and then to construct the inherent linkages between the key ideas and concepts in the style of knowledge and concept mapping [15]. Such initiatives may generate an environment of participation and self-learning among the teachers, which is at the root of school improvement. In this sense, even a limited use of the computer in a proactive role, in contrast with its present largely reactive role, may have much profound and long-term impact on the existing educational scene.

The concept of the computer as a major educational resource has been gaining ground with the growing realization that it is not the number of educational software packages nor even full coursewares which act as the major stimulus in integrating the computer with the curriculum, but how the teachers and students can use the technology in widely diverse situations and contexts. Searching a vast information base stored in a CD-ROM to explore the chronological overlap of the ancient human civilizations by sequencing the important landmarks in each civilization as an exercise in history, using a database as a research tool in the analysis of press information as an exercise in language learning, and plotting a local weather chart using the actual data recorded by the school computer as a lesson in practical physics, are some of the numerous uses one can make of the computer as a major educational resource base in a school setting. It is also not difficult to visualize the new technology as an on-line source of customized instructional material or as 'advance organizers' as defined by Ausobel [16].

There is in-built flexibility in the use of the computer in this kind of utility mode. The immediate attraction to use the utility in a school setting may be the ease with which the individual teachers and students will be able to fulfil some of their urgent teaching and learning tasks which either cannot be achieved without such a resource or would require more time with less effective outcome.

The conceptualization of the New Information Technology as an Education Utility to satisfy the felt needs fo the secondary school in fact abandons the approach of piecemeal reform in education in favour of a renewal of the system with a vision. While Jack Taub visualized Education Utility as a new application of technology in education that could be important for teacher education, the idea turned out to be equally if not more exciting for the students [17]. Taub felt that 'the Utility could help address issues of equity, urban education, integrating higher order thinking skills into the school curriculum, and other challenges'. Giving shape to such a vision may not call for larger investment in computers for schools. It essentially draws our attention to the urgency of removing the traditional gap between the elements that constitute the mosaic of the learning environment and the culture of new technology. It also calls for bridging the gap between theory and practice, and more importantly cognition and action. All agencies and individuals responsible for making the present-day school more self-directing and capable of adjusting itself to the fast-changing physical and technological environment may find the Utility approach to educational computing a practical means of bringing about immediate change. Education Utility is of much greater relevance to developing countries today who may not be in a position to offer all resources to individual schools, but may be willing to consider networking the schools with a centrally located resource base. The other alternative would be to set up community-based Education Utilities which would benefit schools in the neighbourhood.

Education Utility enfolds within it a larger vision of freedom, where schools will release themselves from the bonds of textbooks and examinations and emerge as the most enjoyable environment, not only for learning but for creating ideas and knowledge. This transformation will take place only when we put everything we have in the name of education in a melting pot and look for a new world image afresh.

REFERENCES

[1] Joyce, Bruce R., Hersh, Richard H. and McKibbin, Michael, The Structure of School Improvement (Longman, New York, 1983).

[2] Goodlad, Job I., Foreword in: Joyce, Bruce R., Hersh, Richard H. and McKibbin, Michael, The Structure of School Improvement (Longman, New York, 1983).

[3] Development Education and Communication Unit, Computer Literacy and Studies in Schools

Project - Evaluation Report (Indian Space Research Organization, Ahmedabab, 1956).

[4] Centre for Educational Research and Innovation, Information Technologies and Basic Learning, General Report (OECD, Paris, 1986).

[5] Becker Henry J., Instructional Uses of School Computers 4 (1987) 2.

[6] National Council of Educational Research and Training, National Case Study - IEA Computers in Education Study (NCERT, New Delhi, 1989).

[7] Loc. cit. 5.

[8] Temple-Fry, Jerry, Moving Molecules (Cambridge Microsoft, Indian edition, New Delhi, 1986).

[9] Papert, Seymour, Microworld: Transforming Education, in : Evans, Susan and Clark, Peter (eds.), The Computer Culture (White River Press, New York, 1984), pp. 1-16.

[10] Bork, Alfred, The 'History' of Technology and Education, in print.

[11] Collis, Betty, Using Information Technology to Create New Educational Situations, Proceedings of International Congress on Education and Informatics - Strengthening of International Cooperation (UNESCO, Paris, 1989), in print.

[12] Jalaluddin, A.K., Educational Technology Yearbook 1988 (All India Association for Educational Technology, New Delhi, 1989).

[13] Thornburg, David D., Computers & Education, 12 (1988) 11.

[14] Novak, Joseph D. and Gowin, D. Bob, Learning How to Learn (CUP, Cambridge, 1984).

[15] Ausubel, D., The Psychology of Meaningful Verbal Learning (Grune & Stratton, New York, 1963).

[16] Gooler, Dennis D., The Education Utility - The Power to Revitalize Education and Society (Educational Technology Publications, Englewood Cliffs, New Jersey, 1986).

[17] Ibid.

Computers in Education
A. McDougall and C. Dowling (Editors)
Elsevier Science Publishers B.V. (North-Holland)

CD-ROM INFORMATION SOURCES FOR STUDENTS: ANTICIPATED OUTCOMES AND UNEXPECTED CHALLENGES

Donna J. BAUMBACH

University of Central Florida, College of Education, Educational Media/ Instructional Technology, Orlando, Florida USA 32816*

CD-ROM, which stands for **compact disc - read only memory**, offers students access to massive amounts of information through personal computers and a compact disc player. This paper will briefly describe CD-ROM technology and provide an overview of advantages and disadvantages of this information technology for secondary students as well as lessons learned in working with CD-ROM based products in secondary schools.

1. OVERVIEW OF THE TECHNOLOGY

CD-ROM, which stands for **compact disc - read only memory**, offers students access to massive amounts of information which is easily and quickly retrievable in a variety of ways and is contained in a small space. A close relative of the audio compact discs that have been providing listeners with high quality music for the past few years, CD-ROM contains digital data which has been pressed onto a 4.72 inch optical disc. The disc is encased in plastic for protection and read by a low powered, narrowly focused laser beam. Because the disc is read by a laser beam, it is not vulnerable to surface wear and has a long shelf-life.

A special CD-ROM player, either IBM-or Apple-compatible, is required to read the CD-ROM discs and must be connected to a computer and monitor. Using special search and retrieval software, the information on the CD-ROM disc is displayed on the computer monitor. The CD-ROM disc is read-only. Data cannot be added, changed, or erased after the disc is produced. And even though retrieval is faster than traditional manual methods, those who have worked with hard disk drives will find CD-ROM slow and tedious by comparison. While there are some challenges and problems to be overcome in working with CD-ROM, the potential of the technology for instruction and information management is most promising.

Large storage capacity is the primary advantage of CD-ROM technology. A single disc can hold over 250,000 pages of text, roughly 1500 times the capacity of a floppy diskette. The disc can store other digital data as well, for example 15,000 images, one hour of sound, or any combination of text, graphics, and sound. Although CD-ROM technology is only a few years old, hundreds of applications are already available. CD-ROM is changing publishing, libraries, and the way information is accessed.

Most CD-ROM databases allow the user to search in at least two ways — the browse search and the analytic or Boolean search. A browse search will allow the user to look through an alphabetical index of words or titles (or both) until he or she finds something of interest. A search conducted in this manner is relatively broad because a combination of words or techniques cannot be used.

The analytic or Boolean search is more complex, allowing the user to combine keywords in a variety of ways to narrow or broaden the search. In these searches, three simple and familiar words (and, or, not) are used as logical connectors to define the relationship of the keywords in the articles. Other advanced search techniques include the use of truncation and wildcards. Truncation allows the user to locate all occurrences of a root word with different endings. Wildcards allow for variations in spelling within a word.

More sophisticated searching can involve nested Boolean logic, combining new searches with previous ones, and moving from CD-ROM to online searches to update information using the formulated search strategy.

2. POPULAR APPLICATIONS OF CD-ROM IN U.S. SECONDARY SCHOOLS

While virtually any type of information can be stored on CD-ROM, the major applications currently used in U. S. secondary schools fall into

*Dr. Baumbach is an Associate Professor of Education and Director of the UCF/DOE Instructional Technology Resource Center which is funded by a grant from the Florida Department of Education to disseminate information about technology to Florida educators.

the following categories:

- *Online Catalogs* - If the "card" catalog is on a CD-ROM, students can quickly determine what materials are available in their own school library media center and elsewhere.

- *Reference Sources* - With references like dictionaries and encyclopedias on CD-ROM, the students can get instant answers to specific questions.

- *Indices* - Students also need to know where they can find additional information on a topic for their research. This can be provided with indices to periodicals, or by indices combined with full-text articles on CD-ROM.

- *Multi-media Materials* - Because students are individuals with different learning styles and preferences, they need information and recreational materials in a variety of formats — visuals, sounds, graphs, and maps.

- *Public Domain Software Programs* - These programs will meet the needs of today's computer-oriented youth who want materials they can legally copy, take with them, and share with a friend.

- *Integrated Learning Systems.* Systematically designed and developed basic skills curricula, including pretests, postests, tutorials, and drill and practice programs combined with management software and other utilties have been provided on CD-ROM for delivery on a network.

3. ADVANTAGES OF CD-ROM

While the primary advantage of CD-ROM is its large storyage capacity, the introduction of CD-ROMs into the secondary school offers several important benefits for users. These include:

Speed. Finding information with CD-ROM databases is faster and more efficient than manual searching, providing more time for analyzing and assimilating that information.

Feedback. Users can tell immediately whether or not they have sufficiently defined their search strategies. They can use this information to refine the search until an adequate quality and quantity of information is located.

Confidence Building. There is much satisfaction in accomplishing a successful search, and doing so builds confidence in the student's ability to find and use information. Since the discs are "read-only," users feel more confident in knowing they cannot damage or alter the information in any way.

Motivation. Students enjoy working with CD-ROM materials and recognize that technology is helping them to accomplish their tasks more efficiently and effectively — exactly what technology ought to do!

Increased Language and Problem Solving Skills. Students who use CD-ROM quickly discover that proper spelling, grammar, and typing are important keys to successful searches. Following directions, identifying problems and possible solutions, classifying information, editing, refining, and modifying are skills which lead to successful searches.

Increased Opportunities to Explore Information. Students using CD-ROM are more likely to explore cross references and to browse through related titles. Word and title indices allow students to browse through massive amounts of information, and the hypertext capabilities of many programs allow a sort of "stream of consciousness" exploration.

Ease of Compiling Bibliographies. Users can use information retrieved by their searches to build bibliographies. Students can save information to disk for later use as references for a research paper, editing their work with a word processor. Library media specialists can easily create bibliographies for teachers on a specific topic or area of interest.

4. DISADVANTAGES OF CD-ROM MATERIALS

New technology, however exciting, is never without its disadvantages. For secondary schools these include:

Cost. The price of a CD-ROM can range from about $20 for a single hypermedia story on disc to thousands of dollars for specialized databases which are updated frequently and provide on-line capabilities at no extra cost. In addition to the cost of the disc, library media centers must provide a computer, monitor, CD-ROM drive, printer, and paper. In the case of CD-ROMs which also provide access to an online database, a dedicated phone line must also be available.

Lack of Access and Availability. While several different students can use the printed encyclopedia at any one time, only one student at a time can access the CD-ROM version. Although many applications can be used on one workstation, it is difficult for more than one student to use the workstation at a time. The popularity of CD-ROMs may require multiple dedicated workstations in order to allow students adequate access to information.

Lack of Standardization in Search Protocols and

Screen Design. The commands and symbols used to conduct a search vary widely from program to program. Users will only be able to memorize those they use most often and may be frustrated by the lack of uniformity in commands and function keys when moving from database to database. Programs may offer screen "prompts" or help screens, but there is little consistency in the location of these aids.

Lack of Documents or Delay of Documents. Students may find that items identified in the search are not available in the library media center and/or will be delayed by interlibrary loan. Media specialists may have to increase the number of periodicals available or develop new, faster interlibrary loan procedures such as using facsimile machines (FAX) in order to keep up with the demands of students.

Lack of Information, Scope or Coverage. While CD-ROM technology is designed to increase the amount of information available, the database is only as good as the information it contains. Most databases provide indexing from the 1970s on, limiting their use for historical information. Many databases are quite narrow and specific in scope, hindering the student who may need information which crosses the lines of several disciplines.

Lack of Electronic Reading Skills. The majority of CD-ROM material is text-based, and students who have difficulty reading print material will also have difficulty reading material from the computer monitor. In addition, we read information from the computer at only about 75% of the speed we can read printed information (Gould and Grischkowsky, 1984). And because much of the search software for CD-ROMs takes you to exact points where search words occur in an article, information is often retrieved which is out of context (Barlow, Karnes, & Marchionini, 1987).

Lack of Keyboarding Skills/Computer Literacy. Students who lack basic keyboarding skills will find this can greatly hinder their ability to search databases on CD-ROM. Most programs look for exact spellings and have very specific criteria for entering search words and combinations of words. Students may become frustrated with the results of their searches not because information is unavailable, but because they do not have the basic skills needed to retrieve it. Students who are are not computer literate, who fail to understand the power of the computer in accessing information or who do not have the skills required to save, manipulate, and format information will not be likely to find CD-ROM based materials to their advantage.

4. POTENTIAL IMPACT ON SECONDARY SCHOOLS AND STUDENTS

As with any new technology, the introduction and integration of CD-ROM is likely to bring about change in the school, the students and the curriculum. Change can be positive or negative in effect, but there will be change.

The Curriculum. The ability to conduct a successful search is a skill that is becoming essential in schools. It is becoming an important part of many professions, too, since most businesses access databases on a daily basis. The foundation for teaching CD-ROM search skills already exists in the information skills curriculum. We teach students early to identify titles, authors, and subjects. We help them to identify keywords and synonyms, and we assist them in evaluating the search. These general principles for searching are also important in CD-ROM searches. Students need assistance in conducting searches that are more efficient and more effective.

Students also need an understanding of different databases, the hardware and software being used, and protocols and commands specific to each database. These specific skills will vary with the databases available.

Students must also have an understanding of the subject being searched. This provides an excellent opportunity for integrating CD-ROM search skills with classroom instruction, and like other information skills, they are most effectively taught this way. Students can see the value of CD-ROM and internalize the skills when they are used to meet a specific need. While these skills can be implemented and reinforced at various grade levels and in many subject areas, a review and revision of the information skills curriculum is in order as a school moves into CD-ROM based reference and indexing materials.

While students do not show a clear preference for either the analytical or the browse search (Barlow, Karnes, & Marchionini, 1987; Marchionini, 1989; Liebscher and Marchionini, 1988), instruction for students in formulating and executing search strategies provides greater success and more confident users. With students having access to more and more information, students need instruction in finding pertinent information, filtering it, and using it appropriately. Analysis, synthesis, and assimilation of the information are higher order thinking skills which must be addressed by the information skills curriculum.

Increased Demand for Equipment. A school using CD-ROM will quickly discover that a single workstation is inadequate. More and more students and faculty will want access to a single database, and with the addition of more applications, more workstations may become necessary. Coping with increased demand for use of CD-ROM workstations is a problem that becomes compounded when this resource is promoted to ensure that all students are aware of it (Taylor, 1989).

Utilization of School Library Media Center Materials. Schools with CD-ROM based indices such as *Reader's Guide* are reporting increased circulation of materials indexed and increased demand for interlibrary loan (Taylor, 1989). In addition, several have reported increased use of print indices, indicating not only that searching CD-ROM databases has provided students with a better understanding of indices, but also that students may not want to wait in line to use the CD-ROM workstation (Barlow, Karnes, & Marchionini, 1987).

Staff and Faculty Training. As with any new material or equipment, provisions must be made for training library media center staff so that they feel comfortable with the equipment and knowledgeable in its use. School library media center staff need time and practice to learn each application thoroughly enough to assist users. In addition, inservice training for faculty is needed to ensure that they will use the new technology, incorporate it into their curricula, and encourage their students to use it.

Controlled Costs. While online services such as DIALOG, BRS, CompuServe or other vendors may provide information to meet students' needs, costs cannot be predicted or controlled without limiting student access. CD-ROM applications can be searched without the time or cost limitations of online services. Phone lines, modems, passwords, and accounts are usually not necessary with CD-ROMs (unless online access is included in the subscription cost, as is the case with Wilson Discs). However, updating of information may not be as frequent with CD-ROM. Fortunately, if a school decides to offer both CD-ROM and online searches, the same search techniques and skills can be used for both technologies. The ability to determine an effective search strategy while working off-line with CD-ROM databases saves money when that same strategy is used in on-line searches.

Role of the School Library Media Specialist. As CD-ROM users increase their abilities to retrieve information independently, the school library media specialist can assume more responsibility for enrichment activities, consulting with teachers and students, and integrating information skills into the curriculum. The presence of the CD-ROM in the library media center provides a more positive perception of the school library media specialist as an innovator, as a leader in the area of new and emerging technologies, and as an educator interested in meeting the needs of the school's students and faculty (Epler, 1988).

5. FLORIDA SCHOOL IMPLEMENTATION PROJECT

The Florida Department of Education funds four Instructional Computing Centers to provide information and services to Florida educators. One center is the UCF/DOE Instructional Technology Resource Center at the University of Central Florida in Orlando. Originally charged with providing information and resources related to "computer literacy," the Center expanded its focus approximately two years ago to include the broad spectrum of instructional technologies. Special attention has been placed upon new and emerging technologies for instruction and information management, including CD-ROM.

A CD-ROM Preview Center has been established at the University of Central Florida for educators to come and review over fifty CD-ROM applications as well as a variety of CD-ROM drives and workstation configurations. The UCF Center has produced and distributed three versions of a computer-based CD-ROM tutorial (IBM, Macintosh, and Apple//) which provides an overview of CD-ROM technology, an introduction to search strategies, a simulation of a CD-ROM program, and a listing of the names and addresses of several CD-ROM vendors. In addition, brochures on CD-ROM, optical media, and several other new and emerging technologies for educators have been produced and distributed by the Center.

In an effort to collect data about the educational use of CD-ROM and to provide access to this new technology for many of Florida's students, the UCF/DOE Instructional Technology Resource Center obtained additional funding from the Florida Department of Education, Office of Educational Technology and the Florida Information Resources Network, to install CD-ROM players and software for 18 selected middle and high schools in Florida.

Because the largest number of the CD-ROM applications are available for the MS-DOS environment of the IBM and compatible computers, we chose to purchase IBM-compatible CD-ROM players (Hitachi). Each school agreed to supply an computer with 640K RAM and a color monitor. The UCF/DOE Center supplied the CD-ROM players, and the New Grolier Electronic Encyclopedia on CD-ROM. Schools also agreed to place the CD-ROM workstation in the school library media center so that the maximum number of students in the school could have access to the information. A school library media specialist in each school is the UCF contact. Training was provided at the University of Central Florida during the summer months for the media specialists and teachers involved in the project. The CD-ROM program was first introduced to students during the fall semester, 1989.

In December 1989 the UCF/DOE Center distributed its first survey to the project schools to obtain data on the initial response to the CD-ROM by the students, teachers and media specialists. Participants reported that students love working with the CD-ROM based reference. Adjectives such as "exciting," "fascinating," and "stimulating" were used to describe students' response on every survey. The media specialists report that students especially like the ability to produce a printout that they can take with them. When queried about the purpose and subject areas of

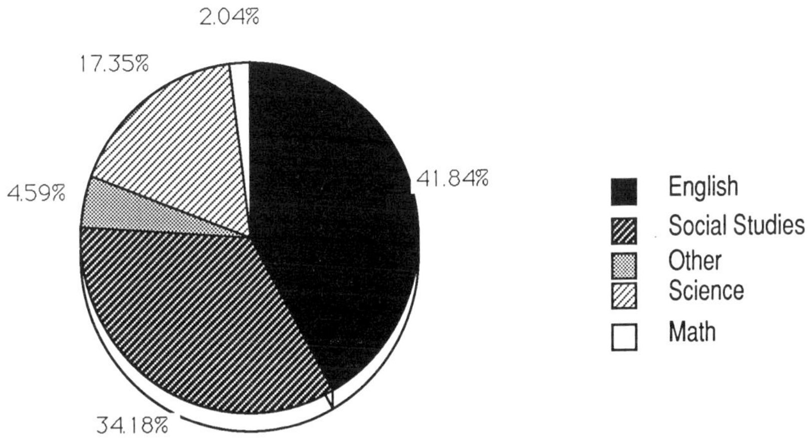

Figure 1. Uses of CD-ROM in Secondary School Curricula

the students' use of Grolier's, the surveys indicated that 65% of the students use CD-ROM for a research assignment and 35% use it "out of curiosity." Figure 1 provides an overview of how the CD-ROM is used in the secondary school curriculum. The schools also reported that teachers are also beginning to use the CD-ROM for research, curriculum planning, and exploration of a new technology. While it was reported that only about 16% of the teachers had used the CD-ROM, no formal instruction or introductional to the technology had been offered by the media specialist. The number is expected to increase during the second semester of the project when formal staff development programs are offered.

When asked about training techniques for this new technology, the majority of the media specialists reported success with small group instruction. They have also found it to be beneficial to train a core group of student assistants, who then help others. The UCF Center, in conjunction with one of the project schools, has produced a videotape demonstrating many of the features of Grolier's Electronic Encyclopedia. A "help" brochure for quick reference has also been provided.

The UCF/DOE Instructional Technology Resource Center will continue to work with the Florida Department of Education to promote the use of CD-ROM, as well as other new technologies, in Florida's schools. Future projects include additional research studies, the introduction of a variety of CD-ROMs for student use in the schools, the production of other appropriate training/educational materials, and formal evaluation reports of CD-ROM products and workstation components.

REFERENCES

Barlow, D., Karnes, B. & Marchionini, G. (1987). CD-ROM in a high school library media center: A research project. School Library Journal, 34(2), 66-68+.

Epler, D. (1988). Networking in Pennsylvania: Technology and the school library media center. *Library Trends*, *37*(1), 43-44.

Gould, J., and Grischkowsky, N. (1984). Doing the same work with hard copy and with cathode ray tube (CRT) computer terminals. *Human Factors*, *26*(3), 323-337.

Liebscher, P., & Marchionini, G. (1988). Browse and analytical search strategies in a full-text CD-ROM encyclopedia. *School Library Media Quarterly*, *16*(4), 223-233.

Marchionini, G. (1989) Information-seeking strategies of novices using a full-text electronic encyclopedia. *Journal of the American Society for Information Science*, *40*(1) 54-66.

Taylor, D. (1989). Reference ROMS: Six implications for libraries building CD-ROM database services. *American Libraries*, *20*(5), 452-454.

Computers in Education
A. McDougall and C. Dowling (Editors)
Elsevier Science Publishers B.V. (North-Holland)

COMPUTER SCIENCE IN BASIC EDUCATION: CURRICULAR ISSUES AND SCHOOL PRACTICE PROSPECTS

Rosa Maria Bottino (*) and Fulvia Furinghetti (**)
(*) Istituto per la Matematica Applicata - C.N.R - Genova - Italy
(**) Dipartimento di Matematica - Università di Genova - Genova - Italy

Via L.B. Alberti 4 - 16132 Genova - ITALY - Tel. +39-10-515510 Fax +39-10-517801

In this paper we consider the possibility of introducing computer science elements in the basic education of students aged 14-16 years. Educational and disciplinary considerations support our opinion that this introduction may be fruitful if performed within mathematics courses, as, at present, occurs in Italy in many experimental mathematics classes. The underlying problems of teaching computer science, in this particular framework, mainly concern: contents, degree of depth, balance between theory and practice and the relationship with mathematics. The way teachers face these problems leads to different orientations in teaching computer science elements and, eventually, to different images of the discipline in school practice. We examine the main lines of these orientations by means of a questionnaire and interviews addressed to mathematics teachers who are experimenting with the introduction of computer science in their courses, for the age group under discussion.

1. INTRODUCTION

It is widely recognized that the impact of computers in school, at any level, affects both the design of curricula and the teaching methodologies. This impact has been widely discussed according to different points of view.
Researches on computers in education mainly concern the orientations (represented as nodes of a tree) stressed in fig. 1, in which the basic problems related to the different roles of computers in school practice are also underlined.
The discussion about the aspects shown in fig.1 is strictly related to the framework in which it is set. In this paper we consider the introduction of some *elements of computer science* in the course of *mathematics* in the first two years of upper secondary school (*14-16 years*).
By the expression *elements of computer science* we intend a set of contents that may be reasonably taught at the school level under discussion, taking into account the available time (which we can estimate in about 40 hours per year, according to the results discussed in § 3).
The school level of the first two years of upper secondary school *(ages 14-16)* is characterized by pedagogical aims which focus on giving students a basic education and not yet a specialist one. It is our opinion that some elements of computer science have to be introduced as a part of this basic education.
There is, however, the problem of introducing such elements into a curriculum which is already quite full. On the grounds of our research experience in the field [1], [2], [3], we think that a solution which, when implemented, has a good chance of success, is to introduce computer science elements as a part of the *mathematics course*.
This way is, at present, the one adopted in Italy for school pupils aged 14-16. In fact, the new curricula for the first two years of upper secondary school, which are proposed by the Italian Ministry of Education (which are still under discussion) explicitly contemplate the introduction of computer science elements in the mathematics program. Moreover, since 1985, a national plan for in-service mathematics teacher training in computer science has been carried out, which has provided teachers with a minimum of knowledge in this discipline. In these training courses an algorithmic oriented approach has been followed and Pascal programming language has been mainly used. On the grounds of these initiatives, several *experimental courses*, officially supported by the Ministry of Education, have been carried out all over Italy in upper secondary schools, in which the introduction of computer science elements has been achieved inside the mathematics program.
It seems interesting to analyse *the orientations which emerge from these experimentations,* in relation to the problems involved with the introduction of computer science in the basic education, at the school level under consideration.
We base our analysis on the *results of a questionnaire* we designed especially for the mathematics teachers who have performed experimental courses concerning the introduction of computer science. Interviews with teachers helped us to enrich, in some cases, the information obtained.

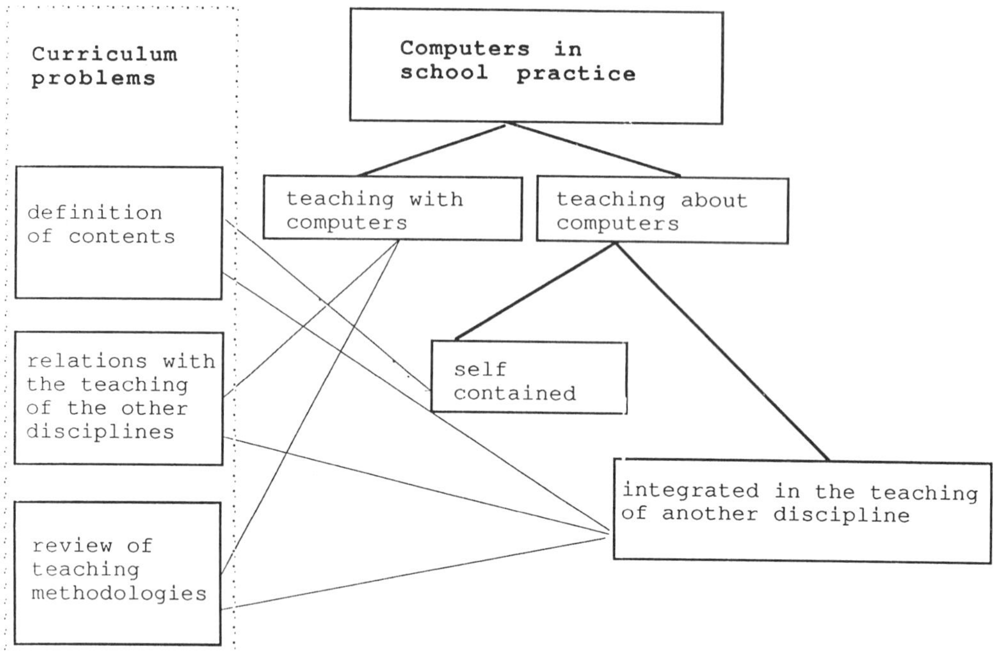

Fig.1: Computers in school and related curriculum problems
The lines relate the different orientations (nodes of the tree) followed in classroom to curriculum problems

2. COMPUTER SCIENCE AND MATHEMATICS: A CHANCE FOR NEW TEACHING PROGRAMS

The introduction of computer science inside the mathematics course is motivated by both cultural and pedagogical considerations.
The history of computers and computer science and the history of mathematics prove that *natural links* exist *between the two disciplines* [4]. Pascal's calculating machine was conceived for computing purposes, say for helping mathematicians to solve problems. Conversely mathematics offered the ground for the birth and the development of computer science. The links are emphasized both by the developments of outstanding researches in theoretical computer science and by the applications of computers in solving classes of mathematical problems.
Indeed at university level, the importance of mathematical contents present in computer science curricula is recognized (see for example [5], [6], [7]), and some mathematical subjects (algebra, numerical analysis, logics, etc.) are considered to be a necessary background in computer science education, thus providing their teaching of further motivations. This aspect is less influential in the design of the curricula for the school level which we are considering, because, at the ages in question, the development of these propaedeutic mathematical topics with a degree of depth suitable for illustrating the links between the two disciplines, is a difficult task which requires a great deal of time to the detriments of more suitable objectives for basic education.
The links of which we are more concerned in our work are those coming from the *affinity of certain methodologies and abilities peculiar of the two disciplines*. In fact the underlying educational objectives of the two disciplines, at the ages under consideration, are, for the greater part, similar: decoding problems, modelling of situations, use of correct and not ambiguous language, passage from natural languages to artificial languages (of mathematics and computer science). Some research works, see for example [8], show that this approach offers good educational opportunities.
The previous considerations suggest that it is possible to introduce computer science elements in the mathematics course, at the ages in question, without relevant additions in contents and radical substitutions. We note that this introduction offers not only the chance of approaching a new discipline and of reviewing mathematics concepts [9], but it also fosters a more critical view and a better mastery in the use of computing machines. So we can conclude that the previously recalled links, synthesized in fig.2, may be completed by the further link represented by the dashed line. This last aspect enriches the mutual educational opportunities between mathematics, computer science and the use of computers.

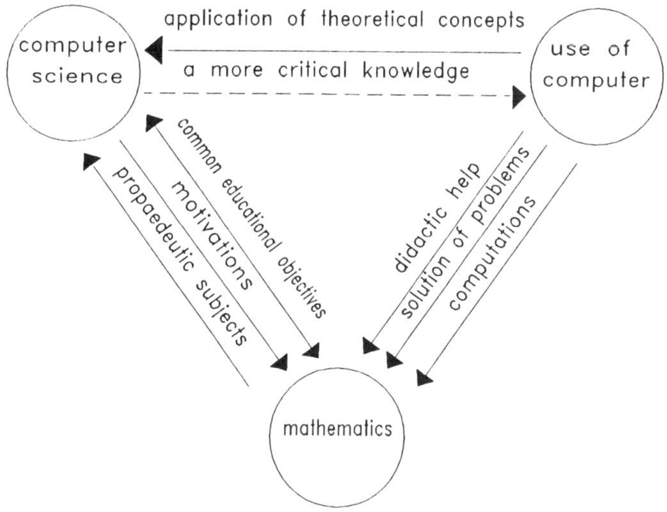

Fig. 2: illustration of the mutual educational opportunities among mathematics, computer science and the use of computers. Arrows show the opportunities given by a topic (indicated in the circle) to another one

3. COMPUTER SCIENCE IN SCHOOL PRACTICE

In the previous paragraphs we have discussed the opportunity of introducing computer science elements in basic upper secondary school education. In particular we consider the mathematics course as a good framework to perform this task.

The aim of this paragraph is to analyse how this introduction has been implemented in *school practice*. As we previously observed, in Italy, a number of experimental courses, fostered by the initiatives of the Ministry of Education, have been running for the last two years. They contemplate the introduction of computer science elements inside the mathematics programme in the first two years of upper secondary school. We carried out our analysis by means of a *questionnaire* addressed to those mathematics teachers developing these experimental courses in our region (approx. 120 teachers).

The sample of teachers is sufficiently wide to be considered significant with regard to school biases (humanistic, scientific, technical, professional, etc.), social context (from industrial town reality to provincial one) and teachers' characteristics (age, cultural background, etc.).

The questionnaire we have designed addresses both the teaching of computer science elements and the teaching of mathematics in the first two years of upper secondary school (age 14-16). In the following, we focus our attention on the results which are linked to the introduction of computer science, while the aspects specifically related to mathematics are more deeply considered in [10].

The analysis we have performed through the questionnaire was aimed at investigating the following elements, which we considered central to characterize the teachers working methods:

a. *time dedicated to the introduction of computer science in the mathematics course;*
b. *distribution of computer science contents during the year;*
c. *role of computer science laboratory (dedicated time, type of activity performed, tools used);*
d. *developed computer science contents;*
e. *approach followed;*
f. *type of evaluation performed;*
g. *role of computer science and of the use of computers in the teaching of mathematical topics.*

3.1 Results from the questionnaire

We obtained answers to the questionnaire from 79 teachers from all the schools considered (except 3).

a. 60% of teachers assign approximately 30% of the total number of hours per year of the mathematics course to the introduction of computer science. We can consider an average number of 120 hours associated with mathematics course in the first two years of upper secondary school, differences in this number depend on the kinds of subjects studied at the various schools.

b. The introduction to computer science is carried out throughout the year by 88% of teachers. The others concentrate this introduction in one or more periods of time. This result reflects not only an attitude in the practical organization of the work, but also gives a significant hint, confirmed by further aspects, on the teachers orientation as regards the relationship between the teaching of mathematics and computer science. As a matter of fact, teachers who prefer to concentrate computer science introduction, in general, develop it as self contained, without emphasizing an actual integration with mathematics.

c. 74% of teachers set aside more than a half of the time available for computer science to laboratory activities. The computer science laboratory is, in general, used to apply the concepts of computer science (81% of teachers) and mathematics (68% of teachers) discussed during the theory lessons (obviously the possible choices are not totally exclusive). During computer science laboratory work almost every teacher (90%) makes the students write programs directly. Some of them (45%) use available software: 36% didactic software, 18% spreadsheets, 18% word processors (not totally exclusive choices). The number of available computers in each school varies widely (range: from 3 to 55). In general, professional and technical secondary schools have a higher number of computers than other schools.

d. Figure 3 shows the results concerning the computer science contents which have been developed (in terms of a percentage of teachers who develop each topic in their experimental courses). The topics considered are mainly those indicated in the new mathematics programmes for the first two years of upper secondary school. It must be stressed that teachers are not requested to develop all the different proposed subjects, but to make a choice from them. We note, in fact, that in the situation we are considering teachers are allowed to assume a more active role than usual with regard to the building of didactic itineraries through the teaching programmes.

Since in the questionnaire we ask also to indicate the order in which the various topics are introduced and the time dedicated to them, we note that the results obtained indicate that the prevailing orientation is to follow the approach: problem decoding, algorithm design, programming. Programming, in particular, assumes a central role in the teaching aims. In fact, as it will be pointed out later, this is the only topic on which a learning evaluation is performed in all situations. On the one hand, this orientation seems justified, at the ages in question, by the teachers' wish to acquaint students with the operative aspects which are peculiar of the discipline. But, on the other hand, we think that, if this attitude will be emphasized too much, it can leave students with the illusion that coding in a particular language is computer science [11]. Moreover it must be stressed that in school practice there is a diffused habit of teaching fixed schemes for the resolution of a given category of problems. In this respect, solving problems can be reduced to the repetitive activity of dealing with "routine" exercises. Also programming, if considered without a critical attitude, can assume the role of the "old" routine exercises, for example, the exercises on literal computation in mathematics. With regard to the used programming language, we note that every teacher, with the exception of five, introduce Pascal as the first programming language (of the others: three introduce Basic, one Logo and one HP-11C programming language, with three of them introducing Pascal as the second language). Moreover Pascal is the first and only programming language which is introduced, at the ages in question, in 94% of the cases. This trend corresponds to the training courses, followed by every teacher who has answered the questionnaire. It may also be a sign that there is no effort towards interdisciplinary work among teachers. In this case the introduction of other programming languages can help the applications in different disciplines, see for example, [12].

Considering other computer science contents, we observe that a considerable number of teachers introduce elements of computer architecture, number systems and operating systems. We interpret this trend as a symptom of the worry they have of giving students some ideas (even if superficially) on the technological aspects of computer science. On the contrary, we observe that a small percentage of teachers develop contents such as data structure, automata, or elements of some other programming language. To interpret this fact it is necessary to take into account the limited image of the discipline teachers have had, in general, from the training courses.

topics	teachers'%
•*construction of algorithms*	94%
•*automata*	20%
•*structured programming*	82%
•*data structure*	38%
•*elements of a programming language*	100%
-*Pascal*	93%
-*Basic*	4%
-*Logo*	1%
-*Other (...HP-11C...)*	1%
•*syntax elements*	74%
•*semantics elements*	48%
•*elements of a command language*	46%
•*graphics elements*	29%
•*elements of computer architecture*	46%
•*number systems*	75%
•*numbers representation and approximate computation elements*	48%
•*elements of a high level programming language different to the one introduced as first*	4%
•*views on assembler type languages*	2%
•*other topics*	3%

Fig.3: Developed computer science topics in the first two years of upper secondary school and percentage of teachers who develop each of them

e. The analysis about the approach which has been followed to introduce computer science elements is based on some aspects which we considered particularly interesting, namely the way in which they introduce algorithms and the software tools used. With regard to the introduction to algorithms, we note that teachers usually use more than one representation with a preference (65%) for the employment of a design language (the other, not totally exclusive answers, are: flow charts 54%, G.N.S. diagrams 38%). These data are coherent with the programming language adopted and, in our opinion, are a symptom of the prevalent orientation towards programming. At the outset, the approach to algorithms is carried out by discussing both numerical and non numerical problems (i.e. problems related to everyday life: kitchen recipes, road routes, etc.). 33% of teachers only discuss non numerical problems. This percentage is high with respect to the ages of the students; indeed our impression, which is also confirmed from talks with teachers, is that the non numerical problems usually discussed are quite easy to resolve with words but that their operative automation is difficult. Thereafter, carrying out these topics can falsify the real problems which underline the subject.
72% of teachers do not feel that it is better to begin using available software to enable students to acquire a working knowledge of the computer. This result is consistent with that corresponding to the utilization of the computer science laboratory, where the majority of teachers try to make the students write programs directly and where less than an half of them use pre-programmed software. We also note that the teachers who answered the questionnaire have already had some training in the use of spreadsheets (Lotus) during the training courses.
38% of teachers think that students could benefit from a working knowledge of a pocket calculator before using a more powerful computer (one of them only uses programmable pocket calculators throughout the year).

f. An aspect which is carefully considered in the questionnaire is the way and the weight teachers give to the evaluation of the learning of computer science concepts. We feel that this is a significant sign of the actual importance that they attribute to the introduction of the subject. Nevertheless, in considering the following data, account must be taken of the fact that for many teachers this is the first time in which they have faced computer science as a teaching subject, so they proceed with care. 58% of teachers carry out qualitative assessments in computer science. The others carry out a quantitative evaluation by means of individual class work, oral tests and tests on the practical use of a computer. The evaluation is carried out on all the topics introduced by 57% of teachers. In the other cases, they only evaluate the writing of programs and tests on a computer.

g. The introduction to computer science for 67% of teachers means that they have given up or reduced the time dedicated to the development of some topics of the traditional mathematical programme (especially in the fields of literal computation and euclidean geometry).
Computer science is usually considered as a means to update mathematics teaching, though teachers have different, and often not clear, opinions in distinguishing contents which are affected by this renovation. Some teachers indicate topics such as logics, approximated computations, numerical sets; other teachers indicate concepts such as variables /constants, recursion, mathematical models; and some indicate methodologies such as problem analysis. We note that, in general, problem solving is the methodology mostly associated to both disciplines, but that there are many different opinions on how to develop it, for instance type of problems, discussion of the results (and related problems of approximation), degree of depth. Moreover, some teachers indicate topics such as statistics, probability and analytical geometry. These last topics give us the impression that they regard computer science as a service subject. Possibly, in some cases, the misleading idea of identifying computer science with the passive use of a computer persists.
A more widely discussion about the role of computer science in the teaching of mathematics can be found in [10].

4. CONCLUSIONS

This study addresses the general discussion about the teaching of computer science elements in basic upper secondary school education. We focus, in particular, on the way in which this teaching has been implemented in school practice by a sample of teachers.
The results of our investigation allow us to determine three main orientations in teaching which we have arranged according to some peculiar aspects which, in our opinion, characterize them, as follows:

• *Technological orientation*

(1) computer science is introduced as a self contained subject and mainly concentrated in one or more periods during the school year;
(2) a lot of laboratory work is dedicated to the use of computers, with an interest in applications such as word processors, graphics, etc.;
(3) emphasis is given on intuitive notions of computer architecture, operating systems, etc.;
(4) the evaluation of students' learning is qualitative.
The outlined pattern of behaviour seems to be the result of the wish to give some views on the practical utility of computers. For this reason, on the one hand, it can capture, from the start, the interest of the students, but, on the other hand it can lead to emphasize the

aspects which are more related to the computing environment. This approach is affected by changing technologies, and, in this sense, can be misleading for students.

• *Service-subject orientation*

(1) computer science is not introduced in concentrated periods of time, but it starts later in the school year;
(2) laboratory work is oriented to the use of educational software and to the writing of programs aimed at illustrating mathematical notions, and mainly to perform computations;
(3) applications are performed also in collaboration with teachers of other disciplines;
(4) the learning hierarchy of topics is focused more on mathematical difficulties than on computer science ones;
(5) the evaluation of students' learning is qualitative.

This orientation seems to be the result of the wish to update mathematics teaching through the use of computers. It is followed especially by professional and technical secondary schools teachers. We note that, even if the first two years of these schools are not, as the following years, oriented to give a specialist formation, teachers are probably influenced by the pressures which arrives them from the needs of the successive years.

• *Educational subject orientation*

(1) computer science is introduced throughout the year;
(2) laboratory work is mainly devoted to the applications of computer science concepts discussed during the theory lessons, possibly in the resolution of mathematics problems;
(3) the prevailing orientation is towards problem decoding, algorithm design, programming;
(4) emphasis is given on common methodologies and skills of computer science and mathematics;
(5) the evaluation of students' learning is quantitative.

The outlined pattern of behaviour seems to be the result of the wish to enlighten general underlying ideas of the discipline (even if the concepts are introduced at a quite intuitive level). Results of our investigation show that this is the orientation apparently followed by the majority of teachers.

We add a last remark which is linked to the pioneering situation in which our investigation is performed. As a matter of fact, aspects of increasing importance both in computer science and education research, such as declarative approach to programming and modelling of cognitive processes, we discussed for example in [11] and [13], did not emerge from our investigation.

REFERENCES

[1] Bottino, R.M., A course for secondary school teachers concerning the use of programmable calculators, Computer & Education, Vol.7, N.2, (1983), pp. 125-130.

[2] Bottino, R.M., Forcheri, P., Molfino, M.T., Computer science in new school culture, in: Alloway, B.S. and Mills, G.M. (eds), Aspects of Educational Technology XVIII (Kogan Page, London, 1985), pp. 87-91.

[3] Bottino, R.M., Forcheri, P., Furinghetti F., Molfino, M.T., An attempt to integrate mathematics and computer science in High School, in: Bowie, P. (ed.), Proceedings of the 38th CIEAEM's meeting, (The Cotswold Press Eynsham, Oxford, 1987) pp.115-120.

[4] Goldstine, H.H., The computer from Pascal to von Neumann (Princeton University Press, Princeton, 1972).

[5] Ralston, A, The first course in computer science needs a mathematical corequisite, Communications of ACM, Vol.27, N.10, (1984), pp. 1002-1005.

[6] Berztiss, A.T., A mathematically focused curriculum for computer science, Communications of ACM, Vol.30, N.5, (1987), pp. 356-365.

[7] Bradley, J., The role of mathematics in computer science curriculum, in: Papers of the 19th SIGSE Technical Symposium on Computer Science Education, (ACM-SIGSE 1988) pp.100-103.

[8] Soloway, E., Lochhead, J., Clement, J., Does computer programming enhance problem solving ability? Some positive evidence on algebra word problems, in: Seidel, R. (ed.), Computer literacy, (Academic Press, New York, 1982) pp.171-185.

[9] Howson, A.G., Kahane, P. (eds), The influence of Computers and Informatics on Mathematics and its Teaching (Cambridge University Press, Cambridge, 1986).

[10] Bottino, R.M. and Furinghetti, F., Computer science and mathematics education in upper secondary school (age 14-16)", to appear in: Proceedings of the 41st CIEAEM's meeting, (1989).

[11] Denning, P.J., Comer, D.E., Mulder, M.C., Turner, A.J., Young, P.R., Computing as a discipline, in Papers of the 19th SIGSE Technical Symposium on Computer science Education, (ACM-SIGSE, 1988) pp. 42-43.

[12] Bottino, R.M., Procedural and declarative languages: a discussion from an educational outlook, in: Proceedings of 6th Canadian Symposium on Instructional Technology, (1989), pp. 185-189.

[13] Bottino, R.M., Prolog experiences in classrooms: possibilities and problems - the PICO project, in: Nichol, J., Briggs, J. and Dean J. (eds), Prolog, children and students (Kogan Page, London, 1988) pp.84-90.

Computers in Education
A. McDougall and C. Dowling (Editors)
Elsevier Science Publishers B.V. (North-Holland)

INFORMATION TECHNOLOGY IN THE 5 TO 16 CURRICULUM - A CROSS CURRICULAR THEME

Walter BURKE

Southern Education and Library Board, 1 Markethill Road, ARMAGH, Northern Ireland, BT60 1NR

ABSTRACT: This paper discusses the proposal that Information Technology in the 5 to 16 curriculum should be a cross curricular theme and examines some of the implications of such an approach for schools and teachers.

1. BACKGROUND

In Northern Ireland (NI), compulsory schooling starts at age five when children attend primary school, At age 11, all children transfer to secondary or grammar school and must remain in full-time education until the age of 16. At 16 a child may continue in full-time education or leave to seek employment. For both the primary and secondary phases of education there are broad guidelines about what children should be taught and this normally culminates in children sitting General Certificate of Secondary Education (GCSE) examinations at age 16 in a number of subjects.

In line with education policy in the rest of the United Kingdom (UK) the NI Under Secretary of State for Education has proposed that all children should follow a common curriculum. This proposal for a draft order in council [1] describes the curriculum for 5 to 16 year olds as composed of six areas of study, namely: **English; Mathematics; Science and Technology; the Environment and Society; Creative and Expressive Studies; Language Studies in relation to schools which are Irish speaking, - and the third and fourth key stages in other schools, ie age 11 to 16.** In addition, six educational themes: **Information Technology, Education for Mutual Understanding, Cultural Heritage, Health Education, and in relation to the third and fourth key stages, Economic Awareness and Careers Education are proposed.** Thus, Information Technology (IT) is described as an educational theme or more commonly called a cross curricular theme.

In January 1989, the Under Secretary of State set up a working party for each of the six cross curricular themes with a report date at the end of April 1989. The IT Working Party (ITWP) reported [2] making recommendations on the appropriate content, delivery and assessment of IT.

The aim of this paper is to highlight the main points of the report and to examine the implications for schools and teachers.

2. INFORMATION TECHNOLOGY AS A CROSS CURRICULAR THEME

When the six educational themes named above were first proposed, it was generally agreed that this meant that none of these justified the status of a subject as did say Mathematics or English, or indeed Home Economics which appears in the Science and Technology area of study. Rather it was assumed that the content associated with an educational theme could be adequately delivered through various compulsory subjects. It should be noted that four of the prescribed areas of study have a number of associated subjects.

In the case of IT there was not universal agreement that it could be dealt with adequately and properly as a cross curricular theme. There are a number of reasons for disagreement. Historically, IT in schools had, particularly in the secondary phase, been a subject with a growing number of children entering for a formal examination at age 16. A community of Computer Studies teachers had been trained and their future employment would be in jeopardy if there was no longer a subject to teach. Also highlighted were two other major difficulties associated with IT as a cross curricular theme, namely, that non Computer Studies teachers had neither the confidence nor competence to include IT in their own subject discipline and that the organisation and management of resources in schools would need to be completely revised.

In the opposite lobby, there was a growing number of practitioners who felt that Computer Studies as a subject was inappropriate for many children in the 5 to 16 age range and probably more importantly that IT had a dual function in the curriculum. It is this dual function that on the one hand provides and justifies the case for IT as a cross curricular theme, but on the other creates a major difficulty. In Section 4, I propose to return to this issue.

The ITWP was asked to make recommendations on: the content and processes of Information Technology so as to ensure that all essential areas of learning experience and understanding were adequately covered; how the recommended content would be incorporated into the various compulsory subjects; ways by which the recommended content could be reinforced through the other curricular subjects. In addition, the group was asked to suggest how IT should be reflected in appropriate attainment targets within prescribed and other subjects and to recommend a basis for a coherent exploration of IT for all pupils between the ages 5 and 16. The recommendations of the group have at this time (September 1989) been passed to a number of subject working groups for consideration. The Under Secretary of State has advised that the IT report be circulated as widely as possible and invited comment up until 8th September 1989.

3. FRAMEWORK FOR INFORMATION TECHNOLOGY

A detailed framework for Information Technology was proposed which defines the knowledge, skills and understanding which all pupils are expected to acquire during their primary and secondary education. The framework is based on five strands or areas, namely: **Communication, Information Handling, Modelling, Measurement and Control, Evaluating the Impact of Information Technology.** Associated with each strand are expected learning outcomes and these are related to four key reporting stages: Key Stage 1, Age 8; Key Stage 2, Age 11; Key Stage 3, Age 14; Key Stage 4, Age 16.

The recommendations within the framework are summarised below:

3.1 Key Stage 1

Communication. Pupils should: be able to create and use pictures, phrases and words to communicate; know that text, pictures and sound can be produced and stored electronically. This to be delivered largely through English with contributions from Mathematics, Art, Music, History, Geography and Science.

Information Handling. Pupils should: be able to talk about the different forms which information can take and be able to use a variety of appropriate devices to enter information into a computer; be able to search a database for information using a single criterion. This to be delivered through Mathematics with potential contributions from English, Science, History, Geography and Art.

Modelling. Pupils should: be able to explore both simple and complex environments using direct commands. This to be delivered largely through Mathematics, with contributions from Technology and Design, and English.

Measurement and Control. Pupils should: be able to control a device using commands. This to be delivered largely through Technology and Design, with contributions from Mathematics and English.

Evaluating the Impact of Information Technology. Pupils should: be able to talk about their use of IT at home and in school, and co-operate with others when using IT. This to be delivered largely through English with a contribution from Home Economics.

3.2 Key Stage 2

Communication. Pupils should: be able to perform simple editing tasks in the creation of a piece of work; be able to create and present information, in the form of text, sound, and images, for a variety of audiences. This to be delivered mainly through English with contributions from Science, Technology and Design, History, Geography, Art, Music, Home Economics, and Religious Education.

Information Handling. Pupils should: be able to collect, classify and order information and design a structure within which the information may be held; be able to add information to a database and retrieve information using two criteria. This to be delivered through Mathematics, with contributions from Science, Technology and Design, English, History, Geography, and Home Economics.

Modelling. Pupils should: be able to use stored procedures to carry out a given task; be able to explore computer models and predict the effect of changing the rules in such models. This to be delivered through Mathematics with contributions from Technology and Design, English, Art, Music and Home Economics.

Measurement and Control. Pupils should: be able to use a computer to create a sequence of instructions to control a device and know from experience that devices can be controlled by computer. This to be delivered through Technology and Design, with contributions from Mathematics, Science, English and Home Economics.

Evaluating the Impact of Information Technology. Pupils should: be able to identify and talk about the uses of IT in the home, school and local community, and compare their experiences and judgment with others. This to be delivered through English, Technology and Design, Geography, with contributions from Home Economics and Religious Education.

3.3 Key Stage 3

Communication. Pupils should: be able to

choose and use a variety of IT tools for communication including electronic communication; be able to integrate text and graphics in communicating with wider audiences; understand how different forms of electronic communication impose limitations on presentation and content. This to be delivered through English and Art with contributions from Science, Technology and Design, History, Geography, Music, Home Economics, and Religious Education.

Information Handling. Pupils should: be able to establish the purpose for which information is required and the need for accuracy; be able to prepare data structures such as spreadsheets and databases and manipulate the information contained to investigate patterns and relationships; be able to identify tasks for which the use of IT-based information handling is appropriate, and cost effective; be able to use spreadsheets to manipulate mathematical functions. This to be delivered through Mathematics, Science, History, Geography, Home Economics, with contributions from English and Technology and Design.

Modelling. Pupils should: be able to create and use procedures; be able to construct models using procedures and understand the limitations of computer models. This to be delivered through Mathematics, Science, Home Economics, with contributions from English, Technology and Design, History, Geography, Art and Music.

Measurement and Control. Pupils should: be able to use a sensor to detect and measure changes in the physical environment; be able to construct procedures in order to make use of a number of sensors. This to be delivered through Technology and Design, Home Economics, with contributions from Mathematics, Science, Geography and Music.

Evaluating the Impact of Information Technology. Pupils should: be able to use their skills and experiences to make appropriate choices about the use of IT tools, including making comparisons between IT tools and other methods. This to be delivered through Technology and Design, with contributions from Mathematics, Science, English, History, Geography, Art and Home Economics.

3.4 Key Stage 4

Communication. Pupils should: be able to design and produce a presentation using a variety of audio-visual media including IT; be able to make use of a range of IT tools to refine the style, accuracy and presentation of ideas; be able to critically evaluate the impact which IT has had on communications at local, regional, national and international level. This to be delivered through English and Art, with contributions from Science, Technology and Design, History, Geography, Music, Home Economics, and Religious Education.

Information Handling. Pupils should: be able to present information in the form of tables, graphs, diagrams, and text; be able to design and create complex data structures and implement solutions to problems using appropriate database management software. This to be delivered through Mathematics, Science, Technology and Design, with contributions from English, History, Geography and Home Economics.

Modelling. Pupils should: be able to model complex situations including creating computer models; be able to collect relevant information from real experiments and use the information to investigate relationships between variables; understand the limitations of computer modelling. This to be delivered through Mathematics, Science, Technology and Design, with contributions from Geography, Music, and Home Economics.

Measurement and Control. Pupils should: be able to explain that the measurement of analogue quantities can be recorded as digital information and that this involves approximation; be able to construct a control system using sensing, monitoring, measuring and feedback mechanisms. This to be delivered through Science, Technology and Design, with contributions from Geography and Music.

Evaluating the Impact of Information Technology. Pupils should: be able to demonstrate a knowledge of a range of IT applications including IT in teaching/learning; be able to refer to the consequences (economic, moral, social, environmental) of IT applications. This to be delivered through Technology and Design, History, Geography, Religious Education with contributions from Mathematics, Science, English and Art.

The full recommendations are very detailed and are consistent with recent publications [3], [4], [5]. However, if implemented, these pose a number of fairly fundamental questions regarding IT in schools and the implications for teachers. In the next section, a number of these issues are elaborated upon, and some guidance is proposed on the resolution of some of the difficulties.

4. IMPLICATIONS FOR SCHOOLS AND TEACHERS

A number of the issues raised by IT as a cross curricular theme are appropriate to the other cross curricular themes. For example, how can a school ensure that there is breadth, depth and continuity, when the content is delivered through a range of subject areas and by a number of teachers? The answer to this question lies in the development of a well planned and co-ordinated whole curriculum.

Schools need to plan for continuity and progression at the following levels: the whole school; class/year group; individual group;

between schools in the same phase; between schools in different phases.

It is fairly well accepted in some schools that such curriculum planning is beneficial and essential and indeed some teachers have developed the appropriate expertise to carry out such activity. However, there are other issues which relate specifically to IT as a cross curricular theme, and where solutions are not readily available or perhaps not even acceptable.

4.1 Resources

The provision of an appropriate IT experience for all children is resource dependent, ie requires IT resources including computers and software, and a range of other electronic devices. Such provision is very patchy, with a few schools well provided for, but with most very much under resourced.

Even with a considerable increase in resource provision, there are organisation and management issues to be addressed in the short term.

Lack of resources has in the past meant that many teachers move computers around the school, sometimes on trolleys, which is both difficult and unsafe. Furthermore, where there are stairs and temporary classrooms, it is impossible. Rather than move computers around the school it is more appropriate to provide the teacher with a computer for a month/six weeks at a time. This has implications for when topics are taught and how they are taught.

4.2 Delivery and Assessment

Until now there has been no IT curriculum to follow, and this has allowed teachers to develop their own. These new recommendations not only require teachers to be competent to teach IT but to resist teaching some topics before the appropriate stage.

A profile component is proposed for IT which will require a child's IT competence to be extracted from a range of areas and aggregated. This raises questions of management, co-ordination, progression, and moderation, (both internally and externally). If IT is mainly about the process children go through, how is it possible to moderate when only the end-product is being examined?

The consultation document "The Way Forward" [6] described the proposed curriculum as consisting of prescribed areas of study and cross curricular themes. However, the Draft Order talks about prescribed areas of study and educational themes.

It is assumed that these educational themes will normally be taught on a cross curricular basis. The proposed legislation states:

ARTICLE 8 (1) "THE CURRICULUM OF A GRANT AIDED SCHOOL SHALL NOT, IN SO FAR AS IT RELATES TO PUPILS OF COMPULSORY SCHOOL AGE, BE TAKEN TO SATISFY THE REQUIREMENTS OF ARTICLE 4 (2) UNLESS IT PROMOTES, WHOLLY OR MAINLY THROUGH THE TEACHING OF THE CONTRIBUTORY SUBJECTS AND RELIGIOUS EDUCATION, THE ATTAINMENT OF THE OBJECTIVES OF THE FOLLOWING EDUCATIONAL THEMES, NAMELY, (A) INFORMATION TECHNOLOGY, (B) EDUCATION FOR MUTUAL UNDERSTANDING" etc.

Does this mean that an educational theme cannot be delivered and assessed through cross curricular activities? It will be very important that schools develop a policy for a consistent approach to the delivery of the educational themes. What is fairly clear even now is that these educational themes should not be delivered via timetabled modules - common practice in many secondary schools.

4.3 Quality of Learning

Information Technology has a dual function in the curriculum ie on the one hand there are skills, knowledge, and understanding that all children should have and on the other there is the contribution that IT can make to the quality of learning. These two functions are not necessarily compatible or indeed of equal weight particularly in the primary phase of education. The potential contribution of IT to the quality of learning has been promoted both in the IT report and numerous other documents. One of the problems of having to assess IT is that teachers will see it as a burden, something to be put out of the way once the assessment bit is finished. If this happens, then the real value of IT in the curriculum will be lost.

4.4 Training

The jargon of IT is intimidating for many teachers. What is meant by simple, complex environments? The translation exercise, ie the in-service training programme appears to be colossal! The training of teachers, both to develop their confidence and competence to use the technology and most importantly to know when IT can enhance and support other work in the classroom is a priority.

4.5 Computer Studies

One of the main arguments for a profile component in IT is that industry/commerce and the community generally wish to know how a child performs in this important area of the curriculum. This has been the strong argument for the development of Computer Studies as a subject. The proposed new curriculum has no 'room' for Computer Studies, it is not listed as a contributory subject. Many of the more academically orientated schools do not believe that IT as a cross curricular theme is a real substitute for a 'proper' study of computing. The ITWP passed this issue to the Technology and

Design Working Party (not yet established). Schools will have to decide if they can 'fit' Computer Studies on to the new curriculum and indeed if they have sufficient resources to support both IT as a cross curricular theme and Computer Studies.

5. CONCLUSIONS

It is generally accepted that it is necessary to define an appropriate 5 to 16 IT curriculum. What is not clear is how such a curriculum should be implemented. On the one hand, and since IT has particular benefits in supporting the teaching and learning in many subjects, a cross curricular approach appears very appropriate. On the other hand, experience of such an approach is fairly patchy with many teachers having difficulties coping with a resource which is unfamiliar. The other factor at this time is to what extent subject working parties are prepared to insist IT has a central role in the range of activities associated with the delivery of the subject. Much of the debate may be resolved when all the programmes of study have been published, however, some issues will only be resolved after the curriculum has been implemented, this will require about five years. The interesting fact about IT is that many changes take place in such a time period both in content and the skills needed to use the IT tools.

REFERENCES

[1] Proposal for a Draft Order in Council Under Paragraph 1 of Schedule 1 to the Northern Ireland Act 1974. Education Reform (Northern Ireland) Order (1989).

[2] Information Technology: A Cross Curricular Theme. Report of the Cross Curricular Working Group on Information Technology to the Under Secretary of State for Education (1989).

[3] Information Technology from 5 to 16. Curriculum Matters 15 Department of Education and Science (Her Majesty's Stationery Office) (1989).

[4] Government response to the ITAP report "Learning to live with IT" Department of Education and Science. (Her Majesty's Stationery Office) (1988).

[5] Design and Technology for Ages 5 to 16. Proposals of the Secretary of State for Education and Science and the Secretary of State for Wales. Department of Education and Science and the Welsh Office. (1989).

[6] Education Reform in Northern Ireland, "The Way Forward", Department of Education for Northern Ireland (1988).

APPENDIX

The subject working groups on English, Mathematics, and Science have each produced draft proposals. These proposals have at this time (January 1990) been sent to schools and other educational establishments for consultation and comment. Considerable interest has been shown in the draft documents for a number of reasons. English, Mathematics and Science have always been regarded as forming the core curriculum, both in the primary and secondary sectors. These are the only subject proposals published to date and hence most schools and teachers are keen to ascertain what the 'new curriculum' requirements are likely to mean for them.

All three working groups have addressed elements of the six cross curricular themes and in particular all identify the benefits that can accrue from the appropriate and effective use of Information Technology. However, different approaches have been taken, and this has created much concern amongst teachers.

This author comments on the three draft proposals as follows:

English

These proposals acknowledge the positive contribution that IT can make to the attainment of objectives in English. The report states that IT 'allows pupils control of the processes of composing, revising and presenting text, thereby illuminating the very nature of the writing process'.

However, it must be understood that this 'approach' does not appear to be reflected in the Programmes of Study[1], or in the Attainment Targets[2]. The ITWP have strongly argued that English should be the main subject through which the Communication strand of IT would be delivered. Unless, there is considerable revision of the proposals, doubts will remain as to the likelihood of children receiving a coherent and balanced IT education.

Mathematics

The Mathematics Working Group acknowledge that IT 'considerably enhances the processes of learning Mathematics' and 'envisages pupils making wide use of computers and other computer controlled devices'. These statements are developed well in the Programmes of Study, however, they do not sufficiently manifest themselves in the proposed Attainment Targets. This latter point raises a very fundamental question in relation to the legislation. What will be the statutory requirements relating to Programmes of Study and Attainment Targets and will schools and teachers be expected to demonstrate that the recommendations in both are covered? It is strongly recommended that the Mathematics Programme of Study should be mandatory for schools, otherwise, it will be difficult to ensure that teachers make appropriate and beneficial use of IT to enrich Mathematics learning. Furthermore, many aspects of IT will not be covered if only the Attainment Targets are obligatory.

Overall, the Mathematics Group has, as expected, addressed much of the relevant IT cross curricular theme material.

Science

The Science Working Group states that 'pupils should be able to use Information Technology appropriately and effectively to communicate and handle information in a variety of forms and for a variety of scientific purposes'.

It is proposed that a single separate Attainment Target be used to identify the appropriate elements of IT in Science. There are advantages and disadvantages in this approach. On the one hand, a separate Attainment Target allows freedom for Science teachers to identify the appropriate context for their use of elements of IT as scientific tools. On the other, because the IT elements are made so explicit, there is a real danger that the Attainment Targets would be addressed, or delivered independent of the scientific context. It will be essential that the latter does not happen, otherwise, the enrichment and enhancement of the Science curriculum will not materialise.

A feature of all three proposals is the recognition that schools need further Information Technology resources, and teachers will require considerable in-service training if the benefits of Education Reform are to materialise.

(FOOT) NOTES

[1] Programme of Study means the matters, skills and processes which are required to be taught to pupils of different abilities and maturities during each key stage.

[2] Attainment Target means the knowledge, skills and understanding which pupils of different abilities and maturities are expected to have by the end of each key stage.

Computers in Education
A. McDougall and C. Dowling (Editors)
Elsevier Science Publishers B.V. (North-Holland)

DESIGNING SOFTWARE FOR SECONDARY MATHEMATICS

Douglas BUTLER

Head of Mathematics, Oundle School, Peterbough, England, and Head of Software Development Panel, The Mathematics in Education and Industry Schools Project, England, Yorke House, 33 West Street, Oundle Peterborough, PE8 4EJ, England.

1. INTRODUCTION

Low-price computers for school mathematics have been with us for nearly 10 years now, and the first attempts to write software for them were ambitious and effective, but severely constrained by low memory.

This Paper reviews the design of a second generation of programs which has evolved from classroom use at Oundle School, England. They incorporate the use of *standard mathematical notation*, and greater ease of *data handling*. At the same time a range of numerical options raises the question of a new approach to the teaching of Calculus.

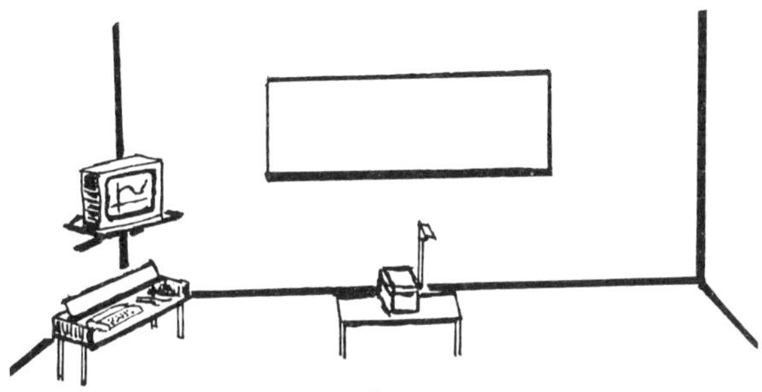

FIG.1

2. MATHEMATICS CLASSROOM COMPUTERS

At Oundle School, England, the need for one computer per mathematics classroom was established five years ago, and the program of purchases was completed last year. The computer is now seen by the teachers as an aid to instruction that is permanently available, rather like a calculator. The major use is to illustrate functions and graphs, so a single colour-TV screen in the corner has proved an adequate and cost-effective solution to the problem of visibility.

This, combined with a white writing board and an overhead projector, completes our 'teaching wall', as illustrated (FIG.1).

The prospect of such an arrangement becoming widespread is of course limited by costs, and it could be argued that the need will in time be replaced by the next generation of hand calculators. At present U.K. costs, one teaching computor per classroom costs about £800, whereas a single graphic calculator costs about £40.

The hand calculator is unlikely ever to match the computer display in terms of resolution and colour (see FIG.2).

3. CHOICE OF MEDIUM FOR A NEW SOFTWARE PACKAGE

Software written in the early 1980's was bold and creative, mostly written in BBC BASIC. It was inspired by the introduction of the BBC MICRO into British Schools. This computer had a tiny memory, however, and many of the programs had little claim to being 'user-friendly'.

The decision to write a new package (see list in APPENDIX A) for classroom use would not have

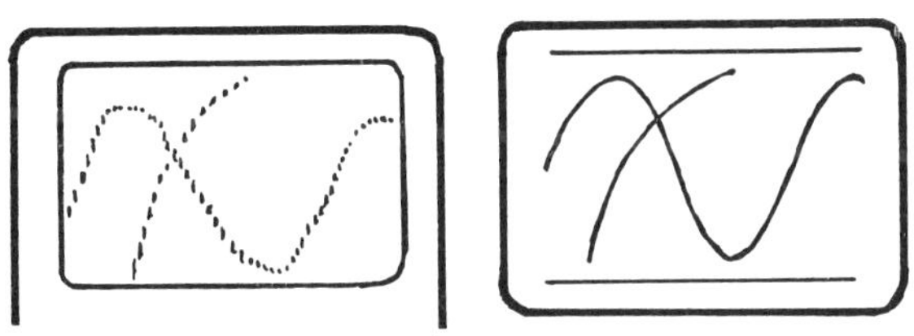

Graphics Calculator screen *Computer screen (colour)*

FIG.2

been taken if the number of man-hours involved had been known! However the following criteria were used as a basis to proceed in BBC BASIC rather than, say, 'C' or Turbo Pascal:

a. The BBC MICRO was being upgraded all the time and now comes with a 32-bit RISC processor (The 'Archimedes'). It is ideal for school mathematics use, offering affordable colour and high-resolution graphics. With the exception of Australasia the manufacturers, Acorn Computers, have had little success outside the U.K. where the IBM PC (or clone) is dominant. The PC offers a far less friendly environment for mathematics software, being predominantly a text-based machine, and there is a confusing multiplicity of graphics cards.

b. The popularity of BBC BASIC has led to successful emulations being written for other micros, including the IBM PC and Apple Mac. This gives rise to prospects of portability.

c. BBC BASIC is a sophisticated, structured BASIC which has been single-handedly responsible to the U.K. taking such a leading role in educational software. It has a wealth of graphics commands, most of which would have to be specially written in any other language.

d. Most importantly, BBC BASIC is one of the only BASIC languages to offer the 'EVAL' keyword, enabling any string of mathematical terms to be evaluated instantly (see FIG.3)

The difference between 'VAL' and 'EVAL'

Most BASICs offer only VAL:

eg: PRINT VAL("PI") will return 0 (zero)

but: PRINT EVAL("PI") will return 3.142...

In BBC BASIC more detailed mathematical expressions can be evaluated:

```
eg: X=PI
    Y=EVAL("2*SIN(3*X/2)∧3")
    PRINT X              will return -2
```

FIG.3

---

e. It is vital that students and teachers are not confronted with expressions in BASIC like the example in Fig.3 above, which would be hand-written as:

$$x = \pi\ ,\quad y = 2\sin^3(3x/2)$$

The first requirement was therefore to write an interpreter that would accept standard notation through the keyboard and convert it into BASIC. Again, the BBC MICRO proved to be a good choice with its ease of defining new characters, and new mathematical BASIC functions.

4. THE GRAPH PLOTTER

The cornerstone of the new package is a single program to perform all the plotting and graphical calculations that relate to school mathematics, from the simplest straight lines to advanced work on differential equations (See APPENDIX 'B').

Throughout its development students have been involved - both in the classroom, debating about the success of the new features and discussing the limitations of the methods involved, and offering programming help. The important procedure to translate true mathematical notation into BASIC was, for example, written by a pupil.

Conic entered implicitly. Eqns of asymptotes found in the Cursor Mode

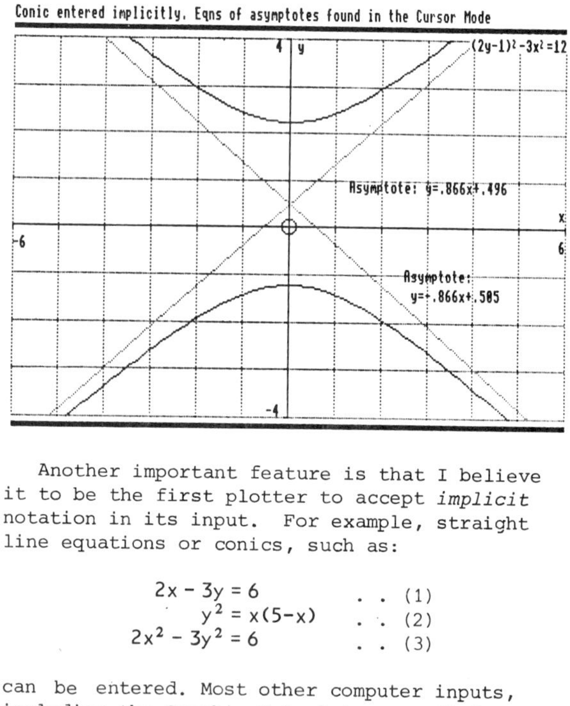

Another important feature is that I believe it to be the first plotter to accept *implicit* notation in its input. For example, straight line equations or conics, such as:

$$2x - 3y = 6 \qquad . . (1)$$

$$y^2 = x(5-x) \qquad . . (2)$$

$$2x^2 - 3y^2 = 6 \qquad . . (3)$$

can be entered. Most other computer inputs, including the Graphic Calculators, call for y = ... only, and in the case of Differential Equations y' = ...

Both 1st Order and 2nd Order Differential Equations can be studied without rearrangement, for example:

$$2y' - y = e^x \qquad . . (4)$$

$$3x'' - 2x' - x = e^{-t} \qquad . . (5)$$

In order to achieve this it has been necessary to 'teach' the computer several levels of algebra. The above equations (1) - (6) are first rearranged as y = ... and then converted into BASIC.

eg: (3) becomes $y = \pm\sqrt{((6 - 2x^2)/(-3))}$

then y = ±SQR((6 - 2*x∧2)/(-3))

(5) becomes $x'' = (e^{-t} - (-2x' - x))/(3)$

5. IMPACT OF NUMERICAL METHODS OPTIONS

The new M.E.I. Graph Plotter has also been programmed to undertake a wide variety of numerical methods, to the extent that all the operations in school level mathematics that require the use of Calculus can now be solved on screen: the list includes -

Solving equations — Areas and volumes
Solving intersections — Arc Length, Surf.Area
Maxima/minima problems — Mean Value, R.M.S.
Tangents, normals — Centroid, 2nd Moments
Fitting quadratics/cubics — Envelopes, Evolotes

If this list is taken with the ability to solve numerically any 1st or 2nd Order Differential Equation, it is surely time to reconsider the role of Calculus in the curriculum.

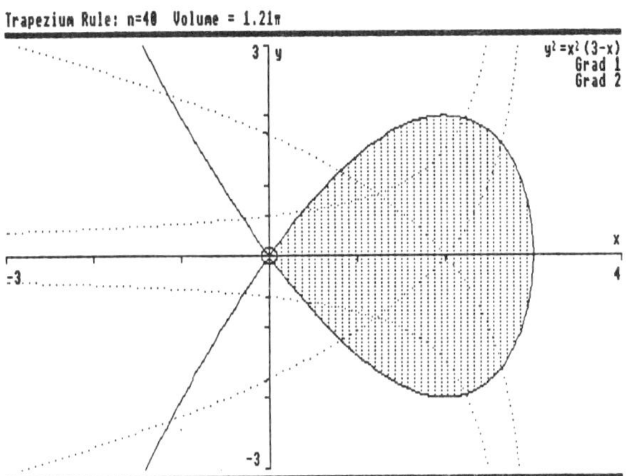

A facility like this can firstly be used to demonstrate graphically the *concepts* behind the Calculus, but then drill and practice routines that usually follow can give way to investigating solutions of equations that would normally be way beyond the capability of the pupils.

Furthermore, the move to learning more about mathematics through *modelling* can be accelerated. At present, a typical modelling situation may be readily understood, but it can present the pupil with an impossible differential equation to solve. With this plotter, not only can the equation be solved, but a variety of starting points can be tried. The problem can be analysed to a far greater extent than before.

Graphical solution sets to 2nd Order Differential Equations can be used to investigate problems concerning oscillations, or motion under gravity. In the latter case, simply enter x" = -9.81 (plotting x against t), and observe solution sets for different starting values of x and x' (velocity).

6. PURE MATHEMATICS PROGRAMS

The programs in this section (see details in APPENDIX 'D') illustrate graphically various aspects of the pure mathematics curriculum.

For example the solutions to simultaneous equations, quadratics and cubics are all accompanied by graphs (drawn automatically), to help enhance the link between the algebraic and graphical concepts that are at the heart of a firm understanding of these topics.

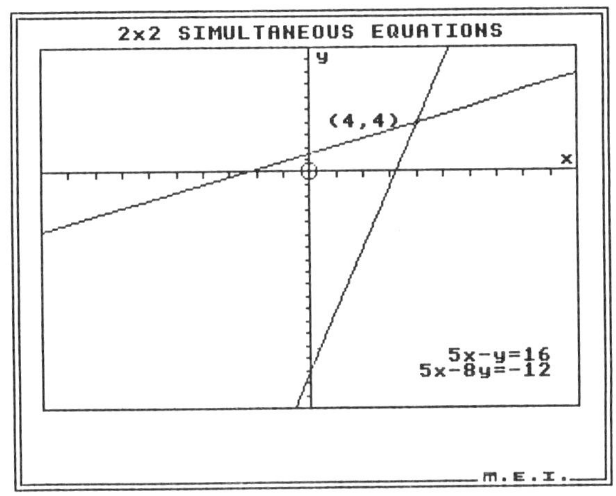

Many of these programs have been used successfully both in a teaching environment and by students in a 'laboratory' of computers. For example their understanding of the Maclaurin Series is considerably enhanced through a personaly exploration of the expansions on the screen.

7. STATISTICS AND DATA HANDLING

Here the approach is to make data entry, saving and loading files, and all aspects of data handling as simple as possible.

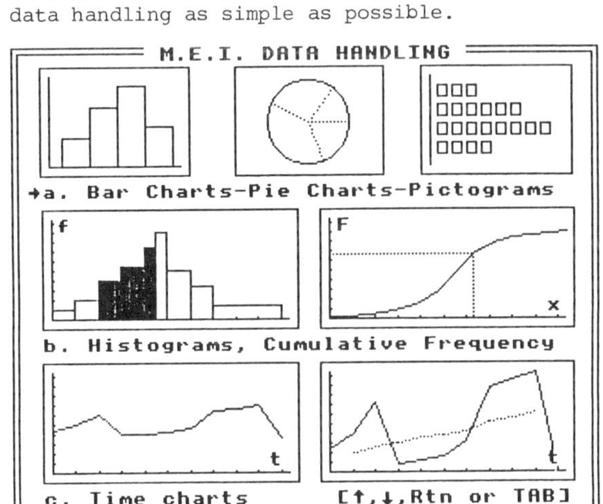

Again, fundamental statistical concepts can be explored on screen by varying parameters. With an increase in the teaching of statistics in schools and the accompanying growth in project work, these programs offer a quick method for pupils to enter data and investigate the results. (See further details in APPENDIX 'D').

8. IN-SERVICE TRAINING

Persuading colleagues to use the new technology and software is a long process, and they need a gentle introduction. In particular they need to feel confident that they will not be upstaged by more confident pupils!

Regular departmental meetings to compare applications are recommended, and where possible colleagues should sit in each others' lessons.

9. CONCLUSION

Computer usage in mathematics departments is still low. Many schools may well have computer 'suites' but they are rarely used for mathematics. The case for computers to be installed in the maths classrooms is strongly supported by our experience at Oundle School.

Teachers can use graphics to demonstrate new concepts, and pupils now have the freedom to solve a variety of problems on the screen. At the end of their courses the pupils will quite simply have 'seen' so much more mathematics than those who have not had this exposure.

It is to be hope that this package, the first major package to be written within a school department, will help a number of mathematics departments to take up the battle for funds to equip each of their classrooms. Funds can come from a variety of sources once the need has been established, notably Government Departments. It may however be time for the manufacturers to turn their attention from Information Technology to Mathematics - their machines are ideally suited to the subject, but rarely promoted as such.

Polar, Parametric and Cartesian

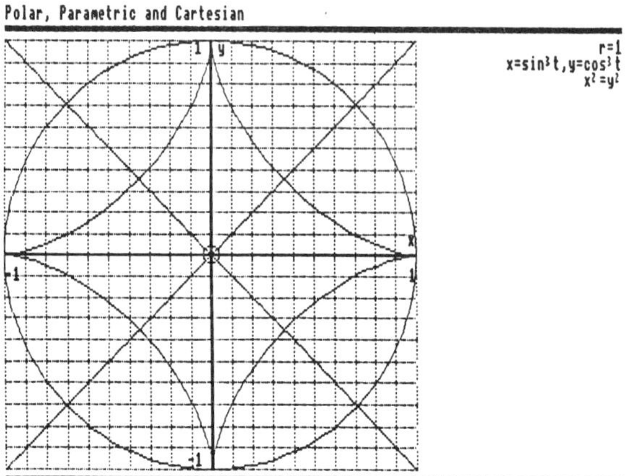

APPENDIX-A: LIST OF PROGRAMS (single disc)

M.E.I. 21 Programs for Mathematical Computing

(*) GRAPH PLOTTER

10 PURE MATHEMATICS PROGRAMS

	1. ALGEBRA	6. MATRICES
	2. TRIGONOMETRY	7. TRANSFORMATIONS
	3. GEOMETRIC SERIES	8. BASES (Binary/Hex)
	4. MACLAURIN SERIES	9. COMBINATIONS
(*)	5. VARIATION	0. CIRCLE

5 STATISTICS PROGRAMS

(*) 1. HANDLING DATA (Pie Charts to Histograms)
(*) 2. HANDLING BIVARIATE DATA
(*) 3. BINOMIAL, Poisson and Normal
4. 2-DICE Simulation
5. CENTRAL LIMIT THEOREM

5 MISCELLANEOUS PROGRAMS

(*) 1. TABLES (Mental arithmetic entertainment)
2. ALLMODES (Investigation of BBC modes)
3. ALPHA (typing timing)
(*) 4. GRID (a game of racing vectors)
5. CROSSFIRE (math. landscape shoor-out)

(*) Programs with associated Data files

APPENDIX-B: SUMMARY OF INPUT NOTATION

As far as possible, equations are entered into the GRAPH PLOTTER using standard mathematical notation, including the superscripts -1, 2 to 7, and powers of x and -x.

TRIGONOMETRY:

sinx, cosx, tanx, cosecx, secx, cotx
$\sin^{-1}x$, $\cos^{-1}x$, $\tan^{-1}x$, $\mathrm{cosec}^{-1}x$, $\sec^{-1}x$, $\cot^{-1}x$
also: arcsinx, etc.

HYPERBOLICS:

sinhx, coshx, tanhx, cosechx, sechx, cothx
$\sinh^{-1}x$, $\cosh^{-1}x$, $\tanh^{-1}x$, $\mathrm{cosech}^{-1}x$, etc
also: arsinhx, etc.

OTHER:

e^x	lnx	logx	$\lvert x\rvert$	intx	sgnx	%
E (10^)	!	nCr	nPr	rnd	div	mod

The Calculator feature also accepts this notation, so it is possible to enter in and evaluate expressions such as:

$$23 \sin^2(3\pi/5) - \arctan(1/e)$$

Computers in Education
A. McDougall and C. Dowling (Editors)
Elsevier Science Publishers B.V. (North-Holland)

A COMPUTER PROGRAM TO ENHANCE THE RECOGNITION AND PRODUCTION SKILLS OF NATIVE AND SECOND LANGUAGE LEARNERS OF CHINESE AND JAPANESE

Eric Chappell

Griffith University, Nathan, Queensland, Australia 4111

This paper describes the development of a product designed to teach the writing of Chinese and Japanese on an IBM[1] PC/XT, PC/AT, or 386 compatible computer. The pedagogical principles upon which the product is based, as well as the language learning principles incorporated into the program structure are also detailed. The product is described as it relates to the demands of learning characters and how it offers learners possibilities which could not exist without the computer.

1. INTRODUCTION

The product called JIEJING[2], translated into English it means Shortcut, was designed to give people easy and quick access to accurate machine written Chinese and Japanese characters. The principles of this program simplify the process for learners while they develop necessary usable skills.

This paper will describe:

a) the pedagogical principles upon which it was designed;
b) the linguistic principles of the product;
c) characteristics of the product;
d) the operation of the product;

2. A PROGRAM TO HELP CHARACTER WRITING

Within Chinese speaking countries and Japan, the difficulty of mastering the writing of characters has long been recognised. The evolution of the characters themselves has been strongly influenced by such difficulty. In recent times, the recognition that modern society demands a large literate population has prompted wholesale simplification of the characters. It was felt that this would provide greater access to literacy in Chinese and Japanese.

The Japanese have attempted to simplify the kanji by issuing a standardized approved list in order to reduce the total number of kanji. They have also introduced simplifications of some of the characters. In the Japanese school system kanji are introduced in ever increasing numbers as children master the hiragana and katakana syllabaries.

Western countries take for granted the use of machine written language. It is not common place in countries using Chinese and Japanese. This is in large measure due to the fact that the principle of the typewriter is not well suited to non-alphabetic languages. The logic inherent in traditional systems has required a clearly defined set. Thus the transfer to computer has been slow as well. For example, Taiwan which is a major producer of computer technology, has very low market penetration of that same technology.

As a number of western countries begin to increase their contact with countries using these languages many students are faced with the task of learning these characters. Learning to write a large number of Chinese and Japanese characters can be a daunting task.

Traditionally the problem is met through teaching pictographic mnemonics, through associations and above all through long hours of practice. Unfortunately, the majority of people who attempt the task through this combination of methods achieve limited success. JIEJING addresses this difficulty directly.

3. BACKGROUND ON LEARNING CHARACTERS

The written Chinese language has some fascinating characteristics. It is visually complex and displays a wondrous diversity of forms. The construction of characters makes use of picture based symbols, sound components, and classifiers. The beauty of the form plays an important role in oriental art. While aesthetically pleasing the complexity of the written characters is difficult for both native and non-native language learners.

Within The Peoples' Republic of China there have been several attempts to help students improve their rate of learning to write; one system emphasises extensive writing drills; another system has experimented with teaching students alphabetic representations of the sounds.

In learning Chinese as a second language and Japanese as a second language, and this is consistent with the teaching programs used in Australian schools, students are trained in English letter approximations of the sound equivalents. There are several problems with this approach:

1) The sound approximations are already English for the students so they cannot accurately represent oriental sounds;
2) there is always a sense that one is not learning what is really used;
3) many memory cues, which at first glance give the learner a sense of progress, become an encumbrance to further success in the language.

Beginning with alphabetic representation with the second language learner does enhance language skills in the short term, however it does not often lead to mastery of reading or writing. Interpreting a picture is different from interpreting a letter of the alphabet; it is a cognitive operation of another order. The complexity of the problem often overwhelms the individual who attempts to learn Chinese or Japanese characters. The result of this approach is that many accomplished second language speakers are unable to recognise even simple, necessary signs in the language. Many language teaching programs attempt to augment this shortfall through various methods of exposing students to the most common written characters .

In language learning, we know that the most efficient way for students to learn a language is for that language to be real and for it to serve communicative ends. The problem with learning an English transcription for Chinese or Japanese is that it is simply not a part of the language. A brief trip to Chinatown or a Japanese restaurant will be disconcerting. What you are learning at class is not related to those beautiful drawings. Language learning is most efficient when the task is stimulating and real. Language learners learn best when the context, situation and content are authentic. In China people read and write in Chinese; they use complex characters. In Japanese, one uses hiragana, katakana and kanji. To learn these languages one must learn to read and write in these forms.

There are a host of challenges when learning to write Chinese and Japanese characters. The effort and investment of time required to master a large number of characters discourages many and reduces one's confidence to use the written language. There is the difficulty of learning to recognise and produce the shapes of the strokes. Another level of difficulty is encountered when attempting to put these together in a recognisable composition. Because it is ideographic and characters are composed within an imaginary box, the sense of proportion is crucial to being able to read what has been written.

JIEJING is designed to help students meet these numerous demands.

4. DESIGN OF JIEJING

While the information and programming which make up the program are complex, the guiding design principles have been derived from pedagogy not from technical theory. That is to say that the design stems from theories grounded in language teaching and language learning. The technology has been adapted to theories of learning rather than the reverse.

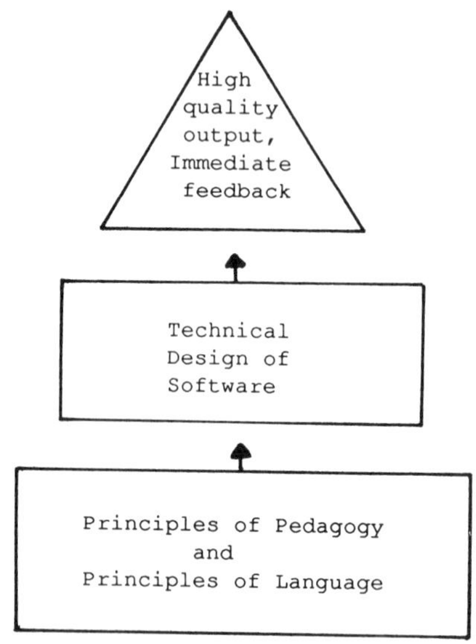

Figure 1

4.1. Pedagogical principles

The development was organised around the following concerns;

1) that the work which is produced must be real, it should not be simplified or made as a stepping stone towards the real thing. Producing written work should immediately be readable and recognisable.

2) use of the product should provide immediate feedback and lead to immediate success. When you constantly feel a sense of progress it is fun and you are more likely to continue.

3) the program should develop real skills. As learners use the program they should establish habits and knowledge which do not need to be corrected as they increase their mastery of the language;

these are the skills which native writers employ.

4) that the product offer support for a variety of cognitive learning styles; learners often employ different strategies on the same task; also different learners employ different learning strategies.

5) that the computer should be used to enhance the learning opportunities and the learning environment in ways beyond the abilities of a single teacher; the teacher will be able maximise strengths in areas in which she or he is best suited.

4.2. Linguistic Principles

The above pedagogical principles were applied to the following information which was developed from existing data and from specifically designed research projects. The following aspects were undertaken:

a) analysed components of known characters;
b) analysed according to common usage;
c) examined writing styles;
d) examined systems used to teach reading and writing of Chinese and Japanese; e) developed a theory of character recognition;
f) developed a structure of character interpretation;
g) semantic relationships between characters were identified;
h) the relationship of semantic cues within characters was analysed with regard to custom and personal writing habits.

In order to best reinforce recognition skills, each character has been hand drawn to clearly show the correct stroke within the finished character. The strokes are clearly visible on on-screen displays and printouts.

This research established the need to isolate and describe parameters involved in recognition versus production of Chinese and Japanese characters. The difficulty of learning the characters in terms of recognition included the following components: a) the ability to recognize the distinctive features of characters; b) the ability to associate the characters into word units; and the ability to remember a large number of characters.

In order to best reinforce recognition skills, each character has been hand drawn to clearly show the correct stroke in the character. On-screen displays and print outs clearly show these strokes.[3]

Difficulties in producing characters relates to: a) learning the types of strokes and the correct order of strokes; b) the placement of strokes relative to other strokes; and c) the correct proportional writing of strokes to create a readable total character.

The computer program had to be written to incorporate all of these variables into an executable form. Each of the above components was defined within a logical structure and then incorporated into a program unit. It was important that each variable be recalculated at each instant the user made some input. The overall design took its direction from the pedagogical principles mentioned earlier.

With the basic structure thus determined, the pedagogical principles also demanded that various learner strategies be supported, thus enabling diverse avenues to rapid success. The guiding belief here was that users apply different strategies at different times. Also different users employ different strategies based on divergent cognitive learning styles. All strategies share the aim of producing the correct character. Therefore the following components were built into the program structure as ways of helping the correct production of the character:

a) visual cues which are both distinctive and generative;
b) semantic cues within characters;
c) the semantic relationship of characters to words;
d) mnemonic help through consistent displays according to semantic components, stroke and order components. This works towards increasing the accuracy of educated guessing.
f) creating a visual track which is available at all times and which is based on the input from the user.
g) access to stroke review and display.
h) ability to create personal lists with strokes printed.

The approach to stroke use, stroke order and the relationship of strokes to the character was derived from resources on the teaching of Chinese and Japanese writing. The resources covered teaching programs of both native and second language courses. The basic structure of the program was designed to incorporate these into directly executing commands. It was then extensively field tested by native speakers from Taiwan, Hong Kong and the Peoples Republic of China.

Examination of the writing and reading process used by native speakers helped to isolate the appropriate semantic and mnemonic cues. Here the emphasis was on internal components of characters and/or word relations as they relate to meaning.

It was important to establish what native speakers do, so second language students could be developing those same skills as they go about using JIEJING.

The program provides students a visual track related to each stroke and the five most common characters which contain the order and combination thus far typed. As each stroke is deleted, the display is immediately updated. Students learn the stroke shapes and stroke orders associated with common parts of characters. Thus students learn strokes as they are distinctive to isolating meaning <u>within</u> characters.

The program was also designed to deal with the second essential cue which native speakers used; that was identification of meaning units greater than one character. JIEJING provides a second display area which calculates the likelihood of a particular character going with the preceding character or characters. The display is arranged according to the shape as it relates to meaning. The program was designed to produce characters in this area by calculating frequency of use, fundamentals of syntax, and semantic relationships. To remain true to the native speakers knowledge, this is cued by the correct stroke and correct stroke order.

Thus the program encourages students to use a number of strategies to make increasingly accurate guesses when producing characters.

When learning to write Chinese, the recognition of characters involves focusing on many strokes which create an ideographic symbol of the intended meaning. Recognition and production of characters is further related to the ability of the learner to focus on the relative proportion and relationship between strokes within a defined space.

JIEJING always produces correctly made strokes within the characters. In recognition this means that students always see correct characters. As learners type they are developing the ability to distinguish variations in strokes, and how this influences meaning.

In writing, the problem of correct proportion is complicated by the need to produce the marks correctly. That is, one must be able to remember and then produce (write) the strokes correctly, in order and in correct proportion. For the learner, this requires accuracy of thought, recognition, memory and production skills all at once. This often overwhelms the learner and failure at first is common. The computer program separates these skills and thus aids learners so they experience success as they develop a command of all of the skills.

JIEJING separates this problem into distinct areas: character recognition and character production. While the program structure required this distinction, using the program develops skills necessary in both, so that individuals can produce characters immediately.

a) Character Recognition

Characters are always displayed as correctly produced perfectly formed characters. The relative length and shape of strokes within characters is always correct.

In terms of stroke order and stroke shape, the program is built upon the basic rules used the world over for the writing of characters; priority of top to bottom and left to right. This program utilises ten strokes types. Each is readily recognizeable. The basic principle is to use the computer in the same way as you would a pen or a brush, writing each character from a series of strokes.

The program gives immediate feedback from every stroke as it is entered. Thus the notion of stroke and order are integrally related. The use of the backspace key to remove the last stroke makes it easy to see the effect of employing various strokes.

b) Production of characters

In writing, besides having to know the correct stroke and stroke order, the accuracy of strokes in terms of length, slope, formation and thickness is crucial. Stroke styles often signal a variation in meaning. Learners often have difficulty accurately manipulating each variable for each stroke. The program only allows correct strokes so the student cannot distort the completed character. Every character produced is an accurate real character. It can be read.

In the production of words, the computer uses algorithms to decide the likely combination of characters. The program structure is based on usage, syntax and meaning. These appear automatically based on the stroke and stroke order of the following character. Thus JIEJING offers a method to test the semantic relationship of characters based on the first stroke of a character which follows another. JIEJING has over 12,000 relationships incorporated into its structure.

This computer program will place at the learner's disposal a range of information which can impact his or her learning which no single person can ever hold. That is, several modes of learning will be readily available at all times. Access to more information than available in a common dictionary is immediate.

The skills learned through using the program are the same skills as those required in reading and writing Chinese. The system is structured to work toward the successful production and recognition of characters and words.

As learners apply strategies to achieve the desired output, they are learning how to write Chinese and Japanese characters. The program has incorporated the various strategies into executable commands. In short, the above program works to cue the cognitive system of learners in as many areas as possible, on a fully consistent basis.

5. USING JIEJING

You must first acquaint yourself with the ten keys which have the stroke types printed on them. These are printed on stickers which can be placed on your keyboard.

W = ㇚ E = ㇏ R = ㇐ U = ㇔ I = ㇕ 0 = ㇈

D = ㇀ F = ㇑ J = ㇒ K = ㇗

Start JIEJING by typing JJ, then open a file. Once you are in a file you must decide which language you wish to work in and what you would like to type. The following will apply.

ENGLISH - Toggle with Scroll Lock

CHINESE TRADITIONAL - Toggle with Caps Lock
CHINESE SIMPLIFIED - Toggle with Caps Lock

JAPANESE - Toggle with Shift+ TAB (Hiragana)
- Toggle kanji with TAB
- Toggle Katakana with Caps Lock

The system of stroke entry and placing characters on the screen is fully consistent across both Chinese writing systems, Kanji, Hiragana and katakana.

When you press the first stroke five characters will appear at the bottom right of the screen. The one in the middle has the highest frequency of occurrence and those on each side are the next highest.

All five characters begin with the stroke you typed. As you press more stroke keys the five characters will change. Again these are ranked according to the stroke chosen, the order in which the strokes are typed, and frequency of use. The strokes you have pressed are displayed in the bottom left of the screen.

The following example is from traditional Chinese. The same process would be true in each of the other languages although the characters will be different.

Press the stroke on the "j" key. You will see the following five characters.

會公人我分

Now press the "r" key and the "w" key which represent other strokes. This will give you the following display on the bottom line of your screen.

㇒㇐㇚ 我鵝

Only two characters remain as these are the only two with this stroke combination. As you add more strokes there will only be the single character you are after left on the screen. You will notice that the line cursor is under one of the characters. You can place any character into your text by moving the cursor under it and pressing the space bar.

Since the cursor is under the character we want, press the space bar. Now press the j key to begin the next character. You will notice that besides the five characters on the bottom right of the screen, another box in the center of the bottom line has appeared. This is the word and syntax box. From the character on the screen JIEJING has calculated the characters with which it is often associated to form a meaning or syntax grouping. This display is also arranged according to frequency of use.

㇒㇐㇚ 等們的 會公人我分

The calculation in this box is cued from the first stroke of the character which follows the one you have placed into your text. It will continually be re-calculated as you enter or delete strokes.

You will see that only three characters form such a pair with the word you have already put into your text and which begin with this stroke. Press the space bar and place the character into your text.

In JIEJING you always have the option to place any character in either of the display boxes into your text or to continue typing.

The boxes in both the word display and the character display react immediately to every stroke, so you can use the backspace key to see how different strokes and different stroke orders produce different sets of characters. This also gives you an instant display of the different words which will be created.

JIEJING is very efficient when bringing characters to the screen. While many characters in both Chinese and Japanese have 18 or more strokes, simply using the 10 stroke keys will uniquely identify characters long before you have typed all of the strokes. On individual strokes characters will be unique on an average of less than 4 strokes. Using the word and grammar box, the average to bring up Chinese characters and kanji is 2.7 strokes. This is much less than the average for typing words in English.

Typing in hiragana and katakana uses this same system of strokes. You type the strokes which you learn in order to write each character. When you are typing you are reinforcing the correct writing technique for each syllable. As you enter the strokes, the syllables are presented in the character box at the bottom right of the screen. Fewer strokes are needed for hiragana and katakana than the kanji as they are both comparatively very small sets. In Japanese, as with Chinese, typing is quick and can be accomplished without looking at the keyboard or the screen. The 10 key strokes, when typed in the correct order, will uniquely identify the characters. This means that when you have typed the character correctly you can be confident that when you press the space bar, the correct character will be placed into your text. You do not have to scan the screen to select from a group the character you want. It is easy to mix hiragana, kanji and katakana. Simply press the toggle and continue to use the same 10 key strokes.

6. CONCLUSION

Learners will experience immediate success. The strategies learned through using the computer will be the SAME strategies which are used by native writers and readers of Chinese and Japanese. The program will accomplish a pedagogic role which cannot be accomplished by an individual teacher. Teachers can devote their time to other aspects of language teaching. JIEJING can easily be incorporated into existing Chinese Language curriculum for both first and second language learners. It will readily complement the programs which are in use at the moment.

This product clearly demonstrates that the cueing system of native writers of chinese can be accurately defined and can be translated to work on a personal computer. This computer technology incorporates visual cues, semantic aids, and mnemonic cues, to build recognition and production strategies in students learning to read and write Chinese and Japanese.

The structure of JIEJING rests soundly on language learning principles and the strategies used by native speakers of Chinese and Japanese. A statement of the success to which it has succeeded in doing this, is the use JIEJING has found by native users. Native writers of Chinese and Japanese are quickly adopting it as their own word-processor. The typing rules are simple; they already know the rules for strokes and stroke orders. JIEJING has given the Chinese and the Japanese the first true touch typing system in the world.

7. HARDWARE SPECIFICATIONS

IBM PC/XT, PC/AT, or 386 compatible (640K recommended); operating system required: MS-DOS 3.0+, PC-Dos 3.0+, DR-DOS, Concurrent DOS or equivalent to support MS-DOS 3.0 or above.

JIEJING comes with a floppy disk, PC board, and manuals. It will run on dual floppies; hard-drive recommended.

It uses a standard IBM keyboard. Colour screens support auto detect type, EGA or VGA; monochrome uses a hercules graphics or equivalent.

NOTES

[1] IBM PC, PC/XT, PC/AT, VGA, EGA are the registered Trademarks of International Business Machines.

[2] JIEJING is the registered trade mark of JIEJING Australia PTY. LTD.

[3] Following is an example of the print in each of the languages.

Traditional Chinese:

我們很少想到自己擁有什麼、
卻總是想著自己欠缺什麼。

Simplified Chinese:

我们很少想到自己拥有什么、
却总是想著自己欠缺什么。

Japanese:

あの日本の本は何返ですか。
つぎの上いは何時何分ですか。

[4] MS-DOS is the Trademark of Microsoft Corporation; DR-DOS and CONCURRENT are the trademarks of Digital Research, Inc.; Hercules is the Trademark of Hercules Computer Technology, Inc.

Computers in Education
A. McDougall and C. Dowling (Editors)
Elsevier Science Publishers B.V. (North-Holland)
IFIP, 1990

THE G.E.R.EX. METHOD TO COMBAT SCHOOL FAILURE

François CHIRIVELLA, Danièle VALENTIN

Education, Youth and Sports Ministery, Department of secondary schools (D.L.C. 15), 107 rue de Grenelle 75007 PARIS FRANCE.

G.E.R.Ex. is a distinctive system to bring up students to a standard ; this system, built by a group of teachers, is used in eight hundred technical schools, for students at the beginning of their technical training. Using the computer as a medium facilitates the setting up of a differentiated teaching method.

1. INTRODUCTION

G.E.R.Ex. is a system built and developed by a group of teachers to bring students up to standard. It started as an experiment in continuous assessment and was later extended to more and more schools. Now it is used in about eight hundred technical schools and in one hundred secondary schools for students starting technical training.

A national and regional framework allows the coordination of training sessions for teachers, the drawing of conclusions from field experiments, the setting up of procedures to assess the students and of system evaluation.

The main goals of this system are to allow the largest number of students to reach the level required to start studying for a qualification and to stimulate students to acquire knowledge and techniques themselves, to take responsability, to make a personal effort and to learn self-evaluation.

G.E.R.Ex. includes three successive stages :

- The diagnosis stage during the first month of school year.

- The training stage (of two hours a week during the rest of the year).

- The evaluation stage which takes

2. THE SYSTEM COMPONENTS

2.1. The Diagnosis Procedures

- **A collection of 56 tests called "*LABYRINTHE*"** allows the evaluation of the students' knowledge during the initial stage of the course.
Each test is described by using the three-dimensional model invented by GUILFORD, i. e. each situation combines "operations","knowledge" and "products", and is characterized by one or more "skills". One particular "skill" can appear within different tests, that allow interrelated networks to be built which are used to analyse the students' work. The tests are designed according to students' knowledge and pre-requisites. The methodology used in these tests is inspired by the works of A.BONBOIR as well as didactic strategies developed by BLOCK and ANDERSON.

- An initial evaluation of each student's work is given as follows :
"+" represents answers in agreement with the requirements necessary to start the training program ;
"-" represents answers which do not meet the necessary requirements.

- Then a second evaluation is made taking into account the approaches used by each student, and the correlated study of answers to different questions. This enables each individual student's needs to be identified. The result of this work is the "INDIVIDUAL NEEDS TABLE".

This is very close to the work done and published by others in this field especially CARDINET, ALLAL and PERRENOUD.

2.2. Training stage

A compilation of exercises aimed at increasing students' capabilities called ***"AILES DE DEDALE"***. At present, there are about 2000.
Each student is encouraged to choose between a large variety of exercises according to his/her personal tastes, interests and needs.

The principles of the training stage are as follows :
- The reconstitution of knowledge and abilities cannot be restricted to basic subjects (maths and native language). Specific support is provided whenever a student has problems in one particular area of study. This support method which is called "punctual support" is characterized by simple exercises, with only one method of solution.
- The highest degree of efficiency is reached only if the exercises which are offered to the student do not emphasize his/her particular problem (for fear of discouragement), but rather induce a more practical constructive approach which refers to his/her socio-professional environment (see Henri WALLON's works).
- Activities and exercises of support do not have to be restricted to cognitive aims, but include larger educative concerns and can be resolved in many different ways. These support methods which imply an active involvement of the students, are called "more thorough support methods".
- These exercises are done under supervision : the students are encouraged either by the teacher or by more competent fellow students.
- The mistakes are considered to be linked to discovering the right answer and at the same time the methods used to find the correct solution. (see BACHELARD's works).

2.3. More advanced work

These are interdisciplinary folders which are offered to students who do not need to follow the training stage or who have reached their pre-requisite level. These folders are expected to help students to establish cognitive links between all subjects.

2.4. Evaluation Procedures

Tests similar to those in ***"LABYRINTHE"*** are offered to students at the end ofthe school year. There are called ***"FIL D'ARIANE"***.

These tests are built on the general principle of diagnosis used in *"LABYRINTHE"*, including the same number of tests of which only the content was changed whilst the objectives, requirement levels and forms in which the answers were given, were retained.

The goals are :
- to proceed to a comparative study of results at the beginning and at the end of the school year.
- to evaluate effectiveness of the system.

3. THE COMPUTER AS A MEDIUM

In addition to written exercises, G.E.R.Ex. offers students educational software programs. Thus, by making the pupils familiar with computing and its cultural surroundings, they are able to assimilate modern techniques of communication, and it becomes easier for them to be integrated into society.

G.E.R.Ex. system also aims to meet in a better way the students' diverse needs by varying the media with written material, audio-visual aids and computers, which are either used separately or together.

The computer :
- facilitates the drawing up of exercises where controls are necessary, for example time limits.
- makes the activities more easily manageable and quicker : the learner can control immediately on the screen the validity of his answers, come back to the initial stage (without having to use a rubber), begin again and so on.
- permits helpful comments or an evaluation to be adapted to the learner's approach or to the kind of mistake pointed out by the analysis of the answer or to previous performances.

Computing is associated with G.E.R.Ex. theoretical and methodological choices concerning personal learning and development. Therefore, the facilities offered by computing such as producing a range of similar exercises from different data are not exploited. The objective is not to train students always to apply the same method, but to develop by different exercises and ways to solve problems, different kinds of understanding and the mastering of knowledge and abilities.

4. CHARACTERISTICS OF EDUCATIONAL SOFTWARE PROGRAMS

These software programs are original scenarios [1] designed for computers (and not the transcription of written exercises).

These programs are organized in "packages", i. e. a group of exercises dealing with the same problem, but on different levels and according to varied and complementary procedures. For example, **"MEMO"** combines eight programs presented in growing order of difficulty, of which the aim is to extend the field of vision and to practise talent for observation and memory. **"LOGICIRCUS"** contains thirteen programs which have the same objective, to develop logical reasoning.

Each "package" fits in with the series of exercises which students follow in the training stage and conforms to the general strategy and the pedagogic objectives of the system.

4.1. Agreement Between Teacher and Student

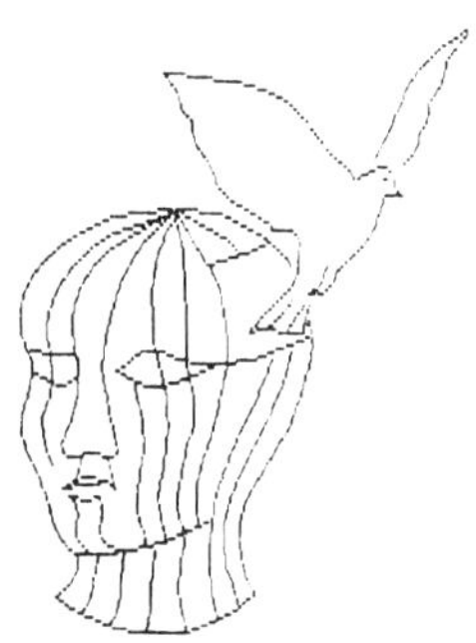

Each "package" starts with a definition of the objectives. Then, each program explains the agreement, presents the task to accomplish, makes sure of learner's acceptance of the task, specifies the form the solution is to take and offers a procedure which is adapted to the learner's type of development in his ways of finding the solutions.

[1] The programs we quoted are from Annie Couderc, Paule Knerr, Mireille Louis, Richard Tran Dang and Danièle Valentin.

Many means are used to evaluate success. Throughout the learner's development, comments emphasize the more positive elements, avoiding depreciating judgement.

An attempt is made to develop the learner's capacity to make a self-evaluation Each program ends with :
- an evaluation : Does the learner's performance fill the requirements or not ?
- instructions which are adjusted according to the student's results and to the method he followed. The main characteristic knowledge and abilities are recalled so that the student can verify his understanding of the problem and assimilate the knowledge he has acquired and the new skills he has learnt.
- ideas of continuation.

4.2. Integrated Education

- Programs are built upon an active dialectic : the observance of data on the screen is followed by the student's action to facilitate the understanding of the problem.

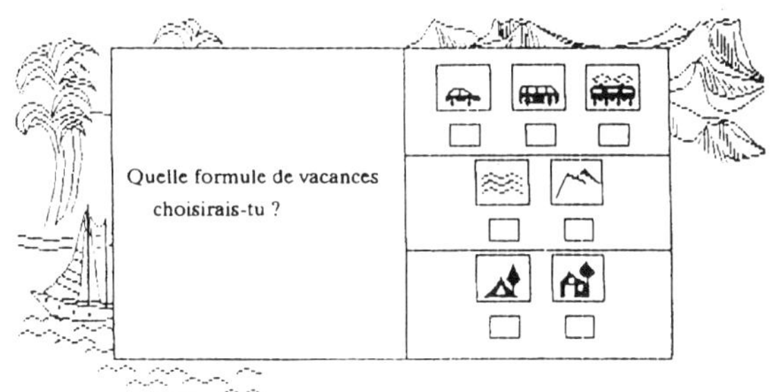

After observing the form offered by the travel agency, the student is invited to choose his own holiday form, which allows him to understand how a form is composed and what makes two forms different. His choice is stated (graphic representation is translated into written language). Then, he is asked to solve the problem. If he wants, he can ask for methodological help (**"COMPTES CHOISIS"**).

- In each program, we try to mark immediately or later the learner's actions. For example, a puzzle is given to the student and he has to reconstruct it by finding out the logical order of paragraphs. A word-processor allows him to shift, insert paragraphs, and so work on the text and see it put back into the right order (**1789**).

- In the same way, a mistake is not only pointed out by a comment, but there is an attempt to make it more obvious by emphasizing the effects it has.

- The students have access to methodological and lexical help. They decide themselves on their capacity to solve the problem.

4.3. A Differentiated Teaching Method

- The pedagogic dialogue takes into account the fact that students are not on the same level : the problem to solve is not formulated in its entirety, but divided into units of meaning to stimulate the student's attention, arouse his interest, and suggest a reading method which the learner will then be able to put into practice in other exercises. By the juxtaposition of different and complementary languages (iconographic and textual), the understanding of problems is made easier.

- An attempt is made to establish a relationship between the level of competence of different learners, answer requirements and the manner of keyboarding the answer in order to neutralize what is irrelevant to the aims being sought.

- The right answer is always justified.

4.4. An Individualized Procedure

- In each "package", the student's run depends on his success or lack of it. The programs are less or more difficult according to his previous performances.

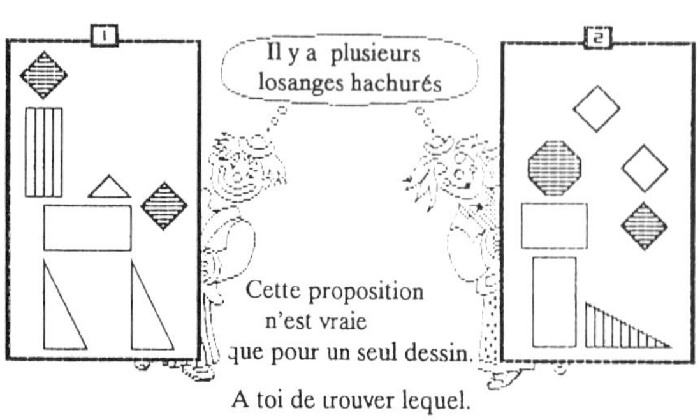

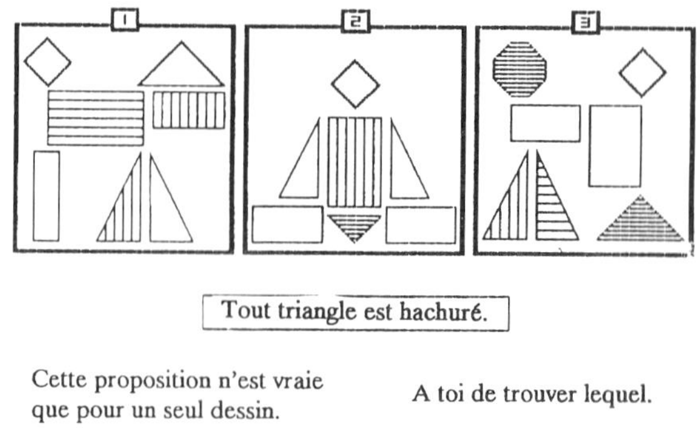

According to his success in the preceding exercise, the learner chooses the right picture from two or three (**"LOGICIRCUS"**).

- Each program takes into account the student's previous acquirements (speed of reading, success).

5. TESTING THE EDUCATIONAL SOFTWARE PROGRAMS

Eighteen technical schools using the G.E.R.Ex. system volunteered to test the "packages".
A booklet has been produced for teaching teams presenting a chart showing the composition of each "package" and defining the total objectives. It requires too a description of each program : its goals, development, forms of evaluation and ideas for continuation.

The programs are offered to volunteer students. Each of them answers a list of questions during and at the end of the testing period. This list includes questions about :
- the contents of programs (difficulties encountered in understanding of statements, help, comments) ;
- the quality of computing achievement (clarity of instructions, pictures, animations...) .
- whether the programs are interesting.

Each teacher, involved in the testing also, answers a list of questions about the progress of experiment, the reactions and the difficulties which are most often encountered.

After necessary adjustments, the programs are considered to be ready.

Computers in Education
A. McDougall and C. Dowling (Editors)
Elsevier Science Publishers B.V. (North-Holland)

GIRLS AND COMPUTING: DISPELLING MYTHS AND FINDING DIRECTIONS

Valerie A. Clarke

Department of Psychology, Deakin University, Geelong, Victoria, Australia, 3217.

Drawing on research literature both locally and overseas, seven myths about women and computing are identified and dispelled: (1) girls are no good at computing; (2) the computing culture is male-oriented; (3) gender differences in computing experience are substantial; (4) experience differences have long-term implications; (5) computing is sex-typed as a male pursuit; (6) to use a computer one must understand the technicalities; and (7) girls are not interested in computing. Six clear directions are suggested: (1) distinguish computing from computer use; (2) redirect self-fulfilling prophecies; (3) recognize girls' need for relevance; (4) change male-oriented values; (5) focus on changing men's attitudes; and (6) attract girls into computer science.

1. WHY BE CONCERNED?

Frequently we hear politicians, parents, teachers, psychologists and employers express a concern that girls have less computing experience and less computing ability than do boys. It is argued that girls' lack of computing expertise reduces their opportunities to develop thinking skills, logical reasoning skills, mathematical competence [1], and positive attitudes to learning [2]. It reduces both their employment prospects [3] and their capacity to function effectively as citizens in our increasingly technological society. But do girls lack "computing ability"? Are girls' disadvantages due to a lack of computing experience? What is meant by "computing experience"? This paper will look at some of the myths about gender differences in computing and offer some directions.

2. MYTHS

2.1. Myth 1:Girls are no good at computing

Girls are no good at computing as they lack "computing ability". This myth probably owes its origins to the dual beliefs that computers are number crunchers and hence inherently mathematical, and that boys have greater mathematical ability than do girls [4]. This myth is readily dispelled.

First, computers have a multitude of purposes unrelated to mathematics, being used as conveyors of information, word processors, office organisers, educators and even entertainers.

Second, purported gender differences in mathematical ability are derived from research showing gender differences in mathematical achievement, which are, in turn, merely reflections of gender differences in mathematical experience [5]. When the data were re-analysed treating experience as a co-variate, gender differences in mathematical achievement disappeared. It is not surprising that students (in this case girls) who have taken fewer courses in mathematics perform less well on standardised tests of mathematical achievement. If this were not the case, why enrol students in mathematics courses?

Turning to studies of gender differences in computing ability, the problem is similar. In the absence of a clear concept of "computing ability", so-called tests of computing ability are essentially tests of achievement in some specific aspects of computing. Reported gender differences in computing achievement are also reflections of gender differences in the relevant type of computing experience, and hence have nothing to do with ability.

Further, when the definition of "computing achievement" shifts from an emphasis on the mathematical and technological aspects of computing to a recognition of the role of communication, girls not only perform as well as boys on computing achievement tests, but often perform better [6,7], being more willing to pay attention to detail and markedly more competent at writing and following instructions [6].

2.2. Myth 2:The computing culture is male-oriented

The nature of the computing culture has been frequently documented, perhaps most carefully by the Carnegie Mellon University team which demonstrated that women are essentially "second class citizens" in a male-oriented culture. Games arcades and computer clubs are male preserves [8]. University terminal rooms are inhabited by males, doing battle with mainframe computers that are frequently going down in the middle of assignments, unavailable due to the pressure of student numbers, and only responding to commands that are idiosyncratic and user-unfriendly [9]. Males occupy most staff positions in computer stores and computer advisory centres. They more frequently read computing magazines, write for computing magazines and are depicted in the decision-making roles in the illustrations. They feature in the major roles in films and videos about computers [10]. This all reflects a male-oriented culture.

Obviously this myth arises from a focus on specific aspects of the computing culture, aspects that are rapidly becoming outmoded. How many of us sit in terminal rooms? Do battle with over-stretched mainframes? Frequent games arcades? Spend our waking hours writing code for computers? If we do none of these things we may still spend a great deal of our working and leisure time using computers. Perhaps we should ask, how many of us work on our own PC's, using menu driven, user-friendly software, to achieve specific goals, while enjoying the peaceful surroundings of our private offices or homes?

Further, the greater reliance on PC's and telephone networks enables a greater number of women to work effectively on computers choosing times and locations that are compatible with their other responsibilities.

2.3. Myth 3: Gender differences in computing experience are substantial

There is a wealth of empirical data documenting the greater participation of boys in computing courses, computing summer camps, and games arcades, as well as self reports of greater use of computers at home, in computing rooms in secondary schools, and terminal rooms in tertiary institutions, while girls report less involvement [10].

At primary and secondary schools, minimal gender differences in children's computing experience and computing prowess are often associated with marked differences in expectations and confidence, which in turn magnify initial differences in both experience and achievement on class computing tests. Those with greater confidence in their ability are more willing to ask questions, are less concerned by their seeming lack of competence, experience less stress in their work, and are more frequently given the opportunity to further this experience [11,12]. The introduction of additional computing resources into the schools further widens the gap [12].

But how great are the real differences in experience? How much are these boys learning in these environments and to what extent is it merely the location of their social interaction? The place where they play together, using the computer as yet another toy? To what extent are they merely spending time repeating the same types of activities? Most studies assess number of hours spent in so-called computing environments, or numbers of students enrolled in particular types of courses, with little attention paid to the quality of the experience or the learning outcomes of those experiences.

Although there may be gender differences in experience, the differences may be less substantial than initially believed. Reported experience differences partly reflect the types of experiences which are considered relevant. Thus this myth is partly an extension of the previous one. What often happens is that the hallowed name of "computing" is reserved for the particular types of computing that men choose to do, enjoy doing, and hence allocate a higher status: games, programming, playing with the latest gadgetry. Observations and questionnaires place greater emphasis on these areas. The types of activities for which women use computers are not seen as "computing": word processing, communication, completion of projects, general organization. If our society were dominated by female values, rather than male values, the female-dominated areas of word processing and information entry would be seen as the more important work, and the programming, and technical maintenance of computers as the secondary "support" services needed to achieve the real work. Then it would probably be reported that women spend considerable time using computers.

2.4. Myth 4: Experience differences have long term implications

Given that there are some gender differences in computing experience, are there any long term consequences of these differences? Possibly not.

Data from our study of tertiary students entering a compulsory introductory course in computing indicates that the benefits of prior computing experience are short-lived and the greater male confidence is misplaced [13]. On entering their course, the men had greater computing experience, having engaged in a greater number of different types of computing activities, spent more hours using computers, and used a greater number of different types of computers. They had more confidence in their computing ability, were more likely to expect to enrol in further courses in computing, and expected to gain relatively high grades. But at the end of semester, there were *no* differences in the final results obtained by the men and the women, and little relationship between anticipated and achieved grade.

Similarly, in a comprehensive assessment of gender differences in enrolments and achievement in accredited computer science courses, Kay and her colleagues [14] found that men entered these courses with considerably more computing experience. In the early stages they outperformed their female counterparts, but once the students were a year or two into their courses and the female students had the opportunity to gain a minimum level of hands-on experience, gender differences in achievement disappeared.

It seems that men may have greater computing experience when they enter tertiary institutions, but when women are required to enrol in computing courses, or choose to enrol in these courses, it takes very little time for them to perform equally as well as their more experienced male colleagues.

2.5. Myth 5: Computing is sex-typed as a male pursuit

In noting the male predominance in computing stores, magazines and classrooms, it is often argued that computing is sex-typed as a male pursuit, and as such, alienates females. At our last World Conference I presented a paper noting that in co-educational schools both boys and girls believed that boys liked computers more than did girls, and that boys were better at computing than were girls. On the other hand, girls in a single-sex school saw computing as sex-typed as a female pursuit and believed that girls were better at computing. This was interpreted as showing that the perceptions of computing depended on the social context in which computers were introduced [15].

In a more recent paper of sex-typing of occupations, I have reported that four computing occupations are in fact sex-typed. Data entry is sex-typed as female, while computer programmer, computer operator, and university computing lecturer are sex-typed as male. However, such sex-typing is significantly greater among men than among women, and among the older rather than the younger members of the population. A re-analysis of the data focussing on the women under thirty showed that they do *not* sex-type any of these occupations [16]. This suggests that such sex-typing of computing occupations is a male phenomenon, serving to boost the male ego. The lack of sex-typing among the younger women may be interpreted as demonstrating that this is *not* a major factor turning women under thirty away from computing courses and careers.

2.6. Myth 6: To use a computer one must understand technicalities of computers

This myth is best considered by drawing on a common analogy, the motor car. Recently I was involved in a discussion with a number of mothers of teenagers who reached the conclusion that the only requirement of a mother was to drive a car, to provide a taxi service to lessons, rehearsals, sports and social functions. We all drive cars daily, but know nothing about their technical features? I could quote the make and colour of mine, but beyond that, if it doesn't go, I contact the RACV.

I see computers similarly. Like automatic cars, computers, especially P.C's., are relatively easy to drive. If the software is user-friendly, it can be menu driven to achieve the desired goals, without any need to be concerned about programming or the technical features of the hardware. If the software is *not* user-friendly, the main skill required is that of deciphering the manual, a skill generally dependent on language skills, an area in which it is generally believed, rightly or wrongly, that women excel [4].

2.7. Myth 7: Girls are not interested in computing

The differential enrolments in computing courses, the observations of gender differences in time spent in computing rooms, and answers to self-report questions about liking of computing may well show that girls are using computers less often that are boys [10]. But does this mean they are less interested in using computers? Do their replies depend on how we define the term "computing"?

To turn from empirical evidence to my observations of two relatively typical girls in a home environment, some light can be shed on this issue. Both my daughters would claim to be disinterested in computers. After all, they live in a society where computers are seen as mathematical, technological and masculine. If completing measures of attitudes to computers, they would gain very negative scores. They would tell you that they rarely use the computer at home and only do computing at school when required by the timetable to do so. But observations of their behaviours lead to different conclusions. For brevity, three examples of their behaviour will suffice.

Example One: They showed no interest in hearing about my new piece of software, but within half an hour of my playing *"Where in the World is Carmen Sandiego"*, I was pushed off the computer. For the remainder of the school holidays, both girls struggled separately and together to improve their detective skills, battling to see how rapidly they could be promoted from rookie to ace detective, emerging with a comprehensive knowledge of tracking techniques and information seeking skills. But if asked about computers, they would tell you "Computers are boring." If asked about Carmen Sandiego, they would tell you "It's great".

Example two: Heather had no interest in learning typing, or to use the word processor in school computing classes because this is "boring", until it suddenly occurred to her that Mum's Mac was a useful way to present a neat, tidy project and get that A she so desperately wanted. Stimulated by the need to have a project in by Monday, a girl who claimed to be disinterested in computers spent the week-end "discovering" print types and font sizes which would allow each topic to carefully fill the allotted space, leaving room for diagrams and a crossword puzzle to be added.

Example three. Rosemary was a Munchkin in the local drama group's production of the *"Wizard of Oz"*. It is customary among the members of the group to give each other cards and little gifts on opening night. Rosemary rushed in babbling about some programme she had once seen. Obviously she was referring to *"Print Shop"*. For the next two weeks I had to battle to gain access to the computer outside school hours as one very busy little Munchkin proceeded to make sixty-five individually designed greeting cards. The child who hated computers, daily begged to be allowed to do "just one more card" before going to bed.

Clearly, these examples show that both girls spend considerable time using the computer when then have a reason to do so, but they rarely fool on it to fill in time. They do not describe their activities as "computing", but as "playing detectives", "completing class projects", and "making greeting cards".

3.DIRECTIONS

3.1. Direction 1: Distinguish computing from computer use

The examples of my two daughters show that it is not always reliable to depend on people's self-reports about their computer interests or activities, as the term "computing" means different things to different people. We need to distinguish between the use of computers as tools and the more hard-nosed computer programming and technicalities. Just as few of us are mechanics, and yet live in our cars, few of us need technical and programming skills to spend our waking hours using computers for a multitude of activities. It might be more accurate to say that some girls are disinterested in computer programming and computer science, than to say that they are not interested in using computers. To assess computing experience, we need to ask questions about a wide range of uses of computers in a wide range of different contexts.

3.2. Direction 2: Re-direction of self-fulfilling prophecies

Rosenthal [17] documented the tremendous impact our expectations can have on the maze running ability of rats and the intellectual development of children, but these effects probably pale into insignificance when compared with the effects we can have on the development of our children's attitudes and expectations about computers. As long as teachers, parents and school counsellors, especially male teachers, parents and school counsellors, believe that computing is mathematical, technical and essentially masculine, with little to appeal to girls, we will find that girls will meet these expectations and find little to interest them in computers. On the other hand, if we expect girls to use computers for a wide variety of activities and to become interested in both their potential as tools, and even in the more technical aspects, they are more likely to respond positively to our expectations.

3.3. Direction 3: Recognize girls' need for relevance

Girls often differ from boys in that they are less likely to tinker for the sake of tinkering. Research into gender differences in science, and craft design and technology indicates that girls are more interested in developing skills if they can see the practical applications of those skills. Certainly, my daughters will spend hours using the computer if they are trying to accomplish a specific goal and see the computer as a useful tool to achieve that goal. Rather than teach computing in a vacuum, it must be introduced to girls within the context of the broader curriculum, as a tool to achieve other ends.

3.4. Direction 4:Replace male-oriented values

Because we live in a society dominated by male-oriented values, activities which men and boys find interesting are allocated a higher social status and greater prestige than activities which girls find of interest. It is generally recognized that the majority of girls are interested in the use of computer applications while a greater proportion of boys are interested in computer technology and programming. But there is no objective reason why we should not see the technicians and the programmers as the low status "support services" which facilitate the work of those using computers as tools to achieve other ends.

3.5. Direction 5: Focus on changing the attitudes of men

Generally those concerned about increasing the participation of women focus on the so-called "deficits" of women, and try to remedy these by providing girls-only classes, or workshops for female teachers and mothers to provide the experience necessary to overcome this deficit. The out-moded, non-productive deficit model must be replaced by a recognition that girls' experiences, although different, are equally valid. These experiences must be the basis of further development. As shown by the occupational stereotypes, this "deficit" view, or sexist perspective, is essentially a male phenomenon, and hence can only be changed by focussing on modifying male attitudes and expectations.

3.6. Direction 6: Attract girls into computer science

Why are we concerned if girls are disinterested in programming and computer science? If it is because there is a shortage of talent in these areas, it is essential to demonstrate to girls that the acquisition of these skills is a means to achieving a desired goal, possibly that of a rewarding and lucrative job. They need to be aware of the purposes for which they are learning these skills, but more importantly, the skills need to be taught in a way which appeals to girls. Certainly, the evidence shows that girls are competent in these areas once they embark on them either in response to course requirements, or to their own choice of area of study, but girls need to be made aware of these findings. More women need to be involved in the planning and development of these courses, not only to provide female role models, but because they are more likely to recognise the needs of girls and present the courses in a way which they find conducive.

REFERENCES

[1] Clements, D.H. , Effects of Logo Programming on Cognitive, Metacognitive Skills and Achievement. Paper presented at The American Educational Research Association Conference, Chicago, April, 1985.

[2] Clarke, V. A., The Impact of Computers on Abilities and Attitudes: A pilot Study Using Logo. Journal of Computers in Mathematics and Science Teaching, Winter (1986) 32-33.

[3] The Commonwealth Schools Commission, Girls and Tomorrow: The Challenge for Schools. (Canberra, The Commonwealth Schools Commission, 1985).

[4] Maccoby, E.E. and Jacklin, C.N., The Psychology of Sex Differences (Stanford, Stanford University Press, 1974).

[5] Fennema, E. Success in Mathematics, in: Marsland, M. (ed.), Sex Differentiation and Schooling (London, Heinmann Educational Books, 1983).

[6] Linn, M.S., Fostering Equitable Consequences From Computer Learning Environments, Sex Roles, 13, (3/4),(1985) 115-122.

[7] Anderson, R.E., Females Surpass Males in Computer Problem Solving, Journal of Educational Computing Research,3,(1),(1987), 39-51.

[8] Kiesler, S., Sproull, L, and Eccles, L., Poolhalls, Chips and War Games, Psychology of Women Quarterly, 4, (1985), 451-463.

[9] Kiesler, S. and Sproull, L. (eds.), Computing and Change on Campus (Cambridge, Cambridge University Press, 1987).

[10] Clarke, V.A., Computing in a Social Context, Deakin University, 1986.

[11] Carmichael, H.W.et al, Computers, Children and Classrooms: A Multisite Evaluation of the Creative Use of Microcomputers by Elementary School Children (Canadian Ministry of Education, 1985).

[12] Chambers, S.M. and Clarke, V.A., Is Inequity Cumulative? Journal of Educational Computing Research, 3, (1987) 493-516.

[13] Clarke, V.A. and Chambers, S.M., Gender-based Factors in Computing Enrollments and Achievement Journal of Educational Computing Research, 5 (4), (1989),

[14] Kay, J., Collings, P., Lublin, J., Poiner, G., Prosser, M., Bishop, R. and Watson, K., Investigation of the Status of Women at the Early Stages of Professionally Accredited Tertiary Computer Science and Data Processing Programmes. (N.S.W. Basser Department of Computer Science, University of Sydney, 1986).

[15] Clarke, V.A. Computing in a Social Context, in: Duncan, K. and Harris, D. (eds.), Proceedings of the Fourth World Conference on Computers in Education (New Holland, Isevier Science Publishers, 1985).

[16] Clarke, V.A. Sex-typing of Occupations: A Declining Phenomenon. Psychological Reports, 1989.

[17] Rosenthal, R., Self-fulfilling prophecy. Psychology Today, September (1968) 46-51.

Computers in Education
A. McDougall and C. Dowling (Editors)
Elsevier Science Publishers B.V. (North-Holland)

THE FELSTED SYSTEM: AN EDUCATIONAL PHILOSOPHY DEPENDENT ON A COMPREHENSIVE NETWORK

Christopher DAWKINS

Head of Computing, Felsted School, Dunmow, Essex CM6 3JG, England*

Felsted School has had a comprehensive and highly utilised network system since 1984, based on the idea that effective informatics education is a byproduct of extensive use of computers in all spheres of school life. This paper describes both the system and the philosophy behind it.

1. INTRODUCTION

This paper describes an educational philosophy and its practical implementation. The philosophy is such that it can only be implemented in a school equipped with a comprehensive campus-wide network and the paper describes the system built up at Felsted School to support it.

The philosophy consists basically of ignoring "computer education", instead, making USE of computers to assist the life of the school in a wide variety of areas [1]. Making computers so much a part of the very fabric of school life that everyone is using them all the time (arcade games, incidentally, are totally forbidden). The result is that everyone becomes skilled in the use of computers and "computer education" occurs as a byproduct. The main product is a more efficient and effective school. Since the most valuable applications within the school require communications, a campus-wide network is the fundamental requirement of the philosophy, and this is the main feature of life at Felsted school.

2. THE HARDWARE

I propose to start with a paragraph describing a fictitious school of the future, and then compare it with the current provision at Felsted. Imagine a school with a local area network extending to every academic, residential and extracurricular area, including the homes of every member of both the teaching and the non-teaching staff, and of the pupils if they are day pupils. With present technology this is thus only possible in a boarding school where all staff live on the campus or very close to the school, but during the next ten or twenty years it should become feasible for all schools. All places of work or leisure in the school have a network terminal, and most classrooms have a full set. With current terminals this would imply an overall number approaching three per pupil. However, with fully portable terminals linked to the network by a wire-less method, the number required would drop to not much more than one per head. Note that the philosophy requires equal treatment of all members of the school whether student, teacher or ancillary worker. All users have their own passworded directory on the school's central filestore, and all make considerable use of the communications facilities on the system, particularly the electronic mail. All pupil records are on the system and can be consulted by the pupils, and although there are security features to restrict what information is available to whom the general philosophy is biased to freedom rather than restriction of information.

The Felsted network, just before the catastrophic lightning strike of July 1989, used 6km of cable to link about 80 terminals in sixteen buildings to central services consisting of two 137 megabyte fileservers, a Unix system and a teletext server. It was far from new: in 1984 it had used 1.5km of cable to link about 30 terminals in five buildings to two 8 megabyte fileservers and the same teletext server [2]. All pupils have automatically had their own directories since 1987, and by 1989 there were few staff without. Most of the terminals are neither multitasking nor WIMP driven, but the menu system leads to most applications with only two or three key-depressions and thus provides faster access than many modern environments.

Unrestricted access to the system is one of the key features at Felsted. Until a machine was stolen the Computer Centre was never locked. Since 1986 there has been an electric lock on the main door, operated by magnetic cards freely issued to pupils. The cards hold the

*July 1989 to July 1990: Scotch College, 76 Shenton Road, Swanbourne, WA 6010

owner's name, and each use is recorded in a file which can be displayed at any network station. However, about 70% of the school's machines are located outside the computer centre so that pupils can and do access the network at all times from around 7 a.m. to midnight seven days a week. The "open system" aspect is obvious to any visitor to Felsted: computers have been scattered around the school in corridor-type locations since May 1980, and there are usually a few pupils (as well as at least a dozen staff) who have machines in their private accommodation.

3. THE SOFTWARE

This can be divided into four areas, which are listed in descending order of importance as far as this philosophy is concerned:

Communications
Document processing
Information services
Software for use in teaching

3.1. Communications

There are four main items of communications software at Felsted. First is the "**Notice-board**". This is a single screen-full of messages, 40 characters by 25 lines, with six of the lines occupied by status and heading material such as the time of day. It has four independently editable areas. The first three are protected by passwords so that they can only be amended by the Headmaster, the teaching staff and the sports staff respectively but the fourth is available for anyone. Fixed screens mounted at strategic points around the school display the current set of messages, which can of course also be displayed and edited at any network station. This "noticeboard" is really a civilised version of a Tannoy system. The restriction to a 40-column display with only nineteen useful lines is necessary to ensure that messages are always worth reading and that occasional cursory glances at the public display screens are adequate to keep up to date, so however technology improves the "Noticeboard" is unlikely to change its capacity. The system has been operational since May 1984 and eliminates large numbers of irritating inefficiencies that are inevitable in schools that do not have a means by which the Headmaster, any member of staff or any pupil can communicate a message to all corners of the school within a few minutes. The Felsted philosophy insists on making available the "General" area: a six-line part of the screen available to all pupils. This does get misused occasionally, and these occasions cause the area to become password protected for staff use for a period.

The second communications application is "**Mail**": an electronic mail system used by all members of the community for private messages and internal memos: particularly useful for communications between pupils and staff. During the 1988/89 academic year this system averaged around 400 messages a day, mostly between pupils. This is a good example of the way the Felsted philosophy eliminates the need to teach "electronic mail", and in the process provides a useful facility for the school.

The third is "**Chat**", a set of "bulletin boards" covering various topics, and the fourth is "**Converse**", an interactive seven-station conferencing capability.

3.2. Document processing

Document processing is merely word processing with full graphic and pictorial capability, and it needs to be an improvement on the current top range of DTP packages with integrated hypertext, database and spreadsheet facilities too. The current Felsted system is based on "Wordwise", a very simple word processor of 1983 vintage. Simple, yet useful because everyone has access to it and everyone knows how to use it. Useful also for system work because it can produce plain ASCII files. There are other word processors and DTP packages available, and a Postscript laser printer attached to the Unix system is accessible from any network station, but Wordwise still caters for the bulk of "document processing" work.

3.3. Information Services

"**Information services**" includes both local databases and access to public ones. The main local databases are

on unrestricted access:

the current nominal roll
the Old Felstedian records
athletics performances
sports teams and their performances
the daily menu

with restricted access:

nominal rolls up to twelve years ahead
absentee/illness/off-exercise records

Some of these items illustrate ways in which the Felsted system provides advantages not available in other more restrictive ones.

First example. From power-on at any network station it takes not much more than five seconds to obtain the nominal roll data (e.g. address) for any pupil - indeed, the information can be on the screen before the monitor has warmed up sufficiently to display it. From one pupil to any other takes less than a second. The fact that all this is available so easily means that all (well, most) pupils check it and submit corrections for it. They do not, of course, have write access to the files but can use a special "Chat" file, or the "Mail" system, to communicate the correction. However accurate the data entry personnel are they cannot compensate for entry forms incorrectly completed by parents, and a number of these have been identified as a result of corrections supplied by pupils. I do not believe parents at other schools are any more proficient in this respect.

Second example. The "Absence" system allows staff at any point on the network to enter information on any pupil's absence. Information on illnesses and medical restrictions on exercise are entered on a terminal in the school Sanatorium in "real time". The network records all this on a central transaction file which can of course be interrogated from any point. A teacher finding a pupil absent can thus instantly find out whether the absence is legitimate - and can also check up on past and (pre-planned) future absences too. I used the word "instantly" above: compared with most other Felsted software this application is rather slow. A query takes at least ten seconds from scratch. This is largely because the files are structured to allow a number of terminals to be updating them at the same time, and I feel justified with "instantly" only because I know of no faster systems anywhere near the same price bracket.

Early in this document it was made clear that the network existed for all members of the school, whether academic or ancillary. The Catering Manager has a machine on the network, which he uses to record the menus. The current menu is displayed on a screen mounted above the entrance to the dining hall, and it (or any other) can be consulted from any point in the school. This is one of the many unnecessary things the network does, but not ineffective: he would have to type it out anyway and the file he creates is used to make the printed copies. Meanwhile many people find it interesting, if not useful, to be able to consult the menu from the comfort of their own location in the school and some time in advance of the meal.

Access to public databases. Only one has been available: the teletext magazines transmitted by the BBC and ITV, amounting to about 500 single-screen pages of generally current-affairs information. These have been available to all network stations since March 1984, and have been one of the main attractors the system has offered to those who would not normally be seen near a keyboard. The educational value of the system is hardly vitiated by the observation that most of the accesses by boys are to the sports pages and by girls to the horoscopes! The teletext server machine has a number of other functions, two of which are worth a special mention. It keeps system time locked to BBC time, so that the times displayed on the noticeboard screens around the school can generally be relied on to be precise. Second, it records the temperature every fifteen minutes on a central file, so any network station can look up a temperature graph covering the past few days. Note how both of these facilities really depend for their utility on the fact that they are provided on a campus-wide network.

Access to remote public databases via a modem server has always been planned: implementation has awaited the availability of suitable control software. It may be that the Unix system will be able to provide this.

3.4. Software for use in teaching

I have placed this last because it is the least-used aspect of the computer system at Felsted, and to a substantial extent it is a byproduct of the philosophy and not the main aim. Placing it last does not mean there is little use in teaching: just that there is a lot more use in the other spheres. There are many hundreds of items of content-specific subject-teaching software on the system, most of them accessible in a few key-depressions from the top menu. These are used when appropriate by subject specialists.

4. THE CHARACTERISTICS OF THE SYSTEM

There are seven characteristics of the Felsted system:

a) Staff and pupils share the same system. This is a security nightmare, since staff are writing examination papers (and their answers), internal memos, reports and so on on the same network that pupils are using - and sharing the same Winchester disc . One short word - the "system password" - keeps them apart, and some of the pupils are expert hackers. The advantage of sharing lies in the economies of scale, in that services provided for pupils are available to staff and vice versa, and it does of course facilitate communications between staff and students.

b) Staff do not necessarily get better facilities. Admittedly the first laser printer was placed in the staff common room, but the second one, a much superior Postscript device, was placed in a pupil area. This was because staff needed the first one, but pupils had more time to learn the necessary DTP techniques to make good use of the second.

c) Risks are taken. For example, machines are loaned out during the holidays. Felsted would much rather equipment was used and broken than not used and not broken. Pupils are also encouraged assist with both hardware and software development and maintenance. Though there have been some losses from this policy, the gains have vastly outweighed them.

d) Students are encouraged to work on real, live and useful applications: artificial exercises and projects form no part of the philosophy (although there are times when it is unrealistic to be rigid about this). This is one reason why there has been little work in Comal, Pascal or other respectable educational languages, because it is a fact of life that the most efficient way to get applications running on the network hardware we use (BBC machines) is to write in the native language, BBC Basic.

e) The system is largely used for non-curricular purposes. Looking up today's menu or the afternoon's cricket scores, arranging parties, having an electronic natter or making up an athletics team: these are some of the hundreds of activities facilitated by the system. Chemistry, Physics, Biology, Maths, English and so on are also assisted, and probably as much as in any other school, but the extracurricular activities far outweigh the intracurricular ones. Though this is largely so because the school is a boarding school, once all homes have fully digital telephone lines such activity will become possible, and presumably inevitable, in day school communities.

f) Felsted has had a full-time computer technician since 1982. A network such as this will only work if it is used, and it will only be used if it works, and a teacher cannot be simultaneously fixing network faults and taking classes. Faults arise every day with a network of this size and age, and they need to be fixed immediately. Of course, if a lightning strike should knock out 83 machines on the day after the Head of Computing has left the UK for a year in Australia it may take a few months for the single technician to get everything back in order again, but lightning does not strike often.

g) The network is extended to every part of the school, as well as to several private houses near the school, and terminals are supplied to all who might make use of them - whether staff, student, or ancillary worker. To be more truthful, this is the policy. Actuality is a little way behind. There are still parts of the school unconnected, and people who need terminals unsupplied.

5. THE EFFECT

The main effect of the network has been to involve the whole school in the computer system. Few members of the teaching staff can resist a system that enables them to summons pupils from the comfort of a chair in the staff Common Room, and few pupils one that enables them to initiate - or terminate - a romance from the safety of a computer keyboard. For more than five years now pupils at Felsted have had immediate access to a computer network offering communications, central filestores, local and remote databases and shared printers. The success of the system is not to be gauged from the few who have learned a lot about it - there will always be pupils who learn a lot without being taught - but from the many who have learned about computers while enhancing their lifestyle and progress in other subjects. "Experiential learning" was the term used by an American visitor, and though only a few pupils have learned the distinction between "data" and "information" many have learned the value of regular backups (when they were able to retrieve a file they had corrupted) or the power of the system manager (his ability to trace misdeeds, and disguised copies of games software). As for the "few", pupils at the school wrote the Noticeboard, Mail, Chat, Converse, temperature display, menu display and Sports systems, and contributed parts of the Teletext and Old Felstedian software.

What is the purpose of computer education? A question with innumerable valid answers: one is "to arrange that students learn how to make effective use of computers". And what is the purpose of computers? "To enrich life, and make it easier"? The Felsted system has fulfilled both purposes.

ACKNOWLEDGEMENTS

Amongst those who have burned the largest quantities of midnight oil developing the Felsted system are Andrew Gordon, David Bisset, Tony Engeham, Stephen Lawrence, David Deacon and Robert Marven. The most unfair job in the world, however, was taken by Barney Clarkson, normally Director of Computing at Scotch College, Perth, Western Australia, who took over the Felsted system in July 1989 just after it had suffered a direct lightning strike and managed it for the year I have spent in Perth.

REFERENCES

[1] Dawkins, C.C.H., The Use of Computers in School, "Computer Education" No.8, (1971), p24.

[2] Dawkins, Christopher, "The Econet Micro Guide" (Longman, 1985, ISBN 0-582-36215-6)

Computers in Education
A. McDougall and C. Dowling (Editors)
Elsevier Science Publishers B.V. (North-Holland)

A CASE STUDY ON COMPUTER-BASED INSTRUCTION FOR PROBLEM-SOLVING IN GEOMETRY

Bainian DONG and Jiqing WANG

Department of Mathematics, Shaoxing Teachers' College, Shaoxing, Zhejiang Province, 312000, China; Institute of Educational Technology, East China Normal University, Shanghai, 200062, China.

In this article we describe a case study on CAI for problem-solving in geometry. We developed a kind of guided-discovery style of software for training the proving skills in geometry for second-grade students in junior high school, and investigated its effect on learning and on students' attitudes towards the learning style.

1. INTRODUCTION

Proof is one of the important problem-solving skills in geometry, and its training is one of the difficult parts in geometrical education. There are several ways to solve a problem of proving, and different students have different ways to work on it, so it takes a teacher more time and higher skills to introduce and train the proving skills. Routinized drill-and-practice CAI software is not helpful for training or testing the proving skills in geometry, as the problem can not be answered with simple "yes/no" or numbers; moreover a step-by-step way will stereotype students' thinking. We developed a kind of CAI software in a guided-discovery method, and tried to evaluate its effect on classroom instruction.

2. SOFTWARE

McArthur indicated that there are two principles in development of educational software:

* Identify specific skills, concepts, or knowledge that you want to communicate to the students.

* Design computer-based learning tools that support the specific cognitive processes involved in learning those skills through practice.

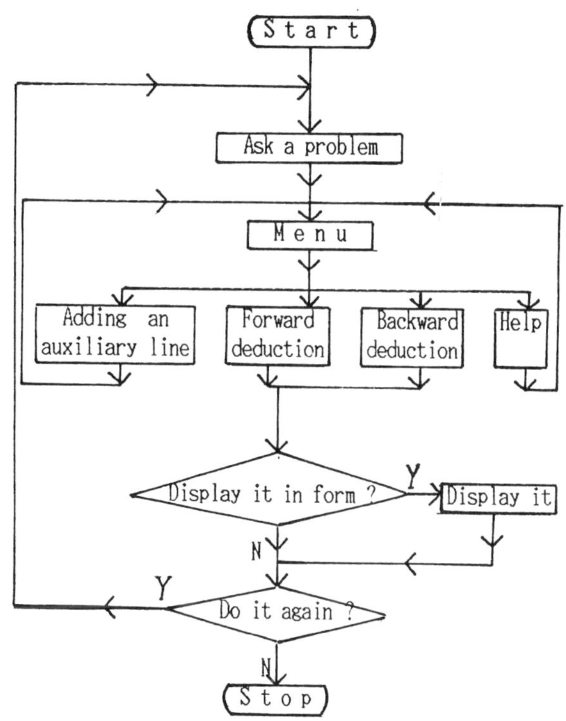

Figure 1

The proving skills can be identified as three parts: adding an auxiliary line, forward deduction, backward deduction. With AI techniques, every problem of proving can be represented in a network of some statements. The structure of the software (see Figure 1) is:

1) planning ways to solve the problem;

2) displaying them in the normal form.

When running the software, the student will make choices in each step, and the computer will follow its choices closely through the deductive network until the goals are reached, then the computer will show up the normal proving form in geometry if the student wants to see this form. All choices will be evaluated and fed back. If a choice is not reasonable, the computer will give a feedback such as "More conditions are needed here for proving that triangle ABC and EGF are congruent" or "It is not helpful here to add a line for proving". In this way the student has some freedom in solving the problem and meanwhile gets the normal form in the end.

The purpose of our case study is to investigate the student's achievements in proving skills in geometry when the software is used. Two questions are posed:

1) Does it exert an influence on their proving skills and other abilities?
2) What are their attitudes towards the application of the software in geometry education?

3. METHOD

The subjects, 49 students in a class, were randomly selected from the second-grade students (similar to the eighth-grade students in western countries) in a junior high school - the Affiliated Middle School to Shaoxing Teachers' College (Shaoxing, Zhejiang Province) and the other 148 students in the same grade were the control group. Students in both treatment groups used the same textbook, and took similar instructions on the geometry concepts, rules and knowledge. The computer group used the software to train their proving skills while the control group did their classroom exercises under the guidance of the teacher. The post-test was the terminal test in mathematics, and one part of it was to test their proving skills in geometry.

The subjects used the software in a computer laboratory equipped with 16 Apple II microcomputers. The subjects were asked to respond to an attitude assessment. The questionnaire was designed as a five-point scale table with about 20 items, and its target objects included motivation, effect, evaluation, etc. Basing on the results, we made the effect analysis and relation analysis.

4. RESULTS

In our case study some interesting facts were found:

A. The subjects made more progress in their mathematical achievements. In Table 1, a main significant difference is observed in our case study ($t = 2.503$, $p < 0.02$), and it clearly shows that using our software is helpful to train the proving skills in geometry and to increase students' mathematical achievements.

Group	Subjects (n = 49)		Control group (n = 148)		Total (n = 197)	
	M	S D	M	S D	M	S D
Score	68.57	37.29	55.28	29.43	58.53	30.07

Table 1

B. The results of correlation analysis based on the attitude assessment after the "congruent triangles" lesson are shown in Table 2.

Remarks:

SR: Scores in running the software;
TR: Time for running the software (the control group spent 90 minutes);
ST: Scores in the terminal test in mathematics;
SP: Scores of the proving skills in the terminal test;
US: Like to use the software;
WI: Wish to increase its difficulty;
UA: Like to use similar one for another lesson;
UC: Helpful to understand the concepts of geometry;
AJ: Helpful to improve the ability of judgement;
AD: Helpful to improve the ability of deduction;
LT: Helpful to form the logical way of thinking;
SM: Stimulate the motivation to learn geometry.

Significant differences:

Mark	*	**	***	****	*****
p <	0.1	0.05	0.02	0.01	0.001
CC >	.2355	.2789	.3284	.3613	.4519

	Coorelation Matrix												
	SR	TR	ST	SP	US	WI	UA	UC	AJ	AD	LT	SM	Attitude Coefficients
SR	1	-.1771	+.6243	+.8420	+.1136	+.6117	+.0314	+.0524	-.0703	.0770	+.1296	.2995	
TR		1	-.1398	-.0117	-.1091	-.3092	-.1087	+.1447	-.2130	.1378	-.1483	.0821	
ST	*****		1	+.6902	-.0981	+.5818	-.1784	-.0360	-.0395	.0218	-.1019	.0205	
SP	*****		*****	1	-.0618	+.3761	-.2886	+.0684	-.1040	.0107	-.1243	.1163	
US					1	+.1667	+.5532	+.4682	+.2595	.3755	+.5186	.4536	0.8680
WI	*****	**	*****	****		1	+.1851	+.2742	+.0514	.3217	+.0647	.3462	0.8133
UA				**	*****		1	+.3321	+.3612	.2675	+.2930	.3944	0.8560
UC					*****	*	***	1	+.1936	.4250	+.3302	.3500	0.8360
AJ					*		***		1	.2001	+.4283	.4825	0.8760
AD					****	**	*	****		1	+.6034	.6242	0.8520
LT					*****		**	***	****	*****	1	.6343	0.8560
SM	**				*****	***	****	***	*****	*****	*****	1	0.8760

Table 2

After analyzing the students' attitudes in our case study we get the following results:

* Most students in the treatment group liked to use it very much (C = 0.8680), and wanted to have another lesson using the same kind of software (C = 0.8560). Their interests did not depend on their scores in using the software (Correlation coefficient CC = 0.1136) or their terminal test scores (CC = -0.0981). In fact, many students with lower scores hoped to learn geometry in this style. One of them said, "The teacher can not watch me closely, but the computer can. The computer not only guides me to find the correct way to solve the problem of proving, but also raises my interest and self-confidence in learning geometry."

* The three scores (That of using the software, that of the total terminal test in mathematics, and that of the proving skills in the terminal test) of subjects have higher correlation coefficients (0.6243 and 0.8420). So our software can train the proving skills and can serve as a reliable self-test for students.

* The reasons that the subjects prefer this style of learning the proving skills are significantly related to the following:
  1) Stimulating their motivation to learn geometry (CC = 0.4536);
  2) Helpful to understand the concepts (CC = 0.4682);
  3) Helpful to improve the ability of judgement (CC = 0.2595);
  4) Helpful to improve the ability of deduction (CC = 0.3755);
  5) Helpful to form the logical way of thinking (CC = 0.5186)

* It took more time to run the software for the lower-score subjects (CC = -0.1771), and they did not want to increase the difficulty of the problems in software (CC = -0.3092).

We are still conducting our case study so that we can find more effective software.

5. ACKNOWLEDGEMENTS

The authors are grateful to Shaoxing Scientific and Technical Committee, Professor Ruifen Tang, Miss Zhongying Yin and all colleagues for their help in this case study.

REFERENCES

[1] McArthur, D., Developing Computer Tools to Support Performing and Learning Complex Cognitive Skills, in Applications of Cognitive Psychology: Computing and Education, K. Pedzek etc. (Lawrence Erlbaum Associates 1986).

[2] McArthur, D., Stasz, C. and Hotta, J., Learning Problem-Solving Skills in Algebra, Journal of Educational Technology Systems, Vol. 15(3), 1986-87.

[3] Wang and Zhang, The Method of Developing CAI Softwares (Science Press, Beijing, 1988).

[4] Polya, G., How to Solve It (Doubleday Anchor Books, New York, 1957).

Computers in Education
A. McDougall and C. Dowling (Editors)
Elsevier Science Publishers B.V. (North-Holland)

THE QUEST FOR QUALITY SOFTWARE

PIERRE DUGUET

Centre for Educational Research and Innovation, Organisation for Economic Cooperation and Development,2 Rue Andre-Pascal,75775 Paris, Cedex 16, France

and JOHN WINSHIP

Curtin University of Technology, GPO U 1987, Perth 6001, Australia

Early in 1988 the Centre for Educational Research and Innovation of the Organisation for Economic Cooperation and Development (OECD) invited John Winship to undertake a comparative analysis of the mechanisms set up in Member countries in order to review and evaluate educational software and disseminate information about it. His report was the working document of an International Seminar on Software Review and Evaluation: Trends and Issues held in October 1988 at OECD Headquarters in Paris, which was attended by national representatives and invited experts from 20 Member countries and has since been published by OECD [1]. The paper describes some of the discussions and conclusions of the OECD Seminar.

1. THE INFORMATION TECHNOLOGIES IN THE CURRICULUM

Although studies conducted by the OECD in 1986 [2] and 1987 [3] have shown that the potential of the microcomputer for education is unprecedented in content as well as in scale, that potential has not been realized to date in most schools in Member countries even where microcomputers are now relatively commonplace. Evaluative studies conducted in Australia [4], England [5], France [6], Norway [7], Scotland [8] and the United States [9] have shown that computers are not yet major tools in the classroom.

The Office of Technology Assessment [9], for example, reports that in the United States only half of the country's teachers say that they have used computers in instruction and that few teachers have found ways to exploit their enormous potential. OTA concludes that although many instances of exemplary use of computers in school can be given, "...... this remarkable achievement in the schools pales in comparison with the rate and magnitude of entry into the age of information experienced by business, the military, higher education and medicine. ..... in general, classrooms today resemble their ancestors of 50 and 100 years ago much more closely than do today's assembly plants, scientific laboratories and operating rooms. A number of information technologists point out that if business organizations today evolved at the same rate as the schools, they would still be using quill pens instead of electronic word processors."

There is no simple answer as to why the potential of the New Information Technologies has not been realized. There appear to be a number of factors which occur in various combinations and inhibit the use of computers across the curriculum in schools. They include the lack of adequate hardware facilities in schools, the lack of quality software which meets the curriculum needs of teachers, the lack of adequate support facilities for teachers to find out about software and assess its relevance to meet their needs, the lack of appropriate training for teachers and the more general problem of how education systems can be made more responsive to innovation.

2. SOFTWARE, THE CENTRAL ISSUE

Among these factors, identifying and selecting high quality software which can be integrated into the curriculum remains a central issue. However, whilst in most sectors of the economy the progress of computer technology has been coupled with the development of powerful and matching software, this has not been the case in education. Why not? Although there are a number of straightforward reasons such as the cost of designing software packages and the re sulting narrowness of the market at present, the real problem is far more complex.

First, the aim of educational software is to improve not only the teaching but also the learning process. Educational research has revealed how to improve the teaching process and thus how to design drill and practice software, tests and certain types of simulation, and also how to use professional software for word processing, spreadsheets or access to databases - but for the learning process, that stage has not yet been reached. The cognitive sciences have provided a clearer understanding of the active nature of this process, but no one has yet perfected a methodology which will allow the examination and detailed explanation of how knowledge is structured. So far, little is known about how students learn or exactly what they learn when they interact with computer-based materials.

Second, software must be adaptable to the wide range of educational methods and strategies used by teachers. The variables in software developed for educational purposes and the facilities it requires are therefore quite different from those which apply to software designed for a known process such as, for example, improving production in industry, commerce or administration.

Thirdly, the problem is compounded by the vast amount of educational software available compared with the number of textbooks available. It is estimated that there are currently thousands of programs on the market.in certain OECD countries: over 10,000 in the United States produced by over 900 companies, and between 1,000 and 4,000 each in Australia, Canada, France, Italy and the United Kingdom - and these numbers are increasing all the time.

In addition to this, teachers cannot 'thumb through' a computer program as they would a textbook, to get an idea of its content and methodology. How can teachers who want to use the computer as a teaching aid select the products that best suit their teaching requirements and their students' learning requirements? When they are looking for information about software, teachers want to know whether a program corresponds to what they require for their curriculum, what its content and methodology are, for what kind of students it is designed, how much it costs, whether any further hardware or software is needed to use it, how they go about previewing it and obtaining a copy and, especially important, whether it has been evaluated and by whom. Teachers want to know the answers to all these questions if they are to use the software effectively. If they do not, they are liable to become discouraged after trying inappropriate products brought to their attention by commercial advertising, and are apt totally to reject the computer as a teaching aid.

Recognising this situation, many OECD countries have set up - or are in the process of setting up - software information and evaluation centres. What sort of information do these centres provide and how do teachers have access to them? The OECD Centre for Educational Research and Innovation (CERI) tried to find out, prompting Member countries to respond to the results of its investigations during the course of an international seminar on "Software Review and Evaluation: Trends and Issues" held in October 1988 at OECD Headquarters in Paris and attended by high level national representatives and invited experts. The Seminar came to five main conclusions:

3. TEACHERS' NEED FOR INFORMATION ABOUT SOFTWARE

Conclusion: We cannot afford not to provide teachers with information about available teaching and learning software.

Although there has been progress in the range of software available in many countries, many teachers are not aware of what is available to them. Comprehensive and reliable access to information about effective pedagogical practices, whether in the form of software packages or of examples of "good teaching" using the new information technologies across the curriculum, is not readily available to teachers. Teachers seeking software consequently face a daunting task in making responsible selections. If we want teachers to use software effectively in their teaching, therefore information about existing software must be made available to them so that they can select the software appropriate to their needs.

A view expressed at the Seminar was that teachers should be provided with the best possible factual information and appropriate training and allowed to decide for themselves what software meets their needs. Several participants suggested, however, that such information by itself is insufficient. One does not, after all, buy a car or a seat at the theatre without having first read the motoring correspondents' comments or the reviews of the theatre critics. Likewise teachers will get a far better idea of a software program if, in addition to factual information about the software, they have some critical comments to go on - comments not only on the technical qualities of the program (for example, reliability under normal conditions, visual presentation, ease of use, colour, quality of graphics and animation), but also on its educational qualities (the effectiveness of the educational strategy adopted, for example, as well as compatibility with curriculum requirements and the degree of student-machine interaction).

The participants explained how information about software has been provided in their countries in the form of printed catalogues or electronic databases. Some of the countries, Australia, Canada, France, United Kingdom, United States, have had considerable experience in this area. Others, Dutch-speaking Belgium, Germany, the Netherlands, Norway, have recently set up reviewing agencies or are about to do so.

All the centres try to provide a factual description of software; many also provide a critical commentary on the software together with a rating from 'not recommended' to 'highly recommended' with some going so far as to award a 'quality label' to what they consider to be the best programs. In the United States, the Educational Products Information Exchange (EPIE) publishes a catalogue of 11,000 packages of which it has reviewed over 1,000 whilst the Microcomputer Software Information for Teachers (MicroSIFT) has a database comprising 3,500 titles. In Canada the database of the Council of the Ministers of Educations lists 1,600 titles and York University over 3,000. In the United Kingdom, the National Educational Resources Information Service has reviewed some 2,000 packages. In Australia the National Software Coordination Unit's database lists over 2000 titles and Curtin University over 2,700. In France the Ministry of Education has published its 'official' catalogue of 700 selected programs as part of its campaign "Informatique pour Tous".

A number of the agencies are part of larger operations providing support services to schools and teachers. Other services provided include the professional development of teachers and the provision of resource or preview centres which by various strategies provide teachers with the opportunity to view the available software and curriculum materials in order to evaluate them for use in their own schools. Some agencies are actively involved in the development of software or in advising developers of software and therefore conduct formative evaluations in order to assist the software developers as well as conducting summative reviews and evaluations to assist teachers.

Overall, however, the evidence of what is actually happening in many countries to provide for the needs of teachers is not very encouraging. Information about available software is generally not easily accessible to teachers or is not used by teachers for a number of reasons even when databases have been created specifically for this purpose. Agencies have been set up to review software but even now they are unable to keep up with the flood of software becoming available and provide teachers with the critical appraisals of software they need. Not all such agencies continue to survive. A common strand running through the account of activities in OECD countries is of projects and agencies being left without continued funding, like so many ships left stranded on the beach when the tide has gone out. Both pre- and in-service training to date has been largely unsuccessful in meeting the needs of teachers for training in the selection of software and its use across the curriculum. Support services including the provision of software previewing facilities for teachers are often largely non-existent.

A number of other concerns about the information needs of teachers were expressed. Teachers need information not just about software in terms of its existence and quality but also about how it can be used in the classroom. Their needs are dynamic and constantly changing and evolving. Time is the significant barrier for teachers who, as more and more information becomes available, are drowning in it. Moreover, it is important to recognize that they are not just recipients of information but also contributors to it.

4. THE VALUE OF SOFTWARE REVIEW AND EVALUATION

Conclusion: Although opinions apparently differ, there is in fact a broad degree of agreement at the international level on the feasibility and value of the educational review and evaluation of educational software.

In any international gathering there will always be differences of opinion due to barriers of culture and language which are more apparent than real. This is especially so when the same terms have different meanings for different authors and speakers and in different countries. This was the case with the terms 'software review' and 'software evaluation' which caused a fair amount of confusion at the Seminar. They are often used to describe a form of critical appraisal of a piece of software. In some countries, for example, the United States and Australia, the terms are used synonymously as a judgement about the value, worth, appropriateness and usefulness of a piece of educational software and are used loosely and interchangeably for activities ranging from sales descriptions of software in magazines to in-depth critical appraisals conducted by academic researchers. In other countries, for example, the United Kingdom, the term 'software evaluation' is reserved in the classical meaning of evaluation for critical appraisals of software involving in-depth testing and anything less than that is called a 'software review'. In other countries, for example, France, only the term 'software evaluation' is used to describe any kind of critical appraisal and the term 'software review' is not used at all. Thus, what one author calls software review another calls software evaluation; what appears impossible to one author is perfectly reasonable and feasible to another, and what is a purely subjective opinion to one author has a level of objectivity for another. Because of these differences in terminology and usage between different countries in the use of the terms the following definitions of terms have been adopted by OECD:

'Software description' is an objective and informative description of a piece of software; 'software review' is a critical appraisal by one or more persons of the educational value of a software package as a teaching or learning tool and 'software evaluation' is a judgement about the value and usefulness of a piece of software involving an in-depth analysis and observation of the use of the software by means of quantitative and qualitative measurements and methodologies.

Both reviews and evaluations normally include both technical and pedagogical descriptions. The technical description gives bibliographic information such as author, publisher, distributor, length of software program, cost, required hardware, including type of screen, peripherals such as mouse, light pen and joystick. A pedagogical description indicates the subject, type of software (tutorial, drill and practice, simulation etc), the target audience, objectives, content, curriculum congruence, interactivity and user support materials.

Reviews and evaluations can be technical or educational: technical review or evaluation is an appraisal of the technical aspects of the software, whilst educational review or evaluation is an appraisal of the educational value of the software.

Evaluations can be either formative or summative: formative evaluation is intended to provide evidence which can be used in the further development of the software, whilst summative evaluation sets out to make a judgement about the value of the software as an instructional tool in terms of its success or failure to achieve its objective as an instructional tool.

Despite the differences of usage, it was clear at the Seminar that there was a broad underlying level of agreement. Despite their drawbacks and shortcomings, many participants considered that software reviews can be very useful guides to teachers in making their decisions regarding the selection of educational software. Like any critique, however, whether of a work of art, a book or a software package, the experience and expertise of the reviewer has to be taken into account before any credence is given to the critique. No matter how reliable the reviewer, in the final analysis it is the teacher who must decide whether he/she can use that particular software package and how he/she will use it.

5. THE NEED FOR TRAINING IN SOFTWARE SELECTION

Conclusion: Teachers need training in the selection of software as well as prior training in the pedagogical uses of computers.

After considering many of the issues related to software review and evaluation and the dissemination of information, the participants agreed that the training given to all teachers, whether at the pre-service or the in-service stage, should include training in assessing and selecting software. Such training should be part of the in-depth training in the pedagogical uses of the information technologies, which is needed by all teachers to supplement the introductory training usually given them in the operation of microcomputers and the setting up and managing of the hardware available in their classrooms. Given such training, teachers would be able to translate the potential of computer based learning into the actuality of instructional use which meets their objectives and curriculum needs. Participants agreed on the necessity of such training but were concerned about the numerous problems involved in the training and support of teachers, for example, the lack of appropriate training, the lack of time, the lack of suitable teacher educators and the lack of appropriate support services.

How should teachers go about selecting software? Once they have short-listed a number of possible programs either by looking through catalogues and journals that both describe and review them in detail, by consulting their colleagues (the 'grapevine' is often a good source of information), through teacher associations in their own particular field or by consulting electronic databases, teachers should preview software before buying it. This they can do either by paying a visit to a software library (some countries have a number of regional and local centres) or by a telesoftware system by which the software is transmitted direct to the school by means of an on-line service from the software library. Although special training is required to be able to use telesoftware systems, they appear to be by far the quickest and most convenient method of allowing teachers to preview software. After this previewing operation which can take several hours, a teacher will have a good idea of how valuable a particular program would be.

6. OPPORTUNITIES FOR INTERNATIONAL COOPERATION

Conclusion: There are opportunities for international co-operation in the review and evaluation of software and in access to educational software.

Although the diversity of curricula, cultures and languages between countries would appear to preclude close cooperation in the actual reviewing and evaluation of software except between countries with close geographic, cultural or language ties, many participants saw that advantages were to be gained by the Member countries of OECD cooperating in a number of areas to realize the potential of the information technologies in education.

In view of the cost of software review and evaluation, it would certainly be worthwhile for countries which are developing databases to pool their information. Where languages permit, there has been some pooling of information between English-speaking, French-speaking and Scandinavian countries. Detailed commentaries and some in-depth evaluations are particularly important for countries that have to rely on others that are more advanced in software production, either because they are not big enough to justify the creation of a home-based industry or because most of their resources have gone into purchasing microcomputers for schools. In this case, before buying foreign software programs, the best would have to be picked out either for use virtually unchanged or for adaptation to suit the social and cultural characteristics of the country concerned.

OECD is looking at a number of ways in which further cooperation might take place.

7. THE QUALITY OF SOFTWARE AND THE FUTURE

Conclusion: The quality of software depends on a number of interrelated evolving variables and the quality of software and software review and evaluation should therefore be considered in the light of past and future developments.

The concept of quality in educational software, of what makes a piece of software an effective teaching or learning resource, is elusive and difficult to define. It is the result of the interaction and interplay of a number of variables, including the subject matter being taught and the curriculum, teaching and the teacher, learning and the learner, the technology itself and the type and design of the software being used, all of which are subject to extremely rapid change and development. At the international level these factors are compounded by national and cultural differences which can cause a piece of software considered excellent in one country to be considered of little value in another.

In his opening address Professor Jacques Hebenstreit, the Chairman of the Seminar, emphasised the importance of 'references to the past which explain the present and references to the future which allow us to put things into perspective'. Twenty years ago, given the state of the technology then, some evaluators considered the drill and practice type of software available at the time as being of high quality, whereas nowadays it is regarded as very poor.

In the next ten years every student will have a pocket computer. This would imply radical changes in the use of computers in schools and a radical change in the software market. The software market would be a mass market in which successful programs would sell by the millions. Hardly a textbook would be published without a set of programs offering a wealth of examples, drill and practice exercises, simulation activities, relevant databases, interactive concept exploration and hypothesis testing, all organized and planned in keeping with an instructional strategy complementary to the content of the book. In the classroom as well as at home, students would be able to make rapid calculations, check the validity of a formula, look up statistics, review a lesson, type a report, take notes, communicate with other students or teachers. Today teachers decide what software is to be used at a given time. In the near future children will be using all kinds of software with or without the teachers' permission and will in fact create a software market which does not exist today.

In this context, what will software evaluation mean? We should use our past experience with pocket calculators. Because they had not kept abreast of rapid technological developments in this area and were unaware of the implications of the rapid drop in cost and widespread use of calculators in society, numerous decision makers and teachers found themselves in a difficult position. We must keep in mind that the children entering school today will still be in the compulsory education system in the year 2000. We are right in the midst of a transitory period and the most radical changes are still to come. "The wisest thing to do, therefore, is probably to try to build a reasonable view of what is coming and to use every area which we can act upon (teacher training, research, evaluation) to prepare our educational system as well as possible for the inevitable changes which lie ahead."

REFERENCES

[1] Winship, J.A., Information Technologies in Education: The Quest for Quality Software (OECD, Paris, 1989).

[2] OECD/CERI, New Information Technologies: A Challenge for Education (OECD, Paris, 1986).

[3] OECD/CERI, Information Technologies and Basic Learning: Reading, Writing, Science and Mathematics (OECD, Paris, 1987).

[4] Bigum, C., Bonser, S., Evans, P., Groundwater-Smith, S., Grundy, S., Kemmis, S., McKenzie D., McKinnon, D., O'Connor, M., Straton, R., & Willis, S., Coming to Terms with Computers in Schools (Deakin Institute for Studies in Education, Australia, 1987).

[5] Department of Education and Science, England and Wales, Aspects of the Work of the Microelectronics Education Programme, Report by HM Inspectors (HMSO, London, 1987)

[6] Ministère de l'Education Nationale, Note sur les Applications Pédagogiques de 'Informatique dans 'Enseignement secondaire (Paris, 1985)

[7] OECD/CERI, The Introduction of Computers in Schools: The Norwegian Experience (OECD, Paris, 1987)

[8] Scottish Education Department, Learning and Teaching in Scottish Secondary Schools: The Use of Microcomputers (HMSO, Edinburgh, 1987)

[9] OTA, (1988) "Power On! New Tools for Teaching and Learning", Congress of the the United States, Office of Technology Assessment

Computers in Education
A. McDougall and C. Dowling (Editors)
Elsevier Science Publishers B.V. (North-Holland)
IFIP, 1990

PROGRESS WITH IT
A summary of curriculum developments in Information Technology

Peter Dutton, IT Adviser, TVEI Unit, Training Agency, Sheffield, England

The British Government is funding the Technical and Vocational Education Initiative (TVEI) over 15 years (1983-97), so that ultimately all students aged 14-18 years in all schools and colleges will follow a curriculum which will enhance the capabilities they require in the modern, highly technological world of work. Information technology (IT) plays a major role as a subject in its own right, as an aid to learning and teaching, and as an aid to managing education. Students' progress is enhanced by using IT, especially where that use has direct relevance in their own learning and in relating their learning to industry and commerce. Teachers progress similarly with IT in their personal and professional capabilities. Improved understanding of learning leads to new roles for the teacher, working alongside student with IT. Imaginative curricula are taking the very nature of information technology to enhance learner involvement and collaborative working, all of which provide excellent grounding for students' enterprise. Industry and commerce are actively supporting these, and future, developments as they see the benefits of more capable young people entering adult society.

ORGANISATIONAL FRAMEWORK

1. In November 1982, the Prime Minister announced in the House of Commons that the British Government was funding a new initiative in technical and vocational education. The first 14 local education authorities (LEAs) started the pilot phase of the Technical and Vocational Education Initiative (TVEI) in September 1983, with all 121 Authorities in England, Wales and Scotland following in succeeding years. Each LEA followed a five year planned and managed pilot programme of development, involving cohorts of about 250 students per year in a small number of schools and colleges. Pilot programmes saw four cohorts entering in the age range 14-18 years, generally at a costs of £2M additional to the normal education budget for each Authority. The later entrants followed a modified approach at less cost.

2. In a White Paper published in July 1986 [1], the Government decided to extend the scale and scope of TVEI, such that in the period 1987-1997 all students aged 14-18 years in all schools and colleges in England, Wales and Scotland would eventually benefit from a TVEI development programme. Authorities that had completed at least three years of pilot development were eligible for additional funding to enable a planned further programme of 5-7 years to extend the principles and practices of TVEI to all schools/colleges and to all students. 11 LEAs started their extension programmes in September 1987, and this will increase to all Authorities by 1992 (see fig 1).

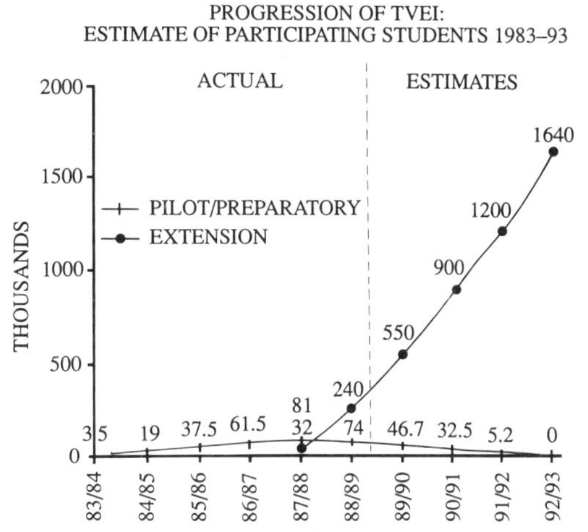

Figure 1

EDUCATION FRAMEWORK

3. The seven education aims of the TVEI pilot programmes were summarised as being to equip young people with the knowledge, skills, competences, qualifications and attitudes which they will need at work in a rapidly changing, highly technological society. Each Authority's programme differed in detail to meet the local situation, but the emphasis was always on ensuring a broad, balanced curriculum, containing science, technology, and information technology for all students, at least up to the age of 16 years. Programmes also had to ensure equality of opportunity for all, irrespective of gender, race or ability.

4. With the emergence of the National Curriculum for students aged 5-16 years in schools in England and Wales, as defined in the 1988 Education Reform Act of Parliament, and with the gradual movement from pilot to extension programmes within TVEI, the main educational emphasis of TVEI has changed to ensuring

that the WHOLE CURRICULUM for students aged 14-18 years is related to the capabilities they will require in the modern world of work. The latter is illustrated by the predicted changes in patterns of employment shown in Fig 2. TVEI operates within the National Curriculum, looking at both educational content and processes so as to increase students' responsibility for their own learning, including how to work in teams in enterprising and creative ways.

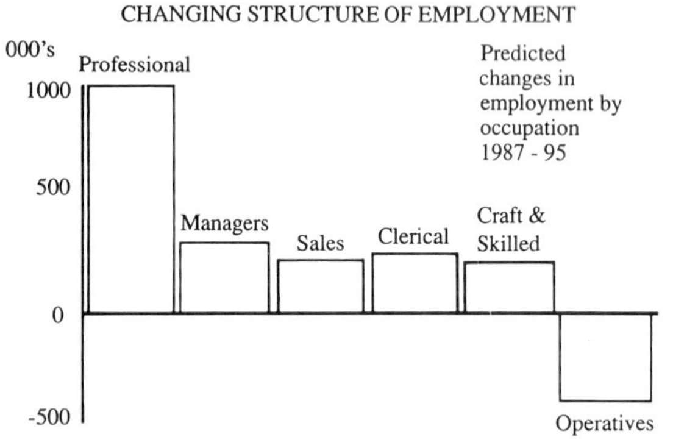

Figure 2 Source: Warwick Institute of Employment Research

5. Within this educational and organisational framework of TVEI, information technology (IT) has played a major role in the pilot programmes as a subject in its own right, as an aid to teaching and learning, and as an aid to managing and organising the new education programmes. Analysis of data from the first four years of pilot programmes shows that IT as a fraction of total curriculum time had increased from 0.5% for non-TVEI students to 3% for TVEI students, with 64% TVEI schools operating new IT courses. Nearly 20% of all TVEI students took IT subjects, compared with only 1.1% for non-TVEI students. Preliminary figures from the TVEI extension programmes show more than half of all students are now taking a technological subject at age 16, including about 40% of all girls. The major role for IT is continuing, although there does now appear to be a shift away from emphasis on IT as a subject more towards IT as an aid in teaching and learning.

STUDENTS PROGRESS WITH IT

6. The National Curriculum for England and Wales (and the corresponding regulations for Scotland) describes capability in information technology thus:

> Students should be able to use IT appropriately and effectively to communicate and handle information in a variety of forms and for a variety of purposes, to design, develop, explore and evaluate appropriate models of real or imaginary situations, and to measure physical quantities and control movement. [2]

Progression in the development of IT capability is only concerned to a limited extent with the accumulation of specific skills in operating IT tools such as spreadsheets or graphics systems in isolation. Progression comes more through the increasing demands of the context in which the IT is applied, and also through a decrease in the level of intervention by the teacher. This progression will necessitate the use of a wider range of IT skills, a more complex application of those skills and the integration of several aspects of IT into solving a specific task. It also requires a growing independence by the student in selecting appropriate IT tools, including those required to aid her/his own learning. TVEI adds an extremely important dimension to this concept of progression. Not only may the educational contexts increase in complexity, but also those outside education. IT has a unique place in this 'double' view of progression, as it is so widely used to real purpose both within and without school and college.

7. Research evidence from careful evaluation of a sample of TVEI pilot schools and colleges shows the increasing emphasis given by teachers to such applications outside education [3]. This is found to be one way of attracting and retaining more girls on IT courses. One example of such external applications is the value of good relevant work experience using IT for some post-16 students. A teacher said that she believed the classroom was "a false situation" which inhibited "personality and presentation". She was particularly concerned to find challenging work experience placements for her students. Responsibility was placed on them to find placements in which they were interested, and her 'bank' of placements was only used at the last minute to help those who could not arrange their own. It was reported that many of her students had displayed only average ability previously, yet examples were given showing very considerable progress being made, not only with using IT but as people: "They go out as children and they come back as little adults".

8. TVEI students also progress using IT as a resource in their learning of subjects other than those directly connected with information technology. One school TVEI co-ordinator said "Our aim is to use the technology in such a way as to allow all students to see useful out-comes. ... The emphasis, therefore, is on word processing and programs available on the school network, particularly graphics programs". The 'narrow' view that word processing was primarily a labour-saving activity and/or an aid to presentation rather than composition was common in early pilot schemes. But there is evidence that a 'broader' view is gaining ground. One teacher "had been staggered by how much pupils love to work on the machines" and saw computers as "extending capability". Another said "Before, she came to the lesson and you knew there was going to be a lot of trouble. Now she

even stops me in the corridor with extra work she's done on her own. The change came when the work progressed from being an 'exercise' to writing History and Geography projects". Another development scheme, involving LEAs in North West England, has produced a way in which students aged 16-18 years can enhance their normal academic work with projects involving local industry and/or higher education. The reports of all such projects have to be word-processed, and most use other aspects of IT in the presentations that have to be made by the students to their peers and senior staffs from school/college, companies and university. Some projects have had specific IT content, including data logging and computer control.

9. In their conclusions about progression made by pupils using IT within and across the curriculum, the researchers reported that "what is learned and the motivation for what is learned are very different (when using IT). The advantages are that the development of user familiarity, expertise and knowledge will be more directly relevant to the learner's immediate needs and so the learning is likely to have purpose and direction. The technology also offers to a wider range of students the possibility of greater control of their learning." Her Majesty's Inspectors, in a report on one of the TVEI Pilot Authorities, recorded similar findings about the uses of IT to encourage and support learning, saying that "the best practice was when the learning was closely integrated with a mini-enterprise project".

10. A survey of over 15,000 TVEI students showed that they did value the schemes that bring increased breadth and overall relevance to their studies, and for the opportunities for off-site learning [4]. They might start at age 14 thinking that IT within TVEI was solely concerned with vocational aspects, to help them develop job specific skills. But by age 16 and beyond, TVEI students saw that the main progress they had made had been in the enhancement of their 'social and life skills' and in their general vocational preparation including learning how to learn.

TEACHERS PROGRESS WITH IT

11. Although the previous section has outlined ideas of students' progression, there is a parallel situation for the progress made by teachers. Many times, the two progressions overlap through shared experience in using or learning about IT. Professionally, teachers need to consider (a) the curriculum approach(es) being used for particular groups of students (considered in detail in the next section), (b) their own role and style vis-a-vis their students' progression (including the recording of, and reflection upon, that progression), and (c) the potential impact of IT upon their subject discipline and/or age phase, including the necessity to consider carefully the impact of relevant uses of IT outside education. Such a pattern of professional development is not unique to information technology, but the nature of that technology itself, plus the scale of recent changes together with increasing understanding of the fundamental nature of learning, has meant that IT has been in the forefront of many changes in teacher training. Behind this analysis is the implication that the changes needed to be implemented in schools and colleges will have to be introduced by the present teaching force: the institutions cannot wait until there are sufficient numbers of new entrants into the profession trained in new approaches and techniques. Thus the bulk of any professional development has to be offered to practising teachers, although changes must also be reflected in initial training programmes.

12. Research evidence culled from TVEI pilot programmes showed that many more classroom teachers than previously had been brought into curriculum development work, made contact with employers and outside agencies, and accepted opportunities for professional development [4]. For example, one Authority published a five year plan for the overall development of IT in all its schools and colleges, with TVEI funds being used specifically to support teachers of students aged 14-18 years. The in-service teacher training part of that plan described the carefully structured training for senior managers to raise the level of their awareness, both in educational terms and in terms of the impact of IT upon the whole community including the 'world of work'. At the request of the Headteachers and Principals, that led to comparable training for members of their staffs selected on the basis of being able to take delegated responsibility for IT across and within the whole curriculum. That in turn led to an enormous amount of training, some formal some informal, some organised for subject teachers across the Authority, some organised for groups of teachers from one particular school or college. A key finding of the effectiveness of this and similar schemes was the considerable advantage in training a natural group of teachers TOGETHER. This might be a whole department, say, teaching English, followed later by other departments (eg Science, Modern Languages, Technology). Such a 'critical mass' ensured the effective introduction of IT across and within the curriculum in a comparatively short time.

13. In moving from TVEI pilot to extension programmes, Authorities have more than just an increased number of teachers to train; they have to consider the most effective strategies for introducing the changes in teaching and learning contained within the aims of TVEI. The emphasis has moved from training teachers in relatively simple IT skills (important though that is, of course!) to detailed professional consideration

of a pedagogy that incorporates understanding of the nature of learning. For example, interactive video (IV) tape systems have been shown to be extremely effective for school-based in-service teacher training [5]. For whole school and/or whole department staff development, the use of such a system encourages group interactions and focusses analysis onto real issues raised by the IV programme. This in turn helps teachers to foster a common purpose, identify agreed goals, and move towards consistency in approaches to learning and teaching. Key issues can be raised in a non-threatening manner, for the teachers can be encouraged to analyse issues and practices in a neutral way before moving to critical examination and evaluation of their own experience and practice. Such an approach encourages 'possibilism' rather than 'impossibilism', for when using IV programmes, teachers see other teachers working with just as limited resources, equally large classes, and equally complex pressures that make it difficult to ensure effective liaison with industry and other external agencies. This particular technology itself encourages active, participative learning; it also can encourage several forms of interactivity (amongst peers, between teachers and students etc) as well as with the machine itself. And although interactive video tape can never compete technically with IV disc, it does enable teachers (and students) to gain very considerably from the production of their own IV programmes.

14. The TVEI Head Office has initiated a major programme of teacher training development in information technology. The overall aim is to prepare teacher training materials, ideas, techniques and experiences that will support the uses of IT within the whole curriculum that reflects the world of work. Some projects are producing teacher training ideas in specific subjects (science, maths, modern languages, design and technology), whilst another is using generic software such as spreadsheets in different forms of modelling. Two projects are developing materials and ideas to train teachers in the effective management of IT, developing policies which can be put into practice using good, relevant industrial experiences. One project will prepare training for support staff in schools. Another has produced training materials in microtechnology, and the final project is working with interactive video tape systems as already described, but now focussed on training teachers in matters connected with all aspects of economic understanding. This programme includes central professional evaluation. Each project reflects the nature of TVEI in that it is operated by an active consortium of an institution of higher education, several LEAs each involving several schools/colleges, and local industry.

PROGRESSIVE CURRICULA WITH IT

15. Intimately connected with the progress of students and of teachers are issues of the curriculum framework and how that can be managed within the whole management and administrative structure of the school or college. Some management issues will be tackled in the next section, whilst this one concentrates on changes in learning and teaching. Information technology both aids such changes and, by its very nature, sharpens the need for the changes. This accords directly with the intentions of TVEI, with the emphasis on educational processes as well as content. One of the great strengths of IT is that it encourages iterative approaches to tasks. The processes of analysis, design, implementation and evaluation are naturally cyclic. Because the computer allows changes to be made easily and quickly, these processes can occur more rapidly and more often that previously. Moreover, in helping to reinforce the notion that learning itself is iterative, IT turns errors from something negative, to be avoided at all costs, into something which can be natural stepping stones on the journey to success. The need to share computer facilities can be used positively to encourage collaboration between students, rather than necessarily be a major constraint. Obviously not all groups work equally together, and somtimes the keyboard operator dominates rather than facilitates. Yet this sort of participative working, when guided by a skilled teacher, can empower students to progress in their personal capacities as well as in gaining knowledge, skills and experiences. For example, the ability to establish and test hypotheses in science, business studies or economics is helped by adding to the usual laboratory or classroom work the possibilities of efficient information handling systems and simulations. This is especially true in processes that parallel those in industry and commerce, where clearly practical experimentation by students is unlikely to be encouraged!

16. Several Authorities in Scotland have worked together within TVEI programmes to integrate the uses of IT across the whole curriculum. This pattern is also found elsewhere, but one interesting aspect of the Scottish developments is the Silicon Society Course for 14-15 year old students. The preceeding two years in secondary school provide a bridge with the work done in primary schools, a careful induction into the whole range of IT possibilities (word processing, spreadsheets, graphics, communications, video, control etc), and a planned and systematic approach to uses of IT resources for learning. The Silicon Society course then provides an opportunity for students to reflect on the effect that IT is having on their lives, and in the workplace and at home. It involves a lot of practical work in groups, including presentations to peers and to adults from outside the school. Another example is of a TVEI Authority which has reviewed the ways in which

IT can support the learning of students with special education needs. Its policy is to integrate the treatment of the student with the work of the school as far as possible; to seek as many interactive tasks as possible; and to negotiate individual targets appropriate for each student. Thus IT is not installed and left, but a commitment is obtained from the whole school community to give access for such students to the whole curriculum. A final example is from a TVEI school that had been involved in a national Newspaper Day Competition, and had in fact won on three successive occasions. The teacher in charge of IT said:

> "TVEI is responsible for our success. It is not simply a funding mechanism, as only 5 out of 81 computers in the school were paid for from TVEI funds. Rather it has changed our thinking of what students can do. They are in charge of their own curriculum, judging their own performances for themselves against known and agreed, external criteria. The whole philosophy of the staff towards the students now is 'Can do'!"

Interestingly, the students decided to produce their last newspaper commercially and to distribute it throughout their neighbourhood. They raised £1700 from selling advertising, the cost of the 12,000 copies was £1300, so they not only learned about producing a newspaper but were commercially successful as well!

PROGRESSIVE MANAGEMENT WITH IT

17. A recent analysis of the views of senior managers from TVEI schools and colleges about the key developments of IT in the near future shows three main areas in which planned progress is needed. One whole area involves the provision of physical resources, and the management of access to them by students and teachers. Lessons from early TVEI programmes shows that, whatever the professed intentions of teacher concerning access to IT when used within the whole curriculum, logistic problems of gaining access to a central resource were a hurdle too high to be surmounted either comfortably or regularly. Similar lessons show how successful many colleges for post-16 students have been in using some TVEI funds to establish or enhance the implementation of 'open access' facilities for both students and staff. Thus, progressive management needs to plan not only the technical aspects of networks, portability of software and transferability of data and information etc, but also an approximate mix of central resources and specialised facilities.

18. The second major concern of senior managers is the development of appropriate policies and practices for IT for all within the whole curriculum. This links back to the progress summarised in the previous three sections, involving clear thinking about the progression expected of the students, a definite programme of staff development, and a curriculum strategy which incorporates appropriate learning and teaching styles for different subject areas and age phases. Linked to these matters is an increasing awareness of the educational validity of 'flexble learning'. Much work has been done within TVEI and elsewhere on open learning, distance learning and supported self-study. A major programme has been started in TVEI to pull these various strands together, and to see where further developments may be needed.

19. The third area of concern of managers involved managing effective links with organisations outside school and college, and the uses of IT to aid effective administration. There are many excellent examples in TVEI pilot and extension programmes of liaison with industry, commerce and the community which has influenced the learning of the students. This includes an example of the secondment of an industrialist full-time for a short period to a group of TVEI schools to help teachers prepare teaching schemes using IT that will develop and enhance skills and qualities required in young people working in modern industry. Another example was where the Business Education Department in a school organised work experience for the students in the local Council's Computer Centre, and with several banks and other firms using computers so that the students had opportunities for transferring skills that they had gained in school into the working environment.

POSSIBLE FUTURE PROGRESS WITH IT

20. As the number of schools and colleges involved in TVEI extension programmes reaches a peak in 1991/92, so the number of imaginative examples of how students progress through good uses of IT will grow. Perhaps the only real limitation on such growth will be that of human imagination, coming mainly from the students themselves but also from those charged with organising and managing such a major educational initiative. However, there are four further developments within TVEI connected directly with IT.

a) A consultation in May 1989 on the theme 'From teaching to learning' identified the main issues facing a school or college wishing to change the emphasis of its way of working as being:

- accepting that the key to change is to concentrate on the learning rather than the teacher;

- making careful decisions about suitable styles and pace of change;

- opening up visions of wider educational partnerships with the whole community with less domination by the education profession yet retaining high academic qualities;

- improving resourcing wherever possible, but also looking to improve the management of all present resources.

These ideas are now being taken into all parts of the TVEI system (and into many other networks) so that ideas may influence policies and practices. IT is both a stimulant of, and an important resource for, such changes, although experiences point to the greater importance of the people than of the information or the technology!

b) The ideas and experiences implicit in the phrase 'From teaching to learning' will form a major part of the TVEI input to the international conference 'School Year 2020' organised by the International Movement Towards Educational Changes (IMTEC) to be held in September 1990 in Oxford, England. Delegates will have opportunites not only to hear major speeches, and to join in discussion groups on various topics within the overall theme of the school of 30 years hence, but also will be able to visit schools and colleges in different parts of the United Kingdom, including TVEI organisations using IT in a variety of ways.

c) Mention has been made earlier to ways in which interactive video is being used within TVEI as a powerful aid in in-service professional development. Many industrial and commercial companies also use the technology for their own staff training, as well as for promotion and presentations. Some further possible developments are being considered involving close collaboration between selected companies and TVEI school/colleges. They will consider learning theories appropriate to using interactive media in schools and in firms; managing learning effectively when using interactive media; exchanging industrial/commercial and educational materials; and an analysis of trends in industrial/commercial uses of interactive media and their relevance to education.

d) The importance of effective management of learning is being highlighted by many of the changes in education. Some work is just starting which will look specifically at the management of effective learning across a whole school community. Preliminary discussions have shown that many TVEI schools are considering 'learning issues' but rarely perceive the potential of IT in helping to resolve those issues. Meanwhile, many other schools are introducing IT within and across the whole curriculum, but have not yet considered how all the different learning experiences might be managed most effectively.

POSTSCRIPT

21. This brief summary cannot do adequate justice to the many achievements and very considerable professional developments of all who have been, and are, involved in the Technical and Vocational Education Initiative. It is a pleasure to acknowledge this work with gratitude, and to trust that the necessary brevity of this paper does not appear to diminish such achievements.

ACKNOWLEDGEMENTS

Most of the information summarised in this paper comes from documents that are for internal use within the Technical and Vocational Education Initiative. Reference has been made to the following public documents:

[1] Government White Paper 'Working Together - Education and Training', HMSO, July 1986;

[2] National Curriculum Council Consultation Report: Technology, November 1989

[3] Technology in TVEI: IT in the TVEI Curriculum 14-18, National Evaluation Report by University of Leeds, April 1989;

[4] 'Perspectives on TVEI', National Foundation for Education Research, 1988;

[5] Developments in interactive video in TVEI, TVEI Unit, January 1989.

A full list of TVEI publications may be obtained from the Enquiry Point, TVEI Unit, Training Agency, Moorfoot, Sheffield, S1 4PQ, United Kingdom.

Computers in Education
A. McDougall and C. Dowling (Editors)
Elsevier Science Publishers B.V. (North-Holland)

FIELD WORK ON A GRAND SCALE: USING DATA FROM EARTH ORBITING SATELLITES IN THE GEOGRAPHY CURRICULUM

H.B. FIELDING and M. FOLLAND

Educational Computing Centre Birmingham, Balden Lane, Harborne, Birmingham B32 2EH, U.K.; Swanshurst School Birmingham, U.K.

The use of data from orbiting satellites is having an impact in the area of Geography Education. The paper outlines the impact at two levels, the school level and the Local Authority level. The introduction of the National Curriculum in England and Wales has raised many issues. One common thread is the appropriate use of new technology. Whilst the Geography Curriculum has not as yet (Autumn 1989) been published, it is likely to contain reference to similar threads.

1. INTRODUCTION

There are many satellites in earth orbit that carry sensors to scan the surface below. Some of these transmit data that can be received easily by relatively simple and inexpensive equipment. The data transmitted may be in the visual range, infra-red or even specific atmospheric material such as water vapour.

There are two types of satellite orbit, polar and equatorial. The polar orbiting satellites follow a general path from pole to pole. The equatorial orbit follows the equator.

Polar orbiters are generally of the order of 800 km above the surface of the earth and consequently orbit the earth in about 100 minutes. The orbit is fixed in position in space but as the earth turns one complete revolution in 24 hours, the satellite orbit appears to move from east to west on each successive pass. Generally these satellites produce two or three overhead passes every day.

The equatorial satellites are much further away, at a distance of 36,000 km. At this distance, a complete orbit takes 24 hours. If the satellite moves in the same direction as the earth's rotation, the satellite will appear to be stationary. This type of orbit is sometimes called geostationary.

There are several uses for satellite data in the Geography curriculum:

a) Land use.
The changes that take place during the year can be seen and compared. This could be linked to agriculture and farming activities.

b) Weather.
The geostationary satellite can provide whole earth or large sections of the earth that can be used in weather forecasting. The polar satellite, with its lower orbit can complement and give close detail of local weather conditions.

c) Physical studies.
The progress of the ice caps in the Polar regions can be followed as well as thankfully rare events such as volcanic eruptions.

One of the most exciting aspects of these systems is that pupils can now have and use the same data with which the Weather Bureaux work. This situation fits well with current educational philosophy of open-ended investigation and problem-solving activities. Whereas, previously, pupils may have been given data that was already partly processed.

2. AN EDUCATION AUTHORITY PERSPECTIVE

In an ideal situation, this sort of data should be available to any pupil. This then leads us into the area of data handling. What software is available and what equipment is needed to run that package? The quantity of data concerned can be very large, for example, a 15-minute pass from a polar orbiting satellite can occupy anything up to 4.5 Mb. Clearly, this is too large for computers in the school. Floppy disks can store about 700 Kb with ease and with computer memories of 1 Mb, can provide a workable system.

As far as the City of Birmingham is concerned, it has some 350 primary schools and another 100 secondary schools and colleges. The primary sector is now being equipped with Research Machines Nimbus computers. These have a basic specification of being MS-DOS compatible with 512 Kb memory and 16 colour graphics capability. The secondary schools have similar machines but with 1 Mb memory and the general ability to connect to a network system.

Many computer systems used for satellite data manipulation need special cards or boards fitted to them. The associated software packages needed to process the data may bear little relation to the general costs of educational software. This may nearly double the cost of the original computer. As a consequence, systems set up for this type of use are invariably in fixed locations. If a general purpose curriculum machine could be used, this would mean a financial saving and give flexibility of access to pupils. Savings could be made if the process of collecting satellite data can be removed from the processes of using that data. A number of centralised satellite receiver stations could supply data to a large number of users. The data could be supplied on floppy disks for use on the school's computer systems.

Birmingham is moving in this direction following the installation of two receiving stations capable of receiving both polar and geostationary satellite transmissions. One is at the Martineau Education Centre where the Education Support Service is located. The other is at Swanshurst School and was financed by Industry as part of their Education and Industry partnership. Both installations are capable of converting the raw satellite data transmissions onto floppy disks. Having access to the raw data is only the first step. Software to process the data needs to be available. The Educational Computing Centre in Birmingham has produced a software package called "IMAGES" that can run on any of the Nimbus "curriculum" machines. The data can be read into the computer and displayed as a picture preserving all 256 brightness levels. The Nimbus computer can only display the 16 colours and so the groups of the 256 levels are assigned to one of these colours. Any one of the 256 data levels can be assigned to any of the colours. Figure 1 shows a colour index table. Each of the 256 data values can be assigned a colour. In this case values 0 to 15 are assigned to black, 16 to 31 to dark blue and so on.

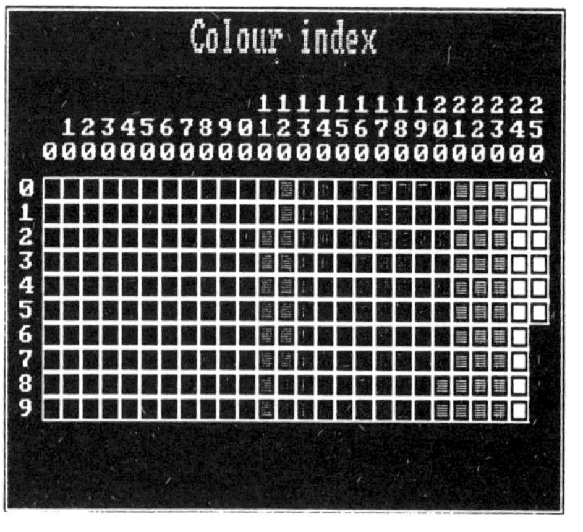

Figure 1

On the initial display the screen shows an averaged pixel picture from the full data file of 640 Kb. (The program will run on the minimum 512 Kb machine.) There is a facility to "zoom" into the display until the maximum resolution is reached. At any stage, there is the facility to scroll the display in any direction, up/down/left/right. There is a further option to "enlarge" an area if required. At any stage there is an option to print out the display. Colour and monochrome printers are supported as well as an option to print out in colour for photocopy reproduction to gain a better grey scale than with a monochrome printer alone. As the image from the satellite is in monochrome, a monochrome monitor should be used together with the colour display. The monochrome display is the starting point for any process work. Colour can then be used to bring out any required feature. For instance, the eye cannot distinguish between brightness levels 128 and 129. However, if level 128 is assigned a colour and 129 a different colour, the result is obvious to the eye. The colours assigned to a value or a set of values are under the complete control of the user. The actual data value of any picture element can be found by moving the cursor onto that element. Most of the actions required by the package can be done by means of a mouse.

Figure 2 shows a satellite view over the UK in May 1989 at 14.00 GMT. The lower area of the screen has the colour index, whilst down the right-hand side are all the possible options at this level. The arrow (cursor) points to an area near the West Midlands, and the data value of 136 is displayed in the top right corner of the screen. It must be said that this was a particularly good view, a virtually cloudless sky due to a high pressure zone over Northern France.

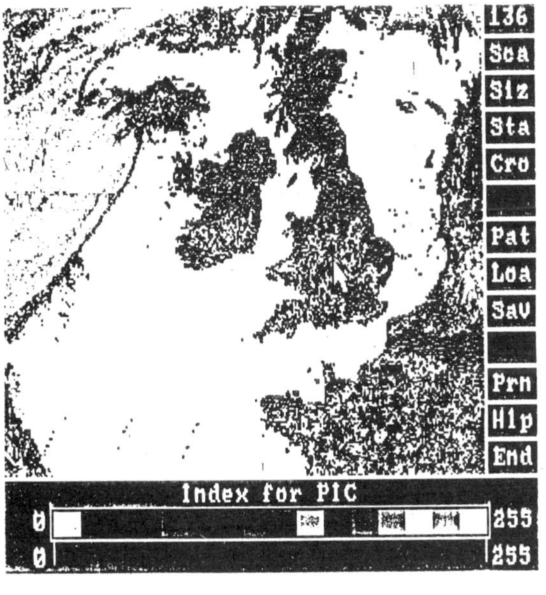

Figure 2

A colour set can be saved for use at a later date, or on a different picture file. This has particular use where a series of pictures is being processed to produce an animation sequence. Whilst this software package will not directly handle this, the pictures produced can be used in other graphics packages to add text and animation.

There are several advantages to this system, for instance, support for teachers and schools on both technical and curriculum uses.

3. A SCHOOL PERSPECTIVE

The cost of a complete receiving station for both polar and geostationary satellite transmissions is relatively high; about double the cost of the associated computer system. Faced with this situation, Swanshurst School in Birmingham made a plea for finance to the West Midlands Engineering Employers Association. The school has had a long history of Education and Industry links through this organisation. The Association readily agreed to finance a complete system comprising:

1. Satellite receiving station, with associated software.
2. Antennae for both polar and geostationary transmissions.
3. Nimbus computer system.
4. Colour printer.

This was installed in the Geography room, which, as luck would have it, is on the top floor of the school building. The dipole and dish antennae were installed on the roof directly above, connected to the receiver by low-loss cable. Late afternoon on April 20, 1989 produced a strong signal from an unknown polar orbiting satellite.

It is still early days yet but it seems that live satellite pictures have had a considerable impact on the way that Geography can be taught. The reality of "catching" the information on a dish on their roof, bringing it down a visible cable into their classroom, controlling the input themselves on their computer is proving a breakthrough in classroom technique. It enables the working from the general to the particular. You can look at a satellite picture of a place that is planned for study, to see what it is like in that place NOW! Discussion about the place can be followed by the ability to zoom in for a close, detailed view. Many topics that used to be uphill work are covered in a few minutes. For example, place name recall used to be an anathema to many staff and pupils. Now it is obvious to all that the picture data must be interpreted! The globe has come into its own and atlases are grabbed, and used effectively, without any teacher instruction. Continents and countries are recognised very quickly. Day and night or the seasons were not popular topics of study in the past. Now the changes can be seen graphically they are taken in the pupils' stride. Pupils are ready to go on to air masses, fronts, convergence/divergence, ridges/troughs, the circulation of the atmosphere, recognition of weather patterns and weather forecasting.

Staff and pupils alike quickly gained confidence in using the system; technology is seen to be working for us in the classroom. Staff and pupils learn together which induces a natural rapport and a partnership in learning between them.

Children take the world as they find it. Between the end of May and mid-July 1989, some second and third year pupils, 13 and 14 years old, became sufficiently confident to operate the system and explain what they were doing for the benefit of TV and Radio networks. Their weather forecasts and interviews were handled competently and calmly, demonstrating considerable communication and presentation skills. Incidentally, although a local story, it was taken up by the national news, much to the pupils' delight.

4. FUTURE PLANS

Central receiving and distribution of satellite data can never give the immediacy to the classroom. It has a place in many areas of Geography education but can never be a replacement for the in-house receiving station. The costs of electronic systems generally fall and it would be hoped that this will happen also for satellite receiving equipment.

One of the needs that was identified early on was a resource and training pack for teachers. There is a need for help in the strategies and techniques needed to interpret satellite data. A group of Geography teachers were sufficiently interested in this area that they have decided to research and produce such a pack. This will take the form of examples of satellite data, on disk, together with associated materials; for instance, in weather studies actual ground station observations and measurements for a range of atmospheric conditions. Links have been made with the Weather Centre at Birmingham University which will bring valuable expertise during this development.

Contacts are being made with schools overseas with a view to establish exchange of satellite data from polar orbiters. Recordings of direct satellite transmissions onto ordinary audio cassette tape mean that there are no incompatibility problems between hardware and software.

Can primary schools make use of the data to back up environmental studies? As yet, there has been no work done on a large scale in this area within the city. It remains to be seen if there is such a use. All that can be said is that the city has an infrastructure that could service that need, should it be desirable or necessary.

5. CONCLUSION

This is very much an initial report on the first steps we are taking into the use of satellite data in Geography Education. We expect this to be an expanding area as time goes by. New satellites are replacing existing ones and these may have enhanced sensors that could give us much more information than we have at present. New information that is made available, and new ideas on how it can be used, should provide us with an exciting and interesting future in Geography Education.

Computers in Education
A. McDougall and C. Dowling (Editors)
Elsevier Science Publishers B.V. (North-Holland)

GEOGRAPHIC INFORMATION SYSTEMS - HOW CAN EDUCATION CATCH UP WITH TECHNOLOGY?

Diana FREEMAN

The Advisory Unit for Microtechnology in Education, Endymion Road, Hatfield, Hertfordshire AL10 8AU, U.K.

The latest buzz word on the software scene is GIS (Geographic Information Systems). After educational computing in schools has been offered word processing, spreadsheets, and desktop publishing from the business and commercial world, Geographic Information Systems are on the horizon to expand the base of British educational software. What is GIS and how has it come about? What are the pressures for its introduction at school level? How should educationalists respond to commercial arguments in such a technology-led field? Although these questions relate mainly to geographers and other users of spatially related data, the arguments put forward are at the heart of debates on whether we are serving children best by merely responding to technological advance, often with little consideration of the implications or consequences from an educational point of view. This paper suggests an approach for introduction of new technology through consideration, identification and elucidation of skills and concepts already being taught.

Geographic Information Systems are a product of the computer age and have stemmed from the advances made in computer-aided cartography in the 1960's, the parallel advances in acquisition and manipulation of spatially-related data in digital form, and the dramatic fall in computer costs. ''GIS' is the biggest step forward in the handling of geographic information since the invention of the map.' (H.M.S.O., 1987). The impetus for these advances has been a world wide need for a scientific understanding of the earth at a detailed level by a number of different agencies concerned with resource management and planning. The need for spatial data and maps has not been restricted to earth scientists. Urban planners, civil engineers, police, sales and marketing companies and public utilities, such as gas, water, electricity and telecommunications, all require information that can be recorded and manipulated in map form. A paper map is no longer the best way to represent information because it is expensive and time consuming to prepare, and is a static, qualitative document. Today's rapidly changing circumstances require fast, accurate representations. For example, weather maps, plans of gas mains and electricity cables or landuse maps of desert margins, need constant updating if they are to be relevant and useful. With the appropriate data and GIS software, computers are able to generate maps that exactly match the users' specification, and aid in modelling and planning changing situations.

The Chorley Report, 'Handling Geographic Information', (H.M.S.O., 1987), was the first attempt in the UK to clarify the situation with regard to the use and potential of GIS. The report was commissioned by the Department of the Environment and canvassed factual evidence in the field of GIS from providers, users and educators. These included Government Departments and other public bodies, utilities (gas, electricity, water and communications), academic institutions, private organisations, local government authorities and professional societies. A major part of the report examined current uses of GIS and identified factors likely to influence its take-up. The theme of education and training was addressed as part of the measures aimed at increasing awareness and familiarisation with geographic information technology and the report recommended that this should be encouraged throughout the education system. This aspect will be discussed later.

The most problematic area at the moment is to decide exactly what GIS comprises. The end users mentioned above have specific demands and applications to which GIS provides an answer, but the answer is different according to each purpose. Many users have developed their own GIS as a response, while others buy off the shelf, and the choice is becoming wider all the time. In recent surveys, Fisher (1989), evaluated eleven MS-DOS GIS packages under $5000 in current use, and Whitehead (1989), evaluated nine packages for the Apple Macintosh. The first national conference of the Association for Geographic Information (AGI) had 36 exhibitors in the GIS software, hardware and consultancy fields. The criteria for the functions of a GIS laid down by Rhind, 1980, (Figure 1) is all embracing, but any one example of a GIS may not contain all the elements of the full implementation that Rhind suggests.

Functions of a GIS

Geographical database:	transform data from one co-ordinate system to another;
	convert data from raster to vector and vice versa;
	build polygons from line segments;
	aggregate and disaggregate geographical entities;
	update records automatically given correct information
Query:	capability to retrieve data by name, co-ordinates or combination of attributes;
	Internal decision rules to assess which operations are feasible with the available data.
Data transformation:	statistical mapping and summation, reformat data for other statistical or modelling packages.
Data display:	ability to generate graphs, histograms and maps
Interactive access:	through a WIMP interface

Figure 1: Functions of a GIS, after Rhind, 1980

A GIS consists of an integrated software package which has five essential modules: data acquisition and input; data storage and database management; data output and presentation; data transformation and a means of interacting with the user (Figure 2). This description is taken from Burrough, 1987.

Data Input: any data used in a GIS has information about the position and attributes of an area. This includes a digitised representation of the earth's surface plus other spatially referenced information about that area. This data can be obtained from a variety of sources and by different methods. For example, remote sensing of terrain by satellite provides a wealth of accurate, up-to-date information about the earth and is in many cases the only way data can be obtained for inhospitable areas. Many automated systems of collecting data such as remote sensing are grid based, but this data may not be the best way to represent the world. Much of the information users require is about points, (i.e. towns), lines, (i.e. road networks or boundaries) or areas, such as counties or districts. Here data has to be collected from existing sources such as maps, and transferred to digital form. This process takes time, money and effort. In the UK the programme of digitised mapping still has far to go and is expensive to obtain. So this type of prepared data may not be available for the area under investigation. Point, line and area data is known as vector data, data based on a rectangular grid is called raster data. Fisher identified one vector-based MS-DOS package out of eleven. Whitehead had six vector-based Macintosh packages out of a total of nine.

Data storage and database management: the core of the system is the geographical database which may hold two types of data: either information about the position and attributes of the points, lines and areas that make up the earth's surface, (vector data); or as information about each rectangle on a regular grid overlaid on the earth's surface, (raster data). The detail at which the data is held depends on the desired scale of the output map, and the capabilities of the computer that runs the GIS. The database also has information on the attributes of the area, in a spatially-referenced database. There is no recognised format for such a database structure, so each organisation or GIS management system has devised their own that relates either to the type of data or to the type of map that is desired. Data sets may be held in hierarchical, network or relational databases.

The database management usually has a powerful Query language to select and match data with particular attributes for mapping. This is a vital component that allows the user to select the data appropriate to his problem.

Data output and presentation: is concerned with the way the results are displayed as maps, tables or diagrams to the user. As more users have large, good quality VDUs, the screen output is becoming a more important method of display, although high quality printed output is the ultimate aim for the commercial users of GIS.

Data transformation: is carried out to present maps at different scales, perform calculations on areas or perimeters, or to

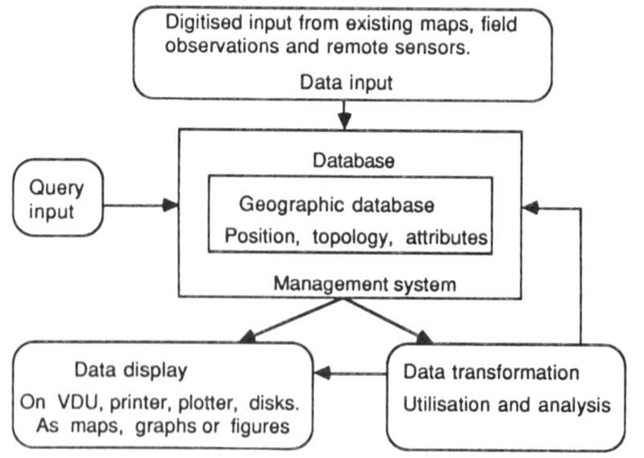

Figure 2: Diagram of a GIS system, after Burrough, 1987

combine these uses to achieve spatial modelling. Many of these calculations will involve predictions over time. Some of these transformations, such as changing scale or map projection or calculation of areas and boundaries, would be expected in most GIS, but others may be application specific, for example, calculating and displaying a map showing the allocation of roads to a fire station based on travel time. A critical aspect of a particular GIS is whether it will allow the user to input and retrieve correct information and present transformations that are required.

User interaction: a WIMP interface is now common on GIS through on-screen menus or icons, whether the system is based on mainframe terminals or micros. Driving a GIS has become a much easier task, although many mainframe systems have little error trapping and lack a user-friendly approach.

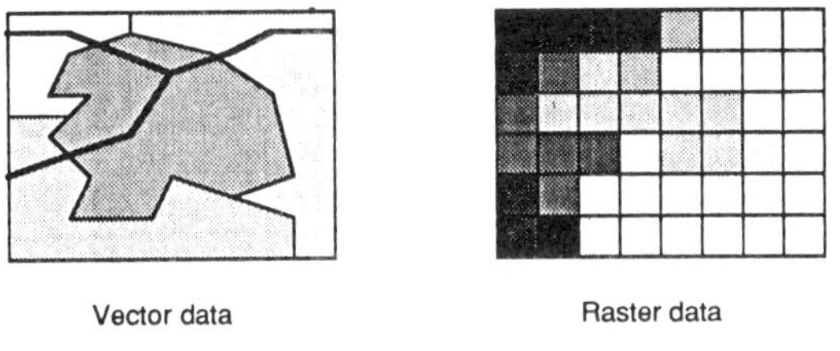

Figure 3: Diagram of raster and vector data

The main development on the technological side is the dramatic and continuing fall in costs compared with the rise in computing speed and power. This has meant that GIS is available on microcomputers and is within the reach of organisations that would not have considered its use a few years ago. One of the consequences of these developments is the fact that there is now a shortage of personnel familiar with GIS and able to exploit its potential. The repercussions are felt in a number of ways: there are only a handful of higher education establishments in the UK that offer degree or post-degree courses in GIS; there is no pool of lecturers that have the background and capability to deliver such courses, and no concensus about the content of courses.

What are the pressures for the introduction of GIS at school level?

The aims and use of GIS in schools are different from those in higher education. Three aims can be identified in courses offered by higher education:

- using GIS as a tool to help describe, explain and plan the environment in Geography Honours courses;
- using GIS as a vehicle for computer cartography in Mapping Science courses; and
- providing a wide practical knowledge of GIS and its applications in Geographical Information Systems courses.

The latter courses are relatively new and at the time of writing there are only two of this type on offer in the UK. The current trend seems to elaborate the training component of GIS and update practitioners accordingly so that they are able to contribute to the shortage of personnel that can understand and cope with this technology in industry.

At school level in the UK there are two trends that need consideration, one in Information Technology and the other in subject teaching and learning. Generic software, fostered by bundling of expensive commercial packages by some educational computer manufacturers, has instilled two cultures in schools: teachers belonging to the IT elite and the IT naive teachers. These two cultures were identified ten years ago. It is not that in-service training has been lacking or inadequate; it is that the goalposts have been shifting. An IT naive teacher nowadays knows more than an IT elite teacher ten years ago, but the packages have proliferated, and become more intricate. Commercial packages which would not be introduced into industry without a staff training programme are put into schools without this support and without educational materials. Curriculum materials have to be provided by teachers groups or educational publishers (now fewer in number). Will GIS be part of this scenario?

Rapid developments in education in the UK have run parallel to advances in technology. Guidelines for the content, skills and concepts for core subjects in the new National Curriculum, which covers all pupils from the ages of 5 to 16 years, have crystallised thinking on how IT can be incorporated into the mainstream of education. The National Curriculum Council Consultation Report for Technology, (NCC, 1989), states that 'pupils should develop information technology capability through activities which arise in other curriculum areas'. There are three attainment targets in information technology capability that are practical manifestations of this aim. These are the ability to:

- communicate and handle information;
- design, develop, explore and evaluate models of real or imaginary situations;
- measure physical quantities and control movement.

The programmes of study set out guidelines which mean that by the time pupils have reached the age of 11 years they are expected to have used wordprocessing, graphics, databases, spreadsheets, Logo, teletext and control technology in the course of learning maths, English, science, technology and humanities, and will go on to use the evaluate these programs at greater depth from 12 to 16. Each subject has also recommended certain skills and concepts that can be enhanced by Information Technology to ensure a progression of learning.

Can the strands already proposed for IT, science, history and geography offer a sound basis from which to introduce GIS into schools? Unwin in an unpublished paper (June, 1989) has listed five characteristics of GIS which make it difficult to teach adequately in university courses:

- differing conceptions in the field. (What is GIS?)
- defining the scope. (What should a GIS syllabus contain?)
- technological dependence. (High costs of introducing GIS.)
- differing needs. (Servicing education or training?)
- speed of development. (Problems in resourcing.)

A Working Group set up by the Geographical Association is considering these points and those recommended in the National Curriculum and will be making recommendations on how GIS could be implemented in schools. At an initial meeting of the group it was agreed that GIS should not be an add-on extra to the curriculum, but be integral to subjects that involve skills of information handling and graphicacy (presenting information in map form).

The group will be:

- carrying out a survey of hardware and GIS software suitable for the school environment;
- identifying GIS 'building blocks' to form the basis upon which to proceed. These will include linking a progression of information handling skills and skills of graphicacy;
- surveying which existing educational packages offer elements of GIS 'building blocks';
- raising teachers' awareness of GIS through articles and regional meetings;
- encouraging suitable examples of practical applications for demonstrating GIS at school level.

It is significant that the Interim Report of the National Curriculum Geography Working Group has already listed a progression of skills in graphicacy which culminate in GIS, and the maths curriculum also encourages spatial awareness. An enquiry learning approach has been recommended for sciences and the humanities whereby children instigate their own investigations from primary and secondary sources. In the primary school children collect, classify and enter information into simple database programs in order to transform data into graphs, tables or maps and interpret the results. At secondary level children are using more remote and complex databases, and combinations of sources, including satellite imagery, interactive video and CD-ROM, to accomplish similar ends, and then evaluate their results.

It is now an exciting time of transition and innovation in UK schools. It is hoped that when the GA Working Group reports in July 1990, and when the other National Curriculum subject groups have reported, it may be said that GIS has supplied a unifying metaphor for information handling and graphicacy in schools.

REFERENCES

Burrough, P.A. Principles of Geographical Information Systems for Land Resources Assessment, Clarendon Press, Oxford, 1987.

Fisher, P.F. Geographical Information Systems software for university education and research, Journal of Geography in Higher Education, Vol.13, No.1, 1989.

Handling Geographic Information, Report to the Secretary of State for the Environment of the Committee of Enquiry into the Handling of Geographic Information, chairman: Lord Chorley, H.M.S.O., London, 1987.

Mounsey, H. Building Databases for Global Science, Taylor and Francis, London, 1988.

National Curriculum Council Consultation Report, Technology. NCC, November 1989.

National Curriculum Geography Working Group, Interim Report, DES, November, 1989.

Rhind, D.W. Geographical Information Systems in Britain, in Quantitative Geography, ed. N. Wrigley and R. J. Bennett, Routledge, 1981.

Unwin, D. Curriculum for Teaching Geographical Information Systems. Report to the Education Trust Fund of AUTOCARTO, Royal Institute of Chartered Surveyors, June 1989.

Whitehead, C. Paper presented to the British Computer Society Conference, Cambridge, 1989.

Computers in Education
A. McDougall and C. Dowling (Editors)
Elsevier Science Publishers B.V. (North-Holland)

TEACHING SPATIAL CONCEPTS USING GEOGRAPHICAL INFORMATION SYSTEMS

B.J. Garner and Q.M. Zhou

School of Geography, University of New South Wales,
PO Box 1, Kensington NSW 2033.

The paper discusses with examples, the way in which recent developments in geographical information systems may be used to assist the teaching of spatial concepts in geography classes at the senior secondary level. The use of computers in geography is briefly reviewed, geographical information systems explained, and demonstrations of their application in the teaching of the concepts of spatial association and accessibility are presented by way of illustrating how the new technology may be used in classroom activities.

1. INTRODUCTION

Computers have been used in research and teaching in geography since the mid 1960s largely as a tool for the statistical analysis of spatial data. Today, as Maguire [1] has documented, few areas of the discipline have not already been substantially affected by the revolution in computer technology. The rapid development in computer graphics technology has been especially significant by making it possible to produce maps by computer and to manipulate spatial data in map form in computers. Rhind [2], Monmonier [3], and Burrough [4] provide useful reviews of these developments.

This paper focuses on the application of computer graphics in teaching spatial concepts in the geography curriculum using geographical information systems technology. The emphasis is on computer assisted learning (CAL) which in geography is typically restricted to teaching *with* computers rather than teaching *about* computers and this is the emphasis adopted here (see Shepherd *et al* [5]).

2. GEOGRAPHICAL INFORMATION SYSTEMS

The term geographical information systems (GIS) is used to describe a family of computer-based systems in which *locational* identifiers constitute a key component in the data base for individual observations. Technically a GIS is a configuration of hardware and software for the capture, storage, manipulation, retrieval and display in cartographic form of spatial data. Marble and Peuquet [6] and Clarke [7] provide useful reviews. GIS are differentiated from, for example, computer aided design systems (CAD) by virtue of their analytical capabilities which make it possible to perform the *cartographic* as distinct from mathematical modelling of geographical data.

In essence a GIS is a collection of software modules which perform a range of transformations on geographical data to generate answers to queries, examples of which are given in Table 1. Many of these are difficult to answer using conventional methods of spatial analysis. Not surprisingly, therefore, interest in the application of GIS has burgeoned during the past decade. In a very real sense, as Tomlinson [8] has argued, GIS constitute today an exciting new frontier in the application of computers to the handling of spatial data.

Table 1: Examples of questions and tasks addressed by a GIS. [4]

- A Where is object A?
- B Where is A in relation to place B?
- C How many occurrences of type A are there within distance D of B?
- D What is the value of function Z at position X?
- E How large is B (area, perimeter, count of inclusions)?
- F What is the result of intersecting various kinds of spatial data?
- G What is the path of least cost, resistance, or distance along the ground from X to Y along pathway P?
- H What is at points X1, X2, ...?
- I What objects are next to objects having certain combinations of attributes?

The use of GIS in teaching is not yet widespread and is still restricted effectively to tertiary level institutions. However, given the current rate of technological development, the diffusion of GIS technology downwards to lower levels in the educational hierarchy will certainly be rapid during the 1990s. The School of Geography at the University of New South Wales is at the forefront of the application of GIS technology in its teaching at the tertiary level in Australia. Based on its experiences, it is currently engaged in exploring ways in which GIS can be used to teach basic spatial concepts as an integral part of the geography curriculum at the senior secondary level.

3. TEACHING SPATIAL CONCEPTS

Geography is recognised as an important component of the secondary school curriculum because of its valuable role in teaching young people to gain a better understanding of the world in which we live. Students are concerned with answering questions about where things are and why and how they are there. The first is essentially concerned with *description*; the second with *explanation* and ultimately with a concern for concepts, models and theories (see Chorley and Haggett [9]). The former is essentially concerned with developing factual knowledge; the latter with developing abilities for logical, abstract thought. The application of computers, and particularly GIS, is particularly relevant in teaching a range of basic concepts used by geographers as building blocks for explanation. Two of these are used by way of illustration: spatial relationships and accessibility.

3.1. Spatial relationships

These are understood by examining the way things vary together geographically. The analysis of information presented on maps is an important component in the identification of spatial relationships. The most effective way of teaching students about spatial relationships is to take them out of the classroom into the *field* where patterns in the association of things may readily be recognised through actual observation. This is costly, time-consuming and in most situations impracticable. An alternative is to bring the 'field' into the classroom in the form of maps and photographs. Even then, however, the use of analogue materials poses a number of difficulties in establishing the existence of relationships between things spatially. GIS offer a novel way of overcoming these problems in the classroom.

3.2. Accessibility and relative space

The concept of accessibility is fundamental for understanding spatial patterns and is used as a basic building block in many theories of spatial organisation. By accessibility is generally meant the "ease of reaching a place". All places are accessible to some degree but some are more accessible than others. Accessibility is thus not synonymous with proximity. Teaching the concept of accessibility is also difficult in the classroom. Resort is usually made to personal experiences in moving around the countryside to identify locations which are easier to reach than others. This empirical approach is satisfactory but is not appropriate for handling the more abstract thinking required in spatial analysis. In this regard, the use of GIS also offers a powerful tool for use in teaching the concept of accessibility and developing logical thinking about spatial organisation.

4. DEMONSTRATIONS

In terms of the questions listed in Table 1, the examples which follow illustrate in different ways the results of intersecting various kinds of spatial data (i.e. question F). The data are stored in the computer as a series of thematic maps for the chosen study area. Given the raster structure of the GIS software used in this demonstration, each map consists of cells coded with a number from 0 to N which identifies either the location of a specific feature (*e.g.* a watering point) or the dominant characteristic (*e.g.* a particular type of vegetation cover). A descriptive label is attached to each code as well as a shading or colour for the purposes of displaying the map on a graphics screen (see Figure 1).

It is assumed that the spatial data bases have already been created for use in the classroom although it would not be difficult for students at senior secondary level to build their own from scratch as part of the development of general computer and related geographical skills. The former would involve data entry and the creation of data files; the latter procedures for encoding data, the principles of classification, and questions of an appropriate map scale.

Questions addressed to the GIS are expressed as a series of simple statements. The syntax is straightforward and easily learned. Additional details about the software used in the examples are given in the Technical Appendix to the paper.

4.1. Example 1

The problem is to identify the association between the level of risk of bushfires and type of forest cover in an area. Two distributions are involved: the timber map which shows the distribution of two types of forest cover (Figure 1), and the firerisk map on which cells are classified as low, medium and high firerisk (Figure 2).

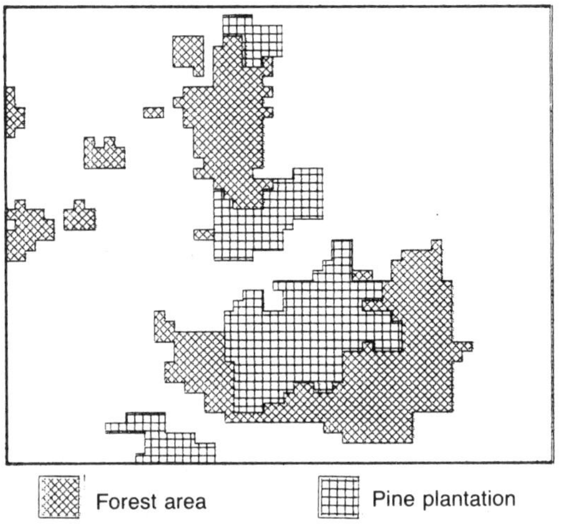

Figure 1

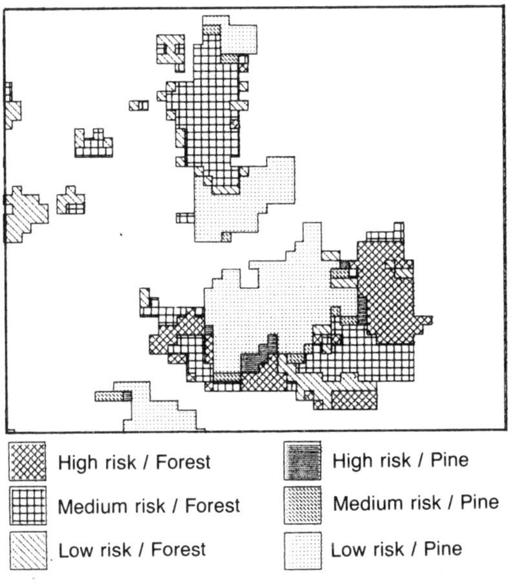

Figure 2

Students are asked to answer the following typical questions: Is a greater proportion of pine plantations subject to high firerisk than forest areas? Which of the two types of forest cover is least affected by firerisk? How many square kilometres of forest areas are subject to high firerisk? Answers to these questions involve the process of map overlay, a technique developed many years ago by McHarg [10] in landscape planning. It requires that one of the maps be drawn on a transparent surface and involves the difficult task of manually recording the covariation between the categories mapped. Experience has shown that the results of answering such questions manually are subject to high levels of error.

Answers to the questions are obtained quickly and accurately when performed by computer. Combinations are retrieved using the GIS software. The result is a new map (Figure 3) showing the distribution of the association between the two types of timber cover and the three categories of fire risk and an accompanying table which shows the extent of the association in absolute (cell counts) and relative (percentage cover) terms. Knowing the scale of the map it is a straightforward task to calculate the required areas (*e.g.* to answer question E in Table 1).

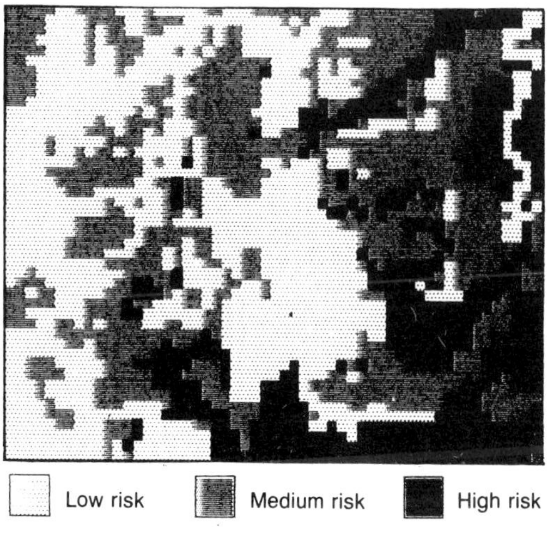

Figure 3

Not Classified	0	2098	76.29
Low Risk / Forest	1	90	3.27
Med. Risk / Forest	2	187	6.80
High Risk / Forest	3	109	3.96
Low Risk / Pine	4	233	8.47
Med. Risk / Pine	5	19	0.69
High Risk / Pine	6	14	0.51

4.2. Example 2

This illustration demonstrates the more advanced concept of accessibility. The example is taken from research undertaken by Zhou [11] which was concerned with the utilisation of rangeland vegetation for sheep farming at the University's arid zone field station at Fowlers Gap, NSW. The model used to develop an understanding of the concept of accessibility is shown in Figure 4. The field station covers about 400 km^2.

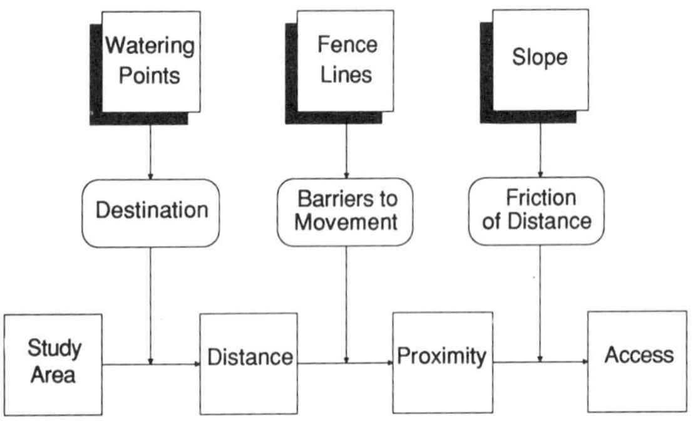

Figure 4

The utilisation of rangeland vegetation resources is very much dependent on the availability of drinking water, which at Fowlers Gap Station is largely provided by man-made supply facilities. Given the fact that sheep need to drink water at least once a day, it is clear that land closer to the water supply facilities is likely to have more frequent visits by sheep than further away and as a result the sparse vegetation there is likely to be overgrazed.

To start, students assume that the location of the watering points occurs on what is known as an *isotropic plain* - a common assumption in spatial theory. An isotropic plain is like a tabletop; a flat surface, devoid of any landscape features or barriers, on which movement is possible in all directions at the same cost per unit of distance. Under these abstract conditions, the only factor determining the choice of a particular watering point by sheep is distance.

Sheep, like people behaving to minimise effort, would therefore move to the nearest watering point. The result is a map of equidistance zones around each watering point (Figure 5). Students would be asked to deduce this from logical thinking under the assumed conditions. The map showing the disposition of the distance zones in the study area would then be produced on the screen by the teacher for examination. The computer is thus being used to generate solutions which students can compare with their predicted outcomes.

Real world landscapes are much more complicated than that portrayed in the simple isotropic model. An important impediment to movement is the existence of barriers. In this particular example, paddocks are fenced such that the movement of sheep is constrained and therefore drinking water can only be obtained from selected watering points. This limitation can be introduced by superimposing the fence lines on what is still considered to be an otherwise featureless plain. Students are now asked to predict how the pattern shown in Figure 5 will be modified as a result of introducing barriers to sheep movement and then to compare their expected outcome with the map showing *proximity* to watering points. Comparisons can again be made between the two maps.

Sloping land, rough surfaces, or dense bush give rise to additional impediments to the movement of sheep. These act to slow down movement by exerting a frictional effect. The concept of the friction of distance is thus introduced as a further factor affecting the movement of sheep to watering holes. Here slope is used as a surrogate to measure this. Students are then asked to predict how the introduction of slope will further modify the pattern of proximity to watering holes. Again, comparisons can then be made between expected outcomes and the map showing *accessibility* to watering points produced by the computer (Figure 6).

5. CONCLUSION

This paper demonstrates the way in which computer-based geographical information systems may be incorporated into the teaching of spatial concepts in geography classes at the senior secondary level in an exciting and novel way. The examples presented briefly indicate, but sufficiently, the way in which teachers and students can engage in a structured learning process in a computer graphics environment as well as the way in which the teaching of geography might be integrated with that in elementary computing subjects.

From the perspective of the vocationally oriented teaching activities we are engaged in at the University level, it is

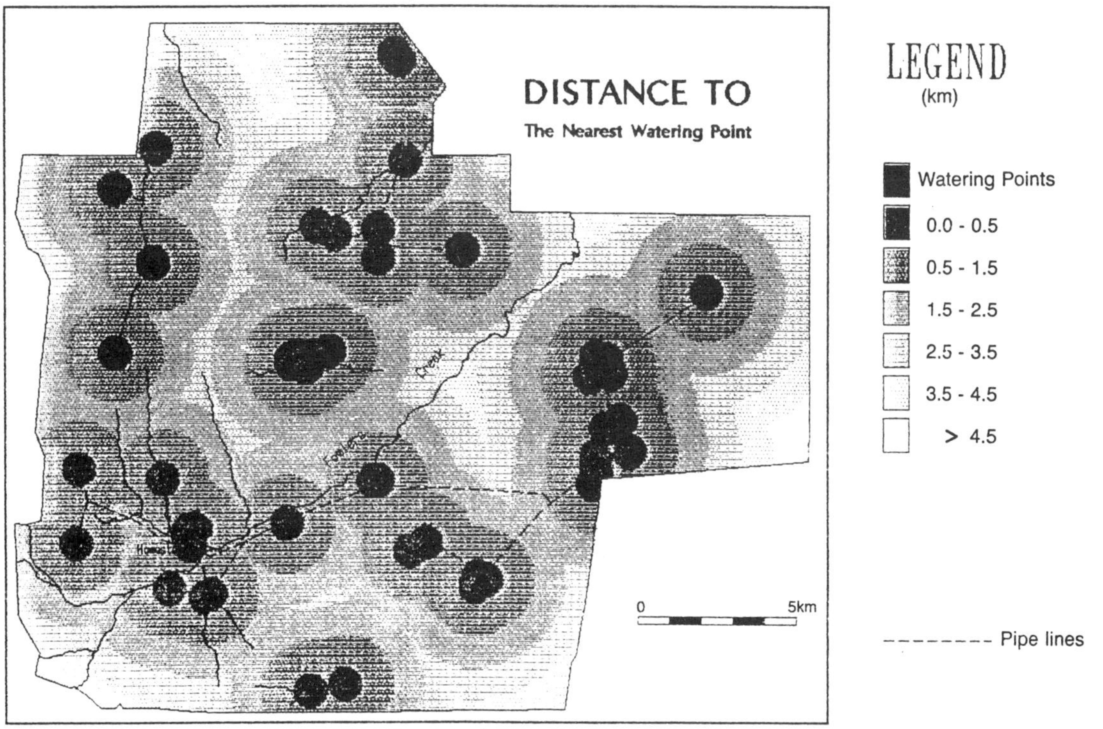

Figure 5

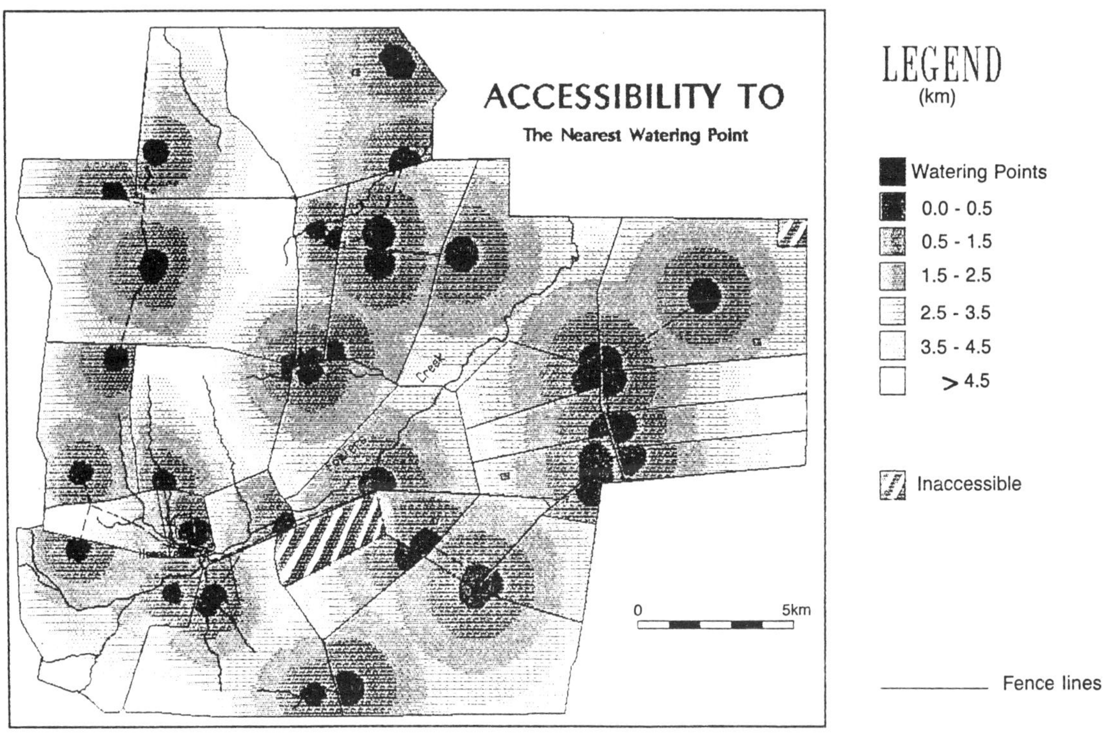

Figure 6

clear that the next generation of students will need to be considerably more computer literate than those who have gone before. Geographical information systems are a powerful new technology to be mastered in this regard and represent a new and challenging frontier for curriculum development in teaching geography at the secondary school level.

6. TECHNICAL APPENDIX

Two GIS software packages have been used to generate the illustrations in the paper. Both are mainframe versions operating at the University on VAX 11-785 with GKS graphics interface software. The original maps were produced in colour on a Tektronix 4691 inkjet plotter with 4510 rasteriser.

The MAP software handles up to 200 maps simultaneously each of which can have a maximum of 800,000 cells depending on the system hardware capabilities. Up to 256 categories may be included on each map. The software is capable of performing 70 different spatial data management, analysis, modelling and display operations.

REMAP has been developed by Zhou [11] as part of research for the PhD degree in Geography at the University of New South Wales. It is based on a substantially modified version of MAP linked to the INFO relational data base management system. The software is interfaced to the ARC-INFO GIS software. A PC version of REMAP is currently under development. The software contains four major modules and is capable of performing 90 different operations supporting system and database management, data integration, analysis and modelling, and the display of data.

ACKNOWLEDGEMENTS

The assistance of Helen Kam and Kevin Maynard in producing the Figures and Lynne Illidge for typing the paper are gratefully acknowledged.

REFERENCES

[1] Maguire, D.J.,*Computers in Geography* (Harlow: Longman Cheshire, 1989).

[2] Rhind, D.W., "Computer assisted cartography", *Transactions, Institute of British Geographers,* 2 (1977) 71-97.

[3] Monmonier, M.S., *Computer-aided Cartography: Principles and Prospects* (Englewood Cliffs: Prentice Hall, 1982).

[4] Burrough, P.A., , *Principles of Geographical Information Systems for Land Resources Assessment* (Oxford: Clarendon Press, 1986).

[5] Shepherd, I.D.H., Cooper, Z.A., and Walker, D.R.F., *Computer-assisted Learning in Geography: Current Trends and Future Prospects* (London: Council for educational Technology with the Geographical Association, 1980).

[6] Marble, D.F., and Peuquet D.J., "Geographic information systems and remote sensing" in R.N. Colwell (ed.), *Manual of Remote Sensing* (Falls Church: American Society of Photogrammetry, 1983) pp. 953-978.

[7] Clarke, K.C., "Advances in Geographic Information Systems", *Computers, Environment and Urban Systems,* 10(3/4) (1982) 175-184.

[8] Tomlinson, R.F., "Geographical information systems - a new frontier", *Proceedings, 1st International Symposium on Spatial Data Handling,* Zurich, (1984) 1-4.

[9] Chorley, R.J., and Hagett, P., *Models in Geography* (London: Methuen, 1967).

[10] McHarg, I.L., *Design with Nature* (New York: Garden City-Doubleday, 1969).

[11] Zhou, Q., *The Integration of Remote Sensing and Geographical Information Systems for Land Resources Management in the Australian Arid Zone* (School of Geography, University of New South Wales, Kensington, 1989).

Computers in Education
A. McDougall and C. Dowling (Editors)
Elsevier Science Publishers B.V. (North-Holland)

META MENTAL MODELLING: A TEACHER TRAINING IMPERATIVE

Pam GIBBONS

Catholic College of Education Sydney, 521 Old Northern Rd, Castle Hill, N.S.W. 2154 Australia.

This paper considers the place of mental modelling and the constructivist philosophy in modern education. It is particularly concerned with strategies which can be used to draw on teacher trainees' own experiences as learners. A case study which used a Logo environment to help trainee teachers explore their own mental modelling is briefly described, with particular attention to the implications that the study might hold for education in the future. It is proposed that through personal experiences in educational situations which encourage metacognition, trainee teachers might develop a thorough understanding of the role of mental modelling in the learning process. Later, as teachers, they may then be in a better position to facilitate active learning and the construction of mental models in their own students.

1. INTRODUCTION

The general educational philosophy of constructivism is in the process of developing a much higher profile on the teacher training agenda. Experiential, active and discovery learning and the purposeful development of metacognitive skills are becoming more widely recognised as potential facilitators in a learner's "process of constructing new representations" (Newell, 1989). Traditional teaching strategies such as chalk-and-talk explanations are now more constantly being called into question, building on the work of theorists such as Jerome Bruner. Bruner (1974, p.406) proposes that discovery learning leads the learner

"to be a constructionist, to organize what he is encountering in a manner not only designed to discover regularity and relatedness, but also to avoid the kind of information drift that fails to keep account of the uses to which information might have to be put."

Carroll (1964, p.111) also states that

"The possession of particular concepts acquired through past experience is a major factor in the solution of problems or the performance of tasks."

It is likely that the majority of current and potential practitioners have themselves been on the receiving end of traditional, passive teaching strategies. It is therefore likely that this is the approach that they will be inclined to apply to their own teaching. Theoretical knowledge about constructivism, mental modelling and active learning are unlikely to shift a lifetime's exposure to what is often perceived as 'real teaching.' It is too often assumed by trainee teachers that passive learning is what education is all about. Keeping a class quiet continues to be the ultimate yardstick used by trainees in assessing their own practicum performances. When nervously facing their early teaching situations, young practitioners are most likely to revert to the security and the familiarity of the type of teaching they received at school: it is unlikely that fourteen years of learning what education is about from their own experience will be usurped by the educational theory propounded by three or four years of tertiary education. It is perhaps in this respect that tertiary teacher education can begin to 'practice what it preaches.'

2. META MENTAL MODELLING

The question must therefore be put: in what ways do models of teacher training need to be reviewed to enable the spread of constructivist models into the everyday reality of classroom practice? What mental models of the nature of teaching are likely to be developed in teacher trainees if the knowledge is imparted through lectures and content-based examinations? The words may be loyally memorised by the next generation of teachers, but their real education about education (that is, what they have learnt from experience) will be more and more ingrained in the school of passive learning. It is ironic that if they were to recognise this tendency in themselves they might be more convinced of the power of experiential learning.

If teachers are to be facilitators in the building of mental models it is important that concepts pertaining to mental modelling be included in the trainee teacher curriculum. The imperative and the difficulty of its implementation are well described by Newell (1989, p.7)

"We [teachers] need to know something about mental models, and how they can be built, if we are to understand the process of learning and how we can assist learners. But the study of mental models is, to quote Heil (1983), a 'hideously complex' topic. We can easily become bogged-down in a detailed, and futile, discussion about the actual characteristics of our invisible representations and the neurophysical basis of their operation."

The concern expressed by Newell regarding the difficulty of understanding mental modelling is perhaps well justified if its understanding is indeed to be dependent on 'detailed..discussion.' It is the proposal of this paper that teacher training institutions should be taking immediate steps to ensure that the teachers of tomorrow are given every opportunity to understand the concept of mental modelling through tertiary education which is also active, experiential and geared towards students constructing their own understanding of educational theory. A continual source of amazement is the practice which sees education students often being lectured on the ineffectiveness of lecturing: the adage 'do as I say and not as I do' is too frequently applicable. In contrast, an approach which emphasises the building of mental models could be implemented in the teaching of the academic content throughout all disciplines, thus providing teacher trainees with the opportunity to construct their own mental models of the process of mental modelling, hence the term, meta mental modelling.

In addition to providing opportunities for tertiary students to construct their own mental models, the importance of developing the language with which to describe such modelling is also recognised. This view is supported by Vygotsky (as summarised in an introduction by Jerome Bruner, in Vygotsky, 1962, p. ix)

"Concepts and the language that infuses and instruments them give power and strategy to cognitive activity."

As stated by Carroll (1964, p.111)

"Language symbols - or rather, the internal processes that underlie given language symbols for the individual - may figure prominently in thinking and often determine its direction. The concepts named by language symbols - that is verbal mediating processes - are "tools" of thought."

Thus it is proposed that the development of the appropriate language to describe the obscurities of one's own mental models should accompany the active learning of tertiary students, lest students fall prey to that common experience so eloquently described in the poetry of Mandelstam (in Vygotsky, 1962, p. 119).

"I have forgotten the word I intended to say, and my thought, unembodied, returns to the realm of the shadows."

Bruner (1974, p. 406) also recognises the two-edged sword of mental model building in his description of the learner who is able to

"...work things out for himself, to organize evidence so that he is able to go beyond it to novel conjectures and insights, and to participate in an active dialogue with his teacher."

3. A CASE STUDY USING LOGO

The subject of the remainder of this paper therefore is to reflect upon the author's practical experiences in her attempts to address the demands of modern teacher training as described above. These experiences were also documented in part in Gibbons (1989). In 1988, a group of first-year teacher trainees were involved in a project which aimed to: develop skills in metacognition; enhance students' recognition of the processes involved in constructing their own mental models; and develop a language of description for mental modelling. The project was repeated in late 1989 and whilst this postdated the deadline for the submission of papers, it is intended to incorporate these most recent experiences into the 1990 conference presentation.

An open-ended problem solving environment using Logo was the vehicle for the study: hence the interest for computing educators. A Logo environment was considered appropriate to meet the objectives of the study, because it provided opportunities to design learning experiences which were active, student centred, and demanded attention to one's own thought processes. In particular, Logo is conducive to building mental models about one's mental models - in a carefully fostered environment, thoughts can become almost tangible. If Logo is able to assist children in building mental models, then it should also be able to assist tertiary students to build mental models about mental modelling. In designing specific, appropriate tasks to meet the project objectives, the words of de Bono (1967, p. 13) were readily acknowledged:

"Thinking about something is the only way to think about thinking, and having something to show for thinking is the only way to judge its worth."

With this truism in mind, the booklet "Turtle Confusion" (Newell 1988) was used as the primary 'problem posing' resource as it provided a variety of integrated computer and non-computer problem solving tasks. It encouraged a variety of approaches to the overall project, this maximising students' chances to construct their own knowledge in a manner which suited their individual learning styles.

In the first instance (in 1988) the sample size was small (eleven students), making an intensive case study approach both feasible and appropriate. The sample size was able to be trebled for the second implementation (in 1989). Students were required to document each stage of their problem solving and periodically reflect on changes to their attitudes and approaches to the project in a journal. Likewise, a journal was kept of implementation techniques and observable classroom behaviours. Students' solutions, documentation and journals were required as components of an assessable piece of work.

Each student was availed of a copy of the booklet Turtle Confusion. They were given five weeks of a twelve week semester to complete the assignment: this included all class time over the period (4 hours per week). Students were encouraged to work together in any configuration they wished: they were able to change their partner(s) at any stage during the project; whilst jointly prepared puzzle solutions were acceptable, each student was required to submit individual documentation and journals. Previous experience with Logo was minimal (approximately 12 hours) however if students were able to clearly describe a specific solution they wished to attempt (pseudo-structured English?), they were given instruction as to how their solution could be coded.

Students were made aware of the emphasis on metacognition through the early distribution of assessment criteria. These criteria indicated equal weighting to the puzzle solution and the document/journal, with the individual requirement of the document/journal making it the more significant component in discrimination between students. No indication of assignment 'length' was given; equal credit was to be given for the in-depth analyses of fewer problems as for brief analyses of many problems. 'Dead-ends' were to be fully documented and were indicated to be valuable components in investigating the thinking that takes place in the problem solving process.

Without exception, students felt uncomfortable about the unusual nature of the project. They were uncomfortable with the freedom they were given in terms of organisation of class time, working in groups, and assignment length. In particular, they had difficulty in coming to terms with the concept of the process and description of problem solving being more highly valued than the product. Despite being briefed as to the value of variety in solutions, they were still anxious to have either 'the right answer' or, at least, the same solution as the rest of the class. It became obvious that the risk of being the only one 'wrong' was a far too ingrained fear to be quickly supplanted by the prospect of being the only one with a different solution. Students usually lacked confidence in the validity of their own solutions or the robustness of their own mental models.

As the project continued, it became apparent that the solution of problems was very new to the students. One observed that he had never before been asked to solve a problem that he did not already know how to solve; by Clements' (1988) definition, he had never tried to solve a true problem. Lateral thinking, probing a variety of sources, following hunches and recognising dead-ends were foreign strategies. Frustration was apparent if any particular problem took longer than 30 minutes to solve (the impression that all problems should be solvable in less than one hour is undoubtedly reinforced by a lifetime of watching commercial television and being taught in 40 minute periods). When it occurred, however, the joy of achievement was overwhelming.

Of equal concern to the difficulties that students encountered in solving problems were the difficulties that they experienced in keeping a journal. At first it was suspected that the problem lay with the discomfort of personal disclosure; it later became apparent that the difficulty was again one of novelty. The newness related not only to the task of journal writing but to the content of what they were being asked to write about: their own thinking. As with their problem solving skills, students' journal writing skills improved dramatically as the project proceeded. In addition to the simple gaining of experience, classroom discussions assisted the development of students' language to describe the processes they were being asked to document. In brief, they needed to develop the ability to recognise their own thought processes as well as the vocabulary to describe them.

4. CONCLUSION

Students therefore experienced many difficulties in adjusting to such a different approach and to such different demands from their 'normal' coursework. Predictably (in hindsight) dialogue and journal writing regarding their own mental modelling also proved gruelling. The apparent novelty of the project (for the students) and the difficulties that it posed raises important issues regarding the effectiveness of traditional educational approaches to developing an understanding of mental modelling and the nature of learning. As a body, tertiary educators should be in touch with current theory regarding effective teaching strategy: it is time to put the theory into practice and let teacher trainees experience what mental modelling is all about if there is to be any real impact at all on classroom practices of the future.

REFERENCES

Bruner, J.S. (1974) Beyond the Information Given, George Allen and Unwin Ltd, London.

Carroll, J.B. (1964) Language and Thought, Prentice-Hall, Englewood Cliffs, New Jersey.

Clements D.H. (1988) "Problem Solving: Beauty and the Beast," Logo Exchange, Vol. 7, No. 2, , pp 28-29.

de Bono, E. (1967) The Five-Day Course in Thinking, The Anchor Press Ltd, Tiptree, Essex.

Gibbons, P. (1989) "Confusion, Cognition and Metacognition: The Agony and the Ecstasy" in: Backup the Future, Proceedings of the Seventh National Australian Computers in Education Conference, T. Dupe, (ed.) The Computer Education Group of the A.C.T. and The A.C.T. Schools Authority, Canberra.

Heil, J. (1983) Perception and Cognition, University of California Press, Berkeley, California.

Newell, B. (1988) Turtle Confusion, Curriculum Development Centre, Canberra.

Newell, B. (1989) "The Crowded Curriculum" in: Backup the Future, Proceedings of the Seventh National Australian Computers in Education Conference, T. Dupe (ed.), The Computer Education Group of the A.C.T. and The A.C.T. Schools Authority, Canberra.

Vygotsky, L.S. (1962) Thought and Language, The M.I.T. Press, Cambridge, Massachusetts.

Computers in Education
A. McDougall and C. Dowling (Editors)
Elsevier Science Publishers B.V. (North-Holland)

TOWARDS A DEFINITION OF BASIC LITERACY SKILLS FOR AN INFORMATION AGE

Richard GRICE, Peter GALBRAITH, Marjorie CARSS, Lou ENDEAN, Merle WARRY

Department of Education, University of Queensland, Brisbane, Australia, Q4067

This paper reports the findings on literacy from a futures study conducted from 1987 to 1989 at the University of Queensland, Australia. Interim results on reading were reported in *Unicorn* Vol 15-4 and are reproduced here with permission. The overall aim of the project was to identify the basic skills and abilities in the areas of literacy, numeracy, and scientific knowledge that are likely to emerge as important attributes within secondary education during the next decade as a result of the burgeoning information society. Particular emphasis is put on the impact of information technology on curriculum, lifestyles, and the workplace. The findings suggest that more complex views of literacy incorporating information technology will be needed by the turn of the century, but not at the expense of traditional print skills.

1. BACKGROUND

The needs of individuals and society with respect to literacy and numeracy are subject to continuous change, particularly in an environment of rapid technological and social development. From time to time studies report on levels of literacy and numeracy within the school population. These reports naturally reflect the perspective of the sponsors of the studies and tend to report on levels of competence as measured for the traditional skill structures of the existing status quo, both with respect to curriculum content and with respect to perceived work-force and life skills needs. Increasingly rapid developments in information technology mean that the concept of "competency" will undergo continuous and accelerating change as industry, commerce, and the social context change. It is therefore important to identify target skills and abilities so that new expertise can be developed and exposed deficiencies addressed within a dynamic, rather than a static, view of education. Robinson and Versluis (1985, 39-40) noted:

> In years to come there may well arise strong economic, ecological, social, psychological or political arguments for a further transition from conventional to electronic print creation, storage, retrieval, manipulation, and transmission. Some replacement has already taken place, particularly in commerce. Yet at the same time, this replacement has involved innovation in the way that information is represented and transmitted. Over time, it is quite likely that the new medium will develop its own stylistic conventions whenever textual information is stored and presented in an electronic form. It is likely to be accompanied by its own literacy, even by its own verbal art form.

This report sets out to identify skills and abilities in literacy that are likely to emerge as important foci within secondary education during the decade ending 1998. Of particular interest are those changes that will be stimulated by a burgeoning information society in its interaction with the school curriculum, lifestyles, and the workplace.

2. METHODOLOGY

The study used the Delphi technique in which information is obtained from experts over several interactive rounds. In this technique the research team designs an initial questionnaire that is sent to the selected group of respondents. The first round of responses is summarised, additional items suggested by respondents are evaluated and, based upon the results, a second questionnaire is circulated. In this questionnaire, the respondents are given the opportunity to re-evaluate their thinking based upon an examination of the group response, and to respond to new and altered items.

Since significant differences of opinion remained, a third phase questionnaire was used to confirm differences or to allow respondents a chance to reconsider their positions.

3.RESPONDENTS

Unlike methodologies that are based on responses from random selections of "average" citizens, the Delphi procedure seeks to identify respondents who have particular interest in, and/or expert knowledge of, the topic of the study.Ten categories of respondent were used in the study: Professional Educational Associations(First round,6;Second,2; Third,2); Business(5,2,2); Colleges of Advanced Education(20,19,15); Curriculum Officers (5,4,4); Department Heads (9,9,8); Federation of Scientific and Technological Societies (5,4,4); Politicians(1,0,0);Universities (19,15,12); Science Teachers (16,10,9); and Mathematics Teachers(10,10,9).

Ninety-six experts responded to the first round literacy questionnaire and reasonable retention rates of 78% and 87% were achieved for the second and third rounds respectively. While this sample formed a satisfactory expert base, representation within the categories was uneven, and in the case of a few groups, somewhat disappointing.

There was strong support from the tertiary education sector, state education departments, FASTS, and educational associations. Considering their often vociferous statements about basics and standards in schooling, business and union groups were tardy to participate. Fourteen unions were approached; six agreed to participate; none did. Thirty-three business organisations were approached, fourteen agreed to participate. In the event, five responded to the literacy questionnaire in the first round, while only two remained in the second and third rounds. Four politicians agreed to participate: only one responded and then only to the first round. Despite this unevenness in representation of planned groups, a sample size of ninety-six experts, reducing to sixty-five in the third round, is a sound basis on which to give considerable weight to the findings of a Delphi probe.

4.THE LITERACY QUESTIONNAIRES

The first round questionnaire in 1987 contained structured items derived from the literature and other sources. In addition, it provided respondents with an opportunity to add qualitative comments and to suggest new items if they wished. The respondents were asked in the structured parts of the questionnaire whether nominated items/issues will be of greater, lesser, or the same importance in 1997 as compared with 1987, whether items will become obsolete and if so what will subsume or replace them, which items/issues will be the first to undergo major change, what new kinds of learning will be possible by 1997, how particular items/issues will influence (be influenced by) the rate of uptake of information technology, which skills will be basic requirements for blue/white collar workers by 1997, which items/activities will survive as basics (but with major changes) in 1997, and how particular items will contribute to the quality of life in 1997.
The responses were analysed and used to construct the questionnaires for Round 2 which was conducted in early 1988. Similarly a third round took place in late 1988 when the prediction time in the questions was extended to 1998.

5.DEVISING LITERACY ITEMS

The derivation of a set of items provided a serious challenge. The problem arose out of the necessity to reconcile the many, often conflicting, concepts of literacy and to establish a degree of specificity in defining aspects of reading and writing which might lead to worthwhile outcomes.

Definitions of literacy range from the simplistic to the highly abstract. Compare "ability to read and write: the ability to use language proficiently" (Concise Oxford) with "an ability to participate socially and culturally and consequently be a constituent element of life-long education" (Lauterbach 1988, 88). Watkins (1989) in the context of developing literacy assessment within a political framework reports facing a similar problem. The answer would seem to lie in beginning with a working definition such as that found in the Beazley report (1984, 123):

> A person is considered to be literate and numerate when he has acquired the skills which enable him to function effectively in his group and community, and when his attainments in reading writing and mathematics make it possible for him to continue to use these skills to

> further his own and his community's development.

This kind of definition does not provide a precise or quantitative answer but can easily give rise to specific behavioural aspects of the reading and writing processes such as those used in the traditional print items and their supportive activities which are listed in the first two groups below. In supporting a pragmatic definition, Watkins (1989, 10) notes :

> In contrast to any "ideal" definition of literacy, if in reality one can exist which has universal or even very widespread acceptance, one which is pragmatic bears more relation to notions developed in working definitions.... That is to say: a pragmatic definition of literacy must show evident concern for matters of fact rather than hypothetical constructs, it must be readily understood by those with only a limited grasp of educational terminology and it must effectively test the truth through practical consequences.

Another important consideration was to raise the issue of the impact of information technology on literacy. Carcia (1986, 83) in a paper called "Information Technology and Education: Public Policy and America's Future" noted:

> Increased literacy and information skills will also become the primary means by which people gain access to income, status, and authority. To participate fully in the economic, political, social, and cultural life of such a society, it will not be enough to receive and transmit information with the new technologies. Individuals will have to know how to evaluate information and to make it relevant for their own particular needs.

Lauterbach (1988,91) highlights one of the more specific aspects of new technology when he draws attention to user-friendly software offering icons which can enable quicker orientation than any text; and mouse, light pen and touch screen that are faster and less tedious than writing. Perhaps for an increasing number of semantic functions, reading and writing may become obsolete because they are less effective and in some cases less powerful than icon referencing.

Accordingly the third group of literacy items introduced a set associated with the new media of an information age, while the fourth group covers various psychomotor skills such as handwriting and keyboarding. Given that respondents presented with structured items are prone to stay within those limits, one strength of the Delphi technique is that it allows for modification of those items and the introduction of new ones, which in turn can be tested on all participants. The items in the fifth section below reflect this process.

6.THE LITERACY ITEMS

1. Items associated with traditional print

(a) Reading

•*selecting sources of information*

•*evaluating sources of information (discerning fact from fiction, relevant from irrelevant)*

•*comprehending information (scanning for main idea, seeing sequence of ideas, making inferences)*

•*appreciating aesthetic values of text*

(b) Writing

•*recording information (note-taking,summarising)*

•*reporting information*

•*generalising, theorising*

•*speculating, predicting*

•*persuading, directing, controlling*

•*reaching agreements and understandings*

•*amusing, entertaining*

•*expressing imagination*

2. Items supportive of reading and writing

•*directory skills (index, glossary, contents)*

•*library research skills*

•*structuring skills (cohesion, coherence)*

•*spelling, punctuation, paragraphing*

•standard English usage

•morphology (prefixes, suffixes, roots)

•variation of language to suit audience, purpose, context

•computer graphics (static, dynamic)

•techniques of filming/videotaping

•editing and proofreading

3. Items associated with new media

•wordprocessing

•reading screen-based text, graphics

•interrogating electronic data bases

•composing on film or videotape

•comprehending information on film or videotape

4. Items involving psychomotor skills

•handwriting

•typewriting, keyboarding

•operating machines (VCR, computer hardware)

5. Items added in the second round

•reading for pleasure

•oral communication skills

•communication skills associated with social interaction and co-operative and collaborative behaviour

•accessing on-line information systems (e.g., Viatel, data bases, catalogues)

•skimming and scanning for information

•drafting, polishing, publishing skills
•writing critical evaluations of non-literary text

7. CURRICULUM DILEMMAS

The findings of this study show that the experts believe not one of the original thirty items (i.e. groups one to four above) will be obsolete in 1998. Agreement was exceptionally high, with over 94% agreement on every item. When the seven respondent-nominated items included in the second round are added, it can be seen that curriculum designers will have great difficulty in finding time in the years of schooling to develop a literacy to cope with an increasingly complex society: items associated with the new media of an information age call for urgent inclusion, but not at the expense of traditional print skills and their supportive activities. Indeed, the items associated with traditional print reading (except for "appreciating aesthetic values of text" which is to have the same status as now) are to have greater importance in 1998. An emphasis on the necessity to develop critical and evaluative processes is evident. Those items associated with the new media also qualify for greater stress in the curriculum with the exception of composing on film or videotape.

In 1998 all writing items are expected to be as important as they are now but for writing to reach agreements and understandings. Its greater importance is reflected in items nominated by respondents in Round 1, viz. oral and communication skills associated with social interaction and with co-operative and collaborative behaviour. Both of these new items are expected to require more attention, as are skimming and scanning for information and accessing on-line data systems.

Directory skills, library research skills, and computer graphics are to be accorded more importance, while other supportive activities such as spelling, punctuation, standard English usage, variation to suit audience, purpose, and context, editing, proofreading and morphology are still to receive no less attention than now. Only handwriting will be of less importance, but more weight will need to be given to keyboard skills and operating machines.

Curriculum planners may be helped in addressing such dilemmas by another section of the study which asked respondents to rank on a one hundred point scale the importance of various educational media for the present, as they expected it to be in 1998, and as they felt was desired in ten years time. The summary of their responses, shown in Table 1, indicates that books, chalkboards, and discussion groups are still very high on the list in 1998, but there are considerable jumps in importance for satellite links, home terminals, data bases, computer-assisted instruction, and microcomputers. None of the latter group reach the weightings of the former except the microcomputer; nevertheless, the fact that the experts see these contexts becoming more and more important would seem to call for increased attention to them in the curriculum.

TABLE 1: Weightings on a one hundred point scale for educational media as they are now, as expected in 1998, and as desired in 1998

MEDIA	NOW	EXPECTED	DESIRED
Books	99.5	98.5	97.7
Chalk board	79.4	71.5	60.8
Discussion groups	52.5	54.3	57.7
Micro-computers	23.9	53.8	64.9
Data bases	18.0	39.3	52.4
C.A.I.	16.9	42.7	48.4
Home terminal	5.6	33.3	37.8
Satellite link	5.6	18.3	22.3

8.SCENARIOS

Educational goals may also be addressed by constructing profiles for blue and white collar workers, and for the quality of life as a whole.
In the consensual vision of the respondents, essential to the quality of life in 1998 are selecting and evaluating information, comprehending information, reading for pleasure, writing to reach agreements and to develop understanding, and oral communication skills, especially those involving co-operation and collaboration. It will also be important to be able to

- wordprocess
- record and report information
- use writing to generalise, theorise, speculate
- use writing to persuade, direct, control
- use writing to entertain and express the imagination
- appreciate aesthetic values of text
- read screen-based text
- interrogate electronic data bases
- access on-line information systems, and
- comprehend information on film and videotape

Directory skills and the structuring skills involved in cohesion and coherence will be the most important of the support skills, but spelling, punctuation, paragraphing, editing, proofreading, standard English usage, and the ability to vary language to suit a context will still be necessary. Only morphology, computer graphics, drafting and polishing, and techniques of filming or videotaping will be of minor importance. Handwriting skills will be needed, but so will keyboard skills and the ability to operate video-recorders and computer hardware.

For the potential blue collar worker, the ability to report information in writing also becomes essential. Writing for other purposes, however, joins the items of minor importance, along with editing, proofreading, composing on film or videotape, appreciating aesthetic values of text and library research skills. Selecting sources of information, reading for pleasure, and oral communication skills remain important but not necessarily essential.
With the exception of composing on film or videotape, it is essential, however, for the prospective white collar worker to have all the skills associated with the new media in addition to the first three traditional reading items and the first six writing skills. Essential also will be all supportive items except morphology, computer graphics and techniques of filming and videotaping, which will remain of minor importance. Editing and proofreading will remain important. Finally, a person entering this sector of the workforce will be expected to have oral communication skills, be able to access on-line information systems, to skim and scan for information, and to be proficient in keyboard skills and operating video-recorders and computer hardware. Nevertheless, reading for pleasure and writing to express the imagination will remain important for this person.

9.CONCLUSION

The "back to basics" view of literacy has traditionally undervalued the place of oral skills in the curriculum. Their importance in their own right and to language development, albeit well established in the professional literature (e.g., Olson 1984; Wells and Chang 1986), saw oracy and an associated emphasis on co-operation and collaboration emerge as new items which subsequently received the consensual support of respondents.

Indeed, the standards debate has continuously diverted attention from a future-oriented view of the skills required in an information age. Marginson (1986) explores the controversy and illustrates the confrontation. Some try to build bridges (Kress 1988), others to bury the hatchet and develop a more complex concept of literacy development (Boomer 1989).

Kennedy (1989, 12) believes that the complexity is being more and more recognised and discerns a rise in level of discourse about literacy:

> Indeed there is evidence that general community views are showing an increasing sophistication. In a recent community survey by Piper and Miller (1987), while English was seen to be a priority area in the curriculum of the junior secondary school, there was no endorsement of a narrow "back to basics" approach. Language education was seen to be much more complex.

Meantime Lauterbach (1988, 87) reminds us that we know from history that the possibilities of information and communications were always used first by those in power to maintain and extend their power; that the time has now come to make the new think-tools and communication channels available for everyone for personal and societal development. The present study reinforces the need to incorporate the technology of an information age in our more complex views of literacy. Morever, this emerging view of literacy also places more emphasis on the critical and evaluative processes served by reading and writing. Hopefully it is pragmatic and specific enough to help curriculum designers. Of course, one always has to remember that the Oracle at Delphi was prone to dispense its wisdom in the form of a riddle.

REFERENCES

Beazley, K.E. (1984) *Education in Western Australia – A Report of the Committee of Enquiry*. Education Department of Western Australia, Perth.

Boomer, G. (1989) *Literacy: The Epic Challenge Beyond Progressivism*. Paper delivered to First Joint Conference of The Australian Reading Association and The Australian Association for the Teaching of English, Darwin.

Carcia, D.L. and Weingarten, F.W. (1986) Information Technology and Education: Public Policy and America's Future. In Topics in Education, *SIGCUE Bulletin*. 18(2-4) 80-83.

Kennedy, K.J. and Rousch, P. (1989) Literacy Policy, Politics and Practice: An Australian Perspective. *Monographs in Literacy Studies* Number 2. Australian Reading Association, Melbourne.

Kress, G. (1988) Barely the Basics? *Education Australia*. Term 1, 12-15.

Lauterbach, R. (1988) New meanings of literacy. In Sendov, B. and Stanchev, I. (Eds.) *Children in the Information Age*. Pergamon, Oxford.

Marginson, S. (1986) The Standards Debate and the Curriculum Debate. *Professional Magazine, Queensland Teachers Union* 4(1), 11-14.

Olson, D.R. (1984) "See! Jumping!" Some Oral Language Antecedents of Literacy. In Goelman, H., Oberg, A.A. and Smith, F. (Eds.) *Awakening to Literacy*. University of Victoria, Victoria, British Columbia.

Piper, K. and Miller, H. (1987) *Priorities in Language Education – A Survey of Community Views*. Australian Council of Educational Research, Melbourne.

Robinson, B. and Versluis, E. (1985) Electronic Text: A Choice Medium For Reading? In Chandler, D. and Marcus, S. (Eds.) *Computers and Literacy*. Open University Press, Milton Keynes.

Watkins, R. (1989) Literacy: The Politics and Practice of Assessment. In *Across the Borders: Language at the Interface*, Proceedings of First Joint National Conference of The Australian Reading Association and The Australian Association for the Teaching of English, Darwin.

Wells, G. and Chang, G.L. (1989) From Speech to Writing: Some evidence on the Relationship Between Oracy and Literacy. In Wilkinson, A. (Ed.) *The Writing of Writing*. Open University Press, Milton Keynes.

Computers in Education
A. McDougall and C. Dowling (Editors)
Elsevier Science Publishers B.V. (North-Holland)

THE ELECTRONIC SCHOOL DISTRICT PROJECT: WIDE AREA NETWORKING FOR PRIMARY AND SECONDARY EDUCATION

Michael Halla

Indiana University, University Computing Services, 1000 East 17th Street, Bloomington, Indiana 47405, USA

This paper contains a project description, progress report, and discussion of some of the findings from the Electronic School District Project, a joint study underway in the state of Indiana among Indiana University, Purdue University, and the International Business Machines Corporation (IBM). The study is investigating the benefits to be gained in primary and secondary education by using a computer network to link school districts with the Indiana Department of Education and with state universities for the exchange of ideas and information. Personal computers on local area networks at participating secondary schools are connected into a wide area network that includes minicomputers and mainframe computers. The hub of this network is an IBM 4381 mainframe computer running the Student and Teachers' Electronic Productivity System (STEPS). A variety of research projects make use of this network. Those described in this paper include distance learning, peer/mentor networking, and process writing.

1. INTRODUCTION

Wide area networks (WANs) have demonstrated their value to business, industry, and to institutions of higher education. Instant access to distributed data, transfer of electronic mail and files, and access to computer systems around the world have significantly increased the value of the workstations that are a part of the WAN. The application of WANs to primary and secondary education is the next logical step. In the state of Indiana (in the USA's Midwest), an experiment is under way to explore the education-enhancing benefits of a statewide network that connects schools to one another, schools to institutions of higher education, and schools to the Indiana State Department of Education.

The experiment is known as the Electronic School District (ESD). The ESD project is a joint research effort among Indiana University, Purdue University, and International Business Machines Corporation (IBM). IBM has committed hardware, software, and personnel to the project. Purdue University, Indiana University, the Indiana State Department of Education, and a group of pilot schools have all committed personnel, space, and funding to the project. This cooperative effort, started in July of 1987, has given birth to a large-scale, innovative project that has the potential to benefit the entire state of Indiana and to serve as a model for other states, regions, provinces, or nations.

2. ESD STUDY OBJECTIVES

The mission of the ESD project is more specifically defined by the following objectives:

To investigate the utility and effectiveness of various computer network applications for use by students and teachers;

To develop, adapt, and evaluate network tools for distance learning course delivery;

To develop, adapt, and evaluate applications that increase the productivity of school administrators;

To promote the infusion of computer networking technologies into the primary and secondary schools through demonstration projects on the ESD network;

To evaluate various communications protocols and network topologies for interconnecting student and teacher workstations into a wide area network.

3. ESD RESEARCH PROJECTS

Guided by the ESD objectives, the participants in this project have created in Indiana, an experimental computer network simulating both the academic and administrative functions of a school district. Through this network participants can test ways to improve the school system using computer technology. Participants in the network include computing center staff at Indiana University, education faculty from Indiana University and Purdue University, staff at the Indiana Department of Education, and faculty and administrators in several Indiana school districts.

Research projects are conducted on this model network under the direction of Dr. J. Dudley Herron of the Purdue University School of Education. A brief description of three of the projects follows.

3.1. Peer/Mentor Network

One key to the success of the electronic school district is easy access to information and to people. The peer/mentor system focuses on providing users with access to those resources that best answer their questions. For example, university resources can use the network to provide expert supplementary curriculum material to classroom teachers, Department of Education personnel can respond electronically to policy issues and state services, and school-based teachers and administrators can use the network as a tool for addressing more immediate issues.

The peer/mentor network provides easy electronic communication among participants and a pool of diverse resources that support peer, mentor, and external requests for educational information on curriculum design.

3.2. In-service Training

This project has created a model for electronic in-service instruction and for delivery systems that relay instructional material through the network. Teachers at several sites around the state participated in a computer training class that was delivered through the network. Communication between instructor and learners was provided through electronic mail, video and document image scanners, graphics packages, and word processing programs, all using the capabilities of the ESD network.

With the successful completion of the network-based teacher in-service training course, the model can be extended to courses for homebound and adult learners, as well as to college credit or advanced placement courses for high school seniors.

3.3. Process Writing Exchange

An important part of the "writing as a process" training model is peer evaluation in which a student's written material is shared with his/her peer group for discussion and revision. This project adopts the "writing as a process" technique and extends the pupil's peer audience through the use of electronic mail.

The purpose of this project is to quantify the influence of peers on student writing. The greater number of students available through the network provides a broader demographic base from which to draw additional conclusions.

4. THE ESD NETWORK

An IBM Systems Networking Architecture (SNA) network was implemented to support ESD projects. This network consists of an IBM 4381 mainframe computer running STEPS (the Student & Teachers' Electronic Productivity System) and IBM System/36 minicomputers located at Indiana University, Purdue University, and one of the school districts. Completing the network are local area networks (LANs) of IBM PS/2 series personal computers in special classrooms in the participating school districts. Using knowledge gained from the network's first six months of operation, the network was streamlined. It was reduced in cost as well as complexity, taking advantage of new telecommunications technology not available at the beginning of the project.

Rather than continuing a system of isolated individual computers we have in ESD created, through the network, a system of individual workstations and host processors connecting student to student, student to teacher, teacher to administrator, and so forth. As has been demonstrated in manufacturing, computing and networking technologies, if applied correctly, can be important tools for improving our schools.

The applications we are now adding to the network reflect the diverse information needs of the constituencies of a school system. For example, the administrative arm needs solutions in areas such as accounting and student records. Teachers need applications in curriculum design, lesson planning, and research. All these uses (and many others) must be available on the same network to maximize benefits and minimize costs.

This same network can also provide interactive learning opportunities for students. Recently developed interactive learning programs complement the traditional "drill and practice" applications and emphasize self-learning in basic skills such as arithmetic and reading comprehension. Such software gives the student, rather than the computer, control over the learning process by using the learner's thoughts, experiences, and language creatively. Students and faculty are demanding that such exciting use of the network become an integral part of their daily activities.

Another major benefit of this network can be in reducing the drudgery that consumes much of a teacher's time: taking attendance, updating and copying tests and exercises, keeping grade books up to date, planning lessons, and teaching basic skills such as reading, writing and arithmetic again and again and again. The computer can assist in many of these routine tasks, freeing the teacher to spend more time in productive ways, such as evaluating individual student progress and one-on-one coaching.

Network technology is also necessary for integrating the currently separate parts of the school system, providing opportunities for increased communication and interaction among various groups. Network applications such as bulletin boards and electronic mail have increased the exchange of information in other organizations and can do likewise for schools.

Use of the network can create new groups and new forms of social interaction, reducing the isolation many teachers experience. With such a system, the teacher can use a personal workstation to obtain direct, immediate access to information from any other network participant, whether a student, an administrator, another teacher, a university faculty member, or a curriculum specialist at a state or national department or ministry of education.

In building the ESD network for the public school system, certain guidelines have been followed. First participation in the system is voluntary. Second, the system has a strong professional orientation; participants are learning that the network is valuable in their daily work. Finally, the network architecture reflects the social structure of the school system. Rather than apply the typical hierarchical structure in which one computer controls all communications, we are using the newer "peer-to-peer" structure that allows communication between any of the individual computers.

5. ESD NETWORK SUPPORT

University Computing Services at Indiana University is responsible for network support. Located at the Indiana University campus in Bloomington, Indiana are the IBM 4381 computer, one IBM System/36 minicomputer, and the ESD Network Operations Center (NOC).

The NOC staff is equipped with electronic aids that can pinpoint and help resolve the network difficulties encountered by ESD participants. The staff also disseminates information to ESD participants about system hours, system outages, and so forth. ESD clients can contact the NOC through a local telephone number or through electronic mail. The Network Services support group assists the NOC with problem resolution, performing any required "hands on" troubleshooting and technical remedies. They also provide technical assistance with equipment installation.

The NOC has gained several insights that will lead to better overall service. For example, we have learned not to place obstacles in the way of clients attempting to contact the NOC. We did so by giving clients access to the NOC through a toll-free telephone number and by using call holding and a recorded message when all telephone lines are busy.

We have also learned that having accurate and complete records containing the names, addresses, and telephone numbers of ESD clients is important when the NOC staff member cannot immediately resolve the problem and must call the client back. Callers have at times actually given the NOC a wrong telephone number. They then waited in frustration for the return call. Up-to-date client records make it easy for the NOC staff member to locate correct client information.

We have also determined that use of an expert system or some sort of problem determination tree would be advisable. Such a system is not yet in place at the NOC.

6. STEPS MENU SYSTEM

It was necessary to tie together the ESD programs and services by some easy-to-use system. How would services be accessed after a teacher or student logged on? The options were a command-driven system or a menu approach. We chose the menu approach with these two objectives in mind: (1) the menus must support the intuitive use of the system and (2) the menus must provide sufficient assistance to the novice or occasional user, while not hindering the experienced user.

To make the use of the menus intuitive to teachers and students, a scheme was developed that corresponded to a school building, using a generic model of a typical school building. Services or activities in a school building are typically located in clusters of rooms. For example, science labs are often located near one another, as are industrial arts shops. Students and teachers go to rooms to participate in an activity or obtain a service. One goes to the library to conduct research or to check out a book. One goes to the guidance office to meet with a counselor.

Services in STEPS are selected from within "rooms" grouped within "building wings" that are accessed via "hallways" from a "main entrance". Upon logging onto STEPS, a teacher or student is presented with an initial menu. This menu, or "main entrance", lists the various wings: administrative, math and science, general classroom, language lab and so forth. Selecting a wing takes the teacher or student to the next level of menu selections: the rooms within that wing. For example, one would find the physics and chemistry labs, the weather station, and the MAPS classroom in the math and science wing. (Note: MAPS is not related to geography but is instead a curriculum for ninth grade math, Mathematics Achievement through Problem Solving.) This type of menu structure provides the necessary landmarks and pathways for novice users.

Experienced users however, could find a menu system inconvenient and frustrating. For them we've created a "shortcut". As in a school building each ESD room is assigned a three digit "room number". By typing the room number, the user can go directly to that room, bypassing any intervening hallways or wings. Room numbers also serve as a memory aid for using STEPS in the same way that most students and teachers know the room numbers in their school buildings.

The room number concept has been expanded to include a "homeroom". Each user can specify which menu will appear first upon logon. This "homeroom" replaces the main entrance menu. Students and teachers are free to change their "homerooms" at any time.

7. PROJECT GOVERNANCE

Two standing committees are responsible for the ESD project. The ESD Policy Committee, chaired by Dr. Arthur J. Lindeman, Vice President for Information Technology, Indiana University, meets on a quarterly basis. This committee establishes priorities for project implementation and sets policy. Day-to-day operational issues are managed by the Operations Committee which is chaired by Mr. Ed Qualls, IBM. The Operations Committee is responsible for all issues related to both network and research operations. Each of the ESD joint study partners have seats on both committees.

As noted earlier, University Computing Services (UCS) of Indiana University has operational responsibility for the ESD network. The Institutional Coordinators consisting of a coordinator from each of the ESD partners, has been appointed to assist UCS in managing day-to-day problems.

8. SCHOOL DISTRICTS, THE LOCAL EDUCATION AGENCIES (LEAS)

The LEA partners are the primary and secondary schools (K-12) invited to participate in the project. The following criteria determined the selection of the initial LEAs:

A broad geographic and demographic distribution;

A willingness of the school to commit to the project in terms of: staff (particularly a "visionary and dynamic champion"), operating expenses, curricular change, network equity, and physical facilities;

A range of "computer sophistication" among students and faculty; and

A familiarity, or rapport, with one or more joint study partners. (Although not required, this criterion was seen as helpful.)

From these criteria, and following in-depth consultation with all parties, high schools in the following school districts were initially brought into the project: Harrison and McCutcheon High Schools in the Tippecanoe School Corporation, at Lafayette; Triton Central in the Northwestern Shelby County School Corporation, at Fairland; and Lake Central in the Lake Central Community School Corporation, at St. John.

Using the above criteria we have added the following additional schools from other districts: Lawrence North High School and Franklin Central High School, both in the Indianapolis metropolitan area, and Batesville High School in Batesville.

9. IN THE SCHOOLS

At each of the participating schools, electronic classrooms have been set up consisting of IBM Personal System 2 (PS/2) Model 30s connected to an IBM local area network (LAN). A system administrator initially enters into the system the name of each student, individually or from a master data base, enrolled in each class. From any workstation on the LAN the teacher of a class may log the entire class onto and out of the system. (This procedure saves the statistics for one class and starts the next class automatically, without each student entering logon information, thus saving valuable class time.)

Students use the IBM courseware according to the class level or subject level being taught. They may progress at their own pace and can be tested at any time throughout the course. A standard function of the courseware programs is to retain records of the progress of each student. Student progress and grades can be viewed by both the teacher and the system administrator.

Additional PS/2 workstations serve as teacher productivity tools and aid in administration of the LAN. The teacher's workstation may be located in the teacher's office, a teacher workroom, a teachers' lounge or any location designated by the school. The workstation's connection to the LAN provides the teacher with access to both the student system and to the statewide network. A teacher may use his or her workstation for word processing, preparation of tests and handouts, preparation of projection transparencies, or searching the school or statewide databases. Teachers can write letters to parents, administrators, or to peers within the statewide system and send the letter electronically or on paper as appropriate.

As mentioned in the section on in-service training, a teacher may use his or her workstation to take a university class delivered electronically. Through electronic mail on the ESD network the teacher can quickly and conveniently communicate with the professor and with other class participants without leaving his or her classroom.

10. RESEARCH STATUS

Purdue University has responsibility for establishing an Administrative Information Network, a Peer/Mentor Network, an In-service Training Network, and a Process Writing Exchange Network. Purdue has also assumed responsibility for the development and documentation of instructional support materials. The following sections provide information on the status of three of the ESD projects as of January 30, 1990.

10.1. Status of the Peer/Mentor Network

The first Peer/Mentor group is in operation and consists of ninth-grade mathematics teachers who are using MAPS, an experimental general mathematics curriculum developed by the School Mathematics and Science Center (SMSC) at Purdue. MAPS (Mathematics Achievement through Problem Solving) is a problem-centered curriculum using non-traditional content and a cooperative learning classroom environment. The SMSC, however, is able to provide only limited support for MAPS users. As teachers begin using the materials, they inevitably encounter difficulties with some of the lessons and need assistance that may not be immediately available. By connecting these teachers via the ESD Network, they now have an efficient means of gaining access to consultants at the SMSC as well as a mechanism by which ideas may be shared, making the program more successful. This group of teachers had a clear need to communicate and constituted an ideal test group for the Peer/Mentor Network.

There were not any MAPS teachers located in the schools with LANs physically connected to the ESD Network. Consequently, it was necessary to provide dial-up capability from IBM personal computers to STEPS via modems. Because of its commitment to support teachers implementing the MAPS curriculum, the SMSC purchased modems and is loaning them to teachers who participate in the Peer/Mentor Network. Thirty-five MAPS teachers in nineteen schools currently make up this Peer/Mentor group. Twenty more teachers from five more schools will become participants by the end of the current school year.

To further support the Peer/Mentor project, electronic conferencing software has been installed on the ESD IBM 4381. In addition, communications software on Apple computers was tailored widening the base of computers that may dial into the network. The second conference to be set up was a weather conference for earth science teachers. Additional conferences have begun for users of video technology, guidance counselors, and physics teachers.

10.2. Status of the In-service Training Project

Twenty-four teachers participated in the first phase of this project under a grant from the Indiana Department of Education. The grant provided financial support for tuition and materials for the teachers.

A Purdue course, Education 573, "Microcomputer Applications to Education and Training," was taught electronically by Professor James Lehman. This course is the introductory graduate level course in educational computing offered by the School of Education at Purdue. As designed, the course used electronic mail for student/teacher interaction, computer-mediated conferencing for group discussion, word processing for homework assignments coupled with electronic file transfer of completed assignments, and computer-based training modules available on each of the LANs.

Between the interest in the course itself and the reimbursement of tuition to the teachers, it was not difficult to attract enough teachers to the class. Keeping all of the teachers in the class, however, was difficult because of problems in delivering the class through the network as originally designed. First, there were delays in establishing the network. Then equipment chosen for the gateway from the LANs at the high schools to the ESD network proved to be unreliable. New equipment improved reliability. Two of the high schools had multiple IBM System/36 minicomputers on their path into the network, which made file transfers impossible between STEPS and the personal computers on the LANs at each of these schools.

At the two high schools where file transfer was not a problem, electronic mail was used successfully as planned for student/teacher interaction. Professor Lehman reported among his findings that the participants using electronic mail were less inhibited in their comments than were students in the actual classroom.

10.3. Status of the Process Writing Exchange Project

Professor Edward Jenkinson of the School of Education at Indiana University, Bloomington, is examining the workings of peer review and editing as done by people who know each other only through the network. Students at three of the ESD high schools are using the network to submit some of their writings to college students in Professor Jenkinson's methods class. The written pieces include compositions, short stories, poems, and song lyrics.

Using word processing on a personal computer the high school students convert their pieces to ASCII text files, which are then transferred to the electronic mail system on STEPS. The college students add their comments to the text and send them back electronically to the high school students. All of the exchanges are logged by the system, providing an audit of how the high school student responds to the review. Professor Jenkinson also uses the audit trail to track the most frequent errors made by the high school students and plans to design simple exercises to help them improve their writing.

An interesting side benefit of this project is the technical preparedness gained by the college students through using a computer network, rather than paper copies, to learn how to review and comment on student writing.

11. ADDITIONAL FINDINGS AND COMMENTS

So much new technology was brought into the ESD project that the technical support staff were at times overwhelmed. The selection of hardware and software was done at the beginning of the project. As time passed we discovered that some of the selected equipment could not be used and other equipment that was needed could not be acquired because it had not been listed in the original grant proposal. It would have been beneficial to all if the flexibility to select equipment as the project progressed had been an option.

A serious problem involved the conflicting needs of the two implementation groups. The team was given two years to complete the project. To accommodate this short time span, the project was divided into two parallel efforts that would develop independently, then converge. One group conducted research on network topology and implemented the network design while another group developed network services.

This division proved to be counterproductive. The network designers were pressured to get the network up and ready to deliver services before it was known whether the network would function as designed. In addition design changes during implementation caused developers to abandon and restart various efforts. It was discovered that sequential, rather than parallel, development of these areas would have been appropriate. Development of services should have been delayed until a fully functioning network was available.

Given the broad scope of the project and the substantial effort required to install the large quantity of computer and communications equipment, the project plan should have allowed three or four years for completion. Fortunately, perseverance overcame frustration, and we decided to continue the project.

12. PROJECT CONTINUATION

In June of 1989 the ESD partners agreed to extend the project's termination date to June 30, 1991. More schools, including elementary schools, are likely to be added to the network. New research project proposals are under consideration at the time of this paper's writing. These include the addition of more peer/mentor groups, an advanced placement Pascal course to be taught over the network, and use of the network to provide career information about the nursing profession.

Further research will explore other network protocols for possible support of the ESD network. This will involve the implementation of TCP/IP access and comparison of TCP/IP functionality and cost/benefits to those of SNA. Additional mainframe computers will become a part of the network, adding to the collection of services the network can provide to students and teachers.

Another exciting research effort under way involves the development of PC-based graphical interfaces to services in the network. The intention is to place between the user and an existing application on a remote computer an easy-to-use interface that incorporates graphics, images, spoken prompts, and context-sensitive helps.

The ESD project provides researchers a unique opportunity to test new ways of delivering existing educational services while providing totally new services. Many research projects spanning the entire K-12 curriculum are made possible simply by the network's existence and availability. The most exciting uses for the ESD network may yet remain to be discovered.

ESD PROJECT TEAM

Purdue University faculty and staff.

Michele Akridge	Weather Project,
Jean Boddy	MAPS Project,
Beverly Cox	Process Writing Project,
J. Dudley Herron	Research Coordination,
James Lehman	In-service Training Project,
Bill McInerney	School Administration Project,
David O'Brien	Process Writing Project,
James Russell	Instructional Support,
Dennis Sorge	LEA Selection,
Mark Whitman	LEA Coordination.

Indiana University faculty and staff:

Michael Enyeart	Network Design,
Jeff Christopher	Network Design,
Teresa Cummings	STEPS Menu Development,
Michael Halla	Project Manager,
Estelle Huston	Peer/Mentor Support,
Edward Jenkinson	Process Writing Project,
Michele Lebrasseur	Hypermedia Development,
Arthur J. Lindeman	Executive Director,
Gary Moss	Videodisc Project,
Agnes Tsang	STEPS Technical Support.

IBM staff: Larry Halbach, Al Terrones, Ed Qualls.

Computers in Education
A. McDougall and C. Dowling (Editors)
Elsevier Science Publishers B.V. (North-Holland)

INFUSING TECHNOLOGY INTO THE HIGH SCHOOL CURRICULUM - A FIVE YEAR REPORT FROM THE BLAIR MAGNET PROGRAM

Michael R. HANEY

The Science, Mathematics and Computer Science Program Coordinator,
The Blair Magnet Program, 313 Wayne Avenue, Silver Spring, MD 20910, U.S.A.

Computers have now been available to schools for over ten years. Software and hardware of all types proliferate. Nevertheless, there are few models where computers have been completely infused into the curriculum of a program for an extended period. The Blair Magnet Program is a high school science, mathematics, and computer science magnet which has an extensive five-year experience implementing a curriculum which not only accommodates but depends on the use of computers. No drill-and-practice and no tutorials are used. Little canned software is available to the students. Instead, at the onset of the program, they are taught to use computers as tools for thinking and creating. In the years which follow, they use and adapt computers to fit their own needs. These uses include information retrieval, model building, student-written simulation, mathematical testing, science interfacing, controlling robots, composing music, manipulating data, and much more.

Significant changes in the curriculum have been possible because of computers. What science and mathematics are taught and how these are learned depend on the students' access to and understanding of computers.

Because of its success, this program has been a model for other programs and schools who wish to infuse technology into their curriculum. The successful practices have been emulated elsewhere. Through the computer and with local and national organizations, the classroom has been redefined to include the larger community with its many resources.

1. INTRODUCTION

To think of computers as the exclusive domain of computer science teachers is to lose half the benefit and all the purpose of bringing computers into the high school. Micro-computers have evolved so rapidly in the last ten years because they open new and fascinating areas of science, mathematics, art, music, engineering, and research among others. They offer tools for divergence in a society where individual goals are in vogue. They are a medium which applies to all facets of understanding. They transcend discipline boundaries, make mathematics relevant and physics real. For ten years, educators worldwide have been pioneers doing innovative things in isolated schools. There is enough evidence now that computers are an answer, but only to the right questions. They are not a panacea allowing us to teach traditional topics with more interest or efficiency. They are a revolution changing what should be taught, how children should learn, and who should control that process.

This is the description of a program that took a different approach. Instead of asking how we could teach what we have been teaching better or more effectively, the staff revised the courses to meet future needs. It was a high risk venture that meant redesigning the curriculum from Grades 9 through 12. It meant building on each year's successes and letting the program evolve in spite of many preconceptions. It meant disregarding our notions about what colleges or parents expect. It meant meeting the needs these children must have to survive in tomorrow's world.

The key is simple. Make computers useful. That begins by teaching each student to use a computer and all basic software for word processing, spreadsheets, information retrieval, data collection, statistics, graphics, and beginning programming. It is sustained by rewriting every course in the program to expect children to use this technology whether it be for a chemistry paper (word processing, information retrieval, graphics) or mathematics (spreadsheets, graphics), or journalism (page layout, word processing, spell checkers). Finally, it is not enough for the students to perceive computers as essential time savers in their work. Computers must be readily available. They should be a medium as natural as spoken language.

2. BACKGROUND

Montgomery County Public Schools decided its first high school magnet program would open in September, 1985. Since the purpose of a magnet is to attract students, the program needed to be one which would entice students from affluent neighborhood schools to endure bus rides beginning at 6:15 a.m. to attend a 67% minority, low socio-economic level school. After community surveys and some political soul searching, a science, mathematics, and computer science magnet was selected to be placed in Montgomery Blair High School. Although the purist may not see this beginning as altruistic, it did solidify a long-range support system and establish an undeniable "raison d'etre" that has resisted subsequent attempts to dilute the program's mission. A steering committee of university, community, and school system professionals set the tone of drastically changing traditional standards while offering a special high technology setting for motivated and capable students. These are the same students who traditionally are not considered risk takers. Despite skepticism and transportation difficulties, the program has grown and strengthened over the past five years. All of the initial goals have been met. Enrolment is approximately 100 students per grade level. Colleges and universities have accepted our curriculum with enthusiasm. The host school has stabilized. Over 50 groups of educators per year, from national school districts and foreign countries, visit the program. The staff works with many other schools across the country. They offer summer training and seminars for other teachers on the interdisciplinary techniques implemented in the program.

3. THE PROGRAM

Since education is usually conducted under tremendous restraints, asking teachers to be architects of change is difficult for them. So the first charge the teachers inherited five years ago was "Forgetting what you teach or what you think students expect you to teach, redesign the curriculum to contain what you feel students need to know." The first obvious question is "Know for what?" That's quickly followed by "Will whatever we do be approved by the State?" Neither of these are very important questions if you believe that good teachers have developed an intuition and an understanding for what should be learned and how it should be taught. Removing these constraints, teachers re-invent many of the old concepts, but they strive to teach in radically different ways. In fact, it is surprising how deeply teachers get into this process of rethinking what they do for a living. They appear to have serious reservations about traditional schools. (These neo-educational revolutionaries are the same teachers who daily stand in front of traditional classrooms lacking ownership for what they are doing even though they are doing whatever they do very well.

The basic required courses for a high school education were redefined. Science would included four courses taught in two years (double period); mathematics would go through Analysis I (Calculus); and computer science should include a year of the basics including tools, structured problem solving, and applications as well as a year of programming. A two-year sequence entitled Research & Experimentation was added to help students build the experiences they need to solve long-term problems and to complete projects and experiments.

Even five years ago, it was clear that computers were essential to what could make such a program work. They would be the glue that binds, the common language of all courses. They would provide the incentive to "twine" the courses producing an interdisciplinary curriculum. With this in mind, each course was redesigned to reflect the needs of the students of the '80s and '90s.

Science was the first curriculum area to be scrutinized. As the steering committee had recommended and the staff supported, science was inverted. Physics now comes first followed by Chemistry, Earth Science, and then Biology. All of the objectives could not be covered in any one course. For example, some Physics objectives would be deferred until Chemistry (thermodynamics) or Mathematics (geometric optics) where they better belong. Each science course would build on the content of the previous course. Chemistry would use and assume what was taught in Physics. Earth Science and Biology would use what students carried with them from Physics and Chemistry.

The advantage of the science sequence is obvious to any science teacher. Each course logically progresses from the former with the more fundamental and less complex sciences first. The difficulty of this approach has always been in the mathematics background of ninth grade students and in their interest in the physical science at a time in their lives when biology is a natural lure for them. With the close cooperation of the mathematics and computer science teachers, the transition is relatively painless.

4. COMPUTER INFUSION

The most important decision the staff made regarding computers was that they should be infused into every course. All students should develop facility with computers. That meant designing an introductory computer science course for all 9th grade students. What should such a course contain? What information or computer skills are so important that all students should have them? The result of six months of planning and two months of curriculum writing is "Introduction to Computer Science A & B".

This innocuous sounding course is quite different from anything else taught in other schools. It is "Computer Organization" taught backwards. It is an introduction to the computer at seven levels. Instead of beginning with hardware logic and building towards systems, it begins with systems and peels layers off the computer like layers off an onion until the core is reached. The outer layer is software. To students who are 13 and 14 years old, this layer is concrete because it can be manipulated. The innermost layers, the digital circuits, are abstract black boxes which are left to last. (This seems to be the reverse of what we find with older, college-level students.) At the software level, students study useful packages including integrated word processing, spreadsheets, databases and information retrieval, graphics, and statistics.

At the next level, students study the algorithms, or broad logic, which underlies the software. This progresses into more manipulable software such as the modeling and simulation package STELLA. Formal rule systems are encountered in True BASIC and in the list processing aspects of LOGO. This is followed by an examination of the structures which are indigenous to all programming languages - data and control. Storage (data structures) and Boolean algebra (control structures) are then implemented in digital circuits.

The strength of this course is in its practicality. Even though it provides a foundation for studying structured programming later, it more importantly arms students with all the tools they need to use computers in every course they take. Information retrieval for background on reports, word processing for all writing and editing, graphics and spreadsheets for number crunching and statistics, etc.

Because of the students' comfort with computers, teachers soon become dependent on the computers as ways of helping students accomplish more work, more meaningfully in less time. Complex environmental processes can be simulated and predictions verified. Simple but tedious operations can be carried out on large groups of numbers allowing students to do analysis of real world problems. Data can be collected through interfaces using shorter and longer intervals than were practical before, thus revealing new relationships which were previously hidden. In fact, students find many applications of computers that were not in the new curriculum. They have made the curriculum fluid, in constant need of change. There is more of a partnership relationship within a classroom, or at least a sense of mutual dependence, when computers are involved. Students learn more and become more self-directed.

5. TWINING

One of the primary features of all courses taught in Grades 9 and 10 is that they be interdisciplinary. The computer lets this happen. The data a child collects in physics on free fall, probably through a computer interface, is taken to computer science class. There, the students are studying, not coincidentally, spreadsheets. The physics data is entered, graphed, and analyzed. The techniques for finding the "curve-of-best-fit" were recently completed in mathematics so the students can generate an equation which approximately describes the motion. That equation is a model of the phenomenon they measured. This lab is extended in "Research & Experimentation" where students are challenged to find the terminal velocity of a falling object such as a ping-pong ball in air or a steel ball in oil. Although they can devise, build, and carry out their own investigation of this problem, it is not surprising so many turn to the computer for help.

Similar examples can be drawn from other combinations of disciplines. Mathematics ties into computer science where Boolean logic is implemented in digital circuits. Students write Pascal programs in Grade 10 to merge red, blue and green satellite data into one picture. They also write their own statistical package to be improved and expanded in later grades. For biology, students write simulations or use the statistical packages available on the computers. They build presentations using video disks controlled by the computer in slide shows. There are many similar examples. The list grows each year as rapidly as students with motivation and imagination move through the program. The teachers have implemented similar ideas into courses at all grade levels. Students have grown to regard what is learned in one course as useful throughout their education.

6. INDEPENDENT LEARNERS

The goal of education is to make students independent. It is to help students become life-long learners. For that to happen effectively, the curriculum should be very different in Grade 9 from what it is in Grade 12. In many schools, the difference is in content and difficulty. In programs which promote academic maturity, the difference is also in approach. This is most apparent in the types of problem-solving techniques available to them. The degree of success of education is largely measured by the student's ability to solve all types of problems.

It is the computer which gives students the independence and the ability to build a personal repertoire of useful skills. Over four years, most students develop the computer as an extension of themselves. They begin by trying to force the computer to follow their personal schemes. They eventually begin to modify their own way of viewing problems to more fully utilize these powerful machines. A series of project skill-building activities unfolds over four years. Most of these entail using the computer.

In Grade 9, students first write a formal proposal for a project. It could be SSSIP, Science Fair, JETS, etc. In fact, they do not have to do the project. They simply plan the project, thinking through the time and resources needed. They must examine the feasibility of their own proposals. Some students elect to do the project. The Research & Experimentation teachers help with this process. A second stage occurs during Chemistry when the students use the Media Center, Information Retrieval System, and other resources to search for literature on a Chemistry topic. In Grade 10, students do one full application project for Earth Science. They design and build a module which fits into a mock space or oceanic capsule. Much of the work is done in Research & Experimentation using computers for design, some basic electronics, and robotics combined with simple programming.

In Grade 11, all students take R. & E. 3, Research Methods. This course explores research designs and areas of possible student project interest. Computers are used for data collection and analysis. It is in this course that students begin formalizing their proposals for a later one-year Research Project. Naturally, the teacher will help students select topics and design the project.

In the second semester of Grade 11 and in Grade 12, students do the Research Project. Students can work alone or in teams depending on the project. They can work in school or in local research facilities. Each student has a faculty advisor, a project coordinator, and a mentor to help. Seniors gain confidence and maturity from the Research Project. They have the opportunity to interact with the adult scientific community where students can discuss their talents and become aware of job opportunities within their chosen field. This experience leaves the student better prepared to choose a college, a course of studies, and even a career.

7. THE SUM AND THE SUPPORT

Innovations in education are always slow to unfold. No vision is so clear that one can anticipate all the needs and nuances for four years. By letting the Blair Magnet Program grow one year at a time, the staff was able to build on the successes and modify the failures. Basic goals were kept intact as specific techniques and activities evolved over the past five years. The single aspect which grew the most was the use of computers. It was spurred on by the students who had learned basic tools and gained the insight to see extended possibilities.

The current computers that support these activities are quite extensive. For the four hundred students in the program, there are approximately eighty computers. This includes a large MacIntosh lab with 50 SEs. They are connected to a MicroVAX II and a Cyber 910 minicomputer. The latter was won by the student SuperQuest team in the ETA-sponsored competition in 1988. The next year, the team won an IBM networked mini-lab which serves as a gateway to the Cornell Supercomputing Center. In the years to come, students will be accessing mainframe computers across the country via this network.

Another dimension to computing at this level is the emerging network, both formal and informal, among schools. In the last two years a consortium of similar schools has emerged. This is the National Consortium for Specialized Secondary Schools of Mathematics, Science and Technology, NCSSSMST. Many of the major academic high schools which specialize in technology are members of this organization. In the past three years, their staffs have gathered for three conferences held in the suburbs of Washington D.C., in North Carolina, and near Chicago. The students have also had conferences at the first two sites. Through this group, students do joint projects, share their ideas and experiences, and have access to the computing facilities of schools which may be thousands of miles away.

8. CONCLUSION

At the Blair Magnet Program, computers have changed both what is taught and how it is taught. Problem-solving techniques, creative and technical, have become more important than ever. The curriculum has been redesigned to meet the capabilities of students who have access to computers. The results have been very encouraging over the first five years.

There are many successes and lessons from a program as committed to innovation as this one. Some are based on teacher insight and design, but many others come from the high energy and interest of students thoroughly involved in their own education. For schools who feel they have found successes, it is important that we share these. A network of schools concerned about similar problems involving the appropriate use of technology is beginning to emerge. Through organizations like this, we can sustain the momentum to continue evolving the curriculum.

Computers in Education
A. McDougall and C. Dowling (Editors)
Elsevier Science Publishers B.V. (North-Holland)

SYSTEM DYNAMICS AS AN EDUCATIONAL METHOD

Harald HAUGEN

Adviser to the Royal Norwegian Ministry of Education and Research, P.O. Box 8119, Dep, 0032, Oslo 1, Norway.

Our surrounding world consists of *complex systems,* too complex to be grasped by our minds without assistance. Nevertheless, people are forced to handle and manipulate these real systems. Building and manipulating *models* help us to understand the dynamics of such systems. *System thinking* and *dynamic simulations* are closely related and complementary to one another. *Computer technology* has made manipulations and calculations much easier, while *authoring systems* for simulations have made model construction simpler. *Simple models* are suitable for understanding fundamental principles, and students are able to *build and handle models* in the computer. Through the building of models they discover the need to know more about *subject matters,* facts and relations between variables. Most dynamic systems require work *across the curriculum* and will thus stimulate a more integrated aspect of problem solving

BACKGROUND

Following a Norwegian white paper on *Computers in Education* and a 4 year Programme of Action (1984-88), several of the previously initiated software projects have now been completed into applicable versions, adjusted to new hardware standards, and extended to include more advanced functions. The concept of a consistent set of software tools, made for educational purposes, has been given high priority. One has come up with a Norwegian concept for CASE (Computer Assisted Software Enginee-ring), at the moment consisting of the following components:

* GrafTrix - a programmer's tool-box for handling graphics, fonts, screens, printers etc., all on a PostScript basis
* Mosaikk - a unifying interface between hardware/GrafTrix, users, different programme modules, external devices like video, CD-ROM, telecommunications, databases, sensors and measuring equipment etc. It was initially constructed as a prototyping tool, but has now been developed into a very powerful programming tool, the central and most important part of the Norwegian CASE concept.
* SimTek - a programming tool for dynamic simulations, more powerful and user-

friendly than traditional PC-tools for the same purpose. Has the possibility to generate Pascal code for the whole model if integration with other program modules is desired. A special interface to Mosaikk has been developed through a powerful SimMos library, enabling users to construct and manipulate models through graphical interfaces. Libraries are also constructed for incorporating external data (from physical sensors etc.) into models, and to export data from simulations to external devices (switches etc.).

* The Director - a tool specially intended for work with *interactive literature*, adventure stories, concept learning, instruction etc. Has been constructed by Mosaikk, has a simple user interface and handles dynamic relations between different screens/situations. May thus be used for "simulations" when mathematical models are too difficult to come by, showing pictures of the next situation when a certain action is taken - or not taken. Handles video discs, photographs and computer graphics from standard software tools.

Other background material of major importance for further work on system dynamics, are the software *design concept*, the "Grimstad Model" with the market diagrams etc., and the integrated software package for communications, databases and distributed education, the "Pegasus". These two concepts are both linked to the other tools, and will play central roles when system thinking is introduced into schools and other parts of society.

PRESENT ACTIVITIES

In the educational system the main task will now be to integrate technology into curriculum, as a natural part of teaching. New topics or subject areas may also find their way into schools, perhaps outside or across traditional subjects. One of the possibilities that has caught attention on an international basis, is the application of computer simulations in order to study complex, dynamic systems. Several seminars and courses have been arranged throughout the world over the past few years. In Norway the method has caught special interest within universities (e.g University of Bergen) and colleges (e.g. Stord College of Education), but is now also finding its way into secondary schools, vocational training - and even into primary education. From 1988 a Nordic project group has been set up to study the possibilities and challenges of system dynamics in education, from primary through secondary to higher education. The group is presenting its findings now in 1990.

From 1989 some projects have been started in different Nordic schools, and a preliminary report will be available in early 1990. Some teacher training institutions have been engaged to support the experiments, and a set of coordinating guidelines set up for others who want to try it out. In addition to introductory courses of system dynamics, more advanced courses in *model construction* has now been arranged, the first one in February this year.

A NEW EDUCATIONAL METHOD

System dynamics seems to be a new way of engaging students at different levels into studying complex systems, challenging their ability to "find out" facts, relations, equations and perhaps less accurate information about subject related matters. Experiences so far seem to indicate possible applications in primary schools, secondary schools and for higher education in several subjects - plus for decision makers at all levels: politicians, economists, business managers, farmers etc.

SimTek and Mosaikk have been applied for some time, and turn out to be suitable authoring tools for model building. The SimMos library is an important link between the two. Models are constructed by software designers who want to incorporate them into more elaborate packages, as well as by teachers who only need rough models for demonstrating or discussing certain topics within their subjects. In both these cases the more or less complete model is presented to the students, individually or as a group. It may then be studied at different levels of insight and complexity.

Level 1, the simplest way for students, is a piece of simulation software, containing a model that is hidden for the students. A more or less sophisticated user interface will then let the student(s) run the model, demonstrating a certain sequence of *events* and *relations*. The same things will happen each time he/she runs the model, e.g. free fall under gravity. An optimal adjustment of one or two parameters is, however, normally included. Actually no computer is necessary for many of these applications; a video or film would do as well - and perhaps even better. But if the computer is available anyway, why not use it for illustration of certain laws or relations? And perhaps it has given the *programmer* certain challenges and satisfaction to manage it . . .

Level 2, a bit more advanced, but still not very complicated. It is still based on a piece of software where the model itself is hidden to the students. The user interface now allows the student(s) to *vary parameters* of the model, one, a few or several. The *system* to be presented may itself be simple (e.g. bank interests) or complex (e.g. algae growth in the Norwegian Sea). The model representing it may still be a simplified version to demonstrate only a few principles, or it may be a serious attempt to present a - more or less! - "correct picture" of the real world, involving a lot of variables and complicated equations. Both kinds of models are becoming rather common in the design and construction of educational software, and may be implemented through software tools (Stella, SimTek), by 3rd generation languages (Pascal, C) or by more advanced assembler or bit coding to speed up the processing.

From an educational point of view both kinds of models have their advantages and drawbacks. The mere use of models in teaching introduces a new dimension into the profession, and will in many cases offer the students better ways of studying composite systems. Through interactive work they may discover important relations between actions and resulting changes in the system. The simplified model has the advantage of considering only a few, important variables, restricting the student to study the most dominating features of a system. The more elaborate model gives a better representation of the real system, and allows the student to make a more advanced and detailed study of it. Both models, however, will be criticized for not giving correct representations in all possible situations. The more advanced model being worse off, because it *pretends* to give a correct model of the world, while the simpler one openly admits that it only takes a few factors into account.

Level 3 also provides the students with already constructed models. In addition to the applications mentioned for Level 2, it offers the model itself open to the student(s). It is no longer a "black box", hidden model, but an open set of relations and equations. The different parameters may still be handled from a graphical (icon) or menu-driven interface, and the behaviour of the system studied through userfriendly presentations on the screen, tables, graphs, colourchanges etc. The new offer to the student is now to choose "MODEL" from the menu and have a closer look into how the different variables are related.

If the model is implemented in a low level programming language, the student will need to know some programming in order to find and interpret the equations. Most likely they will also contain advanced calculus, coded into some cryptic language. Moreover, if there is a desire to change certain parts of the model, a good knowledge of programming is needed to avoid messing up the whole program. Everyone who has tried compiling complex programs after having made minor changes, knows how easily error messages pop up. Of course there may be cases of simple models where constants and factors may be altered without any further complications in a C-or Pascal program.

This is where the advantage of authoring tools come in. In stead of cryptic, coded equations, the model can be laid more open to the user in a simpler language, where words and symbols represent variables and relations. The graphic representation of Stella (Macintosh) with *"levels"* and *"rates"* hides much of the mathematical formulae behind the screen, while the symbols still allow for study of quantities, relations and results. Mathematics is of course still the same, but it is expressed in simpler equations, avoiding for instance advanced calculus. (Actually returning to the Newtonian way of representing infinitesimal calculus.)

In the Norwegian and Nordic projects SimTek has been the main authoring tool for simulations. It offers the same simplifications of mathematics, words are basicly used in stead of symbols, and it has the advantage of generating pascal code that can be compiled and/or combined with other prog-ramme modules. The graphical interface can be obtained through the use of Mosaikk. When students study models, they will normally go into SimTek codes where they meet equations of this kind

```
$ Herd: Initial-Dead-Sold+Born+Bought
% Born: Herd * 0.2
```

-or perhaps

```
$ Temperature: 100 - Tempchange
% Tempchange:  Difference * 0.1
```

-and slightly (!) more complicated

```
$ OxygenProduction: (AlgaIncrease *
NormOxProdFactor * EffectOf-
AlgaDensity) * OxPot.
```

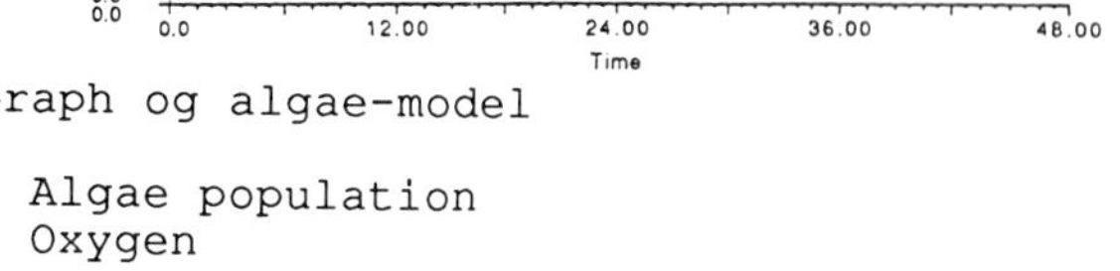

Graph og algae-model

1 Algae population
2 Oxygen

Since the language is fairly simple, students will be able to interpret and make the desired changes in equations without major difficulties. Their challenge will be to investigate the model - and the system it represents.

The educational importance of this simplification, is that the emphasis is shifted from the ability to handle the computer to that of supplying enough *knowledge of the subject* area(s!) in question. Problem solving changes from reproducing facts and formulas to *understanding* relations, seeing interdisciplinary connections, looking for more information and experimenting with new hypothesis. This is perhaps best obtained when students work in groups, may be the whole class together, with the teacher not as a knowledge base, but more as an Oracle or a Hevraklit (ref. the hevristic method of teaching), guiding them to where knowledge can be found. Group discussions are important aspects of the method. This implies a completely new way of teaching, a new role for the teacher, and hopefully a better way to train students for realistic problem solving.

The models and problems may of course still be treated in a superficial manner, altering factors, variables or equations arbitrarily, learning no more than keyboard skills from the exercise. If the models are not adequate, being too different from reality, lacking sufficient testing or flexibility, the students are likely to be more occupied by trying out its weak points than exploiting its strong features. Asking them to improve the model may then give them the challenge needed for serious efforts to be put into action.

By letting the students look into and work with open models, they will also to a higher degree understand the uses of models in the society around them. Models are very often used as a basis for political, economic and other strategic decisions, without informing about weaknesses built into the them. Politicians and others may very often be caught in the net of arguments from a technical "specialist" who presents his views through the use of a simplified model, being far from realistic - perhaps even principally wrong. The knowledge of how models are constructed, how arbitrary formulations may be made, and how unex-pected consequences may arise from certain actions, ought to be a sound background for judgement of models in general.

Level 4 is the most advanced and challeng-ing work with dynamic simulations. This is where the students themselves study the whole dynamic system, they design the model and may - or may not - implement it on the computer. When they are at this level, they very often get so fascinated by the modelling process itself, that they may forget all about computers and final products. The discussions about how things are interrelated, what the connections are and how consequences may be interpreted are of much more interest than a running computer model.

There is not a sharp distinction between levels 3 and 4. You gradually move from patching on existing models to making up your own. In both cases it takes a good portion of understanding to handle the system dynamics. At level 3 one may be more occupied with the computer's simulation language to alter the model, while at level 4 the dynamics of the system itself becomes more important, one focuses more on how to represent the real system by a model.

In the modelling process the computer is initially kept in the background, while one works with paper and pencil, with *causal loop diagrams* or similar tools and methods for illustrating the rules and relations. This is not relevant for more details at computer conference, but is nevertheless a very interesting field of work.

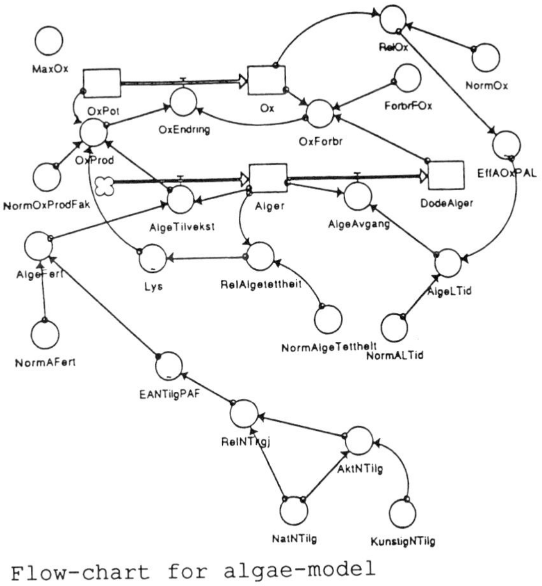

Flow-chart for algae-model

In schools - as well as a university level - dynamic simulations will not necessarily have to involve complex models. Students may very well work at level 3 or 4 with simple systems and simplified models, and still learn a lot about complex, dynamics systems. A central issue is to demonstrate the need for interdisciplinary work and knowledge, as well as the possibility to consider a complex system from a wholistic point of view, where "everything" can be included. When it gets to the point of implementing the model into a computer program, however, one very often ends up with problems that can hardly be quantified to mathematical relations. So far students have had to be satisfied with a simplified model. But a lot of research and development work is put into the field on a world wide basis, perhaps resulting in new methods or tools that are able to interpret causal loop diagrams directly into computerized models?

If relations can not be found from theoretical considerations, perhaps experiments and measurements in some cases may solve the problem? Deriving equations from empirical data is already a well known method in traditional disciplines. With the aid of a computer such derivations may be even simpler. The Stella program has this possibility of accepting an empirical graph as input for a relation between two same variables, and SimTek may collect empirical data from the surroundings directly from physical sensors. A sufficient set of data may then be used to generate the desired relations or equations. This ability is being applied in several projects on POLLUTION, some initiated through Nordic cooperation.

CONCLUSION

The intention is to present a new method for teaching complex topics, that very often go across curriculum. The method has been under development over the past 3-5 years. System dynamics has been studied for much longer. But it is only through the introduction of powerful, fast, personal computers into schools that the method has caught general interest from teachers. Previously it has been considered a university discipline. Now it may be a new opening for presentation of more advanced topics into schools, and bring about some deeper understanding of our surrounding world.

Through presentations and demonstrations we want to share experiences from Norwegian and Nordic work on system dynamics and simulations, hoping to initiate further discussions and cooperations across the borders and hemispheres. So far the work has indicated this as a possible new way of applying computes for innovation in teaching.

Computers in Education
A. McDougall and C. Dowling (Editors)
Elsevier Science Publishers B.V. (North-Holland)

COMPUTING AND THE SECONDARY SCHOOL MATHEMATICS CURRICULUM

Barry V KISSANE

School of Education, Murdoch University, Murdoch WA Australia 6150.

This paper highlights the technology available to students of secondary mathematics over the past two decades, and suggests that the computer is the most recent, and most powerful tool for mathematical work. The special relationship between mathematics and computing is examined, and some of the unfortunate recent history of the partnership is outlined. A number of mathematical metaphors for the computer are presented, together with a detailed review of the associated ways in which the computer is best used as a tool for mathematics. It is claimed that one effect of the computer is to change the nature of mathematics itself. The paper concludes with suggestions for the near future, including policy directions.

1. INTRODUCTION

With increasing trends towards computing across the curriculum, rather than a narrow concentration in the area of educational computing or information technology, it is time to reconsider the traditional school disciplines. This is especially so for mathematics, since recent developments in computing technology have changed the possibilities for schools considerably, and arguably even begun to change mathematics itself.

This paper begins such an analysis with some observations about the past availability and use of technology in the mathematics curriculum, then suggests some of the ways in which presently available computing technology might be put to good mathematical uses. The paper concludes with some policy directions for the future, together with some unanswered questions.

2. OBSERVATIONS ABOUT THE RECENT PAST

2.1 Technologies for mathematics

It is helpful to see the potential deployment of computing in school mathematics in some perspective. In what follows, I argue that the proper role of computers in school mathematics is as a tool for students to use. It is helpful to consider first the increasing sophistication of the high school mathematical toolkit routinely carried by students in recent times:

The Table Book (from the 50s)
The Slide Rule (the 60s)
The Hand Calculator (the 70s)
The Scientific Calculator (the 80s)
The Graphing Calculator (the 90s)

The effect on the curriculum of these changing tools for mathematics has been surprisingly slight. If one examines school curricula at the senior levels today, and compares them with those of twenty or thirty years ago, the similarities are greater than the differences. Some topics have suffered a shift in emphasis (notably logarithms and trigonometry), and much of the curriculum is now able to deal with realistic situations, unfettered by messy computation, but the essential mathematics has remained more or less intact. It seems that we have had a technology-resistant curriculum in mathematics, despite widespread public opinion to the contrary. It is well to take careful note of this when forecasting the likely directions of mathematics education as far as computers are concerned, as unrestrained optimism for change seems unwarranted.

There are two major reasons for this technology-resistant curriculum. Firstly, teachers and others have not yet been convinced that symbolic paper-and-pencil computation is not the main business of the mathematics curriculum. An emphasis on arithmetic and basic skills in mathematics is as widespread as it is damaging. The second reason has to do with the nature of mathematics itself. To date, the technology that has been available to secondary schools has offered essentially *numerical* help to schools. This has had relatively slight impact on school curricula, especially for stronger students. In fact, the stuff of mathematics is *not* computation, as any mathematician will verify. As Davis [1] suggests,

> "If mathematics is not primarily manipulating symbols, then what on earth is it? Real mathematics deals with finding problems, conceptualizing problems, inventing strategies for attacking problems, considering someone else's alleged "solution" and asking if there are any gaps in the reasoning process, recognizing ambiguities and resolving them, and many other matters of that sort." (p.55)

We have seen massive changes to the available technology for mathematics, with little evidence of their impact on the curricula of schools. We should be careful to recall that technological change is not by itself sufficient to bring about educational change.

2.2 Mathematics & Computing: A Special Relationship?

Conspicuous by its absence from this list of technology for mathematics is the computer. Over the past two decades especially, computer hardware and software have become more accessible to schools and some of their students. Indeed, many of the active participants in this process have been mathematics teachers, or ex-mathematics teachers, at least in Australia. Yet, the mathematics curriculum has been remarkably unaffected by the developments. This is an especially curious observation, given the community conception that mathematics and computing were kindred spirits, and hence deserves some scrutiny.

The word 'computer' connotes the act of computing, which also means dealing with numbers. Early uses of the computer dealt entirely with numbers, rather than with text, and there was even a time when we thought that teaching children about binary numbers would be helpful to them in dealing with computers. (Hopefully, no-one still believes this.) As computers have become more sophisticated, the numbers with which computers deal have been hidden deep within the infrastructure of the machine and hidden far from the user-friendly interface, laden with words and images. But the old ideas have remained.

Part of the relationship between mathematics and computing is serendipitous, to do with computer programming itself. When computing facilities first began to be available to schools in the early 1970's, it was necessary to know something about computer programming in order to operate them, and at that time, mathematics teachers typically had a smattering of such knowledge. In practice, when schools first experimented with computers, it was usually mathematics teachers who did the experimenting. Some of them later left mathematics teaching to devote all of their time to computer education, in fact.

Alleged relationships between mathematics and computing have also been accentuated by the view that teaching computer programming would be useful for mathematics education. This argument seems to rest in part on the premise that, in order to write a good computer program, one must first understand well the mathematical ideas involved, so that the computer provides a powerful incentive for this depth of understanding. An example that has appeared in countless mathematics books is that of solving a quadratic equation. Sloppy analytic procedures will lead to computer programs that overlook possibilities such as complex roots, and thus unexpectedly fail. But it seems to me that such an exercise is more concerned with good programming than with good mathematics, and the latter of necessity precedes the former. I always felt that it would be smarter to use a claculator to manipulate the quadratic formula than to write a computer program to do so. However, many, if not most, of the programming problems presented to students in mathematics classrooms have been of this kind. The computer has been used to do things that are already possible with conventional procedures. It is thus not surprising that it has usually been regarded as a frill. There has been surprisingly little attention devoted to solving with computers those mathematical problems that are not otherwise solvable, although this would seem a much more sensible activity. All this is not to say that computer programming might not be of some benefit to mathematics education. The parallels between using an algebraic programming language and algebra itself have not yet been exploited, and we are reminded often by Logophiles that there is an untapped potential of immense significance available through the serious implementation of Logo into mathematics curricula. But these things have not yet happened, and it is not clear that they ever will. What *has* happened has so far been disappointing.

In summary, it is not clear that a special relationship between mathematics and computing has really existed, and, further, whether the excursions of mathematics into the world of computing have been helpful, especially in the secondary school. In comparison with other subjects in the secondary school, mathematics seems not to have been as affected as is commonly thought.

2.4 Educational Computing

Two trends of considerable importance to mathematics education and computing have occurred lately. The first of these is the availability to schools of a great deal more computer hardware. The second is the rise and dominance of educational computing in schools to make use of that hardware.

Over the brief space of the last fifteen years or so, Australian schools have progressed through a cycle of hardware availability that began with central batch processing of students' computer programs, progressed to centralised computing facilities to which schools had dial-up access and thence to the acquisition of computers in schools themselves. Some schools in affluent countries like Australia now speak seriously of having a microcomputer in every classroom, and it is now feasible to imagine a microcomputer on every desk, although this is still some distance away.

The effects of these changes on mathematics in secondary schools have been negligible, and mainly unfortunate. Computing resources generally have been concentrated for administrative reasons in the educational computing areas of the school (both conceptual areas and physical areas). Thus, the access to computing for students within the mathematics curriculum has not always increased, and in many cases has actually diminished.

In Australian secondary schools, many mathematics departments have simply given up the ghost, as far as computing is concerned, and have decided to leave the computers in the computer education area of the school and to continue teaching mathematics in their own part of the school as if computers have never been invented. Thus, there has been little experimentation with computers in mathematics over that time, save for a few zealots here and there. There have certainly not been many serious attempts to reconceptualise the mathematics curriculum to take computers into account, since their inaccessibility has rendered the problem irrelevant.

At the same time, it seems likely that mathematical applications have been neglected in computing courses. One reason seems to be that there are not enough mathematicians teaching in the courses to be interested in the problems. In addition, the least common denominator, speaking in a mathematics educational sense, of most classes is rather low, making it unlikely that a teacher of computing would want the class to concentrate on mathematical areas.

Finally, a good deal of emphasis seems to have been placed on the role of the computer as a tutor and as a tutee, and much less on the role of the computer as a tool in mathematics, to use the metaphor popularized by Taylor [2]. No doubt, the major reason for this has been the limited availability of hardware and software to make the tool concept a viable one. To a lesser extent, too, the emphasis reflects the limited recent role of mathematics teachers *as mathematics teachers* in educational computing in schools.

The administrative convenience of educational computing has thus not worked to the betterment of the mathematics curriculum of late, and it seems that little progress has been made for some time. I was intrigued to find, as a member of a team developing a new mathematics curriculum for the US high school (Rubinstein *et al* [3], that it was easier for mathematics teachers to get continuing access to a room full of computers than it was to get occasional access to computers for particular parts of a course. The reason, of course, was administrative. The computers were typically controlled by educational computing personnel, and it was easier to schedule the room for mathematics purposes for the *whole* year than for parts of it.

Having looked at the recent past, I now turn to the present, in an attempt to highlight the ways in which computers might profitably interact with the school mathematics curriculum.

3. TODAY'S TECHNOLOGY

It has taken me some time to realise that, when people speak of the computer as a tool, they don't all share the same meaning for the term. This was highlighted for me recently when a mathematics teacher talked of using the computer as a tool for storing and manipulating students test scores. It was clear that she thought of the tool as a tool for herself. Likewise, when a mathematics teacher is using the computer to demonstrate something, say how the tosses of a coin converge so that about 50% of them are heads, the computer is being used as a tool for the teacher. Indeed, there are many ways in which teachers might use the computer as a tool to help them do the job of teaching, and it is even arguable that a careful use of a drill and practice program might be a tool in the hands of a thoughtful teacher.

However, I want to think of the computer as a tool for the person using it to achieve their own ends, in rather much the same way that I think of a screwdriver as a tool when I am trying to turn a screw. In my view, the proper way to think of the computer as a tool is as a tool for the *student*, not the teacher, and that is the way I shall use the phrase in the rest of this paper. Perhaps the distinction is nicely cast in the form of the computer as an educational tool *versus* the computer as a mathematical tool. It is the latter I wish now to highlight.

3.1 Mathematical metaphors for the computer

Before we can use the computer as a tool, we need to know what it can actually do. Only then are we in a position to judge whether or not we want to do such things. It is helpful to think metaphorically of the computer, and this section of the paper outlines appropriate metaphors (suggested in part by Zalman Usiskin of The University of Chicago) with some suggestions about present possibilities and their impact on the mathematics curriculum.

The computer as a number cruncher.
This metaphor highlights the fact that computers can manipulate numbers very rapidly, and thus suggests that we may deal differently with some aspects of mathematics with a computer than without one.

The computer as a data analyst.
This metaphor refers to the extensive statistical possibilities opened up by the availability of computers.

The computer as a randomiser.
Simulations have different purposes in mathematics and the natural world, but the essential underlying idea of controlling and taking advantage of random phenomena is common to them all.

The computer as a graphics device.
The computer can represent many mathematical concepts (such as the concept of a function) that have strong visual elements.

The computer as a symbol manipulator.
Many computers are routinely used to manipulate text, but recent software advances allow for algebraic text to be manipulated according to the laws of algebra so that much of what is presently taught in elementary algebra and calculus curricula is now available on a microcomputer.

The computer as a spreadsheet.
This might be regarded as another form of data analysis, but it is convenient to regard it separately, especially since its origins in the financial world locate it within different domains of mathematics.

It is of passing interest to note that there are now calculator approximations to all but the last of these computer metaphors. Also, there may be other useful metaphors for the computer in mathematics education. For example, Willis & Kissane [4] suggested that *the computer as a catalyst* for stimulating student activity and concept development has not yet been well exploited.

We now examine the implications of the computer as a tool for mathematics from the vantage point of each of the above metaphors. These are not discussed in order of priority; rather, all are important, but in different ways.

3.1.1. Number cruncher

The major implication of the computer as a number cruncher is that we may tackle some mathematical problems in new ways. A stunning example of this was the 'proof' of the four colour theorem in 1976 by Hakken and Appel. An example of this, closer to the everyday curriculum of students, involves the summation of series directly rather than through the use of an algebraic formula. Similarly, the divergence and convergence of series might be addressed. The capacity of the computer to approximate the solutions of an equation by merely evaluating a function at many points near a root offers a powerful numerical tool. Many equations that cannot be solved analytically can be quickly solved to arbitrary precision in this way, removing the misconception that many students develop that only linear and quadratic equations have solutions.

With such possibilities easily available, the mathematics curriculum needs to be reconsidered, since it is constructed on the premise that certain mathematical ideas are accessible only to older and more sophisticated students, and hence the foundations for these are not laid earlier.

3.1.2 Data analyst

With computer help, statistical analysis focuses on data quality and on interpreting the results obtained, rather than on the mechanics of manipulating the data itself. It is not accidental that the field of 'Exploratory Data Analysis' is no older than the modern microcomputer, since it was the latter invention that made the former possible. Students rarely see statistics as concerned with answering real questions using real data, since it is too hard for them to perform the manipulations themselves. With the computer as a tool, the curriculum can shift emphasis to data collection (formerly almost totally neglected), data editing and the purposes of statistical analyses of data, such as summary statistics and graphs.

To give a small example, until recently, scatterplots were rarely drawn to get a feel for the nature of the relationship between two variables, since it took much too long to actually draw them in any realistic case. (That is, although a picture may well be worth a thousand words, it took almost as long to produce so that here was no nett saving!) As well as teaching elementary arithmetic as if the calculator had not yet been invented, we also teach elementary statistics as if the computer had never been invented, which is arguably just as silly.

3.1.3 Randomiser

The facility to generate pseudo-random numbers is a useful mathematical tool for simulating otherwise intractable problems. The use of Monte Carlo procedures is fairly recent in mathematical history, but that is not to say that it should be excluded from school mathematics curricula. Often, problems can be simulated fairly easily, but only solved analytically using rather more sophisticated mathematical ideas.

3.1.4. Graphics device

The major advantage of the computer as a graphics device arises from its ability to depict the graphs of functions very easily. (Kissane [5]). The computer is a very powerful tool in this regard, if the appropriate software is available. From the graph of a function, students can explore the roots of the function (how many there are and their approximate values) and study the points of relative maxima and minima. In this way, equations in one variable can be approximately solved, and functions can be optimised. Both of these are very important mathematical tasks, but at present the latter is not dealt with until students get to the calculus (because it requires differential calculus) while the former is possible only for a very limited set of functions (notably only linear and quadratic functions). Of course, an additional bonus of such a facility is that students acquire a feeling for the shapes of graphs of functions that they do not normally acquire. When two graphs are simultaneously drawn, students can use these to solve systems of equations or their associated inequalitite.

An extensive example of how the computer as a tool to graph functions can be integrated into a secondary mathematics curriculum is provided by Rubinstein *et al* [3].

3.1.5 Symbol manipulator

Software is now available to allow the microcomputer to be used to perform the routine manipulations characteristic of elementary algebra and calculus, perhaps providing the most powerful mathematical tool of them all. Such software has been around for a decade now, although it has required a lot of memory and has been awkward to use. Although these restrictions are still partly true, they are becoming less true with time, and elsewhere I have argued (Kissane [6])that all of the manipulations necessary for high school algebra can now be performed by microcomputers. Such a tool provides a new perspective on the appropriate contents of the high school curriculum. Just as the hand calculator has demanded some rethinking of what is worth spending time on in the elementary school, so does symbol manipulation software demand the same kind of analysis for the high school and beyond.

The fundamental questions here are whether it is worth spending a lot of time developing skills that computers can more reliably perform, and how much time should be spent doing things by hand to ensure that students know what they are doing when they use such powerful tools. As I argue in Kissane [6], both extreme views are probably wrong: it is naive to think that we should spend no time at all on skills that computers can perform, and no better to claim that we should pretend that these computer facilities do not exist. The very existence of these tools poses powerful questions for us to consider.

3.1.6 Spreadsheet

A computer used as a spreadsheet reduces the need for students to complete tiresome calculations, particularly those concerned with financial planning. It seems appropriate to allow the use of this tool to deal with such situations, which are as likely to occur outside the mathematics classroom as inside. Creative use of spreadsheets gives rise to the possibility that students might solve problems that are ordinarily difficult to solve. An example is the use of a spreadsheet to solve equations by listing many values of an expression, and successively refining the choices until a close approximation to a solution is found. This is in fact rather like the example given above of solving an equation by listing values of the function and by closely inspecting a graph of the function.

3.2 Using the new tools

There are several likely effects of the increased availability of these new tools for mathematics. One possibility is that the computer will permit us to remove much of the dross from the curriculum, and thus frees more time to use for newer material, or for better treatments of the existing material, such as problem solving and mathematical modelling. Another possibility is to deal with existing content, but in new ways. Yet anoth involves adding new mathematical content and experiences to the curriculum. It is timely here to recall Usiskin's observation [7] that the curriculum is a zero sum game: if we wish to add material into the mathematics curriculum, we must also be prepared to say what we will first remove to make room for it.

The challenge now is to take note of the lessons of the past and to take account of the possibilities of today's technology to move the mathematics curriculum forward, and the last section of this paper is a step in that direction.

4. THE WAY AHEAD

Taking note of the previous section, it seems that a major effect of the computer is to change, irreversably, the nature of mathematics itself. Unlike some of the previous tools for mathematics, the computer does much more than make easier our present ways of doing mathematics; rather, it suggests and even demands that we use new ways. To move from our present state to a newer one that takes advantage of these new tools will not be easy, however. If we have learnt anything at all from post war curriculum experimentation, it is that it is a very difficult task to change the curriculum.

In fact, most of the barriers to curriculum change are psycholgical, economic and political, rather than technological, which accounts in large measure for the difficulties of making changes. For example, the technology referred to above is already available, in the restricted sense that it can be purchased provided you have sufficient funds, although the means of accessing it is less available in many cases, notably developing countries and less well resourced districts in western countries. In a similar way to the present feeling among many elementary school teachers, we might reasonably expect that secondary school mathematics teachers will feel threatened and deskilled when the computer-laden future is contemplated. In a society that continues to be ambivalent about the place of computers and the balance between 'basic skills' and other desired outcomes of schooling, it is difficult for teachers and curriculum developers to solve the many practical problems associated with using this technology in school mathematics curricula.

Most importantly, in mathematics, the computer must not be the object of instruction. A paradigm shift is needed. 'Educational computing' has not been a helpful route to thinking about the computer in mathematics. Now a major shift towards the use of computers as mathematical tools is needed. At the same time, it is important that mathematics teachers get personal experience with computers, to judge for themselves how they might be inforporated into the curricula of the future.

4.1 Policy Directions

To help the important process of reconsidering the curriculum from the perspective of the technology available to support it, I offer below some policy directions for the near future.

(i) First priority should be given to the use of computers as mathematical tools.
(ii) Computers should be used only when they provide clear advantages over alternatives.
(iii) A computer should be available to a student of mathematics whenever she needs one.
(iv) Every mathematics department should have its own computing facilities under its own control.
(v) Students should become computer aware and computer literate through using computers for real purposes, including mathematical purposes.
(vi) Inservice education is urgently needed.
(vii) A minimal collection of tool software for mathematics includes:

- a function grapher
- a symbolic manipulation program
- a statistics package
- a spreadsheet
- a programming facility (Logo, Pascal, BASIC)

4.2 Some Fundamental Questions

Before we will learn to take advantage of the opportunities provided for the secondary school mathematics curriculum by computer technology, we need to deal with some rather fundamental questions.

Can we afford to change incrementally?
Curriculum change is always a slow affair. Regrettably, the development of computing technology does not wait for us to catch up: rather, it continues to change while we are trying to change the curriculum.

Which comes first? The new curriculum or the technology to support it?
There is a serious dilemma reflected by this question. It is difficult to press claims for adequate provision of computing facilities in mathematics when the curriculum is written under the assumption that such facilities are not necessary. Contrariwise, it is difficult to try and change the curriculum to take better account of computers, until such time as teachers (at least) have a greater familiarity with their use.

Should students learn to do things that machines can do (much) better?
This question will continue to bother us, especially as computers become more available in mathematics. If long division is a good example in the case of calculators (and I think that it is), we might expect that it will be very difficult in practice to remove things from the mathematics curriculum, long after their usefulness has been supplanted by a machine.

What should be the relative emphasis on mathematical content and mathematical processes?
In recent years, there have been substantial attempts to concentrate more attention in secondary school mathematics on the process aspects (such as problem solving). Computer uses will influence this question.

What is mathematics? Why is it important? Why are we teaching it to children?
These three questions will, however, remain paramount. It is well to remind ourselves that, while the questions will remain, their answers must be expected to change, and perhaps dramatically, under the influence of computing.

REFERENCES

[1] Davis, R. B. (1988) The world according to McNeill. Journal of Mathematical Behavior. 7, 51-78.
[2] Taylor, R. S. (1980) The Computer in the School: Tutor, Tool, Tutee. New York: Teachers College Press.
[3] Rubinstein, R. et al (1988) Functions, Statistics and Trigonometry with Computers. Chicago: The University of Chicago School Mathematics Project.
[4] Willis, S. & Kissane, B. (1989) Computing Technology and Teacher Education in Mathematics and Science, Canberra: Australian Government Publishing Service, Volume 3, 57-92.
[5] Kissane, B. (1989b) Some implications of function graphers for the mathematics curriculum. The Australian Mathematics Teacher, 45, 3, 2-4.
[6] Kissane, B. (1989a) Symbolic manipulation on a microcomputer: Is algebra dead? Cross Section, 1, 2, 18-23.
[7] Usiskin, Z. (1980) What should *not* be in the algebra and geometry curricula of average college-bound students? The Mathematics Teacher, 73, 413-424.

Computers in Education
A. McDougall and C. Dowling (Editors)
Elsevier Science Publishers B.V. (North-Holland)

COMPUTER-ASSISTED THINKING SKILLS INSTRUCTION: CURRICULUM PRINCIPLES, TEACHER PREPARATION, AND STUDENT OUTCOMES

S. Kim MACGREGOR

111 Peabody Hall, Louisiana State University, Baton Rouge, Louisiana 70803-4721, United States

This paper describes a project designed to develop, implement, and evaluate a computer-assisted thinking skills curriculum at the secondary level. The project was funded by the Board of Elementary and Secondary Education and was a joint effort between academic personnel and school-based practitioners. The learning activities were subject-matter based and integrated into existing science, social studies, and mathematics classes. Evaluation of the first year indicated some positive outcomes for critical thinking, social studies achievement, self-esteem, and attitude toward school.

1. INTRODUCTION

The purpose of this paper is to discuss the project, outline the principles upon which it is based, describe the curriculum development process, and present the results of the program evaluation. The project began in 1988 in two pilot secondary schools serving approximately 1500 students, and will continue through 1990. The goal of the project is to provide challenging and motivational instruction that enhances students' ability to solve problems and think critically in existing content areas.

2. CRITICAL THINKING AND COMPUTING

It is believed that critical thinking and information processing skills are required for subject matter competence as well as for employment in an increasingly technological and information-based society. Critical thinking is a process, and critical thinking skills require more of the student than recall of knowledge or comprehension. Commonly identified features of this process include problem identification, information seeking, identification of relevant information, exploring and evaluating alternatives, and reflecting on one's thinking, or metacognition [1].

Critics of current educational practice believe that insufficient individualized attention and narrow curricula and teaching practices which discourage active participation in learning are barriers to student development [2]. The computer used with appropriate software is a method of instructional delivery which provides individualization, motivates students to learn, and promotes active learning behavior. In addition, there is evidence that computer-based instructional activities can be designed to enhance the development of higher level thinking skills [3]. Thus, the computer was chosen as the vehicle for the thinking skills instruction.

3. CURRICULUM PRINCIPLES

Seven principles were identified to provide the pedagogical foundation for this project. They are listed and described in the following section.

Integrate computer activities into the existing curriculum
Eliminate boundaries between content areas
Use software without an internal

instructional agenda
Make teaching of thinking skills explicit
Encourage collaboration among students
Provide support and training for teachers
Document student involvement

It was determined that existing subject material would be the core of instruction for a variety of reasons. Experts in thinking skills instruction recommend that subject matter be used as the vehicle for thinking to give purpose to the thinking process [4,5], and research indicates that background knowledge of a subject is essential for higher level thinking in that content. In addition, research suggests the motivation to learn thinking skills is enhanced when the skill is needed to achieve subject matter objectives. Specific thinking skills relevant to the three subject areas were identified by the teachers and university personnel.

Another important curriculum consideration was that the boundaries between content areas be eliminated where appropriate. Frequently, in school environments, artificial, forced lines are drawn between subjects. For example, arithmetic is taught only in the math class, and geography is taught only in the social studies class. However, in reality, these boundaries do not exist. One applies math skills in a variety of settings, and science and social studies are related along several dimensions. In this project, an emphasis was placed on creating instructional activities that had relevance across content areas. For example, data collected and organized with a data base in the science or social studies classroom is analyzed with a graphing package in the math classroom.

The software selected was that which could be categorized as having no internal instructional agenda. This included word processors, data managers, spreadsheets, graphing packages, desktop publishers, and puzzle generators. A common concern about the use of commercially available instructional software is the lack of curriculum fit. Teachers find themselves adapting their curriculum to the software rather than the reverse. Moreover, much of the available CAI is not appropriate for thinking skills instruction as it is primarily drill and practice or linear tutorials that encourage convergent thinking. By using software that is adaptable, the computer is an alternative methodology for attaining existing curriculum objectives. In addition, information processing software of the type selected allows students to apply thinking skills in an interactive environment and presents students with motivating and complex situations for problem solving and thinking [3].

The teacher is a critical element in successful thinking skills instruction [4]. Teachers learned to make their thinking skills instruction explicit. Each skill was introduced by giving it a name, providing examples of how the skill can be or has been used in school and in personal experiences, and describing the specific operations that are involved in executing the skill. Students are required to practice the skill, verbalize the process of using the skill, and reflect on how they used the skill. In addition, framing and bridging components are included as part of each activity [6]. Framing activities provide the subject matter setting for the application of the skill and relate a specific skill to a broader context of problem solving. Bridging activities provide a link for the transfer of the skill from the computer-based activity in which it is learned and practiced to a traditional classroom activity.

The thinking skills instruction was organized to facilitate collaboration among pairs of students. The value of collaborative learning has been stressed over the years [7,8,9,10]. Vygotsy [8] proposed the existence of a "zone of proximal development" to explain the role that social interactions play in student learning. The zone of proximal development is defined as the distance between actual developmental level and potential developmental level. The level of actual development is the student's independent problem solving ability and can be measured by an achievement test. The level of potential development can be measured by assessing the student's problem solving capabilities when collaborating with an adult or peer. True peer collaboration takes place only when two or more students work together to solve a problem or create a product that could not have been completed independently. An expanding body of research indicates collaborative learning has a positive influence on content area achievement, problem solving skill, and ability to verbalize thinking strategies.

Teacher training and support was emphasized throughout the project implementation. It appears that extensive training is needed before teachers are able to use computers as effective teaching tools. Management of learning presents a challenge to teachers, and when computers are added to the learning environment, the challenge is increased. Both formal in-service sessions and bi-weekly support meetings were held. Teachers and students were requested to keep journals documenting their experiences with the computers and their reactions to project activities.

4. PROJECT COMPONENTS

The project was organized into four major components including curriculum development, teacher in-service, implementation, and evaluation. Although a specific beginning and end point to each component was planned, formative evaluation activities resulted in ongoing curriculum revision and in-service training to meet teachers' needs.

4.1 Curriculum Development

This phase included the identification of target critical thinking skills, the creation of instructional units that could be coordinated with each of the content area curriculum guides, and the selection and purchase of software. The following thinking skills were identified as the target skills for the curriculum:

Problem Analysis
Interpreting Data
Identifying Relevant Information
Alternative Representation of Data
Identifying Supporting Details
Recognizing Attributes
Drawing Inferences
Decision Making
Gathering Information
Generating Hypotheses/Predictions
Designing Projects/Investigations

Software including a word processor, data manager, spreadsheet, graphing package, desktop publisher, and puzzle generators was purchased. Although the instructional activities were designed to utilize specific brand packages, the lessons can be used with any package of the same generic type. A set of 30 fifty-minute instructional activities was created for each subject area [11]. The instructional modules evolved over the course of the year and were revised as a result of teacher input and student reactions.

4.2 Teacher In-Service

The purpose of this component was to prepare teachers to operate the computing equipment, to model how to teach with computers, to instruct teachers on the use of the software selected for the program, and to demonstrate strategies for teaching critical thinking skills. Although a small percentage of the participating teachers had used the computer for personal reasons, none had experience using the computer for instruction. Four eight-hour in-service sessions were conducted each year. Funds to pay substitute teachers were provided by the project so that the training sessions could be conducted during the regular school day in the computer labs located at the school sites. In addition, informal meetings and individual help sessions were held with teachers as needs arose. The teachers were encouraged to take the computers home during holidays and semester breaks to become familiar with the equipment and the software in the comfort of their own homes. The teachers who took advantage of this opportunity demonstrated greater confidence in using the equipment at school.

4.3 Implementation

A computer lab with 16 computer stations was set up at each school. Each station consisted of an IBM PC Junior with 256k of memory, a color monitor, and a printer. Students went to the lab for one fifty-minute period per week in each of their science, social studies, and mathematics classes. In the lab, the students were supervised and instructed by the classroom teachers, but graduate students from the university were available to provide assistance.

4.4 Evaluation

The students were assessed on a variety of dimensions including content area achievement, critical thinking ability, self-esteem, and attitude toward school.

The Cornell Critical Thinking Test, Level X, was used to assess critical thinking ability. This test is a 71-item, multiple choice test which emphasizes induction, deduction, and assumption identification. Reliability estimates range from .67 to .90, depending on sample and scoring formula used [12].

Content area achievement in science, mathematics, and social studies was assessed through use of the Comprehensive Tests of Basic Skills (CTBS), Level H, Form U [13]. These tests assess content area knowledge and have well-established reliability and validity.

Self-esteem was evaluated with the School Short Form of the Coopersmith Self-Esteem Inventories. All items are short statements that are answered one of two ways: Like me or unlike me. Four self-esteem sub-scales (General, Social, Home, and School) can be derived from the instrument. A reliability coefficient of .89 (based on internal consistency) has been calculated for grade 7. Construct validity of the instrument has been established through several extensive research projects [14].

Attitude toward school was measured by a 39-item questionnaire [15]. The questionnaire focused on student perceptions of the benefits to be derived from attending and completing high school. Items are short statements to which students respond on a 7-choice Likert scale. Two examples of questions are "Staying in school will lead to my being a success in life and 'being somebody'." and "Education helps a person use his or her leisure time to better advantage."

5. EVALUATION RESULTS

Pre and post test data were collected on a total of 560 students (378 project and 182 control). The students in the control group were comparable to the students in the project group with respect to race, socioeconomic status, grade level and ability. A comparison of pre-test scores on all formal measures yielded no significant differences between the groups. The following sections describe the analysis of the data.

5.1 Effect on Academic Achievement and Critical Thinking

Gain scores (posttest minus pretest score) were computed for each subtest (Science, Social Studies, and Mathematics) of the CTBS. Univariate Analyses of Variance (ANOVA's) were used to test for the effect of the project on gains made on each content area subtest. Mean gain scores are exhibited in Table 1. A significant difference ($p<.05$) was found for gains on the social studies subtest. The students in the project group demonstrated larger gains than the students in the control group. No significant differences between the project and control groups were found for gains in mathematics or science.

Mean gain scores were computed for performance on the Test of Critical Thinking. An ANOVA was computed to test the effect of the project on these gains. A significant ($p<.01$) difference was found between the project and control groups. The students in the project classes made significantly larger gains in critical thinking than the students in the control classes. Mean critical thinking gain scores are also displayed in Table 1.

Table 1

Mean Gain Scores for Cognitive Abilities

Group	SS	SC	M1	M2	CT
Project					
M	2.7*	1.7	2.4	2.5	2.9**
SD	0.90	0.77	0.71	0.68	1.01
Control					
M	-2.6	2.4	3.2	2.7	-2.4
SD	2.04	1.34	1.66	1.65	2.74

* p<.05, **p<.01

5.2 Impact on Self-Esteem and Attitude Toward School

The scores from the Coopersmith Inventory were utilized to assess self-esteem. The four sub-scales (General-, Social-, Home-, School-Self) were summed to form a total self-esteem score. Gain scores were derived, and univariate ANOVA's were computed for each subscale gain score as well as for the total gain score. Only one difference between the project and control groups was found to be statistically significant. Students in the project group demonstrated a significantly larger gain, ($p<.05$) in the Home-Self subscale.

The school attitude survey was administered to the project students and a _t_-test computed to compare the pre-project scores with the post-project scores. The post scores were significantly ($p<.01$) greater than the prescores indicating the students' attitude about the benefits of school improved.

6. SUMMARY

The most significant outcome of the evaluation is the effect of instruction on critical thinking. Students in the project classes outperformed control students on a norm-referenced measure of critical thinking ability. It is important to note that, although the thinking skills were taught in the context of specific subject matter, students were able to transfer the skills to a more general type of thinking skills task. Research on the generalizability of thinking skills provides mixed findings [16], and there is evidence that students are not able to transfer skills or strategies spontaneously from one domain to another. However, when certain conditions are present, decontextualization of the skill can occur [5]. In this project, the same set of thinking skills was taught in the context of three different content areas and was embedded within a variety of software environments. Practice with the skills in different subject domains and computer contexts may have allowed the students to establish the skills as general heuristics that they applied to the testing task.

With regard to the effect of instruction on content area achievement, mixed results were obtained. A significant effect on social studies achievement was found, but there were no measured effects on science or mathematics. The primary objective was to develop higher level thinking skills, thus, it is possible that the effect for social studies was simply a by-product of the thinking skills instruction. It is important to note, however, that the use of one day a week for the computer-based thinking instruction did not result in decreased content area performance in math and science.

Students' self-esteem is another important factor to consider in the educational process as there is a positive relation between self-esteem and academic achievement. One assumption for this project was that the computer-based instructional program would enhance the participants' self concept because it creates an empowering environment. There was a significant difference on the Home-Self subscale in that project students perceived their home environment as being more desirable and supportive of their school work. During interviews, the project students described the computer activities to be more relevant and interesting than traditional classroom activities. Teachers reported that on Monday mornings students usually asked what computer activities were planned for the week ahead and if they could use the computer lab more often. Further evidence of an improvement in attitude toward school was provided by the school attitude inventory. At the end of the first year, the project students indicated that they believed school was more important to their self-esteem and future success. It is possible that students' increased interest in school activities led to more discussions with parents resulting in more parental support.

Dropping out of school is major problem in the United States, and enhancing the learning environment with computers appears to be a potent strategy for motivating students to learn and stay in school. The ability to think critically is given increasingly more importance in the scope and sequence of curriculum recommendations made by national and international educational task forces in all content areas. As a result, it is necessary to identify successful methods for teaching critical thinking skills and facilitating the transfer of those skills to new problems. Combining computer-based information processing activities with teacher-directed explicit thinking skills instruction appears to provide a vehicle for achieving this goal.

REFERENCES

[1] Bransford, J.D., Sherwood, R., Vye, N., & Reiser, J. (1986). Teaching thinking and problem solving. American Psychologist, 41, 1078-1089.

[2] Glasgow, D.G. (1985). Statement for the record before the Subcommittee on Education, Arts and Humanities on the Dropout and Prevention and Reentry Act of 1985. (pp. 120-127). Washington, D.C.: U.S. G.P.O.

[3] Perkins, D.N. (1985). The fingertip effect: How information processing technology shapes thinking. Educational Researcher, 14(7), 11-17.

[4] Beyer, B. (1987). Practical strategies for the teaching of thinking. Allyn & Bacon.

[5] Ennis, R.H. (1989). Critical thinking and subject specificity: Clarification and needed research. Educational Researcher, 18(3), 4-10.

[6] Bransford, J.D. & Stein, B.S. (1984). The IDEAL problem solver. N Y: W.H. Freeman & Co.

[7] Dewey, J. (1902). The child and the curriculum: The school and society. Chicago: University of Chicago Press.

[8] Vygotsky, L.S. (1978). Mind in society: The development of higher psychological processes. Harvard University Press.

[9] Johnson, D.W., & Johnson, R.T. (1983). The socialization and achievement crises: Are cooperative learning experiences the solution? Applied Social Psychology Annual, 4, 119-164.

[10] Slavin, R.E. (1989). Cooperative learning and student achievement. In R.E. Slavin (Ed.), School and Classroom Organization (129-156).

[11] MacGregor, S.K. (1989). Developing critical thinking skills: A computer-assisted intervention program for at-risk students. Final Project Report.

[12] Ennis, R.H., Millman, J., & Tomko, T.N. (1985). Cornell Critical Thinking Tests Level X & Level Z--Manual (3rd edition). Pacific Grove, CA: Midwest Pub.

[13] CTBS examiner's manual, Forms U and V, Levels F,G,H,J,K. (1983). Monterey, CA: CTB/McGraw-Hill.

[14] Coopersmith, S. (1981). SEI: Self-esteem inventories. Palo Alto, CA: Consulting Psychologists Press.

[15] Ajzen, I. & Fishbein, M. (1980). Understanding attitudes and predicting social behavior. Prentice-Hall.

[16] Perkins, D.N. & Salomon, G. (1989). Are cognitive skills. context bound? Educational Researcher, 18(1), 16-25.

Computers in Education
A. McDougall and C. Dowling (Editors)
Elsevier Science Publishers B.V. (North-Holland)

PEDAGOGICAL, PSYCHOLOGICAL AND SOCIOLOGICAL ASPECTS CONCERNING THE INTRODUCTION OF COMPUTER PROGRAMMING IN A PUBLIC SECONDARY SCHOOL IN VENEZUELA

José Manuel Martínez & Anne Benko de Rotaeche

Universidad Central de Venezuela. Escuela de Computación. Apt. 47002. Caracas. 1041A. & Universidad Nacional Abierta. Unidad de Postgrado. Apt.2096. Caracas. 1010A. Venezuela

Possible intellectual benefits, development and evolution of programming strategies, cognitive strategies, metacognitive resources, beleifs, attitudes, motivations and myths of the students at the introduction to computer programming learning are studied and analyzed as well as observations and results of introductory courses offered to the administrative and educational personnel.

1. INTRODUCTION

This paper presents the results of a descriptive and exploratory research identifying certain pedagogical, psychological and sociological aspects that may characterize learning situations (*) [1].

The research was undertaken at a high school - "Liceo Carlos Soublette"- between November 1986 and November 1988. It was divided into three main sub-projects: pedagogical, psychological and sociological

The equipment used consisted of 5 microcomputers ATARI 520-ST, each one with one micro floppy disk of 360 Kb., color monitor and mouse, plus 2 printers STAR NP-10.The main software used with the students was: ATARI-LOGO and GFA-BASIC . The operating system (TOS) was permanently installed in ROM and provided GEM Desktop facilities. For the observation work during the sessions, audio and video recording equipments were used.

In our country, private education has been first in incorporating computers, specially in Caracas - the capital -, where more than 80 schools use computers for educational purposes, as a mean of capturing new clients and satisfying pressures and initiatives from parents, who are willing to facilitate the adaptation of their children to the use of new technologies. The public sector is now promoting a plan to introduce computers into the public basic education. These results may facilitate decisions about introducing the computer at the basic school level in Venezuela. [2]

2. OBJECTIVES

The focus of the pedagogical work was to describe the evolution of the programming strategies used by the students. Also to detect the main factors affecting them and the most common difficulties found for the acquisition of the basic computer programming notions. In addition, the possibilities of assistance from teachers to help students overcome these obstacles were also analyzed. The didactical method was based upon the constructivistic knowledge theory derived from Piaget [1].

The psychological research tried to determine: a)whether the existence of certain abilities (e.g. verbal, abstract and numeric reasoning) constituted a pre-requisite facilitating the learning of a programming language, b)the cognitive strategies used by the students to solve programming problems, c) the meta-cognitive resources they employed or developed during the process, d) to assess whether the programming course produced any

(*)This research was possible due to a grant given by the CONICIT (The National Council for Scientific and Technological Research). The research team was formed by Anne Benko (coordinator), José Manuel Martínez (engineer), Beatriz Mejías and Martha Arteaga (pedagoges), M. Fabiola Gutiérrez and Nola Hidalgo (psychologists) and Carlos E. Colina (sociologist).

evolution or modification in the planned behaviour, the abilities for categorization and logical and verbal reasoning. [1]

From a sociological point of view, the research tried to investigate, based upon Fishbein's theory [3], the beleifs, attitudes, myths and ideologies carried by the students and to study students' motivation through several behavioural indicators.[1]

Along those two years, some introductory courses (LOGO, word processor, spreadsheet, data base management packages) were given to the educational, administrative and directive personnel, in order to create an appropiate atmosphere around the experience and to get a close view of what happens when computer is introduced to school [1].

3.METHODOLOGY

The research approach was exploratory with a case study design. Work was organized in two different steps: During the first year a pilot study was realized, teaching LOGO to 40 students of 10th. grade, with the purpose of defining in detail the methodology and for testing the instruments and techniques to be used for data analysis and interpretation at the second phase. In the second year a GFA-BASIC language course was given. This central research was developed between September 1987 and November 1988, over a sample of 50 students, not owning microcomputers, in the 10th. grade of the secondary school, of both sexes, whose ages ranged from 14 to 19, . The students were organized in pairs per computer and the course had a duration of 81 hours, distributed in 27 sessions during 17 weeks.

The main instruments used in the pedagogical study were the following: an initial diagnostic test, two knowledge tests during the course and one at the end; in the psychological study the Differential Abilities Test (TDA) was administered and the following tests of the Instrumental Enrichment Test (PEI) proposed by Feuerstein [4]: instructions, categorization, transitive relationships and silogisms. Systematic direct observation of students behaviour was the main instrument in both the pedagogical and the psychological sub-projects. A register sheet and the support of audio and video recording were used to follow the evolution of the teaching-learning process, the development of cognitives strategies and the interaction modalities between the subjects. Survey, interviews and observation techniques were used to collect and study sociological aspects.

4. MAIN RESULTS OF THE CENTRAL RESEARCH

4.1 Pre-requisites for the learning of BASIC programming.

The research studied the relationship between the results shown by the students after a course in structured BASIC and the capacities suggested by the literature as being related with the learning of this language: abstract reasoning, spatial abilities, numeric reasoning, verbal reasoning. Another test of speed and precision was added. The results obtained agreed with those already outlined in the literature:

- Between abstract learning and programming -.that can be compared to the relationship between intelligence and programming learning studied by Marcia Linn [5] - no significant relationship was found.

- Spatial abilities did not show to have any correlation with the general results in BASIC learning. It should be remembered that studies showing such a relationship were based upon graphical LOGO learning, where spatial relationships are important. Global qualifications obtained at the end of the course do not permit us to establish whether the first part of the course - where some simple designs had to be done - had any correlation with the spatial abilities test.

- Numerical reasoning did not show any correlation. Nevertheless, we consider important Richard Mayer's observations indicating that the existence of very specific abilities related with mathematics and language mastering (as the capacity for translating verbal problems to equations and the facility for understanding procedures) might influence programming learning. [6]

- Verbal ability was the only ability that showed a significant correlation with the BASIC programming learning. Quantitative results obtained with the test agreed with the qualitative observations. Subjects with difficulties in language expression had difficulties for error detection and correction, and failed evaluating the resolution process. We think that programming requires a variety of linguistics abilities, such as reading comprehension and capacity for translating short sentences from English into Spanish.

It seems to be important to study in more detail the hypothesis of the existence of a relationship between verbal ability and computer programming. These results agree with and confirm the repeated calls about the importance of mastering the mother language, for ensuring an adequate performance in a variety of contexts.

As the test used to evaluate this ability included several items related with analogic reasoning, it seems that we agree with the opinion of Pea and Kurland [7] and with the studies by Mayer [8] and Clement [9], who using more specific tests found a positive relationship between the ability for analogic reasoning and the learning of programming.

- Speed and precision tests seem to indicate that the quicker subjects in the execution of routine tasks are not always the best in computer programming. In our research these fast subjects tended to be less efficient for error detection and correction and often made use of cut and trial techniques instead of more reflexive strategies. Although a specific test for measuring impulsiveness and reflexibility was not administered, these subjects showed greater anxiety than the others during the qualitative observations. All these facts show that less impulsive subjects tend to give better results in computer programming learning. It may be important to say that our study was not focused in measuring the effects of a programming course in the students' ability for reflection, as that of Clements and Gullo [10].

4.2 Computer programming learning

- Learning levels: In agreement with previous studies about this topic, we may say that the level acquired corresponds to the first levels of the "chain of cognitive achievements" (Linn [11]). Nevertheless, there is a perception of certain "chunks" of organized patterns of information, although the teaching of "chunks" was not our specific objective. It would be interesting to study in our country Marcia Linn's methods [11], about the relationship between the gain of "chunks" and the global comprehension of the problems, and those of Richard Mayer [8] referring to the advance organizers. The method used in our investigation is closer to the mediational method described by Delclos, Littlefield and Brandsford [12], but with less stress on the verbalizations of the third phase. It seems to be important to put more emphasis about verbalizations in a new study. Numerous authors underline that, for learning, in general, it is very important to promote elaboration activities with the students, stimulating them to express the concepts acquired and the discovered relationships in their own terms.

- Programming strategies: We could not find that the students developed real processes of hierarchical planning; they normally used a down-up approach, characterized by the use of an inductive method and ad-hoc decisions. The majority of the problem-situations were approached using strategies developed for the solution of previous problems having similarities in their statements. Nevertheless, we observed the design of sequential strategies (algorithms) in a natural form.

The subjects who planned, reviewed and evaluated programs frequently arrived to the right solution. Impulsive erasing tended to decrease, in partial agreement with the literature (Clements and Gullo [10]), where it is recorded an eventual decrease of impulsiveness by means of computer programming learning. A more complete specific research would be needed to clarify this hypothesis.

- Evolution of the programming strategies: The most influencing factor in modifying subjects strategies was the partial execution of programs before ending their writing, practice that was facilitated by the software itself, which permitted step by step program execution. The second important factor was the instructor with his interventions, with explanations or key comments, but only in some cases. In general the students became more instructor independent. Even though the pairs of students communicated with each other, we cannot say that these verbal interchanges had any effect on the modifications of strategies, either did spontaneous detection and correction of errors seem to influence modifications of the strategies.

- More frequent errors and difficulties:
. Troubles using the instructions PRINT AT and PRINT TAB to place words or geometrical figures in a definite location of the screen (selection between type or character coordinates).
. Misuse of the instructions PRINT and INPUT.
. Bad interpretation of the meaning of the part ELSE at the conditional

instruction IF..ELSE..ENDIF.
. Lack of comprehension of the use of cumulative variables.
. Incorrect identification and handling of the variable that determines the stop condition for loop construction.
. Confusions for establishing what instructions should be inside the loop.
. Lack of precision to establish the right place to locate the label for closing the GOTO loop.

- Syntactic errors were quickly overcome. Nevertheless logical errors remained, reflecting the difficulties for the logical conception of a problem solution.

4.3. Metacognitive strategies.

The more advanced subjects show the following common characteristics:
Planning:
. Ability for designing their own programs before running them.
. Conciousness about the previous knowledge they needed.
. Easy verbalization during the whole process, demonstrating better conciousness than the others about the strategies they use.
Supervision:
. More frequent spontaneous reviewing.
. Ability for anticipation, that is to make predictions about the consequences of what they have designed.
. Ability for translating the instructions into Spanish.
. Correct identification of one's errors.
Evaluation:
. Efficient evaluation of one's results.

The more anxious subjects showed difficulties to evaluate their results and to recognize that they did not have enough relevant information to identify their errors. The subjects with expression difficulties tended to have problems in error detection and correction, and also in evaluating their results. In general, time estimations to solve the exercises were not done in terms of the problem and evaluated capacities, but in terms of the duration of the sessions.

Summarizing, the more advanced subjects demonstrated that they had more developed strategies than the other subjects; but this does not mean that it was influenced by the programming course. Nevertheless our findings do not show a significant effect of computer programming over the metacognition.

Following Brandsford Delclos Littelfield & Brandsford [12], we beleive that the attempts to teach to think by means of computer programming must focus specifically on this purpose. Thinking about one's own problem solving processes, trying to see them as usable strategies in new, different contexts is very important. But, in our opinion, systematic help to the students enhancing them to do that, does not have to be an exclusive responsibility of programming teachers, it should be a general purpose and approach underlying the whole school curriculum. Obviously, this will have direct implications on the way teachers are going to be trained.

4.4. Interpersonal relationships

Interpersonal relationships between the pairs of students were difficult at the beginning, in almost all the cases; with the exception of one couple, they tended to improve and increase integration and cooperation. This result agrees with the specialized literature that shows the same tendency when the didactical approach favors team work.

The sociological sub-project also showed an increase in the positive attitude towards computer sciences among the students attending the whole course. Tendency to stay working with the computer after class was very important (45.2 % of the students). This is a very objective behavioural indicator about the motivation towards computer programming. Nevertheless, this tendency was not general, we have to mention some dropout cases and the refusal of some selected students to attend to the course.

4.5. Teaching method

The teaching method used was very effective, as it was shown by the results: an important number of students could prepare their own programs as a final activity of the course. The students were surprised and satisfied with the possibilities of personal participation, spontaneous comments, teachers' help and direction to reach a real comprehension of their errors, and also by the possibility of applying their knowledge of English to a practical situation. On the other hand, the school teachers were also interested and wishful to analyse the teaching methodology, since it was less directive than the one they used, and apparently more effective.

4.6. Institutional response

After our experience the school, by its own, introduced computing to official courses and to the administrative tasks. A large number of students (345) is now enrolled in those programs.

5. CONCLUSIONS AND FINAL COMMENTS

•The use of hierarchical planning in an introductory course is difficult for the students.
•Alink seems to exist between verbal ability and programming learning.
•The subjects who use metacognitive strategies are better planners and programming problem solvers.
•Impulsiveness tends to be negatively related to programming learning.
•An active method seems to be a good way to acquire "chunks", an important objective in good programming.
•The computer is a very powerful instrument, but it is not the main tool for stimulating cognitive processes. For this has to be the concern of all school curriculum, since transfer of general abilities is not an easy matter.
•Teachers' training is of upmost relevance in order to make them aware of the possible applications and benefits of such a technology.
•This leads us to assert that enhancement of teachers preparation on pedagogical and psychological areas is a necessary condition to improve the quality of teaching, even in computing.
•As teachers training in computing requires time and efforts, they should be helped to get conciousness and self-confidence about their own abilities to use it in the classroom, so their actual needs and motivations should be taken into account.
•Computing demands many and special financial, logistic and prepared human resources, hence implementation decisions should be taken based upon cost-efficiency studies.
•The experience highlights the importance of implicating the whole organization into a computing program when the purpose is to obtain long range effects.
•Introduction of computers to the Venezuelan basic school should be a slow and progressive process, periodically evaluated and initially located at certain restricted points of the country, taken as pilot centers.
•A center of research on informatics and education, serving as a reference point in policy design and implementation of new plans will be very useful.
•Concerning teaching contents we conclude that learning how to program computers may be useful and beneficial for the classroom.
•Computer literacy for the students and the other members of the educational community may be possible using the same infrastructure, with a convenient schedule. The use of CAI packages may permit the participation of other teachers.
•Administrative applications will also permit staff and teachers of the institution begin to get acquainted with computer use and its possible applications.
•Computer use in basic education seems to give many benefits to the classroom, but its implementation is not easy. Difficulties should be never underestimated.
•Finally as it was concluded in Varna Congress: "No educational system can disregard the problem of computerization"...but,..."no computer can replace the teacher; it is only a tool"..."the final purpose of computerization should be to make people more human". [13]

REFERENCES

[1] Benko, A., Martínez, J.M.,Arteaga, M., Mejías, B.,Gutiérrez, M.F.,Hidalgo, N.,Colina, C.E., Informe Final. La Enseñanza y el Uso de la Informática en la Escuela Media Venezolana, CONICIT, Proyecto S1- 1770, Caracas, 1989.
[2] Martínez, J.M., "La Informática en la Escuela Venezolana Venezuela". Estadística e Informática, Año 2, No.3, Junio 1988, pp. 109-127.
[3] Fishbein, M., "Comunicación Persuasiva: Una perspectiva Psicosocial acerca de los factores que influyen en la efectividad de la comunicación", Psicología, Vol. IV, Nº.3 y 4, Universidad de Illinois, Diciembre, 1977.
[4] Feuerstein, H., Instrumentos de Enriquecimiento Intelectual, University Park Press, USA, 1978.
[5] Linn, M., "Fostering Equitable Consequences from Computer Learning Environments", Sex Roles, Vol. 13, Nº. 3, August, 1985, pp.229-240.
[6] Mayer, R., "Learning to Program and Learning to Think: What's the Connection", Communications of the ACM, Vol. 29, Nº. 7, July, 1986, pp.605-610.
[7] Pea, R.D., Kurland, D.M., "On the Cognitive Effects of Learning Computer Programming", New Ideas Psychol., Vol. 2, Nº. 2, 1984, pp. 137-168.

[8] Mayer, R., "The Psychology of how Novices Learn Computer Programming", Computing Surveys, Vol. 13, Nº.1, March, 1981, pp.121-141.

[9] Clement, C.A. and others, "Analogical Reasoning and Computer Programming", Journal of Educational Computing Research, Vol. 2, Nº. 4, 1986, pp.473-486.

[10]Clements, D., Gullo, D., "Effects of Computer Programming on Youngs Children's Cognition", Journal of Educational Psychology, Vol. 76, Nº. 6, 1984, pp.1051-1058.

[11]Linn, M., "The Cognitive Consequences of Programming Instruction in Classrooms", Educational Researcher, May, 1985, pp. 14-29.

[12]Delclos, V.R., Littefield, J., Bransford, J.D., "Update of Microcomputer Use in Instruction - Teaching Thinking through LOGO: The importance of Method", Roeper Review, Vol. 7, Nº 3, pp. 153-156.

[13]Sendov, B.," Children in an Information Age", in Sendov, B., Stanchez, I., Children in an Information Age, Pergamon Press, New York, 1986, pp.195-200.

Computers in Education
A. McDougall and C. Dowling (Editors)
Elsevier Science Publishers B.V. (North-Holland)

DESKTOP PUBLISHING IN A SECONDARY SCHOOL

Paul Matray

Robert Louis Stevenson School
Box 657
Pebble Beach, CA 93953 USA

Desktop Publishing (DTP) has changed the way in which secondary schools are now able to produce their written communications. The student newspaper is the most obvious publication to be produced using this new technology, but other school publications can also be produced: yearbook, literary magazine, student handbook, faculty guide, college counseling guide, and programs for football games, music programs, and drama productions. A review of the available solutions is presented with a specific description of the way in which a Macintosh computer, laser printer, word processing program, Pagemaker program, Adobe Illustrator program, and various clip art programs were used to produce these documents at a secondary school in the United States.

1. INTRODUCTION

Desktop publishing (DTP) utilizing a personal computer will allow you to prepare documents which look like they have been typeset. It has revolutionized the way in which business now does business and its power is beginning to be felt in education. With the introduction of the Macintosh computer in 1985, and its superior graphics capabilites, DTP took off. The key question is why should an educational institution utilize the technology and are the costs worth it? Arcellana (1988) and Shapiro (1988) evaluate if DTP is worth it - financially and otherwise.

During the past two years I have utilized this technology at the Robert Louis Stevenson School in Pebble Beach California and have been able to not only produce a number of documents for the school, but have also taught the technology to a small group of students and teachers. Stevenson School is an independent K-12 school with a student population in the secondary school of 500. I am a biology teacher who purchased a Macintosh in the summer of 1988 and learned how to use the machine as a hobby, but realized very quickly the power of this machine in producing hardcopy which approaches that of typeset publications.

2. GETTING STARTED

Why bother learning this technology? In my opinion there are five compelling reasons to justify the monetary outlay:

- educationally, it is an integral part of the journalism enterprise.
- it will ultimately be cost effective.
- it is the most efficient way to produce typeset materials.
- it eliminates a number of middle men.
- it can lead to career oriented skills for college bound and non college bound students.

Purchasing a DTP system from scratch can appear to be a costly acquisition. However it may not be as expensive as one might think when the cost of typesetting charges are factored in. At Stevenson I sold the idea to the business manager in terms which are readily understood by people who are responsible for the financial well-being of a school -*money*. We had spent over $3000 dollars in type setting charges for the school newspaper during the 1987-88 school year. A DTP system totally eliminates this expense. In that the system we ultimately ordered cost us a total of about $6000, the payback period was only two years. It doesn't take a financial genius to figure out the benefits of such a purchase.

The Robert Louis Stevenson School purchased a Macintosh SE/20 computer, Apple Writer NT Laserwriter, Pagemaker, and Microsoft Works during the summer of 1988. I spent a few weeks familiarizing myself with the Macintosh and the software programs during August. In September when the students returned I sat down with the two layout editors of our student newspaper for about three hours and taught them what I had learned during the previous two weeks. In that these students were familiar with computers, they understood the basic operations and could quickly acquire the skills necessary to layout the first issue of the paper four weeks later. During the remainder of the year I spent very little time guiding them but continued to consult with them on more efficient and interesting ways to produce page layouts. One of the layout editors actually began his own DTP business and charged $10 per hour to do layouts for local businesses and other schools. He also convinced his parents to purchase a system which he eventually took to college.

One of the major changes in our journalism class became the necessity of having all of the reporters prepare their articles in a format which could be directly imported into Pagemaker. Students had previously handed in hardcopy and the editors would proof it and then the student would rewrite it and it would then be sent to the typesetter. When the typeset material returned there would inevitably be errors which had to be sent back. In addition the layouts were rather sterile and uninteresting and our newspaper became less than late breaking news. DTP allows for immediate revisions and makes it rather easy for the original author to go back and revise his/her work.

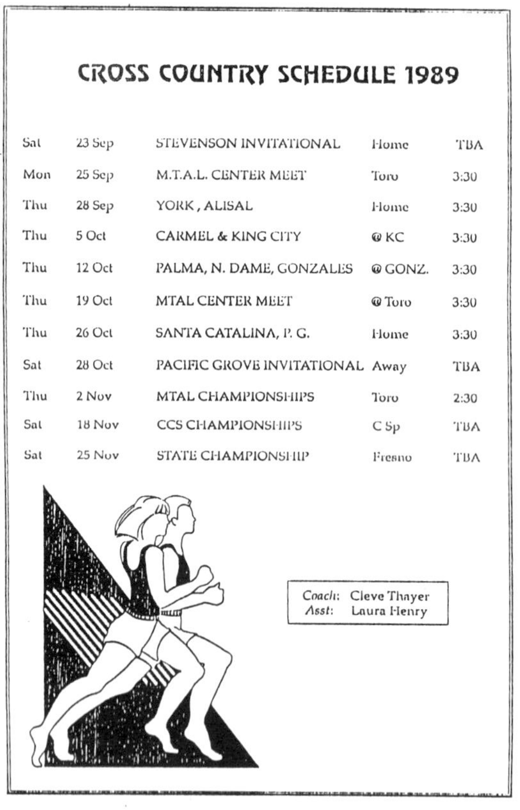

We now had the ability to produce camera-ready proofs which lacked only the halftone photographs. We still go to a print shop to have them done for about $6 each. In my opinion the scanner technology which has been around for a number of years is still inadequate and until it is we will continue to use halftones rather than scanned images.

If you have a copier which can produce 11 by 17 copies you can produce an entire newspaper in-house without going to a commercial printer. Our students prefer the tabloid format on newsprint so we continue to use a local printer. I would personally prefer them using the newsletter size format which would allow the school to produce a paper which would carry stories from the previous day. In addition, by doing it on your own copier, you eliminate the cost of having someone else print your paper and reduce the cost outlay to the expense for halftones and eliminate the headaches associated with working with middlemen.

3. OTHER IN-HOUSE PUBLICATIONS

After the faculty at Stevenson saw the student newspaper, they realized that there were other applications which could make their life less complicated. The athletic director asked me to prepare the program for the home football games and various sports posters (to the left). This poster is 11 by 17 and is done in two colors. The graphic is green and the text black. I produced it on our copy machine, which kept the cost to a minimum. The music director asked me to prepare the program for the winter and spring music concerts. The drama department asked the layout editor of the newspaper to prepare the program for the school plays. The layout editor also was responsible for the layout of the school's literary magazine. These projects were obviously an educational experience for the student involved and in addition it saved the school additional dollars in charges that would have been encumbered due to typesetting and printing charges. In addition, the publications produced appeared every bit as professional as the ones used in previous years, and in some cases is a marked improvement.

During the summer of 1989 I contracted with the school to produce a number of publications and to instruct a number of staff members in the use of Pagemaker. I produced the College Counseling Guide, Student Handbook, Parent Guide, Prefect Guide, Resident Masters Handbook, and Faculty Guide. Some of these documents had been prepared by outside sources and had cost the school in some cases a considerable amount of money. The most striking comparison is our 1988 Faculty Guide which cost the school $1250 for 100 copies. Those same 100 copies cost the school about $150 in 1989 with the costs being related to copy charges, binding (which we do in-house using Velo-bind), and material costs.

Other in-house publications had been prepared by simply copying typed pages and stapling together the desired document. They took on a somewhat informal appearance and were probably not viewed as important communications. By producing professional looking documents, I suspect that they were received as important reading rather than another memo from the administration.

I also produced two documents (the cover the AP Biology Manual is shown to the right) for my biology classes (sophomore biology and AP biology) . Each year I prepare a number of handouts which include lab exercises, review sheets, problem sets, syllabusses, etc.. This past year I included these handouts in a single document for each class, which eliminated the need for me to be copying materials throughout the year and reduced the likelihood of the loss of one page handouts. If the student loses his biology manual, he has to purchase a new copy.

In additon, I also produce a test vehicle called *Biotimes.* My tests are presented in a newsletter format with a leadoff article which pokes fun at one of my colleagues (we team teach in biology). We have gotten some positive feedback on this testing format and feel that it reduces the tension often associated with test taking.

4. HARDWARE DECISIONS

4.1. Computers

Our DTP can be conducted on various computer systems. There are software programs available for the Macintosh, IBM, Tandy, and Apple II series. I chose Macintosh because of its ease of use and graphics capability and am pleased with that decision. (It is also the computer used by **USA Today** – a national newspaper in the United States.) There are several different computer configurations which can be chosen and this decison is based upon cost and needs. The Macintosh presently is available in six basic machines: Macintosh Plus, Macintosh SE/20, Macintosh SE/30, Macintosh IIcx, Macintosh II, and Macintosh IIx. For DTP you need consider only the first four machines even though you can utilize the latter two if you already own one.

Stevenson now owns two Macintosh Plus computers with external hard drives (20 MB), three Macintosh SE computers with 20 MB internal hard drives, and a Macintosh IIcx with a 40 MB internal hard drive and a portrait display monitor. All three systems can produce comparable documents but they differ in their speed and convenience of use. As would be expected, the more costly the system the faster and more efficently it operates. The Macintosh Plus with the external hard drive costs approximately $1600, while the Macintosh SE/20 costs ~ $2100 and the Macintosh IIcx system costs ~ $4600 (prices are educator buy prices) . The Macintosh SE/30 costs about $3100 and is comparable to the SE/20 but has a different micro processor which allows it to run about 4 times faster than the SE/

20 or the Macintosh Plus. It operates like a Macintosh IIcx but lacks the expansion capability and large screen monitor.

Any of the Macintosh series machines will do the job. At Stevenson I have used three of the six systems and have been pleased with all three. Given a choice where money was not a primary consideration (An unlikely possibility?), the IIcx is clearly the machine of choice.

4.2. Printers

In order to convert the information stored in the computer to hard copy it is necessary to have access to a laser printer. A dot matrix printer can produce readable hard copy, but it will not appear to be of typeset quality. This can only be acheived with a laser printer or via a linotronic machine (very expensive). We use an Apple Writer IINT ($3500) and have found it to do an excellent job. There are a number of other laser writers available which are comparable. Two excellent reviews of the available systems can be found in *MACWORLD* (Heid, 1989) and *Publish!* (Cummings, 1988).

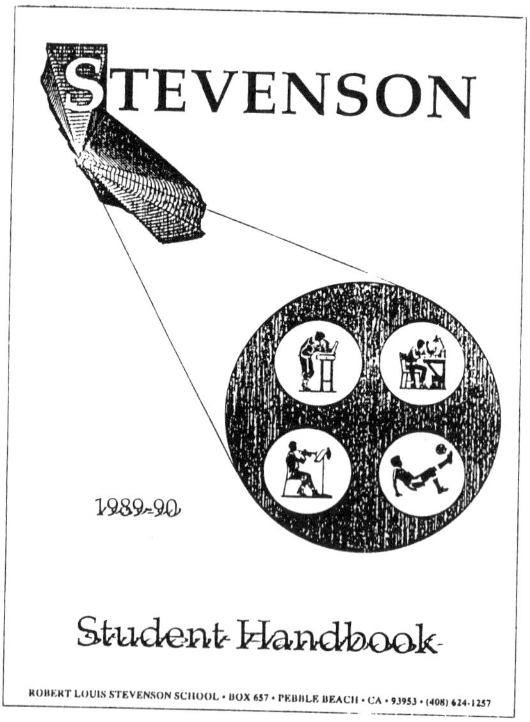

If the cost of a printer seems beyond your budget there is a way around the purchase. There are service bureaus available in most towns which rent time on their laser printers. You simply bring in your disk and load your file into their computer and print it out on their laser writer for a fraction of the cost. If you require a higher resolution printout (most laser writers print at 300 dots per inch(dpi)), there are bureaus which specialize in high resolution output (Linotronic is probably the leader although there are a number of competitors.). Documents can be printed at up to 2400 dpi and the improvement in sharpness is noticeable and makes the computer generated material look typeset (see *Student Handbook* above). Fenton (1989a) provides some recommendations in finding an appropriate service bureau.

If a service bureau does not exist in your vicinity, you can send your file via mail or a modem over normal phone lines to a service bureau half way around the world and they can mail back the hard copy. Although this is not the most convenient manner in which to produce your camera ready documents, it does avoid the large initial monetary outlay.

5. SOFTWARE DECISIONS

5.1. Word Processing Programs

Before you begin to create interesting layouts, it is necessary to type your text in a word processing program. DTP programs are not designed to be effectively utilized to input text. It is also possible that if your desktop publishing needs are relatively simple you can get by with simply using a sophisticated word processing program which includes page layout features.

Seiter (1989) reviews eight of the leading Macintosh word processing programs. He reviews Wordperfect 1.0.2, Mindwrite 2.1, Microsoft Write 1.0, Microsoft Word 4.0, FullWrite 1.0, MacWrite II 1.0, Nisus 1.0, and WriteNow 2.0. Eckhardt (1989) reviews the following midrange word processors: Macwrite II, Microsoft Write 1.0, and WriteNow 2.0. I would recommend Word, Macwrite II, or WriteNow because they can all be easily imported into most DTP programs. At Stevenson we use all three because our students and faculty individually own these programs and we can take their files and import any of the three into our DTP documents.

We have chosen Microsoft Works 2.0, rather than any of the aforementioned word processing programs, for two significant reasons: it is an integrated program (word processor, data base, and spreadsheet) and Appleworks files created on an Apple II computer can be easily converted over to Microsoft Works and then then imported into a DTP program. There is a file exchange program which comes with the Macintosh which allows for the conversion in a few simple keystrokes. Our teachers use the data base of Microsoft Works to compute grades and merge data with the word processing part of the program.

Choice of word processing program is largely up to your own personal needs and preferences. The cost of these software programs range from about $195 to $395. They are necessary.

5.2. Desktop Publishing Programs

The big three of DTP on the Macintosh are XPress, Ready, Set, Go!, and Pagemaker. Ventura and Pagemaker are probably the big two on the IBM. Kelley and Cummings (1989) discuss why they prefer XPress and Ventura to Pagemaker. Taub (1989) compares XPress, Ready, Set, Go!, and Pagemaker and points out how Ready, Set, Go! is attempting to 'stake out the middle ground'. This article does a good job of comparing the big three.

We use Pagemaker and I have been very pleased with its power and ease of use. In the September 1989 issue of Macworld the readers preferences for their favorite Macintosh products was tabulated. Pagemaker received 66% of the votes, Ready, Set Go! 18% ,XPress 12% and others 4%. Pagemaker retails for $595 but there are mail order houses which offer it for well below the advertised retail price. It is my opinion that you will be very satisfied with this program which will be the heart of your DTP needs.

5.3. Clip Art

The purchase of clip art collections is a valuable addition to your software library. It will enable the DTP publisher to enliven his presentations and make his work more interesting and eye catching. The availability of clip art has mushroomed in the past two years and there is a considerable amount to choose from on the market. The most difficult aspect is choosing packages which are well done and meet your needs. Aker (1988), Fenton (1989b) and McCloy (1989) each present a comprehensive guide to what is available. Their presentations are in tabular form with the companies and their respective collections listed in relation to the type of images found in each package.

Clip art is created and saved in two basic formats: draw or bit-map format. Each has its own advantages. Draw formats include those images stored as Encapulated PostScript (EPS). They tend to be sharper and can be imported and edited in sophisticated drawing programs like Aldus Freehand and Adobe Illustrator (discussed further in the next section). Bit-mapped clip art give richer textures and realistic shadings and can be screened behind text unlike EPS clip art. The young man working at a computer is an example of an EPS graph while the soccer player is bit-mapped and saved in a 300 dpi format.

We have purchased six clip art packages from the following five companies: Adobe Systems, Dubl-Clik Software, Dynamic Graphics, Metro ImageBase, 3G Graphics and T/Maker. The software packages range in price from $50 to $150 and include anywhere from 40 to 200 images per package. EPS clip art costs more than bit-mapped clip art and tends to be sized more easily and has a crisp, professional look.

5.4. Graphics Program

Eventually it will be necessary to purchase a PostScript graphics program when you are ready to produce sophisticated art work or modify EPS clip art. It is my opinion that bit-mapped drawing programs (such as MacPaint, MacDraw, and SuperPaint) lack the professional appearance required for typeset quality presentations. The two leaders in the draw format (EPS) field are Adobe Illustrator and Aldus Freehand and each has its own advantages. Fenton(1989c) and Burns and Venit (1988) have done a good job listing the pros and cons of each. We have purchased Adobe Illustrator and I have used it to produce some interesting affects such as shadowing, blending, shading, etc. (see the Student Handbook on the previous page).

Each program retails for about $400 and requires at least 2 MB of RAM memory to be fully utilized. Most Macintosh computers are equipped with 1 MB of RAM. You will need to add an additional MB of RAM if you wish to utilize the full capability of the program. This will cost about $400 to $600 based upon supplier and the type of computer.

SUMMARY OF THE START-UP COSTS

(Minimum)	
Macintosh Plus	$1000
20 MB Hard Drive	500
Pagemaker	400
WriteNow	125
Total	***$2025***

(Ideal)	
Macintosh IIcx with full Page Monitor	$4600
Laser Writer IINT	3400
Microsoft Works	190
Pagemaker	400
Adobe Illustrator	350
Clip Art	300
Total	***$9240***

6. CONCLUSION

DTP can be carried out by anyone, anywhere in the world. It is a technology which has immediate and obvious applications and will eventually be taught as a distinctive offering in many high school curricula. I taught a course to 6 students this past year and they received credit. They were mainly the layout editors of the school newspaper, yearbook, and literary magazine, but two of the students were simply interested in learning the application. These students had the responsibility of preparing documents which I had prepared the previous year. Several universities in the United States already offer DTP courses as part of their curriculum (Crismond, 1988; Webb,1988).

For educational institutions the application of this technology has far reaching implications. It is a recent development and will become an integral part of most institutions in the next decade. It is an obvious choice because it saves money, teaches a skill which is readily marketable, and it can be used for our profession to take on a more professional air.

LITERATURE CITED

Aker, Sharon
1988. You Gotta Have Art. *MacUser* 4(8): 180-190.

Arcellana, J. E.
1988. Is Desktop Publishing Worth It? *MACWORLD* 5(10): 106-115.

Burns, Diane and S. Venit
1988. Call It A Draw. *MacUser* 4(10): 200-212.

Crismond, David
1988. Desktop Publish or Perish *Publish!* 3(10):52-57.

Cummings, Steve
1988. Attention, PostScript Printer Shoppers.... *Publish!* 3(11):60-72.

Eckhardt, Robert C.
1989. Write, Write, Write. *MACWORLD* 6 (10):130-137.

Fenton, Erfert
1989a. At Your Service (Bureau) *MACWORLD* 6(10): 154-159.
1989b. The Clip Art Buyer's Guide. *MACWORLD* 6(10): 138-145.
1989c. The Big Match: Illustrator 88 vs. Free Hand. *MACWORLD* 6 (2): 180-187.

Heid, Jim
1989. Paging All Printers. *MACWORLD* 6(10): 120-129.

Kelley, Donna and Robert Cummings
1989. True Confessions of Former Page maker Users. *Publish!* 4(9): 50-54.

McCloy, Marjorie
1989. Is It Art Yet? *Publish!* 4(7): 46-52.

Seitzer, Charles
1989. Words, Words, Everywhere. *MACWORLD* 6(9): 180-187.

Shapiro, Ezra
1988. Publish or Perish. *MacUser* 4(8): 149-156.

Taub, Eric
1989. Room To Grow. *Personal Publishing* 5(7): 51-59.

Webb, Craig
1988. Making the Grade. *Publish!* 3(10):58-60.

Computers in Education
A. McDougall and C. Dowling (Editors)
Elsevier Science Publishers B.V. (North-Holland)

CURRICULUM INNOVATION WITH COMPUTERS: REDRESSING INEQUITIES OF ACCESS AND USE IN THE FREYBERG INTEGRATED STUDIES PROJECT

David H. MCKINNON and Patrick C.J. NOLAN

Massey University, Palmerston North, New Zealand

This study examines gender and ability differences in computer attitudes and experiences of a group of high school students exposed to a curriculum innovation involving three components: integration of core subjects; out-of-class activities which are the basis of in class studies; and extensive use of computers using applications software. Comparison data were obtained from a class not involved in the programme but who had access to computers at school. The sample comprised 176 students who provided data on: attitudes towards and uses of computers, preferences for and uses of various software packages; keyboarding skills; frequency of computer use, and subject preferences. Males, overall, had significantly more exposure to computers based primarily on access to computers in the home. There was no significant difference in exposure to computers when home computers were excluded. With the exception of one class, there was no significant gender difference in attitudes towards computers. There were significant differences in preference patterns for school subjects and software packages. Interaction between student ability, gender, and teacher variables appears to result in differing attitudes towards computers, and preferences for school subjects and ways of using the computer. Within the Project the meaningful use of computers creates an environment within which students appear to be positively orientated toward learning, and commonly reported ability and gender related inequities are reduced to the point where any differences are not significant.

The Freyberg Integrated Studies Project is a three year educational research programme which is developing alternative curriculum models and pedagogical approaches for implementation in New Zealand secondary schools. The project is based upon educational principles known to enhance the educational effectiveness of schools. These include mastery learning, small group and individualised instruction, peer tutoring, thematic studies and a broad range of motivational strategies. The principles are being implemented in courses of study through the introduction of three main elements. One of these is the widespread student use of computers as information processing tools. The other two components involve the integration of core subjects and the use of out of class activities to generate data for later analysis, within the integrated subject context, using computers (See Nolan & McKinnon, 1990). The use of computers in this way stands in contrast with the traditional approaches involving programming and computer awareness courses. Within the traditional context, both New Zealand and overseas educational research report widespread inequities in computer access and use across ability, gender and socioeconomic divisions (see e.g., Latika, Hesketh & Podd 1987, Chen 1986, Becker and Sterling 1987).

Use entails access and traditionally access is influenced by ability (in reality, by academic achievement), gender and socioeconomic status. In general, the research studies have shown that: more able students have significantly more access than less able students (Becker and Stirling, 1987; Niebauer, 1985); male students have significantly more access than female students both at home ad at school (Lockheed & Frakt, 1984; Chen, 1986; Becker & Sterling 1987; Latvika, Hesketh & Podd, 1987; Ramsay, Katterns and Lillas, 1987; Collis 1988), and; students from affluent backgrounds have significantly more access than students from less affluent backgrounds (Becker, 1982; Dubois & Schubert, 1986). Interaction effects compound each situation. For example, more able students tend to come from affluent homes and therefore have greater opportunity to own a computer. Less able students tend to come from less affluent homes and are less likely to get access at school and they are also much less likely to have a computer at home. Being a female is a barrier to access across all social levels both at home and at school. Generally speaking, less computer time is given to lower achieving students and females in schools which emphasise programming and, high achieving male students dominate computer use in all types of schools (Becker and Stirling, 1987).

Once access is achieved then computer use is further influenced the latter case a number of interaction effects complicate the situation. In general, high ability students engage in computer programming, problem solving activities and use applications software. By contrast, lower ability students spend the bulk of their time using drill and practice programs (Becker and Stirling, 1987). While males predominate over females in any use of computers they typically employ them in different ways, e.g., programming and game playing, whereas female use is highest for "work processing" (Becker & Sterling 1987) and applications software (Lockheed & Frackt 1984). Becker and Stirling (1987, p. 303) conclude their study with the comment that "...except for high school word processing, schools where girls dominated any aspect of computer usage were rare".

Socioeconomic status interacts with both ability and gender in determining patterns of computer use. For example, affluent students will tend to have greater access to computers, have higher personal levels of academic achievement and have more opportunity to use computers both at home and school. Whether this leads to differences in use patterns over less affluent, lower ability students with less access to computers is still problematic. That this difference in opportunity will lead to different patterns of use, however, is a tenable hypothesis.

Research literature world-wide focuses on gender as a key factor in addressing inequities of computer access and use. Gender inequities are also evident in New Zealand primary and secondary schools (Latvika, Hesketh & Podd, 1987; Ramsay, Katterns & Lillas, 1987). Typically, males have significantly greater past experience with computers and they have access to, and make more frequent use of, computers than females. The difference in access and use between males and females exists in both coeducational and single sex schools (Latvika, Hesketh & Podd, 1987). When affirmative action is taken, however, girls still do not gain equitable access. When positive discrimination occurs the evidence suggests that it takes females some time to adopt the view that they have a right to equitable access and to use computers in accord with that right. Learning to exercise this right best occurs in an environment which is supportive of females (Chen, 1986; Lloyd, Loyd & Gressard, 1984; Macrae, 1985).

This paper presents the findings of Freyberg Integrated Studies Project survey research regarding student attitudes towards computers and the extent of computer access and use in terms of ability, gender and socioeconomic status.

METHOD

Subjects and Setting

The school in which this study was conducted is a typical New Zealand coeducational secondary school drawing pupils from both country and urban areas. The student population is broadly representative of the population as a whole in terms of academic achievement, ethnicity and socioeconomic status.

Students elect to participate in the Integrated Studies Programme on entry to high school (Form 3). Integrated Studies involves the students using the computer for a minimum of three hours per week. Word processing is the most commonly used software package and is used by all classes for approximately 75% of the time they are using computers. Top classes in both the normal and Integrated Studies programmes are streamed on ability in Mathematics and English. The remainder of the classes are parallel.

Two questionnaires were administered to 176 students in six third and fourth form classes. All students involved in the Project who regularly use the computers were surveyed. An additional class, not involved with the Project, but who used computers for word processing in English, acted as a comparison group. The Integrated Studies classes surveyed included the top third and fourth form classes, two parallel third form classes and a second level fourth form class. The comparison class in Form Three was the top class in the normal school programme.

One questionnaire comprised 49 questions seeking information on eight pertinent factors: socioeconomic background of parents; gender; time spent using computers; applications used; application preferences; educational and vocational goals; perceived keyboard competency, and; the value of typing courses. A second questionnaire comprised the 26 items taken from the Bath County Computer Attitude Scale questionnaire BACCAS (Bear et al, 1987). The questionnaire has not as yet been validated for New Zealand schools. Preliminary analysis of the questionnaire indicates that the instrument is a useful measure of attitudes towards computers. The results of the validation for New Zealand Schools are to be published at a later date. The questionnaires were administered by Project researchers during normal class time.

RESULTS

Within the sample, there were slightly more girls (55%) than boys (45%). This reflects the gender composition of the school as a whole which is due to the presence of a nearby high status boys' secondary school.

Class	(*)1	2	3	4	5	6	Row Total
female	17	10	18	17	22	12	96
male	10	17	14	11	10	17	79
Column Total	27 15.4	27 15.4	32 18.3	28 16.0	32 18.3	29 16.6	175 100.0

(Chi-square = 9.21292, D.F. = 5, p = 0.1009)

Table 1: Gender Composition of the Classes, (*) - normal programme

Table 1 shows that there was no significant difference in the gender composition of the classes surveyed.

The Elly-Irving Socioeconomic Status Scale was used to determine the SES of both parents. A cross tabulation of both parents' SES against the presence of a computer at home revealed no significant differences between groups, i.e., SES of mother and father makes no difference as to whether students have a computer at home (Chi-Square = 7.732, D.F.= 5, p = 0.17). This finding is somewhat surprising and stands in contrast with earlier research studies both in New Zealand and overseas concerning access to computers in the home. Closer inspection of these data, however, indicate that students from higher SES levels (1 and 2) do in fact have greater access to computers at home compared with students in the lower SES levels (Chi-Square = 7.23, D.F.= 2, p < 0.05). The numbers of computers in the home reported in this study, in both absolute and relative terms, has increased compared with an earlier New Zealand Study. In particular, ownership of a home computer in the lower SES levels has increased dramatically (Ramsay et al, 1987). The relevant data are summarised in Table 2.

SES--->	1 & 2	3 & 4	5 & 6	Row Total
yes	23 (58%)	33 (38%)	9 (27%)	65 (41%)
no	17 (42%)	52 (62%)	24 (73%)	93 (59%)
Column	40	85	33	158

(Chi-Square = 7.23, D.F.= 2, p < 0.05)
(17 missing cases)

TABLE 2: Fathers' Socioeconomic Status against Presence of a Computer at Home

Table 3 shows the mean socioeconomic status of each class. A one-way analysis of variance of SES against class membership revealed significant differences in the socio economic composition of the classes (F = 4.834, p < 0.0005). The Scheffe multiple comparisons test further revealed that the high ability fourth form Integrated Studies class (5) had a significantly higher average SES than the other lower ability classes (2 and 4) (P < 0.05). In addition, within the Integrated Studies cohort, the higher the ability of the class then the higher the average socioeconomic status. The comparison class, which is the highest ability class in the normal programme, had the lowest average SES (mean = 4.000).

CLASS	MEAN SES	σ	N
1*	4.00	0.82	19
2	3.89	1.63	27
3	3.27	1.51	30
4	3.93	1.15	28
5	2.33	1.21	27
6	3.27	2.09	26
GRAND MEAN	3.42	1.57	157

(19 missing cases)

TABLE 3: Mean socioeconomic status of the classes (* - indicates normal programme)

Crosstabulations of time spent using a computer at home and school combined and at school under teacher direction with SES, revealed that there were no significant differences across tie socioeconomic groups (Chi squares = 6.56 and 10.53, df=5, not significant). A further crosstabulation of class membership by presence of a home computer revealed that there were no significant differences across the classes (Chi square = 8.54, df = 5, not significant). On average, 39% of all students had access to a computer at home.

Table 4 shows the crosstabulation of presence of a home computer by gender. This revealed that boys have significantly greater access to computers in the home than girls (Chi square = 9.58, df=1, p < 0.005). A further series of crosstabulations of SES by gender revealed that this pattern of differential access to computers in the home is maintained across all SES levels.

Count	Home computer? yes	no	Row Total
female	27	70	97
male	41	37	78
Column	68	107	175

(Chi-Square = 11.13, D.F. = 1, p <0.001)

TABLE 4: Crosstabulation of Ownership of Home Computer by Gender

Examination of data for the entire group revealed that girls spend significantly less time in using computers at home and school combined (F = 13.58, p < 0.0005), with males using the computer almost twice as often. When access to computers at school is examined, and the use of home computers excluded, the difference is all but eliminated. Further analysis of these data revealed that in the comparison class there is no gender difference either in the use of computers at home and school or solely at school. This result was somewhat surprising given that this class has the lowest mean SES and that boys tend to be favoured with greater access to home computers. When the comparison class is excluded, it was found that there was a significant gender difference in the amount of time spent using computers at home and school combined (F = 15.44, p = 0.0001) and also at school under teacher direction (F = 4.80, p < 0.05).

This result was also surprising given the amount of time that the lntegrated Studies classes had scheduled in the computer laboratories for regular class work. An ANOVA, of these two access variables by gender and class, was carried out in an attempt to explain the apparent gender inequity of computer access in the Integrated Studies classes. This revealed that there was a significant interaction effect between class and gender for both access at home, and at school. A oneway ANOVA with multiple comparisons revealed that the highest ability fourth form class had significantly less access, both at home and at school, than all of the other Integrated Studies classes (Scheffé, p < 0.05).

A series of oneway ANOVAS was carried out to examine gender differences both within this fourth form class and between classes. This revealed that there were significant differences within the fourth form high ability Integrated Studies class. The females (n=20) used computers significantly less often than the males (n=8) both at home and school combined (F = 5.34, p < 0.05), and at school under teacher supervision (F = 8.71, p < 0.01). Moreover, they used them significantly less than females in all of the other classes, comparison group included, (Scheffé, p < 0.01) and appeared to skew the results for the whole group. Exclusion of the high ability class from further analyses revealed parity of access for males and females across all remaining classes. One class (class 6), however, had significantly more access for both males and females ($F = 4.226$, $p < 0.005$). The class variable (and hence the teacher?) appears to be an important factor influencing access especially when interactions with gender are considered. The ability of the class may be equally important in determining the amount of access. Interactions between class ability, the teacher, gender and access were not able to be fully investigated. In a subsequent study these interactions were able to be more thoroughly explored.

The importance of the class (teacher) variable was highlighted by an analysis of the students' attitudes towards computers. Table 5 shows the mean scores and standard deviations, by class and gender, for the computer attitudes questionnaire scores (BACCAS). Overall, the results from BACCAS show that girls were significantly less positive than boys in their attitudes towards computers ($F = 9.88$, $p < 0.002$).

CLASS	Class mean	σ	FEMALE mean	σ	MALE mean	σ
1	36.48	6.71	36.87	7.35	35.75	5.70
2	45.12	5.62	43.10	5.00	46.38	5.76
3	40.28	5.33	39.69	6.37	41.00	3.81
4	37.36	7.81	36.07	6.52	39.00	9.26
5*	32.14	10.85	29.45	10.70	38.11	9.05
6	44.11	6.20	44.75	5.79	43.63	6.64
Overall	39.26	8.57	37.36	9.05	41.50	7.42

Table 5: Mean computer attitude score by gender and class (*) - high ability Integrated Studies class

Multiple comparisons (Scheffé), however, revealed that one class had significantly less positive attitudes towards computers than all of the other classes, including the comparison group. This was the same high ability Integrated Studies class comprised of 20 girls and 8 boys. Within it, the girls had a significantly less positive attitude than the boys ($F = 4.44$, $p < 0.05$). Moreover, the girls in this class had significantly less positive attitudes towards computers than the girls in any of the other classes ($F = 8.123$, $p = 0$, Scheffé, $p < 0.05$). By contrast the boys in this class differed significantly from only one other class, a third form lower ability group which happened to be taught by the same teacher. Reasons for this difference are considered in the discussion. When the high ability Integrated Studies class was excluded from the analysis, boys still had a more positive attitude than girls but the difference was no longer significant.

Three interesting observations can be made from an examination of the BACCAS scores in Table 5 above. These are: i) third form Integrated Studies classes (classes 2, 6 and 3) have more positive attitudes than fourth form classes (classes 4 and 5); ii) lower ability classes in each form have more positive attitudes than higher ability classes, and; iii) the third form high ability Integrated Studies class (class 3) has a more positive attitude than the high ability third form comparison class (class 1). The Scheffe multiple comparisons test revealed that the two lower ability third form Integrated Studies classes had significantly more positive attitudes towards computers than the fourth form classes and the third form comparison class ($p < 0.05$). In addition, the third form high ability class had a significantly more positive attitude than the fourth form high ability class.

Gender and ability differences are also apparent in the patterns of software program likes and dislikes and patterns of software use.

Students were asked to list the three computer applications that they most and least liked using at school. Table 6 shows the pattern of likes and dislikes by gender. From the table it is evident that more girls than expected like word processing. This is not to say that boys dislike it. Similarly, more boys report that they liked using utilities and Dr Halo (a graphics drawing program), and more girls report that they disliked using utilities, spreadsheet and database programs than expected.

SOFTWARE	LIKES female	LIKES male	ROW TOTAL	DISLIKES female	DISLIKES male	ROW TOTAL
Word processing	79	53	132	5	12	17
Utilities	10	33	43	20	9	29
Arcade Games	4	7	11	0	1	1
Dr Halo	36	52	88	0	2	2
Typing Tutor	23	2	25	4	9	13
Strat/Adv games	1	1	2	1	4	5
Spreadsheet	12	14	26	24	9	33
Database	19	7	26	34	21	55
Math games	5	4	9	1	10	11
Graphing	10	4	14	14	3	17

(LIKES - Chi-Square = 46.03, D.F. = 9, P = 0)
(DISLIKES-Chi-Square = 38.02, D.F. = 9, P = 0)

TABLE 6: Pattern of Software Likes and Dislikes by Gender

In an attempt to map the pattern of software use, students were asked to list five computer applications that they commonly-used. For each package nominated they were asked to estimate the percentage of time spent using it. A crosstabulation of package used with SES revealed no significant differences across groups (Chi-square = 30.46, df = 45, not significant). A series of crosstabulations of the percentage of time for which packages were used with SES also revealed no significant differences across groups.

Table 7 shows the pattern of software use for males and females, and the mean percentage and standard deviation of time that students reported using the different packages. There is a significant gender reported in Table 7 does not appear to be congruent with the pattern of likes and dislikes shown in Table 6. For example, Arcade Games are reported as being used by 60 males for a mean of 36% of the time while only 7 males actually report "enjoying' these games. It seems rather incongruous that males should engage in computer activities that they do not report as enjoyable.

SOFTWARE	FEMALE n	FEMALE % use	FEMALE σ	MALE n	MALE % use	MALE σ	N
Word Processing	90	57	24	68	40	28	158
Utilities	34	18	15	71	15	10	105
Arcade Games	24	25	17	60	36	22	84
Dr Halo	37	15	10	45	13	9	82
Typing Tutor	54	16	13	10	12	5	64
Strat/Adv games	16	15	10	41	14	8	57
Spreadsheet	28	18	12	10	10	8	38
Database	26	17	9	7	12	7	33
Math Games	19	13	9	6	19	17	25
Graphing	13	10	6	2	10	7	15

(Chi-Square = 106.39, D.F. = 9, P = 0)

TABLE 7: Pattern of Software Use by Gender

Table 8 shows that there are significant differences between the classes in their pattern of computer use and, moreover, that these differences seem to be due to differences in the pattern of female use. Taking Table 8 in concert with Table 7, males seem to be more stereotyped in their use of computers whatever their ability.

SOFTWARE	CLASS 1 f	1 m	2 f	2 m	3 f	3 m	4 f	4 m	5 f	5 m	6 f	6 m	Row Total
Word processing	17	10	8	11	16	10	15	11	22	9	12	17	158
Utilities	9	5	8	17	5	8	1	9	3	11	8	21	105
Arcade Games	1	3	6	16	5	13	4	9	7	7	1	13	85
Dr Halo	0	5	2	13	13	3	3	4	9	3	10	10	82
Typing Tutor	3	1	6	1	15	4	8	2	12	0	11	2	65
Strat/Adv Games	2	4	2	8	3	12	5	8	3	2	2	7	58
Spreadsheet	5	1	0	0	0	0	14	2	4	4	5	3	38
Database	0	0	2	0	0	0	15	2	5	2	4	4	34
Maths Games	5	1	6	2	5	1	2	1	0	0	1	1	25
Graphing	2	0	0	0	1	0	9	1	1	1	0	0	15

by Class Chi-Square = 152.9, D.F. = 45, p = 0
by Class by gender = female Chi-Square = 135.7, D.F. = 45, p = 0
by Class by gender = male Chi-Square = 50.7, D.F. = 45, p = 0.26

TABLE 8: Pattern of Computer Use by Class by Gender

If frequency and duration of typing tutor are any measures of the students' task orientation with computers then females are significantly more task oriented than males. Participation in a typing class was highly correlated with gender ($p < 0.001$) with twice as many girls than boys taking typing classes. Females also used the typing tutor significantly more frequently than males (Chi-square = 18.623, D.F. = 6, $p < 0.005$), and spent significantly more time in each typing tutor session ($F= 4.665$, $p < 0.05$). On average, females spend 15 minutes per session, while males only spend seven minutes. As expected, females have significantly higher typing speeds as measured by both the typing tutor and traditional methods ($F= 9.828$, $p < 0.005$).

In summary, this research presents results indicating a reduction of inequities relating to computer access at school to the point where there are no significant differences across ability, gender and socioeconomic divisions. With computer use, there was no significant difference across ability and socioeconomic divisions. There were, however, significant gender differences with regard to the pattern of software use.

DISCUSSION

The Freyberg Integrated Studies project has attempted to incorporate computers within the school curriculum in a way that best serves the interests of the full range of secondary school students. An important means of achieving this aim was to create conditions that would encourage, and in may instances require, that all students have access to and use computers on an equitable basis. The computer was, in a sense, regarded as a general purpose educational resource required for use by all students in much the same way that they use text books, pen and paper and pocket calculators for school work. While, at tie outset, there was a discernible Hawthorne effect, increasing student and teacher use and familiarity has led to the computer being perceived as a normal, and perhaps even a taken for granted, part of the school programme.

This acceptance of the computer at school appears to have had important effects on the issue of access to computers both at home and at school. Previous research has indicated a marked disparity in the home ownership of computers across socioeconomic levels. While the present study revealed differences, it also revealed a closing of the gap both in absolute and relative terms. For example, the study by Ramsay et al (1987), with a similar sample size, revealed a home ownership pattern of 50% for SES groups 1 and 2, 25% for groups 3 and 4, and 8% for groups 5 and 6. Comparable figures for the present study are, 58%, 38% and 27%. In the Ramsay study, 23% of students had access to computers at home, compared with 41% of students in the present study.

This almost doubling of home computers may be the product of the different socioeconomic circumstances of the schools involved in each study. More importantly, however, the sustained access to computers at school may be impressing upon parents the value to their childrens' education of having access to a computer at home. Anecdotal evidence supports the view that the latter reason is correct. The magnitude of the difference is reflected in the fact that, in the Ramsay study, the top two SES groups had a home ownership rate more than six times greater than the bottom two SES groups (50% compared with 8%). In the present study, this gap has markedly closed and stands at almost two to one (58% compared with 27%). It is alarming, however, that within this changing ownership pattern, parent are out chasing computers for their sons and not for their daughters.

While females have significantly less access to computers in the home environment, inequity of access at school has been reduced for females in all but one of the classes surveyed to the point where the difference is not significant. The exception demonstrates that the presence of computers available for student use at school on a one to one basis is an important, though not a sufficient, condition for the establishment of equitable access. In the computer learning environment, as in the conventional classroom, the teacher has emerged as a key variable not only in resolving the issue of access but in promoting positive attitudes towards educational uses of the computer. This is especially so where equity of access and use for boys and girls is at stake.

As McKelvey (1984) reported, teacher expectations can have differential gender effects on attitudes and performance, benefiting males and adversely affecting females. In the present study, one of the teachers working with a high ability class was neither confident nor particularly competent in using computers. This was primarily due to inexperience as a teacher. One effect was that she tended to withdraw from personally using a computer and she expected the students to virtually teach themselves. In addition, this class had significantly less access than all of the other classes. In this environment and lacking explicit instruction and teacher support, the boys were able to call upon prior experience and their apparently "natural" interest to master various applications. In contrast, the females confronted with a negative female role model and denied access, developed negative attitudes awards using the computer which remain to this day.

In another, lower ability class, the same teacher had the opposite effect on female attitudes. Females in this class had the second highest computer attitude rating and the males had the highest. In this case, the demands being placed upon the teacher with regard to computer use were within her capabilities. Here, she provided a positive role model for the females. The highly positive attitudes of the males can in part be accounted for by the frequency of their access to computers and the fact that they were allowed to play games for part of the time. This is the class where the males report the greatest use of arcade games.

In a similar lower ability class, with a female teacher who was highly task oriented and highly confident and competent in using computers, the female students had the most positive attitudes of the sample surveyed. Only in this class did the females have more positive attitudes than the males, though not at a significant level. Students in this class had significantly greater access to computers and they tended to use task oriented programs more often than any of the other classes.

While the data revealed a measure of equity in the use of computers at school across ability and SES levels, there are relatively clear cut gender differences. This is reflected in girls' professed preferences for such computer programs as word processing and typing tutor which contrasts with boys' preferences for utilities, games and machine oriented rather than task or work oriented programs. One interpretation of this preference outcome is that prior sex role socialisation works to the benefit of girls who perceive the computer as tool for work whereas boys see it as akin to a plaything. In the context of the Project, where task orientation is highly regarded, females are well in advance of males in their ability to use the computer as a learning and productivity tool.

In classrooms generally, but especially in classrooms where computers are used, teachers must be constantly vigilant in resisting males' almost incessant demands for attention and look to create environments where females' talents are nurtured equally and permitted to flourish. As mentioned at the outset of the paper, both affirmative action and positive discrimination are required. Only in this way will girls gain access to and use computers equitably in accord with their rights.

In general terms, there can be little doubt that the prospect of getting access to and using computers elicits positive attitudes and motivates students. Computer activity occupies students and engages their attention for long periods. Analysis of computer laboratory observation data, also being collected in the research project, has revealed sustained on-task behaviour in excess of 95% of the time for both females and males. In this environment, there is frequent communication between students and between student and teacher. This communication is business like and task oriented in character.

Results from the present study do not permit any conclusions to be drawn regarding patterns of computer use in the home. It could be hypothesized that, in time, school policies on computer use may filter through and influence use patterns at home. An implication is that the school may play a useful role educating parents about ways in which computers can be used for educational purposes at home. Such a role may facilitate closer home and school relationships, and thus go some way towards redressing inequities of computer access and use in the home.

Prior socialisation at home and in primary school has helped make girls into good workers and boys into good seekers of attention. While the computer is an admirable tool for the enhancement of work it is also an excellent giver of attention. A major task facing teachers now is to develop programmes that will enable males to increase productivity and develop task orientation and females to develop powers of command and realise their potential as leaders.

It is unrecognised and unstated assumptions held by both parents and teachers and based on archaic sex-role stereotypes about the future roles of females and males which is at the heart of the inequity question. These unrecognised assumptions embodied in the covert curriculum of schools inevitably come to be "assumed" by the pupils and are reproduced from one generation to the next. Unless they are confronted by teachers, parents and administrators, little will be done to redress inequities now, or in the future.

REFERENCES

Bear, G., Richards, H. C. & Lancaster, P. (1987), Attitudes Toward

Computers: Validation of a Computer Attitudes Scale, Journal of Educational Computing Research, Vol. 3(2).

Becker, H.J. (1985), Final Report: The Second National Survey of Instructional Uses of School Computers, Report by the Center for Social Organisation of Schools, Johns Hopkins University, Baltimore, Maryland.

Becker, H.J. & Sterling, C.W. (1987), Equity in School Computer Use: National Data and Neglected Considerations, Journal of Educational Computing Research, Vol. 3(3), pp. 289-309.

Chen, M. (1986), Gender and Computers: The Beneficial Effects of Experience on Attitudes, Journal of Educational Computing Research, Vol. 2(3), pp. 265-281.

Collis, B.A. (1988), A Multidimensional Study of Adolescent Gender Differences in Computer Use and Impact, Paper presented at the Annual Meeting of the American Research Association. New Orleans.

Dubois P.A. and Schubert J.G. (1986), Do Your School Policies Provide Equal Access to Computers? Are you Sure?, Educational Leadership, 43, 6, 41-44.

Latika, V., Hesketh B. & Podd J. (1987), Sex Differences in Computing Behaviour Arnong Secondary School Pupils, New Zealand Journal of Educational Studies, 22 (2), 201-215.

Lockneed, M.E. & Frakt, S.E. (1984), Sex Equity: Increasing Girls' Use of Computers, The Computing Teacher, 11 (8) pp. 16-19.

Loyd, B.H. and Gressard C.P. (1984), The Effects of Sex, Age and Computer Experience on Computer Attitudes, AEDS Journal, 18 (2), 67-77.

McKelvey, cited in Patterson L. (1984), Sexual Stereotypes Taint Computer Classes, Instructional Innovator, 29, 9, 27.

Macrae Kerry (1985), No Boys to Bug US, Paper presented at the NSW Computer Education Conference, Leura, NSW, Australia).

Nolan C.J.P. and McKinnon D.H. (1990), Curriculum Innovation: Subject Integration, Computers and Out of Class Activities in the Freyberg Integrated Studies Project, Paper Presentation at WECC 1990, Sydney, New South Wales, Australia.

Ramsay P. Katterns R. and Lillas C., (1987), Children, Computers and Equity, Delta, 29, 4-18.

Computers in Education
A. McDougall and C. Dowling (Editors)
Elsevier Science Publishers B.V. (North-Holland)
IFIP, 1990

THE ROLE OF TEXT AND DYNAMIC GRAPHICS IN KNOWLEDGE ACQUISITION

Janni NIELSEN

Copenhagen Business University Institute of Informatics and Management Accounting, Howitzvej 60, 2000 Copenhagen F, Denmark

The purpose of the paper is to contribute to the development of a cognitive model, which will make it possible to capture an enriched understanding of human-computer interaction.

An analysis of videotapes of adults respectively youngsters working with programming serves as point of departure for a discussion of knowledge acquisition. From this a cognitive model in which the concept of visual operational thinking is essential is developed and discussed.

It is argued that the enriched model of cognition may serve as a tool in qualitative analysis of human-computer interaction, and it is suggested that the enriched model may also serve as a tool and an enhancement for system development.

I. INTRODUCTON

The integration of icons, pictures and/or dynamic images with text offers new possibilities, but it is not an unknown approach. Through human history, images have been used to express knowledge, (e.g. cave drawings). In contemporary life, we encounter it daily in advertisements, on television, video etc. It has been/is used extensively in education, for example when introducing words together with images.

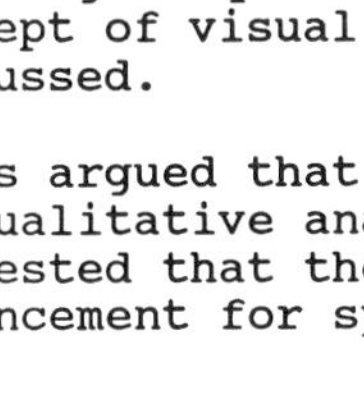

CHAIR

1.1 Computer graphics

The combination of words and images or icons has found many different uses in computer graphics.

Adventure games is one example. The connotations of fairy tales or adventures [1] have served as a basis for introducing computer games. Playing these games often demands metacognitive qualifications such as the ability to work through and see through the embedded story logic. Besides that, and perhaps of greater importance, imagination is a prerequisite. Space Invaders, which in a couple of years acquired millions of users, did not rely on a user's manual. The graphic interface enhanced the computer-user interaction and facilitated the learning and enchanted the playing of the game.

Icons have also been used to make up the basis for the interface in a database. The BOOK HOUSE (Pejtersen 1989) is a unique database developed to assist library users in finding the literature they want. It is built upon the understanding that "efficient navigation in a database by a casual user will be greatly enhanced if the database structure can be embedded in a context which can be represented directly on the interface display surface"(p.472). The opening icon is a graphically-designed image or picture of a house, made up of books (like when one builds a house from cards). Here the illustration of reality is contextualized via the metaphor. It is an icon which has its basis and mode of functioning in the connotations [2] acquired through the experiences of everyday life. This is the foundation for the significance of context.

Also in education, computer graphics have found extensive use. One of the well known examples is Logo, developed at Massachusetts Institute of Technology. It is a very simple programming language [3] combined with Turtle graphics, which has been introduced not only in primary schools but also in kindergartens. The aim of Logo is that a child, without too much trouble, should be able to learn it quickly.

Whether in games, in databases or in the teaching of programming, the underlying question in the development and application of icons is human cognition. The application of graphics has been used in order to enhance understanding and the process of knowledge acquisition. In adventure games it is the ability to imagine and to become cognizant of the embedded logic which is essential. This is also the case with the database. The direct representation of meaning in icons on the display surface aims at promoting easy access for most users. In the teaching of programming in education, it is the learning process which is in focus.

1.2 Programming and knowledge acquisition

The research on pictures which accompany text is extensive. Thus it has been argued that pictures enhance memory (Reid, et al, 1983, Nelson et al, 1984, Pesdek & Stevens, 1984). Also in relation to computer graphics, it has been argued that they enhance learning (Hammond, 1971) and the acquisition of basic knowledge (Baltz 1977, Reif, 1986), because they contribute to the process of imagining topics otherwise difficult to grasp.

The extensive introduction of computers at all levels of education is partly due to the promise of generalized cognitive gains. Programming and the necessary debugging have been ascribed significance for the acquisition of formal operational thinking.

The LOGO group from Massachusetts Institute of Technology has advocated this in numerous publications on children's work with computers. (Lawler, 1985, Papert, 1971, Papert, 1980, Papert, 1986). [4]

However an investigation carried out by Hoyles and Noss (1987) on 13-14-year-old pupils with approximately 120 hours of programming experience with Logo shows though this it not a conclusion they make explicit - that even after 120 hours of hands-on experience, their pupils had problems with very simple exercises. A study by Nielson and Roepstorff (1985) found that pupils were seduced by the graphics. And Nielsen (1988), in an investigation of 30 pupils' work with computers, found a clear preference for graphics as opposed to programming among novice learners. She suggests that the role of dynamic graphics be investigated.

11. THE RESEARCH

In my research project, aimed at investigating how pictorial representation influences cognitive development, I wanted to look more closely at the role of visual dynamic graphics in the process of knowledge acquisition through the use of computers.

I chose to use a software program which embodied both text and dynamic graphics. This allowed for both a programming approach and/or a dynamic graphical approach to problem-solving. At the same time, it enabled me to investigate the role of both text and of dynamic pictorial information in knowledge acquisition.

Thirty youngsters (age 14-16) and 16 adults (age 34-60) participated in the study. They had no, or extremely little, experience with computers. The participants worked in pairs. This setting demanded communication, and to some extent (where cooperation functioned) extensive and explicit verbalization of their problem-solving. The participants were videotaped during their work at the computers, at which time they had

approximately 4-6 hours hands-on experience.

I used two cameras and two visual display units connected with the user station. In this way, one camera was on the extra display unit, taping the products on their screen. The other camera taped the pair viewed from the front. By superimposing the two images, it became possible on the videotapes to see what the participants saw, hear their discussion, and follow their reasoning, (e.g. what information they built on, how they used it etc.).

2.1. Presentation of empirical data

In this section I describe two working processes, one of adults and one of youngsters. To ease understanding and ensure coherence in the reading process, I have carried out continuous analyses through the descriptions.

2.2. The adults: Relying on illustration

James and Bob had just copied the following program from the exercise book, and seen it executed (Neilson 198).

```
SPIRAL(H)
 FORWARD(H)
 RIGHT TURN(90)
 SPIRAL(H+2)
END
```

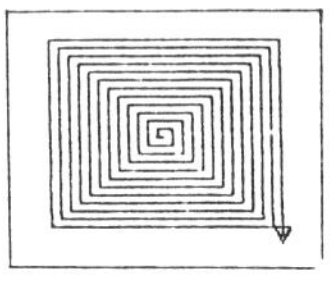

The instruction was to continue working with the program, but make a change in order for it to execute a graphical shape [5] resembling the illustration [6] in the book.

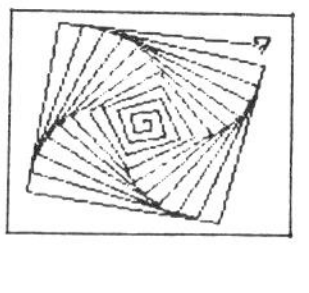

After reading the instructions, they concentrated their attention on the illustration. "A bigger angle, maybe," suggests Bob hesitantly. James continues, at the same time reasoning aloud, "the interior angle is less than 90.... and the one we have seems to be... 90... that is why it becomes smaller and smaller...".

They take the illustrations as their point of departure. By comparing the two, James concludes - as does Bob - that it is the angle. However, James wants it to be smaller than 90 - because he reads the illustrations from outside and inwards (this becomes important later on). Thus it is the illustration they debug, the change of the text order comes second.

Relying on the dynamic graphics

They attend to the SPIRAL program shown on the screen (a variable is missing in their program name). "We just have to change it... and then we have to figure out how large H is to be... which value should we give H2?" ends James with a question.

Their eyes move from screen with program text to illustration, forwards and backwards again and again. Finally in the first attempt the angle is changed to Right Turn 80. And H is given the value 2, though not - after some discussion - in the subroutine.

```
SPIRAL
 FW(2+2)
 RT(80)
 SPIRAL(H+2)
END
```

At the execution of the program the cursor bips noisily around, and Bob breaks out laughing, placing his hands over his eyes (yes, it is too much to watch). "Ha, ha... that will never turn into anything sensible." James follows the cursor around with his eyes, then looks at the illustrations, and back again. "I think we have made H too small." In the second attempt the variable is changed back to H again. [7] Again the cursor moves around noisily. "Well, at least it is different", Bobs laughs, then he sighs deeply.

It is the cursor movements, the dynamic graphics which he compares with the illustration, that is: the-debugging procedure is to read the length the cursor draws, compare it with the length in the illustration, and on the basis of this he reasons that the variable has been given too small a value.

From graphics to program text

They both stare at the cursor which continues to move around for a long time. Not a word is said. Then finally, "That... eh, hey just take a look here (pointing to screen). What was this before (illustration), H+2, and 90 right... And that produced that beautiful shape," exclaims Bob. At the same time he shows the exercise book to James. James leans back, he lets his eyes follow the movements of the cursor. Then they move back to the illustration. "Do you know what... that angle, it becomes smaller and smaller, it must be the exterior angle we have to get hold of, because we are coming from the inside going out... what is 360-80?" he finishes.

The resulting figure causes a long period of absolute silence while they keep looking at the screen. From what is happening here Bob turns to the earlier program, because it produced a beautiful shape. And James, who follows him, reads the movement of the cursor - realizing that the execution moves from the inside and out.

Again it is the dynamic graphics they rely on. This leads to a correction of their earlier understanding, the illustration comes second. Not until then do they turn to the program. On the basis of the graphics James also concludes that the value of the angle should be different (360-80=280). However, he does not realize that the new value will result in the cursor turning to the left.

Dissonance and cognizance

At the third attempt they change the angle to RT(280). At the fourth attempt they decide to substitute H with the value 10. This time they have their eyes glued to the screen. They follow the cursor. Then Bob laughs, "I think it moves the other way around... to the left... it says RT in the program... it moves left.... it is a leftist.....". Discovering the full meaning of his statement, he laughingly repeats, "it is a leftist". James comments "It does not move far enough out ... eh.. When it does not move far enough out... what do we have to do?"

They discuss whether the angle should be changed, but, "No.. it is that one, it changes the length all the time... right," (referring to the illustration) Bob continues his reasoning. James finishes, "... the length H+2... if only it changes all the time... It has to get bigger, right?"

Again the solution is found by carefully following the cursor movements, and Bob reads a left turn. He then mentally refers to the program - realizing that it says RT. Not until then does he fully understand, as he becomes cognizant of the fact that the cursor does draw to the left.

Thus they have a point of departure in the dynamic graphics, which is related to the program order. Reading the dynamic graphics was prior to moving on to the program. Realizing a dissonance between the two, he seems to finally come to grips with his initial visual perception.

James, who is able to continue, also follows the movements on the screen. He reads the length, refers to the program order and defines the problem: that the length does not grow continually. Again they take point of departure in the dynamic graphics, and the problem is defined as a consequence of reading the figure.

2.3. The youngsters: Programs do not trigger imagination

Fifteen-year-old Cecily and Tine's way of working is normally to skip instructions, and mechanically copy programs and ask to have them executed (Nielsen 1987a). With excited expressions the girls follow the cursor movements, and they express enthusiasm when new unexpected results appear.

The Spiral program was copied mechanically and they then asked to have it executed. "Good Lord," exclaimed Tine and smiled happily as the figure gradually unfolded. Cecily smiled quietly at the same time as she followed the execution of the graphic shape closely.

They succeeded in changing the Spiral program and started reading the instruction to the next problem posed. As they did not understand the problem they did as usual: skip a couple of instructions, and move on until they find an illustration they like.

It is the graphics and the illustrations which fascinate them, and ensure motivation. Surprising figures are expected because they do not create mental images on the basis of the text. As opposed to the adults, the girls do not seem to perceive a clear relationship between text and graphics. Yet they move through the same phases.

Intuitive understanding based on visual perception of dynamic graphics

The instruction tells them to write a program which turns a triangle around, at the same time making it bigger.

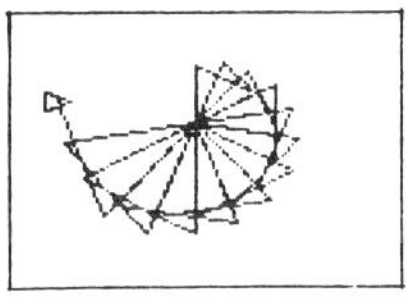

Cecily's attention is caught by the Spiral which is shown on the screen and intuitively she takes this as point of departure. "Then we just have to do it with a triangle, right" she states as a question.

Initially it seems that the girls realize that if the Triangle is to become bigger the Forward order must contain a variable, and also the Right Turn angle has to be given a different value.

```
Tentatively they move on,
"Yes.... key                   TT
Spiral, no key RT........ no,
just wait                       FW(A)
a minute..... RT 120":          RT(120)
Then a long break in which the
girls clearly are deliberating.
Cecily looks front screen
text to illustration and
back again. "Yeah,              SPIRAL(A+2)
but it won't be right......
but let's key Spiral A+2"
she concludes.                 END
```

One problem is that in order to execute a triangle, a program for a triangle must be included. However she knows the variable which she changed to A has to be included in the subroutine. But the recursion creates problems. The Turning Triangle program (TT) has to call itself (TT) in order for the recursion to function.

It is interesting that Cecily, on the basis of a visual perception of the dynamic figure, intuitively reasons from this. She also realizes, though this is expressed very hesitantly, that to call the subroutine SPIRAL in the TT program will not produce the wanted figure, though how and why she knows that is not clear. However, as she has no idea what else to do, the subroutine is keyed.

<u>Debugging figures by reading dynamic graphics</u>

They ask to have the program executed, "Yes, but look at that, it makes quadrangles," exclaims Cecily, and Tine agrees with a very tired and disappointed voice. Hypnotized, they stare at the screen and comment upon the cursor's step-wise drawing. When it starts executing the subroutine Spiral, (Cecily does not realize that this is what it does) she gets all excited, "Yes, but look, then it has to go FORWARD, and TURN, and FORWARD and TURN ....could we not put in a repeat order?", she ends up suggesting.

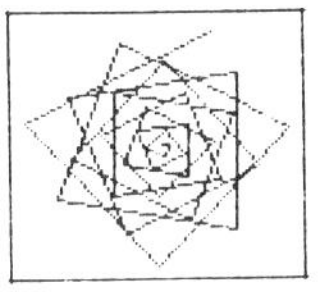

Little by little, and with their eyes glued to the screen, reading the figure which unfolds gradually, they succeed in writing a program for a Triangle with the use of repeat. But they keep the subroutine. "Why does it keep drawing quadrangles", one of them voices in despair.

For the final corrections they have to ask the teacher for help. It turns out that Cecily has contextualized the subroutine directly in the visual dynamic movement. To her, SPIRAL(A+2) = TURN/GET BIGGER.

It is the graphics the girls rely on, and it is the figure they debug by reading the icons and interpreting the dynamic information. In their debugging they rely on their intuition and make inferences from what their eyes see. The movement and the change which takes place in their programming work is the movement from being fixated in the figures, where the visual perception rules, to beginning figure/text analysis on the basis of a perceived dissonance. But their point of departure remains the visual pictorial information, and the text: the language is contextualized directly in the dynamic graphical information.

3. DISCUSSION OF KNOWLEDGE ACQUISITION

Looking at James and Bob, the process they go through may be described in this way. Initially they read the illustration, but they quickly move on to relying on the graphics. This they do by attempting to read the dynamics (movements). They do compare graphics with illustrations, but it is not until the last step that they read the dynamic graphics - relate these directly to the program text - and become aware of a dissonance between the two. One may say that at this point they become cognizant. It is visual perception which rules their work, and though they have a very clear perception of the relationship between text and graphics, the dynamic graphics are the deciding factors in their problem-solving. They try to operationalize their reading of images, but the programming text only comes in second.

The same is true with Cecily and Tine. The girls are fascinated by the dynamic graphics, but their relationship to programming text is - as opposed to the adults - as distant as can be. They do not seem to be able to create mental images on the basis of text. On the contrary, to them the programming text seems meaningless, because they do not see programming language as carrying figurative information. Nevertheless they are able to work with the computer and solve problems. It is because they rely on their visual perception of the dynamic graphics, and on their intuition. By drawing upon both, they are able to move from reading to actually debugging the dynamic graphics.

Despite the differences in perception of relationship between text and graphics, whether adults or youngsters it is the visual perception - that which first meets the eye, be it illustrations or graphical figures - which rules. And the dynamic graphics are the deciding factor in their approach. They move from the immediate perceivable and seem to read the graphics - like when one reads a text - and acquire information from them. This information they use in their on-going work.

4. INFORMATION CARRIER

As a new image technology, graphics is a carrier of information, like the written and spoken word. But the form and way in which they carry information is radically different. This is important, as different types of information carrier seem to demand different qualifications from those receiving them.

Graphics are read not only more often, but also more readily (and easier?) than the program. But how may this be explained? And how may one understand the role of dynamic graphics in the process of knowledge acquisition, and the cognitive qualification which the reading of it requires?

4.1. Imagery

I will suggest, in view of the empirical data presented, that in order to catch the difference in the roles of text and dynamic graphic in the process of knowledge acquisition, it may be fruitful to view the use of pictures or icons in learning processes in connection with the question of whether imagery representation plays any role in cognition.

Kosslyn (1983) describes in his experiments how people can follow a verbal description to assemble different memories into a single imaged display. "Virtually everybody claims to be able to envision George Washington riding a surfboard down a giant wave..."(p. 100). Other descriptions or representations may not promote images as readily as the above example.

4.2. Contextualized/decontextualized

Wason and Johnson-Laird's (1972) research among university students of the rule IF P THEN Q may serve as an example of the different representations and the readiness for provoking imagery, hence demands on our imagination. Their investigation of the rule IF P THEN Q was introduced thus: If there is a vowel on one side of the card, there is an even number on the other. Four cards were introduced, and the question was which cards to turn in order to decide if the rule counted:

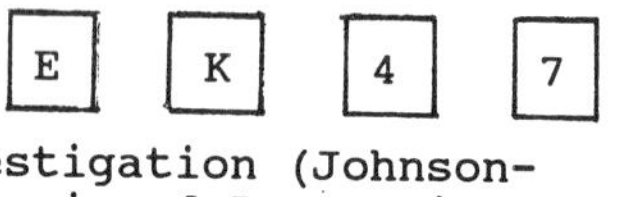

In a later investigation (Johnson-Laird and Legrenzi and Legrenzi, 1972) this was changed to the rule: If the envelope is closed it has a 5-penny stamp. Four envelopes were introduced, and again the question was which envelopes to turn:

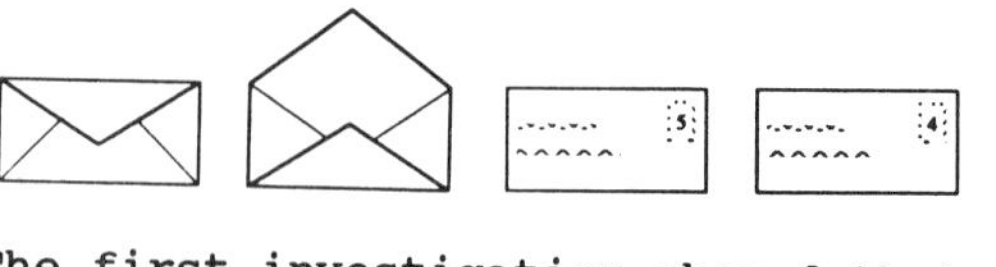

The first investigation showed that the problem was rather difficult to solve for the university students, whereas more than 80% of the students solved the problem when posed as in the second investigation. The difference, it is concluded, is due to the level of abstractions.

I should like to voice it differently in order to bring forward other connotations: When the content of meaning has been rationalized away, one cannot speak of context but only of decontextualization.

Inferential quality

Thus it is a question of contextualization, or as Lindsay has pointed out, the inferential quality of the representation, which must be considered. The presidential example may be characterized as an example of a very figurative language. lt paints images so readily that it demands "only" the general qualification of "assembling different memories into a single imaged display". The two examples of the If P then Q rule do not promote pictures that easily, though the envelopes ease access to imagery, that is, they encourage the person to visualize the problem more readily than that of the cards. The difference between them may be described as contextualized representation (the envelopes), referring directly to context, being concrete language, and decontextualized representation, (the cards) where the reference is in-direct, being abstract language [10].

I should like to argue that this same differentiation is significant in relation to icons. Computer graphics may be more or less contextualized/ decontextualized. Using the concrete/abstract distinction from language on images, 1 will now return to the question of knowledge acquisition in relation to programming and dynamic graphics.

V. COGNITION AND THE ROLE OF DYNAMIC GRAPHICS

The empirical description showed that the girls do not seem to perceive the relationship between programming language and dynamic graphics. Therefore they cannot see the language as carrying figurative information. James and Bob know there is a relationship, and they do their best. But they have difficulties in "seeing" the embedded information in the text, and they also have problems in inferring from one to the other.

Clearly, it is the programming language which creates problems for novices. I will suggest that it is the inferential quality of the programming language which must be considered. In the case of novices, the programming language appears abstract and decontextualized. No meaning can be derived from it, therefore there is nothing to build imagination on, and no inference is possible.

Yet the two pairs are able to write programs. Actually the girls succeed at the fourth attempt by finally relying on a question the teacher asked. Bob and James move through seven attempts, and with explicit definition of the problem by the teacher, they finally succeed.

But they succeed only when they allow their visual perception to rule. They actually operationalize their visual perception by reading the dynamic graphics. The reading allows them to move from immediate perception to a preliminary understanding, as they acquire visual knowledge. In this process the dynamic graphics function as a mediator for knowledge acquisiton and the ability to read dynamic pictorial information provides a means for understanding, when working with the image media.

Visual operational thinking

If one cannot see the embedded information in the graphics, one cannot make use of their inferential quality. But it is not sufficient to merely see the graphics, one also has to be able to operationalize the visual knowledge gained. However from the empirical data, it is obvious that this is not experienced as a problem. On the contrary, both the adults and especially the youngsters are supreme readers of the inherent information in the graphics.

When Cecily intuitively, though hesitantly, takes her point of departure in the Spiral program, in order to create a Turning Triangle, she seems to perceive a relationship between the two. Though she is not quite clear as to why she knows, and what she knows, I venture that she applies the "general qualification of assembling different memories into a single dynamic image display".(Kosslyn, 1983). This general qualification is the ability to operationalize the read information in the dynamic graphics. I suggest that the process underlying this ability is that of visual operational thinking. The special qualification of visual operational thinking is its prerequisite for, and function of, connecting link between concrete operational and formal operational thinking.

Earlier I suggested that icons, dynamic graphics etc. are carriers of information like the spoken and written word, but that their design is different, and that this demands different qualifications from those who read (interpret) their meaning. The empirical material appears to confirm the reasonableness of this assumption. The qualifications are different. However it seems to me that the underlying processes are the same. The dynamic graphic is read sequentially, just like words. It could be argued that this has something to do with the dynamic: the figure is executed step by step, it is not displayed in one move. This special facility certainly promotes the reading. However it is probable that also pictures and paintings are read this way. The English-born American painter David Hockney (1988) describes how discussing the art of painting during a visit to China gave him new ways of understanding paintings. He suggests that the reading is sequential, and argues that the way to understand cubistic paintings is exactly to read them as a movement - not as cubes. Because, he says, in our perception is always that which we perceived a second before. This understanding he has explored extensively over the last years (cf. Hollywood Hills House). Psychological analyses of art may be unknown to Hockney, but years ago Amheim wrote, in his book Visual Thinking (1963) "A review of what is known about perception, and especially about sight, made me realize that the remarkable mechanisms by which the senses understand the environment are all but identical with the operations described by the psychology of thinking".

VI. SYSTEM DESIGN AND DEVELOPMENT

In system design and system development of the future it will become important to take the interplay between text/dynamic images into account. The trend is for more and more people to work with image technology. The change rate in development is high, and new cognitive qualifications and new knowledge of how to handle the systems will have to be acquired, at the same time as the systems are applied. Without greater knowledge of the demands these media technologies put on the user, and without improved knowledge of human cognitive processes, the development may miss the point - and the systems will not promote easy access. These new systems are designed and developed and applied at great cost. If they do not promote easy access, the major investments are thrown into the wind. System design without due knowledge of human cognition may, at worst, have very severe effects, not only on the users' cognitive abilities, but may also result, as they may promote mistakes, in large-scale damage.

ACKNOWLEDGEMENTS

This paper would not have been written without help from Marianne Andersen and Birgitte Bush. They put their skills together and translated the first version from Danish into English.

Birgit Thejls gave extraordinary help when it was badly needed.

Hugh Willmott, University of Manchester, who is a visiting professor at the institute, helped polish the English. But Hugh's help went beyond the translation as he was able to follow my thoughts where others got lost, and sharpened my arguments. Paul Lindgreen read with great care and gave valuable suggestions. For all this help I am very grateful.

FOOTNOTES

[1] Fairy tales in another role than that which they play in the conventional stories. Adventure games may be seen not as a substitute for, but as offering other possibilities for the world of imagination.

[2] It is of course not only a question of connotations, but also of accepted conventions. Thus a library denotes a building with books, which one may visit in order to look for books (one still does not sit at home and go to the library). It is not a place for loud voices and playing around.

[3] Exactly because it has been developed for children who are novices in programming Logo is, in terms of

software development, a very advanced tool.

[4] This has been questioned in a number of investigations, see e.g. Perkins, 1985 and Pea and Kurland, 1983.

[5] The concept: figure, or shape, refers to the dynamic graphical form on the screen.

[6] The concept: illustration refers to the drawing, the illustration in the exercise book, or sheet.

[7] On-going research where the same group of participants were videotaped one year later, and after approximately 45 hours of hand-on experience showed no significant difference with relation to the preference. Neilson, J. (1989a) unpublished empirical data.

[9] The solution is E and 7.

[10] Abstract language may be further differentiated into signs, no reference at all. It is decontextualized, but of course may be used as a tool, like mathematics.

REFERENCES

Arnheim, Rudolf(1963) Visual Thinking, N.Y.

Baltz, B.L. (1977) Computer graphics as an aid to teaching mathematics. Unpublished doctoral dissertation. Ohio State University.

Hammond, (1971) Computer graphics as an aid to learning, Science, 172, p. 903-908.

Hockney, David(1988) David Hockney - a retrospective. Los Angeles County Museum of Art. Harry N. Abraham Inc. publ. New York.

Hoyles, C and Noss R.(1987) Children Working in a Structured Logo Environment: From doing to Understanding. Working Paper, University of London, Inst. of Education.

Johnson-Laird, P. & Legrenzi, P. & S. Legrenzi(1972) Reasoning and a sense of reality. British Journal of Psychology, 63, p. 395-400.

Kosslyn, S.M.(1983) Ghosts in the Mind's Machine: Creating and Using Images in the Brain. New York, Norton.

Lawler, Robert(1985) Computer Experience and Cognitive Development. A Childs Learning in a Computer Culture. Ellis Horwood, New York.

Lindsay, Robert K.(1988) Images and inference. Cognition, 29, p. 229-250.

Nelson D.L. and D. Castano (1984) Mental representation and words: Same or different? American Journal of Psychology, spring, vol. 97, no. 1, p. 1-15.

Nielsen, Janni(1987a) "Jeg fatter ikke spor, gør du?" spurgte han. "Nej, nu prøver vi bare", svarede hun.
15 kommenterede procesbeskrivelser. The Royal Danish School of Educational studies, PPP41.

Nielsen, Janni(1987b) Datamater og erkendelsesprocesser (Computers and cognition), The Royal Danish School of Educational Studies, PPP 42. (english summary).

Nielsen, Janni(1988) THE ROLE OF DYNAMIC GRAHICS WHEN LEARNING PROGRAMMING - implications for cognition. in Lovis, F. and E.D.Tagg (eds) COMPUTERS IN EDUCATION, Elseviers Science Publishers, IFIP.

Nielsen, Janni (1989a) Et år efter - (One year after - unpublished empirical data).

Nielsen, Janni(1989b) Adult novices working with computers. 8 commented proces descriptions from videotapes. Unpublished.

Nielsen, Janni and Lisbet Roepstorff(1985) Girls and Computers -worlds apart? Revised edition of paper presented at the THIRD GASAT CONFERENCE, London, april.

Noss, Richard(1985) Creating a Mathematical Environment through programming: A Study of Young Children Learning Logo. University of London. Doctoral Dissertation.

Papert, S(1971) Teaching Children Thinking. Logo Memo no. 2, Mass Inst. of Technology.

Papert, S.(1980) MINDSTORMS, Children, Computers and Powerful Ideas. Basic Books, Inc. New York.

Papert, S.(1986) Computers are Objects to think with, in Electronic Computing, 5, April.

Pea, R and M. Kurland(1983) On the cognitive effects of learning computer programming. Bank Street College. New York.

Pejtersen,Annelise Mark(1989) INFORMATIONS RETRIEVAL WITH AN ICON BASED INTERFACE. NordData 89, conference documentation, p. 471-478, Denmark.

Perkins, D.N.((1985) The Fingertip Effect: How Informations Processing Technologoy Shapes Thinking. Educational Research, vol. 14,7,aug./sept. P. 11-17.

Pezdek, K and E. Stevens (1984) Childrens memory of auditory and visual information on Television. Developmental Psychology, vol. 20, no. 2, p. 212-218.

Reid, D.J., Briggs N., and M. Beveridge (1983) The effect of Picture upon the readability of a school science topic. British Journal of Educational Psychology, 53, p. 327-335.

Reif, F.(1986) Scientific approaches to science education. Physics Today, Nov. p. 48-54.

Wason P. and P. Johnson-Laird(1972) Psychology of Reasoning: Structure and Content. London.

Computers in Education
A. McDougall and C. Dowling (Editors)
Elsevier Science Publishers B.V. (North-Holland)

CRITERIA BY WHICH PUPILS CAN BE SELECTED TO OFFER COMPUTER STUDIES IN THE SENIOR SECONDARY SCHOOL

D.A. NORTON, P.N. WILLIAMSON and P. WAKER

CAPE EDUCATION DEPARTMENT, P.O. BOX 13
8000 CAPE TOWN, SOUTH AFRICA

Concern over the high drop-out rate of Computer Studies pupils prompted an investigation into the reasons for this with a view to determining criteria for selecting pupils so as to reduce the drop-out rate. The search for the reasons for pupils dropping out was not restricted to questioning the pupils who gave up, but included questioning the principals of schools, Computer Studies teachers and pupils, both past and present, who had completed or were still on the course. It was found that available computer aptitude tests are unreliable and while a certain minimum academic ability and the ability to think logically are needed, factors connected with the applicant's personality have a very important influence. A suggested profile for selecting Computer Studies pupils, based on a points system, was developed.

It is very desirable to be able to predict whether students will be successful at and suited to a field of study before they begin a lengthy course in that subject. The younger the students the more difficult it is to determine their suitability, and in the case of Computer Studies, especially at school level, this has proved particularly difficult.

This Education Department began offering Computer Studies in 1977, but was faced with two problems: exorbitant hardware costs and a critical shortage of qualified Computer Studies teachers. The solution to these two problems was the establishing, over a period of time, of 22 computer centres to serve the approximately 250 high schools. Each centre would serve the needs of all the schools in the surrounding region, and pupils from these schools would attend Computer Studies classes as an optional and additional subject after normal school hours. As only approximately one pupil in forty could be accommodated on the course, applications for places on the course far exceeded the available accommodation. Considering the large investment in time and money made in these pupils and the number of pupils turned away, it was essential to pick suitable candidates. Prior to this research project being undertaken it had been felt for some time that the selection criteria were inadequate, as a large number of the chosen candidates failed to complete the course.

This paper summarises the research into selection criteria for Computer Studies pupils undertaken during 1988 under the leadership of D A Norton [9], presents its findings and reports on the subsequent follow-up. The research suggests some new and important criteria which are widely applicable and, if these prove successful, it will enable 13 year old pupils to be singled out as suitable Computer Studies students wherever Computer Studies is offered as a subject.

The paper first looks briefly at the previous selection criteria and examines how successful they were, then summarises a survey of the literature and the experiences of this and other educational institutions, proposes a set of selection criteria and reports on the practical application of these criteria.

PREVIOUS SELECTION CRITERIA

Previous to this study candidates were selected according to the following criteria:

1. Academic ability: Standard 7 results in Languages (at least 60%); Mathematics (at least 80%); and aggregate (at least 70%)
2. Principal's recommendation: A subjective judgement based largely on knowledge of the pupil; taking into account factors such as motivation, perseverance, involvement in extramural activities and interest in computers. The candidates from each school were ranked according to the principal's recommendation.
3. Superintendent of Education's recommendation: Using the candidate's current results, IQ and the principal's evaluation, the Superintendent of Education assessed the candidate's ability to cope with an additional subject.

Using these criteria an average overall drop-out rate of 77% was experienced in the following way:

Year one: 35%
Year two: 46% of those left on the course
Year three: 20% of those left on the course
A total drop-out rate of between 50 and 66%, although not desirable, was considered acceptable.

The question which must be asked is: "How well did these criteria discriminate between candidates who completed the course and those who did not?"

Academic results: The results obtained in Standard 7 (whether in Mathematics, Languages, General Science or aggregate) did not distinguish between those who dropped out of the Computer Studies course and those who stayed on or completed it. This does not suggest that a certain level of academic achievement in Mathematics or Languages is not a prerequisite for Computer Studies, but what cannot be concluded is that pupils who obtain 90% in Mathematics are more likely to succeed than those who obtain 80%.

Potential ability as measured by IQ: Again virtually no difference was observed between the drop-outs and the stayers.

Experience of computer programming prior to starting the course was also not found to be a separation criterion. In fact marginally more drop-outs than stayers had had previous programming experience.

Data obtained on ability to offer 7 subjects, motivation and perseverance were so vague as to be of no use as discriminating criteria. This is unfortunate because it becomes clear from later research that these are critical factors.

The average number of extramural activities in which successful candidates participated did not differ markedly from those taken by unsuccessful ones, but it was a weakness of the study that pupils did not always indicate the number of activities, nor the amount of time involved. Therefore no definite conclusion could be drawn.

THE SEARCH FOR SUITABLE CRITERIA

It is generally accepted that a good grounding in mathematics and the logical use of language are prerequisites for success in Computer Studies. However, the results above appear to suggest that even candidates with a strong academic foundation may not be successful at Computer Studies. To test this question further, the Senior Certificate results of Computer Studies candidates were compared with their results in their First Language, Mathematics, Physical Science and their aggregate. The First Language and Mathematics marks were chosen as computer aptitude tests generally centre on language and mathematical abilities, these being regarded by many to be good predictors of ability in Computer Studies. While many of the subjects have a high correlation one with the other, their correlation with Computer Studies was found to be low in all cases, which leads us to conclude that the intrinsic abilities being measured by Computer Studies are different in essence to those abilities being measured by the other subjects, or there are extraneous factors impinging on the pupil in Computer Studies which do not occur when other subjects are studied, or both these factors are relevant.

Results from other institutions indicate that skills contained within certain subjects are good indicators of computer ability. The University of Port Elizabeth and the Cape Technikon found that ability in languages, especially with regard to comprehension and logical sequencing of events, is a good indicator of programming ability, and Webb [12] found that a combination of numerical skills and numerical reasoning was also a good indicator. Our results show that the global result in these subjects do not correlate with results in Computer Studies.

To examine further those extraneous factors which may impinge on the pupil in his study of computers, a questionnaire was addressed to pupils presently at school who were still following or had followed the Computer Studies course. Those who had dropped out were asked to indicate why they had discontinued their studies. In order to facilitate the analysis of the data, 23 suggested reasons were given and pupils were asked to indicate those reasons that applied to them. Space was also provided to enter reasons not given in the list. Principals and Computer Studies teachers were asked to rate each of the reasons given to the pupils on a scale of one to five, from not important to very important. The response to the questionnaires was statistically analysed and the following reasons for dropping out of the course were found to be relevant. For the purpose of this analysis the reasons were listed in three categories: demotivating reasons, pressure reasons and ability reasons.

(a) Demotivating reasons
- -- The theoretical work is boring/lessons were not interesting (Rated as a major reason by 45% of the pupils)
- -- I lost interest in working with computers (Ranked highly by principals, teachers and 43% of the drop-out pupil group)

(b) Pressure reasons
- -- My extramural programme is full or clashes with lesson times. (Rated as most important by principals, teachers

and 60% of the drop-out pupil group)
- -- The amount of work in my other six subjects has increased. (37 % of pupils cited this reason)
- -- Travelling to the centre is awkward. (37% of pupils)

(c) Ability reasons
- -- I am not achieving on the course/I am unable to master the practical work. (42% of pupil respondents)

Secondary analysis using the Response Levels Method, performed to ascertain which reasons are associated with one another, revealed that, while there is a strong association within each group of reasons, the inter-group relationships are limited. It would seem therefore that pupils give up because they are demotivated or because they find the pressures too great to withstand or if their ability is suspect. However, more sophisticated analysis using Multidimensional Scaling showed that the two ability reasons are, not surprisingly, closely associated with the demotivating reasons, but confirmed that the pressure reasons are not closely related to the demotivating reasons or the ability reasons.

It can be seen that factors other than ability play a very large part in the decision whether to continue with Computer Studies or not. Demotivating factors and the widely recognised pressure factors must be taken into account. Unless effective measures are taken to counteract these "other than ability" factors the drop-out rate will remain high no matter how refined the aptitude test becomes.

At first glance none of these reasons seem easy to predict before the candidate begins the course. However, we hope to show that it is possible to predict which pupils will find the theoretical work boring and which pupils will lose interest in working with computers.

It seemed logical to examine the reasons for pupils' staying on the course as well as the reasons for their dropping out. Therefore a similar questionnaire was sent to candidates still on the course and to those who had successfully completed it. The results of candidates still on the course were as follows:
Reasons for remaining on the course:

(a) Motivating reasons
- -- I am interested in working with computers. (82%)
- -- I found the equipment provided to be sufficient for my needs. (60%)
- -- The course is relevant to my future career. (59%)
- -- I was encouraged to continue by my parents. (59%)

(b) Pressures that have been overcome
- -- My academic standard has been maintained. (59%)
- -- My social life was not unduly affected. (56%)
- -- I can handle the increased workload at school. (54%)

(c) Ability reasons
- -- I am mastering the practical work. (57%)

Notice that four out of the top five factors were motivational. It must also be mentioned that only 16% of the respondents considered their extramural programmes to be minimal. Note also that the candidates felt that they had mastered the practical work.

The pupils who had completed the course gave the following reasons for completing the course:

(a) Motivating reasons
- -- I am interested in working with computers. (86%)
- -- I found the equipment provided to be sufficient for my needs. (64%)
- -- The course was relevant to my future career. (68%)

(b) Pressures that have been overcome
- -- Seven subjects did not demand too much work. (76%)
- -- My academic standard was maintained. (72%)
- -- Amount of work expected on the course was reasonable (69%)
- -- I could handle the increased workload at school. (73%)

(c) Ability reasons
- -- I mastered the practical work. (72%)

Unlike the present pupils, the past pupils regard pressures that have been overcome as the dominant reasons for their having completed the course. The results of this are in contrast to those of the other two groups and from this it would seem that motivation plays a very important role while on the course, but as one becomes detached from the course one retains an awareness of the pressures exerted from outside.

Should ownership of a home computer or easy access to a computer be a prerequisite for course acceptance? To answer this question present and past pupils were asked to give information on whether they were in possession of a computer at home and what they used it for. Interestingly, forty-two percent of those who dropped out of the course had access to a computer at home and thirty-two percent of those who completed the course had no access to a computer at home. Nevertheless respondents to the questionnaires were unanimous in the view that continuing with/completing the course is assisted if pupils have access to a computer at home.

Three main uses of the home computer were common to both those who remained on the course and those who dropped out. They are "to develop programs", "to explore the possibilities of the computer" and "to make use of developed software".

The computer industry has long relied on aptitude tests when recruiting computer staff. These tests are fundamentally unsuitable as they are designed for adults and not for school children. The Natal Education Department used the ICL programming aptitude test to rank and select its Computer Studies pupils. They have found it not to be a reliable indicator of either ability or interest in computers. The University of Port Elizabeth have in the past used aptitude tests designed by IBM, ICL and Burroughs to select candidates for a degree course in Computer Science. Even though they are dealing with young adults they found no correlation between the test scores and the final mark obtained in Computer Science. It must be concluded that existing computer aptitude tests are not reliable indicators of computer ability.

While commercial concerns use aptitude tests to assist in recruiting their computer personnel, they also rely heavily on a number of other criteria. This prompted an investigation into which criteria experts in the field, educationalists and the computer industry consider important. All the groups considered that the following criteria were important:

- -- Motivation
- -- Perseverance
- -- Ability to reason logically
- -- Mathematical ability
- -- Language ability
- -- Spatial ability
- -- IQ

Research by Sorge [10] and Madden (referred to by Calitz [2]) revealed that data processing professionals exhibited a surprisingly low social need and that people with gregarious personalities were not attracted to the computer industry.

Coupled to this is the observation that field-independent learners do better at computer programming than their field-dependent counterparts. The concept of field-dependence/independence is defined by Witkin et. al. [15]:

> "The individual, who, in perception, cannot keep an item separate from the surrounding field, in other words who is relatively field-dependent, is likely to have difficulty with that class of problem, ... where the solution depends on taking some critical elements out of the context in which it is presented and restructuring the problem material so that the item is now used in a different context."

Furthermore (p. 41), "the preponderant interest of the field-independent person is in the analytical-impersonal domains, ... field-dependent persons express interest in interpersonal domains that particularly require social skills."

It is contended (Stevens [11]) that programming and technical knowledge is generally precise, sequential and requires specific concepts to be combined in a variety of ways, thus corresponding more to the theory of analytical preference of field-independent learners. Field-independent students will perform better when allowed to work independently and field-dependent students will learn more when they have extra guidance from the instructor. By its very nature computer work requires a lot of independent learning, and the instructor does not have the time to get around to everyone in order that field-dependent people can get all the help that they need.

Other researches [Webb [13] quoting Testa (1973), Cherry (1980) and Snow (1980)] also come out in support of the contention that field-independent subjects do better at computer programming than their field-dependent counterparts.

From the aforegoing it would appear necessary to consider various personality factors such as field-independence and the need for social interaction in the selection of candidates. Field-independence can be measured by means of a Hidden Figures Test, but, even without going to these lengths, the teacher-counsellor at a school should be able to rate a pupil on independence/dependence of learning style, and in this way provide some clue as to whether the pupil is field-dependent or field-independent. Similarly, with regard to the need for social interaction, it will probably be better to ask the teacher-counsellor for an opinion on a candidate's need for social interaction rather than to rely on the pupil profile as indicated by psychological tests since a pupil's social awareness is often not sufficiently developed at a Standard 7 level to provide the definite pointers.

Computer programming can be classified into four components (Webb [13] quoting Pea 1983):

- -- understanding the problem
- -- designing and planning the programming
- -- coding the program
- -- comprehending and debugging the program

Webb [12] also found that these different components are best predicted by different abilities. Measures of mathematics ability, spatial ability, non-verbal reasoning, field-independence and previous experience were positively related to most of the components of computer programming and must therefore be considered as selection criteria.

Having identified all the above criteria the researchers combined them using a weighted points system which is used to draw up a "pupil profile" for each candidate. This points procedure is summarised below.

CRITERIA FOR SELECTING COMPUTER STUDIES PUPILS

The pupil profile must be drawn up to take into account the academic background of the pupil and also apposite affective factors. Each factor is allocated a certain number of points and candidates should be accepted on the basis of the total number of points scored.

The academic background of the applicant is divided into two aspects:
- proven ability, as shown by the pupil's Standard 7 academic results
- potential ability, as indicated by the candidate's IQ

The suggested points structure is as follows:

POINTS / SUBJECT	0	1	2	3
First Language (home language)	< 60%	60-69%	70-79%	> 80%
Mathematics	< 70%	70-79%	80-89%	> 90%
General Science	< 60%	60-69%	70-79%	> 80%
Aggregate of all subjects	< 60%	60-69%	70-79%	> 80%
IQ	< 112	112-118	119-127	> 127

Maximum number of points: 15

The affective traits of the applicant are also divided into two main areas:
- Personality traits of the pupil: Judgement on each apposite trait is provided by the principal/teacher-counsellor on a 5-point scale.
- Interests of the pupil: Information as to the pupil's interest in Mathematics and Science is obtained from a standardised interest questionnaire (Cape Education Department [5]) and the scores thereon transformed to a 5-point scale.

The nine affective factors that will be taken into account are
- Motivation
- Perseverance in tasks
- Ability to handle 7 subjects
- Demonstrated interest in computers
- Dependent/Independent learning habits
- The need for social interaction
- Attention that pupil pays to detail
- Interest in Mathematics
- Interest in Science

The points thus gained are to be scaled down to a third so that the maximum number is 15, thus giving equal weighting to these factors and the academic background of the pupil.

As far as the authors are aware, no pupil profile drawn up for Computer Studies combines the affective and the cognitive in the way that this one does. It is an experimental profile which must be tested against the results achieved by the pupils in Computer Studies and the drop-out rate obtained.

It can be argued that there is no reference in the criteria to logical thinking ability and that this is a serious omission. This is an omission but it is hoped that part of the marks that are gained by pupils (in Mathematics especially) are obtained because the pupils think logically. It has been suggested that an aptitude test consisting of questions in Mathematics and the pupil's First Language which centre on logical thinking ability be developed. This test would have to be standardised for Standard 7 applicants. It was estimated that this standardisation process could take up to 3 years, and the test would have to be evaluated continually. This has not yet been attempted.

PRACTICAL APPLICATION OF THE SELECTION CRITERIA

The profile selection procedure as outlined above was used in 1988 to select the pupils to start the course in 1989 and is being used to select the candidates to begin in 1990. Of the 641 candidates accepted in 1989, 96 candidates (14.9%) dropped out during the course of the year. This compares very favourably with the previous drop-out rate in Standard 8 of 36%. It is possible that some candidates will decide during the summer vacation to discontinue. The final figures, which will include these candidates who do not begin Standard 9, will be available in March 1990.

Preliminary analysis of the drop-out group leads to the following two observations:

Sixty percent of candidates gave "pressure reasons" for giving up Computer Studies, 16% "lack of ability reasons" and 14% gave "demotivating reasons". A comparison of these results with those obtained previously (as outlined above), appears to show that the selection criteria are working, but closer analysis suggests that candidates (intentionally or in an act of unconscious selfdeception) may supply an incorrect reason for leaving. The pupil profile of many of those candidates who gave a "pressure reason" for leaving, revealed other, perhaps more likely, reasons.

The amount of interest in computers demonstrated by pupils before starting the course (one of the affective factors measured on a scale of 0 to 5), was noticeably less (0.49) in those pupils who dropped out of the course than in their counterparts who remained on the course. From this it would appear that interest in computers is of great importance in the first year.

CONCLUSION

While the initial results of this research are promising, the drop-out rates in subsequent standards will only become known with the passing of time. Naturally the authors hope that the present low drop-out rate will be maintained and will present the very latest position when the paper is presented.

BIBLIOGRAPHY AND REFERENCES

[1] Anon, Aptitude Tests Abused and Not Taken Seriously Computer Week 10(33) (1987), 9.

[2] Calitz, P., Evaluation of the Aptitudes of Prospective Computer Science Students with a view to the Development of a Computer Aided Testing Program (University of Port Elizabeth, Port Elizabeth, Unpublished treatise, 1984).

[3] Cape Education Department, Taking a Seventh Subject (excluding Computer Studies) Circular No. 81 (Cape Education Department, Cape Town, 1987).

[4] Cape Education Department, Senior Secondary Course Syllabus for Computer Studies Higher Grade (Cape Education Department, Cape Town, 1985).

[5] Cape Education Department, KODUS Interest Questionnaire (CED Psychological and Guidance Services in collaboration with the Bureau for Student Counselling, University of Stellenbosch, Cape Town, 1978).

[6] Konvalina, J. et.al., Identifying Factors Influencing Computer Science Aptitude and Achievement, AEDS Journal 16(2) (1983) pp. 106-112.

[7] Mohamedali, M.H. et.al., Factors Affecting Microcomputer Use and Programming Ability of Secondary School Children, Journal of Computer Assisted Learning 3 (1987) pp. 224-239.

[8] Mulder, J.C., Statistical Techniques in Education, (HAUM, Pretoria, 1982).

[9] Norton, D.A., Criteria for Selecting Pupils for Computer Studies in Standard 8 (Cape Education Department, Cape Town, Unpublished project report, 1988).

[10] Sorge, D.H. and Wark, L.K., Factors for Success as a Computer Science Major, AEDS Journal 17(4) (1984), pp. 36-45.

[11] Stevens, D.J., Cognitive Processes and Success of Students in Instructional Computer Courses, AEDS Journal 16(4) (1983), pp. 228-233.

[12] Webb, N.M., Microcomputer Learning in Small Groups: Cognitive Requirements and Group Processes, Journal of Educational Psychology 76(6) (1984), pp. 1076-1088.

[13] Webb, N.M., Cognitive Requirements of Learning Computer Programming in Group and Individual Settings, AEDS Journal 18(3) (1985), pp. 183-194.

[14] Wileman, S. et.al., Factors Influencing Success in Beginning Computer Science Courses, Journal of Educational Research 74(4) (1981), pp. 223-226.

[15] Witkin, H.A. et.al., Field-dependent and Field-independent Styles and their Educational Implications, Review of Educational Research 47(1) (1977), pp. 1-64.

APPENDIX A

THE LOCAL EDUCATION SYSTEM

Twelve years of schooling are given, starting in Substandards A and B and followed by Standards 1 through 10. Pupils start school in their sixth year and the average school-leaving age is approximately 18. The 12 years are divided into four phases: Junior Primary (Substandards A and B and Standard 1),; Senior Primary (Standards 2 through 4); Junior Secondary (Standards 5 through 7); and Senior Secondary (Standards 8, 9 and 10).

Computer Studies: A Senior Certificate examination subject. Pupils are selected at the end of the Junior Secondary phase to take Computer Studies in their final three years of schooling.

Extramural activities: It is customary for schools to provide their pupils with facilities for and to organise and run sporting and cultural activities (such as debating societies and amateur dramatics) after normal school hours.

First Language: Many of the pupils in the sample group do not have English as a home language. The pupil's first language is considered to be the pupil's home language.

Senior Certificate: An external examination which Standard 10 pupils write as the culmination of their twelve years of schooling.

Standard 7: The final year in the Junior Secondary phase at the end of which pupils choose the subjects that they are going to take in their final three years of schooling. This choice more often than not determines their life direction.

Superintendent of Education: School inspector.

Teacher-counsellor: a teacher who has been trained as a psychologist.

Computers in Education
A. McDougall and C. Dowling (Editors)
Elsevier Science Publishers B.V. (North-Holland)
IFIP, 1990

A PROPOSAL TO ANSWER THE NECESSITY TO EVALUATE COMPUTER SOFTWARE

M. Angélica OLIVARES. Z.; Pierina ZANOCCO. S.; Marta RIVEROS. R.; Sofía ROEPKE. D.

Pontificia Universidad Católica de Chile. Facultad de Educación. P.O. Box 114-D
Santiago, Chile.

The incorporation of computers in the educational centers has meant the acquisition and use of software usually sold in the market as educational SW, without actually satisfying educational demands, mainly because their educational quality has not been analysed. Many of these pieces of software supposed to be useful in developing learning, some of which refers to the subject content of de compulsory study plan for students at different levels. This work presents a set of principles that must be taken into account to give an educational quality to a SW. This would be based on such principles -intentionality, technicality, communicability, action, effectiveness, feedback, moderation.
An instrument was built which enables the user to determine the degree in which the SW has the condition of educational. The evaluating categories and operative criteria are previously precised. This allow to establish which is the educational valve of SW on the basis of the opinions already gathered and analised.

1. INTRODUCTION

A requirement that must be attended before developing an educational process, in which computer software is used as the only and master means, specially in at a distance educational strategy, is that related to the establishment of qualities, restrictions and possibilities that such resource offers to the achievement of a highly efficient and absolutely effective educational process.
It is important to attend such requirement due to the increase in the use of this resource, which often has not been produced with enough direct share of teachers. However, it is offered in the market with an increasing agressive publicity -considered as educational as appointed to the objectives achievement of official programs.
In relation with those SW that are sold under the qualification of educative, there are opposite opinions related to their real quality of such, then it appears as necessary to look for a procedure that permits to judge specially the software educational value of those that will be used either as the only or as master means in a distance educational process.

2. BASIS TO ELABORATE A DESIGN FOR EVALUATION

The objective to be evaluated is a computer software as regards its educational character, therefore we have to keep in mind the following as a basis:

· The principles, were these considered, it would be easer to regard the object, as educational.
· The object analysis perspectives from the different people involved in the process.
· The moment and the way of using the means in the educational strategy.
· The purposes of the evaluation.

2.1. Which are the postulated principles for an educational SW?

Taking into account that the educational process must make its ultimate aim explicit through one more purposes, that these must tend to desireable changes in the students, that the achievements of these purpose demands a significative and achieved communication process, an active share, an appropriate, convenient feedback, and a moderate use of means. Then in order to consider a computer software to be educational, it must respect the following principles: intentionality, technicality, communicability, action, effectiveness, feedback, sobriety.
The principle of "intentionality" refers to the relatively permanent change of conduct that the user experiences as a result of the acquired knowledge and experience through the SW use. This change must be the one explicitily desired and stated to be obtained in the learning process and if other changes are achieved, these must enhance the personal development of the user.
The principle of "technicality" refers to the practical and correct, rational use of the technical resources, and information that the computer engineering offers, the science of the audio-visual communication and the pedagogic science.
Some aspects that come from this principle -and which must be regarded as an element to be evaluated- are the following: included means, screen contents, programming structure, didactics organization.
By "communicability" it is understood the cacapacity that the software must have to trans-

mit with clearness, adjustment, opportunity, significance and fitting the message, using the language in an adequate way, so that the user can decode it without problems, to perform the various actions that can take him to achieve a learning process.
The principle of "action" is related with the fact that it is the person who learns, the one who must act. Since it is by his performed action, through which the desired change will be carried out, then we have to demand the performance of certain activities from the user and enable him to perform others.
By "feedback" it is undertood the effect that is present in terms of the user conduct; such effect is useful to regulate the learning process according to the reached results. It constitutes and enhancing element of the learning process when it is performed in an adequate and convenient way.
The principle of "effectiveness" is related to the control of results achieved by the user when he interacts with the SW.
The principle of "moderation" is related to the simplicity both in the equipment as well as in the activities, requirements and demanded efforts.
An educational software is, therefore, that which respects the principles mentioned above. One which enables an efficient learning in the user who is meant to use it.

2.2. Which are the analysis perspectives of a SW?

The perspectives from which a computer software can be observed and analyzed are too many to be able to make any statements about it. One could be interested in, for example, the used way in the means (code), the content, the present dynamic (rhythm), the possibilities of action that it offers, and that demands, interactions that allow with the user, necessary attached resources...
Undoubtedly, no matter which the perspectives might be, these must be performed having as basis and basic ideas the postulated principles for an educational software.

2.3. SW mode and moment of use

Another basic element to consider is related to the mode and moment of using the computer resource. If its use could be developed to constitute the master means, or maybe the only one, then two evaluating formative moments would be necessary for a self-learning process.
One performed by the "external" evaluators or teacher, and the other by the user himself. On the other hand, if its use were incorporated to a strategy that demands other complementary or master means, and an interpersonal an group interaction, then the evaluating process may turn more complex. Additionally, all these participating in the educational process will be able to take part, besides external evaluators, specialists in learning methodology and audio-visual communication, among others.
The SW could be used in different moments of the process and in each one of these with a prevailing intentionality. Thus, at the beginning it may be used with a motivational purpose, or else, to solve the lack of necessary learnings. During the development, it may be used as a means to provide students with learning as a source or practice. It may be also used to reinforce and eventually to check the reached achievements in each opportunity of use. Its fundamental aim may be different and that would lead to focus the evaluating process on certain aspects. However, in all of them it would be necessary to judge its effectiveness for the achievement of the expected purpose.

2.4. SW evaluation purposes

Unquestionably, the evaluation purpose constitute a high outstanding aspect inside the set of principles to be considered. It will depend, to certain extent, on the complexity level and involvement of these, the greater or less complexity of the evaluating process itself.
A purpose could be to determine the real educational quality of these in order to recomend its use at national level in a teaching-learning process for a certain course or level. This constitutes a purpose that demands the performing of a long and complex evaluating process, in which different people, at several stages, will take part.
Other more specific purposes, are related to the up dating degree of the methodologic approach, with the content truthfulness, with the use effectiveness, etc. These are less complex than the above mentioned and therefore imply less complex evaluating processes.

3. WHO WOULD HAVE TO JUDGE A COMPUTER SW?

- Specialist in informatic communication (programmer).
- Specialist in audio-visual communication.
- General extern evaluator.
- Methodologist.
- Subject Teacher.
- Student.
- Etc.

4. EVALUATING QUESTIONS

Many questions demanding the development of an evaluating process can be asked by the different actors involved in the educational process. Maybe, the most outstanding could be those that arise from teachers and that are related to the aspects that can be judged before using the SW with the students. Others arise when using the SW, and others deal with the reached achievements as a consequence of SW use.
The above, does not eliminate the possibility and importance of considering evaluation ques-

tions that arise from other users, and among these, students themselves. Some questions that can be stated, or that could be answered by the students themselves this being quite interesing, are refered to their when they are using the SW and to what they are reach or learn through this computer means.
The following sketch is shown as an example. The people who constitute a source of evaluating questions, and some questions stated stages. In order to be answered they would demand the development of a previously planned evaluating process.

4.1. Which aspects would be interesting for the evaluators to judge?

1. Specialist in informatic communication
   - Does the SW make use of equipment potentiality?
   - Is the programming technique used appropriate?
   - Is the language and programming technique correct?
   - And...

2. Specialist in audio-visual communication
   - Is the use of technology correct and adequate?
   - Is there any originality in the communicative approach?
   - Which are the most outstanding technographical and communicative aspects on the positive and negative side that offers the SW?
   - And...

3. General external evaluator
   - To what extent are the postulated principles considered for an educational SW?
   - And...

4. Metodologist
   - Is the methodological approach up to date and significant?
   - Is the SW content truthful?
   - When and through which strategy it is advisable to use SW in a learning-teaching process?
   - Is the SW adequate for the offered level?
   - Which present methodologic aspects in the SW are related to the positive reached achievements by the students?
   - And...

5. Subject Teacher
   - Does he make acquisition of programming aims easier?
   - What requirement does he demand from the students so use can be effective?
   - Is the interaction that he provides the most adequate to each student?
   - Which adventageous and harmful reactions are developed in the students through SW use?
   - Do the students get the expected aims?
   - Which effects (results) are obtained?
   - Is the SW content truthful?
   - And...

6. Student
   - What did I learn in SW?
   - What usefulness did I get from the SW use?
   - How do I feel when I use it?
   - To what extent was I encouraged by the SW?
   - And...

5. INFORMATION SOURCE

The different evaluating questions require to get in touch with various information sources. These can be the following:
a. Persons: teachers, students, specialists in technography and informatic and audio-visual communication, methodologists, etc.
b. Documents: tests, student mark reports.

6. PROCEDURES TO COLLECT THE INFORMATION

To get the necessary information of the different sources, various procedures may be necessary. The following may be some of them:
a. Polls.
b. Observations.
c. Tests.
Thus, for the questions that the external evaluators or teachers, can state themselves, regarding aspects to be judged before using the SW with the students, the most relevant procedure is the poll. Whereas, for those related to the reactions developed during the use of SW the most suitable is the observation. On the other hand, to detect the achievement of expected learning processes the most appropriate procedure could be the test.

7. NECESSARY INSTRUMENTS TO RECORD THE INFORMATION

The working process of the necessary instrument(s) involves the fulfillment of the following:
- Clear definition of the field to be evaluated.
- Setting up the conceptualization that will be the basis of the following stages.
- Identification of the dimensions involved in the concept.
- Identification of the descriptive and valve aspects that arise from the evaluating problem and the correspondant conceptualization.
- Validity of the concept(s), dimensions and registers. Perhaps, the most convenient procedure is the judges criteria.
- Development of the that may be necessary according to the results of point precedent.
- Working of reactives or elements that will

form constitute the instrument. If this is a pattern to register the observed, then it will be necessary to write proposals in relation with the matters that must does not mean that the proposal is formulated negatively but that includes a non-desirable aspect to be observed.

If the required procedure corresponds to a poll of opinion, the elements that constitutes the instrument can be either questions or Likert type, or semantic differential types scales.

If the necessary procedure corresponds to a test, the questions or reactives will have to be written in such a way that when students answer them, it will enable to infer the learning of the stated aims which constituted one of the basic purposes of the learning-teaching process that considers the computer SW as an important resource.

In any case, the reactives or elements that will make up the instrument must be submilted to a validity process and also to one that allows to be sure to a great extent that the information to be collected will have at least an acceptable objectivity and releability.

8. ANALYSIS OF THE COLLECTED INFORMATION

The required depends directly on the stated evaluating questions. However, they often use to be stated in such a way that is not clear which the evaluating contitions are. Therefore, it will be necessary to define the categories to be used in the given statements regarding the quality considered. Having done this it is necessary to specify the operative criteria.

For instance, if we ar interested in judging the "Identification" given by the SW authors, then some of the evaluating categories to be used might be: complete, sufficient, insufficient.

The corresponding evaluating criteria for these may be: if an 80% or more of the element necessary to identify a SW, then it would be classified as "complete".

If there is only a range between 85 and 50% of the element a present it would be classified as "sufficient".

If there were less than a 50% of the elements required for the identification, then it would correspond to an "insufficient" category.

As regards both descriptive and value aspect the following criteria may be used in order to give a comprehensive value judgement from the previously mentioned.

Categories	Operative criterias
Excellent	90-100 of the principles in the "excellent" category and the rest in the "good" category.
Good	At least 75% of the principles in the "good" category an the rest in the "fair" category"
Fair	At least all the principles in the "fair" category.
Deficient	Some principle in the "deficient" category.

In order to give a global judgement of the SW the following operative criteria may be used:

Categories	Operative criteria Part				
	I	Ex D.	Des.	Of V.	G.J.
Ex.	C	C	E	Ex	HP
G.	S	S	G	G	FP
F.	S	S	F	F	FN
D.	I	I	D	D	HN

Ex = Excellent
G = Good
F = Fair
D = Deficient
I = Insufficient
C = Complete
S = Sufficient
Des = Descriptive
Of V = Of Value
GJ = Global Judgement
HP = High Positive
FP = Fairly Positive
FN = Fairly Negative
HN = Highly Negative

9. FINAL COMMENTS

Undoubtedly, the necessity of evaluating the educational SW must be taken into account. This imply a complex work which under no circunstances can be improvised, it must be throughly planned. This is specially neccessary when the SW is used in distance education systems.

Computers in Education
A. McDougall and C. Dowling (Editors)
Elsevier Science Publishers B.V. (North-Holland)
IFIP, 1990

COMPUTERS AND GENRE: A PEDAGOGY OF EMPOWERMENT

Bob Pendreigh

Learning Technology Services, Department of Education, Education House, 30 Mary Street, Brisbane, Queensland, Australia. 4000.

Hope was expressed in 1985 that computers would be used as liberating tools in schools as they are today. This paper compares the hopes of 1985 with the realities of 1990, especially in regard to the teaching of writing. A teaching model is developed whereby the technology of computer is allied to genre-based writing methodology.

1. INTRODUCTION

In 1985, Daniel Chandler [1] in the publication 'Computers and Literacy' observed that 'the critical factor is our attitude towards both technology and the nature of learning'. Furthermore, he foreshadowed that 'in schools as they are today, it is amongst primary school teachers and teachers of English in the secondary school that some hope may lie for the appropriate use of the computer as a liberating tool...'

The field of study encompassed by the terms 'computers and literacy' is a truly fascinating enterprise, perhaps because of the emerging and temporal nature of our learning - what was not feasible even a year ago, may now be entirely practicable and manageable. Of particular consideration here is the effectiveness of computers to the teaching and learning of writing.

Firstly however, we need to examine what evidences are available, either from published educational research, or from observed educational practice, that would indicate that writers in primary or secondary schools are appropriating the technology offered by the computer as a liberating tool?

2. WORD PROCESSING AND WRITING IMPROVEMENT: CURRENT RESEARCH

Much has been made of the value of a word processor to the improvement of writing skills. However an examination of recently published research papers reveals a mixed bag of results.

Claims for positive connections between word processing facilities and writing improvement are that:

- word processing has a positive effect on the quality of writing: McAllister & Louth [2];
- reluctant writers tended to write longer word processed stories: Outhred [3];
- word processors are shown to be effective tools in encouraging students to write: Little [4];
- word processors eliminate the physical barrier that young writers experience as they struggle to make letters: Snyder [5];
- word processing and spelling checker programs improve spelling skills: Elkins [6];
- word processors generate student interest and involvement in learning to write: McGarvey [7];
- microcomputers change student writing behaviour, create a writing community, cause teachers to learn with students: Muldrow [8].

Conversely, there are contemporary publications that indicate:

- computer science students used more sophisticated program features of the word processor but student writing did not improve significantly with program use: Monahan [9];
- results suggested that word processing did not encourage students to write more extensively: Harris [10];
- while word processors may have increased writing speed they cannot ensure improved writing quality: Booth [11];
- results of revision analysis revealed that there are more changes in essays written entirely by pen than those written by computer: Freedman & Clarke [12].

While attitudinal data from teachers and students favoured computers, it seems that the quality of the writing might not necessarily or automatically improve because of the employment of a word processor. I would suggest here that the liberating effect of computer tools as hoped for by Chandler in 1985, especially as regards the writing process, has been minimal to say the least. I would further suggest that two factors which have minimised the expected liberating effects of computer technology in regard to writing are strongly connected to writing methodology and are:

(i) the limitations within the prevailing interpretations of the process approach to writing as proposed by Graves [13] and Walshe [14]; and

(ii) poorly based writing instruction, not only in secondary English, but across all areas of the secondary curriculum

3. THE COMPUTER AND CURRENT WRITING METHODOLOGIES

In primary schools particularly, the process approach to writing as proposed by Graves has had a transformational effect on the earlier traditional approaches of the seventies that focused exclusively on marking and correction of the students' texts by the teacher. The process approach has forever wiped out the notion of 'one shot' writing and, in addition, may have made an immense contribution to the improvement of understandings between teacher and students. Unfortunately, the over-arching tendency for students to write narratives, especially personal narratives, is a direct result of the prevailing interpretations of Graves' methodology. Skill in writing narratives alone does not necessarily empower writers or give them command and control over the forms of writing that are a pre-requisite for success across all curriculum areas. While the narrative may be individually meaningful and personally relevant to the writer, it is an inappropriate form for communication in most curriculum areas, in the workplace and between various groups in a society.

Further limitations of the Graves methodology have been pointed out by advocates of the genre-based approach to writing such as Christie et al [15] who maintain that 'the process approach with its preoccupation at leaving children alone to work things out for themselves actually sells children short, denying them all the practical advice, modelling, guidance and direction that good teaching is supposed to be all about'.

The genrists take their theoretical base from the social theories of language, particularly systemic linguistics. They point out that language is social in origin and nature (rather than individual and psychological) and that certain forms of language, genres, have arisen within various cultures and sub-cultures in order to make meaning and to get things done. These practitioners have developed teaching models to give students knowledge of, and control over, the powerful written genres with a view to the development of social literacy. The teacher as caretaker/writer and the students as learner/writers jointly construct the stages of the written genre. Most importantly, the teacher provides overt modelling, guidance and instruction as to the appropriate linguistic features of the genre under construction before the students begin the required writing task.

I would suggest here that the possibilities for computer technology to empower learners under the Graves' process approach are minimal because of the limited range of genres it generated and the lack of direct teacher guidance provided during production. However, the application of computer technology to the genre-based approaches has huge possibilities for both social literacy and learner empowerment. There is however, one very important pro-

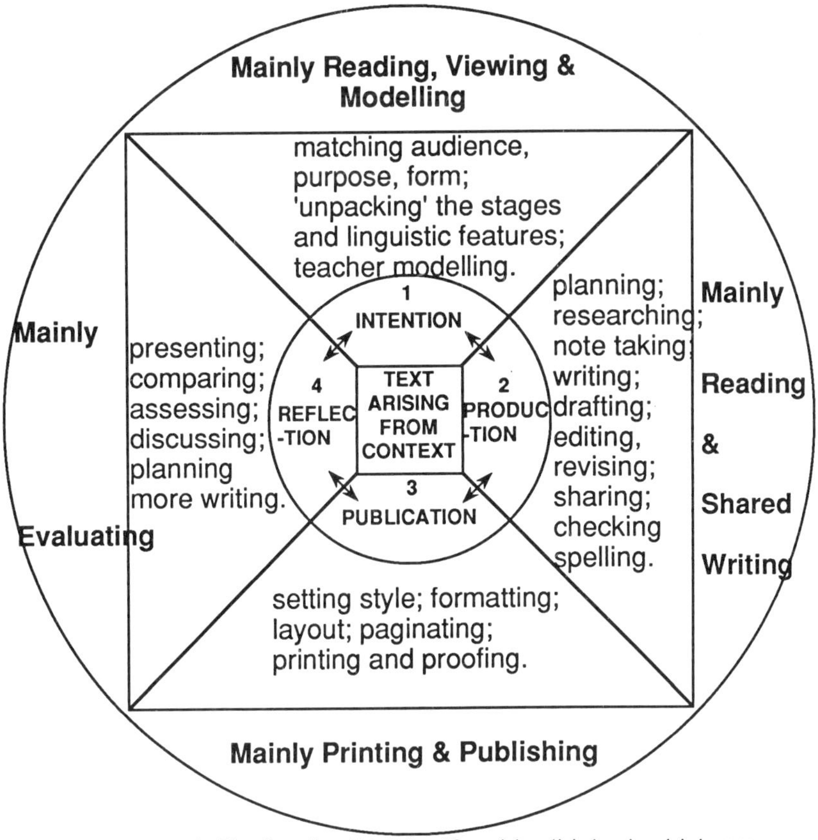

Figure 1. The Reading/Writing/Speaking/Listening Linkages In the Genre-based Approach.

viso, namely, that the advocates of genre-based approach recognize that the powerful written genres that are passed between groups in today's society are 'computer mediated'. The term 'computer mediated' is used to suggest that the influence of the computer is not neutral. It has its own pervasive effect on the written forms as they stand. The computer also affects the processes by which written texts are produced and the way that they are passed from one place to another. Computers and literacy are thus inextricably linked. Computers are changing the dimensions of literacy and literacy education is making functional demands on computers. In one sense, each is in the process of re-defining the other.

4. A TEACHING MODEL AND THE COMPUTER TOOLS

While genre theory is founded on extensive studies in systemic linguistics, what is required is a teaching model that translates such theory and methodology into manageable classroom practice. Such a teaching model appears as Fig. 1. Most significantly, it assumes and utilises the computer as a writing tool to understand, produce, publish and disseminate the particular genre under consideration in any curriculum area.

Any teaching model is of course an incomplete and imperfect description of the action and interaction of writers in a classroom or workshop situation. The word 'mainly' is used to reflect what is the predominant form of communication at any stage. It is of course impossible in real terms to disassociate speaking from reading from writing from listening.

Both the teacher as caretaker/writer and the student as learner/writer need to understand the four stages of the process - intention, production, publication and reflection. While these stages are sequential, they are not lock-step. In the real classroom situation there would be much 'to-ing' and 'fro-ing' between the stages according to such factors as the writing ability and progress of the learners, their degree of familiarity with the genre to be written, the amount of time available to complete the task and one hundred other considerations particular to any classroom. There is, as well, an important assumption that speaking by the teacher and by the students will occur throughout, but this is difficult to show on the model. The whole process is recursive as further attempts are made at writing in the current genre or exploring new genre.

5. THE GENRE AND THE DEMANDS OF THE CURRICULUM

One of the advantages of introducing the genre-based model to secondary teachers from all curriculum areas, not just teachers of English, is that such teachers already have an inherent (if not overt) understanding of the genre which they expect their students to employ - the science teacher expects a science experiment to be written in a certain way, the history teacher has an expectation of the written structure of a biography, the geography teacher has expectations of how the results of a field trip should be presented and the commerce teacher has an expectation that students will use the written genres that are employed to make meaning in the commercial world.

Under the present writing methodologies observed in secondary schools, many teachers have great expectations of how written work should appear, but students have almost the sole responsibility for the generating the written product. In many cases because of a shortage of time or a lack of understanding of the dimensions of the writing task, students are required to undertake the written assignment for homework. This might be minimally sufficient for students who have had some exposure to the requirements of the genre or who can gain some guidance from parents who already have some understanding of the generic demands. It is however almost impossible for those students who have never encountered such generic textual demands either at school or in any part of their normal home life.

Practising teachers can make a useful start to using the methodology and the teaching model by focusing on those curriculum genre whose operation they already understand. With practice and experience, the teacher can gradually understand, collect and add many more useful genres as different demands arise in the curriculum areas or beyond. Such collections of information on generic forms could be assembled as instructional materials produced under hypermedia packages. Jonassen [15] describes hypermedia as a knowledge representation format that empowers instructional design and has special application in building active structural networks and generative learning.

The advantages of using such powerful and empowering software are that the teacher (or the student) can exert two levels of control over the text. The first level of control is over the text itself. By using the facilities of a modern word processor, the teacher can engage in a process of dynamic text modelling. The text becomes almost like clay in the hands of a craftsperson as the teacher models how to construct the stages of the genre. Then, using hypermedia packages, the second level of control is over information about the genre - the stages and the linguistic features. These second-level facilities - questions, comments, suggestions, teaching notes and reminders, may be scattered around the text itself as it appears on the screen, but they are not usually printed when a paper copy is produced. Such second level text control can in fact act as 'scaffolding' to aid both the teacher and the student in the construction of the genre. They may appear as icons under a control toggle that lead us to virtual libraries of information about how, when, where or why such genre have an application. Such icons or questions may toggle access to other related technologies such as video-disk presentations or to mountains of information stored under CD ROM. The possibilities are immense and the technology is available now.

Dynamic text modelling and hypermedia collections of written genres are of greatest value when both the teacher as caretaker/writer and the students as learner/writers have access to the same configuration of hardware and software. Thus it is possible for the teacher to work in the mode of 'do as I do' rather than 'do as I say'. This is a very powerful idea that has thus far been ignored under the current writing methodologies described earlier. The situation whereby the medium of instruction by the teacher is also the medium of composition by the students offers a very powerful learning technology for the teaching and learning of writing.

6. GENRE, COMPUTERS AND THE CHANGING NATURE OF LITERACY

The fascinating thing about genre is that they emerge from social settings or discourses and, while some are of ancient origins eg the doctoral thesis, others are constantly being created as communicating humans have a need to create shared meanings in new contexts. The way one might search out and become familiar with generic types is almost the same process as the way that an anthropologist collects cultural artifacts. The artifact, in this case, the written genre, says as much about the society from which originated as it does about itself.

It is at this point that we again introduce the fundamental connection between computers and literacy - not only are computers the powerful tools by which powerful groups in today's society construct and disseminate the paper-based publications of written genres, the computer and its related technologies are conducive to the creation of new genre. Further, we can to some extent become anthropological observers of our own age.

The apparent assumptions in the model above is that at some stage or other the writing is going to be 'committed to paper' as we commonly say. However, especially in an electronically networked society, this is not always the case. There are new possibilities for genre to emerge that are created on the screen and serve their meaning making functions on the screen without ever having to be committed to paper. The possibilities in such curriculum areas as film and media studies are enormously attractive. By adapting the teaching model above and by using such commonly available pieces of software such as Show Partner (a Microsoft product) or Hypercard (an Apple product), teachers of media studies can guide students in the creation of scripted, dynamic, colourful presentations of mobile text and graphics that communicate in a way that paper based publications can never hope to match.

This adds another dimension to our intention to empower learners and use liberating tools. When a student comes to understand what makes a genre 'tick', as they say, he or she can better understand the techniques whereby such people as the professional creators of TV commercials or persuasive authors, skilfully position the viewer or the reader towards the acceptance of the message - no matter how subtle or vulgar or biased the message may be. Christie [17] suggests that 'we must teach our students both to explore and to challenge what written authorities offer them, and to become in a sense what Kress [18] has called 'resistant readers'. In addition we must teach them to behave responsibly themselves, carefully researching whatever is to be written, and freely acknowledging the problematic and/or unknown aspects of the fields with which they are dealing'.

7. CONCLUSION

The teaching model described in this paper was designed to promote such a healthy critical approach. For teachers and students in classrooms with computer facilities, it provides for the opportunity to become engaged or immersed in the text, and to see where such text might be usefully employed, either in the school context or beyond. The model has been specifically designed to provide the opportunity for teachers to overtly model the textual demands of the genre, to provide feedback to individuals and groups as they begin to make progressive approximations to the required genre.

What is required is the opportunity for practising teachers with access to computers to make the connections between the opportunities offered by the technology and learning possibilities described in the model. When secondary teachers in particular, make the connections between the technology and the learning, we might again have cause to be hopeful that computers will be appropriately used as liberating tools - both for the teacher and the student.

REFERENCES

1. Chandler D and Marcus S, 1985, Computers and Literacy, Open University Press, p11.
2. McAllister C & Louth R,1988, 'The Effect of Word Processing on the Quality of Basic Writers' Revisions', Journal of Research in the Teaching of English; B22 N4 P 417-427 Dec 1988.
3. Outhred L, 1987, 'To Write or Not to Write; Does Using a Word Processor Assist Reluctant Writers?', Australia and New Zealand Journal of Developmental Disabilities, Vol 13 N4 p 211-217, Dec 1987.
4. Little C, 1988, 'Teaching Writing with Word Processors' in Teaching Sociology Vol 16 N3 p 272-274, July 1988.
5. Snyder L, 1987, 'Computers Can Improve Your Children's Writing Skills', PTA Today; Vol 12 N3 p28-29, Dec-Jan 1987.
6. Elkins J, 1986, 'Self Help for Older Writers with Spelling and Composing Difficulties; Using the Word Processor and Spelling Checker' Exceptional Child, Vol 33 N1 p73-76. March 1986.
7. McGarvey J, 1986, 'Word Processors Let Our Kids Relish Writing Class', American School Board Journal, Vol 173 N10 p34, Oct 1986.
8. Muldrow E, 1986, 'On Writing and Word processors in the Ninth grade Classroom', English Journal, Vol 75, N5 P84-86, Sept 1986.
9. Monahan B D, 1986, 'The Relationship Between Previous Training in Computer Science and the Acquisition of Word Processing Skills', Educational Technology. V 26 N3 P22-25, March 1986.
10. Harris J, 1985, 'Student Writers and Word Processing; A Preliminary Evaluation', College Composition and Communication, B36 N3 p323-330. Oct 1985.
11. Booth W, 1984, 'Catching the Overflow', College English, Vol 46 N2 p140-143, Feb 1984.
12. Freedman A and Clarke L, 1988, 'The Effect of Computer Technology on Composing Processes and Written Products of Grade 8 and Grade 12 Students', Education and Technology Series, 1988.
13. Graves D H, 1983, Writing: Teachers and Children at Work, Heinemann Educational Books, Exeter.
14. Walshe R D, 1981, Donald Graves in Australia - Children Want to Write, PETA, Roselle, NSW.
15. Christie F, 1989a, Writing in Schools; Study Guide, Deakin University Press, Geelong. p62.
16. Jonassen D, 1986. 'Hypertext Principles for Text and Courseware Design', Educational Psychologist, 21, 4, p 269-292.
17. Christie G, 1989b, Writing in Schools; A Reader, Deakin University Press, Geelong, p27.
18. Kress G, 1985, Linguistic Processes in Sociocultural Practice (ECS806 Sociocultural Aspects of Language and Education), Deakin University Press, Geelong.

Computers in Education
A. McDougall and C. Dowling (Editors)
Elsevier Science Publishers B.V. (North-Holland)

COMPUTER EQUITY FOR GIRLS: WHAT KEEPS IT FROM HAPPENING?

JO SANDERS

Women's Action Alliance, 370 Lexington Avenue, New York, New York 10017, United States

This paper explains a number of everyday, human, and real-life reasons for the difficulty in achieving computer equity for girls, or the rough equality of computer use between boys and girls, based on the author's many years of experience in technology equity work in the schools.

Among the many things I have learned in ten years of working on sex equity and technology in the schools, perhaps the most significant are the everyday, human reasons for the lack of progress in equalizing girls' computer use in schools with that of boys. The lack of progress is especially frustrating in view of the fact that it is far easier to close the computer gender gap in a school than to get a faculty started on addressing the problem in the first place.

Equity and technology work is an excellent vantage point from which to make observations about the state of sex equity in our schools, focusing as it does on academic courses (computers, science, and math), career exploration and preparation, and employment issues for girls and women. This work has taken me into elementary schools, junior high and middle schools, high schools, and postsecondary community colleges, technical institutes, and vocational-technical schools. I have worked with -- and listened to -- students (children to adults) classroom teachers, administrators, counselors, recruitment and placement staff, and employers; researchers and analysts, policy developers, and government officials.

This paper, then, is a report from the front lines, from someone who "translates" theoretical education research into programs and materials that are used in schools for enabling girls and women to lead lives of self-respect and economic self-sufficiency.

A recent incident provides the context. A math and science magnet high school history teacher invited me to teach a lesson won women in modern society to his students. After the class I showed him the material I had brought with me on women in the labor force, housework, women in politics, science and business, and more. I showed him the figures on women in technology occupations: in 1987, 7 percent of engineers, 33 percent of systems analysts, 8 percent of physicists and astronomers, 11 percent of geologists, 35 percent of science technicians, 4 percent of airplane pilots. I showed him how men outearned women in every case. He seemed pleased to have all this information, saying he would use it in his classes.

Suddenly, he looked up and exclaimed with great consternation, "Hold it, I think I'm getting the picture. You're not talking about equality of opportunity. You're talking about equality of results!" It is a profoundly important distinction.

Behind what he said is a conflict at the heart of the historic American ideal of equality of opportunity, our conviction that like Horatio Alger, each of us can rise as high as our talent permits. Recognizing that this ideal was gravely flawed in practice, the civil rights movement of the sixties expressed itself in legislation promising that e=henceforth all artificial barriers to citizens' accomplishments in public life would be removed, freeing everyone to attain the best education and job she or he was capable of, regardless of race, sex, national origin, or disability.

Special educational and employment programs for groups at the bottom of the national scale were initially approved as a means of dismantling the artificial barriers of discrimination.

After a decade or two of civil rights legislation and special programs, equality of opportunity is now widely thought to be a reality. Any remaining differences in educational, occupational or economic attainments among individuals or groups are seen by many as due to inborn factors which are unchangeable, their outcomes simply a fact of life. Any further attempts to raise the attainment level of underachieving groups is now given the pejorative term "social engineering," meaning the artificial enhancement of an undeserving group usually at the expense of a deserving one. This is where the consternation in the teacher's voice came from.

Many people are certain that males and females are innately and genetically different in ways that extend far beyond our reproductive systems because there is plenty of "evidence" for it: in the aggregate, males are interested in computers and females are not, males are good with machines and females are not, the world's great scientists and mathematicians have been male and not female, and so forth. However, the difficulty I have with the premise of innate inequality is that it is unprovable: we have not, nor will we ever, observe male and female children grow from birth to maturity without any environmental influences whatsoever.

I freely admit that my assumption that females and males are, in the aggregate, equal in their abilities is just as unprovable. It is precisely the unprovability that makes me assume it. After all, if males and females are unequal at birth and we try to make them equal as adults, all we have done is give ourselves useless trouble. If, however, they are inherently equal at birth and we permit environmental conditions to make them unequal as adults, we have committed a great injustice. We are therefore obliged to assume that equality of results is the norm. Special efforts and programs designed to equalize male and female achievement in technology are thus necessary for as long as it takes.

To my mind, equity is what we do to achieve equality of outcomes. The process of equity is quite straightforward: *awareness* of a sex imbalance to the detriment of girls and women, *concern* about it, *action* to correct it, and *results* that eliminate it, thus achieving equality -- of educational, occupational, and economic attainments, and therefore equality in self-fulfillment, self-reliance, and the ability to create a decent life for oneself and one's children.

It is because these goals are essential that vigorous sex equity efforts in schools are critical. And because technology is the key to our economic future, equity efforts to encourage the full participation of girls and women in technology education and careers simply must be accomplished in our schools.

Nevertheless, equity is often quite difficult to carry out in schools. Although in my experience computer equity is the easiest kind of educational equity effort to accomplish, there are many real-life problems that get in the way of achieving computer equity. I've grouped them into four areas: the legacies of history, sex-biased attitudes, how the way schools operate hinders equity, and some thoughts about value, choice, and responsibility.

THE LEGACIES OF HISTORY

We are who we have been. Here are a couple of ways I have noticed the impact of the past on the present, with results that are not helpful in equalizing the educational and occupational potential of girls and women.

Generational Lag

In my computer equity work, I've spoken with many classroom teachers about the educational and especially the occupational value of computer knowledge and skills for girls. I've discussed the changes in the economy and the labor market, and presented figures on the salary and sex differences between jobs that involve computers and those that don't. I've asked them for male/female enrollment breakdowns in their own schools for elective computer classes and optional computer clubs, and they nearly always come up with substantial imbalances. To my mind, the case is pretty clear.

It may be clear, but frequently it's not compelling. Many teachers leave the room *aware* of the computer gender gap, but fewer of them are *concerned* about it. It's natural to gauge the importance of an issue by the role it plays in our own lives. A person who plays the stock market, for example, will pay much more attention to the Dow Jones average than someone who has no money to invest. Similarly, 50-year-old classroom teachers have managed to grow up quite well without computers. They learned how to read, write, and do arithmetic without any software at all. They don't need to spend a great deal of time considering the impact of computers on their future careers -- they already have careers and get along nicely without computer skills. Their districts may be spending fortunes on computer hardware and software and the teachers may be "encouraged" to learn how to use it all, but they know they will not be fired if they don't. Computers are obviously not a burning personal issue for many teachers.

Their students, however, will live in a society in which technology plays a vastly more pervasive role than it does today. Communications, health care, finances, entertainment, production, consumption -- all will be increasingly affected by technology. In ways we cannot imagine today, tomorrow's adults will need to be technologically literate as citizens and technologically skilled as workers.

If I am correct in my conjecture that teachers who live quite comfortably without computers and other modern technology are the least likely to encourage girls' computer use, I wonder whether a substantial introduction of technology into their personal lives would have a positive effect on their motivation to achieve computer equity.

New Converts Are All Alike

Sex equity in education is a delicate topic. It raises the most personal of issues in each of us: how we feel about ourselves and the opposite sex, our role in the world, how we bring up our children. It is understandable that educators don't exactly welcome upheaval in these areas. However, I and other sex equity advocates may have contributed to the problem of sex bias in the schools years ago when we were new converts to the women's movement.

We were angry because we saw so clearly the myriad ways that schools unintentionally mirrored and institutionalized sex discrimination -- the readers that showed little boys exploring and little girls waiting, the math texts that had boys solving velocity problems and girls solving recipe problems, the assignment of boys to shop class and girls to cooking class, the much higher athletics budgets for boys' teams than girls' teams, and on and on.

In the heyday of schools' attention to the sex equity issue in the mid- to late 70's, many sex equity trainers fell into the new-convert trap: our passion and our anger at the unfairness of it all and the damage to girls came through clearly to the teachers who were required to attend these in-service sessions. With hindsight, the result was predictable. Since no one likes to be yelled at or blamed for oppressing poor defenseless little girls, teachers who had been neutral about sex equity distanced themselves from it, and teachers who had been actively sexist found in their resentment justification for being so.

Any computer equity trainer working in the schools today must remember that some groups of educators, particularly those attending mandatory sessions, may be angry before the workshop even begins. Because of past experience with an accusatory trainer (or perhaps because of a guilty conscience!), they;re probably expecting us to call them bigots and point out their faults one by one, even faults committed by textbook publishers or parents or television. This means that a sizable amount of time must be spent defusing their resentment before computer equity trainers like myself can hope to convey our message.

SEX-BIASED ATTITUDES

While it's nice to say that educators are entitled to all the sexist attitudes they want as long as their behavior with students is sex-fair, in reality attitudes tend to control behavior. Here are some of the ways it happens.

Don't Lift That Stool!

Most teachers believe that sex bias is overt and easily recognizable -- the counselor who says "A pretty girl like you doesn't need to take programming," or the teacher who always gives the boys first crack at the computers. Since most teachers rarely if ever witness such scenes or even hear about them (and they *know* they haven't done such things themselves), teachers often don't believe people like me when we say that sex bias occurs all the time.

This is perfectly illustrated by one of my favorite cartoons, which I've shown here. It may be funny, but it's no joke. For the most part, sex bias is in fact the daily accumulation of all the individually trivial references to ladylike behavior and fiddling with one's hair and lifting stools. It is when only boys are computer assistants, and when teachers make more eye contact with boys than girls when referring to technology, and when female teachers exclaim prettily, "I just have no mechanical sense!"

Recently a friend told me about just such an incident. Her daughter, a high school senior, had after much hesitation chosen to take advanced physics rather than advanced biology. She came home from the first day of school very upset. "I'm the only girl in the class, Mom. I hate it. And after class a bunch of the guys and I

were walking down the hall when we ran into our physics teacher from last year. He called out, 'Well, here's the advanced physics group -- and here's the advanced physics groupette!' I don't think I can stick it out, Mom." I can't believe the teacher intended to pressure this girl to drop the course, but nevertheless that's what he was doing.

The Equity Trap

It's obvious to me that since girls are socialized differently from boys, schools that want to equalize girls' and boys' computer behavior have to take sex differences into account. Many educators are now sensitive to sex differences. This sounds like progress, doesn't it? This sensitivity, however, can be a big trap, and here is how it works.

Let's say I'm talking with teachers about girls' computer avoidance -- how girls observe that it's mostly men and boys who use computers in school, at home, in the media, in video arcades, and so forth, and how they conclude that computers are a male thing. I talk about the importance of increasing girls' computer participation, for educational and especially occupational reasons.

One of two things can then happen. A teacher will triumphantly tell me that in his or her school they no longer have a computer equity problem: since many girls like to write, the faculty now encourages girls to use the computer for word processing. Or else a teacher will hear me say that an effective computer equity strategy is to use the computer for writing (which many girls really *do* enjoy), and triumphantly accuse me of sex bias for not having suggested spreadsheets.

One way to get out of the trap is to say that since many girls like to write, it's sensible to use writing *initially* to establish their interest in computers and go on to spreadsheets once that interest is hooked. It's also essential to remember that some girls will initially be far more interested in spreadsheets than word processing. I'm not totally satisfied with this solution, however.

To illustrate why, I am told that there is cosmetics software on the market. You select a face shape, then you experiment with lighter or darker lipstick, eye shadow only on the eyelid or up to the eyebrow, and such. I strongly suspect that a lot of computer-avoiding adolescent girls would love to use this software, and presumably a competent teacher could move them on at some point to spreadsheets and programming. Although I do believe that all good teaching starts with where the student is and then moves her on, I admit that I can't stand the idea of using a cosmetics program, as successful as it would be, to get girls interested in computers.

The fundamental problem is that a sex-biased society teaches girls to have sex-stereotyped interests. When we initially appeal to girls' interests in writing, or heaven forbid, cosmetics -- even when the appeal is a ploy to get them eventually to move on to spreadsheets and programming, are we buttressing the very sex-biased attitudes we are trying to eliminate? If so, then we must propose spreadsheets and programming directly, to bypass the traditionally female, stereotyped interests. But most girls won't be interested in these traditionally male activities, which thus buttresses their computer avoidance. Where is the way out of the equity trap?

THE WAY SCHOOLS OPERATE HINDERS EQUITY

Into this category I place a few situations which, although they may have nothing to do with computer equity *per se*, nevertheless hinder or prevent it from happening in a school.

Acute vs. Chronic

Computer equity progress is often hindered because equity is only one of many programs, initiatives, and concerns that schools would like to address: beef up the library, get more computer hardware, revise the language arts curriculum, expand the health services, create a family life course, get new uniforms for the football team, patch the roof, hire more science teachers, develop a better discipline policy, and on and on. Since most public schools are underfunded in relation to what the state and the parents expect them to accomplish, it is inevitable that the "squeaky wheel" rule prevails and the most acute or crisis-laden needs are addressed first.

Equity in technology is in a sense a negative issue, an issue about what *isn't* rather than what *is*. When advanced computer electives are completely enrolled (with mostly males) and when girls, who are socialized to believe that technology is something men do, avoid technology courses themselves and thus don't complain about the imbalance, there is no squeaky wheel to be heard. It is hard to perceive such a quiescent and superficially acceptable situation as a problem, especially compared to a roof that leaks and parental complaints about drug use in the schools.

To exacerbate the difficulty, it takes no effort to maintain the imbalanced enrollments while it may take substantial time, energy and possibly some money to balance them. It's hard to challenge this *status quo*.

It Doesn't Always Trickle Down

When I worked with teams of junior high classroom teachers and administrators to develop strategies for encouraging greater computer use by girls, they reasoned that it was necessary for teachers and parents to become familiar with computers first in order to encourage girls to do so. Accordingly they carried out a variety of formal and informal sessions with both groups to teach them how to use computers, stressing the need for special encouragement for girls

These indirect strategies turned out to have very little effect on girls' computer use, compared with others that targeted girls directly. I finally figured out that the teachers and parents got sidetracked before their new computer knowledge ever reached girls. In one pattern, the adults became so enamored of the technology for their own needs that they forgot about the girls. In another pattern (especially frequent among teachers!), adults felt they had to be "expert" before actually teaching computing to their female (and male) students, and kept delaying until they were really expert. You can imagine how long *this* can take.

When sex equity progress depends on increasing teachers' skills or changing their behavior, it often falls into the trap of assuming that the new skills or behavior will be conveyed to the students, which in turn will lead to the desired changes in student behavior such as higher female enrollment and completion of computer electives. Without built-in plans and schedules for the adult-to-student transmission, the assumption isn't always justified.

The Lack of Followthrough and Followup

One of the reasons we often accomplish relatively little from all the time and effort we spend on educational innovation is that provision for followthrough is rarely made. This year's successful school program is displaced by next year's new program: educators don't have enough time to do both of them well, and the current one usually has a more insistent constituency. In this way the benefits of the successful program stop with this year' students.

The followthrough problem also relates to the fact that children move on through the grades. Next year's 8th grade teacher may not care as much about Katie's' interest in computers as her 7th grade teacher does. When Katie enters 9th grade in the high school building, those teachers may not even be aware that computer equity is an issue. Without active and continued encouragement from all her teachers during the years when traditional sex-role influences are at their most powerful, Katie may well decide to leave the computers to boys after all.

Follwup is a problem as well. Educational program development grants rarely include funds for longitudinal followup. I am not the only program developer who uses control groups to test the effectiveness of a model program rather than comparison over time because of funding constraints. As a result, we know when new programs are effective in the short run but often have no idea whether the effect remains or dissipates in time.

While the lack of followthrough and followup is a pervasive problem for educational research in general, it is even more critical for equity research. Girls constantly receive messages from society -- parents, peers, teachers, the media -- that technical subjects and careers are more appropriate for males. Without followthrough or continued active encouragement, society's male-only message ceases to be counteracted and many girls are likely to take the path of least resistance. Without followup, we can't document that this is happening.

VALUE, CHOICE AND RESPONSIBILITY

Beyond the legacies of history, sex-biased attitudes, and school operations, I would like to conclude my consideration of equity and technology in schools with a couple of broader issues of value, choice and responsibility.

Required vs. Optional

Beyond the required introductory course of a few weeks to a year that is usually given in the middle school grades, computer instruction in the United States is offered on an optional basis thereafter. Preparation for careers in technology at any level is also elective. The result of all this free choice is that girls take fewer computer courses than boys do, repeating the pattern we have seen for years in math and science.

After twenty years or so of research, we know a great deal about why so many girls drop math and science as soon as these courses are no longer required. Some girls are overtly or subtly discouraged by teachers, counselors, parents, and friends. Most, however, are simply allowed to fulfill the societal expectation that math, science, and technology are male endeavors. When the deck is stacked, no great effort is required to reach the predictable outcome.

I think the unbalanced outcome in computer study should make us reconsider required vs. optional courses. We already make the distinction in some educational environments. We don't let kids choose between reading and recess because we know that reading skills are essential to all children if they are to function in our society -- and also because we know that given the choice, most kids would choose recess. So reading is required. On the other hand, courses such as advanced programming and music composition develop skills and interests that vary from person to person, and as such are properly optional.

Where should computer study be placed on this spectrum? If we believe that computer ability is essential -- occupationally and/or in terms of one's ability to understand and participate in the world around us -- for a fully functioning adult in the first half of the twentieth century, then a semester's course in the 7th grade is grossly inadequate. If we believe that most people will be able to get along just fine without any knowledge of computers, then why do we require children to study computers at all?

This fence-straddling is perhaps inevitable, given the newness of computers and the extremely rapid changes technology has made in our lives. At some point, however, we are going to have to come down on one side or the other of the question. Until then I suspect that the computer equity issue will remain one of personal philosophy: since boys' society-taught enthusiasm for the computer leads them to take more computer courses, to what extent do we have an obligation to ensure that girls obtain computer knowledge and skills on a par with boys?

Swimming Up Streams

In asking educators to promote computer equity for girls, we are asking them to operate in a manner that runs counter to the sexism that permeates all of society. Parents call their newborn son "the big guy" and their newborn daughter "the little doll." Toy doctor kits show boys on the package; toy nurse kits show girls. Children's books and television programs present boys who have adventures and girls who passively admire the boys who have adventures. In elementary school kids have women teachers. They read in their textbooks about more men than women and more boys than girls. The authoritative voice-overs in TV commercials are male. The principal is male. Mommy is the parent who reminds the kids to take their lunch money. And this is only the world of children. The sexism continues into the adult world, perhaps more subtly but not less powerfully.

This is not to blame anyone. Because society has been sexist, it inevitably leaves us a sexist legacy. Adults can only teach children what they know themselves.

The educational equity movement is built on the belief that beyond simple justice our society can no longer afford sexism (if it ever could). Computer equity promotes the equal participation of girls and women in computer studies and jobs because we are unwilling to discard half of our talent pool, because unfulfilled, dissatisfied women benefit no one.

But to accomplish equity -- in this case, to encourage girls' interest in and involvement with computers, to encourage girls and women to enter technology careers -- schools swim against the current of many streams. For every teacher who insists that girls become knowledgeable about computers, girls are receiving the constant message from television, the print media, families, friends, other teachers, even the video arcades, that computers are *really* for males. The full of all these forces is very strong. Educators who resist them need a great deal of support, and where are they to find it?

* * *

If we had answers to some of these questions, I and other computer equity advocates could do a better job of helping educators to recognize that sex bias has causes which lie in the past but have present consequences, such as parents who put the children's new computer in the boy's room, or causes which are subtle but have powerful effects, such as teachers who call on boys for interpretative answers but girls for fact answers. We want to help educators refuse to accept the stacked deck, refuse to permit girls to say "no thanks" to technology just because the stereotype leads them to say it. Finally, we want to help educators insist on nothing less than equity: determined, persistent efforts to overcome the consequences of sex bias, so that every single one of us has a real shot at being superior.

Computers in Education
A. McDougall and C. Dowling (Editors)
Elsevier Science Publishers B.V. (North-Holland)

A METHODOLOGY FOR EDUCATIONAL SOFTWARE ENGINEERING

Jan Schoenmaker, Erik Nienhuis, Jeroen Scholten, Jan Titulaer

Division of Research & Development, Educational Computing Consortium,
P.O. Box 217, 7500 AE Enschede, The Netherlands

ABSTRACT: Educational software development is seen as a branch of software engineering with special characteristics such as a strong emphasis on interactivity and the use of multi-media data. The need for a structured and general development approach has arisen from the demand for bigger applications, ease and efficiency of maintenance, and support for a broad range of types of educational software: drill, tutorials, inquiry, simulations and microworlds.
A methodology is proposed, which is based on the notion of different abstraction levels (from analysis to implementation), each level having aspects such as goals and the three dimensions in which software is modelled: the processes (functionality), the entities (data) and the dynamics (interaction).
The methodology has been tested in different courseware production projects, covering the whole range of educational software types.

I. INTRODUCTION

As courseware becomes more and more complex, courseware design should follow and should become accordingly more advanced. In the past, courseware design meant little more than designing a few screens and specifying their sequences. This approach was appropriate for simple courseware such as drills and tutorials, but not for the sort of courseware required today, such as open-ended systems, complex simulations, information retrieval systems or intelligent tutoring systems. Besides, the size of programs became so great that regular problems of software development such as maintenance, flexibility, modularity and extendibility became issues in educational computing as well. We, therefore, need a more sophisticated courseware design methodology.
To this end, we can build upon software engineering (SE). SE is a branch of computer science that has achieved considerable results in structuring the process of developing business software. We have tried to transfer as much as possible from SE to courseware engineering, making alterations where necessary.
Courseware engineering as a branch of software engineering should address a number of activities and problems:

- design
- implementation
- project management
- production
- maintenance
- evaluation
- classroom use

In this paper we will focus on design and, to a lesser degree, on implementation and project management.

2. A FRAMEWORK FOR COURSEWARE DESIGN

2.1. Introduction

One of the most important notions we can learn from SE is that of separating design decisions. This means that during design we limit ourselves to one part of the software at a time. However, in doing this, one must be aware not to lose track. In order to be able to make the right design decisions at the right time, we have developed a framework for courseware design, based on a framework for information systems design [1].
The framework is based upon two partitions of the design process. One partition is derived from the fact that the designing of systems needs to be done on different levels of abstraction, the other from the fact that designing a system is done through modelling different aspects of that system.

2.2. Abstraction levels

A system is designed by looking at it at

different levels of abstraction, ranging from the very abstract, concentrating primarily on the problem domain, to the very implementation-oriented, concentrating on the concrete solution, i.e. the program.
For our purposes, we distinguish the following four abstraction levels:
- OSM, object system modelling, which depicts the contribution of the courseware to its environment, the educational organization.
- ED, educational design, which describes the educational processes the courseware should perform or support.
- FD, functional design, which describes the architecture of the software.
- TD, technical design, which describes the implementation of the software.

We shall return to each of these below.

2.3. Aspects

In general software engineering can be seen as modelling in a three dimensional space. There are three characteristic dimensions (or aspects) of software: the functionality (active components), the entities (passive components), and the dynamics (behaviour in time). For example, at a technical level these aspects would be procedures, data and interfaces, respectively.
As a consequence, modelling a system should be carried out in every dimension and thus cover every aspect. This is depicted in figure 1 below:

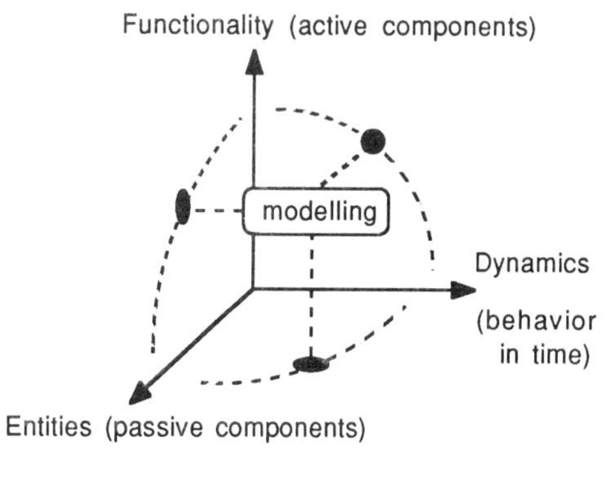

Figure 1: modelling dimensions

Besides these three system aspects, it is important to model two additional aspects, the goals of the system and the realisation considerations, because the two latter often play an important role in making design decisions but are not modelled explicitly.

2.4. The framework

The framework covers the four abstraction levels and five aspects, which together constitute a matrix, providing a taxonomy of design decisions:

	goals	dynamics	functions	entities	realization consider.
OSM					
ED					
FD					
TD					

Figure 2: the framework

This is a model of the software design process. It states that the system should be modelled completely at each level. Here modelled completely means modelled in full detail and in all design aspects.
Below we will discuss each of the abstraction levels seperately.

3. THE OBJECT SYSTEM MODELLING

3.1. Definition

Object System Modelling (OSM) has the purpose to clarify the desired contribution of the courseware to the educational organization and its activities.
The Object System can be seen as the environment of the courseware. Modelling this environment helps to define the objectives of the courseware. The object system is modelled by specifying:
- the goals of learning (in terms of desired knowledge and skills of a target group, i.e. the learners), thus the learning objectives.
- the overall strategy of instruction and more detailed tactics.
- the learning situation (classroom organization, learning tasks, etc.)
- the actors involved and the role they play. We usually distinguish the following actors: a courseware system, a learner, a teacher, an author of contents, conventional learning material (e.g. books), and other media (e.g. video).

The instructional strategy represents the way in which the learning objectives are met. A major variable is that instructional strategies can be more or less learner controlled.
Instructional tactics are more detailed sub-approaches within this overall approach. Therefore, the overall learning

objectives are broken down into manageable pieces (aims). Examples of instructional tactics are: modularisation, phasing, backward chaining, concentric build-up of learning contents, and clustering of learning contents.
These modelling activities can be placed in the framework, resulting in figure 3:

goals	dynamics	functions	entities	realization consider.
learners know-ledge, skills	instructional strategy & tactics	tasks	actors	classroom organiza-tion

Figure 3: OSM aspect modelling

It is necessary to write down the contribution of the courseware to the instructional practice explicitly. Not only will the communication with users (teachers etc.) be more effective, but subsequent design activities will also be performed more easily. For the design of interactive systems in particular, it is essential to have a notion of the system's context.

3.2. Example

The following model gives an idea of the nature of object system modelling. In figure 4 below, the context of a simulation courseware product is depicted:

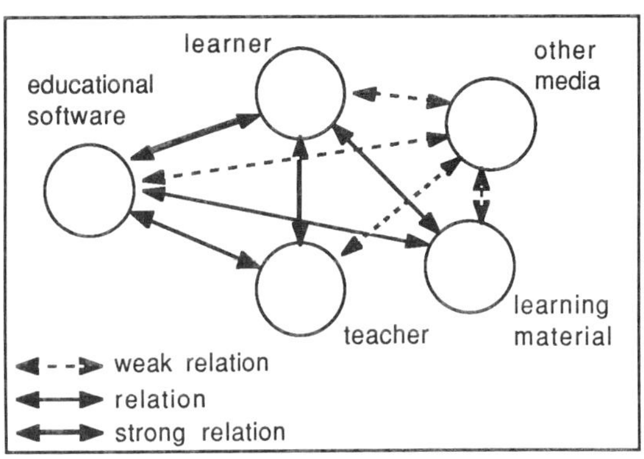

Figure 4: OSM for simulation courseware

Of course, much more has to be modelled in an OSM than is presented in this diagram. More open ended software results in more complex object system modelling. This indicates that it is very important to do something in the nature of object system modelling.

4. THE EDUCATIONAL DESIGN

4.1. Definition

Educational Design (ED) is a central and essential activity in our methodology. It constitutes the semantic level of software specification.
ED consists of modelling the required system, given the context of the OSM, at a very conceptual level, abstracting fully from information science and programming concepts such as dataprocesses, interfaces, data transactions, datastores, etc. Therefore, an essential notion is that the system can be modelled only in the language of the problem domain, namely educational psychological notions such as theories of instruction. Summarizing, an ED is still modelled in terms of education and instruction, but is more specific and detailed than the OSM.
In ED the aims of the system are derived from the OSM-objectives, the instruction process is written down, using instructional transactions as basic building blocks, and the contents of the system, content structure and support for other actors (tasks of teacher and author) are modelled. All this is done with the technical possibilities and limitations of the environment in mind. Placed in the framework it looks like this:

goals	dynamics	functions	entities	realization consider.
aims of system	instruc-tional modules & trans-actions	tasks supported	contents (infor-mation)	technical limita-tions

Figure 5: ED aspect modelling

We are trying to formalise ED, in so far as is possible, in order to make it easier to transfer specifications to a lower design level. To this end we make use of the concept of instructional transactions. We have taken the work of Merrill [2] as a basis for this, but here worked out the idea for our own purposes.
Instructional Transactions (ITs) are dynamic interactions between the system and the learner, in which exchange of information occurs, directed towards some learning task. An IT forms the smallest unit of interaction that is still educationally relevant. It always consists of a presentation part, performed by the courseware, and an execution part, performed by the learner. An example of such an IT is presented in

section 4.2 below.
ITs function as basic building blocks for the real design problem, namely organizing relevant ITs into a structure that fulfils an educational goal. Such a structure is called an <u>Instructional Module</u> (IM). IMs eventually model the system dynamics, and, therefore, the structure of the instructional process, addressing important design issues such as learner control etc..

4.2. Example

To illustrate the concept of the IT, an IT is shown, characterizing instructional elements, which might appear in a hypermedia system.

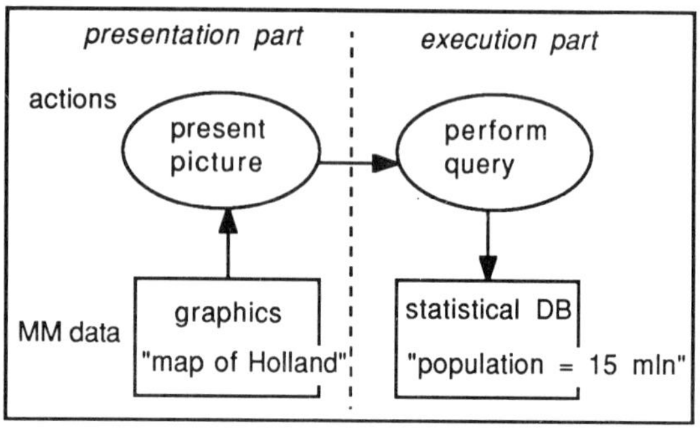

Figure 6: IT for hypermedia system

Here we can see that in the presentation part an operator 'present picture' presents a multi-media data (MM data) operand, then hands over control to the execution part (the learner), where a query on the operand 'statistical database (DB)' is performed.
This example is characteristic of the fact that the basic structure of ITs is always the same, while the educational meaning can differ considerably. The notion that ITs transfer multi-media data is essential.
For our designing practice, we have defined a set of 16 standard ITs. These ITs form the basic building blocks for designs. To give an impression, we recognize for example:
- IT 11: answering a question
- IT 10: making a classification
- IT 16: adjusting program parameters.

ITs are further defined by basic transactions. These transactions are no longer educationally relevant, and will, therefore, be addressed at the functional abstraction level.

5. FUNCTIONAL DESIGN

5.1. Definition

With functional design (FD), the design of the software begins. For designing software, existing methods from software engineering can be applied. These methods are formal, well-defined, established, very often supported by tools (CASE), and successfully used in practice. Software engineering methods are sufficiently generic for every type of software, and can, therefore, be used for our purposes as well. The greatest problem in using software engineering methods is their inadequate user interface design capabilities. In practice this continues to be a problem.
While ED constitutes the semantic definition, FD is the syntactical definition of the software, concentrating on designing the architecture.
This architecture is defined by:
- a user interface design,
- data-processing functions and process logic, and
- a conceptual (or logical) data model,

taking limitations into account by a <u>type</u> of implementation environment (hardware and tools), and criteria such as flexibility of the architecture, completeness, correctness and consistency of the modellings.
These modellings can be filled in in the framework as follows:

goals	dynamics	functions	entities	realization consider.
flexibility consistency, completeness, correctness	transactions, user interface design	process logic & structure	logical data model	limitations by type of hardware and tools

Figure 7: FD aspect modelling

A transaction is any interaction pattern between the system and its user, in which data is exchanged. Transactions are used to define ITs at ED level. They function, therefore, as general interaction building blocks. A basic set of transactions is defined in much the same way as is done for ITs.

5.2. Example

In our designing practice we use Pirbhai & Hatley [3] as a functional design method. This method is based on Yourdon Structured Analysis and Design, but more directed towards modelling the dynamical aspects of software. It uses data flow diagrams (DFD) for process modelling, and control flow diagrams (CFD) for control modelling.
Additionally, we use entity-relationship diagrams (ERD) as a technique for data

modelling, and state transition diagrams (STD) for user interface design.

6. TECHNICAL DESIGN

6.1. Definition

Technical Design (TD) is a precise description of the implementation. It specifies how technical problems are to be solved, given the limitations and possibilities of the actual implementation environment. Goals for the design are usually maintainability, efficiency ('speed'), portability, and modularity. The TD specification contains:
- the exact user interface design (keys, layout, resources, etc.).
- program descriptions in module-structures and pseudocode, and
- internal database scheme.

This can be filled in in the framework as follows:

goals	dynamics	functions	entities	realization consider.
modularity, maintainability portability, speed	event handling, windows, etc.	modules, procedures	data schemes DBMS	limitations by actual hardware and tools

Figure 8: TD aspect modelling

7. THE SOFTWARE DEVELOPMENT PROCESS

Thus far we have considered the design activity of the software development process. In this chapter we will shortly discuss two other development activities, which are closely related to design, namely implementation and project management.

7.1. Implementation

The implementation activity concerns the transformation of the (technical) design into a working software product. This process is usually supported by a number of tools. Types of tools used during implementation are:
- UIMS (user interface management systems): systems that handle the user interface of a program independently of the application functionality. Examples of UIMS are windowing (WIMP) environments.
- third generation programming languages with libraries and fourth generation languages (4GL) are means for greater efficiency in programming the functionality of the application.
- MMDBMS (Multi-media database management systems): DBMS are systems that manage the data of an application independently of the application software. MMDBMS are DBMS that are capable of handling multi-media data.

A general model of this is presented in figure 9 below:

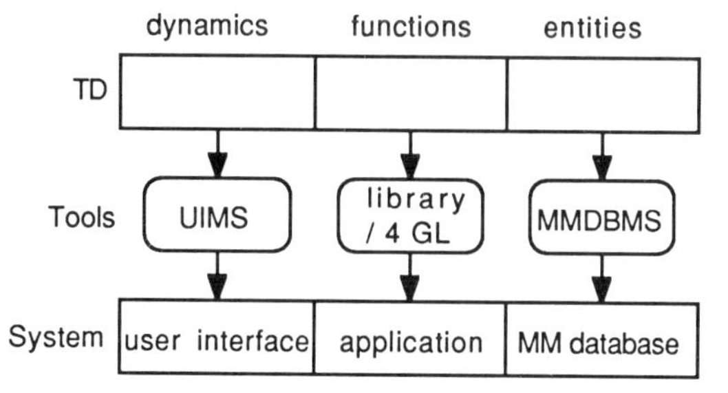

Figure 9: the implementation process

7.2. Project management

In an educational project different types of expertise have to be combined, e.g. expertise in teaching, in educational technology, in computer science, and in the subject matter itself. It is difficult to manage teams speaking different 'languages'. Furthermore, the development of a program often calls for iterations because it is very difficult to define specifications of interactive applications beforehand and because creativity is important in designing CAL. Therefore, project management of CAL development has to take aspects into account that may prove less amenable to formalisation (compared to other branches in software engineering), but that are nonetheless important. Furthermore, for those involved in courseware development a learning curve can be observed with respect to the system being designed. This too leads to a need for iterating design decisions. Nevertheless, the use of formal methods in solution oriented modelling is very important. It facilitates the application of quality control before the system is actually built, which may lead to considerable savings in the overall development process.

8. EXPERIENCES AND CONCLUSIONS

The methodology as described has been developed and put into practice in the past 4 years, especially since '87 in the Dutch POCO-project , a major courseware production project for primary, secondary and vocational education of about 160 manyear. In this project coop-

eration was organized between teachers, educational psychologists, educational technologists, computer scientists and programmers, educational publishers and projectleaders.
In short we can state the following experiences and conclusions:

1. The methodology is suitable for different types of applications: drills, tutorials, simulations, open ended software, embedded training.

2. In general it takes more time - initially - to design small and simple applications according to this methodology (one has to model different abstraction layers according to certain rules). However if one wants to change the design or re-use parts of it in another design one benefits from this approach. Big and complex applications should be modelled according to a methodology of this kind.

3. The separation of design decisions in different aspects and at different abstraction levels is an important instrument in order to design a consistent, complete and meaningful application , for communication between different people from different disciplines and also to strike a balance between project management restrictions and designers freedom.

4. The methodology as such does not contain much semantic knowledge about how to design.One knows very well what to design, but less how to design. Reference models can act as low level support tools at the semantic level.

5. The quality of courseware is dependent on environmental variables as classroom organization, the role of other learning materials and the expertise and attitude of the teacher. The object system model is a useful communication model that pays attention to these aspects.

6. The modelling of the interaction (dynamics) aspects like instructional strategies, instructional tactics, and instructional transactions is still a problem, primarily due to a lack of good educational models.

7. An essential part of the proposed methodology is the formalization and linking of problem-oriented modelling (educational design) and solution oriented modelling (functional design).

8. The major weakness of current software engineering methods is the interaction-modelling. The focus of methods has always been on the data and process aspects, not on the interaction aspect. For courseware engineering we need methods with adequate interface design capabilities.

9. Object oriented design methods might be more adequate to model educational software, especially simulation type and open ended software, but are still underdeveloped. Object oriented designing is something else than object oriented programming.

10. In general, the training of designers is a problem. It will take a period of at least 1- 2 years to become a professional courseware analyst and - designer. However, the training is facilitated by the use of a structured framework such as is presented here.

11. The model of combining user-interface, functionality and datastorage resp. with the help of WIMPS-environments, third or fourth generation programming tools and multi-media database management system is a useful implementation model.

12. As with regard to the use of current authoring tools, we see two important restrictions:
a. They are not general, but specific for certain types of educational software. Furthermore, in general they do not support portability.
b. They do not support the earlier phases of design (object system modelling and educational design)

13. This methodology helps in finding a balance between a more or less linear project management based approach to development, and an iterative and less formal approach (leaving room for creativity).

REFERENCES

[1] Essink, L.J.B., A modelling approach to information system development, in: Olle, T.W., Sol, H.G. and Verrijn Stuart, A.A. (eds.), Information system design methodologies: improving the practice (North Holland, Amsterdam, 1986).

[2] Merrill, M.D., Prescriptions for an authoring system. Journal of computer-based instruction, vol.14, 1, 1-10.

[3] Hatley, D.J. and Pirbhai, I.A., Strategies for real-time system specification (Dorset House, New York, 1988).

Computers in Education
A. McDougall and C. Dowling (Editors)
Elsevier Science Publishers B.V. (North-Holland)

CONCEPTS AND STRATEGIES CONCERNING INFORMATION TECHNOLOGY EDUCATION FOR GIRLS AND YOUNG WOMEN

Dr. Renate Schulz-Zander

IPN - Institute for Science Education, Olshausenstr. 62
D-2300 Kiel 1, Federal Republic of Germany

Girls are less ready to take part in information technology courses in schools than are boys. There is a long term danger that women may be excluded from skilled work in the field of information and communication technology. How can this gender related behaviour be explained? What concepts and strategies might lead to equality for girls and young women? In the following, two projects are described which are intended to prevent discrimination against girls and young women in the field of information technology:

1. A concept of holiday computer courses for girls, which combine information technology with aesthetics.
2. Curriculum recommendations for training in the field of information technology in schools.

1. HOW CAN GENDER-RELATED DIFFERENCES BE EXPLAINED?

There is a wide consensus of opinion that the attitudes and behaviour of the sexes are influenced by socialisation processes which are in turn determined by social structures, especially by the division of work between the sexes (family - career). A theoretical explanation of gender-related behaviour can be seen in the varied concept of the self. This means all an individual's attitudes, judgements, and value judgements concerning his/her behaviour, abilities and qualities. The self concept involves both the perception of these variables and value judgements made about them. Presumably the preservation of the feeling of self esteem is of fundamental importance both for the development of the personality of the child and for that of the adult [5]. The self estimation and appraisal of girls and boys is dependent on value judgements about the roles of the sexes in our society. As "male" roles with the supposedly male characteristics such as the ability to think independently, behave instrumentally, and act in a technically competent way are estimated as being more important than the "female" role with the qualities of sympathy, emotionality, gentleness, passivity and the readiness to be submissive which are assigned to it, girls have no alternative but to become aware of their disadvantages and learn to estimate them at an early age. An example of this is that while boys and men tend to have a positive feeling of self worth in comparison with other less competent rivals, girls and women consider their ability to be socially sympathetic to be stronger [8]. The development of the identity of girls takes the form of a permanent active conflict between the contradictions of the "femininity" which is required and self respect (ANYON after [9], pg. 28). Showing oneself to be competent in predominantly male areas - also in the field of information technology, then - would mean leaving the well trodden path to the increasing of self esteem for girls and women.

Female and male peers play an important role as they form an important group where breaking away from parents is concerned. If there is a danger of loss, traditional norms are strictly adhered to: girls look for reassurance and reaffirmation of their identity above all from their male peers [9], [10]. Studies show that young men also cling to sex specific ideas relating to ability in the area of information technology, and that in doing so they make it more difficult for girls to get involved in it - though this may well also be due to the fear of competition [2], [6].

The following drawings done by girls on the theme of "girls and computers" who took part in the computer holiday course are an expression of this conflict as they experienced it. No discussion about what they had experienced took place before the drawings were done, yet they were almost all concerned with the attitudes of the boys to them. The necessity and desire to assert themselves was in the forefront (figure 1).

Figure 1: The girl is struggling against the boys' arrogance, knowing well that they often only act as if they know more. Sadness and anger are visible.
(The comments in the figures are translated by the author.)

At the end of the holiday course the girls were given the opportunity to discover what they thought it would be like to be technically highly skilled by means of an imaginary journey. The story ended with the following idea: "You are a girl who is very good at using computers - boys ask you for advice too ...". At the end they were asked to draw what they had imagined. About half of the girls could enjoy the idea of being successful (figure 2). Other girls felt isolated, left out, emotionally overtaxed and annoyed. In their imagination, behaviour which deviated from traditional roles was "punished" by their female contemporaries; as such it was seen to make excessive demands on them (figure 3). The conflict experienced will vary in degree according to self esteem and self con-

Figure 2: Success is a positive experience: The others are happy with the girl that she can handle computers competently and do not put her down. She is the focal point of attention.

Figure 3: This girl no longer accepts the successful role. She is not working at the computer. The boy and girl (bottom right) have obviously turned away from her and shut her out. Success is being punished.

fidence. Female and male educationalists must therefore be ready to support girls and women in overcoming socially determined roles, and in altering their self concepts. Esteem for traditional sexually determined roles can also be found in the attitudes of male and female teachers, however, and affects the interaction between male/female teachers and male/female pupils (cf. [3], [7], [12]). This means that both changes in outlook and behaviour must be brought about in female/male pupils and female/male teachers.

What concrete conceptions and recommendations can be made concerning information technological education in the Federal Republic of Germany so that it is suitable for girls and young women?

2. CURRICULUM CONFERENCE ON INFORMATION TECHNOLOGY EDUCATION FOR GIRLS

Information technology education currently available in schools in the Federal Republic of Germany needs to be thoroughly revised so that girls are given equal access to information technology. For this reason a five day curriculum conference was led by the author in 1988.

The conference started from the assumption that acquiring specialist knowledge in informatics formed the basis for increased self confidence, for an appropriate choice of career, and for the ability of girls and women to influence the use of information technology.

Women with very varied skills were invited to the conference: teachers, programmers, women trained in informatics, women involved in research, unions, industry, adult education, cultural projects and in one branch of the media*. The result of this was the production of recommendations for information technology education with four lesson proposals primarily for informatics in grade 11 and 12 and strategies for implementing it. The following were planned:

- a teaching model for the basics of information technology, "Computer and Creativity",
- the concept of an introductory course for informatics,
- an "Expertise and Expert Systems" unit, and
- a project for the use of information technology in the textile business.

Excerpts of the recommendations and strategies which were developed by the female conference participants are reprinted in the following.

2.1. Recommendations for Aims, Contents and Methods

Teaching the basics of information technology should not be the exclusive province of a single subject. The concept of the Bund-Länder-Kommission [1] on the teaching of information technology, which is a basis for the Länder, requires the following additions:

- Influence on the Formation of Systems

The basics of information technology is concerned with user software, not necessarily with the learning of a programme language. As users of user software, female pupils should learn how they can influence the development of software, hardware and the organisation of work.

- Ethical Responsibility

Demystification is necessary for the realistic assessment of the opportunities created by and the limits of information technology. The inscrutability, uncertainty, and fallibility of (network) systems should also be stressed. The ethical responsibility of people and political decisions (which also involves the limitation or removal of information technology in certain areas) must be dealt with in lessons.

- The Use of Computers in the Creative Area

The creative use of computers in the area of the plastic arts (graphics), music, literature, also in connection with sensual perception and the fine arts should be involved in lessons to a greater degree.

- Historical and Philosophical Aspects of the Relationship between Human Beings and the Machine

Lessons should make it possible for female and male pupils to experience the relationship between human beings and technology as a historical and philosophical question. The implications of change must be treated on the one hand from the point of view of the relationship between the sexes, and on the other hand the role of science and technology should be considered where social developments are concerned.

- Formal Thought versus Intuitive Thought

Lessons should make it possible for female and male pupils to get to grips with their relationship to the computer as a machine. In this process sexually different attitudes are thematised; in addition to this a discriminating attitude to formal thought should be created in connection with this. A sex specific moulding of technology should be reflected.

- The Effects of Information Technology on the Relationship between the Sexes

The effects of information technology on the relationship between the sexes should be made clear as well as its social and economic effects (the employment of women, housework, the representation of men and women in the media in connection with information technology, the social allocation of roles).

- The Role of Women in the History of Data Processing

In the representation of the development of data processing the role of women in the history of data processing should be made clear.

- Models for Girls and Women

Models should be introduced especially for girls, e.g. qualified women who are successful in typically male professions. In this way they can also include "typical male professions" in their career decisions.

- Holistic Education

In addition to purely cognitive aspects, care must be taken that physical and emotional aspects are allowed to play a role in lessons as part of a holistic concept of education. This should be applied both to social contents and to algorithmic problem solving.

2.2. Strategies for the Implementation of Recommendations

Several studies have shown that the coeducational approach does not lead to the equality of girls and to the destruction of undermining sexual stereotypes. This is especially true of mathematical, scientific, and technical teaching. New, more flexible forms of lesson organisation should be tested which take the various different approaches and ways of working of the sexes into consideration. Lessons should be organised in such a way as to enable both a limited, situational division of the sexes and teaching in mixed groups. In each teaching phase it should be considered whether

- specifically female/male interests, ways of working or roles should be encouraged and dealt with in separate groups;
- typically male/female themes should be dealt with by the opposite sex;
- a theme can be dealt with in a mixed group in the same way.

All thoughts about the changing of organisational forms, the content and methods of information technological teaching and the inclusion of girls' interests cannot have any effect if women teachers are not able to understand and implement these considerations. New concepts must be developed especially for inservice training. More women should be allowed to attend inservice training courses and to lead courses themselves. In addition to this, courses for women only should be made available. More courses in the areas of the development of the personality and interaction training should be made available and ways of supervising lessons should be created; the cooperation of female/male movement educationalists, female/male psychologists and others is to be recommended.

2.3. Short Term Requirements

- Model experiments and projects should be encouraged in which teaching material is produced and new forms of teaching information technology are tested;
- Women must be given priority where qualifications and in-service training are concerned;
- Teacher training and in-service training for women must be changed.

3. HOLISTIC CONCEPT OF A COMPUTER HOLIDAY COURSE FOR GIRLS

The proposals referred to at the beginning concerning supporting girls and young women where changing their self concept is concerned, formed the basis for the conception of an extra curricula course. The basic concept was that of combining information technology education with aesthetics. Here aesthetics is seen in the broad sense as a philosophical theory which is concerned with sensual recognition as opposed to conceptual recognition (the abstract conceptualisation of the awareness of the intellect). It aims to preserve and possibly improve sensual recognition on the basis of personal theoretical efforts. Aesthetics means confronting nature (both external and inner physical occurences) with all of one's senses, perceiving it with all of one's senses, and in so doing opening up the possibilities for sensual awareness and change.

A stabilisation of identity should be encouraged in girls by the inclusion of the aesthetic (here physical movement, dance, theatre, and video work) and of Gestalt educational approaches. The feelings of self esteem and self confidence can be strengthened by using Gestalt educational approaches, for example, like the imaginary journey and painting. This is achieved by becoming aware of negative feelings and being able to deal with them. Gestalt therapy assumes that "awareness of one's body" is important for high self esteem. "Breathing and relaxation exercises, together with movement help one to become more aware of one's body. The image that a person has of his body is an important part of his self image" ([11], pg. 352; translated by the author). It is important to develop a positive feeling about oneself.

The course was carried out by the author in collaboration with Marion Engmann (movement/dance), Margret Hamann (video) and Gabi Stein (information technology education). Girls aged between 13 and 16 years from secondary modern and grammar schools took part in the 7 day course in 1988.

The course contained the following components:

3.1. Information Technology Education

The introduction to progamming with Logo was carried out by means of turtle graphics. First of all the girls made imaginary drawings. Only once they had done this did they write programmes. At the end they used the computer to write greeting-postcards. By doing this they got to know how to work with Logo objects and recursive programming. Video material was used as a basis for learning about the uses and effects of information technology. They were given an insight into the production of computer graphics and their importance for military purposes in connection with turtle graphics. The question "Is computer graphics art?" was also discussed. The above drawings formed part of the theme of "girls and computers" in the theme complex of "girls/women and technology/ computers"; they formed the basis for a discussion group about subjective experiences. They examined the problem of the role of women in the media by means of a collage which they made from pictures and printed material from computer magazines, and about which they wrote commentaries. A short introduction about the role of women in the history of data processing was designed to make the specialist skills of women in this area clear. At the end of the course they had the opportunity to express their imaginings and feelings concerning the successful use of computers in an imaginary story. The aim was to admit to possible fears and in doing so to overcome them.

3.2. Movement, Dance and Drama

Imagination and creativity, human communication and interaction, emotion and sensual awareness are the central themes of the physical work in the course. The aim of dancing and drama is encouraging and equipping people to improvise - to be able to perceive themselves, others and their environment in a new way at each moment, to be able to do the unexpected, react spontaneously, accept the process which results from this and to be able to move as they wish during the whole process ([4], pg. 24 ff.). Sensibility and physical awareness are promoted by methods from the areas of "rhythmics" and "creative dance"; by expressive playing and "free drama" improvisation is possible within a short span of time which make the spontaneous expression of fleeting moods possible by means of free role play.

3.3. Video - The Use of Technology for the Expression of one's own Perceptions

Video was included as a useful combination of technology and artistic work. The girls used video cameras to find their own means of expression and to express themselves. During the course those taking part experimented with the camera and made small film sequences. Their technical knowledge was schooled by practising zooming in and panning, trick shots, constructing a plot, and by getting to know what materials are used in film making ([4], pg. 25).

* The following took part in the curriculum conference:

Gertrud Effe-Stumpf, Dr. Uta Enders-Dragässer, Prof. Dr. Hannelore Faulstich-Wieland, Ingrid Hölz, Dorothea Jöllenbeck, Edith Krieger, Dipl-Phys. Karin Lindner-Vogt, Maria Meyer, Dr. Cillie Rentmeister, Gabriele Rupprecht, Heidi Schelhowe, Dr. habil. Christiane Schiersmann, Dr. Renate Schulz-Zander, Uschi Stumm, Dr. Esther Tamm, Sigrid Werner

REFERENCES

[1] BLK: Bund-Länder-Kommission für Bildungsplanung und Forschungsförderung (ed.): Gesamtkonzept für die Informationstechnische Bildung. Bonn: Typoskript 1987.

[2] Brandes, U.; Schiersmann, Ch. und BRIGITTE; Institut Frau und Gesellschaft (eds.): Frauen, Männer und Computer. Eine repräsentative Untersuchung von Frauen und Männern in der Bundesrepublik Deutschland zum Thema Computer. Berichte und Tabellen (2 Bände). Hamburg: Gruner + Jahr 1986.

[3] Enders-Dragässer, U.; Fuchs, C. u.a.: Interaktionen und Beziehungsstrukturen in der Schule. Eine Untersuchung des Feministischen Interdisziplinären Forschungsinstituts an Hessischen Schulen im Auftrag des Hessischen Instituts für Bildungsplanung und Schulentwicklung. Frankfurt/Wiesbaden, März 1988.

[4] Engmann, M.; Hamann, M.: Mädchen & Computer & Kreatives. In: päd. extra & demokratische Erziehung, 2 (1989) no. 2, pp. 23 - 25.

[5] Epstein, S.: Entwurf einer Integrativen Persönlichkeitstheorie. In: Filipp, S.H. (ed.): Selbstkonzept-Forschung. Probleme, Befunde, Perspektiven. Stuttgart 1979.

[6] Faulstich-Wieland, H.; Dick, A.: Mädchenbildung und Neue Technologien. In: Fauser, R.; Schreiber, N. (eds.): Sozialwissenschaftliche Überlegungen, empirische Untersuchungen und Unterrichtskonzepte zur informationstechnischen Bildung. Reihe: Projekt: Informationstechnische Bildung. Konstanz: Universität 1986, pp. 83 - 95.

[7] Frasch, H.; Wagner, A.: "Auf Jungen achtet man einfach mehr ...". In: Brehmer, I. (ed.): Sexismus in der Schule. Weinheim, Basel: Beltz 1982, pp. 260 - 278.

[8] Gilligan, C.: Die andere Stimme. Lebenskonflikte und Moral der Frau. München 1984.

[9] Horstkemper, M.: Schule, Geschlecht und Selbstvertrauen. Eine Längsschnittstudie über Mädchensozialisation in der Schule. Reihe: Veröffentlichungen der Max-Traeger-Stiftung, Band 4. Weinheim, München: Juventa Verlag 1987.

[10] Macoby, E.; Jacklin, C.: The psychology of sex differences. Stanford University 1974.

[11] Oaklander, V.: Gestalttherapie mit Kindern und Jugendlichen Stuttgart: Klett-Cotta 1981.

[12] Spender, D.: Frauen kommen nicht vor. Sexismus im Bildungswesen. Reihe: Die Frau in der Gesellschaft. Frankfurt a.M.: Fischer Taschenbuch Verlag 1985.

Computers in Education
A. McDougall and C. Dowling (Editors)
Elsevier Science Publishers B.V. (North-Holland)

THE DESIGN OF NETWORK BASED MULTI-USER CAL

David SQUIRES

Director (Science)
Computers in the Curriculum Project
Educational Computing Unit
Centre for Educational Studies
King's College London
552 Kings Road
London SW10 0UA

This paper suggests five paradigms for computer network based computer assisted learning. These paradigms are based on descriptions of earlier software development in this area and on recent work by the Computers in the Curriculum Project, King's College London. This work of the Computers in the Curriculum Project is described in detail. Major issues concerned with the design of network based computer assisted learning are identified through a consideration of these paradigms.

1. INTRODUCTION

Networks of microcomputers are becoming commonplace in schools. The justification for installing computers as networks rather than as stand alone machines is often given in terms of efficient and cost effective resource provision. In particular claims are made that storage and printing resources can be shared and that it is easier to maintain an extensive library of software. These are compelling arguments in a context where funding and staff time are limited, as they generally are in schools. However these arguments do not provide an educational rationale for using networks in schools. This paper addresses the educational issues concerned with the use of networks in schools, suggesting some paradigms for the development of network software which it is hoped will assist thinking about the use of networks in education and provide guidelines for the design of appropriate software.

2. NETWORK CAL DEVELOPED BY THE COMPUTERS IN THE CURRICULUM PROJECT

Two network based programs have been developed by the Computers in the Curriculum Project with funding from the British Telecom Education Service. NEWSNET [1] has been recently published by the British Telecom Education Service and COMNET is currently being trialled in schools. Both programs run on an Acorn Level 2 or above Econet system. An RM Nimbus PC network version of NEWSNET is currently being prepared and there are discussions in hand about the possibility of producing an IBM PC version.

NEWSNET is a role playing activity in which students are required to assume the role of newspaper reporters employed as foreign correspondents for a national daily newspaper. Each network station simulates the newspaper office facilities available in one of up to seven countries. These facilities consist of a word processor, a wire service, a local and global database and an electronic mailbox. In addition students have access to a desk top publishing package.

The aim of the package is to encourage students working at different workstations to co-operate in the production of a front page for the newspaper. As the software runs the same sequence of headlines appears at the top of each workstation screen. There are stories in the sequence that are relevant to each of the countries represented in the package. These are intended to act as a basis for each student to write front page articles. Links exist between the various stories which are intended to prompt students to communicate with each other while they are writing their articles. For example the same character, using various pseudonyms, appears in a number of the head-lines with each local database containing some information on him.

NEWSNET provides students with an integrated software environment for investigation, communication, writing and presentation. Students can investigate ideas for stories by using the wire service to request information on any one of the headlines. They can use their local database and the global database to research the stories in more depth. If they require information from other students they can send and receive messages via the electronic mail system. "Copy" for proposed front page articles can be written using the word

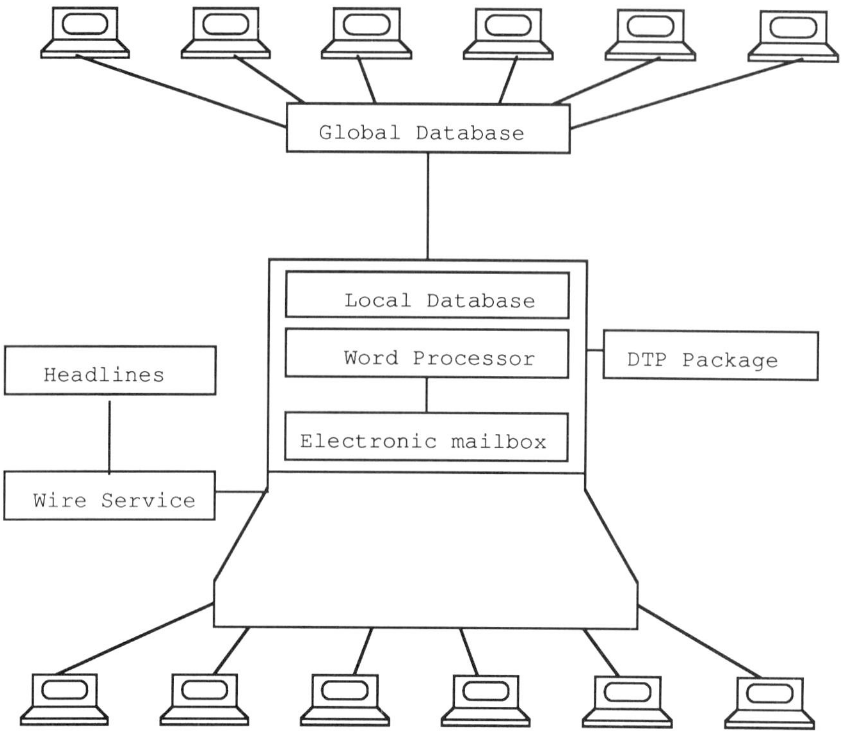

Figure 1: The composition of NEWSNET

processor. Copies of these articles can be sent and received as files using the electronic mail program. Wordprocessor documents can be imported to the desk top publishing package to form the basis of a front page. At this stage page formats can be specified, headlines added and pictures inserted from a picture library supplied with the desk top publishing package. Figure 1 represents the composition of NEWSNET.

COMNET is concerned with the historical development of communications. The package consists of four separate programs. Each program simulates a particular form of communication: semaphore, telegraphy, electronic mail and teleconferencing. Although each package can be used in isolation, it is intended that they are used in sequence to convey a feeling for the historical development of communications.

The semaphore program automatically pairs students so that a given student is communicating exclusively with one other student in the network. Initially each student has to complete an exercise in which they decipher a semaphore message from the captain of a sailing ship. The flag positions that they assign to the letters of the alphabet during this exercise are used by the program to interpret messages that they receive from their partner.

The telegraphy program links network stations together in a linear sequence, with each station representing a railway telegraph office in the USA during the nineteenth century. Messages are sent and received by using morse code. Each student is only able to communicate with students located at the two adjacent railway station offices.

The electronic mail program and the teleconferencing program are intended to highlight modern methods of telecommunications. Most of the features available in real electronic mail systems are available in this network simulation. Using the system students are able to communicate privately with any other student. In contrast the teleconferencing system provides a public means of global communication.

3. SOME PARADIGMS FOR THE EDUCATIONAL USE OF NETWORKS

The experience gained in the development of multi-user network CAL by the Computers in the Curriculum Project, King's College London is used as a basis to propose five paradigms for network based CAL. Earlier work described by

Wilton [2] is also relevant to the specification of these paradigms.

The guiding principle that has been adopted in formulating these paradigms is a consideration of peer interaction in learning. The paradigms are based on the extent and character of communication between students using network based software; not on the resourcing features of different types of network environments.

Many teachers have observed that significant verbal interaction can occur between students who are working in groups with CAL programs. These groups could be using a stand alone computer or a workstation in a network. It follows that much of the network specific communication that is referred to in this paper could be augmented by verbal discussion within groups of students located at a workstation. For the sake of simplicity the term "student" is taken to refer to an individual or a group located at a workstation.

same program. In some cases different programs will be used at different network stations.

The advantages associated with this paradigm are not fundamental in terms of educational philosophy. They are to do with maximising resource provision and effective classroom organisation. For example, using a network in this way enables scarce printing resources to be used more effectively and does not require multiple disk copies to be produced.

3.2. Independent work in a common workspace

Here access to the same copy of a program from a number of workstations is provided. When access is provided in this way all the students will be working on the same task in an independent fashion. When any one of the students interacts with this copy of the program they will change the state of the model and/or data that the program is based on, both for themselves and for other students using the

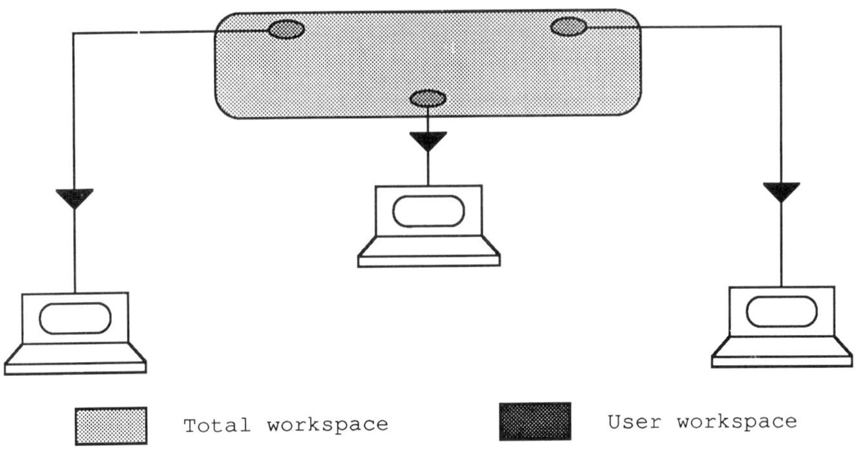

Figure 2: Multiple stand-alone use

3.1. Multiple stand-alone use

This paradigm is the simplest educational use of networks. Access to copies of a program are available to students at their individual network stations. Each student uses her copy in isolation from students using other copies at their workstations. The access to the software is private with the actions of other students in running their copy of the program having no effect of any other copies. In fact in terms of interaction with the software the situation is equivalent to a group of stand-alone microcomputers each using a copy of the program supplied on disk. This paradigm is represented by Figure 2. For clarity only three workstations are shown in this figure and following figures. Obviously it is not essential for all students to run a copy of the

program from other workstations. Students will be unaware of the origin of changes made by other students - they will simply experience an environment which they can only attempt to control on a partial basis. Wilton [2] quotes a stock-market model in which each student plays the role of a stockbroker as an example of this paradigm. She also notes that airline reservations systems provide an example from the real world. Figure 3 represents this paradigm.

It is important to note here that the program will not run on a co-operative basis as there is no communication between the students using the program. Students will have to react to the decisions of other students simply by interpreting their actions through the behaviour of the program; discussion and

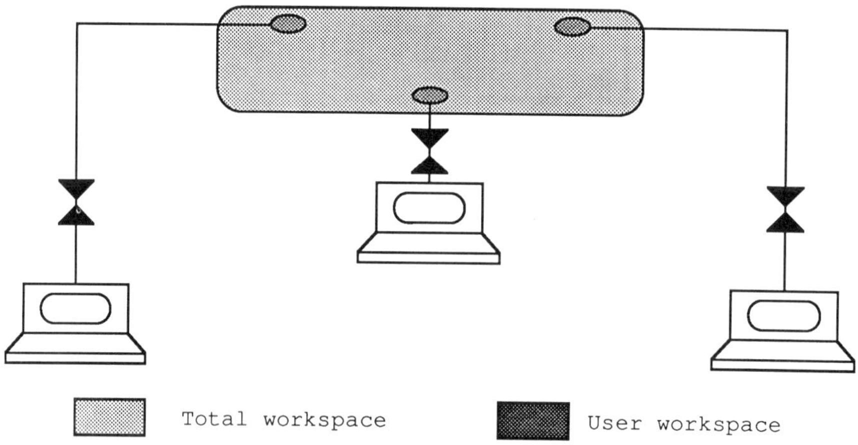

Figure 3: Independent work in a common workspace

collaboration in making decisions are not part of this paradigm

3.3. Individual contribution to a shared task

It is possible for students to use a common program which presents a task which is dependent on the collaboration of students. The work of each student will have some effect on the overall completion of a common task. Typically students would be required to assume roles related to the task in hand. An example of this type of application is provided by NTRECK, produced by the Solo/NET/Works project [3,4]. In this application students assume roles in the management of a spaceship. Obviously the successful management of the spaceship will depend on successful completion of these roles by individual students. Figure 4 represents this paradigm.

Although there is no explicit communication between the students via the network the actions of the students are related through the observed results of their actions of their peers. This contrasts with the second paradigm where the effects of peer action are seen as perturbations on the state of the environment which are accommodated according to an individual student's personal needs. Here the state changes, viewed in the context of the role each student is assuming, are a form of implicit communication between students.

3.4. Group work with the same or similar task

Here students are able to communicate with each other as they work independently on the same or similar task. Communication is effected via the network and they may have access to shared resources via the network. NEWSNET is an

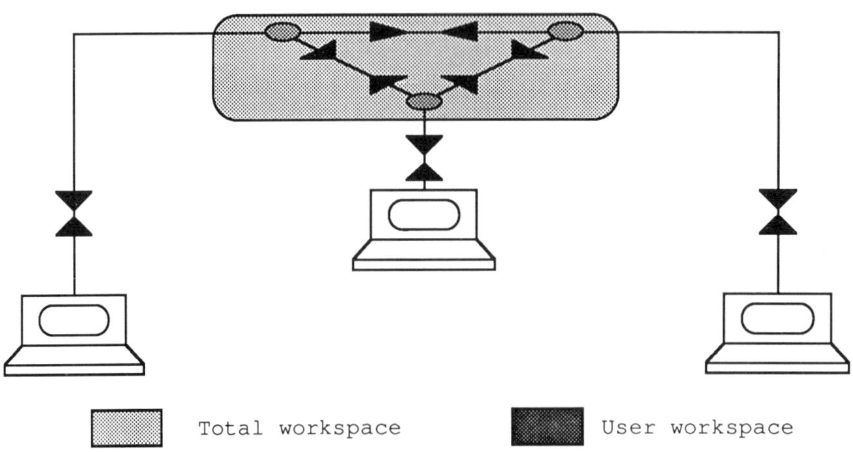

Figure 4: Individual contribution to a shared task

example of this paradigm, where the software provides a framework for students to collaborate in the completion of a shared task; the preparation of the front page of a newspaper. Although the students can collaborate by communicating via the electronic mail system work on their individual tasks is not directly affected by other students. Figure 5 represents this paradigm.

A major aim of software in this paradigm is to sponsor collaborative learning by providing a mechanism for communication via the network. However students can work in an autonomous fashion, only communicating with their peers when they want to.

3.5. Group work with a shared task

Here students are able to communicate with each other as they work together on a shared task with communication effected via the network. COMNET provides examples of this paradigm. The form of communication in the semaphore program and the telegraphy program require the students to work in a dependent fashion, with the actions of students directly influencing each other. Figure 6 represents this paradigm.

As in the fourth paradigm, a major aim of software in this paradigm is to sponsor collaborative learning by providing a mechanism for communication via the network. However, here the software requires the students to work in a dependent fashion.

4. CONCLUSION

The most obvious difference between a network CAL program and a conventional stand-alone CAL

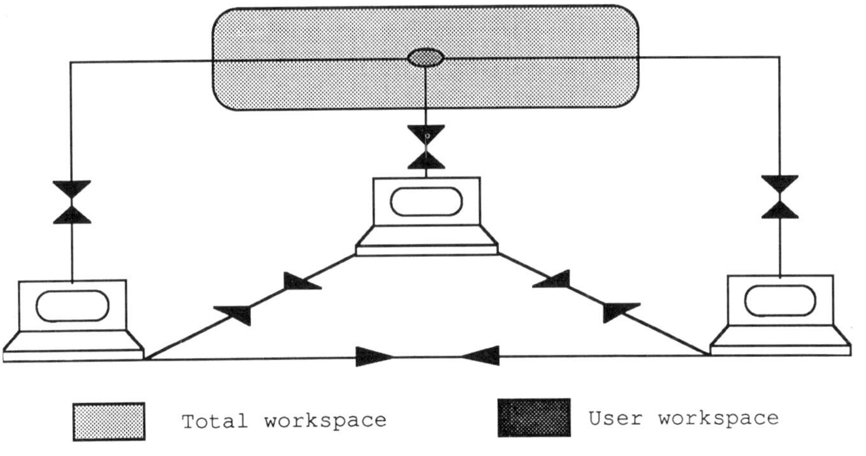

Figure 5: Group work with the same or a similar task

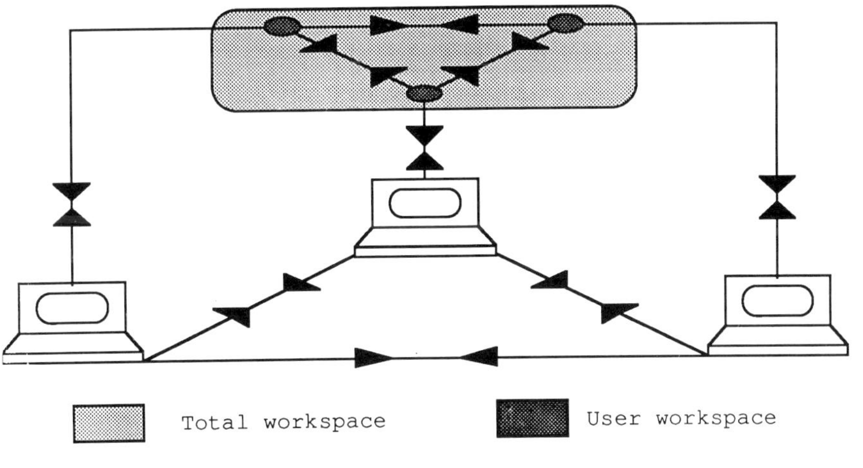

Figure 6: Group work with a shared task

program is that a network program involves a number of separate groups or individuals using different linked computers whilst a stand-alone program involves one group or individual using an isolated computer. In this sense there is no educational difference between stand-alone use and the first paradigm. However the remaining paradigms can be used to illuminate innovative features of network CAL; identifying relevant design issues. In particular two issues emerge: communication style and task definition.

A fundamental aspect of networks is communication between users. In CAL packages this communication is used to encourage educational activities. Consequently the style of communication that the software makes available is important, as the style should be consistent with desired learning outcomes and teaching approaches. Two distinct communication styles emerge from a consideration of the paradigms described in this paper. In the fourth and fifth paradigms the form of communication is explicitly defined by the software. This can be contrasted with the third paradigm where the communication style is implicit. In this case the software does not provide clear protocols for communication as in the fourth and fifth paradigms. Now the communication style is mediated by the character of the task in hand, with students communicating with each other indirectly by interpreting and responding to the actions of other students.

Tasks in a network based environment can have different levels of student autonomy. Students or groups can be given personal responsibility for a task or sub-task as in the second or fourth paradigm. In the second paradigm there is no co-operation between students in the completion of tasks. However, the fourth paradigm does not preclude co-operation between students; rather it allows children to work independently in a co-operative environment. The third and fifth paradigms involve task sharing. In the third paradigm sharing is through implicit communication, whilst in the fifth paradigm sharing is through explicit communication.

Networks are destined to become an increasingly common feature of computer provision in schools. If we are to realise the educational benefits of networks, rather than simply use them as convenient hardware configurations, it is essential that a significant number of high quality network CAL packages are developed. The concepts of communication style and task definition which emerge from the paradigms described in this paper should assist in the specification and design of quality network based CAL.

REFERENCES

[1] Preston, C. and Squires, D., NEWSNET (British Telecom Education Service, London, 1989).

[2] Wilton, J.A., Structured Learning Networks: The Possibilities for Networked Software, in: Duncan, K. and Harris, D., (eds.), Computers in Education (Elsevier Science Publishers B.V. 1985) 491-496.

[3] Dwyer, T.A., Multi-Micro Learning Environments: A Preliminary Report on the Solo/NET/Works Project, Byte (1981 (1)) 204-216.

[4] Dwyer, T.A. and Crichfield, M., Multi-Computer Systems for the Support of Inventive Learning, Computers and Education (1982 (6)) 7-12.

Computers in Education
A. McDougall and C. Dowling (Editors)
Elsevier Science Publishers B.V. (North-Holland)

MAKE ENDS MEET WITH A SPREADSHEET

Eric VISCH

Model School Project West-Netherlands, Vrije Universiteit Amsterdam, Department of Cognitive Psychology, De Boelelaan 1111, 1081 HV Amsterdam, The Netherlands

Within the scope of the Model School Project West-Netherlands the possibilities were explored for the application of a spreadsheet to teach household management. The starting-point in the development of the experimental lessons was the Economics curriculum. The spreadsheet was used successfully as a tool for calculating the expenses of a household, for checking the calculations and for analyzing the expenses of the household. The use of a spreadsheet surprisingly results in more detailed concern for the quantitative aspects of the topic.

1. INTRODUCTION

In 1987 the Netherlands Ministry of Education, together with the Institute for Educational Research (S.V.O.) initiated the Model School Project West-Netherlands (PWN). The main objective of the project is to study the effects of large-scale introduction of computers in a secondary school. A secondary school with 1400 students has been equipped with 49 computers and 50 release hours per week. A team of 5 researchers from two universities was established. In five departments (Mathematics, Dutch Language, English Language, Geography and Economics) a development team was composed. Each team consists of two teachers with release hours, a subject matter specialist, a computer co-ordinator of the school, and a researcher.

There are many possibilities for the use of a spreadsheet for teaching Economics. Porozny [1] describes, as possible spreadsheet activities in education, the first year costs of owning an automobile, vacation budgeting and the cost of family weekly or monthly food bill. Milks and Bell [2] refer to the use of a spreadsheet for budgeting the expenses of a household. They explored the introduction of a spreadsheet in Mathematics. Their goal was to teach the operation of a spreadsheet for illustrating mathematical concepts.

The development team of Economics of PWN chose to experiment with the use of a spreadsheet for managing a household: Make Ends Meet [3]. This topic is taught in the second form. Successively housekeeping money, pocket-money, fixed charges, and replacement expenses arise in the curriculum. In conclusion the total amount of expenditure in a household is compared with the incomings. The goal is to make students aware of the advantages of arranging complex information systematically. In addition pupils have to be prepared to use calculation instruments in their later jobs. In our opinion a spreadsheet could be a tool in the realization of goal. A spreadsheet can make the arrangement of the information more well-ordered and also do a part of the arithmetic. The introduction of the operation of the spreadsheet is necessary, but it is a subgoal. This is in contrast with the order of the goals in the research of Milks and Bell.

In aid of the experimental lessons about 'Make Ends Meet' the development team made templates in the spreadsheet PC-CALC [4] and worksheets. The try-out of the first version was carried out in May 1988. On the basis of the experiences with the first version, the templates and worksheets were revised. This paper describes the framework, the performance and the conclusions of both versions of the experimental lessons.

2. THE CURRICULUM

The curriculum of 'Make Ends Meet' was the starting point in the construction of the templates and the worksheets. The goals of 'Makes Ends Meet' were converted to the following learning activities:

a. Education about the concepts.

   The categories of the expenses are covered qualitatively by short written texts and exercises.

b. Calculation of the amount of expenditure.

   Students process the expenses in well-ordered tables. They calculate the amounts for a fixed period. In the lessons the calculations of students are reviewed. The students respond passively. In the best case they correct their answers, but they don't correct their calculations.

c. Drawing conclusions about the amount of expenditure.

   The amount of expenditure, the distribution of the expenses over the year and the relation to income are discussed. In the tasks the students have to remodel the expenses in order to be able to analyse the financial

Figure 1 - The use of computers in the classroom.

situation of the household. The expenses have to be re-aligned, re-calculated or re-displayed in another form. The students pay most attention to the remodelling of the information and they have only a little time for drawing conclusions.

3. THE FIRST VERSION

3.1. The framework (first version)

In the first version the spreadsheet supports the second and third learning activities. The first activity is not supported with a spreadsheet. The categories of expenses are discussed in the class during the experimental lessons. In aid of the second and third activities the spreadsheet is used in the following ways:

1. Reviewing (activity 2).

   In the first version the students have to do the calculations on paper by hand. In the lessons they have to put the data in a loaded template. The right formula for the calculation is placed in the template by the authors. The spreadsheet calculates the right answer with the formula. The students have to check their answer and to correct their calculation by studying and explaining the formula.

2. Drawing conclusions independently (activity 3):

   a. by sorting the data.

   The students have to sort the data. The data are displayed in the template as numbers. The students have to examine the relations between the sorted quantities.

   b. by experimenting with variables.

   The students have to vary the value of a variable, through which the value of another variable changes. The students have to draw a conclusion.

3.2. The performance (first version)

The first version of the experimental lessons was tried out in three second classes. The students had had no experience in school with the operation of computers. Before the experimental lessons the students were being taught to work with PC-CALC.

The lessons were given by two teachers. Both teachers had no experience in the use of computers in education. The researcher had followed the lessons in one class. In the lessons he observed a group of two students working with the spreadsheet. He assisted other groups regularly. The students had operational problems as well as problems concerning the content. The observations of the researcher and the experiences of the teachers were discussed in the development team.

3.3. Conclusions (first version)

In section 2.1 the ways in which the computer supports the education in 'Make Ends Meet' were described. After the performance of the lessons the role of the computer was evaluated.

1. Reviewing
The students checked and corrected their answers only. In their opinion studying and explaining the formulae was boring. They had responded passively and often they explained a formula by copying it to the worksheet. So they had not corrected their calculations.

2. Drawing conclusions independently
   a. by sorting the data.
   The operation of sorting the data with a spreadsheet was difficult for many students. After sorting the data, the relation between the quantities was not at all clear for the students.

   b. by experimenting with variables.
   The way of experimenting with a simple arithmetic model was not clear for many students. The students didn't make the distinction between the imported variables and the exported variables. As soon as the meaning of the task was clear, the students were able to draw the right conclusion.

4. THE SECOND VERSION

4.1. The framework (second version)

Based on the experiences with the first version, the ways in which the spreadsheet support the learning activities, were changed in the second version.

	A B	C	D	E F	G	H	I J
1	MAKE ENDS MEET - House keeping money (in guilders)						
2							
3	MONTHLY SUM TOTAL			FRIDAY PURCHASES			
4							
5	quan	article	total	quan	unit	costs	
6	tity	and unit	amount	tity			
7							
8	9	whole meal bread	20.70	2	bread	4.60	right
9	2	packets butter	2.90	1	packet	1.45	right
10	5	packets margerine	2.95	1	packet	0.49	wrong
11	1.35	kg meat-products	20.25	200	g		
12	3.9	kg meat	35.10	500	g		
13	5	kg fruit	14.75	1	kg		
14	3	bottles of wine	14.94	2	bottles		
15	2	bottles of cola	2.70	1	bottle		
16	2	bottles of sherry	12.90	1	bottle		
17	1	bag of nuts	4.75	1	bag		
18	4	cakes	9.00	2	cakes		
19						________ +	
20					TOTAL AMOUNT		
21							

Figure 2 - the template 'house keeping money'.

1. Reviewing

In the second version students make calculations using the spreadsheet. For each calculation they have to construct a formula in a template. The spreadsheet calculates the result with the formula. Furthermore the spreadsheet compares the result of the calculation with the right answer which is hidden in another part of the template. Depending on the results of the comparison the students receive feedback about the answer. The expectation was that the students would check and correct their calculations more actively. Figure 2 contains an example of a template which is used for calculating the housekeeping money. The students have to construct a formula for the calculation of the costs of the Friday purchases in column H.

2. Drawing conclusions independently

a. by sorting the data.
In the first place the operation of sorting is described in the second version as a cookbook recipe in the worksheets. In the second place the data are not displayed just by numbers, but they are displayed in bar graphs too. The expectation was that the graphical appearance of the data would make the relation between the quantities more clear.

Figure 3a contains an example of a template which is used by showing the distribution of the fixed charges over a year. For each month the balance and the total amount of fixed charges are displayed in bar graphs. After sorting the balances the template of figure 3b appears on the screen. The students have to relate the balance and the height of the fixed charges.

b. by experimenting with variables
In the second version the students have to fill in the results of their experiments in a table on the worksheet. The expectation was that in this way the task would have more structure and so the task would be more clear for students.

Figure 4a contains an example of a template which is used for experimenting with the replacement-time of the furnishing of a household. In the cells H9, H10, J9 and J10 the authors have placed the formulae for the amount of money to be set aside each year and each month. The students have to investigate how many years John and Ada have to keep their furniture if they are to be able to set aside 200 guilders each month. The students have to experiment with the arithmetic model in the spreadsheet by varying the number of replacement years and they have to fill in their results in the table on the worksheet (figure 4b). They have to draw their conclusions as a result of their analysis.

MAKES ENDS MEET - Fixed charges (in guilders)

MONTH	BALANCE
jan	-12.00
feb	208.00
mar	-162.00
apr	157.00
may	-87.00
jun	-200.00
jul	-12.00
aug	208.00
sep	-135.00
okt	184.00
nov	-180.00
dec	31.00
TOTAL	.00

BALANCE
debit credit

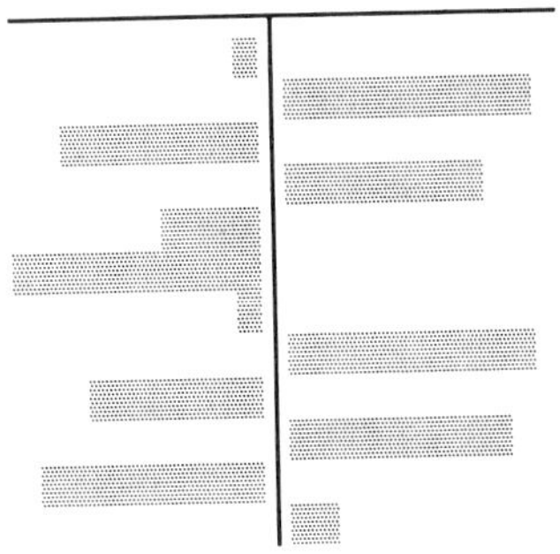

FIXED CHARGES
684.00
464.00
834.00
515.00
759.00
872.00
684.00
464.00
807.00
488.00
852.00
641.00
8064.00

FIXED CHARGES

Figure 3a - the template 'fixed charges' (before sorting).

MAKES ENDS MEET - Fixed charges (in guilders)

MONTH	BALANCE
jun	-200.00
nov	-180.00
mar	-162.00
sep	-135.00
may	-87.00
jan	-12.00
jul	-12.00
dec	31.00
apr	157.00
okt	184.00
feb	208.00
aug	208.00
TOTAL	.00

BALANCE
debit credit

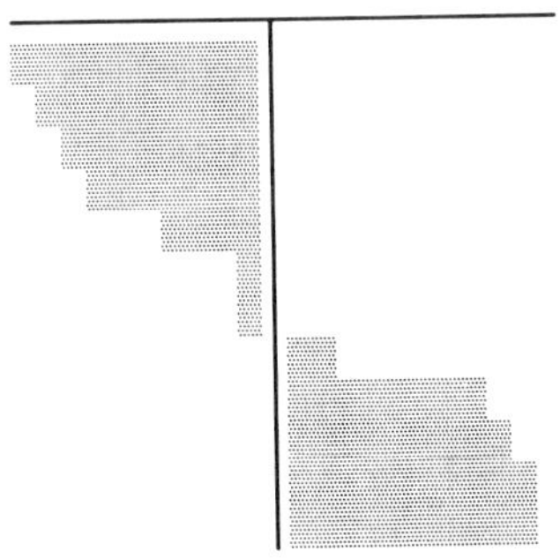

FIXED CHARGES
872.00
852.00
834.00
807.00
759.00
684.00
684.00
641.00
515.00
488.00
464.00
464.00
8064.00

FIXED CHARGES

Figure 3b - the template 'fixed charges' (after sorting).

MAKE ENDS MEET - Replacement expenses (in guilders)

	furnishing costs	number of replacement years	money set aside per annum	money set aside per month
John and Ada	18000.00	5.0	3600.00	300.00
Ernest and Ann	48000.00			

Figure 4a - the template 'replacement expenses'.

4.2. The performance (second version)

The second version of the experimental lessons was tried out in four second classes. The students had followed an introduction in the operation of the computer of ten lessons in the first class. Before the experimental lessons the students had learned to use PC-CALC. The lessons were given by two teachers. In the meantime both teachers had acquired some experience in using a spreadsheet in education.

John and Ada Furnishing costs: f. ______________		
number of replacement years	money set aside per annum	money set aside per month
3	f. ________	f. ________
4	f. ________	f. ________
__	f. ________	f. ________
__	f. ________	f. ________
__	f. ________	f. ________
__	f. ________	f. ________

Figure 4b - the worksheet 'replacement expenses'.

The researcher had followed the lessons in one class. In the lessons he had observed one group of two students working with the computer. In addition he had made inventories of special activities of the students. The observations of the researcher and the experiences of the teacher were discussed in the development team.

4.3. The conclusions (second version)

In section 3.1 the changes of the way in which the spreadsheet supports the activities with respect to the first version have been described. In this section the effects of the changes are discussed:

1. Reviewing

The direct checking of the formulae constructed by the students was very accurate. The feedback 'right' was for the students a stimulus to go on. The students responded to the feedback 'wrong' differently. Some students would look at the right formula on the screen of other students and mostly they were able to construct the next formula by themselves. Other students looked at the formula they had constructed themselves and they were able to improve the formula as in the case of the next observation:

"Marc and Eric are filling in the amounts on their worksheet and then they are going on to calculate the amounts per month. The Jazz-ballet costs 21 guilders per quarter.

Eric constructs the formula: E22*12/4: f. 63,-.
The spreadsheet displays 'wrong' on the screen.
Eric: "The amount is already per quarter!"
He constructs the formula E22*4/12 and the spreadsheet displays 'right' on the screen."

2. Drawing conclusions independently

a. by sorting the data.

Describing the operation of sorting on the basis of a cookbook recipe worked. The impression is that by the graphical display of the quantities the students made the relation between the quantities more easy. An observation to illustrate this point:

"Marc and Eric sort the balances by following the instructions on the worksheet. They look at the screen to see what is happening. After that they draw their conclusions about the relation between the balance and the fixed charges.
Their conclusion is:
'The balance is going from low to high; the fixed charges are going from high to low'."

b. By the addition of the tables in the worksheets the task had more structure. Which variable the student had to vary, appeared from the table. The students filled in the results of the experiments. They discussed the results and made predictions about the further experiments.

Of that the next observation is a good example:

"Marc and Eric read the worksheet. They vary the number of replacement years in the template: 3, 4, 5, 6, 7, 8 years. They fill in the amounts for setting aside for the furnishing of John and Ada's home in the table on the worksheet. For 8 years the amount to be set aside is lower than f 200,- per month. Their conclusion is that John and

Ada have to keep their furnishing for 8 years. After that the same task follows for the furnishing of Ernest and Ann's home.

Eric: "I think they have to keep their furnishing for more years; the cost of their furnishing is higher."
Marc: "I think the opposite."
Eric: "Let have a try!"

They vary the number of replacement years: 3, 4, 5, 6, 7, 8 years. For 8 years the amount to be set aside for the furnishing of Ernest and Ann's home is f 500,- per month.

Eric: "There you are! They have to keep their furnishing longer."

They try: 10, 15, 16, 17, 19, 20 years. For 20 years the amount to be set aside is f 200,- per month. They draw the conclusion that Ernest and Ann have to keep their furnishing for 20 years."

5. DISCUSSION

The goals of the curriculum of 'Make Ends Meet' were translated in section 2 to three learning activities. In these three activities the management of the household was considered quantitatively as well as qualitatively. The concepts are covered qualitatively. By the calculation of the height of the expenses the students learn quantitative skills. In the case of drawing their conclusions the students have to remodel the quantitative expenses in a form in which they were able to draw qualitative conclusions. In support of the quantitative activities a spreadsheet is used in the experimental lessons. The presentation of the data is well-ordered and the spreadsheet takes over a part of the arithmetic.

It is remarkable that by the use of a spreadsheet in this part of the curriculum the students spend more time and pay more attention to the quantitative activities. The spreadsheet may take over a part of the arithmetic, but the use of a spreadsheet gives many possibilities to compose the quantitative activities. In addition the students are more actively engaged in the experimental lessons. They improve their calculations and they discuss the consequences of the amount of the expenditure.

To integrate the use of a spreadsheet to teach Economics, it is recommendable to take the curriculum as the starting-point. Analysis of the curriculum results in the specification of the learning activities. The use of a spreadsheet can than be considered. It is important to give the students an active role. One possibility therefore is to let students construct formulae themselves. Another possibility is to let students experiment with a spreadsheet to make analyses. The instructions in the worksheets have to be clear. The graphical presentation clarifies the data for the students.

REFERENCES

[1] Porozny, George H.J., Electronic Spreadsheet and Database Applications Across The Curriculum, in: Collins, J.H., Estes, N. and Walker, D., The Fifth lnternational Conference On Technology And Education (Volume 1) (Edinburgh, 1988), pp. 569-572.

[2] Milks, Nancy and Bell, Norman, Spreadsheet Math For Middle Schoolers, in: Collins, J.H., Estes, N. and Walker, D., The Fifth International Conference On Technology And Education (Volume 1) (Edinburgh, 1988), pp. 561-564.

[3] Linden, H. Van der en Peters, L., Economisch Bekeken (Den Bosch, 1986), pp. 145-194 (in Dutch).

[4] PC-CALC - version 3.0, Buttonware Inc. (1985).

Computers in Education
A. McDougall and C. Dowling (Editors)
Elsevier Science Publishers B.V. (North-Holland)

INNOVATION IN SOFTWARE DEVELOPMENT

Deryn M WATSON

Educational Computing Unit, Centre for Educational Studies, King's College London, University of London, 552 Kings Road, London SW10 0UA, United Kingdom.

There is a real tension in software development between the needs to serve both innovation and the status quo. This coincides with a growing interest in issues and methods of software development. A case study of one four and a half year project, that has produced three units is described. This work has made heavy use of a variety of prototyping tools. The impact of this, and other aspects of change, are explored with respect to their resulting innovation, in both the nature of the product and the development process.

1. INTRODUCTION

Software development is characterised by the need to resolve conflicting pressures. One major tension resides in whether development should be technologically or pedagogically driven. Although it is increasingly recognised that software development can only be successful if it is underpinned by a clear educational philosophy (Bork [1], Burkhardt et al [2], Watson [3]), there still remains fundamental differences in the way the work is executed. Who should be involved in the development process? What determines the technical specifications and who draws them up? What relationship is there between the authoring, design and technical specifications? (Ramburg [4], Schoenmaker et al [5], Hojsholt-Poulsen [6], Haugen [7], Watson [8]). Overriding these questions about an appropriate development model lies the issue of innovation.

Should software support innovation or should it reflect the status quo? Thus, should software:

- support the existing curriculum or open up the new;
- sustain traditional teacher-centred classroom delivery or radical student-led collaborative learning environments;
- use standard patterns of user interface, or explore the new;
- be developed for hardware environments known to be in schools or for the new?

Since all innovations involve change, and the introduction of software into schools would categorise computers as a major potential change agent, software developers should have a clear perception of their position between the two poles of innovation and status quo, as this will drive their response to development decisions. Moonen [9] suggests that software should support established approaches, because of financial constraints and because educational innovation and change are slow.

It is certainly true that growing interest in methods of software development are related to the length and costs of development, and the problems schools appear to have in incorporating software into the curriculum. But if we want software to have a long term impact, we should surely veer towards innovation, and innovation in both methods of development as well as the nature of the outcome.

One major innovation that has affected the development of courseware over the past few years has been the significant growth in the availability of tools to aid the development process. While the idea of using tools and prototyping is not new, the current variety and availability for appropriate hardware has enabled them to have greater impact. Tools could therefore enable one to streamline the development process, making it both more efficient and cost effective. However, what are the other effects of using prototyping tools?

This paper reports on one particular development project, over a four and a half year period, in which conscious and deliberate use of tools was made throughout the development process. It provides therefore a case study from which one can observe the real and detailed impact of these tools.

2. THE PROJECT CONTEXT

2.1. Aims

The Educational Computing Unit based at King's College has been developing software for some 16 years under the umbrella of the Computers in the Curriculum Project. A clear philosophy has underpinned this work, that software should be developed to support, enhance and extend curriculum delivery and learning within schools; a model for operation emerged to implement this philosophy. Both the model and its shifts through time have been documented, and in particular the role of teachers as authors in the development process (Lewis and Want [10], Watson [11]).

British Gas commissioned the Computers in the Curriculum Project in 1986 to develop software that explained the complex workings of their business and was clearly related to the curriculum framework of secondary schools. In particular they wanted innovative material that illustrated:

- the complexity and challenge of a problem to the gas supply industry;
- the technological nature of the industry;
- the business and economic nature of the industry.

Computers in the Curriculum welcomed the opportunity to:

- develop software that has a distinct cross-curricular unity, after many years of developing material with a single subject focus;
- use the openings promised by the new environments (that is 16 bit computers) and to utilise commercial software tools for development.

2.2. The team

A team was established to explore these ideas and develop the software to run on machines found in schools. The team consisted of subject specialists in the areas where we anticipated ideas might emerge (mathematics, physics, geography and economics), CAL developers, programmers and systems analysts. This team differed from those previously set up, however, in two crucial respects.

Firstly, teachers who were still classroom based were not an integral part of the development team. A deliberate decision was taken to use one experienced and creative CAL developer, with many years association with the project, for each discipline. This enabled us to reduce the delivery time of the first product by six months and develop a new cross-curricular focussed team based at King's. In order to mitigate one of the effects of this decision, that is the removal of practical and recent classroom understanding of delivering the current curriculum, a panel of teachers was drawn together to discuss and review the curriculum idea during the development stage.

The second major change was that the CAL development team had to familiarise itself with the workings of the industry to be able to stimulate ideas and choose appropriate topics for curriculum development. This familiarisation with aspects of the industry required access to a variety of parts of its operation not normally available to the public, an understanding of issues sensitive for commercial or political reasons, recognition of the cost for key officials to discuss their work with the development team, and for a regular working dialogue to emerge. In this way, members of the industry in effect became part of the development team. But some of the time gained by using experienced CAL developers was spent in researching the industry itself.

Interestingly, a new style of software has emerged directly influenced I believe by the time the CIC team spent exploring and examining British Gas operations, in an attempt to gain an insight or window on various activities within the industry. The style is based upon a simulation where the overriding focus is a work shadowing environment, where pupils shadow the role of the operator within the system. This idea was half-formed in the first unit, and fully developed in the rest. The learner responds not to questions or prompts in menus, but to demands generated and illustrated within the screens themselves. This innovation therefore came from the context of the work.

2.3. The curriculum units

The overall theme Network for the Nation was chosen, based upon the network of gas pipelines that cross the country, carrying gas from coastal reception terminals to the customer. This was to be mirrored in the networks of people and facilities which made the whole operation work. Three units emerged, each with their specific curriculum focus.

Working Under Pressure places pupils in the position of planning a pipeline to take natural gas, from a variety of shore terminals, to the customer. They need to balance issues such as the diameter of the pipes, the location of various compressor stations, and seasonal variations in demand, to produce the most efficient design for the task. This supports the design/technology curriculum. Delivering a Service places the pupil in the role of the work shadow, following a gas engineer who services customers' appliances. The whole operation, from receipt of call, job allocation, collection of spare parts, to fixing the appliance itself is reflected in a series of screens which the student works through as if they were operators in the various compartments. This has been designed to fit into the economics/business studies syllabus. Consulting the Community is a planning exercise, such as those that lie in the heart of many geography syllabuses. Rather than simulate a typical planning debate or enquiry between various parties or locations, the unit follows a year in the life of the planner in the industry whose job it is to promote and prepare the building of a plant in an area so that by the time it comes to making outline planning application, there is a good chance of success.

These three CAL units reflect:

- the range of operations, from business management to direct customer contact;
- the modern technological nature of the industry, and in particular the way IT is used during the work;
- the current concerns in three syllabus areas, physics/design and technology, geography and business studies.

All three units incorporate using IT within them, e.g. a calculator, computer aided design package, a database and a project planner. For each the pupil uses such packages within, rather than separate from, the educational simulation.

2.4. Management, costs and the flow of work

The development of these three units took four and a half years. The team was formed in May 1986; the completed software and manuscript for the third unit will be handed over to the publisher in September 1990. Each unit went through the documented key stages for both the technological and curriculum aspects of the work; a significant amount of tight scheduling was required to achieve a proper flow of work.

The cost of this operation in person/years were as follows:

Director/CAL developer	0.1
Coordinator/CAL developer	0.4
Programmer	1.0
Systems Analyst	0.1
Authors/CAL developers	0.2
Office support	0.1
Illustrator	0.2
Institutional support	0.5
Total per annum	2.5
Total for project	11.25

These figures indicate that, despite the wealth of experience in software development, the costs and time involved were equal to, or greater than those of earlier developments. An explanation can be found in the next section.

3. PROTOTYPING TOOLS

Within the context of this work, prototyping tools were used for a variety of tasks.

3.1. Using tools for prototyping design

All three units were designed not just with pencil and paper, but with active use of software to aid the design process. This prototyping fulfilled four functions;

- the specification of mathematical models and range of appropriate costings;
- the sketching out of the flow of the unit and its interrelating parts;
- the planning in detail of the screen design to illustrate the ideas determined by the structure;
- the development and cross referencing of the user interface and potential paths through the structure.

Thus after the initial identification of the idea, the functional and structural design of the unit was determined through exploration; tools used at this stage included DMS (a modelling system) and Logostix for testing models and results, Macpaint and Macdraw for screen mapping, and Hypercard for structural relationships.

In the past this stage of the development, that is, the ideas, exploration and design specification, has involved the drawing up of charts and comic strips which were implemented in code direct onto the final host machines. These first draft programs inevitably required rewriting as the designs were refined. This was time consuming as it involved wasteful rewriting of code. Prototyping enabled this route to be short circuited so that principle design discussions and explorations could take place before implementation.

Various hidden implications however emerged.

- Firstly, two of the three authors did not have regular access to all the tools. The demands of hardware availability meant time was still spent drawing screens by hand or briefly sketching on machine, which the programmer then implemented.
- Learning to use these tools efficiently takes a considerable amount of time, which easily matches the time gained by reducing recoding.
- The capabilities of these tools inevitably directly influenced design considerations.

CIC has paid a significant amount of attention over the years to the design of educational software (Alderson and DeWolf [12], Millwood and Riley [13]). We feel strongly that each design should properly reflect the educational aim of the unit and the learners' routes through it, rather than the underlying model and internal logic of the program structure. We recognise that structural design of the user interface takes as long as model design to execute. The users' interface was now however being directly influenced by the facilities offered by prototyping tools. How much is this design ahead of the interface pupils will meet on the host machine in schools? Our use of active buttons to supersede pull down menus has been influenced by the design environment; it is not what pupils are currently used to.

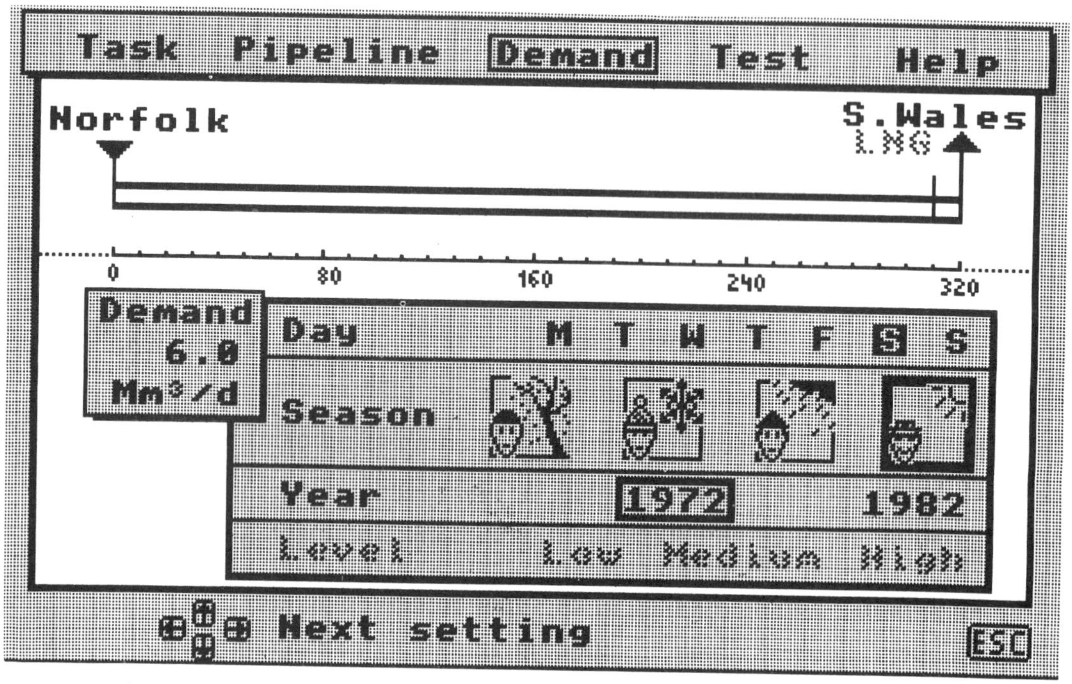

Figure 1: Icon and screen graphics for Working Under Pressure

Figure 2: Pictorial screen for Consulting the Community

3.2. Developing tools for implementation

It would appear to be inevitable in software development that the host machine on which the software is destined to be implemented are not necessarily those that carry the most efficient or greater range of development tools. Thus features of the design environment that become desirable through familiarity with the development tools place demands upon the implementation strategy.

The CIC implementation strategy is based on using languages and tools to ensure that the software is relatively hardware dependent. Thus a philosophy that led initially to the development of a BASIC subroutine library, has resulted in the development of a procedural library based on Turbo Pascal. This enables the software to run on a variety of 16 bit MS DOS hardware. It has been the expectancy of the project that a significant number of tools to aid the development and transfer of code between environments would make our own tool developments redundant. This has not proved to be the case. The procedural library had to be expanded to cover features demanded by the design prototype including a mouse interface, active window buttons, picture file storage, and proportionally spaced character sets for use within the graphics environment. Thus while the design work was proceeding, implementation tools had to be developed in parallel. Note that these implementation tools have not been developed in isolation away from the dictates of design. It is I believe a mistake to suppose that the functional and structural demands of software creation can be served totally by a pre-existing set of tools. If the implementation tools and defined environments are too strongly determining factors, then software design will not progress imaginatively and innovate.

3.3. Tools for graphics

A need emerged to either find or develop a graphics drawing tool that would emulate the illustrative facilities of the Macintosh environment. One author frustrated by his lack of a Macintosh turned to a piece of schools' commercial software, NEWSPA, that emulates the various functions of a newspaper production unit. His drawings were imported as picture files using new picture encoding tools developed for this purpose. These subsequently included facilities developed to read and display the data in compressed form, thus saving disc space and reducing display time. At this stage the screen prototyping moved from the Macintosh to NEWSPA. Because of the specific skills required by the increased emphasis on pictorial representation, an illustrator was employed to translate the author's rough drawings and sketches into polished illustrations.

There is no doubt that the availability of graphics tools has had a specific influence on the overall screen design of the second and third units. Comparison between Figures 1 and 2 clearly indicate a move from the more traditional icon and screen graphical representation with pull down menus, to a more radical and realistic pictorial basis with information and active buttons incorporated into each screen's visual image.

4. CONCLUSIONS

This particular development work therefore resulted in change both in style of unit but also in the methodology for development. The units are much more substantial than those previously developed, e.g. c90 megabyte of code for a 16 bit machine compared with 10-12K for an 8 bit - a direct influence of the greater capacity of the environment for which they have been designed. They also reflect reality in industry through offering a simulation that is not just about an area of operation, but places the pupils in the position of being a participant in the environment itself. Their design has been critically influenced by the nature of the prototyping tools used. These in turn have led to the development of further in-house implementation tools to adequately reflect the demands of the design.

There is a ready temptation when using prototyping tools to choose a host machine because of the design environment inherent within it. But the choice of host hardware for educational software must be determined by the technology likely to be available in schools. By the time the two do occur together, it is more likely that different tools have emerged with newer technologies. As long as software is aiming to be innovative in both curriculum and design terms, working in different environments for prototyping and implementation is likely to remain with us. Using such tools also makes it very tempting to assume that they remove the need for both professional programmers and creative teacher/authors. This project has reinforced for us both the vital creative skills that subject based authors have, and the need for professional programmers to implement ideas and structures put together from using a variety of tools.

This development work has been no shorter or cheaper. The use of tools while speeding up one aspect of the operation, has opened up new possibilities for innovation. We are not a software factory but a curriculum research and development team; we are now concerned to explore further the implications of such innovations in both technological and pedagogic terms.

REFERENCES

[1] Bork, A., Education Technology Centre at the University of California, California, in: Lewis, R. and Tagg, E.D. (eds.), Computer Assisted Learning - Scope, Progress and Limits (Heinemann, London, 1981).

[2] Burkhardt, H., Fraser, R., Clowes. M., Eggleston, J., and Wells, C. Design and Development of Programs as Teaching Material (Council for Educational Technology, London, 1982).

[3] Watson, D.M., A Model for the Production of CAL. Computers and Education (1983) Vol. 7, No. 3.

[4] Ramburg, M., A Model for Designing, Developing and Testing Educational Software, in: Moonen, J. and Plomp, T., (eds.), Developments in Educational Software and Courseware (Pergamon Press, Oxford, 1987).

[5] Schoenmaker, J., van der Mast, C., and Moonen, J., A Methodology for the Development of Educational Software, in: Developments in Educational Software and Courseware (Pergamon Press, Oxford, 1987).

[6] Hojsholt-Poulsen, L., Production of Educational Software: the situation in Denmark. Education and Computing, (1985) Vol. 5, Nos. 1,2.

[7] Haugen, H., Development Tools for Educational Software: Open Ended Software and Creative Programming Tools. Education and Computing (1989), Vol. 5, Nos. 1,2.

[8] Watson, D.M., Software Development: the Challenge of Change. Education and Computing (1989), Vol. 5, Nos. 1,2.

[9] Moonen, J., Courseware Development at the Crossroads? Education and Computing, (1989), Vol. 5, Nos. 1,2.

[10] Lewis, R., and Want, D., Educational Computing at Chelsea (1969-79), in: Lewis, R. and Tagg, E.D. (eds.) Computer Assisted Learning - Scope, Progress and Limits (Heinemann, London, 1984).

[11] Watson, D.M., Developing CAL: Computers in the Curriculum, (Harper and Row, London, 1987).

[12] Alderson, G. and DeWolf, M., Guide to Effective Screen Design, (Computers in the Curriculum, London, 1984).

[13] Millwood, R. and Riley, D., Design Guide for Procedure Library, (Computers in the Curriculum, London, 1988).

Computers in Education
A. McDougall and C. Dowling (Editors)
Elsevier Science Publishers B.V. (North-Holland)

ALLEGRO CON TECHNOLOGICO E PEDAGOGICO - 6 YEARS OF RAPID DEVELOPMENTS IN TEACHER SUPPORT FOR MUSIC EDUCATION WITH COMPUTER TECHNOLOGY

Colin WELLS

Lecturer in Information Technology Education, Department of Arts and Humanities, Faculty of Education and Community Studies, University of Reading, Bulmershe Court, Earley, Reading RG6 1HY, United Kingdom

Abstract: This paper will illustrate the rapid developments which have occurred in the area of Music Education and Computer Technology, particularly over the last 6 years: the changes in curriculum thinking, in relevant hardware and software systems, in methods of classroom use, and in teacher education. It will also show how the various activities of the Music Education Centre Microtechnology Unit at Reading University have developed to support these changes.

1. INTRODUCTION

If the use of computers and other forms of high technology in particular curriculum subjects is to be properly integrated and effective, then it is essential that the people involved in its promotion and development are specialists in those curriculum areas. The focus of thinking must be the needs of the children in that subject area, and ways of enhancing their education, rather than technical issues of computer operation or programming.

It was for this reason that, in September 1984, Dr Anthony Kemp and myself, with financial support from the Government's Microelectronics Education Programme (MEP), founded the Microtechnology Unit as part of the Internationally acclaimed Music Education Centre in the University of Reading.

Over the six years since its founding, the Microtechnology Unit has attracted over a third of a million pounds of Government support, though its Microelectronics Education Programme (MEP), and its Microelectronics Education Support Unit (MESU), (now a part of the National Council for Educational Technology (NCET)), has produced a range of curriculum materials, provided a free information service for music teachers and advisers, and has undertaken over 3,500 teacher-days of in-service teacher training in the uses of microtechnology in music education in the United Kingdom and in several other countries. It is this range of activities, together with the Unit's experience in teaching in the University's pre-service teacher education courses and in the unique Master's Degree course in Microtechnology in Music Education, that have resulted in International recognition for the Unit, and that now provide a firm foundation for the discussions presented in this paper.

2. DEVELOPMENTS IN THE MUSIC CURRICULUM

It is only too easy for people working in the field of computers in education to have their heads so filled with thoughts of the rapid changes in available computer systems, modifications in peripheral devices and in the design and availability of software, that they fail to perceive that the curriculum areas in which they are seeking to apply the computer technology are in themselves evolving and developing, often at a significant rate. This is particularly true of the music curriculum, which has been undergoing a period of radical re-thinking and re-evaluation over the last few years.

Ten years ago it was not uncommon for music education in schools to consist mainly of listening to records, learning about famous composers, singing some songs and learning some musical notation. Those few pupils who took music as an examination subject, usually those having private instrumental lessons, went on to learn about the rules of harmony and counterpoint, which could be applied in composing music on manuscript paper, generally in silence; study a few 'set-works' of music in analytical detail; learn about the history of music and musical forms; and practice notating short pieces of music played to them. Thus the emphasis was on learning about music, with most practical music making being left to the school (or district) orchestra, band and choir.

In the late 1970's and early 1980's, there were many experimental moves to try and change school music into a much less elitist subject, by placing the emphasis on doing music, and asserting that everyone was capable of performing, composing and listening perceptively. This approach was fostered by the Schools Council Project, 'Music in the Secondary School Curriculum', based at York

University during this period, and by books such as those by John Paynter [3] and [4], and by Keith Swanwick [5]. The publication of guidelines for 'Music from 5 to 16' by the Government's Inspectors of Schools in 1985 [1] formalised this approach, stating that 'music education should be mainly concerned with bringing children into contact with the musician's fundamental activities of performing, composing and listening'.

It was therefore not surprising that the new UK National examination syllabus requirements (GCSE), which were published in 1986, were built around these three activities, with a high proportion of the assessment being for coursework, consisting of group and individual performances, and a series of composing activities. Furthermore, the examination criteria stated that all pupils should be cabable of taking the subject of music as an examination subject, and not simply those who were taking extra instrumental lessons. The other major innovation was the lack of emphasis on 'standard' staff notation, which allowed pupils with no written musical skills to hand in compositions recorded on cassette tape, accompanied by written descriptions or graphic (pictorial) scores.

These changes, whilst welcomed in principle, were a source of great worry to music teachers, particularly the large numbers who had never engaged in practical composing activities, apart from the 'silent manuscript writing' type. It was therefore fortuitous that suitable microtechnological aids were becoming available to help enable pupils with limited performance and notational skills to build up and develop compositions to an acceptable standard, and these were seen as a 'god-send' by many teachers. Over the last few years, because of these various developments, it has become not uncommon to see 25 pupils in a school's music examination group, compared to the three or four pupils one would often see under the old examination system.

There is therefore now a radically different environment in school music in the UK, and this needs to be reflected in changes in the type of support available from computers and other forms of technology.

3. DEVELOPMENTS IN HARDWARE AND SOFTWARE

In the early 1980's there were numerous music education computer programs available, notably for the Apple IIe computer, but these were mainly of American origin, and very much geared towards learning music notation, music theory, harmonic rules and aural skills - topics which were being given lower profiles in the UK. In any case, there were hardly any Apple IIe computers in schools in the UK - the common system being the Acorn BBC model B. Many people wrote music programs for this system, but large numbers of these were still concerned with learning about aspects of music notation and theory. A few programs did try and follow the general trend in being more open-ended, being useful as teaching aids in promoting discussions and explorations on certain topics or concepts. However, these still had two important draw-backs: the first being that the quality of sound for any programs involving aural development was very poor, and was unacceptable for many musicians, and secondly that the topics involved were still often concerned with the academic and notational elements of music.

Two different solutions to the problem of sound quality were produced, which were designed to enable the use of more creative music programs. The first of these was the development of sound boards or sound boxes dedicated to particular computer systems, for example the Alf boards for the Apple IIe, the Hybrid Technology sound box for the Acorn BBC, and the integral synthesiser box for the Yamaha CX5M computer. Initially, the Yamaha system was more appealing to music teachers, as it had a music keyboard attached, rather than the other systems with which music had to be entered in coded form via the typewriter-style keyboard. However, even the Yamaha system only had a 'step-time' composing program, where one had to define lengths of notes, rather than playing the required rhythm naturally, as many pupils would prefer. Thus this system still favoured pupils with a good knowledge of music theory and notation.

The other approach, which started to become available in 1984, was to use MIDI. This is an Internationally agreed system of interchanging coded musical information between a range of musical devices, including computers, synthesisers, sound samplers, rhythm machines and various controlling devices. At the simplest level this meant that one could attach a synthesiser via a MIDI interface to a computer, and, with suitable software, could store music in the computer which had been played on the synthesiser keyboard. Furthermore, the computer could replay this music on the synthesiser whilst an additional part of the music was being added, thus allowing a complex piece of music to be built up part by part. Because the information was stored in coded form, rather than sounds being recorded, this kind of system allowed various kinds of editing to be done, for example to change the tempo without altering the pitch of the sounds, or to select different sounds for replay. These features alone were of enormous benefit to the kind of children being attracted into music through the new guidelines and examination system, who perhaps had ideas for composing that they were not capable of performing adequately themselves.

The earliest MIDI systems had some drawbacks, however, which made them less attractive to prospective users in schools. Firstly, although the MIDI standard allows for up to sixteen channels of information to be sent in order to play back music with up to 16 different instrumental sounds, the early MIDI synthesisers could only accept one MIDI channel at a time, and thus be only able to play one sound at a time (though with many simultaneous notes). Thus to build up an orchestral composition with, say, 6 parts for different instruments, would have required 6 different synthesisers or sound sources, each using a different MIDI channel. This, of course, was prohibitively expensive for most schools. The second drawback was the lack of memory size in the 8-bit computer systems then being commonly used, which resulted in very poor editing facilities being available in the programs, and a capacity to store only very short pieces of music.

It soon became clear that 16 or 32-bit computer systems were needed for this type of composing program, and examples appeared in 1986 and 1987 for such computers as the Apple Macintosh, Atari 1040ST, IBM PC, Commodore Amiga and Apple IIGS. There was still this division in thinking as to whether the high quality sound should be internal to the computer or externally accessed via MIDI (or other interface). The Commodore Amiga and the Apple IIGS were two examples of systems which were built to include high quality sounds, but for musicians, who generally required a musical form of input - typically a music keyboard - the MIDI route was a simpler way to meet this need and also provide a sound source. Fortunately by this time the MIDI synthesisers were being produced with multi-timbral facilities, that is, they could play back several different MIDI channels at once, allowing fully orchestrated music involving many different instrumental parts to be created - though still limited to the overall polyphony of the synthesisers (typically 8 or 12 notes).

The music peripherals to use with MIDI then started to become modularised, with separate sound boxes (without keyboards) providing for addition parts of music, and various forms of musical controllers (without sound), to allow for a range of performance skills to be used to play or compose with the sounds. These controllers included keyboards, percussion pads, and those in the form of guitars, woodwind or valve instruments, complete with the normally expected level of touch or breath sensitivity to enable control of such things as volume or vibrato.

The increase in the desire of musicians and music pupils to use music peripheral devices has been recognised by software writers, and some recent packages being produced for systems such as the Atari 1040ST and Apple Macintosh allow full control over all aspects of the program from a controlling music keyboard (or other instrumental controller), with perhaps some use of the mouse on occasions. Certainly the move is away from the use of the typewriter-style keyboard, which can be very inhibiting when using a musical program. (Further descriptions and ideas for using music computer systems can be obtained from the 'Music Computer Cookbook', written at Reading, and published by NCET [7].)

Of course, what is being described above is, to some extent, a speading out from general-purpose computer systems into a range of dedicated and interlinkable modules using computer technology. These modules can provide synthesiser capability, allow acoustic sounds to be sampled and stored digitally for later playback, provide sequencing and editing facilities for music, allow drum patterns to be built up and played, add various effects such as reverberation or delay, provide control over the mixing or spatial placing of sounds, and control over inputting and editing notes or musical phrases. Although disguised as intuitive musical items, these are really dedicated computers which can be linked together into a kind of network using the MIDI system. It is worth stressing again that the majority of technological devices currently being used in schools in the UK for music education are not general purpose computers, but are these dedicated musical computer devices, or other forms of technology, such as tape recorders.

4. DEVELOPMENTS IN THE USE OF MICROTECHNOLOGY FOR MUSIC EDUCATION

Moving from the state of music education described at the beginning of this paper to one which integrates a large amount of technological devices in an effective way is obviously a major change, and one which inevitably takes time. There are many schools in the UK which already have large amounts of technology for music education, thanks to special funding from schemes such as the Government's Technical and Vocational Education Initiative (TVEI), but there are also large numbers of other schools still taking their first tentative steps in this direction.

As music is fundamentally about sound, the most important provision for the practically based music curriculum is that of an adequate, exciting and motivating range of sounds or tone colours, from which the pupils can choose appropriately for the activities they are undertaking. This should include acoustic sounds from classroom instruments, but is being enormously enhanced through electronic sounds produced by electronic keyboards, synthesisers, sound boxes, sound samplers and computers. Many of these devices offer fixed choices of sounds from 'libraries', whilst others allow the sounds to be modified or edited to form new tone colours - both these require careful listening descrimination. Some modern forms of synthesis are quite complex, and these can be made considerably easier by the use of sound editing programs on computers, which display the various parameters graphically.

Whilst the choice of sound is important for music activities, it is the dynamic control of these sounds that makes the difference between a collection of notes and a sensitive musical performance which communicates some aesthetic feelings. Many controlling devices now exist, for example to allow movements of wheels or sliders to subtly adjust the volume or vibrato of sounds being played, to allow the breath pressure on a wind controller or the kind of touch on a keyboard or drum pad to modify the resulting sound in some way, or to allow synthesised sounds to slide in pitch in response to singing a portamento into a special microphone. Such devices can allow pupils to undertake sensitive musical performances, or engage in composing activities 'playing' instrumental sounds that they would otherwise not be able to play.

Having chosen appropriate sounds and methods of control, it is often necessary to combine sounds - acoustic and electronic - by using mixers, which allow the component sounds to be balanced and placed spatially in terms of stereo listening. Other sound processing units are also important, for example to add reverberation, boost certain frequency ranges, and to provide echoes or controlled levels of distortion for special effects.

Of course, the other major contribution of technology to the process of composing, is the provision of storage facilities. By enabling children's compositions, improvisations and performances to be recorded for later playback, this facility allows the children to listen in detail to the whole musical performance in a way that is not possible to do whilst performing, particularly as part of a group. It also enables valuable activities such as discussions, self-criticism and sharing of ideas to take place.

The most obvious kind of storage device for music is the tape recorder, with more sophisticated compositional activities being enabled by those with multi-track facilities. Much use is made of these devices in schools. However, the more important and liberating features are provided by recording music in digital form, as is the case when using MIDI devices in conjunction with a computer-based (or dedicated) sequencer. These can accept input from any form of MIDI control device, played in at a reduced tempo if necessary; can combine and build up parts of music; can speed them up to the required tempo; allow changes in sounds for any of the parts; display the score in staff notation or graphics; and enable expression, i.e. subtle changes in volume or tempo, to be added by using various forms of simple, intuitive control device. This last feature is extremely important, as it allows the user to feel the music he or she is composing, enabling them to interact with the composition in a dynamic way.

It should now be clear that although computers can play a very important part in enhancing music education, there are many other forms of dedicated musical technology which are required for any sense of balanced support, and which are often essential as computer peripherals. In the UK it is still difficult to establish this point with the Government and Educational Authorities, who have helped with the funding of basic computer systems for schools, but who generally leave the school and its staff to purchase their own special peripheral devices. This makes it particularly difficult for the music teachers, who, along with all other subject teachers, are expected to follow the Government's guidelines in integrating the use of computers into the curriculum in appropriate ways, but who often lack the appropriate and necessary additional supporting equipment.

5. DEVELOPMENTS IN TEACHER TRAINING AND SUPPORT

Apart from the problems of equipment provision, the other major area of concern is that of training the teachers. As explained at the start of the paper, this is not just a matter of training them in effective uses of computers and technology, but often also training them in the whole philosophy and approach of the new style music curriculum.

The Government's Microelectronics Education Programme (MEP) was required to undertake in-service teacher training, and most of the training in music (over 3,000 teacher-days during two years) was undertaken by the MEP sponsored Music Education Centre Microtechnology Unit at Reading University.

Most of this training was organised through Education Authorities in the UK, and, because of various management and financial constraints, normally consisted of from one to three days. With so short a time, it was perhaps inevitable that the first reaction was to make the equipment the dominant focus, and allow little time for detailed curriculum considerations. But it soon became obvious that the use of microtechnology could only be put properly into perspective by talking about curriculum needs.

In fact the most successful courses run were one lasting a week, and a specially funded phased course of four separate weeks, allowing time to try ideas out in the classroom. These longer courses provided the time required to discuss curriculum issues in depth, and to find out how the new technology would affect teaching styles, classroom management and types of educational activities. They allowed the teachers on the course to follow a more exploratory approach to their own learning about technology, rather than being given didactic lectures or factual demonstrations. The teachers were encouraged to present simulated lessons for discussion, and to make video films of their music classes using technology for consideration later on in the course. They allowed time to present microtechnology in a balanced and integrated way with the other resources in the music classroom, and enabled discussion of particular target groups of children.

Courses such as these serve to emphasize the need for curriculum subject specialists to undertake the training activities of their colleagues in the effective uses of microtechnology, rather than have courses run by 'computer specialists', as was all too often the case in the earlier days of the development of computers in education.

The Microelectronics Education Support Unit, set up in 1986/87, built on this approach, and commissioned various groups of curriculum specialists to develop support materials. MESU were also given the brief to train Advisory Teachers, who were to be good curriculum practitioners, rather than 'computer experts'.

As one of the two Music Curriculum Projects funded under MESU, (the other being based in the University of Warwick), the Music Education Centre Microtechnology Unit at Reading University has been heavily involved with the training of these Advisory Teachers in music. It helped with their initial course and then it organised and ran the second follow-up music course after the Advisory Teachers had been doing their support job for a year. It is perhaps interesting to observe, from this second course, that many of the Advisory Teachers had become pre-occupied by details of computer operation, seemingly to the exclusion of other ranges of technological support for music education, and one wonders if this is a reflection of the Education Authorities' policy of providing schools with computers, but not the more specialised peripherals. This has seemed to have resulted in the Advisory Teachers trying to do too much with the computer systems - using them when other resources would have perhaps been more appropriate - and in spending the majority of their time helping teachers with the operation of these computer systems.

There is an important lesson to be learnt here - that one must start with the curriculum and see what resources are required, rather than make a global management decision to purchase a certain type of equipment, and then try and apply it in a range of diverse educational situations (remembering that the majority of technological equipment best suited to support music education does not consist of general purpose computers, but a wide range of other devices).

In terms of pre-service music teacher training, this is generally lacking in microtechnology content, due to the lack of resources and staff training in most training institutions. The Government is trying to improve the situation by insisting that all pre-service teacher training courses should contain appropriate uses of information technology, but compulsion in itself will not provide the needed resources and staff experience.

The few training colleges with expertise in this field, including the University of Reading, are mounting useful introductory courses for their students, but available time is very short during a year's post-graduate teaching course crammed with a multiplicity of lectures, discussions, school experience and other activities. To provide teachers with a good understanding about how computers and microtechnology can enhance the music curriculum, as well as providing an adequate knowledge of the range of relevant musical devices and systems, really requires at least a full year of study, and to this end Reading University started its M.A. course in Microtechnology in Music Education.

A third of this M.A. course is devoted to music education curriculum methodology, to provide the necessary underpinning. Then the practical module concerning the range of relevant devices and software is put firmly in context by a major section on educational applications, which involves not only several visits to schools for critical observation, but also a series of group teaching experiences in local schools, to apply ideas where it matters - in the classroom with children. Everyone that has so far completed this course has commented that they now realise that they have so much more to learn about this field of work!

6. FURTHER SUPPORT FOR TEACHERS

Where and how can teachers find out more about the use of computers and microtechnology in music education? One answer is to contact the Music Education Centre here in Reading University, where part of the role of the microtechnology team is to offer an information and advice service to teachers and advisers not only in the UK, but also from any other countries.

Secondly, the publications which the staff have produced may provide much needed information and ideas. Apart from the general guideline USPEC booklets [2] and [6] which they helped produce for the National Council for Educational Technology (NCET), the team were commissioned by MESU to produce a series of six packs of material between 1987 and 1990. The topics for these packs were:

- Creative music activities using a range of microtechnology
- Using a music computer system
- Using electronic keyboards in primary schools
- Aspects of multi-cultural music and microtechnology
- Using non-keyboard technology devices (e.g. the microphone)
- Music microtechnology for children with special needs

These have been (or will be) published by NCET, and should provide some help to teachers embarking on this still new and exciting field of work.

7. CONCLUSION

Much has been achieved in the last few years, but much is still to be done, particularly in terms of adequate resource provision and a major programme of long courses for teacher training. It is hoped that readers of this paper, who may not have known much about musical applications of computers and technology before, now realise that this field is of major importance, and not just another 'fringe' subject dabbling in computing. It is also hoped that the various lessons and messages presented in this paper are considered carefully, so that the progress made so far can be continued in a positive and fruitful direction, for the good of education.

REFERENCES

[1] D.E.S., Music from 5 to 16 - Curriculum Matters 4. (HMSO, London, 1985).

[2] Ellis, P., Ibbs, S. and Wells, C., Electronic Music Systems (USPEC 24). 2nd Ed. (NCET, London, 1990).

[3] Paynter, J. and Aston, P., Sound and Silence. (C.U.P., Cambridge, 1970).

[4] Paynter, J., Music in the Secondary School Curriculum. (C.U.P., Cambridge, 1983).

[5] Swanwick, K., A Basis for Music Education. (N.F.E.R., Slough, 1979).

[6] Wells, C. and Kemp, A.E., A Guide to the Selection and Use of Electronic Musical Instruments (USPEC 24). 1st Ed. (CET, London, 1985).

[7] Wells, C., Music Computer Cookbook. (NCET, Reading, 1990).

Computers in Education
A. McDougall and C. Dowling (Editors)
Elsevier Science Publishers B.V. (North-Holland)

PROGRAMMING AND PROBLEM SOLVING

Joan Frances WILCOX

The University of Sydney Institute of Education,
PO Box 63, Camperdown, NSW 2121 Australia.

Programming and Problem Solving is the name of a strand of the Post Graduate Diploma in Educational Studies (Computer Education) offered to practising teachers by Sydney University's Institute of Education. This strand was introduced in 1989 to replace an introductory course in BASIC programming - the emphasis being on programming concepts, good design and problem-solving applications, rather than on the features of a particular language. Logo is the language which has been chosen to illustrate most concepts. The course attracts teachers from all levels of schooling and all disciplines, and has no computing pre-requisites, so an attempt has been made to find an approach which will, if possible, be new to all participants, and one which will be relevant both to those whose interests lie in enriching their own classroom teaching and to those aiming to become computer consultants or teachers of computing studies. This paper outlines the content of the strand, giving a justification for each aspect as well as an analysis of its difficulties and its successes.

Programs are not uncommon in everyday life - at concerts, for television and radio, and as a teaching plan. Such examples were mentioned by the students at the beginning of this one-semester subject of the Computer Education diploma. It was agreed that their common feature was the ordering of their component parts, and this led us to a first look at computer programming as a *sequence* of specialised instructions. To highlight the importance of this aspect, a number of activities were selected using graphics, music and practical 'hands off' written work.'

The first of these involved the use of a program 'Kiddie Art' [1] written for the BBC computer and implemented solely through the function keys. The program allows the creation of pictures involving only squares and right-angled isosceles triangles (in a 'roof-like' orientation which cannot be rotated). The current shape may be translated as required, its colour changed and its size enlarged or reduced, but once a next shape has been generated, no previous one may be altered. With a little ingenuity, quite elaborate designs may be created, and the user is forced to plan each successive stage. The final result may be saved to disk under a chosen name and loaded back as required. Students were given the task of presenting a sequence of up to ten diagrams, with brief wording if required, for another group member to implement. All successfully completed this activity, and seemed to enjoy it, some producing quite elaborate pictures within the given constraints.

Their next encounter was with the Logo primitive TOOT, (as implemented on the Apple IIe). TOOT takes two inputs - frequency and duration; for example Toot 262 60 sounds the note Middle C for one second. It may be accessed in immediate mode, but students very soon requested a means by which a sequence of notes could be saved, and our *Logo programming* segment began. Nursery songs are usually based on obvious patterns - for example, each line of 'Frere Jacques' is composed of a repeated bar, whereas the structure of 'Jingle Bells" may be denoted

```
JINGLE.1 JINGLE.2 JINGLE.3
JINGLE.1 JINGLE.2 JINGLE.4.
```

A means of implementing a fixed number of *repetitions* arose naturally from such examples,and the value of a *modular structure* was apparent. A number of tunes were developed using previously-created sub-procedures

DO, RA, MI, FAH, SOH, LAH, TE, DOH, RAY.

One student tried out her tunes on an Apple IIGS, whose speed of execution is many times greater than that of the Apple IIe; her comments opened the way for the introduction of the idea of a *variable* (for a note's duration). This idea pleased those who had been dissatisfied with their first attempts at estimating an appropriate speed for the tunes, and made possible some variations in the tonic solfa modules mentioned earlier. A single variable DUR is sufficient for all notes as the different types may be represented :DUR / 2, :DUR / 4, and so on. The students' next request was for the addition of words, and this led to the introduction of list processing.

This introduced a variety of new ideas, including *output* statements (PRINT and TYPE), further work with variables (*inputs* using READLIST, READWORD and READCHAR and *assignment statements* using MAKE), *selections* (IF . THEN . ELSE, and IF THEN), *simple calculations*, *random numbers* and *recursion*. The last of these was the means by which a request, say, could be repeated if the user's response made such a necessity. Non-tail recursion was introduced later with the inclusion of variables in recursive procedures, using both TOOT and PRINT commands. Both REPEAT WHILE and REPEAT UNTIL structures were encountered in this way.

The writing of a computer 'poem' as described below showed clearly how procedures can implement the thought processes required to achieve the desired result. Some learned the hard way how careless naming of procedures can create misunderstandings. The poem was to be of this form:-

> I went walking one fine day
> And took a *adjective.1 noun.1* ,
> Not too far along the way
> I met a *adjective.2 noun.2* .

where *noun.1* and *noun.2* rhyme and are chosen at random from sets

CAP	COAT	HAT	SCARF	and
CHAP	GOAT	CAT	CALF	

and *adjective.1* and *adjective.2* are different and randomly-chosen from the set

HAIRY HANDSOME HEAVY SHABBY TINY

(an idea similar to that described in [2]) A typical top-level structure produced by the students is shown here:

```
TO VERSE
MAKE.DICTIONARY
CHOOSE.NOUNS
CHOOSE.ADJECTIVE.1
CHOOSE.ADJECTIVE.2
WRITE.POEM
END
```

When asked to comment on the advantage(s) of using a modular approach to programming, students suggested the following:

'allows for an orderly sequence of instructions to solve the problem',
'make structure easy to see',
'modules can be individually tested',
'modules can be re-used' and
'saves typing and uses less space'.

Others have written about the advantages of introducing programming through Logo music. (See [3] and [4].) The ease with which errors in Logo programs may be located and corrected, as emphasised by Papert [5], is as obvious with TOOT as with Turtle graphics, and, unlike the latter, no problems occur with the interfacing of one module with another. Quoting from a previous paper, Masterson [6] claims that

> Two requirements for a student programming language are *simplicity* and *power*. . . A third requirement for a student language is *cognitive efficiency:* the extent to which the language facilitates *thinking about* problems.

He later claims 'Logo has the distinction of being *one of the few programming languages designed to meet the above requirements* . ' Writing in the same journal, Bennett and Walling [7] insist that

> the real measure of the ease of writing a program . . . is to determine to what degree the language being considered allows its user to make use of the principles of
>
> 1. sequential operations,
> 2. IF-THEN-ELSE logic,
> 3. iteration, and
> 4. modular program construction.

They warn that this will not automatically follow if Logo is the chosen language; the teacher must so select activities that these principles become apparent.

In the past, I have used the 'Turtle' approach with adult learners in order to either develop or recall inherent mathematical ideas (angles, polygons and variables), but have found that such immediately divides such a group into those who 'know' and those who 'have forgotten', with the latter being often those for whom even the *mention* of mathematics is daunting. Turtle Geometry had also been the approach for those who had had a previous encounter with Logo. The 'musical' approach was new, and seemed to require very little other than an 'ear' for the simple tunes. A table of note frequencies, and a diagram showing the correspondence between notes on sheet music, piano keys and the tonic solfa were given to each student. In general, they worked individually, but shared successes and difficulties, and occasionally created a joint effort, such a canon production of 'Frere Jacques'.

In parallel with the 'hands on' Logo programming, the students undertaking 'Programming and Problem Solving' encountered a number of ideas through written activities. 'Mazetalk' [8] is a 'language' (using the four major compass directions and a specified number of steps) for instructing imaginary robots to traverse a maze from a given entrance to a given exit. It is written in a form akin to *pseudocode* and involves a wide variety of programming concepts, from which only a limited number were presented to the students. These included both a fixed repeat and a 'repeat . . . until' instruction. Students were asked to devise a program for a given maze, keeping secret the names of entrance and exit, and present this to a fellow student for decoding. As with the Kiddie Art activity, this highlighted the need for accurate, unambiguous instructions.

Other 'hands-off' activities were borrowed from Lynch [9] to introduce the use of both flowcharts and structured English. A first activity involved the writing of a sequence of eight instructions (one per small piece of paper obtained by folding then dividing a larger sheet) for making an afternoon snack. Each person's set was shuffled then exchanged with that of a neighbour, who attempted to rearrange the set. This provided a physical representation of a flowchart, and also highlighted the fact that the sequencing of instructions need not always be unique. Flowchart representations for the programming structures encountered were used to illustrate each Logo procedure in problems such as the writing of VERSE (described above).

The group consisted of twenty students, thirteen of whom had a secondary school focus (grades 7 to 12) with the remainder involved with primary school (grades K to 6). Twelve had had no programming experience; three of the others had some knowledge of BASIC only, while the other five had met both BASIC and Logo. Two hours per week were devoted to lectures and group laboratory activities for this subject; a further hour of supervised individual laboratory work was provided. One of the group had no outside access to a computer, and only a minority of the others had Logo available Lack of time for practical work was commonly-felt constraint.Halfway through the fifteen-week semester, a one-hour written test was undertaken. Results indicated that previous programming experience had not been of great advantage; but clearly some newcomers had taken to the ideas more readily than others.

Turtle graphics were introduced in the latter half of the course,firstly using a floor turtle and then a screen representation. The students were given the task of producing a computer 'quilt' (an idea borrowed from Moore, [10]). They divided into groups of four people - each person to be responsible for a design (to fit within a square of given size), and each group one section of the total quilt. The aim of the project was to consolidate previous concepts and to force the students to solve the problems of interfacing the modules, an essential part of the planning of any large programming project. Turtle designs do not necessarily require either a modular structure or the use of variables, but students were encouraged to consider designs involving these concepts (with examples from Newell, [11]).

Commenting later on this project, the students described the importance of group consultation at each stage. In designing the procedure for 'joining' the pieces, the value of uniformity in the choice of a first and final position of the Turtle in each design, and the necessity for unique names for distinct procedures were realised. Most used variables to allow them to adjust their designs to achieve a pleasing result. One group implemented a theme (the four seasons) for their set of motifs.

The final assignment for the course was an individual one involving sound, text and graphics. Many students were not content to use previously-developed ideas (as was suggested), and embarked on most ambitious projects, often with spectacular results. Throughout the course, students kept their own 'dictionary' of both system commands and language features, and a Logo reference sheet was incorporated into their final written examination paper.The course concluded with a brief look at a few 'parallel' sets of simple programs written in Pascal, BASIC and Logo, to provide a perspective on programming ideas which they had encountered.

The results of this new approach seem pleasing; both the students and I, their lecturer, enjoyed the sessions, and their appreciation of the various concepts was apparent. I found it interesting to compare my plan with that of Dalbey and Linn [12] when implementing a first course in computer programming for junior high students. They invented a special interactive 'robot' language, Spider World, which allows the creation of coloured patterns. It was provided with a built-in editor, the possibility of subroutines, and a Repeat-Until looping function. They concluded that this software 'had a strong motivational effect on the students' and speculated that 'it is likely that it was beneficial in helping students overcome any initial anxiety they may have had about using the computer.'

I suspect that some of my adult learners may well have been more apprehensive than any junior high school student about learning to program, and so I sought to select activities which were enjoyable, did not depend too greatly on any specialised previous experience, provided a new approach for those with some knowledge of programming, and emphasised fundamental concepts and good program design. The students appear to have found the course a challenging one - in many cases because of the tasks they set themselves. Indeed, a Logo environment encourages the learner to do this, and to experience the value of breaking down any problem into smaller tasks. I found it difficult to pace the course so that it might be of value to all members of such a diverse group, but look forward to improving my strategies with the next group. A set of worksheets, assignments and tests is available to any interested persons upon request.

REFERENCES:

[1] King, J. C., Big, bright and beautiful. The Acorn User No 54 (1987) 87-91.
[2] Cooper, C. C. H.,Computer Programming, Exploring Mathematics on Your Own Series Number 18. (John Murray, London, 1969)
[3] Fox, C. and Gomilschak, U., Exploring music through Logo. Paper presented at the Logo day associated with ACCE87 (Adelaide, 1987)
[4] Gibbons, P., Logo through music: Yet another approach. in: Making it happen.- Proceedings of the 6th Annual Conference of the NSW Computer Education Group . (N.D.E.C. Cheltenham NSW.,1988) 31-35.
[5] Papert, S., Mindstorms. (Harvester Press,Sussex,1980)
[6] Masterson, F. A., Evaluating Logo: a case study for student programming languages. Computers in the Schools 2(2/3) (1985) 179-195.
[7] Bennett, H. and Walling, D., Once again, structured programming: Is it necessary ? Computers in the Schools. 2(2/3).(1985) 171-178.
[8] Goodnow, J., Mazetalk discoveries: Getting ready for computer languages.. (Creative Publications, Palo Alto,1984)
[9] Lynch, I. J., Concepts & exercises in computer studies. Unit 1: Algorithms. (Mentone Educational Centre, Ashburton, Victoria, 1988)
[10] Moore, M., Logo discoveries: Explorations and programming activities for beginners. (Creative Publications, Palo Alto,1984)
[11] Newell, B., Turtle confusion: Logo puzzles and riddles. (Curriculum Development Centre, Woden, ACT,1988)
[12] Dalbey, J. and Linn, M. C., Cognitive consequences of programming: Augmentations to BASIC instruction. Journal of Educational Computing Research.2(1).(1986) 75-93.

Computers in Education
A. McDougall and C. Dowling (Editors)
Elsevier Science Publishers B.V. (North-Holland)

USING SCHOOL BASED COMPUTERS FOR INSTRUCTIONAL SUPPORT - IS IT WORTH THE BOTHER?

Dr. Peter W. WRIGHT

Adult Career and Technology Education, Faculty of Education, University of Alberta, Canada, T6G 2G5

In discussing curriculum trends of the future, Ornstein (1989) affirms that "a school that does not emphasize technology will mis-educate students for the future". But how can a school go about achieving this emphasis on technology? One strategy is for school administrators to lead by example. The use of microcomputers for instructional support provides an excellent opportunity for the school principal and his assistants to demonstrate leadership in the application of computers. After reviewing the process for evaluating and selecting the most appropriate software system, this paper presents the findings of a survey of the first ten Edmonton Public High Schools to implement microcomputer based student information management.

1. INTRODUCTION

There is no truth to the rumour that the computer was invented in the mid-nineteen seventies - it just seemed as though it was. For all that matters, it might just as well have been since it was about then that mere mortals sat up and took notice. Prior to this time, the only people who were really interested in them were technophiles (whose first language was COBOL), businessmen who already knew that they couldn't do without computers even though they couldn't speak COBOL themselves, and executives with a propensity for blue, pin striped suits.

All of a sudden, however, with the advent of the microcomputer, computers seemed relevant to almost everyone, including educators. And so it was that the schools began to fill up with microcomputers. At this stage in the history of educational computing, we worried a lot about where the money would come from to buy more computers and we counted them often. While we were still trying to figure out what to do with them, pseudo religious wars broke out over which computers should be used - there were casualties. Despite the losses, however, we were not deterred from attempting to make everyone computer literate, even though there was little agreement on what that really meant. Recognising that commercially available courseware of the day was either rubbish or non-existent, we began to teach teachers how to program in BASIC since this was surely where all of "the good stuff" was going to come from. By the time it was realised that this was not the thing to do, better, general purpose software had become available, notably, the productivity tools and Logo. A problem solving cult emerged. And just imagine! Word processors appeared which didn't require special add on hardware, which would display all eighty characters on a line and which did not require a vivid imagination (or a printer) to understand what things would come out like. And so, amid emerging equity issues regarding student to computer ratios, we began to focus our efforts on the productivity tools, spawned in large part by the miracle of Apple Works.

Today, we are all databasing, spreadsheeting and even desk top publishing - pouring words into columns so that they run around pictures and engaging in endless font fiddling. The authoring system, which seemed to hold a great deal of promise, has re-emerged with a vengeance. We may be on the verge of encouraging teachers to put all of their lessons into CAI (again). Recent developments are teaching us that the computers that we have never been quite sure how to exploit are not powerful enough for the job anyway.

In 1986, the last time that computers in Alberta schools were counted (extrapolation showing there to be 22,751 in 1,489 schools), principals were asked what they saw as the burning issues/needs. Overwhelmingly, principals wanted to know how to integrate computers into the teaching/learning environment (specifically, the curriculum).

So what does this all tell us? That we have a very large number of obsolete computers which are being used by relatively few and which are not powerful enough to achieve objectives that we are not sure of or which, at least, appear to be moving targets? This would be an overly pessimistic view of what has transpired. The time is (still) right, however, for meaningful leadership, but where should this leadership come from? There is growing evidence to suggest that school administrators can and should play a key role in the implementation of technology in schools. Jorde-Bloom & Ford (1988), for example, cite research which identifies the "admistrator as the catalyst that senses the need for change, sets the pace for the change process and then monitors its progress as each new idea is translated into a program of action". Bosch (1988) is more specific in identifying the assistant principal as a key player expressing the belief that, in light of their high level of motivation towards the use of computers and of their typical mobility within a school system, assistant principals could act as "the catalyst to the assimilation and dissemination of microcomputers throughout the entire educational enterprise".

Are these observations so surprising? They surely shouldn't be. Aren't the school principal and his or her assistants supposed to provide educational leadership, and wasn't this a key reason why they were so appointed? Miller (1988) acknowledges this and advocates that administrators should do more than just support innovation and act as role models noting that "administrators' verbalisations to their staff about the virtues and advantages of computer use may well fall on deaf ears, unless the staffs can observe that administrators themselves practice what they preach". So how can principals accomplish this? Before attempting to answer this question, it is worth defining the potential areas of application of computers in education (and as with most other things to do with computers, this too has been fiercely debated). For this author, a continuous spectrum of opportunity exists. At one end of the spectrum are the purely administrative (business) applications of computers which have little or no direct impact on students and about which few teachers even care. These applications, which as are typified by accounting and inventory systems, are undoubtedly cost effective. At the other end of the spectrum are the instructional applications of computers. These are the ones about which we all care because they have the most direct impact on the students. They are also the ones which present the greatest challenge as the foregoing suggests. In the middle of the spectrum are applications which can be defined as instructional support. While these applications are not instructional they nonetheless have a very profound impact on the teaching/learning environment and the student. Typified by what has become known as the student information management system (a system which addresses the functions of student records, scheduling, attendance and marks) these applications provide an excellent opportunity to exercise the role model type of leadership referred to earlier. Research has long suggested that student scheduling, an often obsessive preoccupation of the beleaguered assistant principal, can be cost effectively carried out on school based microcomputers (Brown & Reusse, 1983). Isherwood & Blackwood (1988) have observed that "many school principals have discovered that microcomputers can do most of what they want done when they want it done". The best part of all, however, is that if you do it right, it works. So how can you do it right? This paper describes the successful approach employed by Edmonton Public Schools (one of the largest school districts in Canada or North America (with approximately 195 schools serving some 65,000 kindergarten to grade 12 students). Henceforth, unless differentiation is appropriate, the term principal is used to refer to the principal or one of his or her assistants; the term computer is synonymous with microcomputer.

2. CHOOSING THE BEST SYSTEM

Choosing the best (most appropriate) software system is considered to be critical to overall success. While the "best" system will depend to some degree on whether a school is a relatively independent entity or a part of a large district, it is important that the selection of the system result from a well conceived process. Conventional wisdom suggests that software should be chosen first (for its functionality) and then the hardware. Today, however, a school that is part of a large district (or one for which communication between the school and either another school, a district office or a department of education is important) may be able to decide upon the hardware first and then seek out the best available software. Evaluation of student information management systems for Edmonton Public Schools was carried out by a team. This team consisted of data processing professionals from the district's Information Services (computer) Branch and school administrators with assistance from support staff. Five software systems were evaluated, two minicomputer based and three microcomputer based. In the space of about a year and a half, all five systems were subjected to full scale testing in both junior and senior high school pilot sites under the watchful eye and guidance of (typically) the assistant principal. Whether evaluation data is acquired directly or indirectly, it is imperative to define the expectations to be met. This should be done very early in the process. In Edmonton Public Schools case, a very detailed set of evaluation criteria was developed as follows.

i) The evaluation team's data processing professionals developed a questionnaire and a detailed checklist/interview guide. These instruments were developed as a result of extensive contact with schools and took into account the existing modus operandi as well as the capabilities of currently available systems.

ii) The questionnaire was revised and validated, then mailed to eighteen schools (including both junior and senior highs) for completion. Principals were requested to rate the relative importance of items.

iii) After allowing adequate time for completion of the questionnaire, the eighteen principals were interviewed to confirm and clarify their responses and to add any new insights and items.

iv) Information from the questionnaire and the interviews was used to develop a detailed set of weighted criteria against which all systems were evaluated.

The implementation of school based systems for instructional support was only one component in a district plan for a distributed (not decentralised) approach to the use of computer technology in general. It is accurate to say, however, that this component topped the priority list. Several innovative principals already knew that there were better ways to do things and intended to pursue them and while they were pleased that district attention was going to be focussed in this area, they were apprehensive at the prospect of a lengthy evaluation process. Aware that disenchantment with the status quo might be replaced by impatience, a thorough and detailed testing process was pursued. As it turned out, this approach served the District well since one of the systems of immediate interest to some schools not only didn't meet the criteria developed by the schools, it didn't even meet its own specifications. This phenomenon has been noted by others, such as Brown & Reusse, and confirms the value of having at least one trustworthy technophile on an evaluation team. A great deal was learned about relationships with vendors/developers as a result of evaluating this system.

All five systems were evaluated against the same set of criteria which were organized under the following six major headings:

i) System scope and function (what a system does and how well it does it).

ii) Ease of use.

iii) Technical merit (system design, operation etc.).

iv) Support and services (after sales support and service).

v) System qualifications (credibility and viability).

vi) Vendor (who stands behind the product?).

The detailed evaluation criteria, and the information gathering instruments that led to their development, can be referenced in an Alberta Education report entitled Selection Criteria for Integrated Student Information Management Systems (1985). The highly flexible selection procedure which was used in making the final choice has been described in detail by this author. Highlights of the process are reviewed here. During testing and evaluation, the performance of each system was scored against the weighted criteria. A zero to ten point scale was used for scoring with zero indicating either that performance was unsatisfactory or that a required function or feature was not present. For each system tested, weighted scores were calculated and summed across each of the six major headings. The weighted scores were then normalised to the maximum possible weighted score for corresponding sections thereby yielding fractional measures of system performance in each of the six areas. These performance indicators, which vary between zero and one, were entered in the parentheses of a decision table of the type shown.

Decision Table

MAJOR EVALUATION CRITERIA	EMPHASIS (%)	REL. SUITABILITY (=EMPHASIS x PERF.)		
		System		
		1	2	n
Scope and Function	45	()	()	()
Ease of Use	10	()	()	()
Technical Merit	10	()	()	()
Support and Services	15	()	()	()
System Qualifications	10	()	()	()
Vendor	10	()	()	()
TOTALS	100			

The next step in the decision making process was to determine the emphasis to be placed on each of the six major areas. This is referred to as the percent emphasis distribution which should total one hundred over the areas of interest. Individual table entries are the product of the emphasis and the performance indicator. These entries define the relative suitability of a system to the users' needs in the corresponding area of interest.

Column totals will be numbers less than or equal to one hundred and can be interpreted as percentage measures (or scores out of one hundred) of the extent to which a certain system is suitable to users' needs. The strength of this approach to decision making is flexibility. All key variables such as the criteria, weighting factors, and the percent emphasis distribution are at the discretion of the decision maker. The final decision making phase allows the quick and easy simulation of different user perspectives by varying the emphasis. For Edmonton Public Schools, one microcomputer based system proved to be the most suitable to the needs of both the junior and senior highs.

As soon as a system under evaluation began to show potential, serious contractual negotiations with the vendor were initiated to determine the most favourable terms of acquisition. It isn't wise to get caught liking a system too much before knowing whether it's affordable. A lot can be learned about the vendor (and potential support) during the negotiation phase.

Some key points to keep in mind when discussing contracts (particularly to multi school districts) are:

i) Availability of a "one time" district level licence which can be entered into at any point in time. The fee for this licence should represent a reasonable maximum cost for use of the system by the district. Individual (school) site licence fees should accrue towards the cost of the district licence.

ii) Availability of individual site (school) licences according to a sliding scale of cost. These costs should accrue to the cost of the district level licence.

iii) Transferability of individual site licences from one school to another (in the event of school closure for example).

iv) Provision of maintenance at reasonable cost to a maximum district total. The provision for reduced maintenance costs in the event that a district is able to provide in-house support.

v) Provision of training and customization services at reasonable cost.

vi) Access to systems documentation and/or file layouts if interfaces to other systems are planned.

vii) The existence of an appropriate disputes arbitration procedure.

viii) The deposit of documentation and machine readable source code in trust. These items should be released to customers holding valid licences in the event of either the demise of the vendor or of serious breach of contract.

The first ten (six senior and four junior high) schools to use the recommended system were surveyed to determine their reasons for implementation and to gather information on first experiences. The following are the findings of the survey.

3. WHAT THE SCHOOLS WERE LOOKING FOR

As a result of the evaluation process and detailed consultations with school principals, a number of perceived benefits of the use of school based student information management systems were identified. Using a four point Likert type scale (4=very important; 3= fairly important; 2=fairly un-important; 1=very unimportant), principals were requested to rate the importance of these benefits in their decision to implement a local system. Table 1 shows the mean importance of specific objectives to both the senior high school (Sr.) and junior high school (Jr.) administrators.

4. DID SCHOOLS GET WHAT THEY WANTED

The bulk of the survey instrument was devoted to gathering information on the outcomes of the early months of implementation as perceived by the school principals.

Table 1 - Reasons for Implementation

Objective	Mean importance	
	to Sr.	to Jr.
Control of student demographic info.	2.83	3.50
More comprehensive student info.	3.00	3.50
More up to date student info.	3.67	4.00
Immediate access to student info.	3.83	4.00
On site scheduling	4.00	3.50
Improved student scheduling	4.00	3.25
School based attendance	4.00	3.75
School based mark processing	2.33	2.25
Better quality of info. for teachers	3.67	3.25
Better quality of info. for students	3.50	3.75
On demand reporting capability	3.50	4.00
Better overall service to students	3.67	3.25

4. 1. General Outcomes

Overall, the level of satisfaction with the use of a local system was very high. Nine of the ten schools indicated that they were satisfied with their use of the system and the results obtained through its use. Of these nine, six indicated that they were very satisfied. One school (a junior high) indicated that it was very dissatisfied with its use of the system. Nine of the ten schools indicated that they were comfortable with the use of the system (the exception again being a junior high school). Seven of these nine indicated that they felt very comfortable. Seven of the ten schools reported that integrating the use of the system with school operations was easy. Integration posed more of a challenge to the junior high schools two of which reported the task to be only fairly easy while the other two reported it to be fairly difficult. Six of nine schools that responded indicated that more time was required to support normal school operations than in previous years. This outcome is almost certainly associated with lack of experience with a local system exacerbated by the fact that the first task undertaken was organization for instruction, the most complex of the functions addressed by the system. This assertion is supported by the fact that seven of the ten schools indicated that they expected the time required to support school operations in the future would be less than in previous years. In response to the question "were you better able to prepare for school opening than in previous years?", three of five senior highs respondents said "yes" while two of the four junior highs said "no". Despite the fact that some difficulties were encountered by the junior highs, all ten of the schools responded affirmatively to the question "In retrospect, do you feel that the use of a local system for the purpose of student information is viable?"

4.2 Access to Information

Using a four point scale to measure the level of satisfaction (4=very satisfied; 3=fairly satisfied; 2=fairly dissatisfied; 1=very dissatisfied), schools were asked to indicate the extent to which they were satisfied that access to information had improved through the use of a local system. Table 2 shows the mean level of satisfaction with access to information in general.

Table 2 - Access to Information

How satisfied were you that information was	Mean satisfaction of		
	Sr.	Jr.	Both
easier to access	4.00	3.50	3.80
available when needed	4.00	3.25	3.70
more accurate and current	4.00	3.50	3.80
available in more detail	3.60	3.00	3.33

Using a five point scale (5=much better; 4=better; 3=the same; 2=worse; 1=much worse), schools were asked to rate their capability to meet the information needs of specific client groups through the use of a local system. Table 3 reports the capability of schools to meet the information needs of students, parents, teachers, support staff and administrators.

Table 3 - Information Needs of Client Groups

Capability to meet information needs of	Mean capability of		
	Sr.	Jr.	Both
students	4.33	3.50	4.00
parents	4.17	3.75	4.00
teachers	4.50	4.00	4.30
administrative staff	4.83	4.00	4.50
support staff	4.33	3.25	3.90

4.3. Student Scheduling

The first major task to be addressed by the schools was student scheduling. School based student scheduling has always been a priority of the senior high schools who were confident that there was a better way to operate. In the past, the senior high schools had been particularly dissatisfied with both the results of scheduling and their inability to perform an appropriate number of scheduling runs. Survey results indicated that although slightly more administrative time than in the past was spent on scheduling by the senior highs, all six indicated that they were able to complete as many scheduling runs as they required. This result is consistent with observations by Brown (1984) who noted that participants in his study cited the capability to run numerous simulations in a short period of time with the flexibility to change blocks, times, instructors and class size as significant advantages of microcomputerized scheduling. While scheduling has also been high on the priority list of the junior highs, past experiences seem to have led them, reluctantly, to the perception that the organizational patterns of such schools renders them less susceptible to computerized scheduling. Survey results indicate that the junior highs did use the local system to organize for instruction though their approaches clearly differed from those employed by the senior highs. Using a five point scale (5=much better; 4=better; 3=the same; 2=worse; 1=much worse), schools were asked to rate their capability to complete student scheduling processes through the use of a local system. Table 4 reports on the scheduling experiences of the schools.

Both junior and senior high schools considered that the overall scheduling outcomes achieved from their first time use of a local system were better than they would have been from using their respective former approaches. Nine of the ten schools indicated that they expected even better results from the system in the future.

Table 4 - Student Scheduling

How would you rate capability to	Mean capability of		
	Sr.	Jr.	Both
schedule (overall)	4.67	3.67	4.33
accommodate course requests	4.33	3.25 *	3.90
balance semester loads	3.83	4.00 *	3.89
accommodate late registrants	4.67	4.00 *	4.44
accommodate timetable changes	4.17	4.25 *	4.20

* Three of four junior highs responding

5. PROBLEMS ENCOUNTERED

Using a five point scale (5=never; 4=rarely; 3=occasionally; 2=frequently; 1=very frequently), schools were asked to indicate the frequency that specific problems were encountered during their use of the local system.

Table 5 shows the mean frequency with which specific problems were encountered.

Table 5 - Problems Encountered

How frequently did problems occur due to	Mean frequency in		
	Sr.	Jr.	Both
hardware failures	3.33	3.50	3.40
application software failures	4.00	3.00	3.60
processing time constraints	3.00	3.25	3.10
printing time constraints	2.67	3.50	3.00
availability time for staff use	3.20*	3.00	3.11
lack of staff skill/confidence	3.33	2.50	3.00
difficulty using the system	4.50	3.33**	4.11
loss of data	4.67	4.50	4.60

* Five of six schools responding
** Three of four schools responding

6. DISCUSSION

The results of this study clearly indicate that the implementation of student information management systems in Edmonton Public High Schools was successful. In general, the results indicate that implementation was more rewarding for the senior high schools than for the junior highs. With one exception, indicators of performance/satisfaction reported by the senior highs were more positive than those reported by the junior highs. The survey which formed the basis for the results reported here was administered in the Fall of the first year of use (of the system). At this point in time, respondents had gained significant experience with the information management and scheduling capabilities of the system (having used them to organize for instruction) but not with the attendance component. Information acquired informally following the administration of the survey has confirmed the effectiveness of the attendance component. The following observations by a senior high school assistant principal exemplify the feedback received. "If I get a phone call from a dad who wants to know why we are concerned about his son, I can pull a profile from the computer right away and have his attendance right up to the day before the call. That's very impressive when you are talking to parents. Parents also appreciate the detail and frequency of attendance reporting. Along with showing whether a student is absent, the computer records why the student was absent. As well, there is a record of every time the student is late. Everything is wrapped up in monthly attendance reports sent to parents. We were never able to do this before" (see Classroom Connections, 1986).

The ten schools which chose to implement the recommended student information management system did so under challenging circumstances. The lead time between decision making and implementation in the schools was approximately six months during which time, hardware and software needed to be acquired and installed and training sessions conducted. As well, databases needed to be established in the schools.

The initial versions of the school databases were created by downloading from the district's centralized data base via telecommunications links which were established between central office and the schools. Subsequently, the telecommunications links were used to automatically update the centralized pupil records system and to ensure concurrency of school and district level information.

As well as being asked to report on their initial experiences with school based, computerized student information management, schools were asked to project into the future. Eight of nine schools responding indicated that they expected future scheduling outcomes to be better - seven of these eight expected the outcomes to be much better. Nine of the ten schools surveyed foresee the use of a local system to be of benefit to both school support staff and administrators. Eight of the ten schools foresee the use of a local system to be of benefit to teachers. Nine of the ten schools indicated that, in retrospect, they would do it all again. The six senior high schools would do so without hesitation and further, would recommend that other schools pursue the same course.

Perhaps the single most significant question which could have been asked was "comparatively speaking, was this a better way to do things?". The unanimous response of the senior highs was "much better". Both of the junior high schools responding to this question felt that the new approach was better, one indicating it to be much better.

REFERENCES

Bosch, K. A., (1988) A Microcomputer Literacy Training Model for School Administrators, Journal of Research on Computers in Education, 20(4), 331-338.

Brown, D. J., (1984) The Change to Administrative Computing in Schools. AEDS Journal, 18(1): 17-30.

Brown, D. J., & Reusse, M. (1983) User Perceptions on the Cost-effectiveness of Microcomputers for School Administration. The Canadian School Executive, 3(1), 1216.

Home Grown: Edmonton Public School District's answer to the information merry-go round (1986). Classroom Connections, Educators and IBM.- Creating new learning environments.

Isherwood, G. B., & Blacklock, T. (1988) The Politics of Computing. Journal of Research on Computers in Education, 20(4), 339-346.

Jorde-Bloom, P & Ford, M. (1988) Factors Influencing Early Childhood Administrators' Decisions Regarding the Adoption of Computer Technology. Journal of Educational Computing Research 4(1), 31-47

Miller, H., (1988) An Administrators Manual for the Use of Microcomputers in the Schools, Prentice Hall, Englewood Cliffs, New Jersey.

Ornstein, A. C., (1989) Curriculum Trends: An Agenda for the Future, NASSP Bulletin, 73 (514), 37 - 48.

Petruk, M., Microcomputers In Alberta Schools. - 1986. An Alberta Education Report (1986).

Wright, P., Choosing a Computer Based Instructional Support System: An Evaluation/Selection Model. Computers and Education (in press).

Wright, P., & Vemik, I., Selection Criteria for Integrated Student Information Management Systems. An Alberta Education Report (1985).

INFORMATICS EDUCATION AT THE UNIVERSITY LEVEL

Computers in Education
A. McDougall and C. Dowling (Editors)
Elsevier Science Publishers B.V. (North-Holland)

RECENT DEVELOPMENTS IN COMPUTING CURRICULA IN HIGHER EDUCATION

Doris Keefe LIDTKE

Computer and Information Sciences Department, Towson State University, Baltimore, Maryland, 21204, USA

The computing sciences continue to change rapidly, unlike the more traditional fields of mathematics, science and engineering. Thus, in addition to developing high quality curricula in this relately new field, continual revision has been necessary to reflect the rapid advances in computing. Current research and development continue to drive the field, so that most of the material taught to undergraduates only ten years ago is out-of-date today. There are no indications that the rate of change will abate, so faculty must expect to continue to expend considerable effort updating courses and curricula. This paper presents the major, current curricular activities in North America.

1. INTRODUCTION

The most recent, major developments affecting curricula include a wide-range of activities: the establishment through the joint efforts of the Association for Computing Machinery (ACM) and the Computer Society of the IEEE (CS-IEEE) of the Computing Sciences Accreditation Board; the Denning Committee Report defining the discipline of computing; the establishment of the ACM/CS-IEEE Joint Curriculum Task Force, the establishment by the National Science Foundation (NSF) of the Directorate for Computer and Information Science and Engineering; the sponsorship by NSF of a workshop "to identify major problems facing undergraduate computer science education and to advise NSF on ways to solve those problems"; the recent announcement of a program within the Directorate of Science and Engineering Education of the NSF to fund undergraduate curriculum development; and the establishment of the Software Engineering Institute (SEI) at Carnegie-Mellon University.

While these important activities provide guidelines and some support materials for computing sciences curricula, the implementation is primarily dependent upon the faculty, staff and administrators at individual institutions. Thus programs in North America vary widely in quality, depth, breadth, and emphasis. The strength of each program rests upon the quality of its faculty and the ability to acquire and/or develop the infrastructure [equipment, software, laboratory and team projects, etc.] needed to implement the curricula. The new NSF program holds promise for the development and dissemination of curricular materials for undergraduate computing courses. The SEI provides a model for developing and disseminating curricular support materials (for example, detailed course outlines, case studies, software, and video tapes) that can be used in a variety of institutional settings.

2. HISTORY OF COMPUTER SCIENCE CURRICULA IN NORTH AMERICA

Computers have had a tremendous impact on higher education in the recent past. Unlike other fields, a computer discipline was virtually unknown forty years ago. Thirty years ago only a few universities had computers and these institutions generally offered only a course, frequently not for credit, in scientific programming. The first major curricular activity began in 1962 with the formation of the Curriculum Committee on Computer Science as a subcommittee of the Education Committee of ACM. The first report was published in September 1965 [CURR65]. In 1968 the culmination of the efforts of this committee resulted in the influential report commonly referred to as "Curriculum '68." [CURR68] The Computer Society of the IEEE, recognizing the need for improving the curriculum, formed the Model Curriculum Subcommittee and published a major report in 1976 [IEEE76]. This report was influential because it melded what previously had been almost entirely separate areas of computer science and computer engineering into a unified curriculum for computer science and engineering.[MULD75] This report was updated, revised and published in 1983 [IEEE83].

Recent developments in computing make it necessary for nearly every college student in the USA to have some familiarity with computers and to be able to use them in essentially all fields of study. Some universities even require all students to purchase their own computer. Many students on every college campus own computers. To meet the needs of students, some computing departments offer service courses for non-majors and encourage students in allied majors to earn a minor in computing. This paper will not address the issues involved in curricula for non-majors. It will concentrate on the areas of a) computer science and b) computer science and engineering, with some mention of software engineering, which is regarded by many as a subset of these fields.

* Computing is used here as it is used by the Computing Sciences Accreditation Board (CSAB) to include computer science, computer science and engineering, and titles which cover this subject area.

3. A TIME OF CHANGE

While Curriculum '68 won wide acceptance, almost universal acclaim, and was the basis for nearly all programs in computer science, Curriculum '78 was not as influential. Curriculum '68 had filled a great need. It was published at a time when there were very few computing programs in colleges and universities and nearly every institution which had or was considering a program welcomed the recommendations.

By the late seventies and early eighties, the situation was different. There were many more programs in place.[HAMB84, HAMB85] The faculty members came from diverse backgrounds, some with degrees in computing, but a very large number were self-trained or retrained and shared no common foundation. It became virtually impossible to develop curriculum guidelines which satisfied the growing diversity of institutions. Faculty from colleges and universities with widely differing sizes, quality, resources, missions, and procedures for implementing programs, were unlikely to embrace the same recommendations. It was also a time of rapid innovations in hardware and software, with nearly every institution acquiring microcomputers and beginning to teach structured programming in introductory courses.

These changes required intensified attention to curriculum. Since 1970, a substantial body of literature dealing with curricula and its implementation has been published by the ACM Special Interest Group on Computer Science Education (SIGCSE) in their quarterly publication, SIGCSE Bulletin. The first issue of each year contains the refereed proceedings of the annual SIGCSE Symposium. Only a few years after the publication of "Curriculum '78" [AUST79] the Education Board of the ACM established a committee to develop a first course in computer science [KOFF84]. The next year this committee developed the second course in computer science [KOFF85]. Both reports contained revised course content with many more explicit details to guide their implementation.

The Computer Society was also active in curriculum development. Their Education Committee recognized the need for colleges and universities to provide students with an education which "bridges the gap" between computer engineering (hardware aspects) and computer science (software aspects) of computing:

> In far too many situations, the student is placed in the position of choosing between computer science or computer engineering rather than computer science and engineering curricula. The unfortunate result is that a student ventures into industry ill-prepared for the challenges he will meet. [MULD75]

The Model Curriculum had a major influence on programs which had developed in engineering schools, while Curriculum '68 and Curriculum '78 were more influential on programs which grew out of mathematics departments.

4. THE EIGHTIES AND BEYOND

In the early eighties ACM and the Computer Society focused on cooperative endeavors, even to the point of discussing the possibility of merging the two organizations. Their endeavors in the area of education have been among the most successful joint undertakings and have exerted a very positive influence on the curricula of the computing sciences.

4.1 THE COMPUTING SCIENCE ACCREDITATION BOARD

The first major joint undertaking of ACM and CS-IEEE was the establishment of the Computing Sciences Accreditation Board (CSAB). [MULD84] Since the USA does not have a standard curriculum for all institutions as some countries do, nor an accreditation body for each field of study as in some other countries, it is very difficult for students and parents to evaluate the quality of a program or for employers to judge the caliber of the graduates. Regional accreditation bodies accredit institutions of higher education, but do not examine individual programs in detail. State agencies may control what programs can be offered at particular institutions and exert control through the funding provided for state institutions, but seldom do state agencies exercise control over the content or the quality of the curriculum. Since virtually every institution has its own procedures for approving programs and courses, standards in computing were virtually non-existent. The need for assuring students, parents and employers that the programs meet some standard led these two major professional societies to establish CSAB. A joint committee with equal representation from each society 1) established the criteria for accreditable programs; 2) developed the procedures for all facets of the accreditation process; and 3) persuaded the societies to fund and legally establish CSAB. CSAB and its first commission, the Computer Science Accreditation Commission (CSAC), are now firmly established. CSAC recently received recognition by the Commission on Post-Secondary Accreditation (COPA). The first year in which programs in computer science were accredited was 1985-86. There are now eighty schools with accredited programs. Accreditation of programs has a major impact on the curriculum, since the criteria for accreditation very clearly require substantial course work to insure both breadth and depth in computing; appropriate supporting course work in mathematics, science, and communications skills; qualified faculty; and an adequate infrastructure to support the program.

4.2 THE DENNING REPORT

For some years there had been a misconception on the part of many non-specialists that computer science equals programming. This unfortunate misconception was one of the motivating factors which led to the formation of an ACM committee to define the discipline. The committee also included a representative from CS/IEEE. The report of this committee, "Computing As A Discipline" [commonly called the Denning Report for its chairman, Peter Denning], provides the following definition of computing:

> the systematic study of algorithmic processes that describe and transform information: their theory, analysis, design, efficiency, implementation, and application. The fundamental question underlying all of computing is, 'What can be (efficiently) automated?' [DENN89a, DENN89b]

In a further elaboration, the report divides computing into nine subject areas and three processes. The subject areas are:

algorithms and data structures
programming languages
architecture
numerical and symbolic computation
operating systems
software methodology and engineering
database and information retrieval
artificial intelligence and robotics
human-computer communication.

The three processes are: theory, abstraction and design. The report emphasizes that each of the processes is essential in all of the nine subject areas.[DENN89a, DENN89b]

4.3 THE ACM/CS-IEEE JOINT CURRICULUM TASK FORCE

In the spring of 1988 the ACM and the CS/IEEE appointed a Joint Curriculum Task Force to develop recommendations for undergraduate curricula in computing. [The term "computing" is used here as it is in the Computing Sciences Accreditation Board.] These recommendations of the Task Force are to replace the current guidelines of the ACM [AUST79] and of the CS/IEEE [IEEE83]. The many cooperative education projects of the ACM and the CS-IEEE have led to the realization that, in spite of many basic differences in institutions and departments, there is a large body of material which is essential in every computing curriculum. The Task Force has identified this common body of material, referring to it as "common requirements." The Task Force has held five meetings from May 1988 to July 1989. An initial draft report was reviewed by about sixty educators and subject matter experts in February 1989. This same group reviewed the revised draft in the fall of 1989. Public presentations of the preliminary work of the Task Force were made at the ACM SIGCSE Symposium (February 1989), IEEE CS COMPCON (March 1989), and NECC (June 1989). The Task Force will meet in January 1990 to revise the report and work on a few remaining sections of the report. Another public presentation has been announced for the ACM SIGCSE Symposium (February 1990). The final report should be available in 1990.

The work of the Task Force builds on the Denning Report; it uses the subject matter areas exactly as defined in that report with one addition, "Social, Ethical and Professional Issues". By building the curriculum on "common requirements" drawn from each of the subject areas of the discipline, the plan introduces a comprehensive view of the discipline and an appreciation of its interrelatedness. This provides the essential foundation for all students who major in computing. The Task Force recognizes that different institutions will incorporate the "common requirements" into their curricula in a variety of ways. Therefore, the recommendations are not in the form of courses, but are in subject matter modules, called "knowledge units." This flexible approach allows institutions to combine knowledge units in various ways to meet their own particular goals. The report includes a discussion of how to organize the knowledge units into courses, samples of such courses, and samples of complete programs that might be offered in various academic settings. [An appendix contains a description of the format for and an example of a knowledge unit.]

In addition to delineating the knowledge units, the report focuses on other essential aspects of successful implementation of the undergraduate curriculum. It addresses the roles of programming and laboratories, the need to emphasize the recurring themes which underscore the interrelatedness of the discipline, the importance of professionalism, and other educational experiences which are essential to a quality program. The latter include: team work, large program design and implementation, interpersonal communication skills, research skills, and participation in local professional activities.

4.4 NSF SUPPORT FOR THE INFRASTRUCTURE FOR COMPUTING SCIENCES CURRICULA

Recognizing that there are serious problems in science education at the undergraduate level, the NSF held a series of workshops to develop recommendations for the improvement of science and engineering education. In March 1988 a Workshop on Undergraduate Computer Science Education was held at George Washington University. [FOLE88] Four major problem areas were identified: curricula, faculty, laboratory infrastructure, and instructional delivery. The problem in curricula was identified as the continual need for revision.

> This need has been partially satisfied by the efforts of professional societies. ... [However] these efforts [do not] create the necessary instructional materials, such as case studies, work books, instructional software, and solution sets.[FOLE88]

The workshop participants recommended that

> NSF should dedicate resources to continual renewal of the computer science curricula ... for the development and dissemination of computer science curricula and high-quality teaching support materials.[FOLE88]

NSF has responded positively to these recommendations by announcing a program in the Directorate of Science and Engineering Education to fund proposals to develop curricular materials to improve undergraduate computer science education. The first proposals are due in April 1990 and some should be funded by the fall of 1990. This fortunate timing should allow many institutions to develop materials and software artifacts to support implementation of the recommendations of the Joint Curriculum Task Force.

By the establishment of the Directorate for Computer and Information Science and Engineering the NSF recognized the importance of the discipline and placed it on a par with the other sciences. This recognition should have positive implications for the funding of research in the computing sciences.

4.5 THE SOFTWARE ENGINEERING INSTITUTE

SEI was established in 1985 under a contract from the Department of Defense (DoD). Its purpose is "to serve as a focal point for developments in software engineering education and as a catalyst that influences computer science and software engineering curricula." [GIBB89] Because ten percent of the SEI budget is earmarked specifically for education, its Education Program has a permanent staff which "works with affiliated instututions to develop, test, and implement curricula. ... it also serves as a central source of information for teaching software engineering and maintains a growing store of educational materials that are regularly reviewed and updated." [Gibb89] Curriculum modules prepared at SEI are unlike those prepared by the professional societies. The SEI modules are prepared by computing professionals who usually spend a month or more at SEI producing "a document that outlines a body of knowledge, describes educational objectives and prerequisites, suggests effective methods of teaching the material, and provides an annotated bibliography of relevant literature." [GIBB89] The module is thoroughly reviewed and additional instructional aids, such as worked examples and case studies, are included in a kit for public review at a faculty development workshop sponsored by SEI. While the Education Program of SEI focused initially on graduate curricula there is now considerable emphasis on undergraduate education. This effort focuses on providing support for teaching a senior level project course [TOMA87], supporting the teaching of software maintenance, using Ada as the primary language of instruction, and monitoring "the software engineering profession to determine appropriate times and places to establish an undergraduate software engineering degree." [GIBB89]

The model developed at SEI points the way for developing and disseminating quality instructional materials. SEI has developed and disseminated quality print and videotape materials. This effort is particularly important in a field where rapid changes in hardware and software methodologies require constant updating of the courses and curricula, where there is little if any reward for faculty who spend time in developing such quality materials, and where a full-time staff of professionals can work with highly qualified "outside experts and educators" to assure quality, state-of-the-art materials.

5. CONCLUSION

There has been exciting progress in the past few years in the development of computing curricula. Many organizations and individuals have made important contributions of talent, time and money. Within the next few months the Joint Curriculum Task Force Report should be published. NSF has funding to support some projects which will provide the basic infrastructure for curriculum implementation. CSAB and CSAC are functioning to assure quality programs. SEI serves as a model for curriculum development, implementation and dissemination. But it would be mistaken to regard curriculum development as an accomplished task. It is essential to look to the future. Preparation for the computing environment of today is not enough for our students. It is in that future that our students will be functioning. As faculty members and curriculum developers we must continually examine current research and practice. We must prepare our students for an environment of change, an environment where visualization of data is a matter of course, where the common programming paradigms of today are replaced by the new paradigms of tomorrow [SHU89 is a fine tutorial on visual programming], where program design does not include line-by-line textual development but uses "off-the-shelf modules" for a large percentage of the work, where intelligent tools assist in all aspects of the development of software systems, and where reliable software is routinely developed for the life-critical systems upon which we all depend.

Much has been accomplished. An excellent foundation upon which to build has been provided, but our field continues to change rapidly and we must be the agents of change to insure that our students are well-prepared. We must impart the importance and joy of learning, the value of having learned how to continue learning, for as they complete their studies they will join us in our rapidly changing profession.

APPENDIX

The curriculum that is being worked on by the ACM - CS/IEEE Joint Curriculum Task Force does not describe courses, but rather presents "knowledge units" which can be put together in a variety of ways in order to meet the needs of a particular institution. By special permission information on the knowledge units, as described in the September 27, 1989 Draft Report [TUCK89] is quoted below. This Draft Report was circulated to reviewers in Fall 1989. Since this is a working document, the final publication could be considerably different in both content and form.

KNOWLEDGE UNITS

"... a 'knowledge unit' is understood to designate any coherent collection of subject matter that is so fundamental within one of the nine subject areas of the discipline, or within the area of social and professional issues (SP), that it must be mastered by every undergraduate major."[TUCK89]

"For cross-referencing purposes and brevity, we use the following 2-letter tags to identify each of the nine subject areas, and the additional area of social, ethical, and professional issues, for the discipline of computing.

Algorithms and Data Structures	AL
Programming Languages	PL
Architecture	AR
Numerical and Symbolic Computation	NU
Operating Systems	OS

Software Methodology and Engineering SE
Database and Information Retrieval DB
Artificial Intelligence and Robotics AI
Human-Computer Communication HU
Social, Ethical, & Professional Issues SP

The collected knowledge units are organized by subject area. ... Each individual knowledge unit ... has the following style of presentation:

TAG#:KNOWLEDGE UNIT NAME
(Paragraph describing the goals of the knowledge unit.)
Recurring Themes:
(List of recurring themes that appear within this knowledge unit.)
Lecture Topics:
#. List of topics
Suggested Laboratories:
#. (open or closed) List of exercises and goals
Connections:
Overlaps:(List of TAGS for ku's that overlap this one)
Prerequisites: (List of TAGS for prerequisite ku's)
Requisite for: (List of TAGS for ku's that follow this one)" [TUCK89]

SAMPLE KNOWLEDGE UNIT

This is only an example taken from the Draft Report. The final report of the Task Force may be considerably different.

"AL: ALGORITHMS AND DATA STRUCTURES

The knowledge units in the common requirements for the subject area of Algorithms and Data Structures emphasize the following topics: abstract data types, basic data structures, recursive algorithms, complexity analysis, sorting and searching, computability and undecidability, problem-solving strategies, and parallel and distributed algorithms. Their content, lecture topics, and suggested laboratory work are summarized in the paragraphs below.

AL1: Abstract Data Types (2)

Introduction to the concept of abstract data type (ADT), and motivation as a methodology to separate implementation details from applications, thus promoting reuse.

Recurring Themes: complexity of large problems, conceptual models, formal models, levels of abstraction, reuse.

Lecture Topics:
1. Purpose of ADT's
2. Implementation of ADT's in a higher-order language, with illustrations

Suggested Laboratories: (open or closed)
Develop a program using an ADT provided by the instructor, and then run it using alternative implementations. Students gain an appreciation for abstraction, modularity and substitutability of different implementations.

Connections:
Overlaps: PL3, SE3
Prerequisites: Discrete Math
Requisite for: AL2, AL6, OS2, OS7, PL5, PL11" [TUCK89]

BIBLIOGRAPHY

AMAR71 Amarel, S., "Computer Science: A Conceptual Framework for Curriculum Planning," Communications of the ACM, 14:6 (June, 1971), pp. 391-401.

AUST70 Austing, Richard H. "A Lower Division Course Sequence in Computer Science," Proceedings 1970 World Conference on Computer Education. Science Associates/International, New York, 1970, Vol. II, pp. 167-170.

AUST77 Austing, Richard H., Barnes, Bruce H. and Engel, Gerald L., "A Survey of the Literature of Computer Science Education Since Curriculum '68," Communications of the ACM, 20:1 (January, 1977), pp. 13-21.

AUST79 Austing, R. H., etal., "Curriculum '78: Recommendations for the Undergraduate Program in Computer Science," Communications of the ACM 22:3 (March, 1979) pp. 147-166.

BARN70 Barnes, Bruce H. and Gotterer, Malcolm H., "Undergraduate Education in Computer Science: Some Fundamental Problems and Their Solutions." Proceedings 1970 World Conference on Computer Education. Science Associates/International, New York, 1970, Vol. II, pp. 171-174.

COSI67 COSINE Committee. Computer Science in Electrical Engineering. Commission on Engineering Education. Washington, D.C., September, 1967.

CURR65 Curriculum Committee on Computer Science (C^3S). "An Undergraduate Program in Computer Science, Preliminary Recommendations." Communications of the ACM. 16:12 (September, 1965), pp. 543-552.

CURR68 "Curriculum '68: Recommendations for Academic Programs in Computer Science," Communications of the ACM, XI (March, 1968), pp. 151-197.

DENN89a Denning, Peter, J., Comer, Douglas E., Gries, David, Mulder, Michael C., Tucker, Allen, Turner, A. Joe, and Young, Paul R., "Computing As A Discipline," Communications of the ACM, 32:1 (January, 1989) pp. 9-23.

DENN89b Denning, Peter, J., Comer, Douglas E., Gries, David, Mulder, Michael C., Tucker, Allen, Turner, A. Joe, and Young, Paul R., "Computing As A Discipline," Computer, 22:2, (February, 1989) pp. 63-70.

ENGE75 Engel, Gerald L. and Barnes, Bruce H., "The Revisions of 'Curriculum '68': Background and Initial Development," Proceedings of IFIP Second World Conference on Computers and Education. American Elsevier, New York, 1975, pp. 263-272.

FAIR87 Fairley, R. E., "Software Engineering Education: An Idealized Scenario," Software Engineering Education: The Educational Needs of the software Community, New York, Springer-Verlag, 1987, pp. 52-60.

FREE87 Freeman, P., "Essential Elements of Software Engineering Education Revisited," Software Engineering Education: The Educational Needs of the software Community, New York, Springer-Verlag, 1987, pp. 61-77.

FOLE88 Foley, J., T. Standish, N. Dale, G. Engel, N. Gibbs, D. Lidtke, R. Miller, M. Shaw, J. Werth, Undergraduate Computer Science Education - Report of a Workshop, National Science Foundation, DCCR, Washington, D.C., 1988.

FORD87 Ford, G., Gibbs, N., and Tomayko, J., Software Engineering Education: An Interim Report from the Software Engineering Institute. Technical Report CMU/SEI-87-TR-8. Pittsburgh, PA, Carnegie Mellon University, May, 1987.

GIBB89 Gibbs, N. E., "The SEI Education Program: The Challenge of Teaching Future Software Engineers," Communications of the ACM, 32:5 (May, 1989), pp. 594-605.

HAMB84 Hamblen, John W., Computer Manpower - Supply and Demand - By States (Fifth Edition), Quad Data Corp., Tallahassee, Florida, 1984.

HAMB85 Hamblen, John W., "Status of Computer Science Education in USA Higher Education: Thru 1982-83," Proceedings WCCE 85 of the 4th World Conference on Computers and Education. (1985) pp. 867-869.

HSIA73 Hsiao, T. C., ed. Directory of Computer Education and Research, Vol I: Senior Colleges. Washington, D.C., Science and Technology Press, Inc., 1973.

IEEE76 IEEE Computer Science Model Curricula Subcommittee. A Curriculum in Computer Science and Engineering. Committee Report (RW1). November 1976. IEEE Publication. EH 0119-8.

IEEE83 IEEE Computer Society Educational Activities Board, 1983 IEEE Computer Society Model Program in Computer Science and Engineering. IEEE Cat. NO. EHO 212-1, 1983.

KOFF84 Koffman, E. B.,Miller, P. L., and Wardle, C. E., "Recommended Curriculum for CS1, 1984," Communications of the ACM, 27:10 (November, 1984) pp. 998-1001.

KOFF85 Koffman, E. B., Stemple, D., and Wardle, C. E., "Recommended Curricula for CS2, 1984," Communications of the ACM, 28:8 (August, 1985) pp. 815-818.

MULD75 Mulder, Michael C., "Model Curricula for Four-Year Computer Science and Engineering programs: Bridging the Tar Pit," Computer, 8:12 (December, 1975), pp. 28-33.

MULD77 Mulder, Michael C., "Current and Future Trends in the Development of Computer Science and Engineering Curricula." Proceedings of the Computer Science and Engineering Curricula Workshop, June 6-7, 1977, Williamsburg, Va. IEEE Publication EHO 126-3.

MULD84 Mulder, M. C. and Dalphin, J. F., "Computer Science Program Requirements and Accreditation," Computer, 17:4 (April, 1984), pp. 30-35.

RAMA76 Ramamoorthy, C. V. "Computer Science and Engineering Education," IEEE Transactions on Computers, 25:12 (December, 1976), pp. 1200-1206.

SCHE83 Scherlis, W. L. and Shaw, Mary, "Mathematics Curriculum and the Needs of Computer Science," The Future of College Mathematics, Anthony Ralston and Gail Young, eds., New York, Springer-Verlag, 1983.

SHAW85 Shaw, Mary, ed., The Carnegie-Mellon Curriculum for Undergraduate Computer Science, New York, Springer-Verlag, 1985.

Shu89 Shu, Nan C. "Visual Programming: Perspectives and Approaches," IBM Systems Journal, 28:4 (1989), pp. 525-546.

TOMA87 Tomayko, J. Teaching a Project Intensive Introduction to Software Engineering. Tech. Rpt. CMU/SEI-87-TR-20. Software Engineering Institute, Carnegie-Mellon University, August, 1987.

TUCK89 Tucker, A.B.(Editor and Co-chair), Barnes, B.H.(Co-chair), Aiken, R.B., Barker, K., Bruce, K.B., Cain, J.T., Conry, S., Engel, G.L., Epstein, R., Lidtke, D.K., Mulder, M.C., Rogers, J.B., Sapffordk E.H., and Turner, A.J., "Curriculum '89," Draft Report of the ACM/IEEE CS Joint Curriculum Task Force, September 27, 1989.

Computers in Education
A. McDougall and C. Dowling (Editors)
Elsevier Science Publishers B.V. (North-Holland)

MORE THAN TWO VOWELS: PUTTING AI INTO COMPUTING SCIENCE EDUCATION

Dr. Robert M. Aiken
Computer and Information Sciences Department
Temple University
Philadelphia, PA 19122

The theme of this paper is that key aspects of Artificial intelligence (AI) are integral to an undergraduate computing science education. Ideally they should be included in a required AI course, or at a minimum, integrated throughout the curriculum. This paper provides a framework for examining why, when and where the central AI concepts and tools could be interwoven into such a program. Moreover, a capstone course, or a sequence of two courses, is advocated as a means for tying together fundamental principles of computing science, including AI, in the design and implementation of a real, large scale project.

1. INTRODUCTION

Our shrinking world inundates us with increasingly more complex problems, and we need better tools to solve them. Artificial Intelligence (AI) and Software Engineering (SE) are two emerging disciplines which attempt to provide new perspectives and methodologies for looking at large problems. Thus, it is not surprising to learn that software professionals who can design and develop AI systems are in great demand [1]. The goal in this paper is to examine the "what, where and why" surrounding AI topics which every undergraduate in computing science should know before graduating. (Note: Throughout the remainder of this paper computing science will be used to denote Computer Science and Computer Engineering programs. Many of these points also apply to Information Systems/ Science programs and will be discussed in this context as well).

The magnitude of the problems that students will encounter in designing and maintaining large software systems is central to re-shaping our thinking about how we teach the principles of computing science. We know that large problems are many times more complex than smaller ones - it is not a matter of taking double the time to write a program of 10,000 rather than 5,000 lines, it's more likely to be an exponential increase.

Parnas has argued eloquently for a return to the classical engineering approach in the education of computing professionals [2]. In his words,

> "Computer Science programs have become so inbred that the separation between academic computing science and the way computers are actually used has become too great. CS programs do not provide graduates with the fundamental knowledge needed for long-term professional growth." p. 19

In addition, there is a strong movement to establish separate programs in Software Engineering [3]. The majority of the effort thus far has been in designing a Master of Software Engineering Curriculum. However, as Ford and Gibbs [3] note;

> "As the distinctions between computer science and software engineering become clearer (in the longer term), separate undergraduate programs may emerge. Initially, the two programs might have one or two years of common studies, much as the traditional engineering disciplines share an engineering core. The third year might also have some common courses, but the fourth year might be entirely different for the two programs." p. 70

In this paper the author argues for a different, but central role for Artificial Intelligence coupled with Software Engineering in the education of computing science students. The impact of Artificial Intelligence research specific to education is discussed in [4].

2. COMPUTING SCIENCE AND ARTIFICIAL INTELLIGENCE

Let me first define what I mean by computing science and Artificial Intelligence. For computing science I will adopt the definition given in the Association for Computing Machinery (ACM) Report, "Computing as a Disicipline":

> "The discipline of computing is the systematic study of algorithmic processes that describe and transform information: their theory, analysis, design, efficiency, implementation, and application. The fundamental question underlying all of computing is, 'What can be (efficiently) automated?" [5, p. 12]

For the definition of Artificial Intelligence we turn to the text, "ARTIFICIAL INTELLIGENCE and the Design of Expert Systems" by Luger and Stubblefield,

> "Artificial Intelligence may be defined as the branch of computer science that is concerned with the automation of intelligent behavior" [6, p. 1]

In adopting this definition one is also subscribing to the assumption that, at some level, what the brain does may be considered to be a type of computation.

Though one might choose other definitions, these provide a starting point from which to discuss the role of artificial intelligence in computing science education.

3. WHY IS AI A CENTRAL PART OF COMPUTING SCIENCE EDUCATION?

The authors of the "Computing as a Discipline" report recognized that AI topics are an integral part of the discipline, listing them as one of nine subareas that cover the field [5]. A major curriculum effort currently underway in the United States, "Curriculum '89", is based on this report. It describes in detail what the common requirements for computer science and computer engineering students should be. As one part of this report the committee discusses how the central topics from AI fit into the undergraduate major [7]. The two major units they suggest which should be included in the common requirements for AI (and Robotics) are History and Applications of AI and Problems, State Spaces, and Search Strategies [pp 56-57]. However, I believe that AI concepts are even more basic than either of these studies suggest. Furthermore, these same ideas apply to Information Systems (Science) programs that have a quantitative or technical flavor.

What seems to be missing from these programs is the "glue" that can tie the key concepts and various tools and techniques together. The "Curriculum 89" report does a good job of identifying important topics from each subarea that need to be included as common requirements in a computing science program, but there remains the problem of how to connect these topics in courses. My proposal is that students should have at least one experience where artificial intelligence and software engineering models and methods are used to build a complex project, thus providing an overview of the discipline.

This proposal is consistent with the viewpoint expressed in the "Computing as a Discipline" report which noted that experiemental aspects of computing science are crucial in having students successfully understand and integrate the fundamental concepts of computing science. This means that design techniques effective for large systems must be discovered and used by students in a controlled environment. This view has been suggested by others [8,9,10,11]. As noted in Wilson, et.al.

> "...the overall cohesiveness of computer science is best presented by including the design and engineering of software as a major component of a framework which includes theoretical computer science, and that acquisition of software engineering skills requires experience with software design and development prjoects." [11, p.43]

The author would add to this statement the importance of including "artificial intelligence" to the description of the skills.

As noted by Tichy, many of the AI tools, such as frame-based representation languages, sophisticated Lisp programming environments, and natural-language parsers not only increase programmers' productivity but also extend their creative horizons for building novel software systems [12]. Others, such as Carando [13], have shown the possibilities of combining AI techniques with facilities such as hypertext. The AI culture fosters development of smart systems in the sense that these systems are more sophisticated, more automated, and more user-oriented (e.g. user-friendly) than comparable large systems designed for other environments. These programs are "clever" in the sense that they often use heuristics, or "tricks", to achieve a solution in a reasonable amount of time. AI tools and techniques are not magical, but they can play a critical role in identifying automatable functions. In addition, they can stimulate the necessary creativity so that once automatable functions have been identified, they can be implemented and refined quickly.

Moreover, many new ideas and systems now commonplace in the computing sciences stem from AI research, e.g., object oriented programming (SMALLTALK) and design methodologies, graphic user interfaces, and sophisticated development environments. Thus, we come to the question of what are the key aspects of AI that should be included in a computing science curriculum and how can they be used to help tie fundamental principles together?

4. WHAT ARE THE CORE TOPICS IN ARTIFICIAL INTELLIGENCE?

Any student completing an undergraduate Computing Science major should know the following key concepts and tools normally presented in an introductory AI course:

1. Introductory predicate logic - Students need to appreciate the power, potential, and limitations of expert systems built using declarative as well as procedural tools (e.g. Prolog). This material is also useful for understanding database and program verification techniques as well as some of the logical specification languages under development for Software Engineering. In addition, predicate logic is a very useful tool for representing problems and reasoning about them.

2. Natural language components - There is an increasing awareness of the importance of user friendly systems. The ultimate goal is to create systems that would allow the end user to communicate with the computer in a flexible, non-prescriptive manner; the best means for accomplishing this would be with a reasonable subset of natural language.

3. Knowledge representation schemes - Organizing data to permit easy access to required information is a critical ingredient of effective software systems. Moreover, modeling complex systems (especially expert systems) entails representing the inherent semantic properties of these systems. Knowledge representation schemes, such as semantic nets, frames, and scripts are needed to organize semantic information for easy retrieval.

4. Problem Solving Methods - There are basic search strategies and heuristic methods which can be applied to a wide variety of problems. These include standard, weak search techniques such as hill climbing, and generate-and-test, as well as depth-first and breadth first strategies. Though much of this material is taught in Analysis of Algorithms courses it is important for computing science students to obtain a better overview of when and why to use these methods in the solution of real problems.

To best understand the importance of this material students should be exposed to large, real-world problems where these methods facilitate a solution, as well as to small, contained problems that exercise only one method at a time. In addition, these ideas should be presented in the context of social issues. Many of the large, complex systems being designed have tremendous impact on the public, whether they be business, government or military applications. Some further thoughts on this issue can be found in the article by Aiken and Aiken [14].

5. LABORATORY COMPONENT

Students initially learn an AI tool or technique by writing simple, focused programs, but having students work on one or more large problems builds appreciation for how AI techniques can be integrated into the design of software systems. Moreover, used in conjunction with software engineering methodology, this could serve as a means for connecting important curriculum components including user-interface issues, database design, knowledge representation schemes, and time and complexity considerations.

In order to solve large "real-wrold" problems, students need access to a laboratory with a variety of equipment and resources, including AI workstations with good graphics and software development resources such as reusable software libraries, programming environments, CASE tools, expert system shells, and on-line tutors where needed and available. There should be scheduled lab time with an assistant available to answer technical questions. In addition, there should be enough computers available for students to "walk in" and use at their convenience.

6. "LARGE" PROJECTS

The benefits of assigning large programming projects are well known. For example, having students work in teams on such projects promotes learning to work together to first specify and design a software system, and then build and integrate separate systems components. Furthermore, having to combine modules written by several members of a team (or in some cases a different team) reinforces the importance of good documentation.

In assigning large-scale projects that require use of AI tools and techniques the instructor should also keep in mind the following points:

1. Projects that are complex enough to require AI techniques do not "scale-up" from small projects; they require much more effort to understand and solve.

2. One can give students a "toolkit" of programming aids (e.g. expert system shell) which they can use for tackling such a project.

3. Divide-and-conquer techniques do not work well in AI. In complex problems, progress in solving a subgoal often interferes with previous gains elsewhere.

4. Practical applications are a good source of AI projects, although it is difficult to supervise them correctlly, in particular to avoid much busy work of educationally doubtful value.

One should not automatically equate a large or complex project with implementation of an entire software system. One means for providing experience with a large project without having students write an entire program is to provide them with a program that is already written and ask them to modify or write a part of it. Another is to have students implement a portion of an existing system (e.g. MYCIN, PROUST, etc.). The resulting module(s) can then be compared to the actual code that was used. This approach is borrowed from Physics and Chemistry where students are often required to replicate pieces of large experiments. Also, very useful projects can be designed around performance analysis, requirements specification, etc.

7. WHERE SHOULD AI CONCEPTS, TOOLS, AND TECHNIQUES BE TAUGHT?

The ideal solution is for instructors to integrate the concepts, tools and methods in appropriate courses throughout the curriculum which would reinforce the material presented in a required Introductory AI course. Though some programs are taking the lead and offering AI Applications courses (particularly programs emphasizing expert systems) these courses are usually offered only at the graduate level. Moreover, there should be a concerted effort to require students, perhaps in a senior projects course, to design and implement a large project using AI and software engineering methodologies and tools.

Others have discussed various ways to provide students with this type of experience. For example, Little, et. al. [15] discuss an undergraduate course in applications of AI that was sponsored by an industry/academic partnership. In this course teams of four students each worked on one of three AI projects which had been proposed by three participating corporate partners. Each of the projects focused on electronic systems diagnostics. The problems ranged from troubleshooting an electronics board, to isolating faults for a specific subsystem within a large scale communications network spread over several sites. An instructor and a technical liaison from the company were assigned to work with each team. The evaluations from the students indicated they enjoyed the course and learned a great deal. One of the suggestions made by students was that topics such as project management and software engineering principles should be available in courses which could serve as pre-requisites for this course - something that is advocated in this paper in a different way.

Another model that could be adopted is one described by Bolz and Jones [16]. In this article the authors discuss a two semester, senior level sequence of courses in large scale software development. The courses incorporate the element of realism by having an actual user supply an actual project. In the first course students develop a functional specification of user needs and in the second course students design a system from the specifications and implement at least a portion of the project. With respect to the success of the course the authors stress the element of realism and the two semester length. Other articles that describe approaches for introducing large scale projects into courses include [17, 18, 19].

Thus, the problem of <u>where</u> to offer AI concepts and tools in a computing science curriculum must include a component of <u>how</u> to most effectively do so. While most undergraduate programs do not have the flexibility to include a two course capstone sequence that would require writing the specifications and then implementing at least a portion of the system (sometimes with a different team of students), those who have tried this approach have found it very successful. Having a sequence like this would allow the faculty to provide an in-depth experience for students which would incorporate their use of AI methods and tools with engineering large scale software. If a two course sequence is not a viable option then a one course option has proven to be a successful compromise.

At the least I would argue for including central AI topics in various computing science courses to supplement a required, rigorous introductory AI course. Adding a large-scale experiential component would provide students an opportunity to use this knowledge in a way that ties together important fundamental principles.

8. CONCLUSION

One might be tempted to argue at this point that if AI principles are so important then perhaps we should consider designing an undergraduate major based on them. I would argue strongly against this approach. An undergraduate program should concentrate on breadth and the fundamentals of the discipline. What has been proposed in this paper is consistent with this philosophy. AI principles deserve a more prominent role in a computing science curriculum than they have so far received, but not an independent existence of their own. The in-depth exploration of a subject should remain the province of graduate programs. In a recent paper Gibbs has stated that due to government and industry needs there is increased pressure to offer an undergraduate software engineering degree, something that he sees as, "prematurely fragmenting the still young and evolving field of computer science.' [20, p. 596] I agree and would make the same point with respect to any efforts to build an artificial intelligence undergraduate major.

However, given the fundamental nature and importance of these principles, I would argue that, every undergraduate major in mathematics, the sciences and engineering should learn the basic problem solving methodologies and knowledge representation schemes embodied in AI. These ideas provide a context for exploring and solving complex problems that can not be easily solved using typical algorithmic processes. The AI approach stresses creativity rather than efficiency and focuses on concept versus implementation. As problems continue to become more difficult to define and solve, students will benefit from an educational thrust that will help them to be more creative!

ACKNOWLEDGMENTS

The author would like to thank Judith Wilson and Giorgio Ingargiola for their insightful comments. Also, Christine Aiken, as usual, was a superb editor.

REFERENCES

[1] "AI Experts in Short Supply", News Item, Communications of the ACM, Dec. 1989, Vol. 32(12), p. 1384.

[2] Parnas, D. L., "Education for Computing Professionals", IEEE COMPUTER, Jan. 1990, pp. 17-22.

[3] Ford, G.A., and Gibbs, N.E., "A Master of Software Engineering Curriculum", IEEE COMPUTER, Sept. 1989, pp. 59-71.

[4] Aiken, R. M., "The Impact of Artificial

Intelligence on Education: Opening New Windows:, Invited Paper for UNESCO Conference on AI and Education, Oct. 1989, Proceedings to be published by Springer-Verlag.

[5] Denning, P. J., et. al., "Computing as a Discipline", Report, Communications of the ACM, Vol. 32(1), Jan. 1989, pp. 9-23.

[6] Luger, F. G., and Stubblefield, W. A., "ARTIFICIAL INTELLIGENCE and the Design of Expert Systems", The Benjamin/Cummings Publishing Co., 1989.

[7] Tucker, A., et. al., "Curriculum '89", Draft Copy, Sept. 27, 1989.

[8] Denning, P. J., "Educational Ruminations", (Editorial) Communications of the ACM, Vol. 27(10), Oct. 1984, pp. 979-983.

[9] Nelson, D. A., "Relevance vs. Rigor", Communications of the ACM, Vol. 30(7), July 1987, pp. 585-586.

[10] Scragg, G. W., "A Crisis in Computer Science Education at Liberal Arts Colleges", ACM SIGCSE Bulletin, Vol. 19(2), June 1987, pp. 36-42.

[11] Wilson, J., et. al., "ALGORITHMS AND SOFTWARE: Integrating Theory and Practice in the Undergraduate Computer Science Curriculum", ACM SIGCSE Bulletin, Vol. 21 (1), 1989, pp. 42-46.

[12] Tichy, W. F., "What Can Software Engineers Learn from Artificial Intelligence?", IEEE COMPUTER, Nov. 1987, pp. 43-54.

[13] Carando, P., "SHADOW: Fusing Hypertext with AI", IEEE Expert, Winter, 1989,pp. 65-78.

[14] Aiken, R. M., and Aiken, C. U., "Better Education-Different Tools", Invited Respondent paper, in Proceedings of IFIP 11th World Computer Congress, North-Holland, 1989, pp. 107-108.

[15] Little, J., et. al., "An Industry/ Academic Partnership Experiment: A Course in Artificial Intelligence", ACM SIGCSE Bulletin, Vol. 20(1), Feb., 1989, pp. 171-174.

[16] Bolz, R. E., and Jones, L. G., "A Realistic, Two Course Sequence in Large Scale Software Engineering", ACM SIGCSE Bulletin, Vol. 15(1), Feb. 1983, pp.21-24.

[17] Bullard, C. L., et. al., "Anatomy of a Software Enginerring Project", ACM SIGCSE Bulletin, Vol. 20(1), Feb. 1988, pp.129-133.

[18] Kurtz, B. L., "A Course Project to Design and Implement the Kernel of a Real-Time Operating System", ACM SIGCSE Bulletin, Vol. 19(1), Feb. 1987, pp. 115-119.

[19] Tam, W. C., "A Multi-level Approach to Undergraduate Software Engineering Education", ACM SIGCSE Bulletin, Vol. 17(1), Feb. 1985, pp. 332-341.

[20] Gibbs, N. E. "The SEI Education Program: The Challenge of Teaching Future Software Engineers", Communications of the ACM, Vol. 32(5) May, 1989, pp. 594-598.

Computers in Education
A. McDougall and C. Dowling (Editors)
Elsevier Science Publishers B.V. (North-Holland)

THE INTERDEPENDENCE OF DISCIPLINES: COMPUTER SCIENCE AS A FULL PARTNER

Lillian N. CASSEL, Robert E. BECK and Richard AUSTING

Department of Mathematical Sciences, Villanova University, Villanova, PA, U.S.A.; Department of Computer Science, University of Maryland, College Park, MD, U.S.A.

Cluster courses combine topics in two or three disciplines to create a synergistic effect among the individual courses in the cluster. This paper describes in detail a cluster on the topic of text analysis and suggests other possible clusters which involve computer science and other disciplines. These clusters demonstrate how computer science can play a full role in general education requirements.

1. INTRODUCTION

Computer Science contains a wealth of material that is useful in many disciplines. Much of this material is at the advanced level and is generally not available to students in other disciplines because of the typical prerequisite structure within computer science undergraduate programs. Commonly, the kind of material offered in courses by computer science departments for other majors is programming, literacy, societal impact, or application software. As valuable as these courses might be, they do not open up the field to students in other disciplines.

A different approach is presented in this paper. We advocate offering courses with the following design goals. The courses should:

* be offered at the advanced undergraduate level;
* be accessible to targetted audiences of students in specific disciplines;
* be suitable for students in computer science;
* contain advanced computer science material; and
* have appropriate prerequisites to assure qualified students without unnecessarily limiting access to the course.

We highlight a design that leads to the development of courses distinct from the typical computer science courses in a program for majors. In particular, we apply the concept of cluster courses to achieve the design goals. Details of a specific cluster are included to illustrate the kind of upper-level computer science course that is beneficial to both majors and non-majors.

2. CLUSTER COURSES

One goal of general education, or core, requirements in a degree program is to provide breadth in the subjects studied. A course cluster is a mechanism by which this breadth can be obtained. A course cluster consists of a set of courses, usually two or three, linked by a common theme. The topic of a course cluster is one which is not exclusively a part of one discipline. It is one that accommodates several perspectives and viewpoints. For example, one could devise a cluster to address the art, philosophy, and literature of a period in history. One could link biology and philosophy to explore the question of life, its nature, its value, its purpose, and its meaning. When a student enrolls in the cluster, the student must enroll in all courses simultaneously.

The courses are taught by individual

instructors, but the order of the lecture topics in each course is carefully coordinated with those in the other courses in the cluster to obtain the synergistic effect of the simultaneous study of several aspects of a topic. Since each lecturer is discussing topics within his or her own field of expertise, the presentations can reflect an expert's assessment of the current work in the area. It is important to note that a cluster is not a team-taught course, and consequently does not have the disadvantages of that arrangement.

The course cluster provides opportunities for faculty interaction that may not be generally available. Clearly the faculty teaching the courses in the cluster must work closely together; they must become conversant with material in the other courses in the cluster besides the one that they are teaching. Thus, the cluster promotes the cooperation of a joint appointment, but at the undergraduate level. It allows the development of collaboration on material to be presented at lower levels, rather than at graduate and research levels.

3. EXAMPLE - THE STUDY OF TEXT

To illustrate this approach to multidisciplinary study, we describe a cluster of two courses on the topic of text. The computer science component deals with problems of text processing, storage, retrieval, and recognition. The English, linguistics, or communications arts component deals with linguistic and stylistic issues in written material. At times this material is described as text linguistics or discourse. The computer science course is not a collection of computer-supported tools to study topics in English. It is a study of topics in computer science that are relevant to the effective use and manipulation of text, topics that are of interest and importance to computer science students and also students who have different reasons for interest in text handling. Central to both parts of the cluster is the concept of text; each discipline is posing questions about text that can be answered better by including ideas and techniques from the other discipline. In this way the study of literature gains the perspective of computer science in defining and analyzing text. Likewise, computer science gains the perspective of the nature of study in English: the need and ability to deal with subtlety of expression and extraction of meaning. We expect that students in their second or third year of university study would have completed the necessary prerequisites to enroll in the cluster.

In the following two sections we describe each of the courses by giving a course outline and a narrative on each of the major points in the outline.

3.1. Computer Science Component

Title: Computer Methods for Text Manipulation

Description: A study of topics relevant to the computerized storage, retrieval, and manipulation of textual data. Appropriate algorithms and data structures, comparison of techniques, characteristics and limitations of storage devices, indexing techniques, inverted files, searching, sorting, recognition and understanding of strings.

Prerequisites: knowledge of elementary data types and data structures including strings and programming using procedures with parameters as might be obtained from a beginning computer science course. Familiarity with a word processing package.

Topics:

I. What is text?
   A. Definitions of string, word, sentence
   B. Text files as a sequence of strings of characters

II. Text storage and retrieval
   A. Coding of characters (ASCII, EBCDIC, Huffman, Hamming)
   B. Data structures for string and general text storage
   C. Indexing and inverted files
   D. Compression; estimates of size

E. Hardware considerations
    1. Disk technology including CD ROM and laser disk
    2. Optical character recognition
    3. Transfer rates
    4. Error rates; error detection and correction

III. Text processing
  A. comparing strings
  B. More general patterns and regular expressions
  C. Searching
  D. Preparing a concordance
  E. Sorting

IV. Meaning in text
  A. Ambiguity
  B. Understanding
  C. Measuring computer comprehension

The first three sections deal with the storage and manipulation of symbols where the symbols have meaning only to the writer. That is, the computer is not asked to assign or infer meaning from the strings of symbols. In the fourth section, however, the computer in some way responds to the meaning of at least some of the symbol strings.

The first section is designed to raise issues and questions that will be answered or addressed later in the course. The goals of the first section include having the students understand the differences between the human view of text and the computer view of text. Specifically the student should learn the difference between the computer definition of a word in a text file and the human definition of a word in a sentence. Issues that must be dealt with in the computer environment are the treatment of punctuation marks and sequences of blanks. Note that computer text systems (editors, word processors) do not all use the same definition of word.

The discussion would build from the data type character to strings of nonblank characters, called words by most text editors, to sequences of words terminated by some natural delimiter, to sequences of these structures that are stored as text files. The natural language structures - English words, paragraphs - are lost in file storage.

The complexity of text processing is first encountered in section two in answering the question, "How big is text?" Types of hardware for storing large volumes of information are described or even better demonstrated. These can include floppy and hard disks and CD ROM. The hardware for making text storable is also included with examples of OCR equipment. A little bit about character representation (EBCDIC and ASCII, maybe Hamming and Huffman codes) is included. We consider how to estimate the space required and how long it takes to store and retrieve a document of a particular size at x characters per second. Students investigate volume capacity and access speeds of various devices including CD ROM, laser disks, and OCR equipment. We include indexing techniques and their importance in retrieving data quickly from large files, and introduce inverted files.

Section three deals with algorithms for common tasks in the context of string use, maintenance, and manipulation. We compare strings (inclusion or exclusion of punctuation, is can't the same as cannot?, case sensitive or not) which leads to the topic of pattern recognition, which brings up regular expressions, which leads to searching techniques, which are simplified if you have a concordance, which had better be sorted. We would not go into all of the sorting techniques in detail, of course, but would survey the methods somewhat and look at the particular characteristics of sorting character strings. We compare algorithms and show the importance of faster algorithms on large volumes of data.

The fourth section is an opportunity to connect the study of text with the area of natural language processing. Two of the many problems that arise are dealing with ambiguity at the word level by recognizing the correct meaning for words that are spelled the same (for example, bore means to drill and to tire) and locating particular parts of speech or structures. In the latter case one may be searching for verbs or for comparisons. In general, the issue is to find something that cannot be defined in terms of strings to be matched. In this section we also treat the meaning of understanding and ways of measuring how well a computer understands.

Problems from the English course to challenge the machine include finding all moral judgments in Jane Austen or references to science in Ben Jonson's works.

Possible exercises:

1. How many characters can be generated on a standard keyboard?

2. For a particular piece of text from the library, estimate the number of characters needed to store it.

3. Locate and correctly expand all contractions.

4. Given two sets of strings and some text, locate all occurrences of a pair of strings, one from the first set and one from the second.

3.2 The English Component

Title: Textual Issues in Literature

Description: Methods, tools and problems in literary analysis. The characteristics of text. Stylometry. Implications of style in identification and description of authors' techniques and effect on reader response.

Prerequisites: A course in literature and composition as an introduction to analytic writing. A survey course in literature of a culture or period to provide familiarity with various styles of writing.

Topics:

- I. The analysis of literature
    - A. Traditional categories
        1. Historical periods
        2. Themes
        3. Models for cultural understanding
    - B. Nontraditional categories
        1. Textual analysis
        2. Intentionality
- II. Approaches to textual analysis
    - A. What is text?
        1. Coherence
        2. Cohesion
        3. Authorship
        4. Acceptability by readers
        5. Meaning
    - B. What is style?
        1. Semantic analysis
        2. Syntactic analysis
        3. Metrical analysis
            - a. Computational stylistics or stylometry
            - b. Collocation
    - C. Problems
        1. Attribution
        2. Verbal signatures
        3. Differences between human-generated and machine-generated text
    - D. Examples
        1. The seemingly spare style of Hemingway
        2. The authorship of the Federalist Papers
        3. Automatic abstracting and summarizing
        4. Machine translation

The first section is to set the background, fundamental definitions, and possible approaches to the study of text linguistics. It is designed to allow students with various depths of knowledge to be on an equal footing at the start of the course.

The second section forms the majority of the course. It starts with a consideration of structural linguistics, including an analysis of what makes a text and what holds pieces of text together (punctuation, conjunctions, prepositions).

Style is an elusive quality of text, yet there are clearly distinctive styles among writers not only of literature but of text for business or other everyday pursuits. There are many questions that can be raised in the process of defining theoretically and operationally the style of text. Operational definitions are important for tying the analysis of text to the computer science part of the cluster, since algorithms need operational definitions. Among the questions are: What is distinctive about samples of text? What information do readers extract from the style of some text? would they respond differently if the style were changed? What measurable quantities can be extracted from text for statistical analysis? What can be counted? What makes parody work?

The course will require a project on

4. An optional detailed Cost Analysis can be used as a capstone to the Alphabet Project. The general question to be addressed is: "To procedurize or not to procedurize?" and the answer depends on a careful analysis of the computer costs: memory space plus execution time costs when we encapsulate a proposed command sequence as a procedure vs those costs when we just repeat the command sequence whenever and wherever needed. Of course, when programmer time (and sanity) costs are included, there is only one answer to the question: always procedurize as it is the only mechanism we have to create the necessary independent, sharable modules required by the principles of top-down design.

3. ALPHA0

Figure 1 is a facsimile of the student handout describing the ALPHA0 project.

(Due to space constraints, the Figures referenced in this text are not present. For a copy of the figures, contact the author who will be happy to provide them for you)

Ten points charged for each core shape which represents a fixed block memory storage cost whenever a procedure is created. One point is charged for each line or segment of each core shape which is an additional memory space cost representing instruction storage cost (as these segments will have to be generated by Logo commands in ALPHA1). Finally, a one point cost for each stamping operation represents the execution time cost.

For example, if two of the core shapes (embedded within a stamp) looked like this:

Then they could be combined via two stamping operations to produce the letter A in our abridged alphabet:

At this time, the instructor can bring these analogies to the students' attention without elaboration.

The collaboration here is easy to facilitate. The instructor can form the students into groups of three to five to address the problem. As groups finish their designs the instructor can display their scores on the blackboard and the "winning" design can be displayed in detail. This cooperative project fits nicely into a typical fifty-minute class period.

Figure 2 shows a blank cost accounting sheet for ALPHA0.

4. ALPHA1

Figure 3 is a facsimile of the student handout describing the ALPHA1 project.

We now wish the student to make the transition from the hypothetical child's game of ALPHA0 to the Logo program required by ALPHA1. The space-time costs have now been made very explicit: storage costs are ten points/procedure used and one point/Logo command; execution time costs are two points/subprocedure call and one point/Logo command.

This project is assigned prior to the introduction of Input parameters in Logo to mitigate its apparent complexity. The assignment requires that only calls to core shape, letter, and "MOVE" procedures are allowed as modules for the letters in order to discourage solutions that use no core shape modules at all (given the values for the space-time costs, substantially lower costs can be achieved by not modularizing at all).A MOVE procedure, like a main program or driver procedure is exempt from one of our Logo rules of top-down design which stipulates that all procedures must restore the Turtle to its original state.

This phase of the alphabet design project puts the students back into the Microcomputer Laboratory using Logo. As most of the course time is purposively scheduled in the Microlab, the design groups formed in ALPHA0 can evolve into programming implementation teams. Because the top-down discipline is enforced, the implementation can be broken down into tasks (some can do core shapes, some can do the client letter procedures) which can be solved when the group is altogether, but the main advantage accrues when the work is decoupled in space and time. This is especially advantageous in a General Education course as the students' schedules tend to be very disparate. Different groups can be required to swap core shapes and check their adherence to the rules of top-down design.

The costing algorithm can be confusing for some students and care must be taken to spend some time in class clarifying any questions or misconceptions the students may have. The instructor must make clear that this tradeoff between space and time is an important problem in computer science and that tradeoffs of this sort are common to many other "real-world" problems.

Figure 4 shows a blank cost sheet for ALPHA1.

5. ALPHA2

Figure 5 is a facsimile of the student handout describing the ALPHA2 project.

In addition to expanding the scope of the assignment to include the entire alphabet, Logo Inputs are required and, as a further reinforcement of the importance of top-down design, the students must supply their procedures as modules to the instructor-supplied driver program.

Note also that since this is a General Education course, the instructor may have to supply a lecture on how to apply Pythagoras' theorem and how the built-in arctan function must be used to construct many of the letters (Y,M,W,V, etc.). Most college freshmen are "naive empiricists" [3] and will spend countless fruitless hours using a trial-and-error method because it appears easier than applying deductive reasoning. One of the most important jobs for the teacher in a course like this is to convince the students that if they only redirected the time and effort they spend avoiding the hard work of deductive reasoning, their lives would be a lot easier.

If the student programming teams can make class presentations of their finished products, some interesting discussions can ensue. Aesthetic issues are not considered in the costing algorithm; in fact since it must take more commands to make "prettier" letters, beauty is not just not rewarded, it is punished! Shouldn't a "nice" looking alphabet garner some reward? Since the finished product is a "Turtle Typewriter" where the letters of the alphabet are drawn procedurally, it also seems that the costs associated with the most frequently used letters (e.g. the vowels) should be higher; this can easily be implemented via a supplied set of weights when computing the costs of each letter.

Perhaps because ALPHA2 represents the culmination of much hard work, it tends to become intensely absorbing to most students. The instructor must take care the students do not neglect other Logo projects and even other courses.

6. COST ANALYSIS

In this phase of the project we analyze the computer costs in a more detailed way and from a more general perspective. By this time, many of the students have realized that it can be more economical in terms of the computer costs to just provide in-line code rather than subprocedures, even if the code is used several times in the program. Some even resent having to procedurize when they know it's going to cost them more (the competition for the best design is a very powerful motivator). At this point, it can be useful to examine these issues and engage the students in a broader analysis of the costs.

The general question of whether "to procedurize or not to procedurize" a given sequence of Logo commands will, of course, depend on the values of the parameters which measure storage space and execution time. We can generalize the situation as follows: Let

- P = (one-time) space cost for creating a Procedure
- S = space cost per command
- E = execution time cost per command
- J = execution time jump cost per subprocedure
- N = number of commands in the sequence under consideration
- M = number of times the sequence will be used in the program.

Of course we oversimplify the actual situation. In reality, the space-time costs (S and E) would not be constants as they would depend on the instruction type (In Logo, a FORWARD command must take longer than a PENUP). The J parameter is also oversimplified --- it represents not just the time to locate the subprocedure and jump back to the calling procedure, but any parameter passing time as well as the extra time to insure state invariance. However, at the level of a reasoning skills course for college freshman, the above six parameters represent a good aggregated or lumped model to simulate the space-time tradeoffs.

Now we can cost the alternatives as follows:

When we procedurize, the total space cost will be P + NS + MS, and the total time cost will be M(J + NE).

When we do not procedurize and just replicate the commands as an in-line sequence, the total space cost will be MNS, and the total time cost will be MNE.

Thus, we may conclude that Procedurizing is less costly (we choose to minimize the sum of the space and time costs for simplicity) when the following relationship holds:

$$P + NS + MS + MJ < MNS$$

It is at first puzzling to see that E (execution time) is missing from the above relation but, on reflection, it is clear that execution time for the proposed command sequence must be the same whether we procedurize or not.

Solving the relation for M, we get:

$$M > (P + NS) / (NS - J - S)$$
$$(\text{when } NS - J - S > 0)$$

Using the above relation we can answer the original question, "To procedurize or not to procedurize?". Given values for the parameters P, S, and J, we can determine the relationship between the variables M and N that makes procedurizing the least costly alternative. For example, when P=S=J=1 (with no loss of generality) we have:

$$M > (N + 1) / (N - 2)$$

(When explicating these relationships, the instructor should not assume that the students can manipulate inequalities and should be prepared to spend a small amount of class time on this topic.)

Thus a proposed sequence of five commands (N = 5) gives M > 2; i.e., the five commands must be used by the program three or more times to cost justify procedurizing.

It is also instructive to plot the equation:

$$M = (N + 1) / (N - 2)$$

which represents the case where the cost of procedurizing is equal to the cost of replicating in-line code (see Figure 6). The inverse relation between M and N is quite clear: points in the region above the curve represent value-pairs of M and N where procedurizing is the least costly alternative and points below the curve where it is not. The shape of the M-N curve is also intuitive: the longer the candidate sequence of commands, the fewer the number of times it need be used to make procedurizing the least costly alternative (and vice-versa).

Two other interesting features of the M-N curve should be noted:

The values for M when N is 1 or 2 are clearly impossible, indicating that no values of M are acceptable when the command sequence is very short and the vertical asymptote at N = 2 is a reflection of this fact.

The horizontal asymptote at M = 1 can be interpreted as meaning: "If you're going to use a sequence of commands only once then it's going to have to be a very very long sequence indeed to cost-justify procedurizing".

After this detailed cost analysis, it is useful for the students to reexamine their previous ALPHA Project designs by identifying which core shapes are not really cost-justifiable. At this point the instructor can reiterate the argument that computer cost justification is not everything --- programmer time and effort must also be considered and if modularization incurs extra computer costs then that is a small price to pay for a programmer's mental health.

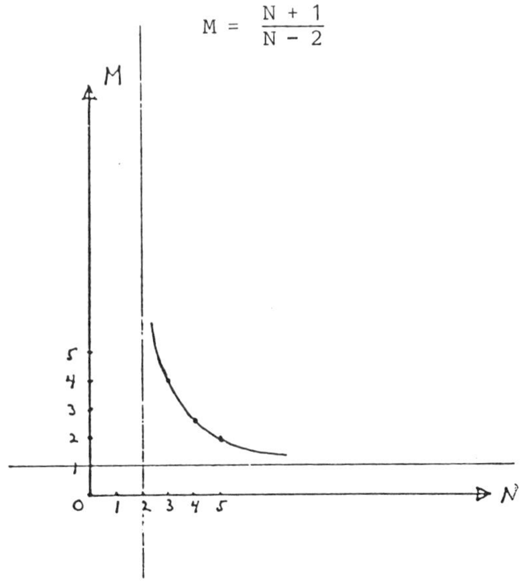

7. SUMMARY

Most students seem to understand the issues involved and profit in terms of improving their problem-solving skills. Many actually become excited and enjoy the creative challenge of producing their own low-cost alphabet. The Logo language and its inherent facilitation of collaborative problem solving makes this otherwise complex project possible and even engrossing to the student. It is also rewarding to the instructor. Unanticipated (and clever) designs are common as students are masters of "beating the system"; i.e. they will stay within the letter of the rules but find incredibly resourceful ways violate the spirit --- perhaps another instance of the all too human inclination to spend a vast amount of time and effort in an attempt to avoid work. Or perhaps it is an affirmation of individuality that a young person is compelled to make. In either case, as Bloom [4] advises, if we can moderate and harness this passion with the virtue of work, we have begun to succeed as teachers. Helping our students acquire a playful, joyful attitude towards work is one of the more important gifts we can impart.

REFERENCES

[1] Denenberg, S. "*Developing Reasoning Skills in College Freshman using Computer Programming, Collaborative Problem-Solving, and Writing*", presented at the XI World Computer Congress, Aug 28 - Sept 1, 1989, San Francisco CA. Published in the IFIP 89 Proceedings, pp 947 -952.

[2] Papert, S. **MindStorms**, Basic Books, 1980

[3] Schoenfeld, A. **Mathematical Problem Solving**, Academic Press, 1985, p43

[4] Bloom, A. **The Closing of the American Mind**, Simon and Schuster, 1987, p129

Computers in Education
A. McDougall and C. Dowling (Editors)
Elsevier Science Publishers B.V. (North-Holland)

VARIED UNIVERSES AND TOOLS TO BEGIN PROGRAMMING

Ghislaine DUFOURD & Jean-François DUFOURD

Centre Informatique et Enseignement, Département d'Informatique, Université Louis Pasteur,
7 rue René Descartes 67084 Strasbourg-Cédex, France.

It has often been said that a good way to interest beginners in computer programming is to have them solve concrete or fun situations within an appropriate hardware and software environment (which is more stimulating than a classical programming language). This article examines different classes of programming tools, their pedagogical contributions and their notional requirements; it proposes three examples of problem designing chosen from different domains, and their Pascal, Logo and Dbase3 programming; it intends to show that whatever the environments, they all fit into a unique conceptual frame: for example a framework with hierarchical types and the deductive method Maiday.

1. INTRODUCTION

It is widely accepted that some programming languages or environments are easier or more *stimulating* for learners than others. It is said about Logo [1,2] because of its turtle-geometry; or about some software systems like DBMS, spreadsheets, graph tools, popular with high school students [3, 4, 5] because their immediate use to them.

Indeed, but how does one assess what they really offer learners and what they require of them ? How does one distinguish between *conceptual* nature assessment criteria (the universe and the problem solving) and *operational* nature assessment criteria (the languages and the tools) ?

This paper means to help bring about some evaluation criteria. It focusses on the *first stages of learning* because of their lasting impact on learners. It concentrates on procedural, functional and object oriented programming, including recursivity but excluding field logic programming (too specific [6, 7]).

Two programming techniques will be used to help present the forthcomming notions:
- *hierarchic constructions of types* [8, 9, 10]: highly desirable notions for teachers, but not to be taught to beginners;
- the *Maiday deductive programming method* [11, 12, 13]: an excellent pedagogical approach [14], if well mastered and, perhaps, simplified.

The following sections will deal with the necessary conceptual framework (section 2) and examine three universes: booleans, numbers and characters in section 3 (Pascal), turtle-geometry in section 4 (Logo) and databases in section 5 (Dbase3); section 6 will discuss their advantages and disavantages, trying to bring out the essential elements for initiation in programming. Section 7 will conclude and suggest further developments. The examples used to illustrate these points are taken from a computer course for second year high school in France.

2. A CONCEPTUAL FRAME: a short reminder

2.1. Object and operation universes

A *universe* is a set of types and operations which account for the objects of the field under study.

A data *type* is a named set of objects. For example, the sets of relative integers, of reals and of unlimited character strings are respectively called *integer*, *real* and *string*. They are *basic* types. Other types are constructed with them, or with others which have been constructed previously, thanks to parametered *generic* types (or type constructors), for example the use in section 5 of the generic type *set of* T, which designates the set of the parts of type T. T is here a formal type which can be replaced by every known type, at the time of *instanciation*. An other way to construct types with others is *inheritance*, but it will not be used here. Those two mechanisms allow the construction of type *hierarchies*, translating their mutual dependencies into a *semantic network*.

Operations between types can be defined. Some of them are called *generic* operations because they apply to generic types. So, the operation set union $\cup$ applies to two sets of the same instance of the generic type *set of* T. Other operations can be *inherited* with the type inheritance mechanism.

In fact, the universe notion is in relation with the mathematical notion of *heterogeneous algebra* [15]. Today, it is widely used in computer science, particularly by means of generic type languages, such as Ada, or of object oriented languages, such as Smalltalk. Eiffel is a good compromise between these two trends [10].

2.2. The Maiday deductive method

This method fits in with the following problem solving process [11]:

```
                                                      data
                                                        ↓
informal → formal →  solving→  program →  calculations
statement  statement process                            ↓
                                                      results
```

The essential phase of this diagram is the working out of the formal statement, written with *algorithmic definitions* belonging to three categories:

- *simple definition* of x: x = <simple expression>
- *conditional definition* of x:
  x = *if* <condition> *then* <expr. 1> *else* <expr. 2>
- *iterative definition* of a sequence (x_i):
  x_f = *while* <condition> *repeat* x_i = <expression>

The two first forms have an obvious meaning. The third is the definition of a sequence (x_i) of which the final term is x_f, from a first term x_0, until <condition> is false. When <expression> contains x_{i-1}, the sequence is *recurrent*, and x_0 has to be defined separately (initialization). To simplify, x_i and x_{i-1} will be respectively noted x and @x. It is the same for the iterative diagram which is used when the number n of x_i is known in advance: x_f = n *times repeat* x_i = <expression>. When *result* takes the place of x or x_f, it is a simple, conditional or iterative *writing*, on a suitable medium, here the screen. When <expression> is replaced by *data* [<string>], it is a *reading* by a suitable medium, here the keyboard, after the sending to the screen of a message <string> to the user.

In fact, the formal statement is a set of *modules* (one of them is a *program*), with a heading and two parts: on the left a *lexicon* and on the right the *algorithmic definitions* of the lexical elements, written as they were needed. A central column allows the final numbering of the definitions in order to get an *algorithm* (cf. figure 3.1). When a definition needs secondary definitions, they are grouped into a module which takes the place of one of the expressions in one of the previous diagrams (cf. figure 3.1). Several definitions can be merged as shall be shown with iterations.

This expression form [12, 16] is suited to a structured, modular, downward or upward, declarative design: it tries to express object *definitions* rather than *calculations* [11]. According to the principle of *unique assignation*, a different name is given to different values, which leads to the use of suffixes for sequences, or the simplified notations presented above [17, 18, 19]. The lexicon is a good guide and a significant help with documentation.

		program BRACKETS
d : *integer* : difference between the number of "(" and the number of ")", for the examined part of the expression;	6	*result* = *if* $d_f = 0$ *then write* ('WELL BRACKETED') *else write* ('BADLY BRACKETED')
	5	d_f, i_f, c_f = *while* $c \neq$ ';' *and* $d \geq 0$ *repeat* ONECHAR
c : *character* : ith character of s;	2	$d_0 = 0$
i : *integer* : place of c in s;	4	c_0 = char (s, i_0)
ONECHAR : *module* : defines current d, i and c;	3	$i_0 = 1$
s : *string* : to examine;	1	s = *data* ['INPUT A STRING:']
		module ONECHAR
	1	d = *if* @c = '(' *then* @d+1 *else if* @c = ')' *then* @d-1 *else* @d
	2	i = @i+1
	3	c = char (s, i)

Figure 3.1 Algorithm of the brackets problem

3. A TRADITIONAL UNIVERSE: booleans, numbers and strings

3.1. Objects and operations

This traditional programming universe will be used to illustrate section 2. Basic types are *boolean*, *integer*, *character* and *string*, with predefined operations: respectively usual logic and integer arithmetic operations (booleans, integers), character constants -operations with 0 variable- (characters), empty string and concatenation (strings). Other operations are mixed: so char (s, i) gives the ith character of string s, and x=y, where x and y are of the same type, is a boolean.

3.2. Problem solving: an example

- *Informal statement*: verify that an arithmetic expression, starting at the beginning of a non empty string, and stopped by a ";", is well bracketed: each ")" is always linked with a "(" which precedes it.
- *Formal statement and algorithm*: they are given in figure 3.1. The sequences (d), (i) and (c) are jointly defined in a merging of iterations. Please note the mechanism of "forward reading" of character c in string s, which is a clearly identified difficulty in algorithmics [20].

3.3. Programming tools

At this stage, a number of programming languages may be used: for example, Basic, Logo, Pascal (see below a programm in T-Pascal™). Suffixes and "@" have been suppressed, ONECHAR has become a unit, instructions have been rearranged, function "copy" has replaced "char".

```
program BRACKETS;
var s: string [255]; d, i: integer; c: char;
begin
  write('INPUT A STRING:'); readln(s);
  d:=0; i:=1; c:=copy(s, i, 1);
  while (c < > ';') and (d > = 0) do
  begin {ONECHAR}
    if c='(' then d:=d+1 else if c=')' then d:=d-1;
    i:=i+1; c:=copy(s, i, 1)
  end; {ONECHAR}
  if d=0 then writeln('WELL BRACKETED')
  else writeln('BADLY BRACKETED')
end.
```

4. A GRAPHIC UNIVERSE: turtle-geometry

4.1. Objects and operations

Basically, the *turtle-geometry universe* [21] is an *extension* of the universe of section 3 to a new type of objects: a screen, fitted with a turtle. The characteristics of a turtle on a screen are: its position [x,y] in the Euclidian plane (abscissa, ordinate), its heading a (angle in degrees in relation to the north), its appearance or not on the screen, its color, etc. These elements are featured on top of the general screen specifications: boundary text-graphics, background color, etc. All these characteristics are defined by operations acting on the screen. Other operations generate screens, possibly from other screens, with the help of some parameters, especially to move the turtle.

In the usual vision of turtle-geometry, there is of course only one screen -and one turtle- considered as *global*, and therefore they do not appear as an operator or a result of screen or turtle operations. These operations are then *procedures* which *modify* the turtle screen by side effect. Such is the case with the *primitives* used and explained later: MS, CT, CS, etc. For more convenience, the names of these primitives are those of Logo. But, in the next paragraph, these operations are used as usual (functions-) procedures, with the usual mathematical notations, especially with bracketed parameters.

4.2. Problem solving: an example [22]

- *Informal statement*: write a program which draws several similar triangles ABC, right-angled in A, this point being situated above the hypotenuse BC, which is parallel to the axis of x. The number of triangles is given, as well as the measure of edge BC and of angle B. The point B of each triangle is localized by the light-pen.
- *Formal statement and algorithm*: they are given in figure 4.1.

4.3. Programming tools

A program can now be written. Although many languages now feature turtle-geometry possibilities (T-Pascal, for example), Logo [1] remains the most obvious "turtle language". See below the program: the module TRIANGLES becomes a procedure and the module ONETRI a block.

```
TO TRIANGLES
  MS (5)  CT  CS
  PR [MEASURE OF ANGLE B:]  MAKE "B RW
  PR [MEASURE OF EDGE AB:]  MAKE "AB RW
  PR [NUMBER OF TRIANGLES:]  MAKE "N RW
  MAKE "AC PRODUCT :AB QUOTIENT SIN:B COS:B
  REPEAT :N
    [PR [POINT ON THE SCREEN THE PLACE OF THE
  NEXT TRIANGLE] MAKE "BXY POSOPT
    PU SETPOS :BXY PD RT DIFFERENCE 90 :B
    FD :AB RT 90 FD :AC SETPOS :BXY]
END
```

Clearly, the conceptual turtle-geometry universe should be distinguished from its implementing tools, among which Logo is only the most famous.

program TRIANGLES: draws a given number of triangles		
MS (p): *procedure*: allows both text (p lines from bottom) and graphics on the screen;	1	*result* = MS(5), CT, CS
CT: *procedure*: clears text portion;	6	*result* = n *times repeat* ONETRI
CS: *procedure*: clears graphical portion, initializes the turtle;	4	n = *data* ["NUMBER OF TRIANGLES:"]
n: *integer*: number of triangles;	2	B = *data* ["MEASURE OF ANGLE B:"]
ONETRI: *module*: draws one triangle;	3	AB = *data* ["MEASURE OF EDGE AB:"]
B: *real*: measure of angle B;	5	AC = AB * sin (B) / cos (B)
AB: *real*: measure of edge AB;		
AC: *real*: measure of edge AC;		
module ONETRI		
PU: *procedure*: puts turtle-pen up;	2	*result* = PU, SETPOS (BXY), PD, RT (90-B), FD (AB), RT (90), FD (AC), SETPOS (BXY)
PD: *procedure*: puts turtle-pen down;	1	BXY = POSOPT ["POINT ON THE SCREEN THE PLACE OF THE NEXT TRIANGLE"]
SETPOS (L): *procedure*: sets turtle to coordinates specified by L;		
RT (n): *procedure*: turns turtle n degrees right (clockwise);		
FD (n): *procedure*: moves turtle n steps forward;		
BXY: *list*: coordinates of point B for the current triangle;		
POSOPT: *function*: returns the two coordinates of the place pointed by the light-pen;		

Figure 4.1 Algorithm of triangle drawing

5. A RELATIONAL UNIVERSE: databases

5.1. Objects and operations

Again, the *relational universe* appears as an *extension* of the one in section 3 to new types of n-tuples (or structures) and relations [23]. So *type* $U = <u_1: U_1; \ldots ; u_n: U_n>$ is the definition of a new type U as a cartesian product (order apart) of the types $U_1, \ldots , U_n$, with the *field selectors* $u_1, \ldots , u_n$. The elements of U are *n-tuples* or *structures* (in the meaning of "records" in Pascal). Then, *type* rU = *set of* U is the definition of a new type rU as a set of parts from set U. The elements of rU are *relations* or (under-) *sets* (in the meaning of Pascal).

In this universe, the *operations* on the n-tuples are: construction of a tuple, projection onto one (or several) components; the operations on the relations are the usual set operations and the relational algebraic operations [24]. So, the selection in a relation r of the n-tuples verifying a predicate $p(u_1, \ldots , u_n)$ is noted $r|p(u_1, \ldots , u_n)$; the set difference is noted -; {x} is the relation reduced to tuple x and card(r) is the cardinal of relation r. It is also possible to go over all the elements of a relation in a given order, to define indexes, to have direct access to a tuple with a given index, and so on. So, eor(r) is *true* if and only if the going all over r is reached at the end; first(r) [resp. suc(r)] returns the first tuple [resp. the next tuple] of the relation r, in accordance with the increasing inner numeration. These operations give to the relational universe a great power, but also a real complexity.

5.2. Problem solving: an example

Our frame is an easy simplified application of library management, with relations about the books, the pupils, the borrowings, and so on [3].

- *Informal statement*: create a transaction to count the books by Victor Hugo published by Gallimard.
- *Formal statement and algorithm*: See on figure 5.1 two versions of transaction COUNTING. The first one uses all the power of relational model primitives, the second one is closer to traditional file management, where one can once again notice the "forward reading" technique.

The type of the books and the type of the relations about the books can be described by:

type book = < n : *integer*; {book number}
a : *string*; {author} t : *string*; {title}
e : *string*; {editor} ... >;
type rbook = *set of* book;

program COUNTING: version 1		
rb : rbook : set of the library books;	2 1	*result* =*write*(card(rb|a = 'HUGO' *and* e ='GALLIMARD')) rb = *data*

program COUNTING: version 2		
t : *integer* : number of pertinent works found before;	5	*result* = *write* (t_f)
	4	t_f, x_f = *while not* eor(rb) *repeat*
rb : rbook : set of the library books;		t = *if* a(@x) = 'HUGO' *and* e(@x) = 'GALLIMARD' *then* @t+1 *else* @t
		x = suc(rb)
x : book : current tuple;	3	$t_0 = 0$
	1	rb = *data*
	2	x_0 = first(rb)

Figure 5.1 Two versions of COUNTING

5.3. Programming tools

For such a universe, the best implantation tool is clearly a relational DBMS. As an illustration, see below version 1 of COUNTING in the handling language of a widely used system: Dbase3TM. Of course any relational DBMS will do. Indeed, in the Dbase3 language, the implicit writings are numerous and reduce the amount of text, but they are a source of wrong interpretation or programming mistakes.

```
TEXT COUNTING : version 1
ENDTEXT
USE RB
COUNT FOR (A='HUGO') .AND. (E='GALLIMARD')
RETURN
```

6 - A DISCUSSION ABOUT THE DIFFERENT APPROACHES

- Stimulating "fun" or "real" problems,

Obviously, the richer the universe, the more stimulating the problems. However, this quest for "interesting" programs may have an *overflowing effect*. For example, in the turtle exercise in section 4, the Pythagorean theorem or trigonometric functions will soon be needed. Indeed, lists might even have to be introduced. Everyone has in mind the misled attempts to impose untimely notions on young pupils and the ensuing abuse. Further more, a true *"real" problem* is often very complex. If one wished to handle the exercise in section 5 in a really comprehensive way (managing a full-scale library), one would have to choose between two evils: wasting time or eventually turning up with a still unsuitable program. Indeed, a real database is often a collection of relations, and not an isolated relation. Moreover, it has to permanently fulfill *integrity constraints*.

- involve thorough teaching and experimentation,

In fact, the richer the universe, the more complex the environment, and the more numerous the necessary prerequisite notions. More often than not, immersion in a new universe requires an object and operation *learning* period. At that stage, the computer is used as an assistant by learners, for example by direct handling of the tools which will later be used for programming.

So, the interest and the difficulties of turtle-geometry initiation for young children as a help to find their bearings and to move in the plane are wellknown. Today, the *floor-turtle* is a widely used educational tool in primary schools, and the immediate execution of Logo procedures, in direct handling mode, allows the systematic exploration of this universe. A good understanding of relational primitives also requires direct handling of the DBMS orders. Moreover, it is necessary to speedily construct relations as testing examples to try out transactions such as in section 5. It means a lot of hours dedicated to this system learning, which have to be prepared by the teacher in a methodical and progressive way.

On the other hand, everyone will admit that initiation is especially fast with a numerical universe, a little longer with strings, therefore direct handling is essential here as well. Since they are the basis for the construction of any richer universe, one cannot do without them.

- but may lead to forgetting the basic points,

Designing the proper blend of *theory* and *practice* is a commonplace problem in computer science teaching (as it is indeed in teaching in general). Emphazing concepts (universe, problem solving method) may lead to forgetting real implementation (computer, system, language). Conversely, too practical an approach may impede a good structuring of the mind [25] and further developments.

To be effective, an algorithmic and programming initiation emphatically supposes interest in the *whole process* leading from problem statement to concrete resolution on a computer. If pupils have to acquire both concepts and tools at the same time, time will have to be wasted on unnecessary and untopical teaching. This has got to be taken into account when choosing a universe or a programming environment.

- and getting overwhelmed by technical trivia,

Concentrating on a particular programming tool, investigating it down to its minutest details could hide the fundamental behind a screen of anecdotal trivia. One may easily be deluded into believing one is dealing with specific concepts and analysis methods. Thus the dithyramb about "Logo processes" and the bombast about DBMS as "4th generation languages".

- whereas basically, everything rests on the notion of universe,

The notions of *universes*, object *types* and *operations* offer a unified conceptual scheme [8, 9], which makes it possible to understand, to classify, to organize into a hierarchy the elements which occur in design-programming.

Yet, in computer science, the type notion has been discussed a lot, especially in relation to non typed applicative languages, such as Lisp. In fact, the Lisp programmer does not apply his functions at random on any object [8]. And, most often today, before setting about programming, he begins to define an "object oriented layer" allowing him to describe his working universe in the form of a semantic network with hierarchic types (or classes).

So, each environment used for programming initiation is based on a universe in which description is always the concern of the *same basic notions*. This universe can then be implemented with the help of different tools or programming languages. Therefore, it is important that the teacher always keeps in mind this dichotomy between universe and concrete environment, and that he communicates this idea to his pupils, without theoryzing it.

- and recurrent problem solving methods.

Indeed, whatever the universe or the programming tools, problem solving rests on *identical mental and methodological processes*. It is true with the three universes described in this paper, but it could be generalized [26, 27].

The essential stage is the *formal statement*: the deductive method could be the suitable tool for teaching beginners how to make formal statements [6], providing one shuns dogmatism, avoids "too much formalism" [28], and sticks to basic concepts: simple, conditional (including recursive) and iterative definitions. The *implementation* phase, the actual programming, is then only a translation of the formal statement into a particular language (pratically any language will do). At this stage eventual problems should only be technical, not conceptual or algorithmic.

7 - CONCLUSION

This paper wanted to fight the always deep-roated tendency to want "to learn programming in..." Basic, Logo, Pascal, Lisp, Ada, APL, Dbase, etc., instead of trying simply "to learn programming". If it is vital to master those tools, it is not less vital to be able to define, to formulate and to solve problems in a clearly identified universe. And it is possible to converge to a unique way to formulate the algorithm statements in all universes.

This basic level of problem solving can later be enriched, remaining always in the same conceptual scheme [29]. The next levels consist then in learning to *supplement* universes with new operations (functions and procedures), then to *conceive* and to *construct* them (construction of types by genericity and inheritance).

In this paper, three universes have been examined, but what has been said fits easily into other universes underlying other kinds of applications and programming tools, such as files, spreadsheets, to some extent tools for computer-aided geometry [30], or computer-aided designing [31]. Experiments are being carried out in the Strasbourg area with a large range of tools, and Maiday as a pivotal way to define objects.

Such experiments have to be extended: to improve the concepts, the methods and the programming techniques (including logic programming); to teach them to varied pupil publics who are easier to stimulate with some universes and some classes of tools. But one always has to keep in mind the deep unity of the concepts of designing and programming!

ACKNOWLEDGEMENTS

The authors would like to thank Pierre Frath and Daniel Frizot for the considerable improvement of the English style of this paper, and Jacques Cardon for his precious help with the editing.

REFERENCES

[1] Papert S., *Jaillissement de l'Esprit*, Flammarion, 1981.

[2] Shaffer D., *The Use of Logo in an Introductory Computer Science Course*, ACM-SIGCSE, 18 (4), 1986, p. 28-31.

[3] Jamm F., *Démarche Pédagogique pour une Initiation à l'Algorithmique à travers l'Utilisation d'un SGBD*, projet pédagogique CIE, ULP Strasbourg, 1985.

[4] Bailey G., *Spreadsheets and Databases-Alternatives to Programming for Non Computer Science Majors*, 18th ACM Tech. Symp. on Comp. Sc. Educ., St Louis, 1987, p. 499-503.

[5] Favre-Nicolin R. & Maraninchi J.B., *Tableur et Récursivité en classe de Seconde*, Pratique et Savoir-faire des Elèves de l'Option Informatique, CRDP, Poitiers, 1987, p. 82-88.

[6] Arsac J., *Des Pédagogies pour l'Option Informatique des Lycées*, Pratiques et Savoir-faire des Elèves de l'Option Informatique, CRDP, Poitiers, 1987, p. 1-13.

[7] Lin F. & Hunt E., *LCD-Reification: A Formal Method for Developing Prolog Programs*, ACM-Sigplan Notices, 23 (5), 1989, p. 249-256.

[8] Cardelli L. & P. Wegner P., *On Understanding Types, Data Abstraction, and Polymorphism*, ACM-Comp. Surveys, 17 (4), 1985, p. 471-522.

[9] Goguen J.A., *Rewriting and Interconnecting Software Components*, IEEE-Computer, 18 (2), 1986, p. 16-28.

[10] Meyer B., *Genericity versus Inheritance*, 1st ACM Symposium on Object Oriented Syst., Lang. and Appl., Portland, 1986, p. 391-405.

[11] Pair C., *La Construction des Programmes*, RAIRO Informatique, 13 (2), 1979, p. 113-137.

[12] Ducrin A., *Programmation*, vol. 1 et 2, Dunod, 1984.

[13] Finance J.P. & Souquières J., *A Method and a Language for Constructing Iterative Programs*, SCP 5 (2), 1985, p. 201-218.

[14] Bana C., Dufourd G., Jaray B. & Finance J.P., *Using Computer Science in Order to Teach Mathematics*, IFIP WCCE 81, Lausanne, 1981, p. 171-176.

[15] Goguen J.A. & al., *An Initial Algebra Approach to the Specification, Correctness and Implementation of Abstract Data Types*, in Current Trends in Programming Methodology 4, R.T. Yeh (ed.), Prentice Hall, 1978, p. 80-149.

[16] GRECO Programmation du C.N.R.S., *Bilans et Perspectives*, Talence, 1986, p. 45-47.

[17] Arsac J., *La Construction de Programmes Structurés*, Dunod, 1977.

[18] Ashcroft E.A. & Wadge W.W., *LUCID, a Non-procedural Language with Iteration*, CACM, 20 (71), 1977, p. 519-526.

[19] Turner D., *An Overview of MIRANDA*, ACM-Sigplan Notices, 21 (12), 1986, p. 158-166.

[20] Wirth N., *Systematic Programming: An Introduction*, Prentice Hall, 1973.

[21] Abelson H. & Di Sessa A.A.,*Turtle Geometry*, MIT Press, 6th edition, 1984.

[22] Dufourd J.F., *Construction of Iterative Programs In Computer Graphics*, Comp. Graphics Forum, 7 (3), North Holland, 1988.

[23] Dufourd J.F., *Types Abstraits et Bases de Données Relationnelles*, TSI, 4 (4), 1985, p. 339-349.

[24] Date C.J., *An Introduction to Database Systems*, 3rd ed., Addison-Wesley, 1981.

[25] Henderson P.B., *Modern Introductory Computer Science*, 18th ACM Tech. Symp. on Comp. Sc. Educ., St Louis, 1987, p. 183-189.

[26] Gram A., *Raisonner pour Programmer*, Dunod, 1986.

[27] Bauer F.L., Moller B., Partsch H. & Pepper P., *Formal Program Construction by Transformations-Computer-Aided, Intuition-Guided Programming*, IEEE-Trans. of Software Eng., 15 (2), 1989.

[28] Ferchichi A. & Joua A., *Teaching First Year Programming: a Proposal*, ACM-SIGCSE, 19 (3), p. 48-52.

[29] Dufourd J.F., *Vers un Cadre Unique pour Spécifier et Construire des Programmes*, TSI, 7 (3), Dunod, 1988, p. 281-293.

[30] Fuller N. & Prusinkiewicz P., *Geometric Modelling with Euclidian Constructions*, Proc. Comp. Graphics Int. 88, Springer Verlag, 1988, p. 379-391.

[31] AUTODESK, *Autocad™, v. 2.1., User Ref. Pub.* 106-006F, 1985.

Computers in Education
A. McDougall and C. Dowling (Editors)
Elsevier Science Publishers B.V. (North-Holland)

MULTI-LAYERED MULTIMEDIA: A NEW LEARNING EXPERIENCE

Kay FIELDEN

School of Information Sciences & Engineering, University of Canberra, P.O. Box 1, Belconnen, ACT 2616, Tel. 062-522410

The emerging wave of multi-media products becoming available to wider cross sections of the community has far reaching implications for education. The creation of a multi-layered learning environment, making multimedia tools available to many levels within the higher education field has been phased in over the past two years at the University of Canberra.

The layers of learning include access to multimedia for first semester students with little or no computing experience for project presentation, final semester computing students for project development, higher degree students and academics for research into the implications of learning in an enriched sensory environment, and a selection of short courses on multimedia subjects to the wider community.

1. INTRODUCTION

The emerging wave of multi-media products becoming available to wider cross sections of the community has far reaching implications for education. The creation of a multi-layered learning environment, making multi-media tools available to many levels within the higher education field has been phased in over the past two years at the University of Canberra.

The layers of learning include access to a multi-media laboratory by first semester students with little or no computing experience. Incorporating multi-media presentation tools for projects at this level enriches the learning environment for a wide variety of students as well as spreading knowledge about multi-media across the campus and out into the wider community.

Development of multi-media projects by final semester computing students has the advantage of increasing the human resources in the multi-media field. Another layer in this learning environment is provided by higher degree students and academics to study the implications of learning in an enriched sensory environment. Research areas of interest include: the barriers to accepting high technology and changes to technology perceived by academics, new styles of learning made possible by multi-media and the spread of multi-media into non-traditional computing areas such as fine arts.

A selection of short courses on a variety of Hypermedia subjects offered to the wider community provides yet another layer to the learning environment.

2. MULTI-MEDIA AND HYPERTEXT

Hypertext systems (Conklin,[1]) feature machine supported links, both within and between documents, that offer exciting possibilities for using the computer as a communication and thinking tool.

As laser disc technologies like video disc CD-ROM and DVI (Digital Video Interactive) come of age there is growing interest in the extension of the hypertext concept into one of multimedia, or hypermedia, in which the elements linked together include not only text but also graphics, digitised speech, audio recordings, still pictures, animation, film clips and so on.

The first stage of phasing in multi-media as a learning environment involved exploring the design issues in developing multi-media systems, in an endeavour to develop an understanding of how to achieve the most appropriate tool to improve computer based training.

3. THE MULTI-MEDIA LABORATORY

The School of Information Sciences and Engineering and the Centre for Media Studies at the University of Canberra jointly established the Multi-media laboratory in the first instance with the following general aims:

(i) to teach students how to develop multi-media applications;

(ii) to develop expertise in the design and production of multi-media applications; and

(iii) to provide facilities for research into multi-media environments.

A joint laboratory was considered necessary because the skills and other resources required for the development of multi-media applications transcended those normally available within tertiary institutions (Fielden & Steele,[7]).

This was later extended by the School of Information Sciences and Engineering in conjunction with the Computer Centre at the University of Canberra to allow wider access to multi-media facilities via the use of a Computer Centre Macintosh Laboratory with add-on equipment such as video disc players, scanners and recorders supplied by the School of Information Sciences and Engineering. This allowed first year students college wide to have access to the multi-media laboratory, as well as offering facilities for short courses to the general public outside of semester.

4. NEW LEARNING ENVIRONMENTS

Nielsen [8] sets out five criteria for the use of hypermedia systems. These are:

(i) Easy to learn: The user can quickly get some work done with the system.

(ii) Efficient to use: Once the user has learnt the system, a high level of productivity is possible.

(iii) Easy to remember: The casual user is able to return to using the system after some period of not having used it, without having to learn everything again.

(iv) Few Errors: Users do not make many errors during the use of the system, or if they do make errors they can easily recover from them.

(v) Pleasant to Use: Users are subjectively satisfied by using the system.

The environment provided by the Multi-media lab, with Macintoshes and Hypercard with appropriate Xcmds to drive devices such as laser disc players, scanners and recorders, satisfies these criteria to the extent that novice users such as first year non-computing students can quickly learn to use the tools, to allow them to develop projects which 'come alive' with the use of the most appropriate presentation devices. As these students quickly become familiar with the use of the available tools, the tools themselves fade from the cognitive process, allowing students to concentrate on the problem to solve, rather than the tool at hand. Hypermedia tools allow for the development of applications which give control back to the user. Hypermedia applications as a learning aid can be compared to a book. The reader of a book can read any page at random, in any order. Information on a subject may be found from the index, a topic list, the table of contents, or by browsing. Such is the case with Hypermedia applications, with the added benefit of using the most appropriate media and form for the presentation of ideas. An advantage with a Hypermedia system is that the links establishing in navigating through hyperspace can be retraced. It is a very disciplined reader who does this with a book.

Using the most appropriate media and form heightens the learning experience by appealing to more than one sense.

The next learning layer to be considered is final semester computing students who have developed a variety of multi-media and graphic applications as part of their course work. Projects undertaken successfully include:

(i) Careers advice for public information display up to year 12 level. Two versions of this project have been completed. The first using a Macintosh, Hypercard and a Laser disc player. The second implementation was completed on a PC using Turbo Pascal and Meta Windows, with a MIC Board to interface a touch screen;

(ii) Computer Aided Design tool for Textiles. This project was completed, as a computer graphics project on a PC driving a colour printer, and

(iii) Astronomy public information display for Australian observatories. This project used two screens, and a laser disc player on a PC. The Software languages and tools used were Turbo Pascal and Meta Windows.

In all of these projects motivation was high in each small group. One of the main contributing factors in such project work is the development of graphic interfaces. (Fielden & Steele [7]). As the product being developed took shape, this provided motivation and enthusiasm to continue. It was as if the project itself took over the motivating force.

Another layer to the learning process is provided by higher degree students and academics studying the implications for learning in an enriched sensory environment. Research areas of interest are:

(i) The barriers to accepting high technology and changes to technology perceived by academics, particularly those with little or no computing skills; and

(ii) New styles of learning made possible by multi-media and the spread of multi-media into non-traditional computing areas such as fine arts.

It is interesting to note that the Computer Aided Design package for textiles provides a greatly enhanced productivity tool at the design stage for weavers, as well as offering aids to creativity that were not possible with the use of manual design tools.

Finally, in an endeavour to spread knowledge about multi-media and its many applications and uses to the wider community, short courses on a variety of topics such as HyperCard scripting, classroom training, authoring systems and multi-media tools and applications are offered to non-computing academics, public service personnel and industry trainers.

5. LEVELS OF LEARNING

Interaction within and across these levels of learning provides a new and enriched environment in which to study and use the learning process. When the tools fade from the cognitive process, and the task at hand becomes the main focus, the multi-media environment offers a number of new learning experiences. These are:

(i) The ability to trace the learning path via the use of links in hyperspace.

(ii) The use of hypermedia applications as a brainstorming tool to aid the creative process; and

(iii) The use of more senses to reinforce the learning process. For instance, graphics from videodisc, scanner or computer graphics or the use of sound, as well as text.

Hypermedia systems have been shown to be most appropriate when there are a large number of short information fragments that cross reference each other, and when the users need to view only a small slice at a given time.

6. COURSE STRUCTURES

All of the innovations to the learning environment at the University of Canberra in using multi-media have taken place within existing course structures. This was seen to be an advantage, in keeping up with the leading edge of technology. Restructuring courses takes time, and the leasing edge marches on.

7. CONCLUSION

The venture into using multi-media within existing course structures can be considered to be a success in developing a rich and new learning environment. This is just the beginning, and much work needs to be done to improve the user interface for multi-media systems.

REFERENCES:

[1] Conklin, J. (1987): *Hypertext: An Introduction and Survey.* IEEE Computer, September, pp.17-41.

[2] Fielden, K. (1989) (a): *People: The Driving Force in Human Computer Interaction.* Proc. 3rd Int. Conf. on Human Computer Interaction, Boston, pp.612-619.

[3] Fielden, K. (1989) (b): *A Collaborative Approach to Computer Aided Design for Textiles.* Proc. ACEC 89, Canberra, October 1-4.

[4] Fielden, K. (1989) (c): *Computing and Creativity: Bridging the Gap.* Presented at ASCILITE 89, Bond University, December 12-15.

[5] Fielden, K. (1988): *Educating for Improved System Design: The Key to Better End-User Development.* Proc. Australian CAE 19th Annual Computer Conference, pp.280-287.

[6] Fielden, K. & Steele, J. (1988) (a): *HyperCard and Interactive Video.* Proc. Ed. Tech.'88, Canberra, September, pp.43-60.

[7] Fielden, K. & Steele, J. (1988) (b): *A Multi-media Approach to Computer-Based Training.* Proc. ACC'88, Sydney. September 21-23, pp.41-56.

[8] Neilsen, J. (1989): *Introduction to Hypertext and Hypermedia.* Workshop Notes, 3rd Int. Conf. on Human Computer Interaction, Boston, September 18-22.

[9] Seeley, D. & Leadbetter, M. (1988): *Supporting Group Innovation with a Hypertext Authoring System.* In Towards 2000, Proc. ACC'88, Sydney, pp.133-158.

[10] Shneiderman, B. (1989): *Future Directions for Human-Computer Interaction in Designing and using Human-Computer Interfaces and Knowledge-Based Systems.* G. Salvendy and M.J.Smith (eds)., Elsevier Science Pub., Netherlands, pp.2-17.

Computers in Education
A. McDougall and C. Dowling (Editors)
Elsevier Science Publishers B.V. (North-Holland)

TEACHING NEURAL NETWORKS

John Alan FULCHER

Department of Computer Science, University of Wollongong, P.O. Box 1144, Wollongong NSW 2500, Australia.

There has been an enormous amount of research interest in the area of Neural Networks during the last few years. However this has not been matched in the teaching arena, at least not until very recently. More and more support for neural networks is beginning to appear in the marketplace, from software simulators, plug-in boards for PC/ATs, Macintoshes and Sun workstations, through to VLSI chips and complete neural network development systems. This paper surveys some of the more notable products available in this area, and comments on their suitability for use at the undergraduate (and graduate) tertiary level.

1. Introduction

There has been a huge upsurge of interest in neural networks in recent times. As Prof. Andrew Barto, keynote speaker at the University of New South Wales Connectionist Modelling Workshop remarked: 'Prior to the early 1980s, it was generally thought that neural networks could not do anything interesting. Since then, *anything* a neural net can do is considered interesting!' - Barto [1]. This observation accurately summarizes the current situation; a lot of people are touting neural nets as a panacea (and thereby inevitably courting disappointment).

The applications best suited to neural nets are those in which rules are difficult to establish, either because they are unknown or too complex. Pattern recognition (of voice, image or other signals) is such an application; indeed, any random, unstructured, non-linear problem is a good candidate.

Artificial neural networks (ANNs) comprise large numbers of simple (and often slow), non-linear Processing Elements (PEs) or 'neurons', interconnected by various 'weights' (either 'excitatory' or 'inhibitory'), to form a massively parallel distributed processor (PDP). Moreover, these weights can be adapted (changed) during use to improve system performance. The outputs of the individual neurons 'fire' if the sum of their inputs exceeds a certain threshold, as indicated in Figure 1.

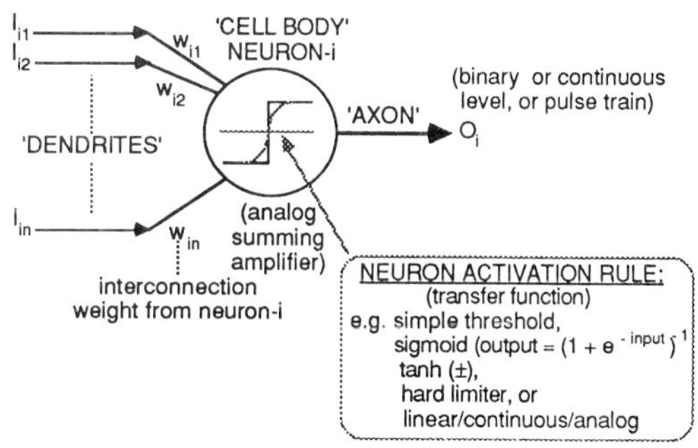

Figure 1

The neuron model can range from the simple McCullogh & Pitts [2] type, through to ones using tanh or sigmoid activation functions (where output = $(1+ e^{-input})^{-1}$), to continuous (analog)-input models. Networks of such neurons can be constructed which, to varying degrees, mimic some of the capabilities of the human brain. The latter contains around 10^{15} neurons, each of which has a response time of the order of milliseconds (which should be compared with *nano*seconds for the PEs of present day computers); the speed of individual neurons is not critical to overall system performance.

Information is encoded via different interconnection patterns; these different patterns constitute the network's (long term) 'memory' (the neurons themselves act as *short*-term memory). Neural nets are more accurately described as distributed, one-to-many, associative memories, rather than conventional, discrete computer memories (in which there is a one-to-one correspondence between addresses and contents).

Neural nets are not programmed in the familiar algorithmic sense. Rather than executing a sequence of instructions, as in a conventional Von Neumann computer, they 'learn' by adjusting their weights in response to various training runs. In this manner, appropriate connection patterns are built up for the task at hand. Following this (time consuming) initial training phase, the net is capable of (quickly) recognizing or responding to inputs it has not previously met. In other words, the performance of the network can be improved dynamically. The 'programmer' (trainer/supervisor) does not need to understand system characterisitcs in any formal or mathematical sense.

ANNs are inherently robust and noise (and fault) tolerant; if some neurons 'die' (in other words, if the memory 'forgets'), the overall network function is maintained (much in the manner of localized damage in the human brain).

2. Neural Net Types

ANNs can be classified in terms of the type of constituent PE (or node characteristics - i.e. binary or continuous/analog input), the connectivity pattern (net topology), the neuron activation rule, the learning (training) rule, whether fixed (predetermined) or variable (adaptive) weights are used, and whether the network is capable of supervised or unsupervised learning (variable weight neural nets are capable of learning, in either a supervised or an unsupervised sense).

In supervised nets, the weights are adjusted during an initial training period, using sample input and desired output training pairs. Widrow's [3] Adaline and Rumelhart's [4] multi-layer feedforward (backpropagation) nets are examples of such associative nets. The Adaline is shown in Figure 2.

Perceptrons (Rosenblatt [5]) fall into the supervised, continuous-valued input category (both single- and multi-layer). Single-layer perceptrons are capable of being trained to recognize simple patterns, the weights being either fixed or adaptive. In the latter case, Rosenblatt's convergence procedure can be used for weight adjustment. The

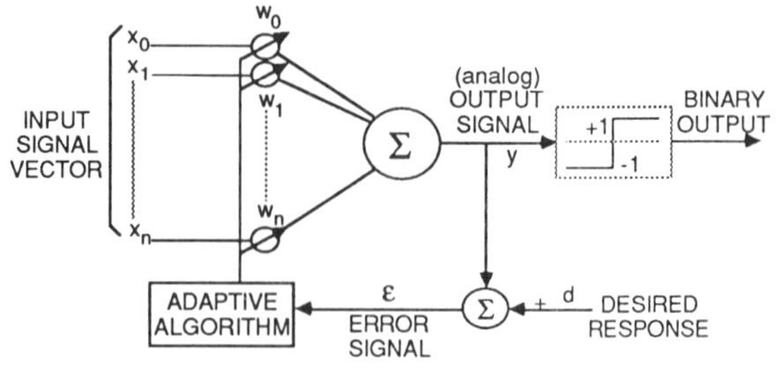

Figure 2

capabilites of multi-layer perceptrons stem from their use of non-linear (sigmoid) neuron models. A 3-layer feedforward net is shown in Figure 3.

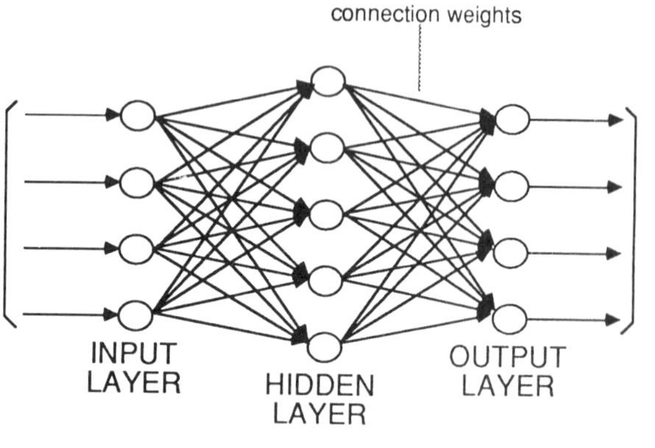

Figure 3

Hopfield [6] and Hamming nets are examples of supervised, binary input nets, and generally use fixed weights. They can be used as associative memories or as pattern recognition classifiers. The Hamming net is a 2-layer feedforward net, useful in maximum-likelihood classification of binary inputs corrupted by noise - Lippmann [7]. The Hopfield net is shown in Figure 4.

Boltzmann machines are essentially adaptive Hopfield nets of analog nodes, with hidden units, and in which a Monte Carlo method is used to reach a *global* rather than a local minimum - Hinton & Sejnowski [8]. Random configuration changes are made at various intervals in order to 'escape' from local minima and/or metastable configurations.

In unsupervised, or self-organising systems, an inbuilt algorithm is used to adjust weights, but there is no 'training' involved. Grossberg's Adaptive Resonance Theory or ART [9] is

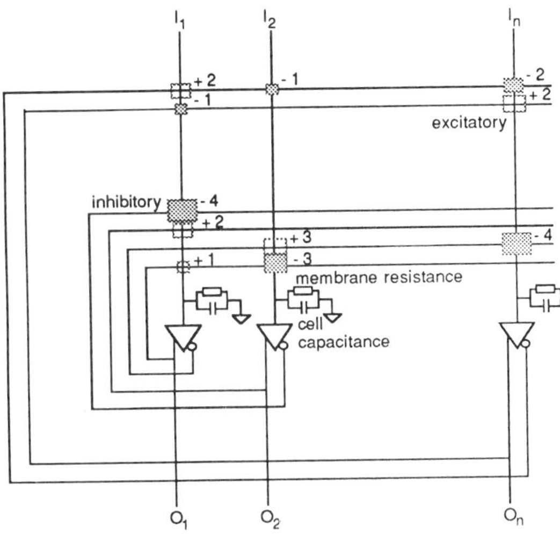

Figure 4

an example of a binary input, unsupervised net. ART can be thought of as a (simple) 'follow-the-leader' clustering algorithm.

Kohonen's [10] self-organizing feature map is an example of an unsupervised, continuous-valued input network. It is used either as a vector quantizer or to form clusters, by adjusting its weights from common input nodes to n-output nodes, arranged in a 2D-grid, as shown in Figure 5.

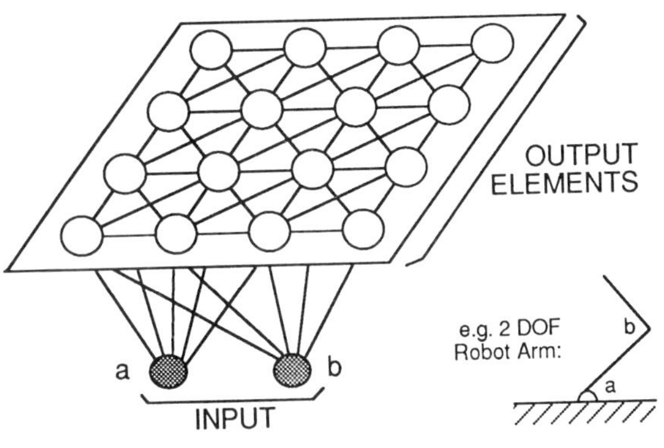

Figure 5

A neuron's firing rate is a function not only of the input signal frequency and coupling strengths, but also on the amount of feedback coupling. Moreover, the adaptive learning process involves both Hebbian [11] learning as well as forgetting (just as with human memory). Typical applications of such self-organizing feature maps include pattern and voice recognition.

Bidirectional Associative Memories or BAMs use both forward and backward search in order to recall associated (bipolar) vector pairs from an input pair - Kosko [12]. Thus, they are sometimes referred to as 'hetero-associative' content addressable memories (CAMs).

It can take a considerable amount of time to train a neural net, however once trained, they can converge to a collective decision within a few time constants. The *full* potential of ANNs may however only be realised using the high speed processing capability of VLSI (WSI perhaps?), or optical computers (Abu-Mostafa & Psaltis [13]).

3. Software Simulators

Researchers tend to write their own neural network simulators from first principles, thereby regularly 're-inventing the wheel'. The type of neural net most often simulated is the simple, feedforward multi-layer perceptron (MLP). Popular magazines such as Dr. Dobb's Journal and AI Expert have even published simple neural net simulator programs. King's [14] program is written in C, and models a simple 3-layer feedforward net, in which the number of neurons within each layer can be set at run time. Simple linear networks (voting), linear threshold nets (XOR) and optical character recognition can be demonstrated using this program. Reece's [15] simulation for the IBM PC is written in Basic. It models a simple neuron (perceptron), and is used for classifiying images drawn on the PC screen into one of two different categories.

The Rochester Connectionist Simulator - Goddard, Lynne & Mintz, [16] is written in C, and is designed to run under Unix on Sun Workstations. It is based on the Rumelhart backpropagation algorithm. It is available at nominal cost to educational and research institutions, and comes with a comprehensive user manual.

Mirrors/II is a connectionist simulator developed at the University of Maryland. It is written in Franz Lisp and runs under Unix on VAX, MicroVAX and Sun-3 workstations. Several different learning paradigms are supported via library calls, such as spreading activation, Hebbian learning, competitive learning and backpropagation. Support is also provided for both synchronous and asynchronous control strategies (for determining which nodes should have their weights updated during any particular iteration).

Some simulators which began life in the research laboratories have been subsequently enhanced and released commercially, bundled together with instructional texts. Typical of these is Explorations in Parallel Distributed Processing or EPDP for the IBM PC (McClelland & Rumelhart [17]), and the Network Demonstration software for the Macintosh - Durbin, Miall & Mitchison, [18]. Figure 6 shows a pole-balancing example from the latter.

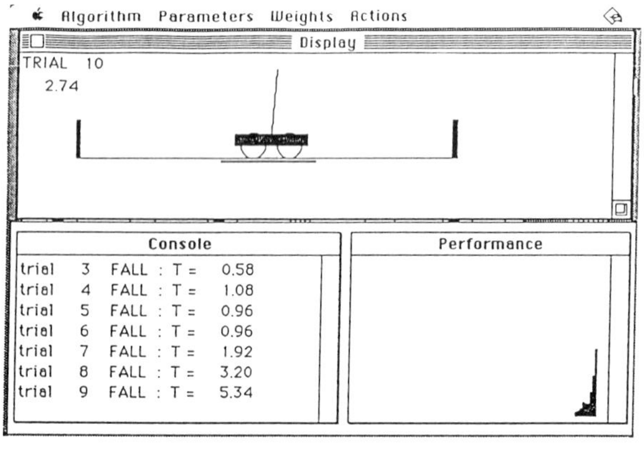

Figure 6

Commercially available simulators include BrainMaker, the Brain Simulator, NeuroShell, Owl and RABAM for the IBM PC, ExploreNet, Netwurkz and NeuralWorks for the IBM PC and Sun Workstations, and Cognitron, MacBrain and Network Demonstration for the Macintosh.

4. Plug-in Boards, Workstations & Neural Computers

The Neural Accelerator (VME) Board (NAB) for Sun workstations was developed by the Australian Defence Science & Technology Organization, Salisbury, SA. It can perform 30 million (pipelined) sums-of-products per second, and is intended to be used as a high-speed classifier. NAB is currently implemented as a systolic array of ASIC processors. Both data and microcode can flow through the array, which can be configured as either SIMD (with shared microcode), or MIMD (with independent microcode). Each of the 64 custom ASICs contain 16 8-bit Neural Accelerator Processors (NAPs). NAB is based on the Hopfield Net paradigm.

The Delta II Floating Point Processor from Science Applications International Corp. (SAIC), San Diego, CA runs at 22 MFLOPS on an IBM PC/AT board. It has a multi-staged Harvard architecture, and supports both integer and floating point arithmetic. Up to 3.1 million Processing Elements (PEs) and weights can be supported. 11 million connections per second can be sustained, but this falls to 2.7 million when backpropagation is included in learning. SAIC also produce Sigma Neurocomputer workstations, based on i802(3)86/87 PC/AT-compatible computers.

Hecht-Nielsen Neurcomputers (HNC) of San Diego, CA offer the Anza VME plus neurocomputing coprocessor for the Sun-3 & Sun-4 workstations.

Micro Devices offers a PC/XT card which contains a neural chip called the Fuzzy Set Comparator neural computer (fuzzy sets cater for innacurate and noisy data, and thus are more appropriate for use with neural networks.

Cognitive Software's Neurocomputer is a Macintosh-II based development system, which uses a plug-in T800 Transputer-based array processor to produce up to 120 MIPS performance.

Apart from such plug-in neural processor boards, complete neural network computers are also under development. For example, the Martin Marietta Corporation is currently developing such a machine for the US Air Force. Another neural computer, the NEC Neuro-07, is capable of performing character recognition tasks, without the need for a scanner. Mitsubishi Electric Corp., meanwhile, is reported to have developed an *Optical* Neural Computer.

5. VLSI Chips

Apart from the NAP chip mentioned in Section 4, other VLSI chips developed to date include the CMOS NNet model developed at AT&T (Graf & deVegvar, [19]; Jackel et.al., [20]), and Carver Mead's [21] SeeHear and Silicon Retina systems (Seehear is used by blind people to form representations of their environment).

A startup company has recently been formed by ex-Intel engineer Carlos Tapang to produce commercially viable NNet chips. Intel themselves have also recently developed a neural net chip.

Dendros-I is a neural net chip that produces the dot product of inputs and connection weights of 22 synapses. An evaluation board is available from Syntonics Systems Inc. of Portland, OR, comprising eight such chips and which can be used as the basis for developing hardware-based neural nets.

6. Laboratory Support for Teaching Neural Networks

One's choice in neural net software/hardware will obviously be constrained by budgetry considerations. This is especially true for University educators attempting to provide laboratory support for the teaching of neural networks. Commercially available systems range from $100 simulators to $50,000+ development systems. A potential purchaser of such systems must ensure that the relevant neural net paradigm of interest is supported; many of the simpler neural net simulators support multi-layer feedforward nets only. Another important consideration is that the simulator actually works! (or to put it another way: how good is the simulator?) - Fulcher [22]. Moreover, does it run under all permutations of host hardware and operating system? Furthermore, can the routines as supplied be separately compiled and loaded into different compilers, indeed into different languages (such as Fortran, C and Ada, say)? Oftentimes it is also important that the software actually does what it purports, and in the manner claimed; commercial vendors of necessity need to maintain some edge over their competitors, after all (the 'hidden layer/factor', as it were?).

If, for financial reasons, commercial simulators and/or plug-in boards are beyond one's reach, one can always 'reinvent the wheel' and write one's own neural net simulator. At least such a simulator will be tailor-made to the application at hand, providing one has access to programmer support (or alternatively is competent oneself in this arena). A cost/benefit analysis should be undertaken in order to determine whether the man-hours (days, weeks, or months?) can be justified, when an off-the-shelf product could quite adequately perform the same task.

7. Conclusion

In summation, as with many other spheres in life, with neural networks, it is largely a question of 'horses for courses'. The old adage in the commercial world of 'let the buyer beware' also applies here. In other words, a thorough evaluation must be made of both demonstration programs and software proper, preferably on data from the application of interest if at all possible. Educators desiring to provide laboratory support fot teaching neural networks will need to reach some form of compromise between (expensive) hardware and (cheaper, but often limited) software; again, how good is the simulator? Some decision will also need to be reached as to whether to develop simulation software in-house, or whether to purchase an off-the-shelf commercial product. Such educators will also be constrained by the need to provide *multiple* laboratory sets of such equipment. Ultimately, it becomes a financial consideration.

Acknowledgements:

The author would like to acknowledge the financial support of both the Basser Department of Computer Science at the University of Sydney, and the Automation and Engineering Applications Centre (AEAC) within the University of Wollongong Technology Centre.

References:

[1] Barto, A.G., Keynote Address, Foundations of Connectionist Modelling Workshop, University of New South Wales, 1-4 July, 1989

[2] McCullogh, W.S. & Pitts, W., Bulletin Mathematical Biophysics (1943) 5

[3] Widrow, B. & Hoff, M.E., IRE WESCON Convention Record (1960)

[4] Rumelhart, D.E. Hinton, G.E. & Williams, R.J., in: Rumelhart, D.E. & McClelland, J.L. (eds.), Parallel Distributed Processing: Explorations in the Microstructure of Cognition - Vol.1 Foundations (MIT Press, Cambridge MA 1986)

[5] Rosenblatt, F., Principles of Neurodynamics (Spartan, New York, 1959)

[6] Hopfield, J.J., Proc. National Academy Sciences (1982) 79

[7] Lippmann, R.P., IEEE ASSP Magazine (1987) April

[8] Hinton, G.E. & Sejnowski, T.J., in: Rumelhart, D.E. & McClelland, J.L. (eds.) Parallel Distributed Processing: Explorations in the Microstructure of Cognition - Vol.1 Foundations (MIT Press, Cambridge MA, 1986)

[9] Carpenter, G.A. & Grossberg, S., in: Davis, J. Newbury, P. & Weiman, E. (eds.), Brain Structure, Learning and Memory (AAAS Symposium Series, 1986)

[10] Kohonen, T., (1988) Self-Organization and Associative Memory (2nd ed.) (Springer-Verlag, Berlin, 1988)

[11] Hebb, D.O., The Organisation of Behaviour (Wiley, New York, 1949)

[12] Kosko, B., IEEE Trans. Systems Man & Cybernetics (1988) 18

[13] Abu-Mostafa, Y.S. & Psaltis, D., Scientific American (1987) 256

[14] King, T., Dr. Dobb's J. (1989) 14

[15] Reece, P., AI Expert (1987) January

[16] Goddard, N.H. Lynne, K.J. & Mintz, T., University of Rochester, Dept. Computer Science Technical Report (1988)

[17] McClelland, J.L. & Rumelhart, D.E., Explorations in Parallel Distributed Processing: A Handbook of Models, Programs, and Exercises (MIT Press, Cambridge MA, 1988)

[18] Durbin, R. Miall, C. & Mitchison, G. (eds.), The Computing Neuron (Addison-Wesley, Wokingham UK, 1989)

[19] Graf, H.P. & deVegvar, P., in: Losleben, P. (ed.) Proc. Stanford Conf. Advanced Research in VLSI (1987)

[20] Jackel, L.D. Denker, J.S. Graf, H.P. & Howard, R.E., in: Jabri, M.A. (ed.) Neural Networks - Their Implementation in VLSI, University of Sydney, Dept. Electrical Engineering Workshop, (1988) November

[21] Mead. C.A., Analog VLSI and Neural Systems (Addison-Wesley, Reading MA, 1989)

[22] Fulcher, J.A., Intl. J. Applied Engineering Education (1989) 5

Computers in Education
A. McDougall and C. Dowling (Editors)
Elsevier Science Publishers B.V. (North-Holland)

DESIGN AND IMPLEMENTATION OF INTELLIGENT COMPUTER ASSISTED CHINESE INSTRUCTION SYSTEM

He Ke Kang, Li Xiu Lan, Xie Yong Gui

Beijing Normal University *

According to the particularity analysis for computer assisted Chinese instruction, the design and implementation for an Intelligent Computer Assisted Chinese Instruction (ICACI) system are presented. The domain knowledge representation, teaching knowledge representation, student model and teaching decision are discussed. A new representation method adapting to the Chinese domain knowledge,i. e. ," network–relation structure" representation is presented. In order to make an integrative evaluation of students' performance and optimal teaching decisions, we constructed a" fuzzy logic model" on the basis of fuzzy set theory. For the requirement of teaching Chinese spelling we developed a Chinese speech synthesizer, the articulation of the voice produced being adequate.

1. INTRODUCTION

The traditional computer assisted instruction (CAI) is from programmed instruction. The early forms of CAI were strongly influenced by Skinnerian behaviorism [1]. Later on, multi–branch CAI was developed; with it you can select different learning tracks according to different conditions. A characteristic of the traditional CAI is that its running process is completely decided by algorithm determined in advance and by the input message. It cannot be adjusted on the basis of the actual needs of different students; neither can it be dynamically adjusted on the basis of the different stages in the teaching process. So it cannot realize individualized tutoring.

The development and application of artificial intelligence (AI) techniques offered the possibility of overcoming the aforesaid limitations of traditional CAI [2]. Since 1970 intelligent computer assisted instruction (ICAI) systems, a highly individualized tutoring systems, have been developed by computer education researchers in order to apply AI techniques (for example,knowledge representation, building knowledge bases, inference engines and machine learning, etc.) to CAI, and explore the function of AI techniques in the process of learning and teaching. ICAI systems can greatly improve the learning and teaching environment in which the student can freely develop his own interests and markedly raise his learning efficiency. ICAI systems can adapt themselves to each student's individuality and demands, and make the teaching contents and methods different for different students.

In consideration of the foregoing advantages of ICAI and the foreigners' requirement of learning Chinese language, from 1987 to 1989, we developed an intelligent computer assisted Chinese instruction (ICACI) system for teaching foreigners Chinese.

Computer assisted Chinese instruction is considerably different from other subjects' CAI in the respects of teaching purpose and courseware type. For example, the teaching purpose of physical or chemical subjects with CAI is to make the microscopical and transient processes showing intuitively and imaginally,i. e. , to make some knowledge which is hard to be described with words and sentences imaginal and understandable. The courseware types in the CAI systems on these subjects are mostly simulation and demonstration. In this case, we must make the graphic functions in computer exactly and quickly display the variance caused by each parameter, so it will be optimal to use dynamical graphs. While the teaching purpose of computer assisted Chinese instruction emphasizes students' ability training (e. g. , colloquial expression ability training and written expression ability training). The courseware in the ICACI system correspondingly emphasizes drill and practice so as to create language environment in a planned way and lead students on to do more and realistic language drills. That makes the computer assisted Chinese instruction system possesses two distinct properties:

a. The Chinese articulate device is an indispensable component in the computer assisted Chinese instruction system to conduct the teaching and practising Chinese phonetics. For this purpose,we developed a speech synthesizer and a speech library with which we can generate satisfactory Chinese speech.

b. It is necessary to use more man–machine interactions. Through the interactions the ICACI system will know the students' knowledge level and learning ability, and conduct individualized tutoring. This individualized tutoring can freely select different levels of learning contents and different teaching methods. In the process of computer assisted Chinese teaching, the graphic, acoustic and literal effects are combined to increase the flexibility of the teaching process, make the learning process interesting and make the learner use his brain, eyes, ears and hands simultaneously so as to intensify his memory and achieve the optimal learning and teaching effects, On the basis of the foregoing analysis about computer assisted Chinese instruction we designed and implemented the ICACI system.

2. ARCHITECTURE AND TEACHING FLOWCHART

Our intelligent computer assisted Chinese instruction (ICACI) system is implemented with IBM–PC / AT. The block diagram of the system

* He Ke Kang et alii are with the Institute of Modern Educational Technology, Beijing Normal University, Beijing 100875, PRC. This work was supported by national "7–5" research program under contract 67–6–12.

architecture is shown in Fig. 1. It follows from the diagram that the system consists of four principal modules: a knowledge base module, a student model module, a teaching decision module, a Chinese speech synthesizer and a Chinese speech library. The knowledge base comprises two parts: the domain knowledge base (in which the domain knowledge of the subject to be taught is kept) and teaching knowledge base (in which the knowledge about how to teach is kept). Since the teaching knowledge representation in the ICACI system is to employ production rules, the teaching knowledge base is also called "rules base".

The student model module is composed of the base of students' cases and the unit for generating the student model.

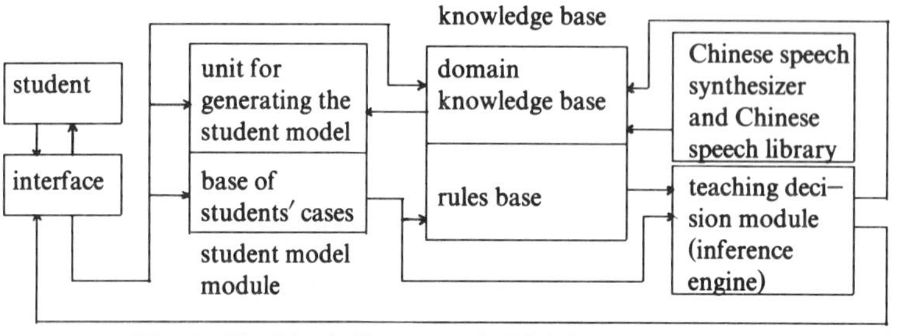

Fig. 1. The block diagram of ICACI system architecture

The teaching process in the ICACI system can be described as follows:

(1). Once a student enters the ICACI system, the computer will first inquire the preceding learning cases of the student from the base of students' cases to determine what teaching content should be selected. The computer is also able to select the teaching content directly from the domain knowledge base without inquiry of the student about learning cases (e. g. , for the student entering the ICACI system the first time).

(2). In the whole teaching process, the unit for generating the student model records the student's learning content, the way the student studies. The unit is also able to test the student's ability and records the type of questions, the marks in the test, and then stores these records into the base of students' cases. Later on, these records will be one of the main bases for making teaching decisions.

(3). According to the data from the base of students' cases, the ICACI system refers to the rules in the rules

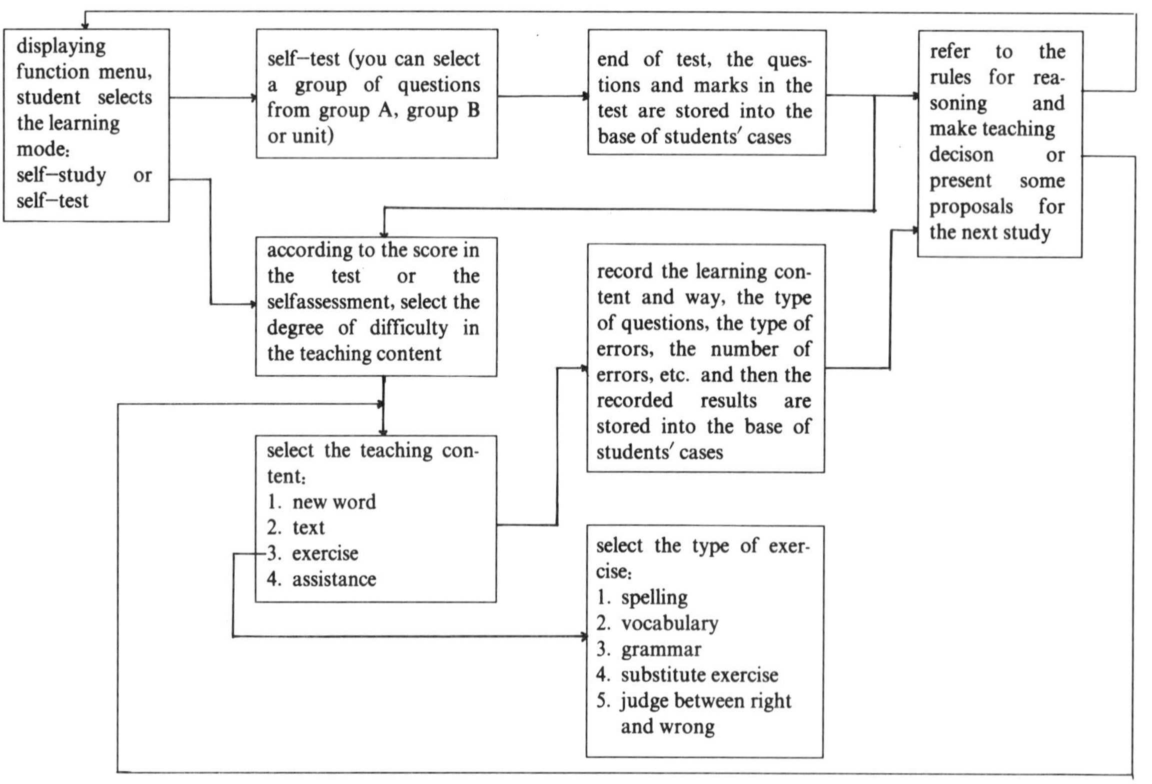

Fig. 2. The flowchart of teaching process in ICACI.

base and does forward reasoning and backward reasoning, then works out the teaching decision on the basis of the reasoning results, and returns the decision to the student in an advisory way.

(4). According to the teaching decision made just now, the ICACI system activates the domain knowledge base and refers the contents of the base to individualized tutoring in a suitable way, or provids some proposals about further learning for the student.

(5). The student who is studying with the ICACI system can either study by himself or test by himself. In the mode of self–study, the student is also able to do exercises and check up his learning cases. The process of self–study or self–test and the results of study or test will be recorded by the unit for generating student model and kept in the base of students′ cases.

The flowchart of the teaching process in the ICACI system is shown in Fig. 2.

The following sections will discuss the idea and methods of our design for four principal modules in the ICACI system.

3. KNOWLEDGE BASE

As mentioned above, the content of the knowledge base is supposed to comprise two parts: domain knowledge and teaching knowledge. The domain knowledge means the teaching content i. e., teaching materials, exercises, questions for test, and the materials for remedial instruction and so on. The teaching knowledge means the teaching idea, ways, and the organization form for teaching materials. Since the content and functions of the two kinds of knowledge are quite different, we use the different methods to represent them.

a. Domain knowledge representation

Considering the particularity of Chinese teaching, we use a method of ″ network–relation structure″ to represent the domain knowledge of Chinese. The domain knowledge in Chinese teaching generally comprises four kinds of knowledge i. e., raw data,questions,solutions and remedial instruction knowledge. The action among the network is able to be represented by substances and attributes of the relation among the network. An example of network–relation structure containing the knowledge datail is shown in Fig. 4.

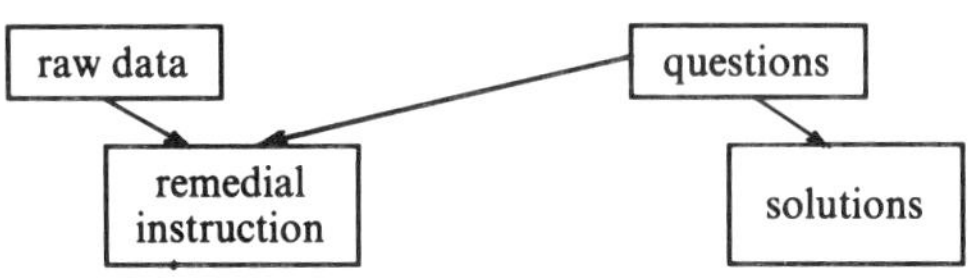

Fig. 3. network–relation structure of knowledge

After the knowledge detail was represented by the relation among the network, there will be various links among the knowledge, and the function relations will exist between the attributes.

The nodes in the knowledge network link together through the characteristic codes of common attributes. We may consider a text, a new word, an exercise, or a paragraph of remedial instruction knowledge as a substance. Then the keywords are formed from multiple attributes in the interior of the substance. We can handily refer to the knowledge in the network through the

raw data knowledge

content	type	character-istic code	the mode of teaching
lesson 1 Welcome Jane: Excuse me, could you please tell me if this is the reception room?	text	1	display Chinese text and ask if any help is needed. refer to the remedial instruction knowledge when student needs help.
welcome		1	display the Chinese word and give its Chinese pronunciation
Could you please tell me		1	display and give the Chinese pronunciation

remedial instruction knowledge

content	type	character-istic code	the mode of teaching
1. Chinese teacher is welcoming foreign students 2. The scene is laid in an airport	text	1	display
中(zhōng) 钟(zhōng) 国(gúo) 郭(gūo)	text	1	display and give the Chinese pronunciation
四(sì) 十(shí) 一(yī) 七(qī)	spel-ling	1	display and give the Chinese pronunciation

questions knowledge

content	type	character-istic code	the mode of teaching
Is you name (Jone)? Are you from (U. S. A)?	substi-tute exercise	1	ask a student and give a reference answer
1 2 3 4 5 yī èr sān sī wǔ 6 7 8 9 10 lìu qī bā jǐu shí	spelling	1	display the word and give its pronunciation
粉红凤凰花凤凰	spelling	1	display and give the Chinese pronunciation
The office building lies to the ( ) of the library	vocabul-ary	2	display and judge right or wrong

Solutions knowledge

content	type	character-istic code	the mode of teaching
name, country Is your name (John)? Are you from (England)?	substitute exercise	1	give a reference answer
left, north	vocabulary	1	display

Fig. 4 An example of network–relation structure containing the knowledge detail

match between the keywords, we can also handily access the other related knowledge by using the attribute values of the characteristic codes.

b. Teaching knowledge representation

As mentioned above, the teaching knowledge representation in the ICACI system is to employ production rules, so the teaching knowledge base is also called "rules base". Some rules in the base are shown in table 1.

The certainty factor (cf)in table 1 represents the degree of the trueness of the conclusion when some hypotheses exist. The value of certainty factor (cf) is given by the experience of educationalists. The range of value of the cf is within the closed interval [−1,1]. cf>0 means the conclusion is true when some hypotheses exist; cf=0 means the conclusion has nothing to do with the existence of hypotheses; and cf=−1 means the conclusion is false when some hypotheses exist. The greater the value of certainty factor, the higher the degree of the trueness of the conclusion.

Table 1

rule number	IF	THEN	Certainty fector(cf)	proposal number
1	70<FX<85	ND=2	o. 4	2
2	DJ=1 OR DJ=2	ND=3	0. 4	1
3	DJ=4 OR DJ=5	ND=1	0. 3	3
4	FS=85	ND=1	0. 8	3
5	FS=95	ND=1	0. 95	3
6	right rate in spelling <80%	Text number= 1,5,7,8,10	0. 9	4
7	total right rate >=90%	ND=ND−1 OR ND=1	0. 9	5
...	...	...	...	...

In table 1, DJ represents the class of knowledge level, ND represents the degree of difficulty of the teaching content, FS represents the mark.

4. STUDENT MODEL

The main function of the student model is to record the learnirig cases of students and assess the learning ability of students, and then supplies the results of assessment for the inference engine as a reasoning basis [2] [3]. When a student once enters the ICACI system, the student model begins to record his learning cases. The learning cases of a student comprise the way he studies, the degree of difficulty of the teaching content, the marks (in self−test), the type of questions, the number of questions, the type of errors and the number of errors. When a student once exits from the system, the student's learning cases just recorded will be stored into the base of students' cases. The data in the base of students' cases refelects not only the current knowledge level of the student but also the student's ability in learning. Comparing the student's learning cases with the behavior proposed in the teaching design, the ICACI system will adjust or modify the teaching strategy, content and method in due time.

How can a computer evaluate a student's performance as a tutor? At the initial stage of ICACI, the investigation method or test method is adopted. The investigation method gives a rough evaluation of the student's performance through the student−computer interaction. The test method requires at first that the student should answer a group of complex questions, and then gives a rough evalution of the student's performance according to the marks of the answers. On the basis of the rough evaluation a suggestion for the student to select an appropriate teaching content can be made.

Using the data in the base of students' cases,the ICACI system will give further evaluatuion for a student's performance. In order to accurately evaluate a student's performance, we may use a "fuzzy logic model".

It is a fuzzy concept when we say a student's performance in learning is better. If we evaluate a student's performance according to mark, the mark from 85 to 100 belongs to Class A (excellent). In this case,95 is excellent, 85 is also excellent; both belong to Class A. We cannot see any difference between 95 and 85. If we adopt the concept of fuzzy set [4] and select a value within the closed interval [0,1] to represent the degree of excellence in learning, it would be much more explicit. For example, when we suppose that the domain of discourse U is a set of marks, "excellent in learning" is a fuzzy subset in the domain of discourse U and is denoted by A,its membership function is denoted by $U_A(u)$. If $U_A(95)=0.9$ and $U_A(85)=0.7$ are given, we can see that the degrees belonging to the fuzzy subset A for the mark 95 and 85 are different. Now, we suppose that the domain of discourse U is a set of different kinds of knowledge, "excellent in learning" is a fuzzy subset in the U and is still denoted by A, then as an example, the evaluation of the student's performance can be given by

$$A=\frac{0.8}{spelling}+\frac{0.7}{vocabulary}+\frac{0.9}{grammar}+\frac{0.88}{sentence}+\frac{0.95}{text} \tag{1}$$

From (1), we can easily estimate a student's degrees of mastering the different kinds of knowledge. In this case, the evaluation of the student's performance is explicit and quantitative.

When we evaluate a student's performance, we should consider not only the student's marks but also his learning ability so as to give a more overall evaluation.

Let the domain of discourse U= {spelling, vocabulary, grammar sentence, text}, and let the domain of discourse V= {test1, test2, learning ability}. U is associated with the state of student's knowledge and V with the factors affecting the evaluation.

We may suppose that the evaluation by single factor (e. g. , by the factor i) is Ri=(ri1, ri2, ri3, ri4, ri5). Here rik represents the role arising from the evaluation by single factor i and represents the influence upon the kth term in U; while rik is the degree of membership in the fuzzy subset A.

Thus the evaluation matrix relating to three factors can be written as follows:

$$R = \begin{bmatrix} r11 & r12 & r13 & r14 & r15 \\ r21 & r22 & r23 & r24 & r25 \\ r31 & r32 & r33 & r34 & r35 \end{bmatrix} \quad (2).$$

It's a fuzzy matrix. Now we suppose that the evaluation by the first factor (i. e. ,test1) is R1=(0. 8, 0. 7, 0. 6, 0. 9, 0); the evaluation by the second factor (i. e. ,test2) is R2=(0. 9, 0. 9, 0. 8, 0. 9, 0. 4); and the evaluation by the third factor (i. e. ,learning ability) is R3=(0. 9, 0. 85,0. 8, 0. 9, 0. 4), then we obtain the following evaluation matrix

$$R = \begin{bmatrix} R1 \\ R2 \\ R3 \end{bmatrix} = \begin{bmatrix} 0.8 & 0.7 & 0.6 & 0.9 & 0.0 \\ 0.9 & 0.9 & 0.8 & 0.9 & 0.4 \\ 0.9 & 0.85 & 0.8 & 0.9 & 0.4 \end{bmatrix} \quad (3).$$

For evaluating the student's performance, it is necessary to consider the magnitude of function of different factors, which forms a fuzzy subset F in the factor domain V, and F=(f1, f2, . . . , fn).

For the case that there are only three factors, we can suppose F= (0. 3, 0. 5, 0. 2), adopting the weighted–average algorithm and we shall obtain

$$B = F * R = (0.3, 0.5, 0.2) \begin{bmatrix} 0.8 & 0.7 & 0.6 & 0.9 & 0.0 \\ 0.9 & 0.9 & 0.8 & 0.9 & 0.4 \\ 0.9 & 0.85 & 0.8 & 0.9 & 0.4 \end{bmatrix}$$

$$= (0.87, 0.83, 0.74, 0.90, 0.28) \quad (4).$$

The computing result in (4) is an integrative evaluation of a student's performance, considering the two tests and his learning ability. Obviously,this evaluation can reflect more exactly the student's level of mastering the different kinds of knowledge. For example, from the fifth term in (4), we can see that the student's understanding of texts is bad. According to (4),the ICACI system will present some proposals to the student for further study (e. g. , do more reading of the texts and remedial materials to enhance comprehension).

5. TEACHING DECISION MODULE (INFERENCE ENGINE)

As an intelligent tutor, the ICACI system not only gives the appropriate evaluation of the student's performance, but also make the individualized teaching decision on the basis of the student's cases and the results of inference [5].

The content of teaching decision consists of two parts: to select the right teaching method and the appropriate degree of dfficulty of teaching content. The teaching method generally comprises discourse and explanation, question, heuristic, drill and practice, and demonstration, ⋯. In order to represent the degree of difficulty of teaching content, we grade the teaching materials into several groups.

Through the integrative evaluation of the student's performance the computer is able to know the learning ability and knowledge level of the current student. Consequently, the teaching decision made by the computer can shoot the arrow at the target. That is the main reason why we can realize the individualized teaching with the ICACI system.

The ICACI system employs a mixed method of data–driven and plausible reasoning to make an inference. At the beginning of the reasoning, the data in the base of students' cases is compared with the facts after IF of each rule in the rules base,if the data matches the facts after IF of a rule, the conclusion after THEN of the same rule would be fetched, and this rule would be recorded. Thus, with the different data we can record and select some different rules from the rules base. Then according to the certainty factor contained in each rule, a logical combination for the different conditions will be made to find out a more applicable rule from the selected rules. For example, we may suppose that a student's case contains three items in the base of students' cases: FS=73, QN=20, EN=2 (Where FS represents the mark; QN the number of questions; EN the number of errors). Since FS=73 matches the fact after IF of rule 1

"IF 70<FS<85 THEN ND=2"

(where ND represents the degree of difficulty of teaching content), the conclusion after THEN ND=2 will be recorded. Then QN=20 and EN=2 will match the fact after IF of rule 7

"IF total right rate>=90% THEN ND=ND–1 OR ND=1"

since EN / QN=2 / 20=10%. So the conclusion after THEN ND=ND–1 OR ND=1 will be selected. and the ICACI system will suggest that the student should select the teaching content with ND=1 for his next study. In the meanwhile, if the student assesses by himself the knowledge level at DJ=2, then according to the rule 2

"IF DJ=1 OR DJ=2 THEN ND=3"

the conclusion ND=3 will be selected. In this case, how can we determine which conclusion is more believable, ND=1 or ND=3? In order to answer this question we should just inquire the certainty factor of related rules and find out the conclusion of the rule having a bigger certainty factor. It follows from the table 1 that the certainty factor of rule 2 is o. 4 and that of rule 7 is 0. 9. It means the conclusion in rule 7 is more believable. So in this case the suggestion made by ICACI system is still to select the learning content with ND=1 for the next study.

6. CHINESE SPEECH SYSTHESIS AND SPEECH LIBRARY

We use speech synthesis technology in our ICACI systam to produce speech sound. Original speech is an analog signal. In its digitized process the sampling rate must be more than 8KHz according to the sampling theorem of signal processing. If we use 8 bits of binary code (one byte) to represent each sample, the bit rate is 64K bits / second (b / s). So, it must occupy a large memory space to store and playback the speech signal. Speech synthesis technology is mainly compressing encoding for original speech signal. There are two kinds of method for speech compressing encoding: Waeform encoding and parameter encoding. Waveform encoding uses the correlativity of neighbour samples, such as Adaptive Delta Modulation (ADM) and Adaptive Differential Pulse Code Modulation (ADPCM). The rate of compression with waveform encoding is not good (compress the original speech data to 1 / 2 – 1 / 8 of one), but the synthetic speech quality is better. It is necessary for the parameter encoding to do short time analysis for original speech signal. The relatively stable characteristic parameters during 20ms or so, such as Linear Predictive Coefficients (LPC) or formant parameters are extracted. The rate of compression with parameter encoding is much better (1 / 8 – 1 / 40 of original speech data), but the synthetic speech quality is a little worse.

To fit in with different applications,we sequentially developed two types of Chinese speech synthesizer. The first one adopts the Linear Predictive Coding (LPC) technique. Its bit rate is 1. 6K b / s (200 bytes / sec). So the memory capacity needed for speech data is very small. In LPC analysing and encoding, we chose proper algorithms and adopted filtering, interpolating and smoothing technique. Because the shortcomings inhere in LPC technique, there are often some errors during analysing LPC parameter. Especially, the errors of short time pitch detecting seriously influence the synthetic speech quality, Therefore,we designed a powerful Parameter Editor Software. It can correct evident errors of the parameter by using phonetics knowledge. All of these make a great improvement for the synthetic speech quality, and the articulation of speech is satisfied by most users. The second Chinese speech synthesizer adopts Adaptive Delta Modulation (ADM) technique. Its bit rate is 12K b / s (1500 bytes / sec). The synthetic speech is more natural than the former one. Meanwhile, in the latter synthesizer we added a new function that makes it possible for the users to input speech and establish speech library by themselves. This has greatly improved the flexibility of application.

In both of the speech synthesizers, we established a Chinese speech library using a word instead of a single Chinese syllable as a working unit. If a syllable is used as a unit to establish speech library, we have to consider lots of connecting rules for words and sentences formation in order to produce natural speech sound. However, the research of a Chinese text to speech system is now still at its beginning stage, we connot use it for practical application. On the other hand, Chinese has its own features(e. g. , there are evident pauses between words). So, if a word is used as a unit in the speech library and when words are connected to form sentences, the result would be much better than when a syllable is used as a unit. In this way the speech is clearer and more natural. Although established speech library is a limited–word library which is suitable for certain situation, it can also be used for other practical applications.

7. SUMMARY

The main problems in building a ICAI system are as follows:

a. how to construct a perfect student model,
b. how to make the optimal teaching decision,
c. how to represent the domain knowledge,
d. how to represent the teaching knowledge.

Problem a and b are especially the keys to building an ICAI system. In building our Intelligent Computer Assisted Chinese Instruction system we explored the above problems and acquired some experience. The actual application of ICACI system shows that this system is welcome by students. The performance of the computer tutor is close to that of a human tutor in some respects (e. g. , in the individualized teaching and intelligent tutoring); and the performance of the computer tutor is better than that of a human tutor in some other respects (e. g. the computer tutor is more patient and flexible) we believe that a deepgoing research on ICAI will not only open a wide application area for computer assisted instruction,but also greatly promote further development of the theory and technology on artificial intelligence.

References

1. Ok–choon Park and Robert J. Seidel, Conventional CBI Versus Intelligent CAI: Suggestions for the Development of Future Systems. Educational Technology, May 1987, 15–20.
2. Halyna Hajovy and Dean L. Christensen, Intelligent Computer Assisted Instruction: The Next Generation. Educational Technology, May 1987, 9–14.
3. John self, Artificial Intelligence and Human Learning. Chapman and Hall Ltd. , 1988.
4. L. A. Zadeh, Fuzzy sets. Information and Control, August 1965, 338–353.
5. Etienue Wenger, Artificial Intelligence and Tutoring System. Morgan Kaufmann publishers, Inc. Los Altos, 1987.

Computers in Education
A. McDougall and C. Dowling (Editors)
Elsevier Science Publishers B.V. (North-Holland)

THE COMPUTERS IN TEACHING INITIATIVE CENTRE FOR MODERN LANGUAGES, UNIVERSITY OF HULL

Frederick William LANGLEY

Computers in Teaching Initiative Centre for Modern Languages, University of Hull, Cottingham Road, Hull, HU6 7RX, England

The Computers in Teaching Initiative (CTI) was established in 1983 to encourage the use of computers in teaching in higher education in the UK. More recently the CTI has established specialist Subject Centres to research in computer-assisted teaching in various subject areas. The Centre for Modern Languages was set up at Hull University in April 1989.

This paper examines some of the recent advances in Computer-Assisted Language Learning and describes the ways in which the CTI Centre for Modern Languages will be of use in this field.

1. THE COMPUTERS IN TEACHING INITIATIVE (CTI)

In 1983 the "Nelson Report" on the use of computers in teaching in UK universities was published. It found that computer-assisted teaching and learning was at a disappointingly low level. In response to that report, the Computers in Teaching Initiative (CTI) was set up, funded by the University Grants Committee and the Universities Computer board.

The fundamental aim of the CTI since its inception has been, to quote Nigel Gardner, "to promote the development of computer-assisted teaching and learning in university-level education in the UK" [1]. Alongside this, and of equal importance, has been stressed the need for critical evaluation of the educational potential of information technology at university level and the desire to raise awareness of the opportunities and possible problems created by IT amongst students and teachers in all disciplines. It must be stressed that it was not the primary aim of the programme to create new educational software, but the development and dissemination nationally of such material has become an obvious and important corollary of the programme. To quote Nigel Gardner again, "the ethos of the CTI was to create new teaching experience for academics, new learning opportunities, and, through effective outreach, to communicate successes to peers in other institutions and disciplines".

The CTI has supported 139 pilot projects, each involving a number of academics with technical support staff. Many of the grants included an element for the enhancement of hardware facilities in the recipient department or institution. Almost all of the projects were firmly discipline-based and sought to demonstrate how computers could be used, again to quote Nigel Gardner, "to represent, communicate and explore scholarly ideas in English literature, modern languages, history, geography, physics, and all the other academic disciplines represented at undergraduate level in the nation's universities".

The success of the programme in raising awareness has been evident. Many valuable innovations have been fostered and the achievements of a number of demonstration projects have been widely publicised. Most importantly, the CTI has emphasised the value of computers in the investigation of problems of teaching and learning which touch most academic disciplines. All of the projects have demonstrated how computers can be used imaginatively in teaching and learning.

Some of the successful projects have developed software; others have generated educational packages which make imaginative use of generic off-the-shelf software which had been designed for entirely different purposes. Gardner again: "there are projects in history which make good use of concordance and database packages, projects in geography which use third-party image processing packages to demonstrate important principles of land use management, and architecture and engineering projects which use the growing range of CAD-CAM packages for educational purposes".

Above all, however, the CTI programme has throughout stressed the importance of evaluation: it is felt that there is an overriding need to look critically at what is available in both soft- and hardware as the advocates of the IT revolution are sometimes blinded by their enthusiasm.

2. THE COMPUTERS IN TEACHING INITIATIVE SUBJECT CENTRES

It was the desire to foster critical evaluation that led the CTI to establish, in April 1989, a number of Subject Centres (nineteen in all and covering a wide range of the academic disciplines current in UK universities) which are to promote, coordinate and support computer-based materials in teaching at degree level. One of these centres is the Computers in Teaching Initiative Centre for Modern Languages (CTICML) in the University of Hull, whose field of activities is that of computer-assisted language learning.

3. COMPUTER-ASSISTED LANGUAGE LEARNING (CALL)

This is not the place to recount the history of Computer-Assisted Language Learning in the UK, but a brief overview might be useful as a prelude to the description of the activities of the CTICML [2].

Ten years ago, CALL was at its embryonic state: there were a few pioneer language teachers valiantly creating unwieldy software to be used on user-hostile mainframes. The wide availability of personal computers changed all that. CALL activity is now so widespread and its future appears so promising that in the UK two major centres have been set up to investigate and exploit its potential: the National Centre for CALL at Ealing College of Further Education (which has responsibility for the non-advanced sector) and the Computers in Teaching Initiative Centre for Modern Languages in Hull (with responsibility for the Higher Education sector). The function of these two centres is to collect and disseminate CALL information within the UK public tertiary sector (a state-funded Centre for Information on Language Teaching - CILT - in London performs a similar, but less specialised, service for secondary education).

The change in the nature and scope of CALL was clearly brought about by the advent of the microcomputer. Two important factors were at play here: first, the widespread introduction of the BBC microcomputer into schools, and secondly the Computers in Teaching Initiative, which facilitated the spread of micros into universities by funding hardware acquisition and the projects in various fields which have already been mentioned. The presence of micros in schools fostered the production of commercial software, which, as far as modern languages are concerned, concentrated largely on French and German. Grammar drills, gap-filling, vocabulary learning and testing, word-games, adventure-based simulations: such were the areas commonly covered by commercial software. Although many of these packages were created for middle-school pupils, some of them had editing facilities which meant that they could easily be adapted for use with and by advanced learners. The CTI funded thirteen language-based projects (in Arabic, Catalan, Chinese, English, French, German, Greek, Italian, Latin and Spanish), all of which, although differing in approach, were aimed at the advanced learner. There have been other initiatives, financed through other channels, in Polytechnics and Colleges of Further Education.

In recent years, therefore, there has been much progress. Achievements can be grouped in three main areas.

First, we have seen the production of more and more sophisticated learning packages relating to grammar, vocabulary and general "cultural knowledge". This approach is exemplified by the Cognate Language Teacher, produced in the Westfield College, University of London, CTI project: the package uses an annotating system in order to introduce the student to a new language (e.g. Catalan, Middle High German) by way of an already acquired language (Spanish, German). Material is being developed elsewhere for other pairs of languages (Spanish/Portuguese, Swedish/Danish, Old French/Modern French). One could quote other examples: the English-teaching programme Grammarland, developed by J. Higgins [3]; The French translation programme Liltre, developed by B. Farrington [4]. A detailed description of some of the work done in this area has been published by Chesters and Gardner [5].

A second area in which much progress has been made is that of the production of interactive video materials. Many teachers of language consider that Interactive Video is by far the most attractive path for CALL to take in the immediate future.

Commercial packages have been marketed by, for example, Eurocentres and Hachette, which have produced videodiscs for teaching English and French as foreign languages. Using the same basic pedagogical approach of simulation as these two packages is one produced by a team at Lancashire Polytechnic (in association with IBM) with impressive videodisc material for secondary-level learners. More recently announced (September 1989) is a collaborative package produced by the BBC, IBM and Vektor, a company spawned by research at Lancashire Polytechnic: the fully interactive video-disc based system is aimed initially at mature students of EFL in a business and commercial context, but will be developed to teach other languages. Another ambitious project is that funded by the Department of Trade and Industry at Ealing and Buckingham Colleges of Further Education: its aim is to produce a videodisc designed to introduce business/commerce-oriented learners to commercial practice and language in the Spanish-speaking world. At present, videodisc, for all its obvious advantages in rapid access, offers relatively little scope to the individual teacher for creating and adapting material. Important work is in progress in the Interactive Video field, however: developmental work in Interactive Video forms part of the original CTI project in the University of Hull, and the inherent attractiveness of Interactive Video will inevitably produce valuable teaching and learning materials in the future [6].

A third area in which interesting and useful developments have taken place is in the adaptation of other computer-based materials for CALL. Some ingenuity has been displayed in the adaptation to language learning processes of software systems that were originally designed with other purposes in mind. Machine translation systems have been used as a CALL tool in the University of Southampton [7], as have word-processing packages at the Universities of Hull and Lancaster. Computational text analysis, too, has interesting possibilities in CALL [8].

In general terms, there remain three major problems in the CALL field. First, the acquisition and updating of hardware. Secondly, the need to convince non-CALL users amongst language teachers that there is genuine potential and value in CALL. Third, and crucially, the integration of CALL activities and developments into the wider area of language teaching methodologies. The first problem has a purely financial solution. The second will be largely solved if the third is firmly grasped. Integration has already made significant progress in some areas: in French, programmes have successfully been developed at Bangor University to support the extensively used course Le Francais en faculte; in Spanish, collaboration between the Universities of Saint Andrews and Hull has provided back-up CALL exercises for the course book !Que bien!; the CTI project at Liverpool University was the computerisation of Learning Latin: an Introductory Course for Adults; at the University of Birmingham the CTI project aims at creating a multi-facet language laboratory, integrating videotapes and satellite broadcasts with CALL; the University of Warwick has extended the usual language laboratory hardware to include a micro with monitor and disc-drives.

There has, therefore, been an exponential increase in CALL activity in the last few years. It cannot be said, however, that it has entered the mainstream of language teaching, either at secondary or tertiary level. The principal reason for CALL remaining somewhat on the periphery is that the majority of language teachers have yet to be convinced of its value. To quote Graham Chesters: "Demonstration of good practice, easier integration into existing syllabuses, encouragement to language teachers to involve themselves in the process of exploration, recognition of the potential of new technical developments (e.g. in speech recognition/reproduction) - all these are ways forward" [9].

4. COMPUTERS IN TEACHING INITIATIVE CENTRE FOR MODERN LANGUAGES (CTICML)

4.1 The Centre

It was in the hope that these ways forward could be made easier that the CTICML was established in the University of Hull on 1 April 1989, with initial funding for three years. The centre has stated that it "will provide a major information service on CALL for learners and teachers throughout the higher education system. It will gather information on work in the field world-wide, and make it available to individuals and institutions in the UK. The aim is to stimulate knowledge and use of computer-assisted methods in language learning."

4.2 The Subject Area

The term "Modern Languages" in the centre's title is to be interpreted loosely: the subject area is intended to be comprehensive, including English as a foreign or second language, Oriental languages and (perhaps paradoxically) Classical languages.

4.3 Coverage

The centre will have as its base activity the evaluation of not only purpose-made CALL packages but also foreign language software (and associated material) which may be useful as learning and teaching material at an advanced level. Such material would include training tutorials, databases, word processors, text archives and other as yet undefined and undiscovered resources.

4.4 Aims and Objectives

In its mission statement to the CTI immediately after its establishment, the CTICML declared that its mission is:
"To promote the effective use of computers in the teaching of languages in higher education; to gather information from workers in the field world-wide and to disseminate it to UK researchers. This it will aim to do through:

1. Directly influencing UK academics;

2. Liaising with relevant organisations in the UK and overseas;

3. Providing an effective information service on research and software developments in the field of Computer-Assisted Language Learning."

More specifically, five principal objectives have been identified:

1. The collection and dissemination of information on existing computer hardware and software for use in the teaching of languages.

2. The promotion and extension of the use of computers and associated technologies in teaching and practice.

3. The provision of information on the effectiveness of CALL materials.

4. Collaboration between providers of courseware both within the UK and internationally.

5. Stimulating the development of courseware within the academic community.

In pursuit of the above aims, a number of objectives have been set in both the short and the long terms.

1. Short-term (period 1 April 1989 - 31 March 1990)

a. Establish contact with all higher education colleagues in the field of modern language teaching (i.e. users and non-users of CALL material) by means of the distribution of 3,000 questionnaires;

b. produce an initial software guide/newsletter;

c. arrange visits to at least 20 universities and give presentations at least three academic conferences;

d. arrange a conference/workshop (by April 1990);

e. prepare an academic article reviewing the current status of computers in language teaching;

f. distribute at least 1500 newsletters (estimated);

g. establish the regular use of the National Information on Software Services (NISS) Bulletin Board, with fortnightly updates of information on the centre;

h. institute a programme of software reviews;

i. establish initial overseas contacts.

2. Final objectives (period 1 April 1990 - 31 March 1992)

a. Maintain contacts with academics (including use of the NISS Bulletin Board);

b. compile a Directory of Researchers in the field;

c. continue the regular production of software guides/newsletters;

d. organise a two-day conference on new technology and language teaching;

e. publish the proceedings of the conference;

f. maintain the programme of visits and conferences;

g. maintain and develop links with relevant organisations in the UK and overseas;

h. provide information on language teaching services to commerce and industry using new technology.

5. ORGANISATION

The day-to-day management of the CTICML is in the hands of the Management Team. This consists of the Director, Professor Graham Chesters, Professor of French and Dean of the School of Modern Languages and Cultures; the Information Officer; the Assistant Director of the University Computer Centre; the Director of the Language Teaching Centre; the School's Computer Programmer; and staff from various language departments. The languages taught in the School are French, German, Italian, Spanish, Portuguese, Dutch, Swedish, Norwegian, Danish and EFL. Specialists in languages not represented in the School of Modern Languages and Cultures will be called upon as necessary.

Overall responsibility for the Centre lies in the hands of the Board of Management, which consists of the Director and some members of the Management Team as well as outside representatives from the Centre for Information on Language Teaching and Research, the National Centre for Computer Assisted Language Learning and the Director of another Subject Centre.

6. CONCLUSION

The CTICML is, at the time of writing this paper, in its infancy, but it is to be hoped that, given wider awareness of its role and activities, it will provide an essential focus for progress in the increasingly important field of CALL.

ACKNOWLEDGEMENTS

[1] I am indebted for my remarks on the CTI to "Technology in Teaching", a paper read by Nigel Gardner at the Association for Literary and Linguistic Computing conference in Toronto, June 8 1989. An abstract of the paper has been published in The Dynamic Text (Centre for Computing in the Humanities, University of Toronto, 1989) pp. 95-96.

[2] I am indebted for this section of my paper to Graham Chesters (Director of the CTICML), Computers in Language Teaching: a Brief Overview (CTICML, Hull, 1989).

[3] See Grammarland: a non-directive use of the computer in language learning, The English Language Teaching Journal, (vol. 39, pp. 167-173).

[4] See Littre: An expert system for checking translation at sentence level (University of East Anglia Papers in Linguistics, pp. 57-74).

[5] The Use of Computers in the Teaching of Language and Languages, eds. G. Chesters and N. Gardner (CTISS Special Publication, 1987).

[6] See the Interactive Videodisc in Language Teaching, ed. J.A. Coleman (Lochee Publications, 1987).

[7] See the CTISS File, No. 8 (April 1989), pp. 52-55.

[8] See Christopher Butler, in Chesters and Gardner (1987), pp. 67-79.

Computers in Education
A. McDougall and C. Dowling (Editors)
Elsevier Science Publishers B.V. (North-Holland)

TEACHING INFORMATION SYSTEMS DESIGN: MISSION IMPOSSIBLE?

Paul A.H.M. Mantelaers and Mike W.F.J. Creusen

Delft University of Technology, Department of Information Systems
PO Box 356, 2600 AJ Delft, The Netherlands

While teaching students to design information systems, it has become obvious to the authors that this is difficult to do effectively, due to the lack of a frame of reference. We therefore report on an attempt to instil this frame of reference into the students, embedded in the 'normal' course material.
The intention of our way of teaching is to produce information systems designers who can be made productive sooner than in the past. The method, a combination of lecturing and realistic project work, consists of
- interaction with officers of an external organization, whose problems are presented in the lecture room, and
- a relatively passive attitude of the teaching staff, i.e. directives are rarely given, but students are encouraged to find feasible solutions by constructive (and sometimes provocative) staff comment.

As there is quite some interest in this way of teaching, we hope to reach a wider, international audience by this report.

1. EDUCATIONAL PROBLEMS IN INFORMATION SYSTEMS TRAINING

An information systems designer must have certain knowledge and skills. A student can only develop these by sharing a certain frame of reference with the teacher. As most students (and, indeed, even some instructors) lack this frame of reference, a few questions are in place:

- which knowledge and skills can a student without a frame of reference be taught?
- to what extent is it possible for a university to make students aware of the appropriate frame of reference?

The answers to these questions are decisive for the expectations of our society and for the aspirations of our educational institutions in the area of information systems design. As there are no simple answers at present, every instructor deals with this in his own way; one could even imagine that what 'must be taught' is replaced by what 'can be taught'.

Considering the current options in information technology, the increasing complexity of applications and the increasing use of computers lead to an increasing need for integrative skills at a higher abstraction level in the area of information requirements, information exchange and in formation processing, as compared to the past. This requires knowledge of the components of information systems and of the context within which these systems are developed in order to function properly. The organizational, sociological and psychological aspects appear to be the most important factor missing in students. They lack knowledge about the way organizations operate, the methods by which their staff deal with information, alternative ways of providing information, and the interaction between the organizational structure and its information systems.

Is it therefore possible to teach these skills before we even begin to discuss information systems? Should subjects like business studies, sociology and behavioural sciences as offered at all universities, be made compulsory, as a preparation for courses in information systems?

We tend to reply 'no', not because of the course content but because we think the benefit for the students would be limited. We offer a few reasons:

- the above courses have usually been set up for wide audiences, while often only a limited part of the curriculum is relevant for a given faculty
- the views presented in the lectures usually originate from the special interests of the teacher
- the effectiveness of the above courses also depends on the students' frame of reference – just the one requiring development.

Another suggestion is to deal with the psycho-sociological elements of the frame of reference in a separate, information technology oriented course. An attempt by one of the authors to try this out, was unfortunately unsuccessful. Lecturing on practical experiences often degenerates to a presentation of amusing anecdotes, certainly for a novice audience tending to think of ideal situations with a mechanistic world view. To these audiences, words like power, autonomy and politics have little or no meaning, let alone any association with information technology. No need was felt to adjust these views prior to running information systems design courses – on the contrary, the subjects taught early on in the course, confirm and reinforce the rational world views.

2. COURSE OBJECTIVES

In the information systems design course we have made an attempt to solve above problems. The objectives of the course are as follows:

a. experience the various phases of the design process as realistically as possible
b. develop skills in the use of methods and techniques
c. integrate experience from earlier courses by problem oriented learning
d. experience and learn to control the design mechanism and the emotional reactions of designers
e. experience the role and responsibilities of the designer
f. appreciate the importance of documentation
g. conduct meetings and interact within groups
h. stimulate interest in new developments
i. appreciate that the designer designs, rather than the user, the owner of the project or the method – in short: act consciously.

Objective (b) continues to be discussed. Differences of opinion concern the meaning of the available methods, as well as their use in the learning process, which is related to design methods, including guidelines for designer behaviour.

The question remains whether the course should be structured around one of the design methodologies; following arguments appear to support the notion:

- students must learn to work with methodologies
- methodologies structure the activities and therefore increase the likelihood of tangible results
- methodologies are used in many external organizations.

We would, however, like to offer following suggestions:

- the choice of a particular methodology in a course should not imply that it is superior to others
- methodologies do insufficient justice to the design process
- methodologies can encourage escapism, which can endanger some of the course objectives because
- students confuse the end with the means
- more time is spent discussing the methodology rather than the design problem
- by relying too much on the methodology, students develop a false sense of security about the relevance of their actions the fame achieved by some methodologies intimidates the students and does not encourage them to to come forward with their often constructive views.

In spite of reactions to the use of methodologies in the course, which are also found in practice, the authors prefer not to structure the course around a specific method. The students are free to choose any methodology, as long as it is not used to justify irrelevant matters.

3. PRACTICE OR CASE STUDY?

With the course objectives in mind, it is clearly preferable to base the course on a practical project rather than on a case study: a case study has only limited 'context' and renders the course less effective; on the contrary, 'context' should be provided with as much reality as possible. Often psychological barriers must be overcome in correcting frames of reference.

A case study has the advantage of being predictable and therefore more controllable, and moreover requires less preparation long term. There are, however, apparent disadvantages:

- only few realistic systems design aspects come into play
- many roles must be played by the instructors
- the feeling that the 'correct' solution must be found
- students feel less motivated and are tempted to copy documents produced in earlier courses
- instructors act routinely and there are fewer 'surprises'
- missing real 'context'
- low reality content – the students' frame of reference risks confirmation rather than adjustment.

In addition, practical projects have several advantages:

- the provision of realistic 'context'
- students are motivated because their efforts may result in products useful to the sponsoring organization
- the wide variety of aspects 'cropping up'
- students experience a larger number of opinions
- students learn to relate – there are no 'correct' solutions, just feasible ones
- fresh problems for both students and staff stimulate the learning process.

Although there are many advantages of practical projects, there is the disadvantage of the effort required to organize and prepare 'the scene' for each separate course; however, the enthusiastic support by external organizations has helped to overcome problems to a great extent. But still, an active recruiting campaign will be necessary if we plan to conduct these practical projects on a larger scale.

A practical project is subject to a number of requirements:

- it should not be high on the sponsor's priority list, because a successful conclusion cannot be guaranteed: students are involved, the available time is limited and teaching aspects have a high priority
- the problem must be well known in the sponsoring organization for it to be meaningfully discussed
- the complexity of the project, including the 'context', should be such that many aspects of the design process come up, without stretching the students' structuring capabilities.

The sponsor should preferably be geographically near and be prepared to

- spend 4 to 8 mandays on the project, without the guarantee of success
- invite student groups for interviews with various persons in the organization
- comment in earnest on reports produced by the students, because this motivates them enormously (they expect to be taken less seriously than they are in reality)
- nominate a contact for ad hoc questions and, if necessary, to provide information during the lectures.

4. THE COURSE AND ITS ORGANIZATION

The course is conducted several times a year and consists of fourteen weekly sessions of about 3 hours. Two instructors are generally required for up to 24 students. There are no formal examinations, but the individual student assessment is based on observations during the formal sessions, during group discussions and interviews, and on the quality of the reports produced. The time spent on activities outside the formal sessions is about 8 hours per week for each student.

The above is a representation of the current situation, influenced by various circumstances and some practical considerations, although more ideal situations are conceivable. The fourteen week period is determined by the length of the term, which is 7 lecturing weeks. The maximum time which can be used efficiently in a session is somewhat less than 3 hours. Taking into account the students' time availability and the amount of time required to achieve our objectives, the total lecturing time has been set at 42 hours. The decision to involve 2 instructors per course was originally intended to acquaint new colleagues with the proceedings, but has now become standard practice, as students were pleased and staff found it less demanding.

The size of the group resulted from an attempt to involve the maximum number of students in a limited number of courses (without jeopardizing the objectives), and to have the opportunity to form balanced subgroups in various ways.

As the course is built around a real life situation, it requires quite some preparation: e.g. identifying an external sponsoring organization with a suitable project (and willing to assist in the course), and making the necessary arrangements for meetings and visits. In order to be able to plan the frequency of courses, early student registration is necessary; this is only taken seriously by the students if sanctions are imposed: in this way students face the real threat of exclusion if they register late. Although the course of events during a project is rather unpredictable, a certain amount of structure can now be identified. In the first session, staff and students make their acquaintance and the rules of the course are explained. Subgroups are normally formed by dividing an alphabetical list of student names, which helps in achieving a statistical homogeneity. We found by experience that otherwise both problem groups and cliques may have strong negative effects on the effectiveness of the course.

After a summary introduction of the problem area and its context, the students are encouraged to decide what activities should be undertaken. Every student is asked to produce a written account of the first session, and to prepare for a visit by the project manager in the second session.

The second session starts off with a discussion of the student reports on the first session: the usual spelling mistakes and factual errors are criticized thoroughly – time well spent, as the occurrence of these mishaps reduces exponentially thereafter. The external representative then introduces his organization and the project to the students, who are also given the opportunity to ask questions. The guest may reserve the right to leave the question unanswered, without having to explain why.

At the end of each session the students are given subgroup tasks and occasionally individual ones. A verbal report on the work done is presented at the next session, in addition to the documents resulting from the task work. Of these, copies for the instructors and the other subgroups must be available at least one day before the next session, to allow adequate preparation. This is especially important for students who try to withdraw from the process because they have difficulty in reacting impulsively. An attempt is made to include certain topics in several assignments, so that alternative views are generated almost automatically, leading to useful discussions quite naturally. Failing this, the instructors normally act as a catalyst.

At their own request, students usually chair the sessions; in case this leads to problems or the discussion wanders off the topic, the staff can intervene. Students also take minutes of the sessions.

In the last session, students voice their opinions about the course, ask for clarification where required and discuss a wide variety of often contradictory evaluations of the course.

5. THE ROLE OF THE INSTRUCTORS

It is the envisaged nature of the course that the sequence of events is determined by the students, but in fact, this is only partly true. The instructors must at least ensure that the course objectives are met, and an assessment of each student is prepared, which requires at least indirect influencing. But staff generally do not take direct initiatives, in concert with the course objectives and the way we try to meet these through highly realistic contexts. Students' reactions and emotions following experiences in the design process are all part of this 'context'.

The instructors play various roles in this respect:

- the likelihood of spontaneously emerging instructive situations is increased by avoiding pre-cooked guidelines – should this fail, then the staff attempt to

create such a situation by selective participation in the discussions
- if appropriate, the staff must draw the students' attention to their reactions to situations
- depending on the situation and the nature of the reactions, the staff take corrective and explanatory action.

Instructive situations, although unpredictable, develop during almost all projects:

- failure to reach agreement on a course of action
- the vicious circle which requires breaking up, because of the interdependence between subjects
- the planning problem
- the interview that failed because it did not produce fresh information
- conflicting information and interests at the various levels in organizations, resulting from different responsibilities
- more interviews do not necessarily clarify the nature of the problem
- high aggregate level discussions and non-committal statements
- inability to reach the stages of structure or design
- operation within unacceptable terms of reference
- the obligation to accept compromises.

Certain aspects of student conduct are under permanent scrutiny:

- making unfounded statements
- drawing premature or false conclusions
- using implicit and often incorrect premisses
- expressing unnecessary value judgements
- using terms which are meaningless in a given environment
- displaying aggression, timidity or defensiveness.

The instructors consider themselves at liberty, where appropriate, to point out grammar and spelling mistakes, uncourteous behaviour and other shortcomings not corrected previously. The second responsibility for the instructors is the assessment of the students. Students have no say in the assessments of their peers, and consequently collective assessments are not given. Each student is marked individually, whereby even 'fails' are possible.

As individual achievements are not judged for each occurrence, students wonder what the actual assessment mechanism is. In fact it is based on observations of student conduct during the sessions and the quality of individual written reports; these include the way sessions were chaired and minutes taken.

This assessment process sometimes resulted in violent reactions in the early courses, because the students were accustomed to discrete assessments and immediate feedback. To render this way of judging more rational, the instructors added a course objective: this is the way the real world does it! Interestingly, the assessments have hardly been questioned in recent years. The remaining criticism points to the subjectivity of the method and the poorly defined criteria, which is equally applicable to verbal and written examinations. It is often pointed out to students that the assessment is mainly based on freely available information, contrary to formal examinations. The openness of this process guarantees a permanent careful attitude of the instructors.

An additional point of discussion are the assessment criteria. According to the course objectives, the staff do not assess a student purely on the basis of intellectual achievements, but include a view of their presentation. Objections do not only concern the subjectivity, but also raise the question whether the course objectives are exceeded. The assessment should be limited to professional knowledge and technical skill. The authors feel that students should be made aware of advertisements euphemistically calling for 'good contactual qualities' and 'social skills', and that even a technical course should be a vehicle to promote this idea without ruining its reputation.

In cases where student conduct derails intolerably, suggestions may be offered for adjustment in a personal discussion. The effect depends on the extent to which the behaviour is determined by personality, lack of experience or inadequate social background. No matter how successful, the authors believe that students should have these matters pointed out to them. At the conclusion of each course the students are encouraged to judge their suitability to the systems design environment. The opinion of the staff is included in the assessment, constituting the last bit of reality context of the project.

6. EVALUATION BY THE STUDENTS

Even though it makes comparison more difficult, we have adopted a rather unstructured written personal evaluation, encouraging spontaneity; we normally did suggest a couple of topics for inclusion, however.

Student conclusion can be summarized by the following:

Working in groups, outside of formal sessions, was found very satisfactory: half of the students felt that useful results were obtained because of efficient work and a sensible distribution of tasks within the groups, while the other half just enjoyed working in a group, even if there was some degree of inefficiency.

It was surprising (not least for the staff) that the appreciation for this type of interaction was based on contacts never experienced with fellow students - third year students - before. There have been isolated cases of criticism of a group member's behaviour, but sofar this has come up only three times. We have always felt that students should solve these problems internally, because this is a common phenomenon which everyone should be capable of handling.

The evaluations gave no insight into adjustments to student opinions of the course objectives during the course.

Some matters considered to be of minor importance by the staff, were valued highly by the students, such as learning to work in groups, conducting meetings, report writing and conducting interviews. Many students complained that the course objectives had not been met, because an information system had not been produced in the end, not realizing that this was not an objective, even in retrospect. The staff's emphasis on the result, also meant as a motivating agent, could well have caused the disappointment.

Two additional statements, often found in evaluations, concerned the feelings of (1) having gained practical experience and (2) having obtained a clearer and less abstract view of a number of concepts presented in theoretical lectures.

During the sessions, differences of opinion between the two instructors sometimes became apparent – which is by no means unfortunate. It did, however, bring about varied reactions from the students: while some felt that disagreements should not be discussed during formal sessions, others found the airing of contradictory opinions enlightening.

The students generally considered working with real life problems stimulating, because they felt that they were learning about real life situations, although many students were disappointed by the low priority nature of the projects. In turn this gave them the impression that they were not taken seriously.

The real life situation situation brought about some completely new and extremely relevant, and therefore surprising experience for some of the students:

- people are not perfect, and they do not present their information needs in a consumable manner
- users change their minds easily
- a wide variety of often conflicting opinions can be found within a single organization – 'very disturbing', in the opinion of some students reports are not always read.

Most students had expected more intensive contacts with the users, but generally not even all of the allocated interviews were taken up – and that normally is the students' decision. There have been numerous occasions where the staff were pressing for an interview, but the students kept putting it off because they felt they were not ready for one.

There were many reactions to the tasks, some of them conflicting. The observation of the problem complexities resulted in the conclusion that it was therefore unsuitable for teaching purposes, while others argued that it was eminently appropriate because of the realism contained in it.

The students also criticized the amount of time required to grasp the complex problems, and that in addition quite some knowledge of the application area was indispensable.

Even the monitoring role of the instructors sometimes led to conflicts, but again, for contradicting reasons: while most students were happy with the involvement of the staff and would indeed have welcomed a greater degree of guidance, some of them were irritated by the extent to which staff influenced the progress of the project. More guidance would have reduced the amount of 'going round in circles'. Less guidance would have increased the motivation. A few students fortunately noticed no staff interference. An interesting quote: 'I was chairman and was given instructions about the steps to be taken in the design process, prior to the session. It was fortunate for the instructors that the groups made the same decision during the session!'. At this stage, the statement was sooner considered as a confirmation of the student's nature than as the basis for behavioural adjustment.

The same applies to reactions to unexpected formal lecturing: some students considered it to be an unsettling transgression, while others valued it as very instructive.

Some thought that too much time had been spent on certain irrelevant topics, at the expense of more important ones.

During many of the courses we have, as mentioned earlier, experimented with student chairmen and secretaries, both functions being performed on a roster basis. The results were unanimously positive, because of the steering capabilities it provided; it also helped some students across the threshold they would never have mastered on their own initiative.

Although no formal examination follows the course, most students were disappointed with the number of credit points awarded to them, because they felt that the reward was not proportionate to the amount of effort required. To alleviate the problem, tasks were slightly simplified during one of the courses, but this resulted in the reaction: 'We are not getting on!', which shows that it is hard to please everybody.

7. EVALUATION BY THE STAFF

Having experienced five years of lecturing on systems design, we conclude that, generally speaking, the effort was well worth spending. Students invariably declare having 'learned a lot' and that they 'wouldn't have missed it', in both formal and informal evaluations. We as the participating instructors, enjoyed equal satisfaction and pleasure, because this type of lecturing, involving a high degree of student activity and immediate feedback, is more stimulating than straightforward lecturing.

Given the above, it remains difficult to assign a more quantitative value to the effectiveness of the course. Student reactions on the course are obviously of a highly personal nature, which applies equally to achieving the individual objectives. Not every student can have picked up everything there was to be learned, nor should this necessarily be so, since they all differ in character and background.

Let us now revert to the individual course objectives. In summary, these were the following:

a. Experience the various phases of the design process as realistically as possible

   Roughly speaking, this objective was met completely; on the other hand, for instance judging the adjustment of the frames of reference, some problems were encountered. Students often attribute the differences between their original opinions and the course experiences to external matters, such as unrepresentative environment, poor organization and incompetent management. For some students, one stimulus does not necessarily set them thinking, certainly if their original concepts appear to be confirmed by other lectures.

   It is impossible to determine the number of students who modified their frames of reference, given the current assesment method. By overly praising achievements in matters of only minor importance, the students gave us reason to doubt complete success of this course objective.

b. Develop skills in the use of methods and techniques

   Various design methodologies were used in the courses. It was surprising that so little use was made of information from other courses or books, even books about methodologies. The application of methodology elements could often not be handled: students were caught in pure formalism, also because they were unfamiliar with certain terms in the handbooks. The required, fundamental experience was missing. We cannot judge whether the course improved this situation.

c. Integrate experience from earlier courses by problem oriented learning

   The objective was met completely, although in a slightly different sense than envisaged. While we were able to define a number of theoretical concepts, we found some discrepancies and gaps. The students appear to lack knowledge of hardware, software and the elementary business concepts, required for the design of even the simplest system.

d. Experience and learn to control the design mechanism and the emotional reactions of designers

e. Experience the role and responsibilities of the designer

i. Appreciate that the designer designs

   The aspects d, e and i have been covered adequately for the design process, the associated reactions and the role of the designer. The extent to which students benefit is as yet unclear, but it follows from the evaluations that it is, again, a purely personal matter. The comments made under point (a) above apply equally.

f. Appreciate the importance of documentation

   Despite encouragement by the staff, students made insufficient use of literature and handbooks, as was noted under above point (b). We feel that this also applies to the documentation generated during the course: answered questions were brought up again, comments in reports were ignored, and little constructive use was made of prior conclusions. As to communication: the medium was more important than discussing the problem itself. We have been unable to determine whether this was due to escapism related to a lack of problem understanding, or to a faulty approach in the course.

   We noticed the reluctance of students to come forward with concrete proposals in all courses; they were regularly caught in generalities instead.

g. Conduct meetings and interact within groups

   This objective scored high in the evaluation. Although the instructors were generally unaware of the proceedings within the groups, personal problems occasionally manifested themselves; the expulsion of a few students by their peers confirms the notion that the individuals are well aware of their personal contributions.

h. Stimulate interest in new developments

   In general there are ample opportunities for the instructors to offer alternative viewpoints in discussions or to make students aware of new ways of thinking, which in our opinion did not always work because their level of understanding of some matters prevented the message sinking in – the impact may become noticeable at a later stage.

From the above we can safely conclude that the mode of teaching as discussed, has generally met with approval. The decision to put the required amount of effort into the courses depends on the circumstances. The authors estimate that 8 hours per week must be reserved per person, including lecturing time, under following assumptions: routine has been built up by running numerous courses sofar, and the authors are experienced practitioners, minimizing the amount of effort required to familiarize them-selves with a fresh project.

Our decision was therefore: the course goes on!

Computers in Education
A. McDougall and C. Dowling (Editors)
Elsevier Science Publishers B.V. (North-Holland)

Graphical Treatment of Anaphora and Ellipsis

Ronald A. Singer

Institute of Educational Technology, Centre for Information Technology in Education, The Open University, Milton Keynes, MK7 6AA. United Kingdom. Tel. (0908) 652397

This paper examines how a well known Intelligent Tutoring System (ITS) Sophie (Brown, Burton et al, 1974, 1976 and 1982) handles discourse phenomena such as anaphoric references and ellipses within its Natural Language (NL) capability. Sophie's use of semantic grammar allows it to handle such phenomena well, although not without some ambiguity. Since its implementation Sophie's NL interface has not really been bettered, semantic grammars remaining the most efficient way of constructing a NL interface.

Most of the ITS's since Sophie have not used NL processing as a mechanism for creating a user-interface because of the difficulties involved in such an approach. Graphical interfaces on the other hand overcome many of these difficulties by allowing the user for instance, to interact either with NL type pull-down menus or directly with objects on the screen. Graphical interfaces also allow the user to express some types of discourse phenomena more easily than is possible in a NL interface.

The macintosh user-interface offers a graphical approach to handling user-machine dialogue. The paper reviews some macintosh applications (e.g. MacDraw, MacPaint, SuperPaint, Word 3.0, and Writenow) in the light of their ability to represent certain discourse phenomena. The results of the review are encouraging since it establishes that all packages, in varying degrees, support discourse phenomena.

Finally, the paper presents an object-oriented prototype system, Circuit I (Singer, 1989), which takes a sample of Sophie's dialogue and attempts to model it graphically. Circuit I demonstrates that it is possible to express simple dialogue graphically. Within the context of the sample dialogue, Circuit I handles anaphoric references and ellipsis well. This implies the possibility that more complicated Sophie dialogue may be modelled in this way, although not perhaps with the same ease.

1. BACKGROUND

Research into Natural Language Processing (NLP) which spans a little over three decades, has encountered many problems which still remain to be solved before it can be satisfactorily integrated into today's computer systems. Important work in this area includes the seminal work of Richard Burton who, in his dissertation (1975, 1976) introduced the notion of semantic grammars into the Sophie systems. This gave Sophie a number of distinct advantages over purely syntactic stratagems, such as allowing the system to accept a wider range of responses from the user, increasing the ability of its parser to recognize irrelevant or missing words from a sentence

A NL interface must be able to handle discourse phenomena, e.g., abbreviations, spelling corrections, context dependent anaphoric references and ellipses within sentences. Anaphoric references and ellipses within sentences are difficult to resolve because the NL interface must be able to solve all problems of reference in the chosen domain. Even in domains such as electronics, where it may be possible to capture all of the necessary knowledge, classification may still lead to ambiguities. In more complicated domains it may be necessary to return more than one possible referent, which is non-trivial and computationally intensive. Given that anaphora and ellipsis are difficult to implement in a NL interface, this paper looks at how a well known ITS, Sophie, and modern graphical packages handle such phenomena.

2. ELLIPSIS AND ANAPHORIC REFERENCES

2.1 Ellipsis

The use of semantic grammars as used in Sophie allows the system to recognize elliptic utterances [1], that is utterances that do not express complete thoughts, a complete question or command. Instead, only differences between the intended thought and an earlier one are given (Burton and Brown, 1986). For example, within the domain of electronics, 2, 3 and 4 below are elliptic utterances which Sophie handles.

1. What is the voltage at node 5?
2. At node 1?
3. And node 2?
4. What about between nodes 7 and 8?

and an example used in everyday conversation might be:

1. What is the time in the U.K.?
2. In Rome?
3. And in New York?
4. What about Moscow?

where again, 2, 3 and 4 are elliptic utterances.

2.2 Anaphoric References

"*In spoken and written discourse, people use certain words to 'point back' in the discourse to people, places, objects, times, events and ideas mentioned there. The use of such a pointing device is called anaphora, and words or phrases used in this way are referred to as anaphors...*" (Sidner, 1986, p. 363). For example, Sophie resolves anaphors such as:

"What is the voltage at it"

where "it" is an anaphor looking for a pronominal referent, by using the semantic grammar to restrict the class of possible referents. In this example, the anaphor refers to voltage measurement points in a circuit, where the occurrence of the word "voltage" in the given context triggers the grammar rule corresponding to the concept of measurement. Once the parser has determined the correct class(es) of referent, a history list is invoked which holds all student interactions for the current session, being searched in reverse order when an anaphor (i.e., *that, it,* and *one*) is encountered enabling the correct conversational context to be retrieved.

An example of anaphor resolution in everyday conversation might be:

1. What is the capital of Scotland?
2. The capital of Scotland is Edinburgh.
3. Is that right?

The resolution of the anaphor "that" in 3 refers to the answer given in 2.

2.3 Graphical Anaphorae and Ellipses

The question this paper seeks to address is: Can such discourse phenomena be more easily expressed graphically than in NL or can it in fact be handled at all?

The results of a recent review of popular packages (MacDraw, MacPaint, Word 3.0 and Writenow) seem encouraging, since all packages handled anaphoric and elliptic references, except MacPaint which only handled anaphoric references. Each of the packages were capable of performing anaphoric and/or elliptic references in a wide range of contexts. The answer to our question, "Can such discourse phenomena be more easily expressed graphically than in NL?" would appear to be yes. This claim can be justified, since the user does not have to type in statements at a terminal to obtain the desired action or response. Instead, the user points to objects or uses a selection window tool (to make them the current objects of interest) and/or commands (pull-down menus) which the user assimilates with written or spoken words in every day person to person communication. The result is that human-computer interaction is much more natural, where users intentions are more quickly expressed, understood and acted upon by the system.

3. CIRCUIT: AN ATTEMPT TO MODEL SOPHIE DIALOGUE

Circuit I (Singer, 1989) was borne out of the necessity to prove, that indeed, Sophie dialogue could be modelled graphically. In an effort to assess the dialogue capability of Sophie in a modern context, a sample of Sophie dialogue (see appendix 1) was selected and modelled in Circuit I, an object-oriented prototype.

In use, Circuit I emulates all of the dialogue shown in appendix I, allowing the user to ask for Voltage, Current and Resistance values of the various components and inspection points of the circuit. In addition, faulted values can be inserted into the circuit. Normal and faulted circuit values share the same three arrays (Current, Voltage and Resistance), normal circuit values being restored by selecting the 'clear' command from the 'Faults' pull-down menu.

Periodically, when Sophie encounters ambiguous user queries, it does not always return the expected answer, and that is a major limitation of Sophie's current technique. For example, when asked:

1. What is the voltage at Node 5 if the load is 100?
2. 10?

Sophie responds to Statement 1 with e.g. 6.0 millivolts. However, in Statement 2 Sophie is presented with an ambiguous situation in trying to interpret what the user is asking. In this example Brown and Burton state that Sophie would tend to favour the 10 in statement 2 as a load because that was the last number mentioned. If Sophie's interpretation of such a question were incorrect the user would have to restate it more explicitly.

Circuit I on the other hand does not suffer from these problems, since the present technique it utilizes allows the user to communicate their intentions either by directly manipulating the circuit components, tool-kit icons, or by using pull-down menu systems popularized for database retrieval, providing the required functionality more efficiently. *"With a menu interface (as used by Circuit I) the user has at least some idea of the capabilities of the system"* (Brown, Burton and DeKleer, 1982, p.243). For example if Circuit I were asked:

3. What is the voltage across R2 if its resistance is 3 ohms?
4. 10?

the user would present Statement 3 to Circuit I by:

(a) Changing R2's normal resistance value from 6 to 3 ohms via the **Faults** pull-down menu (see Figure 1 (a)). Circuit I would resolve the elliptic reference in Statement 4 by allowing the user to:
(b) Change the resistance value of R2 to 10 ohms via the **Faults** pull-down menu (see Figure 1 (b)).

Circuit I also handles anaphors which occurred in Sophie dialogue. For example:

8. What is the voltage across R1?
9. What about its resistance?
10. And its current?
11. If R3 were high what would the voltage across it be?

Circuit I would graphically resolve the anaphors which occur in Statements 9 and 10 by allowing the user to directly point to and highlight the resistance and current buttons, one after the other, once a value has been displayed on the digital display (see Figures 2 (a), (b) and (c)). In Statement 11 the referent to "it" occurs earlier in the same sentence. Circuit I graphically resolves this anaphor when the user highlights the Volts and R3 icons, then sets R3 'high' (to 3 ohms) via the **Faults** pull-down menu (see Figure 2 (d)).

4.CONCLUSIONS

The results of this experiment has shown, as did the review of Apple macintosh packages described above, that graphical treatment of NL is feasible. The application of such graphical techniques in Circuit I seem to indicate that the

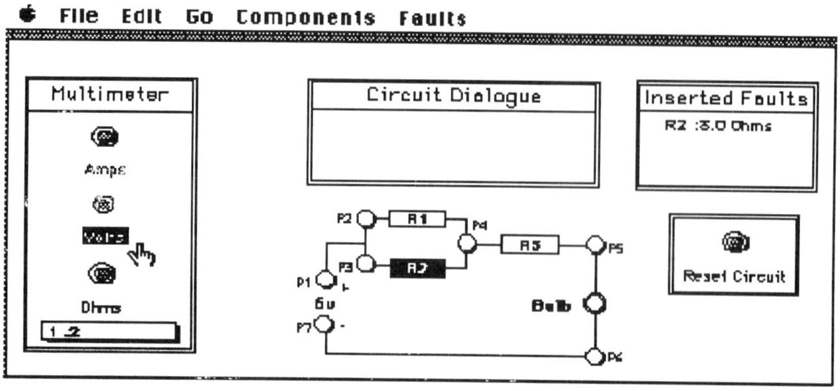

Figure 1 (a) Asking Circuit I "What is the voltage across R2 if its resistance is 3 ohms?"

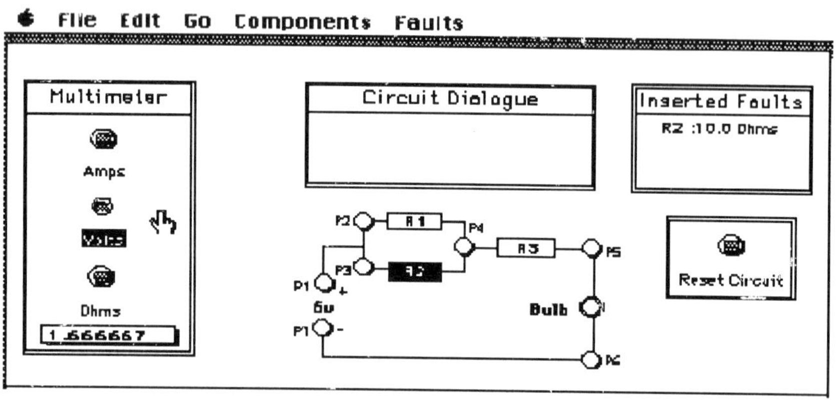

Figure 1 (b) Graphical treatment of an ambiguous elliptic utterance.

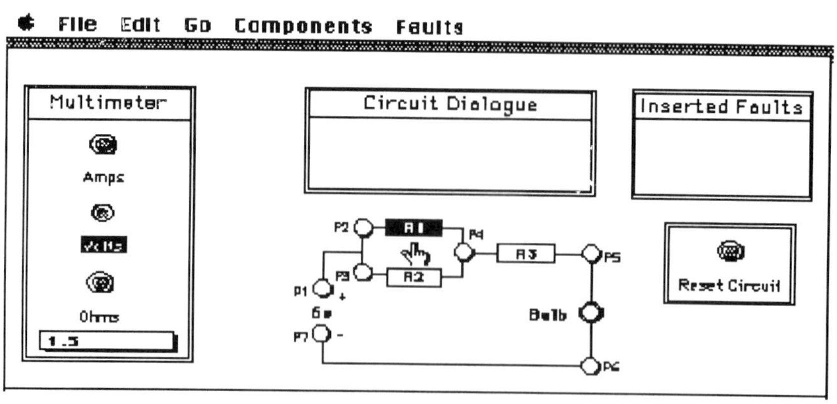

Figure 2 (a) Asking Circuit I "What is the voltage across R1?"

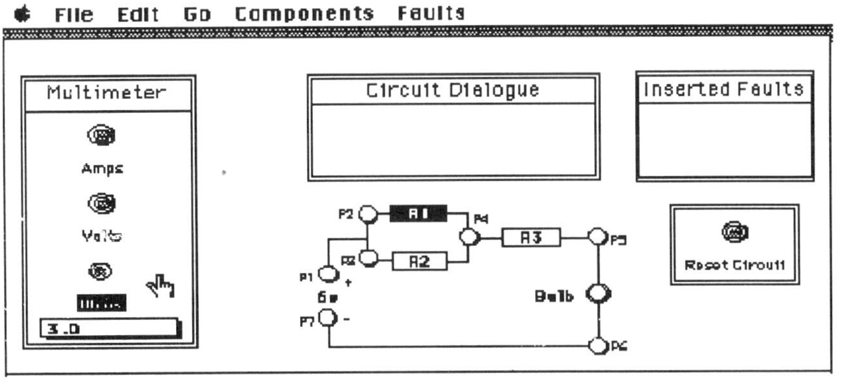

Figure 2 (b) Graphical resolution of the anaphor "What about its resistance?".

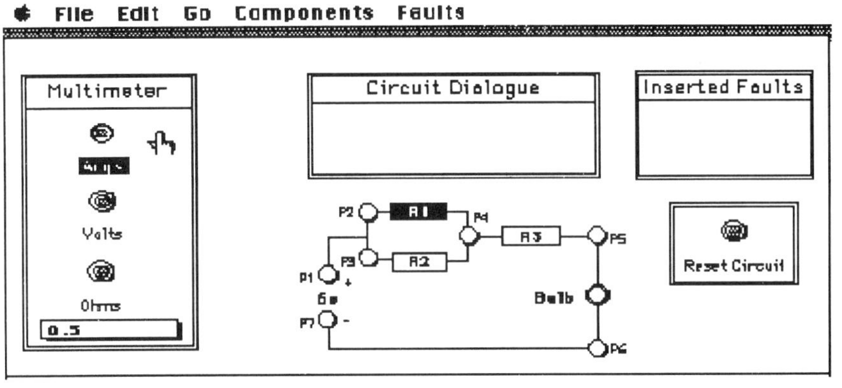

Figure 2 (c) Graphical resolution of the anaphor "And its current?".

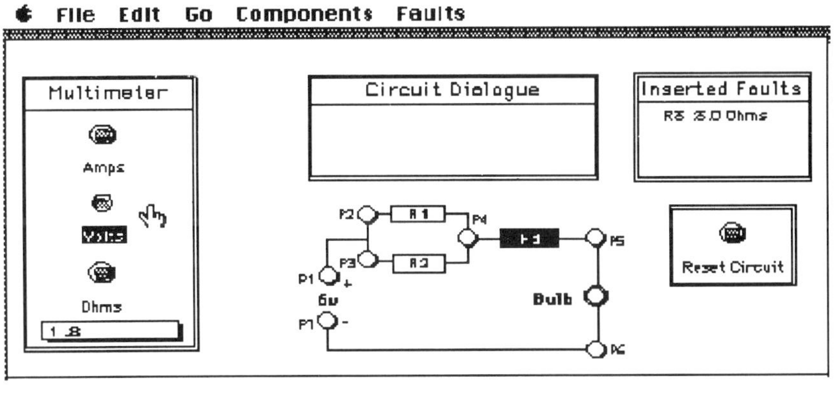

Figure 2 (d) Graphical resolution of the anaphor "If R3 were high what would the voltage across it be?"

interaction between the user and system is more natural.
The resolution of users' anaphoric or elliptic references in a graphical environment as opposed to a NL one is trivial. However, this triviality is encouraging, since it implies the possibility that other more complicated Sophie dialogue may be modelled in this way, although not perhaps with the same ease.

FOOTNOTES

[1] Elliptic utterances refer to any deletion.

REFERENCES

Allen, J. (1987) *Natural Language Understanding.* The Benjamin/Cummings Publishing Company, Inc.

Barr, A. and Feigenbaum, E.A (1983) *The Handbook of Artificial Intelligence, Vols I and II.* William Kaufmann, Inc Publishers, Los Altos, California 94022.

Brown, J.S., Burton, R.R., deKleer, J. (1982) Pedagogical, natural language and knowledge engineering *techniques in SOPHIE I, II and III.*In Sleeman, D. and Brown, J.S. (Eds.) *Intelligent Tutoring Systems.* Academic Press, 1982, p.243.

Brown, J.S., Burton, R.R., and Bell, A.G. (1974) *Sophie A Sophisticated Instructional Environment for Teaching Electronic Troubleshooting.* BBN Report No. 2790. Bolt Beranek and Newman Inc.,Cambridge, Massachusetts.

Brown, J.S., Burton, R.R., and Rubenstein, R. (1976) *Reactive Learning Environment for Computer Assisted Electronics Instruction.* BBN Report 3314 Bolt Beranek and Newman Inc., Cambridge, Massachusetts.

Burton, R.R., and Brown, J.S. (1979) Towards a Natural-Language Capability for Computer-Assisted Instruction. In Natural Language Processing. Morgan Kaufmann Publishers., 1986, p. 612.

Burton, R.R. (1975) *Semantically-centred parsing.* Doctoral dissertation, University of California, Irvine, California.

Burton, R.R. (1976) Semantic grammars: an engineering technique for constructing natural language understanding systems. BBN Report 3453 (ICAI Report 3). Bolt Beranek and Newman Inc., Cambridge, Massachusetts.

Psotka, J., Massey, L., and Dan., Mutter, S.A. (1988) *Intelligent Tutoring System. Lessons Learned.* Lawrence Erlbaum Associates Publishers., 1988.

Sidner, C.L. (1986) Focusing in the Comprehension of Definite Anaphora. In Natural Language Processing. Morgan Kaufmann Publishers., 1986, p. 363.

Singer, R.A. (1989) *Graphical Treatment of Anaphora & Ellipsis in HCI.* CITE Report No. 94. Open University publication.

Wenger, E. (1987) *Artificial Intelligence and Tutoring Systems.* Morgan Kaufmann Publishers, Inc.

APPENDIX 1

Sample of Sophie Dialogue handled by Circuit I

\>> **WHAT IS THE V BETWEEN NODE 4 AND NODE 5?**
THE VOLTAGE BETWEEN N4 AND N5 IS .77 VOLTS.

\>> **OPEN R1**
NOW R1 IS OPEN

\>> **WHAT ARE THE SPECIFICATIONS OF R1?**
THE SPECIFICATIONS OF R1 ARE:
RESISTANCE -- 3 OHMS
POWER/RATING -- .5 WATTS

\>> **WHAT IS THE RESISTANCE OF R2?**
THE MEASURED RESISTANCE OF R2 IS 6.0 OHMS.

\>> **R3?**
THE MEASURED RESISTANCE OF R3 IS 1.0 OHMS.

\>> **WHAT IS THE CURRENT THRU R1?**
THE MEASURED CURRENT OF R1 IS 0.5 AMPS.

\>> **R2?**
THE MEASURED CURRENT OF R2 IS 0.25 AMPS.

Computers in Education
A. McDougall and C. Dowling (Editors)
Elsevier Science Publishers B.V. (North-Holland)

A SYSTEM FOR TEACHING RENDERING AND ANIMATION TECHNIQUES IN COMPUTER GRAPHICS

Kevin G Suffern and Michael J Murray

School of Computing Sciences, University of Technology, Sydney, PO Box 123, Broadway, NSW 2007, AUSTRALIA

A system is described for teaching advanced computer graphics and animation techniques to undergraduate students in Computer Science. The system allows advanced rendering techniques such as ray tracing to be taught, and allows the students to create real time animation sequences.Broadcast quality recordings of these sequences can be made on video tape.

1. INTRODUCTION

Graphics is of rapidly growing importance in many areas of computing, primarily because humans are much more efficient at processing visual information than any other type of information. This is not surprising since roughly half the cells in the brain are involved in processing visual information. Graphics is one of the most rapidly developing areas in computing and has an important role to play in science, engineering, and design (Greenberg [1]), as well as in advertising, and entertainment. An important trend in computer graphics is towards ever increasing realism, which is being achieved through more accurate modelling of the objects being rendered, (including natural phenomena), and more accurate illumination models (Hall [2], Greenberg [1], Peitgen and Saupe [3]). Animation is also important because of the essential four dimensionality of the world in which we live : three spatial dimensions plus time. Physically based modelling is important in animation where the motions of objects are governed by the laws of physics (Barr [4]). In addition, phenomena which can be observed in animation sequences are often not apparent at all in still images (McCormick *et.al.*[5]).

Today, there are increasing employment opportunities for people trained in computer graphics and increasing responsibilities and demands on computer science educators to teach computer graphics. This paper describes recent innovations in computer graphics teaching in the important areas of rendering techniques and animation.

2. BACKGROUND

Computer graphics has been taught for many years in The School of Computing Sciences to varying numbers of students, and we currently teach two subjects :*Introduction to Computer Graphics* in Autumn Semester to approximately 100 students and*Topics in Computer Graphics* in Spring Semester to approximately 40 students.

These are three credit hour elective subjects in the Bachelor of Applied Science Degree, and their popularity has increased markedly in recent years with the result that enrolments have increased dramatically. A difficulty with teaching graphics is the equipment specific nature of the subject; the type of computer graphics that can be taught depends on the type of graphics equipment available, and the numbers of students.

Because of the numbers of students in *Introduction to Computer Graphics*, the practical work for this subject is carried out on IBM PC compatible computers equipped with monochrome Hercules graphics cards. These computers are used because they are present in sufficient numbers on campus to handle the load, but they restrict the type of computer graphics the students can gain practical experience with. Consequentially this subject concentrates on the fundamentals of computer graphics. Topics covered include basic raster algorithms such as Bresenham's line drawing algorithm and region filling algorithms, two and three dimensional transformations, perspective projections, wire-frame views of objects, hidden line removal, interactive graphics programming, and graphic standards. Because most of the students come into the graphics subjects without a background in the applicable mathematics, the mathematical background is taught as part of the subject. This includes two and three dimensional coordinate geometry, matrices, determinants, vectors, and planes and straight line segments using vector techniques. Hard copy of the graphics is obtained on dot matrix printers using a screen dump facility written by one of the graphics students.

At present, the top forty students who pass *Introduction to Computer Graphics* are allowed to enrol in *Topics in Computer Graphics*. This quota will be relaxed in future if our experiences with the new equipment indicate that larger numbers of students can be accommodated. *Topics in Computer Graphics* concentrates on rendering techniques for colour three dimensional computer graphics, and computer animation. Topics covered include illumination models, anti-aliasing techniques, texture mapping, ray tracing, shadows, transparency, radiosity, fractals and animation techniques.

The graphics equipment used for *Introduction to Computer Graphics* is not suitable for teaching this range of topics as the screens provide only monochrome displays, and the ability to do animation is extremely limited.

In 1989 the School of Computing Sciences purchased equipment which will allow rendering and animation techniques to be taught effectively to classes of at least forty students. This equipment is described in the following section.

3. THE EQUIPMEMT

The equipment purchased had to satisfy the following criteria :

(a) The display device must be capable of displaying what is known as *full colour*, which means 24 bit planes for colour. This gives 8 bit planes for each of the red, green, and blue primary colours, and allows up to $2^8 = 256$ shades to be displayed for each of the primary colours. This is necessary for smooth shading because, expressed as a power of two, 256 shades are necessary for a given colour to avoid contouring in the colours. (In practice, less than 256 usually suffice, but if only 7 bit planes were used, the $2^7 = 128$ available shades can result in some contouring). For some critical applications such as medical imaging 36 bit planes may be necessary, Reeves [6].

(b) The display device must be capable of displaying real time animation of three dimensional scenes of a complexity which is suitable for student exercises. Real time animation means the frames are displayed at a rate of 15 or (preferably) 30 frames per second, to avoid flicker. There are basically two ways of achieving this. One way is to use equipment that has sufficient computing and graphics power to calculate and render the scenes at the required rate. The other technique is to calculate the frames and store them in memory. Then, with suitable software, they can be displayed at the required rate. The first way is preferred as available memory usually places severe restrictions on the second method.

(c) The display device must be capable of connection to the School's Ehternet LAN. This was necessary because without networking, multiple display devices would be required to service the number of students involved, and the School did not have the financial resources to purchase more than a single display device with the characteristics (a) and (b). Networking allows many students to use the graphics system through editing and debugging their programs on other devices on the LAN and then transferring the programs or display files to the display device. This requirement necessitated the display device have UNIX as its operating system.

(d) The system must provide facilities for recording animation sequences onto video tape. This can be done using two techniques : real time recording and frame by frame recording, and both techniques are discussed later in the paper. Some means of recording animation sequences is necessary as a means of providing a permanent record of the work and displaying it at other locations. In addition, animation sequences that cannot be displayed in real time must be recorded before they can be seen at all. Video tape was chosen over film for its convenience in both recording and play-back. Video provides immediate play-back, can be edited, and can be played on any compatible video tape recorder.

The equipment purchased consists of the following items :

Silicon Graphics Personal Iris workstation equipped with the Genlock Composite Video option.
Sony BVU-950P U-matic video tape recorder
Acron 606P Encoder.

A schematic diagram of the system appears in Figure 1.

The Personal Iris was chosen because, for the budget available, it provided more computing and graphics capability than any other system available at the time.The Iris employs a series of special purpose VLSI circuits to perform the basic three dimensional viewing transformations and Gouraud shading of polygons in hardware. When these are used in conjunction with the z-buffer for hidden surface removal, the Iris can render approximately 4500 small quadrilaterals per second with hidden surfaces removed and smooth Gouraud shading performed with up to 7 light sources. Alternatively, it can render approximatley 85000 vectors per second. Since all images can be rendered with up to 24 bits of

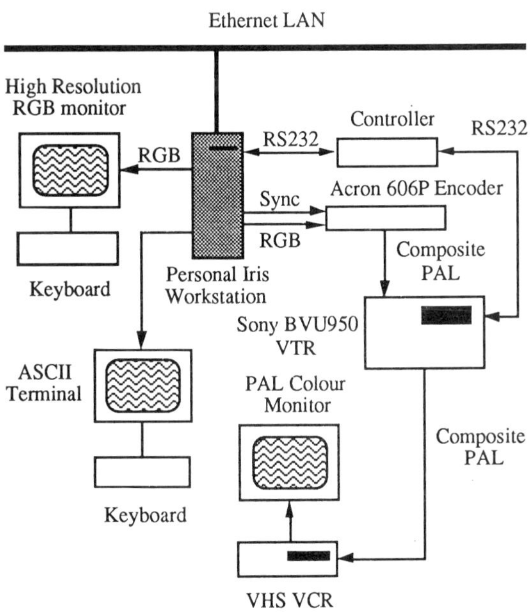

Figure 1 Schematic diagram of the graphics workstation and the video recording equipment.

colour information per pixel the Iris has all the required capabilities for rendering and animation.

To record images on a computer graphics screen to video tape, the RGB (Red, Green, Blue) signals produced by the computer must first be converted to a composite video signal. A problem in doing this on workstations with high resolution screens has been that the RGB signals are not produced at video compatible frequencies. For example, PAL has a resolution of 780 x 575 which is quite different from the 1280 x 1024 resolution of the Iris display. Devices are available for converting high resolution RGB signals to video compatible resolutions, but they are quite expensive. Fortunately, the Iris provides an inexpensive solution to this problem with its Genlock Composite Video board. With this board installed, the Iris can produce RGB signals at PAL resolution as well as at 1280 x 1024 resolution (but not simultaneously), and can also produce a synchronization signal. These signals are fed into the Acron Encoder which converts them to a broadcast quality PAL composite video signal. At this stage they can be recorded on any PAL video equipment. In PAL mode, the Iris uses the lower left hand corner of the display (the lower left 780 x 575 pixels) as output to the encoder.
The Sony BVU-950P video tape recorder is a 3/4" High Band U-matic machine which has extensive editing capabilities. At present it is being used for real time recording where any images in the Iris's PAL window are recorded at 25 frames per second as the tape machine runs continuously. This is the same way the TV programs are recorded on domestic VCR's. In fact, we also record real time animation sequences using a VHS recorder by feeding the signal through the U-matic to a VHS recorder as shown in Figure 1.. However, as expected, the U-matic machine produces higher quality images.

The reasons for buying the BVU-950P were for its high quality images, its editing facilities, and its ability to be used for frame by frame recording in conjunction with an animation controller.

4. TEACHING EXPERIENCE

In *Topics in Computer Graphics* the students are given one assignment on rendering and one on animation. The rendering assignment involves writing a ray tracing program to ray trace a simple scene which consists of a sphere and an infinite plane with a checkerboard pattern on it. The scene is illuminated by a single point light source. As well as teaching the techniques of ray tracing, this assignment gives the students practical experience in other general rendering techniques such as procedural textures, lighting models, shading models, transparency, and object modelling and colour specification. The effects of aliasing are also readily apparent, particularly on the checkerboard.

Ray tracing is a simple rendering technique which produces realistic results for certain types of scenes, but is computationally very expensive. Imagine looking at a scene through a window as in Figure 2 where the window will be the graphics display screen which is covered by a rectangular grid of pixels. An imaginary ray is drawn from the eye position through each pixel and into the scene where it is allowed to bounce between objects. For this scene, some rays such as A will not hit any objects while others such as B, C, and D will be reflected from one or more objects before leaving the scene. The colour of each pixel is calculated from the colours of the objects its ray hits. Pixels whose rays do not hit any objects are assigned the background colour, while rays that hit objects are coloured as combinations of the background colour and the colours of all the objects they encounter. In this way reflections on shiny objects can be modeled as well as specular highlights and shadows. In addition, transparent objects can be rendered by allowing rays to be refracted through them. As a physical analogy, ray tracing adopts a modified pin hole camera model for rendering. The students employed the global illumination model introduced by Whitted [7]. A recent textbook (Glassner [8]) is devoted entirely to ray tracing.

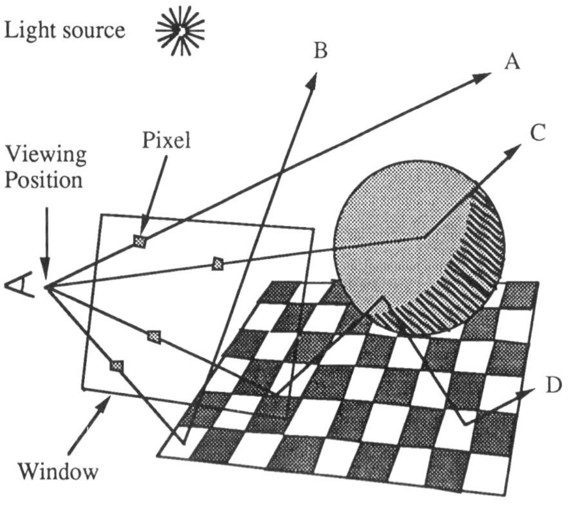

Figure 2 Ray tracing a simple scene showing rays emanating from the eye and hitting objects in the scene.

Figure 3 A 512 x 512 image displayed on the screen of a Sun 3/50 workstation with one bit per pixel. The gray scale is simulated through the use of dithering.

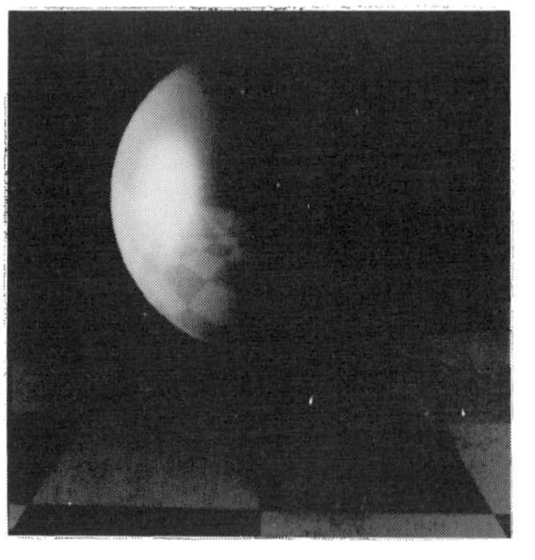

Figure 4 The same image as in Figure 3, displayed on the screen of a Sun 386i workstation with 8 bits per pixel and using 256 gray levels.

Because of the computational expense of ray tracing and the number of students involved, the students wrote their ray tracing programs on a series of 18 Sun 3/50 workstations on the School's LAN, and only used the Iris to display the results.These workstations have monochrome displays and the students also have access to another 18 Sun 386i's workstations which have 8 bit colour displays. This allowed most of the debugging to be done without using the Iris, as the programs store the RGB values for each pixel in a file and a series of utility programs on the Suns and the Iris display the files on each machine. The files are displayed on the 3/50's using a simulated gray scale produced by dithering, on the 386i's using a 256 level grey scale, and on the Iris in full colour. An example from the 3/50's appears in Figure 3 and from the 386i's in Figure 4. In the program development and debugging stages, these images are good substitutes for the full colour image, and give much information about the students' programs. The major computational expense of a ray tracing program is calculating the intersections of each ray with the objects in the scene, and images such as this can show if these intersection calculations are correct. Because a gray scale is produced or simulated, they can also provide information about the shading calculations. In fact, the only thing missing in Figure 4 is the colour. When a student is satisfied with his program on the Suns, the file can be displayed on the Iris. At this stage any mistakes with the colour calculations can be corrected in the program, and the colours adjusted, as is often necessary.

The students are allowed to produce images with resolutions up to 512 x 512, but only after their programs have been completely debugged at lower resolutions. In the debugging stages resolutions down to 16 x 16 or 32 x 32 can still give useful information about a student's program, and at these resolutions the programs take very little time to complete. Running time is proportional to the square of the resolution which necessitates running the programs as background tasks when higher resolutions images are being produced, For example, a 512 x 512 image of a single sphere and checkerboard plane with no shadows or transparency takes 87 minutes to render on a Sun 3/50, (which has no floating point hardware). Transparency and multiple spheres add significantly to the computational time, and the use of files with utility programs to display them on different machines is an important strategy for teaching ray tracing to large numbers of students.

The animation assignment is not specified to the students as precisely as the ray tracing assignment, as the intention is to let the students treat this as a mini project where they have the freedom, within certain constraints, to produce an animation sequence of their own design. One of the constraints is that the animation be smooth, where the Iris can calculate and render the individual frames at 30 or 15 frames per second. The specialized graphics hardware in the Iris can in principle render scenes containing up to about 360 small polygons with smooth animation. Depending on the type of scene being animated, this may not be achieved if the computation time for each frame is too long, because then the CPU cannot keep up. Similar constraints apply to the animation of scenes consisting of wire-frame objects (no hidden surfaces) where about 5500 vectors can be rendered every 15th of a second. The bottle-neck here is usually the CPU.These constraints are very lenient, provided the CPU does not have to perform excessive amounts computation for each frame, and the students are currently producing a wide variety of animations.

The programs for this assignment are also being developed on the Suns, and then transferred to the Iris for running and debugging. Because of storage requirements, the animation sequences are not stored in files, but students may record the sequences on VHS tape as a permanent record of their efforts. The recording may either be done directly on the VHS machine or recorded on the Sony and then dubbed to VHS. The advantage of recording on the Sony first, is the ability to perform editing.

Several students are doing graphics projects on the Iris this semester. One student is writing a package which will allow titles and credits to be recorded at the beginning of the animation sequence. As the Iris uses PostScript for screen display, a flexible package is being developed which displays attractive fonts. Since the Sony is a frame accurate machine, the titles can be recorded first, followed by the animation with no apparent break in the recording. Other students are doing graphics projects on special relativity, mathematical surfaces, and fractals.

5. FUTURE PLANS

An important facility lacking in the present equipment is the ability to perform frame by frame recording of animation sequences on video tape. Such a facility is necessary to be able to observe smooth animation sequences of scenes which cannot be calculated and rendered at 30 or 15 frames per second. To do this, two additional pieces of equipment are necessary. One is a time code generator/reader which is a plug in board for the Sony and places time code signals in the address track of the tape. The other piece of equipment is an animation controller which is shown schematically in Figure 1 and is connected to the Iris and the Sony by RS232 lines. Any program on the Iris which produces a sequence of frames for recording must be written to send a signal to the controller when a frame is ready for recording. The controller then instructs the Sony to record the frame and when this is done, sends a signal back to the program to produce the next frame. The controller uses the time code signals in the address track of the tape to precisely locate each frame on the tape. When the tape is played back at normal speed, smooth animation at 25 frames per second results. This type of recording can only be performed satisfactorily on a frame accurate tape recorder. When properly set up, a system such as this can be left to run unattended, particularly at nights and weekends, and as the following example shows, this may be necessary. If each frame takes one second to calculate and render, 10 seconds of animation requires over 4 hours of computation.

When this facility is in place by the end of the year, it will greatly expand the usefulness of the equipment for both teaching and research. Next year's students will be able to produce more complex animation sequences that could not be rendered in real time.

Other plans include making more extensive use of the Sun 386i's, which support colour. Colour quantization techniques (Burger and Gillies [9]), can be used to display full colour images on colour devices with less than 24 bit planes.

It is also planned to purchase equipment that will allow sound to be added to the video recordings.

The equipment described here is intended to support research in computer graphics as well as teaching, and when it is completed, it will provide a facility where most types of static images can be rendered, and animation sequences from research projects can be recorded on video tape.

6. CONCLUSIONS

This paper has described our experiences in setting up a system for teaching advanced computer graphics rendering and animation techniques. The system provides adequate access for groups of up to forty students to do assignments in ray tracing and animation, and allows students to record animation sequences on video tape. Although the discussion in this paper has naturally been in terms of the specific equipment we purchased and teach on, it is only the functional capabilities of the equipment that is important, and several general conclusions can be drawn.

1. To give students practical experience in advanced rendering techniques, such as sophisticated lighting and shading models, and ray tracing, a graphics system capable of displaying full colour is highly desirable. This is a system with 24 bit planes for colour.

2. Some rendering techniques such as ray tracing are computationally very expensive, and if all the computation had to be done on a single full colour workstation, it would have to be extremely powerful; alternatively, multiple workstations would have to be present. Either of these options is likely to be expensive, but an alternative strategy is to use the networking facilities commonly present in computing science schools. These networks often have multiple workstations attached with monochrome or 8 bit screens. The ray tracing programs can be written and almost completely debugged and tested on these workstations by storing the RGB values for each pixel in files. A series of utility programs can display these files on the different workstations using dithering techniques on monochrome displays and gray scales on 8 bit plane displays. A related strategy is to use colour quantization techniques on colour workstations with less than 24 bit planes. When these strategies are adopted, the full colour system can then be a simple frame buffer which displays the final results. A characteristic of most graphics programs that produce raster images is that they can be debugged using very low resolution images at great savings in computational time.

3. If the colour workstation has hardware support for three dimensional graphics and hidden surface removal, students can gain practical experience in three dimensional animation by producing real time three dimensional animation sequences.

4. Several high resolution graphics workstations can provide lower resolution RGB outputs at PAL or NTSC compatible resolutions. These outputs can be easily converted to a composite video signal to allow animation sequences to be recorded on video tape using any compatible video tape recorder. If the video recorder has editing facilities, and is frame accurate, students can gain experience with video production techniques. If in addition, an animation controller is present, frame by frame recording of animation sequences can be performed.

ACKNOWLEDGEMENTS

Thanks to our students who are acting as the guinea pigs while we get this system developed. Special thanks to Tony McGrath, Systems Programmer in The School of Computing Sciences, without whose efforts the system would not be usable. This project is supported in part by the Key Centre for Advanced Computing Sciences.

REFERENCES

[1] Greenberg , D. P., 1987 Steven A. Coons Award Lecture, *Computer Graphics*, **22**, 7-14, 1988.
[2] Hall, R., *Illumination and Color in Computer Generated Imagery*, Springer-Verlag, 1989.
[3] Pietgen H.-O., and Saupe D., *The Science of Fractal Images*, Springer-Verlag, 1988.
[4] Barr, A. H., *Topics in Physically Based Modelling*, Addison-Wesley, 1989.
[5] McCormick B. H., DeFanti T. A., and Brown M. (Eds) Visualization in Scientific Computing, *Computer Graphics*, **21**, Nov, 1987.
[6] Reeves, W. R., Private communication, 1988.
[7] Whitted, T., An Improved Illumination Model for Shaded Display, *Commun. ACM*, **23**, 343-349, 1980.
[8] Glassner, A. S. (Ed), *An Introduction to Ray Tracing*, Academic Press, 1989.
[9] Burger P. and Gillies D., *Interactive Computer Graphics*, Addison-Wesley, 1989.

Computers in Education
A. McDougall and C. Dowling (Editors)
Elsevier Science Publishers B.V. (North-Holland)

CURRICULUM SUPPORTED BY COMPUTER (CSC)—— BASIC CONCEPT, TRIAL AND EVALUATION

Fumiyuki TERADA*, Takahiro SHAKUSHI**, Naoto NAKAMURA***,
Makoto TAKEYA*** and Nobuyuki KANDA*

*Waseda University, 3-4-1, Okubo, Shinjuku, Tokyo 169, JAPAN
**Bunkyo University, 1100, Namegaya, Chigasaki, Kanagawa 253, JAPAN
***Takushoku University, 815-1, Tatemachi, Hachioji, Tokyo 193, JAPAN

It is necessary to consider the entire curriculum based on the existence of computers in the classroom. Actually in Japan, the existing mathematical curriculum is revised by the government to meet the development of the society. The new curriculum has already been announced and will be implemented in 1994. The 1994 curriculum will take initial steps. To go one step further, the idea of the CSC (Curriculum Supported by Computer) is presented in this paper. First, the detailed design of the CSC is described. Second, the results of the experimental lessons which are designed under the concept of the CSC are reported. Finally, the evaluation of the CSC using SS (Semantic Structure) analysis and factor analysis is described.

1. INTRODUCTION

In Japanese education, particularly mathematical education, the following two themes are pointed out by their importance.

(1) To improve our highly technological society toward the next century, mathematical literacy should be widespread among the large mass of students. It should not be specialized within small groups of students , i.e. gifted students. On the other hand, for the gifted students who will lead the improvement of technology in the future, the contents of mathematics in upper secondary school should be kept at a relatively superior level. In order to cultivate the gifted students efficiently, the mass should be taught the summarized contents of mathematics. It is clear that the accomplishment of this purpose is not easy. But is there any methodology which will accomplish such a task ?

(2) Computer literacy should root itself in the large mass of the people in the growing information society. The education, particularly mathematical education in upper secondary school can play an important role. The coordination of mathematical education and information education contains many tough problems. What kind of solutions should be found ?

The authors have been trying to get at the solution for these difficult problems with effective use of computer capabilities. It is considered that mathematical education should not aim only at teaching mathematical knowledge. The following objectives should be accomplished.

(i) The cultivation of creativity to construct the knowledge systematically from specific or actual facts.
(ii) The ability for logical expression and logical description.
(iii) The ability for analytical expression and analytical description.
(iv) The continuous attitude to demand reasons.

Particularly (i) and (ii) are pointed out. They should be taught to the mass of students more efficiently, not only to the gifted ones.

The CSC is an approach to achieve these purposes using computer capabilities. The CSC tries to reorganize and restructure the existing curriculum of mathematics. Thus the CSC is different from a simple use of computer as training or simulation.

In Japan the curriculum of mathematics for upper secondary schools is under the control of the Minister of Education. The curriculum is revised each 10 years. Thus the next curriculum has already been designed and will be implemented in 1994[1]. A team was organized to prepare the new curriculum, and Terada, one of the authors, is a member of the team. The CSC has not been introduced into the 1994 curriculum yet. The CSC is now a draft plan for the next revision after 1994.

In this paper the detailed design of the CSC is described first. Second, the results of the experimental lessons which are designed under the concept of the CSC are reported. Finally, based on the results of the experimental lessons, the evaluation of the curriculum using SS (Semantic Structure) analysis[2] and factor analysis is described.

2. BASIC CONCEPT AND SPECIFICATION OF THE CSC

2.1. WHY IS THE CSC INTRODUCED ?

Our purpose of mathematical education is not only to cram a lot of mathematical knowledge into the students' heads, but also to cultivate their creativity, or to bring up their mathematical literacy. It is considered that the effective use of computer capabilities is able to help to achieve this purpose. In the following, our approach is described in comparison with the conventional teaching style.

(1) At the starting of the lesson, an ordinary teacher teaches the definitions and/or theorems directly. Aiming at cultivating the students' creativity, it is more important to lead them to the necessity of the definitions and/or theorems.

(2) In the middle of the lesson, the mathematical theorems are taught by the description of their complete proofs. To bring up the mathematical literacy of the mass of the students, it is considered that this way can replace the teaching method by which students' observation of numerical value experiments, graphs, and figures are produced through the students' manipulation.

This ideal mathematical education mentioned above is very difficult to be realized by conventional teaching method using notebooks, blackboards and so on. The CSC is an idea to achieve the ideal education using computer capabilities.

2.2. WHAT IS THE CSC ?

The CSC aims at bringing up the creativity of the students. At the same time, the CSC also aims at making the mass of the students understand the concept of the contents of mathematics. To clarify the creative and mathematical understanding process, it is meaningful to consider a thinking process of a mathematician. First, he/she finds out something through trial and error on papers, then he/she conjectures a theorem, constructs the proof and finally establishes the theorem. This process is creative enough and also essentially general. Therefore this process can be a useful prototype of our method. The above mathematician's trial and error on papers is called *Trial* and *Approach* in the CSC.

Actually it is difficult for the mass of the students to understand the complete proof of the theorem. The proof is able to be replaced with numerical value experiments and manipulation. It is easier for the mass of the students to understand or to hold the mathematical concept through observation of the experiments which visualize the concept into the graphs and/or figures. This educational method through experimental manipulation is named *NATTOKU* in the CSC. The *NATTOKU* comes from a Japanese word meaning *understanding* or *actual feeling*.

The CSC is constructed with six basic elements as shown in Figure 1. They are *Trial*, *Approach*, *NATTOKU*, and three additional elements. In the actual teaching situation, it is necessary to choose some of the elements which are suitable for the objective mathematical items.

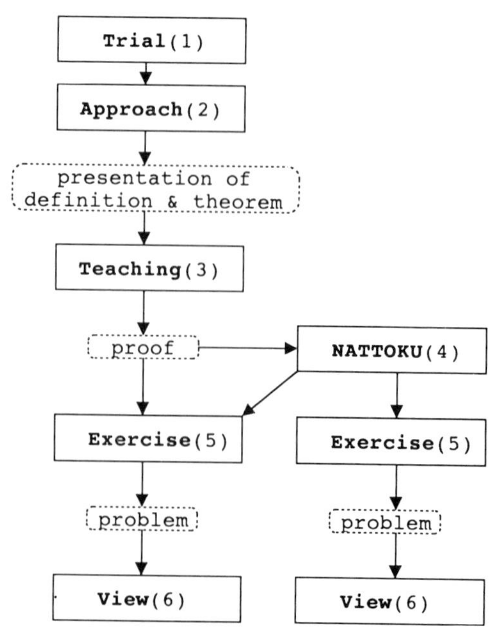

Figure 1 Flow of the CSC

The details of each of the element are described below.

(1) ***Trial***
Trial leads the students to a new mathematical world smoothly. The students are given the margin to put away their sense of incompatibility toward the unknown world.

(2) ***Approach***
Approach leads the students to find something interesting in the mathematical world. A teacher should endeavor to make the students keep their creative attitude with their interest. The creativity should not be given one-sidedly by the teacher. It should be developed by the students experimentally. The activity through the experiment should be able to increase the positiveness of the students to participate in the lesson. Moreover, *Approach* also aims at showing the necessity of the theorems which appear in the mathematical world.

(3) ***Teaching***
Teaching is a usual lesson by the teacher. The students are allowed to use a computer if necessary. The computer assists the students in checking their fundamental knowledge which has already been learned, and/or in clarifying the difficult parts in proofs.

(4) ***NATTOKU***
It is difficult for the mass of the students to obtain full-understanding of the definitions and to make proofs of these theorems. In actuality these students are given a weak consciousness for mathematics by being forced into full-understanding. It can be considered that the general-understanding without complete logical construction is effective enough for the mass. The students can use computers to be satisfied with an outline of the definitions and the theorems through manipulation and experiments without going to full logical understanding. This activity and understanding process is called *NATTOKU*.

(5) ***Exercise***
Exercise makes the students confirm the contents from various angles. The computer is used for drill and practice based on *NATTOKU* activity.

(6) ***View***
View shows in more detail the mathematical world or the utility of the contents to the mass of the students. For gifted students, *View* is able to give extended information on the contents.

3. AN EXPERIMENTAL LESSON

3.1. BASIC PLAN

The authors performed some experimental lessons under the concept of the CSC, particularly aiming at *Approach* and *NATTOKU* wihin in the six elements of the CSC. We picked up 'Quadratic Function' from the mathematical items for the upper secondary school.

3.2. CONTENTS OF THE COURSE

We provided the following four items as learning, objectives in 'Quadratic Function'.

(1) Direction of translation of graph

The student learns the concept of the direction of translation of the graph of $y=ax^2+bx+c$ (where a, b, and c are constants) through the observation of the experiment putting actual values. The computer provides the feature to draw the graph of $y=ax^2+bx+c$ corresponding to the given constant values a, b, and c.

(2) Maximum and minimum

The student learns about the maximum and minimum values of $y=ax^2+bx+c$ with definition domain. Many examples are visualized using computer graphics. Through the manipulation and the observation of the various examples, the student learns the concept of the maximum and minimum values depending on the changes of the given definition domain.

(3) Descriptive solution of the quadratic equality

The student learns about the solution of the quadratic equality f(x)=0. The computer provides the feature to get the visualized image of y=f(x) and to calculate the value f(x) corresponding to the given x. Using the feature, the student observes the graphic image of the quadratic function and perform the numerical experiments assigning the actual values. Through the interaction with the computer, they learn the relation between the visualized graph of the quadratic function y=f(x) and the algebraic solution of the quadratic equality f(x)=0.

(4) How to solve inequality of second degree

The students learn about the inequality of second degree through the similar manipulation as (2) or (3).

4. AN EVALUATION OF THE EXPERIMENTAL LESSONS

The experimental lessons under the concept of the CSC were implemented for forty-seven upper secondary school students. Two questionnaires were prepared. One is for investigating students' attitudes for mathematics. The other is for studying the level of *NATTOKU*. Then they were given the questionnaires before and after the experimental lessons. After comparing the results of pre-survey with ones of post-survey, the effectiveness of the CSC is discussed below.

4.1. INVESTIGATION ON STUDENTS' ATTITUDES

The results of students' opinions on the experimental lessons were analyzed by using SS (Semantic Structure) analysis [2]. The SS analysis shows the relationship among questionnaire items, based on the results of questionnaires. From the results of the SS analysis, we can find out a lot of information for evaluating the students' attitude for mathematics under the CSC. Partial results are summarized below.

(1) Almost every student choose an affirmative answer for the questionnaire items which ask the 'smoothness to hold chart image' and the 'satisfaction in the lessons'. It is considered that the students got the concept of the qudratic function appropriately with the visualized image.

(2) For the questionnaire item which asks 'What items in mathematics computer use is suitable for ?', a large number of the students choose the items of calculation in pre-survey. However, they choose the items of function, and figure in post-survey. It is considered that they evaluated our experimental lessons under the CSC highly.

(3) For the questionnaire item about the effects for the examination score, the students choose middle positioned answers. However, for the questionnaire items which ask their opinions on computer use in mathematical lessons, on their motivation for the further steps, and on their motivation for the computer used lessons, they choose affirmative answers. It is considered that they are released from their weak consciousness for mathematics through the experience of the lessons under CSC.

4.2. INVESTIGATION ON THE LEVEL OF *NATTOKU*

In the questionnaire of *NATTOKU*, the students choose one level from the five levels bellow.

When I read the problem of a quadratic function,

1. I can develope an image of its graph at once and solve it.
2. I can develope an image of its graph after a while and solve it.
3. I can develope an image of its graph at once, but can not solve

Table 1 Average rating score of questionnaire items

	Items	Before	After
1	convexity upwards or downwards	3.4	4.3
2	direction of a graph of a quadratic function	3.1	4.0
3	parallel lines	3.8	4.1
4	lines with same y-segment	3.4	3.9
5	a point of intersection among some lines	3.8	3.8
6	graphical meaning of a linear equation	3.7	3.7
7	points of intersection among a line and a parabola	3.0	3.4
8	translation of a graph		3.6
9	apex and graph of a quadratic function		4.3
10	maximum and minimum of a quadratic function		4.3
11	maximum and minimum of a quadratic function with domain of definition		4.1
12	inequality of second degree		4.1
13	inequality of second degree without solution		4.0

it.

4. I can develope an image of its graph after a while, but can not solve it.
5. I can not develope an image of its graph and can not solve it.

The results of the level of *NATTOKU* comparing the results of pre-survey with ones of post-survey are shown in Figure 2 and Table 1.

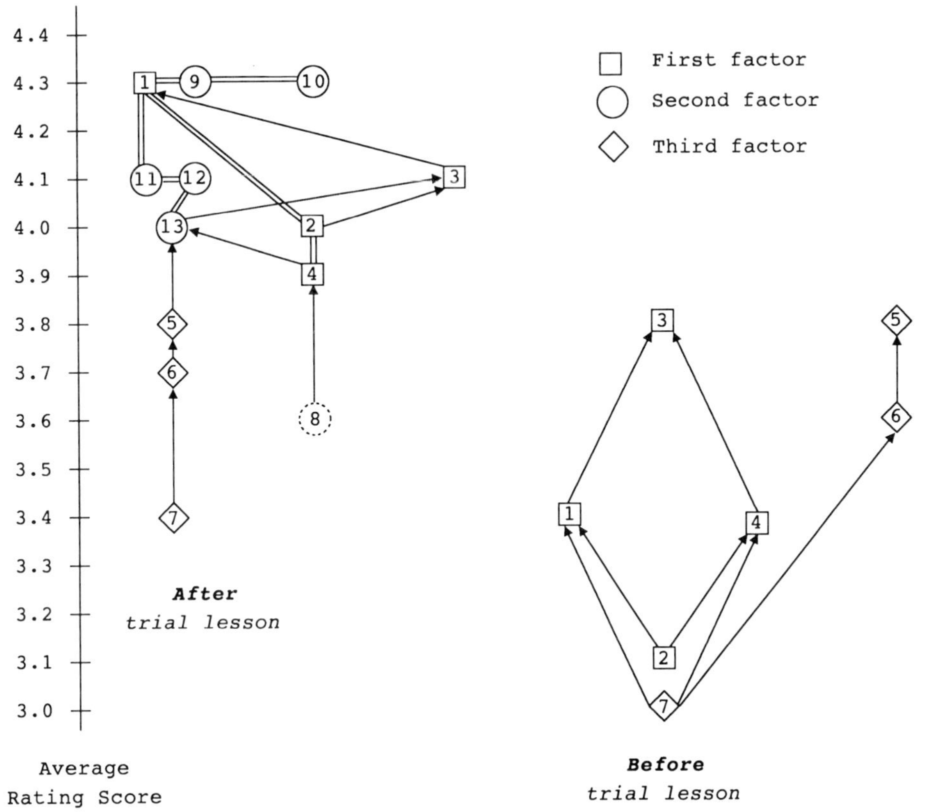

Items

1	convexity upwards or downwards	8	translation of a graph
2	direction of a graph of a quadratic function	9	apex and graph of a quadratic function
3	parallel lines	10	maximum and minimum of a quadratic function
4	lines with same y-segment	11	maximum and minimum of a quadratic function with domain of definition
5	a point of intersection among some lines	12	inequality of second degree
6	graphical meaning of a linear equation	13	inequality of second degree without solution
7	points of intersection among a line and a parabola		

Figure 2 SS graphs for investigating the level of *NATTOKU*

4.2.1 FACTOR ANALYSIS RESULTS

It is effective to use the SS analysis together with the factor analysis. The SS graph can be categorized into three clusters which correspond to individual factors obtained by the factor analysis as shown in Figure 2. That is, all of the items are classified into the following factors.

(1) First factor:
Items that are related to knowledge of functions which had already been studied in junior-high school.

Item numbers: 1,2,3 and 4

(2) Second factor:
Items that are related to knowledge of quadratic functions which were studied through this experimental lesson.

Item numbers: 9,10,11,12 and 13

(3) Third factor:
Items that are related to knowledge of the intersection points of some graphs which had already been studied in junior-high school.

Item numbers: 5,6 and 7

4.2.2 SS ANALYSIS RESULTS

The results of the students' level of *NATTOKU*, based on SS graph, are shown in Figure 2. From the SS graph, we can find out a lot of information about the level of *NATTOKU*. Partial results are as follows:

(1) Items that are related to the quadratic function are all equivalent items, and an average rating score of these items are four or over. Thus it is considered that students can understand it visually, and apply to problems of maximum, minimum and problems of an inequality of second degree.

(2) Comparing SS graph of pre-survey with the one of post-survey, we can obtain that SS graph of post-survey moved to an upper level, and four items (1,2,3 and 4) changed to equivalent items instead of ordered items. From this, it is considered that students understand more deeply.

4.3. AN EVALUATION OF THE CSC

As mentioned above, we could obtain a lot of information to evaluate the CSC. The results of the evaluation are summarized below.

(1) The students who are not good at mathematics, are released from their weak consciousness for mathematics.

(2) The students who are good at mathematics can hope to study mathematics more thoroughly.

(3) The students understand contents of the quadratic function visually, and they are able to apply the contents to the problems of maximum and minimum, and inequality.

As a result, we found out that the CSC is effective for the students, particularly for the students who are not good at mathematics. It is considered that mathematical education through manipulation and experiments instead of full logical learning is suitable for the mass of the students. We also got the analytical results which show the educational effect of the CSC for the gifted students. It motivates them toward learning further, the contents of mathematics keeping their interest.

5. CONCLUSION

This paper described the concept of the CSC, the experimental lessons under the concept of the CSC and an evaluation for the CSC from students' opinions. As a result, we can maintain the notion that the CSC is effective for students of various levels. We hope that our idea of the CSC will be implemented in the near future.

REFERENCES

[1]Terada,F., et al., Computer Assisted Curriculum in mathematics, Proc. of the 14th International Conf. of Improving University Teaching (1988).

[2]Takeya,M., Semantic Structure analysis among questionnaire items using scale method, Behaviometorika (1987) Vol.14, No.2, pp.10-17.

RESEARCH ON EDUCATIONAL APPLICATIONS OF INFORMATION TECHNOLOGIES

Computers in Education
A. McDougall and C. Dowling (Editors)
Elsevier Science Publishers B.V. (North-Holland)

ARTIFICIAL INTELLIGENCE AND IMAGES OF NATURAL LEARNING

Geoff CUMMING

Department of Psychology, La Trobe University, Bundoora, Victoria, Australia 3083

As hardware and software developments arrive it is tempting to explore what they may offer education. But it is also increasingly possible to attempt to support whatever types of learning we would regard as ideal. In an attempt to identify ideal types of learning, and thus give guidance to the design of Intelligent Educational Systems, this paper examines 'natural learning', which is taken to refer to types of learning that have evolved independently of formal education systems. Examples include initial language learning, the learning of games, and apprenticeship. Views of learning from outside the discipline of education, in particular those of film-makers, are also considered. The discussion identifies as significant issues: individual differences among learners, the meaning of the learning tasks for the learner, advice and guidance, and control in a learning interaction. Learning is described in terms of the learner working at the *Task Level*, by undertaking activities or tasks, while simultaneously at a higher level needing a *Discussion Level* interaction. This *refers to* the task activity and includes explanation, guidance, and reflection. A good Intelligent Educational System will provide rich tools for task level work, and will also be able to contribute to a discussion level interaction with the learner.

The aim of this paper is to discuss some conceptions of natural learning, and the ways these might inform our attempts to exploit AI in education.

1. LEARNING PULL OR TECHNOLOGY PUSH?

The education text books recommend that we should nominate the desired learning goal, then choose the best means - whether using a computer or not - to get there. This logic is unassailable, yet the recommendation is rarely adhered to in educational computing. Virtually every investigation is a trial of what the hardware or software possibilities might be. A philosophy of learning may give a general framework, but the approach is essentially exploratory, heuristic, and ad hoc.

This approach is defensible, especially given new tools and new possibilities for learning. We unashamedly adopted it in our Prolog work (Cumming & Abbott, 1988a,b). As enticing new hardware and software possibilities arrive, it becomes ever more tempting to explore what they may be able to offer - observe the boom in hypertext investigations. But there is also greater potential to address whatever learning goal we would really like to achieve. To cast this in slogan form:

Advancing technology gives greater temptation to 'suck it and see', BUT ALSO greater possibility to do what we would really like to do.

'Technology push' is fine, but perhaps it is time to give some attention to 'learning pull': it may be worth standing back and considering what our ideals for learning might be, because now the chances of approaching the ideal may be better than ever. This strategy should not be taken as restrictive: new tools may one day allow us to achieve learning we cannot yet even imagine. Witness Papert's (1980) argument that our view of maths education will be greatly enriched once we learn how to exploit computers appropriately. But as a first step, let us aim for the best learning we can conceive of now.

In this paper I explore the possibility that *natural* learning - types of learning that occur, or have evolved naturally, and separately from the formal education system - may give some useful clues. It may also be useful to examine the images of learning formulated by writers, film-makers, and other outsiders not part of the education system.

1.1. The artificial intelligence context

This discussion can be regarded as part of the current re-appraisal of AI in which more attention is paid to the practical functioning required of a system in its environment than to the techniques available for system building. Winograd and Flores (1986) argue the extreme case that symbolic representations can never be sufficient to embody intelligence. Suchman (1987) is similarly critical, but gives a more positive account by analysing purposeful action and emphasising that it is *situated*, i.e. that it is intimately responsive to immediate context. The aim in both cases is to focus on the performance ideally required of a system, and the practical context in which a system would operate. This is also the aim of the current discussion.

2. IMAGES OF NATURAL LEARNING

2.1. First language learning

The most astonishing human learning occurs in the first few years of life - so astonishing that its speed and success have been taken as sufficient reason to postulate a strong innate component (Chomsky, 1975). First language learning is a prime example.

Besides basic nutrition and biological endowment, successful first language learning seems to require little besides plenty of *examples* of the language in use, and opportunity to practise. Social support and encouragement help, but only a minimum of even these fundamentals seem to be necessary for basic language acquisition.

Innate factors and biological readiness are central. Beyond this, what can language learning suggest? First, the learning is highly *meaningful* or motivated, in the sense that it is integral to the current concerns of the infant: it occurs as part of feeding, playing, exploring the immediate world, and of discovering self and other people. Second, it is *learning by doing*, or practising.

There have to be other language users around, but it is notable that they need not deliberately correct all the infant's attempts, nor need their own language use be especially careful or regular. Compare the haphazard, but copious and meaningful input the infant receives with the aims of early intelligent computer tutors, based on bug and malrule ideas, to give the learner highly detailed diagnoses of fragments of supposed misconception.

2.2. Personal interest learning

If you or I, as enterprising adults, wish to learn something, what do we do? We might talk to someone who knows, buy a book, enrol for a course, or experiment in stumbling fashion by ourselves. Probably we would try some combination, and occasionally change our mind as to what we preferred. Surveying a dozen individuals would probably reveal a dozen different approaches, and each would reflect something about the individual: thinking about a particular acquaintance, you can probably predict whether she would start by reading the instruction manual, or by plugging the new machine in and experimenting with the knobs.

We should have no illusions that any single approach to learning will serve all learners. There probably are quite persistent styles and preferences for ways to learn, although research over many years has so far been able to establish little that is convincing in the area of individual differences in learning.

Consider the products and services that have evolved to serve the individual who voluntarily seeks learning: books and magazines, devices, computer programs, clubs, private tutors, organised courses, and much else. Hazarding some sweeping generalisations, I suggest that important aspects of this vast array are, first, its *diversity* and redundancy. Consider the numerous options if you were to choose to learn gardening, or calculus, or better child-rearing. *Individual differences* are accommodated simply by providing choice.

Second, there is a strong emphasis on coming *to* the learner, and on making the learning activities *meaningful*. Third, *advice and guidance* is usually available in some form, at the request of the learner.

2.3. Games

The advertising of games as 'educational' may be a tired marketing ploy, but many games do lead to a great deal of learning. The learning may be perceptual-motor or factual, but it may also be strategic, or concerned with problem solving, or with inter-personal relations.

One of the most striking aspects of games is again the individual differences in preferences. People vary widely in their general interest in games, and in the types of games they choose to become good at. Turkle's account (1984) of computer game use emphasised these individual differences. Patterns of game participation by any individual also typically vary markedly over time.

Scriven (1987) went beyond noting that games lead to learning, and made a detailed and persuasive case for the educational value of many computer games. His main conclusion, however, was that often some coaching or guidance is required for a person to get full learning benefit from using games. Without this a player may not get far enough to become interested, or may use only some of the possibilities afforded by the game and so derive only constricted learning.

An important aspect of games-for-learning is generalisation from the quite specific skills that often suffice to do well at the game. Scriven's guidance could be important here, by suggesting how general principles can be inferred, and how they can be applied in different contexts, and by pointing out analogies between apparently disparate situations.

Consider Lego for example: it is beautifully designed (Norman, 1988), and uses a highly successful pictorial, language-independent system of giving instructions for constructing complex objects. This approach is, however, highly structured and constrained: would it be beneficial to provide more than the pictures in the 'Ideas Books' to help learners develop more divergent skills of Lego use, and more general, higher-level abilities? This question grows out of the emphasis on guidance, and on meta-level skills in Scriven's analysis, and is worthy of study.

This brief discussion of games suggests again that *individual differences* among learners are vital, and so options and redundancy must be provided. Arousing and maintaining *motivation* and interest are of course central to games, and games are usually set in imaginary worlds. It seems especially valuable to have judicious and sparing *guidance* or advice to accompany game use. This guidance can help the learner to recover from an impasse, and to develop competence, and more generalised abilities. We can think of the guidance arising from a *discussion* between game-player and a mentor that goes on at a meta-level while play continues.

2.4. Apprenticeship

Apprenticeship is probably the richest example of natural learning. It has evolved in many human societies as the mechanism for moving a novice towards expert status in abilities that are important for the society. Study of apprenticeship identifies a broad range of types of learning interaction that occur between student and expert (Collins, Brown, & Newman, 1987). There is some correspondence with the broad range of skills that the expert must acquire.

It is worth noting that an idealised notion of apprenticeship is being considered here, relating more to the hunting tribe or the small craft shop than to the bureaucratised and unionised factory in which 'apprenticeship' may serve to restrict and control the novice, rather than to promote the flowering of expertise.

Before discussing apprenticeship further, let us consider the nature of expertise, the desired outcome of apprenticeship.

2.4.1. Expertise

Study of human experts has revealed an impressive array of abilities. Experts have a variety of ways in which they can represent and think of a problem, a great deal of subject-specific knowledge, many subject-specific techniques and tricks, and higher-level abilities that allow them to marshall their skills and use them effectively.

As an example of a detailed description of expertise consider Schoenfeld's (1985) identification of four components of mathematical expertise:
(i) Resources: facts, skills, procedures, memory for particular problems seen before.
(ii) Heuristics: not merely the well-known Polya (1945) collection, but specialisations of these to the topic area; 'consider a special case' would for example have different, more specific, versions in geometry, and in various fields of algebra.
(iii) Control: the ability to manage resources, to monitor what is being done, to decide when to shift tack, to judge the prospects of some particular approach.
(iv) Beliefs: a mathematical 'world-view'; expectations as to what is required and acceptable; attitudes to various broad approaches, for example the building of a formal proof.

In the expert these components are closely intertwined but all identifiable. Schoenfeld presents evidence that good mathematical education needs to pay attention to all four aspects of expertise. In particular, components (ii), (iii), and (iv) need to be addressed explicitly. These components are strongly related to metacognition, so Schoenfeld's approach accords well with current educational thinking that, first, metacognition is vital and, second, the best way to promote it is to discuss, model and practise it explicitly.

We could add to Schoenfeld's list a fifth point:
(v) Self-knowledge: positive self-concept, knowledge of own abilities, and a positive attitude about the expert's own skills.

As an aside, we could note the particular importance of (v) with respect to learning with computers. It is important that all learners, of whatever ability, sex, or background, should have the chance to develop their expertise, without the tools being used having a negative effect on the vital component (v). Relevant discussions are given by Norman (1988), in the context of considering the mental models developed by people using all sorts of devices, and by Rosen, Sears, and Weil (1987) in describing research on computerphobia.

2.4.2. Apprenticeship as natural learning

Addressing explicitly the different components of expertise, as Schoenfeld advocates, leads naturally to a variety of types of learning activity. Collins, Brown, and Newman (1987) build on Schoenfeld's analysis to argue that *cognitive apprenticeship* is a good model for a mathematical education that aims to build expertise. More generally, they apply the idea of apprenticeship to basic education areas that have important cognitive components, thus extending its application beyond domains of motor skills.

Consider now the variety of activities apprenticeship includes. The expert may demonstrate a chosen activity to the novice, then the novice undertakes one part of the activity while the expert gives guidance and assistance (provides 'scaffolding'). The learner works at simplified versions of a skill, and practises subcomponents of tasks. The expert evaluates the learner's performance, and guides the novice in developing the ability to evaluate his or her own performance. More and more of any task is taken on by the learner, and tasks tackled gradually increase in complexity. The learner is progressively expected to undertake more planning, control and evaluation. Lower-level skills are practised so as to become automatic, thus releasing attention for higher aspects. The learner's conceptualisations, or mental models are modified and multiplied, coming to resemble those of the expert.

Consider some of the conceptions of learning that are currently advocated widely: for example 'exploratory learning', 'learning by doing', 'constructivism', and 'ownership of knowledge'. Each is worthy, and captures important aspects. With the richness of expertise and apprenticeship in mind, however, none tells the whole story.

'Apprenticeship' emphasises the multifarious nature of natural learning. Aspects of apprenticeship worth singling out include *control* of the learning interaction, the *advice and guidance* needed by the learner, the various *levels* of interaction that occur between expert and learner, and the fact that usually most learning activities are *meaningful*, or relevant for the learner.

2.5. The views of outsiders

If I seek insight into the human condition it may be more helpful to turn to the writings of the giants of literature rather than only to the psychology journals. As part of seeking a fresh view of learning it may be useful to examine the images of learning put forward by writers and film-makers, and by scholars from disciplines other than education and psychology.

In the presented version of this paper some images of learning presented by film-makers will be considered, with the aim of gaining a better appreciation of natural learning. Surveying written sources, with the same aim, would be a daunting task; I merely mention as two examples the analyses from an anthropological perspective by Rogoff and Lave (1984), and Claxton's (1984) account of learning that draws both on academic psychology, and on a wider set of conceptions of human nature.

3. INFERENCES FOR EDUCATIONAL COMPUTING

From the brief and selective sketches of natural learning given above I select five aspects for consideration in the context of exploiting AI to assist learning.

3.1. Individual differences

Beyond the truism that people differ, the great variety of approaches taken to personal interest learning warns that a variety of computing approaches to supporting learning are likely to be found effective. In the absence, so far, of substantial understanding of individual styles for thinking and learning, we can probably do little better than provide diversity and encourage learners to choose.

3.2. Activities mattering to the learner

In every case considered above learning occurs in conjunction with activities that matter to that learner. The activities or tasks may be a means to an end (the infant getting food or affection; the apprentice earning a living), of inherent interest (games), or themselves the object of study (apprenticeship). Our attention should therefore be on computer tools and applications that allow users to do things they wish to do: we need to develop ways to promote learning while users are working in this way.

3.3. Advice and guidance

Most apprenticeship activities involve advice or guidance by the expert, and Scriven (1987) argued that the effective use of games also requires advice and guidance. Provision of guidance in conjunction with the task being undertaken by the learner is the central challenge for educational computing.

The guidance may come from a variety of sources, and it may be simply presented to the learner as an interruption, or may be available on request. This raises, therefore, the issue of control.

3.4. Control in learning interactions

If I engage a human expert to teach me, I may decide to submit to the expert's instruction and do as I am told. The expert has local, momentary control of my learning activities, but at a global level I can take the initiative to change the nature of the interaction, or to end it altogether. The concept of control scarcely applies to first language learning, but an essential feature of both personal interest learning and game playing is that participation is voluntary: the learner has ultimate control. As in apprenticeship, however, the learner may often agree to relinquish momentary control.

These examples show that immediate control in a learning interaction must be distinguished from global, or metalevel control. In addition, degrees of control, and also collaboration or the sharing of initiative must be recognised. In one attractive arrangement the learner would have a large measure of global control, while local control would swap back and forth, frequently being with the expert. To the extent that the expert offers advice that earns acceptance by the learner - who retains global control - a feeling of collaboration can be developed.

From a natural learning perspective, it may seem unnecessary even to consider control as an issue. But in educational computing it is a central concern. For many, especially for Logo and microworld proponents, it is currently an important tenet that the learner should have the initiative, i.e. should be in *control*. In Papert's vision "the child programs the computer" rather than "the computer ... being used to program the child" (Papert, 1980; p. 5).

Surely, however, it is unacceptable to give so great an emphasis to learner freedom that the teacher reneges on his or her responsibility and offers no guidance. Even Papert (1980) stressed that, although his Logo and microworld vision is based on learner initiative, this does not mean "simply 'leaving the child alone.' It means supporting children as they build their own intellectual structures..." (pp 32-33).

It is necessary to go beyond merely asking 'Which party is in control?' The general questions of what constitutes scope for initiative, who decides where the initiative is to lie, and how the initiative might be shared require more detailed analysis than they have so far received in education. Meanwhile it is attractive to try to design computer systems for use by a learner in a collaborative way (Cumming & Self, 1989a).

3.5. Levels of interaction in learning

Focussing on learning that centres on tasks mattering to the learner suggests a constructivist view of learning (Anzai & Simon, 1979). This view adopts the slogan 'learning by doing', but actually describes a learner as *doing* some task, and also as *reflecting upon* the task and the learning. Such an account fits well with apprenticeship ideas, and with an emphasis on the development of metacognitive skills, for which the 'reflecting upon' is vital.

More generally, apprenticeship, games-plus-guidance, and many forms of conventional learning can easily be described as comprising interactions that occur at two distinct levels. We can refer to the 'doing' (or the game-playing) as occurring at the *Task Level* (TL), and the 'reflecting upon' as taking place at the *Discussion Level* (DL) (Cumming & Self, 1989b).

At the task level the learner uses a tool for an immediate objective, carries out an exercise, plays a game, or sees some exposition. The discussion level interaction consists of discussion *about* things at the task level, and so occurs at a metalevel. It can include provision of explanation and guidance, evaluation of task level performance, planning of further tasks, setting the task in a broad domain context, consideration of long-term learning goals and reflection about abilities being developed.

In apprenticeship the discussion level is always important. Early in learning the expert or teacher plays a large part in the DL conversation, but seeks to transfer it to the learner. The aim is that the learner will eventually maintain a 'discussion level interaction' privately, i.e. will plan, evaluate, control and reflect on the task being tackled, just as an expert does. Therefore 'internalising the discussion level' is another way of describing the advance towards expertise.

4. INTELLIGENT EDUCATIONAL SYSTEMS

In Cumming and Self (1989a,b) we apply these ideas to the design of Intelligent Educational Systems (IESs), which we see as computer systems intended to support a wide variety of learning interactions. We see the learner as using some computer facilities - a tool perhaps - to work at the task level. Meanwhile learner and computing system conduct a conversation at the discussion level.

Many of the best existing IESs consist of a coaching or advising component added on top of a game, simulation, or application package. WEST (Burton & Brown, 1982) remains the classic example. From this perspective, building an IES becomes the task of providing a DL for the user of an existing package.

This is an attractive possibility because so many outstanding games and software packages, with excellent user interfaces, are now becoming available. Packages that provide the user with tools for exploration in a domain - whether music, statistics, graphics, some physical system, or a particular subject area - are attractive candidates to serve as the basis for an IES because they give users great scope for initiative at the TL.

A further possibility we discuss (Cumming & Self,1989b) is that the TL and DL might be to some extent *decoupled*, i.e. it may be possible for the system to provide some sort of DL without needing to draw on a complete understanding of the TL interaction. If so the notoriously difficult task of IES development might be eased.

5. LESSONS FROM NATURAL LEARNING

This brief and selective survey gives an image of learning in which the learner is engaged in some task that is of importance to him or her, while at the same time participating in a complementary discussion of the activity that includes explanation and guidance. In these terms traditional education, in its concern for abstraction and formalism, has too often used tasks that lack realism for the learner. By contrast, laissez-faire approaches to learning may allow learners to undertake activities that are personally meaningful, but they neglect the essential guidance aspect of the DL. Education drills, at their worst, suffer from both deficiencies.

Some of the best of contemporary computing developments are giving us splendid tools that learners can use to undertake tasks they want to do. However, to give more complete support for learning, a computer system must also be able to contribute to the DL: it must be able to give at least some explanation and advice about TL activities and how they can serve to build expertise. The challenge is to use the techniques of AI, together with the new perspectives on AI arising from analyses such as those of Winograd and Flores (1986) and Suchman (1987), to provide learners with a useful contribution to the discussion level interaction they need.

ACKNOWLEDGEMENTS

I am grateful for the collaboration of many people, especially Elizabeth Abbott, Jonathan Briggs, and John Self; and Roly Sussex and the other members of the EXCALIBUR project. Support for this research has been provided by the Australian Research Council.

REFERENCES

Anzai, Y., & Simon, H. A. (1979) The theory of learning by doing. Psychological Review, 86, 124-140.

Burton, R. R., & Brown, J. S. (1982) An investigation of computer coaching for informal learning activities. In D. Sleeman & J. S. Brown (Eds) Intelligent tutoring systems. New York: Academic Press. pp 79-98.

Chomsky, N. (1975) Reflections on language. New York: Pantheon Books.

Claxton, G. (1984) Live and learn: An introduction to the psychology of growth and change in everyday life. Milton Keynes: Open University Press.

Collins, A., Brown, J. S., & Newman, S. E. (1987) Cognitive apprenticeship: Teaching the craft of reading, writing, and mathematics. In L. B. Resnick (Ed.) Cognition and instruction: Issues and agendas. Hillsdale, N.J.: Erlbaum.

Cumming, G., & Abbott, E. (1988a) Prolog and expert systems for children's learning. In P. Ercoli & R. Lewis (Eds) Artificial intelligence tools in education. Amsterdam: North-Holland. pp 163-175.

Cumming, G., & Abbott, E. (1988b) Prolog as a medium for learning in the classroom: Assessing a broad range of computer-based activities. In F. Lovis & E. D. Tagg (Eds) Computers in education. Amsterdam: North-Holland. pp 317-321.

Cumming, G., & Self, J. (1989a) Learner modelling in collaborative intelligent educational systems. In Goodyear, P. (Ed.) Teaching knowledge and intelligent tutoring. New York: Ablex. (in press)

Cumming, G., & Self, J. (1989b) Intelligent educational systems: Identifying and decoupling the conversational levels. Instructional Science. (in press)

Norman, D. (1988) The psychology of everyday things. New York: Basic Books.

Papert, S. (1980) Mindstorms: Children, computers, and powerful ideas. New York: Basic Books.

Polya, G. (1945) How to solve it. Princeton, N.J.: Princeton University Press.

Rogoff, B., & Lave, J. (Eds) (1984) Everyday cognition: Its development in social context. Cambridge, MA: Harvard University Press.

Rosen, L. D., Sears, D. C., & Weil, M. M. (1987) Computerphobia. Behavior Research Methods, Instruments, & Computers, 19, 167-179.

Schoenfeld, A. H. (1985) Mathematical problem solving. New York: Academic.

Scriven, M. (1987) Taking games seriously. Education Research and Perspectives, 14, 82-135.

Suchman, L. A. (1987) Plans and situated actions. Cambridge, U.K.: Cambridge University Press.

Turkle, S. (1984) The second self. New York: Simon and Schuster.

Winograd, T., & Flores, C. F. (1986) Understanding computers and cognition: A new foundation for design. Norwood, N. J.: Ablex.

Computers in Education
A. McDougall and C. Dowling (Editors)
Elsevier Science Publishers B.V. (North-Holland)

MONITORING KNOWLEDGE AND PROBLEM SOLVING PERFORMANCE IN MEDICINE

José F. AROCHA & Vimla. L. PATEL

Laboratory of Cognitive Studies in Medicine, Centre for Medical Education, McGill University, 3655 Drummond Street, Room 529, Montreal, Québec. Canada, H3G 1Y6*

This paper describes a study where expert and novice representations of a problem in a semantically rich domain are evaluated against a reference model of the problem. The specific objectives of the study are (a) to extend the use of overlay models to cognitively diagnose problem solving, and (b) to show how novices' own explanations of the problem (other than an expert model) could be used as a reference point to evaluate their interpretations of the problem. The results show that the problems of overlay models based on expert behavior, in evaluating novice perspectives, can be resolved by looking at the development of novice problem representation as a process whereby there is an increase in the degree of explanatory coherence with expertise.

1. INTRODUCTION

Assessment of problem solving from a cognitive point of view has become an area of increasing interest to cognitive scientists concerned with educational issues [5],[8], [11]. One of the main reasons for this renewed interest lies in the need to provide a cognitive theoretical basis for educational assessment and evaluative techniques, which to date have lacked theoretical support. Because of the recent advances in research on human information processing, cognitive scientists are beginning to explore solutions to educational problems, such as those involved in learning and assessment. From this research, several models have been proposed that help us understand the process of educational assessment. One of the main components of these models is the student model, i.e., a model of the domain knowledge possessed by the student, and its utilization.

The models proposed in the literature vary in terms of the data they use (e.g.,trace data, answer data) as well as the domains of application (e.g., subtraction, medical diagnosis). The most commonly used are overlay models where the student's behavior is assessed in terms of the behavior typical of the expert. Expert rules are obtained for a task, and then, the student rules are compared to the expert rules. To the extent that the student matches the expert, the student is successful.

In the area of clinical medicine, one of the aspects more frequently investigated is the diagnostic process. Basically, the diagnosis consists of both a categorization process which maps patient observations (e.g., signs and symptoms) onto a disease and an explanation of the possible pathophysiological processes that account for these observations. One problem is that these two aspects of the diagnostic task require different reasoning strategies and knowledge bases. On the one hand, correctly identifying the observations and the disease that explains them is usually associated with *forward reasoning;* a form of mapping process from the the data given in the case onto a disease category. On the other hand, accounting for the underlying process is associated with *backward reasoning;* a type of causal reasoning which accounts for the pattern of observations in the case in terms of underlying disease mechanisms.

Research has shown that as expertise in diagnosing routine cases increases, a shift takes place from backward reasoning to forward reasoning; such a shift is associated to a change in the knowledge used. Novices tend to reason at a different level of the domain, as they are more familiar with the basic science aspects of medicine than with clinical aspects, and also tend to reason in causal terms. Experts, on the other hand, make use of clinical information almost exclusively, and reason in conditional terms. The shift from backward to forward reasoning involves not only a change in the directionality of the reasoning process, but also a change in the knowledge used to solve the patient problem. Given this, it is necessary, then, to represent the *different levels of description* of the medical domain, which are differently used by medical students and expert physicians. This poses problems, as a novice's representation is different in nature from that of an expert. The result is that one cannot be mapped onto

* This research is supported in part by the Medical Research Council of Canada (Grant MH0004) and by Apple Canada.

the other, and therefore, overlay models cannot be used without substantial modification and extension. In the medical domain, experiments done with MYCIN to implement a tutoring system showed its inadequacy for teaching and explanation (except to the expert himself) as the knowledge was extracted from the expert knowledge base and did not correspond to the knowledge used by the student. The implementation of NEOMYCIN [3] was a complete reconfiguration in terms of the knowledge representation and the inference process, using chaining of metarules via diagnostic tasks.

Given the limitations found with the application of overlay models to student assessment, a number of alternative models have been suggested in the literature [5], [10], [11] designed to overcome the limitations of overlay models, as described by VanLehn [17].

The present research is in a semantically complex domain of medicine. The proposed method is based on techniques that Patel and collaborators [15], [16] have used in the analysis of verbal protocols. The method has been used in analyzing causal-conditional explanations of processes generated by experts and novices. In the analysis, observations in the case are linked to the underlying mechanisms that explain those observations. The method is based on the assumption that subjects develop coherent representations of the cases by attempting to account for all available information pertaining to the case. In this regard, a criterion used for assessment is the extent to which explanations are coherent. The degree of coherence in the explanations depends on the knowledge subjects have of the domain.

However, providing explanations may not show all implicit knowledge subjects have, as it has been recognized by developers of expert systems [7]. Probes or questions are needed about details of particular observations to further explore knowledge that is not immediately accessed. In medicine, this is supported by the fact that medical problems can be organized at different levels of description [2]. For the purposes of determining the diagnostic hypothesis, one may need only a pattern matching process of pure forward reasoning. This is typically the way an expert practitioner [13] would solve the problem. However, less than experts or experts in less-than-expert conditions (e.g., medical students, residents, physician solving cases outside their specialty, and to some extent, clinical researchers), recur to explanations of the underlying pathophysiological process at different levels of granularity, and hence to backward reasoning, when accounting for a case [16].

Notwithstanding their limitations, overlay models are the most commonly used methods of student modeling in systems of computerized instruction and assessment [18], and can be used with extensions to assessment in complex domains. The research presented in this paper explores the use of a diagnostic task together with question-answering to model the different levels and components in experts' and students' knowledge of disease. We present experimental data to show how novices' explanation protocols can be used to evaluate their own understanding of a problem.

2. METHOD

2.1. Subjects

A sample of 6 medical students and 4 expert endocrinologists volunteered for the study. The subjects were all affiliated with the Faculty of Medicine at McGill University. A group of medical residents [1] was also part of the sample, but is not included in the present paper.

2.2. Task

A clinical text describing the history, the results from physical examination, and the results from laboratory tests, concerning a 63 year-old hypothyroidic woman, who comes to the emergency room in a precomatose state, was developed by a physician collaborator, a specialist in endocrinology. The text describes a woman who suffers from an autoimmune form of hypothyroidism called Hashimoto's disease.

2.3. Procedure

An expert model for the case, involving the information that would be necessary to reach the diagnosis, was developed with the help of the physician collaborator [1]. The expert model contains the most important biomedical and clinical information for solving the case.

For the purposes of the analysis, three components were identified in the expert model. The main component, of more generality, is *hypothyroidism*. The second component is *myxedema*. The last component concerns the autoimmune origin of the disease, i.e., *Hashimoto's Thyroiditis*.

The case can be represented at different levels of description. (1) *observations*, which represent the information given in the text; (2) *mechanisms*, which represent intermediate constructs between the observations and the diagnosis at different levels of generality; and finally, (3) *diagnosis*, the problem solution.

The purpose of developing the expert model, as in overlay models, was to map the subjects' responses to it. The expert model was developed as a conceptual network which is composed of nodes, representing the explanatory concepts, and links representing the associations, mostly causal and conditional, among nodes. The model also includes the answers to questions that were developed by the physician collaborator. These answers attempt to provide an explanation of some of the more important underlying mechanisms of the disease. An reference model was then developed by superimposing the answers to the questions on the expert model. Each question is overlaid separately, although more than one answer can be superimposed. One limitation of the reference model in its graphic representation is that all components are represented at the same level, whence what is needed is a multilayer representation that takes into account the depth of case representation.

The subjects were 1) asked to read the case; 2) to give a written summary of it; 3) to explain the underlying disease mechanism; and 4) to provide a diagnosis. Next, a set of probe questions were asked to further explain the disease mechanisms of some of the more important observations in the case.

2.4. Analysis

All of the subjects' protocols were segmented and analyzed into causal-conditional networks, following the method described in Patel and Groen [12]. The network from each subject's protocol was matched against the reference model. The answers to the probe questions were also matched against the reference model.

The analysis begins with the segmentation of the text into its constituent propositions [4], [6]. The propositions are then used to develop the reference model by linking the concepts through causal and conditional rules. The network so obtained is a hierarchical network that contains the elements mentioned above, namely, observations, mechanisms, and diagnoses. Single observations or clusters of them lead to intermediate constructs, which in turn lead to the diagnosis. Typically, links going from diagnosis to constructs to observations are termed *causal rules* and are similar to backward chaining. Links going from observations to constructs to diagnosis are termed *conditional rules* and are similar to forward chaining.

3. RESULTS AND DISCUSSION

3.1. Diagnosis

As a group, only the experts identified all components of the case in their diagnoses. All novices identified the general component *(Hypothyroidism)* but none identified the specific nature of the general component, namely, *Myxedema* and *Pre-comatose state*. It is noteworthy that all subjects could, at least, correctly identify the problem as one of thyroid deficiency.

3.2. Protocol Analysis

In the reference model, the disease was decomposed into a set of observations represented by the nodes on the right-hand side of the model; a set of intermediate constructs or hypotheses which serve as explanations of the observations; and the disease diagnosis, on the left-hand side. The subjects' protocols are assessed by mapping each individual protocol against the reference model.

Figure 1 presents an expert endocrinologist's (E1) explanation of the case and answer to question 1, superimposed on a portion of the reference model. The approach taken by E1 was to account for all the observations by using only the main components of the disease, namely, *hypothyroidism, myxedema plus the effect of the potassium iodine mixture*, and its *autoimmune origin*, i.e., Hashimoto's disease. This expert was able to recognize the pattern of observations in the case, which suggested the correct diagnosis in a forward directed fashion. The explanation mapped well onto the reference model as seen in the figure. The response to the questions were also approached with a high-level answer, in the sense that the expert responded without mentioning many of the intermediate constructs between the diagnoses and the observations. For instance, the question, *What mechanism explains the* PO_2 *and* PCO_2 *levels in this patient?*, is answered by E1 in terms of the effect of hypoventilation without mentioning the other constructs in the reference model (i.e., *respiratory failure,* CO_2 *retention,* and *hypercarbia)*. The same way, question 6 is answered as an effect of dilutional hyponatremia and decreased water clearance, both broad terms that serve to summarize a number of lower level pathophysiological processes. This approach of accounting for a case in general, but clinically meaningful components, has been found to be characteristic of endocrine and cardiologist practitioners in previous research [13]. The researchers rather than the practitioners, on the other hand, tend to give more detailed protocols regarding the intermediate mechanisms. This seems to be the standard way to explain observations at the clinical level [14].

In contrast, Figure 2 presents the pathophysiological explanation and response to the question of a fourth year medical student. This student concentrates her description on the cellular processes occurring inside the thyroid gland. Her description cannot be assessed through the use of an expert model because the level of description used by the expert is more general than the level of description used

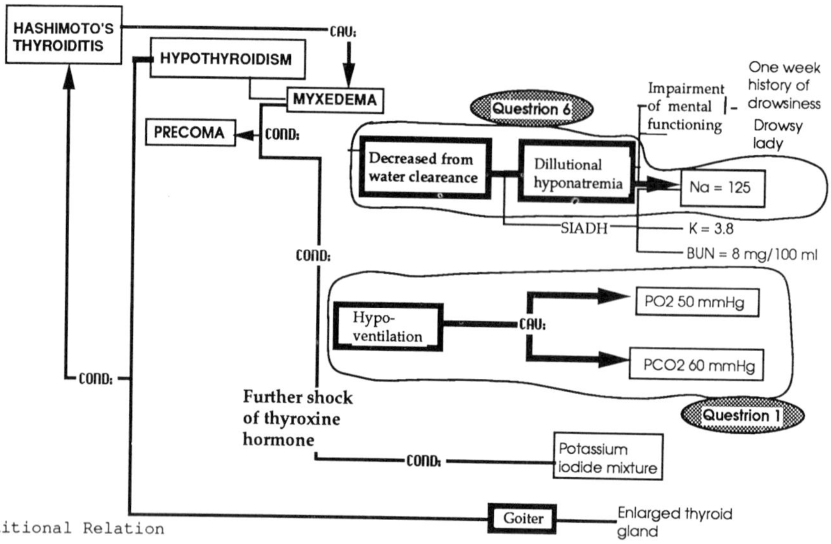

COND: Conditional Relation

CAU: Causal Relation

Figure 1: Representation of Pathophysiology Protocol and Answers to Questions by Expert Endocrinologist Mapped onto Portions of the Reference Model

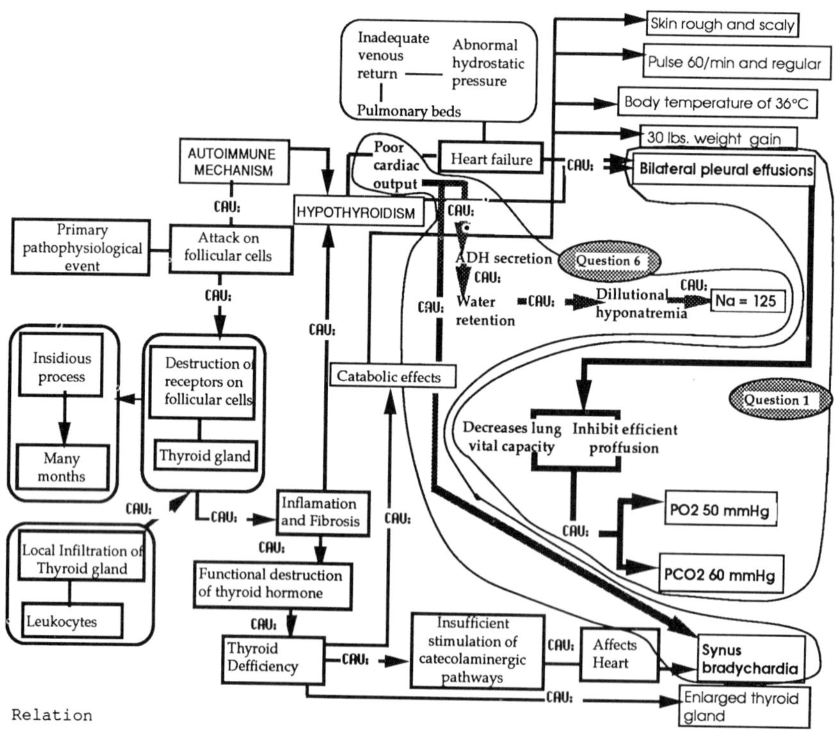

CAU: Causal Relation

Figure 2: Representation of Pathophysiology Protocol and Answers to Questions by Fourth Year Medical Student, Mapped onto Portions of the Reference Model.

by the student. Whereas the expert approaches the case at the clinical level (i.e., at the "shallow" level) the student's account emphasizes more the physiological process that causes the destruction of thyroid hormone production (i.e., at the "deep" level).

Figure 2 also shows the representation of the medical student's answers to questions mapped onto her pathophysiological representation. One feature of this representation is the mixing of levels in the pathophysiology, with a larger number of intermediate components which were not mentioned by the expert. The figure also reveals that this student's representation of the questions seems more coherent with his own pathophysiology protocol rather than with the expert's representation. Although matching more closely the reference model, the expert's representations of the questions are unrelated to one another; contrarily, the student uses common elements in the questions (e.g., pleural effusion common to questions 1 and 3; poor cardiac state common to questions 6 and 3). Students knowledge and problem solving can best be accounted for in relation to their own generated explanations of the process or responses to specific probes.

4. CONCLUSION

With increasing knowledge and expertise, there is a shift in the nature of anchoring points from basic science to clinical in order to generate a coherent explanation. To represent the approach taken by expert clinicians, then, a forward driven, reference model that includes only clinical information seems to suffice. However, less than experts use different sources of information which depart from those used by experts.

A problem arises when attempting to represent the solution procedures and the knowledge used by novice subjects. As pointed out previously, a reference model based on expert knowledge often fail to map novices' case representation. This is so not only because overlays do not capture novices' bugs or misconceptions, but also because they represent an expert's perspective, and therefore an expert's solution of the problem. Whenever there are multiple solutions to a problem (i.e., more than one way to conceive a given problem) it is useful to combine different types of representations.

One way of resolving the issue is to look at the development of novice problem representation as a process of building greater coherence in explanation. Instead of emphasizing the fit between expert and novice, the stress is on the degree of coherence of novices' representation of the explanation provided for the problem. Now, to uncover the coherence in their explanations, one may question further about the knowledge used, through probe questions, as it is done in this research.

The extension of this research can be envisaged in two directions. One is to look at the coherence in the student explanations using computationally oriented programs. We have begun some attempts in this direction. The second is to look at progressions of student explanations within the ITS framework, where the shifts in the directionality of reasoning, e.g., from backward to forward reasoning, with increase in expertise can be studied.

REFERENCES

[1] Arocha, J. F., Patel, V. L., & Frasson, C. (1990).Cognitive diagnosis of expert-novice performance in medicine. (Tech. Rep. No.CME90-CS05) Laboratory of Cognitive Studies in Medicine, Centre for Medical Education, McGill University.

[2] Chandrasekran, B. & Sanjya, M. (1982). Deep versus compiled knowledge approaches to diagnostic problem solving. In: Proceedings of the Annual Meeting of the American Association for Artificial Intelligence.

[3] Clancey, W., Letsinger, R. (1984). NEOMYCIN: Reconfiguring a rule-based expert system for application to teaching.: In Clancey, W. & Shortliffe, E. (Eds.), Reading in Medical Artificial Intelligence: The First Decade. (pp 361-381) Reading, MA: Addison-Wesley.

[4] van Dijk, T.A. & Kintsch, W. (1983). Strategies of Discourse Comprehension. New York, NY: Academic Press.

[5] Ferraris, M., Midoro, V. & Olimpo, G. (1983). Diagnostic testing and the development of CAL remedial sequences. Proceedings of the Educational Technology and Computers in Education Meeting, Winnipeg, Manitoba, Canada.

[6] Frederiksen, C.H. (1985). Cognitive models and discourse analysis. In C.R. Cooper & S. Greenbaum (Eds.),Written Communication Annual: An International Survey of Research and Theory, Volume 1: Studying Writing: Linguistics Approaches. Beverly Hills, CA: Sage.

[7] Gaines, B.R. & Boose, J. (Eds.) (1988). Knowledge Acquisition for Knowledge-Based Systems. New York: Academic Press.

[8] Glaser, R., Lesgold, A. & Lajoie, S. (1987). Toward a cognitive theory for the measurement of achievement. In R.R. Ronning, J.A. Glover, & J.C. Conoley (Ed.), The Influence of Cognitive Psychology on Testing (pp.41-85). Hillsdale, NJ: Lawrence Erlbaum.

[9] Groen, G.J. & Patel, V.L. (1988). The relationship between comprehension and reasoning in medical expertise.

In M. Chi, R. Glaser & M. Farr (Eds.), The Nature of Expertise. Hillsdale, NJ: Lawrence Erlbaum.

[10] Mandl, H. & Lesgold ,A. (1988). Learning Issues for Intelligent Tutoring Systems. New York: Springer-Verlag.

[11] Ohlsson, S. & Langley, P. (1988). Psychological evaluation of path hypotheses in cognitive diagnosis. In: H. Mandle & A. Lesgold (Eds.). Learning Issues for Intelligent Tutoring Systems. New York: Springer-Verlag.

[12] Patel, V.L. & Groen, G.J. (1986). Knowledge based solution strategies in medical reasoning. Cognitive Science, 10, 91-116.

[13] Patel, V.L., Arocha, J.F. & Groen, G.J. (1986). Strategy selection and degree of expertise in medical reasoning. Proceedings of the Eighth Annual Conference of the Cognitive Science Society (pp. 780-791). Hillsdale, NJ: Lawrence Erlbaum.

[14] Patel, V.L., Evans, D.A. & Groen, G.J. (1989). Biomedical knowledge and clinical reasoning. In D. Evans & V. Patel (Eds.), Cognitive Science in Medicine: Biomedical Modeling (pp. 49-108). Cambridge, MA: MIT Press.

[15] Patel, V.L., Groen G.J. & Arocha, J.F. (in press) Medical Expertise as a Function of Task Difficulty. Memory and Cognition.

[16] Patel, V.L., Groen, V.L. & Frederiksen, C.H. (1986). Differences between students and physicians in memory for clinical cases. Medical Education, 20, 3-9.

[17] VanLehn, K. (1988). Student Modeling. In: M. Polson & J. Richardson (Eds.). Foundations of Intelligent Tutoring Systems. Hillsdale, NJ: Lawrence Erlbaum.

[18] Wenger, E. (1987). Artificial Intelligence and Tutoring Systems: Computational and Cognitive Approaches to the Communication of Knowledge. Los Altos: Morgan Kaufmann.

Computers in Education
A. McDougall and C. Dowling (Editors)
Elsevier Science Publishers B.V. (North-Holland)

The Repertory Grid as a Medium for Investigating Teacher/Pupil Perspectives on Educational Software

W.Bell, E.S.Harri-Augstein

Centre for the Study of Human Learning,
Brunel University, Uxbridge, Middlesex, UK

Studies undertaken in relation to education software have generally been of an evaluative nature, and mainly pertained to the teacher or educational researcher. The aim of this research is not evaluation but to investigate how both teacher and pupil perceive the type of educational software in use in schools. The methodology utilises traditional methods combined with the conversational repertory grid technique. The grids are being analysed using the Integrated Repertory Grid Suite of Programs, developed at the Centre for the Study of Human Learning at Brunel University, England. The effectiveness of the conversational method of repertory grid elicitation for this research, the possibility of it aiding the learning process, and its feasiblility for use with children, are also investigated.

The research population initially consisted of teachers and pupils from various schools in England and later included similar respondents from schools in Eastern Canada; hence enabling comparison to be possible.

1. SECONDARY RESEARCH.

The efficacy of educational software has often been of major concern to researchers. Investigators (see Kulik et.al. [1] study), have usually been concerned with evaluative methods utilising control groups and concentrating on measuring performance and achievement. Hooper [2] considered evaluation based on records of achievement was not a valid test of the particular kind of learning experience promoted by computer aided learning.

There have been some who have considered attitudes, such as Beynon [3]. Geyer [4] explored 'cognitive mapping' in an attempt to find out how teachers perceive software, through using a set of provided instructions for analysing a particular item of software. The oonclusion from this exploratory study was that the technique had a place in the evaluation of software. Safrit et.al [5] utilised protocol analysis with verbal reports as data.

While some researchers have considered the views of the pupils, for example Mohamedali et.al.[6] who investigated the beliefs that children hold about computers, a number have concentrated only on the viewpoint of the teachers. Yasdani's [7] opinion on the subject is very clear. He considers that the pupil's views should be seriously taken into account when evaluating software, and that too much attention is paid to the teacher's view. He puts forward the hope that the pupil's view becomes the first and foremost influence in evaluating software.

While results from the evaluation of educational software have often been favourable, there have also been critiques. Self [8] considered that the widespread belief that we already had good educational software seemed to him to be entirely unfounded. The view of O'Shea & Self [9] was that the main effect of the microcomputer revolution was to decrease the average quality of computer software.

Hence, the actual users' viewpoint, and an approach, albeit without an evaluative aim, that takes into consideration the thoughts and feelings of their experience of educational software would seem to be required.

2. PERSONAL CONSTRUCT THEORY.

In this theory, Kelly [10] provided a model in order to facilitate understanding of the manner in which people construe, i.e. place an interpretation on, events. He presented his theory in terms of one fundamental postulate and twelve corollaries. Pope and Keen [11] indicate how certain corollaries can relate to the various educational ideologies. Kelly perceived learning as a personal exploration, and said that in order to participate the teacher must gain some sense of what is being seen through the child's eyes (Kelly [12]).

The repertory grid was developed as a practical means of utilising the theory embodied in personal construct theory. This is the main tool that is used to facilitate this research, combined with its conversational use. The process has parallels with a structured interview, but it is formalised by the use of a two dimensional array to contain relationships of elements -

events pertaining to the subject matter, and constructs - ways of thinking about these events. The elements must be representative of the person's experience of the area being investigated. Meaning is attributed to the elements by specifying relationships between them, their similarities and differences, hence the resulting bipolar constructs. The remaining elements are then assigned to the poles of the constructs.

To understand the views of another individual, the conversational approach is necessary. This is based around the respondent's thoughts and feelings on the grid topic. The elements and constructs are elicited from the respondent in his/her own terms. During and after the elicitation, the researcher encourages reflection, review and development of understanding, again in the respondent's terms. As the conversation develops, the researcher may offer his/her own understanding of the topic as a contribution, but it is the respondent's view that is of primary importance (see Thomas and Harri-Augstein [13]).

3. METHODOLOGY.

For an initial assessment of the situation, a method incorporating elements of the survey and ethnographic type of research was undertaken. This exploratory phase consisted of participant observation in the classroom and questionnaires posted to a wide variety of schools in England. Following this preliminary investigation, repertory grids were then elicited, first from respondents in England, and later from respondents in Eastern Canada. The purpose of the grid was to investigate how teachers and pupils perceived educational software; hence the elements consisted of the various types of educational software most commonly used in schools. Further questionnaires are being devised to enhance the findings.

4. POPULATION.

Teachers who were requested to complete the preliminary questionnaire were from lower, middle, upper, independent and special schools in England.

The respondents completing the grids initially were teachers and pupils mainly from the Bedfordshire area of England. The pupils' ages ranged from nine to fifteen years. Besides those from state schools, pupils from an independent school were selected. Included in the state section was a unit for maladjusted children. Later in Eastern Canada the respondents were teachers and pupils from public schools. The pupils' ages ranged from nine to seventeen years.

5. REPERTORY GRID ELICITATION.

The decision was to provide shared sets of experiences, i.e. elements. This was accomplished by involving teachers and pupils in a brief discussion to enable the identification of these experiences, subsequently to form the elements of the grid. Results from the preliminary investigation revealed that while initially the type of software used in schools followed explicitly the traditional style of teaching, and was very dependent on initial expository learning, teachers had begun to think how the microcomputer could be used to develop children's thinking skills, and to stimulate and involve more child-centered learning. The computer programming language Logo, considered to be more related to pedagogy, was increasingly being used. Word processing was found to enhance communication skills. Database software introduced serendipity learning whereby pupils gained knowledge by being proficient at browsing through a database. Adventure games provided an environment for learning and a break away from didactic teaching methods and receptive learning. These topics related to the following educational philosophies: discovery learning, simulation, game-playing, drill & practice, and tutoring.

The information gleaned from the preliminary research, and discussions with teachers and pupils made the selection of educational software for the repertory grid topical.

Forms containing a two dimensional array were used to contain the grid. The elements, consisting of the various types of educational software selected, were assigned to the column headings. These elements were also written separately on cards and then selected randomly in sets of three, i.e.triads. Verbal statements, specifying in what respect two out of the three were similar and how the third differed, were elicited conversationally in the respondent's own terms. A symbolic rating system was applied to these poles and entered in the grid under the relevant element column headings, and the verbal statements were also entered. The remaining elements were then also rated in respect to these verbal statements and entered in the same row of the grid. These discriminations between experiences are termed constructs. On completion of one row, another three elements were randomly selected and the process repeated for the next row. The ensuing conversation was tape recorded on each occasion.

But it was soon evident how time consuming the grid procedure was; hence a large number of respondents was not feasible. It proved beneficial to make three or four hour-length visits, if possible, for each pupil. This allowed them sufficient time to converse initially about the elements, eventually to fully explain their constructs and to prevent concentration lapse. The difficulty lay in condensing their rather verbose explanations to brief statements for construct pole descriptions, whilst ensuring that they were in agreement with the result.

The teachers stated that while they

considered the grids to be hard work, requiring deep thought, they enjoyed the exercise.

6. ANALYSING THE GRIDS.

While the raw grid clearly shows the person's repertoire of personal constructs, and how each element is assigned to the poles of each construct, it does not display the total pattern of personal meaning that lies hidden within it.

The following CSHL computer programs were utilised to reveal the personal meaning from the grid.

(i) The FOCUS computer program is based on modifications of McQuitty's Cluster Analysis [14]. The software involves re-ordering the rows of constructs and columns of elements to produce a grid in which every pair of adjacent rows and columns has more in common than any other arrangement. The program also calculates a percentage match of both element and construct clusters.

(ii) The SPACED FOCUSED GRID provides a display in which the spacing between columns and rows reflects the degree of similarity between adjacent elements and constructs. Hence, the resulting grid clearly illustrates how particular elements are perceived by the respondent as offering very similar experiences.

(iii) The CHANGE GRID shows how a respondent's view of a topic changes over time.

(iv) EXCHANGE GRIDS reveal the measure of understanding and agreement on the particular topic between two respondents.

(v) SOCIOGRIDS allow the comparison of grids from groups of respondents. This software is being utilised to compare grids obtained from teachers and pupils in England with similar respondents in Canada. Socio-net diagrams can then be constructed showing the system of connections between participants.

7. INTERIM FINDINGS.

7.1. Teacher completed questionnaires.

Total number sent : 172
Number returned : 133

Software considered to be most useful:

- Logo
- Word Processing
- Information Handling/Database
- Adventure Games
- Simulations

The opinion expressed, by the majority regarding other software, was that it had been extremely poor. Some considered it was improving.

Teachers from special schools repeatedly commented on the fact that there was so little software suitable for the physically handicapped.

The comments relating to how the teachers perceived the use of the microcomputer in the classroom, varied according to the type of school.

- Upper schools-mainly enthusiastic.
- Middle & Lower schools- teachers still often apprehensive.
- Special school-teachers keen to learn more, realising the potential for the physically handicapped.

7.2. Observations from schools visited.

Discussions with the teachers revealed disdain at the premise that they were not considered able to distinguish between good and bad software, from an educational stance. While their evaluation was accomplished intuitively, rather than being based on any theoretical implication, Bork [15] emphasises that there is no substitute for the intuition of a skilled teacher.

Teachers were seen to be discarding the drill and practice type of software; even when they recognised a need for it, they were often apologetic about using it. The trend for the types of software favoured in the completed questionnaire was evident.

7.3. The raw repertory grid.

Kelly [16] suggested that grids should first be examined, before being statistically analysed, in order to see something of what the person may be telling us directly. On inspection of the completed grids, thoughts and feelings, via the verbal statements, described the users' perception of the various types of educational software.

The following are examples of recorded statements:

Perceptions-Educational Software in General.

<u>TEACHERS</u>

<u>Canadian</u>
Explorative,investigatory
Good for all age groups
Challenging
Pupil always keen
Majority show interest
Cognitive development
Either sex oriented

<u>English</u>
Stimulates discussion
Teaching asset
Confidence builder
Pupil resource
Trial & Error completion
Many ways of doing things

<u>PUPILS</u>

<u>Canadian</u>
Mainly telling-not asking
Little creative aspect
Good teaching tool for beginners
Teaches less adventurously
Quite simple to grasp
Can't do much with it

<u>English</u>
You decide in a fun way
Variety-many kind of things
Pre-planning often needed

Makes school topics more fun
Gives out facts and also tests
You learn something visually

Whereas the comments from the teachers were similar, the Canadian pupils did not perceive educational software, in general use, as highly as many of the English pupils did.

7.4. Computer analysis of repertory grids.

Grids are in the process of being analysed. The following gives a brief comparison of Canadian and English teachers' and pupils' perceptions, from a mode grid, of software that they consider offers similar/dissimilar experiences. Each construct in the mode grid has been obtained from an individual in the group; hence represents commonality of construing within the group.

TEACHERS:mode grid

Canadian
Highest match-86% Adv.Games/Bus.Games
Lowest match -28% Drill&Pract./Info.Handling

English
Highest match-86% Logo/Word Proc.
Lowest match -41% Logo/Drill&Pract.

PUPILS:mode grid

Canadian
Highest match-91% Word Proc./Info.Handling
Lowest match -35% Logo/Drill&Pract.

English
Highest match-91% Word Proc./Info.Handling
Lowest match - 8% Info.Handling/Games-general

Whereas the pupils differed in how they perceived educational software in general, they showed complete agreement, in their mode grid, in the way they considered word processing and information handling as offering very similar experiences. The high match of 88%, not shown above, for Logo with BASIC from the Canadian pupils' mode grid was rather surprising.

Socio-nets constructed from preliminary Sociogrid runs show the most highly matched participants as follows:

TEACHERS - matched at 59%-53% level
Four English-four Canadian.

PUPILS - matched at 64%-57% level
Predominantly English.

Three of the English teachers and all four Canadian teachers were teaching in schools for pupils in the 9-13 age range. A brief comparison of the software that some of these teachers perceive as offering similar/dissimilar experiences follows. The details were extracted from individual focussed grids; the highest and lowest matches only are shown but the trend in the relationships is apparent. They are listed in order of the highest match to the grid of Canada teacher.1 (Can.1) Can.1 grid was at the centre of a cluster formed from the four English teacher grids.

Highest match.
TEACHERS:individual grids

Can.1	Viewdata/Info.Hand.	100%	
Eng.1	Viewdata/Info.Hand.	91%	
Eng.2	Viewdata/Info.Hand.	90%	
Eng.3	Info.Hand./Logo	98%	(V/I-66%)
Eng.4	Viewdata/Expert Sys.	90%	(V/I-81%)
Can.2	Simulation/Adv.Games	93%	(V/I-75%)

Lowest match.
TEACHERS:individual grids

Can.1	Logo/Games-general	55%	
Eng.1	Info.Hand./Games-general	50%	(L/G-56%)
Eng.2	Expert Sys./Games-general	25%	(L/G-58%)
Eng.3	Control/Drill&Pract.	60%	(L/G-66%)
Eng.4	Logo/Games-general	63%	
Can.2	Info.Hand./Games-general	63%	(L/G-71%)

KEY
English teachers (Eng.1) etc.
Canadian teachers (Can.1) etc.
Viewdata/Info.Hand. (V/I)
Logo/Games-general (L/G)

The highest matching construct across all grids in this group was also in Canadian teacher 1 grid. The verbal labels for this construct differentiated between software for teaching new material and that to encourage memorisation.

The Sociogrid run which consisted of grids from this same group but with the mode grid included revealed the English teacher 4 grid to have the highest match with the mode grid, not Canadian teacher 1 grid.

The English and Canadian pupil grids did not show such a commonality of construing as the teacher grids. The pupil commonality was more evident within nationality.

While the pupil mode grids gave an identical result for software having the highest match, further examination of these grids revealed some disparity.

Example:
CANADIAN RESULT WITH COMPARABLE ENGLISH %.

	Canadian	English
Control/Info.Hand.	81%	46%
Logo/Info.Hand.	76%	58%
Logo/Drill&Pract.	35%	70%
Logo/Curric.Specific	38%	61%

ENGLISH RESULT WITH COMPARABLE CANADIAN %.

	English	Canadian
Adv.Games/Bus.Games	90%	48%
Word Proc./Drill&Pract.	88%	46%
Games-gen./Viewdata	13%	65%
Simulation/Info.Hand.	18%	63%

8. PRELIMINARY CONCLUSIONS.

8.1. Teacher/pupil perception of educational software.

The responses to the first questionnaire completed by teachers from English schools showed that they were not unduly impressed with the educational software available at that time. Data obtained from questionnaires, currently being completed, combined with statements elicited by utilising the repertory grid technique, reveal that teachers from both England and Canada are now viewing the software more favourably. Word processing, Logo, information handling and databases are recorded as being the most used.

Pupils are generally of the opinion that the use of educational software is often an improvement on the traditional method of classroom teaching. But these grids have resulted in a wealth of data revealing how teachers and pupils perceive and discriminate between educational software packages. Much more study is required in its interpretation.

8.2. The effectiveness of the conversational repertory grid technique.

The initial impression was that more information was being obtained from the conversation arising during the elicitation of the grid than from the resulting grid itself. But experience from previous research, which was dependent on methods other than grid usage, shows that extracting detail by conversation alone, compares unfavourably with that employing the combination of conversation and grid technique. Facts emerged without the problem of having to carefully phrase questions in order to obtain the required information. Hence, the use of the conversational repertory grid technique for this purpose is proving viable.

Grid forms and instructional literature were produced to enable grid completion by teachers, possibly without the need for assistance to be at hand. But this distance approach has so far not produced a satisfactory response rate. This points to the benefits arising from the use of the conversational technique.

8.3. Possibility of the elicitation aiding the learning process.

Pupils stated that in completing grids they came to the realisation that they knew so much more about the particular topic than the little knowledge they originally thought they had when initially asked to discuss it. A boy from the independent school was quite surprised when he realised what he had actually stated. He said that he could never have offered such statements if he had been asked directly. On reflection, he agreed with all of it.

While completing the grid a number of teachers, reflecting on educational software, stated that they had not realised they knew so much about it.

8.4. Feasibility of repertory grid use with children.

Fransella & Bannister [17] write that Kelly's triadic method of elicitation had been found to be too complex for children under 10 to 12 years of age. A quickly emerging fact has shown that the apprehension originally expected by attempting to elicit grids from children was misfounded.

The pupils mainly looked on the procedure as a form of game. They were at ease and engrossed when thinking about the grid, and seemed to find it quite easy explaining their feelings about their experiences. Often they were controlling the conversation. In many cases they were more inclined than the teachers to express their personal feelings on the topic. The teachers were apt to point out differences that were more technical and factual than personal.

It had been suggested that it may be impossible to expect pupils from the adjustment unit to complete grids. Initially this was far from being so; the pupils appreciated the one-to-one contact and gave very intelligent responses. Much usage of the computer in this unit enabled the pupils to have a greater knowledge of the various types of educational software than the case for pupils in other establishments visited. When a second grid was required, responses were not quite so enthusiastic and much relied on the conversational aspect. Smaller grids proved less tedious.

Bannister & Fransella [18] considered middle class children related constructs in a more individualistic way. The pupils at the English 'public' school may well be considered to belong to such a class. The responses they gave were distinctive and were offered after much thought and discussion.

8.5. Comparison-Canadian/English respondents.

Teachers

Data, resulting from further Sociogrid computer analysis, will enable much more detailed comparison between Canadian and English respondents to be subsequently carried out.

While word processing, information handling, database creation and Logo were the most commonly used software in schools contacted in both countries, Logo was generally not perceived quite so favourably by some Canadian teachers. They expressed the opinion that previously, when other educational software was extremely poor, Logo had a place in schools. They also thought it was more difficult for teachers to get 'comfortable' with. The respective mode grids showed that the English contributors were in favour of Logo, but this was not entirely so with the Canadians. With the number of computers in the classroom limited in Canadian schools, and word processing viewed so highly, it was pointed out that often there was little opportunity to use the computer for other purposes. The latter statement was often repeated by English teachers too. Drill and practice software was not highly appreciated,

particularly by the Canadian group.
The general impression from both groups of teachers was that educational software had improved considerably over the years.

Pupils

The Canadian pupils viewed certain types of software differently than English pupils. In particular adventure games, simulations and viewdata were mainly considerd by the Canadian pupils as entertainment with little educational value. The English pupils thought these types of software were both fun and educational. Both groups attributed educational value to word processing and Logo.

The English pupils were inclined to place more value on software of the kind that the Canadians associated with mundane school work. The Canadians were more critical and concerned that they should have control and a free hand. While the English also criticised software that was more computer controlled than pupil controlled they often found some aspect of it for appraisal from an educational point of view.

9. SUMMARY.

The responses arising from the elicitations lead to the following impressions of teacher/pupil notion of the ideal educational software.

Teachers: their concern is with the type of learning involved, whether it is a teaching asset, how it enables more self learning, whether it is pupil oriented, whether it holds the interest of a majority, and whether it has the possibility of cross curriculum usage.

Pupils: their major concern is whether it involves a fun element, that they should be controlling it-not just following instructions. They like software that makes them think, is creative, different, and that they can experiment with.

The general opinion was that these labels could be associated with the use of word processing, information handling and Logo, but definitely not the drill and practice type of software.

BIBLIOGRAPHY

[1] Kulik,J.A.,Bangert,R.L. & Williams,G.W. (1983). Effect of computer-based teaching on secondary school students. Journal of Educational Psychology,75(1).

[2] Hooper,R.(1977) National development programme in computer assisted learning:final report of the Director. Council for Educational Technology,London.

[3] Beynon,A.L. (1985) An investigation into the use of CAL and the dialogue strategy in a tutorial context. In Journal of Computer Assisted Learning.1(1),March/April 1985. Blackwell Scientific Publications.

[4] Geyer,T. (1987) Probing a student teacher's cognitive structure of software. In Journal of Computer Assisted Learning.3(2) June 1987. Blackwell Scientific Publications.

[5] Safrit,M.J.,Ennis,C.D. & Nagle,F.J. (1988) The use of problem solving skills in computer-aided instruction:an evaluation. In Journal of Computer Assisted Learning 4(4) December 1988. Blackwell Scientific Publications.

[6] Mohamedali,M.H., Messer,D.J. & Fletcher B.(C).(1987) Factors affecting microcomputer use and programming ability of secondary school children. In Journal of Computer Assisted Learning 3(4) December 1987. Blackwell Scientific Publications.

[7] Yasdani,M. (1988) Tutoring systems:some questions we keep asking ourselves. In the Quarterly Newsletter of the Society for the Study of Artificial Intelligence & Simulation of Behaviour. No.64 Spring 1988.

[8] Self,J.(1985) Microcomputers in Education:A Critical Appraisal of Educational Software.Sussex:Harvester Press.

[9] O'Shea,T.& Self,J.(1983) Learning and Teaching with Computers.Artificial Intelligence in Education. Sussex:Harvester Press.

[10] Kelly,G.A.(1955). The Psychology of Personal Constructs, Vol.1,2. W.W.Norton & Co.Inc, New York.

[11] Pope,M.L.& Keen,T.R.(1981). Personal Construct Psychology and Education. Academic Press. London & New York.

[12] Kelly,G.A.(1970). Behaviour as an Experiment. In Perspectives in Personal Construct Theory. (D.Bannister, ed.) Academic Press, London & New York.

[13] Thomas,L.F. & Harri-Augstein,S.(1985) Self-Organised Learning. Foundations of a Conversational Science for Psychology. Routledge & Kegan Paul plc.London.

[14] McQuitty,L. (1966) Single and multiple hierarchical classification by reciprocal pairs and rank order types. Educational Psychology Measurement 26.

[15] Bork,A.(1989) Suggestions for Developing Technology Based Learning Material. In Interactive Learning International 5(1) Wiley. Jan/Mar 1989

[16] Kelly,G.A.(1955). The Psychology of Personal Constructs, Vol.1,2. W.W.Norton & Co.Inc, New York.

[17] Fransella,F. & Bannister,D.(1977) A Manual for Repertory Grid Technique. Academic Press, London New York San Francisco.

[18] Bannister,D. & Fransella,F.(1971) Inquiring Man. Penguin Books, London.

Computers in Education
A. McDougall and C. Dowling (Editors)
Elsevier Science Publishers B.V. (North-Holland)
IFIP, 1990

A NEW APPROACH: COURSEWARE ENGINEERING

M.N. BESSAGNET (*)(+), T. NODENOT (*)(+), G. GOUARDERES (*)(+), J.J. RIGAL (+)

(*) Laboratoire A.P.I., UPS, 50, chemin des Maraichers, F-31062 TOULOUSE - Tel: (33) 61 52 92 32

(+) LICIAP, Universite Sciences F-64000 PAU - Tel: (33) 59 02 93 93

The low production in the domain of courseware/I.T.S. Software Engineering is widely due to the lack of dedicated CASE tools and to the dullness of existing production tools. In this paper, we present a Software Engineering approach whose objective is to integrate the realization phases in a larger process, involving the life cycle of courseware/I.T.S. Serving this purpose, we introduce an architecture, hierarchically organized on three levels of abstraction: I.C.E.S. (Integrated Courseware Engineering System), M.D.S. (Multimedia Didactic System), courseware/I.T.S.

1.INTRODUCTION

Software Engineering keeps growing. The availability of an Integrated Project Support Environment (I.P.S.E.) is a major change to drastically increase the productivity of software industry and offset the software crisis. The underlying causes of that crisis can be summarized as follows : lack of documentation/traceability, lack of prototyping, lack of software reuse,... In fact, the complexity of large software projects is difficult to manage. In the works of J. Hewett and T. Durham [1], we can note the efforts of US companies for CASE tools development (Computer Aided Software Engineering) to provide environments, supports and automation for software engineering methods.

In the same way, company requirements for Computer Assisted Learning (C.A.T./C.A.L.) and multimedia development are on the increase even though the domain cannot provide to the needs. But, opposed to previous phenomena, if a crisis exists, it is the deep lack of courseware and Intelligent Tutoring Systems (I.T.S.).

In this context, the use of Software Engineering methods and tools applied to C.A.T./C.A.L. would favour courseware/I.T.S. production. *An Integrated Courseware Engineering System (I.C.E.S.)* [2] will allow a more efficient development of courseware or I.T.S : in the first part, we shall analyse the causes of the low production of courseware : regarding software engineering methods and tools, we shall see why the production of courseware is long and difficult. Next, we shall detail an representative I.C.E.S. product : *Multimedia Didactic System (M.D.S.)*. We also shall see the role and structure of an I.C.E.S.

2.THE PRESENT PRODUCTION OF COURSEWARE ITS LIMITS.

There are now two classes of tools from which courseware can be developed : authoring languages and authoring systems which sometimes serve the same purpose but whose methods are different.

2.1. The published studies

In the last few years, several studies have been devoted to courseware in France :

- The study by F. Madaule and col. [3] enables us to know the different functionalities required for courseware development.
- Thanks to the study by B. Diawara [4], it is possible to complete these functionalities by those of Dr Leo's system for the Macintosh.

C.A.T./C.A.L. systems have followed the evolution of computers. They were first developed for mainframes (like PLATO or IMG), then for mini-computers. As regards the courseware for personal computers, more than forty-six authoring systems or languages can be found on the French market. Because of the large variety of such systems, many managers think it is no longer necessary to question the value of the tools themselves since they exist, but rather improve the products (courseware). They think the market will develop only if high quality products exist.

2.2. Limits of the production

We can notice that all the studies published so far, have been devoted to comparing the different tools included in the available authoring systems or languages of the market. These tools are used to implement the courseware. But the life cycle of a courseware can be divided into three main stages :

- *design*
- *realization (mediatization) (*)*
- *evaluation of the product.*

We should add the *distribution and maintenance* stages in the industrial production context. Different documents, software and people are commited to each stage. These studies and an experiment carried out in our laboratory (CLAPER's project) will enable us to analyse the various elements and to show the limits of such a development.

A brief preliminary analysis enables us to define the design process. It consists in making the initial choices (subject, themes, targets) and wondering about the feasibility of the courseware system (cost/benefice study). Most often, this choice will depend on whether the existing courseware are adapted to the problem one has to solve.

2.2.1. The design phase

It consists in a teaching analysis i.e. the description of targets and teaching strategies. There seem to exist three elements in any courseware system[5] :

1- "pedagogic model" : mastery of subject.
2- "didactic model": the strategies to be used
3- "mediatic model" : the different tactics that can be used to respect strategies.

To define the different models, the pedagog generally resorts to a method of analysis which separates the problems linked to the teaching analysis from those due to the means at his/her disposal. Whatever the method adopted [5] [6], the result of this stage is a "paper model" which has the following drawbacks :

- a large and heterogeneous mass of information,
- difficult filing,
- tedious and hazardous updating,
- difficult communication between the users.

Because of the procedure adopted, the freedom of the teacher is limited during the mediatic modelization by the tools he/she will have at his/her disposal. We think this is true whatever the authoring system ; the risk is that the courseware can be limited by the capabilities of the authoring system that has initially been chosen. Moreover, the pedagog will find it difficult to perceive the interactions between the different models.

2.2.2. The realization phase

This is the most concrete phase in the development of a courseware (implementation of the product). What has to be done with an authoring system is to build the screens, standardize the coding of the system (colours, zones,..) and foresee the exchanges between system and learner. This forces the user to know how to use the software and also to understand the principles of mediatization. Difficulties appear which are due to the various ways the paper model (from the design phase) can be interpreted. One can wonder whether it would not be better if the same person was responsible for the two stages ? On the other hand, the pedagog is not necessarily able to implement the principles of mediatization with his/her authoring system.
Other problems may appear :

- The choices made during design can become criticizable during realization. In our experiment (CLAPER), the implementation of one "drill and practice" was not possible, due to enormous quantity of answers to be analysed. This gap between design and realization steps is measured after the mediatization. A return to the previous phase was made necessary which increased the overall cost.
- Pedagogic debugging (to improve the courseware content) assumes that the author-designer can (in a first step) simulate learners' behaviours. The authoring system must include a "learner-mode". But, it is necessary to create screen-pages, dialogs,...
- Quality of documentation and its easy availability can have an effect on lead time. Built-in on-line help-features are widely recommended.

(*) The mediatizeur is for us the specialist who sets up the finish product (courseware) according to the requirements of both the computer scientist and the teaching staff.

2.2.3. *The validation phase*

It can be active during the preceding steps. It consists in validating the courseware on three qualification levels : pedagogic, formal and logic. It is a crucial point within courseware development. The design phase is often questionned and revisions cost a lot. Another team of pedagogs works for real. Courseware and also its related documentation (installation and use) are evaluated. At this stage, problems arise :

- Portability : in France, due to the wide variety of hardware, it was impossible to evaluate an upgraded version of our courseware.
- The lack of reception facilities such as ARDEMI [6] to favour the consistency of courseware production.
- The lack of flexibility of the courseware which prevents the user from making any adaptation.

2.2.4. *The distribution phase*

The product distribution depends on countries. In France, supported by traditional organizations (the book trade channel), the distribution product turned out to be ineffective because there is no mastery of the product specificity [7]. In the United States, this distribution is supported by specialized shops. The same network is not possible in France : the solution must take into account national background.

2.3. Authoring systems and Software Engineering

Nowadays, most courseware are developed from authoring systems. These tools are very succesful with the developers who are teachers more than computer scientists.
In his research, M. Lehman [8] enumerates the qualities required from software. Some of these play an important part in C.A.T./C.A.L. : courseware should be satisfactory, adaptable and versatile.
Unfortunately, courseware computerized with the help of authoring systems do not fill these requirements.

-> satisfactory
Contrary to classical data-processing applications, it is impossible to prove a courseware is correct. Courseware are not bounded by complete and reliable theories but on cognitive psychology. However, a courseware has to be satisfactory : while the system is being used, it must be able to adapt itself to the reactions of the learner. Thanks to the tools integrated in an authoring system, it is possible to achieve the mediatization of the courseware. These tools can be compared to those that computer scientists use to code their programs. Studies in software engineering have shown that the development of satisfactory software depends on the integration of the coding phase in a wider process : the whole life cycle.

Similarly, an authoring system is too narrow a tool. The realization tools have to be completed by a set of educational functionalities enabling us to take into account the life cycle of a courseware. It is absolutely necessary to have tools that can define as completely as possible the different models (pedagogic, didactic, mediatic). To this end, a stage of "modelizing" simulation (a simulation to specify the concepts - Fig. 2) must be integrated in the process of development so as to validate these models before the realization stage. Thanks to validation techniques such as prototyping currently used in software engineering, it is possible to complete such systems.

-> adaptable
In C.A.T./C.A.L., more than in another activity using data-processing, there is a permanent dialog between the machine and the learner, so that any inadequacy will appear as soon as the courseware is being used. This is why the courseware must be thought as something dynamic that can easily evolve if necessary. The structure of the system - and more specially of the process of development - conditions the efforts necessary to transform a partly inadequate system into a satisfactory product.
Most of the existing authoring systems are limited to the tools they include : so that the courseware systems they produce are limited too. Though, they have some weak points (methods, functions), they are frozen. This lack of adaptability is the consequence of their structure.

Since 1983, numerous structures of I.P.S.E. have been offered. Among them, the P.C.T.E. norm [9] seems to be the most successful in Europe. It offers a layer architecture for I.P.S.E. Through this architecture, it is possible to build :

- a quite stable I.P.S.E. in a continually changing technology,
- an "open" I.P.S.E. that can be adapted to varied projects and take advantage of the improvements of hardware and software.

In Europe, research is coordinated in the framework *DELTA* project (Developing European Learning Through Technological Advance). Several action lines are defined to produce a European norm *"Portable Educational Tools Environment (PETE)"* on the learning systems. This large project aims at structuring high technology applications on multimedia learning tools development : the results must give functional specifications about a tool set in a student-pedagog environment [10].

->versatile
The adaptability of a system is an external quality that can be noticed by the users. Only the software engineers realize how necessary it is for a system to be versatile.
The technical characteristics of computers (cards, microprocessors,...) are improving very rapidly, and so it is important to have versatile courseware at one's disposal. At the moment, an authoring system produces courseware for a specific computer. From an economic point of view, this cannot be accepted - because of the high cost of development -. Software engineers are now able to develop versatile programs thanks to configuration and the specification of generic interfaces.

3. COURSEWARE ENGINEERING

These three requirements (satisfactory, adaptable, versatile) are rarely found so that the industrial production of courseware is not yet possible. Some difficulties due to the representation and manipulation of knowledge can be solved by the techniques and tools of "artificial intelligence". Software engineering can help develop tools that authors need. This analysis has led us to introduce the concepts of Multimedia Didactic System (M.D.S.) and of Integrated Courseware Engineering System (I.C.E.S.) [2][11]. They integrate a set of methods and tools enabling us to conceive satisfactory, adaptable and versatile courseware.

3.1. M.D.S. for satisfactory courseware

We divide the courseware life cycle in five steps : design, simulation, realization, validation and distribution. We match each step with different kinds of tools using pedagogic objects, operations and allowing the generation of C.A.T./C.A.L. models (pedagogic, didactic, mediatic). We have already presented these different steps in recent publications [2][11].

Here, we expose the simulation phase whose principles are based on both techniques, software engineering and artificial intelligence. First of all, we remind the reader that two types of tools are provided to the author during the design phase :
- tools allowing conceptualization of pedagogic and didactic models, [12]
- tools allowing pages specification (mediatic model) [11].

These three initial models are kept in a "pedagogic knowledge base" and will be modified or exploited by the next steps (Fig. 1).

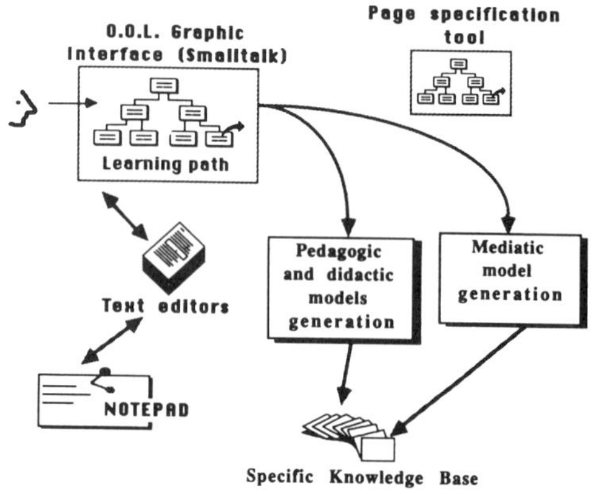

Fig. 1 : Design step

3.1.1. *The simulation phase*

During this phase, the pedagogic knowledge base can be modified and/or ratified by dynamic means. It consists in updating the first version of master model issued from design by testing it on student types defined by the pedagog. We previously mentioned it as a "modelizing" simulation.(Fig. 2)

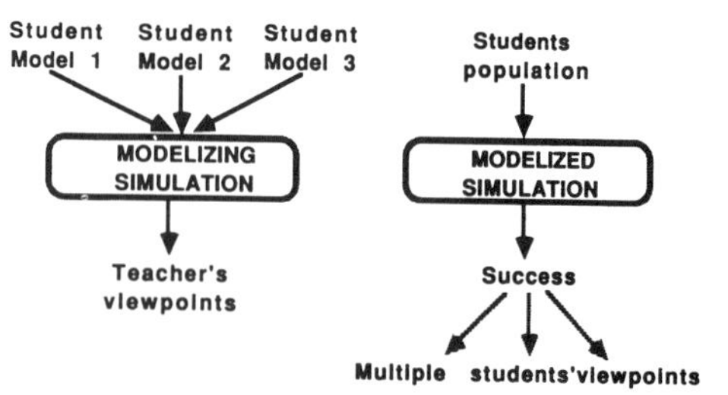

Fig. 2 : Two kinds of simulation

Current research tries to extend this simulation to specify I.T.S.- modelized simulation - (Fig. 2). At the end of this step, we have a ratified knowledge base but the courseware is not yet implemented. Thanks to this base, the author will be guided during the realization.

3.2. M.D.S for adaptable courseware

M.D.S. is made of various toolboxes according to courseware life cycle. Pedagogic constraints stemming from modelizing simulation and economic constraints also impose adaptation on the tools features to pedagogic requirements. Our purpose is not to define a super authoring system with extended functionalities whose cost would be prohibitive and pedagogic benefit, debatable. A second level of abstraction needs to be defined. This architecture (I.C.E.S.) will include computerization tools and supports to produce M.D.S..

3.2.1. The concerned parties

Three levels of users - learner, designer-teacher and courseware engineer - appear. Each plays a specific role in this architecture. At the I.C.E.S. level, only development and integration problems of computerized tools are taken into account. Two abilities are required for the courseware engineer : data processing and C.A.T./C.A.L..

3.2.2. The diagnosis phase

Tools used within the realization phase are diagnosed at the M.D.S. level from the author specifications (pedagogic, didactic and mediatic models).
For this purpose, actually we advocate two tools :

- The first consists in the use of an expert-system operating on the knowledge base (facts-base) and possible functionalities (rules-base)
- The second, an intelligent man-computer interface allows the author to specify his/her requirements.

Two cases may be encountered :

- Functionalities are already existing in the author M.D.S.. The realization step can begin.
- The diagnosis determines a lack of functionalities. The author cannot provide all the information required for an M.D.S. implementation. We need a last step on the I.C.E.S. Here, we need to determine which are the existing tools (market software, interface, specific software) which agree with the expected functions. The features of these tools are stored in a relational database which can be requested in two ways :
  - by the system, thanks to primitives enclosed in a software,
  - by the engineer, interactively.

The choices to be made can be directed by the aggregate knowledge about an existing M.D.S. :

- statistics on author satisfaction,
- knowledge about the target machine and its current tool features,
- knowledge about the author (his/her subject, his/her simulation valuation, ...)

This knowledge makes the adaptation of functionalities and interfaces possible (aids level, friendliness,...) to various users. The works of L.Giroux [13] on user modeling for a text-editor coach seem to be attractive to solve these problems. To end, the adaptability of the tools according to author requirements makes the end-product (courseware) *adaptable*.

3.3. M.D.S. for versatile courseware

The capacity of versatile courseware is obtained in two manners :
-> The software architecture of M.D.S. is based on Sceptre methodology [14] which advocates the portability by a kernel approach. It allows to integrate abstracted machine concepts. This recommended approach induces a three-logical-levels design in order to reduce M.D.S. development to a more general and more regular virtual machine programing. This implementation is non-dependent on the learner target-machine. A specification language (C.A.T./C.A.L. primitives) allows the definition of various M.D.S., whose portability depends on kernel implementation on the related target-machine.

-> Each M.D.S. "brick" is computerized at I.C.E.S. level within an object environnement in ADA [15].
The integration process is as follows :

a) The various bricks, initially are developed and integrated on the development station supporting I.C.E.S. (an meta-system approach for M.D.S. seems attractive). At I.C.E.S. level, we would dispose of an M.D.S. frame, initially empty of tools, but which would feature a user interface like Xwindow (*). The generated M.D.S can be easily tested by the courseware engineer.
b) The transport of the M.D.S. on the target-machine would be performed by cross-compiling, the interfacing problems being solved by the writing of an ADA package which simulates the performance of each Xwindow (*) primitive (such a package already exists in the Macintosh environment).

(*) Registred Trademark of M.I.T.

4. CURRENT DEVELOPMENT AND FUTURE PROSPECTS.

The interactions between both systems are showed after : (Fig. 3)

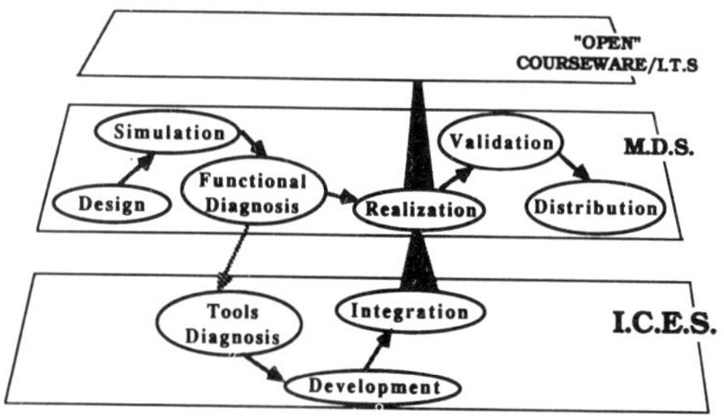

Fig. 3 : Interactions between M.D.S. and I.C.E.S.

At I.C.E.S. level, several remarks need to be made :

- The developed brick standardization brings reusability and therefore influences the potentialities of future M.D.S..
- A current study on C.A.T./C.A.L. systems shows that some invariants appear at the functional level which tends to make us think that the number of bricks required will decrease.

The courseware production advocated by M.D.S. - I.C.E.S architecture reveals different levels of contribution : tools, documents, communication between users,... Pedagogic orientations materialize during design work. They condition the application structure and the tools necessary to its realization, and the other way round.

This two-tiered architecture is an essential element to solve the problems that we raised in our introduction i.e. the fast production of "open" courseware, the lowering of development cost and specificity of each user's part- "the right man in the right place"-.

The I.C.E.S. ends the specification phase. Various tools (prototypes) are yet completed : design tools, simulation tools, standard editors for the realization functions,... We develop now the integration into the definitive system on HP9000 workstations.

The remainding problems are now :

- the development of the diagnosis functions,
- at the I.C.E.S. level, we have two "object-oriented" approaches : the Sceptre "object" approach versus the Smalltalk one. The Sceptre "object" approach introduces kernel supported primitives which allow normalization of each produced M.D.S. tool. The tools used in the design and simulation phases must be formally translated into this norm. On the other hand, we have to translate object formalisms issued from the simulation phase into production rules for the expert-system guide.

REFERENCES

[1] J.Hewett, T.Durham, *Computer Aided Software Engineering : Commercial strategies*, Ovum Ldt - 1987

[2] M.N.Bessagnet et al, *"Un Atelier de Génie Didacticiel Intégré"*, "Le G.L. et ses applications" -Toulouse- Déc.88

[3] F.Madaule et al, *Systèmes d'E.A.O. : étude comparative*, Revue TSI - Vol 6/1 Dunod - Afcet - 1987

[4] B.Diawara, *Etude comparative des langages-auteurs Duo, Arlequin et Dr. Léo*, TSI vol 7/1 -1988- p113-120

[5] G.Gouardères, *Présentation et manipulation des connaissances dans le dialogue Homme-Machine en E.A.O.*, Thèse d'état-Sciences. UPS Toulouse - 1986

[6] R.Guir, *Diagnostic et bilan d'une politique systèmatique de développement de l'E.A.O.*, TSI vol 7 n°1 - 1988

[7] J.P.Domecq, J.J.Rigal, *Etude économique des marchés de l'E.A.O.*, - Lab. CATT- Univ. de Pau - Fév.87

[8] M.Lehman, *Les propriétés souhaitées des produits logiciels et du processus de développement des systèmes logiciels*, Revue G.L. et S.E. N° 14 - Mars 1989

[9] *P.C.T.E. : a basis for a Portable Common Tool Environment. Functional Specification*, CEE, Bruxelles 1988.

[10] M.Lam, *DELTA*, Rapport intermédiaire - DGXIII, CEE - 1987

[11] T.Beltran et al, *"Une approche génie logiciel pour produire des Tuteurs Intelligents"*, "Les S.E. et leurs applications" - Avignon - Mai 89

[12] M.Kriaa, *Une Interface Graphique Interactive en L.O.O. pour le Prototypage et la Simulation de Logiciels Educatifs*, Doctorat d'Univ. UPS - Toulouse - 1990

[13] L.Giroux et al, *"User modelling for a text-editor coach"*, Séminaire IRIT - UPS Toulouse - 13 Avril 1989

[14] *Projet Sceptre : proposition de standard de noyau d'exécutif temps réel*, Rapport BNI n°26/2 - Sept.82

[15] G.Booch, *Ingénierie du logiciel avec ADA*, Interéditions - 1988

Computers in Education
A. McDougall and C. Dowling (Editors)
Elsevier Science Publishers B.V. (North-Holland)
IFIP, 1990

INDICATORS FOR A POLICY IN THE USE OF INFORMATION TECHNOLOGY

Patrick CHEVALIER

Conservatoire National des Arts et Metiers, Centre de Fromation de Formateurs (C2F), Unite Technologies Educatives et Maitrise de L'Information

1. INTRODUCTION

It appears obvious today (1) that the development of Educational Technology in Education relies closely on the expansion of information technology in society as a whole, and in the changes that are implicit in the area of *jobs and professions*, as much as in the *methods of* acquiring information and *learning*.
It is, in part, owing to this late awareness and probably also because of the lack of contact with the evolution of work, that Education has paradoxically been an area somewhat "on the fringe" in the use of these technologies. Whether it is a question of databases or basic knowledge, use of graphics, telematic or cable networks; the use of Information Technology has, until recently been somewhat *artisan and individual*. That may explain why their use has seemed much more to reproduce and reduce existing practices, rather than to construct new answers to the insistent problems in education and training. Under pressures from factors outside of the field of teaching, this use is, at present, tending to become *institutionalized and industrialized*.

The need is making itself felt today for the definition of policies and the facilitating of coordination whether at the level of an institution, a region, a country or even at the level of several countries for a certain type of population or problem.
This will allow a better coordination of efforts carried out in the actual field of training, and will also make training benefit from the efforts carried out in other domains, for example:
- placing in the hands of professional training tools which although not necessarily originally conceived for this purpose, have a very wide distribution in the area of information and can be used for producing, communicating or convincing.
- establishing links with the *research* which is starting to be undertaken on Information Technology in several disciplinary areas (Computer science, cognitive psychology, ergonomics, psychology of work, linguistics and so forth) beyond the strict field of professional training. It is however necessary for that, to have at one's disposal a conceptual framework and common experience which locates the use of technology in its proper context, and which defines in particular:
- the reorganization of contents and aims.
- a general model of the educational situation integrating the use of Information Technology.
- the different educational uses, the sort of devices being able to be set up, and their relationship with the activity of the users.

This is what we propose to outline in this article, adopting our usual point of view and preoccupations. To borrow the terms of Marcel Lesne (2): In the same way that we consider "educational action" as a particular "social action", we propose an analysis of the development of educational technology as a particular use of Information Technology in society.

2- THE REORGANIZATION OF CONTENTS AND AIMS

To repeat the terms of Claude Pair, "if computers rather than cars have a place in education, it's because the computer is not above all an extension of the hand, limited to one field of application, but an extension of the mind, of thoughts and of action"(3).
In the same way, if it is still completely useful to use audio-visual or computer technology for reasons of educational function (for example to demonstrate using graphics or simulation what cannot be shown by reality or by drawing on a blackboard); it is necessary to go further and rethink the aims of training, its content, method, and educational situation while integrating technology and keeping in mind the place that it has taken in work and social life.

2.1 understanding of technology.

Generally, jobs demand a minimum understanding of technology. This

understanding is not limited to a simple knowledge of the functioning of tools, it concerns equally a good understanding of the operations that they carry out. It also concerns new abilities linked to the operations that these tools allow us to carry out today, and to the mass of information that they use.
The use of tools of a similar nature in professional training naturally takes on meaning with regard to the knowledge they are prepared for, and this use allows us to integrate these evolutions directly, organizing the acquisition of knowledge and of professional know-how in the context of the use of new technology.

2.2 Technological culture.

It also takes on meaning with regard to the acquisition of a "technological culture" and the command of varied technology is also a part of the culture and professional identity, for it is one of the indispensable conditions for the understanding of job evolution and of its relationship with the others.
Acquisition of this culture constitutes the second aim and can derive from the use of the minitel for communicating with teachers as much as from access to a cable network for consultation of audio-visual documents. The contents of this culture vary from one job to another, but usually include the acquisition of basic concepts which allow an understanding of the elementary functioning of a computer, the use of automatons, of databases and communication network.

2.3 Skills about information.

The third aim concerns the general skills that need to be acquired. As a general rule, whatever the job may be, new technology through its possibility to store and to access important banks of information, ranks in secondary importance the memorization of information, and enhances the value of the use of tools, the elaboration of strategies and of methods of working.
It is moreover this which is very clearly emphasized in the report of the think-tank committee on the content of education which is chaired by Pierre BOURDIEU and François GROS (4)," We must resolutely give privileges to the teachers who are in charge of assuring the critical and well thought out assimilation of fundamental methods of thinking".."Giving an important place to all the techniques that are seldom the object of a methodic transmission although always demanded by all teachers, the use of a dictionary, the establishment of a file, the creation of an index, the use of databases, preparation of a manuscript, documentary research, use of computer facilities and understanding of tables of figures and graphics. To give every pupil this *technology of intellectual work* and, more rationally, instill them with more rational methods of work (such as the art of choosing between set tasks or distributing them in the time given) would be a way of contributing to the reduction of the inequalities tied to cultural heritage".

3. PATTERNS OF DESCRIPTION OF RESOURCES OF TRAINING USING NEW TECHNOLOGY

The research undertaken in the U.S.A.(5) in the domain of initial training show that the variable" nature of the chosen media" is seldom a proof of the efficiency of education and that, on the contrary, the *educational method* and its *relevance* with regard to the nature of training have a greater effect on the result (synthesis work on the whole research undertaken in the United States of America on the use of media in the teaching for the magazine AERA (American Educational Research Association).

This type of statement, which has been equally made in France and in the U.S.A. regarding the use of computers in children's education (6) can also apply to adults. The problem exists on how to describe and therefore how to evaluate the efficiency of training resources. In our opinion, this problem derives from the fact that media are easier to describe than the educational method effectively made use of. The media have, in fact, a tangible reality whilst the methods can only been characterized by a painstaking observation. The model that we propose below should be an improvement in the description of these methods and in the comparison and evaluation of educational practises using new technology.

3.1 Multimedia feature in its environment

The location of the means of training in their environment is indispensable. The following drawing supplies us with a first approach:

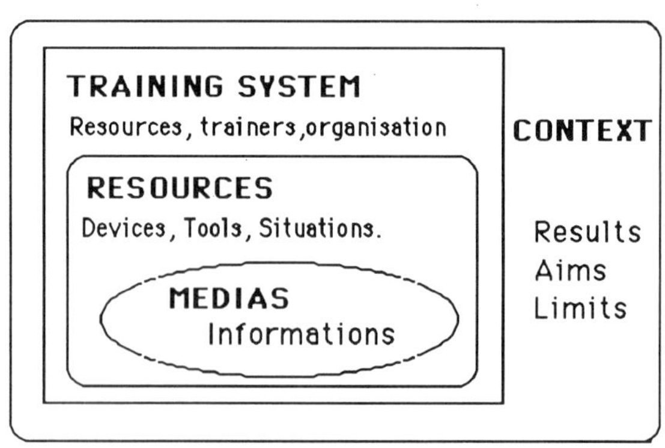

Figure 1

3.1.1 The global context.

Each training device must be referred to the *aims* that it has to achieve (facilitate social adaptation, increase professional mobility, etc.). It must also refer to the results it is supposed to have on the learner (acquisition of working methods, of concepts, of techniques,) as well as to the problems generated by its creation (length of time, budget, number of teachers, etc...).

3.1.2 Nature of the device.

The description of a system cannot be limited to the terms of the resources that it makes use of but must also mention the whole *means* and their *organization* (organization of the courses, organization of the means, mode of management of the "itineraries".

3.1.3 The user's activity.

To characterize the educational devices beyond their appearance and their technical reality supposes to describe the global *training situation*. In the case of multi-media devices, the model should, in our opinion, describe the training situation, locate the technical device in this situation and attempt to specify the link established between *information, knowledge and activity*.
As a first approach, we can describe the educational devices as devices for storage, transmission and processing of information used for carrying out activities or for learning.
We lay great emphasis on action and information processing. Most teachers agree today to say that the transmission of information is not everything and that knowledge cannot be reduced to a series of information or definition, whatever the quality of the layout may be.

3.2 The models of training situation.

This leads us to, first of all, separate a model which currently underlies the description of training situations and which does not take into account the activity of information processing carried out by the user with the help of the proposed device.

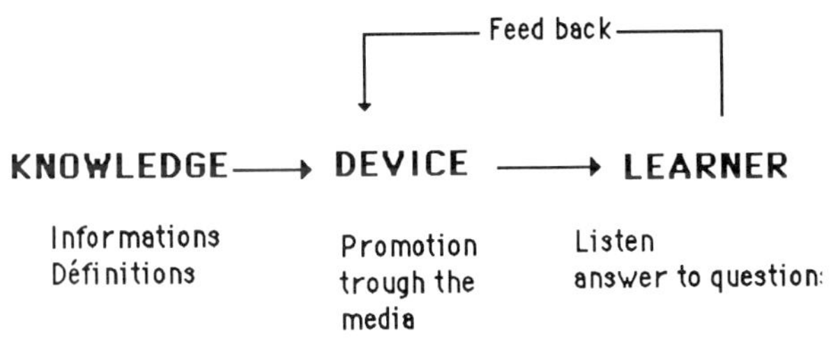

Figure 2

In this first pattern, the training situation is a situation, where knowledge and know how take place in a definitive way. The role of the device and of those who structure it consists of presenting, ordering, mediatizing. This diagram is inspired by the evidence of the processes which are already at work in the media. (T.V., press, communication, publicity and so on..) In this context, the message and its mediatization take into account the situation or the ideas of the reader or of the viewer, but completely condition his activity.

This second diagram is based on the idea that the learner acquires knowledge through his activity.

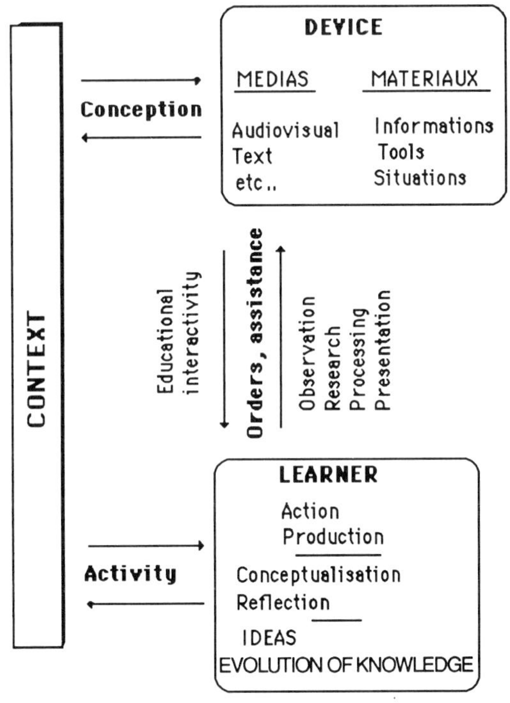

Figure 3

We can note that knowledge is situated on the user's side under the form of ideas ; In contrast, the device itself doesn't contain knowledge but materials, which will help the user to build his own knowledge. This is a fundamental distinction. To consider that a computer or an audiovisual document contains knowledge is a delusion; The pictures or signs are form, which only acquire meaning through an activity or an aim. This show the importance of the context.

These general reflections should help to pick out the educational methods used through devices that can be already seen on the market. This is what we have tried to do during numerous demonstrations and observations, of which the result is:

4. DEVICES AND USES OF INFORMATION TECHNOLOGY.

We resolve to integrate this point of view in our description of the devices, stressing the user's activity. Here is an illustration of these methods of analysis applied to three well known sorts of educational device presenting computers and other tools, such as:
- tutorials
- simulators and micro worlds
- aids for action and decision making

This list of uses is not definitive and must be moreover seen more as an illustration of our method of analyses, rather than as a typology which allows the classification of devices. We can, in other respects bring it closer to the distinction made by Bertrand SChWARTZ (7) between education programmed by computer, simulation and the heuristic approach.

Analysis is made all the more difficult that that new forms taken by multimedia resources are more often observed by automatic reference. The *programmed education*, which is one of the particular forms of computer contribution to teaching. In reality, extreme differences can be noticed between what could be called *automated educational resources* and the resources which have more similarities with the *professional software equipped with educational interfaces*. In these two cases, the computer holds a central place, but its function is radically different. In the first case, the computer comes out in an *automated manner*. The work of a teacher (who asks questions, interprets answers and takes decision). It is therefore the progression of the apprenticeship which is modelled and automated. In the second case, the computer is a *device* which carries out a task and does some of the work of a professional (editor, journalist or accountant). It is therefore in some way the knowledge to be learnt, or the know-how to be mastered, that are modelled and manipulated through the machine. The problem of usage of this device therefore becomes an ergonomic problem in the widest sense, and a problem of the power of the device made usable to the user.

4.1 Tutorials and the programmed education (Knowledge and Know how models)

Information (and here terms like content or subject are perfectly suitable) is divided into simple elements. These units are joined up either by already programmed sequences (automatic or set off by the user), or by decisions taken by the software according to information supplied by the user in the shape of answers to questions, or as a follow up to a choice.

The user looks at the graphics and diagrams and reads the texts, the more often at his own speed but sometimes in a controlled way. He answers questions, (closed or open), carries out procedures and so on although these activities are varied, they are guided and greatly structured by the device. The user can have a wide latitude of choice at a certain time, but he does not have much control over his own itinerary and has very little information about the reasons of the decisions taken by the device.

On the side of the device, the activity presented as being the most spectacular is the "*analysis of the answer*".
The limits of this work are in the nature of the computerized tools which can only *manipulate forms* (in this case, sequences and characters) independently of the meaning. The work of interpreting the user's response is therefore limited to a work of comparison of more or less complexe forms. The meaning floods out of this comparison under the shape of a commentary (sometimes laconic, sometimes humorist) or of a decision and a new action (communication of an information, guidance towards a unit of apprenticeship, etc..).
This generally *univocal meaning* will be confronted with another interpretation, that of the user. One can be sceptic about the convergence of these two interpretations, for the interpretation of the results by the user calls in a great number of parameters which are not communicated to the computer (could it be that it cannot use them without a global model of explanation of the activity of this user). These factors are well enough described in numerous works in the domain of cognitive psychology. It is a question, in particular, of the perception that an individual has of the task he accomplishes, the aims and the minor aims that he sets himself to fulfil this task, and the conceptions that he has on the subject he manipulates.
As J.F RICHARD and E. FRIEMEL show to illustrate the carrying out of operations on a calculator,(8) the *aims* and *input of knowledge* and *procedures acquired* furthermore play an important role in the way the user will represent to himself the task to be carried out, and for instance, will understand the terms of the question. This will also determine the idea that the user will have of the device he is using. The answer analysis should therefore be limited to closed domains where the risk of mistakes in interpretation are limited. In the opposite case, we will have to rely on more important means such as *knowledge database* or on methods of making the user *more active* :
- by proposing that he carries out operations which require the most interpreting work. For example, the analysis of answers, through the making available of information allowing him to interpret his results and to complete those which are provided by the tutorial. Some tools such as hypertext are completely appropriate to this purpose and facilitate the work of the tutorial, while they complete the work of the user.

We can use a resident hypertext (which can be integrated to any kind of computing application such as tutorial or work software) or an electronic notebook such as EBOOK3 (10), which allies the classic functions of hypertext to the possibilities of access to animated sequences, illustrations or exercises.

4.2 Simulators and micro-worlds
(The educational models of reality)

These device propose a *task* to be carried out or a *problem* to be solved with the aid of tools in a particular context. The device can be considered as an *environment* in which the user will work. We can use here the name of micro-world in so far as the aim to be achieved. The subject to be dealt with, the situation, the tools used are supplied to the user who finds himself in an universe with rules he has to accept. Certain devices use simulators in the strict sense of the term, and present the user with a reproduction as truthful to reality as possible.
Sometimes, the device reproduces only the work environment and possibly the shape of the information available about the problems to be solved, but the model does not react exactly in the same way as it does in reality. In this case, the user does not play with reality but he must accept the rules of the game and be aware of the possibilities to transfer abilities acquired from other situations. The educational methods at work can be linked to problem solving, simulation, role playing or case method.

The user finds himself confronted with informations coming from a model of the reality to be transformed, the tools to be used and the actions to be carried out. The production expected of the user is not necessarily limited to decision. It can be a question of intermediary stages in this process of decision making (synthesis rapport, files, arguments, project, article). but the action is always a reference for the user. Some simulations only allow an activity which is strictly working according to the procedure (sequence of precisely defined actions).
In some cases, the activity can be of the heuristic type (the steps and the intermediate aims are not defined at the beginning). Still, the action of the user and the results that he must obtain, are never conditioned by the device. It is twice interesting for the educational approach:
The *activity* of a user will be able to be described from the *use of the device*. That will facilitate the follow up of this activity, the possible aids and a thought on the part of the user on his activity (10). It is the confrontation with these models, and the awareness of the differences between the results expected and the results observed which are at the source of apprenticeship of know how and of the construction of models of the user. In the extreme, one can think that the user takes progressively the possession of the models which control the functioning of the device with which he is confronted. The quality of training depends in the great part on the quality of these models,the aptness of the proposed situations and the efficiency of the methods of communication between the model and the user.

4.3 Aids to action.
(the model tools and the models of use)

Today, these systems still not allow work stemming from the real tasks of the user but the realizations should be considerably developed with the production of aid to the computer tools. It is thus that the processing of texts or of tables has comprised for sometime, directions for use presenting essential functions and consultable aids to the initiative of the user. They integrate today guided visits, and interactive exercises in which the user works on the real tool whilst the training software follow this work, assuring the security of the tool and defining the ulterior steps.

The learner uses the device as a means, a guide which allows him to carry out a task. This device is either grafted or loaded onto the work device of aid and training but, in the two cases, the user must be willing to work. The production carried out takes on meaning in reality that is to say that it can have a use even partial outside of the device-user system, and beyond the time of use.

The user's activity is necessarily complex and global for it is aimed both at the result to be obtained, and on the use of the device. In fact, the aims of the action are not entirely provided and mastered by the device, so that the user has a wide freedom of action and can organize his own activity.
The skills that have to be acquired are not necessarily specified in detail. The aims are global and do not necessarily refer to one specific behavior. In contrast, the know how is, in a certain way, modelled by the tools that the users manipulate, rather than by the reality that has to be transformed.
Difficulties arising from the present knowledge allow us to give an account of human activity. On this point, much is expected from the research undertaken in the areas of ergonomics and cognitive psychology, to describe the activities of the users of computer devices. Let us hope that they will allow us to wider the area of this training beyond apprenticeship in the functions of tools or in the mastery of uses and techniques which are associated to them.

4.4 Interactivity of the devices and user's activity

We can easily imagine that they are a lot of varied uses of resources and training tools. Some research laboratories have therefore had to undertake very great research to modelize the process of training, the resources and to adapt them to this variety.

Bearing this diversity in mind, we can try to propose two tendances:
- The integration of a model of "learner" in the technical devices
- The research of the autonomy and the user's activity.

The first option aims to a maximum of *interactivity* which would make the *device* very *active*. It would take over the numerous functions of the teacher, in particular the follow up, the evaluation and the management of itineraries. This supposes the introduction of the most global pattern possible in the whole mechanism itself. This approach has been developed in the system based on simulation or in the tutorials using artificial intelligence. The principle of programmed education (ie. there is a device in the software which takes the decision concerning itineraries) but today's systems take a great number of variables into account. These variables can be independent and be affected by characteristics such as the age, the school level, the familiarity of the user with the concepts and so on.
They can also be affected by events happening at a certain time of the apprenticeship or be the result of the analysis of the global activity of the user, which is more complex. This would lead to an important complexity of the resources (the costs increase according to the efficiency of the device).

The second option would consist on working on the *ergonomic* and on the use made by teachers of *resources adaptation tools* for the "final user". Most of the time, this go along with the production of resources based on the fact that the user can take in charge his own itinerary. We must then invest on the ergonomic of the device and put the helps and methodological tools *in the hands of the user*.
These two options lead to other different options as far as the management of the training itinerary of the user is concerned in the global system. The decision making mode and the level of transparency of the selection criteria become then very important. Teachers and computers can go on mastering the decisions or, on the contrary, the device because of its structure (ergonomic and ease of use) or its elements (methodological means of training) can give the users the ability to master their itineraries. We shouldn't give more credit to one or the other of these two approaches, since it's possible to alternate them according to the aims, the subjects and the public. We must bear in mind that the inclusion of the learner's model in the device makes the generalization more difficult and requires a bigger investment on the device and on the technical means.
The second approach facilitates the *generalization* of the resources and reduce the cost for the devices. It requires an *investment on the skills* of the user as well as on the setting of methodological means of training and a certain familiarity which give them the autonomy of access to information. Isn't this one of the main aims of training?

5. CONCLUSION

The reflection on the contribution of Information Technology to education and adult training has hardly been outlined. There is still a lot to learn from the use of the first multimedia devices on the field as well as from the works started up in various disciplines and concerning various themes such as information, users' activities of devices of communication and information.
The testing of multimedia devices should contribute to this experiment, provided that there is a contact between the professionals of training and the research laboratories in order to define the fundamental questions, the axes of observation and the aims of development.
On the Educational level, professional of training must have a thorougful thought on the *status of information* and good knowledge in their field. They should envisage the structure, the form and the lay out of the information as well as the methods and the situations meaningful for this information.
This reflection could be based on the setting of observation methods of the real activity of device users. The methods issued in work psychology and cognitive psychology could be used as a basis as well of methods of observation of the real activity of the device's user.
This reflection would be of great help to define means of making the use of the devices accessible to a larger public.

(1) O.C.D.E. : New Information Technology, a challenge for Education : Paris 1986.
(2) Lesne M., Lire les pratiques de formation d'adultes, Ediling (France, Paris, 1984).
(3) PAIR C., Computing and the struggle against scholastic failure, Psychology française, December 1987.
(4) BOURDIEU P., GROS F. Le Monde de l'éducation, APRIL 1989.
(5) CLARK R., SALOMON G. AERA(American Educational Research Association).
(6) DUFOYER J-P., Computerized education and child's psychology. PUF (France, Paris, 1988).
(7) SHWARTZ B.: l'informatique et l'éducation. La documentation Française, (France, Paris,1981).
(8) RICHARD J.F and FRIEMEL E Apprenticeship of the use of a calculator. Psychologie Française, Paris (1987).
(9) SAVOY J. Le livre electronique EBOOK3, Techniques et Sciences Informatiques n°8,1988.
(10) CHEVALIER P., FARGE M., SUCHARD J., TIJUS C.A., Principles for an educational software workshop. I, in print.

Computers in Education
A. McDougall and C. Dowling (Editors)
Elsevier Science Publishers B.V. (North-Holland)

DESIGNING CAL PROGRAMS TO CATER FOR DIFFERENT LEARNING STYLES

John A. CLARKE

Psychology Department, Kelvin Grove Campus, Brisbane College of Advanced Education, Locked Bag No. 2, Kelvin Grove, Qld, Australia. 4059.

Recently, there has been a research interest in examining the effect of learning style on the performance of CAL users. There are difficulties in translating the research findings into practice. This paper is part of a continuing project which is attempting to do that. Earlier work by the author has highlighted the practical problems of identifying and measuring appropriate styles and designing programs to accommodate them. In attempting to address these problems, a style that not only seemed to influence CAL user behaviour but also could be measured quickly and reliably was identified. Data on the reliability of this measure was reported. This paper focuses on the predictive validity of different methods of incorporating the measure into a CAL program and the possible structure of a program. The different methods range from students responding to questions which measure their learning style to simply choosing which type of program they want. Familiarity with the content appears to be a major determinant of how students' styles interact with a program. Possible structures for programs are discussed. Future work will focus on the development of a specific program which does attempt to cater for different learning styles.

1. LEARNING STYLES

One of the most significant developments of the last decade in educational psychology has been the application of the concept of "learning style" or "cognitive style" to the understanding and improvement of how people learn. Although the concept has been around in some form for a long time (e.g. Gillingham and Stillman; 1936) and more explicitly in clinical and general psychology for some time (e.g. Witkin *et al;* 1962), its application to education in general (Kogan, 1971; Messick, 1970, 1976, 1984) and CAL in particular (Hedberg and McNamara, 1985; Sharma, 1987) is of relatively recent vintage.

Learning style has been defined generally by Kogan (1971) as

> ...individual variation in *modes* of perceiving, remembering and thinking or as distinctive ways of apprehending, storing, transforming and utilizing information. (p. 242)

The literature on, and variety of, learning styles is quite extensive. For example, see early reviews by Kogan (1971), Steinke (1974) and Messick (1970, 1976), recent reviews by Messick (1984), Driscoll (1987), Maricic (1987), Sharma (1987) and Joughin (1989) and annotated bibliographies by Barry and Sutton (1973), Nelson (1973) and Martens (1975). In many cases however, the identified styles differ more in name than in nature. The vast majority of learning styles can be classified into either a preference for a reasonable degree of structure and guidance to be provided in the learning situation or a preference for considerable freedom to choose the direction that learning should take. Essentially, this is preference for structured guided instruction versus unstructured discovery learning.

2. LEARNING STYLE AND CAL

Any computer assisted information system consists of three major components - hardware, software and the user. Since users process information in unique and preferred ways as determined by their particular learning styles, it is essential that style be catered for in the production of a CAL program. This aspect of human-computer interface has only received the attention of researchers and writers in relatively recent times. Hale (1981) notes the need for continued support of human factors dealing with human-computer interaction. Moran (1981) and Carroll and Thomas (1982) argue for an objective study of the user and for computer systems to be designed to fit the user. In the context of increasing use of computers for individualized instruction and computer-assisted learning, Barker (1982) in the early eighties noted the need for the development of a variety of interaction techniques that permit users to select modes of interaction that are best suited to their dispositions. Since then, there has been some work in this area e.g. "cognitive and visual style" was a topic at a recent world conference on Computers in Education (Baird; 1986) and there has been recognition of the need to cater for different learning styles in the well established logo approach (Clements and Gullo, 1984; Papert and Reinhold, 1986; Young, 1982). However, there are still consistent calls for the development of such materials (e.g. Chadwick and Watson, 1986; Duncan, 1985; Hammond, 1985; Jonassen, 1985; Phillips, 1986).

3. LEARNING STYLE AND CAL: PROBLEMS AND A POSSIBLE SOLUTION

Clarke (1989) identifies a number of practical problems associated with trying to cater for different learning styles in the production of CAL programs. The "problems" are the plethora of styles, the difficulty of obtaining a quick and reliable measurement, the incorporation of such a measurement into a CAL program and the production of appropriate versions of a given program to accommodate the variety of user styles. He also offers the beginnings of a possible "solution" to these problems in the form of the identification and reliable measurement of a learning style which not only subsumes many of the disparate styles reported in the literature but also is appropriate to CAL presentation.

Based on the earlier comments, such a style needs to range on a continuum from a preference for a reasonable degree of structure and guidance to be provided in the learning situation to a preference for considerable freedom to choose the direction that learning should take. Such a style has been identified by Pask and his co-workers (Pask, 1973, 1976; Pask and Scott, 1972). The two extremes are referred to as "serialists" and "holists". Serialists prefer to learn using a simple step-by-step strategy, focusing on essential facts which are well defined, sequentially ordered and related by simple links. They do not appreciate being distracted by anecdote, illustration and analogy. Holists on the other hand prefer a more global approach to problem-solving using more complex "globetrotting" strategies and, by contrast, thrive on anecdote, illustration and analogy. In utilizing a "global" approach, they concentrate on synthesizing broad descriptions into which details may be added later while serialists use a more "local" approach concentrating on specifics before any total overview emerges. Individuals who are able to use both approaches comfortably are referred to by Pask (1973) as "versatile". Entwistle (1978, 1981) summarizes the research associated with this serialist/holist style.

The style has been measured by various writers (Ford, 1985; Entwistle, 1981; Pask, 1973) using British samples. Clarke (1989) using an Australian sample developed a more reliable 13 item version of Ford's (1985) 18 item Study Preference Questionnaire (SPQ) There are a number of ways of using this information to cater for the different styles of CAL users. These are considered below.

4. INCORPORATION OF THE STYLE MEASURE INTO A CAL PROGRAM

It is assumed in this discussion that the CAL users are entering seriously into the learning task i.e. they wish to learn and they are not behaving as if they were involved in a leisure activity such as reading a book for relaxation purposes. Further, the research focusing on learning styles and CAL has invariably measured the user's style using a non computer-based procedure and independently of their involvement in the CAL activities. A more cost and time effective procedure would be to have any style measurement as an immediate prerequisite to the user's involvement with CAL. On the basis of these assumptions and requirements, allocation of CAL users to different versions of a program designed to suit their learning styles can be accomplished by any of the following procedures:

- Incorporate *one* question at the beginning of CAL lesson and allocate students according to their response.
- Incorporate a *small group* of questions at the beginning of the CAL lesson and allocate students according to their responses.
- Describe the possible ways in which the CAL lesson can be taken (structured vs unstructured approaches) and ask students to choose which they would prefer.

The work done thus far on each of these possibilities is now considered in turn. The empirical results reported in this section are based on the administration of the SPQ to 56 students involved in a one-year postgraduate preservice teacher education course at a large teacher education institution in Brisbane, Australia. All students had completed an undergraduate qualification at a different tertiary institution.

4.1 Allocation based on one question

The rationale here is to achieve the allocation as quickly and efficiently as possible and the process required is two-fold: First, a suitable question has to be found, and second, it has to be incorporated into a CAL lesson. First, the identification of the question:- The process used to reduce the 18 item SPQ to a more reliable 13 item version is detailed elsewhere (Clarke; 1989). The total correlation of the 13 items is a measure of the reliability of the questionnaire and was calculated using the *coefficient alpha* (Cronbach; 1951) procedure. The correlation of each of the items with the *coefficient alpha* is shown in Table 1.

Table 1 Individual Item-Total Measure Correlations

Item No	Item-*Alpha* Correlations
1	0.418
3	0.416
4	0.359
5	0.595
6	0.423
→ 7	0.628
10	0.404
13	0.428
14	0.446
15	0.412
16	0.427
17	0.509
18	0.356

Question 7 has the highest correlation and hence could possibly be used to identify those students with "serialist" or "holist" tendencies. The item is shown in Figure 1 below.

Second, the incorporation of the question in a CAL program:- It is a relatively simple matter to begin any CAL program with a question and allocate students to the version of the program which suits their "serialist" or "holist" style. A procedure for doing that is reported in Clarke (1989) and shown in Figure 1. This could appear as a frame at the beginning of a CAL lesson.

Welcome to the Psychology Department's
Computer Based Learning Series of Programs

PROGRAM 1 - "How Children Learn"

There are two different versions of this program available. The computer will allocate you to Version A or Version B according to your response to this question:

When I'm reading a book (or other information source) for my studies, I prefer to spend quite a long time skimming over and dipping into it to get a clear picture of what it's about and how it will be relevant.	1	2	3	4	5	When I'm reading a book (or other information source) for my studies, I prefer to get quite soon into a fairly detailed reading of it once I know that it's going to be useful, in the knowledge that its precise relevance and contribution will become clear from a detailed reading.

1 = I agree with the statement on the *left*
2 = I agree (with reservations) with the statement on the *left*
3 = No preference for either statement
4 = I agree (with reservations) with the statement on the *right*
5 = I agree with the statement on the *right*

Please place a response (1, 2, 3, 4 or 5) in the space below:

YOUR RESPONSE [ ]

Figure 1. Introductory Frame Preceding a CAL Lesson

Students who choose "1" or "2" will be allocated to Version B, those who choose "4" or "5" will be allocated to Version A while those who choose "3" will be told that it doesn't really matter which version they choose as long as they select one of them! They will then be given the option of choosing "A" or "B".

4.2 Allocation based on a small number of questions

The rationale of this approach is that the validity and reliability of what is being measured can be increased by increasing the number of questions as long as each question is related to the characteristic being measured. The problem here is to identify the appropriate set and an optimal number of questions to again allow allocation to occur quickly and efficiently (Note 1).

Table 1 identifies one of the possible "best" sets of questions in terms of their individual correlations with *coefficient alpha*. Another possible "best set" can be derived statistically by factor analysing the responses to the SPQ and extracting the first principal component. This component and the item loadings are shown in Table 2.

Table 2 Individual Item Factor Loadings on the First Principal Component

Item No	Item Factor Loading
1	-0.269*
2	0.442
3	0.376
4	-0.352
5	0.655
6	0.474
7	-0.583
8	0.334
9	0.286
10	0.496
11	-0.138
12	-0.164
13	-0.278
14	0.569
15	-0.339
16	0.386
17	0.505
18	-0.151

* "-" means that the item has to be reversed for scoring

A good estimate of the optimal "best set" of questions can be obtained by using the intersection of the two sets identified above (Note 2). By comparing the rank ordering produced by the correlation and factor loading values, the important overlapping items are 5, 7, 14 and 17. These are shown in the Appendix and could be utilized in the same way as in the "one question" case with the variation that the responses be averaged before allocation proceeded. An alternative approach as indicated in Note 1 would be to have the set of questions as a separate module which had to be completed before the student could proceed on to the content modules with again their response determining their allocation to the version of the program congruent with their learning style.

4.3 Giving the students choice as to which version they choose

In applying this approach, students are told briefly the difference between the two versions and simply asked to select the one they want to use. This approach is consistent with the "locus of control" approach to motivation (de Charms, 1976; Rotter *et al*, 1972) which places emphasis on the positive effect of learners perceiving themselves to be in control of their own learning. It is also a simple procedure to incorporate into a CAL program.

5. Predictive Validity of These Procedures

Even though the subjective "gut feeling" of the CAL instructional designer may be that one of the above methods (particularly the third) is the "best", to be confident of the choice, the predictive validity of each of these approaches has to be determined empirically.

To measure the predictive validity of these three possible methods of allocating students to an appropriate CAL experience, further data was collected from the subsample (Note 3) of 43 of the original 55 teacher education students used previously. As their responses to items 5, 7, 14 and 17 of the SPQ were already available, they were asked the following hypothetical question (Note 4):

"Consider the following situation:

You are going to learn material by working your way through a computer-based learning package on a topic that is made up of a number of modules. These modules are logically and sequentially related to each other e.g. introductory -- advanced.

I: Assume that you know very little about the content area e.g. psychology of adolescence.

You have the choice of working your way through the modules
(a) in a sequence that has been predetermined and reflects the logical relationship of the modules; or

(b) by choosing the order in which you prefer to complete the modules.

Would you choose (a) or (b)? [ ]

II: Assume that you know quite a lot about the content area e.g. the major in your undergraduate work.

You have the choice of working your way through the modules
(a) in a sequence that has been predetermined and reflects the logical relationship of the modules; or
(b) by choosing the order in which you prefer to complete the modules.

Would you choose (a) or (b)? [ ]

The reason for including the "little knowledge" (I) and "extensive knowledge (II) scenarios is to take into account Gay's (1986) finding that as the knowledge and experience of learners increase, their method of dealing with computer-based material i.e. their learning style, can change from being dependent on structure to desiring more control.

Analysis of the data requires a measure of the relationship between the student's responses to both Item 7 and the cluster of items 5, 7, 14 and 17 and their responses to I(a) and (b) and II(a) and (b) above. Because the former are continuous interval variables and the latter are discrete nominal variables, a polyserial coefficient of correlation is required. These were calculated using the PRELIS statistical package (Joreskog and Sorbom; 1986) and the results are summarized in Table 3. A comment on interpretation: In the analysis, items 5, 7, 14 and 17 have values ranging from "1" (serialist) to "5" (holist) while (a) (structured approach) and (b) (unstructured approach) have values of "1" and "2" respectively. A high correlation therefore means that a student with a serialist orientation generally chooses the structured approach and students with a holist orientation generally choose the unstructured approach.

For the situation where there is little prior knowledge, the responses of the students cannot be predicted by the SPQ items. On the other hand, where students feel that they do have prior knowledge, those who have a "serialist" approach to learning (as indicated by their responses to the SPQ items) choose to work their way through the computer package in a structured guided way while those with a "holistic" orientation choose the more unstructured approach.

In sum, students who have prior experience or feel comfortable with the content can be trusted to choose which approach they prefer while students who are unfamiliar with the content or "flying blind" require guidance as to which approach to take. They should be required to complete some form of learning style pretest. The decision as to whether it should be a single item or a cluster can be guided by the correlations in Table 3. The cluster gives a more significant and hence more reliable result. The incorporation of such a procedure in a CAL program is relatively simple as shown in Figure 2.

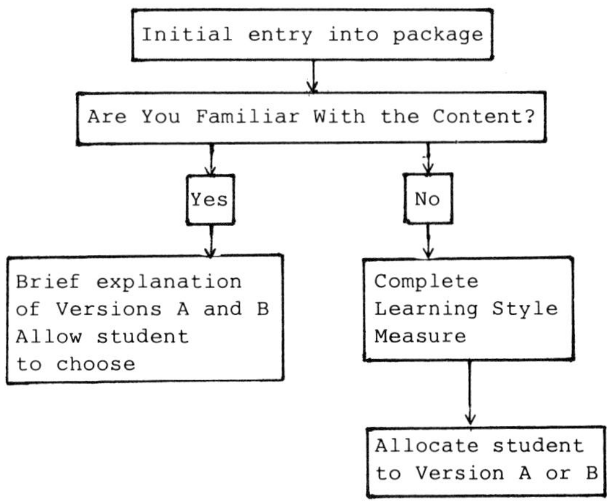

Figure 2 Possible Procedure for Allocating Students on the Basis of Knowledge Level

Table 3 Summary of Polyserial Correlation Coefficients

	No Knowledge Choice (a) str ←→ unstr (b) (low) (high)	Knowledge Choice (a) str ←→ unstr (b) (low) (high)
Item 7 serial ←→ holist (low) (high)	ns	0.36 ($p < 0.05$)
Cluster of Items serial ←→ holist (low) (high)	ns	0.51 ($p < 0.01$)

The remaining "problem", is the production of appropriate versions of a CAL program to accommodate the learning styles of users.

6. The preparation of a suitable CAL program

As far as the delivery of CAL is concerned, the "serialist" or "structured" end of the continuum is catered for by the traditional tutorial-type programs while the "holist" or "unstructured" end is served best by the simulation/game-type programs. This would seem to suggest that the only way to cater for this style would be to produce parallel versions of each area of content (module). Although appealing, this would require a large amount of work.

An alternative approach would be to somehow allow for both approaches within one set of experiences, the difference being that students could be routed through the experiences ("serialist") or could choose their own path ("holist"). Choice could occur at both a macro and micro level. At the macro level, if an area of knowledge were defined by a "concept map" of related topics or "modules", people using the suite of modules could be constrained to move through the set in a preordained manner. Alternatively, they could also be free to choose whichever module they preferred and complete them in any order. At the micro level, that is within each module, users could again be asked at appropriate points if, for example, they wished to be told an answer or preferred to investigate further with the aim of "discovering" it for themselves.

This procedure would seem to be more efficient in a number of ways - production time, utilization of computer memory and hardware currently available on a large scale, and catering for the "versatile" individuals (Pask; 1973) who may prefer to change their approach as they proceed. This versatility notion is important in attempting to cater for learning style because, assuming the conditions of motivation and serious approach to learning identified earlier, the major variable influencing the way students proceed with the learning task, apart from their learning style, is their prior knowledge and/or experience with the content area (Gay; 1986). As the knowledge and experience increases, their method of dealing with the material, or their learning style, changes. The production of a program that will accommodate this approach is an ongoing project (Clarke; in process).

NOTES

1. It could be argued that the more reliable 13 item set of SPQ questions identified by Clarke (1989) could all be used. This could in fact be done as a separate and compulsory prerequisite to any involvement in CAL. The aim here is to produce something manageable which could be incorporated into a CAL program.
2. This process is not based on any statistical procedure but is a legitimate course of action to follow. Personal communication, Dr. D. Chant, Statistical Adviser to the Social Sciences, University of Queensland.
3. Based on availability.
4. Ideally, it would have been better if students could have been exposed to an actual CAL package. However, time has not permitted the production of this. It is in fact the ultimate aim of the total project (Clarke; in process).

REFERENCES

Baird, W.E. (1986) Conference Abstracts: Fourth World Conference on Computers in Education - Part II. *Journal of Computers in Mathematics and Science Teaching,* 5(3), 60-61.

Barker, P.G. (1982) Some experiments in man-machine optimal interaction relevant to computer assisted instruction. *British Journal of Educational Technology,* 1(13), 65-75.

Barry, J.J. and Sutton, T.J. (1973) *The Educational Sciences: A Bibliography with Commentary.* Bloomfield Hills, Michigan: American Educational Sciences Association.

Carroll, J.M. and Thomas, J.C. (1982) Metaphor and the cognitive representations of computer systems. *IEEE Transactions on Systems, Man and Cybernetics,* 12(2), 107-115.

Chadwick, S.S. and Watson, J.A. (1986) Computers and Cognitive styles. *Academic Therapy,* 22(2), 125-132.

Clarke, J.A. (1989) Cognitive Style and CAL: What Can You Do About It? In G. Bishop and J. Baker (Eds.), *Proceedings of the Seventh Annual Conference of the Australian Society for Computers in Learning in Tertiary Education.* Brisbane: Watson Ferguson & Co., 145-153.

Clarke, J.A. (in process) The Production of a Computer-Assisted Learning (CAL) Package for Tertiary Students that is designed to Cater for the Preferred Learning Styles of Students. Report of a Professional Experience Program (PEP) undertaken at the CAL Unit, University of Queensland.

Clements, D.H. and Gullo, D.F. (1984) Effects of computer programming on young children's cognition. *Journal of Educational Psychology,* 76(6), 1051-1058.

Cronbach, L.J. (1951) Coefficient alpha and the internal structure of tests. *Psychometrica,* 35, 509-511.

de Charms, R. (1976) *Enhancing Motivation.* New York: Van Nostrand.

Driscoll, M.P. (1987) Aptitude-treatment interaction research revisited. Paper presented at the Annual Convention of the Association for Educational Communications and Technology, Atlanta, Georgia.

Duncan, M.V. (1985) Computer Programs and learning styles. *Computers, Reading and Language Arts,* 2(2), 8-12.

Entwistle, N. (1978) Knowledge structures and styles of learning: a summary of Pask's recent research. *British Journal of Educational Psychology,* 48, 255-265.

Entwistle, N. (1981) *Styles of Learning and Teaching.* New York: John Wiley.

Ford, N. (1985) Learning styles and strategies of postgraduate students. *British Journal of Educational Technology,* 16(1), 17-26.

Gay, G. (1986) Interaction of learner control and prior understanding in computer-assisted video instruction. *Journal of Educational Psychology,* 78(3), 225-227.

Gillingham, A. and Stillman, B. (1936) *Remedial Training for Children with Specific Disability in Reading, Spelling and Penmanship.* MA: Educators Publishing Service.

Hale, D.J. (1981) Special purpose language for behavioural experiments. *International Journal of Man-Machine Studies,* 14(3), 317-339.

Hammond, M.F. (1985) Cognitive and visual elements of using computers for instruction. *Education and Computing,* 1(3), 155-161.

Hedberg, J.G. and McNamara, S.E. (1985) Matching feedback and cognitive style in visual CAI tasks. Paper presented at the annual conference of the American Educational Research Association, Chicago.

Jonassen, D.H. (1985) Interactive lesson designs: A taxonomy. *Educational Technology,* 25(6), 7-17.

Joreskog, K.G. and Sorbom, D. (1986) *PRELIS A Preprocessor for LISREL.* Mooseville, Indiana: Scientific Software.

Joughin, G. (1989) Adult learning principles and field-dependence/independence in training program design. Paper presented at the Australian and South Pacific External Studies Association ninth Biennial Forum, Gippsland Institute of Advanced Education.

Kogan, N. (1971) Educational implications of Cognitive Styles. In G.S. Lesser (Ed.), *Psycholcgy and Educational Practice.* Illinois: Scott Foresman & Co., 242-292.

Maricic, S. (1987) Information science as interface of the cognitive sphere and society. *Information Processing and Management.* 23(1), 33-43.

Martens, K. (1975) Cognitive style: an introduction with annotated bibliography. Paper presented at the American College Personnel Association Convention, Atlanta, Georgia.

Messick, S. (1970) The Criterion Problem in the Evaluation of Instruction: Assessing Possible, not just Intended Outcomes. In Wittrock, M.C. and Wiley, D.E. (Eds.), *The Evaluation of Instruction: Issues and Problems.* New York: Holt Rinehart and Winston, 183-202.

Messick, S. (1976) Personality Consistency in Cognition and Creativity. In S. Messick, (Ed.) *Individuality in Learning.* San Francisco: Jossey-Bass, 4-22.

Messick, S. (1984) The nature of cognitive style: problems and promises in educational practice. *Educational Psychologist,* 19(2), 59-74.

Moran, T.P. (1981) An applied psychology of the user. *Computing Surveys,* 13(1), 1-11.

Nelson, K.H. (1973) A bibliography of cognitive style research. Working paper, Harvard Graduate School of Business Administration, Boston.

Papert, S. and Reinhold, F. (1986) New views on LOGO and an interview with Seymour Papert. *Electronic Learning,* 5(7), 33-36.

Phillips, M.K. (1986) Approaches to the design of language teaching software. *CALICO Journal,* 3(4), 36-38.

Pask, G. (1973) *Educational Methods Using Information About Individual Styles and Strategies of Learning.* Final Report of the SSRC Project HR 1424/1 (2 vols).

Pask, G. (1976) Styles and Strategies of learning. *British Journal of Educational Psychology.* 46, 128-148.

Pask, G. and Scott, B.C.E. (1972) Learning strategies and individual competence. *International Journal of Man-Machine Studies,* 4, 217-253.

Rotter, J.B., Chance, J.E. and Phares, E.J. (1972) *Applications of the Social Learning Theory of Personality*. New York: Holt Rinehart and Winston.

Sharma, S. (1987) Learners' cognitive styles and psychological types as intervening variables influencing performance in computer science courses. *Journal of Educational Technology Systems,* 15(4), 391-399.

Steinke, R. (1974) Cognitive styles: a review of past and current published research. Unpublished manuscript, Arapahoe Community College, Littleton, Colorado.

Witkin, H.A., Dyk, R.B., Faterson, H.F., Goodenough, D.R. and Karp, S.A. (1962) *Psychological Differentiation: Studies of Development*. New York: John Wiley.

Young, L. (1982) An analysis of the effect of the logo computer programing environment upon the reflective and impulsive cognitive styles of second grade students. Unpublished doctoral thesis, University of Pittsburg.

APPENDIX

"OPTIMAL SET" OF ITEMS FROM 'STUDY PREFERENCE QUESTIONNAIRE' ANALYSES SUITABLE FOR IDENTIFICATION OF LEARNING STYLE

Response Scale:
1 = I agree with the statement on the *left*
2 = I agree (with reservations) with the statement on the *left*
3 = No preference for either statement
4 = I agree (with reservations) with the statement on the *right*
5 = I agree with the statement on the *right*

5. When I'm in the library, I tend to be looking for specific books, etc, rather than browsing (generally speaking).	1	2	3	4	5	I tend to spend quite a lot of time browsing in the library.
7. When I'm reading a book (or other information source) for my studies, I prefer to spend quite a long time skimming over and dipping into it to get a clear picture of what it's about and how it will be relevant.	1	2	3	4	5	When I'm reading a book (or other information source) for my studies, I prefer to get quite soon into a fairly detailed reading of it once I know that it's going to be useful, in the knowledge that its precise relevance and contribution will become clear from a detailed reading.
14. Where a book chapter or journal article includes a separate summary of what it is about, I generally prefer to get straight into the main text since it contains all that is in the summary anyway.	1	2	3	4	5	Generally I prefer to read the summary before reading the full text - even though it will all be found in greater detail in the main text.
17. Where a book or journal has a separate summary of conclusions I prefer to get straight into the main text, where each conclusion is presented along with the evidence on which it is based.	1	2	3	4	5	I prefer to spend quite a bit of time reading the summary of conclusions before going on to a detailed reading of the main text.

Computers in Education
A. McDougall and C. Dowling (Editors)
Elsevier Science Publishers B.V. (North-Holland)

THE ROLE OF EXPLORATION-BASED LEARNING IN THE DEVELOPMENT OF EXPERTISE

Richard COX and Geoff CUMMING

Department of Psychology, La Trobe University, Bundoora, Victoria, Australia 3083

Exploration-based learning (EBL) is increasingly advocated as desirable, and the computer is increasingly being used as a tool for EBL, for example with exploratory microworlds, simulations and coached games. However, any evaluation of EBL must start with specification of the learning that is sought. This paper considers a range of possible learning goals, and adopts 'development of expertise' as an attractive view of learning. The apprenticeship model is identified as a broad package of teaching and learning procedures intended to develop all facets of expertise. From this standpoint we examine EBL, and experimental studies of its efficacy. We conclude that EBL does have great potential, including potential for development of the vital meta-abilities of expertise, but that it must incorporate well-designed domain representations to help the learner develop mental models like those of an expert. It also must be supplemented by advice and guidance; specifying and providing good, sparing guidance is very difficult, and requires intensive study. Study of the guidance given by expert human tutors working with learners using computer-based EBL tools is likely to be especially valuable.

Exploration based learning (EBL) was the subject of educational research in the 1960's and 1970's, and is currently fashionable once again in the context of computer based learning. The starting point for an assessment of the educational benefits of the EBL approach should be a consideration of the goals of learning.

1. THE GOALS OF LEARNING

From the many learning goals that have been suggested in the artificial intelligence (AI) and cognitive psychology literature, we choose five for comment.

1.1. The communication of knowledge

Wenger (1987) uses 'knowledge communication' as the definition of learning on which to base his analysis of intelligent tutoring systems. Miscommunication often results in the development of misconceptions (VanLehn, 1988). Students must interpret instructions correctly. Experts are characterised by, amongst other things, an ability to explain the reasoning underlying their conclusions.

1.2. An ability to structure tasks

A natural and straightforward learning goal is to teach students to structure tasks properly - to develop skills in the student such that he or she can organise and integrate large amounts of information.

1.3. Retention and transfer

Retention as a third view of learning requires that an opportunity for effective practice and performance feedback is available to assist the process of knowledge compilation (Anderson, 1983). Knowledge compilation occurs with practice, transforming initial mental structures into a form that makes performance faster, more accurate and better retained (VanLehn, 1988). The ability to transfer acquired skills to new situations is also important.

1.4. The development of metacognitive skills

Learning should result in the acquisition of problem solving heuristics by the learner. Schoenfeld (1985) suggests that heuristics can be either general or domain specific.

1.5. Progression towards expertise

A view that is more comprehensive than any of the foregoing regards learning as a progression towards expertise. This view is a broad and multi-faceted conception of learning, and one that is in accord with many practical needs. It is the principal view of learning we adopt for our analysis and evaluation of EBL.

2. EXPERTISE

Wenger (1987) differentiates between skill acquisition and expertise. Skill acquisition is assessed by performance measures such as rate of acquisition, retention and transfer. Perceptual-motor skills and cognitive skills can both be assessed in those terms, although with cognitive skills less may be directly observable. Expertise, however, goes beyond the level of skilled performance in several respects.

Experts typically classify problems on the basis of deep structures and underlying principles (Chi, Feltovich & Glaser, 1981; Gilhooly & Green, 1989) rather than on the basis of surface or structural analogies (Anderson, Farrell & Sauers, 1984).

Another characteristic of experts is an ability to reason about a domain from first principles by running mental simulations, a process that de Kleer and Brown (1981) have termed 'envisionment'. Results from studies of novices and experts in knowledge domains such as physics, programming and chess demonstrate that experts are better at organising information in memory and that they chunk stored information in larger units (Bateson, Alexander & Murphy, 1987; Allwood, 1986).

Some forms of expertise are also characterised by an ability to reconsider rules and explain their validity (Wenger, 1987). However, some experts seem to experience difficulty in articulating their reasoning processes - a central problem for knowledge engineers.

We may also add the components of control and attitude which have been identified by Schoenfeld (1985) in relation to mathematical expertise. Control encompasses the ability to decide to alter one's approach to a problem, and the ability to manage resources.

How might 'progression towards expertise' be facilitated? One teaching method that may be of use is that of apprenticeship, a time-honoured method of teaching and learning that has evolved over human history as an effective way to transmit many real-world bodies of skill.

3. APPRENTICESHIP

Four learning stages are posited (Collins, Brown and Newman, 1987):

- modelling (apprentice observes expert performing to-be-learned process, with explanations)
- coaching (expert guides and helps apprentice as he or she attempts parts of the task, then the whole task)
- fading (assistance gradually withdrawn, apprentice becomes more autonomous)
- reflecting (apprentice self-monitors to improve performance).

In practice these stages merge and overlap considerably.

At the modelling stage, the instructor modifies his or her usual behaviour so as to make salient the crucial stages of the operation, proceeds at a slow pace and may select sub-components of the task or a simplified version of the task. In order for the student to learn by observation, he or she must be able to infer the intentions of the expert (Annett, 1989). Learners form internal representations which may be either verbal (symbolic) or visual (analogue) mental models, but the nature of these, as well as the attributes of effective demonstrations, are areas requiring further study.

The coaching stage involves elements of both direct instruction by the instructor and autonomous exploration by the learner. Coaching primarily involves information feedback in the form of hints and tips.
Recent research by Lepper & Gurtner (1989) raises questions about the role of feedback. They found that skilled tutors virtually never provided the sort of corrective feedback built in to many tutoring programs, and that they almost never offered explicit diagnosis of student misunderstandings. Perhaps expert tutors are skilled at contriving situations in which the student discovers and self-remediates errors. Alternatively, the feedback cues of a skilled tutor may involve subtle forms of communication that are not readily discernible by the observer. Clearly, the role of feedback at the coaching stage requires more research.

At the fading stage assistance is gradually withdrawn and the apprentice practises with more autonomy. Checks are required, however, and if an area of misconception or weakness is apparent then coaching can be resumed.

The higher-order skill of reflection requires an ability to self-appraise and to practise the task mentally. Recent work by Foss (1987) suggests that the metacognitive skill of reflection is amenable to training.

Finally, Collins, Brown & Newman (1987) have extended the apprenticeship model to include the cognitive areas of reading, writing and mathematics. To apply the traditional apprenticeship model to cognitive skills requires the skills to be externalized - making the target process observable rather than covert. This skill of making salient the usually covert aspects of cognition may be an essential ingredient of expert tutoring at the modelling stage of the learning cycle.

4. EBL AND THE PROMOTION OF LEARNING GOALS

We shall now consider more broadly the role that EBL might play in the promotion of expertise and metacognitive skills in terms of the goals of learning.

Recent considerable interest in the use of computers as a medium for exploratory learning (e.g. Hollan, Hutchins & Weitzman, 1987; Lepper and Gurtner, 1989) has not, unfortunately, led to agreement as to the definition of EBL. A diverse array of terms confront readers, including 'discovery learning', 'learning by doing', 'exploratory learning' etc. We will continue, however, to use the term 'exploration-based learning' (EBL).

Most definitions of EBL emphasise the initiation and control of learning by the explorer and the importance of what might be termed 'enquiry metaskills', such as reflection and systematic methods of enquiry. Some also emphasise the roles of guidance and hypothesis testing. Generally, computer-based EBL systems aim to be unobtrusive and reticent in the provision of help and advice (Wenger, 1987; Kamouri, Kamouri & Smith, 1986).

The EBL approach has been advocated by many educators for use in both traditional and computer-based instructional settings. Postulated benefits include greater 'intellectual potency', superior motivational effects, propensity to develop metacognitive skills, improved recall, transfer and analogical reasoning (e.g. Bruner, 1961). We now consider EBL in relation to the six views of learning mentioned earlier.

4.1. EBL & The communication of knowledge

Good performance of a cognitive task is not always associated with verbalizable knowledge of that task. Under some conditions 'people can do more than they can tell' (Berry & Broadbent, 1984).

More recently, Sanderson (1989) has investigated the nature of verbal-performance dissociations in subjects who explored a computer-based simulation of a city transport system. The methodology permitted changes in subjects' mental models to be tracked alongside changes in reportable knowledge and control performance. Sanderson (1989) clarifies the roles of practice and training in the verbal and performance modalities. Improvement in ability to report acquired knowledge verbally is associated, *inter alia*, with subjects learning to be precise when finding solutions, responding consistently, and accommodating the system's behaviour within a coherent semantic framework.

In summary, therefore, it seems that EBL does not necessarily guarantee that the learner will subsequently be able to communicate verbally what has been learned. Commentary and reflection additional to the EBL may be needed as well.

4.2. EBL & The ability to structure tasks

EBL, by definition, does not structure the material to be learned in the sense of organising the sequence of its presentation. The student is required to induce structure through systematic exploration. This process can, however, be supported through guidance (eg Brown et al., 1982).

4.3. EBL & Retention and transfer

EBL may produce better transfer to new problems and improved delayed recall (Kamouri, Kamouri and Smith, 1986; Solter & Mayer, 1978; Cronbach & Snow, 1977). Herman (1969), in an early review of discovery learning studies, concluded that the approach favours transfer when compared with 'rule followed by example' methods of instruction. The effect appears to increase with transfer task difficulty. Solter & Mayer (1978) demonstrated that transfer to tasks less similar to the training task was better in a group of preschoolers learning via guided discovery than a group taught in an expository manner. (Note that, once again, guidance was used to complement EBL.)

EBL is hypothesised to allow the learner to generate his or her own mediating links between ideas, a process which leads to better recall than expository teaching methods in which the mediators are those of the instructor or instructional designer. Bruner (1961) claims that students tend to prefer one of a range of mediator styles (thematic [story based], generic [tying using a superordinate concept] or part-whole mediators [made-from, is-a-part-of]).An intelligent educational system which supported a range of representations by the learner would therefore accommodate individual differences in link preference.

4.4. EBL & Metacognitive skills

4.4.1. EBL & reasoning

Reasoning by analogy seems to be a skill that EBL promotes and one which is implicated in the transfer of procedural skills. Kamouri, Kamouri and Smith (1986) studied unguided EBL. They cite several studies in support of the contention that exploration facilitates the use of existing knowledge in the solution of new problems. Kamouri et al. (1986) compared exploration and instruction-based training and concluded that EBL enhanced the trainees' ability to spontaneously notice the relevance of their mental models in the transfer condition.

4.4.2. EBL & the development of enquiry skills

Bruner (1961) advanced the hypothesis that discovery learning promotes in the learner a constructionist approach to knowledge acquisition. This involves the expectation that there will be something to find in the way of regularities and relationships in the explored domain and systematic querying. Also important is the extent to which learners demonstrate connectivity in their information gathering - 'the extent to which questions asked utilize or ignore or violate information previously obtained' (p.25).

4.4.3. EBL & Development of mental models

The work of Sanderson (1989) introduced above provides some support for the effectiveness of EBL in promoting the development of mental models. Practice at the task caused subjects to shift away from their initial mental model towards a more accurate one. Some subjects do not discover all the relations in the system, however, and so do not adopt the 'expert' model.

The STEAMER simulation of a ship propulsion plant (Hollan et al., 1987) aims to provide a representation, not so much of an actual physical device, but of an expert's mental model of the device. The STEAMER icons, though they do not correspond to indicators on any real device, graphically represent aspects of the process crucial to an expert's reasoning. This represents an example of an EBL environment in which the usually covert elements of an expert's reasoning are made salient for the learner.

Some abstract domains, such as electricity, are difficult for non-experts to visualise (Arnold & Miller, 1987) and are commonly represented by a variety of models (Shipstone, 1985; Gentner & Gentner, 1983; de Kleer & Brown, 1981).

The development of mental models is greatly dependent upon experiential knowledge and they are often constructed through analogy and metaphor. The type of analogy used in teaching affects a person's conception of a knowledge domain in ways that can be predicted and demonstrated experimentally (Gentner & Gentner, 1983).

4.4.4. EBL & Encouragement of reflection

Anzai & Simon (1979) studied a single subject's 'learning by doing' - solving the Tower of Hanoi problem. They identified four processes in operation during the subject's gradual transformation of strategy: applying the current strategy, gathering information for later use, recalling prior information and deciding to terminate. Thus there is a degree of task-related metacognition in the form of reflection and strategy change. Another example of effective reflection at the domain level is provided by Foss (1987) who used ALGEBRALAND - a system for assisting students of algebra. She found that students using ALGEBRALAND who reviewed audit trails of previous errors acquired general skills of self-reflection, de-bugging and error avoidance which generalised to solving algebra problems away from the system.

4.5. EBL & Progression towards expertise

The preceding sections, especially 4.4., have touched on EBL in relation to most components of expertise. The discussion earlier of the apprenticeship approach to expertise suggests that expository teaching is important in the modelling and coaching phases, whereas EBL can contribute at the fading and reflection stages. At the coaching stage also EBL has a role, but feedback and guidance to the learner are required as well.

A strong common thread is the need for advice and guidance to accompany EBL; this may not always be necessary, and may be most effective in small, infrequent, judiciously selected doses, but it does have an essential role.

5. EBL, REPRESENTATIONS, AND GUIDANCE

In outline, we have adopted 'advance towards expertise' as a widely-desirable goal for learning.

Adopting the apprenticeship package as a concise statement of the learning experiences we would like our computer systems to support, it is clear that EBL has a natural and central place. In EBL the learner uses computer tools and resources to work at tasks, while having scope to develop and apply initiative in the learning domain. The main additional elements called for by the apprenticeship package are attention to the development of expert conceptualisations, and provision of advice and guidance. EBL supplemented in these two ways should comprise a formidably effective and attractive environment for learning.

Our discussion suggested that EBL seems to be effective in assisting learners with the development of useful mental models, but not necessarily in ways that can be verbally articulated, at least in the early stages of acquisition. Attention is required to the representations provided for use by the learner, i.e. the metaphors used in computer models of knowledge domains. EBL will be most effective in the development of higher order cognitive skills and expertise if the usually covert processes of expert reasoning are made salient to the learner. Computer based EBL environments offer considerable scope for providing this type of information through the use of cleverly designed displays.

This aspect of computer-based systems for learner use has led to considerable work in recent years: we have mentioned some examples of excellent on-screen representations that are tied in with desirable mental models, and scanning of recent literature gives many more. We conclude that the provision of representations likely to help the learner develop expert conceptualisations - has been widely recognised and is receiving a great deal of attention.

The other essential supplement to EBL is the provision of explanation and guidance. This is necessary for the exposition, explanation and commentary functions of the expert in the apprenticeship model; it is also needed to assist the learner carry out exploration most productively, and to develop the variety of meta-skills that are essential components in expertise. Provision of guidance can also be viewed as the way to assist the learner internalise the reflection, monitoring and evaluative commentary that is one hallmark of expertise. (This latter view has been discussed in more detail by Cumming & Self, 1990.)

Provision of advice and guidance emerges as the main issue needing research attention. There are important aspects we have not discussed, including individual differences. We have made little mention also of the difficulty of identifying and assessing the crucial meta-abilities.

There are many perplexing issues relating to the provision of guidance. It is essential, yet must not compromise the scope for learner initiative that is a defining feature of EBL. What form should the advice take, and to what extent should it be intrusive, rather than simply available when the learner asks for it? How sparing should it be, and at what levels - ranging from tiny and local, to broad and strategic - should it be offered. The careful study of expert human tutors working in conjunction with students using computer tools is likely to be a fruitful way of studying these questions.

ACKNOWLEDGEMENTS

Support for this research has been provided by the Australian Research Council.

REFERENCES

Allwood, C.A. (1986) Novices on the computer: a review of the literature. International Journal of Man-Machine Studies, 25, 633-658.

Anderson, J.R. (1983) The architecture of cognition. Cambridge, MA.: Harvard University Press.

Anderson, J.R., Farrell, R.G. & Sauers, R. (1984) Learning to program in LISP. Cognitive Science, 8, 87-129.

Anzai, Y. & Simon, H.A. (1979) The theory of learning by doing. Psychological Review, 86, 124-140.

Arnold, M. & Miller, R. (1987) Being constructive: An alternative approach to the teaching of introductory ideas in electricity. International Journal of Science Education, 9, 553-563.

Bateson, A.G., Alexander, R.A. & Murphy, M.D. (1987) Cognitive processing differences between novice and expert programmers. International Journal of Man-Machine Studies, 26, 649-660.

Berry, D.C. & Broadbent, D.E. (1984). On the relationship between task performance and associated verbalizable knowledge. The Quarterly Journal of Experimental Psychology, 36A, 209- 231.

Brown, J.S., Burton, R.R. & de Kleer, J. (1982) Pedagogical, natural language, and knowledge engineering techniques in SOPHIE I, II and III. In Sleeman, D.H. & Brown, J.S. (Eds.) Intelligent tutoring systems. London: Academic Press.pp 227-282.

Bruner, J.S. (1961) The act of discovery. Harvard Educational Review, 31, 21-32.

Chi, M., Feltovich, P. & Glaser, R. (1981) Categorization and representation of physics problems by experts and novices. Cognitive Science, 5, 121-152.

Colley, A.M. & Beech, J.R. (1989) Acquiring and performing cognitive skills. in Colley, A.M. & Beech, J.R.(Eds.) Acquisition and performance of cognitive skills. New York: Wiley.

Collins, A. , Brown, J.S. and Newman, S.E. (1987) Cognitive apprenticeship: teaching the craft of reading, writing and mathematics. In Resnick, L.B. (Ed.), Cognition and instruction: Issues and agendas. Hillsdale, N.J.: Erlbaum.

Cronbach, L.J. & Snow, R. E. (1981) Aptitudes and instructional methods: A handbook for research on interactions. New York: Irvington.

Cumming, G. & Self, J. (1990) Intelligent educational systems: Identifying and decoupling the conversational levels. Instructional Science. (in press)

de Kleer, J. & Brown, J.S. (1981) Mental models of physical systems and their acquisition. In Anderson, J.R. (Ed.) Cognitive skills and their acquisition. Hillsdale, N.J.: Erlbaum.

Foss, C.L. (1987) Learning from errors in ALGEBRALAND. Technical Report IRL-87-0003. Institute for Research on Learning, Palo Alto, CA.

Gentner, D. & Gentner, D.R. (1983) Flowing waters and teeming crowds: Mental models of electricity. in Gentner, D. & Stevens, A.L. (Eds.) Mental models. Hillsdale, N.J.: Erlbaum. pp 99-129.

Gilhooly, K.J. & Green, A.J.K. (1989) Learning problem solving skills. In Colley, A.M. & Beech, J.R. (Eds) Acquisition & performance of cognitive skills. Chichester: Wiley. pp 85-111.

Herman, G. (1969) Learning by discovery: A critical review of the studies. Journal of Experimental Education, 38, 58-72.

Hollan, J.D., Hutchins, E.L. & Weitzman, L.M. (1987) STEAMER: An interactive, inspectable, simulation-based training system. In Kearsley, G. (Ed.) Artificial intelligence and instruction: Applications and methods. Reading, MA: Addison Wesley.pp 113-134.

Kamouri, A.L., Kamouri, J. & Smith, K.H. (1986) Training by exploration: Facilitating the transfer of procedural knowledge through analogical reasoning. International Journal of Man-Machine Studies, 24, 171-192.

Lepper, M.R. & Gurtner, J. (1989) Children & computers: Approaching the twenty-first century. American Psychologist, Feb., 170-178.

Sanderson, P.M. (1989) Verbalizable knowledge and skilled task performance: Association, dissociation, and mental models. Journal of Experimental Psychology: Learning Memory and Cognition, 15, 729-747.

Schoenfeld, A.H. (1985) Mathematical problem solving. New York: Academic Press.

Shipstone, D. (1985) Electricity in simple circuits. In Driver, R., Guesne, E. & Tiberghian, A. (Eds.) Children's ideas in science. Milton Keynes: Open University Press.pp 33-51.

Solter, A. & Mayer, R.E. (1978) Broader transfer produced by guided discovery of number concepts with preschool childen. Journal of Educational Psychology, 70, 363-371.

VanLehn, K. (1988) Toward a theory of impasse-driven learning. In Mandl, H. & Lesgold, A. (Eds.) Learning issues for intelligent tutoring systems. New York: Springer-Verlag.pp 19-41.

Wenger, E. (1987) Artificial intelligence and tutoring systems: Computational and cognitive approaches to the communication of knowledge. Los Altos, CA: Morgan Kaufmann.

Computers in Education
A. McDougall and C. Dowling (Editors)
Elsevier Science Publishers B.V. (North-Holland)

THE SOCIAL EFFECTS OF NEW TECHNOLOGY IN SCHOOLS - THE SENTIS REPORT

Andrew E. FLUCK

Scholar-in-Residence, Philip Smith Education Centre*

This paper describes a project which measured the actual use 3700 pupils made of computers in school, and compared this with group coherence. The evidence indicates that friendships are not affected by computer use in primary schools. However, the early evidence indicates that computers are having a negative impact on socialisation in secondary schools. The project also discusses the variations in computer use in lesson and free time.

BACKGROUND

When television really took off in the United States, it took just over five years from 1952 to become virtually universal (Lepper, [1]).
In many respects it was socially devastating. Computer technology in schools is taking off at a similar rate, and we have yet to properly assess its impact upon teaching and learning.

The social effects of computers are common themes in most computer courses, with much good material available (Kerr & Heller, [2] and Natali [3]). However, few researchers have had the opportunity to study the impact of the technologies upon the education process itself. In some cases we can see a sweeping change coming into schools, as the possibilities and potential of the new devices increases. On the other hand, the fundamental social organisation of schools and their rationale for existence has changed very little.

It is important at this stage to emphasise what the SENTIS project is NOT about. Claims have been made about the effectiveness of computer aided learning - the economic argument is being addressed by a large project by Dr. Margaret Cox in King's College, London, UK. Further, the twin problems of gender differentiation and technology related social isolation are tangential to the aims of the project. At this stage the SENTIS project is not looking at individual case studies of social effects, but is looking at behaviour in bulk, on a whole school basis. Having said that, the investigation procedure described below rests on three strands, one being the verbal reports from teachers and students.

The potential for change is immense. In terms of computing power, computers are now available at an affordable price with greater processing and memory capacities than ever before. For example, one firm is currently advertising for US$500 a notebook computer which is compatible with the IBM PC, yet fits into a coat pocket. This is just the start of a rush into this area, mimicking a 'dinosaur' which is scarcely a decade old. This kind of development has already been sidestepped by RISC (Reduced Instruction Set Computers) chips, which can use a conventional desk-top interface, but offer significant speed advantages. With software and hardware constantly leaping over each other, education will not be excluded from considerable changes, some

*** This project has been made possible through the support of the Philip Smith Education Centre, Hobart, Tasmania, Australia and the kind permission of the Tasmanian State Education Department. Other thanks go to the project schools for their assistance, and to Richard Gardam(TAS) and Steve Cousins(UK) for vital software development.**

of which revolve around questions of connectivity. Some leaders of this change are even contemplating the end of the teaching profession as we know it.

The majority of schools are still organised on the same lines as those which pre-dated the computer revolution. Thus teachers meet with groups of students on a regular basis, in buildings provided and equipped for the learning activity. The computer provision typically affects students for less than 5% of their school day, and the distribution of the available machinery between students is still a negotiated compromise. Computers are not the learning machines of a previous decade, nor has their potential to enhance learning been fully plotted. Some of the most significant aspects have been discovered when they are used with children with special needs. Children with severe communication problems have been given a voice to the world - and their unfettered thoughts are breaking forth. See for instance the prize-winning novel by Nolan [4].

Several reports have been published which show how the computer can encourage group work, and can become the focus for discussion activities. Heather Govier has used the phrase 'a safe haven for the eyes' to describe work done with disturbed children, where the computer has been used as a stimulus for discussion about sensitive topics (Hope, [5]). Teachers using LOGO and robotic turtles connected to the computer, have found this a good way of encouraging team work. Most of these developments have taken place in primary education, but their worth has been recognised much more widely. This could indicate that the computer can significantly increase socialisation. However, the project interviews consistently found an emphasis on the use of computers for individual word-processing, alongside recognition of their acknowledged excellence as a focus for group work.

PROJECT AIMS AND METHODS

Now the project has reached the end of its first phase, this report describes the investigative process and the main findings. The project has two fundamental aims:

1. To collect initial data on the social effects of computers in schools, at a stage when availability and usage of the technology is at a relatively low level compared to the maximum possible

2. To examine the rough correlation between the sociability of students and the amount of computer use in schools.

It is realised that the comparison with the spread of television is an appropriate one, for the spread of computers into education has only just begun. The reasons for this vary globally, but the new equipment represents a substantial investment in a very large sector of most economies. Political will and educational justification is increasingly being found to support increases in equipment levels, but only in tertiary institutions are there a substantial proportion of students with full-time access to computers. Further, the word 'computer' itself is open to examination, for the gulf between 8 bit processor, 32 kbyte machines and those with full 32 bit processors and in excess of 1 Mbyte is immense. Therefore this investigation has been limited to primary and secondary education (grades 1 to 12, ages 5 to 17 years), and the recording technique effectively restricted to 8 bit micros.

The three strands of the SENTIS project investigation are as follows:

1. Recording of all computer usage in a school, to provide a measure of the actual distribution of human-computer interactions, usually with an automatic network probe.

2. Gathering friendship patterns through the administration of standard sociograms.

3. Collection and collation of recorded interviews with staff and students to compare with the information from the first two stages.

RESULTS

Computer use throughout a school was recorded by a network probe which analysed all traffic on a school-based communication system between the machines. This has given the project a chart of all computer use every five minutes throughout the school. The exceptions to this have been where a school has no network installed, in which case written records have been kept. There are potential faults with both techniques, but the opinion of the computer co-ordinators has been in favour of the automated technique. Analysis of the network traffic can definitely identify operating stations, but it can also omit stations which are in use but not transmitting.

A classroom observation method has been used to identify the systematic error due to this effect. The degree of difference depends upon the type of work being done - the longer the concentration span of the students, the less network traffic. The comparisons indicate that the actual computer use is about 1.3 times greater than recorded by the netprobe. This weighting factor has been used in Table A. Other errors due to the collision of data on the Acorn Econet are estimated at less than 2%. The usage has been analysed according to principles first described by Sid Cumberland [6], breaking down activity according to lesson or free time. Further, an index of total computer use in minutes per student per day is computed.

The standard sociograms have been administered to about 10% of the students enrolled in each project school, generally in home or base classes. From the grid of choosers versus chosen friends, the integration index has been calculated. This integration index is used in the between-school correlation. The classes surveyed were spread over the age range of each school, and are taken to be representative. The integration index has been calculated using the formula

$$I = \frac{R_O \quad q}{U_O \quad p}$$

where R_O and U_O are the observed numbers of reciprocated and unreciprocated choices, and p=1-q is the probability of being chosen, which depends upon the group size and number of choices made by each person. Further details are given by Criswell [7]. Results are expressed as the mean of the integration indices after normalising to group size.

Note that there is no overall correlation between computer use and socialisation. But when similar schools are compared, there is some evidence that higher actual computer use is related to lower group coherence, especially in High schools. This finding is subject to many more investigations in order to isolate any causal relationship.

Table A

School	Type	Weighted mean computer use (mins /student /day)	Mean integration index
A	SecB	3.6	.211
B	SecM	12.0	.334
H	SecM	6.7	.354
C	SecM	7.9	.665
D	Prim	2.9	.214
F	Prim	2.3	.284
G	Prim	4.9	.360
E	Prim	2.6	.372

Table B

School	Students /computer	Free time use	Overall computer utilisation
A	22.9	14%	18%
B	14.4	20%	39%
H	21.7	18%	23%
C	19.2	10%	36%
D	47.1	6%	35%
F	23.5	33%	15%
G	16.9	28%	20%
E	37.9	41%	20%

When the data was analysed, the amounts of time computers were available for use and actually in use were compared to give overall computer utilisation. It is important to contrast the duration of computer use with the entire school day of about 420 minutes. The survey time has included before and after school periods, and also free time such as lunch and morning recess. In some schools, the amount of computer use in these periods is significant, forming a fifth of all use in school B but only 10% in school C (See Table B). School polices vary greatly in this area, with some adopting a card system which allocates lunch-time use on a restricted basis to give fair access to all children. This is one area that would benefit from closer examination in order to identify strategies which maximise the benefits of new technology, whilst reducing any potential risks.

Interviews with students and staff have revealed a wide spread of awareness of the issues and attitudes to computers in general. Some staff weigh the possible social damage against the personal or academic benefits of computer based learning. Other staff agree on the importance of the socialisation taking place in schools, but find it difficult to estimate the likely effects of computer technology. As for the children, they have revealed a surprisingly high degree of access to home computers, rising to 80% even in lower income areas. Some primary school children were particularly emphatic about the way in which computers disturb friendships, though this opinion was restricted to the girls of the class. Another girl commented on the number of 'nerds' who just concentrated on the use of computers.

In the SENTIS project, four high schools and four primary schools have been completely surveyed. Friendship data was collected from over 500 students, and the use of over 150 computers in schools was monitored. Some work in further schools proceeds, particularly in special schools. In special education computer equipment is often installed specifically for individual use. Further, the distinction between health and education related use is very blurred. However, this does not mean that children with special needs in ordinary schools have been excluded from the study.

CONCLUSION

The SENTIS project has identified some possible techniques for investigating the social effects of computers in schools. The systematic approach possible with a whole school network has led participants to suggest that the data is of a high quality. Furthermore, this approach has the merit of being non-invasive. The sociogram basis for measuring group integration has been useful, and was agreed to by the participating schools. However, this is not a properly validated instrument, and a compromise has been made in measuring this dimension. Lastly, the reflections of both students and staff have provided important leads into the nature of attitudes towards computers.

The correlation coefficient between mean daily computer use and group integration for the Secondary mixed schools comes to -0.351, indicating a negative effect upon sociability at the 90% significance level. In primary schools the correlation is virtually zero. The significance of these findings merits further investigation, particularly in geographic areas beyond Tasmania. It should be recognised that Tasmania is well advanced in this field, with computer links made necessary by the dispersion of a small population to a few centres. Most schools are linked to a central computer site, and the mean computer/student ratio is 17.5:1 in High schools, 26.5:1 in project primary schools - compared to 32:1 in UK secondary schools, 67:1 in UK primary schools. Other important research questions have arisen during the project. In particular, why is there such variation in the utilisation of computers in schools (from 15% to 39%), and in their free time use? For those schools with relatively high computer use per student, what distinguishes those with low group integration from those with high integration? In other words, how is it possible to increase learning opportunities with computers and enable socialisation as well?

REFERENCES:

[1] Lepper, M R - Microcomputers in Education: Motivational and Social Issues - IN American Psychologist, January 1985 Vol. 40 No.1.

[2] Kerr, J & Hellier, Y - Social Implications of Technology - Changing Work Patterns. published by the State Computer Education Centre, Victoria 1987 ISBN 0 7241 6167 8

[3] Natali, I - The new technology and the effect on the changes of society - IN Education through Technology, published by Australian Council for Education through Technology Vol. 5 No. 2.

[4] Nolan, C - Under the Eye of the Clock - published by Pan Books 1988, ISBN 0 330 303163.

[5] Hope, M (Ed) - The Magic of the Micro, a resource for children with learning difficulties - published by Council for Educational Technology for MEP, 1986.

[6] Cumberland, S - Investigation of a Special School Network - Teacher fellowship report, Polytechnic of North East London, May 1988.

[7] Croswell, J H - The Measurement of Group Integration - IN The Sociometry Reader by
Moreno, J L published by the Free Press of Glencoe, Illinois 1960.

Computers in Education
A. McDougall and C. Dowling (Editors)
Elsevier Science Publishers B.V. (North-Holland)

QUANTUM CURRICULUM AND CHAOTIC CLASSROOMS: RE-FRAMING EDUCATIONAL COMPUTING

Bill GREEN and Chris BIGUM

Deakin University
Geelong, Victoria 3217
Australia

This paper is the first step in a project of reframing and reconceptualizing computing in education. It draws on the literature from postmodernism and critical pedagogy to situate educational computing in the larger context of curriculum theory.

1. INTRODUCTION

In this paper, we consider questions of culture and framing in educational computing, within a socially-critical perspective on curriculum and schooling. Our larger concern is to bring together the cultural practice of computing in school settings and contemporary theories of critical pedagogy. We seek to do this primarily by drawing upon the discourse of *postmodernism*, as it is currently being developed and debated in cultural and scientific research across a wide range of intellectual fields. More specifically, we intend this account to contribute to the formulation of a post-critical pedagogy for educational computing.

2. (RE)FRAMING EDUCATIONAL COMPUTING

Educational computing as it has developed to date would appear to be an enterprise entirely consistent with the larger field of Western science, and as such reflects the deep and abiding principles of Western culture. In a recent critique, Bowers [1] has argued that, on current trends, the emerging culture of educational computing is intensely problematical, exhibiting many of the ideological and metaphysical dilemmas of the West, as these become more and more apparent in the context of global nuclear tensions, the greenhouse effect, urban crisis, and structural unemployment. Indeed, there is a sense in which the technological revolution associated with computing represents the apotheosis of science as the dream of Reason, the ultimate expression of the classical scientific world-view, within which nature, knowledge and human progress are seen as inextricably linked. Hence, Bowers suggests that there is a particular urgency in the project to reconceptualize the field of educational computing as it currently understands itself, and as it characteristically announces itself on occasions such as this.

Although there are problems in his own analysis, stemming in part from his commitment to a post-liberal version of critical pragmatism, we want to endorse his call to re-frame and re-constitute the field in accordance with new theoretical and political developments. Specifically, we want to argue for the value of bringing to bear contemporary notions of culture, discourse, power and ideology in the curriculum practice of computing, so as to develop a more critical, culturally-sensitive account of what is clearly an area of burgeoning educational interest.

There is a profound and inescapable paradox in the contemporary discourse of educational computing. On the one hand, it presents itself, within the logic of classical science, as the prime solution to the problems facing education today, in a new era of cost-efficiency, accountability, performativity, and instrumental rationality. On the other, it promises a new vision for education, a paradigm shift into a new educational order altogether. Some of these accounts are of the 'more of the same but much, much better' variety, while others seemingly want to change the game-rules entirely, or to shift into another, completely new game. Often, however, they are really simply two faces of the one technicist icon, peddling a common educational project informed by the meta-logic of social efficiency and scientific rationalization.

Bowers [1,2] points to the predominance of what he calls "procedural thinking" in the field, citing the 1987 National Educational Computing Conference in the United States upon which occasion, of some 150 papers, only two could be said to deal with cultural issues, and more generally with "the conceptual, ideological, and cultural side of the technology" (Bowers, [3]). What dominated proceedings was a comprehensive concern with "technical aspects" of the new information technology, in an exemplary instance of what Bowers calls "the technological mind-set", related to which is what Papert [4] has termed "technocentricism". It is not that the field is intellectually moribund, as Bowers [5] is quick to acknowledge; on the contrary, there is a dazzling proliferation of "innovative richness" in the research on educational computing and other forms of information technology, as they impact on the school. However, it would appear extraordinarily narrow and selective, structured by "a narrow epistemological orthodoxy", a "reductionist epistemology which equates thinking with data (information)"; data-driven enquiry which fetishizes information and compulsively accumulates it, in a spirit of almost pathological excess. Bowers [5] points to "areas of silence within the mainstream of educational computing in the United States", something which we are convinced can be generalized to other countries where computing in schools and elsewhere is big business and a major educational priority. It is these "areas of silence"- the 'unsaid' - which must be investigated, those symptomatic absences in the discourse of educational computing that speak to its investments and secret impulses and that must be interrogated and illuminated. What other stories might be told about the field as it currently understands itself? More strongly, what stories have been actively suppressed? Whose stories? What would it mean to formulate different stories, and to tell them on occasions such as this, and elsewhere, in the great forums of the culture?

Bowers presents an eloquent case for the need to "*reframe* our way of thinking about microcomputers", so as to bring new cultural issues and political concerns to bear on curriculum discussion and educational policy. His purpose, as he describes it, is:

to reframe how we think about the educational uses of the microcomputer and, in the process, to establish conceptual boundaries that take account of the broader cultural consequences of this new technology. As long as we approach the microcomputer in terms of technical and procedural questions (How should we interface the software with the regular curriculum? Can LOGO be used by students to write haiku?), the larger cultural context will be put out of focus (Bowers [6])

To this end, he suggests the need to assert the priority of *educational* issues over computing-technological issues. This suggests that there needs to be more engagement than has tended hitherto to be the case with contemporary debates and developments in curriculum studies and curriculum theorising, particularly that concerned with notions of critical pedagogy, the politics of representation, and the social production of meaning and subjectivity (Donald, [7]; Giroux, [8,9]; Lather, [10]). In this paper, our concern is to outline what we propose as an alternative framework for thinking about curriculum, classrooms and computing. Our focus is firmly on the educational and cultural questions that, as we see it, must be asked if the larger political project of educational computing is to be turned towards the interests of social justice and critical democracy.

3. BRAVE NEW WORLD?

In all the excitement and glamour of a new form of educational endeavour, there has tended to be, perhaps understandably, a measure of hyperbole in accounts of the 'Brave New World' that computing technology represents for curriculum and schooling. Some would have it, apparently, that the solution par excellence is at hand for the current educational crisis, as well as for all those administrative and pedagogical problems of discipline, truancy, apathy, boredom, alienation, and burnout, among a host of others. That this is, at best, wishful thinking should go without saying - but of course, unfortunately, can't. The air is thick with the clamour of utopia, more often than not in the negative sense that works *against* the interests of teachers and students now, working together in the crowded classrooms that contain and constrain them. What's more, the versions of educational utopia that are on offer differ greatly. Some bespeak an innocence and a genuine concern for educational change, towards a better, more humane and civilized form of social existence; while others are more cynical and self-seeking, more ready to further the interests of the powerful and the privileged by making schooling an even more effective instrument of social reproduction and class domination.

Much has been said,then, about the educational innovation associated with new forms of information-communication technology. Our concern is with what we want to call the modern, normative concept of the classroom, against which new initiatives and proposals for educational practice are necessarily measured. We suggest that at the very heart of the politics of educational change, and specifically of representing and imag(in)ing classrooms in contemporary public and educational debate, is a conflict between the logic and imperatives of *modernism*, on the one hand, and those of *postmodernism*, on the other. This represents a new agenda for thinking about, among other things, the relationship between curriculum and computing. There is now an increasing body of specifically educational discussion on the implications of postmodern(ist) social and cultural theory for curriculum and schooling (Lather, [10]; Murphy, [11]; Doll, [12]; Giroux, [13]). Specifically, we want to argue that contemporary movements towards process-developmental curriculum and the open classroom are usefully considered in this way, that is, within the shifting dynamics of modernism and postmodernism. In particular, the challenge that these movements present to the normative concept of the modern classroom involves engaging with the radical implications for curriculum of what can be called the emergent culture of postmodernity. This is a matter not just of coming to terms with the pedagogic implications of new forms of knowledge and popular culture and the challenge of "emergent literacies" (Spencer, [14]), although that is most important. It also involves grasping the profound changes associated with the necessary re-framing of modernist projects, which certainly includes schooling and hence the modern classroom system. This does not mean that classrooms as such will simply disappear, although that is something which might well be contemplated; it does mean that, in the conventional, normative form that has lasted now for almost two centuries, classrooms can at least begin to be imagined otherwise, and in the meantime specific changes, modifications and innovations realistically introduced.

We want to explore the possibilities for generating a comprehensive theoretical account of postmodern schooling, and hence of the educational culture of postmodernity, out of a critical engagement with new developments in contemporary science<1>. It seems to us, as educologists, that there is much to be gained in participating actively and self-consciously in the extraordinary cultural and conceptual shifts associated with, and compelled by, the rise into prominence of nonlinear sciences, non-computable forms of mathematics, chaos theory, and notions of structural indeterminancy, relative unpredictability, and irreducible complexity. Prigogine and Stengers [17] begin their account of "Man's new dialogue with nature" with the following: "Our vision of nature is undergoing a radical change towards the multiple, the temporal, and the complex". What such work suggests, above all else, is that our current-traditional forms of educational science, including some of those which might otherwise be seen as radical and innovatory, embody and help perpetuate an essentially obsolete, out-moded system of understandings, a mechanistic world-view grounded in a Cartesian-Newtonian complex of idealist and metaphysical thinking<2>. Increasingly, this constrains and ultimately stifles genuine innovation: new ways of thinking about, and through, educational issues. Hence, there is an need to engage with other forms of research and enquiry, particularly of the kind increasingly identified with the term 'postmodernism'. In an important and influential statement on the status of knowledge in the context of what he calls "the postmodern condition", Lyotard [20] makes the following assertion:

> Postmodern science--by concerning itself with such things as undecidables, the limits of precise control, conflicts generated by incomplete information, 'fracta', catastrophes, and pragmatic paradoxes--is theorizing its own evolution as discontinuous, catastrophic, nonrectifiable, and paradoxical. It is changing the meaning of the word knowledge, while expressing how such a change can take place. It is producing not the known, but the unknown.

What might a postmodern *educational* science look like, on this account? And what would be its value, given the problems and dilemmas that currently face us?<3>

4. A NEW ORDER: THE PROMISE OF CHAOS

We live in a time of awful and exhiliarating promise--the imminence of catastrophe, as it were. This is clearly registered in education, with many new developments and initiatives, all inviting us into a glittering future. Taken together, it can be argued that these various developments participate in a revolutionary event, the historical emergence of a radically new educational paradigm, the effect of which is to challenge at its very heart what has previously been taken-for-granted as the *norm*, as 'normal' educational practice<4>. One way of capturing these developments is to describe them in terms of 'process pedagogy', and in general to see them within the terms of process-developmental curriculum, as a distinct orientation in curriculum theory involving notions of negotiation, transaction and meta-contextualization. It is important, however, to go well beyond current, restricted formulations of these ideas so as to reconceptualize them within the framework of postmodern(ist) developments in contemporary forms of culture and science, and hence to initiate the formal articulation and elaboration of a *postmodern(ist) pedagogy*, appropriate for classrooms of the future and the educational culture of postmodernity.

Central to the new paradigm is a re-assessment and revaluation of the principles of process and time. Prigogine and Stengers point to the emergence of a new sense of time, and to the significance of notions of irreversibility and dynamic open systems: "We are becoming more and more conscious of the fact that at all levels, from elementary particles to cosmology, randomness and irreversibility play an ever-increasing role. *Science is rediscovering time*" (Prigogine and Stengers, [24]<5>. Relatedly, there is a new sense of the concepts of order and disorder, and of the relationship between them. In contrast to the classical, Newtonian world-view, for which order was the privileged term, quantum physics and other forms of the new science are recognizing the primary significance of disorder, of chaos, and of the dynamic, necessary relationship between the two states, between being and becoming, static understandings and perceptions of reality and what can be called nature's open textuality, as the primary, organizing principle of existence. A key statement for the new paradigm is the following:

> We now know that far from equilibrium, new types of structures may arise spontaneously. In far-from-equilibrium conditions we may have transformations from disorder, from thermal chaos, into order. New dynamic states of matter may originate, states that reflect the interaction of a given system with its surroundings. We have called these new structures dissipative structures to emphasize the constructive role of dissipation in their formation (Prigogine and Stengers, [26]

Among other things, what is called for in this new and emerging perspective is a new emphasis on nonlinearity, instabilities, discontinuities and fluctuations. In acknowledging the primary significance of time and change, there is a new sense of the notion of *difference*: "The arrow of time is a manifestation of the fact that the future is not given, that, as the French poet Paul Valêry emphasized, 'time is construction'" (Prigogine and Stengers, [27])

There are profound curriculum implications in these arguments, as Doll [28,29] has indicated<6>. Critically appropriated, they enable the beginnings of a theoretical account of the movement away from the measured, determined curriculum, such as has arguably been characteristic of modern schooling and modern educational science, towards the idea of what can be called *quantum curriculum*, emphasizing notions of process, transaction, instability, undecidability, fluctuation, and relative unpredictability<7>. They provide a basis for reconceptualizing the idea of the open classroom, and of those forms of pedagogy which work with different principles of educational development. In particular, they provide a way of grasping the nature of process-developmental classrooms which, on first glance and to the normative eye, look anything but organized for meaningful and powerful learning. This is succinctly captured in the following comment on process-writing pedagogy: "It looks like unstructured, uncoordinated, unmanageable chaos. The kids are all over the place. 'Confusion writing' would be a better name for it'" (cited in Cambourne and Turbill, [32]). Chaotic classrooms, in short. Classrooms which, in the ordinary course of things, seem meaningless, chaotic, impossibly disordered, messy. And so they are, seen from this perspective - or, to draw upon the terms of this present discussion, framed as they are within a traditional, normative, essentially modernist view of curriculum and classroom learning. Yet it is by no means the case that such classrooms are counter-productive educationally, of necessity; although they are certainly counter-intuitive, within the framework of conventional thinking about education and classrooms. What needs to be grasped, then, is the *productivity* of such forms of classroom organization and curriculum process. This involves understanding how "the perceived 'chaos' [of such a classroom] can become a highly organized and successful centre of language learning" (Cambourne and Turbill [33]), that is, recognizable as productive of "highly structured, organized and robust learning settings" [34]

That this is not at all necessary restricted to such 'deviant' instances of educational practice as the literacy classrooms in question here, or indeed those computing classrooms consequent on the critical-reconceptualist work we are concerned to promote ourselves, may be indicated by drawing on the arguments of Schön [35] and Boomer [36], concerning the practical-professional knowledge of classroom teachers. In contrast to the current dominance of 'technical rationality' in accounts of classroom practice and teacher education<8>, they argue that there is a need to draw in more adequate descriptions of the *complexity* of classroom reality, and to engage entirely different rationalities for dealing with and understanding such complexity. Boomer [37] cites the following:

[Teachers] are not confronted with problems that are independent of each other, but with dynamic situations that consists of complex systems of changing problems that interact with each other. I call such situations messes. Problems are abstractions extracted from messes by analysts... [Teachers] do not solve problems, they manage messes<9>.
In our terms, this is entirely consistent with the notion of quantum curriculum. Teachers are engaged, every day, in realizing the possibility of meaning and order in the 'chaos' of their classrooms; together, teachers and students are "learning the uses of chaos" (Berthoff, [38]). Built into the very nature of such a view of pedagogy, there is a radical uncertainty thesis - a sense of the pragmatic incompleteness of educational action, the essential unpredictability of classroom learning, and the necessarily risky nature of the social praxis of the school.

5. CONCLUSION

Our concern in this paper has been to outline ways of re-framing the current-traditional discourse of educational computing. There is no shortage of 'find-it-and-fix-it' proposals, whether addressing material-technological issues or working on the level of meta-commentary within the existing terms of reference of the field. We have suggested a more radical and adventurous move: a shift into a more openly ideological, critical-pedagogic mode, drawing on the arguments of critical theory and postmodernism. We can't help wondering, however, if anyone is listening.

NOTES

<1> That there is a need to proceed with caution, and critically, is suggested in McHoul [15] and Spivak [16]. They suggest that there is potentially not only a dangerous faddism in making such moves in humanities and social-scientific research, but also, more importantly, they can represent a further encroachment of 'technologic' into the public-cultural sphere.

<2> A point also made persuasively by Bowers [18,19].

<3> We have explored two recent accounts of the classroom in educational computing, one by Michael Scriven [21], the other by Seymour Papert [22], both of which we see as problematical within the specific terms of reference of this paper.

<4> On the power of the norm, see Foucault [23].

<5> A particularly useful reference here is Gleick [25], a scientific-journalistic account of chaos theory and the new science.

<6> See also Weaver [30], with specific reference to reading pedagogy.

<7> There is a deliberate ambiguity in the term 'quantum curriculum' as we employ it here, since there is a sense in which quantum physics has itself been surpassed by postmodern science; see Prigogine and Stengers [31]. A better term might perhaps be 'post-quantum curriculum'.

<8> Educational computing, too.

<9> Actually, Boomer cites Schon citing Russell Ackoff.

REFERENCES

[1] Bowers, C.A., The Cultural Dimensions of Educational Computing: Understanding the Non-Neutrality of Technology (Teachers College Press, New York, 1988)

[2] Bowers, C.A., Journal of Curriculum Studies (1989, in press).

[3] Bowers, C.A., The Cultural Dimensions of Educational Computing: Understanding the Non-Neutrality of Technology (Teachers College Press, New York, 1988) p. 2.
[4] Papert, S., Educational Researcher, 16 (1987) 22.
[5] Bowers, C.A., Journal of Curriculum Studies (1989, in press).
[6] Bowers, C.A., The Cultural Dimensions of Educational Computing: Understanding the Non-Neutrality of Technology (Teachers College Press, New York, 1988), pp. 25-26.
[7] Donald, James, Beacons of the Future: Schooling, Subjection, and Subjectification", in Veronica Beechey and James Donald [eds], Subjectivity and Social Relations (Open University Press, Milton Keynes, 1985) pp. 214-249.
[8] Giroux, Henry A., Teachers as Intellectuals: Towards a Critical Pedagogy of Learning (Bergin and Garvey, Massachusetts, 1988)
[9] Giroux, Henry A., Border Pedagogy in the Age of Postmodernism (Mimeo, Miami University, Ohio, (1989)
[10] Lather, Patti, Educational Research and Practice in the Postmodern Era, Paper presented at the American Education Research Association, Annual Conference, New Orleans, April (1988) pp.5-9.
[11] Murphy, John W., Educational Theory, 38 (1988) 175.
[12] Doll, William E. Jr , Journal of Curriculum Studies 21 (1989) 243.
[13] Giroux, Henry A., Border Pedagogy in the Age of Postmodernism (Mimeo, Miami University, Ohio, (1989)
[14] Spencer, Margaret , Language Arts 63 (1986) 442
[15] McHoul, Alec , Editions, August (1989) 26.
[16] Spivak, Gayatri Chakravorty, Explanation and Culture: Marginalia, In Other Worlds: Essays in Cultural Politics, (Routledge, New York and London, 1987) pp. 103-117.
[17] Prigogine, Ilya and Stengers , Isabelle, Order Out Of Chaos: Man's New Dialogue with Nature (Fontana Paperbacks, London, 1984), p.xxvii.
[18] Bowers, C.A., The Cultural Dimensions of Educational Computing: Understanding the Non-Neutrality of Technology (Teachers College Press, New York, 1988)
[19] Bowers, C.A., Journal of Curriculum Studies (1989, in press).
[20] Lyotard, Jean-Francois, The Postmodern Condition: A Report on Knowledge (University of Minnesota Press, Minnneapolis, 1984), p.60.
[21] Scriven, Michael, Peabody Journal of Education 64 (1986/1989) 27.
[22] Papert, Seymour, Mindstorms: Children, Computers, and Powerful Ideas (Basic Books, New York, 1980)
[23] Foucault, Michel, Power and Norm: Notes, in Morris, M and Patton, P.(eds.), Michel Foucault: Power, Truth, Strategy (Feral Publications, Sydney, 1979) pp. 59-66.
[24] Prigogine, Ilya and Stengers , Isabelle, Order Out Of Chaos: Man's New Dialogue with Nature (Fontana Paperbacks, London, 1984), p.xxviii.
[25] Gleick, James, Chaos: Making a New Science (Penguin, London, 1987)
[26] Prigogine, Ilya and Stengers , Isabelle, Order Out Of Chaos: Man's New Dialogue with Nature (Fontana Paperbacks, London, 1984), p. 12.
[27] ibid p. 10.
[28] Doll, William E. Jr., Theory into Practice 25 (1986) 10.
[29] Doll, William E. Jr , Journal of Curriculum Studies 21 (1989) 243.
[30] Weaver, Constance, Research in the Teaching of English 19 (1985) 298.
[31] Prigogine, Ilya and Stengers , Isabelle, Order Out Of Chaos: Man's New Dialogue with Nature (Fontana Paperbacks, London, 1984)
[32] Cambourne, Brian and Jan Turbill, Coping with Chaos, Primary English Teaching Association (Rozelle, N.S.W., Australia,1987), p. 1.
[33] ibid, p. 4.
[34] ibid, p. 66.
[35] Schön, Donald, The Reflective Practitioner: How Professionals Think in Action (Basic Books, New York, 1982)
[36] Boomer, Garth, The Helping Hand Strikes Again: An Exploration of Language, Learning and Teaching, Opening Address to the International Symposium on Language in Learning, University of Queensland, July 1988, pp. 1-14.
[37] ibid, p. 3.
[38] Berthoff, Ann E., The Making of Meaning: Metaphors, Models, and Maxims for Writing Teachers (Boynton/Cook, Montclair, New Jersey, 1981), p. 68.

Computers in Education
A. McDougall and C. Dowling (Editors)
Elsevier Science Publishers B.V. (North-Holland)

A DIRECT MANIPULATION MICROWORLD FOR VERTICAL MOTION

Sara HENNESSY^, Fiona SPENSLEY^, Claire O'MALLEY^, Malcolm BYARD*, Ros DRIVER*, Conroy MALLEN*, Ramzan MOHAMED†, Tim O'SHEA^, and Eileen SCANLON^

^Institute of Educational Technology, Open University, Walton Hall, Milton Keynes MK76AA, U.K.

The aim of our research project, 'Conceptual Change in Science'§, is to clarify and describe the process of change in learners' conceptual understandings of natural physical phenomena, primarily in the domain of force, motion and energy transfer. A range of intervention strategies is being devised to promote conceptual change, focusing on the identification and development of computer software which could be useful in exploring and challenging children's reasoning. In this paper, we describe the theoretical and empirical steps taken in constructing our first computer-based microworld for linear vertical motion under gravity. It was programmed in Hypercard for the Apple Macintosh IIx and tested with 15-year-old students.

1. INTRODUCTION

1.1 Informal theories and conceptual change

A recurrent finding in studies of science learning is that people develop a powerful and surprisingly extensive set of beliefs about natural phenomena. These 'naïve' beliefs permit us to construct explanations of various phenomena that accord well with our perceived experiences (for example, the belief that motion requires a force is consistent with much experience in a world with friction). Informal or intuitive theories are the inevitable result of a search for meaning and regularity in our environment. They tend to be implicit in the way people interact with and describe phenomena, and to be context bound rather than general. They are also robust over time and resistant to subsequent instruction in new concepts and scientifically supported theories, such as Newtonian mechanics. Research shows that students' prior theories about the physical world can actually interfere with their learning of scientific concepts [1]; they affect what the students perceive to be happening in classroom demonstrations or laboratory experiments.

Instructional methods which tend to emphasise formal expressions of physical laws contribute to students' difficulties too [2]. Successful physics problem solving requires a substantial amount of qualitative reasoning; only after the problem has been analysed and understood in causal terms are quantitative solutions developed and formulae or equations applied [3]. Previous demonstrations of the potent role of naïve theories in science learning and of the central role of qualitative understanding of problem-solving situations, have contributed to a new conception of the learning process. Science learning is now believed to involve a process of conceptual change - a progressive reconstruction of the mental representations of natural phenomena which all human beings construct. This belief is based on the assumption that all learning depends on linking new information with prior knowledge and attempting to interpret new material in terms of established schemata. This consensus on the nature of learning is unfortunately not yet widely reflected in the way that science teaching is conducted in schools.

1.2 Implications for instruction; facilitating conceptual change

Our current understanding of science learning has some clear implications for improving teaching. Successful physics instruction must involve ways of getting students to reassess their conceptual systems or models of the world. The question is, should we ignore prior incompatible conceptions and help students to construct new ones, or directly confront the conflicts between old and new conceptions? We may have to use counter-examples to encourage students to see the limitations of their current conceptions. However, merely confronting learners with such conflicts does not guarantee that they will abandon their naïve conceptions, even when they are actively engaged in exploring the consequences of their own models. (Those models are themselves often inconsistent or conflicting, having been

---

*Leeds University. †Glasgow University.

§This 3-year project is funded by the Economic and Social Research Council through the InTER (Information Technology and Education Research) programme. Other members of the research team who have contributed to the work are Steve Draper (Glasgow University) and Roger Hartley (Leeds University).

derived from different contexts.) Moreover, learners may recognise conflict but be unable to come up with a better model. At least, though, these interventions may help children see the need for change.

We will probably trial a number of specific interventions to see which are most effective in promoting conceptual change. One possible source of help in getting learners to revise their informal conceptions is Socratic discussion, whereby groups of students with or without a teacher explore consistency in the use of their ideas in particular contexts, using different representations (diagrams, graphs etc.). Some insight may also be derived from Karmiloff-Smith's theory of cognitive development, according to which the combination of successful experiences and the opportunity to reflect on these enables changes to take place [4]. Her work indicates that exposing children to problems in a range of contexts will encourage them first to tackle the problems in context-specific ways. Given time for reflection, they will reorganise their conceptions of the problem space to generate a cognitively more economical model.

Other ways of encouraging learners to construct alternative conceptions include introducing new theories using an analogy with a system already known to them; using an intermediate situation to 'bridge' to a new construction; or coaching, whereby a situation is modelled for the student by a teacher or instructional system. In all cases, new procedures and constructions developed in one context will need to be extended to a range of contexts. For this to happen, teaching needs to focus on the qualitative aspects of scientific problem situations so that procedures can take on meaning.

We wish to promote specific kinds of conceptual change in our chosen domain of force, motion and energy transfer. Children's reasoning incorporates a number of conceptions relating to the notion of force which tend to be only partially differentiated, so that to move their reasoning to a Newtonian framework involves differentiating those notions and appreciating how they are related even semi-quantitatively. For example, the idea that a force is needed to maintain steady motion persists in many learners' understanding. Conceptual change involves the identification of friction as a force and a move towards associating force with change of motion rather than with motion per se.

Finally, the classroom is a social context and computers are typically used in schools by small groups of pupils rather than individuals. There is some evidence from developmental psychology research that peer interaction, whether it is computer-supported or not, has advantages over individual problem-solving activity for learning and development [5]. One of the proposed explanations is that collaborators are likely to challenge each other with counter-examples through putting forward alternative perspectives or interpretations. This leads to reflective narratives and discussion. Another possibility follows from Vygotskian theory; benefits may be derived from one (more able) partner providing a scaffolding for the other partner(s). Research into cooperative learning shows that pairs are the most effective grouping for developing improved problem-solving heuristics [6], so our software is intended for cooperative use by pairs of students. In this way we hope to help children learn to do science in a way that reflects an aspect of the way real scientists work - through collaboration and exchange of information.

2. ROLE OF COMPUTER-BASED ACTIVITIES IN PROMOTING CONCEPTUAL CHANGE

What contribution can the computer make to the study of children's scientific thinking and to the promotion of conceptual change? We believe that computer models have an important role to play because they (a) require children to make their implicit reasoning explicit; (b) enable children to visualise the consequences of their reasoning and provide an object for reflection and communication with others; (c) provide dynamic displays of models of phenomena which could form useful bridging analogies; (d) offer rapid data logging and display facilities which represent how variables are inter-related in ongoing situations [7]. We are presently exploiting the computer's potential through two kinds of software development activities.

The first important issue for investigation is the relation perceived by children between computer simulations and the actual physical phenomena they represent. Since real world experience is highly complex and can lead to the induction of incorrect physical laws, we plan to allow students to change and compare the physical laws which govern the real world, in order to explore within a simulation how thev interact with one another. This will be achieved through developing and evaluating ARK-like software: tools with direct manipulation interfaces in the tradition of Smith's 'Alternate Reality Kit'[8].

ARK is an animated environment for creating interactive simulations. It is implemented in SMALLTALK-80 and is built on a physical-world metaphor in which all objects have a visual image, a position, a velocity and are operated on by physical forces. Everything in ARK can be manipulated (with a mouse-operated hand) according to the constraints on physical laws in faithful simulation of the real world. The physical laws - such as Newton's laws of gravity - can, however, be changed. This magical feature permits users to create their own artificial microworlds and carry out counterfactual experiments in alternate realities.

ARK is based on a strong analogy to the physical world, and this literalism enhances learnability of the interface through mimimising the amount of explanation required by the user. Everything of interest is continuously visible and changeable by the user. The ARK interface is designed to be transparent for its users, allowing them to become conscious only of the content domain and not the computer. This is the notion of direct manipulation (DM), developed by Shneiderman [9]. It means that the represented microworld becomes cognitively, directly present to the user, so that s/he develops a feeling of operating directly in the model world ('direct engagement') and can appropriate the concepts modelled by the system. Successful DM - internalisation of new theories and their transfer to everyday life - additionally depends on achieving a mapping from objects and operations in the simulated world to the learner's existing concepts. For instance, teaching a new physical law may necessitate building upon learners' ideas about what an object is and how it typically behaves. Success depends also on using relevant and familiar representations.

We are currently developing and using ARK-like software with DM interfaces to enable pupils to create and manipulate alternate realities. Our aim here is to support the differentiation of conceptions relating to the notions of force, motion and energy. We are constructing computer-based activities in which pupils can make predictions about outcomes and then experiment and hence observe events which may contradict their prior conceptions and experiences. The prototype microworld described in this paper is our first such activity. In developing this work further, we will have to address the question raised earlier: should we introduce conflict in the form of simulations which challenge learners' intuitive models? The danger is that counter-intuitive behaviour may simply rupture the user's belief in the simulated world. We will explore this possibility empirically.

We are also interested in the ways in which students use qualitative reasoning and how they develop more formal and quantitative statements in refining their models [10]. In order to investigate and examine students' progression from informal interactions with our DM systems to formal representations of the behaviour of those systems, our team is developing an interactive software environment called Varilab (based on the STELLA modelling package for the Macintosh). Varilab is designed to facilitate children's development of process-driven modelling; the system consists of a collection of objects, their properties and the relationships between them, parameters being changed through processes which affect objects. We hope that this modelling tool will assist us in our aim of clarifying children's ideas about what processes are causing the behaviour they observe within several key mechanics contexts. This strand of the research also endorses the notion of learning through exploring alternate realities, since STELLA-like software allows the user to build and compare a variety of different models of physical systems.

3. A PROTOTYPE SOFTWARE ENVIRONMENT

In this section we describe the design of our first prototype software tool for linear vertical motion under gravity (not projectile). First, we outline briefly those aspects of the British secondary school science curriculum which are relevant to this domain, and some informal conceptions which pupils of this age are known to develop.

3.1 Pedagogic objectives and prior conceptions

We want our students to develop a detailed qualitative knowledge of how velocity varies for a single body in vertical motion and to go on to connect it to perception of motion, rate of change of position, velocity compared to another object moving with constant velocity, velocity as a variable in equations, velocity as a vector. Then, they need to consider what makes velocity vary and how it varies; this leads to the rate of change notion of acceleration and to terrestrial gravitation as an example of constant acceleration. Thirdly, students require at least a qualitative grasp of the factors that do and do not affect motion in this domain: force/impulse, energy; mass and weight; gravity; elastic bouncing as a function of materials, size and shape; air resistance. Finally, the qualitative aspects of the domain will need to be connected with the quantitative or formal aspects ($F = ma$, $v = u + at$, $KE = 1/2mv^2$). The ability to generate and interpret graphical representations of motion (such as speed-time and distance-time graphs) is also important.

The specific Newtonian conceptions we wanted to reinforce in our development of a microworld for vertical motion include (a) gravitational force is acting all the time as the object ascends and descends; (b) the motion of the projectile is symmetrical (neglecting air resistance). Our team's previous experience of working with pupils aged 8-15 shows that they do not typically hold these beliefs, but tend instead to assert that (c) when an object is thrown up, it is given some 'force' ('energy' or 'power') which gets used up as it ascends. Gravity then takes over and pulls the object down; (d) the time taken to go up may not be the same as the time to come down. Owing to gravity, a body descends faster than it ascends for points at the same vertical height.

3.2 Interface design

A 'pinball' microworld was developed in order to address some of our pedagogic objectives. It was used to gather some data concerning pupils' prior conceptions of velocity and impulse in the context of linear vertical motion under gravity. The animated pinball environment is programmed in Hypercard for the Macintosh IIx microcomputer. (Hypercard is eminently suitable for rapid prototyping; it is quick and easy to use and incorporates a comprehensive variety of useful facilities and features in one application.) Three versions of the activity have been tested with users in the three pilot studies reported below.

Everything in the pinball simulation environment is operated with a mouse-driven hand, which changes shape according to the kind of object it is grasping. Basically, balls of two different masses can be launched upwards with various initial energies by a vertical spring launcher analogous to that found in pinball machines. When launched, a ball visibly ascends, descends and bounces. Features of this microworld include a scale for weighing the balls, a transparent container for storing them, and various meters to measure quantities such as maximum height, time, instantaneous velocity, force and speed. There is also a 'video recorder' for recording an experiment, replaying events at normal or slow speeds, and taking accurate meter readings.

In order to make the microworld believable - and hopefully 'directly engaging' - we decided to make the balls bounce when they hit another object or the 'floor'. This incorporates the commonsense knowledge that on each bounce the ball does not rise as high as it did on the previous bounce. The balls make convincing, fading 'boing' noises as they bounce. Similarly, the handle of the spring launcher is physically pulled down with the mouse-operated hand and an appropriate creaking noise is heard. The video recorder has audible button clicks and tape-rewinding sound effects.

In accordance with DM theory, we wanted to make visible and directly available theoretical quantities such as velocity, so we considered several types of meter and other displays. In order to connect what is represented in the interface with concepts and experiences students already have, we chose to implement first a device similar to an analogue meter, rather than a vector graph which would have been unfamiliar to most pupils in our age group. We in fact represented velocity in four ways during the prototyping: via the analogue meter, a digital readout, a horizontal strip meter, and the motion of the ball itself. The success of our interface design and the usability of a DM system by secondary school pupils was assessed in the following series of experiments conducted by the Open University team.

4. EXPERIMENTS: AIMS, METHODOLOGY AND INTERFACE ISSUES

4.1 Pilot Study 1: Pinball on Paper

<u>Aims</u>: The purpose was to ascertain whether students of this age could detect without substantial explanation what the various objects in the proposed system represented, and to see what changes were necessary before we went on to implement the simulation on the Macintosh. We also wanted to assess pupils' ability to make accurate predictions about the effects of changes in variables such as the initial impulse given the mass of the ball, and whether they could test and refine those predictions through experimentation. Finally, we hoped to gather some data concerning non-Newtonian conceptions in this domain. Our hypothesis was that assertions (c) and (d) outlined above in 3.1 would be the predominant ones elicited.

<u>Methodology</u>: A group of 15-year-olds of both sexes and of mixed ability from a local school (N = 26) took part. The subjects were individually presented with a series of 14 pictures portraying the path of a ball launched from a plunger, and readings on a digital clock, a vertical distance scale, an altimeter and a velocity meter as it reached its highest point. Nine balls of three colours and sizes were depicted in a storage container. Subjects were interviewed using a previously devised set of questions (similar to those described for Study 2) as guidelines before, during and after the pictures were presented. Responses were tape recorded and written notes were taken. Each session lasted about 15 minutes.

<u>Resulting Interface Issues:</u> These can be summarised as follows. It was not immediately obvious to the students what some of the objects pictured, particularly the pinball launcher and the vertical distance scale, were meant to represent. The positions of these two objects were changed for the first animated Hypercard version of the activity to make it more evident that height was being measured (see **Figure 1**). The clock was labelled 'time', and the launcher and all the scales were shown to be bolted to the 'walls'. A 'force on impact' meter was introduced, as was a distance scale showing how far the plunger had been pulled back.

Most students did not know the terms

'altimeter' or 'velocity' (n = 15 in each case). Alternative beliefs included that the meters measured volume, power in ball or weight. The vertical ruler and altimeter were preferred by equal numbers of subjects, so the latter was dropped in the next version. Velocity was interpreted as being equivalent to (non-directional) speed; a horizontal strip meter for speed was therefore introduced, and we added '+' and '-' symbols to the velocity meter. Six subjects did not assume that the largest black ball was the heaviest, so a weighing scale was introduced in the Hypercard version and only two balls were retained: a large, dark (heavy) one and a small, pale (light) one. Finally, most students recognised the utility of the 'video' machine for greater accuracy of measurement and for reviewing events.

4.2 Pilot Study 2: Pinball Hypercard version I

Aims: The purpose was to discover whether students aged 15 could recognise objects and use the interface depicted in **Figure 1** without substantial instruction. Our secondary aim was to determine what, if anything, students learn about vertical motion after using the program; we posed three key questions concerning changes in velocity and the differences resulting when launching balls of large and small mass. We examined whether pupils could make predictions about the outcomes and could test and refine their predictions through experimentation.

Methodology: Seven 15-year-olds from the same school as before took part; all were new to the task. The questions listed below were posed to each individual, with further prompting where necessary. The three key questions came before the students were asked to carry out an experiment to test what happens and they were repeated afterwards. Written notes were taken and the screen was videotaped. Each session lasted 25-30 minutes.

Interface questions: (a) What are all the objects on the screen? What could you do with them? (b) Have a go using the mouse and see if you can find out more about what the objects are for.
Pre-test and Post-test: (c) How fast is the ball going at the highest point it reaches? (d) How fast is the ball going when it hits the plunger again? (e) If the plunger is pulled back as far it can go, what happens if we launch first a very light ball and then a much heavier ball?

Resulting Interface Issues: It was clear that being able to manipulate objects physically in the microworld made the screen objects much more accessible to students. Although not a single subject initially recognised the purpose of the pinball launcher, 6 of our 7 subjects grasped the idea of launching balls using the plunger very quickly. Similarly, some initial misinterpretation of the meters was quickly overcome and students were able to weigh the balls and take appropriate readings from the distance, time and 'speed' meters. Problems with interpreting scale readings were common, however. The 'force on impact' reading caused much confusion and its label was simplified to 'force' for the next iteration. The term velocity was dropped and a new vertical 'speed' strip meter was introduced. Units were added to all meters in the next version.

Experimentation: The video machine was used successfully by nearly all of the subjects and found to be very useful. Our subjects did not however pay careful enough attention to their experimental results and in particular to velocity and time readings - they could have used slow motion more often for greater accuracy. The consequence was that their final responses were at least as inaccurate as their initial predictions (see 5.1.4). A confirmatory bias was also evident, such that students sought to confirm their prior hypotheses. For instance, several persisted in asserting that a ball attains its maximum speed at the highest point that it reaches.

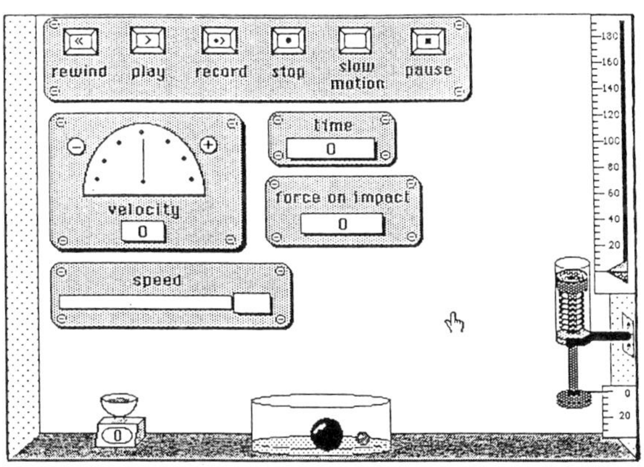

Figure 1: Hypercard Version I of Pinball Interface

4.3 Pilot Study 3: Hypercard version II

Aims: The main purpose of this study was to test the final Hypercard version of our simulation. We also wanted to assess how adequately pupils of this age could use graphs to provide formal representations of what happens with regard to speed and distance during vertical motion under gravity. Again, we examined whether pupils could make and test predictions about the effects of change in mass.

Methodology: A mixed group of 15-year-olds (N = 15) from another local school took part. The method was the same as before, but this time subjects were asked (a) to draw a graph showing what happens to the speed of the small ball over time, from when it leaves the plunger until the moment it hits the plunger again on its downward path; (b) whether there would be any difference in speed if the larger, heavier ball was then launched (representing its speed on the same graph); (c) to draw a graph showing changes in height of both balls over time; (d) to carry out an experiment to test what actually happens in each case and to record their measurements on new graph sheets; (e) to compare these observations with their earlier predictions.

Resulting Interface Issues: The new vertical 'speed' meter proved to be very successful but the height scale with its marker registering maximum height led to some confusion as subjects were unable to take interim readings very easily. Even after a few minutes of interaction with the system, 5 subjects needed some help in working out the function of the pinball launcher. Without an explicit introduction, it seems that this metaphor is not consistently accessible to pupils of this age.

Experimentation: Minimal use was made of the video recorder during the experimentation phase; only 4/15 subjects used it to obtain accurate measurements. The others were either hasty and unscientific or they repeatedly launched the balls, sometimes unnecessarily. Most of the subjects who successfully represented changes in speed or distance over time did not use the clock to obtain actual time readings. (They may have found it difficult to cope with observing two variables simultaneously.) Many subjects were inaccurate in pulling back the launcher to its maximum distance when comparing balls of different mass; most did not even attempt to equalise the force on the plunger. Finally, initial graphs (showing predicted outcomes) were rarely consulted during experimentation although the opportunity for pupils to do so was deliberately provided.

4.4 Summary

The DM microworld we have developed for exploring vertical motion under gravity proved remarkably successful. It was accessible and useable by 15-year-old pupils, the majority of whom were able to identify and execute the pinball task without help. Our subjects enjoyed interacting with the system; they appeared to be engaging directly with it and many were impressed by its realism. However, interpretation of meter readings was often problematic and this highlighted the need to test several different measuring devices in order to connect what is represented in the interface with students' existing concepts and experiences. The video recorder analogy was found to be very effective although many pupils under-estimated the significance of its record/replay/pause facilities. This was a symptom of their generally inaccurate experimental techniques.

5. USING A DM SYSTEM TO EXPLORE CHILDREN'S INFORMAL CONCEPTIONS: RESULTS, CONCLUSIONS

This section summarises our main results regarding the elicitation of students' prior conceptions, including the accuracy of their predictions about the effects of changes in impulse or mass, and their ability to construct formal representations of motion (in graphical form).

5.1 Pilot Studies 1 & 2

1. Students aged 15 years have very hazy ideas about gravity, what 'keeps the ball up' and why it begins to drop. Gravity and impulse were often described in terms of pushing and pulling, e.g. "gravity pulls the ball down and air pushes it so the speed goes up as the ball drops". As expected, a few pupils stated that the ball had been given some force, e.g. "the spring gives the ball power so speed increases, then the ball wears out of power."

2. While nearly all the subjects realised that speed equals 0 at the highest point, some made inaccurate predictions about changes in speed during the ball's flight, indicating a lack of understanding of 'speed symmetry'. Many believed that the speed of an object is different on its downward path to that on its upward path at the same height.

3. Students made many inaccurate predictions and observations when comparing balls of different mass or impulses of different sizes. Over half of the subjects asserted that the lighter ball would not go proportionally faster or higher.

4. Only 2 or 3 subjects (out of 7) gave correct answers to each of our pre-test questions in Study 2 and there was no improvement after students had experimented with the system. However, extensive experience with a system of this kind is deemed to be necessary for promoting conceptual change.

5.2 Pilot Study 3

1. Pupils aged 15 years are not very competent in generating graphs to represent changes in speed and distance over time. Some

subjects recorded only maximum speed or height values, and one expressed worry because she thought graphs were supposed to consist of a line rising from the origin and hers did not conform!

2. Most subjects (8/15) drew two roughly correct graphs representing symmetrical change in height over time, but 5 recorded maximum height values only on at least one occasion. About half of the subjects initially drew graphs showing that speed increases steadily as the ball rises until it reaches its maximum speed at its highest point, and then loses speed until it comes to a stop upon reaching the launcher. 9 subjects did not use the bottom portion of the graph page, labelled 'DOWN', to show speed on the ball's downward path. A lack of speed symmetry was again observed in the pupils' explanations and a couple believed that gravity does not act constantly. Typically, it was said to act only on the way down.

3. In 10 cases, there were significant differences between the speed-time graphs drawn before and after the experimentation phase, and in 3 cases, the height graphs were significantly different. Progression as a result of experimentation is hard to assess quantitatively, although there were some clear instances of more accurate representations being produced when pupils drew the second speed-time graphs. An example of one subject's 'before' and 'after observation' graphs is depicted in **Figure 2**; the second graph even portrays the ball bouncing in the pinball launcher. In some such cases, interviewing indicated that the pupils' interpretation of experimental outcomes had changed too. For example, a few learned through experimentation that at the ball's highest point, speed is 0, rather than at its maximum.

Nevertheless, in keeping with previous findings that naive physical intuitions are very robust, we observed very little actual developmental progression during the experimental phase. (For example, of the 7 subjects who initially drew a graph showing that speed increases steadily as the ball rises, 3 produced a similar graph after taking speed measurements.) Our results confirmed previous findings showing that students' informal conceptions can affect what they perceive to be happening in experiments or demonstrations [1]. Some of our students 'saw' what they expected to see. Similarly, discrepancy between the pupils' verbal explanations and the graphs they drew was common, especially when measurements taken conflicted with prior predictions.

5.3 Summary

Our results indicated that students of this age are limited in their ability to formalise their physics conceptions by generating graphs representing the motion they observe. About a third of our subjects appeared to have no understanding of change in speed or height over time, and some seemed to have stereotyped images of graphs that they simply reproduced. Part of the problem, however, was their common failure to conduct scientific experiments or to take accurate measurements. The software we develop needs to address this problem and to strive to help develop pupils' skills in these areas.

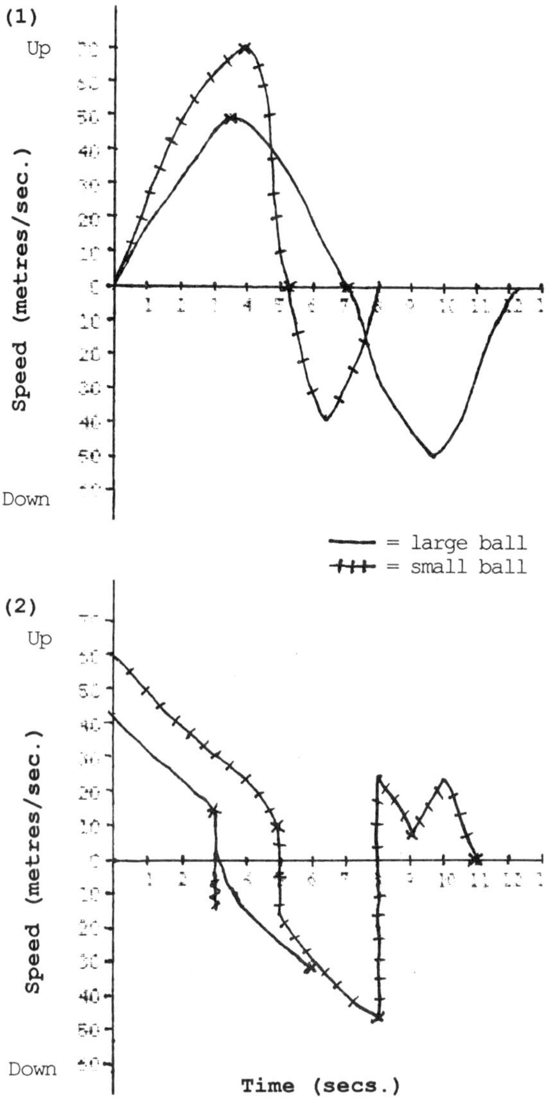

Figure 2

The students were able to make predictions about the outcomes of change in variables such as mass or impulse, but many of these were incorrect. While we elicited Newtonian conceptions relating to constant gravitational force and speed symmetry in some of the pupils tested, others were found to hold common alternative conceptions of the form outlined in 3.1. We can conclude that some students do not understand what makes velocity vary and how it varies and that many have robust, naïve conceptions concerning the factors affecting motion in this domain; particularly impulse, mass, gravity and air resistance. There is evidently plenty of scope for conceptual change in pupils at this educational level.

In conclusion, our DM-based pinball microworld - which dynamically represented vertical motion under gravity - was found to be highly successful in eliciting prior conceptions in that domain. Our subjects were able to make their implicit reasoning explicit, and the interface proved on the whole to be transparent and realistic, requiring minimal explanation to learn.

6. FUTURE DEVELOPMENT OF DM-BASED SOFTWARE TOOLS

DM theory has some implications for further development of this and subsequent microworlds. We will try to link our simulated velocity to different representations, either to connect to the pupils' existing experience of real phenomena, or to the theory and its standard representations which we are trying to teach. We plan to allow students to construct, or at least, to explore alternate realities. We might show a world where objects rise and fall with constant velocity, for instance. This is an extension of DM from the objects to the laws, so that the form of the law of motion can be manipulated too. We will try to tie this variation to commonly observed misconceptions, implementing a situation for each one. Our software will additionally allow pupils to turn on and off velocity, acceleration and forces at different points in a trajectory, their task being to construct behaviour that looks realistic to them.

We have recently developed a piece of software called DM^3 for Direct Manipulation of Mechanical Microworlds. It is being used to create (with SMALLTALK-80) a sequence of further microworlds in the domains of free fall, and horizontal motion (a) without friction, involving both driving and impulsive forces, (b) with friction and (c) with fluid resistance. These microworlds are based on the same simulation engine as *ARK,* but with three important distinctions: all objects are visible in DM^3 but the lesson designer has control over whether they are manipulable by the users; the DM^3 environment does not support visual programming; finally, DM^3 allows multiple interaction units or modules (all different) to be attached to any DM^3 object.

We will be evaluating our software tools with a view to examining both the processes of conceptual change and the effectiveness of our interventions in promoting learning. It is hoped that as a consequence of our interventions, pupils will at least be able to take concrete examples and make predictions, to justify those predictions and to bring more Newtonian conceptions to bear. In developing a sequence of related microworlds, our aim is to get pupils to generalise their new conceptions across a range of contexts and to extend them to increasingly complex situations.

REFERENCES

[1] Driver, R. (1983). *The Pupil as Scientist?* Open University Press.

[2] White, B.Y. and Horwitz, P. (1987). *ThinkerTools: Enabling children to understand physics laws* (Report no. 94480). Cambridge, MA: Bolt, Beranek and Newman.

[3] Larkin, J.H., McDermott, J., Simon, D.P. and Simon, H.A. (1980). Expert and novice performance in solving physics problems. *Science* 208, 1335-1342.

[4] Karmiloff-Smith, A. (1984). Children's problem solving. In Lamb, M.E., Brown, H.L. and Rogoff, B. (eds.), *Advances in Developmental Psychology: Vol. 3.* Hillsdale, NJ: Erlbaum.

[5] O'Malley, C.E. and Scanlon, E. (1989). Computer-supported collaborative learning: Problem solving and distance education. *Proceedings of CAL89,* Surrey University.

[6] Trowbridge, D. (1987). An investigation of groups working at the computer. In K. Berger, D.E. Pezdek and W. Banks (eds.), *Applications of Cognitive Psychology: Problem Solving, Education and Computing.* Hillsdale, NJ: Erlbaum.

[7] Driver, R. and Scanlon, E. (1989). Conceptual change in science. *Journal of Computer-Assisted Learning* 51, 25-36.

[8] Smith, R.B. (1987). *Experiences with the Alternate Reality Kit: An example of the tension between literalism and magic* (Technical Report). Xerox Parc Research Center, Palo Alto, CA.

[9] Shneiderman, B. (1983). Direct manipulation: A step beyond programming languages. *IEEE Computer* 16, 57-69.

[10] Forbes, K. and Stevens, A. (1981). *Using qualitative simulation to generate explanations* (Report no. 94480). Cambridge, MA: Bolt, Beranek and Newman.

Computers in Education
A. McDougall and C. Dowling (Editors)
Elsevier Science Publishers B.V. (North-Holland)

COURSEWARE CAD

Bertrand IBRAHIM, Alain AUBORD, Birgit LAUSTSEN and Michael TEPPER

University of Geneva, 12 rue du Lac, 1207 Geneve, Switzerland

Even though the creation of Computer Aided Learning software (CAL) is always done on a computer, most development phases are still usually done with pen and paper. Authoring systems generally tackle the "coding" phase, leaving aside the specification and design phases and often imposing rather severe constraints on the users of such systems. The specification and design of courseware is not an easy or very formal process. Computer Aided Software Engineering (CASE) can nevertheless be very helpful in such an endeavor. We present here a whole development environment that runs on a graphic workstation. It allows a team of teachers and pedagogues to specify lessons graphically and then makes it easier for the team of programmers to translate these specifications into programs that can run on different target machines. The specification uses a very simple formalism and the programs are generated in a general-purpose programming language such as Pascal or Ada. This development environment includes, among other tools, a graphic script editor, an automatic program generator, a synchronous multi-window editor to hand-code the parts of the CAL program not generated automatically and a translation manager to help maintaining translations of the lessons in different natural languages.

1. INTRODUCTION

The most common approach to the development of computer aided tutoring is to use an authoring system. The problems with such a tool are that it is restrictive in what the developer can do and that it is tailored for individual work. Recent research [6] shows that general purpose (high level) programming languages are still seen as the state-of-the-art for large-scale quality courseware development. Such large-scale projects are the result of a collaboration between teachers, pedagogues and programmers altogether.

Unfortunately, until now, very few tools exist to support large-scale courseware development using general purpose programming languages. Moreover, very little has been done to support the whole development process of such software. There are, however, software engineering techniques [4,7] already used in other fields of software development that can very usefully be applied to courseware development.

Software CAD (Computer Aided Design) is an emerging paradigm of these very last years [8,2]. It refers to automated software design techniques centered around wiring-diagram-like graphical representation of software, with a supporting environment that allows for automatic program generation and fast prototyping.

The project we describe in this document (Figure 1) is based on this paradigm and is the result of a long experience in developing large computer aided learning (CAL)

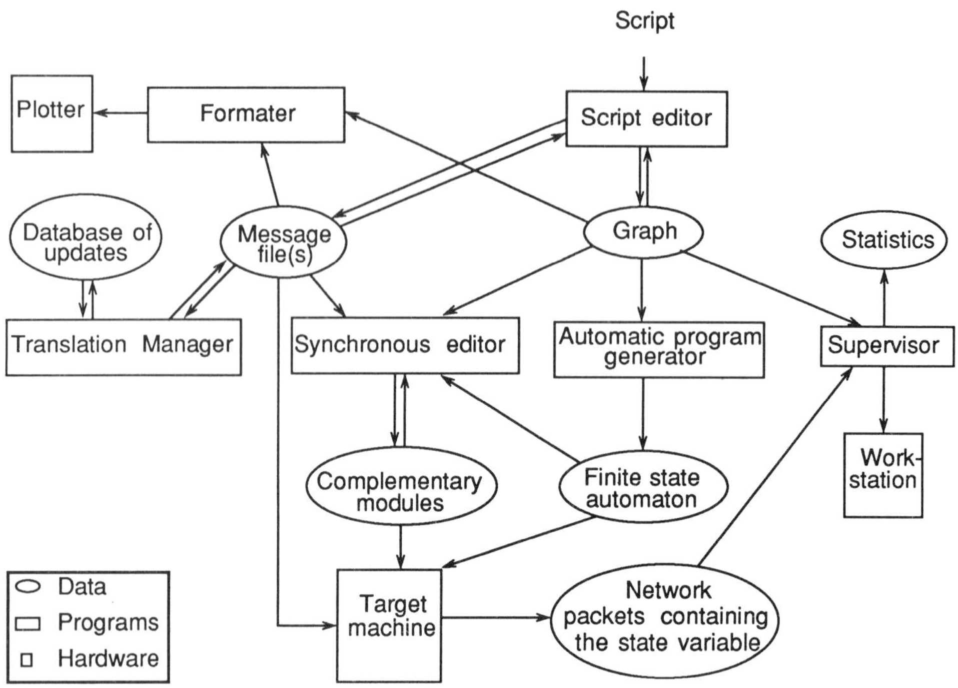

Fig. 1 : Overview of the environment with its tools and data.

applications in a rather traditional way. This project intends to tackle the software development life-cycle of CAL lessons in order to allow the designers to concentrate on the pedagogical aspects of the lessons.

From the very beginning, we made the assumption that the development environment didn't need to be the same as the runtime environment. As a matter of fact, the needs of the designers and coders during the development phases are quite different from the needs of the learners using the final product. It follows from this that the development environment is targeted to run on a large screen graphic workstation when the environment of the learner is more modest and runs on PC-like machines.

Since teachers do not necessarily have a background in programming, it is essential that the tools made available to them to specify and design a lesson be as simple and close to their "universe" as possible. There are different phases in the development of CAL software and teachers or pedagogues are needed only in a few of them. They shouldn't need to be involved in the programming phase and yet a certain continuity is needed from the specification and design phase, then the programming and debugging phase, to the field tests and final use, including reviews all along the development process.

This continuity is ensured by a document that describes in a very detailed way what can happen during the learning process. This document, we call it a scenario or a script, can be considered as a semi-formal specification of the software that will be built thereafter.

2. DESIGN PHASE

The formalism we use in a scenario has been developed by Prof. A. Bork's team [1] at the University of California, Irvine. It allows a complete and detailed description (partially in natural language) of a lesson. Since a good CAL lesson is mainly a dialog between the learner and the computer, the major building blocks of the scenario deal with program output, user input and how the program should respond to user input. All other operations are indicated in free text as instructions to the coder.

This specification formalism is a kind of graphical language. It is precise enough to give an exact description of the behavior of the final product, i.e. the lesson. It is built on just three basic primitives: text that has to appear on the screen, instructions to the coder (in natural language) and predicates (generally corresponding to answer analysis criteria). The specification of a lesson can thus be represented as a directed graph, in which each node corresponds to one of the three basic primitives and where the edges indicate the sequencing of operations (Figure 2). Text to be displayed is written in an ellipse, instructions to the programmer are between curly brackets and predicates are inside rectangular boxes.

The quality of a CAL lesson highly depends on its non-linearity, i.e. its ability to adjust its behavior to the learner's profile. This non-linearity is achieved by using cascades of tests (predicates) to be applied on the learner's answers to questions or on his actions following a task assignment. For more non-linearity, edges originating from a test box are labeled with a number or an interval. At runtime, a counter is associated with the test box. This counter will be incremented each time the criterion specified in the box has been satisfied. The corresponding edge will be followed depending on the value this counter has. Complementary predicates can be put in sequence (like IF THEN ELSIF instructions). If the criterion is satisfied, an edge on the side is followed; if it isn't satisfied, the criterion just below (if present) is then evaluated, and so on. If none of the criteria apply to the user input, the edges originating from the bottom of the last box indicate the actions to be taken in such an unanticipated case.

This formalism does not prejudice who, of the learner or the computer, has control of the other. It has been used to specify very different kinds of lessons, ranging from mastery learning tutorials to microworlds with embedded tutoring as well as self-instructional software.

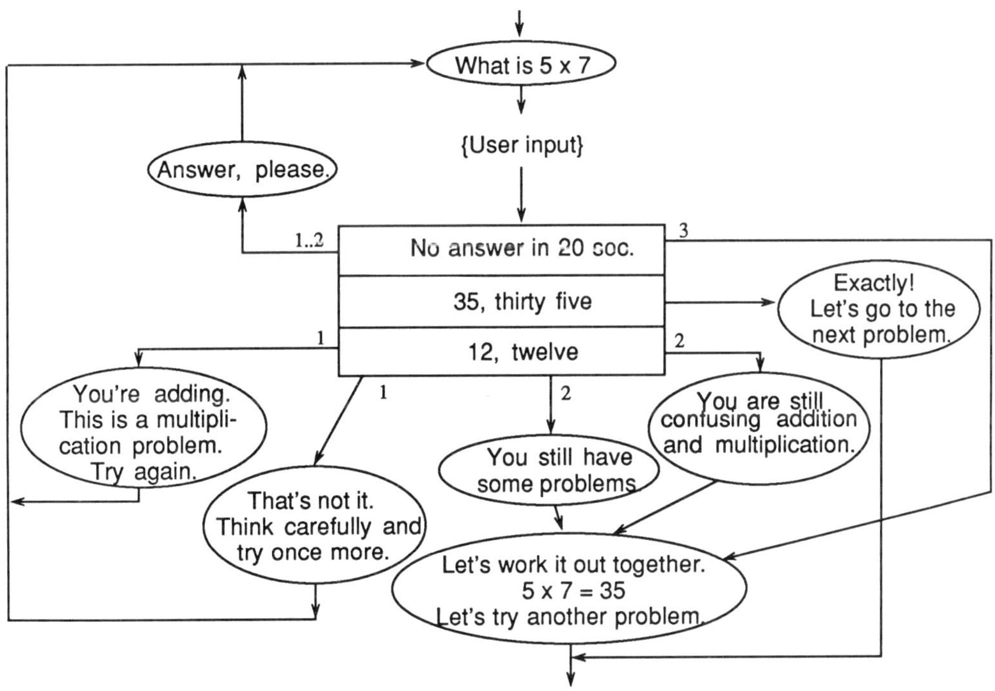

Fig. 2 : Purely academic example of a piece of script

In our environment, a scenario is built using a script editor. This is essentially a graph building editor in which the basic primitives correspond to the formalism we have just described. It is used to interactively enter the detailed specification of a lesson.

Using a mouse and keyboard interface, the designers specify each step of the lesson one by one, edit the textual content of each step and add or change sequencing links as they wish. These links are shown on the graphical representation as arrows, but are not considered by the script editor as simple objects. The user of the script editor can indeed use them to move along the script. He just has to select an arrow on the graph and pick the jump to arc origin or jump to arc end items in the menu to display what is at the beginning or end of a given edge.

As this example shows, the script editor is not just a simple graphic editor. It has knowledge of the structural aspect of a script and, as such, disallows most meaningless operations and offers a few primitives that help the designers check the consistency of their work. There is, for instance, a validation primitive that checks among other things that every step of the script is reachable and that there is no gap in the labelling of the edges originating from a test box.

3. PROTOTYPING PHASE

As we said earlier, the specification we get from the design phase is not purely formal. It includes what we call instructions to the coder that are written in natural language, without any restriction on what they can contain. It is therefore out of question to hope that the environment will ever be able to generate automatically the code for all such elements of the specification. Answer analysis criteria may also be specified in a rather informal way and are thus difficult to generate automatically too.

It is, however, relatively easy to generate code for the formal part of the specification, i.e. the messages and the sequencing of operations. The environment includes for this purpose an automatic program generator that translates the script into a program written in a high level programming language such as Ada, Modula 2, UCSD Pascal, or Turbo Pascal. This tool can be seen as a graphical compiler that transforms a graphical representation of a lesson into an executable program. The target language can be chosen according to what is available on the target machine on which the code will be running.

Since the specification is not purely formal, the automatically generated program does not totally implement it. However, this is not a problem. A node of type message is translated into a call to the text display primitive with the name of the corresponding message as parameter. A node of type test is translated into a call to a boolean function whose body will be defined in a separate module. A node of type instruction to the coder is translated into a call to a procedure whose body will also be defined externally in a separate module.

Even though the body of a procedure corresponding to an instruction to the coder will later have to be "hand-coded", the automatic program generator initially generates a dummy body that displays on screen the text of the instruction. Similarly, the body of a boolean function corresponding to an answer analysis criterion will initially prompt the user for the value the function is supposed to return.

This means that the automatically generated program can already run as is on a target machine without any need for coding. Its behaviour will not fully correspond to the specification, but it will already give a rough idea of how the final product will look.

Running this program on a target machine allows the designers, already at this early stage, to review the text as it is displayed on screen, to work on and tune the screen design and to test the different paths the learner can follow depending on his actions or answers.

As an alternative to program generation, we have contemplated a direct interpretation of the script on the development machine. This solution looks appealing but it is, however, not as easy to implement as it might seem at first. It indeed implies among other things that one emulates the screen and window management of the target machine on the screen of the development machine.

On the other side, the choice we made, i.e. generate source code that will be compiled on the target machine, has the advantage of integrating the prototyping and coding phase.

4. CODING PHASE

The code produced during the prototyping phase includes dummy procedures and functions in separate modules corresponding to the instruction to the coder and to the test elements of the script. The task of the programmers is then to replace these dummy bodies with code that really does what the designers asked for.

One major problem in using code produced by an automatic program generator is that this code is hardly readable by a human being. Most of the symbols used in the code are generated by rather simplistic algorithms and are thus quite cryptic. Isolating the parts that have to be "hand-coded" is already a step in the good direction since the programmers will not have to deal with the automatically generated code.

The use of a modular target programming language is essential here. It allows a complete separation between the automatically generated code and the code added by the programmers, so that the programmers do not need to modify the code produced by the automatic translation.

Programming a procedure when one is not able to see how it fits in the whole application is not an easy task. The programmers can therefore use a specific tool of our development environment to write their code. This tool, a synchronous multi-window editor, allows a programmer to complete, in one window, the automatically generated code corresponding to the part of the script that is showing in another window. The idea is to have different windows show the different aspects or views of the same thing: a regular text editor in one window to edit one of the separate modules that have to be hand-coded and the script editor in another window to show the corresponding specification.

Any script window can be synchronized with a module window, or vice-versa. The script window is read-only in the sense that one can only issue positioning commands in it. One can enter positioning commands in any of the windows and ask for the other window to "synchronize", ie. show the corresponding part of the view it handles. The programmer can thus very easily see, write or modify the code corresponding to a specific part of the script, by finding the location in the script window and then asking for the module window to synchronize, i.e. show the code for that part of the script. One can also find a specific location in the code (e.g. where an error occurred) and then ask for the script window to synchronize, i.e. show the part of the script that is the specification of the corresponding code.

One can have more than one pair of script-program windows at the same time. With this tool, the programmer can always see the specification at the same time as the code he is working on. This specification (the script) should help him understand and manage the code, since it can be seen as a human readable documentation of the code.

5. DEBUGGING AND MAINTENANCE PHASE

Another problem that could arise from the approach we have taken is related to the fact that the development machine is not the same as the machine on which the CAL program will run. If there is an error in the code written by the programmers, it is on the target machine that it will show up.

For this delicate phase, the environment includes a remote supervision tool. It is a program that runs on a development machine at the same time as a lesson is running on a target machine connected to the same local area network (LAN). This tool is used to follow on the development machine the execution of the CAL program. To do this, the automatic program generator has to include, in the code it generates, instructions to send on the network. The informations sent indicate which program is running, which step of the script is currently being executed and possibly the name of the learner (e.g. for automatic curriculum).

The remote supervision tool can thus directly show on the script (which is a human readable specification of the lesson) where in the lesson the target program is. It allows a programmer to find much more easily where in a lesson a given error occurred. The synchronous multi-window editor can then be used by the programmer to move directly to the code that generated the error and correct it.

A similar mechanism makes it possible to collect automatically statistics on the learning process, once the CAL program is operational. The analysis of these statistics is useful for the designers of a lesson to review the pedagogical design. This review can then be carried out with the script editor.

6. TRANSLATION PHASE

In a country that has four official languages it appears natural for us to want to have the dialogues of the CAL programs we develop be translated in different languages. That is why there is in our view another rather important phase: the translation of the dialogues [3,5]. Indeed, all the CAL software we develop is intended to be easily translated into different languages using the Latin alphabet (with some variants for accented letters). This translation phase can happen before, as well as after, design reviews. Therefore, it implies using an editing tool that also has the functionalities of a version manager to handle a database of updates.

We indeed make the assumption that there will not be a canonical language in which the design and all the reviews would be made and from which translations will be made. It may in fact very well happen that the design be done using, for instance, English, then have the lesson translated to French and Italian. Any of these three versions can then be edited with the script editor because some field test has shown a modification to be desirable. The problem is then to make sure that all versions are up-to-date.

In order to help to maintain the coherence of the different translations, a multi-window editing utility manages the modifications that are made to the messages. This tool maintains a database of modifications for the different message files, allowing the person(s) in charge of the translation to find directly the places that need to be updated, showing in a window the original message in the initial language, in another window the updated version of the message for this same language, in a third window the translation of the original message and, in a fourth window, the user can enter the update for the translated message. Only the fourth window is active, i.e. it is the only one in which the user can apply a modification. The other windows are passive (read only), but all four windows are synchronized and moving to a specific message in any of them generates a similar move in the other ones.

This tool is separate from the script editor since it has to be used by different persons. The translations will indeed not be done by the original designers, but rather by people proficient in both the original and target languages. The translation manager has nevertheless to be coupled with the script editor on one version of the messages in order to be able to indicate to the translators where to make updates in the other versions.

7. FUTURE EXTENSIONS

Even though the development of this environment is not yet complete, we are already working on extending its capabilities. As the reader may have noticed, the specification formalism we use is open ended, in the sense that it allows the designer to give part of the specification in natural language (as instructions to the coder). In the first phase, we designed the automatic program generator so that it takes care only of the display of the messages and of the sequencing of the separations. The instructions for the coder are, for the moment, translated into a procedure call and the answer analysis criteria into function calls. These procedures and functions are in a separate module and their body must be written by a programmer.

In a second phase, we intend to augment the translation capabilities of the automatic program generator by using artificial intelligence techniques, i.e. knowledge acquisition and generalization techniques. It will try to detect similarities between different instructions to the coder and query the programmer for a predicate, allowing the generator to associate specific parameters to each instruction to the coder.

Another extension we have in mind for this project is to use groupware techniques for the design phase. We indeed generally have more than one designer work on the development of the same set of lessons at the same time and we often have different people do the reviews. It would therefore be useful if the environment could support such team work either by allowing different people on different workstations to work on the same script at the same time (distributed work) or different reviewers to annotate the original script without changing it in the absence of the designers (asynchronous work).

REFERENCES

[1] Bork, Alfred and Weinstock, Harold, Designing Computer Based Learning Material (Springer Verlag 1986).

[2] Raymond, J.A., Buhr, Gerald M., Karam, Carol J., and Hayes, C. Murray Woodside, Software CAD: A Revolutionary Approach, IEEE Transactions on Software Engineering, Vol. 15, no. 3, March 1989.

[3] Franklin, Stephen D., Levrat, Bernard C., Portability of Computer-Based-Learning Materials across Machines and across Natural Languages (WCCE/85, K.A. Duncan & D. Harris Ed., North Holland, 1985).

[4] Glinert, Ephraim, Tanimoto, Steven, PICT: An Interactive Graphical Programming Environment (IEEE Computer, November 1984, pp. 7-25).

[5] Ibrahim, Bertrand; Kuhni, Christianel, Online Supervision of CBl through LANs, Education & Computing 1985, Vol. 1 no. 4, pp. 243-247, North Holland, 1986.

[6] Karrer, Urs, How to Develop Quality Courseware: Results of a Survey, Journal of Educational technology Systems, Vol. 16(4), 1987-88.

[7] Raeder, Georg, A Survey of Current Graphical Programming Techniques, (IEEE Computer, August 1985, pp. 11-25).

[8] Smith, C.U., Gross, R.R., Technology Transfer between VLSI Design and Software Engineering: CAD Tools and Design Methodologies (Proc. IEEE, Vol. 74, pp. 875-885, June 1986).

Computers in Education
A. McDougall and C. Dowling (Editors)
Elsevier Science Publishers B.V. (North-Holland)

COMPARISON OF CONVENTIONAL AND COMPUTER BASED MEMORIZATION STRATEGIES

Ameeta Jadav, Shashi Rani, Surekha Kishore

CMC Ltd. 115 Sarojini Devi Rd. Secunderabad 500 003 INDIA

The paper discusses the findings of a study with high school students in memorization of twenty-six countries and their capitals using conventional self-learning and computer based strategies. The results show that computer based strategy is more effective than conventional methods but only if the criterion for mastery is set at a high level. Students had a highly positive attitude towards learning from the computer. Issues which need further explorations are discussed.

1. INTRODUCTION

It would seem natural that with the power of random access, unlimited iterations and record-keeping, the computer would prove to be a powerful tool to aid in memorization of paired-association tasks. However, this is the area where experts have expressed the greatest doubts about its efficacy. This may be because many of the computer based memorization programs merely emulate the conventional flashcard strategy in which all the items are learned together and the same amount of time is spent on all items. Experts recommend that for better retention, learners should work on a small subset of items at a time, review unlearned items more often than learned items, do several short spaced reviews and memorize the items in a random order to avoid sequential associations. The capabilities of computers can be easily exploited to meet these requirements for efficient retention.

This paper presents an algorithm (IMPART algorithm) for memorization of paired-association tasks. It then discusses the findings of a study conducted with high school students in India to examine the relative efficacy of conventional and computer based memorization strategies.

2. THE IMPART ALGORITHM

2.1. The Bins

The IMPART algorithm is based on the concept of four types of bins - The Storage bin (SB), Presentation bin (PB), Review bins (RB) and the Learned item bin (LB) (Figures 1 & 2). Each item is associated with a unique state. A change in state signifies movement of the item from one bin to the other. This movement depends on the response of the learners and the criteria for mastery.

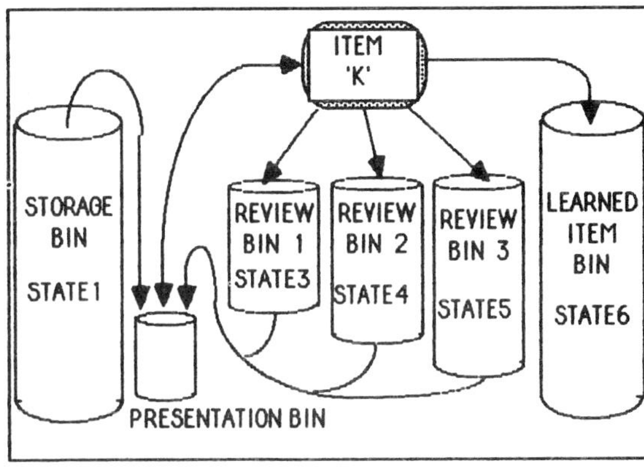

Figure 1

2.2. Movement of Items Between Bins

Initially, all the items are stored in a random order in the Storage bin (State 1). When a learner begins, nine items from the Storage bin are transferred to the Presentation bin. The number nine was determined on the basis of Miller's (1956) contention that human beings are capable of processing five to nine items at a time. The items from the Presentation bin are presented to the learner one by one. If the response is correct on the first attempt that item is transferred to Review bin 3 (State 5). If it is incorrect, the item stays in the Presentation bin (State 2). An item will stay in the Presentation bin until the learner makes a specific number of consecutive correct responses (mastery criterion) after which it will move to Review bin 1 (State 3).

If there are less than nine items in the Presentation bin after all the items have been presented, new items are brought in with priority being given to Review bin 1,

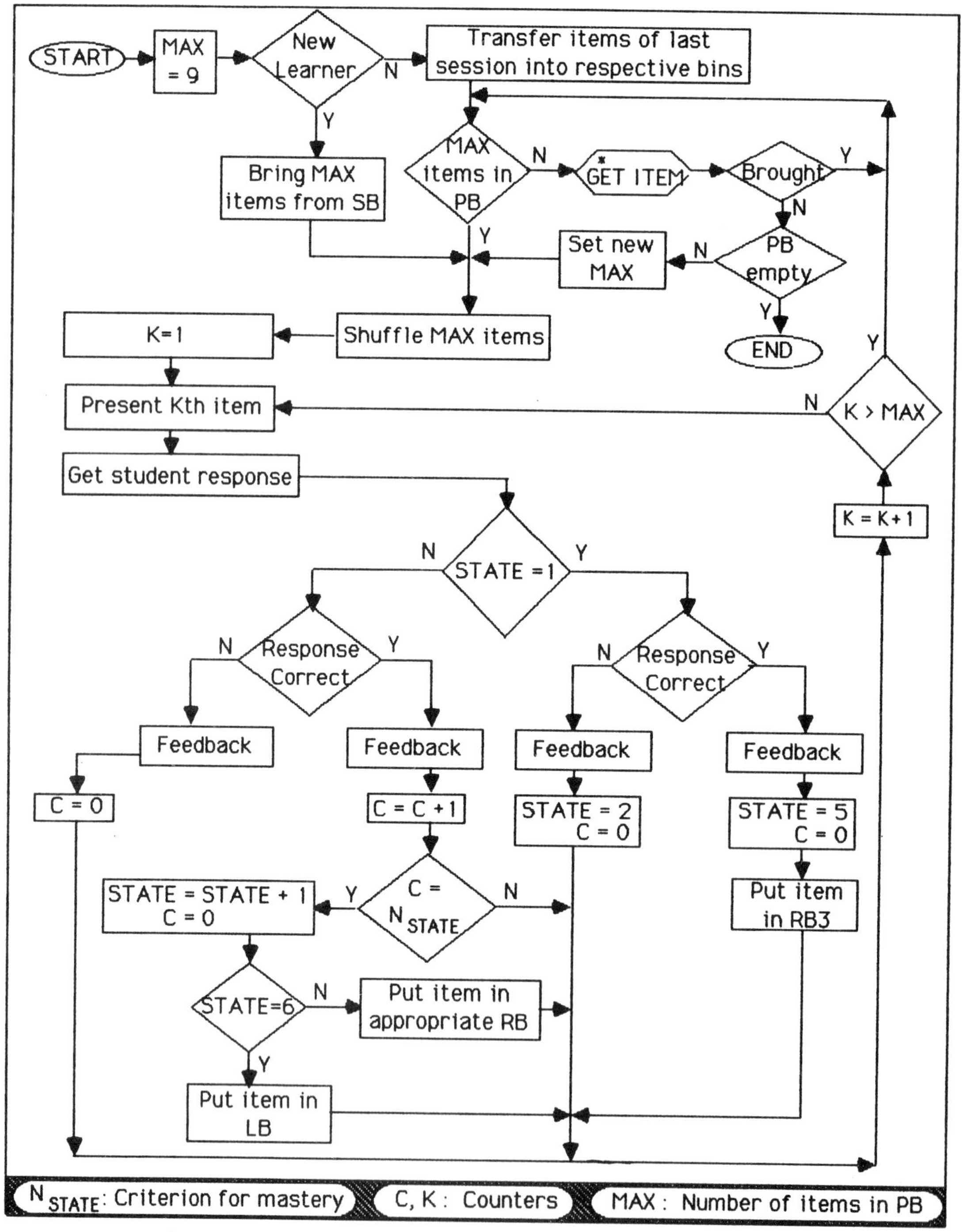
START
MAX = 9
New Learner
Transfer items of last session into respective bins
Bring MAX items from SB
MAX items in PB
GET ITEM
Brought
PB empty
Set new MAX
END
Shuffle MAX items
K=1
Present Kth item
K > MAX
Get student response
K = K+1
STATE =1
Response Correct
Response Correct
Feedback
Feedback
Feedback
Feedback
C = 0
C = C +1
STATE = 2
C = 0
STATE = 5
C = 0
STATE = STATE + 1
C = 0
C = N STATE
Put item in RB3
STATE=6
Put item in appropriate RB
Put item in LB
N STATE: Criterion for mastery
C, K : Counters
MAX : Number of items in PB

Figure 2

Review bin 2, Review bin 3 and then the Storage bin. Items from Review bins are brought only if the bin is overflowing that is, it has more items than its specified size. The items will be brought on the First In First Out basis. An item coming from Review bin 1 (State 3) will move to Review bin 2 (State 4) when the required criterion for mastery is met by the learner. Similarly, an item from Review bin 2 will go to Review bin 3 and from Review bin 3 will go to the Learned item bin. The status of each item for the learner is stored immediately after the response is made. Thus it is possible to go through the lesson in more than one session. The design of the software allows for modifications in the size of the Review bins. The underlying assumption here is that the greater the size of the Review bin, the greater the period between reviews of the item. The software also allows modifications in the criteria for mastery. The frequency of review will be determined by the criteria for mastery. The higher the criteria for mastery, the more often will the learner have to respond to an item.

A simple tic-tac-toe type of game with a four by four cell matrix is played while learning. An item will be presented upon selection of a cell in the matrix. If the response to the item is correct, the cell turns green; otherwise it turns orange. The objective for the player is to get a row, column or diagonal of the matrix in green.

3. STATEMENT OF PROBLEM

Some studies which have compared computer based memorization strategies with conventional strategies have found that while there is no significant difference in the achievement of learners, (Campbell, Peck, Horn & Leigh (1987); Salisbury & Klein (1988)) the attitude toward instruction is more positive for the computer drill groups .

It should be noted that these studies did not compare one medium (computer) with another (print/flashcard) but rather two strategies for memorization. As pointed out by Clark (1983)and Salisbury & Klein (1988), it makes better sense to compare strategies than media. It would thus be worthwhile to compare the various computer based strategies and also variations of the same strategies.

While there are several issues in relation to various strategies which could be examined, we focussed on the following questions:

1. Is there a difference in immediate and delayed retention of subjects using conventional print based self-learning, computer based low mastery criteria and computer based high mastery criteria strategies?

2. What are the affective reactions of subjects using the computer based strategies?

4. DESIGN

The sample was divided into three groups - Conventional, Computer Low Criterion (CLC) and Computer High Criterion (CHC). The Conventional group was given a printed list of twenty-six countries and capitals. The CLC group learned with the help of the IMPART software. The mastery criterion for this group was fixed at one for all levels. Thus, if the first response was incorrect, the learner was presented with an item for a minimum of four times. The CHC group also learned with the help of the IMPART software but the mastery criterion was fixed at two for all levels. Here the learner was presented with an item a minimum of eight times if the initial response was incorrect. The size of the three Review bins was fixed at 5, 10 and 15 for both the computer strategy groups.

Each subject was given a Pre-test, Immediate retention test and a Delayed retention test. The dependent variable for the study was the gain scores for the Immediate and Delayed retention tests.

While the subjects were going through the lessons, their comments, attitudes, method of learning and so on were observed and noted. The subjects in the computer groups were also asked to write down their feelings about using the computers for learning.

5. METHOD

5.1. Sample

The sample consisted of 60 grade ten male students from a high school in a major city in south central India. The subjects were randomly assigned to the three groups of 20 students each. However, because of absences and non completion of learning, the final group sizes became uneven. The data analysis was finally conducted on forty-three subjects for immediate retention and thirty-seven subjects for delayed retention.

5.2. Instruments

The Pre-test, Immediate retention test and the Delayed retention test were paper and pencil tests. The order in which the countries were listed was different in each test.

5.3. Procedures

The study was conducted over a period of two days (thirty subjects each day). All subjects first took the Pre-test.

The Conventional strategy group was given the printed list of countries and capitals. They were told to take their time and follow whatever method they wished for memorization. At the same time, they were told not to talk to each other or to take each other's help. They were instructed that when they were confident about having learned the items, they should raise their hand. When a student raised his hand, he was asked if he was sure about having completed the learning and, on affirmation, given the Immediate retention test.

Both the computer strategy groups first went through a trial lesson. This was done to give them a chance to get familiar with the computer keyboard and the IMPART software. After this, they started the lesson on countries and capitals. The subjects were instructed to raise their hands when the lesson completion message appeared on the screen. They were then given the Immediate retention test. It was estimated (on the basis of a pilot study) that after three hours of continuous learning, the subjects would be too tired to continue and so those who did not complete the lesson by that time were told to quit. Their data was dropped from the analysis.

The subjects in the computer groups were told to write down how they felt about using the computer to learn. There were two observers in each room. These observers took notes on the comments of the students, their expressions, and how they proceeded through the lessons.

Ten days after the treatment, the subjects were given the Delayed retention test. At that time, they were asked if they had actively tried to recall any of the items that they had learned after the initial treatment. None of them had done so.

6. RESULTS

Gain scores were calculated as GS = (Post-test - Pretest)/ (26 - Pretest). The mean gain scores for the Immediate and Delayed retention tests are given in Table 1 and Figure 3.

Table 1
Gain Scores for Retention Tests

Group	Immediate			Delayed		
	N	X	SD	N	X	SD
Conv	18	.73	.26	15	.51	.28
CLC	13	.87	.10	12	.71	.14
CHC	12	.94	.06	10	.80	.14

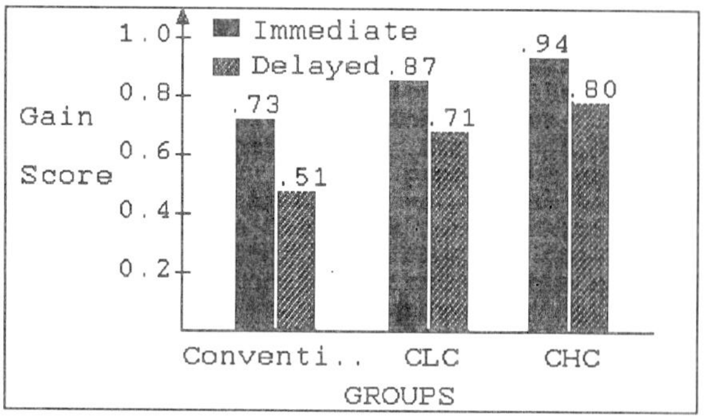

Figure 3.

One-way ANOVA for the Immediate retention test showed significant difference between means ($F = 5.241$, $p < .01$). Fischer's LSD method indicated there was significant difference between the mean gain scores for Conventional and CHC groups. The analysis for the Delayed retention test showed similar results ($F = 6.674$, $p < .01$). Here too, there was significant difference between Conventional and CHC groups.

7. OBSERVATIONS

7.1. Conventional Strategy Group

The subjects in this group completed their tasks in much shorter time than the other two groups. The strategy they used was to cover the responses with paper and try to recall them mentally. Some students wrote the responses next to the stimulus. Others made marks against items they seemed to have learned and then concentrated on the items without marks. Learning was assumed to be over when they were able to go through the complete list and recall all the responses. This process was not repeated more than once.

7.2. Computerised Strategy Groups

The most visible aspect here was that the subjects were thrilled to be working on the computer. Initially, when they were unable to win the game, there was some bit of disappointment. However, as they started winning, their enthusiasm increased and they did their best to recall the responses. This enthusiasm was diminished after they continued to win games. Towards the later part of their learning experience, the game became more of a hindrance.

A high degree of inter-item interference was observed. The interference was not random but specific - certain responses consistently interfered with specific items. For example, Banjul (capital of Gambia) was frequently given as the response for Ghana. The subjects did not seem to adopt any specific method for overcoming this.

The subjects who had not finished after about two hours, experienced fatigue and seemed to have forgotten what they had apparantly already mastered. Some of these subjects did not complete the lesson.

After more than half of the subjects had completed their lessons and walked out of the room, there was unspoken pressure to complete the lesson. This however had varying effect on the subjects. On the one hand, some of the subjects were encouraged to concentrate on their lesson and complete it while the others got distracted and totally lost their concentration.

Virtually all the subjects (even those who did not complete the lesson) said they enjoyed learning from the computer. Some comments from them are given below:

'In the starting I found it very confusing and hard. Then after practicing for a long time I found it easy and exciting. I have also learnt the capitals of many countries.'

'The games were interesting and educative. Simultaneously brain-racking. It required a lot of patience and presence of mind. As it was my first practical on a computer, it was thrilling.'

'I felt it was very interesting. I could learn in a short time and very easily. It is good to learn answers from computer. When I was learning I feel like playing and at the same time learning. This type of learning is very good. I liked it. I like to come next time and sit with the computer and play and learn.'

'I feel it is good way to learn things. Students who are poor must take up this course. Then they could also score good marks. This course is surely worthwhile.'

8. DISCUSSION

The apparent results of this study are in favour of high criterion computer based strategies. However, the study does not give definitive indications about which factors are instrumental in the higher retention for the CHC group; rather, it raises critical questions about the use of computers in instruction, strategies for memorization, learner vs computer control, inter-item interference, role of games in learning and so on.

Learning Time. The computer groups spent considerably more time on the learning task than did the conventional strategy group. If one examines the specific activities of the computer groups, one would see that considerable time was spent on finding the keys on the keyboard, playing the game and figuring out the IMPART software. However, the difference in time taken in self-learning strategy and computer controlled strategy is still likely to be significant.

The question that arises is: Had the self-learning strategy subjects spent the same amount of time on the task as the computer strategy groups, would their learning have been the same ? While the answer to this question could be empirically established, we feel that it would be difficult for a learner to concentrate and stay interested in a learning task for such a long time. Secondly, learners may not be able to use judicious strategies for learning. However, a highly motivated learner could use very sophisticated strategies and exhibit a high level of 'stick-to-itiveness'.

Use of new and exciting medium. The subjects in the CLC and CHC groups were using an exciting new medium and their enthusiasm for learning could be affected by this fact. For many of them, this was the first close encounter with a computer. It would be interesting to examine the relative efficacy of the three strategies with subjects who are familiar with computers.

Fatigue. It is noteworthy that eleven subjects in the two computerised strategy groups had not completed the lesson after more than two and a half hours. These students exhibited a visible loss in learning after about two and a half hours. Ideally, computer based instruction should allow learning at one's own pace and at one's own time. Future studies could be designed to accommodate several spaced sessions for all the groups to avoid a significant effect on the results from fatigue.

The fact that eleven subjects did not complete the lesson could however be examined from another angle. Is it likely that some people just cannot learn with the help of the computer? Would the same subjects have shown a different level of motivation and learning if they were asked to learn through a conventional strategy? Aptitude-treatment interaction may be worth examining in future studies.

Inter-item interference. As was mentioned earlier, significant inter-item interference was observed when the subjects were going through the computerised lessons. It would be possible to enhance the existing algorithms such that they would establish interference indices for each item and use appropriate presentation strategies. Item pairing has been explored as one way of overcoming the effects of inter-item interference (Jadav, 1986). This and other strategies could be explored through development of further algorithms.

Role of Games. Most subjects who went through the computerised strategies mentioned that they liked the game and it was also observed that the game added interest and motivation to learning. However, it was also obvious that after some time, the game lost its 'charm'. Future software could have either more than one game or the same game with different challenge levels.

Conventional vs Computerised Strategies. While the statistical analysis has indicated significant differences only between the Conventional and CHC groups, the trend in the results is in favour of computerised strategy. This trend needs to be further examined with larger sample sizes. The criteria for mastery which was used for the CHC group, did not show evidence of 100 % learning. Would it be possible to establish an optimal combination of mastery criteria and size of Review bins which could lead to near 100 % mastery of the target task? The mastery criteria could also be made a function of the learner's performance. This would lead to a truly individualised method of instruction.

Bias in the Sample. The sample in this study was of only males. Thus the results cannot be generalised across the population. Examination of the same issues with different populations may be interesting.

Cultural Issues. The Indian student in general may have a tendency to respond better to controlled learning environments. Under these circumstances, it would be worthwhile to explore variations of computer-controlled strategies which lead to optimal learning.

Other issues which need further examination are the effects of variation of the period between successive reviews, presentation of options along with the stimulus, and the use of a different size for the Presentation bin.

9. Summary

The study conducted with high-school students in India has suggested that computerised drill may be more effective in retention of paired-association tasks if a high criterion for mastery is used. The subjects showed positive attitudes toward learning from the computer. Further explorations of computer aided memorization strategies could look at factors such as the role of motivation, media, inter-item interference, games, learner control and culture with a varied population.

ACKNOWLEDGEMENTS

We would like to thank our colleagues in the CBT and Video groups, the Principal, staff and students of St. Patrick's High School, Secunderabad and Mr. M. H. Razack for their help during the conduct of the study and writing of this paper.

REFERENCES

Campbell, D. L., Peck, D. L., Horn, C. J. & Leigh, R. K. (1987). Comparision of computer-assisted instruction and print drill performance: A research note. *ECTJ, 35,* 95-103.

Clark, R. E. (1983). Reconsidering research on learning from media. *Review of Educational Research, 53,* 445 - 459.

Jadav, A. D. (1986). *Item pairing and the use of visual mediators in the instruction of paired-associate tasks.* Doctoral Dissertation. Brigham Young University, Provo, UT.

Miller, G. A. (1956). The magical number seven, plus or minus two: Some limits on our capacity for processing information. *Psychological Review, 63,* 81-97.

Salisbury, D. F. & Klein, J. D. (1988). A comparison of a microcomputer progressive state drill and flashcards for learning paired-associates. *Journal of Computer-Based Instruction, 15,* 136-143.

Computers in Education
A. McDougall and C. Dowling (Editors)
Elsevier Science Publishers B.V. (North-Holland)
© IFIP, 1990

Learning Styles and Computer Programming Activities

J. S. James, Lecturer in the School of Education, Tasmanian State Institute of Technology and
L. L. James, Student Administration Officer, T.S.I.T.

This paper concerns a three year study in northern Tasmania using 74 grade 5 and 6 subjects. Children were identified by learning style and administered Lego and Logo activities. The study investigated using these activities to cater for learning style preferences. The results do not support the contention that Lego/Logo activities can effectively cater for learning style preference. However, several areas of further research are identified.

INTRODUCTION

Children have different learning styles. These range from a sequential, step-by-step problem solving approach to an undirected, divergent approach. Activities involving computer programming can be designed which cater for differences in learning styles.

This paper concerns a study which investigated the use of Lego and Logo programming activities in different learning style environments. The purpose of the study was to determine whether teaching methods based around Lego/Logo activities can be identified which effectively cater for preferred learning styles, promoting improvement in reasoning and spatial relations test performance.

The paper includes background on the hemispheric model of learning styles, identification of children's learning style preference, an explanation of the experimental method used, examples of Lego/Logo activities, results of the experiment, and a discussion of the results including identified areas of further research.

LEARNING STYLE

When considering learning styles, it is informative to first look at research which attributes learning style differences to gender. Much has been written concerning the differences between the ways boys and girls process information. In the most general terms, boys tend to process information visually while girls process information auditorially (Helfeldt 1983, 192). Girls seem to outperform boys in reading and language tasks, whereas boys are generally better at visual and spatial skills (Keenan and Smith 1983, 50). Restak (1979) notes that boys have learning styles so different from girls that there needs to be a female correction factor on some IQ tests which compensates for the tests' bias towards one type of problem solver.

While there has been a tendency to explain gender differences in cognitive abilities in terms of environmental influences (e.g., expectations of family and society), there is evidence that there are differences in people's basic information processing styles (Keenan and Smith 1983, 52). The neurobiological model of cognition relates an individual's cognitive style to his/her left or right cerebral hemispheric bias (Davidson 1983, 2). It has been found that females are better at tasks which require processing by the brain's left hemisphere whereas males are superior at right hemisphere tasks (Durden-Smith 1980, 13). The premise that there is a biological basis for behaviour (Restak 1979, 57) is supported by the results of split-brain surgery (Kane 1984, 533), experiments before birth (Durden-Smith, 1980, 10), and experiments from birth into infant periods (Zakariya, 1981).

People who have a left hemisphere dominance tend to be better at language and speech (Levy 1983, 66). They are very analytical and enjoy following directions, ordering, and filling in. They are convergent problem solvers who employ sequential strategies (Kane 1984, 531).

Conversely, those who have a right hemisphere preference are usually superior at visualising patterns, understanding spatial relationships, and images (Haglund 1981, 230). They are divergent thinkers who are inventive and imaginative (Kane 1984, 531). Generally, those who have a right brain preference process information in a simultaneous fashion, while those with a left brain preference process information in a successive (serial) manner.

It is important to note however, that the differences between boys and girls are statistical differences only. We have all seen boys with left-brain and girls with right brain preferences. Therefore, from the point of view of education, it would be far more appropriate to categorise children by learning style rather than by gender.

Patricia Davidson (1983) has developed the Mathematics Diagnostic/Prescriptive Inventory which is designed to assess achievement, ability, and learning style in mathematics. Following are some activities which can be used to help identify cerebral hemispheric preference:

* Giving directions on paper- those with right brain preferences will be more apt to draw a map while those with a left brain preference will give written instructions;

* Estimation- right brain learners are better at estimation and will use the process of estimation in order to identify gross errors in calculations. Left brain learners more often will blindly follow an algorithm and are more likely to ignore gross errors;

* Problem solving- pupils orientated toward a right brain learning style often arrive at an answer without formally working out the solution, and furthermore, are unable to explain how the answer was derived. Those with left brain preference are more apt to follow formal algorithms.

Teachers need to be able to provide varied activities which cater for the different learning styles (Dalbey and Linn 1985, 268 and Loviglio 1981, 11-12). Following are examples of approaches intended to stimulate left and right hemispheres:

LEFT

* Provide activities often using symbols. (Levy, 1983)

* Give children linear (sequential) activities. (Keenan and Smith, 1983)

* Provide excessive verbalisation. Pose problems which require strategies for the transfer of concepts. (Davidson, 1983)

RIGHT

* Give children activities requiring visualisation. (Levy 1983)

* Provide open ended problems. (Haglund, 1981)

* Require and reward general solutions as well as precise responses. Allow children to invent their own problems. (Davidson 1983)

Although children may engage in activities which stimulate left and right hemispheres at different times, it is important that all children receive a combination of activities (Keenan and Smith 1983, 52 and Naour 1985, 104). Stimulating both sides promotes flexibility and problem solving (Kane 1984, 535). Both sides are used in thinking, logic, and reasoning, each from its own perspective and domain of activity (Levy 1983, 69). Furthermore, some activities and conditions stimulate the whole brain. For example, challenges which generate excitement and interest appear to engage the whole brain, and there is evidence that emotional involvement promotes the stimulation of both hemispheres (Levy 1983, 71).

EXPERIMENTAL METHOD

Overview

Figure 1 displays an overview of the experiment. Subjects were tested for learning style preference (1), randomly assigned to four groups (2), provided with different types of activities (3), and tested (4). In order to ensure equity and fairness (especially for the control group), subjects were then provided with activities which were given to the other groups (5). Statistics were computed and analysed (6).

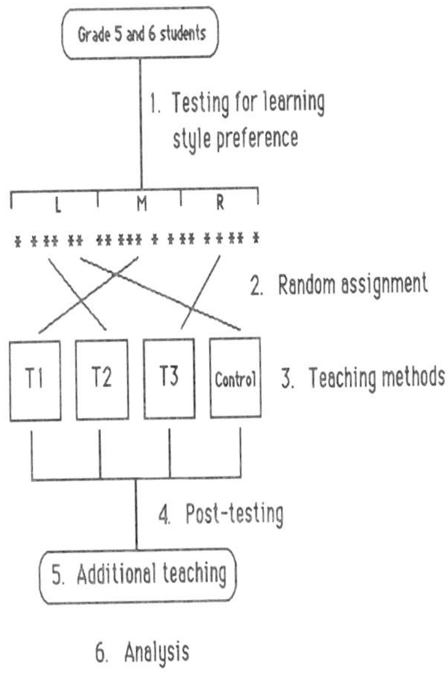

Figure 1. Diagram showing overview of the experiment.

Subjects

Children involved in the study were grade five and six pupils from one country and two city schools in northern Tasmania. There were 35 males and 39 females.

Instruments

Modified MDPI: This test was used in order to determine subjects' learning style preference. The test was designed using 24 items from The Mathematics Diagnostic/Prescriptive Inventory (MDPI). The MDPI was developed by Patricia Davidson of the University of Massachusetts, using over 1200 children ranging in age from five to eighteen. The items were identified as discriminators of learning style. Using raw scores, subjects were categorised as being left brain preferenced (L), right brain preferenced (R) or somewhere between (M).

Raven's Progressive Matrices (PM38, also known as Standard Progressive Matrices): This instrument was used in order to assess subjects' reasoning and problem solving skills. This test identifies the subject's "ability to see relationships and to solve problems" (manual, page 1). The non-verbal form of the test was administered.

ACER Mathematics (AM8): This test was administered in order to measure subjects' mastery of spatial relations. Concepts such as congruence, building of shapes, rotation, reflection, symmetry, and angles are tested.

Procedure

The entire study took place over three years (1987-1989). Four complete classes of grade five and six children were selected as being representative in northern Tasmania. Each child was administered the modified MDPI (about twenty minutes) shortly before beginning the activities. The classroom experimenter was unaware of the results of the learning style assessment. Children were randomly assigned to four groups, one being a control group. Subjects worked in groups of three. Three types of activities were administered (T1, T2, and T3). Sessions lasting for 45 minutes were given once per week for fourteen weeks. Students were then tested (Raven's Matrix and ACER AM8). Following this, less formal sessions of various frequencies and durations were given in order to enable subjects to experience activities not allowed during the formal study. Below is a diagram showing the timeframe, followed by descriptions and examples of activity types.

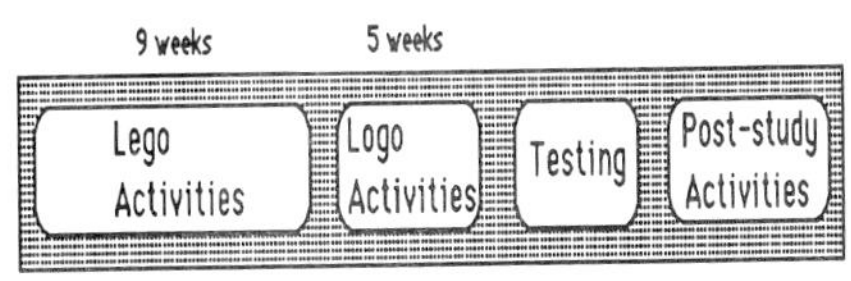

Figure 2. A graphic display of the administration of activities to subjects.

Left brain oriented activities (T1): students in T1 groups were instructed to solve problems in a highly structured, sequential, ordered fashion, often writing down steps.

Right brain oriented activities (T3): subjects in this group were given little instruction. They were set a problem and allowed to solve it in any manner they chose.

Combined left/right activities (T2): students were subjected to less structure than those in T1, but allowed less freedom of solution than members of T3.

Example Sessions

Lego session 5: students were first given a demonstration of using two motors connected to the interface. They were then directed to program models of a car and a boom gate.

T1: Set masking tape markers.
Run car to gate from markers.
Pause for a set time.
Raise gate.
Move car through.
Close gate.
Write computer instructions on paper and test each instruction line by line.

T2: Same as for T1, omitting the last instruction.

T3: Take the car through the gate.

Logo session 2: the basics of Logo program writing were explained, including editing and saving on disk (session 1 involved free play).

T1: Draw a square with sides of 200.
Draw a second square with a perimeter 2 times that of the first.

T2: Draw a square with sides of 200.
Draw a shape that has a perimeter 2 times that of the square.

T3: Draw 2 figures (shapes). Make the perimeter of one 2 times that of the other.

RESULTS

An analysis of variance factorial design was used. Independent variables were Method (T1, T2, and T3) and Learning Style (L, M, and R). The ANOVA was performed first on Raven's Matrix scores, then on ACER (AM8) scores. Following are the ANOVA and incidence tables for each analysis.

Source:	df:	Sum of Squares:	Mean Square:	F-test:	P value:
Method (A)	3	192.002	64.001	1.623	.1932
Style-cat (B)	2	486.176	243.088	6.164	.0036
AB	6	196.901	32.817	.832	.5497
Error	62	2445.207	39.439		

Table 1. ANOVA table for a 2-factor Analysis of Variance on the Raven's Matrix test.

In Table 1 it is seen that the Lego/Logo activities (Method) did not significantly affect subjects' Raven's Matrix results. The learning styles of the subjects (Style-cat) did significantly affect Raven's Matrix scores, however (p=.0036). Main effect interaction (AB) was not significant, thereby not allowing analysis of simple main effects.

Table 2 shows the number of subjects in each Method by Style-cat cell as well as each cell's mean Raven's Matrix score. It also gives numbers and means for Methods (rows in table) and learning style categories (columns).

	Style-cat:	L	M	R	Totals:
Method	T1	6 40	5 36.2	5 47.2	16 41.062
	T2	7 42.143	7 45	4 45.75	18 44.056
	T3	3 43	7 44.714	7 48.143	17 45.824
	Control	8 37.5	7 41.429	8 46.5	23 41.826
Totals:		24 40.167	26 42.269	24 47	74 43.122

Table 2. The Method by Learning Style incidence table on the Raven's Matrix test.

Inspecting Table 3 reveals similar results for ACER (AM8) test results as for the Raven's Matrix scores. Method did not significantly affect scores (p=.6642) whereas learning style did (p=.0119). The incidence table of ACER scores (Table 4) gives subject numbers and means for all Method by Learning Style cells.

Source:	df:	Sum of Squares:	Mean Square:	F-test:	P value:
Method (A)	3	29.808	9.936	.529	.6642
Style-cat (B)	2	178.898	89.449	4.76	.0119
AB	6	12.024	2.004	.107	.9954
Error	62	1165.151	18.793		

Table 3. ANOVA table for a 2-factor Analysis of Variance on the ACER (AM8) test.

	Style-cat:	L	M	R	Totals:
Method	T1	6 20.833	5 21	5 25.8	16 22.438
	T2	7 22.857	7 23	4 25.5	18 23.5
	T3	3 22	7 22.429	7 25.429	17 23.588
	Control	8 21.375	7 20.857	8 24.25	23 22.217
Totals:		24 21.75	26 21.885	24 25.125	74 22.892

Table 4. The Method by Learning Style incidence table on the ACER (AM8) test.

DISCUSSION

The results of the statistical analysis do not support the contention that we can identify teaching methods based around Lego/Logo activities which effectively cater for preferred learning styles, promoting improvement in reasoning and spatial relations test performance. This was due to the fact that Method was not on its own found to account for enough group variance. Furthermore, post hoc tests could not be carried out to investigate simple main effects because Method-Style interaction was not significant.

What is most apparent from viewing the results of Tables 1 and 3 is the highly significant correlation of learning style with test results. This is more evident with the Raven's score than the ACER. Also, it is interesting to note that Method appears to be more effective in relation to the Raven's than the ACER score (although of course "close" doesn't count when dealing with statistical significance).

The incidence tables (Tables 2 and 4) imply that methods T2 and T3 may prove to be superior if examined more closely in further research, especially for those identified as having L or M learning style preference. Also in Table 2, cell T3 by R has a mean higher than all others leading to the question of "do more holistic problem solvers perform better in a least structured environment?"

There are many areas where further investigation may prove informative. The researchers acknowledge that activities performed in groups may have been affected by complex group dynamics. Therefore, subjects working as individuals may provide more information concerning activity type and learning style. Younger subjects who have more distinct hemispheric preferences may provide more definitive results. Furthermore, it could be that only those with extreme learning style preferences react most strongly to different methods.

Other learning style models are beginning to be developed. An investigation of Herrmann's (1988) four quadrant model for example, would be a logical extension to the more standard hemispheric model.

In conclusion, the results of this study tend to encourage the researchers to recommend a mixed-activities approach as one which offers variety and flexibility. Perhaps double open-ended activities can be developed which allow learners to solve problems using both sequential and holistic approaches to problem solving.

REFERENCES

Australian Council for Educational Research, 1979, ACER Mathematics Tests Manual, Victoria.

Australian Council for Educational Research, Manual for Standard Progressive Matrices, Victoria.

Dalbey, J. and Linn, M., 1985, "The Demands and Requirements of Computer Programming: A Literature Review", Journal of Educational Computing Research, vol. 1, no. 3, pp. 253-274.

Davidson, P., 1983, Mathematics Learning Viewed From a Neurobiological Model For Intellectual Functioning, University of Massachusetts, Boston.

Durden-Smith, J., 1980, "Male and Female - WHY", The Collegiate Career Woman, Winter, pp. 9-15+.

Haglund, E., 1981, "A Closer Look at the Brain as Related to Teachers and Learners", Peabody Journal of Education, vol. 58, no. 4, pp. 225-235.

Helfeldt, J., 1983, "Sex-Linked Characteristics of Brain Functioning: Why Jimmy Reads Differently", Reading World, vol. 22, no. 3, pp. 190-196.

Herrmann, N., 1988, The Creative Brain, Mentor Human Resource Group Pty. Ltd., NSW.

Kane, M., 1984, "Cognitive Styles of Thinking and Learning", Academic Therapy, vol. 19, no. 5, pp. 527-536.

Keenan, D. and Smith, M., 1983, "Sex Discrimination and Cerebral Bias: Implications for the Reading Curriculum", Reading Improvement, vol. 20, no. 1, pp. 50-53.

Lego Technic Programmable Systems Teacher's Manual, 1986, Tecmedia Ltd., England.

Levy, J., 1983, "Research Synthesis on Right and Left Hemispheres: We Think With Both Sides of the Brain", Educational Leadership, vol. 40, no. 4, pp. 66-71.

Loviglio, L, 1981, "Mathematics and the Brain: A Tale of Two Hemispheres", The Massachusetts Teacher, Jan, pp. 8-12.

Naour, P., 1985, "Brain/Behavior Relationships, Gender Differences and the Learning Disabled", Theory Into Practice, vol. 24, no. 2, pp. 100-104.

Restak, R., 1979, The Brain. The Last Frontier, Doubleday & Co. Inc., New York.

Zakariya, S., 1981, "His Brain, Her Brain: A Conversation with Richard M. Restak", Principal, vol. 60, no. 5, pp. 46-52.

Computers in Education
A. McDougall and C. Dowling (Editors)
Elsevier Science Publishers B.V. (North-Holland)

PROBLEM SOLVING IN A LEGO-LOGO LEARNING ENVIRONMENT: COGNITIVE AND METACOGNITIVE OUTCOMES

Kwok-Wing LAI

Department of Education, University of Otago, P.O. Box 56, Dunedin, New Zealand.

This paper documents a computer-based learning environment using Lego construction elements and the Logo programming language to foster the development of problem solving of young learners. Twenty-four students (aged 10 to 11) participated in this study for eight sessions (one and a half hours each). The cognitive and metacognitive outcomes, the attitudes of the participants towards this Lego-Logo learning environment, and gender differences in computer use are reported.

1. INTRODUCTION

Using the computer to control external devices has become increasingly important in this technological society. For example, computers have been used to control aircraft, traffic light systems, or robots. The recent advent of programmable systems (e.g. the Lego Technic Control Set) to primary classrooms has provided an opportunity for young learners to acquire an in-depth understanding of the principles underlying control technology. The Lego Technic Control Set (Lego Australia Pty. Ltd., 1987) for example, allows users to build models controlled by microcomputers at a relatively inexpensive price. Fairly complex models could be constructed by using regular Lego elements and special elements such as motors, optosensors, counting discs, light bricks, electric cables, steering elements, and wheels available in the Set. These models could then be interfaced with a computer by using an interface box (or card) and operated by a programming language.

In constructing and programming these models, the learners are engaged in a concrete problem solving activity which encourages them to learn and practise a variety of problem solving skills. It has been suggested by some educators (e.g. Bitter & Gore, 1986; Neighbours & Slaton, 1987; Pearce, 1987) that computer controlled machines enable learners to carry out investigations involving both heuristic (a rule of thumb that often, but not always leads to a solution) and algorithmic (procedures guaranteed to result in the solution of a problem) problem solving, and apply them to situations involving feedback control. Particularly for young learners, robot oriented activities provide a concrete, and a learner-centred environment conducive to concept development. By assembling their own models or machines using kits such as the Lego Technic Control Sets, young learners could have a deeper understanding of machines and control technology, and their skills of planning and co-operation, manipulation, measurement, logical thinking, and evaluation will also be improved. However, very little research has been conducted as yet to document systematically the implementation of robot oriented activities in classrooms as well as their cognitive outcomes.

This paper documents a computer-based learning environment using Lego construction elements and the Logo programming language to foster the development of problem solving skills of young learners. The cognitive and metacognitive outcomes, the attitudes of the participants towards this Lego-Logo learning environment, and gender differences in computer use are reported.

2. THE LEGO-LOGO LEARNING ENVIRONMENT

The Lego-Logo learning environment designed in this study is briefly discussed under the following headings: (1) problem solving approach; (2) metacognitive awareness; (3) cooperative learning; and (4) role of the teacher and the learner. For a more detailed discussion please refer to another report (Lai, in press).

2.1. Problem Solving Approach

The participants in this learning environment were encouraged to use a problem solving approach suggested by Polya (1957) in building and programming their models. There are four main steps in this approach:

1. Understand a Problem - Before building a Lego model, participants were encouraged to think about the problem and identify the goal and subgoals of the task. Also, they were asked to collect information and materials required to build the model. Sketches of the model were drawn to better represent the problem.

2. Planning - Then they were asked to look for a solution. Possible methods were raised and some important problem solving strategies, e.g. breaking down the problem into sub-problems, working backward, etc. were examined.

3. Hypothesis testing - In constructing the models, learners were encouraged to formulate and test hypotheses. They had additional practices on this skill in the programming stage.

4. Evaluation - After they had created their models the participants were asked to evaluate their product and look for other solutions.

2.2. Metacognitive Awareness

The learning environment was also designed to facilitate the development of metacognitive awareness. Metacognition refers to both the knowledge and regulation of cognition (Armbruster & Brown, 1984). Current research on learning suggests that effective learning depends on having knowledge of the repertoire of one's cognitive abilities and being able to regulate one's cognition, e.g. planning, checking, and evaluating learning strategies and outcomes. Brown, Campione, & Day (1981) contend that learners need to be aware of the underlying cognitive processes of the learning tasks, and the importance of applying problem solving strategies to enhance understanding. In this study explicit instruction on metacognitive awareness was given to the participants. They were encouraged to reflect upon their thinking by asking themselves metacognitive-sensitive questions such as "Am I on the right track" or "Do I need more information to solve this problem" and answering questions on their log books.

2.3. Cooperative Learning

It has been evident that computer based cooperative learning is more effective in problem solving (Johnson, Johnson, & Stanne, 1985). The learning environment designed in this study was also a cooperative one. The participants always worked together in small groups even though each member was responsible for a different role in each session. There were four major roles: (1) model builder; (2) programmer; (3) questioner; and (4) record keeper. Roles were rotated in each session.

2.4. Role Of The Teacher And The Learner

Recent advances in cognitive learning research and experimentation support learning as an active, constructive, cumulative, and goal-oriented process (Shuell, 1986). In the learning process learners need to participate actively in the construction of their own knowledge. To facilitate an active learning process, the role of the teacher will be shifted from provider of content-specific information to the facilitator of students' own information organization skills such as finding relevant information, solving problems, asking questions, thinking critically, and communicating ideas (Sheingold, Martin, & Endreweit, 1987).

Recognizing the importance of a learner centred approach to learning, the Lego-Logo environment in this study was designed to encourage active exploration by the learners. Thus except for the first few sessions when the teacher had to take a more active role in demonstrating the use of the hardware and software, she played a relatively passive role in this learning environment. The teacher's role was mainly to encourage the participants to ask questions, and monitor their progress.

3. METHOD

3.1. Participants

15 boys and 9 girls (aged 10 to 11) from a New Zealand primary school participated in this study. These students were randomly assigned to six groups, with four per group. To investigate gender differences, two groups were single-sex groups (boy and girl), and the rest were all mixed. The majority of the participants had some (but limited) experience in using computers (95.7%) and Lego (91.3%) while only less than half of them (43.5%) had used Logo prior to the study. Only one participant had some experience in programmable systems.

3.2. Materials

Two Lego Technic Control Sets each interfaced with a BBC computer were used. Control Logo (BBC Logotron Logo augmented with a library of special procedures) was chosen to drive the models because of its simplicity and because some of the participants were already familiar with the Logo language.

3.3. Procedures

This study lasted for 8 sessions (one and a half hours each). Each group worked with a Lego Technic Control Set and a BBC microcomputer. The teacher served as the leader of the group.

1. In the first session basic concepts of control technology were discussed and the operation of the BBC computer and the interface box was demonstrated. The use of special Lego elements was also investigated. Then the problem solving approach suggested by Polya (1957) was discussed and the participants were encouraged to follow this approach to build their models in subsequent sessions. At the end of each session there was a group discussion on what had been learned and there was also time for the participants to fill in their log books.

2. To familiarize the participants with the use of Lego elements and the hardware, they were provided with instructions to build the first two models - a traffic light system, and a washing machine. The problem solving approach was practised in these sessions.

3. Subsequently the participants were free to build models of their own. They were encouraged to follow the problem solving approach in constructing their models. The role of the teacher was minimal at this stage. Most groups finished two machines of their own design.

3.4. Data Collection

1. Interview - Pre- and Post-interviews were conducted for 12 randomly selected participants to measure their metacognitive awareness on problem solving. Five questions were asked: (1) What does a good problem solver do in solving a problem? (2) What is the first thing you do when you are given a problem to solve? (3) What is the next thing you do? (4) What do you do if you are stuck? and (5) What do you do if you think you have got the answer? The interviews were transcribed and coded, as suggested by Ericsson and Simon (1984). All 12 participants' responses to each of the five questions were examined and categorized to determine the range of responses of each question. Two rating categories on metacognitive awareness were decided: (1) problem solving involves conscious processing of the problem; and (2) problem solving involves continued monitoring and evaluation. A 5-point Likert-type scale was developed to differentiate the range of responses for each of these two categories (Duffy, Roehler, Sivan, Rackliffe, Book, Meloth, Vavrus, Wesselman, Putnam, & Bassiri, 1987.
2. Participant's Log - Each participant was required to keep a log for self-evaluation. They had to answer the following questions: (1) What have you learned today? (2) Is there anything you have learned today which may help you solve problems in future? If yes, what is it? (3) Anything you don't understand? (4) What would you do if there is something in this class that you don't understand? (5) Have you kept track of what you did in this class? (6) Anything interesting in this class? and (7) What do you think about the other members of your group?
3. Questionnaires - Pre- and Post-questionnaires on the participants' attitudes towards educational computing and the learning environment were administered. Questions on knowledge acquisition and problem solving were also asked at the end of the study.
4. Audio- and Video-Tapes - Some groups were audio- and video-taped throughout the study.
5. Researcher's log - A log sheet was completed for each group after each session to record the tasks completed and problems encountered by the learners.

4. RESULTS

An analysis of the data obtained from the interviews, questionnaires, and log books was conducted and is reported here.

4.1. Metacognitive Awareness

Pre- and post-interviews were conducted with 12 participants to investigate gains in metacognitive awareness. Five questions were asked to test the participants' understanding of their cognitive processes involved in problem solving. The scores from the two rating categories were combined and a sampled t-test procedure was used to evaluate differences in metacognitive awareness before and after the study. A significant overall improvement in metacognitive awareness was identified ($t=7.37$, $p<0.0001$). The result clearly showed that when explicit instruction on metacognitive skills was provided and when the learners could practise these skills in a computer based learning environment, their metacognitive awareness could be facilitated.

4.2. Knowledge And Skills Acquisition

A questionnaire was administered at the end of the study to measure knowledge acquisition. When the participants were asked what they had learned from the study the following major categories of skills and knowledge were given: (1) building Lego models (86.4%); (2) programming in Logo (63.3%); (3) working with a computer (54.5%); (4) problem solving skills (50.0%); and (5) working in a group (36.4%).

A few comments given by the participants may provide some ideas of what they have learned:

'I've learned that when you're working with Lego that it is possible to make anything. Because if you think hard you will be able to make anything work. But it is not easy working with Lego and computers.'

'I have learned how to work with Logo a lot better than I used to and learned how to solve problems quicker than I used to ...'

'I have learned a lot about how to put [the Lego elements] together and how to get them going with motors and lights and how they work.'

'[I learned] how to work together as a team and to co-operate together and to decide in thing together.'

The participants were also asked to recall what they had learned in problem solving. The majority of the participants (64%) could recall and elaborate on the four main problem solving steps.

Although the answers written by the participants on their log books were usually very short, possibly due to inadequate writing skill and time (written at the end of each session), some of the answers were revealing. For example, one participant was aware of the importance of planning when he wrote, "We are getting a bit behind because we don't plan what we are going to do". Another example illustrated the development of problem solving strategy of a participant. When he was asked what he would do when he had something not understood in class he wrote:

Day 1: "I would ask the person that was teaching us".
Day 2: "I would ask the teacher or the kids in our group if I really need to".
Day 3: "...ask the other members of the group".
Day 4: "I will try and see if it works and keep trying".
Day 5: "Well I think if it might work and build it and just think if I can picture it in my mind and see how it will run".

From this excerpt one could trace the gradual shift of control of learning back to the learner. Learning has become a more active process. Some insights were also acquired from this learning environment, as apparent from the following excerpt, also recorded on five consecutive days.

Day 1: "I've learned that when you make things with the lego you have to work as a team and cooperate. And when you use the computer it's easy to fix up the mistakes that you do and it's easy to learn".
Day 2: "I learned that help each other when you're playing with the lego and find when the pieces go".
Day 3: "I've learned that when you make mistakes it's easy to fix and you don't have to panic".
Day 4: "I've learned that it was hard and confusing but if you try you can do it".
Day 5: "...[the tutor] doesn't help us, we've got to learn ourselves".

4.3 Attitudes

All participants reported that they enjoyed the project and 95.5% of them would like to spend more time on Lego in future. No gender difference was identified. The participants also reported that the experience they had gained would be useful in future. Major categories reported included general problem solving skills (57.1%), computing concepts (33.3%), and skills in working with others (14.3%). Also, nearly one quarter (23.8%) of them indicated that what they learned would be useful for their jobs in future. The following are some of the comments:

'When you are older you might see a job in the paper for a BBC computer you could get it because you were [taught] how to use one'

'Yes problem solving that will help me in future...to understand the problem...to see the problem and to [fix] it out'

All but one participants enjoyed working in groups. The major reasons reported were: (1) sharing ideas and helping each other (63.6%); (2) group work was more efficient (18.2%); and (3) group work was fun (13.6%).

The following comment is typical:

'Working in a group is a lot easier because you've got other people in your group who may know more than you. It was pretty good when I got stuck because somebody always seemed to know the answer'

4.4. Gender Differences

A question was asked on both the pre- and post-questionnaires of whether it was easier for boys to use the computer than girls. 95.7% of the participants reported that there was no difference at the beginning of the study. Their answer was not significantly different after the study (91%). No gender difference was identified. On the questionnaire they were also asked to rank order their preferences with regard to the four roles they played in the study, namely, model builder, programmer, questioner, and recorder keeper. The most popular role was programmer, followed by model builder. 75% of the girls had ranked programmer as their first choice compared to 35.7% for the boys. As for model building, only 12.5% of the girls ranked it as number 1, compared to 36% for the boys. However, there was no significant difference between girls and boys in their rank orders, although on the basis of literature about sex role stereotyping one might expect that boys would prefer being model builders and programmers and girls being record keepers. As for record keeping, not even a single girl had ranked it as the most preferred activity whereas for boys about one quarter (21%) had ranked it as their first choice. The results showed that girls were at least as positive towards control technology as boys.

5. DISCUSSION

It is no doubt that the Lego-Logo learning environment reported in this paper was highly motivational to young learners. Both girls and boys were enthusiastic about the project and no gender difference was observed in groups. The environment was stimulating because the participants were able to control their learning process and the concreteness of the problem tasks enabled them to relate to what they had encountered before.

From the results reported in the previous section it was also clear that this learning environment was conducive to acquisition of knowledge in control technology and skills in problem solving. It also promoted metacognitive awareness. The cooperative atmosphere encouraged the participants to acquire knowledge in a more active and constructive way, as well as sharing ideas and helping each other. However, it was unfortunate that the participants only worked in small groups, without having an opportunity to work as a whole class.

Although this computer-based learning environment did facilitate problem solving and cooperative learning, the extent to which it may lead to transfer of problem solving skills has not been examined. Further research should be conducted to investigate this possibility. Also, how this learning environment could be integrated into the existing primary school curriculum need to be investigated.

As a final note it is important that computer based instructional activities should be student centred rather than computer centred. In a Lego-Logo environment it is especially important not be overwhelmed by the sophisticated hardware and software. It has to be remembered that the role of the computer is purely instrumental. It provides learners with an aid to try out their ideas and reflect upon their thinking. As for teachers, they should function as facilitators encouraging students to ask questions, formulate and test hypotheses, and be prepared for the challenges raised in the process.

ACKNOWLEDGEMENTS

This study was funded by the Otago Research Grant #DAM802. I appreciate the cooperation provided by the children and teachers of North East Valley Normal School, Dunedin. Special thanks are given to Mr Dennis Hughes and Ms Helen Trevethan. I am also grateful for the support of Gillian Swinney, Paula Vickery, and Dr Bruce McMillan.

REFERENCES

Armbruster, B., & Brown, A. (1984). Learning from reading: The role of metacognition. In R. Anderson, J. Osborn, & R. Tierney (Eds.), Learning to read in American Schools: Basal Readers and Content Tests (pp. 273-281). Hillsdale, N.J.: Lawrence Erlbaum.

Bitter, G. & Gore, G. (1986). Robots in the classroom: Another of tomorrow's teaching tools today. Computers in the School, 2 (4) 15-20.

Brown, A., Campione, J., & Day, J. (1981). Learning to learn: On training students to learn from texts. Educational Researcher, 10 (1), 14-21.

Duffy, G., Roehler, L., Sivan, E., Rackliffe, G., Book, C., Meloth, M., Vavrus, L., Wesselman, R., Putnam, J., & Dassiri, D. (1987). ffects of explaining the reasoning associated with using reading strategies. Reading Research Quarterly, 23, 347-368.

Ericsson, K. & Simon, H. (1984). Protocol Analysis. Cambridge: MIT.

Johnson, R., Johnson, D., & Stanne, M. (1985). Effects of co-operative, competitive, and individualistics goal structures on computer-assisted instruction. Journal of Educational Psychology, 77, 668-677.

Lai, K. (in press). Using robots in primary classrooms. Proceedings of the Third New Zealand Computers in Education Conference.

LEGO Australia Pty. Ltd. (1987). Something about ... LEGO Technic Computer Control Sets. Com 3 Journal, 13(3), 21-22.

Neighbours, D. & Slaton, F. (1987, March). Robots in my classroom? The Computing Teacher, 24-28, 45.

Pearce, J. (1987). Robotics with Lego and Logo. Com 3 Journal, 13(3), 18-20.

Polya, G. (1957). How to solve it: A new aspect of mathematical method (2nd Ed.). N.Y.: Doubleday.

Sheingold, K., Martin, L., & Endreweit, M. (1987). Preparing urban teachers for the technological future. In R. Pea & K. Sheingold (Eds.). Mirrors of minds (pp.67-85). Norwood, N.J.:Albex.

Shuell, T. (1986). Cognitive conceptions of learning. Review of Educational Research, 54, 411-436.

Computers in Education
A. McDougall and C. Dowling (Editors)
Elsevier Science Publishers B.V. (North-Holland)
IFIP, 1990

ON THE PROBLEM SOLVING WITH THE COMPUTER: ANALYSIS OF DIFFICULTIES AND REQUIREMENTS

Enrica Lemut (*), Giampaolo Chiappini(*), Angela M. Martinelli (**)

(*) Istituto Matematica Applicata C.N.R. - Via L.B. Alberti,4 - Genova - Italy
(**) Scuola Media "Lomellini", Piazza G. Ferraris, 48 - Genova - Italy

This paper examines the behaviour of 12 to 14 year old pupils who use the computer in typical problem solving activities, within the context of a curricular project which strongly emphasizes the aspects of thought expression, through the integrated use of different language codes, during problem solving. Several typical difficulties encountered by the pupils are analysed and an attempt is made, through these difficulties, to single out some computer literacy requirements. Several proposals for the construction of such prerequisites and several methodological and theoretical questions under consideration are referred to.

1. INTRODUCTION

Within the research area on problem solving which, as is well known, has gained considerable impetus in the last fifteen years, the research group to which we belong has been involved both in finding some of the more important and frequent difficulties encountered by the pupils, and in defining and testing teaching methods aimed at overcoming these difficulties. The research activities that were undertaken mainly concern compulsory education in Italy (6 to 14 years old). This results from our involvement in curricular projects for two levels of primary schooling, namely for pupils aged 6 to 11, and for pupils aged 11 to 14. Our objective is to enable as many pupils as possible to become good problem solvers.

Within the above research context, this paper deals with the specific researches conducted by us on using the computer for problem solving. These researches have pointed out many types of difficulties that the pupils must face. Some are typical of the introduction to the computer environment, while others are independent, though, inevitable. According to our experience these difficulties may be overcome through long-term teaching activities, which allow the pupils to make in-depth studies and gradually extend their proficiency in the subject.

In section 2 we examine the behaviour of 13 to 14 year old pupils while they are attempting to solve some problems; we also try to point out from the various difficulties encountered, those which can be attributed to:

a) language deficiencies (for communicating and representing solution strategies and using artificial language coding), thus highlighting questions regarding the confusion between different languages, incomplete thoughts or how they are communicated

b) planning deficiencies connected with the internal generation and management of space-time images by the mind, associated with the evolution in time of the resolutions according to a particular working hypothesis.

c) cultural deficiencies regarding the mastery of the relationship between possible reasonings by man, and forms of reasoning incorporated, and/or that may be incorporated, in the computer.

In section 3 we refer to several teaching and research activities, developed within the framework of our curricular projects, which were aimed at overcoming the difficulties met, by constructing suitable requirements for computer literacy. In section 4 we briefly outline a theoretical question connected, in particular but not exclusively, to computer aided problem solving which our group is currently working on.

2. THE BEHAVIOUR OF CHILDREN USING THE COMPUTER DURING PROBLEM SOLVING ACTIVITIES.

In this section we refer to three problems tackled by 13 to 14 year old children stdying the topic of "automation".

2.1. The context

Our projects, in fact, provide for a first and general approach to computer use in the topic of automation. We believe that this form of approach prevents the automation of computation and data processing from becoming isolated from the context of incorporating typical abilities and knowledge typical of man, into machines in general. This context is also motivated by the fact that the computation instruments available in schools today could over-privilege the strictly sequential aspects of problem solving with a computer. Whereas, reasoning on the operating logics of other automatic devices leaves ample room for analysis of operations performed in parallel, concurring together to meet the same objective. It may become extremely useful to consider these devices, in view of the current technological development of computers.

2.2. The problems referred to:

(A) The pupils, who have already had some experience in using non programmable pocket calculators and have already programmed in BASIC with pocket calculators, are asked:

"Try to describe a possible way to determine the area of the irregular polygon shown below using a pocket calculator provided with its own memory [M+] assuming that the figure has been divided into four triangles.

(You may describe the process verbally or use a flow-chart: use letters to help you if necessary.)"

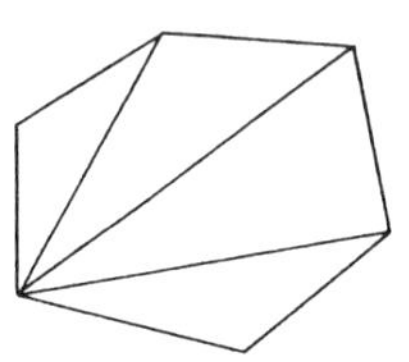

fig.1

(B) The pupils who have already experienced some BASIC programming are asked to find an algorithm with which to calculate the amount of the quarterly telephone bill and to write a suitable program. They are provided with the following information. "Up until 1986 the amount that a family had to pay for using the telephone depended on the following call charges:

- the first 120 units cost Lire 40 each
- each unit from unit 121 through to unit 198 costs Lire 85
- each unit from unit 199 through to unit 399 costs Lire 95
- each unit over unit 399 costs Lire 116

The pupils are advised to find equations such that the amount to be paid by a single subscriber for N units may be calculated for all possible cases.

(C) The pupils are asked to use a commercially available data processing program (not designed for teaching purposes), for example "Superbase" for the Commodore 64 computer or "Microsoft File" for the Macintosh computer, to construct and interrogate data bases. Historic data were used in some experiments to analyse the changes that have taken place during the last three generations. Geographic and economic data were referred to in other experiences to initiate a quantitative analysis of development and under-development in the world. The experiences have involved, for similar lengths of times and under analogous conditions, both classes which had never used the computer, and classes which had previously carried out problem solving activities of the types in (A) and (B) above. The data base is interrogated for answers to open problems, the solution of which requires the pupil to develop mental planning activities (for example, "How has schooling changed in the last three generations ?"; "What opinion would you give on the statement <Rich countries become richer and poor countries become poorer.> ?").

2.3. Problem (A): Emerging Difficulties

The children frequently produce "solutions" from which it is possible to deduce their great difficulty in expressing themselves according to the rules of an artificial language. In fact they tend to mix different languages, as can be seen in the two following answers:

- first answer: (see fig.2)
  "I press the sequence:

0+ (BCxAG):2+(CDxAH):2+(DExAI):2+(LExAL): 2 =

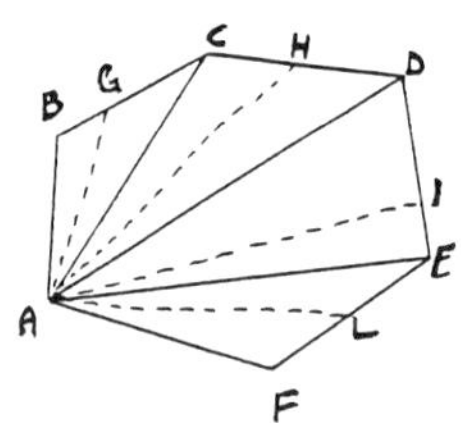

fig.2

- second answer: (in form of flow chart)

Start

BxH:2 = M+

BxH:2 = S + MR = M+

BxH:2 = S + MR = M+

BxH:2 = S + MR = S Total

Stop

Disregarding the geometric errors, several elements of confusion are apparent in the first answer: "I press the sequence" indicates that the pupil intends to express himself in terms of the calculator "keys". "0+", which he probably does not intend to press, indicates that he remembers that, for the sum of addends the sum must be initialized to "0". The pupil uses then a typically algebraic-geometric language and no longer refers to the technical

characteristics of the calculator (it is not provided with alphabetic keys and no indications are given as to the availability of brackets).
As far as the second answer is concerned, the pupil does not respect the typical conventions for a flow-chart (one operation per block) and from the second block on, he mixes algebraic language with the "key sequence" to be entered.

The triangulation problem considered is subsequently generalized into that of finding an algorithm to calculate the area for the case of plane figures divided into N triangles. It was noted that very frequently the pupils resort to a "repeat...(computations)" structure, but very rarely include a syntax marker of the type "until ...". The pupils do not have difficulty in determining the repetition, but do have difficulty in expressing the loop terminal condition.
This type of situation is related to a problem discussed in section 3, that is, whether language deficiencies such as the latter refer to pupils not completing their "thoughts", or more simply to a lack in their manner of expression.

2.4. Problem (B): Emerging Difficulties

The majority of pupils find it difficult to mathematically model (through formulae) the calculation of the amount to pay. The main difficulty is in considering the problem dynamically instead of statically, in other words, realizing that the cost per unit changes with time depending on whether it is the first, the hundred and fiftieth, etc.. The following two modifications to the text were of little or no use at all: in the first case, inter-pretation of the rule of computing the units on a time basis was suggested ("...each unit from the 121st unit to the 199th unit costs ..."), whereas in the second case, a visual and "space-related" interpretation was provided with he above case, in the form of the following table.

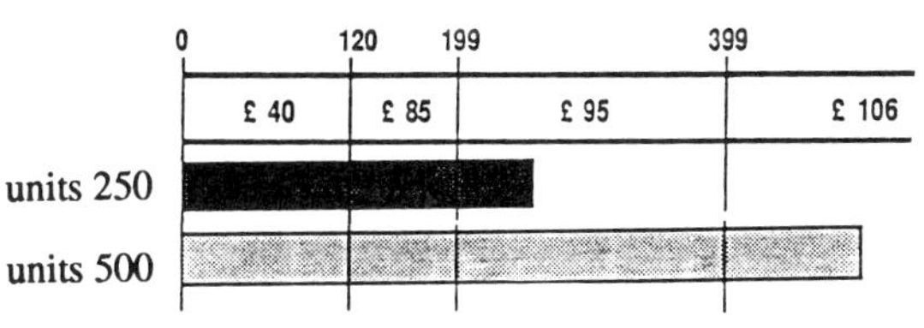

fig.3

Nevertheless, the pupils continued to reason in static terms producing, as explanation for the written formulae, texts such as: "To answer the question, I examined the tables carefully and I noticed that 250 units were worth 95 Lire each. Hence I multiplied them.", or "I thought that multiplying the number of units by the price for each unit between 200 and 399 would give me the amount to pay, as 250 lies between these two", or " I thought that the units between the 200th and 399th unit cost 95 Lire each, therefore I took the 250 units and multiplied them by 95, which is the price of this a unit, and thus obtained the final result.".

It becomes interesting, to analyse the reasoning of the pupils who answered correctly. We quote three texts: "I thought of the 250 units as many coins of different values.", or " I answered in this way because, for example, if a person uses 150 units, he pays 40 Lire for each of the first 120 units and 85 Lire for each of the remaining units.", or " After having determined how much the first 120 units cost, I added them to the cost of the next 79 units. 51 units were left over and I determined their cost and added it to the cost of the previous units, thereby calculating the overall cost for the 250 units".

We have the impression that the pupils who are able to solve the problem correctly are those who construct a mental space-time model of the problem. Further detailed studies should be carried out to determine whether this depends more on the capability of carefully analysing the text, or on the capability of constructing hypotheses that take into account what has occurred before and what is going to occur in the mental evolution of the problem. As far as the conclusion of this phase of the work is concerned, several pupils, even among those who answered the first questions correctly, find it difficult to correctly use the variable N (number of units). In fact they refer to N as the total number of units and as the remaining units within the upper cost bracket. For example, they write that for N=250 the amount is given by 40x120 + 79x85 + Nx95.

At the end of this phase of the work the pupils are able to create the following type of mathematical model:

If $N \leq 120$ then $I = 40 \times N$
If $N > 120$ and $N \leq 199$ then $I = 40 \times 120 + 85 \times (N-120)$
If $N > 199$ and $N \leq 399$ then $I = 40 \times 120 + 85 \times 79 + 95 \times (N-199)$
If $N > 399$ then $I = 40 \times 120 + 85 \times 79 + 95 \times 200 + 106 \times (N-399)$

The difficulties of the pupils in entering into computer logic functioning become apparent when they start writing the program, or when they construct the Basic language oriented flow-chart. It is quite natural for many pupils to translate the mathematical model directly into program language statements. The non availability of some appropriate Basic statements suitable for direct translation of this model, causes the difficulty of having to process a program based on strictly sequential controls. Whereas, for the pupils, the different conditions that express the mathematics problem resolution model are completely independent and may be analysed in any order whatsoever. The difficulty of adapting to a sequential mathematics solution model also makes it very difficult to recognize the redundancy of some controls. The last redundancy "If N>399 ..." is the most difficult to eliminate. This still leaves some doubt that the "else..." logic processing by the computer, even in the other tests, is still not clearly understood. This could be due to the pupils' conviction that the computer does not "memorize" what it has learnt through the "controls" made and, as a consequence, cannot "choose" what to do (this is also confirmed in several accounts written by the 12 to 13 year old pupils. In fact, the inability to choose is indicated in these texts as a difference between man and computer.)

2.5. Problem (C): Emerging Difficulties

We have observed that deficiency in language and logic creates great difficulties at different times in the work, that is: in understanding the text of the problems given, in designing particular tables from those possible, in analysing compliance of a certain table with the hypotheses provided in the text of the problem. In this context, in fact, not only is the command of some important connectives, in informatics such as "if", "and", "or", "not" .... necessary, but also the control of the mental representation evoked by a gerund ("passing from the rich nations to the poor ones ...", "passing from the great-grandparents to parents.."), or of a series of specification complements in Italian natural language ("the comparison of incomes of nations of various continents"). Difficulty in controlling these syntactic structures may be noted, above all, in the pupils who do not seem able to construct and manage their own artificial mental space-time, where they can organize and correlate the data so that a table may freely expand or contract, appear differently (different order within a column, different location of a column,...). When using a Data base, the pupils encounter, at different levels, the problem of dealing with a device that operates according to a logic, different from their own, according to which they are forced to operate in order to attain their objectives. This occurs, for example: a) When the information to be memorized is being encoded (certain code choices which would be "semantically" justified must be modified so that tables that can be interpreted more easily by the pupils may be subsequently obtained, bearing in mind that all the tables are constructed on the basis of a unique order known by the software, namely alphabetic or numeric); b) When defining the criteria by which to order or search for information to be structured as tables (for example to order the nations according to their income and continent where they are located). Many pupils would spontaneously first give the criteria by which to order according to the incomes, as this is reasonable from a semantic point of view, and then that according to the continents. However, the result of a command of this type would produce a table which cannot be used. In fact, all the nations would appear in ascending or descending order according to their incomes, grouped alphabetically, according to the alphabetical order of the continents; c) When choosing procedures to use ("manually" we may think of producing more productive procedures that can be handled by the computer; we may think of the procedure "find and sort" which with the software available was impossible).
The difficulty of knowing how to operate on two levels, emerges when using a data base program. A first level is that of constructing mental space-time models regarding software operation, in terms of single commands; a second level is that of assuming mental space-time models of the effects of using single procedures or sequences of procedures. This second level often requires the ability of mentally separating oneself from the first level.

3. FROM THE ANALYSIS OF THE DIFFICULTIES TO THE CONSTRUCTION OF REQUIREMENTS

Some of the difficulties discussed above have already been considered in our research programme and which we have been attempting to overcome for some years. Others appear to be new types of difficulties which, most probably, are more difficult to interpret and overcome. From the difficulties considered we can indicate those due to some shortcomings in the language, as discussed in our previous paper [1]. In particular, we refer to difficulties in the written and oral verbalization of ones own thoughts in situations where the necessary thought structures are strictly bound to the characteristics of the problem, and/or to the instruments available to solve it. For example, the command of specific connectives and/or equivalent language forms which are of the utmost importance in computer science ("if", "while", "until"), or the command of different languages (natural, algebraic, flow charts and programming) under conditions in which they are used to provide the solution to a problem almost simultaneously. We have already made some proposals in our previous papers [1], [2] regarding contents and methods necessary to overcome these difficulties. We have testing these proposals for several years gaining some highly favourable results.

Some difficulties may be attributed to cultural deficiencies regarding the command of the relationship between human reasoning, separated from that of the computer, and forms of reasoning incorporated and/or that may be incorporated into the computer. For a number of years we have been working both with primary school children [1] and with 12 to 14 year old children [3], trying to overcome these difficulties. We refer to class activities concerning a long-term and systematic analysis, carried out over a number of years, of the use and functioning of a wide range of machines of increasing complexity. Machines which incorporate mechanical functions, computation ability, ability to logically test the values of single variables, procedure tests, and tests of results.

Let us now consider new types of difficulties which we are currently giving our maximum attention, both in terms of interpretation and in terms of teaching strategies aimed at overcoming the difficulties.
From problem (A) emerges the need to support the complementary use of different language codes used as communication and representation instruments, even in the solution to a problem, with a reflection on the specific aims and grammatical and syntactic rules of each of them. By making an effort to adapt to the constraints caused by a particular instrument, the children understand the potential and limitations of the instrument.
A further analysis of problem (A) poses the question of the incompleteness of certain written reports. Some of our research activities and class work are currently oriented towards the analysis of this incompleteness. This concerns the setting up of suitable instruments for investigating and establishing when the insufficiency of the written reports is to be attributed to incomplete acts of thought or when they are to be attributed to the incomplete manner with which the thoughts are communicated. For the specific case of problem (A), we are more inclined to interpret the behaviour of the pupils as "incompleteness of communication". On the other hand, we retain that the incompleteness related to the "if.. then.. else.." structure should be interpreted differently (noted both in the written accounts of the mathematical model regarding problem (B) and in the analysis of numerous automatic devices). In fact, we have ascertained that the pupils often express only the "if.. then" part of the control structure, referring to the aspect which they consider as being the most important for the fact analysed. In these cases we believe that it is more correct to speak of incomplete acts of thought. Very often, however, even when these incomplete acts of thought are overcome, the pupils, even at 12-13 yrs, frequently do not use the "if.. then.. else" structure but resort to using two successive structures, "if.. then", " if, on the contrary,.. then". From these facts it is possible to better interpret the difficulty of the pupils in adapting to the management of conditional structures of the different programming languages.
With regards to planning deficiencies found in problems (B) and (C), segments of class work have been prepared within the framework of our projects and are currently being tested. These segments are aimed at systematically encouraging hypothetical reasoning through activities that highlight, in particular, two types of hypotheses, hypotheses which induce choices from the possible alternatives, implicitly or explicitly, in the problem situations considered, or hypotheses which must or may be generated in the construction of resolution strategies in relation to the constraints that must be satisfied [4].

Two examples of problems which require the first type of hypotheses are reported as follows: Problem 1: the children (8-9 years old) know their own height and have a piece of string representing the length of their shadow at 9:15 a.m.. They are asked: "Explain how you would compare your heights with the lengths of your shadows."
Problem 2: (for 13 to 14 year olds) The operation of a lift which can move between two floors (F1, F2) in a warehouse is examined. The pupils are asked to describe, by using the phrases "if.. then.. else", all that can occur when the user enters the lift cabin with a load less than the maximum admissible load and, once the door has been closed, presses one of the two push-buttons available (B1, B2).
Despite the diversity of the problems, the ages of the pupils, the relationship between the problem and activities directly carried out in the classroom, the accomplishment of a correctly written account passes, in almost all cases, through the autonomous or under the guidance of the teacher phase of constructing a mental space-time model of the situation in which all the possible alternatives, even if only probable, are pointed out.

A problem that requires a hypothetical thought of the second type in our project, concerns 12 to 13 year old children. It is assumed that the San Paolo quarter is a sleeping quarter of a large city and that 30000 people live in it. 8000 of these people work in offices and factories located in other parts of the city. There is only one 3 km long and 7 m wide road linking the quarter to the rest of the city (hence there is only one lane available for each direction of traffic). There are many bends along the road and overtaking is forbidden. It is assumed that the cruising speed of the traffic is constant and that there are no lorries. Every morning, almost 8000 people must travel down this road. Consider that the average length of a car is 4 m and a bus is 9 m. The problem to solve is the following. "At what speed should the traffic move (from the figures provided in an attached table) to allow all the people to reach the city between 7 and 9 o'clock?" Other hypotheses, in addition to those suggested in the table, must be made to solve the problem, and in particular "how" should the people travel (by car, one or more than one person in each car, by bus...).

The difficulty of problem (C), regarding the attainment of a discrete level of general knowledge of procedures, may be overcome by referring to the general question left open in paragraph 4. Here it can be noted that it is helped by the context of solving problems with the computer. In fact, even by giving "incorrect" commands, the reasoning by procedures is assisted by the speed of the computer which initiates an interactive process among the choices made by the pupil and the results given by the computer. Even incorrect results, found while verifying the answers supplied by the computer to the needs of the problem to be solved, are not a cause for frustration, but instead push one to think deeper about the choices made, to detail thoughts and explain the sense of the problem, and explore new ways of reaching the solution.

4. AN OPEN QUESTION

On numerous occasions throughout this paper we have mentioned how important it is for the pupils to construct mental space-time models of the problem situations that they are analysing. In problem solving with the computer, however, very often we have the feeling that many pupils do not have the motivation for resorting to models which they could activate if they were solving the problem with "pen and paper". It is much easier for them to mechanically refer to established computer science models used in previous situations and which, for some reason, are evoked by the text of the problem. We believe it unlikely that these pupils will become good problem solvers with computers, while we feel that the pupils who passed through the phase of constructing mental models related to "computer space-time" will do so. This construction seems to occur by sometimes operating by analogy and sometimes in contrast, even in a space-time relationship, with one's own way of thinking. Finally, we feel that this phase must precede that in which procedures may be used naturally, in order that meanings and effects may be mastered.

However, the question of the "transition" between the two phases, in terms of ascertainment, interpretation and cognitive value, still remains open, while maintaining the need to operate in this manner to resolve or dominate the automatic solution to problems of ever increasing difficulty. Consequently, when solving problems with a computer, a central theoretical question concerning all aspects of problem solving becomes even more important, namely that of the equilibrium to reach between the need to supply the pupil with standard procedures and formal handling ability and the need to operate and preserve full command of the meanings.

REFERENCES

[1] Lemut,E., Ferrero,E., Of the linguistic prerequisites of computing literacy, in: Lovis,F. and Tagg,E.D. (eds.), Computer in Education, IFIP 88, (Elsevier Science Publishers B.V., North-Holland, 1988), pp.139-141

[2] Lemut,E., Ferrero,E., Bonino,M., Methods to establish linguistic and mathematic prerequisites of computer literacy, in Proceedings of Third International Conference "Children in an informatic age", (Sofia,Bulgaria, 1989)

[3] Bonino,M., Lemut,E., Computers and Automation: curricula implications, Proceedings of Second International Conference "Children in an Information Age", (Sofia, Bulgaria, 1987)

[4] Ferrari,P.L., Hypothetical reasoning in the resolution of applied mathematical problems at the age of 8-10,Actes de la XIII Conference Internationale Psychology of Mathematics Education, (Paris, France, 1989)

[5] Hoc,J.M., L'apprentissage de l'utilisation des dispositifs informatiques par analogie des situation familieres, Psychologie francaise, tome 32-4 (1987)

[6] Samurcay,R., Plans et schemas de programme, id.

[7] Rogalski,J., Didactique de l'informatique et acquisitions cognitives en programmation, id.

[8] Martinelli,A.M., Le role de mediation de l'enseignant entre objectifs des programmes,project,theories de l'apprentissage, eleves: un example, Proceedings of XL CIEAEM, (Bruxelles, Belge, 1989)

[9] Gilmore,D.G., Green,T.G.R., Hoc,J.M., Samurcay,R., Psychology of Programming, Academic Press, (in print)

Computers in Education
A. McDougall and C. Dowling (Editors)
Elsevier Science Publishers B.V. (North-Holland)

CHILDREN, RECURSION AND LOGO PROGRAMMING: AN INVESTIGATION OF PAPERT'S CONJECTURE ABOUT THE VARIABILITY OF PIAGETIAN STAGES IN COMPUTER-RICH CULTURES

Anne McDOUGALL

Faculty of Education, Monash University, Clayton, Victoria, 3168, Australia.

This paper describes a study which investigated Papert's conjecture that children in a computer-rich learning environment using Logo might be able to engage in activities involving abstract or formal thinking at ages considerably younger than would be expected from Piagetian theory. It reports the development of understanding and use of recursion, a topic usually considered difficult for undergraduate computer science students, in children of primary school age.

1. INTRODUCTION

This paper reports a study which investigated Papert's (1980) conjecture that children in a computer-rich learning environment using Logo might be able to engage in activities involving abstract or formal thinking at ages considerably younger than would be expected from Piagetian theory. It reports the development of understanding and use of recursion, a topic usually considered difficult for undergraduate computer science students, in children of primary school age.

The study was focused by several themes from Papert's work: the importance of the culture in which children learn in providing suitable resources for building intellectual structures, the power of computing in "concretising" abstract ideas, the idea that learning to communicate with a computer might change the way other learning takes place, and the importance in learning of language and of thinking about thinking.

2. WHY RECURSION WAS CHOSEN FOR THE STUDY

Recursion, as it is used in the study, means the solution of a problem in terms of simpler versions of itself. In this sense recursion is a relatively new word, originating in the mathematics of the 1930's, and subsequently finding wider application in mathematics and computer science. Recursion combines aspects of self reference, repetition with variation, interruption and nesting of levels, and the possibility of continuing infinitely. Some or all of these features can be seen in many areas outside mathematics and computing, in science and nature, in music, language and literature, and in everyday situations (see for example Hofstadter, 1979).

For the study it was necessary to work on a topic which was widely regarded as too abstract or formal for children of primary school age to understand and use. Also, since I hoped to observe the process of development of understanding, it was important that the topic chosen should, as far as possible, be one which was essentially quite new to the children, and not one for which they might have begun learning under-pinning ideas already. For this reason some of the more advanced mathematical ideas made available in Logo were not particularly suitable topics for the study, as I did not know what related workthe children might do in their school mathematics before or during the study. Recursion is one of the very "abstract" powerful ideas made accessible through Logo, but, apart from Logo contexts, it is not normally considered appropriate for presentation to children at primary school level.

3. THE STUDY

A case study methodology was used. Support of Papert's conjecture in an informal, resource-rich case study environment does not imply its necessary transfer to classrooms as we now know them. However if his ideas are not supported in these circumstances, the chances of their being substantiated in real classrooms must be very small.

Two children were provided with a home learning environment rich in materials and opportunities for learning about recursion. Very detailed, though not constant, observations of their programming and other activities in this environment were made over three years. In particular all incidents related to the development of their understanding of recursion were recorded.

In the first part of the study the two case study children worked individually on Logo and some recursion activities. In the second part each child taught Logo to a chosen schoolfriend of similar age. In the third part the elder child and her friend worked on Logo activities specifically involving recursion.

The study aimed to investigate the possibility that children in this environment might be able to engage in more abstract and advanced recursion work than had previously been expected for children of primary school age. The criterion I chose to assess this was confident and independent writing and debugging of Logo procedures using embedded recursion (Leron, 1985).

4. SETTING AND SUBJECTS FOR THE STUDY

I endeavoured to establish a learning environment rich in appropriate resources: a computer and appropriate peripherals, a teacher well-versed in Logo and related issues of learning and teaching, books and other materials, and, as far as possible, unrestricted time for working with these things. The learning environment was to be informal, with a sense of playfulness; clearly there should be no set curriculum to be covered and no assessment, and the role of the teacher should not be in any way authoritarian or prescriptive.

The setting for the study was our home. The resources available to the children included the books, toys and similar materials usually found in a middle class suburban home, as well as an Apple II computer, a robot turtle and Logo, and an adult (and occasionally some of her colleagues) with expertise and a professed interest in computing and Logo.

In a sense the environment was not an ideal Logo culture such as Papert (1980) describes. The ultimate agenda of our activities was inevitably mine - the carrying out of a research project - rather than being completely the children's own. Within that constraint, however, as far as possible the children had control over our activities.

The subjects for the study were my own two children. The elder child was aged 9 when data collection commenced in 1984, and 11 at the conclusion of data collection in 1986. The younger was 6 on commencing the study. Each chose a schoolfriend of the same age to work with for the second part of the study. We worked at our house, mostly after school hours, in weekends, and in holiday times.

5. DATA COLLECTION

I collected data from four main sources. The major part of the data collection was done while I was a participant observer in a series of sessions in which the children worked with Logo. Further data was recorded from interviews with the two case study children, records of time they spent preparing for the Logo sessions with their friends, and notes I made throughout the study of less formal incidents related to the study's aims.

For a considerable part of the study I used a peer teaching technique for data collection. While I planned to obtain data about the two children's learning from sessions in which they worked alone with Logo, greater insights into their learning would be possible if, having learnt Logo themselves, each child were to teach it to a friend. Reports of the discussions occurring with pairs of students working together (see for example Hoyles et al., 1984) gave me the idea that peer teaching could be a very valuable and revealing situation for the Logo researcher. My plan was that first my children should learn what they might about Logo and about recursion. Then each should teach Logo to her friend, in whatever way she wanted.

There were 79 Logo sessions, spread unevenly over the period from March 1984 to September 1986. From March 1984 to October 1984 the two case study children worked individually with me. From October 1984 to December 1985 each child worked with her friend. During August and September 1986 the elder child and her friend worked on projects particularly involving recursion.

Table 1

	No Sessions	Total Time	Longest Session	Shortest Session	Average Time
Younger child	32	17.3 hr	70 min.	15 min.	33 min.
Older child	47	44.8 hr	2 hr	10 min.	57 min.

In 1982, when data collection for the study was being planned, the powerful dribble file facilities which have been built into later microcomputer versions of Logo were not available. A colleague, Tony Adams, wrote from my specification a data collection system in LCSI Apple Logo (Adams, 1986). This was a set of procedures that captured and stored each complete command (not each keystroke, as most dribble systems do) as it was typed by the user. The data file of Logo commands for each session was saved on a disk, and printed out for inclusion with the other records of the session.

All of the sessions were audiotaped, using a small cassette recorder placed on the table where the children worked. Data from the Logo sessions are in four forms: audio tapes, computer data files, printed pictures, and the children's notes and other written materials. The children also kept work books.

6. DEVELOPING UNDERSTANDING OF RECURSION AND SKILLS IN RECURSIVE PROGRAMMING

A detailed description of the case study children's development of understanding of recursion and skills in recursive programming is reported elsewhere (McDougall, 1988) and part of the material has been published earlier (McDougall, 1985). I shall present a very brief summary here.

The case study children's early work with recursion did not involve programming at all. Both children recognised and made many situations involving self-reference, repetition with small variation, and nesting of levels, with pictures, story fragments, toys and everyday materials.

Since the younger child's programming work did not involve procedure writing, she did not use recursion in Logo. The elder child's first recursive programming project was the development of a tail recursive procedure to draw a nested squares design, which she completed with help in August 1984 at age 9. Early in 1985 I wrote for her an embedded recursive Logo-like procedure for the story "The Cat in the Hat Comes Back" (Seuss, 1958), and showed her a graphics procedure emphasising the unwinding part of embedded recursion.

In 1986 the elder child and her friend, then aged 11, worked on a series of recursive programming projects, becoming competent and confident in using recursion in Logo. Various areas of difficulty they encountered during these projects, and their overcoming of these are described in detail in the full report of the research (McDougall, 1988). The difficulties included problems with interpretation of the function of the STOP command, appreciating the scoping of variables, passing of values between procedures, and multiple inputs in recursive calls.

I shall present here two of these children's most advanced projects to illustrate the level of their programming at the end of the study.

7. A GRAPHICS PROJECT: DISPLAY PROCEDURE FOR NESTED REFLECTED POLYGONS

This project stretched over two sessions on consecutive days; the total time was 3 hours and 15 minutes. The children had previously written procedures to create an ongoing "display" of spirals of different shapes, each spiral being drawn by the turtle, then erased before the next was drawn. They planned to make a similar display, built on a procedure they had already to draw nested reflected squares.

Following are the final versions of their procedures for the display of nested reflected polygons. Some of the designs generated by running O 45 5 are shown in Figure 1.

```
TO O :N :T
FULLSCREEN
IF :T = 360 [STOP]
FP :N :T
REPEAT 2000 []
CS
O :N (:T+5)
SPLITSCREEN
END

TO FP :N :T
PU HOME PD
IF :N = 0 [STOP]
PU HOME PD
F :N :T
PU HOME PD
FP (:N-15) :T
PU HOME PD
F :N (-:T)
PU HOME PD
END

TO ABS :NUM
OP IF :NUM < 0 [-:NUM][:NUM]
END

TO F :N :T
REPEAT ABS 360/:T [FD :N RT :T]
END
```

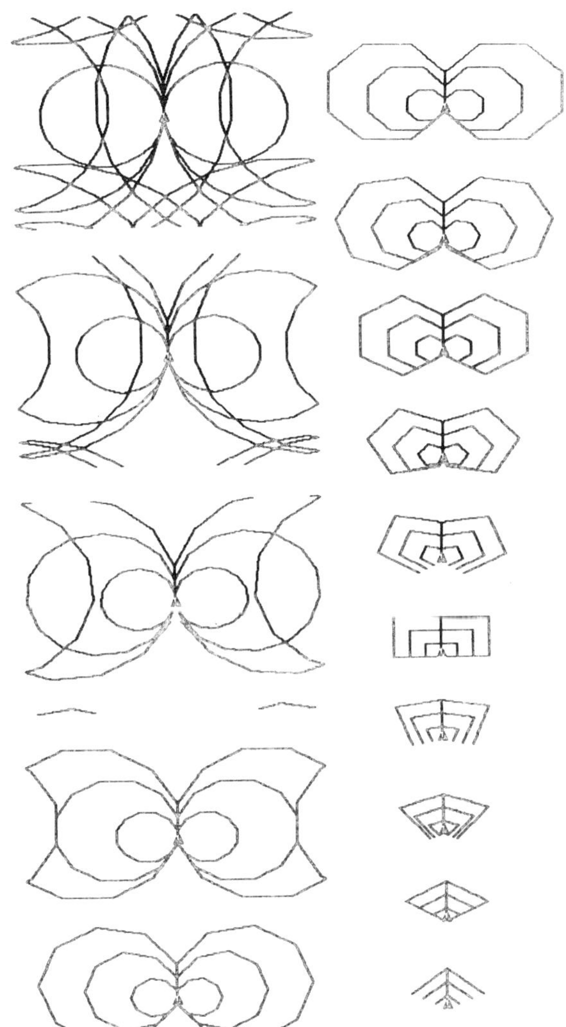

Figure 1

8. A LIST PROCESSING PROJECT: "TOO MANY BEARS"

The elder case study child had previously read the story "Too Many Bears" (Ahlberg and Amstutz, 1983), recognised its structure as recursive, and suggested that her friend read it as well. They planned to "write the story in Logo". This project was done in one one-hour session. I helped with the IF test in the TELL.STORY procedure, suggesting that it test for [GOLDILOCKS] instead of the empty list, and with the syntax of the PRINT statements. The children's procedures for the project were the following.

```
TO CH.1
BEARS.IN.BED
QUESTION
TELL.STORY [ALLAN.AHLBERG DINAH GOLDILOCKS]
SLEEP
END

TO BEARS.IN.BED
PRINT [BIG MEDIUM SMALL]
PRINT [DADDY MUMMY BABY]
PRINT [DINAH'S BED]
END

TO QUESTION
PRINT [???]
END

TO TELL.STORY :L
IF :L = [GOLDILOCKS] [PRINT [GOLDILOCKS TELLS STORY]
                      PRINT [GOLDILOCKS FINISHES STORY] STOP]
(PRINT FIRST :L [TELLS ABOUT] BUTFIRST :L)
TELL.STORY BUTFIRST :L
(PRINT FIRST :L [FINISHES STORY])
END

TO SLEEP
PRINT [GOODBYE]
PRINT [GOODNIGHT]
PRINT [SNORE]
END
```

```
CH.1

BIG MEDIUM SMALL
DADDY MUMMY BABY
DINAH'S BED
???
ALLAN.AHLBERG TELLS ABOUT DINAH GOLDILOCKS
DINAH TELLS ABOUT GOLDILOCKS
GOLDILOCKS TELLS STORY
GOLDILOCKS FINISHES STORY
DINAH FINISHES STORY
ALLAN.AHLBERG FINISHES STORY
GOODBYE
GOODNIGHT
SNORE
```

9. CONCLUSION

Recursion was introduced to these children using examples of self-reference, repetition with variation, and nesting of levels in pictures and stories. Both children, at ages 6 and 9 respectively, were able to recognise and generate examples of the features of recursion in pictures, stories and everyday situations, although they found it difficult to define or talk in general terms about recursion. The elder child, working at first (at age 9) with the researcher, and later with a school friend (until age 11 at the end of data collection for the study) developed Logo programming skills including confident use of controlled embedded recursion.

These children, in an environment rich in opportunities for learning about recursion, were able to understand and use this abstract idea when one of them was as young as 6 years of age. At age 9 the elder child was able to read with understanding, Logo procedures using embedded recursion, and to prepare with help a procedure containing tail recursion. At age 11 she and a schoolfriend together operated as competent and generally independent programmers with full recursion in Logo. Thus Papert's conjecture that children in a culture rich in resources for building intellectual structures might be able to engage in activities involving abstract or formal thinking at ages younger than would be expected from Piagetian theory is supported, in the case of recursion, by this study.

REFERENCES

Adams, T. *The Logo Language as a Tool in Education and Research.* Unpublished Master of Applied Science Thesis, Royal Melbourne Institute of Technology, 1986.

Ahlberg, A. and Amstutz, A. *Ten in a Bed.* London: Granada, 1983.

Hofstadter, D. *Godel, Escher, Bach: An Eternal Golden Braid.* Harmondsworth, U.K.: Penguin Books, 1979.

Hoyles, C., Sutherland, R. and Evans, J. *A Preliminary Investigation of the Pupil-Centred Approach to the Learning of Logo in the Secondary School Mathematics Classroom.* University of London Institute of Education, 1984.

Leron, U. Logo Today: Vision and Reality. *The Computing Teacher,* February, 1985, 26-32.

McDougall, A. Teaching and Learning about Recursion. Paper presented at the Logo85 Conference. Reprinted in Salvas, A. (Ed.), *Communication and Change.* Melbourne: Computer Education Group of Victoria, 1985, 217-21.

McDougall, A. *Children, Recursion and Logo Programming.* Unpublished Ph.D. thesis, Monash University, 1988.

Papert, S. *Mindstorms: Children, Computers and Powerful Ideas.* Brighton, U.K.: Harvester, 1980.

Seuss, Dr. *The Cat in the Hat Comes Back.* New York: Random House, 1958.

Computers in Education
A. McDougall and C. Dowling (Editors)
Elsevier Science Publishers B.V. (North-Holland)

ISSUES OF INTEGRATED AUTHORING/LEARNING ENVIRONMENTS

Max MÜHLHÄUSER

University of Kaiserslautern, Telematics Group
Erwin-Schrödinger-Str., D-6750 Kaiserslautern, W. Germany
Phone [+49](631)205-2992, Internet: max@uklirb.informatik.uni-kl.de

The paper reports about the mutual influences of hypermedia technology and integrated computer supported authoring/learning (A/L). It presents recommendations for adoptions and extensions of hypermedia systems. These lead to a 'hyperinformation machine' suitable as a design center for integrated A/L environments. Highlights of a such an environment are sketched, as currently prototyped in a joint project.

1. INTRODUCTION AND PREREQUISITES

1.1. Overview

A vision will be presented of how the A/L process can be computer supported in an integrated environment (section 2). Section 3 tries to classify the evolution of 'hyper...' systems. Recommendations will be given about how to construct an advanced *'hyperinformation* machine' (3.6). Section 4 will sketch an overall architecture for an integrated A/L environment.

1.2. Background

The concepts presented are related to a project called NESTOR. This project is undertaken jointly by the University and the Digital Equipment Campusbased Engineering Center in Karlsruhe, and by other Universities. The field of research is the use of networked multimedia workstations in computer supported A/L. A prototype A/L environment is prototyped, focusing on a *common environment* for all tools, *overall computer support* (for the authoring process, instructional methods and strategies, group learning, etc.), seamless *integration of media*, and *distribution and collaboration* aspects.

I would like to thank the NESTOR project members for their manifold fruitful contributions to this paper.

1.3. Terminology

Some terms related to computer supported A/L have to be described, abstracting to almost naive definitions, but trying to introduce a common terminology and to meet the different 'world views' of the disciplines involved.

Category: An important process in learning is that of building categories, i.e. the attempt to *unite and distinguish* things, to recognize similarities and differences, to relate new things to known ones by category assignment. Learning often means to build sub- and supercategories, assign several categories to one thing, and relate categories to one another. *Representations* of categories in our mind shall be called *concepts*.

Model: A model *exhibits* some *behavioral analogy* to the concept it represents. Lab experiments, miniature models, computer programs are examples for models. Experimenting with models is accepted as a good way of conveying concepts.

Gestalt: Information as a Gestalt shall denote the entire perception of an information when presented. For textual information, the Gestalt is the sum of actual text, layout, color, presentation medium (paper, computer), font, size, and all other context of the presentation (even hour of day, etc.).

(Information) media: the 'kind of sym-

bols' used to form the information (audiovideo, text, graphics...) are called information media or just media (to be distinguished from storage, presentation, and communication media).

1.4. Technical Assumptions

Recent technical advances open new opportunities for more efficient computer aided A/L environments. We view a well suited <u>*multifaceted computer system*</u> for our needs to comprise *powerful workstations*, capable of coping with *multiple information media*, integrated in a *sophisticated distributed system*, and providing an *on-line information space*.

The *distributed system* should allow real-time long distance media communication and true distributed processing with large numbers of irregularly connected nodes and processes.

On-line information space means on-line availability of most of the 'secondary' information used along with the provision and consumption of a course. More and more, contents of courses will not be recorded to a computer readable medium intentionally for a specific course, but be retrieved at authoring time from *multimedia libraries*. Such libraries start to evolve and will in the long run be on-line accessible. Multi-user and *multilevel* support has to be offered to authors and learners: courses must be extracted from, related to, and merged with the residual online information space, which may in turn consist of private, group or organization wide, or even foreign parts.

2. INSTRUCTIONAL VISION

Many features of multifaceted computer systems have not yet been sufficiently explored in the context of instruction. We want to briefly sketch the envisioned influence of computers on courseware, authoring, and learning, as we want to advocate it.

2.1. Computer support in courseware

In order to understand how courseware on a multifaceted computer systems should look like, we must ask what a computer can provide in an A/L context.

a) Flexible Gestalt: as the Gestalt of the information is of great importance for the learners' performance, the flexibility and power of a multifaceted computer system should be used to keep the Gestalt of the information - in its broadest sense - as flexible and adaptive as possible. Layout, information media used, flow of information (granularity, sequence, iterations...) should allow to be varied and driven by authors, tutors, or learners. Even lower level concepts (literal meaning, specific tactics applied, etc.) might be kept variable to augment the learners' performance in understanding the important 'higher level concepts' of the subject taught.

b) Use of models: the processing power of a computer can help to make much better use of models, (e.g., simulations). The relevant classes of models are: *concept models* (models of concepts to be conveyed, according to 1.3), *instruction models* (instructional strategies, rules, methods), and *student models* (models reflecting the envisioned student population).

c) Human centering: The biggest advantage of classroom teaching lays in the flexibility of human-human interaction. In order for A/L to provide some of this flexibility, too, 'human centered design' and computer supported tutor assistance must be considered. These must try to keep the motivation of authors and learners high and to reflect the individual differences of possible users.

2.2. Computer supported authoring

Traditional authoring processes consist of steps like goal selection, content assessment, determination of objectives, scripting/storyboarding, prototyping, production, evaluation, etc. But the traditional approach has two principal disadvantages:

1) It is badly computer supported:

While the end product (courseware) is a computer program, both the authoring *process* (except for the final generation of the courseware itself) and the description and realization of the *instruction model* are hardly influenced by the use of computer programs.

2) It is inflexible: either the authoring process (and instruction model handling) is fully 'paper based', or it is slightly supported by 'authoring systems'. In both cases, major changes in the process are very hard to achieve (think of introducing a democratic author/learner approach).

Three requirements for the authoring process are stated as follows:

1) Computer supported authoring should be provided throughout the process, offering and well integrating tools which guide through the steps, producing computer-readable data which can be reused in subsequent steps. Special emphasis is to be put on: a) computer support for *instruction model handling* (using generic semantics, enabling reuse) and b) computer supported *collaboration* among and between authors/ learners.

2) Flexibility of the authoring process should be offered via customizable and most freely mixable tools and user-accessible, easily changeable descriptions of the process.

3) Additional support is necessary in order to reflect the requirements of sections 2.1 and 2.3 at authoring time.

2.3. Computer supported learning

The frustration about traditional presentation-CAI lead to the desire to make better use of the computer system, with a strong emphasis on the student model. This lead to 'intelligent tutoring systems' (ITS [7,9]). The enormous complexity of a human, a good model of which is hard to build, and the resulting vulnerability and lack of general applicability of ITS systems developed, recently seem to have lead to a second frustration phase. More and more, people believe that models (student models, instruction models, sometimes even concept models) are largely impossible and should not be tried. Rather, students should organize their own way through the information space and should be provided as much freedom and as little 'determinism' as possible, helping to make the 'free journey' through the information space as easy as possible.

Our vision is that of *'non-intrusive guidance':* Systems should allow flexible combinations of information with instruction models, student models, and concept models, providing limited *freedom* through *navigation assistance* (driven by goals such as performance, motivation, or evaluation).

The worst characteristic of author-based instruction is its 'distribute and forget' nature (authors 'dump' documents onto the learners and forget about the learners). Therefore, electronic mail channels from learners to authors became popular. But we need much more 'broadband' feedback channels, and ways to make their use an integral part of the instruction model.

3. HYPERINFORMATION VISION

3.1. Related Work, Overview

Of the literature about hypertext/ hypermedia, we want to cite [4,2] for open issues, [6] for the instructional use, and [8] as an advanced instructional hypermedia system. The evolution of hypertext/hypermedia was in the past driven by the request for more flexible Gestalt of information. We will show - using an evolutionary approach - how increasing flexibility was introduced, what goals were missed, and how our *hyperinformation* vision can help to lay the ground for a new integral A/L concept (cf. figure 1 below).

3.2. Hypertext

<u>What was added: structure</u>. Hypertext added explicit non-linearity to sequential text. Textbooks had had implicit ways of helping the reader to organize

his/her own path through the information (citations and cross-references, different abstraction levels, etc.

Hypertext gave up predefined paths through the information, made relations, abstractions, and alternatives explicit, and allowed all references to become 'primary' (e.g., direct links to a citation). Gestalt became more flexible. Formerly independent pieces of information started to coagulate.

Three building blocks fell into place: *nodes* (information 'atoms'), *abstractions* (sets of nodes/abstractions), and *links* (references between those).

What was lost: guidance. We saw that freedom without guidance is undesirable: 'not getting lost in hypertext', 'goal-directed learning' and 'learner motivation and evaluation' all imply guidance. Hypertext does usually not provide explicit guidance.

What was left out: categories. Early hypertext systems did not provide system support for categories of nodes and links, and abstractions were pure 'envelopes' around elements.

3.3. Hypermedia

What was added: media. The advent of multiple media on the computer again allowed more flexible Gestalt of information by the use of multiple media.

What was left out: media synchronization. A tough task in coping with multiple media is that of synchronizing different media in order for them to jointly form integrated multimedia information instead of just 'multiple media'. A hypermedia system should offer means for composing different media into 'integrated multimedia' and for their integral manipulation.

3.4. Intelligent Hypermedia

What was added: knowledge representation. Early in hypertext/hypermedia development, the need for representing notions of knowledge-based systems within hypertext was raised. The 'bubbles-and-arcs' structure and static nature of hypertext qualified semantic networks as the most appropriate AI concept, so this one was realized in several hypermedia systems. But concept models, instruction models, and student models are hard to realize using semantic networks only (cf.[1,3]).

What was left out: 'non-procedural programming'. Non-procedural programming concepts, like 'logic programming' (cf. PROLOG) and functional programming (cf. LISP) provide much better possibilities to express dynamic behavior than semantic networks; the few attempts to introduce student models into authoring therefore combined hypertext/hypermedia systems with non-procedural languages, yet without integrating these concepts at the system and semantics level.

3.5. Hypermedia processing

What was added: dynamics. A major strength of a computer system is its *processing* capability. Plain Hypertext, however, uses computers as storage media only. True dynamics here means that links to choose among, even new nodes can possibly show up dynamically at the time the learner 'wanders' through the network, and nodes possibly are programs instead of static information elements.

What was lost: static structure. Some systems have introduced some kind of programmable links and nodes. But by doing this, they reduced the static structuring means (e.g. by giving up static links).

What was left out: common semantics. The few systems which introduced dynamics use different programming languages and paradigms for programming a node, programming a link, creating a static link, creating the user interface, etc. What is missing is an integral semantic framework for all these aspects.

3.6. The Vision: Hyperinformation

To be added: collaboration, appearance, things 'left out' or 'lost'.

a) *collaboration:* Mutual access to and

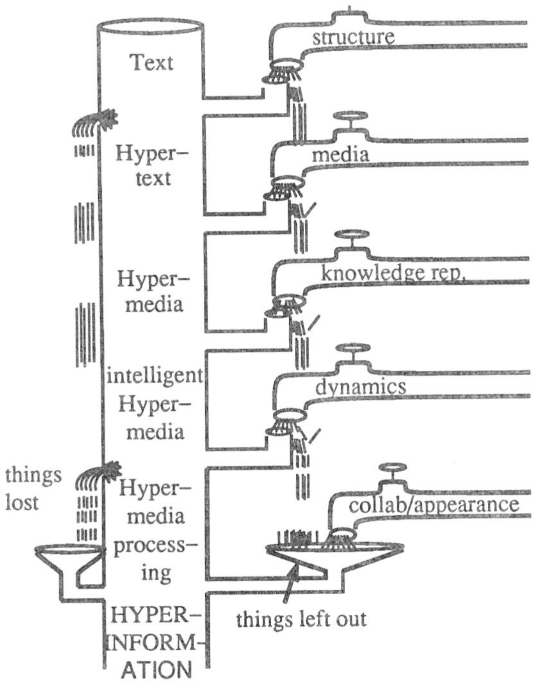

Figure 1: hyperinformation evolution

change of information by different humans, i.e. collaborative manipulation of information, is to be supported [5]. Hypermedia systems are often designed for single-node, single-thread, or single-user access or support client/server-like or 'single-network' distribution only. In our hyperinformation vision, frequently changing combinations of computer network nodes and different hyperinformation networks should be able to be interfered with one another, with partial network transparency and distinction of personal/restricted/public/global access.

b) appearance: we require hypermedia nodes to consist of three parts: *behavior* for procedural (object-oriented) and non-procedural 'dynamics', *status* (usual content of a hypermedia node), and <u>appearance</u> (node-specific human interaction; note that this is orthogonal to the system wide human interface).

c) things 'left out' or 'lost' before: An integrated hyperinformation machine comprises all of the features added in the above described evolutionary steps, but also integrates what was 'left out' or 'lost' in these steps.

The result: hyperinformation. The envisioned system marries the node/link based hypertext paradigm with the object/method-call based object-oriented paradigm. According to section 3, hyperinformation can be characterized as 'intelligent hypermedia processing, including categories, media synchronization, non-procedural programming, dynamics, structure, common semantics, collaboration and appearance'

4. A/L ENVIRONMENT VISION

The ideas of what we called a hyperinformation machine in 3.6 were fed into project NESTOR. The two relevant coarse layers of NESTOR are called BASE SYSTEM and PLATFORM. Built on top of a general multifaceted computer system, the BASE SYSTEM provides all the hyperinformation support necessary. The specific functionality of an A/L environment is delivered on top and is called PLATFORM. The hyperinformation machine offers both the semantics for the A/L environment and tools, and the semantics for the courseware itself.

4.1. Hyperinformation machine interface

The following hyperinformation base concepts are offered:

<u>*Nodes*</u>*:* nodes can be assigned categories ('types' or 'classes' in computer science terminology), we therefore distinguish an *instance* of a node from a node 'class'; Nodes can be either 'basic nodes' or 'abstractions'. Both consist of sections *behavior, status,* and *appearance* (cf. 3.6)

<u>*Links*</u>*:* links can also be assigned categories (types, classes). Link classes can be used in the more elaborate concept of an n-dimensional 'space'. Links can be static or dynamic, and can be instance-, set- and class-based with respect to the nodes they connect (sets are unions of nodes).

Webs: Networks and self-contained subsets of networks compose webs, comparable to the 'view' concept of databases.

Scripts and Policies: Dynamic behavior of and access to webs is expressed using two relevant concepts:
Scripts describe the non-intrusive guidance ('navigation') through a web of nodes and links, using procedural semantics (following the 'object-oriented programming' paradigm), non-procedural semantics, and/or associative means (queries about contents).
Policies regulate cooperative access to webs by groups of people. Policies consist of 'rules' and 'roles', where roles in turn are sequences of 'actions' and 'role interactions'. Both 'humans' and 'threads' may take roles.

4.2. BASE SYSTEM: virtual machine functionality

The components of the BASE SYSTEM together deliver the functionality of the hyperinformation machine. Major components of this layer are NEXUS (the portability interface), COLLABORATION (providing base support for collaborative A/L), the RUNTIME SYSTEM (for code execution and object management), and DATA MANIPULATION (providing persistent hyperinformation and interfacing to 'externally' stored media).

4.3. PLATFORM: authoring/learning environment

The PLATFORM, as mentioned, delivers the functionality of a sophisticated A/L environment:

CUSTOMIZED SCRIPTS & POLICIES: A basic concept here is that of easy customization and extension. A specific NESTOR installation is compiled from generic tools provided in PLATFORM and customized or extended via *scripts* and *policies*. Predefined scripts and policies deliver 'default' functionality.

GENERIC TOOLS: seven major generic tools form the functional building blocks for NESTOR A/L environments, serving for media handling, data storage/retrieval, hyperinformation handling, human interface design, hyperinformation navigation, configuration/revision management, and collaboration management.

5. CONCLUSIONS AND PROJECT STATUS

Issues have been discussed for a next-generation hyperinformation system, to be used as a basis for an integrated (networked, multimedia) A/L environment NESTOR. It is considered a step of many on the path from current, poorly computer-supported authoring techniques to a widely accepted A/L methodology and to related standards. Project NESTOR has left its early conceptual phase and will soon release a first prototype implementation.

REFERENCES

[1] Berger, D.E., et al.(eds), Applications of Cognitive Psychology: Problem Solving, Education & Computing (Lawrence Erlbaum, London 1987).
[2] Conklin, J., Hypertext: An Introduction and Survey, IEEE Computer, V.20 No.9 (1987), pp. 17-41.
[3] Gagné, R.M., Instructional Technology: Foundations (Lawrence Erlbaum, Hillsdale, NJ 1987).
[4] Halasz, F.G., Reflections on Notecards: Seven Issues for the Next Generation of Hypermedia Systems, CACM, V.31 No.7(1988), pp. 836-852.
[5] Johnson, D., Johnson, R., Learning Together & Alone- Cooperative, Competitive & Individualistic Learning (PrenticeHall, E. Cliffs, NJ 1987).
[6] Jonassen, D.H., Designing Hypertext f. Learning, in: Scanlan, M. et al. Directions in Educational Technology (Springer, New York 1989)
[7] Mandl, H., Lesgold, A., Learning Issues for Intelligent Tutoring Systems (Springer, New York 1988).
[8] Russell, D.M., et al., Creating In struction w/ IDE: Tools f. Instructional Designers, Xerox PARC Report No. P88-00076, Palo Alto 1988.
[9] Self, J. (ed.), AI and Human Learning - Intelligent CAI (Chapman and Hall Ltd., London 1988).

Computers in Education
A. McDougall and C. Dowling (Editors)
Elsevier Science Publishers B.V. (North-Holland)

THINKING SITUATIONALLY: RESULTS WITH AN UNINTELLIGENT TUTOR FOR WORD ALGEBRA PROBLEMS

Mitchell J. NATHAN and Emilie YOUNG

Institute of Cognitive Science, University of Colorado, Boulder, CO 80309-0345 USA

We present a theory of algebra word problem comprehension which favors computer tutors that encourage students to think about how problem situations relate to formal equations. Tutors need not be "intelligent" or model students' actions if they allow students to assess their own performance. Problem solving performance with ANIMATE, a situation-based tutoring system, is compared to a tutor identical to it except for its lack of situation-based feedback. ANIMATE subjects score higher on problem solving and transfer tasks. Insights for education and tutoring system designs are discussed.

1. INTRODUCTION

Computer-based tutors for education range from those which give the student full autonomy to those which are highly structured. We examine computer-based tutors in light of a theory of problem comprehension which highlights the importance of establishing a correspondence between the situation described by a problem and the formal expressions students need to produce quantitative answers. Most favorable to this theory are tutors we term "situation-based".

We then describe a situation-based tutoring system for word algebra problems, ANIMATE. With it, students learn to build a formal problem model which organizes problem information and makes explicit the values and relations of a problem through computer animation. Students watch the animation and use their own understanding of the problem situation to "debug" the problem model until they are satisfied the animation is appropriate. Errors in specifying the formal problem model produce incorrect animations, the resolution of which is highly constrained by its relation to the situation. Experimental results (Section 3) indicate that ANIMATE students outperform control subjects on word problems which require an understanding of the situation and interpretation of algebraic expressions. A transfer test shows that students maintain this when solving paper-and-pencil problems. These findings are discussed in reference to computer-based education and instructional design.

2. STRUCTURED AND UNSTRUCTURED CAI

At one end of the spectrum, CAI designers have pursued systems which foster "learning by exploration" by providing a free environment within which students can discover concepts. These systems view the student as a scientist and teacher, capable of performing self-diagnosis and error correction, e.g. [10].

The other end of the spectrum contains systems with highly-structured knowledge about the domain and expectations about student actions. These Intelligent Tutoring Systems (ITSs) are capable of tracking students' actions and providing immediate and meaningful feedback regarding errors, e.g. [3], [11]. Expert systems guide the student through pre-planned lessons to develop problem solving skills [1] and tag student actions as acceptable or not. Anderson [2] demonstrates many positive attributes for this approach but recent work have shows that delayed or selective feedback can lead to better problem solving performance and transfer [8], [14].

Situation-based tutors lie between these two extremes and rely not on a large knowledge base for error detection and teaching, but on the student acting as a planner and diagnostician as well as a problem solver, [4], [12], [13]. They focus on imparting understanding to the student rather than skill acquisition. These tutors support some exploration of a domain, thus engaging the student, but provide some structure as well. In the ideal, this structure reveals to the student the meaning of formal expressions and manipulations in terms of an underlying situation.

3. A THEORY OF SITUATION-BASED PROBLEM COMPREHENSION

In our theory of problem comprehension [9] we assume that students have an informal situation-based representation for understanding and solving real world problems, and that they learn formal methods of representing and solving math problems but do not always coordinate these two representations [5], [7]. Thus, when asked to find formal solutions to real world (i.e. word) problems, students have difficulty. Our goal is a tutoring environment which helps students bridge between formal and informal representations of a problem statement (Figure 1).

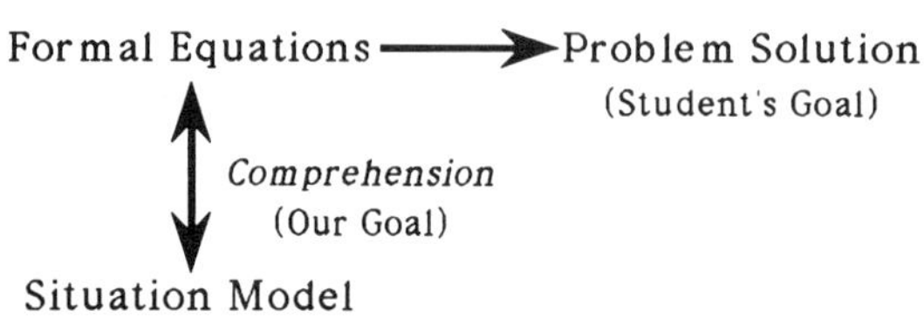

Figure 1: Mapping between formal and informal representations.

Current theories of reading comprehension highlight two informal representations that are extracted from a text: a propositional representation and a situation model [15]. We focus on the situation model as the basis for understanding actions and relations in a problem text.

In addition to informal representations, students learn how to represent math problems formally so that solutions can be found. Formal representations can be viewed at several levels, the most general being mathematics. Below this are the laws of the physical world which hold for real events and rely on mathematics. While one can write an equation that is *mathematically* true, it is not necessarily *physically* true. There is an even more specific situation level. One may write an equation that is *physically* true, but it is not necessarily true for a given situation.

Along with the formal and informal representations mentioned, some researchers propose a third representation which is both mental and formal. This has been termed the problem schema or problem model [6]. Here, solution-relevant information is extracted from the text and reorganized to facilitate problem comprehension. In Figure 2 this is depicted by the arrow which links the "word problem" to the "conceptual problem model". Information relevant to solving the problem but not explicitly stated is inferred from the reader's situation model and real world experience. The problem model is made complete by drawing on representations of the problem passage and knowledge of the physical world which is then described formally.

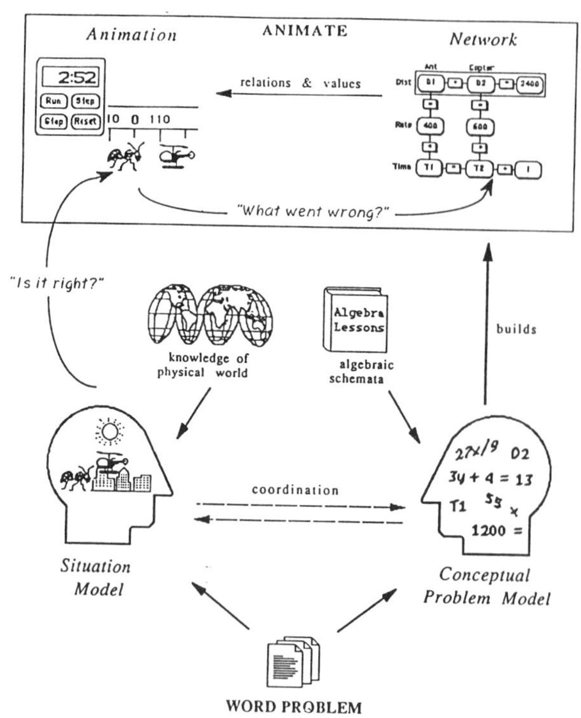

Figure 2: Our theory of situation-based problem comprehension.

For word algebra, a problem model has been suggested by Weaver & Kintsch [16].Its application is explained more fully in [9]. An example network for a typical word problem sentence is given.

"The plane leaves 3 hours later than the train."

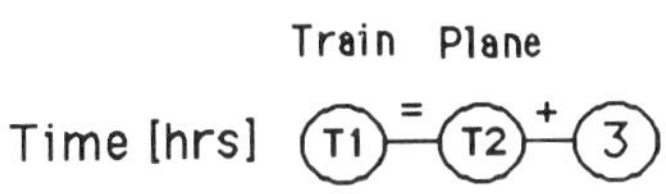

4. THE ANIMATE TUTOR

From our discussion, we have derived requirements for the ANIMATE tutoring system [9]. The tutor is an interactive computer program that runs on the Apple Macintosh. It helps the student construct a formal problem network, which runs a simple animation. ANIMATE knows nothing of the problem being solved and so cannot tell the student if the network being built is correct. We rely upon the student's understanding of the situation described in the problem statement to set her expectations for how the animation should appear, and address the "Is It Right?" link of Figure 2. A mismatch between animation and expectation tells the student how to alter the problem model and create the correct animation. In this way, the student addresses the "What Went Wrong?" link.

4.1. System Use and An Example

ANIMATE gives students complete control over the order they choose to solve the problems. A student may redirect herself to build portions of the network, enter animation parameters, or run animations on partial and incorrect networks. The student may change a network value simply by selecting a node with the mouse cursor.

Currently, ANIMATE only tutors problems in the AMOUNT-PER-TIME RATE family of word problems. These are problems which employ the "distance = rate x time" equation and includes "overtake", "collision" and "distance apart" problems. Here is how a student uses ANIMATE on a collision algebra problem.

A huge ant terrorizes San Francisco. It travels east toward Detroit, which is 2400 miles away, at 400 miles per hour. The Army learns of this one hour later and sends a helicopter west from Detroit at 600 miles per hour to intercept the ant.If the ant left at 2 PM, what time will the helicopter and ant collide (ignoring time changes)?

To describe the ant the student pushes the button "Pick Character 1" and is presented with pictures representing the possible characters. Buttons appear at the bottom of the screen which allow the student to select the ant's starting location and travel direction (see Figure 3).

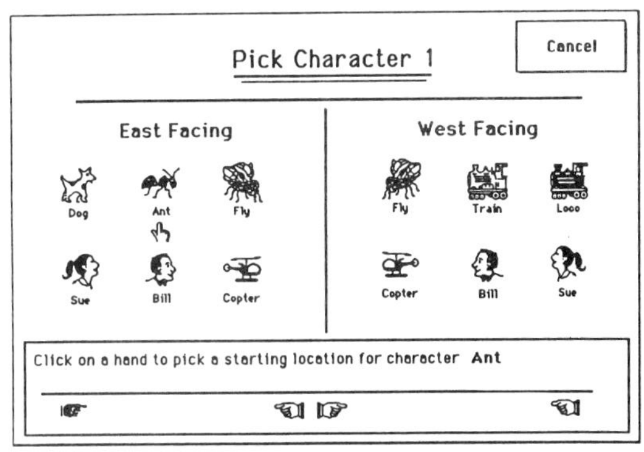

Figure 3: Starting location and direction for ant are chosen.

To specify the motion of the ant, the student must build and customize the ant's problem model. Pushing the "Equations" button causes a palette of suggested network equations to appear. She chooses the equation $D1 = R1 \times T1$ and the first "D = R x T" equation in the network appears. This equation may be made the *stopping condition* for the animation and the animation will stop when it is satisfied by the position and travel time of the ant. The student then selects the rate node (R1) of the network and, in accordance with the problem, enters the number 400.

Pushing the "Run" button initiates a check of algebraic and network errors. Finding none, the tutor begins the animation by moving the ant across the screen. Gauges show the elapsed time and distance travelled for the ant.

To build the rest of the network the student chooses the equations $D2 = R2 \times T2$, $T1 = T2 - T3$, and $D1 + D2 = D3$. The last equation is the stopping condition which appears with a box around it in the network. The student enters the rest of the values given in the problem. From the text she knows the helicopter leaves 1 hour after the ant and so mistakenly portrays this delay (T3) as being *subtracted* from the helicopter's time (T2). She knows also from the text that the ant leaves at 2 PM and so erroneously enters 2 for T1. Since the helicopter leaves one hour later she enters 3 for the T3 node.

The student then enters the distance values by multiplying the rates and times in the network. When she pushes "Check Net", the tutor warns her that **800 + 1800 = 2400** is not correct, and highlights the flawed equation (Figure 4). The student ignores the error and, with no further errors, she selects and positions the helicopter, and pushes "Run".

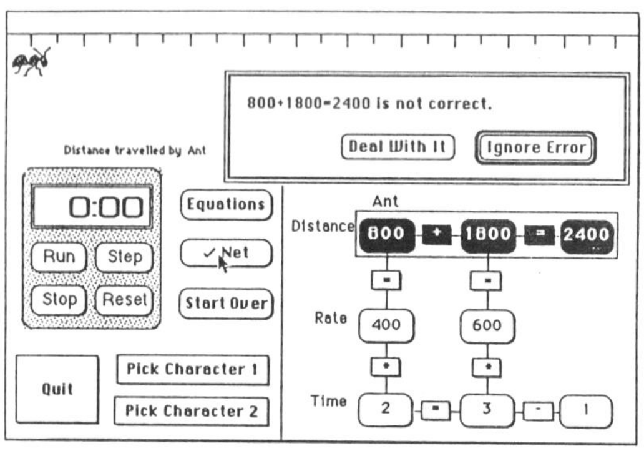

Figure 4: System highlights incorrect network problem model equation.

Right away the student notices that the helicopter, not the ant, starts moving first which is contrary to her situation-based expectations (Figure 5). The mismatch suggests that the delay for the characters in improperly specified in the network. The Time equation in the bottom row is suspect. She stops the animation and picks $T1 = T2 + T3$. The Time equation in the network changes from **2=3-1** to **2=<u>3+1</u>**, which is arithmetically wrong. She realizes now that she has entered in "starting times" for the characters whereas the network needs "travel times". Since these are unknown, she enters variables for the times and distance values.

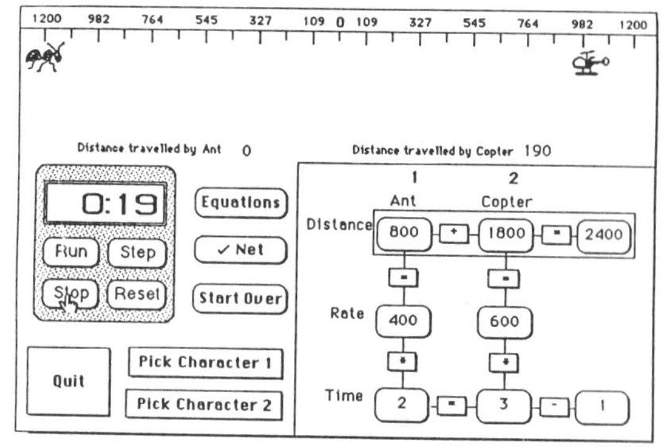

Figure 5: Situationally incorrect problem model, helicopter leaves before ant

When she runs the animation again, she sees that the ant now leaves an hour before the helicopter (Figure 6). As the ant and helicopter near the point of collision she decides that the animation matches her mental picture from the word problem. The following equations are taken from the net, and she is done.

$$D1 = 400 \times T1 \qquad D2 = 600 \times T2$$
$$D1 + D2 = 2400 \qquad T1 = T2 + 1$$

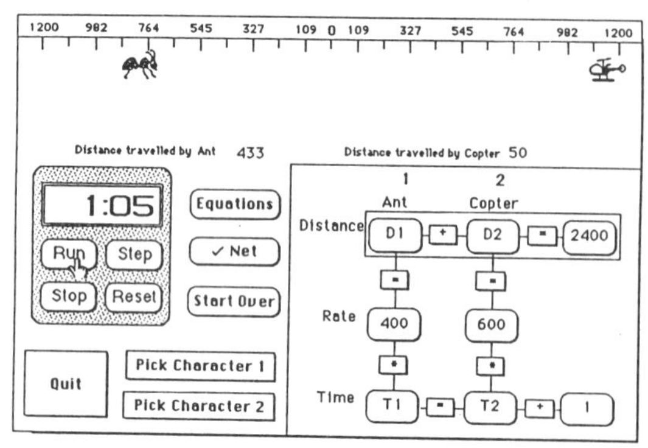

Figure 6: The situationally correct problem model.

4.2. Experimental Findings

<u>Experimental procedure and scoring</u>. Twenty eight undergraduates from the University of Colorado participated in a two hour experiment as part of their course requirements for Introductory Psychology and were randomly assigned to either the NETWORK or the ANIMATE treatment. Both groups were pretested

on their knowledge of algebra. Subjects then had a brief tutorial (30 min) on the network method discussed above. They solved 3 problems in a task booklet using either the complete ANIMATE computer program, or a Network-only program which is identical in every respect except that it gives no situation-based feedback. Finally, subjects took a post test of comparable difficulty to the pretest, without use of the tutors, and were excused.

Results. ANIMATE subjects produced the highest scores on average for the booklets, $F(1,27)=8.367$, MSE=4.13, $p<.01$. All subjects, regardless of condition, improved from pretest to post test, $F(1,27)=33.9$, $p<.0001$ with the ANIMATE group improving more than the NETWORK group, $F(1,27)=6.35$, MSE=9.14, $p<.02$. Analyses of individual test problems indicate that the ANIMATE program helped most on the novel story-writing problem, where students generated a story from equations.

5. DISCUSSION

NETWORK and ANIMATE subjects received the same training and both received feedback from the tutor on the mathematical and physical validity of their network problem models. Only the ANIMATE group, however, was shown a situation depicting the problem model. This feedback helped subjects perform better than NETWORK subjects on problem solving and transfer tasks.Situation-based reasoning appears to be an important facet of problem solving and comprehension. By grounding formal relations in meaningful situations, students obtain a greater appreciation for how mathematics relates to events in the world.

What new insight does situation-based tutoring provide for educators and tutoring system developers? It shows that a tutor for a domain as difficult as word algebra need not be dependent on a large knowledge base for its success as an instructional device. Rather, improvements in understanding can come about when feedback helps students relate expressions to their own experiences.Tutors must be engaging so that they motivate students and make the problem solving process personal and even creative. While strides have been made in providing meaningful feedback to students, the amount and structure of knowledge necessary to successfully emulate an experienced teacher is currently beyond our conception. The ability to sufficiently model a student learning a new field is equally difficult. But, how different the task is when the student is on the designer's side! The student can apply his own reasoning, not only to the problem at hand, but to monitoring his own problem solving processes.
When students are free to explore problems and solution paths in many different ways, "play" with mathematical concepts, and build upon experiences, their comprehension improves. These are things that educators know and tutoring system designers need to support.

ACKNOWLEDGEMENTS

This work was supported by NSF Grant BNS-8608741 to Walter Kintsch whose efforts and contributions made this project possible. We also thank Clayton Lewis for the benefits from our many discussions.

REFERENCES

[1] Anderson, J. R. (1988). The expert module. In M.C. Polson and J.J. Richardson (Ed.s) *Foundations of Intelligent Tutoring Systems.* Hillsdale: Erlbaum.

[2] Anderson, J. R. (1989). Analysis of student performance with the LISP Tutor. In Frederickson, Glaser, Lesgold, and Shafto (Ed.s), *Diagnostic Monitoring of Skill and Knowledge Acquisition.* Hillsdale: Earlbaum.

[3] Anderson, J.R., Boyle, C.F., Farrell, R., & Reiser, B. (1984). Cognitive principles in the design of computer tutors. Carnegie-Mellon Tech. Report ONR-84-1.

[4] Gould, L., & Finzer, W. (1981). A study of TRIP: A system for animating Time-Rate-Distance problems. *Proceedings of the 3rd World Conference on Computers in Education.* (Lausanne).

[5] Greeno, J. G. (1989). Situation models, mental models, and generative knowledge. In D. Klahr and K. Kotovsky (Ed.s), *Complex Information Processing: The Impact of Herbert A. Simon.* Hillsdale: Earlbaum.

[6] Kintsch, W., & Greeno, J. G. (1985). Understanding and solving

word arithmetic problems. *Psychological Review. 92.* 109-129.

[7] Larkin, J. H. (1983). Expert and novice differences in solving physics word problems. In Gentner, D., and Stevens, A. L. *Mental Models.* Hillsdale: Erlbaum.

[8] Lee, A. (1989). Timing of feedback in tutoring systems. Institute of Cognitive Science Technical Report No. 89-10, University of Colorado.

[9] Nathan, M.J., Johl, P., Kintsch, W., & Lewis, C. (1989). An unintelligent tutoring system for solving word algebra problems. In D. Bierman, J. Breuker, and J. Sandberg, (Ed.s) *Proceedings of the 4th Int'l Conference on AI and Education*. Amsterdam:IOS. 169-176.

[10] Papert, S. (1980). *Mindstorms: Children, computers, and powerful ideas*. New York: Basic Books.

[11] Reiser, B., Kimberg, D. Y., Lovett, M. C., & Ranney, M. (1989). Knowledge representation and explanation in GIL, an intelligent tutor for programming. Princeton University Cognitive Science Laboratory Technical Report No. 37.

[12] Roschelle, J. (1987). *Envisionment, mental models, and physics cognition.* Int'l Conference on AI and Education (Pittsburgh).

[13] Scardamalia, M. E., Bereiter, C., McLean, R. S., Swallow, J., & Woodruff, E. (1989). *Computer-supported intentional learning environments. Journal of Educational Computing Research, 5,* 51-68.

[14] Schmalhofer, F., Kuehn, O., Messamer, P., & Charron, R. (1989). An experimental evaluation of different amounts of receptive and exploratory learning in a tutoring system. Proc. of the 19th Annual Meeting of the Society for Computers in Psychology.(Atlanta)

[15] van Dijk, T.A., & Kintsch, W. (1983). *Strategies of Discourse Comprehension.* New York: Academic Press.

[16] Weaver, C.A. & Kintsch, W. (1988). The conceptual structure of word algebra problems. University of Colorado Technical Report.

Computers in Education
A. McDougall and C. Dowling (Editors)
Elsevier Science Publishers B.V. (North-Holland)

ON THE CONCEPT OF DATABASES OF MULTIMEDIA LEARNING MATERIAL (DBLM)

Olimpo G., Chioccariello A., Midoro V., Persico D., Sarti L., Tavella M., Trentin G.

Istituto Tecnologie Didattiche (Consiglio Nazionale Ricerche)

This paper refers to the ESM_BASE (Educational Systems Based on Multimedia Database) project carried out within the EEC DELTA programme. The concepts of ULM (Unit of Learning Material) and of DBLM (Database of multimedia Learning Material) as resources for learning and as bases for courseware reusability in the authoring process are discussed in connection with possible developments of the educational market. A basic architecture for a DBLM is proposed which allows for different personalized views of the same DBLM to be used by different classes of educational applications. Educational processes based on learners' navigation in a DBLM guided by an intelligent tutor are also considered.

1. INTRODUCTION

The increasing use of technology in education and training together with the advances in the field of optical storage and communications are the main motivations for the implementation of the concept of databases of learning material as a resource for educational applications. A database supporting a variety of possibly distributed educational applications makes it possible to share the same material among many different users (learners and authors) and is a key factor in reducing the large amount of resources needed to develop high quality courseware.

A DBLM (DataBase of multimedia Learning Material) can be thought of as a resource which can be accessed and navigated by learners (in order to achieve specific information or educational goals) and by authors (in order to design educational processes based on navigation in the database).

While traditional courseware has a specific educational objective and is oriented toward a well-defined target population, a DBLM is only related to a specific content domain, but not necessarily to a specific educational objective or user [1]. This may depend either on the learner, who can select the units of learning material most suited to him, or on the author who can define classes of paths within the database which relate to specific educational objectives, or on the strategies of an Intelligent Tutoring System (ITS) which can dynamically guide the learner's navigation in the database. The same generality applies to educational strategies which should be defined outside the database by the author of a specific learning process. Finally, the learning resources within the database may be used in different technological contexts, to develop either non-interactive learning material or *traditional* interactive courseware or educational processes based on artificial intelligence techniques.

The hypothesis underlying this concept is that a new wider market is going to develop for educational software involving the distribution of content oriented rather than objective oriented learning material [2].

The use of a DBLM has interesting implications in the authoring and learning processes:

- it modifies the process of designing new learning material which does not have to start every time from scratch: already existing multimedia components can be selected by authors from a DBLM and imported into an application being developed within a specific authoring environment. This allows for actual courseware reusability in the educational design and may dramatically reduce the development costs of high quality multimedia courseware.
- it provides more mature learners with a facility where they can autonomously build their own informative/educational paths [3].
- it provides the basis for a new type of educational system whose core is a database of learning material which fulfils the needs of different courses in the same content area.

2. A DBLM AS A RESOURCE FOR EDUCATIONAL APPLICATIONS

A DBLM can be regarded as:

- *a stand alone resource to be accessed directly by the user for informative purposes.*

This "open" use of the database requires suitable primitives and suitable user interfaces to help the user find the material which is most interesting and best suited to him in an easy, quick and natural way.

- *a resource which can be accessed by any authoring or learning environment.*
  This implies the possibility for virtually any educational application to access a DBLM to retrieve potentially interesting material. For authoring applications this means finding and possibly modifying useful multimedia components in the database and importing parts of them in the application being developed with a 'cut and paste' mechanism or with a run time query.
  For learning applications this means the possibility for the learner to satisfy his needs or to develop his own personal interests by freely accessing the material in the database.
  An interesting example is that of hypermedia navigation, which may be thought of, and implemented, as a specific client application of a DBLM.
- *a pool of learning material where an ITS can select the most suitable units to present to the learner.*
  An ITS may help the learner find a path within the database to reach specific educational objectives. To assist the learner individually, a suitable model of the learner is required (and the related modelling system) as well as suitable representation of the content domain being taught. Given the amount of learning materials and the wide variety of alternative strategies available in a DBLM, the selection of the material most suited to the learner requires sophisticated decision rules based on adequate student modelling facilities.

3. ULM (UNIT OF LEARNING MATERIAL): THE BASIC INHABITANT OF A DBLM

This section aims at clarifying the concept of ULM, whose definition is a critical aspect deeply affecting the actual usability of a DBLM.

ULMs can be thought of as the basic blocks of learning material accessed by learners and by authors. The ULM is an abstraction which collects content segments of various media and types, hides their differences and offers a common and consistent interface in order to accomplish fruition and/or authoring activities [4]. All the multimedia aspects of the learning material are encapsulated in the definition of ULM.

ULMs can be simple monomedial objects, or the composition of other (simpler) ULMs. Simple ULMs may be of two types:

- Multimedia Sequence (MS)
  A MS corresponds to the delivery of a multimedia message to the user possibly including texts, still frames, dynamic sequences and digitized audio. No interaction is included in a MS except the standard one provided by the delivery system (quit a MS, altering the velocity of delivery, replay, etc.)
- Facilities
  A facility is any kind of (possibly interactive) program to be used by the author or by the learner to perform a specific educational function (a test, a simulation environment etc.)

The glue which binds together different ULMs in a composite learning sequence has to be provided by authors using a specific authoring environment. To ease the process of composition of ULMs in a learning sequence, each ULM is endowed with an Events Table which relates possible user actions (i.e. mouse clicking, keystrokes, timeouts, etc.) to activities to be performed by the system. When a ULM is generated only the "event side" of the table is initialized: the semantic actions are specified during the authoring phase.

4. A PROPOSAL FOR A CONCEPTUAL SCHEMA OF A DBLM

In this section an Entity Relationship (E-R) description model is used to describe the conceptual schema of a user view of a DBLM [5]. It should be noted that the choice of the E-R formalism does not entail a particular kind of data model and it is only considered a suitable language for communicating ideas [6].

4.1 A first step into the schema of a view

The two major entities in the conceptual model of a DBLM are the *ULMs*, the multimedia units of learning material, and the *TOPICs*, i.e. the specific elements of the content domain which a DBLM refers to. It should be noted that a set of topics does not involve a specific knowledge structure. On the other hand, many different structures can be imposed on the same set of topics.

ULMs are linked to TOPICs by the relation ASSOCIATED_TO. A ULM may be linked (refer) to one or more TOPICs, and a TOPIC may be associated to (many) different ULMs. The core of a DBLM can be characterized by the E-R diagram in fig. 1.
The diagram also establishes that TOPICs have a single attribute *topic_id*, ULMs have mostly attributes of a rather objective and technical nature while the attributes of the relation ASSOCIATED_TO are of an educational nature and characterize the pedagogical function that a ULM may perform for a given TOPIC.

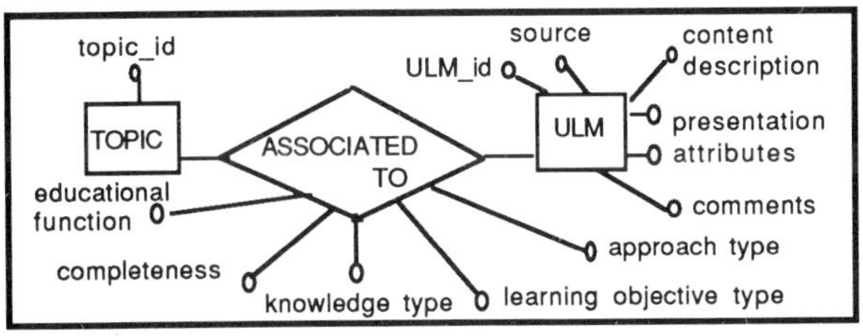

fig.1: a segment of the E-R diagram for the DBLM

4.1.1. ULMs' Attributes

A ULM is designed as an abstract object that hides all the implementation details and exports a set of features which are the only way to access the object. In this perspective a user can show or reuse a ULM without being concerned with all the technical details such as the different media involved, the physical location of the material (text and graphic files, video frame numbers), etc.: the fruition of any ULM is achieved through a small, simple and consistent set of primitives.

As an entity of the database, the ULM class exports values which are seen by the database user as the attributes of the entity. All the attributes of the entity ULM are values returned by methods of the object ULM.

These attributes can be grouped into three categories:

- *ULM identification*
  Each ULM is identified by a unique name, which is regarded as a primary key for the database.
- *content description*
  This category of attributes provides a mean to connote the ULM's content. Composed ULM are defined in terms of reference to the composing ULM and composition criteria (in space and time).
- *presentation attributes*
  The *show* method is redefined for each different medium subclass that a ULM may belong to: a user (human or program) can show any ULM with the same command, regardless the nature of the medium and structure of the material.

4.1.2. ASSOCIATED_TO attributes

ASSOCIATED_TO is a fundamental relation in the database which establishes a link between topics and ULMs making it possible to retrieve the set of ULMs referring to a given topic or the set of topics involved in a ULM. This *many to many* relation has the following attributes:

- *educational function*
  Each association ULM-TOPIC is characterized by the specific educational function which the ULM performs in connection with that TOPIC. Possible values for this attribute are {exposition, explanation, description, assessment, drill&practice, simulation, ...}.
  It should be noted that if we admit that the same ULM may exhibit different educational functions for the same TOPIC, it could be more appropriate to represent the educational function as an entity rather than as an attribute. In this case the relation ASSOCIATED_TO would became a ternary relation between ULMs, TOPICs and EDUCATIONAL FUNCTIONs.
- *completeness*
  The association between a ULM *u* and a topic *t* is characterized by an educational function *e*. If the ULM *u* performs *e* in such a way that nothing more is needed to accomplish *e* for the topic *t* we say that the triple *{u,t,e}* is complete. If *u* performs only part of *e* for the topic *t*, then we need more ULMs to accomplish *e* for *t* and, in this case, we say that *{u,t,e}* is not complete.
  If *{u,t,e}* is not complete, then *u* is of little use to an automatic tutor willing to perform *e* for the topic *t* since no information is contained in the database about how to combine *u* with other ULMS to fully accomplish *e*.
- *knowledge type*
  This attribute specifies the nature of the knowledge that a ULM can transfer to a learner in connection with a given TOPIC. Possible values are {theory, data, facts, hypothesis, deduction, instance, concept, rule, skill,...}
- *learning objective type*
  Traditional classifications of learning objectives usually refer to the affective, psycho-motorial and cognitive domains. For each domain specific taxonomies have been developed. In our case, to specify a set of values for this attribute, it is more interesting and appropriate to refer to taxonomies of cognitive objectives. Referring to Bloom's Taxonomy the set of values for this attribute could be {knowledge, comprehension, application, analysis, synthesis, evaluation}
- *approach type*
  This attribute specifies the way in which a ULM approaches a given TOPIC.
  It should be noted that the set of possible values for this attribute are often domain dependent (as an example think of ULMs referring to alternative theories to explain the same phenomenon).
  A generic set of values for approach type could be {inductive, deductive, concrete, abstract, formal, intuitive, traditional, historical,...}

4.2. Including content representations in the DBLM

4.2.1. Reasons for including knowledge representation in a DBLM

At an earlier stage of this project, keeping the knowledge structure information outside the database was considered a cleaner solution. In this view, a knowledge representation should be considered as a set of links (external to the database) connecting a set of TOPICs (internal to the database).

Eventually it was decided to include structures in the database for two independent reasons: first, the association between ULMs and TOPICS is not an absolute one, but it is relative to a specific knowledge structure, and second, it may be difficult to keep the knowledge structure (outside the database) consistent with the set of topics (inside the database).

4.2.2. How to represent knowledge structures in a DBLM

Each structure can be represented in the DBLM as a set of typed links between topics. To this purpose a relation LINKED_TO between TOPICs and TOPICs has been introduced in the conceptual model of the database (see fig. 2)

The attribute *link type* allows for a variety of different knowledge representation techniques (hierarchies, Petri Net, semantic networks, ...).

It should be noted that the relation LINKED_TO is ternary since it involves also the entity STRUCTURE which specifies the knowledge structure in which two TOPICs must be considered linked. The type of knowledge structure (hierarchy, Petri net, semantic network, ...) is specified by an attribute of the entity STRUCTURE.

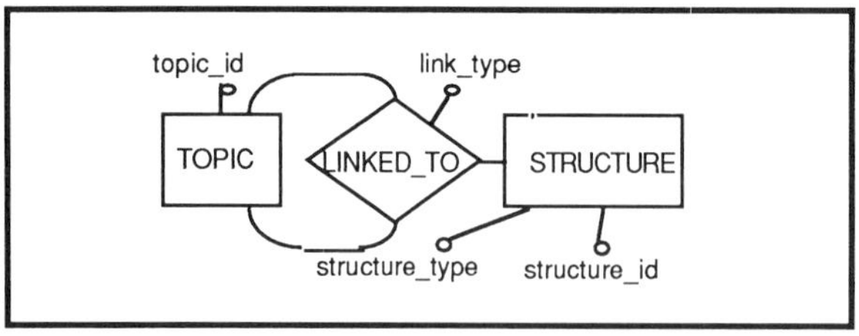

fig. 2: Representing knowledge structures in a DBLM

The users of a view of the database may define different structures according to their needs. For instance, they might need a structure for consultation/navigation purposes, another one for teaching and assessing a subject and a third one for teaching another subject or the same subject from another point of view. Moreover the system could provide a tree structure for the TOPICs in order to make it possible to browse them efficiently.

The E-R diagram in fig. 3 shows the complete skeleton for the conceptual model of a view in a DBLM.

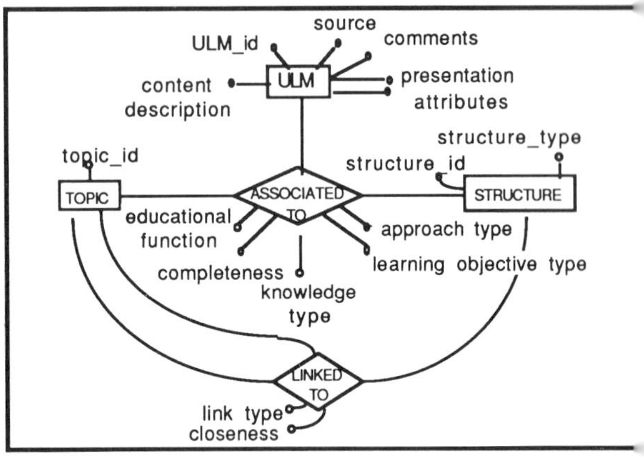

fig. 3: Conceptual schema of a DBLM user view

5. PERSONALIZATION: A DBLM AS A HIERARCHY OF VIEWS

5.1 Hierarchical structure of a DBLM

The idea of a DBLM supporting different users and, therefore, different learning and teaching needs and objectives within the same content area entails a flexible structure allowing for different *views* of the database. For example, an author might wish to enhance the data base (with new ULMs, new links between database entities, new STRUCTUREs, etc.) or to modify the qualification of the material inside the database to make it more suitable to the nature of the application being developed. Besides, among the users of a given view, some might wish to go further in the personalization process, while maintaining that view as a starting point.

This leads to the organization of a DBLM as a hierarchy of databases (views), each belonging to a user or group of users, with a responsible person regarded as the *author* of the view.

Theoretically, there is no limit to the depth or width of the hierarchy. The conceptual scheme of each view is inherited from the root and, for practical reasons, it is assumed that it cannot be altered by the view authors. However, in order to cope with the needs of specific educational applications, view authors may modify the range of possible values for entity and relation attributes. Several problems may arise from this structure such as the integrity and the internal consistence of a view with respect to modifications taking place in other views and the unnecessary duplication of learning material stored in more than one view. These problems require suitable criteria and rules for an efficient management of the collection of views.Such criteria may be referred to as the dynamic aspects of the personalization process, as opposed to the static ones, i. e. the hierarchical structure of the DBLM.

Among the possible solutions of view management problems, we envisage here a combination of a pure inheritance mechanism and a simpler copy and paste approach, which minimises the drawbacks of both.

In this approach a view may inherit part (or all) of its ancestors' content. This means that any modification to the parent view also affects its sons (pure inheritance). In order to prevent unexpected inconveniences resulting from lack of concertation among the authors of different views, this default mechanism may occasionally be overridden by copying and pasting those parts of the data base which are shared by a view and its ancestors.

6. NAVIGATION IN A DBLM GUIDED BY AN INTELLIGENT TUTORING SYSTEM.

This section aims at providing a possible model of operation for an Intelligent Tutoring System guiding the navigation of a learner in a DBLM [7][8].

A tutorial program should first build an initial model of the learner including her specific learning objectives [9]. On the bases of such model it should be able to chose the knowledge structure to be used (if more than one structure is available).

After the initialization phase, the questions that an ITS has to answer again and again during its interaction with a learner are: "what to teach next? how to teach it?". The steps that a DBLM based ITS should go through to answer these questions are summarized below.

a select a set of topics compatible with the educational objectives and with the status of the learner.
  The first step consists in deciding which topics may be taught to a specific learner at a given time. Criteria for making this choice will take into account the model of the learner (especially the domain dependent aspects of the model) and a specific knowledge structure in the current user view.

b select from the set the 'best' topic to be taught first
  Here the word best has no absolute value: it refers to criteria established by the ITS designer. It should be noted that these criteria do not belong to the DBLM. On the contrary, they can be defined in many different ways for different client applications of a DBLM. Possible criteria are: "Teach first the topic having more connections (in the knowledge structure being used) with topics that the learner already masters" or "Teach first the topic having fewer connections (in the knowledge structure being used) with topics unknown to the learner"
  Of course applying these criteria requires the knowledge of the current status of the model of the learner.

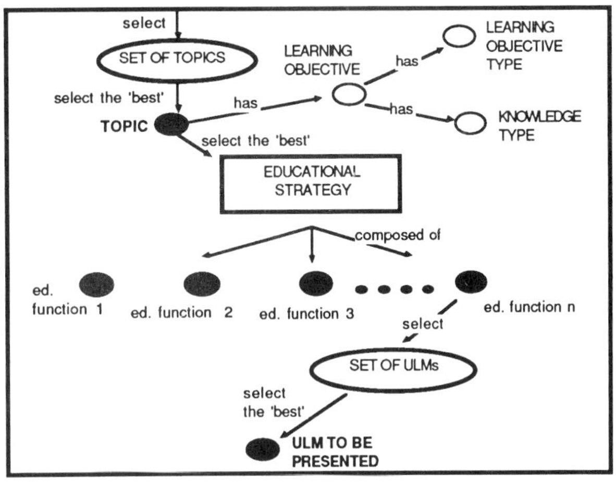

Fig. 4: Mode of operation of a DBLM based ITS

c select the best strategy to teach that topic
  It should be noted that teaching a topic is a generic term which can be defined more precisely by specifying the learning objectives to be achieved by the learner. Moreover, a specific learning objective can be characterized by a learning objective type (for instance with reference to Bloom's taxonomy) and by a knowledge type (theory, data, fact, hypothesis,...). Different educational strategies should be available in an educational system. The choice of the best strategy for a given topic should be based on rules referring to the model of the learner and to the nature of the educational objective associated to the topic (learning objective type and knowledge type). Again, the word 'best' refers to criteria established by the ITS designer.

d select the best ULMs to implement that strategy
  An educational strategy can be decomposed into a sequence (more generally into a structured set) of educational functions. For instance a possible strategy to teach a topic could be defined by the sequence ex

planation, simulation, assessment, (possibly re-) explanation.
To implement a given strategy (composed of educational function e1, e2, ..., en) for a given topic t an educational system should look for the ULMs performing e1, e2, ... for that topic (*educational function* is one of the attributes of the ASSOCIATED_TO relation in the database). Also the type of learning objective to be achieved in connection with t and the type of knowledge to be transferred to the learner should be taken into account (*knowledge type* and *learning objective type* are also attributes of the ASSOCIATED_TO).

e *select the best ULM to perform a given educational function.*
If more than one ULM is available in the database to perform a given educational function for a given topic the choice could privilege the best approach type for that learner (*approach type* is an attribute of relation ASSOCIATED_TO in the database).

The detailed structure of the student model used in the ITS is at present under development. More specifically, it includes a content dependent component (mostly assessable via diagnostic evaluation of the student knowledge) and a content independent one, including such things as affective components and learning style. Information about the latter may partly be directly elicited from the student and partly inferred through a systematic analysis of the history of his interaction with the system.

7. CONCLUSIONS AND FUTURE DIRECTIONS.

We have proposed a conceptual model for a DBLM. This model should be considered as a first step in the exploration of the concept of DBLM as a mean of saving, communicating and sharing knowledge.

This model is now being implemented through the development of a shell and of a specific DBLM in the field of Plate Tectonics.

These prototypes will be used to validate the conceptual model in three different directions:

- experimentation with instructional processes based on learner directed navigation in the DBLM on Plate Tectonics [10]
- implementation of an ITS for guiding user navigation in the DBLM
- experimentation with an author environment linked to the DBLM.

ACKNOWLEDGEMENTS

This research is being carried out whithin the EEC programme DELTA, contract D1012. We would like to thank all the project partners for their contribution to the development of the ideas here presented.

8. REFERENCES

[1] Delta Project D1012, D1, Basic Assumptions, (1989).
[2] Hodges, M.E., Sasnett, R.M. and Ackerman, M.S., A Construction Set for Multimedia Application, IEEE Software, Jan.89, pp.37-43.
[3] Weyer, S.A., As We May Learn, in: Ambron, S. and Hooper, K. (eds.) Interactive Multimedia (Microsoft Press, Redmond, Washington, 1988) pp.87-103.
[4] Horak, W. and Siemens A.G., Office Document Architecture and Document Interchange, Formats: current status of international standardization, IEEE Computer, October 1985, pp.50-60.
[5] Delta Project D1012, D4, Conceptual Model for a Database of Multimedia Learning Material, (1989).
[6] Ulman, J. D., Database and Knowledge-base systems, (Computer Science Press, Rockville, Maryland, 1988).
[7] Burton, R.R and Brown, J.S. An investigation of computer coaching for informal learning activities, in: Sleeman, D. and Brown, J.S.(eds) Intelligent Tutoring Systems, (Academic Press, London, 1982) pp.79-97
[8] Clancey, W.J., Knowledge-Based Tutoring (The MIT Press, Cambridge Mass, 1987).
[9] Clancey, W.J.,1988, Qualitative student models, Annual Review of Computer Science, pp.381-450.
[10] Midoro, V., Chioccariello, A., Olimpo, G., Persico, D. Sarti, L. Tavella, M., Interactive video and artificial intelligence: a convenient marriage, PLET 25/4.(Kogan Page, 1989) pp.299-309.

Computers in Education
A. McDougall and C. Dowling (Editors)
Elsevier Science Publishers B.V. (North-Holland)

AN EVALUATION INSTRUMENT FOR TRAINING SOFTWARE

Michel PARISET as coordinator of the **European MEDA project***

In January 1987, EEC General Direction N°5 asked the REREF (The European Network of Research in Education and Training) to the educational software designed for adult training. The project was christened MEDA (Méthodologie d'Evaluation des Didacticiels pour Adultes).Research teams from the following institutions worked on this project : in England, the Department of Psychology and the Department of Education at the University of Lancaster ; in Belgium, the Technology and Education Department of the Notre-Dame de la Paix Colleges in Namur, and the Experimental Pedagogical Laboratory of Liège ; from Germany, the I.P.N. in Kiel ; in France, the Chair of Adult training at the CNAM in Paris, and the C.N.R.S.-IRPEACS laboratory at Lyon-Ecully ; and in Italy, the FORMEZ in Rome and DIDA*EL in Milan. A double purpose was then set for this project :

- to develop a **practical evaluation instrument** easily adjustable to the various objectives that decision-makers may have in the field of training software. The use of this type of software indeed tends to be more and more widespread and requires ever increasing budgets. That is why it is important to have a reliable evaluation tool.

- to produce a **methodological framework** for this tool allowing the users to take a more objective look at their evaluation.

The MEDA evaluation tool was built in five phases :

1/ **Surveys** were carried out, in several European countries, on the current means of evaluating training software developed by the various actors concerned by the issue (companies, training institutions, research institutes).

2/ Based on these surveys, a **typology** of the main evaluation strategies observed today was compiled : the actors involved, the objectives of the evaluation, the categories of information sought in termes of these objectives, and the tools implemented.

3/ A **functional tool** was designed on the basis of this, which would serve both as a tool for investigating the objectives (the "preoccupations") of the tool's user, and as a mean of making available the categories of collected information (the "foreseeable aspects") and the instruments (the "questions") in keeping with these objectives.

4/ The tool thus designed was **trialled** on an European evaluation sample.

5/ A **software version** of the tool has been developed, improving its decision making functionnalities.

1.A MAJOR JOB OF PRELIMINARY INVESTIGATIONS

The first phase of work was devoted to collecting the necessary data (fig.1).Of

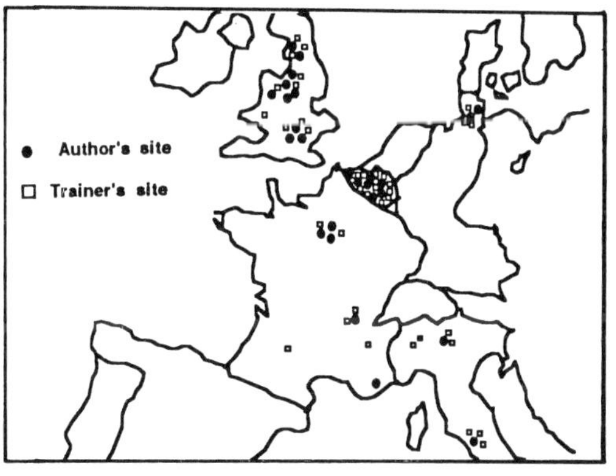

Figure 1

*__MEDA research team__ : J.M. Albertini (Lyon), J.M. Barbier (Paris), J. Donnay (Namur); A. Gammaldi (Rome), W. Graber (Kiel), R. Lewis (Lancaster), J. Machell (Lancaster), C. Martinengo (Milan), M. Pariset (Lyon), R. Peeters (Liège), M.J. Rebondy (Paris), M. Romainville (Namur), D. Salmistraro (Milan), M. Saunders (Lancaster), Y. Souriau (Grenoble), V. Tremp (Kiel), R. Zeiliger (Lyon).

course, this entailed setting out and comparing the grids and methods for evaluating educational software - multimedia or otherwise - but also and espacially, a serious collection upstream, of the intentions and problems dealt with by those who designed these systems, and downstream, of the opinions and practices of those who use training software.

The first job accomplished was to set out and compare **the grids and methods available** for evaluating training software. At this stage, the evaluation grids more specifically designed for primary training were not systematically excluded. Some thirty grids were collected, differing in terms of quality and in terms of the scope of evaluating covered. It rapidly became apparent that this first approach needed to be completed by a two-fold survey (fig.2) :

- **a survey upstream, of those who developed the grids**, so as to better understand the implicit and explicit reasons of their methods ;

- **a survey downstream, of the users themselves**, so as to determine their perception of evaluation, as well as the language and practical criteria they use in reference to it.

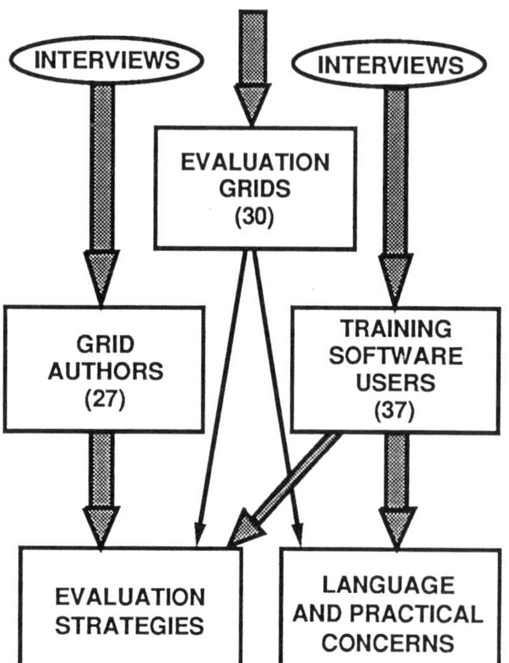

Figure 2

The interview questionnaires of the grid authors made it possible to carry out 30 in-depth interviews with the best authors of evaluation tools in the five countries covered by the study. The results have been partially collated by country, and these reveal that the approaches and the problems dealt with vary greatly from one country to the next.

The second survey addressed 37 European trainers who use training software, and who work solely with adults. The partial national analyses, unlike those above, very definitely converged, which leads one to think that the practical concerns or preoccupations of the users are very similar in the different countries covered by the study.

2.AN ANALYSIS OF EVALUATION STRATEGIES

The analysis of data on current evaluation practices thus collected made it possible to make four main observations :

a/ There are in fact three areas in which the results of teaching software evaluations are used : in **designing** the product, in **using** the product, in **distributing** the product. This is why we devised a question in the tool on the user's position in terms of these three preoccupations. One person may will be concerned with more than one of these areas.

b/ The process of what is termed evaluating training software actually covers three considerably different types of processes (fig.3) : processes whose main goals are to provide information, or **identification** processes, processes aiming at an **analysis and comparison** of the information collected, and finally, processes meant to evaluate per se, that is, to produce a **value judgement**.

c/ The evaluation process in the strictest sense of the terme sometimes works as an evaluation process of the product itself, concerning its purchase and its effects (which generally leads to making decisions about the product), and sometimes works as an evaluation process of the action of those involved in the designing, using or distributing of the product (which generally leads to decisions evaluating that action). This distinction also exists among the strategies which have been defined, either in terms of the notion of tests

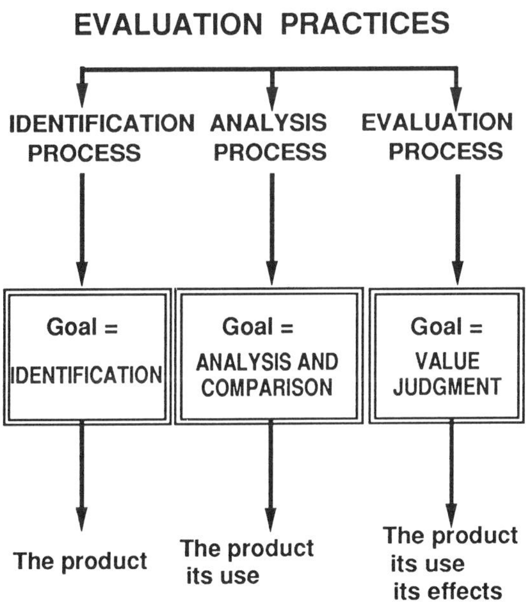

Figure 3

or validation, or in terms of notions of skill and management.

d/ There are two distinct phases in the evaluation process : that of collecting information on assessed situations and that of comparing the objectives and the criteria of the actors involved.

3.THE MANUAL VERSION OF THE MEDA TOOL

The essential features of the manual version of the MEDA tool are the following :

a/ It is an **operative product** which, thanks to its size, the language used, and its internal dynamism, is well adapted to the potential deciders who will be using it. In particular, on the one hand, it leads the person doing the evaluating to define his own position and his own objectives, and on the other, it induces him to build. This is why we can say that the user of the tool is the architect of his own process, process in which three types of activities occur :
- an activity of familiarization with the tool ;
- an activity of building one's own evaluation process ;
- an activity of implementing this process.

The different components of the tool correspond to this three step process : directions for use, questions on the situation and the aims of the tool, and the providing of grids for each of the aspects selected, and finally, documents for explanations and the analysis itself (fig.4).

b/ It is a product which can **evolve**, and which has built-in flexibility, making it possible, in the short term, to take into account new preoccupations and questions from the users, and in the medium term changes, particularly those of a technological nature, which training software will undergo.

c/ It is a product with a **European calling**, as in 1989 it will be distributed in four languages (German, English, French and Italian). Preliminary work has made deciders aware of the opportunity for evaluating training software, and in this way they will soon be able to use the tool in a large part of the European community.

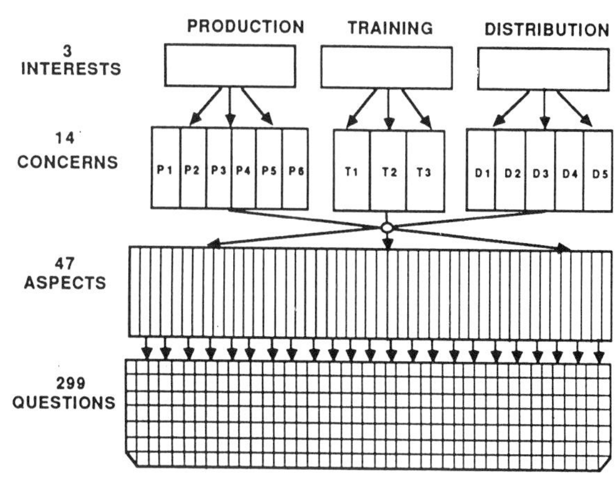

Fig.4 Tree structure of the MEDA tool

4. VALIDATED AT 34 EUROPEAN SITES

The next phase of the project consisted in validating this tool by a series of on site experiments and consequently, improving it, so as make it operative for the various deciders involved in the design, the use or the distribution of training software.

A strictly parallel protocol for experimentation has been developed in the United Kingdom, Belgium, Germany, France and Italy. This was greatly aided by a seminar held in Milan, in April

1988, entitled "New technologies and enterprises : the evaluation of training software", and organized by the REREF. Indeed, as a result, the setting up of experiments was begun in better qualitative and quantitative conditions. This was espacially the case for Great Britain, where the MEDA team of Lancaster was entrusted with a large-scale study over a one year period, evaluating the training software by the Manpower Service Commission, which was thus able to significantly strengthen its means for observation and experimentation. The situation was the same in Italy where, inspired by the Milan seminar, a number of companies joined forces to create a permanent evaluation unit with the coordination handled by MEDA italian research teams.

In all, therefore, there are 34 european companies which accepted, in excellent conditions, the on site experimentation of the prototype of this tool for evaluating training software.

5.A SOFTWARE VERSION OF THE MEDA TOOL

Finally, the last phase of the MEDA project has made a software version to the MEDA evaluation tool possible. Needless to say that this software version keeps the main characteristics of the manual version (self-construction of an evaluation grid according to the user's own objectives, possibility of integrating new evaluation criteria if technological advances make it necessary, availability in four languages using a vocabulary adapted to users). But it also reinforces the handiness and the flexibility of the tool by offering decision-making functionnalities which are both effective and easy to use. Four points should be enlightened :

- the MEDA software offers **a double and continuous representations of the user's choices** ; the first one is textual and displayed on several windows, the second one appears in the form of a graph (fig 5).

- a **complete mobility** within these two representations and beetween them has been achieved.

- a weighing system, simple but which can be easily modified, results in **very effective interactive facilities allowing the user to be closely followed in his choices** (thus avoiding the rigidity often found in expert-systems concerned with this type of problem).

- Lastly, the appropriate use of colours and graphs make **comparisons and synthesis** possible, which definitely improves the conditions of decision making.

Figure 5

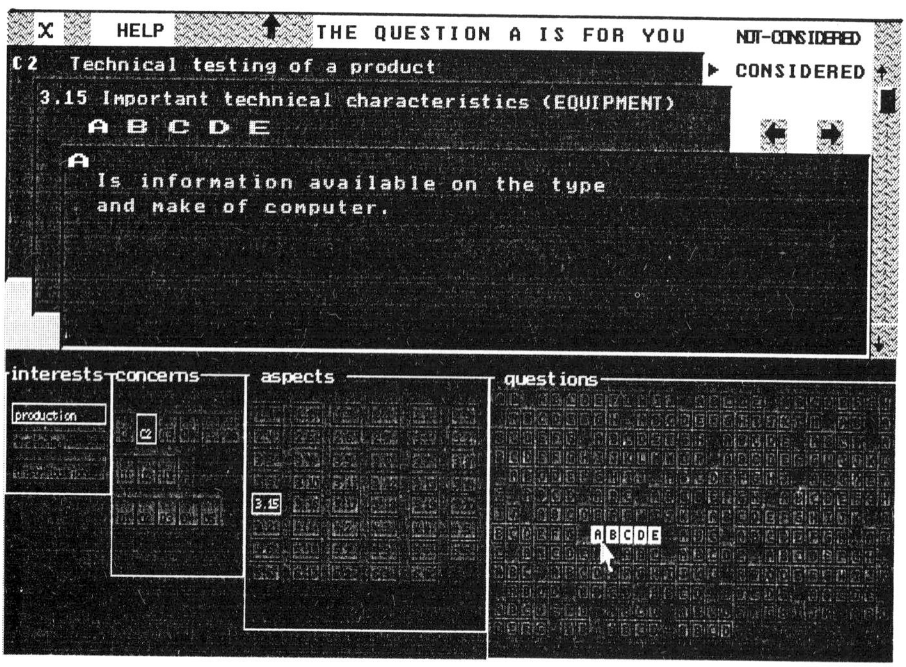

Computers in Education
A. McDougall and C. Dowling (Editors)
Elsevier Science Publishers B.V. (North-Holland)

DESIGN ISSUES FOR A KNOWLEDGE-BASED EDUCATIONAL SYSTEM

Helen PURCHASE and Brent ROBINSON

Engineering Department, University of Cambridge

Although artificial inteliigence techniques have been used for many years in research into effective educational software, few "intelligent" educational systems have actually filtered through to schools for practical use. Intelligent systems are considered here with respect to current educational needs and preferences, resulting in the definition of design criteria for a flexible knowledge-based learning environment which encourages personal expressivity. The aim of the system is to encourage understanding of subject matter, as well as the development of information skills and symbolic processing abilities, through the creation, amendment, manipulation and exploration of an explicit symbolic representation of knowledge. The architecture of the system is described in some detail and requirements for the representational method are considered.

1. INTRODUCTION

Relevant design issues for the creation of a flexible intelligent learning environment intended for children between the ages of 9 and 11 are outlined here. Our aim is to create an educational tool in order to investigate the claims that:

* making the structure of knowledge explicit will foster learning of subject matter;
* the use of a computer can stimulate the symbolic processing abilities of a young child.

We maintain that the use of an expressive representational medium free from the structural limitations of text or tables will both encourage understanding of the subject matter presented, develop the ability to process symbolically-presented information, and foster development of information technology skills.

2. PREVIOUS RESEARCH

The first computer educational systems were based on pre-programmed teaching material, strategy, questions and answers; they resulted in narrow, deterministic systems which gave limited feedback and explanation. The branching, generative and authoring systems of the 1960s were more tolerant, allowed for more varied instruction and enabled efficient production of large tutoring systems. But these early systems took little account of current educational psychological theories, nor of educational needs. Their explanation, remediation and diagnosis facilities were limited, and there was no tailoring of material presented or method of presentation according to the requirements and competence of the user. In addition, the student had no opportunity to take any initiative. Large and unwieldy, these systems were mostly ineffectual.

Carbonnel first proposed that the artificial intelligence (AI) techniques that were becoming more advanced should be used to improve educational software (1). He suggested that the domain knowledge to be taught should be explicitly represented in the system, allowing for questions, answers and detailed explanations to be generated at run-time. An explicit representation of teaching strategy (not embedded in the program code) was first proposed by Hartley and Sleeman (2), who suggested that by using a set of means-end rules and the achievements of the student to date, the system could decide upon the best teaching strategy to apply. Self (3) then proposed that the student model should be represented in the same manner as the domain representation so that comparisons could be made between what the student knows and what the system is trying to teach, enabling improved diagnosis of misconceptions. These proposals resulted in the now widely-accepted architecture for intelligent educational systems: explicit representations of *what* is being presented (the domain knowledge), *how* it is to be presented (the pedagogic strategy), and to *whom* (the student model).

The field of educational systems subsequently divided into a continuum of approaches, from tutoring systems at one end of the spectrum, through simulations, to learning environments at the other end. The differing approaches could be classified according to the relative emphasis placed on the four main components of intelligent educational systems (student, domain and teaching strategy representations, and the communication channel).

3. EDUCATIONAL PREFERENCES AND REQUIREMENTS

3.1 Research and Applications

Not much Intelligent Computer Educational Systems (ICES) research has permeated educational environments to any considerable extent - even sytems designed for particular courses are seldom used (4). The promises and optimism shown in the ICES literature are not reflected in educational documents concerned with the practical use of computers in the classroom. This is not an unusual state of affairs for AI research areas, but it does seem unfortunate that in the interim period between the research and the useful product (when pressure from government departments and parents for the increased use of computers in schools is becoming greater), software is being used which embodies all the basic principles evident in the early educational systems and scorned by ICES researchers.

The most obvious reason for this is resource constraints: the availability in schools of the appropriate hardware required to run sophisticated software is low. Funding schemes tend to underestimate the finances, skill and knowledge necessary for the production and subsequent use of good-quality software. In addition, there does not appear to be much effective collaboration between teachers and researchers (5). School environments may be used in order to evaluate research projects, but teachers are seldom involved in the definition of the learning objectives or the underlying design of the system. This results in systems which are not adequately integrated into a syllabus and which embody a limited and idealised view of the domain (6). Researchers in intelligent educational systems often concentrate on inappropriate domains which are formal, personal preferences, or merely a chunk out of a syllabus. In some cases, the computer is not the best medium of interaction for the domain chosen, and the system produced is little better than a programmed textbook.

3.2 Tools

A prevalent educational philosophy which recognises the importance of self-expression and creation (7) has resulted in many domain-specific computer educational systems being rejected in favour of more general tools (databases, spreadsheets, wordprocessing packages) (see note 1). While this does not imply the redundancy of ICES when they finally reach the classroom, it does mean that domain-specific software must be exceptionally good to justify its use: it must meet specific educational needs, be in a domain for which the computer is the most appropriate medium, be flexible enough for adaptation to the teacher's particular course, syllabus and teaching style, and, most importantly, it must be effective and achieve its aims.

It is not surprising, therefore, that many teachers currently tend to concentrate on the effective use of tools and flexible learning environments. Software that may be used whenever appropriate in any subject area, and allows for personal expressivity and creation by the user is favoured, in spite of the fact that such tools often require more planning and course management by the teacher. In relation to the recognised spectrum of intelligent computer education systems outlined above, it appears, therefore, that computer learning environments (rather than tutoring systems) are the most appropriate area for useful research.

3.2 Learning Environments

Domain-based learning environments

The aim of computer environments that include an extensive representation of a knowledge domain (explicit or implicit) is to teach the user the subject matter. The method of communicating this knowledge is not through explicit instruction, but via exploration, experimentation, manipulation and action within the domain representation.

These environments may take on various forms. "Microworlds" allow the explicit manipulation of objects and variables according to various constraints and procedures whose interaction defines the domain (often by analogy) (8, 9). Simulations provide an explicit (often graphical) representation of a process to be taught and by changing the values of variables and seeing their effect, the user can come to understand how the process works.

Content-free learning environments

These are entirely free from any particular domain; their aim is to enhance learning by giving the user a means of expression and the ability for creation within specified constraints. Information may be entered into the system by the user in accordance with a specified structure or format, and may subsequently be manipulated, or used with a processing facility to produce results.

Programming languages fall into this category. Prolog is used to teach first-order logic, natural language syntax and object relationships (10, 11), and simple languages like APL may be used to write programs which enable the user to have a better understanding of mathematical concepts (12). Other tools used in educational environments are often reduced, easy-to-use versions of commercial tools like spreadsheets, databases and wordprocessors. While requiring more work from teachers than domain-specific software, tools and languages are greatly preferred: they cater for a wider range of abilities within the class and are more flexible in their use.

For AI research to have any immediate effect on educational systems, therefore, we feel that learning environments, and specifically content-free tools, should be considered seriously as appropriate topics of study. The creation of intelligent and flexible domain-independent tools and support systems for tools, as well as environments allowing for powerful representation and manipulation of knowledge could indeed make a worthwhile contribution to the effective use of computers in education.

4. A KNOWLEDGE-BASED SYSTEM: DESIGN ISSUES

4.1 Objectives

We here define design criteria for an intelligent learning environment for children between the ages of 9 and 11. The aim of the system is to encourage discovery learning by making cognitive structures (and corresponding cognitive manipulations) explicit. It is hoped that by providing a suitable representation that could correspond to an internal cognitive structure (see note 2), three learning activities could be fostered: concept acquisition in a particular subject domain, symbolic processing abilities, and information technology skills.

Concept Acquisition

To enable concept acquisition, we propose that the representation of a domain should contain "anchoring concepts" (as defined by Ausubel et al. (13)), to which the user can explicitly relate newly-learned concepts (see note 3). In addition, facilities for organising, manipulating and extending the structure as required during discovery learning should be available, with motivation provided by the discovery of inadequacies within the representation (as suggested by Piaget's process of equilibration, which compensates for discrepancies in the cognitive structure (14)). In addition, the user should have the facility to express and organise (and thus clarify) knowledge already understood by creating a completely new structure. This would encourage personal expressivity and cater for varying abilities.

Symbolic Processing

In order to develop symbolic perception and processing skills as much as possible, we propose to use a primarily symbolic method of knowledge presentation appropriate for the age-range of interest. Popular developmental theories tend to restrict the development of symbolic processing abilities to early adolescence (15, 14). These theories were proposed at a time when the computer was not as flexible and powerful as it is now, and considered development in terms of literacy as the primary tool for communication; we now question whether they are still valid when computers are used to stimulate thought.

Skills

The importance of fostering information technology (IT) skills enabling the storage, retrieval and communication of information is evident. Although Alvin Toffler's book "Future Shock" (16) may be considered radical and over-reactionary, he makes some valid points concerning education in the future, suggesting we should be concerned with teaching ways of manipulating knowledge, rather than the knowledge itself, due to the currently high rate of facts and data.

That the need for the development of IT skills has been recognised is shown by the emphasis placed on the use of computers "across the curriculum" in the new national curriculum in Engalnd and Wales (see note 4). The level of achievement spanning the 9-11 age range emphasises the creation, amendment, organisation and communication of information, particularly using a database. It is hoped that similar skills could be fostered by the manipulation of a symbolic representation of knowledge which is less quantitative than that stored in a database, and that use of such a system will contribute to satisfying these targets.

4.2 Design Criteria

Features which should be considered in the design of the intended system can therefore be summarised thus:

* a flexible, content-free tool which allows for self-expression and which can be used effectively in a mixed-ability class;
* the use of an appropriate symbolic method of representation.
* the capacity for creating, exploring, manipulating, extending, amending, and organising a knowledge structure, and retrieving information from it;
* a facility to highlight discrepancies or incompleteness in the structure.

5. DETAILED DESIGN

5.1 Architecture

We describe here the architecture of a knowledge-based educational system based on the educational and psychological design criteria outlined above, with the aim of encouraging learning by making knowledge structure explicit.

Our system can divide into four main groups: one representation and three process components (Figure 1):

Knowledge representation: The knowledge is represented internally, as well as presented in a visible, graphical form.

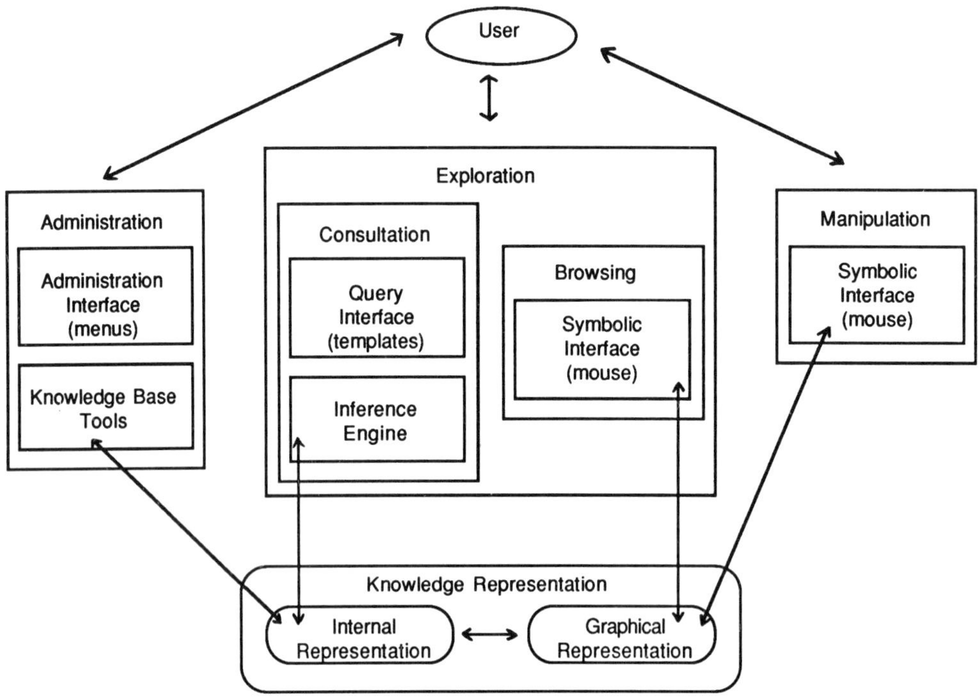

Figure 1: Proposed system architecture

Exploration: The user may access the knowledge either via consultation (requiring inference to be performed on the internal representation) or by browsing the external graphical knowledge presentation.

Manipulation: The user may alter an existing knowledge structure or create an entirely new one.

Administration: Various tools are available for manipulating entire knowledge bases (e.g. loading, saving).

These components are described in detail below.

5.2 Knowledge Representation

The domain knowledge is realised in two ways: an internal representation which can be processed by an inference engine, and an external graphical presentation which may be both browsed and manipulated. In trying to keep our system as transparent as possible, we attempt to make the graphical knowledge structure mirror the internal form closely.

As one of our aims is to develop (and exploit) the symbolic processing abilities of young children, we will use a symbolic rather than iconic method of knowledge presentation. Two conflicting constraints need to be considered and a compromise reached: the graphical form must be simple enough to be understood by children between the ages of nine and eleven, and the representational method should be powerful and flexible enough to be appropriate for a variety of non-trivial knowledge bases (see note 5). In addition, the knowledge base must "mean" something: the representation should have a clearly defined semantics associated with it, and an inference engine within the system should be able to perform appropriate deductions.

Design criteria for the representational method include the facility for adequately representing objects (concepts or exemplars of concepts) and various types of relationships between objects. It is possible that we will use a method of representation which combines ideas from associative and structural methods of knowledge representation: a "semantic network" (named concepts connected by relationship links (17) of "frames" (structures containing labelled slots of information(18)). This would allow important relationships between concepts to be made explicit, while less important ones could be embedded in frame structures so as not to make the network unnecessarily complex. It is felt that such a representation is more appropriate for the modelling of cognitive structures than are production rules or logical expressions, and is therefore more likely to be understood by young children.

5.3 Exploration

The user should be able to explore the domain

knowledge in two ways, corresponding to the two representational forms in the system: there should be facilities for both browsing the graphical presentation and consulting the internal representation.

Browsing

Browsing the graphical presentation entails the direct manipulation of elements in the knowledge structure using a mouse as the interface device. Unlike micro-worlds, where the items manipulated are iconic, our system will use a symbolic representation relating more to cognitive structures than to physical objects.

The means of exploring the symbolic structure will, of course, depend upon the method of representation used. It is probable that the exploration methods made available will be similar to those proposed by Eisenstadt for his TPA system: granularity, scale, compression and abstraction (19).

Consultation

Although it is possible that the student will come to understand the subject matter by merely browsing through the graphical knowledge presentation, it is felt that some motivational influence will be desirable.

We propose to provide an inference engine (similar to that which would be included in an expert system shell to enable expert knowledge to be accessed) to allow the internal knowledge representation to be queried. It is hoped that the discovery of incompleteness or inconsistencies will motivate the user to amend the structure appropriately. A suitable query interface would need to be created; templates which model various query types would probably be appropriate. These templates should allow for both "yes/no" and "wh-" questions to be asked, and "don't know" answers should be given if unavailable information is queried.

5.4. Manipulation

As it is intended that the system should be content-free and suitable for flexible expression of knowledge and that the student should be able to change an existing knowledge structure to compensate for discovered discrepancies, further direct-manipulation facilities for amendment, manipulation, creation, extension and removal of elements in the knowledge structure are necessary. Like the browser, a mouse is an appropriate interface device for this component of the system.

5.5 Administration

The intention is that the system will be an entirely content-free tool similar to databases and spreadsheets, enabling pupils to use knowledge bases created by teachers or other pupils. A menu-driven administrative component is therefore essential in enabling knowledge bases to be loaded and saved. In addition, the user should be able to create an entirely new knowledge base if required, making the system appropriate for users of varied abilities and encouraging expression of knowledge in an alternative form.

6. DEVELOPMENT AND EVALUATION

It is hoped that the computer learning environment described here will be developed over the next twelve months, and appropriate software and hardware have been selected to assist with the development.

Analysis of the system will be undertaken by monitoring its use in an appropriate situation in a classroom. The primary observations will be concerned with the extent to which pupils can come to terms with the symbolic representational method and understand the knowledge embodied in a given structure. In addition, we will also observe their ability (and willingness) to use the explanation facilities to investigate the validity of the knowledge structure represented, to manipulate and amend a given structure, and to create an entirely new structure adequately representing a subject they already know. Qualitative rather than quantitative analysis will be performed, and the response of the class teacher will also be noted.

Evidence that the pupils are able to adequately comprehend and manipulate a symbolic representation will serve as supporting the claim that the use of a computer can stimulate the symbolic processing abilities of a young child. The pupil's ability to transfer the subject matter embodied in a structure to another representational medium (e.g. text) would indicate the extent to which the claim that making the structure of knowledge explicit fosters the learning of subject matter is valid.

In this design, emphasis has been placed on current educational theories and requirements, in the hopes that the completed system will satisfy an educational need for a flexible and expressive representational tool that fosters understanding by making the structure of subject matter explicit. By using this system, we hope to demonstrate that the symbolic processing abilities of a young child can be used effectively when freed from the structural limitations of text and tables.

NOTES

[1]Observations regarding software both used and preferred in schools are based on interviews with primary and secondary school teachers and pupils.

[2]It should be emphasised that the representational method

proposed cannot, of course, correspond exactly to cognitive structures that the brain actually creates and maintains.

[3]Following Ausubel et al. [13], for the purposes of this document *concepts* are defined as "objects, events, situations or properties that *possess common criterial attributes* and are designated in any given culture by some accepted sign or symbol."

[4]The goal of the IT curriculum is summarised thus: *Pupils should be able to use IT appropriately and effectively to communicate and handle information in a variety of forms and for a variety of purposes and to design, develop and evaluate appropriate models of real or imaginary situations* [20].

[5]By *non-trivial* we mean that the structure of the knowledge is too complex for perspicuous representation in a tabular, columnar or textual form. Such structures are currently available in databases, spreadsheets and word-processing packages.

REFERENCES

[1] Carbonnel J. AI in CAI: an artificial intelligence approach to computer-assisted instruction. *IEEE Transactions on Man-Machine Systems*, 11(4), 1970.

[2] Hartley J.R. and Sleeman D.H. Towards more intelligent teaching systems. *International Journal of Man-Machine Studies*, 5, 1973.

[3] Self J.A. Student models in computer-aided instruction. *International Journal of Man-Machine Studies*, 6, 1974.

[4] Woolf B.P. 20 years in the trenches: What have we learned? In *Proceedings of the ITS conference*, 1988.

[5] Self J.A. *Microcomputers in Education*. The Harvester Press, 1985.

[6] Self J.A. A perspective on intelligent computer-aided learning. In Jones A. and Scrimshaw P., editors, *Computers in Education 5-13*. Open University Press, 1988.

[7] Lawler R.W. Learning environments: Now, Then and Someday. In Lawler R.W. and Yadsani M., editors, *AI and Education*. Ablex, 1987.

[8] O'Shea T. Magnets, martians and microworlds. In *Proceedings of the 4th International Conference on AI and Education*, 1989.

[9] Papert S. *Mindstorms: Children, Computers, and Powerful Ideas*. The Harvester Press, 1980.

[10] Kowalski R. Logic as a computer language for children. In Yadsani M., editor, *New Horizons in Educational Computing*. Ellis Horwood, 1984.

[11] Ennals R. Teaching logic as a computer language in schools. In Yadsani M., editor, *New Horizons in Educational Computing*. Ellis Horwood, 1984.

[12] Moss J.M. APL in education. *Computer Education*, February 1988.

[13] Ausubel D.P., Novak J.D., and Hanesian H. *Educational Psychology — A cognitive view*. Holt, Rinehart and Winston, 1978.

[14] Phillips J.L. *Piaget's Theory — a Primer*. W.H. Freeman and Co., 1981.

[15] Bruner J.S. *Toward a Theory of Instruction*. Norton and Co., 1968.

[16] Toffler A. *Future Shock*. Pan, 1970.

[17] Quillian M.R. Word concepts: A theory and simulation of some basic semantic capabilities. In Brachman R.J. and Levesque H.J., editors, *Readings in Knowledge Representation*. Morgan Kaufman, 1985.

[18] Minsky M. A framework for representing knowledge. In Brachman R.J. and Levesque H.J., editors, *Readings in Knowledge Representation*. Morgan Kaufman, 1985.

[19] Brayshaw M. and Eisenstadt M. A practical tracer for Prolog. Technical Report 42, Open University Human Cognition Research Laboratory, 1989.

[20] Design and technology for ages 5 to 16. Department of Education and Science, June 1989.

Computers in Education
A. McDougall and C. Dowling (Editors)
Elsevier Science Publishers B.V. (North-Holland)

A RESEARCH STRATEGY USING MICROCOMPUTERS TO ASSESS THE CONCEPTUAL UNDERSTANDING AND PROBLEM SOLVING STRATEGIES OF LEARNERS USING SCIENCE SIMULATIONS

Patricia E. SIMMONS and Judith F. KINNEAR

The University of Georgia, Athens, Georgia; La Trobe University, Victoria Australia

1. INTRODUCTION

In January, 1986, a national conference involving scientists, science educators, cognitive scientists, mathematicians, mathematics educators, and curriculum and technology experts recommended that "researchers need to explore in greater detail such questions as how students develop a world view, reason about new information, and solve problems in science" [1]. The report also affirmed that "research in science education should reflect and respond to real instructional needs" [1].

Ongoing research studies in science education are needed to enhance understanding of how learners engage in problem solving and how learners employ and develop concepts during problem solving. Detailed studies of problem solving based on conventional problem tasks have been conducted in many domains, including physics and genetics [2, 3, 4, 5, 6, 7, 8, 9, 10, 11, 12]. The problem solving tasks used in many of these studies have involved closed data sets such that all relevant data were implicitly or explicitly given in the problem statements. Fewer studies [13, 14, 15] have addressed problem solving in settings where subjects work in an interactive computer-based medium and where the problems involve more open-ended tasks in which the solution depends in on the generation of relevant data by the problem solver.

There is a need for detailed information that describes reasoning patterns and processes used by learners in solving or attempting to solve problems when the context involves an interactive medium. Learners in these contexts are able to explore the operational consequences of the concepts they hold and to test hypotheses that are generated as part of problem solving in biology, chemistry, and physics. Extracting, analyzing, and comparing common and unique characteristics of groups or of individual problem solvers in settings of this nature should complement the findings from research studies that have employed more traditional and constrained problem tasks. Studies of problem solving in such interactive settings may result in important information about cognitive behaviors and the cognitive patterns of learners [15, 16, 17]. This information can lead to powerful models guiding research in conceptual development and problem solving, and has significant implications for teachers and their instructional strategies. The findings from these kinds of research studies have the potential to inform the development of new instructicnal strategies and enhance existing strategies which stimulate students' growth in problem solving and conceptual development [18].

This paper focuses on a research strategy using microcomputers that was directed towards elucidating conceptual understanding and problem solving strategies employed by learners interacting with an open-ended computer simulation.

2. RESEARCH QUESTIONS

Major research questions which were addressed through the use of a research strategy that employed microcomputers and instructional software included:

What patterns and generalizations can serve as the organizers for the theoretical models in applied research and development?

What testable, theoretical models guiding applied research and development can be generated by the uses of microcomputers and software?

3. A RESEARCH STRATEGY FOR MICROCOMPUTERS

Microcomputers and well designed instructional software, when used appropriately, have the potential to help students learn and elaborate concepts and develop problem solving skills [1, 19]. In addition, computer-based instructional software provides an important medium for studying how students learn concepts and solve problems [19]. The nature of studies on conceptual change during problem solving warrants the use of a research methodology capable of assessing the dynamic character of subjects' cognitive skills and use of scientific concepts and of elucidating aspects of their mental processes [20].

Naturalistic research studies entail the use of fields methods such as case studies, clinical interviews, analysis of documents, and unstructured observations [21, 22, 23]. The field method employed in this study is termed "structured observation" [19]. The use of this method facilitates the generation of data by subjects during a "think aloud" protocol [19, 20]. From these data, patterns of behaviors and strategies can be extracted for comparisons between individuals and between groups of subjects. "Structured observations" provide information that suggest research hypotheses to be tested subsequently by experimental methods. This method enables researchers to study: 1) how learners develop certain concepts, 2) how learners solve problems, 3) how learners interact with instructional software, and 4) how software can be more effective in terms of design and use.

During "structured observations", two types of recordings of subjects' interactions with computer-based software were made. One type of recording made use of a videocassette recorder (VCR) interfaced with a microcomputer. This recording stored both the video output from an Apple IIgs microcomputer and the subjects' verbal commentaries. In terms of information obtained, this type of recording captured subjects' verbal utterances and positioned them simultaneously with the monitor displays that the subjects were viewing. This recording gave detailed information of both the sequence of the computer screen displays and the duration of each display. In a second type of recording, three sets of synchronized information were obtained. These three sets of information, video images of the computer monitor displays, video images of the subjects, and a sound track containing subjects' verbal commentaries, were integrated onto a single videotape. The two video images were arranged to form a composite picture, with the image of the subject occupying the major area and the image of the monitor screen displays inserted in the upper right hand corner. This type of recording supplied the major source of data relating to the subjects' inferred conceptual understanding, their problem solving skills, and their nonverbal behaviors [24]. Problem solving behaviors were based on commonly recognized stages of problem solving [5, 11]. Data for triangulation and analysis of subjects' understanding of concepts were also obtained from written documents (pretests, posttests, and notes made by the subject during problem solving tasks) [24]. Specific directions and protocols were modified for each series of studies. Some subjects required more prompting to speak aloud than other subjects. In this situation, the researchers prompted subjects with comments such as "Please tell us what you are thinking or doing". The researchers provided technical aid to subjects only when difficulties with the hardware or software occurred.

4. SAMPLE INVESTIGATIONS

A microcomputer-based simulation, KANGASAURUS [25], was selected as the vehicle for examination of subjects' genetics concepts and problem solving strategies as they interacted with a model of transmission genetics. In one mode of operation, this program allows users to specify a genetic system through their decisions regarding a number of genetic parameters, including the number of autosomes, sex chromosome system, number of genes, trait controlled by each gene, number of alleles for each gene and their dominance relationship, chromosomal location of each gene, and in the case of linked genes, the distance between gene loci and the precise linkage phase (*cis* or *trans*). Having specified a genetic system, subjects can then formulate hypotheses about gene action and interactions, and then select organisms to be crossed. The use of an imaginary organism in the program KANGASAURUS meant that users were required to focus on genetic principles and could specify a genetic system free from the constraints imposed by their prior knowledge of the genetics of a 'real world' organism (such as a fruit fly). In their interaction with this simulation, users controlled the choice of variables and their manipulation, the genetic models to be constructed, the problem solving strategies to be tested, and the data to be extracted for generalizations about principles and patterns governing inheritance.

To gain insight into how people think and solve problems, an approach focusing on intensive studies of a small number of individuals [20] was employed. A group of problem solvers with varying levels of expertise in genetics was selected as subjects for this study. The subjects included professors and doctoral students of genetics and of education (ten subjects) and two masters level (graduate) students in science education.

As part of the familiarization with the program, each subject undertook an initial problem task. Within the context of a problem situation, subjects were presented with a general cue that embodied a commonplace genetic principle, such as independent assortment or sex linkage. Subjects then attempted to demonstrate their conceptual understanding by translating a general principle into its specific operational consequences by defining a genetic system and carrying out crosses. An example of such a problem is as follows: '*Problem P-1. A friend who is studying genetics says that he/she can't understand what is meant by the term "independent assortment". Try to set up a genetic system and carry out a cross that would allow you to demonstrate independent assortment to your friend.*' The findings were compared with corresponding pretest items, and a ranking of a list of concepts in terms of their perceived difficulty of understanding by subjects. In a later phase of the study, subjects were required to construct a genetic system which drew upon conceptual knowledge and procedural knowledge in order to solve a more open-ended problem expressed in general terms: '*Problem P-4. Two parents are different from each other in appearance. Their offspring are of two kinds. All sons are similar in appearance to the mother. All daughters are similar in appearance to the father.*' and '*Problem P-6. Two parents are different from each other in appearance. Their offspring are of four kinds: two kinds make up the majority of the offspring and they are different in appearance from either one of the parents, Only a few of the offspring are the same in appearance as either of the parents. Set up a genetic system and carry out a cross that shows this pattern.*'

These studies revealed the importance of learners' ability to describe or recognize critical evidence during problem solving. For example, one subject (a masters student with extensive biology background) consistently overlooked the critical evidence he needed to set up the appropriate crosses and solve the problem. An excerpt from his commentary during his attempt to solve Problem P-4 is shown below. In this excerpt, the subject made an unsuccessful attempt, and was attempting to solve the problem again; this excerpt captures the verbal utterances of the subject as he thought aloud about the chromosomal location of a gene and of the consequences of that gene location: *"...well I think that I was wrong somewhere in that I need to give ok the father is going to have to pass a dominant trait to his daughter and the mother is going to have to pass a dominant trait to her son What I did wrong was to let the father pass a recessive trait...so what I'm going to do is...now here's where I messed up last time choosing location now let's see I want to put it on I still want is on the X chromosome of the father...there's no indication that there's anything to do with sex linkage My thinking is still wrong somewhere I'm wondering now if I should put it on the Y chromosome...".*

The following excerpt illustrates the subject's approach to Problem P-1; this approach suggests that the computer program would derive the relevant data or expose an "answer" to the problem. The subject read the initial problem (P-1) and stated: *"I'm not sure what I'm doing is going to show independent assortment cause I know what the general concept is but I'm not sure of the actual mechanics of it in terms of separation of the alleles so I'm going to pick some parents and see what happens and see if it makes sense to me after I get done ok".*

For some subjects, commonly used terminology that is basic to transmission genetics (e.g. 'independent assortment') was poorly understood in terms of its translation into a dynamic genetic system. In some cases, this occurred in spite of subjects identifying this concept as relatively easy to understand. The video tapes also provided evidence that, for some subjects, much knowledge is 'inert' and is elicited only in a narrow context, rather than having much wider applications.

In terms of their performances on Problem P-6, subjects could be categorized into three subgroups; these subgroups did not correspond to groupings based on presumed genetics knowledge. The first subgroup included subjects (masters students and one professor) who did not demonstrate an understanding of the problem, but employed rote algorithms in an attempt to solve the problem. One subject repeatedly reformulated the problem and did not generate any strategies which led to problem resolution. The second subgroup included subjects (doctoral students and one professor) who engaged in several unsuccessful attempts and needed to reflect on the problem and their strategies before satisfactorily solving the problem. One doctoral student generated several cycles of problem reformulation, data gathering, analysis, and evaluation before realizing that the outcomes of the crosses would not result in the desired outcome. The subject returned the following day (after reflecting on the problem) and explained and demonstrated the desired outcomes, strategies, and crosses that led to problem resolution. These subjects typically overlooked critical decisions during their early attempts at problem solving. After several trials and reflection, they realized what actions were necessary and proceeded to demonstrate a strategy which led to problem resolution. The third subgroup (two genetics professors and one doctoral student) were able to efficiently and effectively solve this problem.

In addition to recording data that allowed for identification of problem solving behaviors and strategies, the composite videotape record allowed for the identification of specific nonverbal behaviors. These behaviors were predictable, ideosyncratic in some cases, and characterized or anticipated critical points of decision-making during problem solving. For example, hand-to-face movements by one subject preceded the selection of a specific problem solving strategy. Some nonverbal behaviors which signaled critical decision-making points included furrowing the eyebrows, widening the eyes, and touching of the face with a hand.

5. DATA COLLECTION AND ANALYSIS USING MICROCOMPUTERS

Microcomputer software programs available to aid in coding and analyzing verbal protocol data included: WORDPERFECT [26], ETHNOGRAPH [27, 28] and TEXT ANALYSIS PACKAGE (TAP) [29]. A word processing program, such as WORDPERFECT (available for Apple or IBM), can be employed to serve as a database for coded verbal phrases and statements. Recently, other computer programs have been developed to aid in coding and analyzing qualitative data, such as the verbal and visual recordings generated by the studies described in this paper. ETHNOGRAPH involves coding segments or entire passages of transcripts for analyses. TAP consists of sets of computer program procedures which allow the user to code text files, search for and retrieve patterns among the codes, and generate frequency tables of the codes. An added feature of TAP is its utility of working in any word processing program, converting a file to ASCII, and analyzing the converted file.

For example, transcripts were coded as shown in the following excerpt from a subject's commentary during a phase of problem representation. The subject, a faculty member in biology, read Problem P-6 and then commented: "(PR) (cNAU) *well there was a question like this in the prequiz* (HFc) (HR) (TO) *and there I* (HFc) *said something had to be abnormal about meiosis* (TO) (LP) *to make more* (P) *progeny that are different from the parents as if they are recombinants* (TO) (P) *so if I'm right I'm not sure that I can set up that system here* (LP) (TO) *set up a genetic system to carry out a cross* (HMr) (HFm) *but if I'm wrong I don't see how*" (HFch). The following multiple codes were entered into the transcript: nonverbal behaviors were coded as: HFch = hand to face on the cheek, HFm = hand to face to mouth, HMr = hand motion (rubbing hand), HR = head rests on hand, TO = taps object (pencil), LP = lip pursing, P = 3 second pause; screen displays were coded as: cNAU = choose the number of autosomes; and problem solving behaviors were coded as PR = problem representation. The use of the microcomputer and these kinds of computer programs can aid researchers in analyzing verbal protocols by using a variety of coding schemes [28, 29].

The richness of verbal protocol data, complemented by synchronized visual data, can be explored more efficiently and effectively by searching for emerging or significant patterns. For example, the sequencing of subjects' evaluation strategies can be coupled with the conceptual organizers they employ during their evaluation strategies. These kinds of analyses can reveal if subjects exhibit predictable behaviors during problem solving and aid researchers in examining factors involved in the development of conceptual understanding and the evolution of learners' mental models.

6. IMPLICATIONS FOR INSTRUCTION, CURRICULUM AND RESEARCH

The advent of microcomputers in classrooms brings us to the beginning of a new era in education, and a spectrum of both comprehensive and specific research is needed. "Structured observations", such as the series described here, can serve as important sources of information about cognitive and affective behaviors of students engaged in using instructional software. Research of this kind can enhance our understanding of how learners develop important concepts, logical thinking and problem solving skills, and mental models. Such studies can also provide a rich foundation for the synthesis of instructional models and for their applications to classroom practice.

REFERENCES

[1] Linn, M. 1987. Establishing a research base for science education: challenge, trends, and recommendations. Journal of Research in Science Teaching, 24, 191-216.

[2] Champagne, A. B., Gunstone, R. F., and Klopfer, L. E. 1982. A perspective on the differences between expert and novice performance in solving physics problems. Research in Science Education, 12, 71-77.

[3] Chi, M. T. H., Feltovich, D. J. and Glaser, R. 1981. Categorization and representation of physics problems by experts and novices. Cognitive Science, 5, 121-152.

[4] Larkin, J., McDermott, J., Simon, D. P., and Simon, H. A. 1980. Expert and novice performance in solving physics problems. Science, 208, 1335-1342.

[5] Hayes, J. R. 1981. The Complete Problem Solver. Philadelphia: Franklin.

[6] Hackling, M. W. 1986. Hypothesis Testing Strategies Used in the Solution of Genetic Pedigrees. San Francisco: American Educational Research Association Convention.

[7] Elstein, A. S., Shulman, L. S., and Sprafka, S. A. 1978. Medical Problem Solving an Analysis of Clinical Reasoning. Cambridge, Massachusetts: Harvard University Press.

[8] Hildebrand, A. 1985. Conceptual Problems Associated with Understanding Genetics: A Review of the Literature on Genetics Learning. Manuscript submitted for publication.

[9] Smith, M. U. and Good, R. 1984. Problem solving and classical genetics: succesful versus unsuccessful performance. Journal of Research in Science Teaching, 21, 895-912.

[10] Stewart, J. 1983. Student problem solving in high school genetics. Science Education, 67, 523-540.

[11] Sternberg, R. J. (1986). Intelligence Applied. Orlando, Florida: Harcourt Brace Jovanovich.

[12] Reif, F. 1986. Interpretation of Scientific or Mathematical Concepts: Cognitive Issues and Instructional Applications. Arlington, Virginia: Office of Naval Research.

[13] Collins, A. 1985. Problem-Solving Rules for Genetics. San Francisco: American Educational Research Association Convention.

[14] Rivers, R. H. and Vockell, F. 1987. Computer simulations to stimulate scientific problem solving. Journal of Research in Science Teaching, 24, 403-415.

[15] White, B. Y. and Fredericksen, J.R. 1986. Progressions of qualitative models as a foundation for intelligent learning environments. Cambridge, Massachusetts: BBN Laboratories.

[16] de Jong, T. and Fergusson-Hessler, M. G. M. 1986. Cognitive structures of good and poor novice problem solvers in physics. Journal of Educational Psychology, 78, 279-288.

[17] Bodner, G. M. and McMillen, T. L. B. 1986. Cognitive restructuring as an early stage of problem solving. Journal of Research in Science Teaching, 23, 727-737.

[18] Omasta, E. and Lunetta, V. N. 1988. Exploring functions: a strategy for teaching physics concpets and problem solving. Science Education, 72, 625-636.

[19] Krajcik, J. S., Simmons, P. E., and Lunetta, V.N. 1988. A research strategy for the dynamic study of students' concepts and problem solving strategies during interaction with microcomputers and instructional software. Journal of Research in Science Teaching, 25, 105-120.

[20] Larkin, J.H. and Rainard, B. 1984. A research methodology for studying how people think. Journal of Research in Science Teaching, 21, 235-254.

[21] Easley, J. A. 1982. Naturalistic case studies exploring social-cognitive mechanisms and some methodological issues in research on problems of teachers. Journal of Research in Science Teaching, 19, 191-203.

[22] Neuman, D. 1986. Qualitative Research: What Can It Bring to CBE? Washington, D. C.: Association for the Development of Computer-based Instructional Systems Convention.

[23] Smith, M. L. 1982. Benefits of naturalistic research methods in science education. Journal of Research in Science Teaching, 19, 627-638.

[24] Ericsson, K. A. and Simon, H. A. 1985. Protocol Analysis: Verbal Reports as Data. Cambridge, Massachusetts: MIT Press.

[25] Kinnear, J. 1989. KANGASAURUS: a genetics simulation. Danbury, Connecticut, EME.

[26] Stewart, C. O., Shore, J., and Rosenbaum, D. 1988. WordPerfect Tips, Tricks, and Traps. Carmel, Indiana: Que Corporation.

[27] Tesch, R. 1988. Advances in ethnography: software for qualitative data analysis. Seminar, University of Georgia, Athens, Georgia.

[28] Seidel, J. V., Kjolseth, R., and Seymour, E. 1988. The Ethnograph a User's Guide. Qualis Research Associates. Littleton, Colorado.

[29] Drass, K. A. 1986. TEXT ANALYSIS PACKAGE. Dallas, Texas.

Computers in Education
A. McDougall and C. Dowling (Editors)
Elsevier Science Publishers B.V. (North-Holland)

A TOOL TO PRODUCE COURSEWARE SPECIFICATIONS

Bernard Sodoyer

Delft University of Technology Faculty of Technical Mathematics and Informatics Julianalaan 132 2628 BL Delft - The Netherlands

The development of courseware in a professional and structured way is an iterative process in which a high level of different skills is required.

From each stage in the development cycle accurately working and especially good documenting is a necessary condition to allow in the design stage well considered and well understood decisions, and later to allow review and maintenance under good conditions.

Most of the software tools used in the courseware area are oriented to the production stage and are usually inappropriate to support the activities of a professional team to produce a pedagogical design.

This paper focuses on a script editor (SE) to produce in a structured way a well documented design. SE aims at supporting in an interactive way the major author's activities during the design phase. The produced script, if completely and accurately worked out, can be considered as a functional design on which implementation can be based.

1. INTRODUCTION

A multidisciplinary approach combined with a strong management in order to reach professionalism has been followed in the Dutch National Informatics Stimulation Plan (INSP 1984-1988) [Moonen, van der Mast, 1986].

In the framework of cluster I of the INSP an Educational Software Development Guide has been published [Hartemink, 1988]. The methodology described in this guide is based on:
- the separation of the management activities from the technical activities,
- phasing of the development path,
- the maintenance of documentation wherein the end products for each phase are unambiguously described.

The part of the methodology which concerns the project management: financing, planning and organizing is discussed in [Moonen, 1986].

The part dealing with the courseware development process can be sketched as follows:

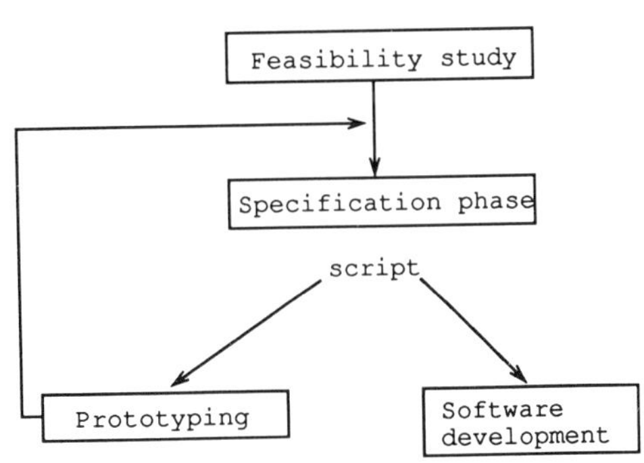

Figure 1: Courseware development cycle.

Within a few steps the design process results in a script. A script describes in full detail the program modules, what is to appear on the screen, how it is to appear, what are the branching sequences, etc...

If completely and accurately worked out, a script is the base document for the software developers.

2. SCRIPT EDITOR ENVIRONMENT

The script editor (SE) aims at supporting a number of major activities of a design team during the process of producing a pedagogical design. It offers facilities to produce a standard document, to define the pedagogical structures, to generate prototypes of interaction and to support the review process.

The basic idea in SE is that a script can be built upon different kinds of components and that a component contains a specific part of the courseware requirements. Because SE is in fact more than a document generator it has some features to extract from the requirements, the parts dealing with the pedagogical issues, and to present them on the screen realizing in fact a screen sequencing.

Each component used in a script is generated from a library of component structure types. These types are defined by the user using the library editor.

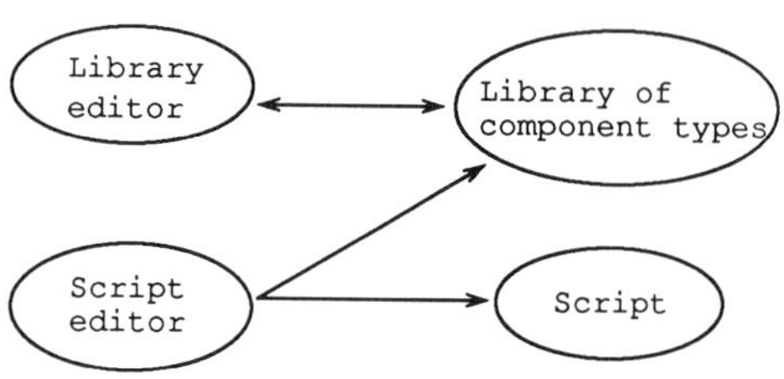

Figure 2: Global conceptual model.

2.1. Library editor.

The library editor is used to define and to collect structure types in a library. This library is used by SE to generate instances of component structure in the script.

Each component type in the library may have its own specific structure. The building stones of the structure are blocks and fields. A block is a logical part of a component structure and may contain blocks and/or fields. A field is an atomic structure item, which has a name, a type and some properties.

A field is of the type text or graphic and is coupled or not to a screen area. Fields coupled with a screen area, are called visible and may be shown during the visualization process of the script. Fields which are not coupled with a screen area, are called invisible. They contain purely text aimed at documenting the script and will never be shown on the screen during the visualization.

A block may have the "repeat" property meaning that its structure may occur more than once in the generated component. This property is handy to realize a screen sequence inside a component of the script.

2.2. script editor

The script editor integrates a number of tools to perform the different tasks in producing a script. There are a structure editor, a text editor, a graphics editor, a visualizator, a command generator and a note editor.

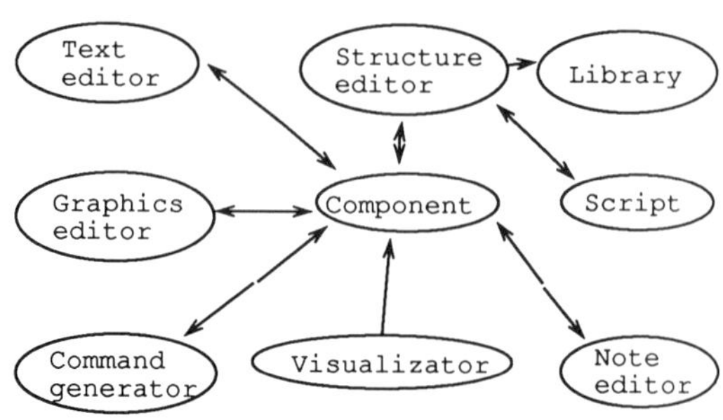

Figure 3: Conceptual model of SE

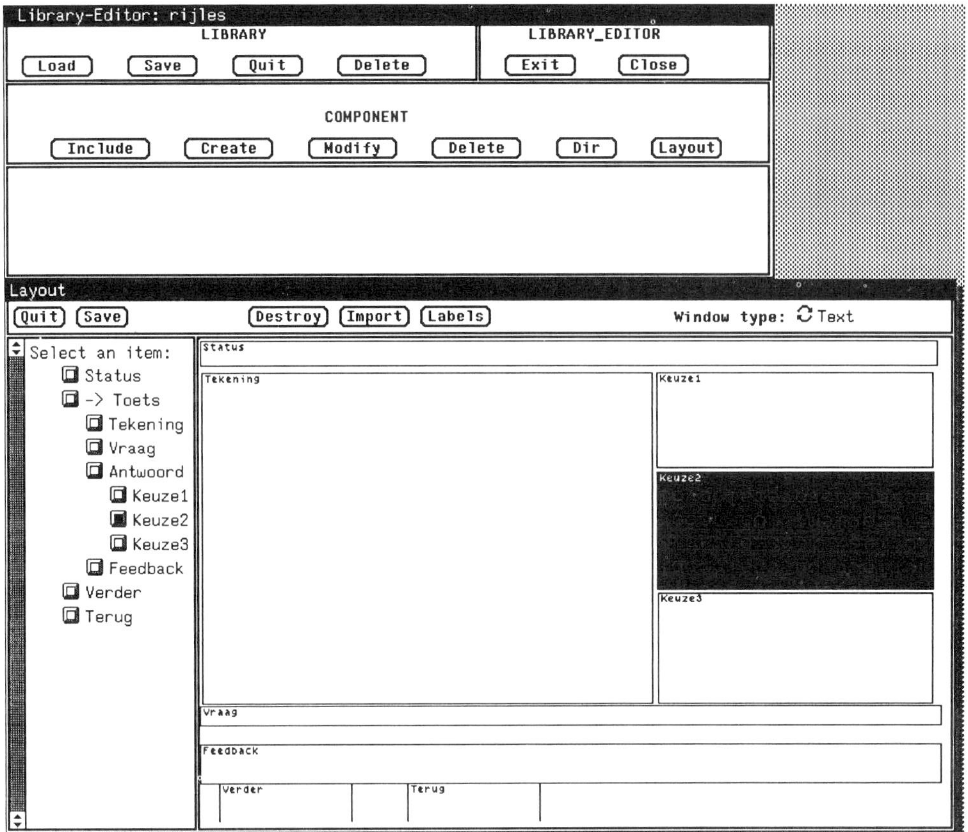

Figure 4 shows the library editor when fields of a component-structure are coupled to screen areas.

2.3. Structure editor

The structure editor offers the possibility of building the script, component per component. From the library it retrieves all the information needed to generate instances of the component structure. Automatically it builds a graphical map of the structure of the script. This map functions as an interface with the user to select, edit or visualize a component of the script. All other tools are working on the current component selected from this editor.

2.5. Text- and graphics editor

When a component is created or selected from the structure editor it becomes immediately available in the working area of the text editor. The structure and its contents are displayed and only the contents of the structure can be edited.

This way of working may be seen as generating a check-list and filling it with text.

If a field is marked as visible, i.e. coupled with a screen area, the text that it contains will be presented in the defined screen area during the visualization.

When a field in the structure is marked as graphic, the graphics editor may be activated to fill that field. Such a field is by default visible.

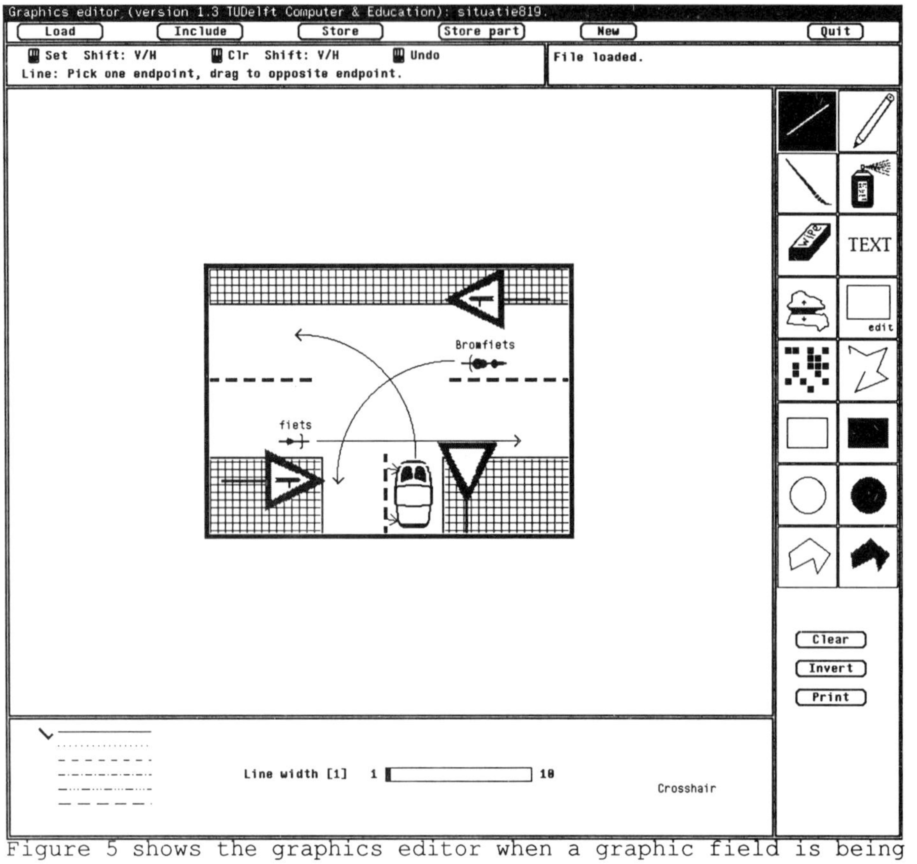

Figure 5 shows the graphics editor when a graphic field is being edited.

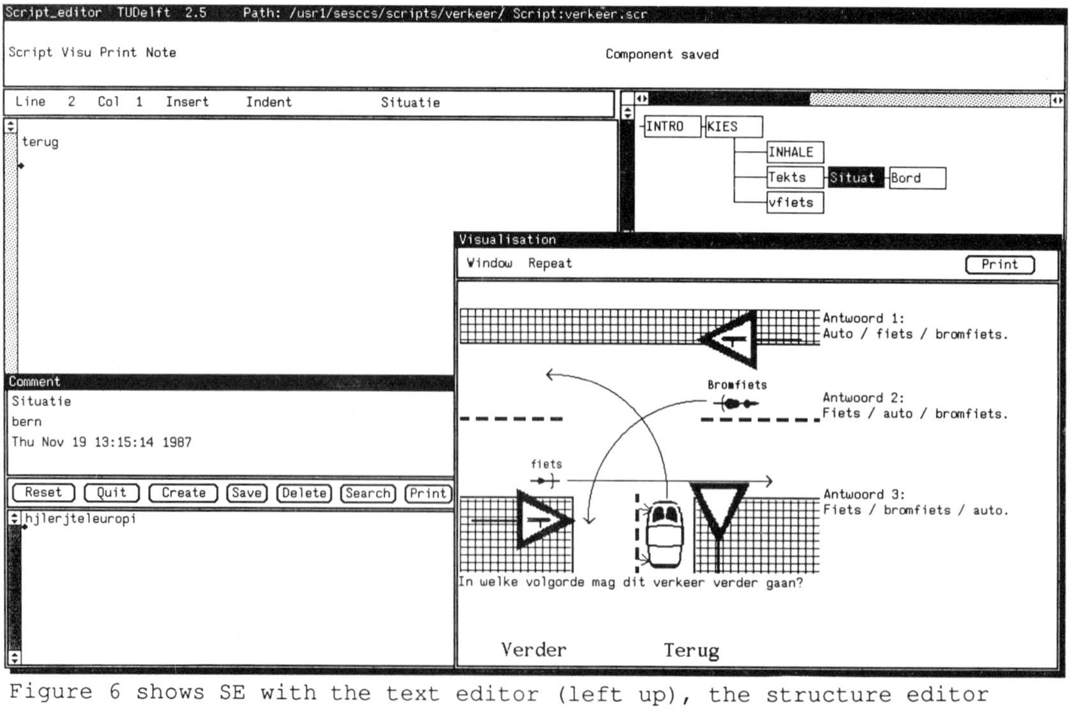

Figure 6 shows SE with the text editor (left up), the structure editor (right up), the note editor (left down) and the visualizator (right down).

2.6. Visualizator and command generator

When started, the visualizator analyses the structure of the current component and presents in the visualization area the contents of the visible fields.

The visualization is made by blocks, forwards or backwards to produce a sequential screen sequence. In this way the contents of the course may be examined in detail. Changes in text, graphics or layout may be done at a glance and visualized again.

Because screen sequencing is too static to get a good appreciation of the interaction, the visualizator has also the possibility of interpreting commands stored in the component to present the course more dynamically and to let the user interact with it.

The commands needed for the dynamic presentation are added to the component at dedicated places with the help of a command generator. There are commands to show and hide screen areas, to detect mouse and keyboard events, to make conditional or unconditional jumps, to compare keyboard input with predefined strings, to start animation.

2.6. Note editor

The note editor is used to notice remarks or comments about a script.

When a note is created the contents of the note and some extra information such as the owner's name are stored in the component. This offers the possibility during the development of a script to exchange information between members of the team, for example about design decisions or to give some suggestions for improvement.

During the review process it offers also the possibility to visualize notes from a specific reviewer and to present them in the contents in which they have been made.

3. IMPLEMENTATION

SE is actually implemented on a graphics workstation SUN and uses the facilities of the window environment SunView.

For historical and technical reasons the library editor and the graphics editor are not integrated in the SE environment but implemented as independent UNIX processes.

4. CONCLUSION

SE is not an industrial product but a prototype that is evolving with research progress.

SE has been tried out in two INSP-projects and is actually intensely used by students at the Delft university. Based on this usage the following conclusions may be drawn:

- the framework of SE forces the authors in an early stage to make clear what are the goals and the structures of the program,
- the visualizator and the corresponding prototyping facilities are essential during the specification,
- the open structure of the component offers the possibility to adapt SE to the standard documentation which is used in an organization,
- it offers also the possibility to use again, from one project to another, component structures which have been improved.

Although the following has not yet been proved I am convinced that delivering a complete script with a running prototype will greatly improve the communication between designers and programmers.

FURTHER RESEARCH

Because a lot of well defined data related to the course is available in a script, there are some potential possibilities to extend SE with a code generator.

The functionality of the library editor may be extended and reviewed in order to create standard and user defined interaction objects which can be used to improve the visualizator.

On the long term SE philosophy can be used to investigate some features and foundations of a CAD/CAI system.

REFERENCES

Hartemink, F., 1988, "Handboek voor de ontwikkeling van educatieve programmatuur", version 3.0, in PMI-reeks no. 12, Center for education and Information Technology, Enschede, The Netherlands.

Moonen, J., 1986, "Educational software development: the pedagogical design", in proceedings of a conference of the European Commission on the development of Educational Software, edited by Tjeerd Plomp, Koos van Deursen, Jef Moonen, North-Holland.

Moonen, J., Mast, van der, C., 1986, "Production of courseware in the Netherlands" in proceedings of the international conference on courseware design and evaluation, edited by Laurin F. Lewis, Benjami Feinstein.

Computers in Education
A. McDougall and C. Dowling (Editors)
Elsevier Science Publishers B.V. (North-Holland)

INTELLIGENT TOOLS AND LEXICAL SUPPORT FOR THE LANGUAGE LEARNER: PROVIDING ADVICE AT TASK AND DISCUSSION LEVELS

Roland SUSSEX
Centre for Language Teaching and Research, University of Queensland, St Lucia, Queensland, Australia 4067

Geoff CUMMING
Department of Psychology, La Trobe University, Bundoora, Victoria, Australia 3083

Lexical access in second language learning provides a fruitful area for the investigation of theoretical and empirical issues of intelligent learning tools in CAL. Interfaces to lexical resources can enhance language learning, and also provide an experimental cognitive vehicle for tracking, analysing and guiding lexical learning and exploration through intelligent help and guidance tools. We combine the framework of lexical toolkits with the concept of the separation of online help and advice into a *Discussion Level* (general cognitive and disciplinary principles of the learning area, and the students' learning strategies) and a *Task Level* (local learning tasks and activities). We investigate the issue of the separation of these two levels, and the ways in which an intelligent system, based on the two levels, can be designed so as to invoke and provide help of both kinds in response to the student learner's needs.

We see the language learner as taking a good deal of initiative while working at computer-based language tasks like comprehension, question answering, transformation exercises or translation. The learner calls on computer-based lexical tools as needed. Tools could include monolingual and bilingual dictionaries, concordances, thesauri, and reference sources for morphology, syntax and discourse.

We describe the learner undertaking such tasks as working at the *Task Level* (TL). Learning is likely to be most efficient if the learner is, in addition, engaged in a conversation at the *Discussion Level* (DL): a DL conversation takes a higher-level view, and refers to more global aspects of the work, including strategies, evaluation of progress, and the development and exploration of general principles.

1. COMPUTER TOOLS FOR LANGUAGE LEARNERS

Students of foreign languages have well-known difficulties in acquiring lexical resources to support their conceptual and communicative needs. Language teaching methodology has not so far made a significant impact on the search problem, though progress has been made with the selection and organization of the vocabulary to be learnt at each stage in terms of frequency, communicative and topic relevance, and active/passive lists. Experienced language users, including professional translators, also often encounter difficulties with bilingual lexical resources.

Language learners derive a very large amount of their lexical knowledge directly from conventional printed dictionaries. But these sources suffer from a number of shortcomings:

- students are not trained in dictionary use, and often fail to establish appropriate search and exploration strategies
- the information provided by dictionaries can be unhelpful, excessive, wrong or obscure
- dictionaries can be searched only in alphabetical order, and do not allow simultaneous multiple-path search
- dictionaries do not allow for different styles of use
- limitations on the volume and quality of contextual (longer text) information in dictionaries.

Information technology, both hardware and software, now presents tools for a radical improvement in the field of lexical search for language learners

(Ahmad, Rogers, Corbett & Sussex, 1985). The increasing availability of large lexical data-bases is resulting in computer-readable and searchable dictionaries; text data-bases are making it possible, with KWIC (key word in context) programs, to extract relevant information on lexical items quickly, and to build concordances. Software packages like Hypercard allow us to establish dictionaries with multiple-path searches (e.g., for synonyms, examples in context, stylistically related words, semantically related words (thesaurus function), rhymes, etc.). In addition, knowledge of lexical distributions, frequencies and functions is making it theoretically possible to tailor lexical resources to the needs of students - in volume and quality of information - at different stages of language learning, and for different language learning tasks. And audio-enhanced response from the dictionary, which can speak as well as provide written information, is technically available as well.

In terms of Computer-Aided Language Learning, these requirements mean that the student is provided with a set of learning goals and assessment instruments to determine when he or she has mastered the material; and a set of texts, exercises, and resources like dictionaries and grammars to support the learning process. The tools-based approach to lexical support provides tools like dictionaries and thesauri, textual tools like texts and KWIC (key word in context) or concordance programs, grammatical analysis tools like parsers, assessment tools, and so on - for the learner to use initiative to exploit. Learners benefit from working in a flexible and open-textured learning context; in addition they usually can benefit from guidance.

The creation of this learning environment and its linked learning tools requires the investigation of a number of key issues in learning patterns and strategies in second language learners.

2. A TOOLS-BASED IES

The EXCALIBUR Project is exploring the development of expert-system shells for intelligent computer-aided learning. In studying the extent to which such shells might be generally applicable, the conclusion of the EXCALIBUR researchers (Girle, 1986), and that of many other workers (Self, 1988), emphasises the great difficulty of meeting the needs of even a limited range of different learning domains with any single system. Creating an intelligent monolithic shell, even for a relatively restricted domain, presents enormous conceptual and software-engineering problems.

This difficulty was one of the reasons prompting Cumming and Self (1990a,b) to describe Intelligent Educational Systems (IESs), in which the distinction is made between interactions at TL and DL. Their suggestion was that some *decoupling* may be possible between the conversations occurring at the two levels, so that the system development task may become more tractable. In other words, the IES should be less difficult to build if it can support a useful DL interaction with the learner, including explanations, advice and guidance, without needing to have a fully complete and detailed understanding of all that is going on at the TL.

2.1. Decoupling of Task and Discussion Levels

To explain the decoupling notion further, consider the example of a language learner engaged at the computer in a translation task. The learner might draw on a dictionary, a thesaurus and some grammatical reference material. The system may be able to give advice, or respond to the learner's requests for help, in a way that is local to the immediate task - perhaps translating a phrase in a sentence. That would constitute TL interaction between system and learner.

The local advice given as part of the TL may, for example:

- point out that a word can be an adjective as well as a noun
- alert the learner to an irregularity of syntax
- alert the learner to multiple meanings of a word or phrase
- alert the learner to a possible idiom
- allow the learner to see how the previous similar problem had been solved, or
- demonstrate the commands needed to call on the thesaurus at this point

By contrast, consider an expert language teacher watching over the shoulder of the learner using the computer system. The teacher may make a range of types of more global comments, such as:

- "Well done. You seem to understand better now; you are doing better than yesterday."
- "That sort of construction can be quite tricky. Remember we had a similar case last week? ... A good rule of thumb to remember is ... "
- "You seem to be going in circles. Try

starting the sentence again, but try another word-order."
- "Fine. I suggest you go on now and try the following tasks ..."

These DL comments may be made either as an intervention at the initiative of the teacher, or could be given in answer to a request for help from the learner.

The important question to consider is the extent to which the expert teacher could make helpful DL comments of this sort without full insight into what the learner has done and is trying to do. Perhaps the teacher is walking around a large class of learners and has paused momentarily to help an individual student. Given established problem-solving abilities of this learner, he or she may be able to make use of teacher comments that are less than optimal, perhaps by asking for a restatement, or by carrying out the suggested operation and trying to interpret the result. This kind of scenario occurs frequently in normal classroom interactions.

This classroom analogy suggests that it is possible to offer useful and relevant DL conversation to the learner, even if the conversation may not be ideal in every detail, and may lack a fully detailed and articulated understanding of the TL activity. Some decoupling has been achieved in such learning scenarios; and even a modest degree of decoupling should make much more tractable the task of developing the IES. Cumming and Self identify the critical issue as being the form of representation for communication between the two levels inside the IES.

2.2. Learner modelling

To be to some extent intelligent, system comments given at the DL need to be based on modelling of the learner's understanding, abilities and styles, as well as some domain knowledge. Developing, maintaining and using a model of the learner's current state of understanding and misconception has always been a central feature of intelligent tutoring systems; the decoupled, two-level IES proposal does not remove the need for learner modelling, although it should make the modelling task more tractable. In a decoupled system the learner information used at the DL would be at least partially separate from the corresponding information used to support TL response by the system. The discussion above of TL interactions suggests that local, short-term learner modelling may largely suffice for maintaining the TL interaction. By contrast, a good DL interaction will probably need to have available more enduring and higher level information about the specific learner.

2.3. Adding a Discussion Level.

Cumming and Self (1990a,b) also argued that, if decoupling is feasible, it may be possible to base an IES on already existing computer-based resources, by adding facilities designed to support a DL. This is an extremely attractive possibility because a great variety of excellent computer-based tools, simulation packages, databases, games and other applications are now available. Many of these are powerful, well designed, and have excellent user interfaces. If in addition a DL interaction could be provided to the user, the learning value of these resources would be greatly enhanced. A gradualist strategy of progressively adding DL facilities to the tools being used to support TL learning activities is especially attractive. More broadly, the add-a-DL strategy could be considered for enhancing other computer-based language learning activities like exercises, extension reading or story writing.

Our aim is to explore these possibilities in the context of providing computer-based lexical tools for language learners. Lexical search is an especially appropriate domain: in addition to the applied importance of the domain, learner initiative is natural and important in undertaking language exercises, new and powerful computer-based tools are becoming available, and language-related tasks lend themselves to protocol-based methods of investigating learners' processes, strategies, and preferences.

3. LEXICAL SEARCH IN LANGUAGE LEARNING

For the beginning learner, the textbook is likely to provide an effectively closed world, with word-lists and appendices covering the vocabulary which falls within the domain of the text. But from intermediate levels, students can experience lexical agoraphobia: the full-size dictionaries of the second language are often large, and contain much information which may be beyond the student's current knowledge. Worse still, from the learning point of view, the student is often unable to determine which information is relevant, and lacks strategies to make that determination.

Consider a simple but common category of example: a student looks up <u>ignore</u> in an English-Russian dictionary, and finds both *ne obrashchat' vnimanie (na)*, literally 'not to pay attention to', and *ignorirovat'*. How is the student to determine whether *ignorirovat'*, having been borrowed, has the same range of meanings as English *ignore*? Or is it like French *ignorer*, which also means 'not to know'? In such cases checking the relevant words in the Russian-English dictionary does not always yield an easy or obvious answer for the learner who is just moving outside the world of the textbook-bound language course of the elementary year. At this point the student may start to "thrash", seeking at random any further information to provide a way out of the impasse.

There are effective strategies which can be articulated and applied to the lexical problem at this point (Sussex, 1989), and discussion of such strategies certainly belongs to the DL level. Ideally, DL intervention would offer guidance, with the specific aim of helping the learner acquire, test and exploit an appropriate strategy to handle this type of situation. Behind this immediate goal is the more general aim of helping the learner develop over-all strategies to cope with the phenomenon of impasse. This aim is related to the highly desirable development of meta-level abilities by the learner, and will be of especial interest to a learner with a broad view and top-down orientation. Our research aim is to track, model and evaluate these lexical search strategies, for incorporation in the DL component of the IES.

4. LESSON AUTHOR AND EXPERT TEACHER

In traditional CAL the lesson author (Merrill, 1985) draws on knowledge of the domain and of teaching to specify the learning experiences and feedback to be offered to a learner. In traditional knowledge engineering for the development of an expert system, an attempt is made to capture salient aspects of an expert's understanding in rule form. These two models for the incorporation of human expertise in a computer system can be considered to merge in the development of the type of tools-plus-DL IES which we are describing. On the one hand, there needs to be scope - and the appropriate interface - for any teacher to enter recommended tasks, activities, or curriculum paths into the IES, while on the other hand, the DL component needs to incorporate expert knowledge about lexical search derived first in a knowledge engineering exercise from a human expert language teacher, and then supplemented as the IES is studied in use.

This analysis identifies learning issues as crucial (Lesgold, 1988); it also suggests a further way to regard the development of the DL component. We could study how an expert teacher advises and guides a learner who is given access to the computer tools that constitute the TL. We could then use knowledge engineering of that teacher to identify useful expertise to incorporate in the DL component.

5. A DECOUPLED IES FOR LEXICAL SEARCH.

The lexical search area offers the promise that search parameters can be specified clearly at both TL and DL, and that a variety of search modes can be made available to the learner, at least in prototype form, in Hypercard or Intermedia environments. The strategies and performances of learners can then be tracked in detail, as the learner works at the TL. We are currently developing icon-and-mouse Macintosh II-based Hypercard prototype interfaces to allow this study of learner behaviour.

In terms of tasks, the present project aims to implement a series of restricted monolingual and bilingual dictionaries and thesauri in a computer environment, and to use this environment to plot and analyze student strategies in lexical search. The parameters of search involve not only traditional dictionary searching, but also:

- monolingual, bilingual and multilingual search
- a choice of search paths
- multiple concurrent search paths.

Both users and instructors will have facilities for setting search paths and parameters, and to tailor lexical and text resources to individual needs.

The system will also cater for levels of lexical access above that of the *ab initio* learner. Language learners in their second year of tertiary study experience a sudden expansion in the volume and quality of lexical information which they need in order to handle advanced texts. The expansion in the computer-based lexical resources will involve not only a quantitative increase, but also a qualitative change in the nature and scope of the links and search paths through the lexical and text material. These changes will be largely driven by the results of ongoing observations of the strategies of students using the system. There is also, in principle, no reason why such tools should not extend to the incorporation of major term-banks, such as those which are being built by ESPRIT-funded projects for special lexical areas. The intention is that intelligent tools will enable these data banks to be searched along multiple paths, and algorithms will be developed to emulate human decision patterns in eliminating unproductive search paths, and to resolve conflict and ambiguity in the information derived from multiple searches. Furthermore, users should in principle be able to extend a lexical search into concordance-based texts, in order to observe the selected word or phrase in syntactic and semantic contexts. Again, this kind of search, and the strategies which drive it, are so far unexplored in terms of task-*versus*-discussion types of advice.

A further extension concerns media: the lexical search support shell should in principle be able to interact with a digital interactive language laboratory for auditorily-cued, as opposed to visually-cued, lexical search.

5.1. Cognitive aspects

Approaching lexical search in this tools-based environment links up with psycholinguistic research (Spolsky, 1988) on lexical access, principally in monolinguals. It is useful, as a starting hypothesis, to conceive of lexical exploration by second language learners as an explicit search through problem space, in the terms of Newell and Simon's (1972) model of Artificial Intelligence. (How far the search metaphor will be valid (as model or heuristic) is in itself a major question.) The input to the help/advisor will require information from the student model, and the ways in which the current state of the student's knowledge can be advanced by intervention from an intelligent discussion level tool.

5.2. Achieving decoupling

The foregoing discussion shows that we regard the lexical IES as a setting for research, especially on cognitive aspects of language learning. From the point of view of developing a decoupled IES that is practically effective in helping language learners, we have identified the design of the communication between DL and TL within the system as a crucial task. We have argued that attainment of at least some decoupling is plausible, by using a loose analogy with human teaching. Demonstrating a possible pattern of links would add greatly to the argument.

Recognising the communication issue as fundamental, we offer a relatively simple example of possible communication fragments between DL and TL. The learner is working on a sentence transformation task involving word-order. This kind of task provides many typical problems of language learning, since highly inflected languages which mark cases (subject, object, etc.) tend to allow more varied word-order than languages like English, where Subject-Verb-Object is the predominant permissible order. The learner has tried three different word-orders, and each time the software has indicated that the language will not accept that order, with messages like "X has to come before Y in the sentence." The learner is obviously starting to thrash. At the Task Level the student can request help, or the system can intervene. The information available on this level will include access to the dictionary, and access to a corpus of the language, where the student can see the word(s) or construction(s) in use in different sentences. Task Level information would also guide the student about basic rules for word order in the language - like the well-known "Time-Manner-Place" rule for German adverbials, supported by examples. But what is the appropriate intervention at the Discussion Level?

The key general issue in the implementation of the Discussion Level is the extent to which it can function without full information input from the Task Level. Cumming & Self (1990b) give the example of a Discussion Level expert in graphics design who is able to offer effective guidance with no detailed information about the detailed operation of graphics software. In the context of our current German language example, the learner could be encouraged to explore more general issues of word-order. Languages lacking morphological case markers – English preserves these only in pronouns like *I/me* – often need fixed word-order in order to help mark functional roles in the sentence: who does what to whom. In German, on the other hand, it is quite appropriate to say the equivalent of "The book have you read?" if there is contrastive stress on "the book". In this instance, a report of "3 successive mismatches for word-order" will suffice to prime the Discussion Level to take up the conversation with the student, and to explore different parameters of word-order in language. The important point is that the Discussion Level can intervene on the basis of very incomplete input from the Task Level.

The Discussion Level is often a macro-level treatment of the learning tasks at the micro-level. But this is not always the case. The Discussion Level allows not only a more top-down approach to the given problem; it can provide rule-driven explanations, example-driven explanations with inductive exercises for the student to explore, and can approach the problem at the meta-level by talking about strategies and solutions. There is a distinction between Discussion and Task Levels. But whether this distinction is to be realized in terms of a clear boundary, and the consequences of this in terms of CAL design, cognitive issues and software modelling, are questions which remain to be solved.

6. CONCLUSION

The development of effective intelligent CAL materials has been hampered in the past by the very heavy requirements on intelligent shells, and their limited generalizability. The current proposal has two advantages. First, it allows the incremental, gradualist evolution of intelligent support shells through the implementation of the toolkit approach, which has some architecturally and structurally well defined exemplars in the field of language learning. And second, by placing this developmental path in the context of Discussion and Task Level conversation, it explores the relation between local and more generalized learning in a way that permits direct access to the cognitive issues of learning.

ACKNOWLEDGEMENTS

We are grateful for the collaboration of other members of the EXCALIBUR project. Support has been provided by the Australian Research Council.

REFERENCES

Ahmad, K., Rogers, M., Corbett, G., & Sussex, R. (1985) Computers, language learning and language teaching. Cambridge: Cambridge University Press.

Cumming, G., & Self, J. (1990) Learner modelling in collaborative intelligent educational systems. In P. Goodyear (Ed.), Teaching knowlege and intelligent tutoring. Norwood, N.J.: Ablex. (in press) (a)

Cumming, G., & Self, J. (1990) Intelligent educational systems: Identifying and decoupling the conversational levels. Instructional Science. (in press) (b)

Girle, R. A. (Ed.) (1986) Report of the first Round Table Conference. Australian Educational Expert Systems Project. Brisbane, University of Queensland: Project EXCALIBUR.

Lesgold, A. (1988) Towards a theory of curriculum for use in designing intelligent instructional systems. In H. Mandl & A. Lesgold (Eds), Learning issues for intelligent tutoring systems. N.Y.: Springer. pp 114-137.

Merrill, M. D. (1985). Where is the authoring in authoring systems? Journal of Computer-Based Instruction, 12 (4), 90-96.

Newell, A. & Simon, H. A. (1972) Human problem solving. Englewood Cliffs, N.J.: Prentice-Hall.

Self, J. (Ed.) (1988) Artificial intelligence and human learning: Intelligent computer-aided instruction. London & New York: Chapman & Hall.

Spolsky, B. (1988) Bridging the gap: a general theory of second language learning. TESOL Quarterly, 22, 3.

Sussex, R. (1989) Issues in computer-aided language learning: Towards an expert-systems learning environment. In C.N. Candlin and T. McNamara (Eds), Language, learning and community. Festschrift in honour of Terry Quinn. Macquarie University, Sydney: National Centre for English Language Teaching and Research. pp 91-104.

Computers in Education
A. McDougall and C. Dowling (Editors)
Elsevier Science Publishers B.V. (North-Holland)

HYPERCARD AS A RELATIONAL LEARNING TOOL

Teresa Van Haalen

Research Assistant, Department of Curriculum & Instruction, University of Houston, Houston, TX 77004

Abstract: Computer programming as a rehabilitation activity for head injured adults is the subject of this presentation. Hypertalk programing language with the Macintosh is addressed given its ability to draw upon prior semantic knowledge. This case study examines the ability of one young adult in utilizing the relational nature of Hypercard as a programming tool.

1. INTRODUCTION

Richard Skemp in 1976 discussed two concepts of "understanding" that are applicable in the Hypercard environment and have special meaning for teachers of handicapped persons. The first, instrumental understanding,is the acquisition of knowledge that relies on rote learning and memorization of procedures. It is limited in scope and does not easily lend itself to memorization of procedures. Skemp describes such understanding as 'rules without reasons', not necessarily involving understanding. Relational understanding, on the other hand, is adaptable to new tasks, easier to remember, effective as a goal in itself and is organic in quality. Relational understanding is what most of us think of when we talk about understanding--to be able to apply knowledge in new and imaginative ways. Skemp applies these definitions to mathematics instruction, but their application enriches other areas of academic interest.

Analogies to Skemp's framework occur within Bloom's taxonomy and provide relevance to educators as they become familiar with the concepts inherent in Skemp's models of understanding. Knowledge and comprehension levels of subject matter presentation are obviously what Skemp would call 33"instrumental" knowledge. Comprehension, analysis, synthesis and evaluation are more similar to his concept of "relational" understanding. This paper will explore these definitions as they apply to the perceived relational nature of Hypercard programming, especially for unique learners.

2. BACKGROUND

For Bruce Roberts, relational qualities of learning tasks are critical if memorial episodes are to survive short term memory and be integrated into the long term schemata. Bruce suffered a subdural hematoma several years ago and was left comatose for six months following an automobile accident. Two years ago I began working with him at the request of his parents who felt that computer programming would be one way to maintain some higher level thought processes following his remarkable recovery. As with many young people who suffer head trauma, he has been able to recover more than medical science would expect, and my primary concern was not whether he could program, but how interesting and meaningful programming would be to him. Would programming for him consist of bits and pieces of instrumental knowledge? Or could we turn the experience into an enjoyable activity in which coded information was linked from lesson to lesson?

Another way in which this dilemma might be illustrated is through paradigms in cognitive psychology, especially Tulving's concepts of episodic and semantic memory. We go through life encountering an infinite number of experiential episodes, linked one to the other by time. The episodes are not necessarily meaningful (or remembered) unless they become integrated into our "modus operandi", that is semantic memory. In this regard, my challenge was to take Bruce's biweekly programming lessons and help him see them as something other than discrete and unrelated episodes, allowing his understanding to extend beyond instrumental knowledge.

An example most people can relate to is the hearing and retelling of jokes. How many have heard a joke in the last two weeks? If I were to tell one now, you would have no problem retelling it a few minutes later because it would surely survive short term memory. One might be able to recall the joke a week later if the circumstances surrounding the telling could be called to mind. But only if the joke were committed to semantic (or long term) memory through some relational means would you be likely to remember the joke in a month.

In remembering events (or jokes) there is a tendency for distortions to occur. Actually, people tend to reconstruct episodes using their existing knowledge--so events are recalled according to what was expected rather than what really happened. Long term memory "helps out" by supplying meaning to discrete events. Thus new information becomes relational learning because of that link to preexisting memorial "data".

3. HYPERTALK

The practical importance of these concepts became apparent as Bruce and I embarked on Microsoft Basic using a Macintosh Plus computer. Many of the commands which could be executed immediately were boring to him (such as PRINT statements), and it seemed as though we were going to have to work through hours of tedious instrumental learning before the information became integrated and relational. Skemp provides analogous situations in his article when he looks at typical and atypical means of instructing students in algebraic concepts.

Bruce's impediments in programming endeavors were twofold. First, the commands were seldom self-explanatory. While PRINT certainly is, commands such as GOSUB or READ DATA are much less so. Few commands have any relationship to the semantic knowledge he already possessed and used with such facility when communicating. Second, if the concepts behind the commands were learned, the length of the programs themselves would tax problem solving ability, Bruce's weakest suit. Debugging appeared to be an unattainable goal.

Enter Hypercard. At the verge of dropping our programming efforts, we found what eventually proved to be the "ideal" programming environment for Bruce. I would like to describe the reasons for Bruce's success in this environment, (despite some stumbling blocks) in hopes that someone teaching people with deficits in short term memory, episodic memory or semantic (long term) memory might benefit from our story. Besides, teaching Hypercard is a lot of fun for the teacher!

3.1 Hardware Considerations

Bruce has a Macintosh Plus which has a custom designed keyboard. The keyboard is arranged alphanumerically with the keys themselves placed into depressions in the surface of the keyboard. The keyboard was designed by Bruce's father who realized that his severe physiological impairments would prevent him from accessing a standard keyboard with any accuracy. When the decision was made to move to Hypercard, Bruce's computer was expanded with a 10 megabyte hard disk to accommodate the program.

Our initial lessons consisted of browsing through the stacks that are supplied with the Hypercard program. While Bruce had previous experience with word processing programs (which he accessed with one index finger), the extensive use of the mouse required by the program was his initial challenge. At the browsing level, there is little need for keyboard us and accuracy with the mouse became a critical issue. Bruce is able to use his left hand to grasp and point, but gross motor movement from the shoulder is inaccurate, and sudden jerks frequently had his mouse losing or dropping objects that he wanted to manipulate on the screen. We began using a track ball, and while not the perfect solution, it seemed to give him more leeway in his movements. For example, when using a track ball, the key does not have to be down to move the cursor. The user merely moves the cursor using a 2" sphere held in a casing, and clicks a separate key when the correct location has been found.

3.2 Hypercard Objects

Bruce began his foray into Hypercard programming through what is known as "browsing". Browsing is the entry level of Hypercard use and merely allows the user to peruse the existing stacks of information. No changes or additions are possible. It was at this level of use that Bruce became familiar with key concepts which later became second nature as he learned to program in Hypertalk. These concepts are tagged with names which are easily retrievable from long term memory by anyone who understands English: buttons, fields, cards, stacks (of cards), home, and message. It is not the intent of this presentation to instruct in Hypercard terminology, but use of the terminology will hopefully illustrate the metaphorical nature of the language and the accessibility to long term memory. A Hypercard browser has access to the Message Box. Accessible from the menu bar, or from a keyboard command, this window is a primary avenue of communication between the user and Hypercard. Single command lines can be entered in the Message Box, many of which are identical to the commands to be used later when writing Hypertalk scripts (programs). For Bruce, this Message Box was an integral part of learning to program because he could try out new commands one at a time while still viewing the current stack.

Once a user enters the second and third levels of Hypercard use, typing and painting, he is able to enter text and manipulate some graphics. At the fourth and fifth levels, authoring and scripting, the user can create new stacks, and begin to understand the hierarchical order that Hypercard objects occupy. While entering text was not a difficult maneuver for Bruce, using the variety of painting tools was a more formidable task. This challenge was due largely to Bruce's motor impairment, however, other factors also served as impediments especially when he was first learning his way around Hypercard. We spent a large amount of time initially just browsing around our existing Clip Art stacks, and using provided art work. Cutting and pasting capabilities were already a part of his repertoire from paint programs he had used previously on his Macintosh. Of course, the ability to "tear off" the paint tools so that they would be accessible was potentially a desirable feature of the program. Surprisingly, it took Bruce several months to remember to tear off his palette consistently when he was using the program.

Hypertalk itself consists of thirty-eight commands ranging from navigation commands to arithmetic and information commands. Reliance on Bruce's prior knowledge was substantial as we learned manipulation of such messages and commands as "mouseDown", "go" and "find". Putting items in "containers" (local and global variables) and retrieving those items using a "get" command, are examples of ways in which Hypertalk reaches out to users of all types. While Bru and I may not be authoring stacks th would interest serious programmers, we are exploring a creative system of programming that will be useful and memorable because of the semantic (meaningful) links to our prior and future knowledge base.

5. COGNITIVE BENEFITS

We began by creating a few Hypercard stacks ourselves using the menu driven commands inherent in Hypercard. We needed to generate a stack to which Bruce could transfer art wo to experiment with painting, as well as stacks to generate original scripts as we began using Hypertalk. Constructive approaches to lesson design throughout the past two years has been based upon the context-embedded design of Hypercard.

The term "context-embedded" was first coined by James Cummins (1983) in his theories of second language learning. He contends that language learning is best accomplished in those situations where a high degree of context is incorporated. This theory certainly applies to computer programming, especially with populations having special learning problems. Hypercard programming has proven a stimulating and rewarding experience for Bruce based upon the following assumptions drawn from the learning theories offered in this paper:

1. The Hypercard environment in this case provides a rich relational learning experience at every level of use. For example, when Bruce began authoring stacks, he was able to customize his own backgrounds to reflect his penchant for anything western in motif. Now at the scripting level, he can import or create sound files that provide auditory embellishment to the stacks he created earlier.

2. Progam-product relationship is more apparent than with other programming languages. Easy accessibility of the script cards enable the programmer to create short routines, and then to run them with two short clicks of the mouse. This immediate feedback confirms (or not) the user's logic, contributing to the learners semantic memory cache.

3. The ease of creating or borrowing picture and sound files creates a far more context-embedded learning environment than traditional programming languages. Additionally, the naming of Hypercard objects which trigger events (through scripts) is encouraged, contributing to a contextually rich programming experience.

6. CONCLUSIONS

The purpose of this paper is to illustrate advantages experienced by closed head injured persons in learning to program on the Macintosh using Hypertalk. Presentation slides used to indicate the correspondence of Hypercard terminology to existing schemata contribute to an understanding of problem solving outcomes. Anecdotal information will be provided to teachers of technology with the handicapped.

According to Bright (1983), academic learning time and involvement of learners with learning tasks are significant predictors of the success of any instructional technology. In this respect, Hypercard programming shows promise in the instruction of programming and problem solving skills for learners who bring unique motivational and cognitive backgrounds to the learning task.

REFERENCES

Bright, G. W. (1983). Explaining the efficiency of computer assisted instruction. Association for Educational Data Systems Journal, 25,144-151.

Cummins, J. (1983). The role of primary language development in promoting educational success for language minority students. In Schooling and language minority students: A theoretical framework (pp. 3-51). Los Angeles, CA: California State University, Evaluation, Dissemination and Assessment Center.

Skemp, R.R. (1978). Relational understanding and instrumental understanding. Arithmetic Teacher, 23(3), 9-15.

Tulving, E. (1972). Episodic and semantic memory. In E. Tulving & W. Donaldson(Eds.) Organization of memory. New York: Academic Press.

VOCATIONAL EDUCATION AND TRAINING

Computers in Education
A. McDougall and C. Dowling (Editors)
Elsevier Science Publishers B.V. (North-Holland)

STRATEGIES FOR VOCATIONAL EDUCATION & TRAINING IN IT - TOWARDS THE YEAR 2000

PATRICK RAYMONT, PRINCIPAL CONSULTANT, THE NATIONAL COMPUTING CENTRE, UK.

A vocational education and training (VET) system ought, by definition, to aim to meet the needs of society (industry, commerce and administration in particular) for skilled providers and users of IT systems. As strategies for the use of IT develop (a focus on mission critical systems and on the management of interdependence is evident), so VET strategies will need to respond. A framework for VET strategies is developed, based on the concepts of lectures, tutorials, coaching, group learning and self-study. Two main strategy thrusts are identified as "employer led, competence based, modular, short" provision on the one hand, and "academic led, understanding based, integrated long" provision on the other. Both thrusts are needed, in a suitable mix to cope with changing needs as a person's career develops.

1 INTRODUCTION

Most countries suffer from a shortage of people skilled in the development of IT systems. For example a 1988 survey by the National Computing Centre [1] showed that in the UK there is a shortfall in the User sector alone of about 20,000 IT development staff (programmers and analysts principally) representing about 12% of the total employed in the field, and that staff turnover rates are typically of the order of 15-20%. It is also a common complaint that the users of IT
systems (from top management to clerical levels) are not able to use their systems as effectively as possible due to lack of the appropriate skills.

With IT systems proliferating (worldwide sales of mainframes show a growth of about 7% pa, PC sales roughly double themselves every two years), this creates a serious problem for those countries which are heavily dependent on IT for their economic success. Such countries need a vocational education and training (VET) system, which will provide a flow of appropriately educated and trained staff.

This paper addresses the problem of devising a suitable framework for a VET strategy in the IT field.

One disclaimer should be made. It is a limitation of the author's background that he is much more experienced in the application of IT to business and administration than to, say, manufacturing or control systems. The author apologies for the bias that will inevitably arise from this.

2 THE CONCEPT OF "STRATEGY"

We adopt the classic distinction between strategic planning and management/operational control put forward by Anthony [2]. It is worth repeating Anthony's definition of strategic planning as "the process of deciding on objectives, on changes in these objectives, on the resources used to attain these objectives, and on the policies that are to govern the acquisition, use and disposition of these resources". We also note that strategic planning is not necessarily "long-range" : some changes of objectives may be pushed through very quickly.

Strategic planning is about identifying possible futures, selecting desired subsets of the possible and planning how to get from the present position to the desired future. The so-called "planning-cone" (figure 1) offers a model which some readers may find helpful.

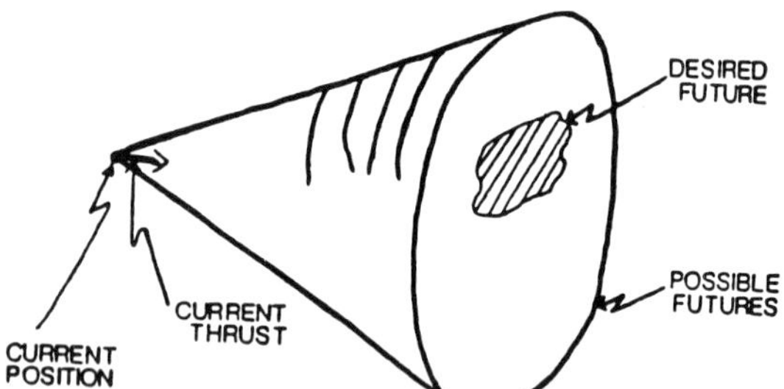

Figure 1 The Planning Cone

3 TOOLS FOR STRATEGIC PLANNING

A number of tools exist to aid in the process of strategic planning. Here we mention only four which we can relate directly to VET strategies. Firstly "models" can be developed (sometimes computerised) which enable options to be explored. Of course, the question of the validity of the model is crucial. But in strategic planning the accuracy of any predictions is of less interest than the insights gained in the modelling process. A simple model of the UK VET funding system [3] is shown in Figure 2.

A second tool is extrapolation from existing trends. Figure 3 shows an alarming extrapolation of demographic data on the supply of school-leavers for the VET system of the UK [4].

Population of 16- and 17-year-olds 1981-2001, Great Britain

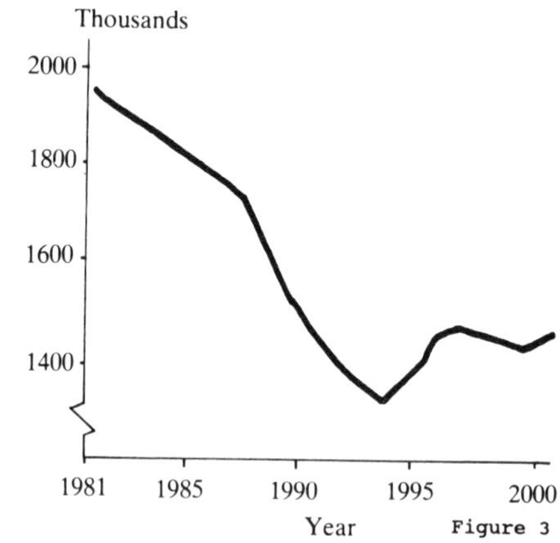

Figure 3

A third tool is the relevance tree, particularly as applied in the Planning-Programming-Budgeting System (PPBS) developed by the USA government in the 1960's and subsequently widely employed in planning public sector strategies [5]. A hypothetical tree related to VET is shown in Figure 4.

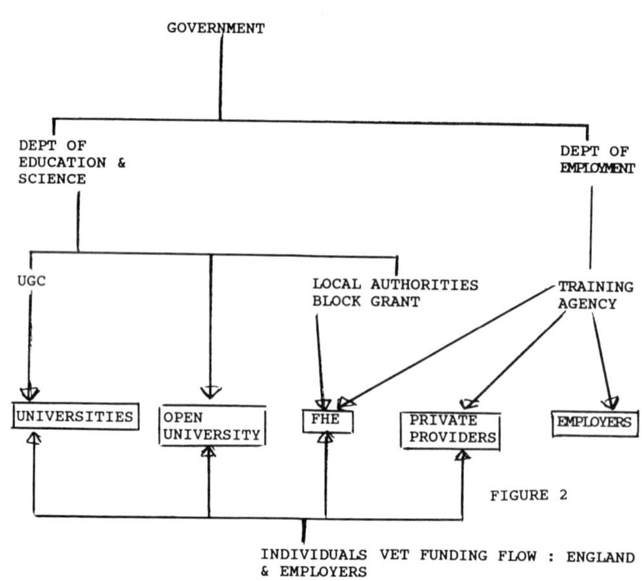

FIGURE 2

VET FUNDING FLOW : ENGLAND & WALES

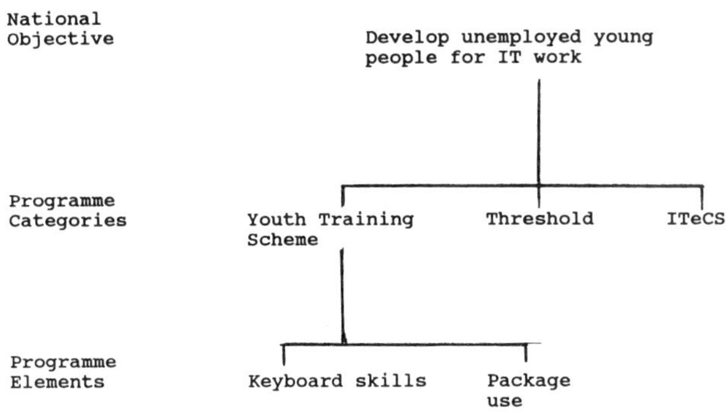

Fig 4 Partial example of a PPBS relevance tree for UK IT Youth Training Schemes.

Scenario writing, our fourth and final tool, is particularly valuable in formulating ideas on possible futures. A short scenario developed by the author based on material at the end of [6] is as follows: Ms X is worried about the health and safety aspects of her new job in the despatch office; she wants to remind herself of company health and safety guidelines; she goes to her nearest "study station", identifies herself using a plastic card and is given a welcome prompt "what do you want?" She responds by voice, "A health and safety update". The screen response is to confirm "You last ran a check on health and safety regulations 10 months ago; you want a refresher?" She responds by keying "y" (or by saying "yes"). The system shows her a short overall video followed by a one screen summary, with the option of following up any particular aspect with further intelligent computer based tutorial material, or, if needed, access by electronic messaging to the health and safety officer. Such a scenario could be the starting point for defining a target system of the future.

4 THREE STEPS IN STRATEGIC PLANNING

Before you can develop a strategy, you must have some objectives in mind, and before you can have objectives you must have a framework of concepts which enable you to articulate your objectives.

Thus the process of strategic planning is a three stage process

- devise a framework
- articulate your objectives
- plan to meet these objectives.

A key concept is that of the architecture of a strategic plan (and architecture supposes one or more architects). There must be a vision of what is required; there must be a means of discussing that vision with the "client" and reaching a realisation of the agreed vision.

An architecture has the following elements

- a language for describing functions, services, features, options etc.
- a design (using the language)
- documents on priorities, schedules, estimating, monitoring etc

We will illustrate many of these concepts in the sections which follow.

5 STRATEGIES FOR THE USE OF IT

If the VET system is to respond to the needs of the IT user, we clearly need to know about strategies for the use of IT. Here the author draws upon some work done by him with the User Panel of the UK Alvey Research programme [7] and on some very stimulating ideas emanating from the Sloan School of Management and MIT, together with some ideas on using IT to secure "competitive edge" developed at Harvard Business School. John Rockart at the Sloan School distinguishes four "eras" of information system [8]

- the accounting era : batch technologies, systems department driven
- the operational era : on-line technology, some user involvement, but systems department driven
- the information era : 4GLs, relational databases, PCs, networking; a partnership between users and systems staff
- the era of the "wired society" : this is the new strategic decision; linking not only within the organisation, but, more strikingly, linking organisations to each other.

Also identified were the move to "mission critical" systems, and the drive towards achieving competitive edge in the ways envisaged by Michael Porter at Harvard emerged as crucial [9]. The UK Alvey work confirmed the applicability of these ideas in the UK.

In terms of the strategy concepts outlined in the previous sections, the framework is the language of the "wired society", (mission criticality, competitive edge,etc). The target is, in Rockart's view, the "management of interdependance" [10]. In spite of seemingly independent organisational units being set up, successful organisations find it increasingly necessary to cut across organisational boundaries; even to link themselves into consortium arrangements with other organisations. IT serves a vital role in enabling this. An "architecture" for this would cover, for example

- IT for better customer service (Otis Elevator is a good example [11]
- IT for more efficient product delivery (not yet fully implemented anywhere)
- IT enabled team support (Groupware - a generic name for aids to support collaboration)
- Interactive budgeting
- The provision of user support (e.g. "Information Centres").

From the point of view of our objectives for a VET in IT system we see that we shall need

- a better understanding of the potential of IT among business people
- a better understanding of business and its strategic aims on the part of IT specialists
- a wider skill and understanding, throughout the workforce, in respect of IT and its use.

6 STRATEGIES FOR VET IN IT

Our framework for VET in IT is built around concepts of some antiquity, except that the use of IT has had some impact on their applicability and economic viability. In fact changes in the "productivity" of the VET system, so far, have been very small (compared with, for example, changes in the productivity of manufacturing industry over the last century). An emphasis on learning as opposed to teaching has become apparent. Framework concepts include

- tutoring (based on the old Socratic methods)
- listening to lectures (not very effective)
- coaching (based on correcting mistakes, usually on- the-job)
- discussions and other group learning activities
- self-study (often using audio/video/CBT technology).

We must use these approaches to meet our aim, through a process of life-long learning (to cope with the rate of change). There is much talk these days of "Human Resource Development" (HRD) to meet the needs of society. To meet the needs of the IT developers and users we need to produce

- more "hybrid" staff i.e. staff having strong experience in both IT and functional disciplines.

- IT staff who are capable of working effectively in teams (both teams of IT people and mixed user/IT teams); so often education fails to develop the skills needed (team working savours of cheating); yet much could be done e.g. in using walkthrough approaches to systems development.

- IT staff capable of developing easily used IT systems, and users demanding of such ease of use; again the academic approach often fails to develop the necessary skills; systems, if tested at all by other than the developer, are tested by fellow IT students; why not make IT students produce e.g. accounting systems which will be tested by accounting students? [11].

Finally, we discuss two very different attitudes to VET which are seldom held in either extreme view, but which do give rise to tensions in trying to develop VET systems. On the one hand we have a very "practical" approach.

A employer led; modular; competence based; short.

Whilst on the other hand we have a "theoretical" approach.

B academic - led; integrated; understanding based; long.

The view of the author is that both are needed, and may alternate in the course of any persons career. In fact approach B may be the most appropriate pre-employment approach. To develop in a first job some type A VET may be needed. For a "career jump", further type B VET may be appropriate, and so on. On a purely practical note, one can understand that employers could be asked to fund type A VET, but there is surely an obligation on the state to fund type B VET, since it is for the benefit of the state that human resources are developed as fully as possible. However both employers and states may view this issue differently according to their basic political standpoints.

7 CONCLUSION

This paper has outlined some approaches to the strategic planning of a VET system for IT. The author hopes that its publication will help to guide those with interests in developing VET systems in whatever context, curriculum, finance, manpower etc. In so far as the paper touches on practical issues of orienting courses of study to meet the needs of employers, the author hopes to encourage also some changes in the practice of VET in IT.

REFERENCES

[1] B Buckroyd & D Cornford
The IT Skills Crisis NCC 1988

[2] R N Anthony
Planning and Control Systems _ A Framework for Analysis. Harvard, Boston 1965

[3] The Funding of Vocational Education and Training
UK Manpower Services Commission (now Training Agency) 1987

[4] Changes in IT Skills - The Impact of Technology .
The Information Technology Skills Agency

[5] E Jantsch
Technological Forecasting in Perspective OECD Paris 1967

[6] P G Raymont
"Towards Fifth Generation Training Systems" in Barta & Raab (Eds). The Impact of Informatics on Vocational and Continuing Education, North Holland 1985

[7] Further User Environment (An Alvey Publication distributed by the IEE) 1987

[8] "The Line Takes the Leadership - IS Management in a Wired Society" JF Rockart Sloan Management Review Summer 1988

[9] "How Information Gives You Competitive Advantage"
M Porter & V Millar, Harvard Business Review July/August 1985

[10] "IT in the 1990s: Managing Organisational Interdependence" J F Rockhart & J E Short, Sloan Management Review Winter 1989

[11] P G Raymont
"A User Perspective on Informatics Education" in Lovis & Tagg (Eds) Computers in Education (ECCE 88) North Holland 1988.

Computers in Education
A. McDougall and C. Dowling (Editors)
Elsevier Science Publishers B.V. (North-Holland)

SITUATED COMPUTING IN PRE-SERVICE TEACHER EDUCATION

Chris BIGUM

Deakin University
Geelong, Victoria 3217
Australia

Computing in the pre-service education of teachers can take many forms. This paper discusses some aspects of the practices of computing in teacher education and describes the work that has been done at Deakin University in this respect.

1. INTRODUCTION

It is not so very long ago there were no computers in schools and there was no computing in teacher education courses. That all changed with the appearance of the first microcomputers. In a manner not unlike the way secondary and primary schools responded to perceived parent and community pressure, institutions with teacher education programs responded, albeit slowly, to the perceived needs of teachers and would-be teachers. Just as schools assimilated computing into the curriculum by creating space for subjects like computer literacy, awareness and studies, so too, in teacher education, subjects were created in the name of educational computing. Computing very quickly became a thing. It materialised in terms of timeslots, rooms, subjects, "expert" staff and assessment. The reification of computing in teacher education was and is still reflected in the steady stream of books, articles and tests offering 'definitive' lists of skills and knowledge for teachers[1].

In a discourse in which the dominant concern is technical, most commonly, how to do it better, computing in teacher education has been grounded in an uncritical acceptance of the new information technologies as a given. Rationales amount to little more than perpetuating the myths and rhetoric of an industry which has more than a passing interest in what occurs in schools. Relatively few engaged in computing in teacher education have asked other than technical questions[2]. The uncritical acceptance of the new information technologies in schools is paralleled in teacher education.

The parallels between what is happening in schools in computing and what is happening in teacher education remain strong. What I attempt to do in this brief paper is to critically examine the nature of educational computing in pre-service teacher education and outline an approach to computing that we have developed in the pre-service teacher education courses at Deakin. I have structured the paper around three questions:

- What is worth knowing in computing in teacher education?
- In whose interests is it that computing is a part of pre-service teacher education?
- How do we teach would-be teachers?

In the following discussion I use computing in place of educational computing. I take the word computing to mean using a computer.

2. WHAT IS WORTH KNOWING IN COMPUTING IN TEACHER EDUCATION

In order to make sense of what is taught under the label computing in teacher education it is worth recalling what was worth knowing in the first computing courses in teacher education. As happened in schools[3], what was taught was largely dictated by the computing experience of the people taking the course: expertise in programming in BASIC was translated into a course in BASIC programming and so on. From these early days, changes in what was seen to be important seemed to roughly follow the boom-bust cycles of successive waves of hardware and software, although strong local movements provided some perturbations to the commercial tides[4]. Teacher educators proved to be no less susceptible to the promise and hyperbole of every new piece of hardware and software than the rest of the computer using community. In fact many aspects of the fiercely competitive computer industry were reproduced in the community of teacher educators who promoted computing: keeping up with the latest became an implicit part of the job description<5>. There is little evidence of teacher education having any control over what was often perceived to be the juggernaut of computer technology that changed shape, price and power seemingly by the day. This sense of helplessness and uncritical compliance is faithfully reproduced in many teachers and schools.<6>

The computing market can therefore be seen as a structuring influence upon what counts as computing in teacher education and in education generally. In one sense, reproduction of what is 'out there' both in terms of schools and in terms of the industry is similar to other aspects of many teacher education courses. What is different is the uncritical manner in which computing new and old is interpreted for teachers and would-be teachers. The *problem* it seems is one of seeing where or how certain hardware or software 'fits into' an existing school curriculum. Questions that might vest teachers with control over computing in education are not asked.

The only level of critique if it could be called that, is the uninformed hostility by teacher educators towards the things with which they are unfamiliar or uncomfortable. This is a form of the loyalty that individuals often demonstrate towards the make of car or camera they own. Individuals can reaffirm their original financial outlay by expressing the view that brand X, which they just happen to own, is by far the best available for the money. In computing, and in teacher education, the same phenomenon works to denigrate hardware or software to which little or no professional commitment has been made. Preference disguised as critique enters the curriculum. The preference is 'justified' by resorting to whatever technocentric arguments are necessary. For instance a commonly held view in parts of Australia is that as a form of organising computers in schools, networks are bad because they support the centralisation of computing resources in a computer room.

While it is instructive to point to the commercial and historical influences and their idiosyncratic mediation in computing courses for teachers, a greater concern is that whatever teachers are taught is taught within an entirely unproblematic framework: the new information technologies are givens and the only problem is the engineering one of seeing how suited different computing technologies can be used in education. There is no awareness of views like Rosen's [9] who argues that this century is the 'Age of Syntactics' in which meaning is reduced to syntax. This perspective is one that many teacher educators would regard as unimportant. Even for the better known critics like Joseph Weizenbaum [10], there seems little evidence that teacher educators have paid anything but scant regard to his warnings about and critique of computing. Beyond Weizenbaum there is little awareness of the work of Dreyfus & Dreyfus [11], Hinkson [12], Chesneaux [13], Aronowitz & Giroux [14], Bowers [15] and Cooley [16] who understand the new information technologies as a good deal more than how best to do it:

> The choices are essentially political and ideological rather than technological. As we design technological systems, we are in fact designing sets of social relationships, and as we question those social relationships and attempt to design systems differently, we are then beginning to challenge, in a fundamental way, power structures in society.
>
> The alternatives are stark. Either we will have a future in which human beings are reduced to a sort of beelike behaviour, reacting to the systems and equipment specificed for them, or we will have a future in which masses of people conscious of their skills and abilities in both a political and technical sense, decide that they are going to be the architects of a new form of technological development which will enhance human creativity and mean more freedom of choice and expression rather than less. The truth is, we shall have to make the profound politcal decision as to whether we intend to act as architects or behave like bees. (Cooley [17])

In contrast to the one dimensional, technical understandings that dominate the discourse of educational computing in teacher education circles, critics of the information technologies point to political and economic understandings of the computerization of society. Understandings such as these do not count as worth knowing in computing in teacher education. These understandings go much further than the innocuous considerations of 'computers in society' that seem mandatory elements of many computing courses for teachers.

3. IN WHOSE INTERESTS IS IT THAT COMPUTING IS A PART OF PRE-SERVICE TEACHER EDUCATION?

Rather than seeing computing in pre-service eacher education in terms of a necessary response to the requirements of a new information age society, it is instructive to see how much of this practice can be reconsidered in terms of a different requirement: the preparation of an education community that is an efficient and effective consumer of the products of the new information technologies. Teaching would-be teachers about the evaluation and selection of hardware and software, and the integration of computing into all aspects of the curriculum and administration of schooling then take on interesting new meanings. There is a symbiosis that has developed between the computing industry and education. It has attracted little attention apart from some comment about the drift of teachers into sales and training positions in the computing industry. While the industry is keen to portray itself as serving the interests of schooling, it is certainly not in its interests to highlight other aspects of the unusually close relationship it has with education. For instance, if the amount of taxpayer's money that directly goes to the manufacturers and distributors of hardware and software were published as frequently as euphoric accounts of computer use in classrooms then the community may be better placed to ask questions about the wisdom of such expenditure. As important as direct sales to schools and universities are the 'flow-on' purchases that occur through the promotion of particular hardware and software that are used in education and that result in purchases by teachers, parents and students.

4. HOW DO WE TEACH WOULD-BE TEACHERS?

It is less than ten years ago that the microcomputers which provided the means for much of computing in education, began to be used in schools in any number. Yet we now find a staggering array of courses and subjects in teacher education with the word computer or information technology in their name. The institutionalising of computing in pre-service teacher education is more than just a means of providing teachers with understandings of computing. Courses convey the message that computing is learned or best learned or most efficiently learned in a course. Computing is thus reified not only in the minds of teacher educators but also in the minds of would-be teachers.

It is useful to ask how the people who designed these courses got on when they began their foray into computing. Did they have the 'benefit' of a course on software evaluation? Did they do a course in word processing before they began to use one? Did they do courses in how to 'apply' a computer to the teaching of History? It seems that the ways that those who introduced computing into pre-service teacher education learned about computing are either too difficult to reproduce, inefficient or simply wrong.

These questions presuppose something about the way teacher educators learned their computing. To fill in the contrast I want to draw upon my recollections of how I learned computing and compare it to what is commonly required of teachers and would-be teachers in computer education courses.

When I learned to use a word processor I did it with a manual, with occasional help from someone who knew more than I about the software and in the context of having a writing task to do. Student teachers have lessons. When I learned a programming language, I did so with a manual, with some help from more experienced friends and in the context of having a real task to complete in the language, a task that was important to me. Student teachers have classes in Logo, Prolog and other unmentionable languages. When I learn a new computing related skill, I do so either from a manual, or having someone who knows how show me but *always* in the context of having a real task to do, a problem to solve. Student teachers on the other hand are given an arbitrary set of skills and experiences that are devoid of any purpose other than fulfilling someone else's agenda for the use of computers. The kind of situated learning about which Brown et al. [18] write seems far removed from the practices of computing courses for would-be teachers. Maybe I am the odd one out. Maybe the rest of my colleagues have spent their lives doing courses in using the new information technologies in education?

There will be some that make arguments about time, timetables and the pressure of both.<7> There will be some who say it is *only* an introduction and the best we can do. 'Only introductions' no matter how only, carry powerful messages to students: they tell students that computing is no different from the rest of the subject matter they have been fed throughout their schooling. They tell students that there are experts and users. They tell the student that when they go into their own classroom that the way to 'do computer' is to reproduce what they have experienced in their teacher education. Importantly 'only introductions' preclude the student from engaging in critical enquiry thereby developing autonomy in dealing with the new information technologies in education.

It is possible to argue for the teaching of computing in teacher education in terms of add-on subjects and courses in that, after all, the rest of the teacher education curriculum is constructed along similar lines, i.e. if we want students to know about X then we need to run a course in X. It is difficult to hold current teacher education practices as some kind of educational ideal. By making computing a part of the structure of pre-service teacher education, a measure of electronic endorsement is given to teaching practices and structures which should have changed at the end of the industrial revolution. As Hamilton argues:

> ... educational practice lies at the intersection of economic history and the history of ideas. That is the pedagogical practices of an epoch are expressions of both material and ideological resources. (Hamilton [20])

Hamilton traces the origins of the present structures of schooling into the eighteenth century and maps the ideological and material resources that gave rise to notions of school, classroom and timetable. He demonstrates that the structure and logic of the *modern* curriculum is grounded in the material and ideological resources of the eighteenth century. As I have argued elsewhere (Bigum [21]) there are considerable problems in recourse to an argument that relies upon claims for an information age, thereby drawing upon *postmodern* ideas and argument in order to locate computing in a what is a *modern* curriculum.

5. COMPUTING IN PRE-SERVICE TEACHER EDUCATION AT DEAKIN

There are *no* computing courses in the pre-service teacher education programmes in the School of Education at Deakin. Students engage in computing in the context of their education courses. Each course has some computing as an integral part of it. This approach to computing is supported in two ways: a professional development program for academic staff, and an open access work space for students.

In order to have students experience computing as a normal part of a course, requires that the staff who teach the course need to have developed their own understandings of computing and are able to exploit computing for their teaching purposes. The professional development of staff has been carried out around computing practices that support their scholarly work, i.e. the preparation, sharing and communication of text, as well as some modelling for some staff. The consequent reshaping of the work practices of the School has been the basis for an on-going debate among staff about the new information technologies, work and education. The debate is also informed by a project which is directed at theorising the new information technologies in education (See Green and Bigum [22]. This project draws upon postmodern literature from a wide variety of fields and disciplines as a basis for reframing our understandings of the new information technologies in education.

When a course team<8> plans future teaching, it invites one of the staff with responsibilities for supporting the use of the new information technologies in education to its meetings. Computing is considered in terms of two conditions: that its use in the course supports the planned teaching and, that its use is such that course team members are either familiar or comfortable with the proposed application. Once a decision has been made, the work to ensure that the application is able to be used by students is carried out by technical staff.

Some examples will convey something of the work that has been done to date. In a third year Education Studies course, the course team had constructed a pedagogy based upon student responses to a curriculum text. The text was in draft form and was being worked on by a colleague in Scotland. The course team wanted tutorial groups to collectively write responses to parts of the text. Sharing between tutorial groups was less of a priority but was seen as useful. The text was divided up so that students would work on a number of chapters during each week of the course. Students used word processing software to prepare their responses and took advantage of being on a local area network to share text and the preparation of responses. Tutorial group responses were posted to an electronic bulletin board. At the end of each week the course team read each tutorial group response and synthesized a class response which was also posted to the bulletin board. The class response was then sent by electronic mail to the curriculum scholar in Scotland who reacted to the class response. His comments were also posted to the local bulletin board. Students were then able to make use of these exchanges in the preparation of essays which were based upon themes taken from the original text.

While such investigations might be regarded as extreme, it nevertheless was the choice of the staff concerned in that year and represents the approach that is taken in all of the pre-service teacher education courses at Deakin. Another example concerned a first year language course in which the staff wanted students to investigate different forms of conversation. Students would tape record short pieces of conversation set in particular contexts and transcribe the material for subsequent analysis. Staff were concerned to allow students to draw upon a wider range of data than they had individually collected. It was decided to set up a research archive on the local area network in which students would deposit their work so that their peers could draw upon the data. The exercise was continued over a number of years so that students in following years could make use of data collected years earlier.

This approach to computing has been in place in all years of the course for the past four years.[9] There are therefore many other examples. In the main, applications involve text preparation and sharing either using bulletin board software or database software. There has been some work with spreadsheets, desktop publishing software, LOGO (See Ellerton and Bigum [23]). and expert system shell software. In the instance of each application, issues and questions about the use of computing arise in the context of the work of the course.

The other part of supporting computing in pre-service teacher education at Deakin is the maintenance of an open-access work space for students which is known as the ECL (Educational Computing Laboratory). Apart from the provision of hardware and software, we have placed considerable emphasis upon creating a climate which is consistent with the view we hold about the teaching and learning of knowledge and skills in computing for teachers. One part of this is having a space in which attention has been payed to offsetting keyboards, screens and printers with plants, ergonomic furniture, partitions and fish tanks. In addition the ECL is arranged to accommodate students who choose to work alone, in pairs or in larger groups.

Students assume a good deal of the responsibility for the management and responsibilities in the ECL. In particular, all students have a responsibility to support other students in solving technical problems.[10] We stress the importance of a human support network in the use of computing in the ECL and while there are inevitably some problems which require the support of technical staff, a high proportion of answers to the 'how do I' questions are provided by students. The ECL has become over time one of the key focal meeting places for students. A convivial atmosphere pervades the space even in the frantic days before an assignment is due.

Apart from having the majority of our computing resources attached to a local area network, the other feature worthy of note is that we have a number of laptop computers that students may borrow in order to input text away from the ECL. When students return to the ECL they transfer text from the laptop to a computer attached to the network for formatting, printing, spell checking and so on.

Because there is at least one computing-based piece of work in each course, all students engage in some computing during their pre-service experience. We take the view that because pre-service teacher education is the beginning of an on-going professional development for the teacher, that decisions to do further computing is the responsibility of the student. We encourage and provide extensive support for students to use the computing resources of the School outside of that required by their courses. Bulletin board software and electronic mail software are used routinely by frequent users of the ECL for many purposes. About a third of the students use the resources of the ECL to support most of their student work. For all students, computing is situated in their work as students. As Brown et al. argue:

Activity, concept and culture are interdependent. No one can be totally understood without the other two. Learning must involve all three. Teaching methods often try to impart abstracted concepts as fixed, well-defined, independent entities that can be explored in prototypical examples and textbook exercises. But such exemplification cannot provide the important insights into either the culture or the authentic activities of members of that culture that learners need. (Brown et al.[24]).

NOTES

<1> See for example Flemister [1], Woodhouse and McDougall [2], Anderson et al. [3].

<2> Troyer [4] reviews the literature in respect of endorsement and criticism of teacher computer literacy education. Bowers [5] presents a detailed critique of computing in education generally. Moursund [6] criticizes Colleges of Education for not doing a good job.

<3> See for example the case study material of the National Evaluation Study, Bigum et al. [7].

<4> In Victoria compared with some other Australian states for instance, there has always been a strong interest in LOGO .

<5> The competitiveness of the industry was also reproduced in the way that individuals would derive kudos from being among the first to have access to a particular piece of hardware or software.

<6> See for example Bigum [8].

<7> Paulo Freire has an eloquent critique of 'educators' who use arguments about time. He shows how such arguments betray a basic assumption about the nature of teaching and learning, i.e. that students are empty vessels. See Freire [19].

<8> Courses are designed, planned and taught in teams at Deakin.

<9> In the beginning it was phased in a year at a time.

<10> It is a condition of having access to the work space.

REFERENCES

[1] Flemister, Michael G., Journal of Research on Computing in Education 20 (1988) 213.

[2] Woodhouse, D., and McDougall, A., Computers. Promise and Challenge in Education (Blackwell Scientific Publications, Melbourne, 1986)

[3] Anderson, R.E., Krohn, K. and Saunders, R.S., The Minnesota literacy and awareness assessment test (Minnesota Educational Computing Consortium, St Paul, Minnesota, 1980)

[4] Troya, M. B., Journal of Research on Computing in Education 20 (1988) 141.

[5] Bowers, C.A., The Cultural Dimensions of Educational Computing. Understanding the Non-Neutrality of Technology (Teachers College Press, New York, 1988)

[6] Moursund, Dave, The Computing Teacher 16 (1989) 4.

[7] Bigum C. et al., Coming to terms with computers in schools (Deakin Institute for Studies in Education, Deakin University, Geelong, 1987).

[8] Bigum, C., Architects of Bees? Understanding the new technologies, in Bigum et al., Coming to terms with computers in schools (Deakin Institute for Studies in Education, Deakin University, Geelong, 1987).

[9] Rosen, R., On the Scope of Syntactics in Mathematics and Science: The Machine Metaphor in Casti, J.L. and Karlqvist, A. (eds.), Real Brains Artificial Minds (North-Holland, New York, 1987).

[10] Weizenbaum, J., Computer Power and Human Reason (Penguin, Harmondsworth, Middlesex, 1984).

[11] Dreyfus, H.L. & Dreyfus, S.E., Mind Over Machine (The Free Press, New York, 1986).

[12] Hinkson, J., Arena 80, (1987) 123.

[13] Chesneaux, J., Arena 81, (1987) 26.

[14] Aronowitz, H. & Giroux, H.A., Education Under Siege (Bergin & Garvey, Boston, Ma, 1985).

[15] Bowers, C.A., The Cultural Dimensions of Educational Computing. Understanding the Non-Neutrality of Technology (Teachers College Press, New York, 1988)

[16] Cooley, M., Architect or Bee? The Human Price of Technology (The Hogarth Press, London, 1987).

[17] ibid, p. 180.

[18] Brown, J. S., Collins, A. and Duguid, P., Educational Researcher, 18 (1989) 32.

[19] Freire, P., Education: The Practice of Freedom (Writers and Readers Publishing Co-Operative, London, 1974).

[20] Hamilton, D., Journal of Curriculum Studies 12 (1980) 282.

[21] Bigum, C., Archiving the past in T. Dupé (ed.) ACEC89 Backup the Future, Proceedings of the 11th Australian Computers in Education Conference, Canberra.(1989), pp. 58-64.

[22] Green, B. and Bigum, C., Quantum Curriculum and Chaotic Classrooms: Reframing Educational Computing, this volume.

[23] Ellerton, N.F. & Bigum, C., Learning Logo as part of the mathematics education program for pre-service education students, Proceedings of the 3rd International Logo and Mathematics Education Conference, Montreal.(1987).

[24] Brown, J. S., Collins, A. and Duguid, P., Educational Researcher, 18 (1989) 33.

Computers in Education
A. McDougall and C. Dowling (Editors)
Elsevier Science Publishers B.V. (North-Holland)
IFIP, 1990

VIDEODISC FOR INTERACTIVE TESTING

Fred BOSMAN and Hans FEENSTRA

Cito, National Institute for Educational Measurement, P.O. Box 1034, 6801, MG, ARNHEM, The Netherlands

The use of videodiscs as a tool for education is quite common in training with an industrial or military background. In the regular (Dutch) education, i.e. in public schools and colleges, only a few applications of videodiscs as an educational tool, are available.

In 1987, the Dutch Ministry of Education published an official document, to promote the use of the so called 'new media and new technologies' in the regular Dutch Educational System. One of the results of the policy based on that document is, that the department of Vocational Education of Cito (the Dutch National Institute for Educational Measurement) has developed a test for the assessment of vocational qualifications of pharmaceutical chemist's assistants. This test is based on the interactive use of a videodisc, under control of a program on a PC.

This test is developed within the context of a number of activities in the field of 'testing and new media'.

1. INTRODUCTION

In vocational education and more specifically in the welfare oriented sectors of secondary vocational education, it is hard to assess the whole complex of the vocational qualifications of students who almost have finished their training. The aims of vocational education are often complex and more practical and attitudinal rather than purely cognitive in structure. In particular, education for a number of specific vocational qualifications at a higher level, is an example of education with a complex structure of theoretical and practical skills. A good way of doing a job involves not only performing a number of practical skills, but also a profound knowledge of the applicable theory. It is a big problem for schools and educators to establish a sound, 'real life' kind of assessment for these skills. An example of such a skill which is difficult to test, is a proper social intercourse with other people, as part of professional duties.

One part in the field of secondary vocational education in Holland, in which the above described problems occur, are the schools for social welfare and public health service. Inside these schools the department of pharmaceutical chemist's assistants is selected for the first application of a new kind of assessment of complex skills. This new assessment consists of an interactively used videodisc based on a computer program. The subject of the program is "dispensing medicines to patients". We suppose that testing based on the interactive use of video is an appealing and efficient way of measuring learning results, see also Sales [1].

In the last months of 1988 a preliminary examination of costs and profits of the project was carried out. The conclusions of that examination were used to ask the Ministry of Education for a subsidy for the development of the program and the videodisc. This subsidy was granted in April 1989 and the actual development started in May 1989. The program and videodisc are scheduled to be ready for use in May 1990. Evaluation in the schools will take place in May, June and September 1990.

2. BACKGROUND OF THE PROJECT

As already stated, it is difficult to make a valid test of the complex practical and theoretical skills required for a chemist's assistant. It is relatively easy to make a reliable test for the cognitive aspects of this subject only. The problem is that the results of those tests only give partial information about a student's ability to do her/his professional job. Interactive use of a videodisc is supposed to be a possible way of solving this problem, see Laurillard [2].

Doing a professional job requires not only a good theoretical background in the subject but also the ability to use this knowledge in the right way. The opportunities for practising skills in health care are present, but only for a relatively short period per student. In an ideal situation each student should have her or his own patients. Those patients should all behave identically for a reliable result. It is impossible to realise this in practice. Using the interactive possibilities of a videodisc solves this problem. A professional actor is required to act as a patient only once. In that case every student faces the same patient in the same circumstances.
Developing a reliable, valid and attractive test is the first important goal of the project, but there is a second even more important aim. This aim is getting experience in developing this kind of materials. In the near future, there will be a great demand for reliable, attractive and easy to use instruments for learning and testing. Therefore we feel that it is necessary for our department to keep up to date with, and explore further, the nature of interactive technologies.

A third goal of this project is to participate in a study on the adjustment of a number of psychometric values for interactive testing. Interactivity means that not every student tackles the problems stated in the test in the same way. That is the reason for different calculations of difficulty, reliability and validity (if it is at all possible to make these calculations in an interactive educational setting). It is not the intention of the project to establish a new kind of test theory, but the results of the evaluation in schools can be used for this purpose in the future.

The educational reasons for selecting the pharmaceutical assistants training as the first subject for an interactive test, were the following:

- educational aims are defined clearly and will not change within the first few years,
- practical skills can be assessed objectively, which means that there is a clear difference between correct and incorrect skills,
- the right behaviour in complex situations is part of the training and the student can demonstrate that behaviour,
- interactive use of a videodisc gives a better representation of reality than present testing methods.

3. FRAMEWORK OF THE PROJECT

The test is based on the requirements in the examprogram. This program is published by the Ministry. From this program the following skills are selected:

problem solving skills:

- point out some specific problems; for instance: possible interaction between different medicines,
- be able to analyse certain problems; for instance: check between medicines delivered in the past and a new prescription,
- gather relevant information and interpret that information correctly; for instance: knowing where to find the rules and regulations for a specific prescription and carry out these rules,
- distinguish between decisions and actions which solve a problem and those which don't; for instance: if a physician has written a prescription with an unfamiliar (maybe wrong!) proportion, decide which person to consult (colleague, chemist, physician's assistant or physician).

determine the correct sequence of actions, work efficiently;

for instance: gather all the necessary information from the client, before starting the prescription's route through the dispensary.

practice a number of social skills;

for instance: react politely to an angry or impatient client.

The examination program is based on skills and knowledge that can be assessed with available testing methods. In the ordinary testing and examination situation it is impossible to assess a number of skills, specifically those that combine theory and practice in a real life situation, as stated earlier. A lot of chemists complains that newly certified assistants cannot handle the work at the counter. Our test contributes towards alleviation of this complaint.

It is clear that an interactive test which is specifically developed for assessing complex skills (for instance a counter with patients) has some learning effects. This is not the place to discuss the consequences of interactivity on learning and testing, but it is becoming more and more obvious that, as a result of interactivity, the difference between 'learning' and 'testing' is harder to pinpoint, as Ives [3] stated.

Examples of skills in pharmaceutical practice, which can be assessed better by means of an interactively used videodisc are:

- consulting the right person at the right time and doing the right consultations,
- processing the route of the prescription in the dispensary with the use of a computer,
- interpreting computer messages,
- making right choices out of the stock of medicines, with respect to the day of decay,
- counting and filling right proportions of medicines,
- delivering prescriptions to the right persons,
- communicating politely with clients,
- giving clients information about the prescription, while respecting the clients own involvement,
- explaining in ordinary language the use of the medicine.

4. THE TEST

The test itself consists of five different prescriptions. Each prescription functions as an independant case. Students have to pass sequentially through the cases. The student has to make decisions on all of the 'build-in problems' of the prescriptions. Every decision is recorded on the PC-disk in a log-file, for later judgement and comment by the teacher. Every decision and every answer results in another path through the test. The computer program in turn, reacts to answers and actions of the student. For every predicted student action an adequate reaction is included in the program. In the case of nonsense answers and random actions of a student the program asks for more details and more information. The program as a whole has a very open structure and in every part of the program a student has the option to choose whatever she or he wants to do next.

An average student needs about two lessons (approximately 90 minutes) to make the test. After the test the student gets feedback. Feedback during the test is contradictory with the purpose of testing. Also it would divert the student's attention from the problems presented and cost too much time. Feedback however, as Cohen [4] stated, is necessary. The feedback shows all the cases again at the end of the testing session. Every case is supplemented with comments and remarks on the student's actions, given by the chemist who is the actor in all the cases. The feedback is composed out of the log file mentioned earlier. A print-out of the log-file gives the teacher the opportunity for more detailed feedback and comments addressed to the student after the test is completed. The teacher is able to give a judgement and/or a mark based on this whole set of actions and choices in the test. For instance a teacher will then give an advice on what to revise and when to resit the test.

5. TECHNICAL SPECIFICATIONS OF THE TEST

In co-operation with Extraware, a courseware development company settled in Amsterdam, a list of specifications was made. Extraware has a wide experience in making videodisc-based

training materials for a number of Dutch companies.
In 1987 Extraware was the winner of the "NVWFT Interactive Media Award" for the program "Per Expresse", made for training of Dutch Post Office employees (NVWFT is the Dutch Association for Scientific Film and Television).
In 1989 Extraware got the "Sony Video Award 1989" for a program developed for training of AH-employees. AH (Albert Heyn) is the biggest chain of supermarkets in Holland.

Program writing, in TenCore, realization of the video materials and other technical affairs on hardware, is put out on contract to Extraware.

Staffmembers of Cito are responsible for all the educational matters in the project. A chemist and a number of assistants are responsible (as external writers) for the pharmaceutical expertise.

Two conditions were superimposed on the project:

- IBM/MS-DOS like computers are, as a result of the government stimulation of computer use, wide-spread in schools,
- many dispensaries in Holland use branch-specific computer software named PHARIAS. This program is also used in the schools. Parts of the program are simulated in the test.

Concerning the hardware, a number of choices has been made (the following is an extract of the hardware chapter of the global design of the test):

- the PC is an IBM-AT (or alike) with MS-DOS as operating system,
- a harddisk and a floppydrive are used,
- a mouse is used as input device,
- the following extra features are added:
- video-overlay (video-output and PC-output on the same screen),
- fieldstore (more space on the disc, quiet image and a far better method of changing from one image to another),
- audio-digitizing (digitized speech is stored on harddisk, giving more and better opportunities for updating, and space saving still-video/audio combination),
- Betacam is used as video-standard with digital editing of the master tape.

The global design (ready June 1989) has been worked out in detail into a micro design (ready December 1989). In November 1989 program writing and video production were started. Direct discs were ready in April 1990. Use and evaluation of the test is started in May 1990 and will be completed in September 1990. A final report about the outcomes of the evaluation in schools will be published in October 1990.

References:

[1] Sales, G.C., The Computing Teacher (May 1989) 27.
[2] Laurillard, D., (ed) Interactive Media, working methods and practical applications (Chichester, 1987).
[3] Ives, W., Educational Technology (29-5, 1989) 50.
[4] Cohen, V.B., Educational Technology (24-1, 1984) 16.

Computers in Education
A. McDougall and C. Dowling (Editors)
Elsevier Science Publishers B.V. (North-Holland)

IT AIN'T WHAT YOU DO, IT'S THE WAY THAT YOU DO IT

Stephen BROWN

Distance Learning Unit, British Telecom Management College, 219 Queensway, Bletchley, Milton Keynes, MK2 2DQ, U.K.

British Telecom has recently implemented a major programme of training courses for managers which integrate open learning with more traditional elements. This paper assesses the effectiveness of one such course. The main conclusions reached are that open learning in general and interactive video in particular is a hugely cost-effective training platform for large organisations but the design of the infrastructure and the ways in which students are introduced to the medium are as important as the design of the training material itself.

1. INTRODUCTION

1.1. Changing environment

Since 1984 the commercial environment of British Telecom has changed significantly. Privatisation, deregulation and expansion have necessitated considerable changes in the way the organisation is structured and run. New technology has added further momentum to such change. These changes require new skills, attitudes, knowledge and ways of working and hence there is an urgent and ongoing need for staff training and development.

1.2. BT management training programme

New managers in BT receive a minimum of 5 weeks training in each of their first two years and 2 weeks minimum per year thereafter. On one hand it is recognised that this represents only relatively short periods of time for training during a working career and it is important therefore to maximise the effectiveness of this valuable time resource. On the other hand, given the size of the company, it amounts to a major training commitment. With over 35,000 managers worldwide the training requirement is currently running at about 66,000 student training weeks per year.

In the past BT training needs have been met largely through conventional face-to-face training courses delivered at a small number of classroom based colleges. But the sheer scale of the task facing the company now requires more radical solutions.

Traditional training methods cannot produce either the quantity or the quality of training needed in this context. Centrally delivered courses are costly in terms of accommodation, travel costs, tutor provision and time away from the job. Managers are reluctant, for a variety of reasons, to attend residential courses and the sheer scale of the training programme ensures that there are always long waiting lists for places.

Locally delivered training eases some of these problems but creates new ones in their place. Regional variations in aims, content and delivery schedules can arise in response to locally perceived needs. Standards of accommodation and delivery can be extremely variable and the scale of the training programme necessitates enormous numbers of trainers to be trained and licensed to teach the same subject nation-wide.

In both cases the quality of training is tutor dependent, with all the variability that inevitably implies, and the training emphasis is on delivery rather than design in terms of resource allocation.

The proposed solution is an integrated programme of face-to-face and open learning components. Company policy is to provide 35% of management training in open learning form by 1992.

Open learning provides the opportunity to decentralise training to local units, thus improving access for large numbers of students while maintaining consistency through centralised design. In combination with other training methods it allows for flexibility while reducing both implementation times and running costs.

2. APPRAISAL AND COUNSELLING

2.1. Course design

One of the first such courses, launched in late 1987 is called Appraisal and Counselling. Originally a three day centrally delivered event, Appraisal and Counselling has been redesigned as a multi-media package comprising a video cassette introduction, an interactive video disc with text support, and a one day follow-up workshop delivered locally with further video and text elements.

2.2. IV Design

The core of the new Appraisal and Counselling course is the interactive video (IV) component. This introduces the knowledge and concepts relevant to the subject and provides opportunities for cognitive skills practice. It is intended to provide background information for managers, to review the purpose and principles of Appraisal and Counselling and to clarify the procedures involved. The IV is also designed to provide a grounding in the skills of Appraisal and Counselling. The follow-up workshop gives managers an opportunity to review and discuss the main points presented in the IV, to relate them to their own particular circumstances and provides an opportunity for behavioural skills practice.

The disc, which is doubled sided, is structured as follows:

Side 1: Appraisal
Introduction
Overview of the course
Attitudes to appraisal
Stages in appraisal
Understanding performance
The appraisal form
Case studies
Summary/test

Side 2: Counselling
Revision
Overview
Attitudes to counselling
The six critical steps in counselling
Preparing to be counselled
Counselling skills
Example interviews
Summary/test

The IV is mouse driven from computer generated menu screens. The modular design allows sections of the IV to be studied in any order although there is an implicit sequence in the way the sections are ordered. A mixture of moving video, computer and video graphics is used to present case material and examples, exercises and information.

From the main menu users can ask for an overview of the course, help, a progress report or exit from the course. During video sequences normal video controls are available via screen icons which appear when the space bar in pressed. These and other features are explained within the course itself.

Other design features include the opportunity to ask for explanations of answers to test questions, alternative phrasings of statements, more detail, examples, review of video sequences, a notepad facility for personal use and a comments pad for comments about the course.

3. EVALUATION DESIGN

3.1. Independent assessment

It was felt that since this form of training would be new to most of those using it, a thorough evaluation of how people reacted to it would a helpful guide to future developments in terms of both hardware and software. We chose the Open University to carry out the study because we wanted an independent assessment from an organisation which understood the issues in open learning. The study, Kirkwood [1], has been conducted in three phases:

3.2. Phase 1a: Survey of trainees.

In phase one 14 regional units (districts) and 2 other BT administrative units were surveyed via a postal questionnaire. The trainees survey was targeted at BT junior and middle managers ie. the target audience for appraisal and counselling training. The threshold for analysis was set at 200 responses and the findings used to devise a structured interview for trainees.

3.3. Phase 1b: Survey of trainers

At the same time twenty local trainers from 11 districts were surveyed to obtain their views on the course.

3.4. Phase 2: Structured interviews

The second phase was designed to collect less formal data on people's feelings and attitudes. A smaller sample of the managers who had completed the course were interviewed (9 managers from 3 BT districts). Most members of the sample had 20 plus years service with BT although the range was from 3-39 years. In addition, follow-up interviews with district trainers were conducted in 2 districts based on the findings of the questionnaire survey.

3.5. Phase 3: Analysis of impact

The third and probably most important phase examined the impact of the training on the behaviour of BT managers. This phase, which at the time of writing was still being conducted, entailed interviews with appraisers and appraisees; line managers and subordinates; and analysis of actual appraisal forms completed before and after training.

4. EVALUATION FINDINGS

4.1. Attitudes to hardware

Most users (76%) had had no previous experience of using interactive video and only 2.5% had experienced more than one, which reflects the novelty of IV as a training medium. More surprisingly nearly three fifths (58%) had had no experience of computer based training of any kind.

Some trainees (21.5%) found using the IV difficult due to the locations of workstations within BT distance learning centres. Typical problems were screen reflections and poor contrast because of ambient lighting conditions, noise, interruptions, poor ventilation, uncomfortable headphones and insufficient table space to operate the mouse or take notes.

A high proportion (39%) reported difficulties with the IV equipment or the IV itself due to unfamiliarity. Use of the mouse in particular was observed to be difficult. However initial hardware and workstation location problems were quickly resolved. Although trainees initially reported low levels of confidence in their ability to use the IV workstation controls, their confidence improved considerably as they worked through side 1 of the IV. Initially men tended to feel much more confident than women but after some practice this difference in attitude disappeared.

4.2. How the IV was used

Most trainees worked through the material in the order presented in the menu. Only about one tenth (9.5%: side 1, 12%: side 2) chose to miss any sections although rather more (55.5% and 39.5% respectively) took the opportunity to view some sections more than once.

About three fifths (61%) made use of the video controls and half (55%) referred to the Help option on the main menu. The other design features were comparatively under used.

4.3. Attitudes to software

Commenting on the design of the IV, trainees reported that they particularly liked having summaries and test sections to check understanding. They also liked being able to work at their own pace and they liked the flexibility of the IV design.

On the other hand nearly two thirds (63%) of the trainees thought that the Appraisal and Counselling situations depicted in the video segments of the IV were rather too straightforward compared with real life and a further 46.5% thought the settings were rather false.

4.4. Attitudes to the course overall

The combination of IV and a workshop was received very well. The IV was seen as good preparation for the workshop which further clarified both the purpose and principles and the procedures and skills of appraisal and counselling. The workshop was welcomed by trainees as an opportunity to exchange views (81.5%) and demonstrate what had been learned from the IV (45.5%).

Overall, trainees felt they learned a lot from the course as a whole, 80.5% reported that they felt more confident in their own ability to appraise and counsel their staff. In addition 61% felt the course was very appropriate to their job and a further 27% said it was highly appropriate.

Approximately half the respondents said the course as a whole was interesting and fun, they liked learning from the IV and for those new to the medium their first experience of IV training was considered to have been successful.

4.5. Cost-effectiveness

At the time of writing this research was still being conducted but preliminary results from interviews suggest that there has been a significant improvement in the way in which appraisals are being conducted. In addition, a comparison of the costs of developing and running the new course during the first 18 months revealed a saving of £1.4 million compared with the previous version of the course.

5. CONCLUSIONS

The result is a highly cost-effective training tool, yet the content of the new course is essentially the same as its predecessor. The differences lie in the way the content is presented to the students and the ways in which they use it. The key issues are:

Ease of access. The combination of IV and locally delivered training makes the new course more accessible to more people.

Flexibility. Students can work through the IV in any order, at their own pace, and as often as they like. The evidence here suggests that the package has more flexibility than the target audience required.

Dialogue. Although many of the design features were under used there is a strong sense of student involvement in the material, arising from the ways in which interactions were built in.

In addition to confirming our belief that open learning is a cost-effective way of meeting our training needs, the study taught us some important lessons about how the way that you do it affects the kind of results you get.

New users should be introduced to the hardware in a sensitive, supported way. The features available to the user within the package should be made clearly visible and their utility fully explained. The levels of support, help and advice given to a user within a package should adapt to the user's level of experience. The design of the workstation environment is crucial to the success or otherwise of media based learning materials.

REFERENCES

[1] Kirkwood, A., Report on the Evaluation of British Telecom Appraisal and Counselling Training Package (Open University 1988).

Computers in Education
A. McDougall and C. Dowling (Editors)
Elsevier Science Publishers B.V. (North-Holland)

COMPUTER-BASED TRAINING AND ADVANCED TRAINING TECHNOLOGIES

S. CHARP

Editor-in-Chief, Technological Horizons in Education, Upper Darby, PA, U.S.A.

Use of advanced technologies in training, information technology professions and computer end-users is growing. Individualized computer-based systems have proven effective to help meet the demand for more education and training.

1. INTRODUCTION

More and more educational institutions are recognizing the need for skilled employees to build and maintain a quality work force and to better provide for the acquisition of new knowledge in a changing world. The complex requirements of our society demand ever-greater knowledge and skills. To help organizations meet the challenges of change, initial training and continuing education have become major concerns. Use of latest developments in technologies is being investigated. Individualized computer-based systems have come into existence. These are used at any location and require minimal involvement by training personnel. The role of the instructor becomes one of administering the training. Students are free at any time to skip over material they already understand or repeat any portions for better comprehension. Administrative and report-generating capabilities permit an instructor to monitor the performance of each student and provide assistance as required. Multi-media presentation makes information come alive for the student, is far more interesting and results in greater retention. The use of new tools and methods, such as computer-aided instruction, satellite programs, and interactive video discs is growing rapidly. However, it must be remembered that productivity gains are not achieved solely by successful technological innovations, and from new hardware and software, but from changes in organization management, human resources and operational objectives.

2. ISSUES AND CONCERNS

Computer-based training of information technology personnel and end-users is being given careful consideration at an international level. To adapt to the changes made imperative by rapidly developing modern technology and the restructuring of industry and services requires new methods and curricula. Education is being criticized for not taking into consideration the changes in technology and the redefining of work needs, and not cooperating to any extent with industry, adversely affecting the real marketable working skills of students entering employment after graduation. Traditional instructional material has not been able to keep pace with expanded corporate and institutional demands. The result of a recent U.S. study on how to develop a strategic plan for the implementation of computer-based training in an organization listed the following as most critical:

* Awareness of need for change - key leaders must understand elements of training methodology.

* Understanding of the real vs. perceived need - looking at successes and failures of competitors' training efforts is critical.

* Recognizing advantages and values of the use of technology in education and training - understanding the value of proper implementation - is utilization technology or need driven?

* Appropriate planning - a trial period provided - people, space, production costs, evaluation component taken into consideration.

* Support of key people - continuous planning for growth - total organization cooperation.

* Education and training must be treated as a strategic investment, vital to a company's future success.

Education and training within corporations in the U.S. is an important and growing industry. It has been estimated that annual costs are around $80 billion, comparable with the total spent by all the country's four-year universities and colleges. Educational programs are especially well developed in the large technically-oriented companies. Computer-based education is growing using networks that link voice, graphics, text and audio.

3. SOME EXAMPLES OF LATEST TECHNOLOGIES

Technological advances in the telecommunication industry have produced rapid growth in its utilization for education and training. Advances in electronics, video, voice, data and facsimile communication are assisting in educational delivery systems. Telecommunication technologies are able to provide education to the end-user through video communications that include broadcast, coaxial cable, fiber optics, satellite, closed circuit television and instructional television fixed services. In addition, video components are combined with audio graphic technologies such as the electronic blackboard, facsimile, freeze frame and plan scan video, computers and telecommunication systems. Across the U.S., examples of institutions sharing programs can be found. For example, the National Technological University (NTU) in Fort Collins grants Masters of Science in Engineering degree programs by offering credit courses by satellite from participating universities to students located at member industry sites across the U.S. In addition, on a nationwide basis, NTU offers non-credit short courses to introduce new, advanced technology concepts to a broad range of technical professionals.

Oklahoma State University Arts and Sciences Teleconferencing Services delivers courses in mathematics, science, foreign languages and staff development to high school sites across the U.S. Technologies of compressed video and fiber optics allow two-way video interactive presentation of material. At California State University - Chico, courses are being delivered to businesses in the local area over a fiber optic network. Companies are using very small aperture terminal (VSAT) networks to train their employees relatively inexpensively. Satellite dishes in conjunction with orbiting satellites are creating point-to-multipoint corporate networks. This kind of satellite network permits the sending of a large amount of data to many locations at a fixed cost. It is being used to exchange data and train people at remote sites all over the world.

Interactive videodisc (IVD) technology is being implemented in traditional and non-traditional education and industry settings. The number of videodiscs and videodisc players has increased dramatically. It is estimated in 1989 more than 60,000 videodisc systems were in use for training. Videodisc programs for entry-level jobs in computers and computer applications are growing. On-disk tutorials have proven particularly effective in job skills training.

The newer tutorials present material that appeals to the ear and eye as well as to the mind. The utility and cost-effectiveness of IVD is being well documented. Every learner has a unique learning experience with the same material, different from everyone else's experience. Depending on the individual's responses and the designer's pre-determined objectives, the learner is not only carefully and systematically guided through the material but is also given opportunity to review, receive assistance as required or to move on when mastery has been achieved. At any time, the learner may stop, may review part or all of the lesson, may move ahead, or may go back to a previous lesson. Many educators and corporate training personnel are extolling the virtue of using videodiscs. The industry is experiencing a growth period. As educators and training personnel become more comfortable with videodisc technology, it is predicted that a stronger demand for more videodisc products will occur. Interactive videodisc training programs are effective and do provide simulations that mimic real job situations. Utilizing interactive videodisc technology in training is resulting in significant savings to industrial corporations in terms of training salaries and long-term retention benefits.

4. EDUCATION AND TRAINING ACTIVITIES OF SOME COMPANIES

The Ford Motor Company made a commitment to emphasize learning and to train veteran workers and new employees who need to be trained for the factory of tomorrow. Interactive Videodisc Technology (IVD) is used in Ford's "high tech learning centers". Many IVD systems (estimated 750) are in operation in Ford Motor Company shops and offices across the U.S. The first course on IVD was a general introduction to transmissions, with everyone in the new Transmission and Chassis Division plant, from general management, engineers, accountants and secretaries required to take the course. Workers are taught "how to observe a problem, how to analyze it, what steps to take to determine what needs to be done, and then set up a method for solving the problem".

IBM has developed a set of courses for each of approximately 85 major jobs plus a company-wide delivery system for training its own personnel and end-users. They use a variety of methods for delivery of instruction - a central classroom, a site classroom and learning modules on individualized workstations. Their use of computerized training and interactive videodisc programs is expanding. In the U.S., the IBM company states that on the average 18,000 employees are involved in some degree of training each day.

Bethlehem Steel Company, a large U.S. steel company, needed to return to profitability after five long years of losses totaling over $2 billion. Implementing on-going cost-effective skills training became an integral part of Bethlehem's strategy and improved its competitive edge in the steel world. Many workers using computer-based learning stations at seven sites receive training in one or more of 36 courses ranging in length from one hour to 40 hours. Interactive VideoDisc Training courses include industrial and technical material as well as mathematics, management development and administration. Workers use the system during the work day because the company believes training is part of the work routine. The IVD training is adjusted to individual skill levels and is highly effective in helping workers to become proficient more quickly and to retain their skills for a longer period of time.

Fiat SpA is one of the larger private industrial groups in Italy with activities in many sectors. The company employs over 270,000 people. The most important education and training services are provided by Isvor Fiat SpA - a Group Company that specializes in industrial training and management education. Isvor's Technological Training Department is one of the most modern and efficient organizations working in the field of technical and technological training in Europe. It sets aside a specially-equipped area where all situations that an engineer could come across in a real factory are re-created. Technical training is carried out for a wide range of trainees; for newly-hired workers and for professional managers. A specific project, "The Advanced Educational Technology Project", is involved in studying, developing and applying new technologies and methodologies in the field of training and education.

5. CONCLUSIONS

The amount of knowledge and number of

skills that must be transferred to others is increasing, and the importance of this situation is growing as demand for education and training soars around the world. According to an estimate by the American Society for Training and Development, U.S. businesses already spend about $30 billion in education and training each year - a number that is expected to rise by five per cent per year over the next five years. It is also predicted that, by the year 2000, about 75 per cent of today's workers will need retraining. Companies are becoming more aware that their current operational capabilities will be impaired by people who can not adequately perform the tasks that need to be done.

Education and training is increasingly being treated as a strategic investment, and utilization of the best tools is not an option but a necessity. Training personnel are:

* Responding to pressing day-to-day priorities for using flexible training systems.

* Training people to perform specific sets of tasks tailored to specific purposes.

* Increasing short-term responsive training as means of minimizing training costs.

* Investigating technology as an asset in the learning process.

The rapid development of information technology, combining the allure of high-quality video and audio, the capabilities of computer graphics, the increasing sophistication of animation and the man/machine integration of expert systems opens up exciting possibilities for training. While some corporations make use of new technologies for technical and job skill training, its full potential has not been discovered. New opportunities and new models for updating and upgrading the skills and competencies of the working public will be forth-coming.

Computers in Education
A. McDougall and C. Dowling (Editors)
Elsevier Science Publishers B.V. (North-Holland)

USING COMPUTERS TO MAXIMISE TRAINING EFFECTIVENESS

COLIN CHESMOND AND KEITH TUCKER

ELMS LEARNING MANAGEMENTS SYSTEMS LIMITED AND
NEW SOUTH WALES DEPARTMENT OF TECHNICAL AND FURTHER EDUCATION (TAFE)

This paper addresses the issue of the use of computer technology, in particular, Computer Managed Learning (CML), within educational and industrial environments. It examines ways in which the educational sector can work with the industrial sector in the production of improved vocational training programmes with a view to meeting the demands of the Australian Government's Training Levy. The paper deals with the issue of exporting education and suggests how educational institutions could be more entrepreneurial in this field. The paper presents a case study which looks specifically at the introduction by NSW TAFE of computer managed learning into their Business Communication courses.

1. INTRODUCTION

Education and training bodies are experiencing considerable pressure to increase learner throughput for little or no increase in financial outlay, and to lift the quality of their product so that Australia may retain or improve its competitive position in a world experiencing accelerating technological change. In a country in which the tyranny of distance exacerbates this problem, it is becoming readily apparent that traditional approaches to the delivery of education and training are inadequate, and therefore need to be either replaced, or at least supplemented, by new approaches using the latest technology in the most cost-effective manner achievable.

This paper will set the scene from industrial and educational perspectives, specify the requirements of typical vocational training programmes, describe a technology-based solution and provide experiences based on the application of this solution.

2. THE INDUSTRIAL-SECTOR/EDUCATION-SECTOR NEXUS

To respond to the Federal Government's training levy, the education sector needs to boost its activity in the areas of industrial retraining and educational upgrading. In order that industry can achieve the objectives intended for the levy, a much more intensive level of collaboration will be needed between Industry and Education.

Such a nexus will need to be exploited to the full, if John Dawkins' prediction - that Education will eventually become Australia's largest export services industry - is to be achieved.

This exploitation will require that educational authorities become entrepreneurial and export orientated, and a consequence of this will mean that these authorities will collaborate extensively with overseas providers of education and training services.

Let us consider the basic requirements of exportable vocational training programmes.

3. SPECIFICATION FOR A TYPICAL EXPORTABLE VOCATIONAL TRAINING PROGRAMME

Firstly, such a programme must be capable of delivery by a variety of methods, if it is to satisfy the requirements of a divergent market. These methods will include:

- face-to-face classroom instruction by a teacher
- self paced classroom learning
- self paced workplace learning
- self paced home study.

Secondly, such a programme must make maximum use of training resource materials, which can take the form of any source of knowledge and/or skill. This use can be maximised by:

- exploiting computer support to manage the learning process
- packaging training resource materials into a readily transported form
- providing learner assistance by a subject expert - be it face-to-face if the expert is close by or by means of appropriate electronic communication if the expert is remote
- providing frequent self assessment to the learner, to reinforce the learning process
- providing instant feedback, with remedial advice, following self assessment, so as to minimise wastage of learner time and activity
- creating flexible training programmes which can be customised to the needs of

each individual learner.

Thirdly, such a programme must be both educationally and commercially sound. This can be achieved by:

- ensuring that programmes are developed by individuals experienced in instructional design
- developing curricula to satisfy demonstrable industry needs
- packaging the programme materials professionally and attractively, and selling them at an attractive price
- authoring these materials to suit the needs of a range of domestic and overseas clients, which may be both industrial and educational
- linking the programmes, where appropriate, to formal accreditation processes recognised in the the recipient geographical region.

Fourthly, the delivery of such a programme must be manageable using computer support, for maximum cost-benefit. Such support should preferably include all of the following features:

- both formative and summative testing and assessment using the computer
- feedback information provided to the learner by the computer, as a consequence of computer analysis of the learner response to testing and assessment
- two-way electronic-mail communication between trainee and supervisor
- full reporting by the computer on trainee activity, rate of progress, and competency level, as appropriate, to the trainee, supervisor and management
- records linkable, as appropriate, to payroll, skills audits, personnel record systems, and the like
- software and databases to be highly portable across a wide range of computer platforms
- software to be user-friendly, requiring no programming skill on the part of the learner, supervisor or manager
- software to be readily customised to suit the requirements of individual user organisations.

Finally, the computer support must be suitable for use with a variety of communication media, including:

- dial-up modem links between a trainee's personal computer and a central mainframe computer
- computer networks distributed across sites
- satellite communication channels, for remotely-situated trainees
- computer bureau facilities, where appropriate, serving dispersed groups of trainees.

4. COMPUTER MANAGED LEARNING (CML)

CML can be designed to satisfy all of the criteria in the above specification, provided that the installation is complemented by the application of 'learning guides' as an integral part of each learning programme.

A learning guide is a small, expertly-authored, printed document related to a unit of study activity, which can involve the transfer of either knowledge or skill from any appropriate source, to the learner. Typically, a learning guide will include:

- an outline of the learning activity
- a listing of the learning objectives
- identification of the appropriate learner audience
- a listing of the relevant training resources necessary to support the activity
- descriptive material to support the use of those resources, but not attempting to reproduce the material contained in those resources
- a self assessment task for the learner.

Potential sources of learning guides and learner support are:

- TAFE/CAE/university teachers
- industrial training staff
- Industry Training Council (ITC) trainers
- employers' federations' trainers
- independent subject experts.

Potential sources of fully-packaged training programmes are:

- TAFEs, CAEs and universities
- ITCs
- employers' federations
- publishing houses.

In respect to the provision of CML-based courseware by TAFE, recent experience with CML in the New South Wales TAFE system will be described.

5. INTRODUCING CML INTO THE NSW TAFE SYSTEM

There are several reasons why the introduction of CML was seen as being beneficial to the learning process in TAFE in NSW. The reasons relate not only to the internal structure within TAFE, which involved a complex centralised system of administration and which focused on the traditional classroom as the primary vehicle for learning, but also to the demands placed on TAFE by industry and the marketplace. While some of the following reasons may seem somewhat removed from the decision-making process that led TAFE to introduce CML, they all contributed to the scenario in which major change seemed inevitable.

5.1. Metal and Engineering Award Restructuring

By the commencement of 1989, it was clear that the major focus of award restructuring was the need of Australian workers to be better equipped to improve productivity. As the government noted in "Skills for Australia", 'education and training will play a vital role in productivity improvement by promoting labour efficiency through the enhancement of workforce skills' [1]. Put simply, Australia required a more skilled and adaptable workforce. As the major provider of post-secondary education and training in NSW, TAFE was ideally situated to respond by meeting this training need.

5.2. TAFE Restructuring

On 15 September 1989, the Scott review of TAFE in NSW was handed down. This review, TAFE Restructuring [2], was highly critical of TAFE's ability to respond to industry's training needs given the centralised, top heavy, bureaucratic structure. Apart from the massive administrative reorganisation which followed the release of the report, there was also a perceived need to provide more flexible means of instruction, including modularisation of course delivery, extension of the academic year, and the provision of courses at the workplace. Read in conjunction with the award restructuring plan, there was obvious congruence between industry's and TAFE's initiatives, and clearly a need for more efficient means of meeting the training and education needs.

5.3. Instruction Within TAFE

Four factors concerning instructional practices in TAFE relate to the introduction of CML in TAFE: the emphasis on the traditional classroom as the major setting for instruction and the consequent inflexibility of course provision; the increasing use of computers and related technologies both in the workplace and as the focus of training and education programmes; the range of programmes being offered by TAFE; and, finally, the provision of external programmes to students unable to gain enrolment in face-to-face courses.

Generally, with traditional modes of instruction, students have difficulty entering a course at a level of knowledge and skill congruent with their current ability (since few courses have challenge tests); and students cannot progress at their own individual rates of achievement. Until recently, the use of computers in the instructional process was limited largely to the use of specific software learning packages used in Individual Learning Centres. Despite the omnipresence of computers in colleges and in the workplace, educators within TAFE have been slow to make widespread mainstream use of them in the instructional process.

One of TAFE's major commitments has been in meeting the needs of students unable to attend classes because of distance, extenuating circumstances, or through course unavailability. It is only in the last five years that there has been any significant attempt to use electronic means of delivery (ie there has been a limited use of teleconferencing and a limited use of satellite broadcast). Based on the experience of organisations and institutions both here and overseas (Guthrie [3]) TAFE acknowledged that CML had the potential to meet the changing needs of industry by providing greater flexibility in its provision of courses, while at the same time providing an enhancement to the more traditional means of course delivery and presentation.

6. CONVENTIONAL DELIVERY OF BUSINESS COMMUNICATION SUBJECTS

Within the School of Office Administration, Business Communication subjects are taught in all mainstream courses and in all traineeship courses. Two main strands comprise the Business Communication offering within the School's courses: an English Language strand and a Communication strand.

Prior to 1989, the Business Communication subjects were offered face-to-face, and in a limited capacity through external studies (not all Business Communication subjects were available to students seeking this mode of delivery). During second semester, 1989, CML was employed for the first time in Business Communication classes.

6.1. Reasons for Introducing CML into Business Communication

The course review process, which occurs every five years in TAFE, ensured that by 1990 a new suite of courses would be offered by the School of Office Administration. The review process itself allowed many of the attributes associated with the conventional delivery of courses, discussed in the previous section, to come under close scrutiny. It also meant that innovations, such as the use of CML, could be accommodated meaningfully within the new course provision.

CML was introduced into Business Communication for numerous reasons, which are reflected in the following objectives:

- to ensure greater consistency in both content and approach than is currently available across the 105 colleges offering the School's courses;
- to integrate the use of computers into students' learning;
- to enable an individual student's learning programmes to be tailored to ability levels, be they remedial or extension;

- to provide a useful and valid resource base through the creation of item banks; and
- to encourage effective time management among both students and teachers.

It is anticipated that by achieving these objectives CML can benefit both teachers/instructors and students/learners, on the following basis.

6.2. Benefits

To instructors:

- allows time to focus on most-needy learners
- provides an alternative mode of instructional management
- provides a valid bank of exercises, tasks and tests
- maintains a consistent orientation toward the achievement of learning objectives

To learners:

- focuses learning at an appropriate level, given language/communication competence
- develops problem-solving decision-making and evaluation skills
- orientates learners towards technology within the learning process
- creates a learner-centred approach to education

7. CML - BUSINESS COMMUNICATION PROJECT

The initial development work for this CML project focused on that subject content which all mainstream students had to complete, regardless of the specific course. The content comprised a range of objectives related to English language usage in the office, including use of language references, the development of an office vocabulary, the use of correct punctuation, and the use of appropriate style.

7.1. Scope of the Study

Three learning programmes were developed for the study:

BUSINESS LETTER WRITING
(four learning units)
VOCABULARY
(nine learning units)
PUNCTUATION
(six learning units)

These areas were chosen because of the importance of the content of the subject and because of the potential for providing scope in evaluating the CML software's ability to handle different types of content.

Learning guides and instructor guides were prepared for each programme. Item banks were prepared for each unit.

Three colleges were invited to participate in the project. Ten classes, eight teachers and approximately 150 students were involved. The colleges were chosen to provide a sample of college types: by location, demographic makeup and size. The colleges are Granville, Wyong and Orange.

7.2. Programme Development Model

Since computer access centres were not available at the colleges, each college was provided with an IBM - compatible PC and printer, plus the CML software and printed support materials. Following initial training in the use of CML and in the project, the teachers at each college decided on:

- the location for the hardware;
- the use that students would make of available learning programmes;
- the integration of the CML learning programmes with syllabus content; and
- the timing and frequency of use within the overall subject duration.

This approach was intended to allow for optimal teacher-directed use of the CML materials. Consistency of approach across classes was conditioned by the use of a set syllabus and the CML item banks and guides. Since conventional class settings were used, teachers were encouraged to determine how students would access the CML programme for drawing tests and exercises, and for marking and feedback.

7.3. Programme Evaluation Model

Since this was the first of TAFE's ELMS-CML projects to get underway, it was important that any evaluation undertaken provided sufficient scope for determining not only the effectiveness of the Business Communication learning programmes, but also the usefulness of the ELMS software package and CML as an instructional mode in TAFE.

Within the evaluation model, information was sought on the adequacy of:

- CML staff development (for teachers) and orientation (for learners);
- materials (including software, learning programmes and written support documents);
- process (of using CML alongside traditional teaching and within fixed syllabus requirements); and
- support (offered by the production team to colleges, and by supervisors and instructors to learners).

The evaluation model, as depicted in Figure 1, allowed for a three-college comparison, but within this framework there was also potential for strengthening the evaluation, by comparing the assessments (where appropriate) made by the production team with those of the college-based staff using CML, and the learners. In addition, the results of the study could be fed back to ELMS for confirmation of perception.

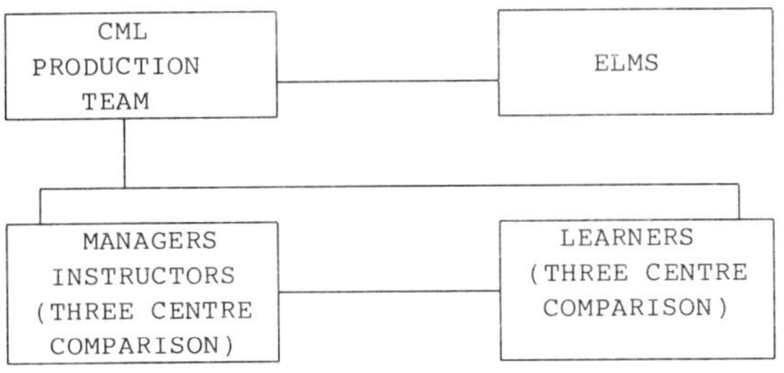

Figure 1: Evaluation Model

Feedback was achieved through:

. monitoring learner behaviour in the use of CML both inside and outside class time;
. monitoring learner results using ELMS-CML management functions;
. interviewing a sample of learners/classes;
. administering a questionnaire to instructors and learners;
. conducting structured interviews with the members of the CML production team and college managers and instructors.

Formative evaluation concentrated on initial training, implementation and the learning process, while the summative evaluation concentrated on learning outcomes and the relevance of content and course duration.

7.4. Results of the Project Evaluation

Within the context of this project, ELMS-CML has been received most favourably by the project managers, the instructors, and the learners at the three colleges. The following results reflect the views of the eight teachers, and a sample of 100 students.

7.4.1. Staff Development and Learner Orientation

An intensive two-day staff development activity, providing orientation to the CML software and to the process of using CML within the learning process, was most favoured by teachers.

A thirty minute in-class orientation was judged by students to be adequate for meeting their needs in using the computer for CML.

7.4.2. Materials

The printed learning guides and item bank software were accepted most favourably by both teachers and students. In presenting language content, teachers felt that the standarisation of rule-based subject matter was a major advantage in using CML-based materials. The ability to draw a randomly generated, and, therefore, individual test or assignment was noted by students as an important aspect of the material availability of CML.

7.4.3. Process

When considering their approach to instruction, teachers indicated that CML brought about a less formal structure in the class, but that it alone had not changed their teaching style. Teachers perceived that CML encouraged students to be: careful in answering questions; responsible for completing work; independent in their approach to work; and that CML assisted weak students who were not confident in working with texts, but who had no inhibitions in using a computer.

In describing changes in their approach to learning, students responded that CML: encouraged them to examine content closely and accurately; challenged them; was not boring; and gave them a sense of independence. Many students indicated that they had not changed their learning behaviour to accommodate CML.

The students indicated that using CML was different to traditional classroom learning in that it: was an interesting way to learn; was relaxing; allowed for self pacing and encouraged self evaluation and revision.

Students most frequently responded that their teacher's approach to teaching had not changed. Most students responded that they used no more non-class time for completing course work than before CML was introduced.

Throughout the evaluation, the only unfavourable rating occurred in the assessment of the computer marking function. Three possible sources of error in the use of this function were identified: bugs resulting from the down loading of the system to colleges; answer, prompt and typographical errors; and the misreading of prompts by students.

7.4.4. Support

Support provided by the CML production team to each of the three centres was considered essential to the success of the project, and both managers and teachers felt that phone and fax facilities provided an adequate backup network.

8. PLANS FOR EXTENDING CML DELIVERY OF BUSINESS COMMUNICATION EDUCATION

This project has been, by design, small-scale both in terms of the learning content covered and the implementation in the educational setting.

The plans for further development include:

- introducing a learner self assessment/evaluation function into the ELMS-CML package;
- extending the use of CML to all language subjects within the School of Office Administration;
- developing a production cell for further learning programme development;
- extending the project to those colleges having the necessary hardware facilities;
- investigating the potential for using CML - Communication content for delivery to distance learners through regional/network centres; and
- determining the marketability of the learning package, both interstate and internationally.

9. CONCERNS IN DEVELOPING CML

There are several issues which may be of concern to anyone wishing to use CML. Failure to find early solutions to the problems may mean that a project fails to meet its objectives. The issues and corresponding solutions are set out as follows:

Issue: orientation towards summative testing by learners;
Possible Solution: use of self assessment/evaluation options.

Issue: ad hoc learning programme development;
Possible Solution: use of expert input; ample lead time; seeing CML as an augmentation to learning, not a panacea

Issue: measurement of achievement being contingent upon the completion of items (eg exercises, tests)
Possible Solution: effective monitoring of the learning process, and human input at appropriate intervals

Issue: ad hoc acquisition of item banks by course developers;
Possible Solution: develop item banks outright, or vet and critically appraise 'borrowed' materials

Issue: adequacy of forward planning;
Possible Solution: allow sufficient lead time

Issue: prolongation of learning sequences;
Possible Solution: use entry/exit tests and limit duration of learning programmes

Issue: bugs in the system
Possible Solution: on-going consultation with software developers.

10. CONCLUSIONS

The introduction of CML-based self paced study into the NSW TAFE system, initially in pilot trials but hopefully on a large scale in the long term, has the potential to act as a significant catalyst for providing low-cost high-quality packaged education on both a national and international basis. Assuming the long-term success of this activity, Australia will have provided itself with the nucleus of a Knowledge Industry, having the potential for exportability on a massive scale.

REFERENCES

[1] Australian Department of Employment Education and Training, Skills for Australia (Australian Government Publishing Service, 1987).
[2] TAFE Restructuring (Sydney, NSW Department of TAFE, 1989).
[3] Guthrie, H., Computer Managed Learning: A Monograph (Adelaide, TAFE National Centre for Research and Development, 1987).

Computers in Education
A. McDougall and C. Dowling (Editors)
Elsevier Science Publishers B.V. (North-Holland)
IFIP, 1990

LOCAL AREA COMPUTER NETWORK FOR CAD TRAINING

Ivan DALBOKOV, Sophia IVANOVA

Institute of Engineering Cybernetics and Robotics, 1113 Sofia, Bulgaria

Some basic principles of Local Area Networks (LAN) used for Computer Aided Design (CAD) training have been considered. These principles have been implemented in the LAN for CAD training developed in 1988 in the Institute of Engineering Cybernetics and Robotics (IECR) in Sofia, Bulgaria. Structural and organisational features of this computer training medium have been discussed. A similar LAN computer classroom for CAD and Computer Numeric Control training has been installed in 1989 in the Advanced Training Institute (ATI) in Madras, India (United Nations Development Programme - International Labour Office project with the first author participating). A comparison between the two classrooms has been made; conclusions and practical solutions have been suggested.

1. INTRODUCTION

A growing number of Computer Aided Training applications has appeared during the last few years. Computerized education is implemented in colleges, higher schools, and in vocational training centres as well. LANs are a suitable technology for building computer classrooms [1]. They offer a lot of advantages for the whole training process. Computer Aided Design is with the greatest potential for computerized training. There are many CAD software packages that could be implemented in CAD training at different levels. Modern professional CAD systems use sophisticated graphics equipment. They are overloaded by a large variety of design activities, thus being inappropriate for training of novices. That is why a standard PC LAN system used throughout a large educational program in the CAD field leads to effective accumulation of basic knowledge of modern CAD systems operation. For implementing such training medium, the main objective should be to define suitable LAN and CAD training software and then to combine them into an efficient training system. Although the training elements used are standard and well known, putting them together for convenient and reliable work of the trainees turned out not to be a trivial task. In this paper, practical aspects of our LAN training solutions have been presented.

2. LOCAL AREA COMPUTER NETWORKS FOR TRAINING

The differences between a stand-alone PC and a networked machine are principally supplied by the network operating system. New multitasking and multiuser features are available [2]. Functionality, ease of use, management, data safety and security are all features of the operating system. It controls the network server. There are two types of servers - a disk server and a file server. With a disk server the control of the directories and files is distributed among the networked PCs. A file server, on the other hand, maintains central control. Distributed control is less expensive since a dedicated central processor is not required. But the server supports multitasking, virtual discettes, access rights, electronic mail and shared peripheral devices. This load can become substantial even when only three or four PCs are networked. Since these functions can easily use up an IBM PC/XT's* processing power, they leave little for foreground processing. Therefore, a person trying to use the server as a local workstation may discover that the system's response time is totally unacceptable. There is another disadvantage of the shared server. A foreground user can be running a program and have the program fail or crash. This freezes the foreground application or causes an exit into DOS. In that situation most users automatically reboot the system by using Ctrl-Alt-Del, or turn the power off and on. In foreground/background environment such actions are disastrous, because the integrity of the files on the disk server can be damaged. In the case of central control, a single network managor can better and safer organise the multiuser activities on a local area network. Since only one dedicated device is performing the management function, less software and network overhead is required. Moreover, the system is more reliable and better structured as a whole, because the server is a special purpose computer and the workstations have no network control functions. Summarizing, we can conclude that a centrally controlled file server is more convenient for use as a LAN training medium because of enhanced integrity and reliability.
Considering the network operating system, NOVELL* is possibly one of the most widely used LAN operating systems with IBM PCs and compatibles. It is hardware independent and can run on a wide variety of LAN hardware [3]. The NOVELL shell is a resident program - extention of MS DOS*, which runs in the workstation and

provides the communication link between the workstation and the file server. The main advantages to select NOVELL LAN software for the computer classroom realizations are the hardware independence and the security features for reliable work of many trainees in the same hardware and software environment.

There are many hardware LAN standards for networking IBM PCs and compatibles. ISNET* is a linear bus network with a raw bit rate of 1 Mb/s. It uses coaxial cable with wave resistance of 75 Ohm, which allows maximum cable length of 1000 m. The network allows up to 50 workstations to be connected to a server and up to two hard disks and three printers per server [4]. The ISNET network is produced in Bulgaria. It has proved suitable for networking IBM XTs and IBM PCs and compatibles for initial CAD training of technicians and college students. The ARCNET* LAN hardware used in ATI, Madras, is superior in some aspects to ISNET. ARCNET is a linear bus network with 93 Ohm coaxial cable and raw bit rate of 3 Mb/s. Maximum cable length is 2000 feet [5]. The training medium in ATI is used for professional training of plant engineers and medium level industrial managers. The CAD package for training in this LAN is more sophisticated. It produces more complex drawings, thus raising the network transmission load and requiring a greater rate.

3. CAD SOFTWARE PACKAGES FOR TRAINING

We have chosen two widely distributed universal CAD packages, which we consider suitable for training.

AutoSKETCH* is a full-function computer aided design package for generating line art [6]. It is suitable for initial CAD training. One can draw with a mouse, digitizer or with the arrow keys, using pull-down menus and dialogue boxes. Lines, arcs, circles, points, polygons, and spline curves are drawn automatically. One can also copy, stretch, rotate, mirror, scale, measure and zoom the drawing. AutoSKETCH drawings are fully compatible with AutoCAD* version 2.5 and higher - they both use DXF file format. This provides a cost-effective way to create preliminary designs which can be further on developed using AutoCAD. AutoSKETCH can run on low-cost IBM PC/XT compatibles and graphics peripherals. AutoCAD can only run on IBM XT/AT or on fully compatibles with 640K RAM and a hard disk [7]. A mathematical coprocessor is desirable for speed acceleration. AutoCAD is a 2.5 dimensional professional package for design automation with a lot of elaborated features. Its version 10 is 3D with three-dimensional primitives. AutoCAD is used in ATI, Madras, for advanced vocational training, where it is run on powerful HP Vectra computers (IBM AT compatible) and enhanced graphics peripherals, networked with NOVELL file server (72 MB) and software.

4. STRUCTURE OF THE COMPUTER CLASSROOM

The environment for CAD training in IECR, Sofia, consists of an ISNET LAN with NOVELL software on IBM PC/XT compatible computers (one IBM XT with 20 MB hard disk is used as a server; seven IBM PCs, with two floppy-disk drives each, as workstations). It offers a possibility for direct connection between the teacher and the trainees. They share common resources (hard disk, printer, plotter), but each student can work independently. The standard computer classroom is for 6 trainees (both in Sofia and Madras), as shown below:

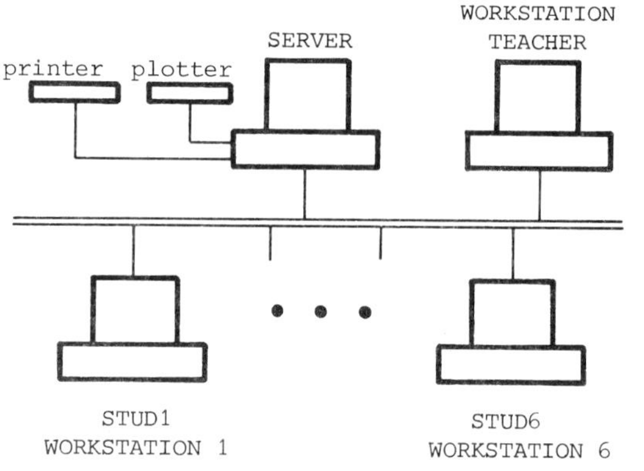

Figure 1

Information protection is one of the main advantages of NOVELL LAN. The teacher should control the whole computer system and the work of the trainees. That is why he is given trustee rights of Supervisor and creates an ASKETCH subdirectory on the file server. AutoSKETCH CAD package is copied there. The ASKETCH subdirectory is assigned rights for creation, writing, reading and deleting files. The trainees should use the information in the ASKETCH directory in a manner that would not destroy it. For this reason the teacher uses the SYSCON network command for registering the trainees as members of STUDENTS user group with rights only for opening, reading and searching in that directory. The structure of the created directories on the Server is given on Figure 2, where:
TRAINING/SYS: is the root directory of the server, formatted in one volume;
SYSTEM, LOGIN, PUBLIC, MAIL are standard NOVELL directories;
ASKETCH - contains AutoSKETCH software package and work area for CAD beginners' course (common resources are shared herein);
READY - directory with restricted rights for trainees' tests;

ACAD - contains AutoCAD software package and work area for advanced course on CAD training (it can contain another specialised CAD package - i.e. for PCB design, architectural design, etc.);
ST1 - ST6 - subdirectories of ASKETCH (ACAD respectively). They supply a work area for individual training and exercises.

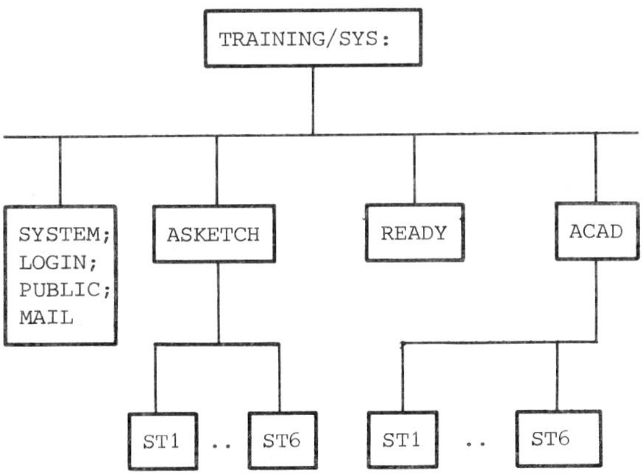

Figure 2

All these directories and files have been created during the initial installation in order to ensure CAD training in the computer classroom in IECR, Sofia.

The file organisation adopted in Madras differs from the Bulgarian one - the ATI system is fully menu driven and it is only the teacher who has limited access to the LAN control to change the LAN parameters. This has proved to be essential for the integrity of the system, although flexibility has been lost, i.e., the LAN system is not transparent for the training staff, because they cannot easily study and change the installed directories and files.

5. TRAINEE SCENARIO

Each workstation in the computer class in IECR, Sofia, has been provided with a system diskette or a hard disk, containing the files:
- system files of MS DOS 3.10 (or higher version);
- the ANET3 program;
- AUTOEXEC.BAT to load ANET3 into the computer memory, to execute it, to switch to the network device F: and to execute LOGIN command. ANET3 is the network shell - it controls the service requests from the workstation to the server.
The trainee puts the system diskette into floppy-disk drive A: and loads the system and the network shell (in the ATI LAN in Madras the local hard disk C: is used for the automatic start-up procedure). After that he registers himself in the server with the LOGIN command by entering his user's name, for example, STUD1. The login procedure reads the login script of STUD1 and activates the search devices. The teacher must first create a login script for each trainee, in which he must assign the individual trainee directory to the activated workstation. Only after logging in the network, the trainee's workstation is ready for starting the CAD package for computer drawing. After finishing the new drawing, the trainee gives it a name in order to save it in his individual directory. "Individual directory for each trainee" means individual work area for those that are present in the classroom at the moment. The teacher usually registers six trainees' user names and the corresponding directories on the server. Therefore, the trainees from the next group will work with the same user's names and in the same directories. The teacher could create a personal directory for everyone but this is not recommended, because it leads to an unnecessary complexity and disk overloading.

In the ATI system in Madras all the trainees work in the same ACAD directory. Their drawings are distinguished by an individual code number for each trainee, which is the identifier of the drawing. Such training structure might be inconvenient when many drawings are created by the trainees and by the teacher in the same directory.

When the drawing is relatively complex and requires several hours work, the trainee should copy it on a diskette at the end of every period. If another trainee, working in the same directory, damages a drawing, it can be restored from the individual diskette.
In the IECR system in Sofia, the teacher organises a special area on the server for collecting the trainees' tests and homework. For that purpose, s/he creates a directory (named READY on Figure 2) and grants trustee rights to the STUDENTS user group only for file creation and writing in it. This means that every trainee can copy his drawing from his own directory to READY only once. He has no rights to open and read files from READY, so he cannot look in the drawings of his classmates and cannot alter his own test later. On the other hand, the teacher has full rights in that directory and he can copy the most successful drawings into the ASKETCH directory. Thus he enables all the trainees to look simultaneously at one of the drawings and to discuss it, but they cannot change or destroy it. It is not possible to Write a drawing from AutoSKETCH mode into the READY directory because of the restricted rights of the trainee. One has to elaborate the drawing in the individual directory and copy it into READY when it is completed.

The input/output devices used by AutoSKETCH or AutoCAD are determined during the initial configuration of the CAD system. Each trainee can determine the output device: either a pseudographic printer for printing the drawing, or a plotter. The configuration data is stored in a special file, called ASKETCH.CFG or ACAD.CFG in the individual directory of the trainee. The presence of the configuration file in every individual directory is very important - although every student uses the same CAD package, he or she can work with different I/O parameters of the system.

Usually the network printer outputs a header before every printed file. The header contains one page of system identification information, which is not really useful but only time and paper consuming. For skipping the header it is recommended to use a parameter NB (no banner) in the SPOOL command in the login script (this has been done in both LANs in Sofia and in Madras).

All workstations in NOVELL are similar - there is no difference between the teacher's and the trainees' ones. In case of a hardware error in some trainee's workstation, the respective trainee can log in his directory from the teacher's workstation and continue his work. This "reserve" in the computer classroom is very useful during the training process.

The NOVELL network has a sophisticated electronic mail. However, our experience with it, while running AutoSKETCH or AutoCAD, turned out to be unsuccessful. If the teacher sends an express message to a trainee, working on a drawing, the latter will be informed of the received mail not earlier than after going into text mode or quitting the CAD package. The messages, sent with the BROADCAST and SEND commands, are not accepted by the workstation while running AutoSKETCH or AutoCAD, the reason being that messages are written on the 25-th row of the screen of the accepting workstation, which row is not accessible during the graphic mode of the screen controlled by AutoSKETCH or AutoCAD. That is why it is not recommended to use SEND and/or BROADCAST commands - they sometimes interrupt the work of the CAD packages.

6. CONCLUSIONS

The computer classrooms for CAD and CNC training in IECR and ATI are good examples of the modern LAN training technology. The system in Sofia uses low-cost hardware and software equipment. It is directed towards training in automated drafting and can be used in colleges and vocational training centres for acquiring initial CAD skills. The system in Madras is more expensive, since it contains professional hardware and software. It is used in higher-level vocational training and in higher schools as well. This is actually a CAD-CAM training system, because it also includes a CNC simulator and post-processor. It is suitable for training of mechanical engineers.

The implementation of the discussed computer networks for CAD training has brought new elements in the CAD training field:
- efficient use of shared hardware and software;
- creation of common libraries with elementary drawings, archives and training examples, etc.

The LAN resource is powerful enough to enhance the information and course support in the training centre, too. Framework II* and Word* software packages have been installed in the LAN in Sofia, and Symphony* - in the Madras LAN. They are used by the training staff for curricula and lessons development. Spelling checkers have been of much help in those cases. Personal data of trainees and course scheduling are prepared in the LAN. Data Bases have been organised for course materials and for analysis of the training process. Managing vocational training has proved to be much easier, because these software packages automatically generate circular letters, address labels, etc.

Our experience up to now shows that LANs with modern personal computers offer new possibilities for training in all computer-related technologies, as well as for computerization of different aspects of course support.

* The following trademarks appear in this paper: IBM, NOVELL, MS DOS, ISNET, ARCNET, AutoSKETCH and AutoCAD, Framework, Word, Symphony.

REFERENCES

[1] McLean, R.S., Local Area Networks in Education: An Infrastructure Perspective, in: ECCE 88 Proc. of the 1-st European Conference on Computers in Education, Lausanne, Switzerland, 24-29 July, 1988, North-Holland, pp. 259-264
[2] Networking IBM PCs: A Practical Guide, IBM Corp., 1986.
[3] LAN Operating System Report, Novell, 1986.
[4] ISNET User Guide, KMPT "Pravetz", 1987 (in Bulgarian).
[5] Netware Installation for ARCNET, NOVELL Inc.
[6] AutoSKETCH, User Reference Manual, Autodesk Inc.
[7] AutoCAD, User Reference Manual, Autodesk Inc.

Computers in Education
A. McDougall and C. Dowling (Editors)
Elsevier Science Publishers B.V. (North-Holland)

NEW ADVANCED EDUCATION AND TRAINING FOR DP PROFESSIONALS IN FINLAND

Lauri Fontell, Terttu Honkasaari

ATK-instituutti, Rautatielaisenkatu 5, SF - 00520 Helsinki, Finland

The paper presents a new advanced curriculum for dp professionals who have passed datanomi education (2.5 years), and who have worked some years in the dp field.

In the curriculum there are five main streams: Information Engineering, Data Management, Data Communications, Applications, and Management. Every stream has many courses. There are three different levels at which courses are located: basic level, general level, and specialized level.

Every student has to plan his/her own study program. A student is required to take 40 study weeks altogether. Basic level courses will take 1 study week, general level courses 2 - 4 study weeks and specialized courses 5 - 8 study weeks. A student must have at least 2 specialized courses with 3 - 6 study weeks of a special project work. Students must finish their studies in 5 years.

The whole curriculum emphasises a students own contribution to the learning process.The re are not many lectures in the program. There is much more group work, group discussions, individual work with guidance and tutored reading programmes. There are some distance learning sections which also make use of new technology.

1. INTRODUCTION

In the years 1988/89 we have planned a new advanced curriculum for dp professionals. The curriculum was planned as a project which started in the spring of 1988 and ended in the spring of 1989. In autumn 1989 we started to implement the plan. The first courses of the curriculum are starting in 1990.

This paper is a presentation of the curriculum of the new advanced dp professional program.

Our curriculum project group has worked together with open minded dp professionals in business, administration, and industry. First we have forecast the future in data processing, what the demands upon dp professionals will be in the future, and which skills dp professionals lack today. After that we started to plan the curriculum.

2. THE CURRICULUM FOR THE ADVANCED DP PROFESSIONAL

2.1. Starting level of students

The advanced curriculum has been planned for a dp professional
- who has passed datanomi education (2.5 years, a post secondary education) and
- who has worked at least five years in the dp area as a programmer or system designer or analyst

In Datanomi education students have had about 1500 study hours in dp subjects and about 300 study hours in Commercial Science. Other dp education of similar content is accepted as an alternative starting level.

2.2. The Aim of Education

The aim of an advanced dp education is to educate practical dp specialists. These specialists will work in different areas depending on which set of courses a student will take. In the next chapter you will find all the educational goals, but a student is expected to pass only a part of those depending on witch courses he/she has taken.

The goals of education are

- An advanced dp professional will work individually and apply his/her own initiative. He has a good over-all picture of Information Systems Management and possibilities of IS Technology in Business Management. He has a deeper knowledge in a certain dp area.

- An advanced dp professional will develop the business action or a product or a service using dp technology with other professionals in different areas. He can lead the project or dp organisational unit or his/her own company in the dp area. He can manage one or many dp applications. He can manage to produce new service or product ideas using dp technology in his/her own business area. He can manage marketing, personnel, purchase, facilities, and equipment in a dp organisation.

- An advanced dp professional is a specialist in one or two areas in data processing. He seeks in-depth knowledge in his/her special area. He will investigate new things in his/her area. He will train, guide, and advise others in his/her special area.

2.3. The Structure of Education

The structure of education is planned so that students are able to work during the courses. The extent of education is 40 study weeks. One study week is 40 study hours. A part of the study hours are lectures, but the main part is the students individual study work - either alone or in student groups.

In the curriculum there are five main streams: Information Engineering, Data Management, Data Communications, Applications, and Management. Every stream consists of several courses. There are three different levels:

- basic level courses (something new in information technology which has come after passed datanomi education)
- general level courses (datanomi education as the starting level)
- specialized level courses (specializing in a certain subject, level after general level courses)

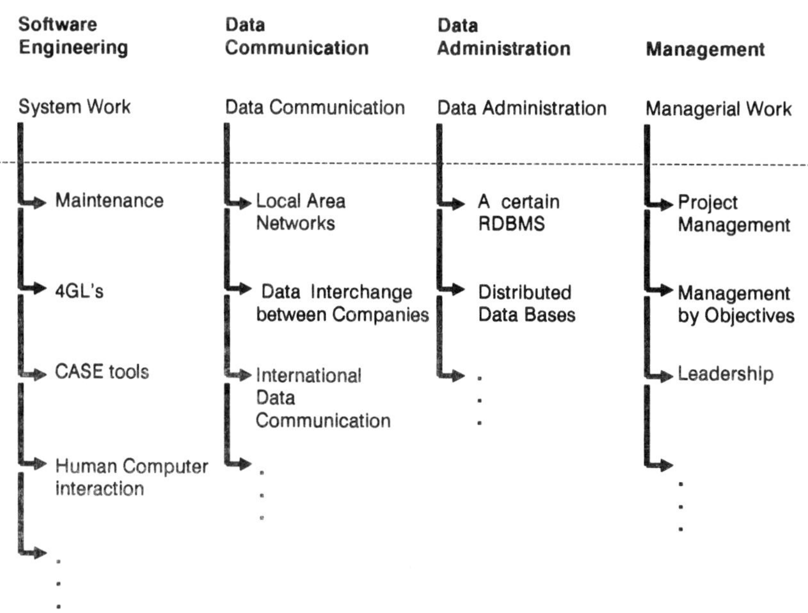

Picture 1: Four main streams and some courses in the general and specialized levels.

Basic level courses will take 1 study week, common level courses 2 - 4 study weeks and specialized courses 5 - 8 study weeks. A student must have at least 2 specialized courses with 3 - 6 study weeks of special project work. The courses are prerequisites for others. Some courses have a entrance test before starting. All courses have a final test.

Every student is expected to plan his/her own study program. A student is required to take 40 study weeks altogether. A student must pass his/her final examination within five years. After a student has passed a course he will get a graded course diploma. After passing a minimum at 40 study weeks a student will get a final diploma in advanced dp education.

2.4. Following a course

Most courses are made up of several units. A unit of a course may be reading a book or study notes, a unit may be an individual work, a unit may be a group work, a unit may be a traditional series of lectures in the classroom. The whole curriculum emphasises the students own active participation in the learning program. The amount of lectures is kept to a minimum. Group work, group discussions, individual work with guidance, reading papers and books with guidance, and so on are considered far more important. There are some distance learning units using new technology. Lectures are also given in the evenings.

The students participating in this new program are adults. They are studying part-time. The role of the educators is that of a tutor, not so much a teacher in the traditional sense.

[1] ATK-instituutti, Peruskoulutetun atk-ammattilaisen jatkokoulutus, opetussuunnitelma, 1989, Helsinki, Finland

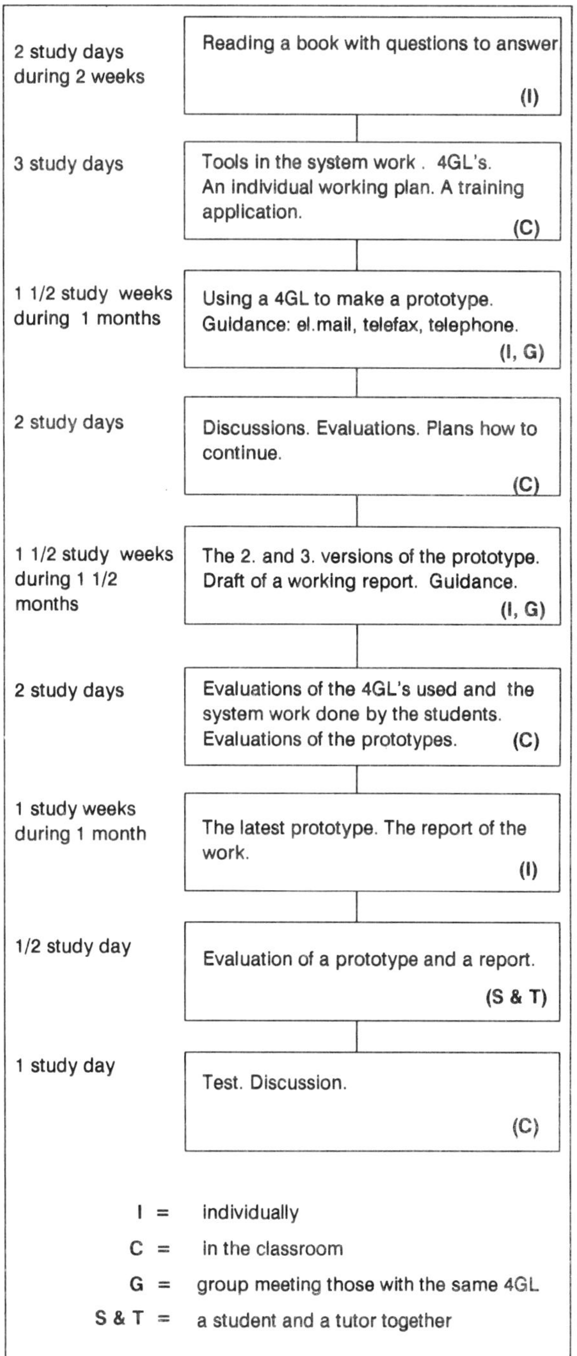

Picture 2: An idea of a cource, first draft.

Computers in Education
A. McDougall and C. Dowling (Editors)
Elsevier Science Publishers B.V. (North-Holland)

DATA PROCESSING EDUCATION IN AN INDUSTRIAL PERSPECTIVE

Bengt Gällmo, Telefonaktiebolaget L M Ericsson, S-126 25 STOCKHOLM, Sweden

ABSTRACT

This paper asserts that DP education must be designed with the needs of the students in their future careers, usually in trade or industry, in mind. To facilitate an analysis of such needs, a structuring of the DP field into a number of subfields is proposed, and competence requirements in each subfield are discussed. From this, it is concluded that DP education should contain not only computer science, but also a number of subjects that can be seen as peripheral to computer science, that sharp boundaries between specialties within the DP profession, e.g. between administrative and technical DP, do not exist, and that corresponding boundaries between branches of DP education should be avoided.

1. INTRODUCTION

"Data Processing" (DP), in this paper, is used in a wide sense. It is not limited to hardware or software, administrative or scientific DP, systems or applications work. On the contrary, the author considers some of the traditional partitioning of the field as obsolete and undesirable.

"DP Education" refers to university education, primarily up to Masters level. The paper deals chiefly with the education of DP professionals, i.e. people with DP as their main competence, but comments also on DP education of people with their main competence elsewhere, e.g. in engineering.

In the software part of DP education, a distinction is made between "computer science" and "programming". Loosely defined, computer science is the advanced, theoretical part of DP, including, among other things, artificial intelligence and database theory. Programming is the practical part, the technique. Numerical analysis is not included in computer science, but in applied mathematics.

2. THE ROLES AND PURPOSE OF A UNIVERSITY

There are different views of the roles and purpose of a university:

Consider a traditional university education in the humanities, e.g. in history. It is not aimed at any particular career outside the university. The only career that can be directly identified is often a teaching career. Certainly, the curriculum is not based on analysis of the student´s probable needs in his or her future career. The university sees as its main tasks to order knowledge, that previous generations of scholars have accumulated, to make it available to the students, to expand it, and to breed the next generation of scholars, who will then order, make available, etc. The university is a Guardian of Knowledge. We will call this type of education "subject oriented".

A student in a subject oriented education typically studies relatively few subjects, but each one in some depth. There may be differences in education contents and quality between universities, because of different interests among professors and because, basically, the university teaches what it is good at, not what the student "needs".

Consider next the education of a dentist. Although it is certainly a professional level education, it is designed from an analysis of what a practising dentist needs to know. There is, of course, research related to dentistry. It is important to the university that some of the students stay at the university, or come back to it after a few years of practice, to become the next generation of researchers. But, the production of dentists is the university´s main goal. We will call this type of education "career oriented".

A student of dentistry will need to study not only dentistry in a narrow sense, but also general medicin, chemistry, materials, law, psychology, maybe ethics, and many other subjects. Students in a career oriented education study many subjects, some of them somewhat superficially. There may be differences in quality between universities, but there will be few differences in education contents, since the contents of all dentistry educations are determined by similar analyses of career needs, sometimes by law.

If history and dentistry are taken as the extremes of a spectrum, where in this spectrum should DP education be positioned?

I submit that DP education should be chiefly career oriented, much more similar to the education of a dentist than to that of a historian. It must be based on a thorough understanding of what the student will probably need to know in his or her future career, outside the university, and it must contain many subjects other than "pure" computer science.

One reason for this is that the majority of students will make their careers in trade or industry, not at the university. This is, of course, true for the humanities students also, but while their future roles are difficult to predict, the probable future roles of the DP students can be analysed in some detail, as will be seen in the following. Therefore, it is possible to design a career oriented DP education with some cogency. Obviously, some students must be enticed to study some subjects in depth and become the next generation of computer scientists. But, it is much easier to allow a few students in a career oriented education to study a few subjects in depth, than to give the majority of students in a subject oriented education all the supplementary courses that they will need for a career in trade or industry.

If the future roles of the students are not taken into account when their education is designed, i.e. if the education is made too subject oriented, the students will experience an unnecessary and painful "culture shock", both to them and to their employer, when they come out into industry (more about this in 3.5).

Basing the curriculum on an analysis of career requirements does not mean that the university should cater to every wish and whim of industry. The education must aim at expected requirements ten years or more into the future, not at requirements today. It must lay the ground for life-long continuing education (one of the career requirements is, in fact, re-educability), which means that basic subjects, as opposed to applied ones, must be weighted heavily. The curriculum should also reflect insight, e.g. about trends in the DP field, that the university has acquired in its research. Curriculum design must start with an analysis of the students' career requirements, but the university should listen both to industry and to its own scientists, then form its own, balanced opinion as to what the relevant requirements are.

3. REQUIRED COMPETENCE IN THE DP PROFESSIONAL

To be able to analyze the competence requirements on DP professionals, we need to structure their field of activity. As mentioned in the Introduction (1), the author considers the conventional ways of subdividing the DP field as largely obsolete. In the following, a different way of structuring the field is proposed, by dividing it into subfields. These subfields are:

- Hardware development (3.1)
- Computer based, autonomous systems (3.2)
- Dialogue systems (3.3)
- Systems programming (3.4)
- Industrial system development (3.5)
- Scientific and technical computation (3.6)
- Computer aided design, etc (3.7)
- Administrative information systems (3.8)
- Product-administrative systems (3.9)
- Cognitive science (3.10)

The first subfield is primarily hardware, the others primarily software. Of the software subfields, the first two (3.2 and 3.3) correspond to two broad types of computer based systems, the others (3.4 to 3.10) are specialisations, with respect to the type of system or the role of the DP professional.

The subfields are not disjunct. One subfield can be regarded as a special case of another, or as a combination of two others. The structure is just a tool for the analysis of competence requirements.

Individual jobs can contain elements of more than one subfield. While working in one subfield, a DP professional will often have to step temporarily into an adjacent one. Also, in his or her life-long career, as personal interests change, or as the job mix of the employer changes, the professional may move from one subfield to another.

For each subfield, the required competence can be described. The competence requirements in two subfields may look similar; the two subfields may require proficiency in the same subjects. The difference, then, is in the emphasis. The competence requirements of the subfields are summarised in table 1.

At the end of this chapter (3.11), some competence requirements common to all or most subfields are discussed.

3.1. Hardware development of computers or computer based systems

The primary competence here is, of course, electronics design. But, programming skills are useful also for hardware designers. They are heavy users of software, they implement their design largely in "firmware", and they get involved in tradeoffs between hardware, software and firmware. However, the broadening of their education with software subjects must not go so far that they lose focus on their primary competence. We still need electronics designers!

3.2. Computer based, autonomous systems

This refers to systems that control or monitor a process of some kind, largely without human intervention. Examples include traditional process control, many so called "embedded systems", modern telephone exchanges, etc.

Work in this subfield requires an engineering education, including mathematics, physics and some physics based subjects, such as electronics design, measurement techniques and automatic control, as well as computer science and programming skills. The emphasis should be on the system aspects of computing.

3.3. Dialogue systems

This refers to systems that primarily present information to a human decision maker and effectuate his commands. Examples include control systems for air traffic or for nuclear power plants, and also advanced information retrieval systems and control systems for large computing centers.

The information to be presented is often complex. It is difficult to give the operator the right amount of information in the right way for optimum decision making. Therefore, human factors (ergonomics in a wide sense) is important. Some subjects from the humanities, so called cognitive science, are useful, such as behavioural science (cognitive and perception psychology), linguistics and logic. Advanced computer science is mandatory, since dialogue systems often make use of it. This includes, more and more, artificial intelligence.

Hardware design ability is usually not required (exception, see 3.7). Therefore, classical mathematics (calculus) and physics are not as fundamental as in other science or engineering education. Discrete mathematics is a prerequisite for the advanced computer science, but the rest of the traditionally "basic" subjects can, in fact, be studied late in the curriculum. Their purpose is general education, so that the DP professional can converse with people in his or her surrounding, but calculus and physics are not fundamental to the main body of education for this subfield.

3.4. Systems programming

This refers to the development of software that administrates the work of a computer (operating systems), or that is common to many applications.

Competence requirements are quite similar to 3.3, although the job contents of the two subfields may seem rather different. The emphasis is, obviously, on computer science. Some cog-

Table 1. Competence requirements by subfield of the DP field

	3.1 hdw	3.2 aut	3.3 dia	3.4 sys	3.5 ind	3.6 sci	3.7 cad	3.8 adm	3.9 pra	3.10 cog
Calculus	xx	xx	x	x	xx	xx	xx	x	x	x
Discrete math		x	xx	xx	x			xx	x	xx
Applied math	x					xxx	xx			
Physics	xx	xx			x	xx	xx			
Electr.design	xxx	xx		x	x	x	x			
Measurem. & ctrl	xx	xx				x	xx			
Computer science		xx	xxx	xxx	xx	x	x	xx	x	xxx
Programming	x	xxx	xxx	xxx	xxx	xxx	xxx	xxx	xx	xx
Economics	x	x	x	x	x	x	x	xx	x	x
Org. & admin.					x			xxx	xx	
Dev. & mfg proc.					xx		x	x	xxx	
Human factors			xx	xx	x		xx	xx	x	xx
Behavioural sci.			xx	x			x	x		xxx
Linguistics			x	xx						xx

xxx = primary competence
xx = strong requirement
x = useful background

nitive science is useful. The remarks on calculus and physics in 3.3 apply. Some understanding of hardware is valuable, more so here than in 3.3.

3.5. Industrial system development

This refers to the design of large computer based systems, e.g. the computers themselves, or large systems for telecommunications or defence. Design of hardware and software often take place concurrently, although the dominating part is usually software. Industrial systems fall into one of the categories described earlier (3.1 to 3.4), or they contain subsystems of more than one of those types. In this sense, industrial system development is not a unique subfield. But, I believe that all industries, that develop really large systems, will agree that largeness itself seems to add something.

To analyse competence requirements in this subfield, first take the union (OR-function) of all requirements described in 3.1 to 3.4. Since industrial systems typically contain subsystems of different types, almost any competence profile within this union is a good base. In addition, the developer of industrial systems must understand how large projects are organised and controlled, and how large systems are specified, developed by large teams of people with different skills, tested, documented and maintained (a long life time is often a characteristic of these systems). He or she needs to understand the importance of standards.

Above all, the DP professional must understand the importance of an orderly, sometimes a bit bureaucratic, development process. This is clearly difficult to convey in a university environment, where one typically handles exercises or projects that are tiny, by industrial standards. Yet, many students end up in this subfield, because developers of large systems are large employers. Recently graduated new employees sometimes experience a "culture shock", that can be quite painful both to them and to their employer, because the university has not prepared them enough for the industrial environment!

3.6. Scientific and technical computation

This refers to the use of computers for advanced calculations.

This requires a good education in calculus and applied mathematics (numerical analysis, mathematical statistics, etc), for many jobs also physics. Programming techniques are important, but the most advanced computer science is seldom used. Some computer architecture may be useful; the professional in this subfield may come in contact with supercomputers, highly parallell processors or other unusual architectures. Hardware design ability is not required, except that an engineering education is useful if the work environment is engineering. Human factors and cognitive science are usually not important.

The old notion that a scientific programmer manipulates numbers but not files, while an administrative programmer manipulates files but does trivial arithmetics, is, of course, obsolete. Also in scientific computation, the DP professional needs to understand data storage, retrieval and communication!

3.7. Computer aided design etc

This refers to technical support systems, such as CAD, CAM, CAE, CASE, and CIM systems.

These are dialogue systems (3.3) that involve scientific computation (3.6). A CAD/CAM developer must have the strong base in calculus and applied mathematics of a scientific programmer, coupled with the ability of a dialogue system programmer to design a good man/machine interface. Therefore, cognitive science is more important than in 3.6. He or she should also understand the development and manufacturing processes (cf. 3.5).

3.8. Administrative information systems

This refers to the design of information systems, where storage and retrieval of data is the main object.

Competence requirements include computer science (e.g. data base theory) and some cognitive science (e.g. for use in the specification of system requirements), but also subjects from business administration, such as economics, organisation, and project management.

Side remark: Education in administrative DP is often provided quite separately from technical or scientific DP education. This is unfortunate! For one thing, the administrative DP education usually pays attention to how system requirements are established and documented. This would be a useful addition to many educations in technical DP. In the other direction, I suspect that some educations in administrative DP could be improved if a more rigorous approach to the subject were taken, starting with discrete mathematics and logic, as is often done on the technical side.

3.9. Product-administrative systems

This refers to the support systems that are used in industry to keep track of products, variants of products, documentation, manufacturing data, etc. They are, basically, administrative systems with complex, technical contents.

The primary competence here is an understanding of industrial development and manufacturing processes. Therefore, previous experience in industrial system development (3.5) is useful. However, the DP professional in this subfield must also have about the same skills as the developers of administrative information systems (3.8). This combination of technical and administrative interest is somewhat unusual!

3.10. Cognitive science

This refers to a subfield that overlaps the border between technical sciences and the humanities, that has just been born, and that may become very important in the future. As mentioned earlier, cognitive science plays a role in several other subfields, e.g. 3.3. Subfield 3.10 differs from the other subfields in that cognitive science is the primary competence. It differs from "pure" cognitive science (in the humanities) in that the application of the cognitive science is technical. The cognitive scientist in this subfield must also be strong in computer science.

The role of the DP professional in this subfield might be that of a "knowledge engineer", for knowledge acquisition and representation in knowledge-based (expert) systems, or he might be part of a team that designs a very advanced user interface.

3.11. Special competence requirements

As stated earlier, education of DP professionals should be based on a thorough understanding of what the students will probably need to know in their future careers. This includes, in all subfields, several subjects other than computer science, that have not been discussed in 3.1 to 3.10. These subjects would not be included in DP education if it were subject oriented, but some of them are indispensable to the practising DP professional. A few examples:

- Oral and written presentation. Many DP professionals spend more time on discussion, presentation, specification and documentation of their work, than on what students may think is the work itself. DP professionals work more with natural language than with programming languages, and must have adequate training also in the use of the former!

- Languages. At least if one of the minor languages of the world is his or her mother tongue, the DP professional must be able to communicate in other languages than his own.

- Economics and organisation. Many DP professionals will work with administrative systems. Even those who won't will be working in an environment that is controlled by such systems, by cost constraints and by profit objectives. They must understand that environment!

- Law. The DP professional must understand a growing mass of legislation, concerning privacy and personal integrity, copyright, and many other aspects of his work.

4. DP EDUCATION FOR NON DP PROFESSIONALS

This paper, in the main, has dealt with the education of DP professionals, but DP education of people with their main competence elsewhere should not be forgotten. It can be argued that this, in terms of volume, is, or will become, the major part of DP education.

The computer is not an end in itself! It is a tool, for engineers, scientists, economists, businessmen, and many others. The time is over, when DP competence was so unique that the DP professional could go out into almost any field and act as an expert, relying on his competence in DP to outweigh his ignorance in the subject matter. The challenge now is to give the real experts in all those other fields so much DP competence that they can take full advantage of the computer. That means a lot more than BASIC courses. It means, more and more, modern computer science!

There seem to be three ways of achieving this. The computer science departments can try to acquire so much understanding of mechanical engineering, civil engineering, or whatever the relevant disciplines are, that they can teach courses like "Computer science for civil engineers" within the computer science department. Or, mechanical engineering, etc, can try to build their own competence in computer science and teach their own DP courses. Or, computer scientists can go out into the other departments, and help them set up proper DP education there. The last solution may be laborious, and implies that the computer scientists will be teaching courses that are considered secondary in the department where they are taught. I still think that is the way to go!

5. GENERAL REMARKS ON DP EDUCATION

A few general points about DP education remain to be discussed:

5.1 Attracting students, especially women

Industry and society in general, in the 90's and beyond, will need many people, well trained in DP. In many countries, the number of young people, ready to enter the universities, will go down in the 90's. This is worrying! DP education must be organised and carried out in such a way that it attracts enough students, with enough motivation and ability.

A special aspect of this is the attraction of female students. Too few girls select a technical education; DP education should be able to attract more of them. This is also a matter of equality: Women, as a group in society, need to understand computer technology as much as men.

It is diffucult to say how DP education should be organised to attract female students. One assertion, that is often made in discussion of this subject, is that women prefer a more "holistic" approach to science than men, and react negatively to a curriculum of many small and poorly interrelated courses. Reorganisation of some curricula in this direction might not be bad for male students either.

5.2 Elective courses vs. compulsory courses

The universities resources must, of course, be used efficiently. One of the most important resources is the mental resources of the students! These are best utilized if the students are given a large degree of freedom to study what they are motivated for. This would seem to be at odds with the assertion in this paper that the curriculum should be based on systematic analysis of the student´s need in his or her future career.

The conclusion is that the students should be motivated, rather than forced, to study the "right" subjects. A large part of the curriculum should consist of elective courses. But, the students should be given as much insight as possible into what their future careers will require. Guest lecturers from industry, projects, study visits and summer work can be used for this purpose.

5.3 Flexibility

The education system must be flexible enough to adapt to changing needs of industry and society (subject to the reservation i chapter 2, last paragraph). For instance, standards (formal or informal) play a very important role in the DP profession. Universities must recognize important standards and reflect them rather promptly in their curricula.

6. CONCLUSIONS

Universities should assess the total need for DP education in their "territory", including the need for DP education of non-DP professionals. They should the assess their ability to satisfy that need.

They should then plan their DP education so that it meets the long term needs of the students in their careers. As an aid in the analysis of these needs, a structuring of the DP field into a number of subfields has been proposed in this paper. One conclusion, already from the structuring, is that DP education should contain also a number of subjects that can be seen as peripheral to computer science.

Every university should not necessarily provide education for every subfield, but it should consider in which subfields demand exceeds supply in the university´s surrounding. In Sweden, for instance, "Industrial system development" is definitely undersupplied.

Sharp boundaries between different subfields of the DP profession do not exist. Therefore, sharp boundaries between different types of DP education, e.g. between administrative and technical DP, should be avoided.

ACKNOWLEDGEMENT

Many opinions in this paper have been expressed also in a study by the Swedish Board of Universities and Colleges (UHÄ), in which the author participated. The report from that study, entitled "Datautbildning inför 90-talet" ("DP Education for the 90´s"), which also contains an analysis of the present situation in DP education in Sweden, and policy recommendations for the future, is written in Swedish, but an English summary is available. UHÄ have concurred in the publishing of this paper.

Computers in Education
A. McDougall and C. Dowling (Editors)
Elsevier Science Publishers B.V. (North-Holland)
IFIP, 1990

A NATIONAL EFFORT FOR CAD/CAM/CIM TRAINING IN SINGAPORE

Dr. Robert K. L. GAY, Research Director, GINTIC Institute of CIM, Nanyang Technological Institute, Nanyang Avenue, Singapore 2263, Singapore

Two distinct phases can be identified in the national effort to develop CAD/CAM/CIM education in Singapore. The first phase involved the introduction of CAD/CAM training into all Engineering and Architecture courses at the universities and the polytecgnics, and the promotion of the use of CAD/CAM in industry. This was the responsibility of the National CAD/CAM Steering Committee between 1984 and 1989. The second phase, which began in 1988, is the responsibility of the National Automation Committee and involves the promotion of training in industrial automation at all levels of education and the use of industrial automation, especially in the smaller industries in Singapore. Through these efforts, the resultant growth of the technology in Singapore has been quite significant and is expected to have some impact on the economic future of the nation. In this paper, the recommendations made and their implementation are described. The ideas and reasoning behind the strategic planning and recommendations are also discussed.

1. INTRODUCTION

The development of CAD/CAM/CIM activities in Singapore can be divided into two fairly distinct phases. In the first phase, between 1983 and 1988, the emphasis was on CAD/CAM training, which in this context meant training in the use of computers for design, drafting, simulation, analysis and the control of robots and machines. The National CAD/CAM Steering Committee (NCSC) was mainly responsible for this phase. The second phase began in 1987 (there was some overlap of the two phases) and is the responsibility of the National Automation Committee (NAC). In this phase the emphasis is on industrial automation, including Flexible Manufacturing Systems (FMS) and Computer Integrated Manufacturing (CIM).

Underlying all of this has been the overall economic strategy of Singapore, formulated in the late 1970s, where high technology and high value-added activities are being encouraged to sustain growth in a tight labour situation. At about the same time, computer aided design and manufacturing (CAD/CAM) was beginning to make an impact on the manufacturing world. It was inevitable that this technology would be identified as a key area for development in Singapore.

The first CAD/CAM workstations appeared in Singapore as early as 1981, but it was only in 1983 that the first major training facility was set up by the Economic Development Board (EDB) of Singapore. As the importance of CAD/CAM became more visible, it was apparent that education in this technology would have to be introduced into the mainstream tertiary institutions in Singapore, i.e. the universities and the polytechnics. These institutions had already begun to make plans for introducing such training in their Engineering and Architecture curricula in 1983. However, it was felt that a co-ordinated effort was required to formulate a national plan for introducing CAD/CAM training in these institutions. As the statutory board responsible for promoting computerisation in Singapore, the National Computer Board was given the task of appointing a national committee to make appropriate recommendations for introducing CAD/CAM training in the four tertiary institutions. The National CAD/CAM Training Committee (NCTC) was appointed in September, 1983 to carry out this task.

Following the recommendations made by this committee in August, 1984, a steering committee (The National CAD/CAM Steering Committee) was formed to direct and monitor the implementation of the recommendations (8).

Progress in the implementation of CAD/CAM training was reasonably good and by 1987 it was felt that it was time to advance to system integration technology and concepts such as Computer Integrated Manufacturing. The problem was that the level of industrial automation was still very low in most of the Small and Medium-sized Enterprises (SMEs) in Singapore. To remedy this, a National Automation Master Plan Committee (NAMPC) was formed in July, 1987, to formulate a plan for accelerating the growth of industrial automation. Their recommendations, announced a year later, are now being implemented under the direction of the National Automation Committee (NAC) (7).

2. THE FIRST PHASE: CAD/CAM

The NCTC was appointed in September to formulate a comprehensive plan for the introduction of CAD/CAM training into the tertiary institutions. The Committee included senior staff from the tertiary institutions, the National Computer Board (NCB) and the Economic

Development Board (EDB). However, there was also input from CAD/CAM users in both the private and public sectors of industry. Advice was also obtained from three consultants from US universities who were engaged under the US Trade and Development Programme.

The NCTC submitted its findings and recommendations to the Committee for National Computerisation (CNC), which was a high level committee chaired by the Minister of Trade and Industry at that time, in August, 1984 (8).

3. THE RECOMMENDATIONS OF THE NCTC

Although the immediate issue for consideration by the committee was the introduction of CAD/CAM education into the tertiary institutions, this could not be separated from the real and wider issue which was the impact of information technology on engineering design methods and the manufacturing industries. Basically there were two problems to be addressed. These were how to include CAD/CAM training into an already packed engineering programme and how to promote the use of CAD/CAM technology in industry in Singapore.

Right from the beginning, the Committee recognised that carrying out a survey to determine how many people to train in CAD/CAM would not be very useful, Without available trained manpower and without sufficient awareness of the technology, there would be very little demand for CAD/CAM manpower. In the end the most useful means of projecting requirements came from a study of dominant trends in factory automation, in which CAD/CAM is a key technology.

Surveys made by reputable bodies such as the CIRP (6) predicted that, before the end of the century, the majority of newly started manufacturing facilities would have a high degree of automation. However, this presumed that there would be sufficient skilled manpower to achieve this. A cursory investigation into the efforts of various universities and national efforts for CAD/CAM training was sufficient to show that the demand for manpower skilled in CAD/CAM and factory automation technology would exceed the availability before long (2,3,5,11, 12,13).

Hence, the growth of computer-integrated factories would be a manpower-limited growth.

In Singapore it was anticipated that by the 1990s suppliers and sub-contractors to large manufacturers would have to be able to produce and read electronically generated drawings and manufacturing data using CAD/CAM systems. This would increasingly be a necessary requirement for qualification to be suppliers or sub-contractors for large corporations who would by and large be highly automated. Hence, the numerous small and medium sized companies in Singapore who were sub-contractors to large corporations would need to take this into account for future planning. In order to implement such plans it was essential that the required manpower be available.

Convinced that the widespread use of CAD/CAM was crucial to the economic development of Singapore, the Committee took a highly pro-active response. This involved the promotion of the technology to industry in concert with the introduction of CAD/CAM training in all the tertiary institutions. In effect this required implementing measures for the creation of a demand for CAD/CAM manpower and measures for fulfilling this demand at the same time. With this in mind, the Committee made the following recommendations:

3.1. The introduction of CAD/CAM training into the curriculum of appropriate polytechnic and university courses.

3.2. The establishment of training schemes for teaching and technical staff of the tertiary institutions.

3.3. The establishment of a CAD/CAM centre for research and development.

3.4. The establishment of a CAD/CAM information centre.

3.5. Government support and funding for training, feasibility studies, and projects for industries.

3.6. The establishment of a steering committee to monitor and direct the implementation of recommendations adopted in the report.

4. CAD/CAM TRAINING FOR THE TERTIARY INSTITUTION

CAD/CAM, which in this context also includes computer aided engineering (CAE), represents the most advanced use of computers in Engineering. It is also potentially the most powerful tool available for engineering education. Without the use of the powerful design capture and simulation facilities available in today's CAD/CAM systems, students can solve only relatively trivial problems which may illustrate some of the principles of design considerations and analyses. However, these often bear little relation to real life engineering problems which are large and complex enough to illustrate the effective applications of engineering principles and procedures. With a powerful CAD/CAM system, students can experiment with different designs and look for better solutions. The implications go beyond just the introduction of more powerful calculators and drafting machines. It will eventually change the way engineers think and work. Hence the introduction of CAD/CAM into engineering curricula should not just be the attachment of a few more new courses. It should be an integral part of all existing courses in which it is appropriate.

In recommending measures to be taken in introducing CAD/CAM training to all the tertiary institutions, the Committee identified four basic levels of training.

Level 1 training is a general appreciation course on CAD/CAM which would require one day to cover at most. In the tertiary institutions this would be included as an introduction to their level 2 training. Such a course would be suitable for management in industry who need to be aware of what CAD/CAM is all about.

Level 2 training is meant to replace part of existing courses in engineering drawing or graphics. This should be compulsory for all engineering students.

Level 3 training should be related to a particular engineering discipline. Hence, a mechanical engineer would have training in mechanical engineering design software and an electronics engineer in electronic design software. Again, all students should be involved, as they would be in one discipline or other.

Level 4 training is meant for students intending to specialise in CAD/CAM. Only some students would require this and such training would be offered as optional courses or projects in the final year at the universities.

The proposed educational structure for CAD/CAM training is shown in figure 1. The estimated cost of the equipment, including hardware and software, for implementing the training schemes proposed was S$35M.

5. STAFF TRAINING

At the time of the proposal, CAD/CAM was a very new area of technology and there were very few staff at the tertiary institutions with sufficient experience to teach the various aspects of CAD/CAM. To remedy this, the Committee recommended short-term and long-term training programmes for teaching staff, the engaging of experts from overseas, the award of scholarships specifically for CAD/CAM training and the encouragement of co-operative training programmes between vendors and educational institutions.

6. A RESEARCH AND DEVELOPMENT CENTRE FOR CAD/CAM

The reason behind the recommendation for an R & D centre was to provide substantial facilities for staff of the various tertiary institutions to carry out meaningful projects in CAD/CAM research. This would enable them to progress further from their initial training and build up a technological resource in advanced areas of CAD/CAM for the nation. Technological transfer from industry to the tertiary institutions and vice versa was envisaged. Technology transfer from overseas would also be possible through the engaging of overseas experts.

7. AN INFORMATION CENTRE FOR CAD/CAM

The role of the proposed information centre was to centralise the collection and dissemination of information about CAD/CAM.

This would include the organising of seminars and conferences, the collection of library material and the publication of a quarterly newsletter.

8. GOVERNMENT SUPPORT AND FUNDING

In 1984 there were already numerous schemes in terms of funding and tax incentives for industries, particularly small and medium-sized enterprises (SMEs), for computerising and automating their activities. However, the Committee recommended that there should be special attention for CAD/CAM development to encourage the propagation of the technology. Funding for feasibility studies, training of technical staff and research and development projects would be essential.

9. THE CAD/CAM STEERING COMMITTEE

In order to ensure that the recommendations of the NCTC would be implemented in a proper and orderly manner, it was recommended that a steering committee be appointed to have responsibility for this. The committee should comprise members from the tertiary institutions, the Economic Development Board and the National Computer Board.

10. ENDORSEMENT AND IMPLEMENTATION OF THE NCTC RECOMMENDATIONS

The recommendations of the NCTC were accepted and endorsed by the Committee for National Computerisation, and a National CAD/CAM Steering Committee (NCSC) was appointed to monitor and direct the implementation of the recommendations which had been made.

10.1 CAD/CAM training

The educational framework in figure 1 shows the distribution of students going into the tertiary institutions. About 7,000 engineers, architects and technicians will be trained per year.

The actual acquisition of equipment, training of staff and re-organising of curricula was left to each of the institutions to implement as appropriate. The steering committee provided a common point of contact for discussing problems in the implementation of the training and a common platform for reporting progress to the CNC annually. It was also a platform for requesting of resources for implementing the recommendations made.

Progress in the first three years was slow but steady. Most of the equipment required had already been purchased by the end of 1986, but the greatest difficulty to face was the reorganising of existing curricula, In already full programmes in the engineering courses, it was difficult to decide what topics had to be discarded to make way for the introduction of CAD/CAM training. Progress has, however, been made and courses have now achieved a fair degree of stability. Over the years there has been a gradual introduction of CAD/CAM content into existing courses, the introduction of new courses and the introduction of laboratories for hands-on use of work stations and project work (9).

10.2. Staff Training

The training of staff proved to be one of the more difficult problems faced in the first two years. Because of busy schedules, staff were often unable to take time off for periods as long as three months to go for training. However, through courses run by the EDB institutes, vendors, visiting experts and in-house experts, a large number of staff had had some exposure to CAD/CAM training of one sort or other by 1987. Teaching staff sent for training overseas in CAD/CAM related subjects have also now returned and enlarged the pool of local experts.

10.3. A National CAD/CAM R & D and Resource Centre

As early as 1983, Nanyang Technological Institute (NTI) had discussed the possibility of jointly setting up a CAD/CAM centre with Grumman International Incorporated. Following the recommendations of the NCTC, the EDB offered substantial additional funding under the Initiative for New Technology (INTECH) scheme to upgrade the proposed centre to a national R & D centre for CAD/CAM. The centre would also be expected to play the role of an information and resource centre. In January 1985, the Grumman International/NTI CAD/CAM Centre (GINTIC) was established. The objectives of the centre were to develop R & D facilities for CAD/CAM and to promote training for the technology through consultancy, and joint industrial projects.

The implementation of the plan began with the sending of nine staff for periods of six months of training at Grumman in the USA. This was followed by the appointment of a director from Grumman for 18 months from the middle of 1986 when premises at the new NTI campus were ready. The first task was the purchase and installation of the computing system, consisting of an IBM 4381, twenty 5080 work stations and twenty PC/AT or compatibles. Following this, the hiring and training of staff began. By 1988, staff strength had grown to forty, a number of projects had been completed and several seminars, workshops and conferences had been organised. GINTIC's quarterly newsletter had reached a circulation of 3,500 and a small library of journals and publications related to CAD/CAM was available to the public.

11. GROWTH OF CAD/CAM IN SINGAPORE

Together with manpower training, there were also several incentive schemes offered by the government to help finance the introduction of CAD/CAM technology into industry. The success of these measures is reflected in the growth of CAD/CAM usage between 1984 and 1988. In 1984 there were 35 major installations with a total of 227 work stations. By the end of 1988, there were 2166 work stations in 400 organisations (9).

12. THE SECOND PHASE: CIM

By the end of 1987, CAD/CAM education has been quite well established in Singapore and attention now shifted to Industrial Automation with CIM as the eventual goal. The concern of the government was that industries in Singapore, especially the samm and medium-sized enterprises (SMEs), were not automating fast enough, although the overall rate of growth of the use of robots and Computer Numerically Controlled (CNC) machines was good by most national standards (see figure 2, figure 3 and Table 1). Enterprises without a reasonable level of automation would not be able to benefit fully from the use of CAD/CAM, so with the growing numbers of trained personnel with CAD/CAM knowledge, it was logical to consider measures to accelerate the progress of automation in the SMEs. This task was assigned to the EDB, which appointed the National Automation Master Plan Committee in August, 1987. The Committee included top executives from industry and relevant statutory boards, and a representative from the tertiary institutions. There was sufficient communication between this Committee and the CAD/CAM Committee to avoid too much duplication of effort and to ensure a cohesive plan. The Automation Master Plan Committee's report was completed in July, 1988 with the recommendation of a five point strategy (7). These were:

12.1. Manpower Development

This would involve building up an adequate pool of automation engineers and technologists within a period of ten years. Industrial automation would be introduced into the curricula of the engineering courses of the tertiary institutions at both undergraduate and postgraduate levels. The retraining of engineers already in industry would also be given more attention.

12.2. Technology Development

Technology development would be encouraged at all levels. At the basic levels, technical assistance would be given to SMEs through the Automation Applications Centre (AAC), and the transfer of technology from multinationals through the Local Industry Upgrading Programme (LIUP). At more advanced levels, existing centres of excellence in the technology such as the German Singapore Institute, French Singapore Institute, Japan Singapore Technical Institute, Design Advisory Service and GINTIC would be expanded. New centres of excellence in appropriate areas would also be established.

12.3. Infrastructure development would involve setting up the physical and technical facilities for encouraging the implementation of automation. The proper environment for consultants, vendors and system integrators should be established. Financial assistance schemes should also be available to SMEs wishing to automate.

12.4. Automation Culture Development

This would involve the education of both management and workers on the benefits of automating. Programmes to educate the public at large and inculcate interest in automation would also be planned. It was important to ensure that everyone understood what automation meant and felt comfortable with its implementation.

12.5. Co-ordination

To co-ordinate and implement the recommendations, a National Automation Committee (NAC) and a special operational unit within the EDB were formed. The NAC effectively took over most of the functions of the NCSC at a higher and more formalised level, and covering a much wider spectrum of activities. The focus would be directed more at upgrading the industrial base of Singapore by addressing the problems of the SMEs directly and in a pro-active fashion.

13. ACTIVITIES IN THE SECOND PHASE

Following the recommendations of the Master Plan Committee a number of studies under various task forces have been carried out. Some of the more significant plans being considered are the setting up of a major Automation Exhibit Centre to demonstrate the concept of automation including CIM, the establishment of an Institute of Automation and the establishment of Advanced Engineering Institutes at the universities. In the meantime activities at centres such as GINTIC have been stepped up.

In July, 1988 a research division was established to carry out joint industrial research projects to address medium to long term problems in CIM. The division would also be responsible for organising a Master's Degree course in CIM. The decision to introduce a MSc course in CIM was based on recommendations of a task force appointed by the NCB in July, 1988 to study specialist manpower requirements for CAD/CAM/CIM and Factory Automation. The course would be launched in July, 1990.

14. CONCLUSION

The introduction of CAD/CAM training into the tertiary institutions was carried out with a supporting programme to encourage the use of CAD/CAM in Singapore Industries. The same formula is being used for the introduction of CIM and factory automation training, except on a larger scale. It is believed that manpower development and propagation of a technology into industry must be planned in concert. In general, the manpower has to be made available first before significant changes can be made in industry. This would seem to be obvious. However, in estimating manpower requirements many committees would have begun by carrying out a survey, which in this case would have been inappropriate. Where there is no skilled manpower in a particular technology, there is unlikely to be a current demand for that skilled manpower in industry. Estimates have to be made based on projected (or required) growth of the technology in industry.

It is interesting to observe that the programmes set in motion in Singapore have been initiated by a multitude of committees and task forces. It is remarkable that a cohesive strategy is possible with such large numbers of diverse bodies. Two main factors have made this possible. Firstly, total commitment and support from the government at the highest levels, and secondly the judicious cross-membership of committees to ensure proper communication between groups.

Time is required in the formulation of national strategies and in the initial stages progress will appear to be slow. However, once an effective strategy is in place, there will be a strong infrastructure to build on. Progress will then be cumulative and there will be sustained growth and advance of the technology. In the long run, having a national strategy becomes a winning strategy.

ROBOT INSTALLATION AND DENSITIES FOR SELECTED COUNTRIES

COUNTRY	NO. OF ROBOT (1986)	ROBOT DENSITY (1985)	ROBOT DENSITY (1986 [EST'D])
JAPAN	118,000	42	53
SWEDEN	2,383	15	17
W.GERMANY	12,400	8	11
USA	25,000	7	9
BELGIUM	1,050	8	8
UK	3,683	6	7
SINGAPORE	227	5.3	7.8

Singapore (1987) : Robot Installation = 309
Robot Density = 9.7

* Robot Density = No. of Robots per 10,000 manufacturing workers

Source : The Industrial Robot October 1986 and September 1987 (International Figures)

EDB Survey (Singapore Figures)

Table 1

SINGAPORE CAD/CAM EDUCATION FRAMEWORK

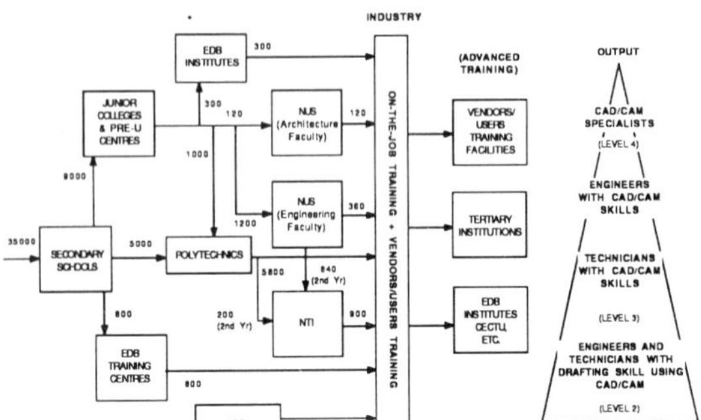

Figure 1

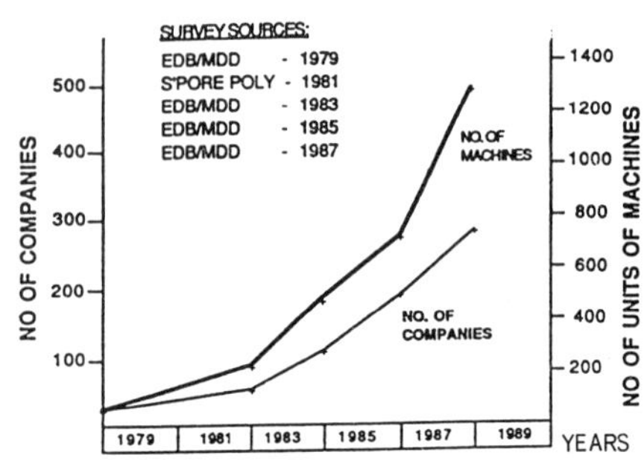

SURVEY TAKEN AS AT:	Jan 79	Nov 81	Sep 82	May 85	Dec 87
No. of Machines	57	209	452	697	1284
No. of Companies using CNC Machines	25	57	125	199	271

Figure 2 : Growth of CNC Machine Tools

INDUSTRIAL ROBOTS GROWTH RATE IN SINGAPORE (AS AT DEC 87)

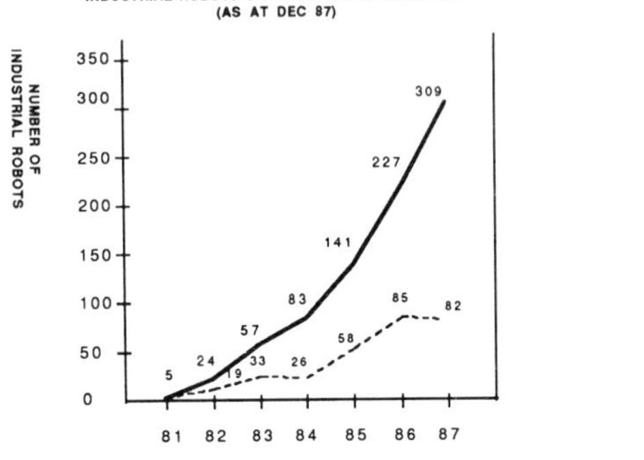

Source : EDB

FIGURE 3

REFERENCES

(1) CAD/CAM/CIM/FA Task Force Report NCB, (Dec.1988).

(2) Canadian CAD/CAM Technology Advancement Council, "Strategy for Survival: The Canadian CAD/CAM Option", (September, 1980).

(3) Freeman, E.M. and Hillier, W.E., "When do you adopt CAE?" Computer-Aided Engineering Journal, November, 1983), pp.3.

(4) Gay, R.K.L., "A National Strategy for CAD/CAM Training in Singapore" IES Journal, Vol 27, (May, 1987).

(5) Gibson, J.E., Richards, L.G., "Redirecting Engineering Education: Computer Graphics and CAD/CAM", Automation Technology for Management and Productivity Advancement through CAD/CAM and Engineering Data Handling. Editor Peter C.C. Wong. Prentice Hall, Englewood Cliffs, N.J. 0732, (U.S.A., 1983.

(6) Merchant, M.E., "Analysis of Existing Technological Forecasts Concerning the Computer-Integrated Automatic Factory". CIRP Annuals, (1980), 29, (2), pp.507-511.

(7) National Automation Master Plan Committee Report. EDB, (July, 1988).

(8) National CAD/CAM Training Committee Report, NCB (August, 1984).

(9) National CAD/CAM Steering Committee Progress Report, NCB (Dec. 1988).

(10) National IT Plan; a Strategic Framework. NCB, (August, 1984).

(11) Renda, R.B., "The Establishment of a CAD/CAM programme within an Engineering Technology School". Report from Purdue University, School of Engineering and Technology at Indianapolis.

(12) Sheldon, D.F., "The present state of the art on computer aided draughting and design". IEE Proceedings Part A, (1983), 130, (4), pp.173-179.

(13) Sheldon, D.F., McTaggart, W, "An affordable CAD/CAM education". Computer--Aided Engineering Journal, (February, 1984), pp. 45-48

Computers in Education
A. McDougall and C. Dowling (Editors)
Elsevier Science Publishers B.V. (North-Holland)

SINGAPORE'S IT PROGRAMME FOR OFFICE WORKERS

Angela GOH

The Centre for Computer Studies, Ngee Ann Polytechnic, Singapore

Kin Chew LIM

Japan-Singapore Institute of Software Technology
Singapore Polytechnic, Singapore

This paper describes a training programme for office workers called IT POWER: Information Technology Programme for Office Workers. The objective is to expose office workers in Singapore to Information Technology(IT), its benefits and its uses. The Singapore National IT Plan is introduced, followed by a description of the training programme. An evaluation of the programme is given, together with the results of a survey of office workers who have undergone the training. A comparison with similar schemes conducted in other countries is then presented. Finally, the paper concludes with some future directions for the programme.

1. INTRODUCTION

In the traditional office, activities such as mail handling, printing, typing, filing, and answering telephone calls are very necessary to the overall running of an organisation. Such activities are labour intensive, not well structured and not well appreciated. The cost of employing office workers such as secretaries, stenographers, typists and clerks is increasing while the prices of office technology is decreasing. As a result, many companies are beginning to use personal computers for many office functions. Consequently, employers are now demanding that their office staff be familiar with and know how to use personal computers.

With increasing business volumes, there is an urgent need to increase white-collar productivity. This means that new ways to restructure secretarial and clerical support have to be looked into.

In Singapore, one catalyst which has prompted many employers to automate their offices and businesses is the Singapore's National Information Technology (IT) Plan.

The National IT Plan consists of the following 7 strategies:

1) IT Manpower
2) IT Culture
3) Information Communication Infrastructure
4) IT Application
5) IT Industry
6) Creativity and Enterpreneurship and
7) Coordination and collaboration.

As can be seen, the second, fifth and seventh strategies are those strategies that address the need to prepare the nation for the information age.

2. IT POWER: Background and Curriculum

Information Technology Programme for Office Workers (IT POWER) is a training course for office workers. It aims at providing office workers with the basic skills in using personal computers. IT POWER was initiated by the National Computer Board (NCB) and the National Productivity Board (NPB). These organisations are statutory boards in Singapore. NCB is responsible for overseeing IT applications and innovation whilst NPB is responsible for promoting manpower productivity in industry.

IT POWER was launched in April 1988, with a target of 10,000 workers to be trained annually. The programme is targeted at office workers who have little or no experience with personal computers. It has been estimated that there are about 200,000 office workers in Singapore.

Currently, the only qualifications expected of the trainees is that they complete their basic secondary education. The entire programme consists of 56 hours of training which has specially been designed to be practice-oriented. Although lectures are used to convey the knowledge, practical exercises, product demonstrations and video shows are also used in the training [7]. Currently, the programme is made up of 6 modules. These are:

* Fundamentals of Information Technology and its benefits
* Introduction to Personal Computers
* Word processing
* Spreadsheet
* Database management systems, and
* Office Automation.

In the first module, trainees are introduced to topics such as Information Technology and the Singapore National IT Plan. In the next module, they are taught the components of a personal computer, and some basic operating system commands. Issues such as the Singapore Copyright Law are also brought up. The trainees spend about 60 percent of the total programme learning how to use a word processing package, a spreadsheet, and a database management system. Only the basic features are taught but sufficient practical exercises are included. The entire programme concludes with a look at the future office which includes PC connectivity, local area network and emerging technologies.

The entire IT POWER programme is offered in the following modes: 14 half-days, 7 full-days, 14 evenings, or over the weekends. Organisations, therefore, can choose the most convenient mode for their staff.

The government also give support in the form of a subsidy given to each staff sent by his/her company. The Skills Development Fund, formed through a levy paid by employers on workers, is used to subsidize 70 % of the cost of the training. Thus, although the course fees per staff are approximately U.S.$400, the sponsoring organisation is reimbursed U.S.$280 from the Skills Development Fund.

3. Implementing IT POWER

3.1 Training Centres

In order to meet the targets projected (10,000 office workers a year), there must be sufficient training centres. To this end, various private commercial schools, unions, associations and in-house training centres are encouraged to conduct the programme. However, in order to ensure that the programme meets and maintains a consistent standard, the NCB sets guidelines. NCB is also the approving body for training centres. Certain conditions have to be met by a training centre before it can be classified as an IT POWER approved training centre.

As of June 1989, there were thirteen training centres, including commercial schools, computer vendors and the Singapore National Trade Union Congress. The National Computer Board holds regular meetings with these centres to obtain feedback and suggestions on how to improve the programme.

3.2 Trainers

Another difficulty faced was the availability of suitable trainers. A special course for trainers, called the Materials Familiarisation Programme, was mounted. This programme covers training techniques and tests the technical knowledge of the would-be trainers. A set of guidelines for trainers was developed by the NCB. Trainers are expected to possess a minimum academic qualification, personal computer working experience and must have passed the Materials Familiarisation Programme before they are certified to be IT POWER trainers. As of mid 1989, there were 62 approved trainers in all the training centres.

3.3 Course Materials

The NCB has also to ensure that certain standards of training are maintained. There is a need to ensure consistent delivery of course material which includes a trainer's guide and a trainee's manual. Since it is not the intention of the programme to promote specific software packages nor to restrict the hardware, all training centres are invited to develop courseware for submission to the NCB. A training centre may propose to develop courseware for software packages on any personal computer. Other centres will be notified, and they may also wish to submit courseware for the same package. The best courseware meeting the standards set would be chosen. This policy will obviously raise the level of consistency in the training across all centres.

The courseware is therefore an important element of the whole programme. A high standard is set for both the trainer's guide and the trainee's manual. The NCB provides guidelines for courseware developers, including a description of the curriculum.

The trainer's guide must follow a given format. This format gives a step-by-step treatment of the material and is sufficiently detailed, in order to promote consistent delivery of the course, regardless of who the trainer is and which centre he is from. The time allocation for each section within the courseware, together with the instruction mode (lecture, demonstration, practical) should be specified. Consistency between the guide and the trainee's manual must be maintained. Additional notes to help trainers clarify certain concepts and terminology should also be included.

The trainee's materials are not to be used solely during the training course. They are intended for use by the trainees on their own thereafter. The materials must therefore be clear and concise. The terminology used should be consistent throughout the courseware and explanation in the form of a glossary should also be provided. Every module comes along with many exercises and end with a review exercise of the entire module. One key feature in the materials is an Adaptability Skills Chart. As its name implies, this chart aids trainees in adapting their skills in one operating system/package onto another. It is of course unrealistic to expect companies where the trainees work to possess exactly the same hardware/software used in the programme. Hence, trainees should know how to transfer their skills onto another environment.

4. A Survey of Trainees who have attended IT POWER

The thirteen training centres in 1989 provided 11,000 training places. However, as a number of these centres are newly approved, only 2600 office workers have undergone training since the programme commenced in April 1988. It is significant that all 2600 trainees were supported by some 600 organisations from both the public and private sectors of industry.

In order to gain feedback on the programme, a survey of 500 trainees was conducted in 1989. The survey consisted of a comprehensive list of 75 questions, covering the overall programme and aspects of each module. The effectiveness of the training, the quality of the training facilities, trainers, and courseware were queried into [5].

93 % of the respondents indicated that they would recommend the programme to others, while two-thirds (66 %) rated the overall programme as above average. The charts shown in Figures 1 to 4 summarise the responses of the trainees to several other key issues. The overall results indicate a high level of satisfaction of the trainees on all aspects of the programme.

In Figure 1, the trainees rate the effectiveness of the IT programme. This

FIGURE 1

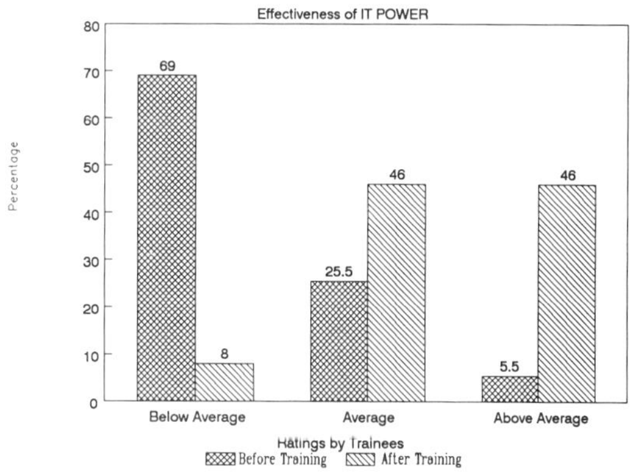

was done by asking them to describe their awareness and knowledge of each module before and after the programme. The chart in Figure 1 shows that 69 % of the trainees surveyed gauged themselves as below average BEFORE the programme, but AFTER the programme, only 8 % felt that they were still below average. Furthermore, 92 % of the trainees felt that, after the training, their awareness and knowledge was average or above average.

As indicated in Figure 2, there is a high satisfaction on the quality of the training facilities. This includes teaching aids such as overhead projector slides, video tapes, and demonstration of packages/information services, etc.

FIGURE 2

Ratings of Training Facilities

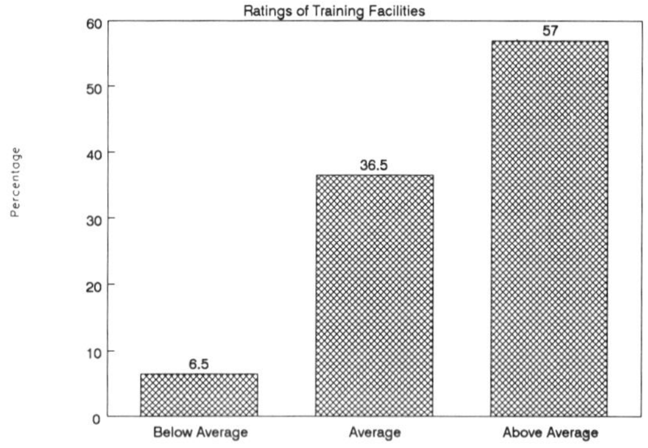

Figures 3 and 4 show the ratings of the effectiveness and knowledge of the trainers. This is broken down by the type of modules, namely, the three which are relatively theoretical, and the other three which involve the learning of application packages. The results of the two charts are very similar. The trainees gave high ratings to the trainers for both their effectiveness and knowledge in the theory-based modules. However, the ratings fell by more than 20 % for the application-based modules. This is not unexpected; it is harder to teach someone how to be skilled in a software package than it is to relate facts concerning general concepts in IT. In spite of this drop in ratings, the overall ratings shown in Figures 3 and 4 indicate that the trainees were generally satisfied with the competence of the trainers.

FIGURE 3

Effectiveness of Trainers

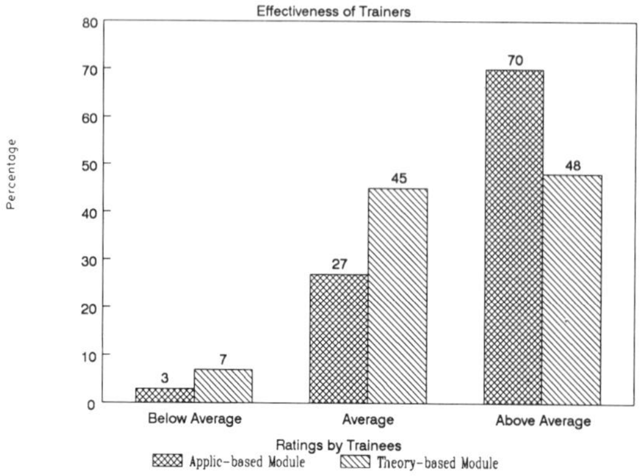

FIGURE 4

Knowledge of Trainers

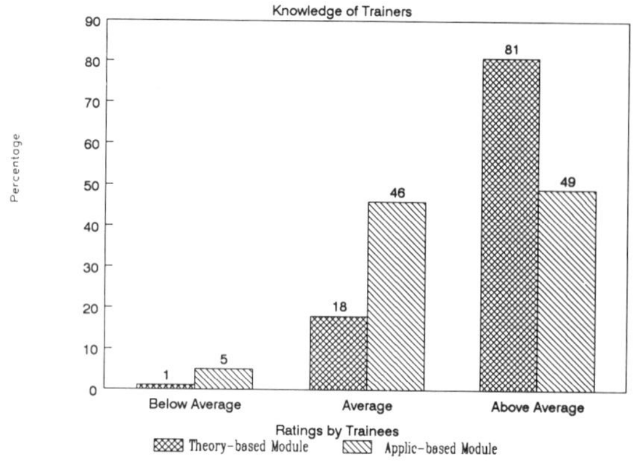

5. A Critical Assessment of the Implementation of IT POWER

This section presents a critical appraisal of the different aspects of how IT POWER has been implemented. The curriculum, the different training modes, the courseware, its development, evaluation and endorsement are also looked into. Finally, the adequacy of training centres and trainers is examined.

At present, there are 6 modules in the IT POWER curriculum. About 40 % of the time is devoted to an introduction of the fundamental concepts of Information Technology, its uses and benefits to the modern office and components of a personal computer. The remaining time is spent on word processing, spreadsheet and database management system software packages. The time allocation appears appropriate, as the objective of the programme is to achieve an appreciation of the uses of IT in the office. In other words, the trainee is expected to know what equipment/applications can aid his/her work. Thus, it is appropriate to spend more time acquiring basic skills in the applications area.

It is interesting to note from the survey that the module which received the least significant effectiveness rating is the database management system (DBMS) unit. In the other modules, nearly 50 % of the trainees had the confidence to rate their knowledge/skills as above average. Only 35 % had the same level of confidence after the DBMS module. Furthermore, this module had the highest percentage (12 %) of trainees rating their knowledge as below average **AFTER** the training. This is not totally surprising as many of the concepts are difficult for an office worker to grasp.

Currently, IT POWER is offered in four different modes: 14 half-days, 7 full-days, 14 evenings or over weekends. One concern of the full-day mode is the short assimilation time given to trainees. It is preferable to stretch the training period, in order to allow the trainees to assimilate better.

In spite of the quality control placed on courseware by a panel of evaluators, there are varying styles of presentation, due to the different courseware developers. Courseware development is a very time-consuming, resource intensive task. Writing, designing, packaging, proof-reading are undertaken by different centres vying for approval. Although competition is healthy in promoting the overall standard of the materials, it has adverse financial effects on all concerned. Furthermore, the current endorsement period is one calendar year, after which further endorsement has to be sought. In the long term, such a system of producing courseware may not be viable. In the short term, it is probably better to extend the current endorsement period of one year. This would give the developers a greater incentive to produce better quality courseware.

There is also the large number of available courseware. At present, there is no limit to the number of packages which can be used for each application. For example, there could be courseware for dozens of word processing packages. This would make quality control even more difficult. Hopefully, the training centres will create a limit themselves by selecting only the most popular packages in the market. As employers are able to choose which centre to send their staff, they are unlikely to select centres which offer relatively unknown products. More importantly, developers may not embark on developing courseware for products which are not widely used, since the sales for such courseware may not even cover the cost of producing the material.

The number of training centres and trainers have been adequate to meet the projected target of 10,000 office workers per year. However, if the estimated total number of workers in Singapore is accurate (200,000), the projected target of staff to be trained per year must be increased significantly. At the current rate, it would take more than decade to ensure that a majority of office workers are introduced to IT. Increasing the target would obviously imply a corresponding increase in the number of training centres and trainers. This may prove to be difficult as training resources are scarce. An alternative is proposed in the section on Future Directions.

6. Comparison with Similar Programmes in Other Countries

At this point, it is useful to see if there are any similar schemes run in other countries. Much of the literature on computer literacy found today concentrates on introducing computer concepts in formal educational systems ranging from primary to university levels and in different courses within tertiary institutes. In conferences such as the IFIP World Conference on Computers in Education (WCCE) [4] and National Goals for Computer Literacy in 1985 [6], there have been many papers on computer literacy programs in these formal education systems. However, there is little written on computer literacy programmes for the general public.

An early report published in 1981 at the third WCCE conference held in Lausanne, indicated that the issue of educating workers is not a new one [2]. The paper described the efforts made in six European countries in offering training to non-management staff. Due to the fact that almost a decade has transpired since the paper was written, and that technology has advanced at an exponential rate during this period, any comparisons with the findings of this report are not appropriate.

De Backer [3] reported in 1985 of an ambitious project in Belgium, which aimed to give opportunities to a large group of people to learn about computers and the fast changing working conditions. The paper also outlined the use of television and radio to reach the masses and the fact that 10,000 people received hands-on experience in applications such as spreadsheets. There were, however, no further details of the implementation of the programme or any report of the consequences of such an undertaking.

7. Future Directions

Although the IT POWER has taken off to a good start, there are a few areas in which the programme can be improved upon.

We believe that CAI (computer-assisted instruction) coursewares can be used effectively in some IT POWER modules. Modules such as Fundamentals of IT and its Benefits, Introduction to the Personal Computer and Office Automation could have their contents developed into CAI courseware.

Another possibility is to form a separate body of curriculum developers. Staff from government training institutions could be seconded to the NCB for a period of time. These staff would help to develop the course materials for all the IT POWER modules.

There is a need to obtain feedback from the trainees a few years after they have completed all the IT POWER modules. It would be useful to find out from them whether the IT POWER has benefitted them and how much of what they have learnt has been put into practice. Such feedback not only indicates the effectiveness of the programme, but can be used to fine-tune various aspects of the course.

At present, when a trainee finishes all the IT POWER modules, he or she is awarded a joint certificate of attendance issued by both the NPB and the NCB. There is no indication of the level of competency achieved by the trainees. Instead of having individual reviews for each IT POWER module, a common test for all the modules should be considered.

Within IT POWER, it is worthwhile considering the possibility of offering options to the trainees. The choice could reflect the industry/department the trainee works in. For example, office workers in public relations departments may well find desk-top publishing very useful in the preparation of brochures, newsletters, etc. Other applications are business graphics, drawing tools, presentation tools, accounting software, etc.

With the "explosion" in information technology knowledge, we should also consider grouping some new modules into an advanced IT POWER scheme, perhaps calling it IT POWER II. The contents of IT POWER II could include desktop publishing, micro-mainframe link, local area networks and bulletin boards. IT POWER I could be viewed as a basic programme whilst IT POWER II could be an advanced programme.

8. Conclusion

As Singapore survives on trade, it has little choice but to exploit IT as widely as possible, in order to compete on a global basis. In short, companies in Singapore must exploit the advances in IT in order to gain a competitive edge. With such a situation, it is even more important that our workers be well trained and work efficiently and effectively.

Computerisation is now seen as a necessity and no longer an option of large multi-national corporations. Amoroso [1] cites several other authors in stressing the importance of education and training of end-users.

IT POWER is a bold initiative especially when it is embarked on a national scale. So far, all the feedback obtained from the participants have indicated that the IT POWER is achieving its objectives. There are plans to extend the IT POWER to those in the manufacturing and service sectors.

References

[1] D.L.Amoroso, Organisational Issues of End-User Computing, Data Base (Fall/Winter 1988, ACM).

[2] C.Ciborra and P.Maggiolini, User-Oriented Education in Informatics: The Experiences of some European Trade Unions, in: R.Lewis and D Tagg (eds.), Computers in Education (Elsevier Science, 1981).

[3] C.De Backer, Large-Scale Multi-Media Computer Courses in Belgium, in: K.Duncan and D.Harris (eds.), Computers in Education (North Holland Pub. Co., 1985).

[4] K.Duncan and D.Harris (eds.), Computers in Education (North Holland Pub. Co., 1985).

[5] IT Focus, IT POWER reveals benefits (Publication of the National Computer Board, Singapore, June 1989).

[6] R.J.Siedel, R.E.Anderson and B.Hunter (eds.), Computer Literacy (Academic Press, 1982).

[7] R.Struckman, A Model to develop computer literacy in Education, in: K.Duncan and D.Harris (eds.), Computers in Education (North Holland Pub. Co., 1985).

Computers in Education
A. McDougall and C. Dowling (Editors)
Elsevier Science Publishers B.V. (North-Holland)

USE OF COMPUTERS IN EDUCATIONAL ADMINISTRATION : A CASE OF ADDIS ABABA UNIVERSITY

Sushma GUPTA

Assistant Librarian, Institute of Ethiopian Studies, Addis Ababa University, Addis Ababa (Ethiopia)

This paper documents the historical development of higher education in Ethiopia, increasing academic activities and the complexity of administration. Administrative objectives, hardware, software and liveware facilities of SDDPC are briefly described. Services rendered by SDDPC - inventory control, purchases, budgeting, accounting, billing, personnel records and management, student records, examination results and records and ESLCE control etc., have been discussed. Future plans to improve its services and operations are stated. The computer network is managed locally with most software either developed or modified locally to suit local conditions. SDDPC has full potential ability and capability for growth and development.

1. INTRODUCTION

"The computing power at the disposal of the average university user has grown in the last ten years in proportions that are difficult to realise." [1] These words were written for the University of Geneva which is located in a highly developed country only a couple of years ago, but here this paper attempts to prove this statement true to a certain extent, in a certain context, for a university located in a Least Developed Country. The university is Addis Ababa University and the country is Ethiopia; fortunately the duration of time is also ten years. The main purpose of this paper is to highlight the history of the use of computers for administration purposes on Addis Ababa University Campus. The data were collected through two brochures published by the Computer Centre of the University for information purposes [2,3], an annual report of 1987 and personal informal interviews with the Director and a Systems Analyst of the Computer Centre.

2. REASONS FOR USING COMPUTERS

Higher education in Ethiopia started with the foundation of the University College of Addis Ababa in 1950. In the following decade a number of colleges and faculties were opened to fulfil the need for higher level manpower in Ethiopia. All these institutions were finally brought together under one central administration in 1961 to form what is today the Addis Ababa University. The new university started with about 1,000 students on its roll and about 100 academic staff members out of which only a handful professional staff members were Ethiopians. [4] Presently Addis Ababa University has nine campuses, five of which are located within the city of Addis Ababa and the remaining four are in other major towns of the country. The number of students is 18,000 and the number of academic staff members is 812 plus 3,194 administrative staff members.

Since 1961 the University has expanded

a lot in many directions such as staff strength, students strength, number of courses etc. Its administrative operations have also become more complex, and academic activities have become multifold. All this expansion means more channels of communication; perfect coordination among staff, students and outside agencies; and full control on all the information, data and statistics to know about the present situation and to plan for the future. To meet these challenges Addis Ababa University established a System Design and Data Processing Centre (SDDPC) through which University policies, procedures and data processing are now effectively streamlined.

3. AIMS AND OBJECTIVES OF THE SDDPC

SDDPC, established in 1979, started with the aim of serving all administrative research and teaching activities of the University by providing:

1. Centralised business system and data processing services;

2. Computer data processing production capability; and

3. Teaching staff and students about the application and uses of computers.[5]

Specifically, SDDPC is a service function of the University whose basic responsibility is to advise, recommend, design and implement those methods of processing data manually, mechanically or electronically which will:

1. simplify the work through:
   *the use of modern manual methods, or
   *the use of mechanical and electronic methods, or
   *elimination of unnecessary operations, or
   *recommendations of improved organisational structure;

2. improve communication through:
   *designing new systems, or
   *writing new procedures and/or computer programmes, or
   *designing and controlling forms;

3. reduce cost by:
   *combining related activities,
   *eliminating unnecessary paper work,
   *providing the focal points for planning, and
   *use of modern reporting methods; and

4. provide expansion capabilities within each system.

4. HARDWARE, SOFTWARE AND MANPOWER FACILITIES

This Centre started with an NCR mainframe V-8250 with 512 Kilobytes of memory. It had two disc units with a capacity of 200 Megabytes each, two tape units, one printer with a speed of 600 lines/minute, one card reader with a reading speed of 600 cards/minute. There were five IBM 29 key punch machines as well as three NCR 7500 magnetic cassette encoders. For online communication there were four terminals - one was devoted to the system, two were used by the central programmers and the fourth one, at that time was for the academic staff community of the University for online programming purpose. There were enough key punch machines available to both staff and students.

After ten years now the Centre has an NCR V-8568 computer with 6 Megabytes of memory. It has now five disc units, two printers with 600 and 2,000 lines/minute speed, one card reader with a speed of 600 cards/minute. There are two IBM 129 keypunch machines and five NCR 7500 magnetic cassette encoders. The number of terminals has increased from four to fifteen hooked to the system. Out of these fifteen terminals, six terminals are used for developing and maintaining programmes and files; the other nine are distributed to some administrative units of the University for online application purpose - four in the Accounting Section, two in the Budget Section, one in the General Services Section and one in the Personnel Section. The Centre has four more terminals which are available to researchers who want to use the online facility on their own. Both staff and students can use them alike.

At present the Centre is using only

one piece of software bought from outside, that is P-STAT, for statistical work. It is normally used by researchers in their statistical applications for their research. The Centre has the compilers for COBOL, FORTRAN, BASIC, RPG and NEAT/3. All administrative jobs are done by indigenous software prepared by local programmers.

There are fifteen people working in the Centre including one Head, five programmers, two systems analysts, one system operator and three key punch operators. The systems analyst said that this staff was enough to do all the jobs they were doing there.

5. SERVICES

The Centre manages the inventory work, budgeting and personnel data for all the nine campuses of the University, but manages payroll data only for the five campuses of Addis Ababa. It does some other petty jobs also for the University.

5.1 Inventory Control

For all the ten campuses of the University, an inventory of every item is controlled by the Centre. A data entry programme records inventory data directly from the requisition and issue slip immediately on arrival. This programme is designed in such a way that it is possible to record data from the store department directly and also to treat invalid entries. There is an online master updating and stock inquiry programme which helps the Centre to generate any kind of report on issues like - monthly consumption report of each department, monthly report showing the quantity received in and issued out from the store, summary report showing the current balance, etc. on request.

5.2 Purchasing by Computer

A piece of software helps the Centre to prepare an indigenous Purchase Requisition Form. It also helps to check the availability of items in stock and that there is a sufficient budget to allow their purchase. Another piece of software compares the proformas of bidders and selects the optimal supplier.

5.3 Budget System

The University's budgeting system is also computerised. This helps the budget to be prepared more easily and efficiently with comparable figures of the last budgets.

5.4 Account Control

The University's accounting system and its analysis have been computerised. This helps the University to know where its money has been spent and how much is left at hand for future expenditure by pressing only a few keys. Its daily cash register is also computerised.

5.5 Telephone Bills

Some software has been developed concerning telephone billing and generating necessary reports about telephones.

5.6 Data Related to Personnel

Various pieces of software have been developed for this purpose. They can produce a staff list, a list of those employees that will receive a pension in any given year, a list of the employees' annual leave entitlements etc. All reports of the Personnel Department have been computerised; now they can generate other consolidated type reports also, as and when required. The University's five campuses located in Addis Ababa now receive their salary slips computerised.

5.7 Class Scheduling by Computer

A package of thirteen programmes helps in class scheduling. It can modify the schedule of lecturers and courses; it can assign lecturers to classrooms and can also find clashes if there are any; it can generate two sections of a class automatically if there are students numbering from 75 to 105 taking any particular course. The output is normally error-free, but if there is an error it is indicated by a message.

5.8 Commission for Higher Education

The Commission for Higher Education is the body under which are all institutions of higher education. The Centre generates and supplies various types of data to the Commission in the form it requires annually.

5.9 Book Centres
The University runs some book centres at its various campuses. Special software has been developed to handle the transactions of these book centres.

5.10 Fixed Assets Control
All the data about the University assets are available on computer for retrieval, updating and reporting purposes.

5.11 Research Assistance to Staff and Students
This service is rendered alike to the staff and students for their research projects. Under this service anybody can come to use these facilities with his own programme and data. Sometimes if the researcher does not have his own programme and needs one to use for his research, the Centre helps to develop appropriate software for him. Many students and staff members come to use these facilities.

5.12 Ethiopian School Leaving Certificate Examination (ESLCE)
This examination is conducted for the students of 12th Grade at a national level. Since both the University and this examination office are under the Ministry of Education, the University helps this office in several ways. The Centre has developed various pieces of software for this office to ease the load of its work. The Centre performs all the jobs from preparation of admission slips based on the candidate's data to issuing the certificates to the students. Approximately 170,000 students appear in this examination every year, thus it is a great help to this office.

6. FUTURE PLANS

Since the Centre has expanded its capacity - in a couple of years - it, at present, has only one major plan to execute as soon as possible. It wants to computerise all the information required by the Registrar's Office about the students. To execute this plan it has already developed all the forms required to capture data and the software required to manipulate these data. It needs only one additional minicomputer system to implement the system. It plans to perform the following jobs for this office:

1. preparing the pre-registration master file records.

2. admission and registration records, sorting, validation programmes for registration data and to check the final registration and admission file against master file,

3. adding new students' records and printing out the list of those students who should not have registered,

4. students' detailed life history and other information,

5. detailed information of the students registered in each course, faculty, semester and their results until graduation,

6. producing a grade roster file and printing out the grade reports,

7. checking for the students who registered for the courses but did not receive the grades, or for those students who have received the grades for courses they did not register for, and

8. printing out the transcripts, etc.

Apart from these jobs, it intends to increase the number of terminals for the use of students and staff from four to 24 so that it can render this service to a larger population of the University.

7. DISCUSSION

During the last ten years the Centre has expanded its hardware and software capacities tremendously to render many useful services to the University. It started with a computer with only 512 Kilobytes of memory, then changed in-between to a computer (NCR 8455) with only 1 Megabyte of memory and now it has been using an NCR V-8568 with 6 Megabytes of memory from about two years. Its disc units and printers have also increased from two to five and one to two respectively; and one printer is a fast one. The number of terminals has also increased from four to nineteen. This shows that more services are offered to more people and more people are using them for their online work and research. It has a further plan to expand its services both to administrative and academic staff and students too.

Asked about the use of terminals in administrative sections and the attitude of those people who are using those terminals towards their use, the systems analyst said that the terminals were heavily used and there were no complaints about their under-use. About the general attitude towards computers, he reported that the people who have been using computers for some time realise their importance and efficiency and prefer to work on computers, but the new people have some inhibitions about using them and still want to stick to their manual applications. However he was confident enough that with time everything will be alright and in future the demand for terminals will increase more.

All this development in just ten years shows a speedy and steady progress in the use of computers and computer services by the educational administration in Ethiopia. The main thing to be proud of among all this development is that, except for one piece of software all software is custom-made locally and all is working very well; the second main thing to consider is that the Centre is managing such a huge amount of data and information with very limited hardware facilities; and the third and most important of all is that it has been able to change the attitudes of the people towards computers and their use. This description from a Least Developed Country may inspire other developing countries to use computers without any hitch in their educational administration, if they have not done so.

ACKNOWLEDGEMENTS

I am highly grateful to Ato Getachew Woldesilassie, the Head of the SDDPC, and Ato Solomon Yewondwossen, the systems analyst for their help and cooperation throughout the study period without which this study could not have been possible.

REFERENCES

[1] Levrat, Bernard, The Impact of Massive Computing Power on the University Environment, in: Lovis, F. and Tagg, E.D. (eds), Computers in Education: Proceedings of the IFIP European Conference on Computers in Education - ECCE 88, Lausanne, Switzerland, 24-29 July, 1988 (North-Holland, Amsterdam, 1988).

[2] Addis Ababa University, System Design and Data Processing Centre (SDDPC), Addis Ababa University, Addis Ababa, 1979.

[3] Ibid. 1989.

[4] Addis Ababa University, General Catalogue: Section I (Addis Ababa University, Addis Ababa, 1965) p. 59.

[5] Addis Ababa University, System Design and Data Processing Centre (SDDPC),...1979. Ibid.

Computers in Education
A. McDougall and C. Dowling (Editors)
Elsevier Science Publishers B.V. (North-Holland)

CAE FROM INDUSTRY TO EDUCATION

Dr. Jan Houben, President of the Managing Board, PTH

Post-box 826, 5600 AV Eindhoven, The Netherlands

The introduction of computer-aided designing, manufacturing and managing methods in technical vocational education in The Netherlands involves a rigorous breakthrough of the existing educational pattern. The basic techniques and basic skills are going to have completely new contents. The applications break through subjects and departments.

STRUCTURE OF THE DUTCH EDUCATIONAL SYSTEM

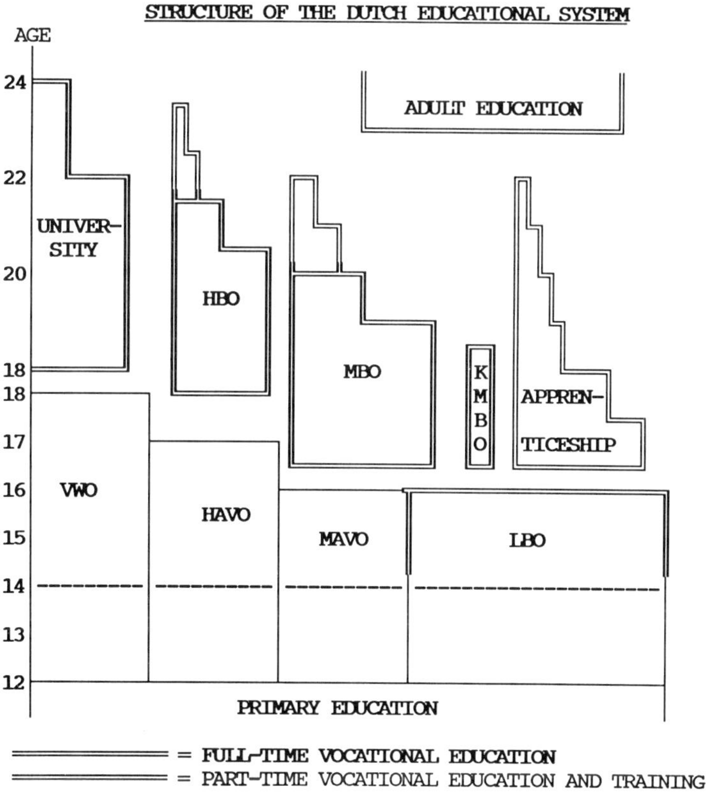

1. CURRENT TECHNICAL VOCATIONAL EDUCATION IN THE NETHERLANDS

In The Netherlands a distinction is made between primary, secondary and higher technical full-time vocational education, with 300,000, 70,000 and 25,000 pupils/students respectively.

Apart from this, there exists the apprentice system with 120,000 pupils and advanced students in a dual education system, i.e. practical experience in a certain enterprise and, in addition to this, a school component for theoretical courses at school.

Primary technical education (LBO) orientates and prepares for craftsmanship.
Apprenticeship trains, in a successively phased dual system, for craftsmanship.
Secondary technical education (MBO) prepares for industrial executive positions, with practical as well as theoretical components.
Higher technical education (HBO) trains the application engineer and technical designer.
At university, the scientific engineer and the researcher are trained for top positions in society.
At the same time, these levels and numbers represent the pyramid of employment in Dutch industry.
These types of training consist of several departments, i.e. mechanical engineering, graphics techniques, construction engineering, electrotechnical engineering, motor-vehicle engineering, etc. Within each department various subjects are taught, being part of vocational theory, practical training, technical designing and practical workshop training. These departments and subjects were linked to the culture of employment 10 to 15 years ago.
Today schools are questioning whether the ratio of the present departments and subjects, flowing from an employment culture of 10-15 years ago, still exists. There is a clear tendency to get rid of isolated subjects and to teach integrated subjects.
By means of projects, several subjects have already been positioned. In the meantime, experience has been acquired in attuning lessons in drawing-offices and workshops, both in theory and in laboratories.
Computer sciences are a separate subject where the principle of the information processing machine is taught and the principles of programming, word-processing, file-processing and process controlling are introduced in general secondary education. A start has also been made with courses in professional applications of the computer like Robotics, CAD, CNC and estimation techniques.

2. DEVELOPMENTS IN INDUSTRY WITH REGARD TO CIM

Analysing the developments in Dutch industry concerning computer-integrated manufacturing (CIM), there is a great difference between large international concerns and medium and small-scale businesses.
The great international concerns like Philips, DAF, HBG and Fokker have automated operations where possible.
First of all, the design departments were been computerized and next, in a modest way, a start was made, where possible, with automated production methods.
Cars are now assembled on production lines. Aircraft parts are made with computerized production machines. System building is realized using robots. Supply companies are being forced to adopt automation.
Drawings are created by floppy. Quality control is automated. At the moment, the international companies are having a lot of trouble in linking their islands of automation.
Medium and small-scale businesses are now automated on a modest scale. There are hardly any integrated CIM systems. Step by step, bridges are being built between islands.
Concerning personnel, internationals take care of their own training possibilities. Medium and small-scale businesses need well-trained employees. This is a very scarce article.
Engineers determine the developments in the enterprises. Then the more highly skilled take over from them. At present, tasks are already being delegated to employees at secondary or primary education level. However, with regard to the latter, regular vocational education has to provide the remedy. The Dutch solution is described below.

3. THE TASK OF TECHNICAL EDUCATION AND TEACHER TRAINING

Adaptation of technical vocational education to the modern requirements of CIM in industry, demands refresher training of teachers in vocational education and adaptation of school equipment. In order to establish a basis for potential adaptation of vocational education, extensive refresher and post-graduate courses for teachers are necessary. But these refresher courses should be offered in the light of:

a. the present and future needs of industry for qualified staff at different levels,
b. prospects regarding the possibility of training at these different levels.

The Vocational Teachers' Training Centre in Eindhoven has developed a perspective based on information from schools and industry.
In The Netherlands, the following structure has been made possible by substantial financial support from the government.

Introduction to companies: the government enables teachers to spend half a year in companies for further training. A good choice of company and teacher provides a double effect. An enthusiastic teacher gets back to school, willing to train himself and to set to work on the curriculum. Relations are made between company and school. Achievements from these contacts can be found in the curricula.
Specialization from companies: schools together with industry can be subsidized for a curriculum development project. According to a plan approved in advance, school and company work out a curriculum. In this way an up-to-date curriculum has been realized, to be applied by all schools. This application demands educational reorientation for the colleagues and course material for the students.

This subject matter then has to move on from the teachers' training to technical education. To this end, the knowledge of the experts, in co-operation with subject didactics, pilot schools and media experts, is transferred in course material. This material is up to date and ideal in many ways. Subsequently, this material is implemented in all schools by means of a refresher project. In this way, innovation is realized in technical vocational education by means of curriculum development and refresher training. The history of CAE is outlined below.

4. DEVELOPMENT OF THE CAE COURSE

The Vocational Teachers' Training Centre applied this strategy in the development of an interdisciplinary CAE course. This course was part of the extensive LERO-TV-project. [1] Computer-aided engineering for mechanical engineering, for electrotechnical engineering and for construction engineering shows a great number of analogies. A condition for using an automated design package is that one is able and free to use the available toolkit. Designing then occurs at three levels:

1. preparing, defining and coding primitive elements in accordance with normal instructions and current standards;
2. defining and preparing the functional units from the available elements;
3. realizing the particular application by combining the functional units and primitive elements and, if necessary, complemented with only once-defined components.

The symbol and macro libraries must be easily accessible to the users.

With the aid of a user computer language, the trainee can relatively easily link the existing basic commands, which gives a new command at the symbol level. Next, symbols can be clustered to functional units at the macro level. It is now possible to make a design by configuration of macros.

For this purpose, dialogue software has been developed so that there is no need for the trainee to face tiresome CAD commands. He can focus his attention on design optimizing by configuration of existing design matrices. The dialogue software has been developed by a designer who is acquainted with this field and its specific products and has knowledge of structured programming in a higher-level computer language.

Knowledge of a structured computer language in CAD surroundings is essential for maintenance and expansion of the use of the application. The computer languages for users are generally unsuitable for structured working. Therefore, standards must be drawn up beforehand. The CAE course includes three total areas each with about five total modules for 228 periods. The areas comprise:

A. A vision of CAE; handling the tools; automated 2D and 3D designing; preparation, input and use of data; the relation to developments in society.
B. Include the different subjects: methodical design; design of product model and product structure; problem analysis and programme structures. Applications within the subject include discipline regarding constructions, production preparation, material tables, print designs, installations for measuring and regulating techniques, etc.

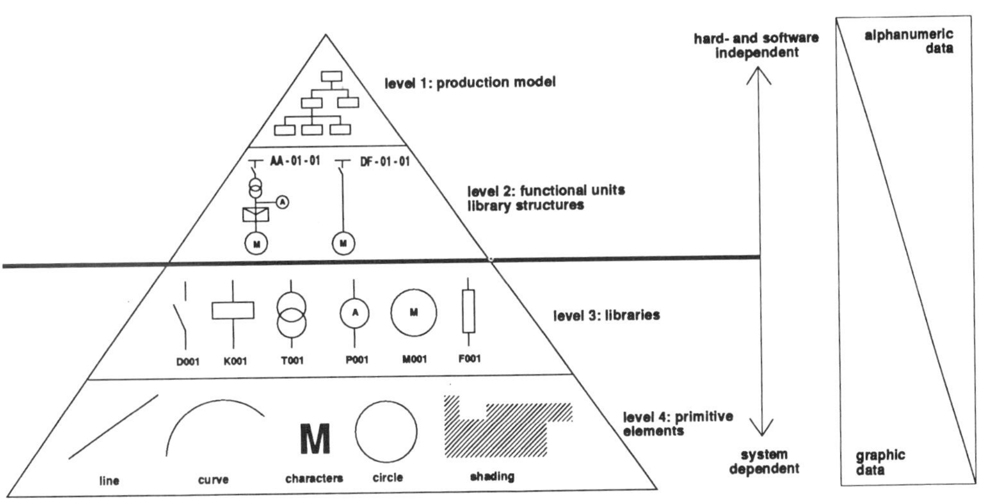

INFORMATION EXCHANGE AT VARIOUS LEVELS OF ABSTRACTION

c. Beyond one's own discipline projects come up, such as building projects, automation projects, etc.

The recommendations of the hardware system-choice adviser showed that the computers must be suitable for the UNIX operating system as well as DOS.
Possibilities in this regard were:

- Apollo-like apparatus alone;
- Apollo-like computers combined with ATs;
- ATs alone.

Taking into account the number of computers and the available budget, the choice fell on ATs alone, namely Type 386 ATs.
Additionally, the possibility of extending the network from 2x12 workstations to 4x12, could not be excluded.

There was also the desire to build a multi-disciplinary graphics and alphanumeric database. This will takeup a number of years, and reliability of the apparatus and service must be guaranteed. We hope to have made the right choice with Compaq.
Tulips were placed in the auxiliary branches. This choice was based on:

- the budget, which was not even big enough to buy Type 386;
- the fact that there were no demands regarding extension of the number of work-stations into a network and the setting up of databases.

5. CONSEQUENCES FOR TECHNICAL EDUCATION

The introduction of the course described above has a number of consequences for technical vocational education.

a. The students have received up-to-date training. The quality is guaranteed by industry.
b. There exists an enormous software problem. Schools cannot use the software from industry and they lack their own didactically based software. This software needs to be developed to international standards by specialized bureaux in cooperation with the educational system.
c. The course can also be taught in industry. Feedback leads to adjustment. Such feedback improves and guarantees quality.
d. The schools will work together on CIM, starting with CAD. To achieve this aim, so-called 'regional centres' have been set up. In these centres, experienced teachers, assisted by universities, carry out experiments in order to integrate design and production. A great deal of money from the Dutch Ministry of Economic Affairs has been put aside to realize these experiments. Standardization of the design package and the production machine are now the 'bottleneck'. In cooperation with the industrial development institute TNO (= Applied Physical/Scientific Research) this will now be dealt with.
e. The subject schemes of vocational schools are currently being discussed. An integrated approach is at the moment the most appropriate.
Some new subjects (logistics) should be introduced. A new approach to the entire industrial production process is necessary. This means: less to learn by heart, but learning how to refer to files, etc.

6. FEEDBACK TO INDUSTRY

By means of the teachers' training college and technical vocational education in general, the leading-edge developments from advanced industries will quickly and effectively move on to other industries and in particular to small and medium-sized businesses. It is only after an optimal link between the distribution of work to preparatory training and capacities of the employees has been set up, that the economic benefits of computerized design through to quality control can be realized.

7. CONCLUSIONS

Our view of the design function in the future can be summarized thus:

a. The design function will be of increasing strategic importance for business undertakings and will form the basis for flexible product automation (FPA) and market flexibility.
b. The need for integration of information demands an open-system approach to the course on fundamental design (inter-disciplinary thinking).
c. Introducing technical data systems assumes expert knowledge (architectural and constructional, mechanical and electrical engineering, etc.) to gain results which can be applied in practice.
d. Involvement of other disciplines (such as business administration) is desirable as part of the transformation processes due to technical automation.

ACKNOWLEDGMENTS

I wish to express my gratitude to all members of the PTH CAE development group for their contributions to the reported study. I further record my thanks to TLO Holland Controls B.V. for the stimulating discussions in the reported field.

REFERENCES

[1] Engelshoven, P.v., LERO-TV-PROJECT, this volume.

Computers in Education
A. McDougall and C. Dowling (Editors)
Elsevier Science Publishers B.V. (North-Holland)

TRAINING THE INFORMATION TECHNOLOGY PROFESSIONAL AS A TRAINER - EXPERIENCES OF AN INDIAN ORGANISATION

Ameeta Jadav

CMC Ltd. 115 Sarojini Devi Rd. Secunderabad 500 003 INDIA

The paper describes the experiences of designing and conducting workshops for training Information Technology professionals as trainers. Recommendations for similar workshops are listed.

1. INTRODUCTION

Like many other technocrats, Information Technology (IT) professionals have a high degree of competence in their field of expertise. However, these professionals are not always proficient in other disciplines such as training, finance and management. In spite of this, during their career, they are often called upon to undertake tasks for which they have not been prepared through formal education. In most such circumstances, they develop the expertise for these tasks through in-service training.

This paper deals with the experiences of training IT professionals to do something they are invariably not trained to do - training.

2. DESCRIPTION OF THE TRAINING ENVIRONMENT

The IT professionals referred to in this paper belong to one of India's largest IT organisations. As a part of its many activities, this organisation conducts several short term (one to three week) courses in a wide range of IT topics through a department of Education and Training. The content in these courses is mostly informational or conceptual but with a practical orientation. The courses are indigenously designed. The teaching aids being used are overhead transparencies, computer aided presentation and videos. Computer based training packages have also been introduced for individualised instruction in some courses.

Each course has a *co-ordinator* who has overall charge of the course (administration, participant profiles, faculty co-ordination, preparation of materials and so on). The courses are conducted with a number of faculty who may each take one or more sessions.

The professionals who serve as *faculty* in these courses hold a master's degree in computer applications, computer science or electronics engineering. They have work-experience of two to fifteen years in the field of IT. As such they are a highly qualified and experienced group of technocrats.

The *participants* in these courses are adults, some of whom are sponsored by their organisations. These participants have varied academic backgrounds and professional experience. While quite a few local participants attend the courses, it is usual to find participants from different parts of the country in a single course.

3. TRAINING OF TRAINERS

In the mid-eighties, the trainers for these courses were prepared for their trainer role through Train the Trainer workshops in which presentation skills were given the major focus. Later, workshops with emphasis on generalised theoretical inputs on classification of learning tasks, systematic design of instruction and so on were tried. However, as more and more workshops were held, a need to shift the emphasis from theory to practice was perceived. The participants in these workshops continually asked for specific examples from their field of training (ie IT). They often expressed doubts about the applicability of theory to actual training situations. This, of course, was not new to training environments! Adult learners are known to be sceptical about new concepts and learn best when given relevant concrete examples (Gilley, 1987; Janov, 1986). It was also found that the sessions which had a high degree of interaction among the participants and between the faculty & participants, were better accepted. This, too, was in keeping with the recommendation of experts that adult training situations should be interactive (Clemons, 1986). As per tradition, the workshops were of five days duration. It was felt that this time was too short for bringing about an effective modification in skills.

In view of these observations, the workshop design was modified several times. Eventually, in the late eighties, a design emerged which was found to cater with a reasonable degree of success to the specific training needs of IT professionals who are called upon to be trainers. In the next few paragraphs, the design of this workshop is discussed and observations which we made as workshop designers and co-ordinators are shared.

4. WORKSHOP DESIGN

Purpose. The purpose of the workshop was to help the participants share information, develop skills and recognize the processes which are essential for effectively carrying out their role as a trainer.

Duration. The workshop was designed for two weeks (10 working days).

Prerequisites. The participants were expected to be familiar with the Education & Training courses. Experience of having been involved in courses as a co-ordinator or trainer was considered to be an added advantage.

Approach. The workshop had philosophical, theoretical as well as practical sessions. The orientation was participative with encouragement being given to the participants to share their experiences and relate their learning to these experiences. At the beginning of the workshop, the participants were divided into three groups and a course topic was identified for each group. All practical exercises in the workshop were carried out in the context of this topic. Most practical exercises involved design and development of materials which could be used in actual courses. Feedback sessions were planned after each exercise. This was done with the assumption that constructive feedback from the participants and faculty would be useful for improvements in the skills of the whole group.

During the workshop, the participants were asked to read various articles and papers which were pertinent to the topics being discussed in class. Some of these were prepared specifically for the workshop while others were articles from journals and chapters from text-books. The participants were also given checklists, job-aids and samples of materials such as course syllabi and lesson plans.

Sessions. The sessions covered in the workshop are given below with a brief desciption of purpose.

Corporate philosophy for E & T: To allow the participants to clarify the organizational perspective for Education & Training.

Issues in E & T : To enable the participants to gain a common understanding of the issues that they have faced or are likely to face in the future and to identify means, if any, of coping with them.

Marketing Perspective in E & T : To appreciate the marketing perspective in E&T courses.

Course Co-ordination: To identify the responsibilities of a course co-ordinator and ways and means of effectively carrying them out.

Course Design: To identify the steps and specific materials to be prepared for a course.

Session Planning: To develop skills in systematic design and implementation of course sessions.

Design & Use of Visual Teaching Aids: To identify the various teaching aids which could be used in sessions, recognize principles of message design to be considered when designing the aids and identify effective methods of using them in class.

Design & Use of Handouts: To design and produce handouts for the courses.

Design & Use of Evaluation Strategies: To design and use valid evaluation instruments.

Training Methods: To identify various training methods that could be used and select the most appropriate method for specific training situations.

Collection & Use of Participant Feedback: To identify methods of collecting formal and informal feedback and to use it to improve the effectiveness.

Micro-teaching: To improve the communication style and gain confidence in making classroom presentations.

Management of Classroom Dynamics: To recognize the role of classroom dynamics in the 'success' of sessions and also identify the role the faculty could play in it.

At the end of the workshop, immediate feedback was collected. Two months after the completion of the workshop, the participants were requested to indicate the extent to which the workshop had helped them to improve their specific training related skills. They were asked to give general comments about its usefulness & relevance, and suggestions for improvement.

5. OBSERVATIONS

The following observations were made during the conduct of the workshop and from the feedback from the participants.

a. The practical exercises were most valuable in developing conviction about the relevance of the 'theory' and in giving the participants a chance to explore the implementation related issues.

b. Group based exercises allowed the participants to learn not only by 'doing' but also by 'discussing'. This method allowed them the opportunity to relate their individual experiences in training, explore the relevance of the 'theory' to their environments and share feelings. The exercise also 'pushed' them to perform because of accountability to each other. In a restricted sense, one could say that the experiment in adult co-operative learning was a success.

c. The participants experienced some difficulty in following the processes of writing objectives and matching evaluation items. To some extent this may have been because of the inherent difficulties in writing 'good' objectives and evaluation items. But there was also the issue of 'So What?' (relevance), a questioning of the eventual utility of this rather time-consuming and 'cumbersome' exercise. However, conviction set in after the practical exercises in which they had to design a complete course and session.

d. When the systematic methods of design of instruction were compared to Structured systems analysis and design methods, there was a quick and easy reception of the concepts and procedures. Seeing examples and non-examples of materials to be developed was also of considerable help.

e. The sessions dealing with Presentation skills, Session planning, Use of teaching aids and Course design were considered most useful and immediately applicable.

f. The period of two weeks was found to be a bit cramped. Specifically, the feedback for practical exercises was hurried, and revisions which the participants made were not presented.

g. Clarification of organizational perspective and discussion of issues were critical at the start of the workshop. This ensured that later sessions could proceed on the basis of some common understanding of the basic values and philosophy of the organisation towards Education & Training.

h. The sessions in which there was considerable interaction, resulted in more significant learning. Specifically, the role of critical, constructive feedback was the most important in the workshop.

i. Initially there was resistance to giving feedback. This was overcome after the participants realised the contribution they could make in improvement of each other's skills and after the faculty members asked for feedback on their own design, presentation skills and so on.

j. There was a tendency among the participants to look for well structured, 'ready-made' solutions to training problems. This may have roots in the basic characteristics of technocrats in the field of IT. However, there was a need for inculcating an attitude towards training as a more creative and personal experience and not a formula driven, impersonal happening. This was found to be critical in view of the high level of trainer burnout which several IT training organisations have experienced.

6. RECOMMENDATIONS

On the basis of the above observations, we have developed the following list of recommendations for the design of similar Train the Trainer workshops:

a. Group/Co-operative learning based activities should be made an integral part of the workshop.

b. As far as possible, theoretical presentations should be followed by activities where the participants can put the theory into practice.

c. Analogies and relationship to processes which participants are familiar with will quicken the conviction and acceptance of relatively new concepts.

d. All activities should be followed by a group review and feedback. At the same time, it is important that the participants recognize and accept the criticality of this process. To some extent this can be achieved if the faculty invite feedback for their own products, procedures and presentations.

e. There may be some issues which cannot be resolved through training (such as organisational values) but at the same time, these issues are likely to affect the functioning of a professional in his/her role as a trainer. The workshop should facilitate a discussion in which a common understanding of the issues could be arrived at. This should be done at the beginning of the workshop.

f. All product related sessions must include samples (both examples & non-examples) of these products.

g. The duration of the workshop should be such that the participants would have a chance to modifiy their work and present it again. This aspect is critical because adults seem to learn the most through doing, sharing and discussing.

h. The faculty for Train the Trainer workshop should take on the role of a facilitator rather than an expert. Adults seem to learn most by discussing and least by listening to discourses from 'experts'.

i. The workshop should include sessions which facilitate exploration of issues such as creativity in training, identification with the role of a trainer, trainer burnout and so on.

While all the above observations and experiences were in the context of Information Technology professionals, it is likely that the recommendations would apply to other situations also. A significant lesson that we, as designers of these workshops have learned, is that each time we think we have finally got a perfect workshop design, we find at least a few things which could make it still better. So this list of recommendations may keep growing as we keep polishing our designs.

REFERENCES

Clemons, H. (August, 1986). How can sub ject matter experts prepare themselves to be trainers? (Four by Four). *Training and Development Journal,* 18-20.

Gilley, J. W. (March, 1987). Adult learners and the classroom. *Data Train ing,* 58 - 59.

Janov, J. (August, 1986). How can subject matter experts prepare themselves to be trainers? (Four by Four). *Training and Development Journal,* 17-18.

Computers in Education
A. McDougall and C. Dowling (Editors)
Elsevier Science Publishers B.V. (North-Holland)

IT ENGINEERS EXAMINATION AND CAROL COURSEWARE

Fumihiko KAMIJO and Masato NAKAYASHIKI

Information-Technology Promotion Agency; Japan Information Technology-Engineers Examination Center.

There will be a serious shortage of Information Technology (IT) engineers in the near future. Self-development and the mass education of engineers are two solutions to the problem. Based on the policy of the Ministry of International Trade and Industry (MITI), several non-profit organizations have set up activities necessary to foster professionals.

This paper describes two such activities which are very popular in Japan. One is the Information Technology Engineers Examination (ITEE), and the other is the CAROL Project for IT courseware development.

1. INTRODUCTION

1.1 Growth of the Information Processing Industry

1.1.1. Continuing Growth of the Industry

The information processing industry has grown into one of Japan's major industries. Its annual revenue approached 3.3 trillion yen (25.4 billion US dollars). The annual growth rate has been as high as 40% (20% in FY1987, 43% in FY1988).

Its revenue is based on contract software development, data processing services, hardware sales, etc. The sale of software products is very small; this is a unique characteristic of the Japanese software market.

The demands of data processing will continue to grow because MIPS and MEGABYTES for general purpose computers will increase, and the use of micros will spread.

1.1.2. The Educational System

The Japanese educational system is well established, but its comprehensive, tightly structured configuration is very difficult to change. It has therefore responded slowly to the dynamic evolution of the computer-based society.

Contribution to the supply of IT professionals by various educational institutions were as follows:

Universities	7,450
Junior Colleges	1,690
Junior Technical Colleges	480
Professional Schools	24,877

(Ministry of Education, FY1986)

1.2 The Short Supply of IT Engineers

An estimate of the additional manpower which will be required by the industry in FY2000 revealed that the Japanese information processing industry will receive 96,000 new professionals in that year. The largest contribution will be graduates of professional schools, approximately 56%. In FY1985, this was approximately 40%.

Professional schools do not have a degree-based educational system. Their curriculum is not regulated directly by the Ministry of Education.

MITI recognized the needs and introduced the exam system, ITEE, to contribute to the enhancement of the skills of IT engineers. It hopes to set a standard for levels of skill.

ITEE has not been able to achieve all its objectives by itself, so a standard IT curriculum was also introduced. This project was nick-named the CAROL (Computer Aided

Revolution on Learning) project. The standard curriculum and a set of IT courseware for Computer Assisted Instruction (CAI) are two major results of the project. Both are to be used by any IT-related educational institution, including professional schools.

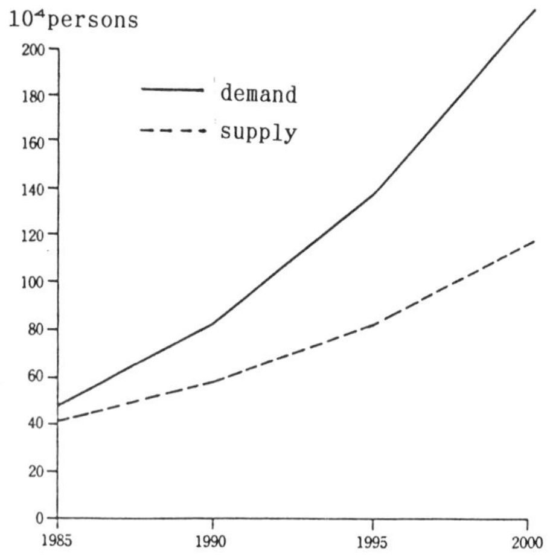

Figure 1: Estimate of Supply of IT Engineers (Human Resource in 2000, MITI)

2. TESTING IT ENGINEERS

2.1. The Japanese IT Engineers Exam (ITEE)

ITEE is a government-sponsored examination. It is an assessment of ability which encourages the development of technical talents. An official certificate recognizes the successful completion of the examination. It is based on the Law concerning the Promotion of Information Processing.

Although it is not an official licensing examination, its acceptance by the professional community has been extremely favorable. In FY1989, there were almost 500,000 applicants. For an examination that allows a pass rate of only 7 to 20% (depending on the type of exam), it seems to enjoy unusual popularity.

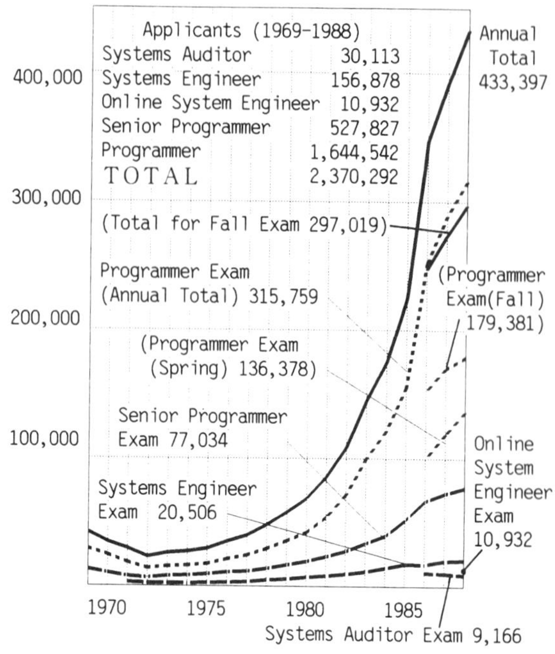

Figure 2: Number of Applicants

2.2. The Objective of ITEE

The objective of ITEE is stated in the law as follows: "To contribute to the enhancement of the information-technology engineer's ability". It is further explained by four sub-goals, namely:

(a) to enhance IT by providing goals and incentives to IT engineers;

(b) to contribute towards the establishment of standard IT-related education programs by defining the various skill levels required for IT personnel;

(c) to provide objective criteria for the evaluation of IT engineers; and

(d) to foster a broad awareness of the information society among the Japanese people by providing them with the opportunity to sit for ITEE tests.

2.3. Organization

ITEE is prepared and executed by the Japan Information-Technology Engineers

Examination Center (JITEC), under the auspices of MITI.

The tests are offered in 38 cities all over Japan. All types of exams, except the Senior Programmer Exam, are offered every fall. Currently, the Programmer Exam and the Senior Programmer Exam are offered every spring.

2.4. History

The first examinations of the Programmer Exam and the Senior Programmer Exam were held in 1969. There were 42,022 applicants, of whom 2,463 successfully completed the exam.

In 1971, the Systems Engineer Exam was introduced. The original plan was fulfilled with the introduction of this exam.

There was a change in the operational environment of the data processing community when the computing System Audit Standard was defined and enacted by MITI in 1986. A new type of test, namely the Systems Auditor Exam, was introduced as a response to the needs of the industry.

The most recent addition to ITEE is the Online System Engineer Exam. It was introduced in 1988 to solve the problem of the shortage of such specialists.

Because of the ever changing nature of IT and the application environment, new types may be added to our list to respond to the needs of society.

2.5. Types

There are five types of examinations in the ITEE. They are the Programmer Exam, the Senior Programmer Exam, the Online System Engineer Exam, the Systems Engineer Exam and the Systems Auditor Exam.

Originally, the category classification of ITEE was oriented to the job type.

Specialty oriented classifications such as the Systems Auditor Exam and Online System Engineer Exam are new additions.

For the Programmer and Senior Programmer Exam, 2.5 hours out of five are allocated to debugging type questionnaires to test practical programming skills. Only one programming language, COBOL, FORTRAN, PL/I or CAPX (an artificial assembly language, now CASL) is required for the Programmer Exam. For the Senior Programmer Exam, CAPX is a required language, together with one other selected language.

Project management experiences are tested by short essay of the Systems Engineer and Systems Auditor Exams. The time allocated for short essay is two hours, and applicants are asked to complete 2,000 to 4,000 characters (1,000 to 2,000 words) from a choice of four case study type questions.

2.5.1. The Programmer Exam

This exam tests competence in programming, based on the given program specification. A general knowledge of arts and science at the high-school level is also required.

There is no explicit prerequisite other than more than one year's programming experience.

The number of applicants in FY1988 was 315,759, out of which 33,864 engineers passed the exam.

2.5.2. The Senior Programmer Exam

The ability to design and prepare programs is the major subject covered by the exam. The ability to supervise a team of programmers is another consideration.

A Senior Programmer is one who has a college graduate's level of knowledge of arts and science. He or she must have more than three years of programming experience.

We had 77,034 applicants of whom 7,158 passed in FY1988.

2.5.3. The Online System Engineer Exam

Competence in online system analysis, design and evaluation, is the major test criteria for the Online System Engineer Exam. The testee must have the knowledge of general-purpose information systems. General knowledge at the level of a university graduate is also required. At least three years of experience in actual systems work is assumed.

This brand-new exam attracted 10,932 people, of whom 902 passed in FY1988.

2.5.4. The Systems Engineer Exam

This exam covers a wide range of computer-related subjects: application, project management, and the operation and control of systems.

The exam tests the ability to analyze and design systems and the professional knowledge of computers and applications. An applicant must write a short essay after completion of the multiple-choice section of problems.

A university graduate level of knowledge of business and industry is also required. It is assumed that an applicant has more than three years of practical experience.

It is required that an applicant be at least 25 years of age.

The number of applicants and those who pass are relatively small due to the high standards required by the exam. In FY1988, the figures were 20,506 and 1,154 respectively.

2.5.5. The Systems Auditor Exam

This exam is one of ITEE's new exams. The first test was given in 1986. The test covers systems auditing skills, abilities in systems planning, development and operation, and the general knowledge of business environments.

Applicants should have at least five years of experience in either auditing or business data processing.

He or she must be 27 years old or older.

We had 9,166 applicants in FY1988, and 341 passed the exam.

2.6. Evaluation

The evaluation of ITEE is a difficult task. A survey of the opinions of employers was undertaken by the Japan Information Processing Development Center in 1988. A summary of 512 responses represents the view of the employers.

The questionnaire posited three criteria for the evaluation of the ITEE system. They were: the evaluation of the engineer's skill, the means for training and the measure of the corporate image.

The answer was classified into five levels, namely "very useful", "useful", "not very useful", "useless" and "no response". We looked at the partial sum of percentages of the two levels, "very useful" and "useful", as the measure.

Concerning ITEE as the measure of examinee's skill level, the figure ranges from 79.5% to 51.5%. This is a very favorable result.

Considering ITEE as the means of training, 90.8% to 54.3% of employers who responded, consider the examination useful.

The number of employees who have passed the test is considered an indirect index of the level of skill of the software company. Eighty-two per cent to 55.7% of the respondents found ITEE useful in this regard.

Another discussion that has been raised by the data processing community on the ITEE system is its low passing rate.

The original thoughts were based on the level of skills required by ADP departments of Japanese computer users. Most of them were users of medium to large scale general purpose hardware. They hire tens to hundreds of ADP personnel. As a consequence, the level of skill has to meet the requirements of large application systems developments.

It may be the reason why the passing skill level was set at a relatively high standard.

Category	As the measure of Examinees' Skill Level (%)				
	Very Useful	Useful	Not Very Useful	Useless	No Response
Systems Auditor Exam	18.9	32.6	10.4	7.8	30.3
	51.5		18.2		
Systems Engineer Exam	25.0	37.9	9.2	6.1	21.8
	62.9		15.3		
Senior Programmer Exam	31.3	48.2	10.4	3.3	6.8
	79.5		13.7		
Programmer Exam	27.9	50.6	14.8	4.3	2.4
	78.5		19.1		

Table 1: Summary of Survey of Evaluation of ITEE

3. STANDARD IT CURRICULUM

3.1. The CAROL Project

The CAROL project was set up by MITI to solve the problem of the shortage of IT engineers. It has four objectives:

(a) Standardization of curriculum. Professional schools have different types of curicula. Some do not meet the requirements of employers. A guideline is necessary to change the status quo so that graduates receive a unified evaluation.

(b) Improving the current educational standards by offering courseware based upon the standard curriculum.

(c) Offering a greater educational opportunity.
The shortage of teaching staff is an immediate problem. Setting a standard for the curriculum and supplying the courseware will greatly help such schools.

(d) Encouraging the software and hi-tech industries to settle in non-urban areas.
The current geographical distribution of the software and hi-tech industries shows a very high concentration in the Tokyo area. This causes an additional shortage of skilled manpower. It is a government policy to provide the means to entice industries to non-urban areas by increasing skilled labor in local communities.

3.1.1. Organization and Functions

The project is carried out cooperatively by four institutions: i.e. MITI as the policy board, the Central Academy of Information Technology (CAIT) as the central educational institution, the Information-technology Promotion Agency (IPA) as the product development organization, and the Association for Professional and Vocational Schools (APVS) as the supporting organization of the potential users of CAROL products.

CAIT has the job of compiling CAROL curriculum, and trains teachers for the beta test sites.

IPA prepares CAROL courseware based on the CAIT curriculum.

Professional schools which have been designated by MITI carry out beta tests of CAROL-based CAI. APVS coordinates the beta test plan and interfaces with CAIT and IPA.

3.1.2. Teaching and Learning Methods

CAROL's approach aims at the education/training of young people who are not knowledgeable with regard to data processing skills.

Three-fourths of IT engineers in Japan start their data processing careers as junior programmers. There aren't any competent educational systems in the computer user organizations except the "on the job training" (OJT) approach. The OJT approach is viable provided there are good teachers available. Unfortunately it is not the usual case to have talented teachers/trainers of basic technical training always available.

Professional schools have been set up to fill the discrepancy of basic technical training. Unfortunately such vocational type education is out of the formal educational scheme. There is neither a formal curriculum or text book validation.

As a consequence, graduates from such vocational educational schools have difficulty in being recognized as professional engineers.

CAROL materials are designed to resolve this unhappy situation for both sides, namely the professional schools and hiring organizations. The approach taken is 1) the standard-ization of curriculum, 2) the ready-to-use teaching materials, 3) the use of the CAI approach and 4) the necessary assistance to train teaching staff.

1) Standardization of Curriculum

CAROL Curriculum is the core of the whole system. It can be used in the entry level classroom and in the more advanced training groups as well. It consists of 30 subjects which are graded to 19 levels.

2) Standardization of Teaching Materials

The standardization of teaching materials is the basis for the assurance of the educational/training level. The materials consist of:

CAI courseware executor CAROL courseware programs

Program manuals
Teachers guides
Student textbooks
CAI courseware authoring system

CAROL courseware has been reviewed with two different view points. One is to validate the contents of programs against the CAROL Curriculum. Ease of use and effectiveness of application are two measures of another view. Such activities will continue for several fiscal years to come.

3) CAI Approach

It is not mandatory for a teacher who is going to use the CAROL system to use a full set of material. Rather he may select any material according to his plan. We recommend that the beta test site schools adopt at least two subjects with full features. For other schools or enterprises, there is no such conditional offer.

The CAROL curriculum is not fully compiled into computer based programs. A subject, "Files", for example, has two sub-divisions, namely "Introduction to Files" and "File System". "Introduction to Files" is designed for fourteen hours of class work with only seven CAI-based study hours. For "File System", all ten hour class hours are covered by the CAI material.

4) Assistance to the Development of Teaching Staff

CAIT has been running short courses to train teachers of the beta test sites. It is not the concern of the government to train all the teaching staff of the professional schools, but a self-learning type of development is expected. The beta test sites will be a good source of information for such teachers who want to acquire relevant know-how.

3.2. The CAROL Curriculum

The CAROL curriculum is divided into two separate parts. The elementary course and the advanced course.

3.2.1. The Elementary Course

The elementary course consists of the following 11 subjects.

(a) Hardware
An introduction to computer hardware. It covers computer types, architecture, IO devices and communication devices.

b) Software
An introduction to computer software. It includes types of software, programming procedures, programming languages, operating systems, service programs, packaged software and software engineering environments.

(c) Information Processing Systems
An introduction to computer systems. It includes purposes, functions and features of systems. Systems concepts, systems performance and systems utilities.

(d) Program Flowcharts
An introduction to the standard flowchart technique with an emphasis on structured programming.

(e) Files
An introduction to file-system technology. Major topics are physical and logical records, dataset layout, file organization, system design considerations, file creation and maintenance, and job control language. Some considerations of the mechanisms of file devices, file access and performance.

(f) Programming Languages
Four languages: COBOL, FORTRAN, Assembly Language, BASIC and C. Language specifications are standard-based. Assembly Language is defined by the ITEE committee.

(g) System Development and Operation

This courseware covers a variety of topics, they do not represent the knowledge necessary to write programs, but are important for understanding operations of data processing organizations. Topics include application program development, program testing, system operation, etc.

3.2.2. The Advanced Course

The advanced course consists of 11 subjects.

(a) Hardware
Advanced study of hardware design, for example, system architecture, internal architecture, interface design and digital circuit design.

(b) Software
Advanced study of software, for example, operating systems, virtual memory and virtual machines, language translators and the UNIX operating system.

c) Database
Understanding database management systems (DBMS), design methods for database, methods for using DBMS, and system performance considerations.

(d) Communication Networks
The role and function of DSS, DSS packages, implementing DSS in business system, etc.

(e) Decision Support System (DSS)
The role and function of DSS, DSS packages, implementing DSS in business systems, etc.

(f) Security and System Auditing
Design considerations to system security, auditing factors of a system, and procedures for auditing.

(g) Project Control
Application of various project control techniques to information processing system development projects. Consideration is given to system standardization procedures.

(h) System Analysis
Methods to understand and analyze end-user requirements and specifications. Techniques to develop system specifications based on the information acquired by the analysis.

(i) External Design
System design methods to develop internal specifications (detailed or program designs). The subject includes the integration and test procedures.

(j) Internal Design
System design methods to develop internal specifications (detailed or program designs). The subject includes the integration and test procedures.

(k) Application of AI Techniques
An introduction to artificial intelligence, its theory and application.

3.3. CAROL Courseware

Courseware programs based on the CAROL curriculum are under development by IPA. The first phase of program development is almost complete. The second phase will be an enhancement of the first phase and maintenance, based on the requirements of beta test users and commercial users.

Courseware is organized in two groups, namely the elementary course and the advanced course.

3.3.1. The Elementary Course

The elementary course is shown in Figure 3. The sequence is self-explanatory. Such subjects as an Introduction to Information Systems, Computer and Information Processing, Introduction to Electronics, and Business Systems are based on conventional teaching methods.

3.3.2. The Advanced Course

The structure of the advanced course is somewhat complex. The sequence on the left side of the Figure is a curriculum for the systems engineer who develops and maintains application-based systems. The sequences at the center and on the right side are for specialist engineers.

Subjects such as considerations for System Development, Migration, and System Operations are covered by conventional educational materials.

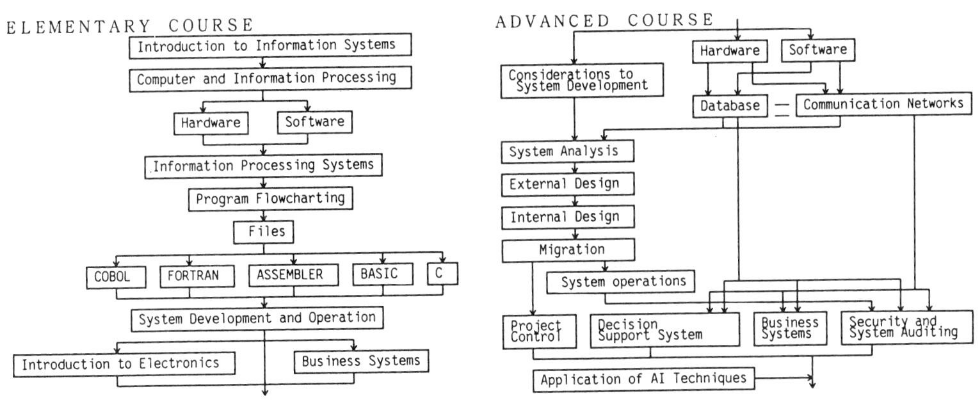

Figure 3: CAROL Curriculum

3.3.3. Development of Course Material

Hardware for CAROL has been selected by IPA so that a large part of professional schools may use the programs without much additional investment. The NEC PC9801 series and the Fujitsu FM-R are two such micro computers. After the initial phase of development, some of the courseware has been converted to several other makes, such as IBM PS/55 series and Univac UP10E series.

The Japanese version of MS/DOS by Microsoft Co. has been selected for the common operating system.

4. CONCLUSION

IT engineers are scarce now, and this demand-supply gap will most likely continue on into the future. It is necessary to attract and educate potential engineers. Although there is a strong need for IT education and continued training, there is a serious shortage of IT teaching staff.

ITEE was designed to encourage IT engineers and prospective engineers to study on their own. The CAROL project has the objective of making better and more efficient IT education possible.

Fortunately, ITEE has had high recognition from IT engineers and their employers. It is an examination that is relatively conservative due to the number of applications and its long history. We do feel that it has to be modernized with more consideration given to microcomputers and workstations.

The CAROL project is under development. We need more responses from the beta test sites and users. Due to the ever-progressing nature of computer technology, a continuous upgrading of the curriculum and courseware are mandatory.

Both projects are accepted by a large number of engineers. We thank the people who have supported us for providing a successful environment, in particular the valuable leadership given by MITT.

5. REFERENCES

"On the Information Technology Engineers Examination System in Japan", Japan Information Technology Engineers Examination Center, February 1989.

"A Report of the Survey on Fostering and Testing Information Technology Engineers", Japan Information Processing Development Center, March 1989, (Japanese).

"CAROL, Courseware for Training Software Engineers", Central Academy of Information Technology, and Information-technology Promotion Agency, March 1988.

"Standard Curriculum for Information Technology Engineers". Information-technology Promotion Agency, June 1987, (Japanese).

*UNIX is the registered trademark of AT&T.
*IPACAROL is the registered trademark of IPA.

Computers in Education
A. McDougall and C. Dowling (Editors)
Elsevier Science Publishers B.V. (North-Holland)

A RAPID AND SUCCESSFUL SYSTEM-WIDE IMPLEMENTATION OF SCHOOL-BASED COMPUTER NETWORKS FOR ADMINISTRATIVE PURPOSES

Jeff MACNISH and Terry MARCH

Schools Administrative Systems Branch, Ministry of Education, 151 Royal Street, East Perth W.A. 6004

1983 saw the start of significant changes to the Western Australian education system. Schools gained far more responsibility. Scope for initiative increased, particularly in addressing local needs through a flexible curriculum structure, but also through the administration of their finances and resources. They also became more accountable for their performance. These changes were the major impetus for the provision of a significant school-based administrative computing system for all government schools in Western Australia.

The first of the changes came with the recommendation from the Beazley and McGraw Committees to allow a far greater amount of choice by students when selecting their courses. The introduction of a unitised curriculum structure in the lower secondary system meant that schools, potentially, would have to create several, separate, complex timetables in the one year to cater for the increased student choice. It quickly became apparent that schools would require some form of computerised support to cope with the increasing timetabling demands.

The second and more recent change came with the implementation of the Better Schools report. This involved the gradual devolution of more authority and responsibility to schools. The aim of this programme was to make schools more self-determining by developing their own educational goals and priorities. They had to manage their own facilities and resources and develop strategies to measure the level of achievement of school-based goals. Schools needed to outline a programme of action for achieving the agreed educational goals. This made them far more accountable for their overall performances both to the Ministry and the community. The Better Schools report also recommended that a new computer system be introduced to minimise the workload associated with these changes and to provide the basis of a management information system.

In 1986 a number of Ministry officers started work on specifications for the new computer system to be installed in schools. Funding was ultimately obtained through a special Cabinet submission and a system selected by tender in 1988.

This paper looks at the highly successful processes that the Ministry of Education has gone through in rapidly installing sophisticated computer networks and applications software into all secondary schools throughout the Western Australian Government system. In addition, the paper also describes how all staff who work in the administrative area of schools have been trained in the operation, use and management of the system within the same short period of time.

1. INTRODUCTION

In recent years many changes have occurred in the Western Australian education system. The roles of educational administrators have also changed and there has been a substantial growth in clerical tasks undertaken by schools. To help manage the changes and the increased pressures on schools, computerised administrative support systems have been installed in all government secondary schools. These systems are perceived as being able to provide gains in efficiency and effectiveness in the areas where schools have been coming under increasing pressure.

As early as 1972 schools were receiving timetabling assistance through the use of timetabling software on the Cyber 72 computer at the Western Australian Regional Computing Centre. The system proved most useful and very popular. It was in fact the first step towards introducing computer technology into the administrative area of schools.

A philosophy of trying to cater for student needs by offering students a range of courses to choose from and then trying to schedule classes so that the majority of students obtain most, if not all, of their course requests has been part of the education system in Western Australia since the late 1960s.

It's a process of fitting the multi-purpose resources of the school to the student course selections rather than making the students select courses which fit the rigid pre-determined use of such resources.

Timetabling a school of approximately 1,000 students in such an environment is a difficult and demanding task and one which cries out for computer assistance.

Rapid developments in computer technology have meant that small businesses and schools are now within the the marketing range for both hardware and software. Early microcomputers, although not powerful enough to handle timetabling, were capable of handling a number of other administrative functions within schools. Some of the larger schools investigated their use and, as the power of the systems increased and their relative cost decreased, more schools purchased microcomputers to help them address their changing administrative needs.

1984 saw the beginning of significant and, by comparison with previous times, rapid changes to the Western Australian education system in both a curriculum and structural sense. The McGaw and Beazley Reports, published in 1984, recommended changes to the secondary education curriculum structure.

The McGaw Committee recommended the division of year eleven and twelve courses into one-year modules and the establishment of more flexible patterns of choice for students in those years (McGaw (1)). At the same time the Beazley Committee recommended that all courses for students studying at the lower secondary school level should be offered as units of study (Beazley (2)). This would replace the fairly structured and limited choice style of education which existed up until then. As can easily be seen, the major change with these new proposals was greater freedom of choice for students when selecting courses.

With the introduction of a unitised curriculum, schools had to try to combine diverse factors such as freedom of student choice, unpredictable popularity of units selected, effective use of their limited resources such as teachers and rooms, and at the same time maintain and balance the educational needs of all students. The introduction of this expanded freedom of choice meant that the administrative task of developing a suitable timetable became an even more complex task. To add to the timetabling woes, there was also the potential for separate timetables to be created for each term or semester instead of the previous process of scheduling classes, once only, for the entire year.

Central support for school-based administrative computing was not in place until 1987 when these curriculum changes began to be introduced. As a consequence, most schools quickly obtained small stand-alone computer systems of their own and began to run a range of locally-developed software to help them with tasks associated with timetabling. They regarded this as a better option than the bureau system, which was limited in its capabilities and time-consuming to use, particularly for remote sites.

With publication of the Better Schools report in 1987 even more significant changes to schools were forecast. The report outlined revised principles that were to provide the foundation for the administration of government schools. This involved the gradual devolution of more authority and responsibility to schools. They were to become more self-determining. Schools would not only have to rationalise their priorities and analyse their relative needs - they would also require some means of determining the success or failure of their school-based development plans. A comprehensive database of student and financial information, together with a sophisticated query and reporting facility, were seen as important componentsin the process of establishing self-determining schools (Ministry of Education (3)).

To address many of these needs which arose from the introduction of a unitised curriculum and the projected devolution of authority and responsibility to schools, the Ministry of Education commenced development of user requirements and technical specifications in 1986. Given the importance of these changes for the education system, an approach was made to goverment seeking funds to support a system-wide implementation where substantial emphasis was to be placed on user training and support. Cabinet approval and support were obtained and a tender let for the supply of hardware and software.

At the same time as these developments were taking place, a major restructure of the administration of the government education system in Western Australia took place. During this process a new branch was formed within the central office to manage and support the introduction of computerised administrative support systems into schools.

2. THE SYSTEM

After an intense evaluation of local and international submissions, an administrative computing system was chosen through the tender process in 1988. It was very sophisticated by comparison with previous computer systems that schools had used for administrative purposes and incorporated, as the major application software, the MAZE school administration system. This was complemented by MS WORD for word processing, PC Anywhere for remote communications, Everex for tape backup and Novell systems software for networking.

MAZE had been developed by a Western Australian company, CAZ Computer Services. It consists of a relational database and software modules specifically designed to assist schools with their administration. As well as the powerful and complex database facility, the software offers users a very high degree of flexibility in designing the data fields, enquiry and data entry screens and reports. Having access to such a powerful tool, which was specifically designed for school administration, allowed the Ministry of Education to quickly customise the system and to address the areas which had been identified as being most in need of computerised assistance. These areas were:

- Storage of student information
- Storage of staff information
- Timetabling
- Booklists and bookshop information
- Academic records and reporting
- Financial records and accounting facilities
- Assets register
- Attendance register
- Flexible query and reporting facilities.

The hardware package was based around a 70 Mb 386 or 286 fileserver, depending on the size of the school, five XT and AT compatible workstations, a modem, letter and draft quality printers and a streaming tape drive.

3. FACTORS AFFECTING THE IMPLEMENTATION STRATEGY

During the planning process it was evident that several factors would play an important part in determining the overall implementation strategy. A large number of sophisticated computer networks had to be operational at sites across a vast geographic area and with a user group that had very demanding and diverse requirements.

Sophisticated multi-user, multi-tasking systems, such as those which had been selected by tender for schools, required considerable skill and expertise to set up and maintain. Schools had neither the staff nor the expertise to manage such an undertaking and so a major role for the central support group emerged. Training had to be the key feature of the implementation. It had to be efficient and large-scale, and address many different needs from a user group with varying levels of expertise.

Coupled with this, one of the underlying concerns to be considered with any system-wide implementation in Western Australia is the vastness of the State. One-third of the total size of Australia, WA has a total area of 2,525,500 sq. kilometres (Pink (4)). It stretches from Albany in the south some 2,500 kilometres to Kununurra in the north. Whilst approximately 60% of the population of the State live in the capital city, Perth, the remainder are scattered through the agricultural, pastoral and mining zones in smaller towns and communities. The climatic conditions vary from tropical humidity and extreme heat in the north to the wet, temperate and very cool temperatures found in the south of the State. The large distances between the capital city and country schools pose problems for the installation and maintenance of equipment as well as for the training and on-going support of users in each school.

Staff in different roles and in different promotional positions in the administrative area of schools each had their own expectations and needs for the new system to fulfil. Principals required management information, Deputy Principals timetabling assistance, Registrars needed help with day-to-day financial management and School Assistants wanted assistance with typing tasks, record storage and management.

These diverse elements created a major skills enhancement problem when the new technology was introduced.

The timing and rate of installations into schools were also important parameters that were considered when the implementation strategy and pan were developed. In order to interlock with other Ministry of Education initiatives, it was important for all schools to develop their timetables for 1990 on the new computer systems. As schools start this complex and time-consuming task in August, a major milestone was predetermined. All of the high and senior high schools had to have their systems installed by were considered when the implementation plan and strategy were developed. In order to interlock with other Ministry of Education initiatives, it was important for all schools to develop their timetables for 1990 on the new computer systems. As schools start this complex and time-consuming task in August, a major milestone was predetermined. All of the high and senior high schools had to have their systems installed by August 1989 and to be operational by that time. To achieve this goal a strategy was designed for the installation of the systems at a rate of three per school week up to August 1989.

4. INSTALLATIONS AND TRAINING

The first of the 86 high and senior high schools received its computer system within one week of the announcement of the tender result in October 1988. Initially, school assistants were trained only in the operation of the hardware and the word processing package. Further training with the MAZE database software and MS WORD was to follow early in the 1989 school year.

This rapid installation of several systems into schools in the later months of 1988 established a high level of confidence in schools about the computer system and the implementation methodology.

It was important that schools had concrete evidence that the system worked and could be installed at a rate fast enough to include all remaining high schools by August 1989. In addition, it enabled them to use their new system immediately in a productive way, albeit only for word processing.

The importance of providing suitably customised software was recognised at an early stage. If the different modules of the software had a similar "look and feel", then a substantial transfer of training from one module to another could be expected.

Whilst a common "look and feel" were inherent in the software, a large number of reports, data entry and enquiry screens, all of which were under user control, had to be set up in the same way. The rapid implementation of systems and the provision of minimal training, in the first instance, kept faith with the users but it bought valuable time for the support team to recruit and train additional support staff and customise the software.

By the beginning of 1989 the central support group, known as Schools Administrative Systems Branch, had reached a total of eighteen staff members, thirteen of whom came from a teaching background. They brought to the branch experience in schools as deputy principals, senior masters, computing teachers, timetablers and primary school teachers. These branch members had the required skills, background knowledge and confidence to liaise with senior Ministry executives and senior administrative staff at all levels, develop and conduct training courses and tailor the software to meet the needs of schools and the Ministry.

As an integral part of the implementation all courses were developed and written by the branch members whose teaching background and familiarity with the role of the course participants provided them with the ideal expertise for such a task. The variety of courses ranged from administration of the system, word processing, data entry, timetabling, principals' seminars and accounting. Most of the courses were held over a two-day period in two training rooms established within the Ministry of Education building in Perth.

This central approach to the training allowed for the more effective and efficient use of staff and facilities and provided the added benefit of allowing ideas to be interchanged between participating schools.

Travel to and from the courses and accommodation of participants was covered by the Ministry. As a further incentive for schools, relief staff were provided for all approved participants attending courses.

Courses were offered in a cyclic manner, thus allowing staff to attend more than one course depending on the needs of each school. The cyclic method of training also allowed the branch to maintain a LOCK-STEP approach with the development of the courses. Schools would all be trained in stages and to the same level rather than fully training one school at a time. This allowed schools time to become familiar with each of the new processes and concepts learned and helped prevent information overload. It also provided a means for the branch to maintain an ongoing assessment of the training techniques and allowed time to make alterations to courses where necessary. Documentation for each of the courses was also prepared by the branch and has been developed in stages to correlate with the level of training being undertaken.

Members of the branch were divided into five teams, each with specific roles related to the training of staff, installation of computer equipment and the provision of ongoing support. One team would supply technical support, another team would provide special timetabling support and training while the remaining three teams would install equipment in schools and provide training courses, telephone support and advisory visits.

Each installation team used two of its members to install the computer systems within the school while the third member was available for training courses or telephone support. Schools were installed by a team in groups based on their location and proximity to each other.

This allowed for the efficient use of branch staff, particulary with respect to travelling time in country areas. The close proximity of schools also provided the possibility for the interchange and discussion of new ideas and administrative procedures. Visits to groups of schools could be accomplished in a single trip.

Each installation required an initial discussion with the principal and associated administrative staff to decide the suitable placement of each of the terminals and the file-server. Once this had been established the computer equipment was installed and tested.

This initial set-up used temporary cabling to allow the school staff to familiarise themselves with the new system and make any necessary changes to the layout before the system was permanently wired. The whole installation process could be completed in half a day depending on the complexity of the layout of the administration building.

Once a school had its system installed two of the staff attended a System Administrator's course. This course provided basic training in the operation of the network software and showed them how to effectively control and run the whole computer system. Once trained these staff were the main link between the school and the branch for all future support.

A second course on word processing followed soon after for two of the clerical staff within the school. Many of the schools already used some form of word processing package and were able to adapt to the new system fairly readily. Initially the courses were designed to introduce the basic skills of word processing. More advanced word processing skills were covered at a later stage. In a similar fashion, schools were introduced to MAZE data entry and timetabling. These courses were followed up at a later date with more advanced training.

The cyclic method of training gave schools a lot of flexibility in addressing their training needs. A variety of dates were available to them and over a period of time all administrative staff could be trained in one or more aspects of the system.

As well as providing comprehensive training courses the branch also provided ongoing support to schools. Once a system was installed the various teams maintained contact with the schools by on-site visits or telephone. A central help desk was also established. Another sophisticated system of contact used the communications package and modem to connect a computer at the central office to the school's computer system as a workstation. Through this facility staff at the central office and the school were able to simultaneously view the same screen. In this way, support staff were able to work directly with a school's database and word processing documents and both the school and support staff could see and discuss what was happening in real time even though they were many miles apart.

5. CONCLUSION

By the end of 1990 all secondary schools in Western Australia will be fully operational with their new computer system. They will be able to use the database to provide reports for their own use and also be able to send relevant data to the Ministry of Education. Reports obtained from the system by schools will play a major part in designing and evaluating school development plans and will be an important component in the accountability process as authority and responsibility are devolved to schools.

During the course of this initiative a vast number of people have been trained in the use of the new computer system. In fact, all staff who work in the administrative area of secondary schools will have been through a substantial skills upgrading exercise by the end of 1990. A major technological upgrade will have been rapidly and successfully undertaken across a major sector of the Western Australian education system.

REFERENCES

(1) McGaw, B., WA Ministerial Working Party on School Certification and Tertiary Admissions Procedures. Assessment in the Upper Secondary Schools in WA (Perth, April 1984) pp. 37-8.

(2) Beazley, K.E., Inquiry into Education in Western Australia. Education in Western Australia (Government Printers, Perth, 1984) 71.

(3) Ministry of Education, Better Schools in Western Australia: A Programme for Improvement (Ministry of Education, Perth, 1987 5.

(4) Pink, B.N., Western Australian Year Book No. 26 (Government Printers, Perth, 1989) 293.

Computers in Education
A. McDougall and C. Dowling (Editors)
Elsevier Science Publishers B.V. (North-Holland)

SWEDISH POLICY ON THE USE OF COMPUTERS IN VOCATIONAL TRAINING

Ph. D. Göran Nydahl

Swedish National Board of Education, S-106 42 Stockholm, Sweden. E. mail (Earn): PCOMGNY at SEUMDC51

Modern vocational training must cover different computer applications relevant to the occupation in question. Access to these creates opportunities for a new methodology and can dramatically affect the syllabus and structure of our training. Well-developed simulation programs can be used for facilitating learning and giving students the opportunity of freely experimenting in an environment that otherwise would not be accessible.

1 INTRODUCTION

In Sweden all students receive nine years of compulsory schooling. The curriculum for this is centrally determined to guarantee equivalent education irrespective of residence and personal financial circumstances.

Almost all students on reaching the age of 16 continue to the next level - upper secondary school "gymnasieskola" - which has different theoretical streams, some of which are preparatory for university studies , as well as a large number of vocational training courses of different kinds. In total there are 26 educational streams. All the streams in the upper secondary school have a centrally determined curriculum.

Specialized vocational training, for example, for economists and technicians is provided in colleges.

2 BACKGROUND

Developments in vocational training in Sweden must be seen in the light of general developments in the Swedish labour market. However, they are broadly equivalent to those in the rest of Europe and other industrialized countries. The labour market has changed and will continue to change both in terms of organization and the type of work to be performed. Technical developments - particularly information technology, demographic changes as well as changing attitudes towards work - these are all factors playing a role in this process. The dividing line between office and industrial work is becoming less clear. Administration tasks such as placing orders, invoicing, etc., will move closer towards production, which in turn implies a needs for "bridging" administration.

Today we have entered a new and technically intensive period, even though large parts of industry may not have undergone major changes as regards the introduction of new technology. The movement towards customer orientation and "just in time" production has to a large extent been satisfied through new technology, particularly in service-oriented activities. Communications technologies of all kinds have reduced the constraints of time and distance.

The service and public sectors, especially the social services, nursing and care, education etc. have, however, tended to remain outside these developments. Even today these activities are highly "labour intensive", although the circumstances surrounding the work have changed considerably. Technical developments have caused a change in the content of the work as well as providing support tools enabling work to be carried out more effectively.

When the computer first was seriously introduced into working life, it was done to automate time consuming processes and to replace human labour. Computer systems often reduced the worker to a "button pusher" controlled by a central computer. Systems were created by specialists without any direct practical experience and knowledge of the working area concerned, and often on the basis of purely theoretical models. This led to reactions against "inhuman" systems, thus starting a healthy debate in society.

The development of computer systems to rationalize and improve company and organizational profitability and efficiency is still being carried out , but with a better insight into the role of people in the system. Besides these information systems, others were developed whose target was in the first instance to extend vocational knowledge as opposed to replacing it. For example engineers extend their range by using computers to perform advanced calculations and quickly design machine parts. Accountants are able to simulate reality through financial models and analyse different alternatives in business. Such computer applications are based on the needs and the knowledge of the professional "non-computer" expert.

Access to systems that increase the opportunities open to the individual are often easy to introduce in an organization. They are not experienced as being threatening since their purpose is not to replace but to enhance the employee, and when they are based on relevant professional knowledge, they are understandable and thus natural.

Computerization, earlier the domain of specialists in information technology, is increasingly being carried out by professional non-computer experts and office workers. This will present the school with new and greater challenges as we approach the 21st century. What follows is an overview of the thinking and direction of vocational education in computer studies for the Swedish upper secondary school sector.

3 THE SETTING OF GOALS FOR THE USE OF COMPUTERS IN MODERN VOCATIONAL TRAINING

Vocational computer training in schools aims at preparing students to be able meet the computer requirements that will be posed in their future occupations. This means:

- that the students should have a certain degree of proficiency in using computer programmes relevant to their future working life.

- that the students, through training in modern technology, should develop an ability and a preparedness to adapt and exploit new computer technology in their future occupations.

- that the students, through concrete experience, learn to evaluate and judge the opportunities provided by computer technology, its limitations and implications in different professional areas and particularly how their own professional roles and working environment are affected.

To reach these goals the school must not only have access to computers, peripheral equipment and computer programs with the same features and functions as in normal working life. The vocational sector in schools must also have skilled computer personnel who can initiate and develop pedagogical methods as well as give vocational teachers support and help in the actual training situation.

4 VOCATIONAL COMPUTER TRAINING - METHODS AND THEORY

Too often computer training is provided in a mechanical way making the user into a "button pusher", without any insight into how the system functions. In unfamiliar situations the user then becomes "stuck" and is often very anxious about pushing the "wrong button".

Computer education aimed at teaching how to operate only a particular system, immediately creates a new educational need when the user is confronted with a similar but new system. The user does not see the similarities, but feels incompetent and uncertain when confronted with the system. New training is thus necessary whenever there is a change in the computer system.

Technological development can be represented by the following diagram:

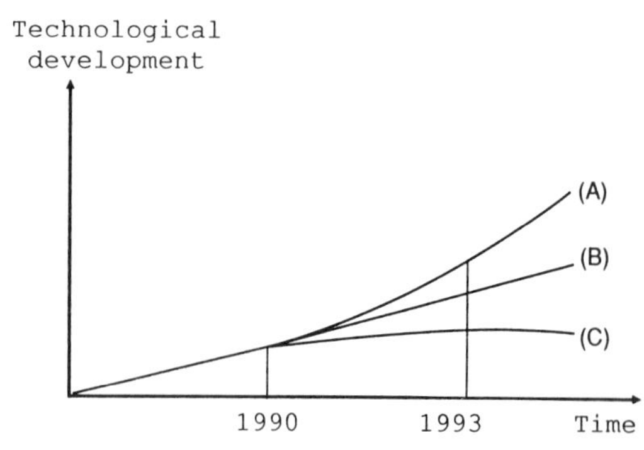

Curve (A) describes "strong" technological development Curve (B) describes generally expected technological development Curve (C) describes technological stagnation

Regardless of whether curve (A) or (B) represents the situation, we can with a very high degree of certainty predict that technological development means that students will usually not be using the system for which they have been trained. Neither can the schools continue to invest in new equipment, nor can we expect or require teachers to "digest" new technologies and design training scenarios for these.

What then shall the school do in such a situation?

One option would be to give up and to transfer responsibility for vocational training to the employer. This may sound drastic, but it might be appropriate in some cases, since it is unrealistic for the school to work with the larger and more complicated technical systems that exist only in some of the larger industries. In these cases emphasis should be put on developing programmes that simulate such systems on the school's computer system.

A word processing system contains a range of different functions that must be present in all systems. The system must contain functions for writing, saving and retrieving texts etc. Besides these basic functions, there also should be other essential functions such as hyphenation, column handling, and others. In advanced systems there can also be other interesting functions such as the ability to draw simple diagrams in a text.

A student who learns a word processing application in an administrative course must learn to recognize these functions. When the student meets a new program he/she will study how the necessary functions for word processing work in the new system. In this way the student is prepared to act intelligently in new situations.

The educational goals of a computer application can be likened to those of a driving licence. The student is not trained to drive a specific type of car but to drive all types of cars, even those that have not yet been developed.

Many of us experience a feeling of temporary uncertainty when we change cars. At the very first crossing the driver puts the windscreen wiper on instead of the indicator. This is not a problem though, since the driver knows the functions that must be present in a car and can thus quickly adapt to the characteristics of the new car.

Vocational computer training should not be given in isolation, but should be naturally integrated into the educational curriculum. The teacher should, through his own use of computers in his daily work, show how computers can be used in different areas. If vocational computer training is given in isolation (sometimes by a special computer teacher), this reinforces for many the picture of the computer as a complicated, exotic piece of equipment for specialists. The need in modern vocational training is to demystify the role of computers.

It is important that the curriculum contains comments and instructions that make it clear that computer applications should be naturally integrated into different subjects. The curriculum must also take into account the fact that the contents of the various subjects can be affected by computer applications. Some of today's skills and knowledge will eventually become less relevant for particular occupations as our knowledge increases. In many occupations, working methods are affected by the powerful tools provided by computer applications and this must, of course, be reflected in the work of the school

Integration in its turn requires general access to computer equipment in ordinary classrooms and not just in computer rooms. Methods for integrating computer training need to be developed and introduced into schools. Schoolbooks must be modified so that they take account of the opportunities provided by computers.

5 THE COMPUTER AS A PEDAGOGICAL SUPPORT TOOL - COMPUTER AIDED EDUCATION

Computers clearly have a role to play in modern vocational training systems. They can also be used to make education more efficient by facilitating the development of new educational methods. This does however raise a number of controversial questions.

It is not obvious that the structure and process of education, as well as its current contents, etc. should be preserved, when new modern techniques are available. It is also not self-evident that education in its future development must be of the "type" we know today. It is more effective to teach students and teachers to actually work on an integrated circuit, instead of beginning with an overview of transistor history. For a teacher this may feel wrong, since one may feel comfortable only in the technological development of which one has been a part. The youth of today take for granted today's technology in a way that should be utilized in education.

Below follow a number of examples on the computer being used as a pedagogical support tool.

Example I. Within the immediate future all technical drawings will be computerized (CAD). What does this imply for education in, for example, technology in engineering courses, if students are taught to draw with a computer, without first learning to draw manually on a drawing board? Experience from earlier projects shows that it does not create any difficulties for the student initially to learn drawing on the computer without having first developed skills in manual drawing. There is even some evidence showing that skills in manual drawing make it more difficult to learn computer drawing and design (experience from a Swedish school "Torsbergsskolan" in the city of Bollnäs). It is easier for students who have learnt "freehand drawing" on computers to learn modern drawing techniques than those who have had no experience of "mouse handling" and the other ways of handling a computer.

This is controversial, since many regard manual drawing skills as the very foundation of an engineering education. To be able to examine more carefully the effects of computer aided education, The National Board of Education here in Sweden started a project where about 150, 16-year old students started using powerful computers right at the very beginning of their first week in technology courses. Initial experiences from the project were:

- Students need about 10 lessons to learn to use the CAD programmmes (AutoCAD) on their own.

- Computer drawing means that the resulting drawings look very good to all students, which is then a source of inspiration and self-confidence for all students.

- Students who could barely create a satisfactory drawing earlier in a purely technical sense and who had to redo the drawing several times, were able produce acceptable looking drawings and thus devote more time to the exercises.

- Training gives the students a number of "Aha" experiences due to the competence that is not only built into the program but appears to the student in its right context.

- Drawing techniques (like many other stages in technical subjects) are of such a nature that the solution to an exercise can be reached in many ways, look different and yet still be correct. Being able to reach the goal in many different ways increases the creativity of the students and their motivation in learning the opportunities implicit in the technology.

- Manual sketching is an important complement to drawing. Computer drawing increases the need for sketching, and also provides more time for training in this skill.

- Clever students advance more rapidly and discover the potential inherent in computer programs for accomplishing different tasks in different ways.

- The role of the teacher in this situation after the introductory phase becomes that of a leader, initiating and encouraging the students as well as sharing his knowledge with them.

Future work in the project will study how students can utilize their skills in drawing in areas such as designing, simulating and making calculations etc. The project also aims to study how far it is possible to go if students have access to a modern engineering environment early on.

Example II. A second example can be drawn from business studies. Is it really necessary to first be taught how to balance the ledger traditionally before studying computer accounting techniques? Many claim this. It has, however, been shown that it is perfectly possible to learn accounting principles directly on a computer and then to use the time saved to simulate and create understanding of different types of accounting systems. This is far easier to do using a computer, since the student can then work with a greater amount of data and be relieved of tedious routine calculations, which would distract attention from the actual problem.

Access to computers can lead to business studies that focus to a greater extent on modern marketing techniques and provide an increased understanding of the different financial conditions under which companies operate. The NBE have initiated a project for studying the use of computers as a pedagogical tool in this area. At this stage, it is too early to evaluate the results.

Example III. A number of projects are studying how knowledge-based systems can be used in vocational training. Today there are a number of systems that provide support for repairing devices of various kinds in different situations. Using such systems can be quite easy. The knowledge in the system is usually built up on the basis of facts and rules where frequency of repetition gives the user a picture of how the knowledge is structured. A larger system can resemble a reference book where knowledge is searched for in a dialogue with the computer and not just based on an alphabetical system. When the information is obtained, it is also possible to find out how and why it was found.

Experience gained from projects based on knowledge systems shows that the knowledge engineer in trying to extract knowledge from the expert becomes the expert himself in the area he is working on. The very process of structuring knowledge in terms of rules necessarily provides knowledge and understanding in the area, even though the final system in itself may not be very impressive. Can a student work as a knowledge engineer in an area and at the same time gain knowledge in different knowledge areas? This is studied in a number of projects.

Example IV. More advanced vocational training implies a greater emphasis on theoretical aspects than before. This is a problem, since many students have chosen vocational training to avoid an orientation that is too theoretical.

Can simulation models be utilized in the computer as an environment for gaining knowledge, which can then later be the basis for developing theoretical reasoning as an alternative to traditional education with models drawn on the blackboard?

A simulated environment is no more than an simplification of reality. On the one hand this presents risks if the student is allowed to interpret the model himself without additional support . On the other hand it can create pedagogical opportunities for studying the effects that otherwise could not be shown in school.

To test these ideas a number of simulation programs are being developed. One works with the distillation of different liquids. The operator of a distillation unit has from experience learnt to work with the system, which in itself is not a trivial task, since the factors involved affect each other. This is obviously a very costly way of learning. A well developed simulation program can take over a great deal of the training input. The idea is not to make a program to train a operator to handle a particular distillation process. Instead the program tries to illuminate operating processes, the environment and the interaction of business factors, at the same time as the distillation process is being studied in different ways.

A different program project with the same goal works with the chemical reduction of a substance, which is then used as the basis for pharmaceutical manufacturing. The reduction is performed under intensive heat conditions, and this means that the process can run out of control, if the students are not able to handle the cooling correctly. This dynamic simulation is aimed at giving the student a feeling for how the related parameters interact with each other.

Many accidents occur due to improper loading of different load carriers (lorries, wagons, boats, aeroplanes etc). The loading must be carried out with care and knowledge as regards the equilibrium point and axle pressure. To illuminate this process, programs have been developed for studying different loding problems.

Already there are programs for studying the effects of pharmaceutical products, conducting experiments with radioactivity and simulating the work of an operator on a nuclear plant.

Finally, using computers as a pedagogical tool can be said to provide experience in using computers, a factor that contributes insight for the student into purely vocational applications.

6 THE NEED FOR COMPUTER EQUIPMENT AND PROGRAMS IN UPPER SECONDARY SCHOOLS

Many in the computer business attempt to develop their own special "niche" to ensure themselves an ongoing market for sales and training. The more unique this is , the higher the fees that can be charged.

Developments are, however, going in the opposite direction. Computer systems have become more similar and they can work together in different ways. The dividing line between personal computers and larger systems is being blurred by modern data communication technology. A Nordic project (Network technology in vocational training) has shown that it is possible to connect bigger systems (Prime), and advanced workstations (Apollo) with a network of IBM and Apple (Macintosh) computers. From the same work ing place, the whole computer network is accessible, in addition to that of neighbouring schools. Development of agreed standards, "de facto" standards, determined by market forces etc., leads to a situation where computers look very similar to the experienced user.

Personal computers and what are called workstations have normally a greater flexibility than large computer systems, since they offer a much greater range of programs. Larger computers are strong in areas where complicated computations and sophisticated database management features are required.

Some specific computer systems, sometimes used in vocational training, do not provide the general knowledge that is necessary for basic education. This applies to systems that in terms of hardware and software are relatively obsolete or whose method of working lies outside current standards. Teachers and students who learn on such systems will be handicapped in comparison with others and unable to use effectively the other computers in the school. Thus in all situations it is necessary to investigate whether a vocational application can be handled by general computers, and only if that turns out to be impossible should we search for "special" solutions.

Knowledge of computers in networks is still very low and many schools are hesitant over choosing relatively complicated networking technology. A special state allowance is given to those schools that want to acquire networks and thus develop knowledg e about network technology in school environments.

7 TEACHER TRAINING AND IN-SERVICE TRAINING

At present admission to teacher training colleges does not require any computer knowledge. As computers are used in almost all occupations, it would be natural to expect future vocational teachers to "bring" with them the computer knowledge gained from their earlier occupations.

Knowledge about the computer as a pedagogical tool is generally sketchy and thus thinly distributed among teacher trainers. This must be changed gradually, since teachers in their basic training should be taught how to use the computer as a pedagogical support tool.

Every vocational area uses the computer in its own specific way. There is an essential difference in using computers in nursing education as compared with machine workshop training. Vocationally specific computer training for the different streams should be developed centrally together with the colleges.

In conclusion, it can be stated that basic training in working with computers should be handled locally with the knowledge that already exists in the individual upper secondary schools. On the other hand in-service training regarding vocationally specific training in computers, should be handled by specialists from the colleges.

Computers in Education
A. McDougall and C. Dowling (Editors)
Elsevier Science Publishers B.V. (North-Holland)
© IFIP, 1990

TEACHING HUMAN-COMPUTER INTERACTION TO COMPUTER PROFESSIONALS BY DISTANCE LEARNING: SOME KEY ISSUES

Jenny PREECE and Laurie KELLER

Computing Department, Open University, Milton Keynes MK7 6AA, United Kingdom

This paper reports on issues needing resolution when developing a course in human-computer interaction.

When deciding what to teach and how, the multi-disciplinary nature of HCI becomes problematic; other issues, some of which stem from this, are: theory versus practice, provision of tools versus knowledge, the nature of design and encouraging human-centeredness.

The paper also draws a comparison between the practices of user-centered iterative software design and the way that our course was developed.

1. INTRODUCTION

Two often stressed aspects of human-computer interaction (HCI) are its newness and its multi-disciplinary nature. These not only provide unique challenges to both researchers and teachers, they are also the source of problems. An obvious problem for those starting to teach HCI is the lack of an established curriculum. Being multi-disciplinary with strong foundations in psychology, computer science and ergonomics also results in diversity of opinion about what should constitute the curriculum. This is manifest as much in terms of how particular processes, such as design, are carried out as in decisions about which topics should be taught. Consequently, developing a curriculum without strong bias can be a problem. Another problem facing those who teach HCI is that many important topics are still only research issues and are thus not well established.

We shall discuss how we dealt with these and other questions in the development of a graduate level course intended for practising industrial and commercial software developers, engineers in telecommunications, software development and manufacturing and technical managers. In addition we shall describe how the development and presentation of this course resulted from a process very like the iterative development of an interface, from idea through design, evaluation and testing. It is taught by distance learning. The teaching materials must stand on their own merits, and the student is in the same situation as a learner interfacing with a new computer system. Distance learning can be considered as covering the various forms of study at all levels which are not under the continuous, immediate supervision of tutors present with their students in lecture rooms or on the same premises, but which, nevertheless, benefit from the planning, guidance, and tuition of a tutorial organisation (Holmberg 1978).

Before discussing some of the challenging academic issues that we encountered while developing the curriculum, we shall briefly paint the scene by describing the nature of the course, how it was developed and how it will be studied.

2. COURSE AS INTERFACE

2.1. Course materials

The primary means of teaching is through written material, which in our case is eight *units*, which are purpose-written booklets each containing material for approximately 15 hours of study and a purpose-compiled reader (Preece and Keller, 1990), supplemented by a 75 minute video entitled 'Industrial Applications of HCI'. The reader consists of from two to four articles and papers of importance in each of the areas described under 'content' in section 5. The video shows real case studies filmed *in situ* and is an excellent medium for demonstrating the dynamic aspects of interfaces and HCI work. Theoretical and practical exercises are provided in the course materials and these are discussed later in the paper.

2.2. The development process

Self-contained support is of major importance in distance learning (Neil, 1981). This is ensured by the development process described below.

The team

The development team reflected the multi-disciplinary nature of HCI: One of us is a computer scientist coming from an educational background with a strong interest in science teaching and psychology. This team was assisted by academics from the Dutch Open Universiteit, consultants, assessors (who assess the academic and industrial suitability of the material), student testers and critical readers who are subject experts in cognitive science, human factors, educational technology, computer science and industrial research and development.

The process

The course team developed the materials through sessions of discussion and intra-team negotiation by working iteratively: criticizing, assessing and testing material as it was developed. This is analogous to user-centered iterative design processes advocated by many HCI specialists (e.g. Gould, et al. 1987). The material passes through five draft stages. Stage one is commented on by the team alone, with stages two and three commented on additionally by the critical readers and assessors. The fourth draft is tested by student testers, and the final draft again assessed by the assessors. This accords well with Jones' (1981) description of the design process: 'Simulating what we want to make (or do) before we make (or do) it as many times as may be necessary to feel confident in the final result.'

At those draft stages where material is commented on by team members, critical readers and assessors, suggested changes are negotiated and incorporated. Students who test the material are selected on the basis of how typically they represent the target audience. These students 'do' the course, including assessment material, reporting on how long it took them, any parts of the material they experienced difficulty with, and any suggestions they have. All this is taken into account in the preparation of the final draft, which then passes to an editor and is published, much as a book is.

2.3. Student interaction style

Material in the units and the reader is broken down into easily assimilated 'chunks' of sections (bands in the video). The student moves from reading a unit to reading a chapter or section in the reader, back to the unit, and thence to a band of the video as directed. The size of such sections and bands has to take into account attentional constraints; the movement from one medium to another helps to keep the student alert and reinforces teaching by restating topics in a variety of ways and introducing variations.

Learning is not merely a passive activity. Each section contains two types of activity for the student. One is the self-assessment question, which is a question that directs the student to *rephrase or integrate* knowledge taught within a unit section or a reader chapter. This helps to reinforce the material. The student who gets a 'wrong' answer (answers are given at the back of the unit booklet) can re-read the material again. The second type of activity (an exercise) asks the student to *apply* the knowledge just taught in a practical way (for example asking the student to read a scenario and then select suitable evaluation method(s) for the situation described in the scenario, giving reasons for her choice). Some exercises call upon the student to relate her own experience to concepts through demonstration (for example, demonstrating running a mental model by asking the student to recall the number and placement of windows in her home or place of work). Others provide real scope for developing concepts. Feedback is provided in a 'comment' immediately following each exercise. The comment may be a firm answer where this is appropriate, an example answer, or consist of a discussion of the issues raised by an exercise.

At three points in the course the student undertakes much more extended exercises in the form of three assignments, which are marked and commented on comprehensively by a tutor. In these, the student selects an existing computer interface with which she is familiar, analyses it for its strengths and shortcomings, selects one aspect of it which is particularly 'poor' for redesign, and then evaluates her new design. This virtually constitutes a project, but it is carried out during the learning process. Feedback from the tutor thus provides more than correction of error - it also provides suggestion for altering the project as it is in progress.

3. MAJOR ISSUES

We found that three aspects of HCI presented us with special problems which had to be solved at the curriculum planning level, although they also had significant effects on such issues as the order of topics and at a fairly detailed content level. These were: the newness and multi-disciplinary nature of HCI, questions of a balance between theory and practice, and whether we would place our emphasis on tools for HCI, knowledge about HCI, or both.

Newness and multi-disciplinary nature

The fact that HCI is new means that there is little in the way of curriculum models for us to follow. Thus we were confronted with the question of what to teach. At the same time we had to be aware that our students would be drawn largely from among software developers, engineers and managers, and that many of these people are unfamiliar with and sceptical of the claims of other disciplines, cognitive science and psychology in particular. We had to find a way around the resistance we expected to encounter from people accustomed to 'hard' disciplines when confronted with a 'soft' discipline. Long and Dowell (1989) have identified and analysed three different perspectives of HCI which they describe as frameworks; these are craft (e.g. the heuristic approach), applied science (a hypothesize and test approach) and engineering (the use of prescriptive knowledge applied to design). Explicitly defined frameworks like these can be useful for explaining and identifying the nature of different perspectives both when examining research issues and when developing a curriculum.

Theory vs. practice

A special problem exists about the relative placing of what we teach on a continuum ranging from pure theory to pure practice. Should we emphasize computer science to the exclusion of psychology, should we supply our computer scientists with a large helping of psychological theory, should we stick to practice? In the case of distance education, theory is probably easier to teach as it is amenable to handling in print and on video and practice is generally the most difficult because of the logistics of providing access to a particular computer system. Our answer was partly influenced by this logistical problem, as our students cannot be brought together in a well kitted laboratory where they can be assisted by technicians. We have assumed, based on marketing studies of our students, that each has access to a computer and software of *some* type, so we chose to involve them in practical work but not in set exercises, allowing them to draw upon their own experience in their own work environment. Thus our course is more oriented towards practice than theory. We most closely meet Long and Dowell's (1989) engineering framework of HCI (ideally constituted of human factors and software engineering principles and practices as (ideally) specifying then implementing designs, p24), but include some aspects of their applied science framework of HCI ('HCI as an applied science discipline uses scientific knowledge (psychology, linguistics, artificial intelligence, computer science) as an aid to addressing the general problem of designing humans and computers interacting to perform work effectively.' p20).

Tools vs. knowledge

Tools include guidelines as well as software and other design tools. We had a choice of teaching a purely practical course which would equip our students quickly to work with tools we provided, or we could equip our students with knowledge about tools, techniques, methods and how to use these appropriately. We chose to equip our students with knowledge, including the knowledge of where to find and how to evaluate guidelines and other tools. As an example, the unit on applied cognitive psychology explains how some laboratory research findings have been distorted and over generalized and it then sets an exercise in which students evaluate a set of guidelines with reference to an architectural CAD system.

4. OTHER ISSUES

A number of subsidiary issues also needed consideration; several of these derived, at least in part, from the multi-disciplinary aspect of HCI and other general issues.

In situ vs. laboratory practical work

Wrapped up in the debate about theory and practice is the issue of practical work. As we have already said, students can analyse, evaluate and redesign systems that they use at work. Studying systems *in situ* like this has some obvious advantages; students are much more likely to see the relevance of the course and their work may even have long term benefits.

Being able to do *in situ* practical work is fortunate because we cannot provide conventional university laboratory work. The interactive style of the course and the assignments more than compensate for what might appear to be a problem. What cannot be compensated for is the team aspect of most system design. Whereas students generally do our design exercises on their own, it is likely that they experience team work in their jobs.

Psychology for a sceptical audience

Another influence of the multi-disciplinary nature of HCI is seen in decisions about the topics that are taught. How much ergonomics, computer science and psychology should be taught and how? Our decision was influenced partly by the kind of students who will do the course and partly by the expertise of the core team and the consultants. A conscious decision was taken that the pure ergonomics content of the course would be low. Also, while we point out the importance of work organizational issues, we could not cover this area of HCI in detail. Nor did we think it necessary to go into basic computer science since our students will have expertise in this area, although they would be unlikely to know much about the way HCI issues can contribute to design practices, HCI prototyping techniques and UIMs. Also, most of them would have very little knowledge of psychology so we needed to teach psychology and show its relevance to system design.

Teaching subjects in an applied way can be problematic; experts often argue that essential topics have to be taught in a relatively theoretical fashion before concepts can be appreciated in *an* applied situation. Our experience is that students must see the relevance of a subject. In addition we have observed scepticism from computer scientists about the value of psychology in system design. Consequently, a great deal of effort was focussed on making the applied psychology units relevant and palatable for these students. A number of strategies were employed to achieve this goal. Firstly, we avoided teaching the psychology and then illustrating it with examples; whenever possible we found examples and showed how the psychological issues applied. Secondly, we used a large number of small everyday examples as well as larger case studies such as the exercise which has been mentioned in which students examined their mental models of their own houses.

We also tried to discourage the 'cookbook' approach to psychology epitomized by low level guidelines. Again, we have observed the appeal of guidelines among non-psychologists, with little concern about how generalizable the information is. Consequently, we developed exercises in which students saw the inappropriateness of particular guidelines for certain design problems.

Order of the topics (i.e. units)

The order of topics covered by the eight units may seem fairly obvious; particularly if it is decided that topics will be taught in roughly the order in which they occur in the design process. However, for various reasons this was not straightforward. For example 'input, output and communication style' is taught before applied cognitive psychology even though there are many important psychological issues to be considered in device selection and the choice of communication style. This is because we recognized that even psychology sceptics identify immediately with the obvious need to make these selections in system design. We took this opportunity to hold these students' attention and to point out the relevance of psychological considerations in, for example, selecting an input device or command, menu and icon design. This also helped to pave the way for the applied psychology unit.

Design - what is it?

There are two units on design because this is the focus of the course - many concepts are brought together and applied in solving design problems. As well as recognizing the importance of these units, it was obvious that their content would be controversial. The different perspectives of the course team members and the HCI community at large were reflected in our debates. For example, should it be top-down as advocated by most software engineers, or should it be holistic? Two related issues tend to arise from these two approaches. Firstly, how much should we reflect idealized theory and how much the practices of the real world? Secondly, how much emphasis should be placed on formal representation? Thus, the 'multi-disciplinary' and 'theory vs. practice' issues discussed earlier were very influential.

Formal top-down approaches like those advocated in Moran's Command Language Grammar (1981) and Foley and Van Dam's Linguistic Model (1982) are not used in practice for a number of reasons. The structure of these models is such that each level is viewed in its entirety and must map and be consistent with layers above and below it. This is achieved through a formal notation. However, the lack of clear distinction between levels and the often cumbersome nature of the mappings themselves (brought about partly by the notation and partly by repetition from one level to the next before the new components specific to that level are introduced) make these approaches unsuitable for large-scale system design. What are the alternatives? Which current practices are sufficiently exemplary to be taught in a course of this nature? After considerable deliberation we developed our own definitions of two approaches to design: a generalized layered approach and a non-layered approach, which we define as:

> A layered design framework is one in which a design is developed through a number of layers in a relatively structured and rigorous way. The main features of such an approach are that: (i) layers are hierarchical and the approach to design is top-down, that is, from the most abstract level to the most concrete; (ii) each layer is clearly distinguishable from the next; (iii) formal notations are or can be applied at each layer; (iv) each layer is itself a complete description of the system from the perspective of that layer; and (v) specific mappings are used to go between layers.
>
> A non-layered framework does not contain an explicit layered structure. The design process appears to focus on the conceptual design of the system and then moves fairly directly to some form of prototyping. Only at a much later stage when the basic conceptual form of the design is sorted out does the issue of notation become central in order (i) to communicate the design to programmers for implementation and (ii) to check that consistency and other agreed design principles are upheld and trade-offs are made apparent.

The non-layered framework might be said to be a 'creative' approach while the layered framework is much closer to approaches adopted by software engineers. Both, however, are user-centered: the first emphasizes the need to take psychological issues into account in a theoretical way, while the latter tends to rely heavily on testing prototypes with users. Thus, the theory vs. practice issue is again raised. Our aims were to illustrate the advantages and disadvantages of the two extremes and to discuss how 'shades of grey' might be useful, such as using the framework of the layered approach without detailed mappings, and to introduce a number of techniques of practical benefit to students. We adopted the motto of 'when controversy exists come clean about the issues and then provide the best possible cases representing each side of the debate; develop exercises in which students are exposed to the strengths and weaknesses of each case, and then let the students judge for themselves having experienced each.'

This debate about teaching design also impinged on several other units in the course. For example, in the unit in which the selection of input devices for use with particular systems for specified tasks and by particular users is discussed we get students to consider how such decisions should be taken: top-down as advocated by Foley *et al*. (1984) or holistically as advocated by Buxton (1987)? Although the Foley *et al*. paper is now old in terms of HCI their top-down approach is consistent with the way many people with software engineering and engineering backgrounds prefer to work. However, Buxton's approach is more in tune with the way many researchers with psychological training might want to work. Hence the multi-disciplinary nature of HCI again made itself felt. Our solution here too was to guide students to evaluate the strengths and weaknesses of each for themselves.

5. WHAT WE DID: CONTENT AND SPECIFIC ISSUES

As we have already said, the course consists of eight units, each with a different area of content. These are:

Unit 1: Introduction to Human-Computer Interaction (scene setting)
Unit 2: Input, Output and Communication Style (devices and dialog)
Unit 3: Applied Cognitive Psychology
Unit 4: Knowledge and Action: Mental Models in HCI
Unit 5: Fundamentals of Design (user-centered approaches and techniques)
Unit 6: Design: Analysis and Representation (analysis of formal design and notations)
Unit 7: Evaluation
Unit 8: Design Support (guidelines, tools, prototyping and UIMs)

The basic content of the course (Open University, 1990) can be inferred from these titles; due to lack of space we shall not discuss each in detail. Instead, we shall discuss some lower level issues related to these units.

Lack of good case examples

There was a problem finding case studies to illustrate particular issues. For example, we needed to satisfy our students with practical software and managerial experience of such questions as why HCI is important in system design. However, as clear-cut conclusions are impossible to draw in complex situations where direct cause and effect relationships are hard to identify, there are few case study examples available. Our way around the problem was to develop hypothetical though realistic scenarios in which students are forced to draw on their own experiences to recall or relive interactions with systems.

Terminology

At several points in the course, we had to define explicitly the terminology that was used in a form suitable for teaching. In such a young discipline and one with multi-disciplinary roots, there is a problem of terminology, particularly when there has been a strong research thrust and until very recently no undergraduate or graduate programs of study. Often when researchers talk to each other it is unimportant whether one, for example, refers to dialog style (discussed in Unit 2) to mean such things as command based systems or uses the term very specifically to mean generic proprietory product styles as the term is used by Newman (1988). Nor does it matter too much if 'direct manipulation' is a dialog style, a collection of styles, an interaction style, a communication style, a set of principles or some kind of hybrid of several of these things. Again experts can identify the important aspects of the conversation, so precise use of terms is not necessary and may even seem pedantic. This is not so in a teaching situation, and particularly not in distance learning where there is no one on hand to rectify misunderstandings. A similar problem arose in discussion about mental models and design - a well known terminological problem.

Other problems include clashing terminology which seems to have arisen from borrowing terms from other disciplines - particularly prevalent in a multi-disciplinary subject like HCI. For example *multi-tasking* has a restricted meaning in computer science (interleaving instructions from different tasks in a processor), whereas in HCI it is used much more generally to mean a person continually switching from one task to another.

How much statistics should be taught in the evaluation unit?

The unit on evaluation teaches Long and

Whitefield's (1986) five categories of methods: Analytic (e.g. keystroke level analysis), observational, survey, experimental, and expert. In order to carry out good evaluation experiments (in the purest sense of the word 'experiment') students need to know some basic statistics. It was a controversial issue how much should be taught about experimentation and statistics. The conflict was that the whole course falls more towards the practice end of the theory-practice spectrum and yet it is a short course. The decision reached was to focus on experimental method and to point those students with no statistics to suitable references elsewhere. However, in future years we may include our own short guide on basic statistics.

6. CONCLUSIONS

The multi-disciplinary nature of HCI has been debated by several authors (e.g. Kammersgaard, 1988; Reisner, 1987; Long and Dowell, 1989) and as we have shown, its ramifications for curriculum development are far-reaching. For example, Figure 1 shows that this issue has an impact on most of the others either directly or indirectly. In this respect it can be thought of as a meta-issue.

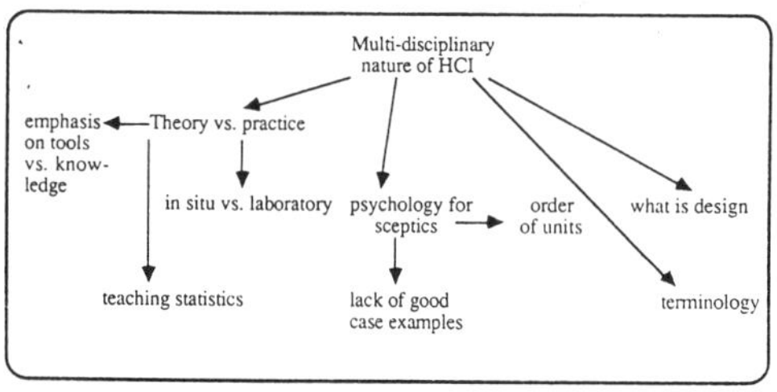

Figure 1: The impact of the 'multi-disciplinary nature' issue on the other issues.

Figure 1 also summarizes our conclusions about the relationships between the other issues, which are not always straightforward; several are inter-related.

The interactive course development process was valuable for bringing as many views as possible into debates about the issues and, as in interface design, the course ought to meet the needs of the users (that is, students) - time will tell.

Acknowledgements

The authors would like to acknowledge the other members of the course team, particularly Yvonne Rogers. We also wish to thank the students who tested the materials and the following people who have been consultants or contributed material to early drafts: Gilbert Cockton, Steve Draper, Ken Eason, Claire O'Malley, Brian Sharratt, Simon Richardson, and Michael Tauber. Many others have also offered advice and suggestions including several people who have critically appraised drafts of the material during its development; others have provided secretarial and administrative support. We are very grateful to all of them.

References

BUXTON, B. (1987) There's More to Interaction than Meets the Eye: Some Issues in Manual Input, in NORMAN, D. A. and DRAPER, D. W.(eds), *User-Centered Design,*. Lawrence Earlbaum Assoc., Hillsdale, NJ. pp 319 - 337

FOLEY, J. D. AND VAN DAM, A. (1982) *Fundamentals of Interactive Computer Graphics.* Addison-Wesley, Reading, MA.

FOLEY, J. D., WALLACE, V.L. AND CHAN, P.(1984) The Human Factors of Computer Graphics Interaction Techniques. *IEEE Computer Graphics and Applications.* (Nov.) pp 13 - 46. Reprinted in PREECE and KELLER.

GOULD, J. D., BOIES, S. J., LEVY, S. RICHARDS, J. T. and SCHOONARD, J (1987) The 1984 Olympic Message System: A Test of Behavioural Principles of System Design, *Communications of the ACM,* Vol. 30, No. 9 (Sept.) pp. 758 - 769. Reprinted in PREECE and KELLER.

HOLMBERG, B. (1978) *Distance Education - A Survey and Bibliography.* Kogan Page Ltd., London.

JONES, J. G. (1981) *Design Methods: Seeds of Human Futures.* John Wiley and Son, New York.

KAMMERSGAARD, J. (1988) Four different Perspectives on Human-Computer Interaction. *International Journal of Man-Machine Studies.* Vol 28, pp 343 - 362. Reprinted in PREECE and KELLER.

LONG, J. and DOWELL, J. (1989) Conceptions of the discipline of HCI: craft, applied science, and engineering, in SUTCLIFFE, A. and MACAULAY, L. (1989) *People and Computers V - HCI '89,* The Cambridge University Press, Cambridge, pp 9 - 32.

LONG, J. and WHITEFIELD, A. (1986) 'Evaluating interactive systems', a tutorial presented at *HCI '86*, York, September.

MORAN T. (1981) The Command Language Grammar. *International Journal of Man-Machine Studies*. Vol. 15, pp 51 - 85.

NEIL, M. W. (ed) (1981) *Education of Adults at a Distance, a Report of the Open University's Tenth Anniversary International Conference*, Kogan Page Ltd., London. p. 98.

NEWMAN, W. N., (1988) The Representation of User Interface Style, *Proceedings. of the Fourth Conference of the British Computer Society Human-Computer Interaction Specialist Group, People and Computers*, JONES, D. M and WINDER, R. (eds.) Cambridge University Press: Cambridge. pp 123 - 137

OPEN UNIVERSITY (publishers) (1990) *PMT 607 - Human-Computer Interaction* , Milton Keynes, UK. ISBN 0 7492 4230 2

PREECE, J. and KELLER, L. (eds) (1990) *Human-Computer Interaction: Selected Readings*, Prentice-Hall, Englewood Cliffs, New Jersey.

REISNER, P. (1987) Discussion: HCI, What Is It and What Research is Needed? in CARROL, J. M. (ed) *Interfacing Thought: Cognitive Aspects of Human-Computer Interaction*. Bradford Book, MIT Press, Cambridge, MA.

Computers in Education
A. McDougall and C. Dowling (Editors)
Elsevier Science Publishers B.V. (North-Holland)

RECENT STATUS ON CAI IN JAPANESE INDUSTRIES

Yasutaka SHIMIZU*, Ryuichi ISHIGURO** and Mitsumasa MORIYAMA**

* The Center for Research and Development of Educational Technology (CRADLE)
Tokyo Institute of Technology, 2-12-1 O-okayama, Meguro-ku, Tokyo, 152 Japan

** Educational Media Development Division, Japan Management Association
3-1-22 Shibakouen, Minato-ku, 105 Japan

The CAI Committee of the Japan Management Association (JMA) conducted a survey in April of 1989 to determine the level of interest and present use of CAI in Japan. More than 4,000 questionnaires were sent to individuals and sections involved with employee training in companies in Japan and 530 responses received. It is significant that the proliferation level of CAI has changed drastically since the last survey. In 1986, only 6.1% of the companies surveyed said they had already introduced CAI; in 1989 the figure increased 3.7 times to reach 22.5%. In addition, 25.5% of the companies indicated that they "are currently considering", "will start considering soon", or "are currently conducting surveys on" the introduction of CAI, which implies that 48% consider CAI as a positive tool in their employee education system.

1. INTRODUCTION

Many now claim that Japan has become an information society on a par with the highest developed countries. A variety of information can be treated by computers and communications systems, and mastering the effective management of these tools will assure a comfortable life for society in the future.

The personal computer has recently drastically increased in capacity and decreased in cost. Because of this, computer applied devices in almost every conceivable category have been developed and put into practical use. It is also utilized in education, particularly in educational research, school management and individual learning systems called Computer Assisted Instruction (CAI).

Determining the current and future potential value of CAI in enterprises is of great interest for those who are in charge of corporate in-house education. The Japan Management Association (JMA) has been conducting surveys in an attempt to clarify the situation since 1985. The first 1985 survey conducted was limited only to regular clients. However, when the second survey was conducted in November of 1986 by the CAI Committee, the results were widely publicized through the media. The third survey was conducted in April of 1989 and questionnaires were sent to individuals in Japan involved with in-company employee training to ascertain the status of CAI. This report presents the results and an evaluation of this most recent survey, and also refers to statistics obtained in the second survey.

2. METHOD OF SURVEY

1989 questionnaires were mailed to 4,423 individuals in educational and training departments of companies listed on the Japan Stock Exchange and those who had attended CAI seminars sponsored by JMA. The list of questionnaire recipients did not include makers of CAI hardware or courseware equipment vendors, since the main purpose of the survey was to learn the system's actual use in company training and the opinions of trainers and educators. Inclusion of those in the business of making and selling the system would not have reflected the real demand by companies.

The survey period was from April 3 (questionnaire mailed) through April 21 (deadline for receipt). The majority of the 530 replies received were from individuals at the level of president, director or manager, the decision-making level, and 44% of these were directly involved with the training and education carried on within the company itself. The percentage of responses received to total questionnaires sent out was 12%, a normal ratio for mail distribution. Table 1 shows the number of subjects and responses.

Table 1 Number of subjects and responses.

Survey period	Subjects	Responses (Response rate)
April 1989	4423	530 (12.0%)
November 1986	4720	609 (12.9%)

3.INDIVIDUAL RESPONDENT OPINIONS

3.1 Recognition of CAI

The recognition of and inclination toward the CAI system by those who are administering it is of interest, because they are really the motivating force behind the increase in its use. Figure 1 shows the percentage of recognition of CAI and the level of interest expressed by respondents. Note that these levels of awareness and interest have increased over the past two and half years to the extent that eight out of every ten individuals have heard of the term. Obviously different from the situation two and half years ago is that the ratio of those who are "aware of" CAI has increased to 65% from 48%, and that the ratio of individuals who "have studied" or "can explain to others" has doubled, reaching 40%, because of its highly promising educational attributes. It can be concluded that CAI has become much more popular and better-known among those responsible for in-house education.

3.2 Affirmation for Company Education

There are two primary and quite opposite opinions regarding the use of CAI for training: one is that it is sure to be good in future because of the great potential of computers; and the other is that human relations are extremely important in education of any kind and that this responsibility should not be turned over to machines.

We asked whether or not CAI is good for company training. The percentage of affirmative replies is shown in Fig. 2, where (a) displays the overall results obtained from all respondents. Those who had heard of CAI and those who had not are represented in (b) and (c), respectively. Note that 61.3% of those who were aware of CAI favored its use in company training; only 7% of this group replied negatively to its implementation. It is impressive to note that the percentage of affirmative answers from those who know of CAI was much greater than the response from those who did not know of it. The more one learns of CAI, therefore, the more positive is the attitude favoring its introduction in companies. This means that CAI certainly has positive future prospects.

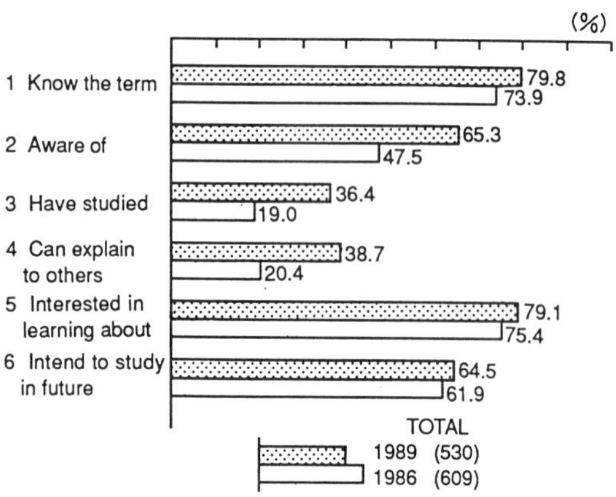

Fig.1 Recognition of CAI and level of interest

3.3 Conditions for Broad Diffusion of CAI

There are certain conditions which were pointed out as requiring attention in order for it to be more widely used (Fig. 3).

Sixty-four percent of the respondents aware of CAI noted that the most important condition for its wider utilization was improvement in the quality of educational software. The second important condition was that individuals in charge of employee education must understand CAI, which had increased from 36% to 60%. Other conditions included a greater variety of educational software and easier-to-use hardware. The percentage of respondents who answered that cost was too high, particularly the software-related cost which had been an important condition for popularizing CAI, decreased drastically from 54% to 35%. The prevailing perception seems to be that quality is more important than cost. At the same time, it was found that it is increasingly important to enhance the understanding of CAI among those who are in charge of education. CAI is now entering a new phase in which the issue of promoting user understanding needs to be addressed, although the quality of the software still remains a challenge.

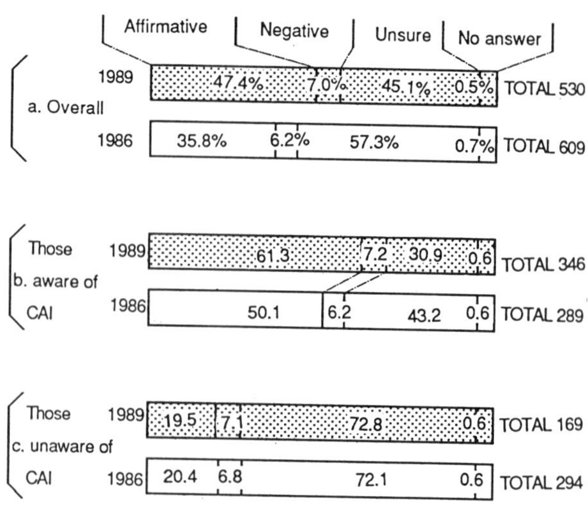

Fig.2 Responses regarding use of CAI for in-house education

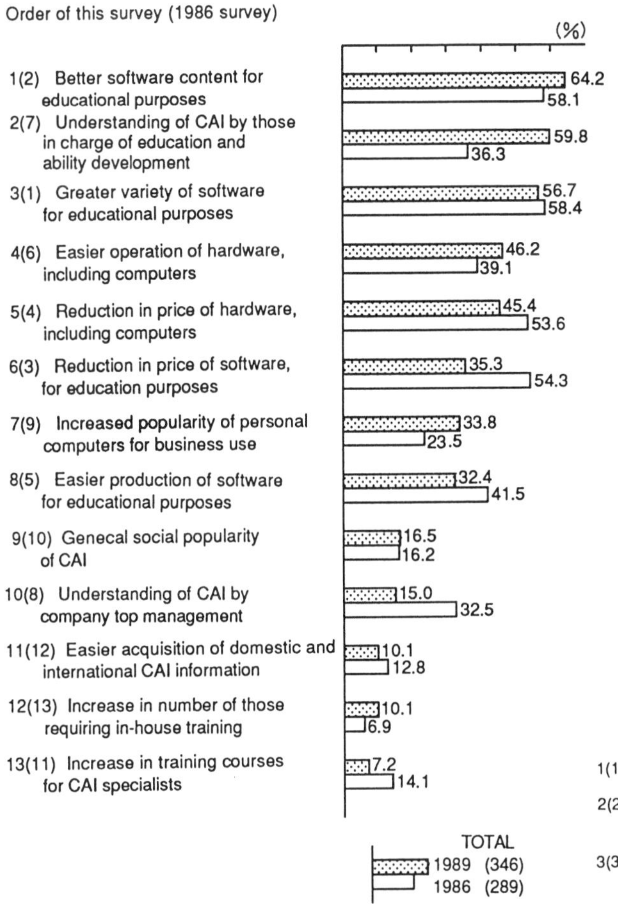

Fig.3 Conditions necessary for CAI diffusion

3.4 Company Opinions on CAI

Company opinions on CAI are compared with results of the first and second surveys in Fig. 4. Note that a dramatic change can be seen between the 83.4% of companies who had no plan to use CAI in 1985 and the mere 8.5% who replied this way in 1986. Comparing the results between 1986 and 1989, CAI is more popularly accepted by companies than ever before, with 22.5% already having introduced it. Considering the fact that only 6.1% had utilized CAI in their education programs two and half years ago, tremendous progress has been made in the level of CAI acceptance. Two and half years ago, 25.2% of those surveyed responded that CAI was "now under consideration", "to be considered soon", or that "a survey was now underway". The fires indicate that a considerable number of these companies during that period made decisions in favor of introducing CAI. It is also thought that some of the companies which had not considered the introduction of CAI two and half years ago are now looking into the possibility.

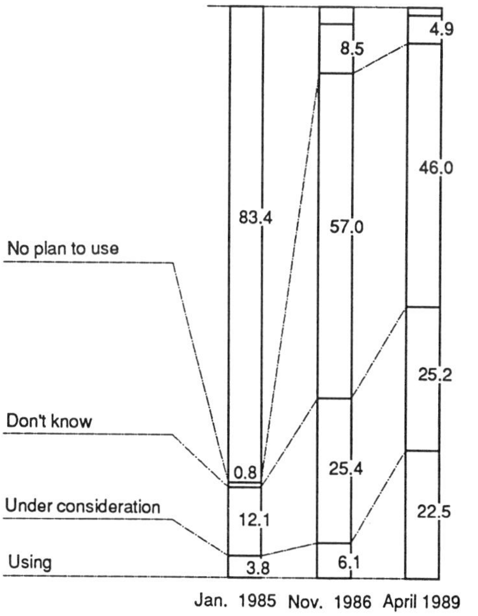

Fig.4 Comparison of CAI survey results

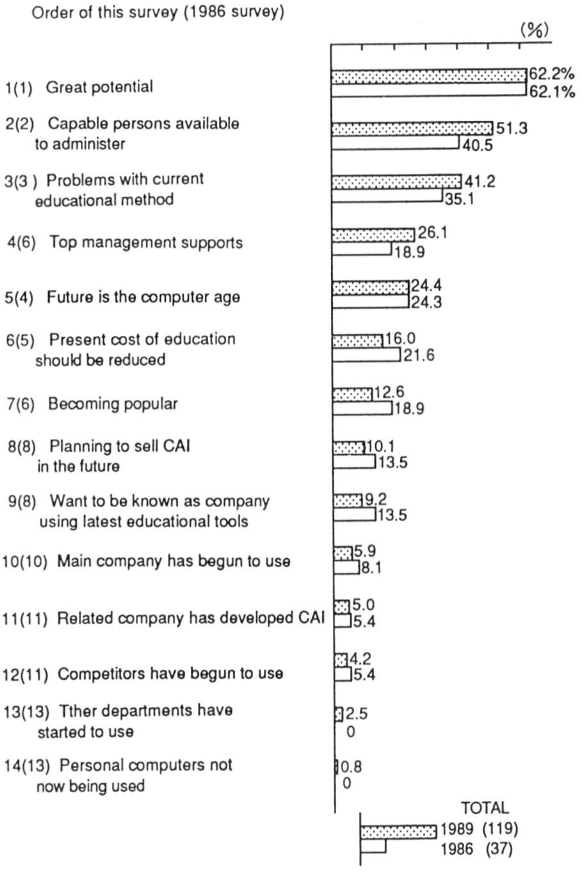

Fig.5 Main reasons for CAI utilization

4. STATUS OF COMPANIES ALREADY UTILIZING CAI

4.1 Motivation behind the Introduction of CAI

Our question was the reason that the company was now using CAI. Figure 5 reflects the finding of why the CAI system is already in use or is being considered by the companies represented in the 1989 survey. Sixty-two percent of the respondents said that the major factor which had motivated them to introduce CAI was the great potential it offers. The second most common factor was that the person in charge of education enthusiastically promoted CAI (51%). This clearly shows the value of having skilled individuals able to oversee the CAI program and, in the author's opinion, indicates that specialized training in CAI administration would greatly advance introduction of the system. Compared to 1986, there was an increased dependence on the enthusiasm of the individual in charge or of top management, indicating that CAI is still supported by the eagerness and foresight of a limited number of people within the company.

4.2 Fields to which CAI is Applicable

For the 119 companies with actual use experience represented by the individual respondents, the use of courseware was then calculated for particular areas and employees as shown as in Fig. 6. The abscissa shows six categories as the aim for which the education is given, while the ordinate classifies the education itself into four kinds and then further breaks down the first two kinds into employee skill groups.

The majority (52% of those surveyed) said that CAI is utilized for enhancing the knowledge of engineers. Compared to 1986, when it was mainly used to improve the English conversation skills of middle-level employees, the purpose of CAI is now shifting towards the acquisition of knowledge, and more engineers and technical specialists are learning by this means. The trend now seems to be its employment in the teaching of highly specialized factual information. In 1986 it appeared that they were starting with areas in which the development of courses was least difficult, but now there is a gradual transition towards areas where the demand is greatest.

	Kind of education \ Aim of education	Knowledge	Technical skills	Technical skills (through experience)	Business /Company attitude	Human relation-ships	Decision making
by position	for new employees	48.7 51.3	31.1 56.7	11.8 16.2	6.7 5.4	3.4	4.2 2.7
	for middle-level employees	42.9 37.8	28.6 59.4	8.4 21.6	0.8 2.7	0.8	4.2 10.8
	for manager class	10.9 10.8	5.9 13.5	5.9 2.7	0.8	0.8 2.7	3.4 13.5
	for managing derectors	2.5		1.7	0.8		0.8 5.4
by professional skill	for salespeople	13.5 13.5	5.8 10.8	2.5 5.4	1.7	1.7	0.8
	for engineering staff	52.1 29.7	34.5 21.6	21.9 8.1	2.5		5.9 8.1
	for technical specialists, researchers, etc.	26.9 18.9	20.2 21.6	4.2 5.4			2.5 8.1
	for personnel, accounting, usual office operation staff	4.2 10.8	3.4 16.2	3.4 8.1	2.7		0.8
Education for changing professional categories		11.8 13.5	6.7 10.8	2.5 5.4	0.8		0.8
Education for retirement preparation							0.8

TOTAL: 1989 (119) (shaded bar); 1986 (37) (open bar)

Fig.6 Courseware being used

4.3 Areas Where CAI is Considered Effective and Areas where it is Employed in Education

The 346 questionnaire recipients who had replied they were aware of CAI were then asked for which particular areas and employees they felt the system was most useful. They were given a chart listing the positions, levels and classifications by the same means as in the previous section and asked to circle the ones they felt important under each reason or "aim" shown. The number of circles was then counted and the percent it represented of the total replies was calculated; these are shown as the shaded figures in Fig. 7.

Figure 7 compares the areas in which the "aware-of-CAI" group felt CAI to be most effective and the areas in which it is actually utilized. The results show that, although many feel that the problem-solving abilities of management can be improved by CAI, the number of courses in this field is still inadequate at present. The number of courses is also inadequate in very hopeful areas such as enhancing the knowledge of ordinary employees, accounting and administration staff, and employees changing their profession; there is a strong demand for the development of courses in these areas.

4.4 Measuring the Effectiveness of CAI

An important part of using CAI is evaluating its effectiveness - that is, how it compares with ordinary methods of teaching. The question was then posed to the recipients in the companies which had used CAI for in-house training in order to measure its effectiveness.

Figure 8 shows the method of measurement. The most common method was through reports or the questionnaires returned by students (72%), followed by evaluations made by instructors (39.7%), implying that the qualitative means of measurement still prevails. However, the use of more quantitative measurement parameters, such as examination results, the number of students or the frequency of attendance, are increasing gradually. In the previous survey, none of the companies answered that questionnaires had been sent or that interviews had been held after a given interval upon completion of the CAI study; this time, however, 11.8% responded that they had. It is assumed that two and half years ago they were not ready to do a follow-up on the effectiveness of CAI in this manner because it was still at the initial stage, but now that they have the necessary experience they are able to obtain data from former students.

Kind of education \ Aim of education		Knowledge	Technical skills	Technical skills (through experience)	Business /Company attitude	Human relation-ships	Decision making
by position	for new employees	75.7 48.7	54.1 31.1	23.7 11.8	21.1 6.7	24.0 3.4	18.9 4.2
	for middle-level employees	52.9 42.9	56.4 28.6	19.4 8.4	16.2 0.8	20.2 0.8	32.7 4.2
	for manager class	31.2 10.9	24.0 5.9	4.6 5.9	9.5 0.8	13.6 0.8	47.1 3.4
	for managing directors	17.9 2.5	12.7	2.6 1.7	3.8 0.8	6.4	31.5 0.8
by professional skill	for salespeople	42.8 13.5	24.0 5.9	7.5 2.5	9.3 1.7	30.0 1.7	18.2 0.8
	for engineering staff	59.5 52.1	55.5 34.5	35.3 21.9	8.1 2.5	5.2	17.6 5.9
	for technical specialists, researchers, etc.	48.3 26.9	49.1 20.2	11.6 4.2	5.2	5.2	18.5 2.5
	for personnel, accounting, usual office operation staff	39.3 4.2	24.0 3.4	6.1 3.4	7.5	10.1	20.5 0.8
Education for changing professional categories		46.0 11.8	36.7 6.7	14.7 2.5	4.9 0.8	6.6	8.7 0.8
Education for retirement preparation		23.4	15.0	7.5	3.4	4.3	5.5 0.8

TOTAL
(shaded) Applicability of CAI by those knowledgeable about it 346
(white) Courseware being used 119

Fig.7 Fields in which CAI is being used and its applicability by those knowledgeable about it

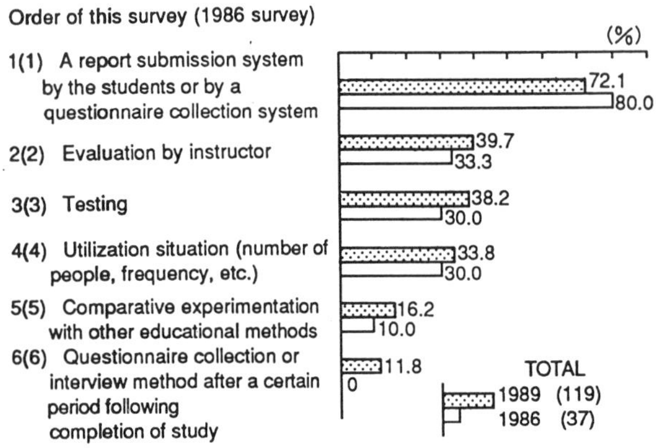

Fig.8 Method of Measurement

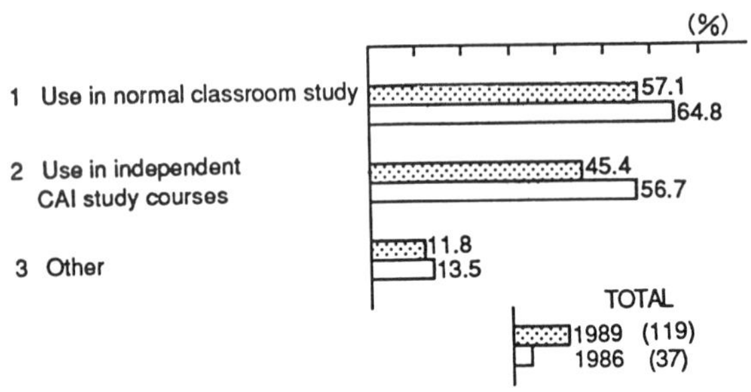

Fig.9 Use of CAI

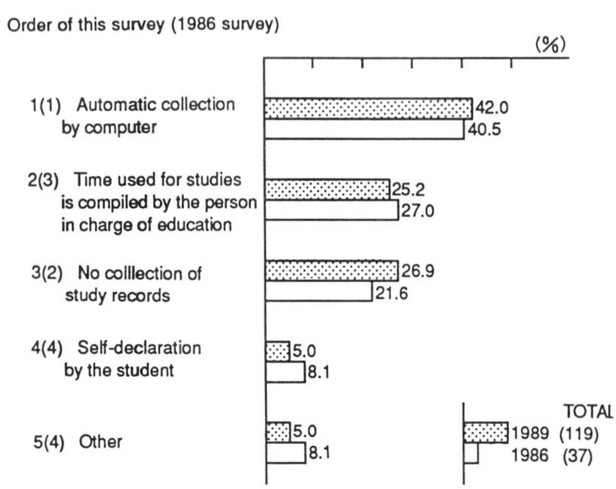

Fig.10 Collection of stydy records

4.5 Position of Education Offered by CAI

As shown in Fig. 9, "How CAI is Used", all of the percentages are smaller than the previous ones. This is due to the fact that in the multiple choices given in the 1986 questionnaire, a variety of uses had been attempted, but the 1989 focus was on fewer uses. The overall trend that CAI is nearly eqvally used in both collective education and independent study courses still remains.

4.6 Operation Administration of the CAI System

It is obviously inappropriate for trainees at higher levels to be made to feel they have clear lacks, or to be forced to ask a trainer who might be in a lower position in the company something which he is embarrassed not to know. It is also well known that the computers can easily manage a student's records. For these reasons, as shown in Fig. 10, forty-two percent of the using companies preferred to automatically collect the learner's records by computer. Another 25.2% had the instructor in charge of the training keep the record and another 8% took the student's word for this. However, 26.9% do not collect records.

5. CONCLUSION

The 1989 survey revealed some known and some unknown facts about the status of CAI in Japan. Despite the limitations of courseware, some companies have already introduced CAI into their in-house educational programs and are recognizing its benefits and potential. We were surprised and pleased to see the increase in awareness which has occurred in Japan. None of us can be unaware of the tremendous influx of computers of all sorts into our daily existence, and yet many of us remain unfamiliar with just how these sophisticated tools can be used to benefit us and enrich our lives--while at the same time making them more simple. CAI offers great potential but much more development must take place before it is a common phrase in our language and everyday experience.

The CAI Committee in JMA will continue to make efforts to collect data on the methods of applying CAI information and its effectiveness so as to contribute to the further proliferation of this educational means.

Acknowledgments:

The author would like to express his gratitude to the questionnaire respondents, who made this survey meaningful, and to the members of the CAI Committee in JMA.

Computers in Education
A. McDougall and C. Dowling (Editors)
Elsevier Science Publishers B.V. (North-Holland)

INTEGRATION OF MICROPROCESSOR AND PERSONAL COMPUTER USES IN DISTANCE VOCATIONAL TRAINING OF ELECTRONICS PROFESSIONALS

Israel SILBERSTEIN

Centre for Educational Technology (C.E.T.), 16 Klausner St. Tel-Aviv, ISRAEL

Extensive integration of uses of personal computers and microprocessor laboratories in our School of Technology's distance learning system of vocational training in electronics has taken place during the past several years.

This paper presents the self-study program in electronics and the ways microcomputer software, courseware and hardware are implemented in various courses.

INTRODUCTION

The School of Technology was established within the framework of the Open University of Israel a few years ago. The school is a nationwide technological training institution offering courses towards the degree of Skilled Worker as well as towards the higher degrees of Technician and Practical Engineer through individualized instruction and distance learning methods.

The development of the curricula, study methods, and instructional means began in 1984 and is being conducted mainly by the Centre for Educational Technology (C.E.T.). The first courses of the School of Technology were offered by the end of 1986.

The main study means and methods are:

1) Self-study written material
2) Personal computers and software packages
3) Computerized home laboratories
4) Project assignments at home and study centers
5) Video programs
6) Group sessions at study centers

As of now, most of the courses in two main professional fields, Electronics and Computer Studies, have been developed.

The following presentation consists of two parts. In the first part, the learning system and "course tree" of the Electronics Program is described. The second part concentrates on study methods 2, 3 and 4 which were listed above and includes a detailed description of the diversified uses of microprocessors and personal computers in the electronics curricula, the courses in which they are used, and the ways some instructional objectives of the electronics training system are reached through the microcomputer applications.

DESCRIPTION OF THE ELECTRONICS LEARNING SYSTEM

The chart in Figure A shows the "course tree" of the Electronics Program. It includes the names of the courses, their interrelation and the courses that are needed for completion of each diploma.

The instructional system consists of modular courses, each lasting one semester. Each course is worth a certain number of credits towards a diploma (i.e., 0.5, 1.0 or 1.5). The number of credits allocated to each course depends upon its complexity and the quantity of material included in the course.

The three levels which are integrated in the curriculum are:

1) Electronics Skilled Worker (6 credits)

2) Electronics Technician (one year post-secondary level - 14 credits)

3) Electronics Practical Engineer (two year post-secondary level - 21 credits) with specialization in one of the following fields: Computer Hardware, Communications, Control or Optoelectronics.

There is almost complete continuity between the levels so that a student can progress from one level to another at his convenience.

In order to receive the Technician diploma or the Practical Engineer diploma, each student must also successfully complete a project which takes approximately 150 hours at the Technician level or 250 hours at the Practical Engineer level.

THE IMPLEMENTATION OF MICROPROCESSORS AND MICROCOMPUTERS IN THE ELECTRONICS PROGRAM

The shaded rectangles in Figure A represent the courses in the Electronics Program in which uses of microprocessors or personal computers are integrated. The uses are somewhat different at the Electronics Worker and Technician levels than at the Practical Engineer level. At the lower level of training, the microcomputer uses are more of the hardware type, while at the higher level, they are more of the software type.

In some courses, the Technician students use printed circuit boards for experiments in which microprocessors control faults insertion and finding, and in other courses, they use applications boards which are connected to a PC. The Practical Engineering students use software packages more than the Technician students for design, experiments, circuit analysis, etc.

SCHEME OF COURSES IN ELECTRONICS

CURRICULUM FOR TECHNICIANS & ELECTRONICS WORKERS

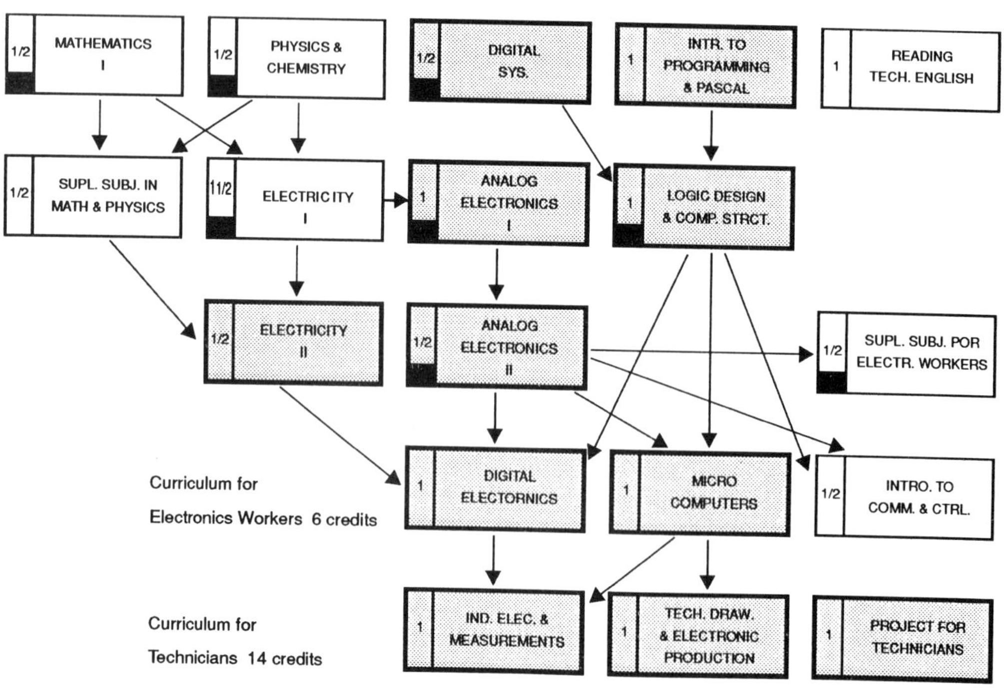

FIG A

SCHEME OF COURSES IN ELECTRONICS

SUPPLEMENTARY CURRICULUM FOR PRACTICAL ENGINEERS

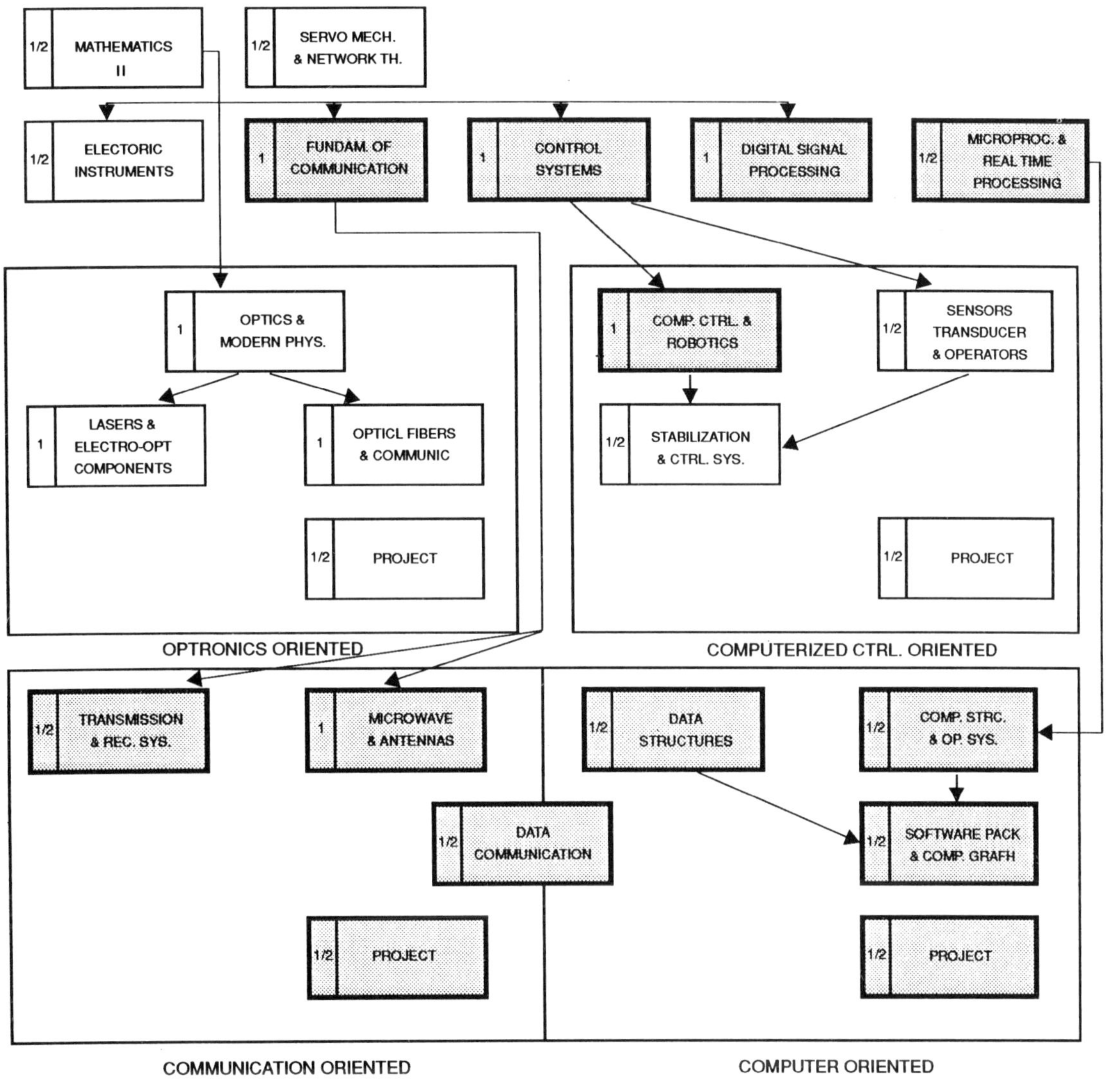

PRACTICAL ENGINEERING CURRICULUM	<u>21 CREDITS</u>
COMPULSIVE COURSES	5 CREDITS
ELECTIVE COURSES	2 CREDITS
PROJECTS	1.5 CREDITS
PREREQUISITES	12.5 CREDITS

FIG A

The "flower" in Figure B presents the various uses of microprocessors and microcomputers in our training system. The explanations that follow describe the types of uses and objectives that are achieved by each of them.

1. Programming and Software Development

In the programming language courses: PASCAL, PC ASSEMBLY and the DATA STRUCTURES course for practical engineers, the PC is used for programming and debugging computer programs. The School of Technology provides the students in these courses with a personal computer to be used at home. The student pays a fee for the use of the computer. If the student already has a PC at home, he receives only the compiler, sample programs and other software that have been prepared for the specific course.

2. Computerized Fault Finding

In many courses in the Electronics program including Digital Systems, Logic Design, Linear Circuits, Industrial Electronics, etc., each student receives a specially designed home laboratory for the duration of the course. The student pays a fee for the use of the laboratory. The laboratory is used for the demonstration of theories, experimentation, and learning and exercising troubleshooting procedures.

The laboratory includes a computerized system for the insertion of faults in circuits constructed on a printed circuit board. There are between five and eight printed circuit boards provided for each course which are plugged into the laboratory one at a time. A microprocessor based system inserts the breakdowns in the PCBs and the student has to find them using fault-finding procedures learned in the course. The faults were planned in advance by our course development teams. When the student finds the fault, he notifies the computer system in his laboratory and if he is correct in his findings, he receives positive feedback from the computer and then goes on to the next fault.

The computerized troubleshooting system also has a test mode in which the student receives a grade. In this mode, the student has to find four faults, each within 15 minutes.

3. CAI & Drill and Practice

In some electricity courses, students receive CAI on a personal computer or a minicomputer at study centers. For example, at C.E.T. we have developed special software for courseware development called SMITH - Self-Directed Mixed Initiative Tutorial Helper. Courseware in subjects in the area of electricity has been developed using SMITH.

Drill and Practice is included, for example, in our Technical English course. C.E.T. has developed exercises based on a matrix of 15 topics and 15 levels. The students are exercising, for the time being, on a minicomputer that we have developed and produced (TOAM System) but in the future, this drill and practice might be done on a personal computer.

4. Connection of Hardware Boards to the PC

In a few courses, the main learning objectives are to design some computer-controlled devices, connect them to the PC, write suitable control programs for them in assembly language or high-level language on the PC, operate the systems and test them. In these courses, specially designed units are connected to the PC. Examples of exercises are control of a motor, measurement of its speed, and microprocessor control of an elevator.

5. Simulation of Lab Experiments

Simulation software packages are being used largely in the electronics industry and the future technician or practical engineer will probably have to use them intensively in his daily life. Therefore, we have decided to teach our students to use such packages in different courses to simulate, as precisely as possible, lab experiments and behavior of circuits and systems. We also considered that the use of such packages is highly cost-effective since the investment in laboratory equipment and instruments, either for home use or for use in study centers, is minimized as a result of the simulated laboratory experiments.

One package we intend to use is the Tess communication system software package. It is used for experiments on receiver systems, transmitter systems, modulation and detection, etc. Another software package which we consider using is a courseware package developed in Israel by Degem Learning Systems Company called the EWB - Electronics Work Bench. The package includes all the components, power supplies and measuring instruments needed for simulating experiments on analogue electronics circuits, digital circuits and logic design.

6. Exercises & Circuit Analysis with Engineering Software Packages

The use of purchased industrial or scientific software packages is integrated in many of our courses, especially the advanced ones for practical engineers. An example of this is the use of PC MATLAB scientific software package for computer exercises in the Digital Signal Processing course. This package is used also for digital filters design and analysis. In the Linear Control course, we use an engineering package called PROGRAM C.C. which enables analysis of control systems when given their transfer function. The analysis includes drawings of Bode plots, plots of the Root Locus, testing stability conditions etc. More packages are now being evaluated in subjects such as transmission lines, microwaves and antennas. The packages that would suit our requirements are easy to learn, menu driven and user-friendly, not expensive, and enable exercises on significant parts of the course curricula.

The main learning objectives are to expose the student to industrial software packages and to teach him the use of packages of the kind that we assume he will encounter in his work in industry.

7. CAD & CAD Applications in Projects Submitted by Technicians and Practical Engineers

The industrial CAD software system

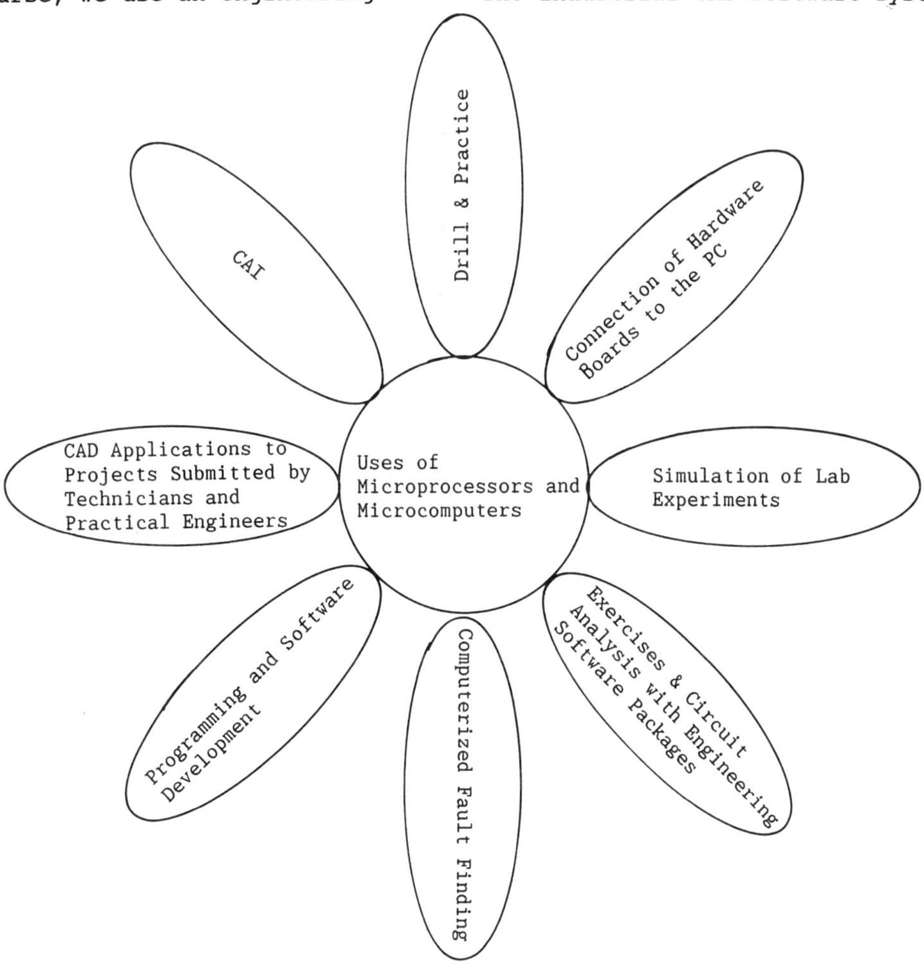

FIG B

which was recently introduced into our electronics learning system is used not only as a learning tool but also as a practical tool to design and implement projects, either by technician or by practical engineering students.

The package purchased was the PCAD System for Personal Computers. The study and exercising of its various parts, i.e. electronic drafting and schematic capture, circuit design and analysis, editing of printed circuit boards (manual or automatic) and preparation of data for board production, are included in our compulsory course for all students -- Electronic Production.

After students have learned to operate the CAD package and are familiar with its options, we encourage them to use it in their work on their final project. In this project, the student is expected to design an electronic product or system, analyze its performance and in some cases, actually build the product and test it. At the end of his work, he has to submit a well-written report on his project.

The PCAD system is a powerful software tool which opens to the student the possibility of preparing large parts of the project on the PC. In this way, much time and expenditures on the electronic design, computations and calculations, and PGB editing and construction can also be reduced.

SUMMARY

We expect that the extensive integration of hardware and software microcomputer uses in our vocational training system of electronics professionals will train technicians and practical engineers to be better prepared for tomorrow's work market as well as increase students' motivation and update some of the means and methods of study.

ACKNOWLEDGEMENTS

I would like to thank my colleague Yakov Schwartz for his suggestions and comments and Eva Stobsky for her devoted editing of this paper.

Computers in Education
A. McDougall and C. Dowling (Editors)
Elsevier Science Publishers B.V. (North-Holland)

DEVELOPMENT OF NEGOTIATION SIMULATOR FOR TRAINING PERSONNEL

Hidenori SUZUKI

Education Division, Systems Engineering Group, FUJITU LIMITED
1-17-25 Shinkamata, Ohta-ku, TOKYO, 144, JAPAN

ABSTRACT

We have developed a CAI (Computer Assisted Instruction) negotiation simulator which uses a personal computer to simulate interaction between a systems engineer (SE) and a customer.
SEs develop most user systems. The larger and more complicated the system becomes, the greater the risks accompanying system development. Problems such as delayed system start, too many development hours, and unrecoverable costs occur because most SEs lack experience in negotiating system development with those ordering the system. Conventional training has not been much help.

This paper describes the two main problems we had in developing the simulator:
1 how to simulate a negotiation and
2 how to model the vague aspects of a negotiation.
The simulator is a tool for training SEs, and has already proven its worth.

1. BACKGROUND OF DEVELOPMENT

1.1. Importance of Negotiation

Problems similar to the following develop in negotiations during system development:
When a customer asks the vendor to modify design specifications without clearly expressing the need for them, the vendor is then forced to negotiate at a disadvantage for negative reasons such as insufficient time and personnel.
Misunderstandings between customer and vendor over who develops what and who supports what leaves the vendor holding the bag when deadlines are no longer possible to meet.
Even events which appear to be minor failures at the time may result in a loss of several hundred million yen.

Part of the problem lies whth the SE, who, despite knowing the necessity of negotiating with the customer promptly and candidly, tends to shun such negotiations as unimportant or somehow beneath SE consideration becacuse such negotiations are nontechnical in nature.

1.2. Difficulty of Training Personnel in Negotiating Skills

Negotiating skill is important, but can it be taught?
The fact those who have participated in many negotiations are usually good negotiators suggests that personnel can be taught how to negotiate.
Conventional training methods are ineffective for the reasons given in Table 1.1

table 1.1

Use of examples	Trainees only superficially understand what a third person has experienced. Relating to another person's experience is difficult.
case studies	Reasons for a trainee's proposals and actions are uncertain. Unexpected events are difficult to create.
Negotiation theory based on game theory	The range of application is narrow. The theory is ineffective in solving actual problems faced by SEs.

1.3. Considerations for Training Using a Simulator

The best training method for negotiating is to serve as a project leader in actual negotiations. The method, however, requires much time and is risky in an actual project which cannot be allowed to fail. Instead, we have developed a negotiation simulator. Characteristics of the user and project are modeled on a personal computer (Figure 1.1). A trainee faces the computer as the user and negotiates with it.
The trainee learns various heuristics used in negotiations by participating in the simulation.

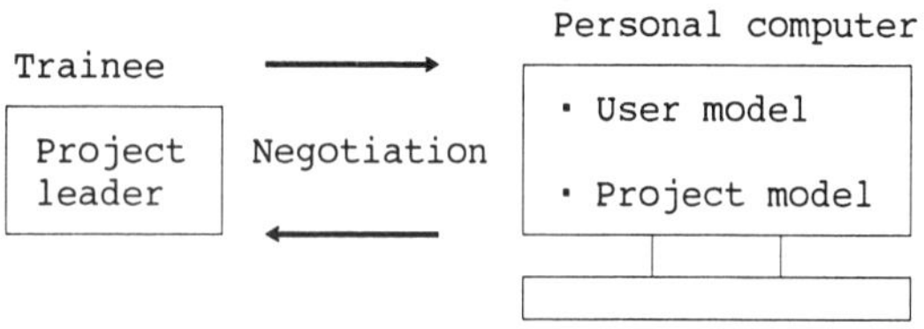

Figure 1.1 Simulating negotiations with a customer using a personal computer

2. PROBLEMS OF DEVELOPMENT

The human elements in negotiations cannot be accounted for with a rational theory. Simulating negotiations with a personal computer is effective only if the following problems are overcome:

① The simulation is designed for trainees.

② The simulation model must include vagueness, especially of the type that models the human elements in negotiations. Quantifying vagueness is difficult.

③ The simulation must be realistic.

3. SIMULATION METHOD

3.1. Image of Simulation

A trainee conducts negotiations with a customer while serving as the project leader of various steps from the start of the negotiations until the start of system operation. He examines the issues and interviews the user, his or her supervisor, and sales department personnel to grasp the problems (Figure 3.1). When negotiations are required, the project leader correctly uses the channels between negotiators and proposes the course the vendor should take.

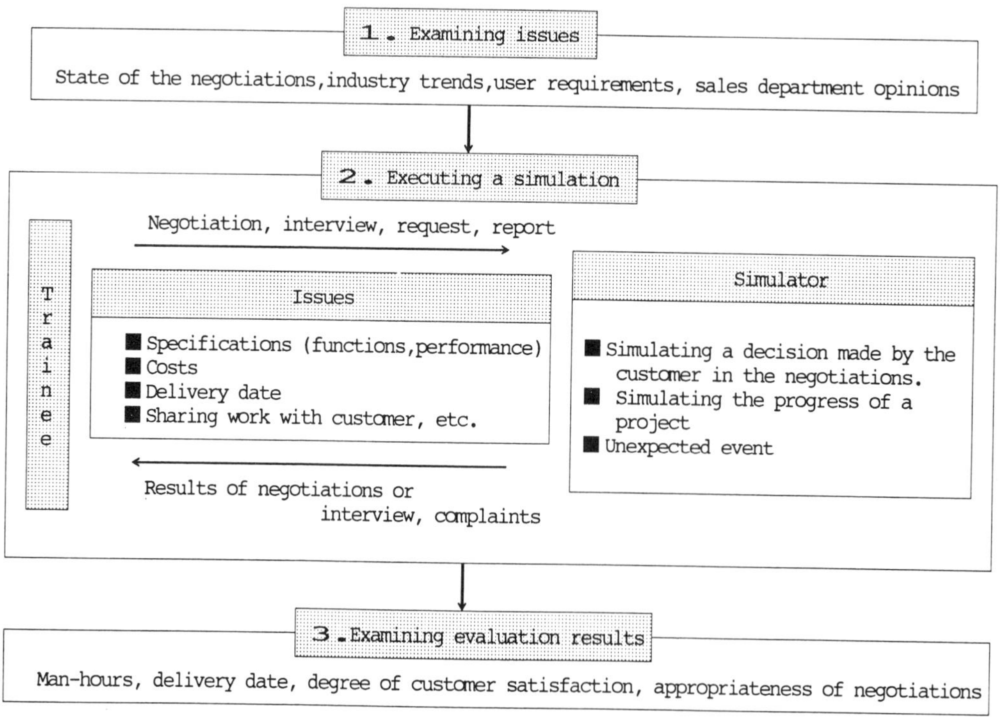

Figure 3.1 Simulation method

3.2. Proceeding a Simulation

When negotiations become unnecessary, a trainee first prepares a proposal (Figure 3.2). The trainee's first hurdle is to understand what the customer really wants, then to win the order in competition with other manufacturers without blindly following the customer's assertions (Figure 3.3). If the trainee wins the order without examining the customer's requirements carefully, he or she will probably failin a later phase as the actual project begins to take shape.

3.3. Evaluation of a Simulation

When a simulation is over, the simulator evaluates the trainee's performance by checking the following:

① The trainee prevented an increase in man-hourse.

② The trainee made sure that the delivery date would be met.

③ Relations with the customer remained good.

④ The negotiations were successful.

< < Work assignment setup > >

Step	User man-hours (man-months)	Vendor man-hours (man-months)	Done by
Project planning	1 0 . 0	2 0 . 0	User
Design	6 . 0	5 0 . 0	User
Programming	0 . 0	4 5 . 0	Vendor
Testing	1 4 . 0	5 5 . 0	Vendor
Total man-hours	3 0 . 0	1 7 0 . 0	

> Enter a menu number.

This is an example of preparing a manufacturer's proposal for job responsibilities. The man-hours for the user are 30 man-months,and for the vendor 170 man-months.

Figure 3.2 Proposal setup screen

< < Negotiation > >

Select action	Select category	Negotiators: User	Negotiators: Vendor
1.Negotiation 2.Modification of proposal 4.Presentation of reasons	1.Functions 2.Assignment of work 3.Organization 4.Prerequisite conditions 5.Delivery data 6.Costs	· Market Planning & Sales Support Department Maneger · Market Administration Department Manager · EDP department Manager	· SE acting as project leader · Sales department Manager · Sales department liaison

Speaker for user:Market Planning & Sales Support Department Manager
I understand how you feel,but you are leaving too much work to us.

> Press the RETURN key. The next speaker's words will be displayed.

This screen displays the Market Planning & Sales Support Department Manager's answer from the user negotiator to the proposal on work assignment.

Figure 3.3 Negotiation screen

4. SIMULATION MODEL CONFIGURATION

4.1. Outline of the Simulation Model

The simulator consists of a model incorporating the characteristics of the user, vendor, and system, logic for making a decision on a vendor's proposal, logic for expressing a decision, and a scenario that controls the story and generates unexpected events. (Figure 4.1)

4.2. Incorporating the Principles and Rules of Negotiations

The word "negotiation" suggests techniques and tactics. However, we adjusted the parameters of the model so that the following principles and rules of negotiations are regarded as more important than techniques and tactics.

① The trustful relationship between the customer and the vendor is the foundation of negotiations. Past actions speak louder than the words of negotiators.

② A one-sided victory in negotiations should be avoided to insure the business. Reaching an agreement through mutual concessions is important.

③ There is more than one method of negotiating. Submit alternative plans and discuss them from many viewpoints.

(Example)
A system can be delivered on a predetermined date, but the functions are inadequate.
--> Submit a proposal, for example, showing how the functions can be expanded step by step.

④ Preventing a problem is better than fixing it after it occurs.

4.3. Simulating a Customer's Thinking Process with AI Techniques

It is difficult to represent a user's thought process in decision making completely by only using a mathematical model. AI techniques have been used where quantification is not possible. To provide realism, we incorporated the techniques in such a way that a personal computer uses natural language to respond to the trainee. The program languages are GCLISP and ESHELL/FM. GCLISP is a COMMON LISP language designed for personal computers. ESHELL/FM is a tool that supports the building of an expert system.

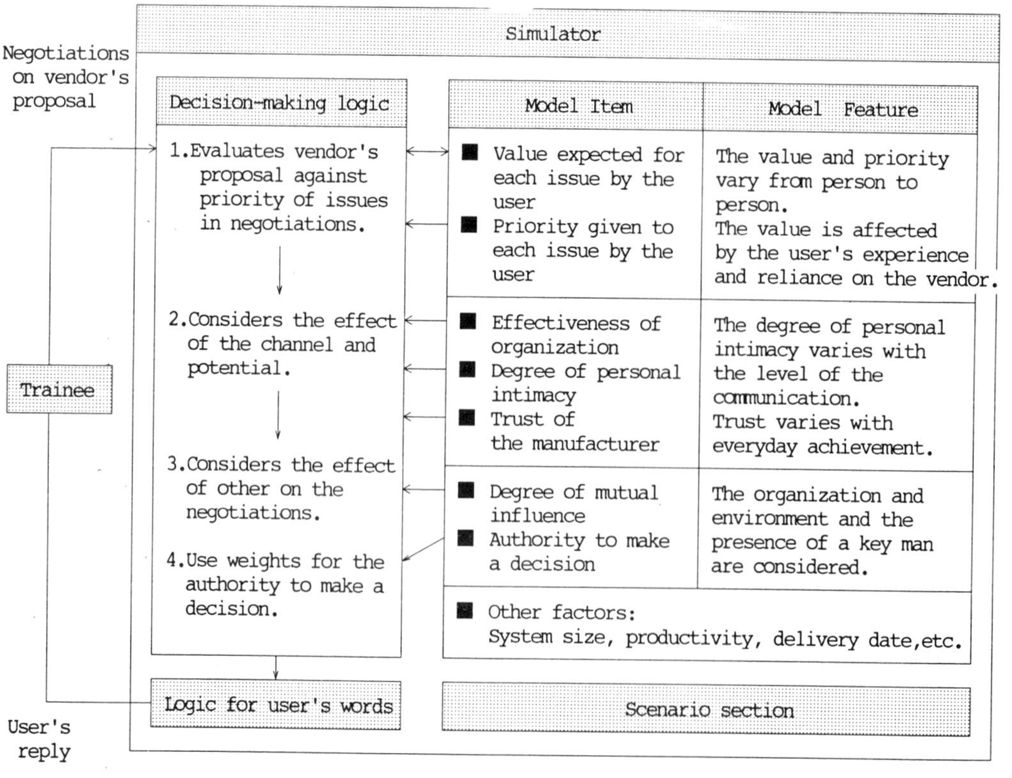

Figure 4.1 Outline of the model

4.4. Example of a Simulation

In the evaluation of a proposal, the user first considers the possibility of adding four new functions. However he determines that it will be impossible to develop all four functions without a delay in delivery. Therefore the user considers the possibility of adding only three new functions. This thinking process, based on trial and error, is simulated by an AI technique in which alternative plans for issues in the negotiations are generated and the plans evaluated (Figure 4.2).

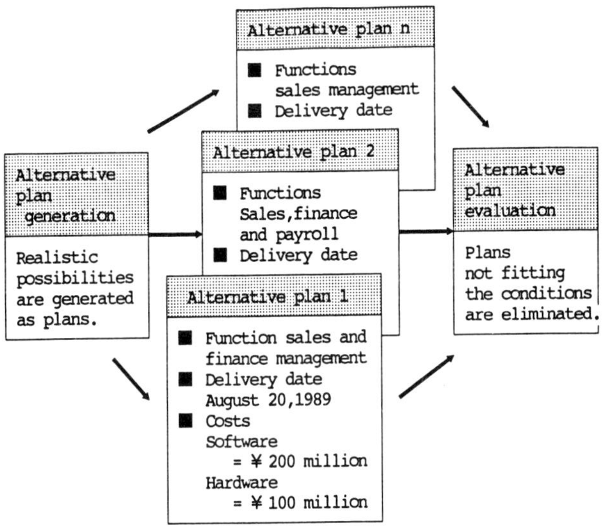

Figure 4.2 Simulating a customer's thinking process by generating and evaluating alternative plans

① Generating alternative plans
Basically, the user and the vendors have widely differing expectations. Alternative plans are generated for issues based on their priority.

② Evaluating alternative plans
Alternative plans that do not fit the conditions of the negotiations are eliminated.
In Figure 4.3, four plans for adding functions were generated in the order of preference, but plan 1, the most desirable and plans 5 and 6 were eliminated because of the delivery date.
The simulation then went to plan 2 (backtrack by using the automatic backtracking function which is part of the inference engine of ESHELL/FM), and alternate plans (plans 7and 8) for the delivery date were generated.

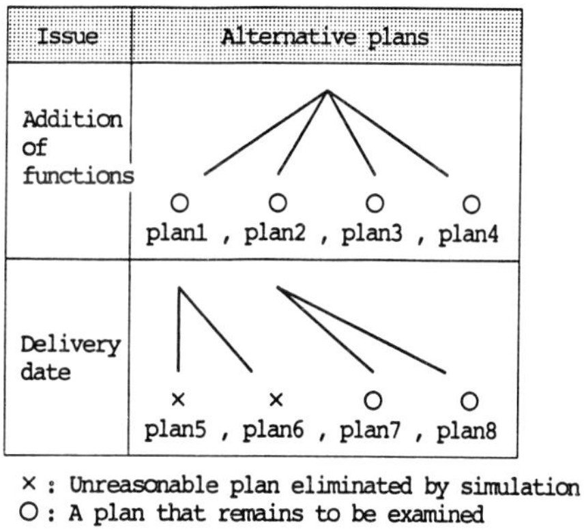

Figure 4.3 Simulating a user's thinking by AI techniques

The alternative plans generated were numerous. In reality, a person finds suitable alternatives by limiting the search: all combinations are not examined one by one. The simulator's alternative plan generation and evaluation sections have enough heuristic knowledge of human beings and knowledge of customer's strategy and character to make it possible for the user to simulate as if he was thinking.

4.5. Customer Response in Natural Language

To enable a user to respond in natural language, the simulator determines the response at the abstract level, then converts it to natural language. The simulator also adjusts the words to show feelings. It first takes the nucleus of the response from the user response dictionary according to the results of decision-making process (degree of agreement or disagreement with the vendor's proposal), then modifies it for nuances, such as the authority to make a decision and the sense of trust. In negotiations, user representatives may or may not speak in character and may not reveal their depth of concern. (Figure 4.4)

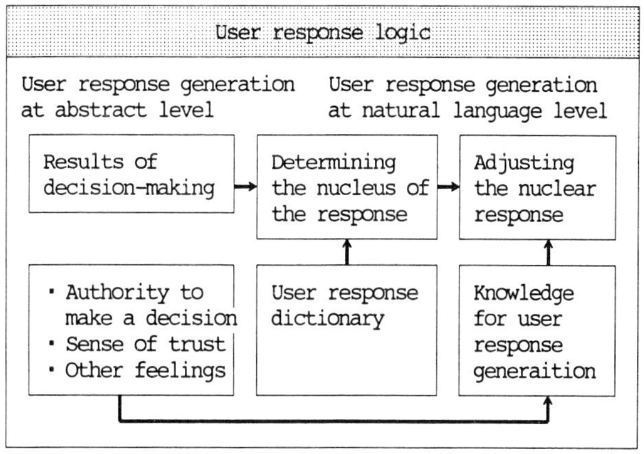

Figure 4.4 Generating user response using AI techniques

5. OPERATING ENVIRONMENT

The simulator requires the following computer resources:

Hardware	- Model FMR-50, 60 - Memory 5 megabytes - Mouse - Printer
Software	- MS-DOS - GCLISP - ESHELL/FM - Simulator (about 30K steps) Simulating the customer's decision-making process requires 3 to 5 seconds.

6. TRAINING FORM

About 20 persons, four or five persons to a group, can be trained at one time with the simulator. The members of the group talk among temselves, negotiate with the user, and decide what the project leader should do.
Training sessions are three days. During the training, the trainer makes the atmosphere more realistic by asking trainees to make interim reports as if they were participating in an actual meeting on estimates or a project evaluation meeting. (Table 6.1)

7. RESULTS OF TRAINING

360 senior SEs have used the simulator during their training in negotiation skills, since it's release.
They are actively exchanging their opinions and introducing fresh negotiation-specific reactions to the actions which they have experienced.

One example is that of a response by the user where the user will order a system from another manufacturer because their development costs are too high.
Many empirical rules learned from many projects have been incorporated in the simulator. Some examples are: the rule that the user's key man should be sought; and the rule that all facts in reestimating costs or lead time should be clearly explained and mutually understood. Trained SEs appreciate the simulator because it allow them to experience the rules through simulation.

8. CONCLUSION

In the past, on-the-job training was used to train SEs in the skills of negotiating with a customer. We have developed an effective training method using a simulator, that is, a computer in which customer and project characteristics are modeled.
Bringing software projects to a successful conclusion will become more and more difficult. Whether a project succeeds or fails depends on the project leader. We will train as many project leaders as possible using the simulator.

REFERENCES

〔1〕 SE training text "Computer Contract and Copyright" (YAS45L) 1987

〔2〕 K. Sakuma, "Strategy of Negotiation," Business Education Publishing Company 1987

〔3〕 T. Fujita, "Age of Negotiation Skill," PHP Library 1984

Table 6.1 Suggested training scheduLe

	First day	Second day	Third day
Morning	-Necessity of negotiations and negotiation concepts -Explanation of issues	-Interim report 1 -Simulation	-Simulation -Group discussion and summarizing of results
Afternoon	-Discussion of proposals -Simulation	-Simulation -Interim report 2	-Presentation and questions and answers -Evaluation and lecture

Computers in Education
A. McDougall and C. Dowling (Editors)
Elsevier Science Publishers B.V. (North-Holland)

MULTIPULE LEARNING ENVIRONMENTS USING THE MULTIMEDIA CAI SYSTEM

Makoto TAKEYA[*], Naoto NAKAMURA[*], Takahiro SHAKUSHI[**], Fumiyuki TERADA[***] and Tatsunori MATSUI[***]

[*]Takushoku University, 815-1, Tatemachi, Hachioji, Tokyo 193, JAPAN
[**]Bunkyo University, 1100, Namegaya, Chigasaki, Kanagawa 253, JAPAN
[***]Waseda University, 3-4-1, Okubo, Shinjuku, Tokyo 169, JAPAN

The THE system(Terada and Hirose Education system) is a multimedia CAI system with a video disc player controlled by a personal computer. This system was first presented at WCCE/1981, and has been improved several times. First, we present our philosophy of the mathematical problem solving process. Our philosophy is based on the evaluation of the THE system from the view point of mathematical education. Particularly great importance is placed on the guidance with *TESSOKU* which is a set of strategies to find deterministic solution. Second, this paper shows a basic learning environment which contains *T & P style* (Tutorial and Practice style) courseware. Third, a new environment is presented. This environment aims at learning *TESSOKU* strategies. Finally, a configuration of the THE CAI system under multiple learning environments is described.

1.INTRODUCTION

The THE system(Terada and Hirose Education system) is a multimedia CAI system with an optical laser video disc player controlled by a personal computer. The THE prototype system was presented in WCCE/1981[1]. The 2nd version of the THE system was reported in WCCE/1985[2]. It provides a large quantity of the voice presentation using SWSD(Still With Sound and Data) unit. It has the Tutorial and Practice style courseware which is called *T & P style* courseware for upper secondary school mathematical learning. The learning effects of the THE system has already been reported[2].

In addition to this evaluation, the relationship between the system feature and learning effects has been analyzed[3]. During the analysis of *T & P style* courseware, the effectiveness of the guidance by *TESSOKU*[4] was pointed out. *TESSOKU* is a set of strategies to find deterministic solution. Particularly in problem solving it is important to apply *TESSOKU* strategies effectively.

In this paper a new learning environment is presented. This environment aims at coaching *TESSOKU* to a student efficiently rather than the existing basic learning environment.

2. OUR PHILOSOPHY OF PROBLEM SOLVING

We would like to present the structure of the problem solving process based on the analysis of an actual student's problem solving process. Figure 1 shows this process. In the understanding stage, a student attempts to understand the contents of the problem, by translating them into a mathematical representation using symbols, expressions and graphs. Furthermore, he/she analyzes the given conditions and the given/unknown target of the problem. In the logical planning stage, he/she plans steps towards the solution on a logical basis. In the description stage, he describes the solution process. In addition to these three stages, there exists another stage, i.e. the thinking stage, where he/she developes problem solving through trial and error using actual values and graphs.

In each stage, a student utilizes two kinds of knowledge, MK(Mathematical Knowledge) and *TESSOKU* which comes from a Japanese word meaning 'ironbound rule'. The MK is a set of mathematical truths, i.e. definitions, formulas, theorems and so on. They are classified into mathematical categories, e.g. 'quadratic function', 'trigonometric ratio', 'finite mathematics' and so on. In the traditional THE system, each mathematical category corresponds to each chapter. On the other

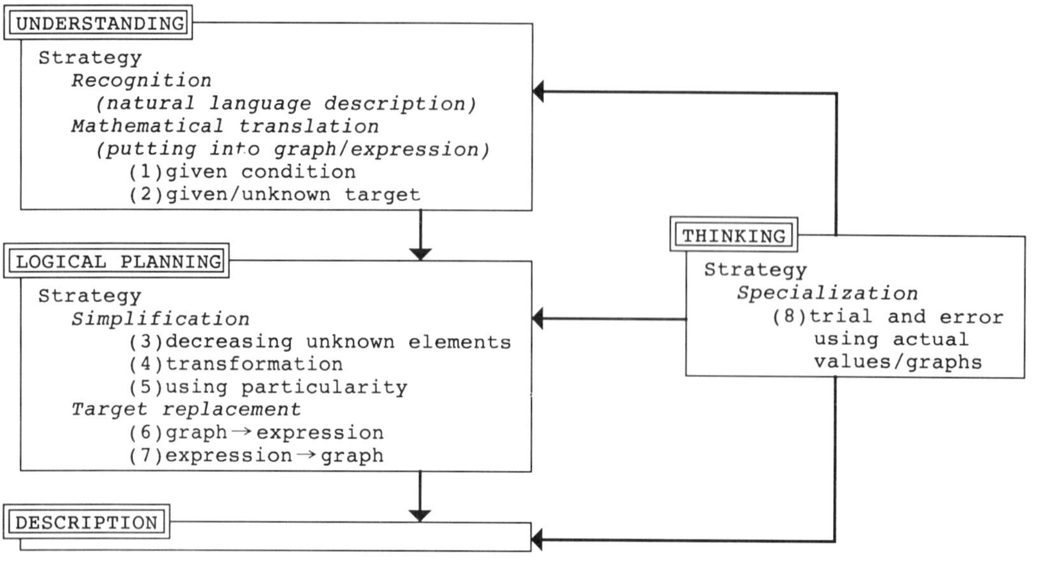

Figure 1 Process of the problem solving

hand, *TESSOKU* is a set of strategies to apply MK efficiently for problem solving. Each *TESSOKU* strategy is generally related to the various mathematical categories. Therefore, *TESSOKU* strategies are necessary to solve difficult or complicated mathematical problems. Considering the above process of a student's problem solving, we classified more than 200 *TESSOKU* strategies into eight categories by analyzing about 2000 mathematical problems included in the THE system, as (1)-(8) in Figure 1. This categorization is called *TESSOKU* categorization.

The *TESSOKU* categorization is essentially different from ordinary mathematical categorization. The concept of the relationship between *TESSOKU* categorization and mathematical categorization is shown in Figure 2. Each problem includes a subset of the MK. All dashed arrows between problems are made explicit in the authoring process. However, the problems within each *TESSOKU* category are located in various mathematical categories. Solid arrows show the connections among these problems. From the view point of the learning process, a student is able to acquire MK through learning in each mathematical category. However, obtaining MK in each mathematical category is not enough for him/her to acquire *TESSOKU* strategies. These analytical characteristics of *TESSOKU* strategies establishes their necessity in effectively solving complicated mathematical problems as opposed to simple ones.

To clarify our philosophy, a few examples are given. An example of a problem is shown in Figure 3. In the mathematical category, 'Trigonometric ratio', there are *TESSOKU* strategies: 'Unify the given angles' and 'Unify trigonometric ratio'. More specifically, the latter strategy means that when sin, cos, and tan are appeared by mixture, trying to apply MK as a formula 'tan x = sin x / cos x' is effective to solve the problem. For another example, in the mathematical category 'Vector', there is a *TESSOKU* strategy: 'Replace all of the given vectors into the linear combination of the basis'. These examples belong to the different categories under mathematical categorization, however they are contained within a common category: 'Decreasing unknown elements' (a category (3) in Figure 1) under the *TESSOKU* categorization. We think that learning *TESSOKU* is very important to bring up a student's creativity level and to improve his/her ability for logical thinking. We present an effective way to learn *TESSOKU* in the section 4.

3.BASIC LEARNING ENVIRONMENT

In this section, we present briefly the basic learning environment of the THE system. The basic learning environment includes the *T & P style* courseware which was implemented within the traditional THE system. This courseware has various modes; lecture mode, training mode, judgement mode, and so on. The detail of

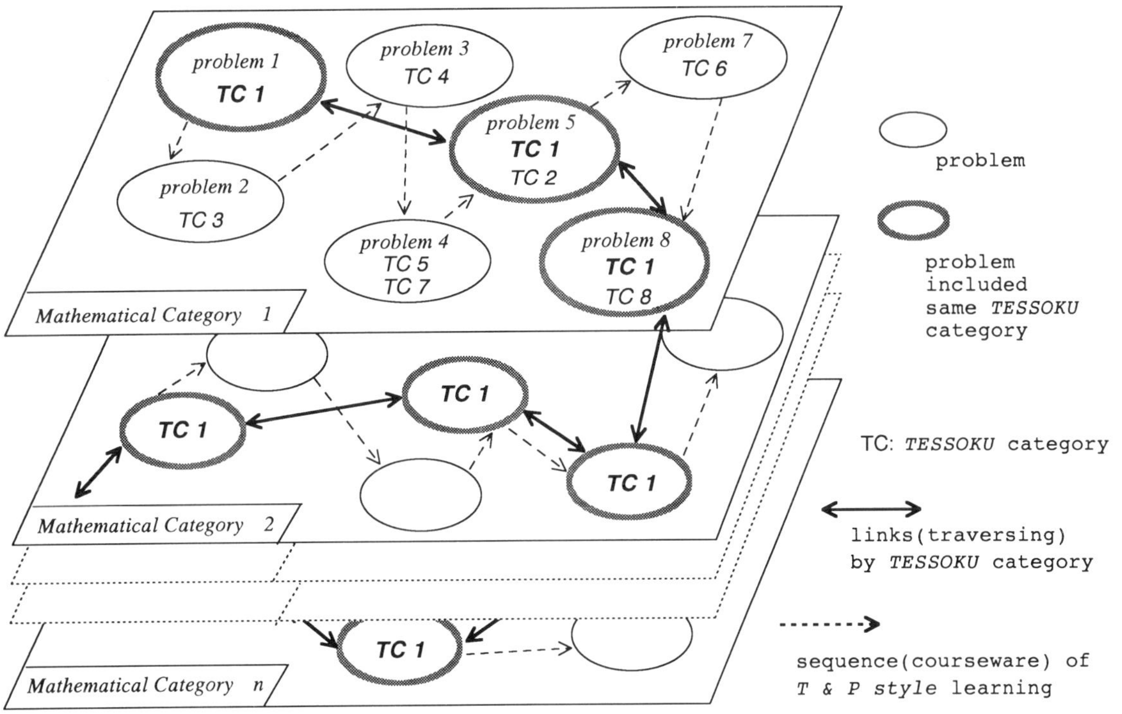

Figure 2 Relationship between mathematical category and *TESSOKU* category

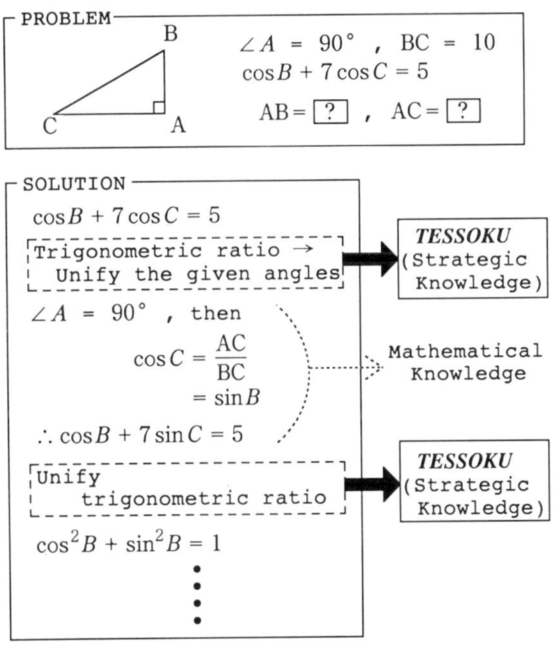

Figure 3 Example of the problem on the THE system

T & P style courseware is shown in Figure 4 and is described bellow.

The Chapter is equivalent to the mathematical category which is described in the previous section. In each chapter the study starts with a survey of the student's performance. Based on the survey, the system is prepared to start with most suitable course among F(Fundamental), S(Standard), or H(High) courses. In the study of each section in that course(F,S,H), the student is given lectures(definitions and theorems), examples of solutions, many problems and a summary, in that order. Each section requires about two hours of study. When the student finishes all sections, he/she has to take an achievement test, and he/she is judged on the understanding level of learning. A short comment and advice to continue or review the contents of the chapter are given at the same time.

This courseware aims at supplementing incomplete parts of MK through problem solving. The method of problem solving was taught through individual *TESSOKU* as in Figure 3. This courseware teaches individual *TESSOKU* strategy which is

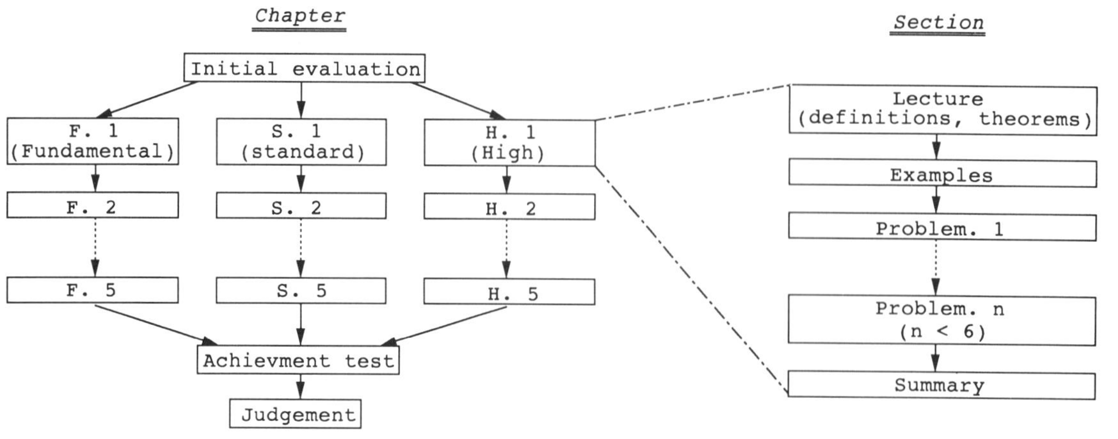

Figure 4 T & P style courseware in the basic learning environment

applicable to the given problem. A student is able to learn *TESSOKU* strategies through Tutorials and Practices. However, it was not enough to teach a student the method to choose the most suitable *TESSOKU* strategy for the given problem from the variety of *TESSOKU* strategies because the course sequence is based on mathematical categorization. Our new learning environment aims at learning *TESSOKU* strategies through traversing some problems within a common *TESSOKU* category. The detail is discussed in the next section.

4. ADVANCED LEARNING ENVIRONMENT

In this section, the new learning environment which is called advanced learning environment is described.

4.1. TRAVERSING

Our philosophy of problem solving is reflected in the advanced learning environment. In this new environment, traversing mathematical categorization plays an important role. Figure 2 shows the relationships among the problems.

The *T & P style* courseware includes the course sequence according to mathematical categorization. In Figure 2, the arrows with dashed lines represents this sequence. Each problem has some applicable *TESSOKU* strategy, for example, the *TESSOKU* strategy TC1 can be applied to the Problem 1, 5, 8. The arrows with solid lines reconnect the problems according to the applicability of *TESSOKU* strategy TC1. Considering the applicability of *TESSOKU* strategies, Problem 1, 5, 8 are similar and related to each other. However they are located separately in the sequence according to mathematical order.

A student must find similarities between problems by himself/herself. Also, each student must learn how to apply *TESSOKU* strategies through problem solving practices. When he/she succeds to categorize problems into *TESSOKU* categorization, it means that he/she can generalize the strategies of problem solving. These generalized strategies take their root within the student's understanding as mathematical intelligence.

Why is it easier to learn MK rather than problem solving strategies? A student can more readily learn MK, because it is taught in a well-organized order. To teach total mathematical intelligence, we have produced a new learning environment in which the following two traversing modes are included;

(1) *Strategic Learning Mode*
(2) *Similar Problem Searching Mode*

The *Strategic Learning Mode* links problems into a sequence according to the applicability of *TESSOKU* strategies. In the *Similar Problem Searching Mode*, some similar problems are presented through interaction with the student. The similar problems are selected from 2000 problems recorded on video disc which are prepared for the *T & P style* courseware. Similarities among the problems are defined by the applicability of *TESSOKU* strategies to the problems. Thus, by utilization of *Strategic Learning Mode* and *Similar Problem Searching Mode*, a student can consciously recognize the problem solving strategies and acquires total mathematical intelligence.

4.2. DATA STRUCTURE AND TRAVERSING METHOD

The data structure implemented within the new environment is shown in Figure 5. The substructures named Mathematical Category and Video Disc Address were prepared for the previous *T & P style* courseware. They are re-used under the new environment to access the information on the video disc. The substructures named *TESSOKU* categories are added to the previous data structures. Each *TESSOKU* category structure has two fields, Category No. and *TESSOKU* No. The Category No. field has the value 1 to 8 corresponding to the category No. of *TESSOKU* strategies (See Figure 1). *TESSOKU* No. field has a value corresponding to each *TESSOKU* strategy.

Using the above data structure, the THE system presents problems corresponding to the *TESSOKU* sequence in the Strategic Learning Mode. Within the Similar Problem Searching Mode, the THE system requires students to access keys which are related to mathematical category, mathematical items, or the *TESSOKU* category. The screen of the interaction of this mode is shown in Figure 6. According to the given accessing keys, the THE system choose some problems from 2000 problems on video disc and presents the similar problems which are effective to lead the students to the generalized problem solving strategy.

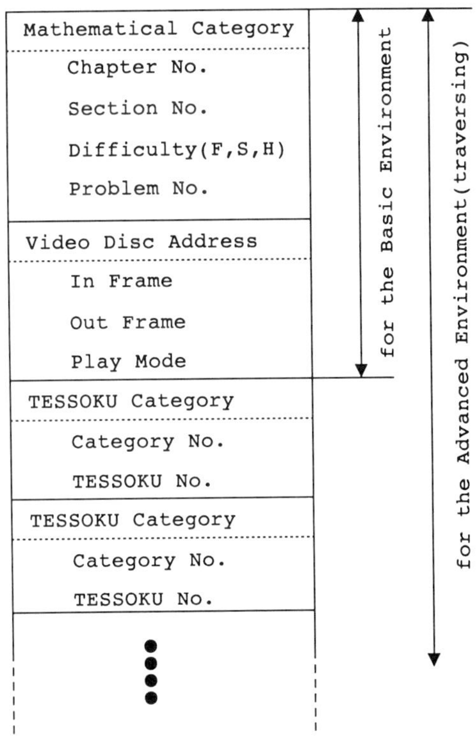

Figure 5 Data structure of a problem

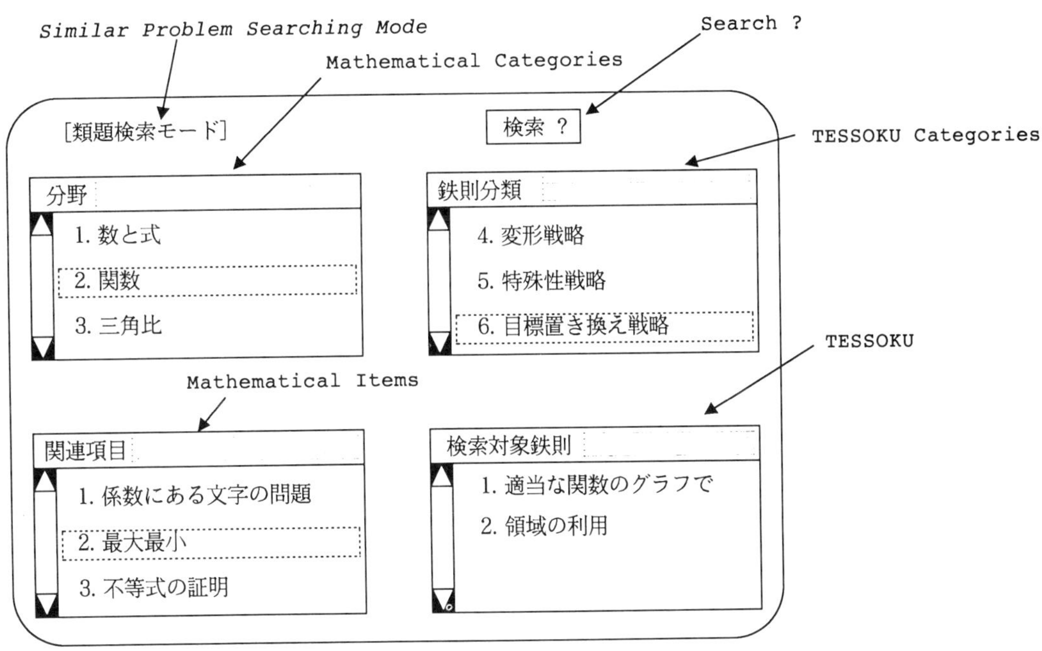

Figure 6 Menu for sarching

4.3. CONFIGURATION OF THE THE SYSTEM

The hardware configuration of the THE system is a personal computer connected to a video disc player as shown in Figure 7. The personal computer UC-V102(MSX-2 type) is made by Universal Pioneer Corp. This UC-V102 includes the interface for the superimposed image. Audio and visual information are recorded on the video disc and played through the SWSD(Still With Sound and Data) unit. This SWSD unit is controlled by the RS232C interface of the personal computer.

The unit has three types of playing methods, i.e. still play, dynamic play, and SWSD play. The previous version of the THE system had only the still play and dynamic play methods. The SWSD play method is a voice synthesized method which was not available for the previous system. This has allowed more voice information to be incomparably obtainable compared to the previous system. Thus more versatility for the courseware is achieved. The previous system allowed 30 minutes of voice information per side, but due to the SWSD method a maximum of 5,400 events (one event is one still image with 28 seconds of voice) per side of information is now available.

5. CONCLUSION

This paper describes about the multiple learning environment focusing on problem solving strategies based on the analysis of the *T & P style* courseware. The following two modes are added to the THE system for this purpose;

(1) *Strategic Learning Mode*

(2) *Similar Problem Searching Mode*

It is considered that these two modes are effective for students to learn problem solving strategies. It is necessary to evaluate and analyze the effects of the new THE system with the new courseware. As additional functions for *Similar Problem Searching Mode* are developed more inteligent accessing methods to similar problems should be prepared.

REFERENCES

[1]Terada,F., Hirose,K. and Ono,T., Instruction technique on using video disc systems, IFIP Proc. of 3rd World Conf. on Computers in Educ. (1981) pp.343-349.

[2]Terada,F., Hirose,K. and Handa,T., Towards a self-paced Learning support system, IFIP Proc. of 4th World Conf. on Computers in Educ. (1985) pp.39-44.

[3]Takeya,M., Nakamura,N., Matsui,T. and Terada,F., An evaluation method of the THE multimedia CAI system using Semantic structure analysis, in: C.,Bell, J.,Davies and R.,Winders (eds.), Promoting Learning. Aspects of Educational and Training Technology Vol.XXII (Kogan Page, London, 1989) pp.289-294.

[4]Terada,F., TESSOKU of Algebra and Geometry (in Japanese, Obunsya, Japan, 1982)

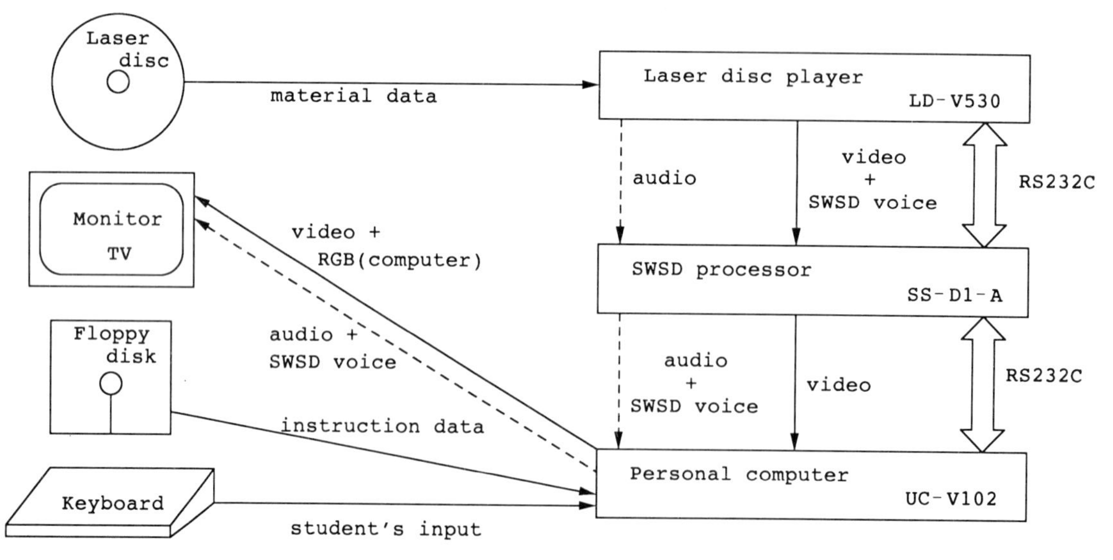

Figure 7 Configuration of the THE system

Computers in Education
A. McDougall and C. Dowling (Editors)
Elsevier Science Publishers B.V. (North-Holland)

A TRAINING MODEL FOR DEVELOPING COUNTRIES

Dr. Ho TATKIN and Mr. Song NAY HAY

Japan-Singapore Institute of Software Technology, 1 Maritime Square, #12-11 World Trade Centre, Singapore 0409

In any developing country, education and technology are the crucial factors for enhancing their standard of living. This article presents a mode of a training Institute where computer software technology was transferred from a developed and advanced nation, Japan, to a developing nation, Singapore. It traces the development where the Institute adopted the standard designed for the computer programmers in Japan to suit the Singapore requirements.

The result of the effectiveness of the technology transfer showed that the method used could be adopted as a model for developing countries to transfer technology from a developed country to a developing one.

1. BACKGROUND

The Japan-Singapore Institute of Software Technology (JSIST) is a technical co-operation project between the government of Japan and Singapore.

The project to establish the Japan-Singapore Institute of Software Technology (JSIST) was formally launched with the signing of the Record of Discussions on 18 December 1980 by the government of Japan, represented by the Japan-International Cooperation Agency (JICA) and the government of Singapore, represented by the Economic Development Board.

Under this agreement, the government of Japan would provide technical assistance to Singapore for the planning, establishment and operation of the Institute via a resident team of Japanese Software Specialists for a period of five years, provide computer hardware and peripherals, as well as training awards in Japan for the Institute's local lecturers. The objective of the Insitute is to prepare trainees for careers in Computer-based data processing, either as application programmers or as Systems Analysts both within the computer industry itself and in the commercial and public sectors.

At that time,the Singapore Economic Development Board (EDB) had identified the computer software industry as a leading edge industry of the future and one which Singapore should develop. Singapore is a small country with no natural resources whatsoever. Software needs no natural resources. Bits cannot be depleted. On that rationale, in October 1980, the Committee on National Computerisation (CNC) identified the shortage of trained Computer professionals as the major single resource in which the government must produce in order to meet Singapore's plan to develop it into a regional software centre by 1990s. The CNC thus recommended that computer education and training programmes which produce the much-needed competent computer professionals be given top priority.

The Institute was thus quickly set up on 2443 square metres of floor space on the 12th Floor of the World Trade Centre Building. This central location is convenient for the students. Right from the start, the Institute planned to simulate the entire working environment for the students while they were under training.

2. ANALYST PROGRAMMERS' TRAINING

The Institute received its first intake of 50 'A' level students in 1982. All the 50 students were selected from a record application number of 938 applicants. The Institute set the entry requirements at two 'A' levels with a least an 'A' level pass in mathematics and a pass in English Language at 'O' level. The requirement of an 'A'- level pass in mathematics was in fact a very traditional approach. Both the Japanese Computer specialists and the local lecturers believed that people who did well in mathematics should possess the right aptitute for computer software training.

Of these 50 ; one was company-sponsored, the rest were sponsored by EDB. EDB paid their training fees to the Institute and at the same time gave them a bursary. In return the students after graduation were bonded to the EDB for three years. During these years, EDB would assign them to serve out their bond in specified organisations which could be in either the private or the public sector. During these three years graduate students were not allowed to leave the organisation to which they had been assigned. In this way, EDB ensured a steady flow of trained manpower to the industry and also prevented job-hopping among the graduates.

The course was based mainly on a framework drawn from the Japan Ministry of Trade and Industry (MITI) Examinations. At that time, MITI conducted three levels of examinations for the Information Technology professionals in Japan.

Table 1 gives a summary of the MITI examinations and a comparison with the JSIST's Diploma Course.

Table 1

MITI		JSIST	
Examination Type II	Pre-requisites High School graduates with at least 5 years of experience in the computer industry	Equivalent Coverage	Pre-requisites Minimum of 2 A-level passes
Type I	University graduates with at least 5 years of experience in the computer industry	Programming & Systems Analysis	
Special Level	University graduates with at least 10 years of experience in the computer industry		

About 50% of the time is spent on practical work to ensure that students are trained with sufficient practical skills relevent to their future employment.

The central theme of the course is computer-based information processing with its main areas of study concentrated in programming, computer systems and systems analysis and design. Communication skills in interviewing, oral presentations and report writing are important aspects of the analyst/programmer's work and students are given adequate training and practice in this area.

To assist the students to attain a better understanding of their future working environment, supportive training in Mathematics, Operational Research, Management Accounting and Business Knowledge were also provided. There is a 17-weeks in-house group project during the second year to train students in Analysis, Design and Implementation of a system. Each project group consists of about six or seven students. Based on the real-life scenarios of a existing application system given by the group supervisor, the students are required to follow the System Development Life Cycle with a structured methodology and transfer it to Design, write the program, do a presentation and demonstrate the system that the team has implemented. The objective is to test the students' analytical and programming skills. The team spirit developed during the group project preparation is an important aspect of their training. At the end of the project each student must be able to communicate effectively through presentation on their part of the work and the whole team must submit a group report.

To provide a more realistic view of their prospective life in the industry, students in the second year are sent to industry on an individual basis to work on a project designed by the industry. This takes place in the last three months of the second-year course. In fact that is a characteristic of all full-time course of the Insitute. Before the student is assigned to the industry, the supervisor of the student will approach computer installations to see if they have any suitable projects. If the scope of the project is too wide, it may be divided into sub-systems/modules so that several students can work on it. In each project the student must be able to demonstrate his or her initiative, creativity and ability to apply what he or she has learned during the course.

The advantage of the industry project is that it exposes a student for a period of three months to a different computer system and also offers a very realistic test of the students' ability to apply what he or she has learnt. This scheme allows the prospective employers of our students three months period to view the students potentials, without obligation or cost, before actually employing them. Companies also regard this as a conversion period where the students whom they intend to employ are exposed to the company's computer system which could be different from the Institute's system and this is done at a time when the company is not obliged to pay him/her any allowance. Because students need to pass the project in order to obtain the Diploma, they are motivated to learn to use a new computer system in a short period of time as to get on with the project proper.

3. THE RESULT

Since the first batch graduated in 1984, many batches have graduated and are now gainfully employed. In 1983 the Institute's Diploma had been validated by the Singapore National Computer Board to be of National Level 1 Standard. Companies to which our students have been attached for industrial project, were asked to give assessments of our students. Appendix 2 shows a summary of the companies's assesments of the students by batches. Most students have in fact done well.

In an unprecedented move, on 1 August 1989, Japan's Ministry of International Trade and Industry has gave its stamp of approval on graduates of JSIST. The JSIST Diploma in Programming ans System Analysis was accredited to the MITI Type II Examination. The much-sought-after accreditation made JSIST the first Institute outside Japan to be given such honours. This MITI accreditation is seen as enhancing JSIST graduates' status not only within Japanese companies, but also with other firms. Multinational Corporations especially those in the information technology industry, would find it advantages to employ JSIST graduates as they can now compare the standards of the JSIST with those in Japan.

Since the first batch graduated, the Institute had been looking for further study opportunities for its graduates. By 1989, 20 Universities and Poly technics in UK and Australia have accepted JSIST graduates for direct entry in their Master Degree programmes.

3.1 Survey

In 1989, our sponsor, the Japan International Cooperation Agency commissioned a survey to find out the effectiveness of the Analyst Programmer (AP) Course. The survey was carried out by an independent Management Consultant and it covered the first nine batches of AP graduates (AP01-AP09) who obtained their diplomas between 1984 and 1988. The following are the results of the survey.

3.1.1 EMPLOYMENT INDICATOR

Of those graduates who responded, 98.8% were economically active. 99.1% of the economically active graduates were employed. Only 1.5% were unemployed at the time of the survey In fact those unemployed were actually on maternity leave or have resigned from the jobs waiting to go oversea for their studies. Generally most graduates found jobs related to their course of study. 98.6% were in information technology (IT) jobs.

3.1.2 EMPLOYED GRADUATES

Job hopping with IT professional used to be a very wide spread problem because of the shortage of supply in comparison to demand. JSIST graduates were therefore asked on their employment history to ascertain whether they were job-hopping.

The Singapore National Productivity Council has defined a job-hopper as a person who changed three or more jobs in twelve months or spent about four months in one job. It is noted that there was no job-hopping among the graduates.

Considering only those who have been in the job market for three or more years (that is, AP01 to AP05), 43.1% of the graduates were still holding their first job. 45.1% of them had changed their job only once since graduation. For these graduates who changed their job once, the average period of time they spent in the first job ranged from 12.7 months for AP05 graduates to 38.1 months for AP01 graduates. (Table 2)

Table 2

Distribution Of The Average Length Of Time Graduates spent In Their Previous Job By Course Of Study And Batch

Course/ Batch	Year Graduated	Presently Holding 1st Job		Average Time Spent In Previous Job: Presently Holding 2nd Job		Presently Holding 3rd Job		Presently Holding 4th Job	
		No	Months	No	Months	No	Months	No	Months
AP01	1984	4	59	11	38.1	1	30.0	-	-
AP02	1985	5	47	8	28.9	3	10.0	1	16.0
AP03	1985	7	41	12	29.1	3	5.0	-	-
AP04	1986	16	35	6	20.0	1	21.0	-	-
AP05	1986	12	29	9	12.7	3	6.7	-	-
AP06	1987	8	24	2	12.5	-	-	-	-
AP07	1987	21	18	3	11.7	-	-	-	-
AP08	1988	16	12	-	-	-	-	-	-
AP09	1988	24	6	-	-	-	-	-	-

3.1.3 Salary

Earlier batches of graduates were earning more than the recent graduates as they had accumulated more than 4 years of working experience at the time of the survey. (Table 3)

TABLE 3

Distribution Of Gross Median Monthly Salary By Course Of Study And Batch

Course Of Study And Batch	Gross Median Monthly Salary (In Singapore Dollar)
AP01 to AP04	S$1500 - $2000
AP05 to AP09	S$1100 - $1400

JSIST AP graduates upon entering the job market were earning slightly more than their `A' level contemporaries with 2 years of working experience. They were also earning just as much as fresh university graduates who had spent 3/4 years pursuing a general degree or honours degree. (Table 4)

TABLE 4

Distribution Of Estimated Gross Monthly Salary By Type Of Graduates

Type Of Graduates	Estimated Gross Monthly Salary (In Singapore Dollar)
AP Diploma Holders	S$ 900 - $1500
'A' Level Holders with 2 Years Working Experience	
General Degree Graduates	S$ 700 - $ 750
Honours Degree Graduates	S$ 900 - $1000

3.1.4 **Present Job's Minimum Qualification**

It was found that 77.4% of the JSIST graduates were able to meet the minimum qualification required by the employers. (Table 5) These graduates were working in jobs that required a minimum qualification of a diploma. Another 6.1% of the graduates' jobs required a degree. Out of the 13 AP graduates who were presently employed in jobs that required a degree, 7 had about 4 years of working experience. These 7 graduates would thus be able to qualify for jobs that required a degree.

TABLE 5

Distribution Of Graduates By The Minimum Qualification Required For Present Job And Course Of Study

MINIMUM QUALIFICATION REQUIRED FOR JOB	N o	%
G.C.E. `O' & `A' Level	34	16.0
Diploma	164	77.4
Degree	13	6.1
Not stated	1	0.5

3.1.5 **Relevance of Training**

JSIST training had helped the graduates in their work as 80.8% were making use of the knowledge they acquired during their training. 13.7% made use of the training to a large extent and 66.5% to a satisfactory extent. (Table 6)

TABLE 6

Distribution Of Graduates By The Minimum Qualification Required For Present Job And Course Of Study

Relevance of Training	AP	
	No	%
Large Extent	42	19.8
Satisfactory Extent	141	66.5
Little Extent	29	13.7
Not Stated	-	-

3.1.6 **Ratings of Graduates on Various Areas of Training**

All the graduates were asked to rate the effectiveness of the various areas of training as required by their jobs.

A total of 212 graduates made use of Programming in their present jobs. Most of them found it effective as 92.0% rated it average and above 78.4% rated it very good or good while only 13.6% rated it as average. (Table 7)

In System Analysis, 186 of the graduates were making use of it in their present jobs. 96.8% rated it average and above. 55.4% rated Systems Analysis average while another 41.4% gave good or good ratings. 176 of the graduates made use of Systems Design in their present jobs, 96 gave average and above ratings for it. Systems Design received more average ratings than very good or good ratings.

In the area of Database, there were 182 graduates who made use of it in their present jobs. Out of the 182 graduates, 92.9% rated it average and above. 51.5% gave average rating while or 41.8% gave very good or good ratings.

There were 136 graduates who made use of Data Communication in their present jobs. Out of the 136 graduates, 79.4% gave average and above ratings (17.6% gave very good or good ratings while 61.8% gave average ratings). About 20.6% gave poor or very poor ratings. Compared with the other four areas of training, the proportion of graduates who gave poor or very poor ratings for Data Communication was larger than for any other four areas of training.

TABLE 7

Distribution Of Graduates By Area Of Training And Ratings

Area Of Training	Very Good /Good		Average		Poor/ Very Poor		
	No	%	No	%	No	%	Total
Programming	189	89.2	21	9.9	2	0.9	212 100.0
Systems Analysis	77	41.4	103	55.4	6	3.2	186 100.0
Systems Design	66	37.5	103	58.5	7	4.0	176 100.0
Database	76	41.8	93	51.1	13	7.1	182 100.0
Data Communication	24	17.6	84	61.8	28	20.6	136 100.0

4. Conclusion

Technology Transfer can be successful only if 3 main factors are satisfied.

1. The trainers must be willing to understand the trainee's environment, including understanding the cultural differences and respecting their culture differences and then adapt their training methods accordingly.

2 The trainees' level of education must reach a level capable of accepting technology transfer.

3. The country's infrastructure must be able to allow technology to be nurtured, this offering good job propects for those trained.

In JSIST and in Singapore these factors were present. Other than some of problems of technology transfer which included language and communication problems [Tatkin (1985)]1, the technology transfer has largely been successful. The concept of bonding students also ensured minimum job hopping.

In this paper we share our experience in technology transfer and believed that our model could be adapted by developing countries who are facing a similar problem in manpower shortage in the IT industry.

Footnote:

1. Ho Tatkin, "The Japan-Singapore Institute of Software Technology - A Case Study in Technology Transfer", Education and Computing, The International Journal, North-Holland, 1985 vol 1 No 4 page 256.

Computers in Education
A. McDougall and C. Dowling (Editors)
Elsevier Science Publishers B.V. (North-Holland)

PREPARATION FOR PLACEMENT AND THE BENEFITS TO EMPLOYERS - A CASE STUDY OF BUSINESS COMPUTING STUDENTS

J. B. THOMPSON

School of Computer Studies and Mathematics, Sunderland Polytechnic, Priestman Building, Green Terrace, Sunderland SR1 3SD, United Kingdom.

Within the wide spectrum of degree courses designed to produce computer studies graduates those concerned with business computing, due to the nature of their subject matter, must be very vocationally orientated. In the 1970s a number of Business Computing courses were established in British Polytechnics to meet the direct needs of the business community. This paper is concerned with the developmental aspects that relate to the placement or "sandwich" year within such a Business Computing course at Sunderland Polytechnic. Details are given concerning the structure of the course, the types of placement that students undertake and the needs of their employers, the ways in which the course has developed so that its students are more attractive for placement, the relevant activities that take place within the course before placement, some relevant results from a nation wide survey of placement organisations regarding the benefits they see from placement employments and finally some conclusions regarding this type of vocational education.

1. INTRODUCTION

The Business Computing degree course at Sunderland Polytechnic is typical of those courses that were established in United Kingdom Polytechnics following the Land Report of 1975 [1] which recognised a "continuing and developing need for high calibre young men and women whose education prepared them for the demanding careers of systems designers and systems analysts". An important feature of such courses is their sandwich nature where the students spend time in industry in addition to that spent within the Polytechnic. The sandwich elements may be for a fixed duration within several years of the course (thin sandwich) or may be for a complete year during the course (thick sandwich). The latter is the more common form and it is the one adopted at Sunderland. The sandwich year is regarded at Sunderland as one of the most important elements of the course. The practical experience gained during the year enables the students to appreciate in a more mature fashion final year topics and also the placement with an employer often leads to a job offer to the student within the same organisation after graduation.

For students to gain placements and for organisations to readily take on placement students year after year it is necessary that the students are well equipped with skills that will make them attractive to the employers. Also the employers must be able to identify very clear benefits to their organisations from the students' placements.

This paper describes the very vocational and practical approaches that have been adopted within the degree in Business Computing at Sunderland which, it is believed, make its students very attractive for placement. It also reports some very relevant results from a recent investigation [2] which has identified the benefits which employers recognise as accruing from the employment of such sandwich students.

2. THE SUNDERLAND B.A. HONOURS/B.A. DEGREE IN BUSINESS COMPUTING

The B.A. Honours/B.A. Degree in Business Computing (originally entitled Data Processing) is a thick sandwich of 4 years duration. In the third year the students undertake a minimum of 48 weeks of relevant supervised training in a commercial, business or industrial environment [3]. In the remainder of the paper this period will be referred to as simply the student's placement.

The original course was introduced in 1979 and it was designed to offer an integrated blend of computing and business skills appropriate to those aspiring to participate in the development and maintenance of major computer based information systems. However, by the time the course was revalidated by the Council for National Academic Awards in 1985 two other additional areas of likely employment had been identified [4] viz. in the computer service industry and as computer specialists in smaller organisations or departments. Thus the revised course scheme was designed also to attract students who could see their immediate careers within one of these areas. That there is an active shortage of skilled staff in the areas of Business Computing to which the course relates has and continues to be well documented [5-10]. This has been further substantiated by the fact that the majority of the graduates take up gainful employment very shortly after completing the course often at very high salary levels.

The first two years of the course have a curriculum centered on the core subjects: Commercial Programming, Systems Analysis and Design and Computer Systems (basically covering hardware and systems software). Also since the 1985 revalidation significant use has been made of block week workshops [11].

3. TYPES OF PLACEMENTS AND THE NEEDS OF INDUSTRY

An analysis [12] of the working environments of 170 placement students who were following either the Business Computing degree course or a parallel Higher National Diploma course in computer studies at Sunderland Polytechnic in the academic years 1984/85 and 1985/86 showed that although the type of work done by students in these placements is quite varied, the following broad categorisation of placement type and work could be made:-.

(a) Central DP placements:- COBOL (and a number of other high level languages), use of Database Management Systems, small amount of analysis and system design work (52% of the students).

(b) User department placements:- micro-based tools (e.g. dBASE) all related analysis and design, training and support (26% of the students).

(c) Computer services placements:- a substantial amount of programming using very diverse languages, little analysis or system design work. However, frequently students are required to support customers in their use of software products (22% of the students).

This analysis of student placements confirms that students should be equipped with two distinct types of system building skills to underpin their placement. These are, for large scale environments, skills typified by the use of COBOL, Database Management Systems and Transaction Processing and, for small scale environments which use microcomputers with quick building tools, skills typified by the use of spreadsheets and simple database packages. The team who redesigned the course in 1985 also recognised that for students to be well prepared for placements there was a need for them experience "real world" situations, at least to the level that could be reasonably simulated in an academic environment. In addition they felt that integration of subjects within each teaching year was most important if students were to operate effectively in industry. Thus there was a need for the students to be presented with exercises during the course which would reflect those activities which they were most likely to undertake during their placements and these exercises should include problems which would require the use of knowledge and skills from various subject areas for their solution.

4. COURSE DEVELOPMENTS WHICH DIRECTLY SUPPORT PLACEMENTS

Several major changes which were directly related to the perceived needs of the students while on placements were made to the structure and content of the first two years of the course in 1985. Subsequently more minor modifications have been introduced to tune the course so that it meets developing business needs. These changes and modifications can be grouped as follows:

(a) Introduction of Block Week Workshops

To achieve integration and provide the opportunity for undertaking in depth practical work in a wide range of subject areas block week workshops [11] are now employed in each of the college based years. This concept was developed to advantage in the pre 1985 course by the final year subject Systems in Practice - a case study built round a pottery company [13] - which had evolved into a programme of five block weeks and which had been found to be very successful in promoting integration of material in a realistic manner. During a workshop all other activities, lectures, tutorials etc., cease and the total time is devoted to the workshop subject itself. The workshops provide the opportunity for extended practical exercises and always attempt to draw upon knowledge from more than one subject. The second year workshops in particular provide essential preparation for the student placements. The use of workshops is discussed further in section 5 of the paper.

(b) Development of Professional Programming Skills

It is essential that the students have a very high standard of professional programming skills by the end of their second year as the majority of them wiil be employed during their placement year primarily as programmers or programmer/ analysts. Many of the students entering the course have little or no useful commercial computing experience and hence to raise their knowledge, skills and abilities to the necessary professional standard during the first and second years of the course approximately 25% of staff/student contact hours (some 260 hours during the two years) are devoted to the programming subject and related block week workshops.

In the pre 1985 version of the course the programming subject was taught in all three college based years. However, it was felt on revalidation that it would be much more beneficial to the students if the programming subject was concentrated into the first two years and that it was centered around specific skills that were likely to be used in during their placement viz. program design for a wide range of environments including on-line and database, an in-depth knowledge of COBOL and an appreciation of other commonly used languages, plus knowledge and abilities in ares such as program testing and documentation.

Major use is made in both the first and second years of the course of workshops that involve the students' programming skills. It is strongly believed that these workshops provide the ideal opportunity for the students to develop their programming skills and that they provide excellent preparation for the students' placement year.

(c) Use of Microcomputer Based Software

A strong element of exposure to microcomputer application software exists within the course's first two years. Many of the workshops provide a means of developing the students' ability to use microcomputer hardware and software to satisfy information system needs. This sort of ability with microcomputer systems is considered important in its own right as well as being a prerequisite for the placement year.

(d) The Adoption of Particular Systematic Design Methods as Course Standards

For the students to be able to operate confidently and effectively in industry it was felt that they needed to have a through knowledge of a well accepted method for commercial program production and of a modern method for Systems Analysis and Design. It is believed by the staff that it is much better to concentrate on one method in each subject and ensure that the students are really competent in its use rather than study a number of methods in a superficial manner. This decision has led to the adoption of Jackson Structured Programming (JSP) [14] and Structured Systems Analysis and Design Method (SSADM) [15] as course standards during the first two years of the course. The teaching of these methods is very practically orientated and attempt, as far as possible, to use exercises and case studies which are typical of the types of applications which the students will be working on in their placements. This teaching has led to the development of text books [16,17] by staff at the Polytechnic aimed specifically at business which reflect the work done within the course. These have been published as the first texts in a Polytechnic Computing Series intended for use both by trainers in business organisations and by academics.

5. INDUSTRIAL PLACEMENT RELATED ACTIVITIES

Although the majority of the exercises carried out by the students during the first two years of the course are related as far as possible to "real world" situations it is within the workshop subject that the most useful work can be undertaken. While carrying out a workshop the students are able to concentrate their minds on one particular set of tasks, which can represent a realistic situation, and they have the opportunity to be stretched and measure themselves against deadlines. There is no doubt an improvement in student ability at the end of workshops and it is probably the most satisfactory means of students practising skills in one particular area e.g. database programming. The workshops also provide the ideal opportunity for students to undertake controlled group work and they therefore can experience much more the situations they will find on placement.

Currently twelve workshops are held in the first two years of the course and of these nine in particular provide the students with experiences that directly relate to their placements. The nine workshops, their duration and place in the course structure are:

a) Data Interpretation and Presentation (4 days in year 1). The students gain practical experience in collecting and interpreting data and in presenting their results to non-mathematicians.

b) Application Package Investigation (4 days in year 1). Small groups of students, working from a typical manual supplied to a small business user, set up, test and demonstrate a business application package on a microcomputer.

c) System Design (4 days in year 1). Here the starting point is source papers (conversation records, existing documentation etc.) and lecturers act as users. Students form a brief statement of requirements, and produce overall design documentation: dataflow, data storage, and input/output specifications.

d) Advanced Programming (10 days in year 1). Each student designs the validation and update COBOL programs for a batch program suite and develops and tests the update program. A tested validation program is provided for the student, who then develops the job control necessary to test the complete suite using associated utility software for file creation and sorting.

e) Systems Implementation Using Spreadsheet Software (5 days in year 2). This provides students with the opportunity to apply their practical skills and knowledge to the solution of a significant business problem by implementing a system using spreadsheet software on a microcomputer.

f) TP (Transaction Processing) Programming (5 days in year 2). The students design and implement application modules for a TP system and form a TP service by linking together a number of modules.

g) Systems Analysis (5 days in year 2). Working in groups of 3 or 4 the students practise techniques used to investigate and analyse a business situation represented by a case study. The workshop culminates in a formal presentation of their findings.

h) Database Programming (5 days in year 2). On completion of this workshop each student will have designed, coded and tested straightforward database enquiry and update programs which navigate an IDMS database.

i) System Design and Specification (5 days in year 2). This provides opportunities for the practical exercising and assessment of system design skills. These are applied to a substantial data processing problem with a realistic set of constraints starting from a model Requirements Statement.

These nine block week workshops represent a significant proportion of the time available for class contact activities during the first two years of the course. However, the experiences of the staff are that the effort expended in running the workshops is very worthwhile. Also the skills gained during workshops, particularly those undertaken in the second year of the course, have been favourably commented on by the employers of the students during their placement year. In addition feedback from the students themselves confirms that they have gained really useful experience during the workshops which has proved invaluable to them.

6. GENERAL BENEFITS TO EMPLOYERS ARISING FROM THE EMPLOYMENT OF SANDWICH STUDENTS

Between June 1987 and April 1989 an extensive investigation [2], financially assisted by the Council for National Academic Awards' Development Fund, has been carried out by staff at Sunderland Polytechnic and Napier Polytechnic of Edinburgh (previously Napier College) into the costs incurred and the accompanying benefits gained by employers from the employment of sandwich students during their placement year. The investigation involved surveying placements which were undertaken by students on computing based courses and non computing based courses from both institutions during the placement year August 1987 to August 1988.

In all survey data relating to 232 sandwich placement students was obtained from 67 different employers. Of this data some two thirds related to students undertaking computing courses and half of that related to placements undertaken by students on the B.A. computing course at Sunderland. Approximately 85% of the computing students worked in departments carrying out purely software development, maintenance and support. Of the remainder, most worked in departments that developed or used software extensively even if this was not the department's main function. However, the results that are reported in this section of the paper are mostly of a general nature and may be regarded as relating to most sandwich placements. The major findings from the survey are:

a) Very few employers were able to give detailed costs relating to 'placement' students. Even organisations that had established procedures for employing such students did not appear to closely monitor these costs. Indeed none of the organisations responding to the survey attempted formally to balance the financial costs of employing students against any real or perceived financial benefits. That a majority of employers do not seem to pay close attention to costs is very surprising since high expense is one of the most common reasons given by employers when refusing to offer placements!

b) The overwhelming majority (98%) of employers who responded to the survey reported that they 'considered placement students to be of benefit'. Further evidence of this positive attitude is the fact that most of the respondents had recruited 'sandwich' students for a number of consecutive years. One of the main benefits declared by employers was that such students complete a significant amount of productive work. Also many found great benefit in having the additional labour available to carry out projects that were not of top priority and which would otherwise probably not have been completed due to the pressure of other work. The abilities of students to inject new ideas and bring additional enthusiasm to the work places were widely recognised. Another major benefit to employers is the facility provided by the placement arrangements for the assessment of the students as potential full-time employees. About four fifths of the companies in the survey made use of this opportunity. Indeed, over 70%, had in the past, offered permanent posts to placement students after they had completed their 'sandwich' experience.

c) Although organisations do not appear to undertake any formal cost-benefit analysis in relation to sandwich student employment they do express a general subjective view that they are getting 'value for money'. The 'value' would appear to be compounded from several elements (productivity, new ideas, impetus for change, potential later employment) which vary in importance from one organisation, and probably department, to another. For example, it is apparent that the ability to integrate into a team is an important feature for commercial organisations.

The results of the analysis of the survey data confirm the suggestions made in the RISE report of 1985 [18] that employers might benefit from taking on industrial placement students in some or all of the following ways:

a) the recruitment of skilled manpower (sandwich education offers the opportunity to assess possible future employees at work and over a period of time, with no commitment);

b) increased productivity, innovative ideas and reduced training costs (compared with full-time graduate recruits);

c) labour (access to a relatively cheap and flexible supply of labour in the form of sandwich students on placement);

d) stimulus (contributed by sandwich students with divergent and potentially innovative ideas).

7. CONCLUSIONS

The results of the survey reported above show that employers are not particularly interested in exact monetary costings of the work that placement students undertake but rather see benefits as coming from many different areas. For example one employer who has regularly employed sandwich students from Sunderland's Business Computing course for their placement year has publicly stated [19]:

"We see the (sandwich) scheme as providing us with a very realistic opportunity of supplementing our resource levels with the right people in the right job at the right price. Our primary objective is to use the scheme as a means of recruiting good graduates onto our permanent staff. A secondary objective is to provide for an immediate need for additional useful staff".

Thus it is necessary to equip students with the knowledge, skills and abilities that will both satisfy and impress placement employers and will enable the students to carry out their duties while on placement in a highly competent and efficient manner. The staff at Sunderland Polytechnic believe that their approach with the Business Computing students is satisfying these requirements. A qualitative confirmation of this may be taken from the facts that:

a) all of the students who have successfully completed the second year of the course have obtained training places - often early in the preplacement year.

b) the majority of placement organisations continue to take students for several years and that it is normally economic pressure or changes in company policy that cause breaks in placement patterns rather than bad experiences with students.

c) that, with the exception of students who have taken up full time employment during their training year, all those student who have entered placements have successfully completed them.

d) that many placement organisations extend post graduation offers of employment to their placement students.

To provide vocationally orientated education - especially vocationally orientated education which involves sandwich placements - courses must be developed so that they match the real needs of employers and students must be provided with the necessary practical experiences. The developments introduced into the Sunderland Business Computing course, especially the use of block week workshops are felt to match these needs and provide the necessary experiences.

REFERENCES

[1] F. Land, Report on degrees in data processing, Computer Journal, 18, 382-398, 1975

[2] J.B. Thompson et al, A comparison of the costs and benefits to employers of providing experiential learning opportunities to students, Preliminary report for Council for National Academic Awards, Sunderland Polytechnic, 1989.

[3] R.T. Bell and I. Potts, Sandwich Students Placed Outside Data Processing Departments, Inf. Tech. Training, November, 1983, 160.

[4] COSIT, A Survey of the Training Needs of the Computing Services Industry, 1982.

[5] A. Gordon and R. Pearson, Shortfall in Skilled Manpower, THES, No. 607, 1984.

[6] COSIT, A Summary of the Training Needs of the Computing Services Industry, 1983.

[7] J. Kavanagh, Director Pleads for More Graduates, Computer Weekly, June 21, 1984.

[8] IT Skills and Shortages Committee, First Report, The Human Factor - The Supply Side Problem, Department of Trade and Industry, 1984.

[9] Information Technology Skills Agency, Changes in I.T. Skills - The Impact of Technology, CBI Eucation Foundation, 1988

[10] R. Pearson, H. Connor and C. Pole, The IT Manpower Monitor, Institute of Manpower Studies, University of Sussex, Brighton, 1988

[11] J.B. Thompson, The Use of Intensive Workshops in the Teaching of Computer Studies Students, Computer Education, 60, 9-14, 1988.

[12] R.T. Bell and E.H. Robson, Some remarks on data processing degrees, Computer Bulletin, 2, 26-29, 1986

[13] National Computing Centre, XYZ Potteries - A Case Study, NCC Publications, Manchester, 1979.

[14] M.A. Jackson, Principles of Program Design, Academic Press, London, 1975.

[15] G. Longworth and D. Nicholls, SSADM Manual, NCC Publications, Manchester, 1986.

[16] J.B. Thompson, Structured Programming with COBOL and JSP, Vols 1 and 2, Chartwell-Bratt, Bromley, 1989

[17] M. Lejk, M. Meldrum and P. Guy, SSADM Techniques, Chartwell-Bratt, Bromley, 1990

[18] Department of Education and Science, An Assessment of the Costs and Benefits of Sandwich Education, Report by the Committee on Research into Sandwich Education (RISE). Department of Education and Science, London, 1985.

[19] R. Williams, One U.K. Employer's View of Sandwich Courses, in The Evaluation and Extension of Euronational Student Exchange and Placement in Industry, E.H. Robson and A.E. Brown (Eds), Sunderland Polytechnic, Sunderland, 1988.

Computers in Education
A. McDougall and C. Dowling (Editors)
Elsevier Science Publishers B.V. (North-Holland)

LERO-TV-PROJECT

Peter van Engelshoven, former project leader

PTH, Post-box 826, 5600 AV Eindhoven, The Netherlands

From 1st August, 1987 to 1st August, 1989, the Technical Teachers' Training College (PTH) in Eindhoven, The Netherlands, realized an extensive project to stimulate informatics in their technical teachers' training courses. Thirty lecturers cooperated with advisers from industry and gained expertise, developed five new courses, and bought equipment to a total value of 1.5 million US$.

1. PREFACE

In 1984, a 5-year national informatics stimulation project (INSP) started, which had to make up Dutch arrears in the application of informatics as compared with other countries. Education, and especially vocational education and the teachers' training colleges, were also to profit from this plan.
The technical teachers' training course in Eindhoven (PTH) is a 5-year full-time training course for prospective teachers of architectural engineering, electrical engineering, mechanical engineering, motor-vehicle engineering, mathematics and physics. At Present, the college has about 700 students and 100 lecturers for training and post-graduate courses.
The institute, opened in 1979, is unique in education. A special feature is the integration of the technical with the pedagogical and didactical aspects of the training. During the first five years we were fully engaged in developing programmes, structuring the training and even designing the new housing. As a consequence there was not enough time to follow developments in technique and information technology.
In 1985, three lecturers of the college were given the opportunity of a sabbatical year of industrial practice in informatics.
The experiences and insight gained during this period were recorded in an informatics policy plan for our own teacher training. The execution of this plan was possible only with an massive financial injection, which had to be obtained from the above- mentioned informatics stimulation plan.

2. ASSIGNMENT OF THE PROJECT

The project manager of the INSP for higher vocational education decided in 1986 to cluster the many requests for subsidies for informatics projects into some 10 so-called spearhead projects.
One spearhead project was assigned to the PTH on the preconditions:

- that the PTH itself would draw up the plan for an extensive project to integrate informatics into the technical vocational subjects;
- that the term would run from 1st January, 1987 to 1st January, 1989;
- that the project would be financed with 6 million Dutch guilders (about 3 million US$).

It was decided to accept this proposal notwithstanding many internal problems. During the school year 1986-1987, the part-time teachers' training colleges in The Netherlands and our daytime training had been merged. At the same time, the financing system for the institute changed, which not merely allows but even obliges the PTH to enter into activities on contract. Furthermore, internal moving of the staff caused housing problems.
Hence there was no basis for legitimization of the informatics project. Only a few people were involved in making the plan, which had drastic consequences for the whole college.

3. OBJECTIVES

All former project proposals were carefully analysed and clustered afresh to four different sub-projects, which were relevant to all the training activities of the PTH:

a. Computer-aided engineering (CAE)
b. Computers in industrial control processes (CIB)
c. Data-communication (DTC)
d. Measuring automation in the laboratory (MAL)

(The sub-projects CAE and CIB will be discussed in separate sessions of this conference WCCE-90 by Jan Houben [1] and Max Cremers [2].)

Each sub-project had three main objectives:

1. Advancement of the lecturers' expertise.

2. Development of teaching material for the lecturers of the teachers' training college, including lessons for students and didactical examples of lessons for their future pupils.

3. The purchase of computers to be used with the developed teaching material.

Besides all this, the project had some secondary objectives which partly laid down procedures and organization in the project:

4. The project had to contribute to the training of lecturers at the teachers' training college (since there is no training for lecturers of teachers' training institutes!)

5. Advancement of cooperation between lecturers involved in the daytime and the part-time training.

6. Exchanging of ideas between lecturers of the various fields, cooperating in the teachers' training.

7. Standardization of the computer equipment within the institute.

8. Preparation of post-graduate courses for inservice training of teachers.

9. Advancement of cooperation with industry and apprenticeship training.

10. Advancement of cooperation with the declining educational field.

This seems a complicated range of objectives, but it ought to be clear from the short summary of this paper, that though integration of informatics into the training was important, the institute also had other priorities which we tried to bring into this unique project.

4. PROCEDURES AND ORGANIZATION

For the realization of the project, four interdisciplinary work groups were formed for which lecturer-employees were appointed from different technical fields: an information scientist, an educationalist, a mathematician and in two cases a lecturer on philosophical and social education. In each development group, 6 or 7 lecturers worked half of their time on the project. Futhermore, they still attended to the teaching of students and/or post-graduate courses for teachers. These lecturers had to become experts in their field; they had to develop teaching material and buy equipment.

At the same time, to every development group an adviser group was appointed consisting of experts from industry in the field concerned. This adviser group was supposed to control the processes in the development groups as regards the contents. Also, some pilot schools from technical vocational education were appointed to each sub-project to cooperate with the development group in developing some pupil examples as a didactical example within the teaching material.

A legitimization group was set up for the total project to legitimize arrangements for our own college but also for the declining educational field. Finally, a steering committee was appointed, comprising delegates from the subsidizer, the authorities of the college, scientific education, the apprenticeships and industry.

A project office had to supply the necessary technical and administrative support. All this all led to a complex organizational scheme.

During the preparatory phase of this project, attention was mainly directed towards recruiting suitable stand-ins for the participants in the project. Many temporary lecturers had to fulfil 20 full-time functions, to which several schools in the region contributed. The students involved in the training did not always consider themselves fortunate with the situation.

During the initial phase of the project, the adviser groups were frequently consulted in order to direct the advancement of expertise and to gain insight into the necessary developments. This process of advancing expertise took more than a year!

After half a year we formed an idea of the necessary equipment, which was then ordered and installed. This stimulated the motivation of the developers and gave a strong stimulus to the development of new teaching materials. The steering committee met every few months, monitored the progress and created favourable pre-conditions.

5. RESULTS

On 1st September, 1989 the project was formally concluded with the following results (in order of objectives):

1. Advancement of expertise to the developers' level:
   7 x in CAE
   7 x in CIB
   3 x in DTC
   5 x in MAL
   Total expenses were about 700,000 US$, which mean an investment per teacher of over 30,000 US$.

2. Five teaching material packages with pupil examples have been developed, which can be used in training and in refresher courses for teachers. The scope of these packages is indicated below:

Title	Volume	
Basic course	64 periods	360 pages
CAE course	326 periods	1400 pages
CIB course	144 periods	700 pages
2 DTC courses	196 periods	800 pages
2 MAL courses	96 periods	200 pages

   The CAE and CIB courses will be explained in separate sessions.
   One DTC course is intended for electronics teachers and the other for all other technical teachers.
   The courses on measuring automation consist of a user course and a designer course.
   The development of this material cost over 1 million US$ in personal effort. Taking into account the necessary advancement of the expertise of the teachers, this averages out at 500 US$ per page!

3. The purchase of the equipment for our institute amounted to 1.4 million US$. The following purchases have been made and are now used in the training:

HARDWARE/SOFTWARE	BASE	CAE	CIB	DTC	MAL
Computer systems	16	59	28	10	12
AutoCAD		49			
Printer	3	5	1		
ORCAD		9			
Plotter		2			5
ULTIBOARD		13			
Digitizers		41			
WP 4.2	15				
PLC's			20		
IEEE					12
Measuring instr.			2	8	12
Lotus Measure					12

   In addition, much specific equipment was purchased, such as a PABX for digital communication, set-ups for glass-fibre tests, IEEE equipment and control equipment.

4. The interdisciplinary cooperation in the project groups, the cooperation with the pilot schools and the orientation toward the new developments in industry contributed to a considerable extent to the education of teachers.

5. We did not succeed in improving cooperation between lecturers involved in daytime and part-time training, because it was not possible to attract part-time lecturers to the project.

6. The exchanging of ideas by and within the various fields has proved very profitable. After some hesitation, the technicians recognized the know-how of the educationalists. Now, the mathematicians and information scientista can, much better than before, refer to technical applications while the technicians realize that they are working in a teachers' training programme!

7. We barely succeeded in promoting standardization in the project. The specialities in the various sub-projects were too extended and, at the decisive moment for purchase of the equipment in the sub-projects, the pressure of work was such that the members of the work groups could hardly pay attention to any sub-project but their own. Possibly, standardization may take place in the next round.

8. The courses developed within the project can nearly all be used directly for post-graduate courses for teachers, and some are already so used.

9. Cooperation with industry was essential for the project. It went quite well and has led to continuing contacts.
   Cooperation with the apprenticeship training was very limited, because this part-time training made cooperation very difficult.

10. Initially, the intention was to start the LERO project in February, 1987, with half a year's time for preparation of the contents. Unfortunately, formal consent for the project was delayed until June 1987. The pilot schools were then under contract, but the programming as regards the contents was not yet ready. Consequentlyt, cooperation with the pilot schools got off to a slow start and the contents of the pupil examples from the pilot schools and the rest of the LERO projects were not optimally geared to one another. As a result, not all pupil examples can be used as an example in the developed courses.

6. EVALUATION

The above-mentioned results showed on the whole, that the project fulfilled the objectives set.
It was clearly proved that the execution of such broad educational projects must be combined with full school years. Stand-ins for lecturers of the college were available only for the duration of one project, which limits the possibilities of such projects.

The preparation of the project could not be optimal. At the crucial moment, nobody was approachable for legitimization of the objectives of the project, so part of this process will have to take place after termination of the project.
As a consequence of the delayed consent from the Ministry, it was not possible to lay down the contents in cooperation with the industrial adviser groups in time.
Consequently, during the first months the project got into its stride too slowly, which was discouraging for the employees.

In retrospect, I must say that the assignment, as regards the contents of the sub-project MAL, was too difficult.
To start on the subject of measuring automation, one must have an adequate base of information technology and digital electronics; otherwise one gets stuck with physical principles, sensors and AD digitizers, without really understanding what it is all about. Consequently, this project will be concluded at a later stage.

Altogether, this has been a special experience which I will gladly discuss with anyone interested.

7. CONTINUATION AND IMPLEMENTATION

Completion of the products and equipment confronts the PTH with the tremendous task of:

a. advancing the expertise of all lecturers to such a degree that they can handle the developed teaching material and base their own lessons on this renewed basis.

b. changing the mentality of many lecturers. They must learn to use teaching material developed by others!

c. inserting the developed teaching material into the training curriculum. The conservative techniques will be superseded. It is already clear that the graduates of our college in technical education are immediately put in a position to work with examination subjects in which information technology needs to be applied.

I hope to be able to report on the follow-up to this project at the next WCCE Conference.

REFERENCES

[1] Dr Jan Houben, CAE from industry to education, in this volume.

[2] Max Cremers, Information technology in all technical fields. Teachers' training course development for information technology. In this volume.

Computers in Education
A. McDougall and C. Dowling (Editors)
Elsevier Science Publishers B.V. (North-Holland)

THE COMPUTER AS MANAGEMENT TOOL: PROMISES AND PITFALLS

Adrie J. Visscher

University of Twente, Department of Education, Division of Educational Administration, P.O. Box 217, 7500 AE Enschede, The Netherlands

1. INTRODUCTION

In this paper we at first (chapter 2) will make an analysis of the various functions of the computer: in which different ways can the computer assist the execution of activities? After that (chapter 3) we will, in more general terms, pay attention to the advantages of computer use. The fourth chapter is devoted to the various conditions for the use of the computer. We finally discuss some problems of the state of the art (chapter 5) and the initiatives that should be developed to realize a better future for computer assisted school administration (chapter 6).

2. COMPUTER FUNCTIONS IN RELATION TO SCHOOL ORGANIZATIONAL PROCESSES

One can describe information systems on the basis of several criteria such as the physical components, the types of computer output, the various data processing functions and the like (see Davis and Olson [1]). Within the scope of this article we will describe the ways in which the computer can be used in schools by distinguishing various data processing computer functions.
We will first mention five computer functions and then illustrate them with an example:

a. *Keeping the data base up to date and consistent* (UPTO): this concerns recording the relevant changes of the situation of the organizational environment and the organization itself
b. *Information retrieval and the production of documents* (IRPD): by this we mean respectively the retrieval of data that are stored in the computer and making standard reports for use within the school. These reports and documents concerning the situation of the organization(al environment) that has been registered by means of the processes mentioned under (a). The information is retrieved on behalf of all kinds of different daily operational activities. The decisions that have to be taken for these activities are of an operational kind. They can be taken quickly, little time is needed for problem diagnosis, the available data directly lead to the decision.
c. *Decision making support* (DMS): this bears upon administrative decisions directed at the coordination of operational activities. These coordinational types of activities are less obvious, of a less routine character than the types of decisions that we mentioned under (b). Diagnosis, searching, and choosing solutions, are important and time consuming activities here. The problems to be solved can vary with regard to the degree in which they are structured. Some problems are very structured, have a limited number of alternative solutions and have a known solving strategy. In this case the computer can generate alternative solutions that can be evaluated on the basis of several criteria. However, finally it is man who chooses a solution.
In the case of less structured problems the computer can analyze the relevant data (e.g. relations between various data) and as such provide the decision makers with important information. This information can as well consist of reports that the information system produces in a standard fashion as of answers to very specific management questions for which no standard report exists.
d. *Decision making* (DM): the computer 'itself' takes a decision on the basis of the available information. Within schools this function probably is not very important.
e. *Communication* (COM): in this case several computers within the school and/or computers of other organizations are mutually connected. These links make it possible to exchange messages with other staff members and/or organizations.

To illustrate the above mentioned computer functions we will discuss the application and admitting of new pupils. When a pupils applies for a school by means of an application form that has been filled in, this form is first checked for completeness and correctness. After that the application data are entered into the database (function UPTO). The secretary of the admitting committee can let the computer produce an overview of the pupils (function IRPD) that have applied, or of the pupils that have applied but still have to hand in certain data that are relevant for the admitting

decision (e.g. previous training, test scores). The admitting decision will probably always be something where man plays an important role, but in fact it is imaginable that, if the admitting criteria have been defined unambiguously, the computer takes the admitting decision (function DM) on the basis of the entered pupil data and, moreover, produces the (standard) admittance- c.q. refusal letters. After the admitting decisions have been taken and the lists with corrections and supplements have been returned, the new data are entered into the database (function UPTO). After that the adjusted lists can be transmitted by means of the computer to the relevant staff members who possess a computer (function COM).
When the admitting procedure has been finished an analysis can be made of the admitting trends over several school years. One can for instance investigate the number of admitted pupils and the characteristics of the admitted pupils (e.g. from which delivering school, which diploma). These characteristics can be related to the school career of pupils. The computer as such provides information with which developments, problems and possible solutions with regard to the admittance can be analyzed (function DMS). On the basis of that kind of information an admittance policy can be developed.

3. POTENTIAL ADVANTAGES

In chapter two we discussed which computer functions can be used. Now we will pay attention to how the use of the computer can improve school efficiency and school effectiveness.

3.1. Improving efficiency and effectiveness

We make a distinction between two types of potential advantages that result from the use of the computer for administrative purposes: a) improvements of the efficiency and b) improvements of the effectiveness.

re a: The amount of data that is registered in schools during each school year is gigantic: among others, data on pupils, personnel, finances, timetables and subjects. Every school often has several partial registration sets (one of the janitor, the school office, the counsellor, the deputee headmasters), that contain an overlap of data. Moreover, the same data often have to be transferred to various internally or externally used forms. This means that if data are registered manually the same data have to be filled in frequently.
If the computer enables the <u>single</u> entry of data (at one central spot) and the multiple use of data for various purposes, enormous efficiency improvements are possible. Clerical personnel can then take care of the entry and updating of the database. The software can take care that the required lists, reports, labels, etc., are produced automatically. Also, it can be predicted that data that are demanded by external bodies will not be delivered by means of (with regard to lay out, frequently changing) official forms, but by means of diskettes that are mailed or delivered or by means of direct data communication between the computers of the school and those of external bodies. If the latter is realized, efficiency improvements are possible at the level of the external body as well at the level of the school.
In general we can state that because the computer can take over a number of clerical tasks and because data can be registered by means of the computer at one spot for subsequent use at various locations, the computer makes it possible to produce the same amount of, or more information with less manpower and in a shorter period of time.

re b: The computer might also contribute to a more effectively operating school, that is, to a better realization of the goals of the school organization. This is possible by providing better conditions for goal realization. An improvement of school efficiency might, for instance, result in the availability of more time for non-clerical (e.g., the development of instructional material, additional training) activities.
Another imaginable effect is that the job quality and satisfaction of the clerical workers and of the managers (who also carry out many clerical activities) are improved because the computer takes over monotonous clerical work. One might expect that this has a positive influence on the satisfaction and functioning of these employees (see e.g. Visscher & Vloon [1]).
Another potential advantage is related to the already discussed facet of single-entry-multiple-use of data. If data are kept up to date at one location within the school, then everybody can always make use of the same up to date data. It is plausible that this will effect the quality of activities (e.g. better decisions) based on these data and as such the effectiveness of these activities.
When we discussed the computer assisted allocation processes, another potential advantage of computer use was mentioned. The computer makes it possible to explore several alternative problem solving activities, to evaluate them and to choose the most desirable alternative. This means considerable progress in comparison with the old manual situation in which one mostly had to be satisfied with one solution that was found. The quality of, for instance, the timetables and lesson groups (the allocation products) during every school day influence the functioning of pupils and employees. For that reason one might expect that finding high-quality solutions for these

allocation problems will improve the functioning of schools.
Moreover, we have seen that the computer can support the control of school organizational activities by the timely observation of problems and by taking care that adjustments are done in time, by the computer 'itself', or by the school management. It is likely that a timely (and adequate) reaction will lead to a more effective organization.
We have already discussed the production of information by the computer, on the basis of which a school policy can be developed and evaluated. Also it seems probable that an improvement of the conditions for decision making will effect the quality of policy making in a positive way and as such, the effectiveness of the school organization (elements).

4. CONDITIONS FOR THE USE OF THE COMPUTER

In this chapter we will describe some conditions for the use of computers for administrative purposes. We distinguish between three types of conditions:
a) technical conditions
b) implementation and logistic conditions
c) structural organizational conditions

Since the first two types are rather familiar and because no or little attention is paid in the literature to the third condition, we will concentrate on the organizational conditions and discuss the other conditions only briefly.

re a: Every information system needs, of course, an adequate software and hardware basis. Important factors in this context are sufficient memory and processor capacity as well as well-structured software (including the database).
The number of computers/terminals that is available within the school is of importance for the speed with which data can be entered and retrieved and for the simultaneous utilization of several applications.
Software characteristics that will influence computer use concern the the number of programming mistakes, the user friendliness (e.g., simplicity, uniformity of commands, availability of HELP-commands), and the like. Finally the accessability and usability of the manuals have to be of such a level that each user can get desired information in an easy way.

re b: A school needs to possess the required implementation facilities in terms of finances, personnel and the like. The concerned staff members should, moreover, have the required knowledge to fulfill their tasks. Knowledge with regard to the computer software but also knowledge with regard to non-computer related activities (e.g. who should deliver which data to whom and how is the computer output distributed) is essential. The latter has to do with the logistic conditions: the conditions for handing in, registering and processing of data. The more those involved are aware of their tasks and the tasks of others and the more everything is done according to an agreed-upon way, the more solid will be the basis for the use of the information system.

re c: Information systems can produce much information that can be used within the policy making process, if the school has a policy making capacity of a certain level. This capacity is related to how the school as an organization functions. Schools differ in the degree to which policy is made and executed (Van der Krogt [2]) as well as with regard to the areas in which policy is made. E. Marx [1] distinguishes between four areas for policy making: the facilities (finance, personnel and the like), the general pedagogic-didactic area, the educational profile of the school (the structure in terms of school type grades and school types) and finally the didactic and contents of the various subjects. Many schools restrict their policy making activities to one or a few of these four areas. Most often a school policy is only developed with regard to school facilities, because this does not touch the contents of the work of the teachers. In schools in which teachers operate less autonomously, policy making in the other three areas is also likely.
Schools should be aware of the fact that buying a computer will not change their organizational characteristics; on the contrary, the characteristics of the organization are the limits for the administrative use of the computer. In schools with only a limited policy making capacity, part of the potential of the computer information system will be unutilized.

4.1. The conditions and reality

Research (Visscher & Vloon, 1986) has shown that the technical, implementation and logistic conditions for computer use often are only partially fulfilled. Frequently available software does not fit with the desires of the users and hardware problems are not uncommon. Implementation often leads to problems because the users are not coached sufficiently or because the new logistic procedures are not clear to everyone.
Even when all the technical, implementation and logistic conditions have been fulfilled, utilizing the potential advantages of management information systems (MIS) still continues to be difficult. The reason for this is that the school as an organization must also be able to make use of the possibilities of a MIS. There are indications that many schools are insufficiently equipped to fully exploit the potential of the computer. We will try to explain this by discussing a number of school

characteristics that are often mentioned in the literature and treat their implications for the use of a MIS.

Research on *(school) manager behaviour* (see Mintzberg [1]) has shown school managers behave only for a very small part according to the stereotypical picture that is often given of them: as rational problem solvers who make a thorough analysis of problems and causes, generate alternative solutions and elaborate the most suitable solution.

In reality, managers tend to base their activities not on solid, objective data but on impressions, conversations and the like. Knowing this, the question rises to what degree the computer will be used to support policy making and evaluation. Although the computer can be an important tool to observe problems and to analyze trends, the previously mentioned research data make an intensive use of computer information less probable.

Schools are organizations with *autonomously operating teachers*. Teachers' knowledge and skills are the most important mechanisms that determine their behaviour. So there is no hierarchical management that continuously gives assignments to the operational staff. For that reason, it is questionable if the increased possibilities to register and control what is happening in schools will effect the functioning of teachers and the school. The work that is done within the professional bureaucracy is complex. It is highly doubtful if this work can be supervised and controlled in a top-down way. Many examples exist that prove that more supervision and standardisation in this kind of organization are counterproductive. More control of highly trained professionals often proves to be demotivating. Will more control, more evaluation of the professional by means of the computer, result in an improvement of teachers' work or in a reduction of teachers' professional feelings of responsibility?

We already mentioned that *policy making capacity* in general can vary between schools. Moreover, there can be variation with regard to the areas in which a school is able to develop and execute policy. A school in which the teaching-training process is a matter of the individual teacher and the mutual coordination on the level of the departments and divisions of the school is minimal, is unlikely to make use of general data related to the educational process. The effect of the data that the computer produces will then be determined by the degree to which the individual teacher is guided by these data in his/her behaviour.

Another problem with respect to policy making concerns *the relation(s) between cause(s) and effect(s) with regard to the teaching-training process*. To give an example, many factors influence the truancy of pupils: the personal characteristics of pupils, their situation at home, societal developments (e.g. unemployment), school factors, etc. We know that these factors are of importance, but we do not know the magnitude of their influence. Therefore, if the computer informs us of high truancy scores, we do not know how we should interpret them. What do they mean and by what are they caused? In which way can the school itself influence the truancy? The computer can show us the relations between variables (e.g. between truancy magnitude and pupil achievements, or between truancy on the one hand and subjects, timetable moments, school type grades, and the like on the other hand), but can not present us with cause and effect. However, this does not mean that computer data are of no value. In former days we did not have the tools to observe the trends and relations among different data, something that is necessary for effective policy making. It will be important to complement the 'solid', quantitative computer data with 'soft' data that can help to explain the backgrounds and causes of the hard data. The risk exists that if this is not done, one draws conclusions too easily.

Characteristics of the decision making processes in schools concern another facet of schools that may influence the impact of a MIS. Literature (Cohen, March & Olson [2]) shows that decision making situations in these organizations often function as "garbage cans" in which every participant throws his individual goals (instead of the school goals) and problems. This phenomenon is connected with the fact that the central goals of the organization often are not defined unambiguously and as such cannot function as a clear guide for the members of the organization. In reality, many individual goals exist in schools that do not always fit with the general organizational goals. In combination with the earlier mentioned problem of determining causes and effects of phenomena, this results in a situation in which decision making situations become more complicated and taking decisions directed to solving problems becomes more and more difficult. This often means that decision making is put off (e.g. to collect extra information) or that decisions are taken that do not threaten any of the participants but do not clearly addres a particular problem. The term "non-decision making" is used in this context.

If we combine the discussed problems with the problem that *the link between decisions and their execution* does not prove to be very strong in school organizations, then it will be clear that in schools in general we do not generally find a decisive policy making and execution process. What will be the influence of the introduction of a MIS on this? Will the availability of more data lead to dramatic changes in these school characteristics? We doubt it, for the short term. If schools will change, it will be very slowly and they will need a long learning process.

So far our discussion has been of the school organizational characteristics. We expect that their restraining influence will especially be important in the area of the control of the educational process by means of the computer. We have tried to relativize the potential influence of the computer in this context. We also have to be aware that only part of the information that is used in schools can come out of the computer. So the support that the computer can give can only concern part of the decision making process. All this does not imply that we do not see the computer as a very valuable tool for the administration of schools. Even if we only look at the assistance that it can give to clerical processing and data communication, already then its value is undisputed. Besides, it can assist the policy makers by analyzing problems. That it does not offer the causes of and solutions for these problems is a pity but not tragic.
The school itself determines how valuable the computer will be for it. The school decides if it retrieves much or little information out of the computer and which information it uses. In other words: the computer cannot be a universal remedy that solves all management problems of schools. However it can help to work at solving these complex problems.

5. LIMITATIONS OF THE CURRENT SITUATION

Research (Visscher and Vloon, 1986) shows that the computer should be considered as an important administrative tool. All kinds of applications have already been developed by enthusiastic teachers, administrators and by software houses: management supporting and clerical applications as well as applications that assist the teacher with his clerical activities. Nevertheless, we have the impression that there is very little cooperation between the various developers. One disadvantage of this is that everybody is developing software on the basis of limited resources (finance, time, know-how). Because of the lack of exchange of information between developers, these limited resources are moreover used very inappropriately; in other words, the wheel is often reinvented.
Besides, we can observe that the quality of the software differs enormously. Some information systems offer possibilities to the user that, given the conditions under which they have been developed, are admirable; others clearly violate the current standards for information systems far too much. In general, the support that the software offers is limited: too often inefficient solutions have been chosen to enter, manipulate and retrieve data.
The maintenance and expansion of the software is often very difficult because of the use of inflexible so-called third generation languages and the little attention that has been given to the documentation of the software.

Many of the applications are almost always tailored for one situation (the school for which it is developed). It will be clear that the developed systems often do not fit with the situation in those schools that were not involved in the development process. Sometimes the software only can be used if one possesses hardware of a certain brand (a specific operating system). The available software is written in a so-called third generation programming language (e.g. COBOL, PASCAL, BASIC) which are inflexible and therefore make it difficult (that is, expensive) to adjust the software to the specific situation and/or wishes of schools.
If the developed software becomes a commercial package, if the developer(s) decide(s) to adjust the software or not it depends on how general the occurring problems are and how difficult it is to solve them.
In our opinion, the currently developed software should be seen as a very partial automation of school administrative activities. In general, what has been done is the computerization of (part of) the directly visible, mainly <u>clerical</u> activities, routine activities that formerly had been executed manually and that are well-structured and labour-intensive (e.g. marks, absentee and financial administration). However, the attention given to the computer assisted registration and manipulation of data has led to comparatively little attention given to the computer assisted support of school managers. This strong accent on the automation of clerical activities in schools is very understandable. Also different organizations started their automation activities with the automation of routine clerical activities, because these activities could be defined well and the return on this form of automation was clear. A major problem of automation in schools, however, is that no careful attention has been given to the question which information is valuable for those who have to run schools and in which way the computer can assist them in getting this information available. In our opinion we should devote more research and development activities to the computer assisted support of school managers. Another problem of the software is that most of it is developed for use in a single-user (one stand alone computer) environment and not for the so-called multi-user, multi-tasking environment (when several staff members can work at the same time in various locations with the MIS via their own terminals). When schools have a decentralized school office and/or when records exist at more than one location, a multi-user, multi-tasking environment is a prerequisite for an efficient and effective school administration. The single-user option probably only works in a situation in which a specific activity (e.g. the processing of data about a specified group of pupils) is only done at one location and when all the mutations are

carried out at that same spot. However, in all types of organizations a trend can be observed from the use of stand alone computers to the use of computers that are mutually connected within a local area network within which each computer/terminal has access to a central database. We expect that in schools the need will also increase for this kind of distributed systems. In the near future several employees of the school will have access to (a part of) the central database by means of their own terminals, and the terminals of this network will be able to operate individually and simultaneously without conflict or interference.

6. SOME RECOMMENDATIONS FOR THE FUTURE

On the basis of our research in this field we would like to present some recommendations for the promotion of computer assisted school administration. In our opinion, we should strive for a situation in which school information systems are developed that:
- are based on the use of professional know how and modern tools for information system development and maintenance;
- are a result of the combined and efficient use of the required knowledge and facilities from various resources;
- are suitable for use in as many schools as possible;
- provide all the possible and useful clerical and management support;
- are appropriate for use in a multi-user, multi tasking environment.

Since the nature of some of the applications is very complex (e.g. timetabling, computer assisted testing, planning) fundamental research in these areas will be necessary.
A next recommendation concerns the evaluation of the available software. The quality of various available packages varies enormously and many schools cannot judge the qualities of the software adequately on their own. For this reason a careful analysis of available software should be made by an independent organization. This analysis should separate the wheat from the chaff and point out the relevant evaluation criteria to schools. Besides, this evaluative information might also be used for the improvement of existing systems and the realization of better software.

Within various countries initiatives are undertaken to solve some of the problems that have been discussed in this article. The future will learn to which degree these activities will result in better school information systems.

REFERENCES

[1] Davis, G.B. and Olson, M.H., Management information systems (McGraw-Hill, New York, 1985).

[1] Visscher, A.J. and Vloon, W.J., Schooladministratie en schoolmanagement m.b.v. de computer: mogelijkheden en effecten [School administration by means of the computer: possibilities and effects] (University of Twente, Department of Education, Enschede, 1986).

[2] Krogt, F.J. van der, Schoolorganisatie en Beleidsvorming [School organization and policy making], Handboek Schoolorganisatie en Onderwijsmanagement (Samsom, Alphen aan den Rijn, 1985) pp. 1615-1 - 1615-31.

[1] Marx, E.C.H., De organisatie van scholengemeenschappen in onderwijskundige optiek [The organization of comprehensive schools from an educational point of view] (Wolters-Noordhoff, Groningen, 1975).

[2] Cohen, M.D., March, J.G. and Olson, J.P., A garbage-can model of organizational choice, Administrative Science Quarterly, 17 (1972) pp. 1-25.

[1] Mintzberg, H., The Nature of Managerial Work (Harper & Row, New York, 1973).

INFORMATICS IN ELEMENTARY EDUCATION

Computers in Education
A. McDougall and C. Dowling (Editors)
Elsevier Science Publishers B.V. (North-Holland)

REALITY IS AN UNENDING FAIRY-TALE

Erling Schmidt

DAKS - Department of Educational Computing
Municipal Authority of Aalborg
Godthåbsgade 8
DK-9400 Nørresundby, Denmark

The technological development has not only introduced the computers as ubiquitous in society, but has also introduced them into the elementary school. This process has been extremely fast and naturally brought about some new tasks to the school.

It has always been the task of the school to prepare the pupils for the society in which they live and are an integral part. The intensive computer application in society has added new dimensions to this task, which must necessarily be taken into account.

Besides, the computer as a tool in the teaching confronts the school with new tasks, too. Especially here is a great challenge to the teachers, who - as we know - hold the final responsibility for the teaching.

Both tasks concern the most proper choice among many possibilities, and then it is vital that as many as possible are given the best possible background for participation in making the optimal choices.

1. Fairy-Tales and Computers

It was so lovely in the countryside; it was summer! The grain stood yellow, the oat green, the hay was raised in stacks down the green meadows, and there the stork walked about on his long red legs, talking Egyptian, for this language he had learned from his mother.

This is the beginning of the fairy-tale by Hans Christian Andersen about "The Ugly Duckling", which is well-known by children all over the world.

Children - of all ages - like fairy-tales: they appeal to imagination and feelings, but also to reason and pensiveness. They can often be interpreted at several levels and contain a moral.

Many fairy-tales - including "The Ugly Duckling" - are built up in such a way that the principal character of the fairy-tale starts with a number of problems, is treated unjustly, abused, exposed to insults, misunderstood, and is left out in the cold. But in a surprising development the situation turns to the advantage of the principal character, qualities, possibilities and connections hidden so far are discovered, and the main character is compensated and given the right and well-deserved place in the world.

In many respects, parallels can be drawn between the fairy-tale of the development of computer applications in elementary school and "The Ugly Duckling":

In a flash they appeared - the computer in the school, and the duckling in the duck-yard. And from the beginning they were misunderstood - in the fairy-tale the ugly duckling was believed to be a turkey and thus could not swim, while the computer was regarded by the school as an over-size calculating machine - the hobby of a few fanatics ...

As it presently turned out that the ugly duckling actually could swim very well, and that computer applications were relevant and interesting in various connections at school - they were to be presented to the world: the ugly duckling to the duck-yard, and the computer to school authorities and colleagues.

The ugly duckling had a mixed reception. Admittedly, it was accepted by the highest authority - after some hesitation - but nevertheless it was immediately exposed to persecution by the other ducks and ducklings and was regularly mobbed in the ordinary turmoil of the duck-yard.

At many places, this applied to computer application at the school, too. Admittedly, the authorities did not reject it, but at any rate it was not broadly recognized at the school itself from the start, and those teachers who did work with computers had a hard struggle to obtain reasonable possibilities for development on terms similar to other activities at the school. The fact that something new and unknown suffers such a fate - in the fairy-tale as in real life - is not necessarily caused by a deliberately evil will. Tradition, inertia, and prejudice have always been known to be powerful factors ...

At a certain point the duckling meets a cat and a hen who want to know immediately whether it can purr or lay eggs. As the duckling must admit to being unable to do this, it is rejected instantly as useless. In this way computers in schools have been exposed to misapplication or assessments based upon irrelevant criteria.

But after a series of such thought-provoking episodes the fairy-tale about the ugly duckling ends at the point where the duckling has become a swan and is recognized as such. Some merry children bid it welcome, offering it bread and biscuits, and thinking that the new swan is the prettiest of all the swans in the lake. And here Hans Christian Andersen choses to end the fairy-tale about "The Ugly Duckling".

The fairy-tale about computer applications in schools, however, has not reached its end. Here, we rather find ourselves at the beginning of a new chapter: Most of the teachers recognize today that we have "swan" in our "duckyard". And where there used to be a good deal of scepticism and resistance, the major trend today is probably positive hesitation.

2. Changes in School and Society

Actually, teachers cannot be blamed for the prevailing feeling of insecurity, for society as well as the school are in the process of rapid and extensive changes as a consequence of the technological development.

One could say that the preconditions of development of human society are on one hand the cultural traditions, ideas, and attitudes, and on the other hand the technical possibilities, the practical, economical, and organizational capabilities, and the resources available. In an interaction between these factors, the continuous development of society takes place. Especially because it is an interaction between the various factors, it is essential that there is some sort of balance between them and that there is ample time for mutual influence in the shape of a parallel development. Only under these circumstances will we experience the best and most stable development.

The school is a function in and of society - a mini society, so to speak, with its particular traditions, ideas, attitudes, and possibilities - in fact furnished with the same set of factors directing its development. And here, too, it is obviously just as important that there is a balance between them.

However, we are probably in a period where technological development especially is so rapid that we need to ensure that it will not disturb the balance of the overall development. It is vital that other factors which cannot always develop at the same pace, are given sufficient consideration that they may contribute to the general development. The factors in question are e.g. changes in traditions and attitudes, and development of new ideas and organizational concepts.

3. Two Tasks

Here are the important tasks of the school - both the internal development of the school itself, and its contribution to the general development of society. In my opinion it is relevant to regard this as two different tasks, simply to ensure that they are both solved.

If you look back upon the development of computer applications in schools you can see in a way that there have always been these two tasks. Besides, there is a long tradition of dividing the application of computers in schools into various fields. It probably started with CAI and Computer Science. (For the sake of completeness I should also mention the use of computers for administration as an independent area, which I leave out completely in this connection.) Gradually the activities developed in two main streams, however with ramifications, of course, as well as entanglements, and quite a few loose ends.

- One stream deals with learning something about computers, their use and implications. These activities have taken place under the names of Computer Science, Computer Studies, Informatics, Computer Awareness, etc. At the beginning, the main importance was attached to algorithms and programming, and through wider sorts of problem-solving the emphasis moved towards a perspective of the computer and its implications for society and the individual. Although the major part of these activities take place with the older pupils, there has been a tendency over the years to place them at increasingly earlier stages of school attendance.

- The other stream deals with teaching and learning with computers. Here, we see the development from drill and practice to a broader use of the computer as a tool in cross-curricular activities. Particularly in this area the school is in a phase of rapid development, owing to new and better programmes and more powerful computers.

4. The Task of the School in regard to Society

Although the former stream originates from Computer Science - and many persons have rightfully questioned the usefulness of a range of the activities in this area - I believe that society makes such demands on the school that a task still exists here.

In summary, one might say that the primary task of the school was previously that of teaching the children writing and arithmetic. Today, the aim is generally broader, and for instance we may see objectives like "training the ability to take an individual attitude" and "preparing the pupils for understanding and taking active part in a democratic society and for sharing the responsibility for the solution of common tasks".

In view of the development in the application of computers and new technology in society, and of its impact on all of us, it has become the task of the school to furnish the pupils with such a background that they are able to estimate and take an attitude towards the possibilities, influence, and consequences deriving from the use of computers.

Through a variety of examples the pupils should be guided in the utilization of electronic data processing and should solve practical tasks with computers, themselves, in order to get an impression of the number of possibilities afforded by new technology.

But they should also experience the problems that are related to the extensive use of EDP, the impact we are subject to, and the consequences created by this still more common use.

An important aspect will be the pupils' acknowledgment of the fact that, in this area, too, the technical development is created by man, and that therefore, as citizens in a democratic society, they will share the influence on and the responsibility for the way in which EDP contributes to changing the development of society and the life of the individual.

A computer is a general tool which may be applied for a variety of tasks, and the consequences of the use of the computer are therefore dependent on the specific application itself, and not on the computer as such. In fact, the computer may be used for directly opposite purposes.

For instance, computers may be used to make information accessible to many people in connection with de-centralization of decision processes and functions, but those very computers might as well be utilized to concentrate knowledge, power, and influence in a few hands.

In general it could be said that, of course, the results and the consequences of the development in the field of EDP are determined by where and how we choose to apply this technique, and how good we are at it, and NOT by the technique itself. But only a few come to this realisation by themselves. A lot of people, adults as well as children, (and teachers, too), regard computers and their application as something beyond their influence, and therefore it is imperative that the school take up these relationships and clarify them in order to stimulate the pupils to participate in choosing how we are going to utilize the possibilities afforded to us by new technology.

The solution of this task cannot be placed in an isolated subject or a brief treatment in certain grades. All subjects - and the intercurricular activities, as well - should contribute, and it is my opinion that it can take place in all grades throughout the school attendance.

Now it is not in my idea, of course, that the task should be solved by taking pains in procuring an enormous programme at a certain stage, which can print out primes or maybe even twinned primes, and at another time by discussing the "big brother" syndrome based upon some of the idiotic computer systems you see examples of occasionally, especially in public authority. That stage is past.

A far better way to approach the task is to work with projects. Project-oriented teaching is not unknown in schools, but somehow this organizational form suits the application of computers particularly well.

(Here, one cannot but wonder whether the shortage of a sufficient number of computers at the school has in a certain way forced the teachers to be extra creative and careful in planning the activities, and that this in fact has been rather stimulating.)

At many places projects concerned with the application of computers in teaching have been started in the more advanced grades. It was wished not just that programming and the computer were to be the subject as such - the tools should be used for the solving of relevant problems, and in this connection the pupils would learn something, about possibilities as well as consequences.

During the past few years similar projects have been taken up in elementary education, among other things due to the fact that the projects as such are a suitable organizational form at these levels, and programmes and materials are now available to facilitate the introduction of EDP in this way.

One of the tools which has contributed a good deal to offering the possibility of making exciting, instructive and motivating projects with computers in elementary education possible is for instance LEGO Technic Control. With materials of this sort a practically inexhaustible world of activities is opened, where teaching of factual knowledge and skills can be combined with development of the children's faculty for problem-solving, collaboration, critical thinking and decision-making.

Besides, it is my point of view that projects where concrete materials (models, measuring instruments, etc.) are combined with data processing, can add in themselves new dimensions to teaching, but also be capable of influencing other instruction in a positive way. If a teacher has had the experience that such a project can bring about, he will inevitably revise to some extent his attitudes - and especially his habits - with regard to teaching in general.

In particular, I would like to point out an important area where the construction and control of LEGO models can contribute to the solution of one of the tasks of the school, viz. to furnish the children with a suitable background to be prepared for participation in a computerized society. For there is the special quality in computer technology that it is incredibly flexible - and that it can be built into other machines in a hidden way.

We surround ourselves with - and make ourselves dependent on - an increasing number of automatic facilities, devices, and machines which are controlled by means of programmes, i.e. built-in micro processors. In order not to end up completely lost and alienated by such a technology, it is vital for us to acquire some understanding of the actually often simple basic mechanisms and principles enabling it all.

The work of inventing, building and modifying various models and controlling them by means of one's own programmes highly supports the formation of such an understanding. And many teachers will be surprised at the speed of even small pupils' understanding of principles, for instance "feed back", and their resulting utilization of them in the work with their models, not to mention the creative imagination which characterizes their work.

Furthermore, it is generally experienced that - based upon the practical work with the models - the pupils are highly motivated to discuss the actual or prospective possibilities and consequences of technology. Here, too, the pupils will often give a free rein to their imagination, but at the same time there is evidently a thoughtfulness and an understanding of the relationships. Of course, there are matters where the younger pupils have no background for discussions, but it has been a positive surprise to realize how conscious they are of many of the sets of problems that we are faced with.

Finally, as a teacher one cannot but feel that something must have succeeded when - at a class visit to a big exhibition of "Intelligence in Industry" - a ten-year-old girl, at her first meeting with an industrial robot of several tons, partly expresses her wish to control it, partly proposes a better way to do it. She at least will be well-prepared to face the challenge from the technological society.

5. The Task of the School for Itself

When the school is to change, time is required. Some compare the school with a supertanker where quite some time passes, and distance is covered, before a change of the wheel brings about a change of course. Others maintain ungraciously that it requires about 40 years to have changes penetrate entirely in schools: meaning the time which passes before the last teacher engaged retires on a pension.

It might be correct to admit that today we find ourselves in the paradoxical situation with regard to the application of computers in teaching that the teacher is the prime mover and the brake at the same time. But indeed, other factors - as for instance financial and political - play an important part, too.

Of course one can - and should - start by asking oneself the question whether the computer has a justification as a tool in teaching, at all. But with the results appearing around us today, and with the potential which the computers have proven to be in possession of, I find this question outmoded.

Then one may ask why computers are not already today used more extensively and better in schools than is actually the case. This question is sometimes raised by the politicians, who have often granted the major part of the money to the computers themselves, believing that a quality application is in direct ratio to the number of computers. (Fortunately, there are also politicians of broader foresight.) There are a variety of explanations for this, some of them more correct than others.

The three typical excuses for a teacher to give when asked this question are:

- There are not enough (good) computers
- There are not enough (good) programmes
- In-service training in this area is missing

Of course, these excuses have been valid - and they still are in many places, but gradually they are losing their credibility. In return, there are other explanations of the relatively slow pace in the development:

- Getting acquainted with completely new possibilities takes time
- Changing traditions and attitudes takes time
- Originating ideas and carrying them into effect takes time
- The teachers' readjustment takes time...

So it is my theory that in various situations it is the teachers themselves who form the biggest obstacle to reaching the most appropriate ways to apply computers in education. There may be many reasonable explanations for this fact, and I shall come back to some of them in a moment. But let me illustrate this theory with a little case history:

In 1985 a group of Danish teachers went on a study tour to England, that is, Greater London. It was a most profitable trip, and as on previous occasions there was a brisk exchange of ideas and experience.

However, one specific event remained fixed in the minds of all participants and could not but invite a good deal of reflection:

One of our visits took place at a small primary school south of London, and prospects were held out to us of seeing eleven to twelve-year-old pupils working with databases of various sorts. For instance, we were told that they had constructed an interactive database of all plants in the neighbourhood of the school, so that names and qualities of plants gathered could be found quickly.

This sounded very advanced to our group, and up to the visit vivid discussions took place as to which database programme was used by the school. Partly it caused a good deal of wonder that such a small school could afford equipment and software to handle such a database, and partly, people were curious to see how children that age could manage to control that system.

Our expectations did not diminish when - on the arrival at the school - we were told that the pupils had made a database of the Vikings' activities in England for the occasion of our visit.

Then it was both a shocking and stimulating experience to have the databases presented by the pupils, for it turned out that they were using a programme known by many under the name of "animal".

In short, the programme works in such a way that it starts by asking whether you think of an animal. If the answer is affirmative, the programme proposes that you think of an elephant. If this is denied, you are asked what then you think of. Here you could reply "a giraffe", for instance, and then the programme wants to know which question should be asked to distinguish between a giraffe and an elephant. Here the answer could be that the question should be asked whether the animal has a long neck, and hereby the programme has divided its world into animals with long necks (where giraffes will be proposed), and other animals (where so far only elephants are known). But if the dialogue with the programme continues, it will "learn about" an increasing number of animals, and can gradually find precisely those animals you have in mind.

The stimulating aspect was to see this programme being applied in such a creative and sensible way in the instruction. The children had no problems in using the programme, and furthermore, they had made print-outs of the search trees incorporated in the various databases. The tool was applied with the use of common sense and contributed to an quality teaching with a computer application.

The shocking aspect of it was that no Danish teacher had thought of this possibility so far. The fact was that this very programme had accompanied practically all micro computers appearing in Danish schools for the previous 7 or 8 years. It was used as an illustration in the manual for Comal80 and was lying on the distribution disks ready for use! This programme was only used to a small extent to illustrate tree structures as sort of a bad example of AI in computer science.

My point is that today we have reached the level at many places where both equipment and software are present at the schools - now the goal is to use it in a creative way.

To start this is the teacher's task, but of course it is a precondition that he actually gets the idea!

Fortunately, the process of change is in full swing. It is a great task, but it is essential that all teachers involve themselves actively and give their contribution to the development of computer applications in schools. If not, we run the risk that the aggregate development of the school may take a less fortunate direction, where we cannot utilize the possibilities afforded to us by the development - or that we shall succumb to it.

The task makes heavy demands on the teachers and, indirectly, on the authorities, who are responsible for giving the teachers genuine possibilities to solve this task.

Of course, the basis is education and in-service training. But experience proves that this is not always enough. There is quite a distance from the first word processing course to a creative and relevant use of word processing in the classroom. Here the teachers should be ensured of support all the way in the shape of advice, good materials, inspiration such as case studies, etc. But the teachers should also be granted time, partly for the revision of methods and and contents of their teaching which lies ahead, and partly for the development and testing of new ideas. The latter is of particular importance, for when teachers have only a limited number of hours to reach some educational objectives, they will often choose the safe rather than involve themselves in something new and unknown.

The teachers themselves must invest a good deal of energy, stubbornness, and will to get on. At the same time they must be critical on a factual and educational level, and above all be open-minded and flexible towards innovations. They must also have the courage to throw themselves into experiments and new activities, despite some insecurity about the result. And they ought not fear that for instance it should turn out that some of the pupils cope with all the novelties far better than the teacher (which will probably happen.). This very fact may show the way for new and positive learning situations.

6. Combining the two Tasks?

To some people it might seem a little far-fetched to talk about two tasks for the school with regard to EDP. But as already mentioned, this division is primarily made to make sure that both tasks are considered. In practice you can easily imagine that the same activity with EDP contributes to the solution of both tasks.

Here I strongly believe that the most appropriate way of involving EDP in instruction is through projects. The projects may form relevant, motivating, and meaningful frameworks for many activities with and without EDP. But projects without some sort of structure or objective can also just consume time without much effect. It is important in this connection that the teacher contributes actively and supports in a flexible way the pupils' ideas and activities, in order that the project may lead to a positive and useful experience.

When we involve computers at the school, a series of choices must be made. What are we going to use them for, when, and how? And where shall we refrain from using them?
Here I feel convinced that all teachers should take part in choosing.

Furthermore, we are faced with many choices in society. How and to what end will we utilize all the possibilities offered to us by new technology?
Here, I am equally convinced that all must participate in the choosing.

A famous Danish architect and social critic, Poul Henningsen, once said:

"You should neither fight against nor yield to development - but choose the best of it."

I believe this is true, and therefore it all ends up with realizing that the two main tasks of the school actually both aim at ensuring that as many as possible are given the best possible background for the participation in making the optimal choices.

Computers in Education
A. McDougall and C. Dowling (Editors)
Elsevier Science Publishers B.V. (North-Holland)

DESIGN AND DEVELOPMENT OF AN ADVENTURE GAME FOR PRE-SCHOOLERS

Alan R. C. Angwin

Monash University Melbourne

In recent years the micro-computer has revolutionised home entertainment and education. This revolution has created concern for some educators, and great excitement for others. DESIGN AND DEVELOPMENT OF AN ADVENTURE GAME FOR PRE-SCHOOLERS, has grown out of a special interest in the use of computers as a teaching tool for very young children.
On the basis of an ever increasing body of literature, as well as personal contact with teachers making use of computer based adventure games with older children, the author was prompted to design and develop a prototype adventure game that would stimulate learning at a pre-reading level.
The paper provides a brief outline of early childhood aims and objectives as a basis on which to develop an adventure game. The author then describes the procedure involved, as well as the problems encountered, in the development of an adventure game aimed at four-year olds using "LOGOWRITER" as a development language.

1. INTRODUCTION

On the basis of an ever increasing body of literature, as well as personal contact with teachers making use of computer based adventure games with older children, the author was prompted to look at the possibility of providing similar learning opportunities for pre-schoolers.
Following a review of a number of adventure or learning games designed in the main for older children (in order to establish an operating pattern), the author proceeded to develop an adventure game aimed at four-year olds and pre-readers.
The aim of this project was to design and develop a prototype adventure game that would stimulate learning at a pre-reading level.
The major objectives of the project included:-
1. To establish a series of learning goals that might be attained through use of an adventure game by pre-readers.
2. To develop the game to a trial stage.
After a brief assessment of the current needs in early childhood education and the introduction of modern technology, the paper then describes the game, procedure used to develop it, and the problems encountered.
In looking forward to the development of suitable software for use as an early childhood teaching tool, I believe it is valuable to review the philosophy behind educating very young children, and then to look at both the current research on the subject of early childhood computing and some of the material already available to homes and schools.

2. BACKGROUND TO THE PROJECT

In recent years the term "discovery learning" has taken on a rather exciting new appearance with the development and use of "adventure games" on the micro-computer. Computer games provide a medium that encourages an active response, and interaction with the plot of the story, Henderson-Lancett and Boesen [1]. Adventure games provide the teacher with a powerful

Footnote: Alan Angwin is currently employed by Community Services Victoria as a Pre-School Adviser.

motivating force towards learning.
The majority of adventure games on the market require that children using the game need to read in order to have a meaningful interaction with the program. This of course is not possible with the majority of four year old children.
I will briefly outline a number of ideas about children and learning as they have been presented in recent literature. While many of the points made are normally taken for granted, a reminder of our aims and objectives often serves to stimulate lateral thinking in the light of more recent discoveries in educative tools and methods.
Pitcher, Lasher, Feinburg and Braun [2] assert that it is important to see each child as an individual bringing to the group different and irregular growth patterns and abilities, different experiences and different perceptions. The teacher needs to remember that children are unique individual, social animals who are not small adults, and furthermore that very young children are different from older children. Young children are usually more active than older children and, while they can be quiet for long periods, they also move around a lot and want to touch and manipulate objects. The child learns from concrete representation and feelings.
There are two particular aspects of a child that provide the teacher with fertile ground for facilitating learning. First, children learn best when they are learning about something real and important to them. Second, children respond readily to sensory stimuli. Through his activity the young child explores, manipulates and practises. These actions result in immediate feedback. In this way one experience builds upon another and the child learns about the world around him. He gradually becomes able to grasp relationships and to apply general rules to particular situations.
In recent years there has been an increasing amount of research conducted into the use of computers as a teaching tool in early childhood education. As early as 1974 writers such as Radia Perlman [3] were looking at pre-school children and the computer. Perlman describes the use of "TORTIS", Toddler's Own Recursive Turtle Interpreter System, as a device to enable pre-schoolers to communicate with a robot turtle. Since this device was developed, microcomputers have reached a size and price that makes them economical for school and home use. Research has shown that three, four and five year old children can manage a keyboard, making it unnecessary to produce button boxes such as was used in the TORTIS project. Similar devices are used in special education but there are also many more sophisticated devices available today such as the simple joystick, touch sensitive pads of various sizes, light pens, through to speech input devices.
Papert [4] describes how he was influenced by Piaget, how the computer language Logo was developed and how it can be used. Papert describes how children learn in general, and how that learning can be enhanced through the use of a computer.
Since the introduction of educational computing for young children, much work has been done in developing appropriate software. A good deal of this material emanates from the United States. From the point of view of this paper, therefore, it is important to clarify some terminology, as the difference in word usage between America and Australia is one of the reasons behind the work contained in this project.
When discussing Kindergarten children in Victoria (Australia), we are talking about four year old children not yet ready for school. In the United States, and many other places outside Victoria, these children are referred to as "pre-schoolers" with Kindergarten children being approximately one year older. The difference may be somewhat confusing for some Australian parents when they find that some of the commercial software presented for Kindergarten children is beyond their four year old's understanding.
While there have been a great many researchers throughout the world investigating and supporting the use of computers in pre-schools, there are also those who do not support it.
Anselmo and Zinck [5] describe their research into early childhood computing, starting from the viewpoint that we cannot assume computers to be essential for early childhood classrooms. Within the paper they affirm the view that children must already have a broad background of concrete experience before they can find meaning in the abstracts of computer activities. Equally important to the educational process then, is the design and objectives of the software used for these computer activities.
Throughout their research, Anselmo and Zinck evaluate software against four areas - Comprehension, Memory, Evaluation (or the ability to make decisions), and Creativity. The priority is to help children learn to use and trust their abilities to

receive information, remember it and make decisions to solve problems.

3. GAME PLAN

For the game to be stimulating for the children, I believe it needed to meet a number of criteria:-

1. Simple, clear yet attractive graphics.
2. Easy to understand screen instructions.
3. The game must contain a simple sequence of events that may be discovered by the player in order to reach the objective.
4. At the commencement of each adventure, the computer should randomly select a secret solution from a pre-determined set of alternative solutions.

In order that the game should meet the requirements outlined above, I set down a game plan see figure 1. For this game plan, I made extensive use of the material obtained in the earlier story trials at Goodwin Estate Kindergarten. To prepare a game plan with a random element I found it necessary to review the number of possible options. The story presents six starting points later narrowed to four - Kindergarten, Park, Shop and Jim's House. In each of these areas, the pre-school children at Goodwin Estate presented me with a number of more specific hiding places.

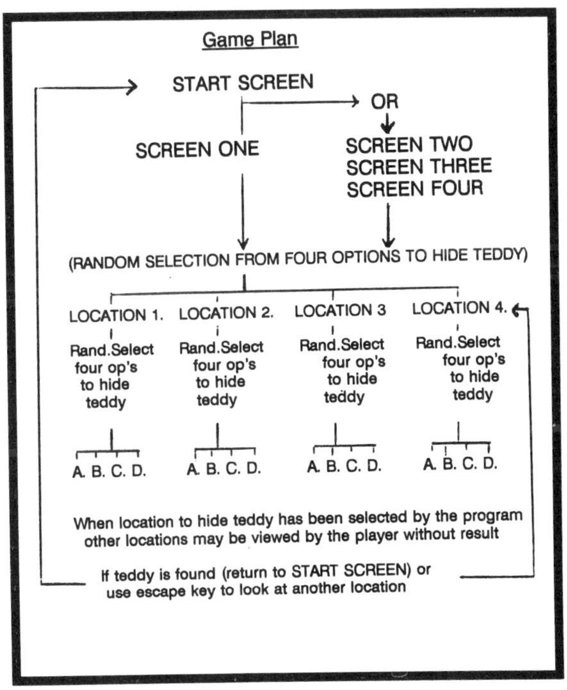

Figure 1

4. THE GAME

The first screen operates as the "startup", providing a display of the game title and author, together with a press-to-continue sequence. From this point there is a random selection by the program from numbered screens one to four. From the player's point of view, there is no difference between these screens. Within the program, each of the screens makes a different choice of the major location in which the sprite will be hidden. The program now randomly selects a specific location from a further four options.
To play the game, the child must use nine keys on the computer. Numeral Keys one to four and seven are labelled as function keys. The main search keys are the alphabetical letters A, B, C, and D. The child is required to locate these without help.
Each try without success produces the first two bars of 'Pop goes the Weasel', a successful find sounds the last bar, as well as flashing the sprite on the screen. When the bear has been found, the program goes back to the first screen in order to start again with a new location.
As this paper is about the process of developing my adventure game "WHERE IS CHOCOLATE?", I will include not only details of my successful work, but also the problems faced in reaching towards the goal.
Armed with a view on the educational needs of young children as well as an outline of the structure and design of other adventure and learning games, I commenced detailed work on my game.
In order to develop an adventure game suitably attractive to pre-school children, I first devised a short story. This story included various elements to which I believed the children would relate. The story included family, a favourite toy, the hustle and bustle of family life as seen by a little boy, and a variety

of events that might result in the loss of the special toy.
The completed story was used to introduce the adventure game consisting of a search for the toy.
Step two of this story and game development, was to trial the story draft with groups of four year old children. The children were from the 1987 Goodwin Estate Kindergarten.
Groups were presented with the story and most were keen to listen and to join in the discussion that followed.
The children were asked to help think of places the toy could have been lost.
The ideas presented by the children, far exceeded my expectations. The children were particularly enthusiastic about finding the toy and in the case of "Story Trial One", it was only because of time constraints that we cut short the discussion. From the discussions with the children there were a total of 9 possible locations given. These locations were subdivided into a total of 34 specific hiding places.
There were six to eight principal locations given by the children, of which most related to the story. Of the major story related items, the first four - "shopping", "Kindergarten", "Jim's House" and "The Park" were broken down to smaller segments and the children supplied further ideas.
The information gained in these trials was used at a later stage for the game construction.
The program was designed to be easy to operate using single key instructions.
There are five function keys designated by a keyboard template. The search keys are A, B, C, and D, and children should be encouraged to find these for themselves. The first four function keys select the general location for a search while the last function key escapes back to the menu. The search keys allow the child to "look" behind each object on the screen.

Major Locations:-

Jim's House	In the garden Behind the wardrobe In the cupboard Under the bed
The Shop	In the trolley On the shelf In the bag In the box
The Park	In the trees Under the slide Under the swings In the play house
The Kinder	The show-and-tell box Under the chair Under the table In the dolls house

Each time the game is used, the program will randomly select a different location to hide "CHOCOLATE" the toy bear.

5. PROGRAMMING LANGUAGE

After discussion with Dr Anne McDougall, my tutor at Monash, it was decided that the best working language available for the development of the game was "LOGOWRITER".
"LOGOWRITER" is a learning tool for students. It provides a creative learning environment in which students can formulate ideas, construct systems, and create images. Logo computer Systems Inc. [6].
A further advantage of this language was its availability for the Commodore C64 computer. As I have a Commodore C64 computer at home, I expected to be able to work on the project at times that did not clash with my day-to-day teaching duties.
The major problem faced with this project was the difficulty in obtaining a working version of "LOGOWRITER" for the Commodore C64. It would appear that there had been some difficulties with the production of C64 disks outside Australia, and with only a small market demand the principal suppliers did little or nothing to resolve the problem. Thanks must go at this point, to Softime Australia for the efforts of their staff and associates to produce a working C64 disk.
Before this disk arrived however, I began a contingency program using "BASIC" as my programming language. To keep track of the direction of the game, I drew up a flow chart as noted in figure 2, and began typing in details of the decision points in the program. It was obvious that this would be a long and involved process, but I did not wish to run the risk of pinning all my hopes on a version of "LOGOWRITER" that may not work.
In late December 1987 it became clear

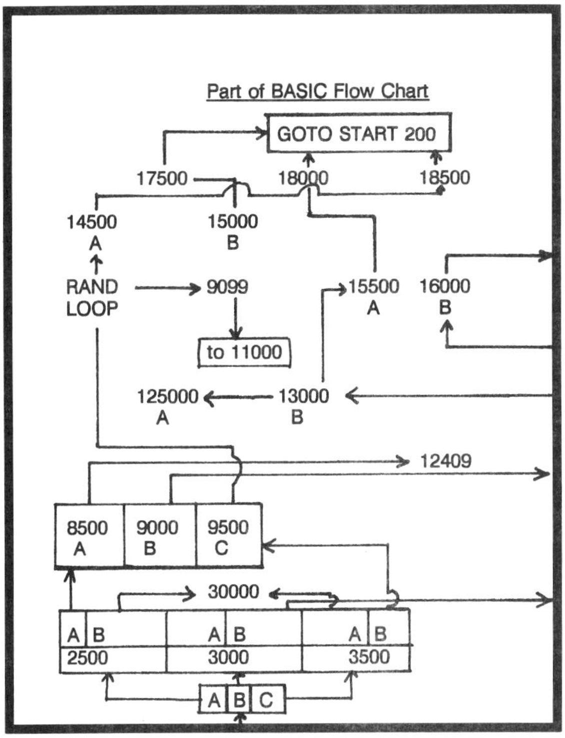

Figure 2

that a working version of "LOGOWRITER" would be available and I set aside the complex "BASIC" flow chart and began work on a more straight forward layout to be used with "LOGOWRITER".
While it would seem that "LOGOWRITER" could handle option one, a more detailed study of its primitives was necessary to ascertain the feasibility of option two.
Coming to grips with a new computer language gave me a few difficult moments, however after discussing the "LOGOWRITER" commands with a more experienced friend (Rob Pitts of Dandenong Nth), my problems were solved, Within the "LOGOWRITER" structure, I had not understood the use of two simple words - "make" and "try". It was these words that would set up the ability to randomly select locations and hide the sprites.
The next problem to face was the method by which "Chocolate" (the bear) should be hidden within the game. It would seem that there were two options.
The first was to provide a "page" of graphics for every possible combination of events. With four main locations, each divided by three or four specific points, there would be in excess of forty screens to develop.
The second possibility was to use a sprite that the computer could "hide" behind any of the items shown on any particular page. The placement of this sprite appeared to be somewhat difficult but on the other hand, the number of screens required would be reduced to around twenty.
With a program solution in hand (see figure 3), it was possible to operate the game with a limited number of screens as proposed under option two above.

Part of "LOGOWRITER" Program

```
to musica
tone 880 1 tone 988 1 tone 1046 2
tone 587 2 tone 698 1 tone 659 2 tone 523 3
end

to startup
hide
end

to hide
setsh 17 sect 1 ht make "try random 4
if :try = 0 [hidea]
```

Figure 3

The graphic screens for this prototype game were produced using the "LOGO" turtle graphics commands. A particular feature of "LOGOWRITER" that I found most valuable in this process was its ability to change the turtle shape and then print or "stamp" that shape and colour on the graphics screen. One problem I found however was the fact that where symbols overlapped, there could be some distortion.
While "LOGOWRITER" has proved to be a good language for a teacher or older student to develop an idea, I believe there are some drawbacks to its use. The major drawback I see is the time involved in loading the program and then changing from screen to screen (this didn't worry the young children however). The problem has been particularly emphasized on the COMMODORE C64 computer which I used (even with a fast load cartridge).

"LOGOWRITER" however offers the opportunity to set something on to the screen. If the idea looks good, I see a teacher passing it on to a commercial programmer to be produced in a programming language that would allow quick changes from screen to screen with all material loaded into the computer memory at once.

6. POSSIBLE EXTENSION TO THE PROGRAM

The game "WHERE IS CHOCOLATE", could be further developed by the introduction of two items to be found, the teddy bear and Frank's kinder bag. As with the "MR MEN" game, Primer Educational [7], these two items should be found in sequence before the game is concluded. This process would extend the development of memory skills for the children.
A further extension of this program for emergent readers could be the use of on-screen large print single words related to the graphics as is done in "DETECT-A-PET", Sherwood [8]. Teaching reading however was not the initial aim of this project, but simply to give young children and other non readers the experience of using adventure games.
Following the completion of an operational version of the game, I first presented it to a visiting four year old and was pleased to find it kept her occupied for some time. With this success I decided to use the program for demonstration at Kindergarten Teacher "in-service" days. The program was well received by the Teachers at Furling Park School and Pre-School for the deaf.
Since obtaining a C64 computer, Furling Park have been trialing the game with their children.
The story and game was also well received by Pre-School Teachers from the Lilydale area in Victoria Australia, as well as a number of Pre-School committees who requested an introduction to Pre-School computing.

7. ACKNOWLEDGEMENTS

I wish to extend by grateful thanks to the following people and organizations:
Dr Anne McDougall, my tutor - Monash University Faculty of Education.
My colleagues Mrs Margaret Sedlins and Mrs Jeraldine Hill, and the 1987 children from the Goodwin Estate Kindergarten, The Basin Victoria.
Softime Publishing - Victoria.
Mr Rob Pitts - North Dandenong Victoria for his advice on programming problems.
Community Services Victoria - Outer East Region.

8. REFERENCES

[1] Henderson-Lancett, Lexie and Boesen, Janice - Dragon World 1: Implementing an Adventure Game"' COMPUTERS IN EDUCATION: ON THE CREST OF A WAVE? Computer Education Group of Victoria. Edited by Salvas, A. D. and Dowling, C. ISBN

[2] Pitcher, Lasher, Feinburg and Braun - HELPING YOUNG CHILDREN LEARN - Second Edition, Charles E. Merrill Publishing Company - A Bell & Howell Company, Columbus, Ohio 43216. Library of Congress Cat. Card No. 73-92244. ISBN 0-675-08818-6. 1974.1 862532 004 1. p. 115 - 117. 1986

[3] Perlman, Radia - "TORTIS Toddler's Own Recursive Turtle Interpreter System"' Massachusetts Institute of Technology, AI Memo 311, Logo Memo 9, December, 1974.

[4] Papert, S - "MINDSTORMS: CHILDREN, COMPUTERS AND POWERFUL IDEAS, Harvester Press, London. ISBN 0-71080-472-5. 1980.

[5] Anselmo, Sandra, and Zinck, R. Ann - "Computers for Young Children? Perhaps", YOUNG CHILDREN, Vol. 42, No.3., National Association for the Education of Young Children, Washington, DC. p.22 - 27. March 1987.

[6] Logo Computer Systems Inc. - "LOGOWRITER" - Published by Logo Computer Systems Inc. New York. Made in Canada. Distributed in Australia by Softime Educational Resources, Victoria. 1986.

[7] Boulton, Richard - "FIRST STEPS WITH THE MR. MEN. - Copyright 1983 by Roger Hargreaves and Mirror Group Newspapers Ltd. Published by Mirrorsoft, Holborn Circus, London ECIP IDQ for Mirror Group Newspapers Ltd. 1984.

[8] Sherwood, Kathy - "DETECT-A-PET" (yet to be published). Kathy Sherwood is Education Officer, Computer Software Development Production Services, Queensland Department of education. Personal contact. 1987.

Computers in Education
A. McDougall and C. Dowling (Editors)
Elsevier Science Publishers B.V. (North-Holland)

MATHEMATICS - JEWEL IN THE COMPUTER CROWN

Mike ASTON

The Advisory Unit for Microtechnology In Education, Hatfield, United Kingdom

Many teachers of mathematics have deserted their subjects to take classes in computer studies or information technology - the pressure to do so coming from a number of sources.

The consequence of this is that mathematics has largely been ignored as a rich area of the curriculum which can benefit significantly from the use of a wide range of software.

This paper gives evidence of changes that are taking place in the curricula in the advent of the computer environment and illustrates the scope for children to gain new insight through investigation.

1. PREAMBLE

During the last ten years computers have come to be seen as an important resource for schools. The number of computers in schools has been growing steadily in the UK and now averages about 32 in secondary schools and just over 3 in primary schools.

Teachers and educationalists in Britain have become increasingly aware of the significance of computers for many areas of the curriculum in primary and secondary schools. There have been major Government initiatives designed to promote and support the introduction of computers into schools.

These developments are to be welcomed. It is now a strongly held belief that computers offer substantial opportunities for those who are teaching mathematics and for those who are learning it.

It is important that the rapid changes in our society in technology, in methods of communications and in knowledge are reflected in changes in mathematics education, both in what is taught and in the methods by which pupils learn.

In the longer term the widespread use of the new technology implies substantial changes to the mathematics curriculum.

As long ago as 1983, Trevor Fletcher, one of Her Majesty's Inspectors, in a Department of Education and Science document 'Microcomputers and Mathematics in Schools' [1] commented that 'the implications of the current technology for mathematics are so extensive that it is difficult to present a balanced appraisal without seeming to exaggerate' and 'the changes which computers have made already are so big that we lack any previous standard by which to compare them'. It can be argued that these comments are even more relevant today - seven years on.

2. THE SITUATION TODAY

One of the aims of recent initiatives taken by the Government is to make the eductional system more relevant to the future social and economic needs of the country; in particular the Government aims to support the information-based sectors of commerce and the technology industries and to prepare young people for life in an increasingly 'technological society'. Many of these aims are embodied in the new National Curriculum.

Mathematics has an important contribution to make in meeting these aims. Pupils learning mathematics should be enabled to develop flexible problem-solving skills, to work cooperatively and to communicate difficult concepts, to extract meaning from complex data and to enjoy and value their own learning processes. [2] Styles of teaching which involve the use of microcomputers can aid greatly the acquisition of these important high-level skills, which are exactly those which will be required in the future by our industries and, indeed, by our citizens.

At present only a minority of both primary and secondary teachers of mathematics are using computers to support these styles of teaching and learning. A recent survey suggests that nearly three-quarters of secondary mathematics teachers use computers either very rarely or never in their work.

Those teachers surveyed who made little or no use of computers gave a variety of reasons for this. These included lack of hardware, lack of software, lack of training and the fact that work involving the use of computers was not on the syllabus. Where computers were being used this was mainly for demonstrations in connection with graphical work, statistics, calculus and numerical work. Only a small proportion of the departments surveyed had computers which were available constantly, to be used as a resource whenever they were needed in mathematics lessons.

As a consequence of the new technology there have been significant changes both to the mathematics being used in industry and commerce, and also to the technology, science and mathematics curricula in further education. These changes imply the need for corresponding changes to school curricula.

Some of the ideas currently being explored by computer scientists, such as the design of expert systems, also have strong links with mathematics and may in the future find their way into school mathematics syllabuses.

Those responsible for taking national initiatives and funding curriculum development projects have placed relatively little emphasis so far on the introduction of computers into classrooms where mathematics is learned. This is particularly true of secondary mathematics classrooms.

Ten years ago the majority of teachers involved with computers were mathematics teachers; mathematics and computing were perceived by headteachers and administrators to be closely linked. In the early eighties teachers and educationalists began to realise that computers could profitably be used to help teach many other subjects of the school curriculum. Consequently projects were set up to encourage teachers of other subjects to use computers and, not unnaturally, these projects placed little or no emphasis on mathematics. Teachers' courses on the use of computers across the curriculum were rarely for mathematics teachers, and little support was provided for the development of software for mathematics classrooms. [3]

The thinking which produced such discrimination is understood, but there is now an urgent need to recognise both the significant value of computers for mathematics education and their far-reaching implications for the mathematics curriculum in the future.

The limited use, thus far, of computers in mathematics teaching might appear disappointing. But, if it is accepted that educational innovation is often slower than technological innovation, and that the past five years have been particularly difficult ones for teachers, a surprising amount has been achieved. Many teachers have already experimented in a variety of ways with the use of computers in their mathematics lessons.

3. THE MICRO AS A TEACHING AID

In the report of the Cockroft Committee "Mathematics Counts" there is a frequently quoted recommendation concerning the desirable range of learning activities:

> Mathematics teaching at all levels should include opportunities for exposition by the teacher;
> Discussion between teacher and pupils and between pupils themselves;
> Appropriate practical work;
> Consolidation and practice of fundamental skills and routines;
> Problem solving, including the application of mathematics to everyday situations;
> Investigational work.

The effectiveness of the role of educational software in the learning of mathematics depends as much upon the imaginative development of classroom use by the individual teacher as the original design of the programs. In the hands of a skilled teacher even a poorly designed program may prove an effective aid.

A criterion often put forward as important in the educational evaluation of a piece of software is: "Could the activity be equally well effected without the use of a computer?" While this makes good sense it has been observed that many teachers who do extend their range of activities to include discussion and investigation when aided by pieces of suitable software (but which could be sustained without any use of a computer) would not have done so if left with conventional teaching aids. Thus the very need to plan out the use of a particular program in the classroom can bring about some of the changes of approach that Cockroft seeks.

An example of the use of a program called "Counter" is quoted: [4]

This lesson with a class of less able thirteen year olds, involved a considerable amount of discussion which was followed by written work. The class worked on this problem:

"Given two counters starting at 20 and 50 respectively, can you select step sizes for the counters so that they will at some point be displaying the same number at the same time? Can you predict what this number will be?"

At first the whole class work on this together. The beginnings of a table is constructed on the blackboard. Subsequently, different groups of pupils show differing amounts of interest in the problem. One group gets particularly interested and spends several lessons exploring it further.

After some considerable time the group is able to predict the "meeting number" and explain, orally, how to find it by working out how many times the difference between the steps (for example, 4-1=3) divides into the difference between the starting numbers (50-20=30). They cannot, however, write this down and "forget" between lessons. It is interesting that the childrens' work draws attention to the patterns in the table, but gives no clues to the deeper insights with which they have struggled.

One girl in the class works away at the problem on her own. She is not normally particularly successful at mathematics. However, she manages to deal with the problem and eventually formulates what amounts to a general solution. The teacher spends a lot of time with this girl during the first lesson; he does not lead her thinking but he does prompt her to open the problem up at each stage. While he is working with her the rest of the class is more or less neglected and several of the pupils who have lost interest in the problem have a far less profitable lesson mathematically!

During this lesson the teacher decided to work with the one pupil who was using the computer. It is perhaps important to be aware that this is a possible choice for the teacher. Publicity material for computer programs often attempts to seduce teachers to the opposite point of view. That the computer is an effective device to occupy a pupil's time so that the attention of the teacher can be given to other pupils in the class.

The above problem is widely adaptable. Younger children would require smaller starting numbers to be selected. For older, more able pupils, there is the possibility of formulating an algebraic equation (for example, if n is the number of steps to the "meeting number" then 20+4n=50+n). Perhaps the pupils could be invited to race with the computer in solving the equation!

Note: "Counter" is a two number counter system which can be altered in terms of speed, step and increment.

4. SHORT PROGRAMS ON THE MICRO

If a teacher of mathematics is able to control a computer to tackle problems in the way illustrated above, then he or she also has the necessary skills to be able to exploit the power of the micro as an aid to mathematics learning inside and outside the classroom. One of the most powerful of such uses makes the micro into a 'test-bed' to facilitate exploration of mathematical behaviour.

There is considerable support, [5] research findings and personal opinion, that programming is best learned by following a sequence of activities which involve:

(a) using 'blocks of code' or short programs to do a significant and/or interesting task: in such a situation the children will see the 'words' working
(b) modifying or extending a short program to do a new but related task
(c) and finally, designing or preparing new programs to solve problems.

These ideas can be illustrated with a simple program to generate multiples of 5 (written in LCSI LOGO):

```
TO MULTIPLES5
MAKE "NO
REPEAT 10 MAKE "N:N + 1
[MAKE "M:N*5 PRINT SENTENCE :N :M]
END
```

The children are asked to type the program into the computer, run it, and observe the output and finally use the program and output to explore some relationships. The following shows some examples:

(a) (i) The multiples of 5 all end in ? or ?. Why?
(ii) Which multiples of 5 end with a 0? What is true about N when M ends with a 0?
(iii) What is the difference between any two consecutive multiples? (Consecutive means they come one after the other.) Why is this so?

(b) Change the program so that the computer prints the first 20 multiples. Are your answers to number 1 still the same?

5. THE MICRO AS A PROBLEM SOLVING TOOL

Undoubtedly the computer is a very powerful and versatile tool in the hands of a mathematician engaged in problem-solving. It is arguable that it is now at least as important for a practising mathematician to be able to program a microcomputer as, say, to be able to use a calculator or a set of drawing instruments. In this context alone there is an onus on the teacher of mathematics to provide opportunities to illustrate this form of mathematical activity.

The spreadsheet is a powerful example of a tool in this context. [6] The following is a classic problem but the method of solution has only recently been available to the young pupil:

"A box to hold small pins (without a lid) is to be made from a sheet of metal 15cm square, by cutting squares from the corners, folding up and joining the edges. What size of square needs to be cut out to give the most volume?"

Imagine cutting out a small square. What will the box look like? Imagine cutting out bigger amounts .... (with less able groups we usually make some boxes using graph paper and sticky tape, with this class it is important that they should visualise).

Imagine we want to fill these boxes. Which will store the most? This provokes a variety of responses. Some think they will all be about the same. Some think the tall thin one will hold the most, because it has "more area up the sides". Others do not have any view on the matter.

After some discussion, the class elect to calculate volumes. Following their instructions, we draw up some headings for a table on the blackboard. Someone wants to start with 1cm cut out, then step up in 0.5cm. We write the numbers in the first column. "Keep to simple numbers", is suggested. We propose that we complete the whole number values, leaving alternate entries blank. Two are done as a class, the rest completed individually. Some have difficulty working out the dimensions of the boxes - they are encouraged them to visualise or sketch each example and avoid any mention of formulae.

Square Cut Out	Dimension of Box	Volume
1cm	13 x 13 x 1	= $169cm^3$
1.5cm		
2cm	11 x 11 x 2	= $242cm^3$
2.5cm		
3cm	9 x 9 x 3	= $243cm^3$
3.5cm		
4cm	7 x 7 x 4	= $196cm^3$
4.5cm		
5cm	5 x 5 x 5	= $125cm^3$

The final stages of the solution offer no problem to the pupils in the class.

6. CONCLUSION

The evidence is there for all to see. The incorporation of new technologies into the teaching of mathematics needs promotion on a grand scale if changes are to be brought about.
Mathematics guidelines and syllabuses in schools should be encouraging pupils to undertake extended pieces of work with the computer being recommended as providing an effective way of supporting such projects. The implications for resourcing mathematics are not insignificant but the rewards are worth striving for.

REFERENCES

[1] Fletcher, T. J. Microcomputers and Mathematics in Schools. Department of Education and Science, London, 1983

[2] Ball, D. et al Will Mathematics Count? The Advisory Unit, Hatfield, 1987, ISBN 0 946039 50 X

[3] Oldknow, A. Learning Mathematics with Microcomputers. West Sussex Institute of Higher Education, Bognor Regis, 1983

[4] Waddingham, J. and Wigley, A. Secondary Mathematics with Micros In-Service Pack. The Advisory Unit, Hatfield, 1985, ISBN 0 946039 21 6

[5] Doyle, M. P. et al LOGOS Supplement. BLUG, Houghton-on-the-Hill, 1989, ISSN 0268 0777

[6] Bufton, N. et al. Exploring Mathematics with Microcomputers. CET, London, 1986, ISBN 0 86184 162 X

Goldstein, R. et al. The Use of Computers in the Learning and Teaching of Mathematics. MESU, Coventry, 1988, ISBN 1 853790 42 7

Tagg, B. et al. A Parents' Guide to Educational Software. Telegraph Publications, London, 1985, ISBN 0 86367040 7

Computers in Education
A. McDougall and C. Dowling (Editors)
Elsevier Science Publishers B.V. (North-Holland)

INVOLVING THE REAL USERS - DEVELOPING SOFTWARE WITH HEARING IMPAIRED CHILDREN

C. Bloor and N. Cavalier-Smith

School of Computer Studies and Mathematics, Sunderland Polytechnic, Sunderland, Tyne & Wear, SR1 3SD England

This paper describes an approach to software development which has been used at Sunderland Polytechnic in collaboration with Local Primary Units for Hearing Impaired Children. A prototyping method has been extended so that the production of an item of educational software is used within the teaching process, and the children with whom the software is intended to be used are involved in specifying and developing that software. The development of three such items of software is discussed. The areas of application of the software have been specified by the unit teacher, and are generally aimed at specific problems encountered in the teaching of the hearing impaired, or at problems which a specific child or children have. The software has general applicability however. Where this is not necessarily so the specific features are described in this paper. In addition to providing software to help solve a specific problem there are other benefits to this approach, the major one being the amount of language work generated in the development of the programs. This is discussed and the benefits derived from the three programs are described.

1. INTRODUCTION

The School of Computer Studies and Mathematics at Sunderland Polytechnic has used final year student projects to develop programs for children with Special Educational Needs for a number of years. This work has been reported elsewhere [1]. During the development of one item of software, the Ghost Hunt program described below, it transpired that there were a number of benefits which arose from the way in which the student was encouraged to work with the children for whom the software was being developed. The prototyping method which was being used to develop the program required the student to visit the school on a number of occasions. The discussions which took place at the time of the visit, and subsequently in the classroom, were providing valuable language work leading to interaction between child and child, child and group, child and younger child, child and unknown adult (the student at the beginning of the project) and child and known adult (the teacher and the student in the later stages). These interactions were as valuable as the final program and so in subsequent projects these interactions, and the generation of language/vocabulary work has been seen as a major part of the project and has been encouraged.

1.1 Prototyping

Bell [2] provides a concise description of prototyping:

After a minimum of discussion with the user, the designer goes away and produces a prototype of the required system. This prototype is not expected to survive very long. During its demonstration the user will correct the designer's misconceptions, discover his [or her] own unstated assumptions and may also be prodded into new and creative thoughts. This generates a further prototype and further demonstrations and discussions take place.

It is hence an iterative process, of presenting ideas to a user, obtaining feedback and using this feedback to develop a further prototype. This is continued until a satisfactory product has been developed. At the early stages the prototype will be very 'quick and dirty', with no provision being made for error trapping or reporting of results, for example. The very first attempt will invariably be a paper prototype or storyboard (see below).

In general terms the method is applicable where there is a high degree of user interaction in the final product; where the system being developed is new, rather than an adaption of current practice; and where the intended user is a 'naive' computer user. We would thus argue that it is the preferred method for the development of educational software. There is a high degree of user interaction with the final product. Indeed this interaction is critical and its design should occupy a considerable part of the development time. Educational software should not be a mere copy of what the teacher does, and can do better than the computer. Hope [3] and Rostron and Sewell [4] argue that the computer should be used to provide a 'micro world' in which the pupil can explore, experiment and test. Whilst the teacher may not necessarily be a naive computer user, it is unlikely that they will have any experience of specifying software. The prototyping approach allows the teacher to develop his or her ideas as the package evolves, and to move towards a final package in easy steps.

2. GHOST HUNT PROGRAM

'Ghost Hunt' was developed as a student project [5] from a fairly loose specification that the program should be written to exercise concepts of position and colour with commonly used household vocabulary. The children in the unit suggested that games involving ghosts were exciting! The idea of the program is that the pupil has to go through three rooms in a house looking for objects, the initial letters of which form the name of a ghost 'SCARIM'. Two objects are found in each room. The pupil is required to type in the name of the object, given a clue of the initial letter, its position given three possibilities, and its colour. The objects are presented on the screen at random from the list given in table 1. If all the objects are collected the ghost is scared away.

The idea of the game was developed from a discussion between the student, the unit teacher, and the children who indicated what they did and did not like about the software being used in the unit at that time. The children also compiled a list of possible objects in discussion with the student. She produced her own list which formed the basis for further discussion with the children. We would emphasise that these sessions formed one of the most valuable parts of the project. Interaction between child and child, and child and student also provided the stimulus for further language extension and vocabulary work before the student's next visit.

Table 1 Nouns used in Ghost Hunt

Shoe	Spectacles	Chair	Radio
Spider	Sock	Apron	Record
Scissors	Candle	Apple	Ribbon
Saucer	Cushion	Anorak	Cup
Ruler	Camera	Aerosol	Rubber
Racquet	Iron	Insect	Instrument
Magazine	Mug	Mirror	Money

The first prototype was a 'storyboard', that is a series of hand drawn sketches indicating the screens that would appear, with the student talking the teacher through the sequencing of these screens. At this stage the teacher also suggested the form the dialogue should take.

The three programs discussed in this paper have all been written for the BBC 'B' machine. The restrictive use of colour and limited graphics resolution make it difficult in some cases to imagine what the final screen will look like. The next stage was, therefore, to produce the screen and text for one of the rooms. The teacher could then comment on the use of colour, the resolution used, and whether the objects drawn were sufficiently realistic. The student was also unfamiliar with the BBC machine at the start of the project. Producing a screen at this stage enabled her to gain familiarity with the machine and allowed her to make a more realistic estimate of the effort required to complete the project on time.

Once the graphics for one room had been agreed upon it was then possible to complete the game for this one room only as a third stage in the prototyping. The next stage was to produce the screens and code for the other rooms. Finally introductory and instruction screens were added, the end screen was coded and the security coding (to disable the escape and break keys) was included.

The guinea pigs for the program were the children in the unit. They commented on the graphics and were observed using the program, with the student noting what mistakes were made and whether these indicated a fault in the design of the program or whether they were just normal learning errors. Not all the 'mistakes' were corrected. One of the items used was a sock hanging from the bookcase in the living room. The student felt the graphics here were not up to the standard of the rest of the program and attempted to produce a better representation. The teacher insisted that the original graphics be left in because of the amount of language produced by the children when they were trying to decide which object on the screen began with 's'. This language was quite complex, and went beyond merely suggesting possible objects. It involved, within complex sentence structures, the suggesting and discarding of ideas. "It cann't be that because..." "It might be a ...." "You wouldn't have a ..... there"

3. THE SPIDER GAME

The development of the Ghost Hunt program described above gives a generalised account of the prototyping approach. It was the first program developed within the units and it lead the teacher to see a number of possibilities and wider applications. In describing the next two programs we will show how the development of a program can be used in the teaching process.

The Ghost Hunt program is a little restrictive in that the number of objects which can be chosen to form the name 'SCARIM' is limited, and the positions in which these objects may reasonably be placed are restricted. The game was also developed with a specific group of children in mind. It does have general applicability but it has been noted above that some 'mistakes' have not been corrected. In addition some teachers might not consider 'aerosol' to be a common household noun. This word was included in the object list because it arose in the discussion between student and children and was then included as a new word which the children could talk about during language extension work.

The Spider game is a development which gets away from these restrictions and provides an environment in which the child can use the computer to explore in a manner suggested above by Rostron and Sewell [4] and used for example by Houldsworth in Wordweb [6], and by Ward et al [7]. The nouns and prepositions used are more general and a larger list of phrases can now be generated in two modes. In one mode the computer generates phrases and asks the user to move an object (the spider) to that position. In the second mode the computer responds to the phrase typed in by the user by placing the spider in valid (and known) positions. Spiders can also get anywhere, so we are again removing a restriction inherent in Ghost Hunt which is that the objects used can only reasonably be in a few positions on the screen.

The same basic screens are used as in Ghost Hunt but the user can choose which room to enter, and may move from room to room by using the function keys. The two modes are then:

3.1 Put

In this mode the computer generates a phrase of the type:

Put the spider <preposition> the <noun>

from a list of prepositions, nouns and allowed combinations.

For example:

Put the spider in front of the fireplace

The full list of prepositions and nouns for the living room is given in table 2. Not all combinations are allowed. In Put the child has to use the cursor keys to move a spider on the screen to within a reasonable approximation of the required position. Thus 'near the table' would be too vague an instruction. The child might know where to place the spider, but the computer (or rather the programmer) would have some difficulty in defining a correct answer. There is a total of 126 allowed combinations for all three rooms. If the child performs the task satisfactorily the message 'well done' is given. At the first incorrect attempt a clue is given, of the form 'move it up and left'; 'move it right'. At the second incorrect attempt the cursor keys are disabled except for the required key and the child is instructed to move the spider horizontally 'move it left' until the correct horizontal position is reached, then vertically 'move it down' until the spider is in the correct final position.

Table 2 Prepositions and Nouns used in the living room for the Spider game

on top of	fireplace
below	tele
under	television
above	light
in the middle of	lamp
to the side of	table
next to	bookcase
near to	wall
on the left of	window
on the right of	corner
in front of	mirror
on	bin
in	plant
behind	ceiling

3.2 Where

In the alternative mode the child is asked 'Where's the Spider?' and given a prompt 'It's'. Even at this first stage the children were involved in a discussion of the grammar. "Shall we say 'Where is the Spider?' or 'Where's the Spider?'" "Shall we say 'It is on the wall' or 'It's on the wall'?". The spider is not visible at this stage. If a valid phrase is typed in, the spider appears in that position. Incorrect (and unknown) phrases result in the message 'Try again'. Because the computer is responding to a specific instruction, the number of allowed combinations is greater in this mode (342). Phrases such as 'near the fridge' are now allowed and the spider may also be placed inside such objects as the fridge, drawers and wardrobe. It is also possible to remove the rug to see the spider underneath.

It is necessary, of course, to define the prepositions and nouns, and the correct positions. This was given to the children to do as part of their language development work. Rather than used squared paper to estimate coordinates (a time consuming and error-prone task) a program was written which allowed the spider to be moved about the screen until the return key was pressed. At this point the program responds with the message 'It is <x> across and <y> up'. The children then generated their own lists of prepositions and nouns and filled in a grid of coordinates. This generated a good deal of discussion of possible combinations and exact positions, and provided a cross-curricula link with maths. They were concerned to ensure that the correct position was chosen. 'Under the light' generated further use of language. "How far up" "How far down" "That's just right"

4. THE 'THAN' GAME

This program was designed specifically for a group of younger, profoundly deaf children who needed reinforcement of the mathematical concepts and language involved in comparisons of length. They needed the opportunity to put this language into sentence form.

The program helps children build sentences of the form:

The <x> is <bigger / taller / shorter / smaller / wider> than the <y>

It provides keyboard practice and uses 15 common nouns to form the above sentences. (see Table 3).

For Example:

The fence is longer than the gate

Table 3 Nouns used in the Than game

man	church	ship	car	gate
lorry	bus	yacht	house	girl
ladder	sign	fence	engine	lighthouse

Again the program was written as a final year student project [8]. The game is designed for use by children with a reading age of 6.5 onwards. It incorporates a tutorial and a vocabulary training section. A series of work sheets is also provided.

In playing the game two of the objects are displayed on the screen and the child is asked:

Which is <relationship>,

the <x> or the <y>?

For Example:

Which is longer,

the car or the lorry?

The two objects are chosen so that their relationship on the screen is the same as their relationship in real life. For example, the screen church is approximately the same size as the screen ladder. This would not be so in real life, so the ladder and church are never compared. The church is always compared with the lighthouse or the house. When the correct answer is recorded, the child is asked to construct the appropriate sentence. As a prompt the relationship and the two nouns (but not the definite article) are displayed on the screen. In the above example the lorry is longer than the car. If the child types in 'car' or 'the car' he or she receives the reply:

No,

Look again.

The lorry is longer than the car.

A correct answer of 'lorry' or 'the lorry' gets the response:

Good,

That's right.

The lorry is longer than the car.

The text screen is then cleared, and the child is asked:

Now can you make the sentence?

Here are some words to help: longer
car
lorry

He or she is then required to type in:

The lorry is longer than the car.

The whole game consists of ten questions with a reward of a gold star for each correct answer. The sentence building is not scored.

4.1 Development of the program

A prototyping approach was used for this project working from a storyboard through to the final package. The student visited the unit approximately every two weeks and worked in the main with two of the older boys. This continuity was invaluable, introducing opportunities for dialogue, "Do you remember what we were doing last week?", and allowing the children's confidence to develop as they became familiar with the student.

4.2 Worksheets

A survey of software already in use in the unit had shown the value of additional worksheet material which could be used to complement the software. A series of worksheets which mirror the operation of the game was thus produced. There are two vocabulary worksheets. Worksheet one has the words across the top of the page and a series of pictures. The child is required to write the correct word under each picture. Worksheet two has the words printed in a series of squares and the child is required to draw the correct object above each word. The final worksheet consists of pairs of drawings. The child is required to answer the same type of question as in the program, and then to write the sentence.

4.3 Evaluation of 'Than'

The object of this paper is to describe the methodology used, not to evaluate the programs in any formal sense. The program was designed for a specific need and the evaluation as far as the unit teacher is concerned is an evaluation of the whole project. The criterion used by the teacher is 'Did the children understand the concepts and did their ability to apply the language improve?'. This is a test of the whole project, including the development stage which has been used in the teaching process. Because of the close working relationship between the programmer, teacher and children a formal evaluation of the program itself would be difficult and would have to be done within another unit. In the case of Than the program was developed using the two oldest children in the unit. There were other, younger children who had not been involved in the development and who were used to evaluate the vocabulary teaching part of the program. Four children were used for the evaluation. They were given a pre-test which consisted of the teacher using the worksheet, pointing at each of the objects in turn and asking the child 'What's this?'. The child's response was noted. The two older children, for whom the program had been designed, then used the program every day for a fortnight, for about twenty minutes each day. The two younger children used the program four times, partly under teacher supervision. At the end of this period the children were re-tested. The results given in Table 4 demonstrate that the children did learn new vocabulary using the program. Although not formally recorded there was also an increase in the speed at which the children responded to the teacher's question. In addition in their answers to the post-test the two older children used the indefinite article, which they had not used in the pre-test. They also, in written and oral form, were able to formulate at normal speed correct sentences such as:

The ladder is taller than the sign.

These findings agree with those of Green [9] who found that the computer was a valid medium for teaching vocabulary to autistic children.

5. CONCLUSIONS

We have shown how cooperation between educational experts and computer experts can produce software which is robust and of educational value. In addition by the programmer working within the unit and involving the children who are the ultimate users of the system a lot of good educational input can be derived from the development process. For the teacher the language work engendered during this process is probably the most important outcome. Nevertheless good educational programs are produced. An evaluation by a teacher of the deaf not involved in developing the Than game concluded that the program was useful in the areas of "reading, writing, spelling, language development, speech

Table 4 Than game evaluation

Child	Age	Pre-test score	Post-test score
Severely deaf girl	6.0	9	14
Profoundly deaf girl	7.4	3	11
Severely deaf girl	7.6	8	15
Profoundly deaf girl	8.11	6	15
Mean	7.3	6.5	13.75

(especially spontaneous speech), maths concepts, trial and error learning, concept development, and working cooperatively".

The disadvantage of this method is that it is only feasible if the programmer is geographically close to the intended users. Only a small group of users are able to participate in the program development. The final product, however, is of wide applicability.

REFERENCES

[1] Bloor, C., Using Student Projects to Develop Materials for Children with Special Educational Needs - Experience at Sunderland Polytechnic, in: Coleridge Smith, P.D., and Scurr, J.H., (eds.), Medical Applications of Microcomputers (Springer-Verlag, London, 1988) pp. 175-181

[2] Bell, R.T., Management of Systems Development, (Hutchinson, London, 1987)

[3] Hope, M., Micros for Children with Special Needs, (Souvenir Press, London, 1987)

[4] Rostron, A.B., and Sewell, D.F., Computers in Special Education, (Croom Helm, London, 1984)

[5] Mitchell, D., Educational software for the Hearing Impaired, Final Year Project, BA Data Processing, Sunderland Polytechnic, 1987

[6] Houldsworth, J., "Wordweb" (ESM Software for Schools, Cambridge)

[7] Ward, R. Lidley, P. Rostron, A.D. Sewell, D.F. and Cubie, R., Computer Assisted Learning and deaf children's language: using the language and thought software in a hearing-impaired unit, J. Brit. Assn. Teachers of the Deaf (1985) 61-66

[8] Cavalier-Smith, N., Software for Hearing Impaired Children, Final Year Project, BA Data Processing, Sunderland Polytechnic, 1989

[9] Green, S.J., PhD Thesis Sunderland Polytechnic, 1990

Computers in Education
A. McDougall and C. Dowling (Editors)
Elsevier Science Publishers B.V. (North-Holland)

USING COMPUTERS TO ACHIEVE LITERACY IN MINORITY LANGUAGES

Paul C.DENCH

Computers in Education Project, Curriculum Programmes Branch,
Ministry of Education, EAST PERTH WA 6004, AUSTRALIA

This paper describes the development of language-controlled software which can be activated by entering the lexical and syntactic information of the chosen language. Students can then compile grammatically correct sentences from a bank of words to control visual images on a V.D.U. Word processors linked to touch-sensitive boards provide an excellent extension strategy for language-controlled software. Overlays placed on the boards display the words from which a selection can be made. Design principles for overlays are discussed for English and several Australian languages. These demonstrate that minority language overlays may offer more potential than is possible from English overlays. The combination of language-controlled software and touch-sensitive boards linked to word processors has immense implications for bilingual education.

1. INTRODUCTION

The combination of language-controlled software with the use of a word processor linked to a touch-sensitive board is a powerful instructional strategy for achieving early literacy skills in English. Language-controlled software allows students to control visual images on a V.D.U. by constructing grammatically correct sentences which are selected, word by word, from a lexicon displayed on a touch-sensitive board or other such device. Touch-sensitive boards can also be used with word processors and, though not self-checking, they too allow students to experiment with whole words. Using these two teaching tools, students are able to focus on the whole words and how they work together in sentences to create meaning rather than having to worry about the mechanics of spelling and/or letter formation. Children thus have '...total control over print long before they can formally read or write...'(Dewsbury, 1989).

The same strategy, using the minority first language, would help to achieve a literacy breakthrough there being '...clear evidence that Aboriginal children who receive bilingual education achieve significantly better academic results than Aboriginal students who receive their education in English only...' (House of Representatives Report, 1986). The skills acquired would be applied later to achieving literacy in the major second language. The problem is to provide language-controlled software for a host of minor languages when only a few such packages have been written for English; there are between 100 and 150 Australian Aboriginal languages surviving (hereafter called Australian languages).

This paper will show how a linguistic approach to this problem has generated a solution. A range of generic, language-controlled software is being developed in which a teacher-linguist will be able to enter the lexical and syntactic information for the minority language they wish to use. The same linguistic concepts can also be applied to the design of touch-sensitive board overlays to supplement and extend the learning achieved with language-controlled software. As demonstrated below with Australian languages, this may result in arrangements that are more powerful than the equivalent purpose overlays written in English.

2. LANGUAGE-CONTROLLED SOFTWARE

Languaged-controlled software is not a new concept. 'Frog and Dog', from the Compass Sofware 'Windows Into Literacy' series is a good example. A limited vocabulary of words is mapped onto function keys or is defined as object areas on a touch-sensitive board. A grammatically correct sequence of assembled words such as 'The spotted frog jumps.' is rewarded by the equivalent visual action on a V.D.U. This may then be printed complete with the sentence that initiated the action.

The affinity of Aboriginal children to learning with computers is commonly recounted in Australia though little research evidence has been presented. Folds (1986) suggests that it is the '...highly visual, graphics oriented type of instruction which appeals to ...(them) and may tap into their learning style...' which Harris (1984) reports this as being characterised by observation and imitation; personal trial and error; real-life performance; successive approximation to an efficient end product; and persistence and repetition. Language-controlled software fits this prescription very well.

2.1. Designing language-controlled software for minority languages

It is relatively easy to write language-controlled software for European languages such as English or Spanish because legal sentences such as 'The spotted frog jumps.' have quite a rigid structure; a definite article, adjective, noun, verb sequence for the former language with the noun-adjective order reversed for the latter. Poetic arrangements such as 'Jumps the spotted frog.' are quite rare for young children and can be readily ignored; the same cannot necessarily be said of all languages particularly Australian languages where many other legal arrangements are possible.

The economics of developing language-controlled software for minor languages can be overcome by designing a software shell which defines a scenario, the things (animate and inanimate) which inhabit it and the possible actions and interactions which can be controlled by language. The shell can then be activated for any language by entering the names of the things and their actions (lexical) and the rules of legal sentences (syntactic).

2.2. A Legal Sentence

The surface structure of a legal or grammatically correct sentence which conveys a certain meaning will differ from language to language. A comparison is made here between English and Watjarri. Watjarri is a suffixing language of the Murchison district belonging to the Pama-Nyungan group, typical of 80% of Australian languages.

Imagine a bush scenario which consists of the following objects: *camp, river, tree, rock, child, emu, dog, and kangaroo;* actions: *run, shoot, jump and chase;* and directions: *on , beside, behind and towards.* Each category is assigned a part-of-speech code: N (noun), D (definite article), V (verb), A (adjective), P (position) etc. The scenario would be caused to react by entering a legal English sentence such as (*The dog chases the emu.*) (D N V D N). No variation in this subject-verb-object order is permissable in English except in rare circumstances. In Watjarri there are six acceptable sequences. This is because the subject is identified by a suffix marker, (*-subj*) (-S), so that the order of the three components then becomes unimportant though the subject-object-verb order is most usual (Kaldor, 1982, p.67), e.g. (*dog-subj emu chases*) (N-S N V)

(*dog-subj chases emu*) (N-S V N) etc.

If the sentence is extended by including a direction phrase, the number of English possibilities increases to two; a (*towards the camp*) (P D N) phrase can be inserted at the beginning or at the end of the sentence though the end is more usual. The number of Watjarri possibilities is increased to twenty-four by creating a (*camp-towards*) (N-P) phrase which can be positioned anywhere within the six simpler sentences without ambiguity though certain arrangements are preferred. The use of adjectives further compounds the number of possibilities.

2.3. Decoding a legal sentence

Consider the following two 'Watjarri' sentences: a legal structure (*camp-towards chases emu two dog-subj*) (N-P V N A N-S) and an illegal structure imposed on Watjarri, (*towards camp dog chases two emu*) (P N N V A N), likely from an English-speaker learning Watjarri.

The decoding or parsing process has three tests: the legality of each code cluster (the illegal sentence above has an unattached 'P'); the attachment of each adjective to a noun phrase; and the appropriate quantity of each cluster (the illegal sentence above has more than one un-suffixed 'N' cluster). Finally, a legal sentence is split into its verb phrase and component noun phrases so that these units can be used to drive the picture generating program.

It is anticipated that this method will be able to cope with Australian languages with the more elaborate suffixing and prefixing systems common in the Kimberley and the Northern Territory. In more complex cases it would be possible to check short sequences of code clusters and in the worst case, where simple decoding rules cannot be formulated, all possible code cluster sequences would be mapped. The latter is a viable strategy because of the limited scale of each scenario and avoids the need for elaborate parsing algorithms which would be beyond the capacity of most microcomputers.

Several scenarios relevant to different Aboriginal communities are planned; these will include bush, coastal, station, and camp scenarios as part of a wider series which could include urban scenarios specifically for Languages Other Than Teaching (L.O.T.E.) and E.S.L. environments. These would assist the teaching of foreign languages to English-speaking students, and English to foreign students learning English as a second language. Mathematical problem-solving scenarios which are language-controlled could also be developed.

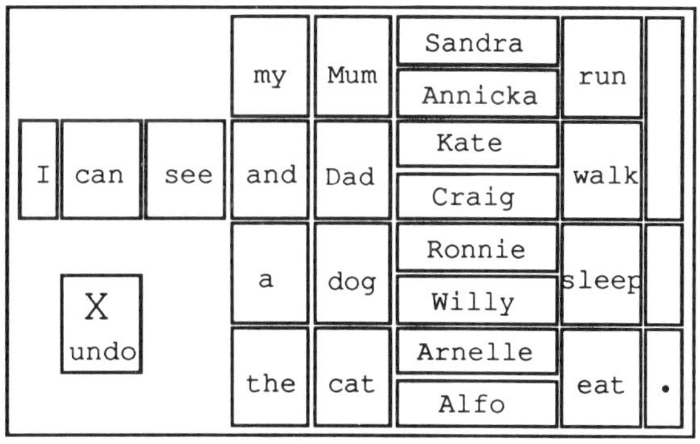

Figure 1. An overlay for a Yr.1 class

3. WORD PROCESSORS LINKED TO A TOUCH-SENSITIVE BOARD

The power of language-controlled software is greatly increased by the concurrent use of overlays designed for use on a touch-sensitive board linked to a word processor. Unlike language-controlled software, overlays do not have a self-checking system, however they can be used to reinforce the work already completed and would include extension vocabulary to allow a wider range of sentence constructions.

The CONCEPT Keyboard is one example of a touch-sensitive board on which the contents of up to 128 rectangular objects can be programmed into meaningful spatial relationships with respect to each other. A variety of object contents are possible with a word processor: letters, phonemes, morphemes, whole words, phrases or even sentences. A natural sequence of pressed objects can provide scaffolding to suggest a grammatical structure. Mediation between what appears on the word processor screen and what is 'printed' on the overlay is an important aspect of overlay design. Object labelling can vary from concrete materials such as feathers, shells, etc, through a range of increasingly abstract labels such as photographs, illustrations, pictographs, ideographs and, ultimately, the letters which appear on the screen itself as the objects are pressed. Johnston (1989) discusses many of these aspects.

An example of an overlay used in a small Yr.1 class in a W.A. coastal community where the children speak Aboriginal English, is shown in Fig 1. These children had a very small sight vocabulary and just able to cope with copying short English sentences. By the end of the first day of use they were constructing, illustrating and reading sentences they had written: as complex as 'I can see my Mum walk and Willy and Ronnie run.' A similar less-structured overlay was designed for the Year 3/4 class using the Salisbury list: a basic English vocabulary. The very first user paused in the middle of constructing a sentence to look for a word that was not there. The overlay was quickly amended to include local words such as dugong, turtle, mangroves, boat, beach and swim. Words not relevant to that coastal community were deleted. This incident demonstrated the need for overlays to be a reflection of self as discussed by McDonald (1986). She adds that the '...need for a real audience and a known audience is of even more significance (for Aboriginal children) than it is for Anglo-Australian children...'(p.13). Touch-sensitive boards with well designed overlays open up many opportunities for Aboriginal children and could be a critical element in their development of literacy.

Some principles for the design of overlays for touch-sensitive boards using alternative 'QWERTY' arrangements and lightly-scaffolded arrangements which deal with more than one verb tense will now be explored.

3.1. Orthography

The relationships between the phonetics of a language and the written symbols we choose to represent those sounds vary from language to language. Orthographies for Australian languages generally share the same symbols as English, however, many of the twenty-six letters are redundant. Ideally the design of a keyboard should take these differences into account.

Many educators believe the QWERTY uppercase keyboard is unsuited to early writers and, instead, prefer a touch-sensitive board with an alphabetically-ordered lower-case overlay. Similar overlays can be designed to suit Aboriginal writers in the orthography of their own language. A basic South-Kimberley orthography will suit most Pama-Nyungan languages (McGregor, 1988); it needs the use of only fourteen of the twenty-six alphabetic characters to depict the necessary phonetic sounds. Rather than organise these alphabetically, other possibilities should be considered e.g. a twenty object Watjarri keyboard with digraphs grouped separately as suggested by Hudson (personal communication), see Fig.2.

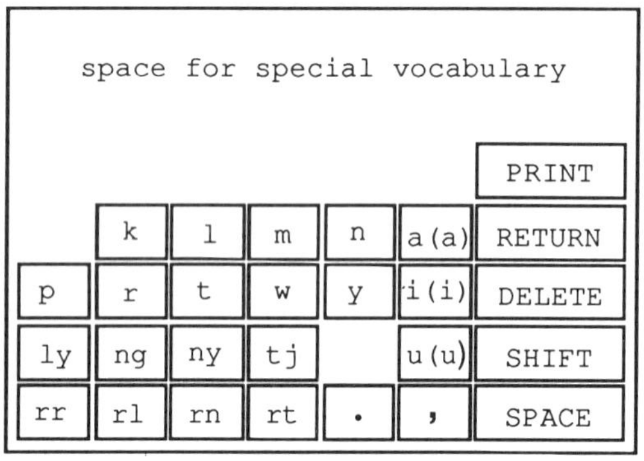

Figure 2. A Watjarri orthography

3.2. Verb tense

A sense of time is shared by all languages; verb tenses, however, differ from language to language. Some Australian languages have only two tenses like English. Many have three tenses: past, present and future. Some are more elaborate; Bardi, for example, having eight tenses (Kaldor, 1982, p.67).

Designing overlays to cope with tense of verbs in English is difficult because so many of the verbs are irregular. These difficulties are further compounded by the need to take into account aspect and mood. Teachers may be detered from attempting the design of similar overlays for Australian languages because they experience difficulty with English overlays; however, verbs in Australian languages are generally more regular. In some languages the main verb root remains entirely unmodified with tense, aspect and mood suffixes being carried on auxiliary verbs. The greater verb regularity of Australian languages will allow more sentence construction possibilities from a given number of overlay objects than is possible for English; hence the greater potential power. This will be illustrated by comparing partial designs for English, Kriol and Watjarri.

3.2.1. Verbs and English

There is always a tension between simplicity and utility when overlays are designed for use with word processors: if too complex, use will be discouraged; if excessively simple, utility is limited. With English overlays, utility is constrained by the complexity needed to cope with spelling rules which modify the verb root to cope with '-ed' and '-ing' suffixes and with the many irregular verbs (Jespersen, 1933, p.232, lists thirteen of the chief irregularities).

A partial English overlay illustrates this tension (see Fig. 3). Verb tense possibilities can be selected by a general, but not exclusive, left-to-right sequence of pressed objects; e.g. 'talk-s', 'do-es talk', 'is talk-ing', 'talk-ed', 'did talk', etc.. Spelling complications of the following sort occur; 'chase*-ing' and 'run(n)-ing' where the asterisk is a cue demanding a last letter deletion and the parenthesis a cue demanding a last letter reduplication when the suffix commences with a vowel.

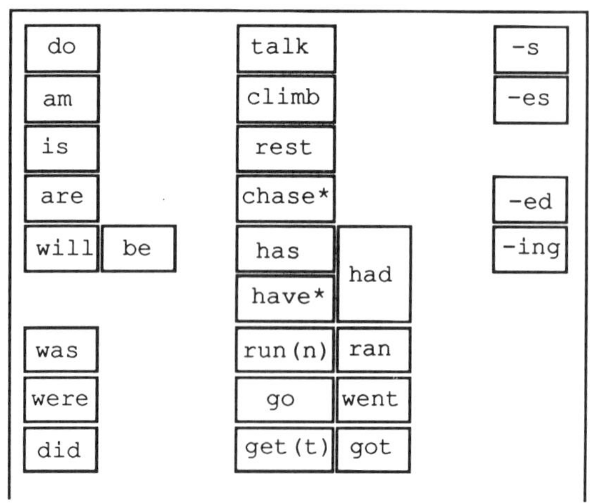

Figure 3. A partial English overlay

3.2.2. Verbs and Kriol

The contrast between the highly irregular verbs of English and the completely regular verbs of the Fitzroy Crossing dialect of Kriol is quite marked. A neater overlay design (Fig. 4) is a consequence of this difference. It offers quite extensive utility and is simple to use with a left-to-right sequence of pressed objects generating a grammatically correct phrase; note, however, that other word arrangements are acceptable in Kriol.

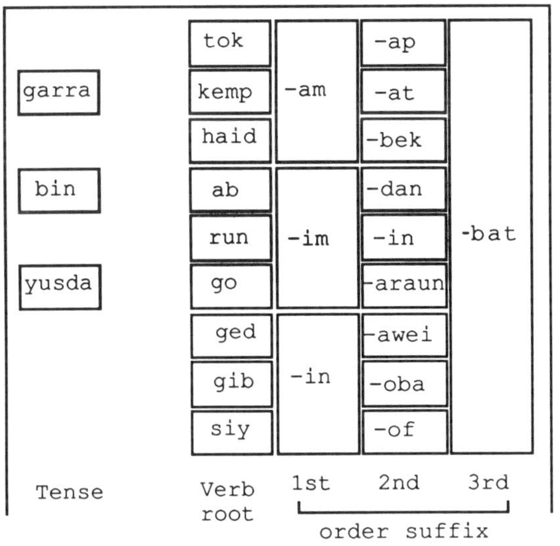

Figure 4. A partial Kriol overlay

A Kriol verb consists of an unmodified verb stem extended by first, second and third order suffixes as appropriate. The first order suffix, *-am/-im*, creates a transitive verb and is chosen for vowel harmony with the verb stem; this link could be established on the overlay by colour cues. The other first order suffix, *-in*, indicates a progressive action as with '-ing' in English. The second order suffixes are historically derived from English prepositions; their meaning, however, has not remained as firm. The third order suffix, *-bat*, indicates an iterative process. *'Fil-im-ap'* and *'grow-am-ap'* are examples of transitive extensive action verbs and *'bin haid-im-ap-bat'* meaning 'was hiding for a long time' is an example of a verb with all the orders of suffixes used. Tense is indicated by a pre-word as follows: *'bin'* indicates the past; *'yusda'*, the habitual past; and *'garra'*, the future. The absence of a pre-word indicates the present. (Note: All Kriol data is taken from Hudson, 1983).

The extension of the partial Kriol overlay to include habituation , mood and aspect words would provide very extensive possibilities and would remain largely used by a left-to-right sequence of presses. To achieve the same results in English would require a much more elaborate overlay design.

3.2.3. Verbs and Pama-Nyungan languages

Pama-Nyungan verbs are not unlike Kriol verbs in their use of suffixes to extend the verb root; however, there is a wide variation in suffixing strategies among the languages of this group. The partial overlay design for Watjarri, Fig. 5, gives some idea of the design principles which can be applied.

Seven irregular verbs have been recorded for Watjarri; these are common verbs and would need to be included with all their variations. The remaining verbs are regular and are divided into two groups, the *'-la'* and the *'-ya'* classes. Verbs may also be created from nouns and adjectives by using the verbalising suffixes, *'-tji'* and *'-ma'*; for example, *'karla'* (hot) is converted to *'karla-ma-la'* (will heat) and to *'karla-tji-ya'* (will become hot). Some *'-la'* class verbs require *'-r-'* to be inserted between the verb root and the tense suffix; this would be cued by colouring the *'-r-'* and the appropriate verbs. No more than three key presses would be needed for any verb or verbalised noun or adjective.

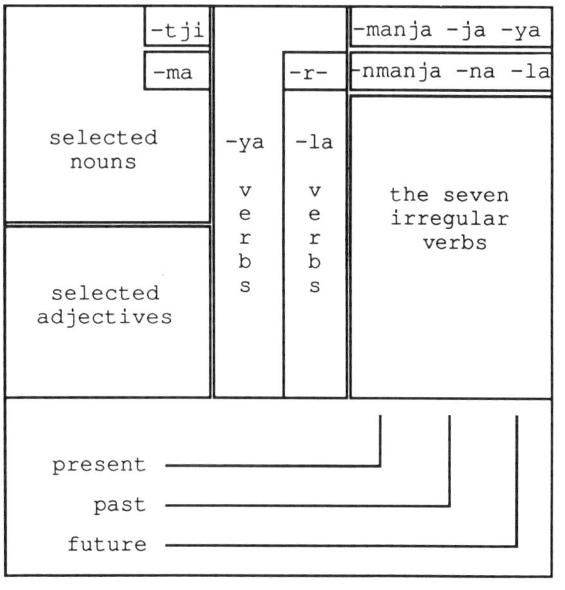

Figure 5. A partial Watjarri overlay

Another organisational feature which could be included would be adjectives clustered in category groups in their normal order of grammatic use: from left to right - number, colour, size and state. (Note: All Watjarri data is taken from Douglas, 1981).

4. POSSIBILITIES WITH ABORIGINAL ENGLISH

The emphasis in this paper has been on early literacy. Hudson and Taylor (1987) have stressed the importance of the oral language of the Kriol home as a bridge to competency in S.A.E. because it facilitates the '...development of skills of prediction, substantiation of that prediction and decoding needed later for reading...'(p.9). A similar case can be made for Aboriginal English, the language of the home in many country and remote areas. As Kaldor and Malcom (1982) note, the Aboriginal English continuum ranges from creole languages to S.A.E. The examples of Aboriginal English they give (p.75-112) suggest there is enough distinction in language for the earliest overlays to reflect home language rather than the language of the school . Eagleson et al (1982), discussing the teacher's task, state that '...whatever the child's mother tongue may be ... it is a cohesive linguistic system with its own grammatic/semantic properties (consequently)... there should not be a sharp break between early childhood language experience and language experience at school' (p.193).

Language-driven software and word processors with touch-sensitive boards can provide early literacy support keyed to the oral transition between Aboriginal English and S.A.E. Once children have acquired early literacy skills, transition to overlays with more formal English would occur.

5. CONCLUSION

The examples above have shown that a detailed study of the grammar of a language can be most informative and can provide scaffolding principles for use on an overlay linked to a word processor. As has been demonstrated, the possibilities with Australian languages are generally greater than they are with English; the same results might occur with other languages.

The combination of language-controlled software with overlays designed to operate with wordprocessors has great relevance for early literacy in English and, arguably, has even greater relevance for acquiring literacy in minor languages particularly where there is no tradition of formal literacy. The combination strategy presented in this paper is an immensely powerful tool for bilingual teaching programs.

ACKNOWLEDGEMENTS

My thanks to Alison Dewsbury for her enthusiastic support for the development of the ideas expressed in this paper, and to Dr. Alan Dench with whom I had many helpful discussions about linguistics.

REFERENCES

Dewsbury, A., 1989: Leaping Into Literacy -Instant Writing in Early Literacy. *Hands ON, Proceedings of the 7th Annual Conference,* N.S.W. Computer Education Group.

Douglas, W., 1981: Watjarri; in Dixon, R. and Blake, B., (Eds), *Handbook of Australian Languages,* Vol. 2, Canberra, Australian National University Press, 196-272.

Douglas, W., date unknown: *Watjarri Experimental Primer No. 1.*

Eagleson, R.D., Kaldor, S. and Malcom, I.G., 1982: *English and the Aboriginal Child.* Canberra, Curriculum Development Centre.

Folds, F., 1986: Desirable Characteristics of Computer Courseware in Tribal Aboriginal Schools. *The Aboriginal Child at School,* 14, 3, 37-43.

Harris, S., 1984: Aboriginal Learning Styles and Formal Schooling. *The Aboriginal Child at School,* 12, 4, 3-23.

House of Representatives, 1986: *Report of Select Committee on Aboriginal Education,* 92-113.

Hudson, J., 1983: Grammatical and semantic aspects of Fitzroy Valley Kriol. *Work Papers of SIL-AAB,* Series A Vol. 8, Summer Institute of Linguistics.

Hudson, J. and Taylor, A., 1987: *Teaching English to Kriol Speakers.* The Aboriginal Child at School, 15, 4, 3-20.

Kaldor, S., 1982: *The Aboriginal Languages of Australia* in Eagleson et al.

Kaldor, S. and Malcom, I., 1982: *Aboriginal English in Country and Remote Areas: A Western Australian Perspective* in Eagleson et al.

Jespersen, O., 1933: *Essentials of English Grammar.* George Allan & Unwin, London.

Johnston, A., 1989: Integrated Language Development with the Concept Keyboard. *LOGIN, The Journal of the Educational Computing Association of W.A.* 3, 2, 26-29.

McDonald, H., 1986: Context and Strategies for Writing with Urban Aboriginal and Islander Students. *The Aboriginal Child at School,* 14, 2, 3-15.

McGregor,W., 1988: A survey of the languages of the Kimberley Region. *Australian Aboriginal Studies,* 2, 90-102.

Computers in Education
A. McDougall and C. Dowling (Editors)
Elsevier Science Publishers B.V. (North-Holland)

INFORMATION SKILLS, INFORMATION TECHNOLOGIES AND YOUNG LEARNERS: A REAPPRAISAL

Toni Downes

School of Education and Language Studies, University of Western Sydney
Macarthur, P.O.Box 555 Campbelltown, NSW 2560, Australia.

It is the conviction of the author that the effective integration of both information handling skills and new information technologies into the classroom curricula for young learners is of the utmost importance. This paper explores a range of critical issues associated with both current practices and current technologies and argues that there is room for improvement in both.

1. INTRODUCTION

In the dynamic social and economic milieu of modern society, increasing demands are being placed on schools to evaluate and modify their curricula. These demands involve a reappraisal of the context in which we develop information handling skills both with the more traditional print-based resource collections, and with the newer electronic information technologies.

Although there is some diversity in the existing definitions of information handling skills, there remains a general concensus that they involve all of the cognitive skills needed to access and evaluate information (Kirk 1988, Wray 1985 and Avann 1985). Such a view moves information skills beyond traditional library or study skills and embraces, yet remains distinct from literacy, numeracy, and other processes such as problem solving and investigating. Recent education policies in Australia (e.g. NSW Department of Education 1989) and in Britain (the National curriculum for British schools, NCET 1989) specifically target the development of these information handling skills from the first years of schooling.

As well as targeting information skills, governments and educators in both countries have strongly argued that new information technologies have a place in classrooms as a teaching and learning tool as well as being a technology deserving attention in itself. It is not surprising that educational authorities are focusing on these two areas at the same time, as both grow out of recognition of the increasing importance of information and information technologies in all sectors of society. However the very fact that they are being targeted at the same time can make a school's task more complex as it grapples with the relative priority given to either area and the implementation of strategies for developing either or both of them.

As computer technology in particular receives a high profile in both the popular and educational press, some schools believe they have discharged their total responsibilities to both information skill development and appropriate use of the technology through computer literacy programs. Many of these programs demonstrate little awareness of the underlying information handling skills that students need in order to harness the powerful information processing capabilities of the computer. On the other hand many information skills programs in schools are firmly based in the print media with little or no recognition given to the role of newer information technologies (Wray 1985).

It is the conviction of the author that the integration of both information handling skills and new information technologies into existing classroom curricula for young learners is of such importance that the present situation must be critically examined and ways be sought to improve both current practices and technologies. This paper explores a range of critical issues associated with the implementation of information technologies in schools and their potential to assist in the development of information skills in young learners (five to twelve years of age).

2. EDUCATIONAL CONTEXTS

That information skills are best developed in a functional environment, that is, when they are needed and can be used in a meaningful context, is a viewpoint supported by several authors. They variously describe this approach as needs driven (Kirk 1988) research driven (Atmore and Craig 1989) or as an integrated approach (Wray 1985). Proponents of this approach believe that skill development should occur from the first years of school (Avaan 1984), that it should involve both direct and indirect instruction within the context of a meaningful task (Elder & White 1989), and that it requires a well structured curriculum plan to ensure all relevant information skills are systematically introduced and developed (Wray 1985). Current policy documents from British and Australian education systems reflect this integrated approach.

Similar arguments exist for the integration of new information technologies into the classroom curriculum as teaching and learning tools. While many secondary schools in Australia have separate computing courses, most secondary and primary schools have also made serious attempts to integrate new technologies, particulary computer technology into a variety of curriculum areas (Fitzgerald 1985). It is interesting to note that with the new National Curriculum in Britain, there is no longer a place for separate courses even in the secondary schools. Such an approach suggests that computer skills are also considered as being best developed on a need basis (such as learning to use wordprocessors in the context of a meaningful writing activity).

Mention must also be made of the nature of the new information technologies being integrated into classrooms in Australia, the U.K. and the U.S.A. Although more and more sophisticated technology is being used in some schools, e.g. CD ROM, online databases, electronic mail, and video-disc. This type of technology remains beyond the reach of most elementary classrooms. In the majority of these classrooms teachers are still grappling with microcomputers, printers and simple software packages such as wordprocessors, adventure games, simulations and drill and practice programs (Fitzgerald 1985, U.S. Congress, Office of Technology Assessment 1988 and Gwyn 1988).

It is within the above context that an increasing number of teachers and learners are using simple data base management packages as information handling tools. Both teachers and learners are using these tools as they undertake a variety of information handling tasks. Underwood (1988) examined 18 classrooms and found a variety of reasons for the use of database packages. The most common reasons given were the development of cognitive and communicative skills. The cognitive component included terms such as formulating questions, testing hypothesis, problem solving and decision making.

Supporting this use is a growing body of literature, most of which consists of descriptive and anecdotal accounts from teachers about how they have successfully used simple database packages in their classrooms (e.g. Ross 1984, Bell 1985 and Coonans 1985). Rarely do these accounts describe situations where teachers have systematically integrated information handling skills and software such as databases into the classroom curriculum. Regardless of this, most of these accounts present good practices of enthusiastic teachers that are consistent with the development of information handling skills (e.g Pon 1984, Sutton 1985 and Jackson 1985). However when studies have been undertaken that investigate a range of teachers, learners and topics, the task of integrating the skills and the technology, usually simple database packages, seems much more problematic.

Freeman, Hawkins and Char (1985), Guttormsen (1986), Carter and Monaco (1987), Rawitsch D, (1987-8), Underwood (1988), Downes (1988) and White(1987) have all reported such studies. Although all of their findings were encouraging, many factors were identified that will require attention, if schools are to successfully integrate the technology and information handling skills into their curriculum. Some of these factors are outlined below.

Freeman et al (1985) found that many teachers lacked a clear perspective or agenda for teaching research and information-handling skills, thus the role of the data base was also unclear. He also found that the extent of the teachers' exposure to tool uses of the computer and the degree to which they were comfortable with database management software influenced their ability to use the data base in creative ways.

Guttormsen (1986) focusing on primary-aged children, found that they needed a basic level of computer awareness before being introduced to database packages, and that the manipulation of databases required the application of a range of skills as yet not well developed in primary school children.

Underwood (1988) found that the nature of the problem being investigated was important. She found that the formulation of an appropriate and relevant research question could make the selection and organization of data relatively easy even for young children. She also found that the approach taken to questionning, to who designs the questions, and to whether they are seeking facts or testing ideas, is of considerable importance in determining the cognitive development of the children.

White (1987) found that merely using a database does not develop information skills, but rather that both direct and indirect instruction in information skills is needed within the context of its use.

Rawitsch (1987-88) found that student learning style may be an important factor in determining effective strategies for working with databases, with some styles more suited to general exploratory approaches rather than structured worksheets.

The author has found that lack of time is an important factor inhibiting the effective use of databases (Downes 1988). In the classrooms studied, both the total amount of time allocated to the topic and the amount of time students actually spent using the database package on the microcomputer were not sufficient to allow the primary-aged students to develop their information handling skills to any great extent. Four classroom studies in this area have been conducted by the author, and two of these have been published Downes (1989). It was found that most students (in groups) had little more than 20-40 minutes a week actually using the database package. Each time students came back much energy was expended in working out how to operate the software again, and often their 'turn' would finish just as they were settling into some significant enquiry. In terms of overall time for the topic, in two classrooms where the students developed their own database in order to answer research questions, the time allocated for the topic expired before the database had actually been completed, hence the purpose for creating the database and the opportunities for analysing the data were lost. In the two classrooms where the students were using an existing data file as a source of information the children did not really progress beyond the point of retreiving specific pieces of information about individuals before the topic came to a close.

All of the above studies highlight factors that may reduce the overall value of using database packages in the classroom. Neither researchers nor practitioners would find any of these factors remarkable yet their range and complexity suggest the extent of the challenge facing teachers who attempt to integrate both information skills and database packages into their classroom. Indeed these factors may begin to explain why Australian teachers are not embracing database packages in their classrooms. A study by Fitzgerald (1985) has found database packages to be the least popular of all software in schools. This contrasts with word processors which have been readily adopted by teachers into their classrooms.

To better understand the lack of success of database packages it may be of value to discuss the success of word processors. Word processors were successful because a context for them already existed. A niche had been unwittingly created by the reshaping of writing classrooms which had taken place five to ten years previously. The problems of implementation were tackled within a curriculum context where most teachers felt confident about putting the theory of process writing into practice in their classroom.

A similar context or niche for the use of database packages is only just beginning to emerge. In general teachers are only now beginning to explore enquiry-based learning. This more student-centred approach places greater demands on the information handling skills of the learner but many teachers have yet to fully appreciate this fact. Tabberer (1987) has found that most teachers in British schools have not yet come to grips with the *need* to develop information handling skills let alone begin to think about *strategies* for developing these skills.

It is heartening to note that some teachers are enjoying considerable success with using database packages even at this early stage. For the vast majority, however, there is much work still to be done in classrooms and most of it directed not so much to the technology as to the curriculum context.

4. CURRENT TECHNOLOGIES

While emphasis must be placed on empowering more and more teachers to reflect on their curriculum decisions and change their practices, there is also a pressing need for the development of new information handling software that is more appropriate for the young learner than the present generation of flat file databases which currently exist in the schools. This section seeks to present the author's response to this need.

A number of reviews have compared existing packages or features e.g. menu vs command-driven (Freeman & Levett 1986). Few investigations have moved beyond this level to question the very nature of the current flat file database packages used with young learners. Mackey (1986) has expressed concern that young learners are using software that reflects the needs and methodologies of business and more significantly assumes the preknowledge of adults. This concern is shared by the author, who, although not doubting young learners' enormous capacities to master almost any software placed in front of them, questions the appropriateness of current information handling software. This concern relates to both the stage of concept and skill development of young learners and the range of information handling activities in which they engage in solving problems and investigating their world.

Rather than fitting the user and task to the existing tools we should begin by closely examining both the learners and their information handling tasks. By doing so we can begin to define, an information handling tool or toolbox which will best support these young learners.

The first insight into such a package may come from thinking about the abilites and experiences most children bring with them to school.

Within the current cultural and educational context of Australia, it is reasonable to assume that almost all young children come to school with a rich experience of putting marks on paper through activites such as scribbling, writing, drawing and painting. Invariably they have had ownership of their tasks and have used a variety of media and tools for a variety of purposes. When these children are confronted with a painting package on a computer they already have a rich collection of mental models that will support their work. Painting packages are generally designed to be consistent with the manual procedures that children and adults use. In addition they allow children to do things they couldnt do before e.g. draw perfect circles or undo the last bit of drawing or shading. Children can do all of this without the worry of spilling the paint. Usually it is not long before children, even as young as five are confidently experimenting with complex operations such as brush mirrors, stamping or colour cycling and independently using these features to create pictures and patterns for the screen or other more traditional media.

Similarly a large number of children come to school with a rich experience in oral and written langauge. Print has played a significant role in their lives and most are ready to dive into the world of reading and writing. These children have been exposed to a wide variety of print for a variety of purposes. They bring to simple word processors a rich collection of experiences and appropriate mental models to use a word processor to write stories or record ideas, even if they are still using invented spelling.

In contrast to these two areas, the mental models and skills assumed by existing database software are poorly developed. Although collections of objects such as dolls, cars, books, rocks and shells are commonly found in homes only a few children come to school with a wide range of experiences with organised collections. Most children's play would not extend beyond grouping objects for a specific purpose and rarely would a child need to describe the ordered collection to another child or an adult, or maintain an ordered collection for the purposes of finding an object when needed (regardless of the wishes of parents!).

A second insight comes from an examination of the information handling tasks encountered in the classroom. Information handling activities in the first years of school build on children's early experiences with language and with collections. In order to do this teachers create new contexts in which children organise, describe and represent their collections in a variety of ways and for a variety of purposes.

Within these contexts, most children have their first experience of using pictures, words or numbers to represent the objects or patterns in their collections. At these early stages, simple packages that provide alternative ways of representing collections through tables, graphs, symbols and codes may be of more value than existing database packages.

Parallel to this early development is the more traditional treatment of information skills within the context of the print media. As children learn the alphabet, and investigate the structure of books, they begin to develop a sense of order about what is in books and how organised collections of books are stored and accessed. During this stage young learners often have trouble finding things, yet we rarely find an information handling tool for young children which helps them "find" an object in an unorganised collection or in a collection whose structure is still a little beyond them. e.g. a simple electronic dictionary with supporting graphics or a graphics library that can be accessed by keywords.

Over time these learners develop a greater knowledge of the world and their problems and investigations lead them to handling information in different ways. Two of the most common tasks relate to collecting information from secondary sources such as books, records, encyclopedias and audio-visual media and collecting information through observing, interviewing or surveying objects or events.

With the former there has been some research into ways that new information technologies can support young learners as they work with these more traditional resources. Some areas that have been investigated include the use of keyword searching of print and audio-visual resources (Williams & Herring 1986), the use of outlining tools, thought processors or knowledge-based tools to help students organise the collected information, and the use of database files as secondary sources of information (Downes 1988).

The second type of information handling activity involves young learners collecting data about individual events, people, places or objects, in order to learn more about the characteristics of the group, subgroups and individuals within the group. The use of computer-controlled devices to aid students in the data collecting stage of investigations is becoming more popular. To analyse and organise this data young learners have used tools such as binary tree programs, spread-sheets, graphing packages and database packages. What seems to be lacking in this area, however, is any research examining ways of improving these tools so that they more readily meet the needs of the young learners.

The author believes that these learners can be well served by an information handling tool with an underlying structure similar to existing data base packages. What needs to be different is the environ-ment in which the students work with the information. Special features which go beyond the needs of business are needed. Listed below are just two examples out of many that have been identified by the author after many hours of observing young learners. These features may also apply to those packages being used as secondary sources of information.

The first feature relates to the frequent need for young learners to refine or rearrange the structure of information as their knowledge of the domain grows or the nature of the task becomes clearer. The feature could be as simple as enabling the learners to add new fields or transform data half way through the analysis or it might involve the development of a front end that structures the refining process (Galpin & Schilling 1988).

The second example takes account of the range and type of information that young learners collect. Most packages allow for text and numeric fields. Young learners need help with a much wider range of data types. Measurement of characteristics such as mass, length, capacity and time needs to be supported through 'typed' fields. Similarly both categorical (e.g. hair colour) and free text data fields (with unlimited length) should exist.

5. Conclusion

Although the above discussion concentrates on problems and may appear to present a less than rosy picture the author truly believes that the integration of information handling skills and new information technologies is important enough to warrant a critical examination of current practices and technologies to improve the information-handling environment of the young learner.

ACKNOWLEDGEMENTS

I gratefully acknowledge Anita Straker who has been a critical friend during the development of my ideas. I also wish to thank the many teachers and students who have allowed me to observe their classrooms and question their practices.

REFERENCES

Atmore & Craig (1989) Exploratory Studies in Educational Computing. SET No 2 1989 NZCER

Avann, P, (1985) Teaching Information Skills in the Primary School. London: Edward Arnold.

Bell, S, (1985) "Data Bases in the Primary School." Classroom Computing, 5(1), pp9-12.

Carter, C & Monaco, J (1987) Learning Information Technology Skills. London: British Library.(LIR Report 54).

Coomans, S., (1985) "A Graveyard Database", Classroom Computing, 2(4), July, pp5-7.

Downes, T, (1988) "Databases in the Classroom: A Tale of a Fourth Classes' Introduction to a Convict Database." in Golden Opportunities, Proceedings of the Fifth Australian Computers in Education Conference. Perth: Educational Computing Association of Western Australia.

Downes, T, (1989) "Integrating Information Skills and Technologies into the Curriculum." Pt 1: Scan 8(4), pp11-14. Pt 2: Scan 8(5),pp11-14.

Freeman, D. & Levet, J. (1986) "Computer Assisted Information Handling as a Tool for Change." in Moonen, J. & Plomp, T. (eds) EURIT 86: Developments in Educational Software and Courseware. Proceedings of the First European conference on Education and Information Technology. Oxford: Pergamon Press.

Freeman, C., Hawkins, J. & Char, C., (1985) Information Management Tools for Classrooms: Exploring Database Management Systems. Technical Report No.28, New York: Centre For Children and Technology, Bank Street College of Education.

Galpin, M. & Schilling, M. (1988) Computers, Topic Work and Young Children: Learning to use information in the Primary Classroom. London: The British Library Board.

Guttormsen, R. (1986) "Computer Based Information Handling in the Primary School: Learning Tool or Simply Awareness?" in Guttormsen, R.(ed) Computers in the Curriculum: Realizing the Potential. The Papers from the 1986 CEGQ Conference. Brisbane: Computer Education Group of Queensland.

Gwyn, R. (1988) "Information Technology and Education in the UK: a Survey of Recent Development." in Harris (ed) World Yearbook of Education 1988 - Education for the New Technologies. Kogan Page.

Jackson M, (1985) in Avann, P (ed) Teaching Information Skills in the Primary School. London: Edward Arnold.

Kirk, J. (1988) "Information Skills: Preparing students for the Information Society." Scan 7(2) pp 2-6.

Mackey, B. (1986) "Effective Educational Courseware (The Microcomputer as a Learning Medium)." in Moonen, J. & Plomp, T. (eds) EURIT 86: Developments in Educational Software and Courseware. Proceedings of the First European conference on Education and Information Technology. Oxford: Pergamon Press.

National Council for Educational Technology, (1989) Information Skills and the National Curriculum: A Summary Sheet. Coventry: NCET.

New South Wales Department of Education (1989) Information Skills K-12.Sydney: NSW Department of Education.

Pon, K. (1984) "Databasing in the Elementary (and Secondary) Classroom." The Computing Teacher, 12(3), pp28-30.

Rawitsch, D. (1987-8) "The Computerized Database: Not A Simple Solution." The Computing Teacher 15(4) pp34-37.

Ross, A. (1988) "How does Information Retrieval Help Children's Learning?" in Jones, A. & Scrimshaw, P. Computers in Education 5-13.Milton Keynes: Open University Press.

Ross, A.(1984) "Learning Why To Hypothezise: A Case Study of data processing in a primary school classroom" in Kelly, A.V. (ed) Microcomputers and the Curriculum, London: Harper and Row Publishers Ltd.

Sutton, D.(1985) "Homemade and Claytons Databases." in Oakley, J. (ed) Computers in Education: Issues and Applications. Bathurst: Computer Education Group of New South Wales.

Underwood, J. (1988) "An Investigation of Teacher Intents and Classroom Outcomes in the Use of Information-Handling Packages. Computers and Education 12(1) pp 91-100.

White, C.S. (1987) "Developing Information-Processing Skills through Structured Activities with Computerized File-Management Program." Journal of Educational Computing Research, 3(3) pp 355-375.

Williams,D.A.& Herring, J.E.(1986) "Keywords and Learning. Ideas on Information Skills and Information Technology from MISLIP." Aberdeen: School of Librarianship and Information Studies, Robert Gordon's Institute of Technology.

Wray D (1985) Teaching Information Skills through Project Work. London: Hodder &Stoughton.

Computers in Education
A. McDougall and C. Dowling (Editors)
Elsevier Science Publishers B.V. (North-Holland)

CHILDREN CAN PUBLISH; ALL IT TAKES IS THE RIGHT PROCESS

Leigh Finney
Kate Fraser

Computer Consultant, Metropolitan East Region NSW Department of Education
Computer Consultant, Metropolitan West Region NSW Department of Education

This session will focus on the development of publishing skills for 8 - 12 year old children and how these can be facilitated by the classroom teacher, addressing the areas of layout and design in relation to the software being used and the learner's own creativity. Principles of desk top publishing will be presented in relation to industry and education.

Power has always been held by those who have superior knowledge. This concept began early in the 15th century when monks maintained the hand written volumes of books, by restricting circulation, held much of the control and power. With the advent of the printing press, the general population began to have greater access to the knowledge that had been previously withheld.

Gradually the monks relinquished much of their power base as the keepers of knowledge when books and other publications began to be produced faster and with more consistency.

Information is increasingly becoming public property as technology gives rise to easy access and manipulation. The technology of today has empowered children with the tools of presentation and publication. The power once associated with privileged understanding of print has shifted to the masses creating an information explosion.

Teachers, who have been the knowledge keepers in the past, are beginning their new role of information skills facilitators. With this change the power of information has been extended to the children.

There is a plethora of information that can be obtained easily by children. The amount available through traditional and electronic means is staggering. Children are now learning to deal with vast amounts of data, not only in its handling but manipulation, storage and presentation. The development of skills such as: selection, skim reading, note taking, summarising, drafting and editing have become a feature of the modern day learning environment.

Emphasis is changing in the education field. More and more the "process" of learning rather than the "product" is becoming recognised as the important learning strategy. The mere learning of facts is now insufficient to deal with the information society and skills for dealing with data must now be learned.

Each skill learned is of great importance to the overall development of the child but the skills which will have influence and power over others are those of information handling and presentation. Those practised in the art of information manipulation and presentation will hold the power in a society such as ours.

The computer has placed powerful, easy to use tools within the hands of children. However, having the tools to publish does not mean that the publication will be effective.

There are many examples of people using the very latest equipment producing less than effective output. Take a look in a few magazines to determine which techniques are most successful. While the computer makes the task of manipulating the layout much easier, it will never replace the creativity that is needed to produce something that is attractive and effective.

The area of creativity can easily be overlooked with the power that the technology generates. It is often all too easy to print out a ready made graphic as it generally tasks a lot less time than hand drawing.

Children need to continue to develop skills of drawing, writing, creating borders, headlines, and manual fonts. By starting with this "manual discovery" they can later apply their skills in electronic presentations.

The planning of a publications layout is a step often left till very late in the production process. Generally it should occur right after the purpose has been defined and the audience targeted. By defining the structure and establishing some rules for layout considerable time may be saved. It is at this stage that the technology begins to play an important role.

Teachers and students need to ask: Does the software have the capacity to mix fonts, size, style? Can I use clip art for graphics or is it more appropriate to draw them? Can the software efficiently combine text and graphics? Is it more efficient to use the computer to create the layout or to manually cut and paste with scissors and glue? Does the publication need colour? What is the best size for the text? What is the best font? Should all headings be the same font? How many different fonts should I put on the one page?

When these questions begin to arise it becomes clear that there is a lot more to publication than writing the story and adding pictures.

Everybody has some idea of what looks good in printed material and what is clear and concise in writing. By providing the children with a few clues at a time they may better learn the techniques employed by professionals when producing a publication.

As computer usage for classroom publishing increases daily, so too does the students understanding of effective presentation.

Are these skills that we as educators should be teaching children? There is a fine line between showing effective layout design and entrenching children in its use.

Followers of Guttenberg will be familiar with his analysis of layout and its specific detail for western writing. All features of the page are considered. The line of vision from the Primary Optical Area (essentially this is the Point of attachment area of the eye) in the upper left hand corner, transferring down to the lower right hand corner or the Terminal Area of the page.

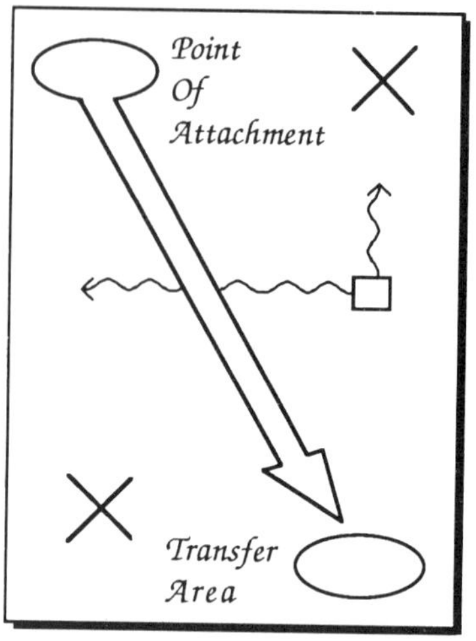

Given that this is the path the eye takes in looking at a page, then clearly the childrens' message will not be as effective if it is hidden over on the centre left hand margin or conversely at the top of the right hand side of the page. Guttenberg describes these as the dead areas. Guttenberg's principles have been employed by media specialists and have tremendous implications on audience impact. Indeed a typical newspaper page layout has each of the characteristics he refers to. It is not then amazing to see that company logos are often positioned in the bottom right hand corner, thus leaving the reader with a message before the next page is given attention.

Guttenberg has many interesting ideas in relation to the readers comprehension and:

These are all issues that need the educators attention, it is clear that the commercial sector has taken advantage of many of these recommendations as these ideas are so clearly reflected in much of the print media that society consumes daily. So what advantage is being taken of these principles by teachers in the publications they and their students generate? However other recent studies suggest quite different recommendations, these too will be addressed during the session.

Children are still producing masses of published work each year and much of this is on lined paper with a margin down the left hand side. This of

	Decreasing Comprehension -> -> ->
characters on a line	more than 60 or less than 20
number of columns	2 columns of 40 to 50 characters
text justification	both 86%, left 60%, right 28%
choice of fonts	serif , san serif, all capitals
mixed fonts	increasing mix of fonts
headlines	mixed case, all capitals
style to enhance text	italics for emphasis, bold sparingly
length of document	50 to 500 words, more if interest demands
leadline legibility	chose font and size carefully

course has its place, however the time has come to once again change the power base and offer children the marketing control over their work.

Not all produced work produced by students need have a huge technological input. In the initial stages of layout and design the technology of scissors, ruler, pens and glue is more than sufficient for the purpose of layout. Introduce the technology slowly and still employ the manual cut and paste method. This will allow the children to blend their own manual creations with that of the new technology.

Show children examples of varying types of print media and encourage them to begin looking critically at what they see. What is the message? How did the page capture my attention? Did I need to read the whole page to get the intended message? Did the page layout or choice of colour influence the way I felt about the product?

Slowly introduce the children to the principles of desk top publishing. Choose those pieces of classroom work that have been deemed by the children as effective and add the principles of publication to the strategies of the authors.

Once the children have mastered the idea of page layout and influence over their audience, a problem will very quickly surface. That is the production of thirty individual pieces of work that all look the same. At least the children will all employ the same principles so that the chance of repetition is greatly increased.

Teachers at this stage can then introduce the next lesson in desktop publishing. That is, the primary principle of layout is to "stand out". The skill comes in knowing the rules so you are able to break them creatively and successfully according to the publication and its inherent features. There are thousands of possible permutations of desktop layout principles and children lack no genius in finding new implementations.

In summary, to teach or not to teach? Yes teach, distribute the power, encourage the children to be divergent thinkers and explorers with their publishing.

The process of publishing begins with a definition of the purpose. This is followed by the identification of the intended audience. The combination of these two factors will largely determine the overall appearance of the publication.

The raw data, which will form the content of the publication, is then collected from an array of sources. The data may come from a wide range of areas including electronic mail, databases, children's own writing, libraries, interviews and other printed material. Data will encompass not only text but illustrations, pictures, diagrams, charts and the like.
Decision making and problem solving then come into play as appropriate and inappropriate information is added or deleted.

Presentation techniques and strategies are then employed to layout the selected data. Following this the text and graphics are combined into the master copies for the print run.

The final step in the process is marketing of the publication to the intended audience. At this stage there is some objective feedback to the students on their relative success.

The following model presents the process through which the children progress in the publication of a specific task

The Publishing Process

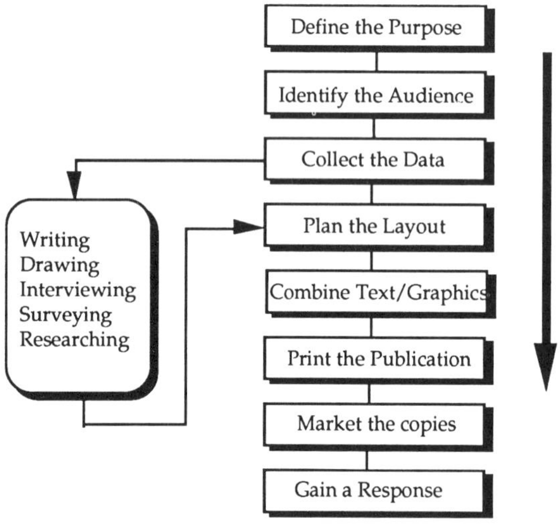

The process offered above is a general approach which broadly encompasses most publications. However, the process may vary when the task is diverse.

Pro's and Con's of specific software packages
After using many software packages for a variety of purposes it soon becomes very apparent that no one software package or computer system will perform all the tasks you require. Given the constraints of the computer system in the school and the available software packages some form of publication can be achieved in most situations. Even the best software in this field will lack some features you may require. In many respects this can be a classroom advantage as it will encourage children to look beyond a single package and in so doing critically evaluate the worth of the software.

Younger children require simple to operate packages but, these by design lack many features. Fully featured packages usually require much more training to operate.

Encourage children to intergrate the technology with their own work. Technology can be used as a tool to enhance the work of the children when used appropriately.

The printing press has enhanced production of the newspaper but it has done little to enhance the actual paper. All newspapers look the same The layout, the format, the font, headlines and the like are standardised to such an extent that often a good article may be buried amongst the presentation features of the paper. In children we need to encourage individual layout and design features which will inspire audiences to read, to find and to investigate the intended message of the text.

By blending the children's own drawings, layout ideas, and information with the technology they will be able to create a piece of published work that is truly unique.

Whatever the work to be published, it must have relevance to the children. This may come through: topical discussion, such as that seen daily on the news, community events, children's story writing, research topics, interviews, sporting events, world news, electronic mail, letters from friends, science experiments or a host of other activities.

An example of this occured around the time of the release of a popular print program that comprises a series of "American" graphics. In classrooms near and far the graphics from this program were displayed in many published forms. The varied use of graphics within itself was a very positive use of the technology. However, the hotdogs, baseball, gridiron players, the American flag, racoons, American eagles and the like did little to enhance the relevance of the work of Australian children.
The use of desk top publishing techniques places control of the final appearance of a published work into the hands of those who are willing to learn the technology. In the past this technology has been beyond the means of most and usually very complicated. Today the same facilities are afforded by computers with relatively cheap and simple to operate programs.

In the classroom this means that students can have full control of the writing and publishing process from beginning to end. The selection of the appropriate technology to use, layout considerations and forward planning are all skill based results of using this process.

Computers in Education
A. McDougall and C. Dowling (Editors)
Elsevier Science Publishers B.V. (North-Holland)

ENHANCING VOCABULARY DURING READING USING ELECTRONIC HANDHELD TECHNOLOGY

Patricia M. Gildea*, Cheryl L. Wurtenberg, George A. Miller**

Microlytics, Inc., 20 Nassau Street, Suite 204, Princeton, NJ 08540, USA.

What is the optimal environment for encouraging reading and vocabulary growth? We explore how dictionaries have been used as tools for children. We then introduce a novel approach to reading using a handheld computer: MicroReader. Vocabulary instruction is embedded in the process of reading classic literature. We report testing comparing MicroReader with standard reading with a dictionary, learning words out of context, and using our context materials without the dynamic aspects related to MicroReader. We discuss the advantages and disadvantages of learning in a rich contextual environment with a handheld computer.

1. BACKGROUND RESEARCH

Every school child learns "dictionary skills" as part of his formal education. And, when asked what a word means, many parents and teachers tell children to "look it up in the dictionary." Since dictionaries are so ingrained into literate cultures, we thought it would be of interest to examine how well children use and understand dictionaries (Miller and Gildea, 1985). To our surprise and temporary dismay, we discovered that children are easily and quite often confused by dictionaries. While they have mastered the skills necessary to locate a word in an alphabetized list, they do not have the understanding needed to apply the written dictionary entry to a given situation. In other words, children have great difficulty extracting from a lexicon the semantic information that is required to understand and remember what a word means.

Since dictionaries were confusing for children, we next explore the effects of learning words in context (Gildea, Miller and Wurtenberg, 1990). We provided a familiar visual and verbal context from which children could learn words: children watched a segment from the movie, Raiders of the Lost Ark, and read a narrative, adapted from the story, that complemented the scene. Embedded in the narrative were vocabulary words. Children learned these words with the help of either a dictionary definition, a sentence illustrating the word in the same context as the story, a picture from the movie highlighting the word, or a combination of these three. Children learned the most words when they were given an illustrative sentence as the only additional tutorial information about the word. When children received a defintion along with a sentence, they focused only on the definition which, as demonstrated previously, was confusing for them, and thus did not benefit from the context sentence. When presented in isolation, however, the illustrative sentences provoked thought and mental guessing games in the children. We concluded that context sentences enhance children's natural work-learning ability. We also discovered that without any additional learning materials, children gained much word knowledge from simply watching the movie and reading the story. That is, we became aware of the importance and absolute necessity of a rich learning contextual environment. Without context to tie words and ideas together, new word meanings are facts which do not build onto anything or into a lasting structure. Thus isolated, word meanings without context are quickly forgotten.

Comparing learning contexts yielded one final result which must be mentioned. We observed that while children's vocabulary growth was greatly facilitated through the use of a narrative context and context appropriate sentences illustrating unfamiliar words, there were occasions when a child's guess about a word's meaning was incorrect, and since no definition was presented, the child was not able to reorganize his thoughts and develop a more consistent hypothesis. Because this was a concern, we experimented with adding information to the context sentences (Wurtenberg, in preparation). Taking into consideration the confusion of presenting a definition and an illustrative sentence together, we presented the sentence first, then added a word or two from the definition. The definition-type information was provided to give the child feedback about his inferences, i.e., to steer him on the right track. The word from the definition replaced the unfamiliar word directly in the sentence; thus, the child saw the sentence written with the unfamiliar word, then saw the same sentence written with a familiar word. The manipulation

*Department of Psychology, Rutgers University, New Brunswick, New Jersey 08903, U.S.A.
**Department of Psychology, Princeton University, Princeton, New Jersey 08544, U.S.A.

in this experiment was the presentation timing of the familiar word. Some children were presented with the definition-word immediately after reading the illustrative sentence while other children were presented with the definition-word after a 20-second delay. The delay was inserted to allow children to think on their own for a finite amount of time before being given some feedback. We hypothesized that when given time to think on their own, children would learn and remember more about new words than when presented with dictionary-like information too soon. Our hypothesis was overwhelmingly supported. Children used the delay to come up with guesses as to what word would replace the new word. They used their knowledge of the story, the context, to "figure out" the meaning of the new word. Then, the familiar word either affirmed their guess or redirected their thoughts in the appropriate direction. This method of vocabulary building (rich context, additional sentence demonstrating correct use of the word in the same context, timing delay, verifying word) has been found to enhance children's word-learning abilities, and has been developed into a handheld computer product.

2. INTRODUCTION TO MICROREADER

MicroReader is a handheld computer that was designed to incorporate the learning principals supported by our research. The computer contains classic novels in their complete form, such as Dr. Jekyll and Mr. Hyde by Robert Louis Stevenson, or Peter Pan by J. M. Barrie, along with a subtext created by trained writers. The subtext is composed of individual illustrative sentences written for each word in the story that is coded as fourth-grade level or above according to the EDL Core Vocabularies list. The sentences are designed to be substitutable in the selected story; that is, the same characters perform realistic actions and thoughts using target words in the same sense as originally in the story. Rather than paraphrase, a sentence is designed to amplify and explain new words within the context of the story. A child using MicroReader can stop at any word in the text that he is unfamiliar with and by pressing the STUDY key, he will be presented with a new sentence using the word written in the context of the story. After reading the new sentence, the child will then have some time to think about what the unfamiliar word means and relate it to the story. Then, a familiar word or phrase replaces the unfamiliar word in the new sentence. After the child has learned about the new word, he can go back to reading the story. The goal of MicroReader is first to promote reading and then to facilitate vocabulary growth.

MicroReader's ability to facilitate vocabulary growth was compared to other classroom methods of vocabulary development in a field test this Spring. Children representing a range of reading levels read a story and were tested on both reading comprehension and vocabulary acquisition. Their scores were compared to the vocabulary scores of children who looked up words in a dictionary format. The comparison between learning words using context-based sentences with specific timing parameters versus dictionary definitions demonstrates the effect of context. Our hypothesis is that if children benefit from integrating word meanings with their surrounding context, then children who look up words in a context-based illustrative sentence will learn more than those who look up words in a context-free dictionary.

Data analysis is ongoing at this time. We expect that children reading and learning vocabulary with MicroReader's basic principles will outperform all other groups on measures of vocabulary knowledge. We plan to discuss MicroReader's benefits in terms of children's natural ability to extract semantic information from context, and the enhancement of that ability with the timing dynamics provided by MicroReader.

3. FUTURE STUDIES

We are currently conducting additional tests of MicroReader. One question concerns the dynamic presentation of information while learning. In other words, what is the benefit of having helpful information instantaneously available while reading? The comparison of MicroReader to reading the story on paper with the additional materials appended will demonstrate the effects of MicroReader's timing parameters for presenting tutorial information. While both groups will receive exactly the same information about target vocabulary words, only the MicroReader group will receive the materials according to specific timing parameters. Subjects who receive written materials will be free to look at the additional information whenever they choose. Our hypothesis is that if children do not benefit from having extra time to figure out a word's meaning, then the two groups' vocabulary scores will not differ. We expect, however, that they will differ: children who are presented with information at the right time on the computer will score higher on a vocabulary test than children who receive the same information without the timing dynamics.

4. RELATED ISSUES TO BE DISCUSSED

*Reading a whole novel on a handheld computer has never been done before. The issues and concerns of reading comprehension when reading is done on a computer screen will be addressed along with the advantages and disadvantages of having a small window in which to scan a page.

Figure 1: Conceptual components of Health Horoscope

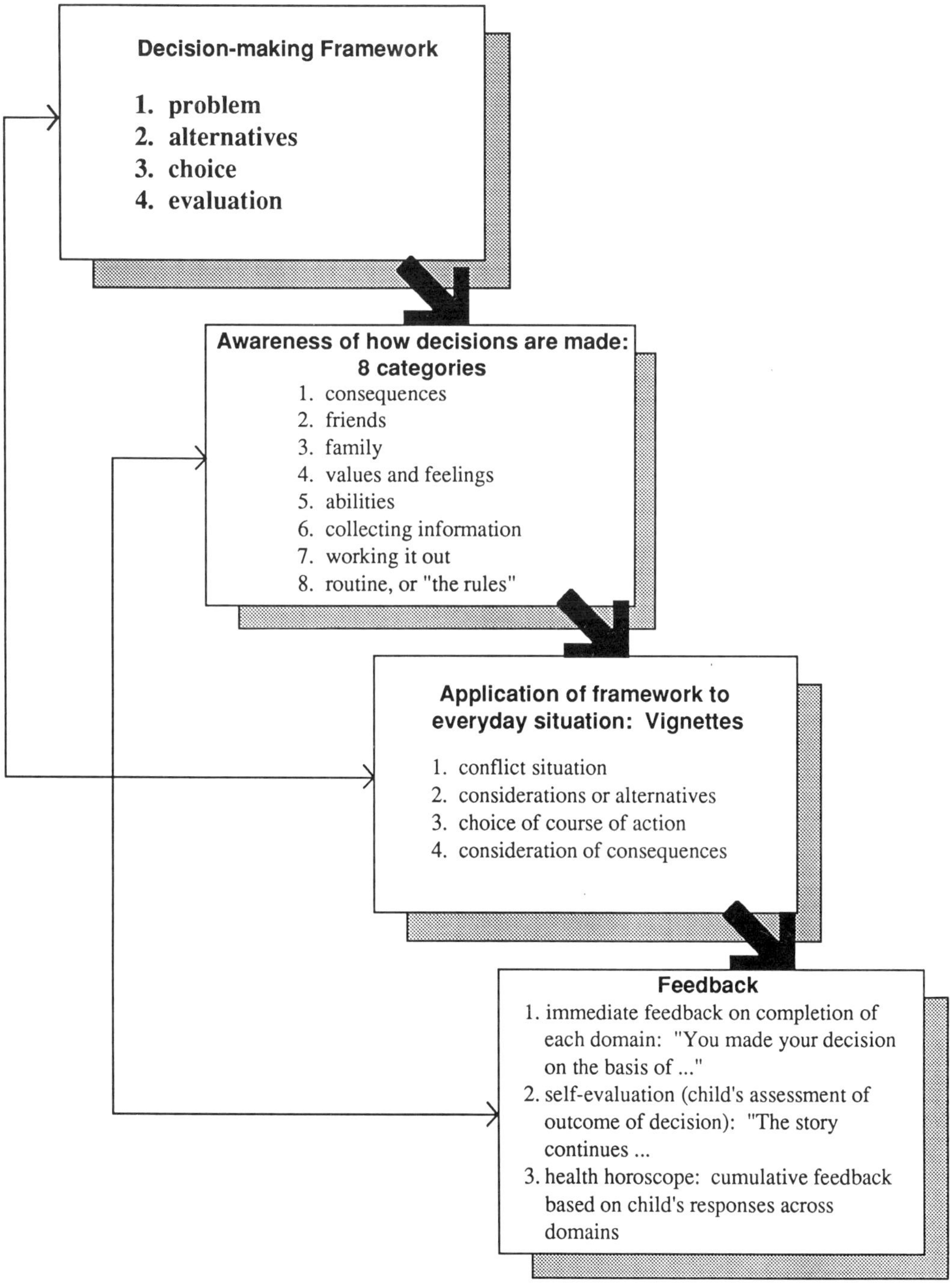

As our primary concern was to ensure that the decision-making framework be perceived by children as applicable to themselves and to their everyday lives, it was necessary to associate the model with (1) the kinds of considerations that typically entered into children's decision-making and (2) everyday situations in which children commonly had to make decisions. This requirement determined the relationships between the conceptual components of *Health Horoscope* (see Figure 1).

The decision-making framework is briefly presented as a four-step model which, as has been discussed, incorporates the major elements of most other prescriptive decision-making models. The self-awareness component introduces the child to the eight kinds of consideration that typically enter into decision-making; these correspond to the eight categories yielded by the research database. The next component is a group of typical conflict situations (also gleaned from the database) in which the child must make a health decision within a structured process that corresponds to the decision-making model. Finally, to encourage the child to reflect on and evaluate decisions, we have built in feedback mechanisms that respond directly to the considerations that informed his or her decisions.

It will be noted that the structure of the decision-making framework is reproduced in the vignette situations, and that the awareness component is reinforced in the feedback. In this way, the abstract and theoretical components of *Health Horoscope* are reflected in its dynamic and interactive components. The manner in which the four conceptual components are combined in *Health Horoscope* results in a unique approach to teaching decision-making. The last three components are of particular interest and will be examined in more detail.

The awareness component is represented by an introductory module concerning "the kinds of things you think about when you're making a decision." This module outlines the eight categories of responses listed previously and instructs the child that any of these is a possible response to a decision-making situation. Figure 2 shows selected screens from this portion of the program.

In order to coherently incorporate the database and the decision-making model in *Health Horoscope*, we constructed a series of prototypic vignettes. Each of these briefly describes a conflict situation identified from the interviews with children. In the course of playing

Figure 2: Sample screens from "Awareness in decision-making" component of *Health Horoscope*.

the game, children are asked to respond to the vignettes by considering all possible courses of action; by indicating what they would do in that situation; and by giving their reasons for the choice. In this way, the steps of the decision-making process are associated with conflicts that children can be expected to commonly encounter. Every effort was made to include the full range of information obtained from the interviews and to preserve, insofar as possible, the children's own wording in describing feelings, choices and reasons. Figure 3 presents a sample of screens developed for the hygiene conflict situation.

Figure 3: Screens from Hygiene vignette

At the conclusion of each health domain, the child is given personalized information about the kinds of considerations he or she employed in making a decision. Consideration of outcome is encouraged by giving the child an opportunity to write a story about "What happened next," describing the consequences of his or her choice. Printouts of the feedback and the story are available for each child if classroom resources permit (see Figure 4). At the conclusion of the game, more comprehensive feedback in the form of a "horoscope" is provided, summarizing each child's individual decision-making pattern. Care has been taken to provide non-judgemental feedback; emphasis is placed on promoting self-awareness with regard to personal decision-making strategies (with reference to the eight decision-making processes outlined at the beginning of the game) rather than on evaluation of particular decisions made by the child.

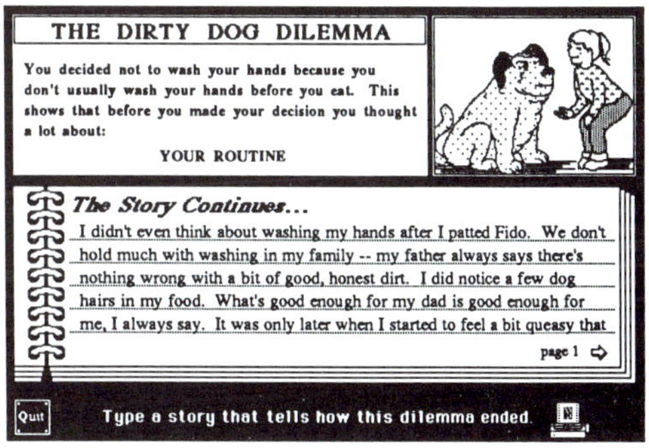

Figure 4: Sample of immediate feedback for Hygiene vignette

It should be noted that, while a conceptual model is useful for the organization of a database and absolutely essential for later evaluation of the program, it creates considerable difficulties in program design. The effective use of a decision-making framework, as it has been described, means that the same format (presentation of the conflict situation, possible choices, choice of one alternative, and reasons for the choice) must be repeated across the different health domains in a manner that is fresh and interesting to the child.

The use of Hypercard as a programming language provided as much mobility within the different components of the game as possible, given the research and educational requirements. Features and enhancements of the program include quizzes related to each of the eight health domains, a help function, a reference module about the decision-making model and a glossary.

Preliminary testing has indicated that Hypercard's graphic, movement and sound capabilities are effective in capturing and maintaining children's interest. However, the difficulty of designing creative and engaging software within the constraints of a theoretical framework should not be underestimated.

4. NEED FOR EVALUATION OF PROGRAM IMPACT

Finally, instructional software must be designed in such a way that its impact on user knowledge, attitudes and behaviour can be tested. Unless positive effects can be clearly and reliably demonstrated, no health education strategy (be it computerized instruction, role-playing, or mass-media) is likely to be adopted.

To meet this requirement, we have incorporated a tracking system in *Health Horoscope* which documents each selection made by the child in response to the components of our decision-making model. Thus, children's patterns of decision-making can be ascertained. They can also be evaluated for changes in response to educational instruction or health education interventions.

With proper safeguards for anonymity, our program can be used in the classroom in a variety of ways. The printout of the decision path and individualized feedback can be used by teachers to discuss the conflicts children face and potential strategies for their solution. The printout can also be used by a health professional on a one-to-one basis to highlight the lifestyle concerns of a particular child. Finally, the child can take the printout home to discuss with his or her family. Research with adults has shown that computerized lifestyle checklists are effective in initiating discussions about lifestyle matters between physicians and their patients (Skinner and Allen, 1983; Skinner, Allen, McIntosh and Palmer, 1985). We can, therefore, reasonably expect that our program will have a similar effect for teachers and students in the classroom.

The program will also become a research instrument to study children's health decision-making. As children go through the program, data about their decision paths will be stored (without personal identification) in retrievable form for further analysis of the patterns of child health decision-making within and between lifestyle situations, and by age, sex, and cultural background. Our aim is to identify children who consistently make poor or unhealthy decisions across lifestyle situations. Such patterns, if evident, may lead to the early identification of children at risk for poor lifestyle health habits and the subsequent development of intervention strategies. Since no investigations of this type have as yet been carried out, the data and findings generated will be unique.

5. CONCLUSION

The creation of a high-quality program in health decision-making is a time-consuming process. Our experience has shown that the key issues include the choice of a conceptual model, the inclusion of a valid database for the model and the development of an evaluation constructed around the model. Each of these requires integration of knowledge about children's health cognition with the potential of computer technology. Further, it demands the collaborative efforts of teachers, health professionals and software specialists. We believe that consideration of these issues is crucial to the creation of high-quality software that meets the health educational needs of children, and that can be evaluated for its impact on the user.

REFERENCES

de la Sota, A., Lewis, M.A., & Lewis, C. (1979). Actions for health. Don Mills, Ont.: Addison-Wesley Publishing Co.

Hamrick, M. H., Anspaugh, D. J., & Smith, D.L. (1980). Decision-making and the behavior gap. Journal of School Health, 50(8), 455-458.

Janis, I. L., & Mann, L. (1977). Decision making: A psychological analysis of conflict, choice and commitment. New York: Free Press.

Skinner, H. A., & Allen, B. A. (1983). Does the computer make a difference? Computerized versus self-report assessment of alcohol, drug and tobacco use. Journal of Consulting and Clinical Psychology, 51, 267-275.

Skinner, H. A., Allen, B., McIntosh, M. C., & Palmer, W. H. (1985). Lifestyle assessment: Applying microcomputers in family practice. British Medical Journal, 290, 212-214.

World Health Organization (1984). Health promotion: A discussion document on the concept and principles. Copenhagen: WHO Regional Office for Europe.

ACKNOWLEDGEMENTS

The development of the research base and the computer program was made possible by the generous support of the Hospital for Sick Children Foundation, the Max Bell Foundation and the University of Toronto Life Sciences Summer Graduate Scholarships. Technical support was received from the Apple Canada Education Foundation and from Computers in Education, Scarborough Board of Education.

Computers in Education
A. McDougall and C. Dowling (Editors)
Elsevier Science Publishers B.V. (North-Holland)

SUPPORTIVE ENVIRONMENT FOR CREATIVE WRITING IN CHINESE

Nancy LAW, W.W. KI, S. TSE, A.L.S. CHUNG

Department of Curriculum Studies, University of Hong Kong, Pokfulam Road, Hong Kong

The teaching of creative writing in Chinese has traditionally been done by getting the pupils to appreciate classic. The essential idea was to learn by modelling good examples of writing. Recent research findings show that writing is a complicated cognitive process involving the employment of a variety of cognitive strategies. This paper describes a computer based writing environment in Chinese which was designed to allow incorporation of teaching ideas and resource support. This supportive writing environment provides a good medium for the learning of different writing strategies in a modular fashion.

THE TEACHING OF CHINESE CREATIVE WRITING

In a survey done by the People's Education Press in 1979 on the standard of Chinese compositions written by junior secondary students in two provinces on Mainland China, it was found that only 24% of the essays examined met the required standard. Most of the essays suffered from wrongly written characters, wrong choice of words, ill-formed sentences, poor vocabulary, lack of substantial content, poor structuring of ideas, etc. There is no evidence that the quality of Chinese essays written by Hong Kong students is better than that of their Chinese counterparts' in the PRC. Chinese language teachers are thus faced with the problem of how to teach creative writing more effectively.

Hong Kong teachers are very much influenced by traditional beliefs about how someone comes to be a good writer: through reading and appreciating examples of good writing, and through frequent practices in writing. There is an age old saying that `if you can memorize three hundred poems from the Tang dynasty(the historical period when this form of literary expression flourished), even if you can't write poems, you can still borrow from them (their form and style)'. This saying summarizes very well the kind of approach that a lot of teachers still believe in: it is an approach that depends primarily on the analysis of forms and syntax of writing and imitation of the written product. Thus the memorization of classic Chinese texts has always been an important part of Chinese language learning. In terms of actual writing exercises, tasks set are normally either rigid productions of sentence patterns according to set rules, or free compositions given a general theme/ title.

Starting with Emig (1971), writing research began to look into the cognitive processes involved and the strategies employed in the course of writing. It was found that there are different stages during the process of writing (Emig 1971,;Stallard 1974,;Pianko 1979; Hays & Flower, 1980) and that there are individual differences in the cognitive process involved in the writing process (Graves 1973). These findings lead many to believe that for effective teaching of writing, one should focus on the writing process and not the finished product.

In two recent pieces of research on the writing processes of Hong Kong students in writing Chinese composition (Tse, 1982; Tse & Chan 1986) it was found that the students generally follow a common sequence of stages: pre-writing, writing and revision. The processes involved in each stage were also found to be largely common, with individual variations for some processes. The kinds of mental activities taking place in the writer's mind for the different writing

This work was supported by research grant #335/053/0012 from University of Hong Kong for the project 'A Chinese Storybook Writer for Pupils'. Special thanks are due to Mr. B.F. Chu of Shenzhen Industrial Park for technical advice on use of the Chinese Operating System.

processes are different, and good writers have a repertoire of effective cognitive strategies for successful completion of each of the different processes. For example, generation of ideas is the first process in the pre-writing stage. Effective strategies for generating ideas include association and retrieval of visual and audio images from memory. It is possible to teach each of these strategies to students so that they become more proficient at writing, through improving performance of one process at a time. Thus, instead of looking at writing as one integral process and demanding that students pay attention to all aspects of what is demanded of good writing at the same time, it should be possible to focus the teaching of writing onto the teaching of particular cognitive strategies and/or skills, offering advice and practice exercises for a particular writing process. This composing processes approach (Tse, 1984) to the teaching of writing therefore advocates a modular, cognitive processes based approach, making it possible to break down the teaching process into the organization of a number of exercises not all of which would be seen as `writing' in the conventional sense. In this project, a computer based writing tool, `Chinese Storybook Writer', is developed to provide a supportive environment to assist students in the modular development of skills and strategies required for the different stages of writing.

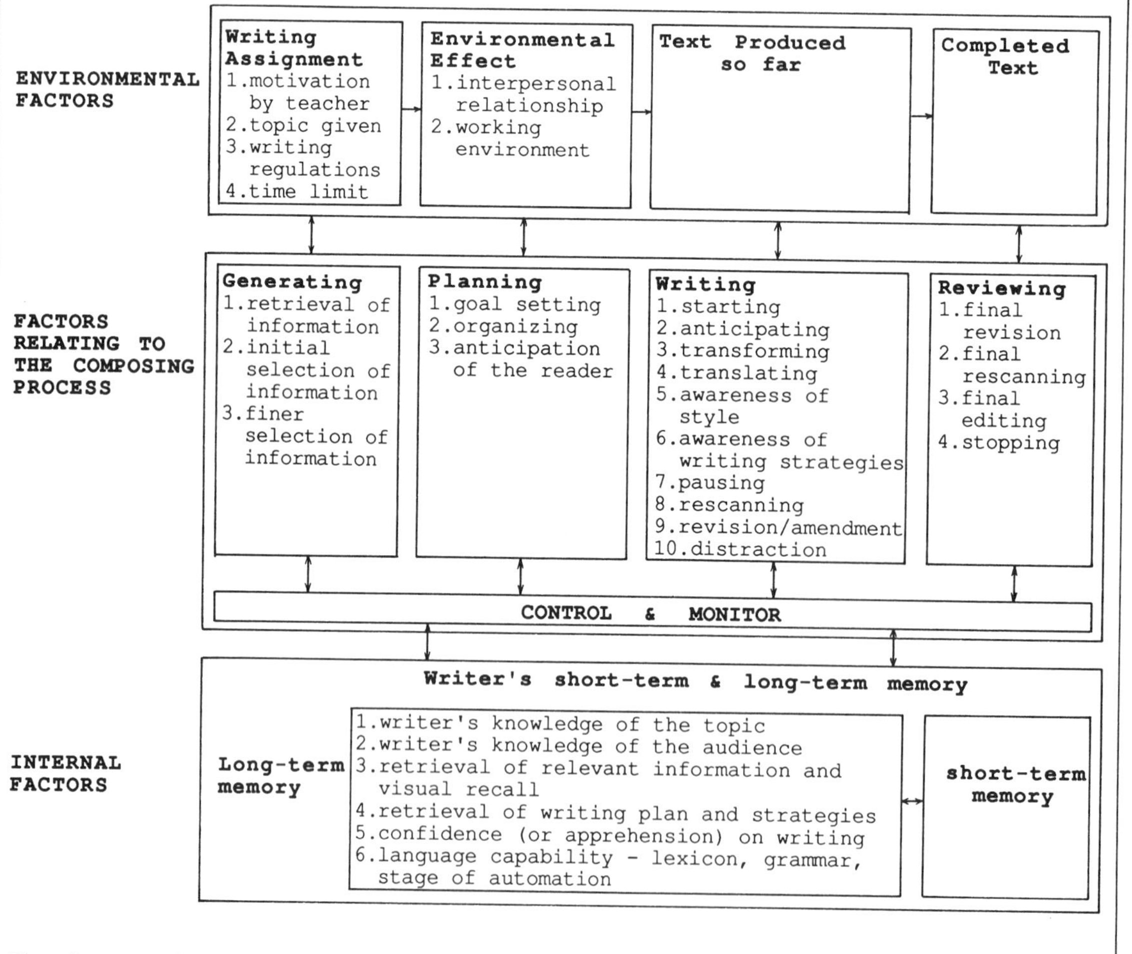

Fig. 1. A Model of the Composing Process.

BASIC FEATURES OF THE CHINESE STORY-BOOK WRITER (CSW)

The CSW is a piece of software implemented on the IBMPC for the creation of story-books in Chinese, with integrated use of text and pictures. The basic design idea of the software is that a student can get access to a number of books through the computer. Each book is composed of `pages' (cf hypercard), with each page being a basic unit of organization. Editing and copying for text and/or graphics can be done freely on the whole or parts of a page. Pages can be easily reshuffled to explore the effects of different sequencing of a story. Pages can be put in half finished form, or with just a pictorial sketch to record the idea for further work at a later stage. Users can also create empty pages to be filled later, or, alternatively they can insert pages at any point in the book. Contents in one page can later be split into more pages to allow for subsequent elaboration.

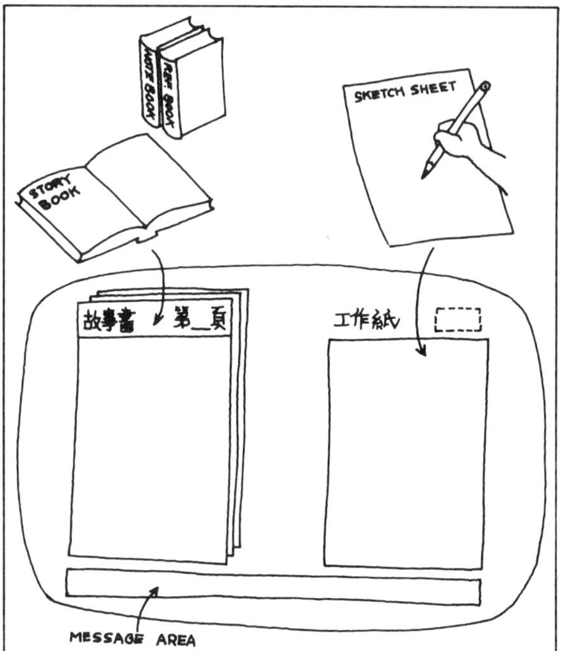

Fig.2 Screen layout of the CSW showing the design concepts of the software.

Another feature of the CSW is that the screen layout (fig. 2) is designed to provide a simple analogy to the familiar pencil-and-paper writing situation for easy understanding and mastery. The screen is divided into three fixed windows. The one on the right is reserved for the `sketch sheet' where the user can do all the writing, drawing and editing. The story s/he is producing is put on the left window and s/he can turn to any page of the story book for reference and other purposes. Direct editing of the story book is not allowed on the left window so that there is very little chance for them to accidentally lose the work they have done. After s/he is satisfied with what's written on the sketch sheet, s/he can then insert that page into the story book at the required position and start work on a new page. She can also copy the whole or parts of a page from the left window to the sketch sheet on the right for further editing. Through the left window, the user can also have access to a number of books s/he wants to open for reference and other purposes.

MODES OF USAGE FOR THE CSW

However, the CSW is not just a wordprocessor with built-in graphic capabilities. With a conventional wordprocessor, what is provided is essentially a typing, revising, formatting, and at times a proof-reading aid for the user. They make it much easier for users to revise their documents and provide valuable assistance to users in producing good looking, accurate essays (in terms of spelling). Many new word-processors also try to provide aids to the users during the pre-writing and writing stages. For example, some wordprocessors provide outlining facilities for users to plan their writing, and they are also designed to allow easy switching between planning and writing. Another useful facility provided on some wordprocessors that is of great help to authors during the writing stage is the provision of a comprehensive thesaurus. However, these facilities are provided with the expert writers in mind and they would seldom be made use of unless the user has already mastered the particular strategy that the facility is designed for.

The CSW is a supportive environment implemented on the computer to assist novice writers in the development of effective cognitive strategies for writing. It is designed to allow the incorporation of supportive resources to aid writers in the various processes of writing and can thus become a good teaching medium for teachers of Chinese creative writing. The CSW is designed for use by pupils learning to write in Chinese (there are more powerful Chinese word-processors on the market in terms of the features demanded of word-processors) and it is anticipated that most of the time it would be available to the users not as stand-alone software but together with teaching resources.

The resource support is provided mainly through the other two books that the user has access to through the left window (fig.

2). It is anticipated that one of them would be a reference book provided by the teacher and the other one would be a note-book used by the student for jotting down ideas, or to make copies of selected words, phrases and pictures for later use. The notebook may also contain items (text or pictures) that the student wants to retain from previous exercises.

The provision of graphics facilities on the CSW is also another important resource. It not only made possible the incorporation of pictorial elements with text in the writings produced by the user. The use of visual imagery is the basis of many strategies that may be used in the pre-writing stage for the generation of ideas. In his work on memory retrieval of "imaginal" information, Kosslyn (1973, 1975) found that many visual properties of concrete objects could be stored in memory in either a propositional or an imaginal form. For writing to be more attractive, the descriptions need to be more detailed and full-bodied. It is possible to retrieve information about properties of concrete objects by scanning a mental image. Strategies like association and information retrieval through successively zooming in on a visual image are effective in generating ideas for descriptive essays. To teach novice writers these strategies, visual cues would be much more effective than textual ones and should be used at least at the initial stages. The graphic feature of the CSW can thus be an important facility for teachers to design exercises on these strategies.

SOME SAMPLE USES OF THE CSW

The following are some possible ways of using the CSW for the development of specific cognitive strategies for creative writing.

An exercise on the association strategy. One useful form of exercise on the association strategy is to give pupils a set of pictures and ask them to exercise their imagination to write a short story involving all of the pictures (see fig. 3 for an example). There are a number of advantages in implementing this exercise on the computer. Firstly, we can easily provide a wide variety of pictures to the pupils, with the possibility of each pupil getting a different set. For those students who can already start making up a story soon after seeing the pictures, they can of course go straight on to further elaboration of details and the other stages of writing. However, for those who find it very difficult to start the imagination rolling, prompting questions can be offered to pupils to suggest ways to start thinking. Pupils can choose to start working with prompts for any of the pictures by typing in an appro-priate number. Another advantage of this computer based exercise is that we can provide prompts to individual pupils so that pupils can ponder upon the cuing questions (which can vary according to the pictures picked) at their own pace and choose their own preferred sequence. When the pupil wants to create links between the various pictures, s/he can turn to a page that holds all the pictures and questions.

1. 這是什麼?
(What is this?)
2. 想像一下，你在什麼場合看見這東西?
(Try to think for a moment, under what circumstances would you see this?)
3. 你可以用它來做什麼
(What can you do with it?)
4. 它是張開著的嗎?
(Is it open?)

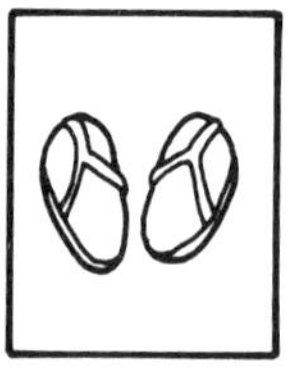

1. 這是什麼?
(What is this?)
2. 想像一下，你在什麼時候會穿著它?
(Try to think for a moment, when would you put it on?)
3. 你見過多少種不同的式樣設計?
(How many different kinds of design have you seen?)
4. 除了保護雙腿，你還用過它來做什麼?
(Besides protecting your feet, what else have you used it for?)

1. 這是什麼?
(What is this?)
2. 想像一下，你在什麼地方，什麼時間看見牠出沒?
(Try to think for a moment, where and when have you seen it?)
3. 見到牠，你有什麼情緒反應?
(What emotional reactions would you have on seeing it?)
4. 牠有什麼特點?
(What special features docs it possess?)

1. 這是什麼?
(What is this?)
2. 它有什麼用?
(What can it bc used for?)
3. 想像一下，你會把它放在哪裡?
(Try to think for a moment, where would you put it?)
4. 它有多大？外型設計是否美觀？能否有效運作?
(How large is it? Does it look nice? Can it work properly?)

1. 這是什麼?
(What is this?)
2. 想像一下，是什麼品種？什麼顏色?
(Try to think for a moment, what species is it? what colour is it?)
3. 你會把它放在哪裡?
(Where would you put it?)
4. 它令你想起什麼?
(What does it make you think about?)

Fig.3
A sample set of pictures together with some prompting questions to be used as an exercise on association strategy.

An exercise on information retrieval strategy.
To encourage pupils to exercise their imagination, perception and to develop their ability of image description, variations of the following exercise would be very useful.

Here the task for the pupils is to write a description of a human face. First of all, a pupil constructs the human face s/he wants to describe by choosing each facial feature (hair style, shape of eyes, nose, etc.) from a bank of such images stored in the computer. S/he then writes a short paragraph describing the constructed image as precisely as possible (the teacher can also offer further help by providing a set of vocabulary useful for the task). This written description would be read by another pupil who would then be required to construct what s/he thinks the described face is like. These two constructed images can subsequently be compared. This is a very interesting exercise which makes a deep impression on the pupils. The CSW enables this task of designing and constructing the human face to be easier and more cheaply available to a large class of students than if it were to be done using non-computer media.

An exercise on different ways of sequencing a piece of writing.
There are different ways of recounting a story besides telling it in sequential order of the episodes that took place. For example, fig. 4a shows the story of the chicken family and the cat in the order of its development in time. However, that may not be the most interesting way to tell the story. Pupils can be encouraged to explore the different possible impacts made by different sequencing schemes on readers by reordering the pictures. For example, fig.

a. Story of the chicken family in sequential order of time development.

b. The same story told in reverse sequence: Why is the chicken family so happy?

Fig.4. An example exercise on different ways of sequencing an essay.

4b shows the same story told in reverse order: starting with the last scene and asking why is the chicken family so happy? Further training in linguistic skills can also be provided through asking pupils to modify the story (the written commentary attached to each picture) according to the sequencing chosen.

How CSW can help pupils learn to plan their writing.
Conventional outliners (cf those provided on some word-processors) may not be useful for novice writers. They tend to look too well organized to be able to reflect the hazy thinking of some writers in their ideation stage. Furthermore, it is designed to capture only the hierarchically organized structures. Pupils can be prompted to put down words, phrases, or even pictures wherever they like on the sketch sheet as they proceed with the generation of ideas. These not only provide a visual reminder for them on what has been passing through their minds. In addition, they may subsequently move these elements to change their positions in order to reflect the sequential time development, spatial distribution of objects, etc. as required when they proceed with the planning. These pages from the sketch sheet can be clipped onto their notebook (c.f. fig. 2) to form a plan for the essay which they can refer back to during their writing process.

LOOKING AHEAD

So far, the CSW has proved to be attractive mainly because of its good graphic capabilities and its design concept of allowing incorporation of resources to aid in the cognitive processes involved in writing. The underlying assumption is that the CSW would be used as an integral part of a writing course where the presence and expertise of a teacher would be mandatory. One important deficiency of the CSW is its inability to offer interaction with the students during the writing process. If the software can be further developed so as to allow different feedback to be provided to a student according to the different responses s/he makes in reaction to the prompts provided, we can see that the scope of application of this software tool can be greatly extended.

REFERENCE

Emig,J. (1971). *The Composing Processes of Twelfth Graders.* Illionis: NTCE.

Kosslyn, S.M. (1973). Scanning visual images: Some structural implications. *Perception & Psychophysics*, 14, 90-94.

Kosslyn, S.M. (1975). Information representation in visual images. *Cognitive Psychology*, 7, 341-370.

Graves, D.H.(1973). *Children's Writing: The Writing Process of Seven Year Old Children.* Buffallo: University. of N.Y.

Hays,J. & Flower,L. (1980). Identifying the Organization of Writing Processes. In L.Gregg & E.Steinberg (Ed.). Cognitive Processes in Writing (p3-30). Hillsdale, N.J.: Lawrence Erlbaum Associates.

The People's Education Press (1982). A Survey of the Writing Abilities of Secondary School Students, *Communication of Teaching of Chinese*, No. 7, p34-36.

Pianko, S. (1979). A Description of the Composing Process of the College Freshman Writer, *RTE*, Vol. 13, p5-22.

Stallard, C.C. (1974). An Analysis of the Writing Behavior of good Student Writers, *RTE* , Vol.8, p206-218.

Tse, S.K. (1983). *The Composing Process of Secondary School Students in Hong Kong.* M.A. thesis, the School of Education , the Chinese University of Hong Kong.

Tse S.K. (1984). The composing process of senior secondary students in Chinese, *Journal of Chinese Language* (Hong Kong), 12, p.43.

Tse, S.K., Shem S.K. (1988). Teaching Chinese Writing by Teaching the Composing Processes. *Proceedings of the International Conference on the Teaching of Chinese,* p153-163. organized by the Hong Kong Chinese Educational Association. July 14-16, 1988. Hong Kong: Hong Kong Cultural and Educational Publishing Co.

Computers in Education
A. McDougall and C. Dowling (Editors)
Elsevier Science Publishers B.V. (North-Holland)

EXPLORING TWO-DIMENSIONAL PLANES WITH A LOGO MICROWORLD

Bruce W. MCMILLAN

Department of Education, University of Otago, PO Box 56, Dunedin, New Zealand

This paper discusses children's learning of a particular mathematics concept. A constructivist perspective on learning (based on the work of Vygotsky and Piaget) is adopted, and it is suggested that these theoretical frameworks are particularly appropriate both for integrating ideas about children's understanding of mathematics, and for investigating the context within which the learning occurs.

The paper outlines a study (which will be reported in more detail in the actual conference presentation) involving twenty eight- and nine-year-old children's use of a Logo microworld which deals with the notion of number planes: that is, with the location of points on a two-dimensional surface. The explicit task involved production of a picture comprising any combination of eight different elements, all of which could be located on the screen (and subsequently printed out) using simple ordered number pairs, or coordinates. The implicit task involved learning about ordered number pairs, and an understanding of map-reading skills.

The results will be presented in terms of the change in knowledge about number planes, and the extent to which this knowledge appears to generalise to map-reading skills. Some implications for mathematics learning will also be discussed.

1. INTRODUCTION

International concerns about the effectiveness of mathematics teaching at elementary levels are reflected in New Zealand. At the same time, new resources are being introduced to accompany recent syllabus developments for mathematics (Department of Education, 1985). These curriculum materials currently see only a minor place for computer-based experience, yet the undoubted motivating power of computers cannot be ignored when attempting to respond to concerns about teaching in this area.

The present study examines an issue related to children's learning of some particular mathematics ideas. First, some theoretical issues are reviewed, and the current context for mathematics learning in New Zealand schools outlined. Then, a study (which is still in progress at the time of writing) is outlined. Data from the study will be presented and discussed when this paper is presented at the Conference.

2. THE BACKGROUND LITERATURE

This paper reflects the premise that mathematics involves thinking based on real or concrete experiences (Saxe, 1988), and that associated cognitive developments derive from integrating and reflecting on such experiences. It is a view which reflects a Piagetian theory of development. Yet attempts to build Piagetian notions into specific curricula are not widely supported. Many writers assume children should only attempt to solve problems "appropriate" to their level of cognitive development. For example, Copeland (1974) claims that conventional reference systems to compare distance and positions are only established around the age of formal operations, and that consequently, map-making tasks should only be given to children in junior high school level. More recently, however, Blades and Spencer (1989) have demonstrated that four- to six-year-old children were able to learn to identify coordinates when they were labelled with familiar symbols.

Arithmetic has been the subject of more investigations into mathematical thinking than has geometry, but there are some clear indications from studies into children's computational abilities. One of the most significant of these (in the current context) is that basic number concepts are constructed by children on the basis of their "ordinary" experience. In part, this reflects the fact that much mathematical learning is associated with the beliefs and practices of particular cultures (Stigler and Baranes, 1988). Yet children's ordinary, culturally specific experiences are often ignored by much "formal" school work in mathematics (Resnick, 1989). Shared discussion of problems in mathematics is suggested by such writers as one strategy for improving children's abilities in the area.

There has been debate recently in New Zealand about curriculum material for mathematics. For example, Young-Loveridge (1987) reports that young children have more understanding of numeracy than is commonly believed. (This is in part because many educators have mistaken ideas about Piagetian "stages" of cognitive development). There is less information about children's understanding of geometric ideas, although such material itself is represented in recent mathematics curriculum development.

"Locating points on a number plane" is one of fifteen geometry sub-topics in the syllabus for mathematics from Junior Classes to Standard Four, and may be introduced during years three and four. The curriculum materials give relatively little attention to the topic, which is introduced in a supplementary booklet for School Mathematics 2 (Booklet B8, Graphs); it comprises 18 pages, three of which deal with row and column coordinates for maps, and six with number pairs. Number planes also appear as a three-page unit of work in School Mathematics 4, where number pairs for locating points on a two-dimensional plane, and map coordinates are again used. All these activities lead to more advanced concepts, such as Cartesian coordinates; but the latter topics are generally introduced at a more advanced level of schooling (secondary).

The advent of computers facilitates a new perspective on children's learning experiences, for they combine great motivational appeal with powerful opportunities for individual or small-group learning. Logo has been described (Papert, 1980) as enabling teachers to establish a learning environment in which children not only use mathematical concepts comfortably, but also think about their own concepts. It can help children learn specific ideas by means of small-scale learning environments termed "microworlds", which enable children to explore powerful ideas of intrinsic interest and discover the more complex meanings they represent. A principle at the heart of Logo is that the computer should provide an environment within which children can explore powerful ideas. Logo language is an example. It is easy to get into; and a few simple commands, expressed in the kind of language they are accustomed to using, enable children to construct simple designs, and develop powerful modifications of those designs.

But children do not need to master Logo commands before being able to benefit from such a learning environment. Teachers may prepare Logo procedures in order to focus children's learning experience on particular concepts. These teacher-made, small-scale learning environments are "microworlds".

The main idea behind a "microworld" emphasizes children being free to explore ideas, and to construct their own meanings for events, concepts, and relations, as they work with Logo. For example, Papert writes:

"A central idea behind our learning environment was that children would be able to use powerful ideas from mathematics and science as instruments of personal power. For example, geometry would become a means to create visual effects on a television screen." (1980, p.212)

The present paper argues that the notion of a microworld needs to be broadened to include more than the learner's interaction with a computer-based environment. One published investigation of microworlds (Thompson & Wang, 1988) indicates that it is beneficial for children to function in pairs, for this enables them to share ideas generated by the microworld. The importance of communication in exploring a microworld signifies that the "learning environment" must comprise not only the computer-based experience, but also the specific learning environment in which the microworld is explored (in this case, the paired learning setting) as well as the general classroom context. Thus the Piagetian perspective Papert contributes must be further elaborated by reference to a Vygotskyian emphasis on the social construction of meaning.

At the heart of Vygotsky's theory is the notion that children's ability to function is influenced both by their "innate ability" and by the social context within which they operate. The range of achievement children can demonstrate (the "zone of proximal development") is thus influenced by the extent to which they are provided with adult guidance, and/or with assistance from "more capable peers" (Vygotsky, 1978, p.86).

There are a number of sources of support for these ideas. A major review of cooperative learning methods (Bossert, 1988) emphasizes the importance of mediating factors (such as cognitive processing and the oral rehearsal of principles and strategies) as well as the motivational power of cooperative learning. A number of studies have also revealed the power of peer tutoring in reading or language work (for example, Wheldall and Glynn, 1989), although these have largely been undertaken from within a behavioural theoretical framework. There are few Vygotskian studies, but a seminal paper by Forman and Cazden (1985) concludes that:

"the Vygotskian perspective enables us to see that collaborative tasks requiring data generation, planning, and management can provide another set of valuable experiences for children. In these tasks, a common set of assumptions, procedures, and information needs to be constructed. These tasks require children to integrate their conflicting task conceptions into a mutual plan." (p.343)

The literature reviewed here suggests that a problem-solving approach to mathematics learning, with the use of a Logo microworld providing a specific area of learning to be encountered, could be profitable.

3. OBJECTIVES

The purpose of this project is to examine the process by which elementary school children explore a number plane microworld, and the extent to which they consequently learn a particular concept in mathematics (that ordered pairs of numbers can be used to locate objects on a plane surface). It is also intended to examine the extent to which this learning transfers from the computer-based to microworld, to map-reading tasks (using a three-dimensional village as a model, which is to be replicated in two dimensions).

It is hypothesized that in using the microworld, the process of discussing the placement of a graphic element within the total picture to be constructed will lead to increased specificity in terminology for positioning, and to a discovery of the role of ordered pairs of numbers. This discovery should also transfer to other map-reading tasks. For this reason, a post-test-only task (translating a three-dimensional model onto a two-dimensional plan) is being used as a dependent measure.

4. METHOD

The sample comprised 20 eight- and nine-year-old children from a small-city primary (elementary) school. The children in this sample were chosen on the basis of their performance on a pre-test of activities related to number plane and map-reading coordinates, such that "more competent" children were paired with those "less competent".

The measures included pre- and post-treatment pen-and-paper tasks to establish children's understanding of number planes and coordinates; and a post-treatment individual task involving reproducing the plan of a village (from a three-dimensional model) in order to test for the generalisation of the coordinate reference system. The children's planning for their microworld explorations was monitored individually.

5. Data

At the time of writing, data collection is still in process. The variables being investigated in this study are: the total number of sessions spent exploring the microworld; the degree of change in planning for the microworld picture construction; and the relationship between number plane activity and map-reading skills. Individual discussions with the children (undertaken as they enter their log-book records) is also expected to reveal the qualitative aspects of the planning the children will follow.

A pilot study for the major project explored this microworld with six eight-year-old children (three boys and three girls) in their fourth year of elementary education. Four learning sessions each from 20 to 40 minutes in duration were conducted. The results showed that all six children grasped the idea of using ordered pairs of numbers to locate points on a plane, both in terms of a five-by-five alphabet grid and a ten-by-ten graph, and coped with the other tasks presented. The final planning task indicated that they had varying levels of success in planning the product (graphic outcome), with most only making a few alterations to their plan in order to produce the picture they intended.

The final plan and its product were rated on a five-point scale (from "excellent" to "not satisfactory"). There was some change in the rank order positions the children attained. There was sufficient change in these children's rank order positions to produce an almost zero correlation (rho = 0.09) between the pre- and post-test assessments, although the pre-test and the final plan scores showed a moderate correlation (rho = 0.54). However, the small size of the pilot group precludes serious interpretation of these results.

It is clear from the pilot study that the microworld can be used with children at this level, and that working in pairs can be productive. It was decided that a greater amount of planning should be encouraged in order to stimulate the articulation and sharing of relevant ideas. A number of amendments were thus introduced into the design of the study to be reported here.

6. DISCUSSION

This study is significant in that it explores a new emphasis within the mathematics syllabus introduced to New Zealand in 1985. It also uses a novel and theoretically significant strategy (based on paired learning) to develop children's understanding of number planes. While this concept plane is familiar within mathematics, it has become a more prominent feature of the recently-introduced mathematics syllabus: the sequencing of ideas, and integration of different mathematical concepts, has become more explicit. Thus an early appreciation of geometric relations is assumed to relate not only to the later use of grid or map references, and to Cartesian coordinates, but also to mathematical relations more generally.

REFERENCES

Blades, M. and Spencer, C. (1989), Young children's ability to use coordinate references, Journal of Genetic Psychology, 150, 5-18.

Bossert, S.T. (1988), Cooperative activities in the classroom, In E.Z. Rothkopf (Ed.), Review of Research in Education, v.15. Washington, DC: American Educational Research Association, pp. 225-252.

Copeland, R.W. (1974), How children learn mathematics, (2nd ed.), New York, NY: MacMillan.

Department of Education, (1985), Mathematics: Junior classes to Standard Four, Wellington: Department of Education, School Publications Branch.

Forman, E.A. and Cazden, C.B. (1985), Exploring Vygotskian perspectives in education: The value of peer interaction, In J.V. Wertsch (Ed.), Culture, communication, and cognition: Vygotskian perspectives, Cambridge: Cambridge University Press, pp.323-347.

Papert, S. (1980), Mindstorms, New York, NY: Basic Books.

Resnick, L.B. (1989), Developing mathematical knowledge, American Psychologist, 44, 162-169.

Saxe, G.B. (1988), Candy selling and math learning, Educational Researcher, 17 (6), 14-21.

Thompson, A.D. and Wang H-M.C. (1988), Effects of a Logo microworld on student ability to transfer a concept, Journal of Educational Computing Research, 4, 335 347.

Wheldall, K. and Glynn, T. (1989),

Effective classroom learning, Oxford: Basil Blackwell.

Vygotsky, L.S. (1978), Mind in society, Cambridge: Harvard University Press.

Young-Loveridge, J.M. (1987), Learning mathematics, British Journal of Developmental Psychology, 5, 155-167.

Computers in Education
A. McDougall and C. Dowling (Editors)
Elsevier Science Publishers B.V. (North-Holland)

SOME RESULTS IN TEACHING MATHEMATICS WITH APPLICATION OF COMPUTER DRILLS AND LOGIC GAMES IN PRIMARY SCHOOLS

Mariana NENOVA

Sofia University, Department for Primary School Pedagogics, Bulgaria

The paper describes some of the results from a longitudinal study whose aim was to find out the contribution of computer-supported education in creating computational habits, in the development of logical thinking and in reinforcing positive personal qualities in children aged 6-8. The emphasis in the paper is on the achievements in giving the children mathematical knowledge and creating in them computational habits and skills.*

BACKGROUND INFORMATION AND ORGANIZATION OF THE EXPERIMENT

The goal of the study was to create a methodology for introducing original specialized software in the teaching of mathematics in the primary school. The experiment was carried out with the pupils in two classes from two different schools in Sofia, giving them computer-supported training for two years using two academic hours weekly. Computer games were used for reinforcement of the mathematical operations included in the standard teaching programme for the primary school. The games were selected in such a way as to enhance logical thinking in the children, to increase their interest in mathematics and to form in them personal qualities like strictness, punctuality, consistency and stability of attension. Along with this, the children were instructed how to use the computer equipment which was quite new for them: how to place discs in the disc-drive, how to control images on the screen using the key-board, etc. These are skills which they will undoubtly need in their further education in a computerized enviroment. More details about the experiments are given in the list of publications below.

GENERAL DESCRIPTION OF THE METHODOLOGY FOR INTERPRETATION OF RESULTS

In order to be able to make our measurements, we compared two groups of children: an "experimental group" which consisted of the children in the computer-trained classes, and a "control group" which included both the chidren from the classes which were selected for the experiment /the experimental group/ and children from the neighbourhood studying in other classes but living in the same social environment. The measurements were made using batteries of classical tests, specially designed tests, expert evaluations, etc. The following tools were used:

a) objective tests (asking the student to identify the error in one of several solutions of mathematical problems) and classical written tests (in which case the student is given mathematical problems and are expected to solve them, as this has been done for years in all schools) for assessment of the mathematical knowledge of children;
b) tests for logical thinking
- comparative analyses
- tests for consistency in thiking
- tests for assciation relations in a given situation;

c) psychological tests: the Pieron-Voser test and labyrinths;
d) subjective assessments of the personal qualities of the children given by their teachers;
e) children's assessments of the communication skills of the other children in a small group;
f) self-assessment of children's interests.

Here we shall present only the aggregate results from the assessment of the mathematical knowledge of the children at the end of grade two (i.e. at the end of the experiment which lasted two years and covered the first and the second grade).

---

* The study was a part of a research project completed with the financial support of the Committee for Science at the Council of Ministers in Bulgaria, contract 658.

The table below contains the nummber of pupils who were studied during the experiment (E - experimental group, C - control group):

	School 1			School 2		
	Class 1		Class 2	Class 1		Class 2
	E	C	C	E	C	C
Boys	10	9	12	13	4	11
Girls	5	7	13	7	4	16

METHODOLOGY OF MEASURING MATHEMATICAL ACHIEVEMENT IN THE END OF GRADE TWO

Our approach to checking the mathematical knowledge in children took into account the presence of two levels in mastering the learning material. Therefore we wanted to find out:

- if the obligatory minimum of knowledge and skills on the basic mathematical operstions has been internalized, and
- if the children are able to apply this knowledge creatively, in standard and in non-standard situations, for solving equations with multiplication and division.

In order to measure mathematical achievement we used both objective tests and classical written tests.

By means of the objective test we wanted both to check the knowledge, skills and habits of the children in the field of mathematics, and to find out and record the eventual ability of the children from the experimental group to make correct decisions in a given situation. The assumption was that as a result of their work with computer programmes and the reading of mathema tical problems on the screen, solving them and receiving a feed back about the correctness of their solution, and also by making their decisions about what is to be done next, the pupils from the experimental group would have improved their decision - making abilities.

The tests were presented on blank sheets where the mathematical expressions or equations were given with their solution but in one of the cases there was a deliberate error in the solution, while the remaining two examples of the same type of problem were correctly solved. The pupils were asked to make corrections where they considered this necessary (see fig. 1.)

The classical written tests contained the same type of problems, only the students were expected to solve on their own, i.e. to perform the necessary mathematical operations.

Both the obective and the classical tests for the first level included the following tupes of problems:

1.a) addition of bi-figural numbers with carrying in, the sum never exceeding 100;
1.b) subtraction of-figural numbers with carrying out;
2.a) general cases of table multiplication;
2.b) special cases of table multiplication;
3.a) general cases of table division;
3.b) special cases of table division;
4.a) addition of tri-figural numbers without carrying in;
4.b) subtraction of tri-figural numbers without carrying out.

The objective and the classical tests for the second level included the following equations:

1.) a.x=b   3.) x:a=b
2.) a:x=b   4.) a.x=b.c
where a, b, c are concrete numbers.

In the interpretation of the results from the objective tests we considered the following alternatives (see fig.1):

1. The arithmetic case contains an error on the blank sheet, but the pupil has not corrected it.
2. The error has been identified by the pupil, but in correcting it he has made another error.
3. The pupil has made an unnecessary correction into a correctly solved problem on the blank sheet.
4. The student had made a right correction in a problem which contained a deliberate error on the blank sheet.

The results from the classical written tests were interpreted taking into account the two possible alternatives-correctly performed mathematical operations, and errors made.

The time for complection of each objective test and each classical test was recorded for all students.

STATISTICAL INSTRUMENTS FOR ANALYSIS OF RESULTS

Classical methods were applied like Student's t-test, analysis of variance and discrimination analysis. The latter two revealed the domination of factors in the experimental and in the control group and the mathematical learning contained in the software (types of problems and methods for their solution). Some special methods of Data Analysis were used as well, like dual scaling, clustering, integral indices, etc.

ANALYSIS OF RESULTS

RESULTS FROM THE OBJECTIVE AND THE CLASSICAL TESTS FOR THE FIRST LEVEL

The special cases which we emphasized more, followin the recommendation of the expermental classes were:1, 2, 3.a and 4.a from the list. The results obtained in the experimental group were better than those in the control group, the difference being statistically significant.

Little attention was given in the development in the computer drills to cases 3.b and 4.b. The corresponding results from the tests do not show statistically significant differences, although the average values in the experimental group are better as compared with those in the control group.

The classical written tests reveal again better averages in the experimental group, although there is no statistically significant domination in all kinds of errors.

RESULTS FROM THE OBJECTIVE AND THE CLASSICAL TESTS FOR THE SECOND LEVEL

The results show a strong statistically significant difference in favour of the experimental group. An interesting fact was observed. The equations of the first type are the most frequented in the mathematical textbooks and the teachers give them more attention in the standart lessons. This is probably the reason why the results for this type of problems had no statistically significant differences. In the case of the remaining 3 types of equations, however, the students from the experimental group showed better results, with statistically significant differences. This means that the experiment has contributed to the formation of skills for applying old knowledge in a new situation.

As to the time needed for solving the problems, in 2 of the 4 cases there was a statistical difference (p 0.05). In the other two cases there was a similar tendency. There are no statistically significant differences between boys and girls with regards to the degree of mastering the new knowledge.

CONCLUSIONS

The application of the software and the methodology for applying it in extra-school activities has a positive effect in the following cases:

1. When it is necessary to make a correct decision in a familiar situation (for example, to identify errors in problems of a familiar type).

2. For development of a new type of "visual culture", i.e. the children from the experimental group internalize and analyze the information better when it is presented in a typed form. This is particularly important for the creation of habits for independent work with textbooks and other literature which is required for the further development of the children into creative and independent persons.

3. It assists the students by improving their abilities in transferring old knowledge in a new situation.

4. The applied methodology for assessing the results from the longitudial experiments makes it possible to identify the role of computer-assisted training, as the results from this training are compared with and differentiated from those from standard teaching.

5. Contrary to the negative influence frequently described in the literature of some software and some computer drills on boys and girls, in our case the results were not influenced by sex differences.

LITERATURE

[1] Nenova, M. Computer Games and Mathematics for the First Grade Pupils (Second International Conference: Children in the Information Age, Bulgaria, May '87, Preprints N 2, 109-124)

[2] Nenova, M. Why Use Computers? Better Use a Piece of Chalk (Informatica i matematika, 1988, N 4) (in Bulgarian)

[3] Nenova, M. Correction of Errors and Feedback Using Software in Primary Schools (7th Workshop on "Problem of Informatics and its Application,'88)

Objective test - level one

<table>
<tr><td rowspan="1">1</td><td colspan="2">34
+ 48
82</td><td colspan="2">26
+ 67
92</td><td colspan="2">46
+ 24
70</td><td colspan="2">53
- 17
35</td><td colspan="2">64
- 57
7</td><td colspan="2">73
- 55
18</td></tr>
<tr><td rowspan="2">2</td><td colspan="4">7 . 5 = 35</td><td colspan="4">8 . 9 = 73</td><td colspan="4">7 . 7 = 49</td></tr>
<tr><td colspan="4">0 . 3 = 3</td><td colspan="4">1 . 5 = 5</td><td colspan="4">a . 1 = a</td></tr>
<tr><td rowspan="2">3</td><td colspan="4">56 : 8 = 7</td><td colspan="4">36 : 6 = 6</td><td colspan="4">42 : 7 = 6</td></tr>
<tr><td colspan="4">0 : 4 = 1</td><td colspan="4">0 : 5 = 0</td><td colspan="4">3 : 3 = 1</td></tr>
<tr><td>4</td><td colspan="2">324
+ 153
477</td><td colspan="2">824
+ 131
965</td><td colspan="2">326
+ 263
589</td><td colspan="2">324
- 121
213</td><td colspan="2">476
- 154
322</td><td colspan="2">572
- 361
211</td></tr>
</table>

Objective test - level two

1	7 . x = 42 x = 42 : 7 = 6	x . 8 = 56 x = 56 : 8 = 7	9 . x = 72 x = 72 : 9 = 9
2	36 : x = 9 x = 36 : 9 = 4	56 : x = 7 x = 56 : 7 = 8	32 : x = 4 x = 32 : 4 = 7
3	x : 8 = 4 x = 4 . 8 = 32	x : 6 = 7 x = 6 . 7 = 42	x : 8 = 7 x = 8 . 7 = 56
4	3 . x = 9 . 2 3 . x = 18 x = 6	5 . x = 10 . 3 5 . x = 30 x = 4	x . 4 = 6 . 2 x . 4 = 12 x = 3

Figure 1

Computers in Education
A. McDougall and C. Dowling (Editors)
Elsevier Science Publishers B.V. (North-Holland)

MEANINGFUL LANGUAGE LEARNING IN THE AGE OF TECHNOLOGY

Bev Pacey

Computer Consultant, South Coast Region, Queensland.

Increasingly, teachers are being called upon to make decisions about computer use in their classrooms. Many of these decisions are made about short-term goals for computer use, and are made by those who see the computer as just another fad, to be placed in an already crowded curriculum. Educators often seek ways to slot the technology into the existing curriculum, rather than looking for innovative ways of using it to restructure their classrooms, and, indeed, education. The empowerment of teachers to make their own choices about how to use technology for improved learning in their classrooms mirrors the need for informed decision-making about long-term goals for computer use. This paper concerns language learning and technology. Its purpose is to encourage educators to reflect on what they are doing to promote language learning in their classrooms and to raise their awareness about the use of technology in language development. Finally, some activities which schools are using to make language learning more meaningful for their students will be outlined.

1. LEARNING LANGUAGE

Language learning should not be viewed as merely an academic task; language is a social function. We learn to speak, read and write to communicate, to fulfil our needs, to relate to others, for pleasure and to make sense of the world. Reading and writing also involve an active thinking process. Boomer and Spender [1976: 13-14] make this point about the use of language as thinking:

> Another aspect of language which is too little understood is its relationship with thought...Language is not just a means ofpenetrating social and cultural barriers; it is the cutting edge of our minds as they confront new experiences,information and ideas.

Holdaway [1985:2] also writes about the importance of reading and writing; he says

> Power resides more than ever in the ability to write. Reading, on the other hand, is essential to participation.

1.1 LANGUAGE LEARNING IN SCHOOLS

Traditionally, children in primary schools engage in a variety of language activities which aim to increase their knowledge about language. Older students copy notes from the blackboard (or, in the age of technology, from an overhead projector), fill in answers in work- books, or on stencilled sheets, "do" projects. But these activities, which deal with parts of language, often have no real meaningful application for students.

Much of the writing which is done in schools is what Johnson [1988] calls "prowess writing" - writing which is done for the sole purpose of demonstrating the writer's prowess. Other writing activities are carried out to demonstrate that the child knows something from previous instruction - to show that the child has learnt certain information. Johnson says that this type of writing is in stark contrast to the language which happens in the real world [ibid,30].

In school, writing tasks have often been presented in isolation, without any real audience or purpose for the students. Johnson names the existence of an audience as "the central feature of all writing" [ibid,26]. He also believes that if writing is to be functional, it must also have a purpose. Johnson talks about children writing invitations to a party which were never sent. He says

> The children learn, once again, that what you do in school doesn't have much to do with the real world [ibid,36].

Smith [1989:354] also comments on the lack of meaningful writing tasks conducted in classrooms:

> Children are rarely taught what *is* worthwhile reading and writing in schools. Instead,reading and writing are used for school chores.

It is interesting to note how people in the real world learn how to read the instruction books, the manuals, the directions that are necessary to satisfy their needs. Smith comments that

> Many students leave school having learned the "basics" of reading and writing but with no inclination ever to pursue these activities voluntarily; they have no understanding of what literacy can do for them (apart from getting them through school) [Smith,1989:355].

He further states that

> Literacy is not a set of skills or a finished state; it is an attitude toward the world. A literate attitude makes learning to read and write both possible and productive [ibid].

Our past attempts to teach language have been criticised by a number of other writers. Holdaway [1985:3] comments:

> Instruction has persistently separated reading from writing in a way which would be insufferable in learning to listen and talk;

while Cambourne [1983] says

> If we taught our children to talk and walk using the same methods (as those used to teach reading and writing) we'd produce a nation of mute cripples. (*1)

1:2 THE SKILLS-BASED APPROACH TO LANGUAGE LEARNING

The use of a skills-based approach to learning - i.e. learn lower level skills, progress to more complex skills - is still in evidence in many classrooms, although this approach is in contrast to whole language theory and to other current research theories being promoted, about how children acquire language. This emphasis on skills attainment seems to be based on the premise that language ability will develop if fragmented knowledge about language is delivered, rather than by children being engaged in a series of meaningful and purposeful language activities. Children engage in filling in spaces with words, circling correct answers, crossing out incorrect answers, all in the name of reading and writing instruction. This gives a false impression of reading as a bottom-up model of learning.

2. COMPUTER SOFTWARE AND LANGUAGE LEARNING - Promises, Promises

There are many software programs available which claim to "teach" language; a survey of the current software catalogues will verify the abundance of such programs. Most of these are based on the subskills theory discussed above, rather than on the holistic approach to language learning. Indeed, Irwin [1987:37] says that "others (programs) seem to be based on no theory at all".

This basic skills approach to learning is probably well accommodated by the use of computers; but while programs may be used to teach children *about* language, concern should be raised about the children's ability to *use* language for meaningful purposes.

It is not my purpose to deny that the teaching of basic skills is important - far from it. Whole Language theory does not say to ignore the basics, but rather to teach them in context, thus making thei learning more meaningful. And I am not say ing that children will not learn the particular spelling, vocabulary, grammar and other skills presented by the computer. But, as in the past, the teaching of skill in isolation may not lead to transfer learning. Forrest, writing in the *Dragon World* manual, explains this:

> We often compartmentalize these skills into particular 'exercises' in school. Isolating a skill can be useful, and even sometimes essential. But it can also lead to learning which never gets transferred to the real world (p5).

A further consideration must be whether the learning of low level skills warrants such an expensive piece of equipment, when many of these types of activities could be carried out just as easily with pencil and paper. And while children may initially be motivated while using the computer, how long will this motivation last, when they realize that they are still completing the same boring tasks, albeit electronically?

3. READING IS MORE COMPLEX THAN JUST SAYING WORDS

Reading is a communicative process. Should we use computers to teach the skills of reading, or should we provide frequent opportunities for children to read and to write, and to help them develop their communicative skills in a meaningful manner? The 70s and 80s have provided us with an explosion of printed materials and a proliferation of software programs with a variety of educational claims. Are we sure that this is all good?

A child who is asked to do the same low level tasks over and over again, e.g. in a computer skills program, may develop a limited range of reading skills and strategies. Cairney [1988:186], referring to the teaching of reading, says

> ...reading laboratories and worksheets may dull children to reading's real potential for meaning making.

Reading comprehension should deal with more than just low level thinking processes. The use of software which encourages students to answer literal questions, in the name of comprehension,fails to develop the thinking strategies which are essential to understanding.

Another problem is that most computer programs do not take into consideration the importance of students making connections between the information presented, and their previously acquired knowledge. There is a need for recognition of the diversity of prior knowledge and understanding that students bring to the learning situation; readers may not have the background experiences to be able to internalize the information being presented. Strategies may need to be used to activate the readers' prior knowledge.

4. WRITING IS MORE THAN JUST PUTTING WORDS ON PAPER

Recent debates have centred around the different approaches to the teaching of writing - the Process approach advocated by Donald Graves, Brian Cambourne and others, the Genrists' approach of Martin and Rothery, Halliday and Christie, and the Environmentalist approach of Hillocks. Johnson [1988] recommends a writing program which includes aspects of all three approaches, with an extra emphasis on a "development sequence based on the observed growth patterns in children's writing" [ibid,24]. The importance of audience, form, and purpose, for meaningful writing activities is also noted.

There are a variety of programs available which claim to promote writing development - poetry writing, style checkers, electronic spelling checks, ideas generators, etc. It is important that teachers critically evaluate the effectiveness of these programs before accepting the claims that the software companies make. For the purpose of this paper, I have limited my focus to word processing.

4:1 Word Processing

Teachers use word processors for a variety of purposes. Many books have been written giving instructions about how to use Software X, detailed lesson plans to familiarize children with Software Y. Books and papers have also been written explaining how students can write, save to disk, recall their work a number of times, making changes, and finally printing the finished product.

Young writers do not write in the same way as adults do; yet teachers often make judgements based on adult writing patterns.Since the introduction of word processing can take away, for the child, many of the physical problems of writing - the physical act of drafting, editing, rewriting - teachers may choose to use the technology to help them gain valuable insights into the way novice writers write.

Recent writings of Daiute [1989] and Hodgkin [1985] have recognized the importance of children's play and exploration in the learning process.

> Free play is often experimental or exploratory - children try out alternatives based on implicit principles of language,the social world, or some other phenomena [Daiute, 1989:3].

Novice writers who are allowed free play with word processors are able to experiment with language in a way which is similar to the one in which they learnt to speak. Risk taking, an important element in language learning, is encouraged as the children identify the ease with which the writing can be entered and edited.

It is my belief that novice writers do not engage in long editing processes; they prefer to engage in instant editing, thinking and editing in their minds, before they commit themselves to print.(*2) This is in contrast to the expert writer, who engages in multi-editing tasks.

4:2 Collaborative Writing

An interesting strategy which is being used more often in classrooms for the teaching of writing is collaborative writing - students collaborating on a piece of text, teacher and student constructing joint texts.

The use of collaborative writing may blur the expert/novice distinction - the roles of apprentice and master may be interchanged at different stages of the process. Children are often the experts and teachers the novices when using a computer. If the writing is about something about which the children have prior knowledge, they may become the experts about the content, while the teacher may provide expert feedback about sequencing and semantics. It is recommended, however, if the children and the teacher work together on a collaborative writing project, that an audience other than the teacher be found.

4:3 Modelling the Process

Johnson [1988] says we need to provide multiple models for children - not just one model. While it is easy to provide models of writing, in books, modelling the writing process is more difficult. Teachers can use word processing to work through the process with the students of their class; and it can be done with one computer coupled up to a television screen, allowing all students to view the construction of text. Teacher and students may choose to work through the process, in a reciprocal teaching situation. (*3)

It is important that teachers are seen as readers and writers. The fact that the teacher is seen writing in the classroom may legitimize this activity for students.

> Children don't learn from what we exhort them to do; they learn from what they see us doing......usually they learn that reading and writing are boring, painful and useless activities...... Wherever do they get such ideas? [Smith,1989:357]

Smith goes on to say

> Most students *never* see their teachers reading for their own pleasure. And what they see is what they learn; that reading consists of a variety of rituals,frequently meaningless and sometimes punitive, engaged in reluctantly by teachers and students. Still fewer students see their teachers writing, certainly not anything a teacher might normally want to write, and they have no opportunity to experience personally the achievement and satisfaction that writing can bring [ibid,357].

How often do children see their teachers writing with a word processor?

It is important that teachers realize that the use of word processing will not solve all the problems of teaching children to write. Writing tools will not, on their own, improve writing. Pea and Kurland [1987:280] say that

> Most current computer writing tools are designed for skilled writers;they are more like production tools for *being* a writer than for *becoming* one.

One must wonder if, by allowing our students to use these computer writing tools, we may be further advancing the inequalities of education.

The promise of future technological developments in writing tools - hypertext, the multiple storage capacity of CD Rom, and Multimedia software - may allow users to create new ways of writing and thinking. Klauser [1986:47] says that

> Many, if not most, writing instructors insist that you prepare an outline before you write. Since the majority of them mean a linear outline, you are doomed before you start. The very problems that plague you in getting words on paper will impede the fluency of your ideas as you outline.

Writers do not plan and write in a linear progression; the brain does not think in an ordered, methodical way. New writing tools should allow writers to explore ways to organize their knowledge in a non-linear way.

5. THE NEW WAVE?

Recently two new projects have emerged which claim they will change the way children learn: the Apple Classroom of Tomorrow [Bowers, 1988], where children spend a considerable amount of their day "interacting with software that "delivers" the curriculum" [ibid, 53], and the IBM Writing to Learn program [Smith, 1989],of which the author has claimed "he can be the teacher of every child and that no other teacher is required" [ibid, 355]. From my meagre understandings of these two projects, I see this type of learning as a backward step, in conflict with current research theories - a return to a way of teaching language which, if we are to believe the media today, was not as successful as it might have been. Teachers who respond favourably to such teaching may find they are moving themselves towards redundancy.

Approaches such as these do not take into account the social aspect of learning language. Smith says you learn from the company you keep; what sort of thinking patterns will develop if students keep company with a computer that organizes information in a digital way? Children interacting with a computer in this way are not operating in a social context. They are isolated from a social setting and from any sort of oral language communication with others.

6. THE INTERACTIVE PROCESS

Traditionally, school language learning has focused on the written word rather than the spoken; oral language has become a low status subject. Considering the importance of oral language in the educative process of our ancestors, we are probably doing our students a disservice by not allowing more discussion in our classrooms. The introduction of technology into classrooms could mean that children engage more often in group activity learning, and thus develop the oral language skills so necessary for them to become contributing members of society.

Teachers must establish an environment which fosters language learning, to create opportunities for interaction. If children engage in group problem solving and conferencing, they are not learning *about* language, but learning *through* language. This will entail more than just putting computers into classrooms - choice of software is important. Research [Clements and Nastasi, 1985] has shown that children who work with software which rewards only 'correct' responses tend to talk about who is winning - low level conversational skills.(*4)

Adventure games and simulations can serve as springboards for a variety of language activities. Whole language learning can focus on a theme suggested by the software, and a range of reading and writing activities can be organized which relate to the theme. Problem solving can become a group process, as children seek to find solutions to help them with the programs. Then comes the negotiation, the argumentative language, the persuasion, the discussion, as children begin to use real language for real purposes.

The use of collaborative writing can help to situate writing in an oral context [Daiute, 1989]. Because of the nature of this activity, Daiute says,

> the collaborative writing context offers the support and elaboration of familiar conversation interchanges around the relatively unfamiliar activity of writing [ibid,5].

7. TEACHERS AND TECHNOLOGY

The importance of presenting a model for the children cannot be denied. Holdaway [1985:16] tells us that

> As literacy teachers we must be observed daily as lovers of reading and writing - people who actively practise and are willing to share its mysteries in fulfilling genuine purposes.

A good starting point for teachers seeking to use technology effectively in their classrooms is knowledge about the current theories about language learning. Their initial concerns should be about how to foster reading, writing and speaking processes, how to motivate children to learn language, how to help writers develop ideas, rather than how to use the new technologies. Bowers [1988] tells us that professional judgements should not concern such questions as - Can students use this program without teacher assistance? or Is the reading level appropriate? He says these answers require low level judgements and common sense of teachers [ibid,28-9]. Instead, teachers need to be more critical of what they read in software manuals, and of the influence of the new technologies in their classrooms.

Computers are changing the role of teachers, pupils, curriculum and education. This change process should be concerned with improving schools. Teachers have to become risk-takers as they try unfamiliar strategies with their students. Teachers may have to become temporarily incompetent as they experiment with the new technology. This has not been the case with other technologies, e.g. television, overhead projectors, videos; these machines easily slot into the classroom and can leave the teacher still in command, with the children sitting passively in rows.

8. CASE STUDIES

In an attempt to show how classrooms have tried to accommodate the new technologies and to make learning more meaningful for their students, to engage in authentic activities rather than classroom tasks, the following case studies of primary classrooms are briefly reported:

Case Study 1. To increase the awareness of audience, form and purpose in reading and writing, a class of year 7 children has set up a publishing company in their classroom. They compose, edit and publish a number of materials - books, sets of instructions - using a number of written and spoken genres, for a variety of audiences.

Case Study 2. A year 1 class has been matched up with a year 7 class for the purpose of joint authorship of a book. On completion, a formal Book Launch takes place. Each pair of authors is presented to the public, together with their books. The books are displayed for all to see.

Case Study 3. A year 7 class has decided to undertake a critical evaluation of the power of the media on their lives. Initially they video and watch news reports. They then list, group, and categorize the different news stories, comparing and contrasting the news reports across different channels; then they compare and contrast television reporting, radio news and newspapers. Finally, they develop their own news reports, creating their own radio news, video and newspapers.

The focus of my reporting of these activities has been the *learning* that is taking place in these classrooms. Each of these case study classes has made use of computers. Depending on the activity, some, or all of the following programs were used - word processing, databases, utility programs, spreadsheets, graphics programs, graphing programs, adventure games, simulations, desktop publishing. The learning tasks have been structured so that they promote meaningful learning for the students.

9. CONCLUSION

Smith [1989] asks are we overselling literacy? while Boomer [1988:16] says that maybe

> Now it is time to look at the changing literacy demands of society, the changing nature of work practices, the changing challenges of the economy and technology and to the raised expectations of our people with regard to quality of life and cultural fulfilment. In many ways,society is outgrowing its literacy clothing. We need a new literacy wardrobe. We need changed literacy aspirations and changed standards of performance.

What would this new literacy in the age of technology be like? Lanham [1989:288-289] warns us that

> Literacy scholars have traditionally resisted and resented technological change. If we decide once again to view technology with a hostile eye, this time we may find ourselves making the pianos while someone else makes the music. But if we put aside our traditional resentments and fears, then we must decide just what our "music" is and how to make it in new ways.

Are teachers prepared to allow software developers and computer companies to be the composers and conductors, while they sit passively in the orchestra, with their students, playing the tune? Or will they believe, as Boomer [1988:16] writes, that

> it is our teachers who must bring it all together with wit and wisdom in the infinitely complex and ever changing context of the classroom community. (*5)

NOTES

1. Brian Cambourne is quoted from *The Australian*, July 12 1983.
2. My findings about children writing with a word processor are as a result of the research carried out for my M.Ed. dissertation.
3. Reciprocal teaching occurs when teacher and student collaborate in a learning situation, both taking turns in making sense of the learning task. The teacher models the expert strategies, providing a scaffold for student learning, and the student then has the opportunity to model his/her strategies. This approach is described in Collins and Brown (1986) and Daiute (1989).
4. The research of Clements and Nastasi (1985) is cited in Dudley-Marling & Searle (1989: p.45).
5. Actually, Boomer's comment is made with reference to Literacy development, but I feel the message is apt.

REFERENCES

Boomer, G. (1988) "Standards and Literacy Two hundred years on the road to literacy: Where to from here?" Directions Literacy, supplement to Education Victoria, State Board of Education, Victoria.

Boomer, G. & Spender, D. (1976) The Spitting Image Reflections on language education and social class, Rigby, Melbourne.

Bowers, C.A. (1988) The Cultural Dimensions of Educational Computing, Teachers College Press, New York.

Cairney, T. (1988) "Teaching reading comprehension: the development of critical and creative readers", Australian Journal of Reading, Vol.11,No.3, August, pp. 184-193.

Collins, A. & Brown, J.S. (1986) "The new apprenticeship: Teaching students the craft of reading, writing and mathematics", in Resnick, L. (ed.) Cognition and Instruction: Issues and Agendas, Lawrence Erlbaum Associates, Hillsdale, N.J.

Cambourne, B. (1983) "Teaching of writing is ignored", The Australian, July 12.

Daiute, C. (1989) "Play as Thought: Thinking Strategies of Young Writers, Harvard Educational Review, Vol.59, No.1, Feb., pp. 1-23.

Dudley-Marling, C. & Searle, D. (1989) "Computers and language learning: misguided assumptions, British Journal of Educational Technology, Vol 20, No.1, pp.41-46.

Hodgkin, R.A. (1985) Playing and Exploring Education through the Discovery of Order, Methuen, New York.

Holdaway, D. (1985) Stability and Change in Literacy Learning, Heinemann Educational, New Hampshire.

Irwin, M. (1987) "Connections: Young Children, Reading, Writing, and Computers", in Blanchard & Mason (eds) (1987) The Computer in Reading and Language Arts, Haworth Press,New York.

Johnson, T.D.(1988) Unriddling the World, Foundation for Research in Literacy, Wesley College, Perth.

Klauser, H. (1986) Writing on Both Sides of the Brain, Harper & Row, New York.

Lanham, R.A. (1989) "The Electronic Word: Literary Study and the Digital Revolution", New Literary History, Vol.20, No.2, pp.265-290.

Pacey, B. (1987) Teaching the Craft of Writing Does the Word Processor have a Role to Play? Unpublished M.Ed. Dissertation, Deakin University.

Pea, R. & Kurland, D.M. "Cognitive Technologies for Writing", in Rothkopf, E.Z. (ed) (1987) Review of Research in Education, 14, American Educational Research Association, Washington. pp.277-325.

Smith, F. (1989) "Overselling Literacy", Phi Delta Kappan, Jan. pp.353-359.

Computers in Education
A. McDougall and C. Dowling (Editors)
Elsevier Science Publishers B.V. (North-Holland)

A COMPUTER AIDED INSTRUCTION SYSTEM FOR DEVELOPING BASIC LISTENING SKILLS IN JAPANESE FOR FOREIGNERS

Izumi SAITA, Yoshiyuki KAWAZOE, Ken-ichi TAKEDA, Yasushi INOGUCHI, and Yuri TAKAHASHI

Intensive Japanese Language Course, Tohoku University, 2-1-1, Katahira, Aoba-ku, Sendai, 980 Japan

A computer aided instruction system for Japanese listening comprehenshion for foreigners has been developed. The system consists of two types of courses : basic listening skills and task-oriented training. The characteristic features of this system are real time sound generation and a friendly man-machine interface. It also has an authoring system and several statistical analysis programs. Some preliminary results have already been obtained and are discussed.

1. INTRODUCTION

Recently it has been pointed out with increasing frequency that quality and quantity of "input" is a key to acquiring foreign languages[1]. In an ideal situation, learners receive sufficient comprehensible input directly addressed to them from teachers. However, when class size is not small enough or when the listening proficiency of learners varies widely (both common situations), it becomes quite difficult for the teachers to give enough comprehensible input to each member of the class. Therefore, it is very important to develop learners´ aural comprehension ability in the target language. For this purpose, it is necessary to provide both "intensive" and "extensive" listening practice. The former concentrates on developing the learner´s ability to distinguish individual sounds, accents, rhythm and intonations; the latter treats how to grasp the essential meaning of the utterance he/she heard based on his/her own knowledge, the social context, and one´s ability to deduce from what one heard. Although both are indispensable for full development of aural comprehension ability, their training methods are quite different. It is very difficult to develop good extensive listening skills without interaction between teacher and classmates, while intensive listening training is much more suitable for computerization. Moreover, we believe that it is better to conduct intensive listening training with computers, as computers can provide practice repeatedly, individually and patiently.

To date, the use of CAI in the teaching of Japanese as a foreign language has not been readily accepted. This is especially true of training listening ability. As far as we know, with respect to the listening comprehension training, there is only one CAI system available: developed by Professor Ootsubo, Tsukuba University and produced by Seiko-Epson[2]. It, however, uses a computer-controlled tape recorder to supply sounds. Therefore, the learner must wait some time before listening to the desired stimuli. The present CAI system developed by the authors stores digitized sound resources on the hard disk of the personal computer, as a means of overcoming this disadvantage. Generating stimuli in real time, even a most impatient learner can enjoy the system[3].

2. COMPUTER SYSTEM

This system consists of a personal computer, Macintosh SE with a 100MB hard disk, MacRecorder, and HyperCard which fulfills our minimum requirements: 1) friendly user-interface, 2) sufficient capability, 3) ease of sound resource handling, and 4)international availability.

To evaluate progress and assist learners, it is necessary to accumulate a large set of learners´ records. For this purpose, we use the statistical analysis package, SAS, available on the IBM 3081, the host computer at the Education Center for Information Processing (ECIP), Tohoku University. The analysis is achieved by transferring the learner files via TAINS (Tohoku University Academic / All-Round / Advanced Information

Network System) from the Intensive Japanese Language Course in another location. This communications network and transfer process is depicted in Fig. 1.

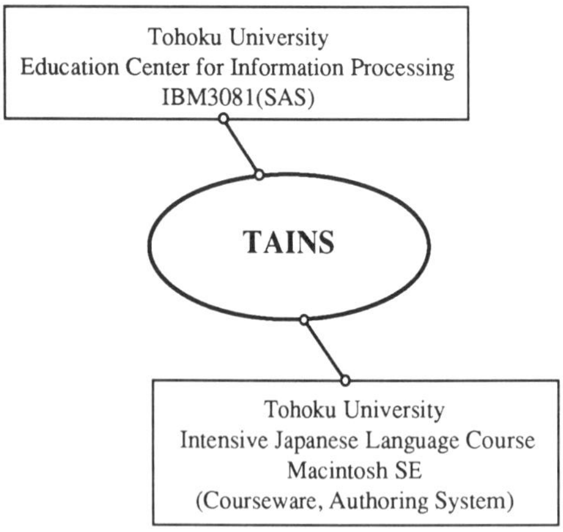

Figure 1. Schematic configuration of the data handling system

3. COURSEWARE

We have developed all of the necessary softwares by using HyperCard on the Macintosh. Several subprograms including file handling and hardware control, which are not supplied by HyperCard, have been written in C language and included as subroutines. The present system consists of 9 courses which can be divided into 2 different types of practice: one is very simple, basic listening skill training; the other is task-oriented training designed like a game.

All 9 courses have "repeat" and "help" functions. The former type gives the sound as many times as one likes, and the latter type gives hints and clues to find the correct answer. The sound to listen to is given in Japanese, and comes out from the computer in real time. Instructions are given on the computer display screen in Japanese as well as in English(1). For the convenience of the new user, the various methods are additionally given in the form of : 1)thorough explanations in English and/or 2) demonstraion practices called "warm-up".

3.1. Basic Skill Training Course

There are 7 courses in this category. Here we list titles of the courses below.

1) Long sound vs Short sound
2) Voiceless sound vs Voiced sound
3) Can you distinguish various sounds?
4) Contracted sound vs Non-contracted sound
5) How many moras?
6) Which one was it?
7) Phrase boundary

The courses from 1 to 4 are similarly designed. They each train the learner to recognize some Japanese phonemes which are considered to be slightly difficult for foreigners to distinguish. As is shown in Fig.2, a set of 4 strings of Japanese hiragana are presented on the computer screen. When a learner chooses an answer which he/she believes corresponds to the given sound, he/she presses the button on the screen by moving the cursor via mouse and pressing a button on it. Feedback in Japanese appears on the screen with the a chime for correct or a beep for wrong.

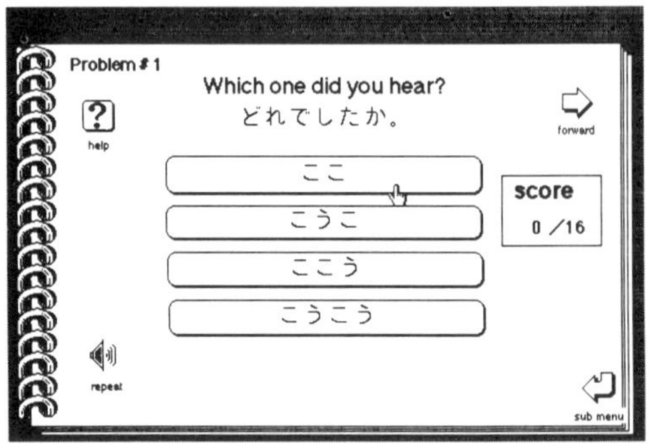

Figure 2. Typical computer display screen for vowel length distinction

Course 5 is aimed at developing recognition of the Japanese mora. Mora is a key phonological unit for Japanese pronunciation and word recognition. It is different from syllable. In the case of a word "kon" (root), it has one syllable but two moras ; "ko" and "n". A word "obasan" (aunt) has 4 moras, whereas "obaasan" (grandmother) has 5 moras. Mora carries significant semantic information.

This course has 3 steps according to the level of difficulty that a student is capable of undertaking. Counting the moras of the stimulus, a student is asked to press one of the six buttons on the screen, which shows numbers from 1 to 6 or 2 to 7 (see Fig.3). If he/she reacts correctly, feedback is given in Japanese along with a chime.

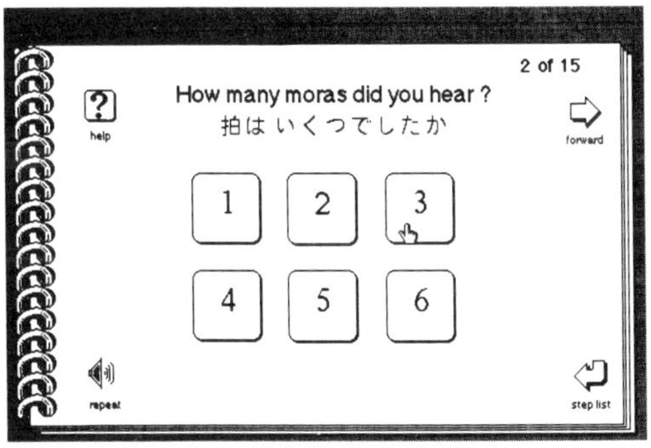

Figure 3. A display screen of Mora recognition course

Course 6 is the one for distinguishing individual sounds. For instance, French speaking learners have difficulty in distinguishing "hashi" from "ashi". For learners from Thailand, there is trouble telling "shi" from "chi". Two buttons with a circle and a cross on them, respectively, appear on the display to judge whether or not the given two stimuli were the same.

In course 7, a learner listens to a sentence. There are 10 pairs of sentences. Each pair consists of the same sound, but carries different meanings, according to the positions of the word or phrase boundaries. This course is also divided into 3 steps with different forms of tasks (see Fig.4, 5, and 6).

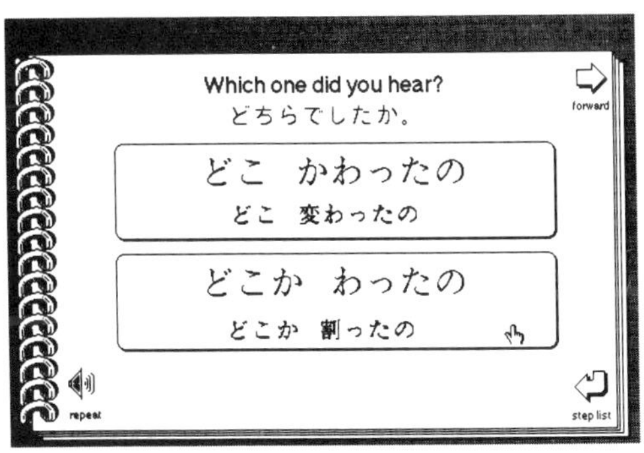

Figure 4. A display screen of Phrase boundary step 1

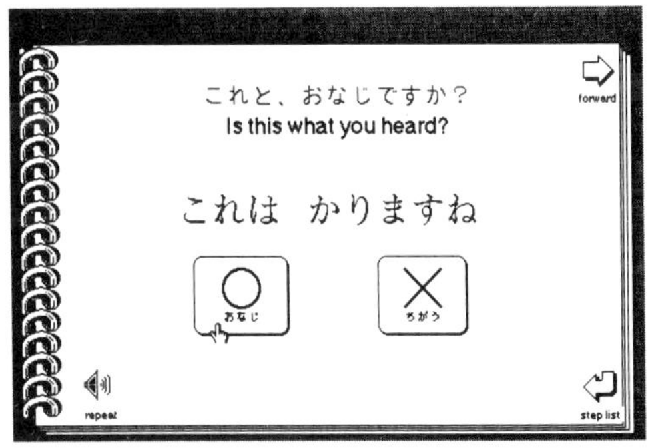

Figure 5. A display screen of Phrase boundary step 2

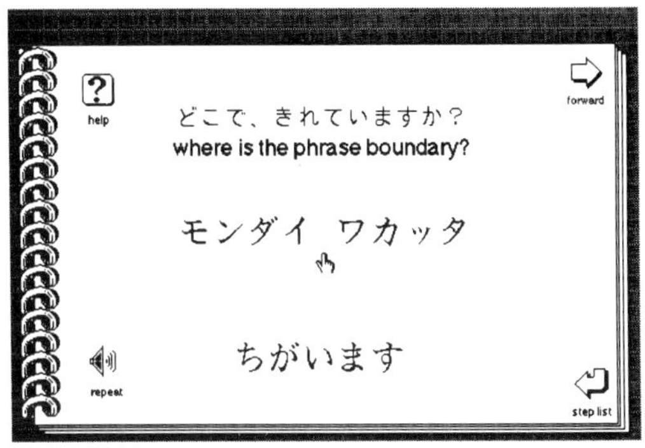

Figure 6. A display screen of Phrase boundary step 3

3.2. Task-oriented Courses

There are two courses in this category.

1) Word Construction
2) Point Hunting

Both of them have game-like structures and can be regarded as modified forms of Total Physical Response[4].

Figure 7 shows an example of Word Construction, in which a learner listens to the sound and lines up the necessary hiragana cards accordingly. This course has two levels -introductory and intermediate- and each level has 3 steps. In the introductory level, no stimulus is longer than a word and when a learner completes the required string correctly, not only is a chime given, but also the English translation of the word. In the intermediate level, stimuli include phrases or sentences and the task becomes more complicated.

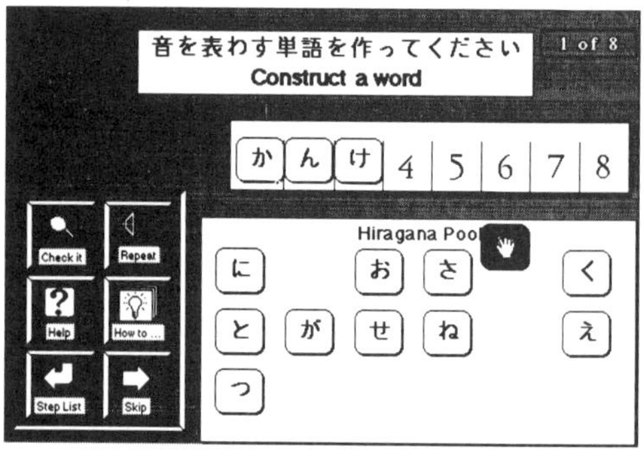

Figure 7. A display screen of Word Construction

Point Hunting is an exercise aimed at recognizing instructions for numbers and directions. As shown in Fig.8, there are several numbers scattered on a 10x7 board. Following the spoken instructions, the learner controls a human figure. If the movement is correct, and if the human figure happens to be placed in a box containing points, the learner obtains the points shown in the box. When a mistake is made, 10 points are subtracted from the user´s total score. The objective is to collect 100 points within 30 operations.

Although the contents of each instruction is quite simple, we have adopted as many forms as possible, in order to provide numerous variations. Additionally, we avoid giving the same number or the same direction in any one series of instructions.

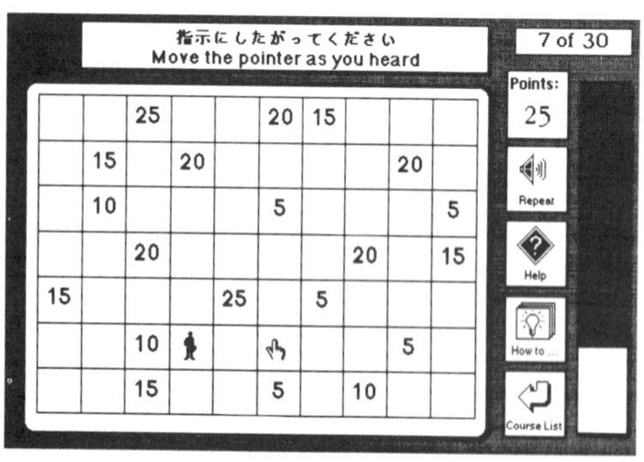

Figure 8. A display screen of Point Hunting

4. AUTHORING SYSTEM

If a teacher wants to change or add sound resources, authoring facilities are available for every basic listening skill course. All that is required is to record new sound resources on a tape, connect a tape recorder and a MacRecorder to the system and run the authoring program. One can choose a course from the menu screen and change it by following the instructions listed in Fig.9.

For the teachers´ convenience, we have also prepared a program for checking students´ records, so that information concerning their progress can easily be obtained.

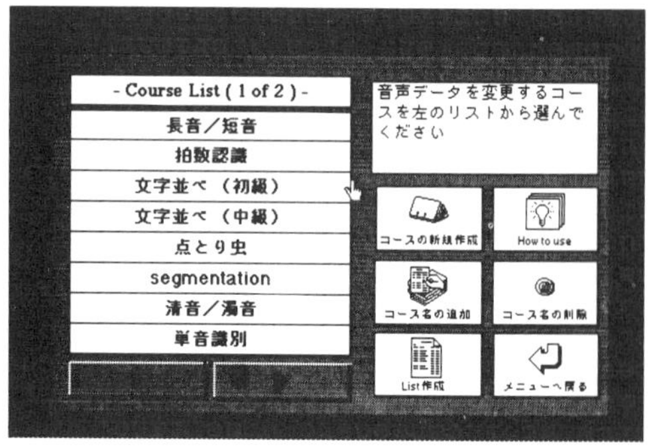

Figure 9. First menu screen of the authoring system

5. DISCUSSION

This system is now undergoing testing with the cooperation of the students in the Intensive Japanese Language Course at the College of General Education, in Tohoku University.

Each student´s record is automatically recorded on his/her own floppy disk. The data consists of the following:

1) student´s name and ID. number
2) the date and the start time
3) the name of the course practiced
4) the problem numbers
5) the task´s correct answers
6) the answers given by the student
7) the lapsed time in answering
8) the usage records of the help and the repeat functions.

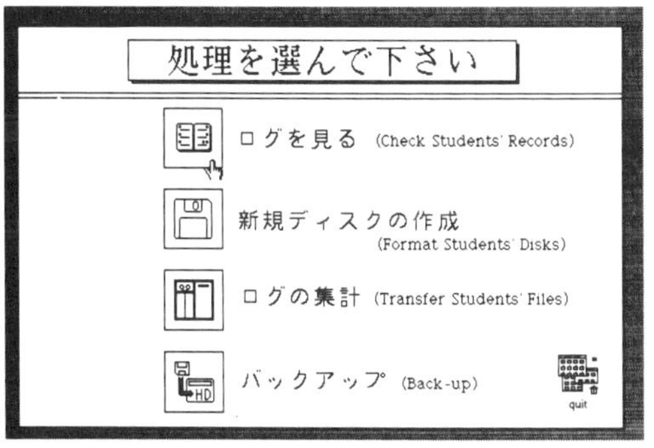

Figure 10. Menu screen to process students´ records

The teacher can see the record by using the program named "teacher". The first menu of this program is shown in Fig.10. The students´ records are sent to the host computer through TAINS, in order to perform statistical processes and obtain final results in the form of various graphs. A typical example is displayed in Fig.11, which indicates the progress of one of our students from The Philippines in distinguishing long vowels from short ones.

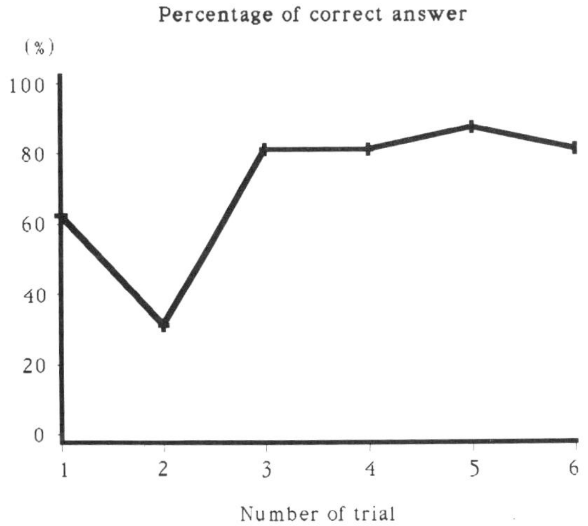

Figure 11. An example of a student´s record in the form of a graph

Although we still don´t have sufficient data to judge the general validity of the training on this system, some very interesting tendencies have already been observed. We would be expected that repetitive use of the exercises by the students will result in them obtaining better marks and using less time to do each tasks, since they are becoming better at recognizing each sound and the numbers of moras. Contrary to this expectations, their use of the repeat and/or help functions and the lapsed time required to answer specific problems increased as trials proceeded. This means that students did not have the ability to recognize the sound or mora differences at the beginning of a test, but with practice, they learned to recognize the differences between sounds and thus pay more attention to each sound in an effort to minimize mistakes. We think the computer is a perfect tool for facilitating or complementing such a careful attitude.

6. CONCLUSION

In theory, if a teacher can ignore each student´s problem in sound recognition, there could be satisfactory time to focus on interactive class-activities. However, it is impossible to do so in practice, because quite a few learners have a tendency to try to pick up every sound they hear. Even if a teacher tells them to ignore the sounds that slip away and to reconstruct the given information from their own background knowledge, they never stop asking the teacher to replay the tape.

The CAI system we have developed provides a good solution to this problem. Through a computer program, learners can practice basic skills as much as they like by themselves, and through classroom activities they can practice extensive listening skills. In short, by adopting this CAI system, teachers and learners of the Japanese language can expect more rapid progress in learners´ communication ability.

ACKNOWLEDGEMENTS

Special thanks to ECIP staff members for their kindness, Professor Todd Holden who checked the English instructions as well as this paper, and Ms. Liu Shu who is working on the Chinese version of instruction.

NOTES

(1) At the moment, we are working on giving instructions in Chinese, due to the large Chinese-speaking population enrolled in Japanese universities.

REFERENCES

[1] Krashen, S.D. and Terrell, T.D., The Natural Approach: Language Acquisiton in the Classroom (Pergamon, Oxford, 1983). Richard-Amato, P.A., Making It Happen (Longman, New York, 1988).

[2] Ootsubo, K., private communication.

[3] Saita, I., Kawazoe, Y., Takeda, K. Inoguchi, Y. and Takahashi, Y. Computer Assisted Instruction System for the Listening Skills in Japanese, in Nihongo Kyooiku Gakkai Taikai Happyoo Ronbunshuu (Nihongo Kyooiku Gakkai, Tokyo, 1989) pp. 83-88.

[4] Asher, J.J.and JoAnne Kusudo, R. de la T. Learning a second language through commands: the second field test, in Modern Language Journal 58 (1974) pp.24-32.

Computers in Education
A. McDougall and C. Dowling (Editors)
Elsevier Science Publishers B.V. (North-Holland)

THE EVOLUTION OF A COMPUTER EDUCATION POLICY FOR GOVERNMENT PRIMARY SCHOOLS

R.A. SCHIBECI and T. BECKETT

School of Education, Murdoch University, Murdoch, WA 6150

Since 1982, there has been an upsurge in the use of microcomputers in primary schools throughout Western Australia. This increased use can be partly attributed to the Western Australian Education Department's release, in October 1981, of a policy on computers in primary schools. The release of the policy was seen by some teachers as supporting the acquisition of computers when in fact it was designed to have the opposite effect, that is, to discourage hasty purchase of computing equipment.

This paper provides an account of the emergence and development of that policy and its transformation to the recently released 1989 policy.

1. THE EVOLUTION OF A COMPUTER EDUCATION POLICY FOR GOVERNMENT PRIMARY SCHOOLS

In October 1981, a document was issued by the Director-General of the Education Department of Western Australia: Computers in primary schools (Education Department of WA, 1981a). This was a plain, single sheet (approximately 21cm x 30cm), printed on both sides. In February 1989, a new document was issued: Computer use in primary education policy (Ministry of Education, 1989). This was a single sheet (approximately 59cm x 42cm), printed on both sides in three colours. The surface contrast between these two single sheets of paper could not be greater: the drab 1981 policy statement with the glossy 1989 policy. On the surface, to use a biological analogy, the "ugly duckling" has been transformed into a "beautiful swan".

What about the substance? The purpose of this paper is to chart the evolution of the policy over the eight-year period, 1981-9. The changes in the policy reflect major structural changes in the WA government's education portfolio, and therefore makes an interesting study of educational change.

2. A NOVEL POLICY

The publication of the 1981 policy was an innovation. Computers in government primary schools simply did not exist for a long time, so that no policy regarding their use was considered necessary. The policy statement observed that technical colleges had computers for 'business-oriented' and 'industry-oriented' training, and that there was a growing computer presence in secondary schools. The document continued:

> The need to consider the relevance of computers to primary education, however, has emerged only in the last year or so. Quite suddenly there has been an increase in pressure to have computers in primary schools. Some of this pressure has come from certain commercial sectors, who see the primary schools as a lucrative market, and some from parents who associate computers with modern society and want their children education for such

> a society. There has also been some pressure from a small number of primary teachers who are computer enthusiasts.

The Department's response to this ferment had been to circulate a policy discussion paper dated March 1981, Computers in primary schools (Education Department of WA, 1981b).

2.1. The Discussion Paper

The Discussion Paper outlined what was occurring in relation to computer education in Western Australian secondary schools, described activities that had been undertaken in some primary schools, and briefly outlined the dimensions of the policy. The discussion paper also put forward the Education Department's perspective, as to the role it envisaged for computer use in primary schools, and then invited responses from interested parties.

The paper also described what the Department regarded as sources of pressure to which primary schools were being, or were likely to be, subjected in relation to the use of computers. Six sources from which pressure was being generated for the use of computers in primary schools were identified: the availability of deceptively inexpensive computer hardware; the "hard sell" approach of some of the retailers of low cost computer equipment; the view of some parents and others, who had a concern for the social and vocational implications of increased use of computers; the view of teachers who thought that the computer is the panacea for all administrative problems in schools; the enthusiasm of some teachers who had a personal hobby interest in microcomputers; and, the enthusiasm of some computer professionals without any knowledge or expertise in education.

The paper noted that "the availability of deceptively low-priced computer hardware" was a factor of concern for departmental personnel; they felt that teachers would be misled into believing that hardware cost would be the most important aspect to consider when buying a computer for their school. The use of the term "deceptively" was intended as a warning to teachers that hardware costs were not the only costs to consider when the decision to purchase a computer was made.

In pointing out "the aggressive stance of the retailers of low cost computer equipment", the department indicated that teachers might be vulnerable to aggressive marketing techniques and be swayed into making "hasty" purchases of equipment which the department regarded as inappropriate.

According to the Discussion Paper, the department felt that many teachers were being influenced by computer professionals who had no expertise and were inexperienced in the field of computer education. People tended to regard computers and computer professionals with a certain amount of awe. According to departmental officers, this perception was unwarranted because very few computer professionals were aware of the requirements of computers for use in primary schools. In such a relatively new field, even officers working in the department's computer branch were often uncertain as to the computer needs of the primary school system. To assist with identifying these needs, a primary school teacher was appointed to the staff of the Schools Computing Branch of the Education Department.

The two phrases "mistakenly believe" and "without any knowledge/expertise in education" (p. 5 of the Discussion Paper No. 9) tends to sum up the general feeling held by some departmental officers regarding the understanding of primary school computing that some teachers and computer professionals displayed in advocating the purchase of computers of primary schools. These people were identified as "likely to have the greatest impact" when it came to encouraging schools to acquire computers. However, the role of parents should not be overlooked. Parents often became aware, mostly through the media, that other schools were purchasing computers. This in turn often led them to put pressure on their own children's school to acquire a computer, in the belief that their children's education would be lacking if the school failed to respond quickly to this technological innovation.

The Discussion Paper went on to outline the educational rationale for use of computers in primary schools as well as "hardware considerations" and "policy implications". The final section, headed "Action to be Taken", listed a number of activities that the Department intended to undertake in its development of a primary computer education policy. These activities included the following proposals (pp. 22-23): (i) the secondment of a primary school teacher to the Schools Computing Centre to assist in a feasibility study into primary school computing; (ii) employment of a programmer to work with a primary teacher on software development; (iii) training and assessment on microcomputers and other peripheral equipment in primary schools; and, (iv) the development of a comprehensive primary school computer education policy.

Finally teachers were asked to "consider the matters raised and submit their comments to the Director-General of Education before June 30th, 1981".

2.2. Responses to the Discussion Paper

The response to the call for submissions to the discussion paper from teachers was very limited. Of the thirty-five responses, only six came from the primary schools. Five of those were individual submissions and one a combined staff submission.

Reasons for this poor response might include the following. First, very few primary school teachers had any experience with computers. Second, many teachers were unaware of the existence of the Discussion Paper as some principals do not make a practice of drawing teachers' attention to the steady stream of materials that arrive regularly at the school unless they personally feel it is important. Third, teachers themselves tend to avoid reading material that comes to schools unless it has immediate relevance or interest to them.

Perhaps barriers erected by computer jargon also helped keep the responses to a minimum. Many teachers, even if they had read the Discussion Paper, would have been left wondering the meaning of such terms as "hardware", "software", "disc drive" and "interface".

One of the major areas of concern was the role of programming languages in primary schools. Some secondary school personnel opposed the teaching of programming to primary school students; however, primary school teachers pointed out that at least some students had already taught themselves programming on home computers.

Although thirty-five submissions were received by the department, very few contained any significant proposals. Many "submissions" were nothing more than offers of assistance from professional bodies, requests for information, or congratulatory articles supporting the department's decision to develop a policy.

Using these limited responses, a draft policy was developed by officers of the Education Department. This draft policy was presented at a seminar for primary school superintendents held in August 1981. A revised draft was then prepared and circulated to all Superintendents and Directors for further comments.

2.3. The Issue of "Standardization"

It would have required a considerable financial outlay for the department to have offered a high level of technical support for the primary school microcomputer system without the high degree of machine standardization which it imposed. To provide free maintenance, free software support and teacher in-service would have been extremely expensive and time consuming if a school had been free to purchase any system that it considered appropriate to its needs.

The department was obviously aware that the approval of two or three machines would spread too thinly the limited financial resources available. To develop software for more than one machine would require either an increase in or reallocation of available funds, or reduced support for each machine.

A combination of pressures both from within and outside the department contributed to the initiation of the development of a primary computer education policy. The department was fortunately in a position to examine critically several international programmes being conducted at the time. The examination of these programmes undoubtedly influenced the department's thinking.

Once the department's policy on computers in primary schools had been published, the machinery for its implementation was set into action.

2.4. Supporting Hardware

Following a series of meetings of various advisory committees, a set of specifications for a desirable computer was drawn up. Suppliers were invited to submit machines which met these specifications. The BBC Acorn Model A with extended memory was chosen to be the approved machine (later to be replaced by the Model B).

Under a subsidy arrangement, schools could theoretically have up to $4000 to spend on computing equipment if they first obtained $2000 of their own funds. However, the funds available in 1983-84 were not sufficient to allow subsidies for all schools which applied for them. In fact, thirty-five primary schools that applied during this period were placed on a waiting list for 1984-85 funding. In some instances, schools which could raise the full amount required to purchase an approved microcomputer did so without waiting to receive subsidies from future funding. These schools obviously felt an urgent need to obtain a microcomputer system. The reasons for such urgency are difficult to ascertain but in some cases it could have resulted from pressure by other teachers and parents.

There were other benefits for schools which chose the approved machine: local software was developed and back-up service was available. Schools purchasing non-approved software were "on their own".

3. A NEW BROOM

The BBC computer remained as the approved machine for government primary schools for some years.

In the meantime, a state election intervened. The government promised, if re-elected, to put at least one computer into every government primary school in the state. The implementation of this election promise led to a number of machines being placed on an "approved" list. Thus primary schools, instead of having to purchase a BBC machine (if they wanted support) could choose any machine from the following list: Acorn BBC Archimedes; Apple II GS; Apple Macintosh; Nimrod XT; and Squirrel. (The Microbee 256TC and Acorn BBC Model B would also continue to receive some limited support.)

At the same time, major changes were taking place within the Education Department. The state education minister proposed, and implemented, major structural changes. The Education Department became the Ministry of Education. The state was divided into 29 school districts. Many head office functions were transferred to districts or to individual schools.

A group at head office was, however, given the task of developing a computer education policy for primary schools.

In 1988, a draft policy document Computer use in K-7 education was published. This document was eleven A4 pages long, and was accompanied by an invitation to schools from the Ministry's Executive Director (Schools) to provide feedback. In addition, a timetable for "consultation/implementation" was published.

In February 1989, the revised policy document, Computer use in primary education policy was published and distributed. This document included two major goals:

"1. For all primary school teachers to be in a position to make decisions about the potential of computers to achieve their teaching objectives and enhance the learning of the students in their care by:

incorporating the regular use of the computer in their own teaching/learning environment as a tool to achieve particular objectives;

using their knowledge about good teaching practice to identify potential software and to evaluate its usefulness in achieving their educational objectives; and

using a computer as a personal tool.

2. For all primary school students to:

become confident about using the computer as a learning tool; and

use a computer regularly across the curriculum to achieve learning objectives and to solve problems in the context of their daily classroom activities."

The document provided the following 'outcome indicators' which could be used to assess the achievement of the goals. For goal 1, the indicators were:

"Extent to which documentary evidence indicates computer use as an integral part of school development plans.

Extent to which classroom practice indicates computer use as an integral part of school development plans.

Extent to which teachers are confident in appraising software to meet their own teaching purposes.

Extent to which teachers use a computer as a personal tool."

For goal 2, the indicators were:

"Extent to which students are confident in routinely using computers as tools.

Extent to which students regularly use computers to solve problems across the curriculum."

3.1. Then and Now

The extent to which the policy has influenced classroom practice is not known.

It is obvious that the decisive action taken by the Western Australian Education Department in 1981 resulted in a controlled introduction of computers into primary schools. Whether it can be claimed that this led to limited experimentation in the field of computer education is doubtful, as the policy itself did not exclude schools from using their own initiative.

The policy, however, did discourage some initiatives by not offering any support for the primary schools that did not adhere to the department's policy. The limited funds available for providing subsidies for hardware purchase ensured that there would be primary schools in Western Australia which purchased computers that were not recommended by the department, and used in applications not supported by the department.

The two policy documents, one published in 1981, the other in 1989, reveal some major changes in perspectives. The 'outcome indicators' of the 1989 policy document reflect a move to a greater 'accountability' on the part of teachers, schools and the system. Few would object to some form of 'accountability'. We will need to monitor the implementation of the policy to determine the extent to which classroom practice has been changed.

REFERENCES

Education Department of WA (1981a), Computers in primary schools (Policy from the Director-General's Office, No. 34), Perth Government Printer.

Education Department of WA (1981b), Computers in primary schools, Discussion Paper Number 9.

Ministry of Education, WA (1989), Computer use in primary education policy, Perth.

Computers in Education
A. McDougall and C. Dowling (Editors)
Elsevier Science Publishers B.V. (North-Holland)

USING COMPUTERS IN WRITING TO READ

Kenneth E. Sinclair and Alan J. Watson

University of Sydney, Sydney, Australia, 2006.
University of New South Wales, Kensington, Australia, 2033.

The paper presents results of an Australian evaluation of Writing to Read, a program in which children's writing becomes the starting point for learning to read, and in which the computer has an important role to play in facilitating the teaching and learning process. The results of the evaluation are based on measures of pupils' reading and writing performance, their meta-cognitive understanding of the reading and writing process, and on attitudes of teachers, pupils and parents towards the program. The results are generally favourable to the program and confirm the findings of other evaluations. The program and results serve to demonstrate that the computer has an important role to play in assisting with literacy teaching and learning.

1. INTRODUCTION

One recent source of teaching practice (Martin and Friedberg [1]) has advocated the use of children's writing as the starting point for learning literacy skills and understandings. The discovery that children can create their own spelling system (Read [2]), the closer study of children's writing behaviours (Chomsky [3]; Clay [4]) and the use of writing in new teaching programs (Turbil [5]; Graves [6]) has helped to bring about the recognition that writing can be an effective means to introduce young learners to reading. This has been further underpinned by the theoretical acknowledgement of the close inter-relatedness of all literacy learning.

An analysis of the writing and reading process indicates that a range of skills and understandings must be mastered in developing the capacity to read and write. These include a knowledge of the graphophonic relationships of print and the use of the alphabetic principle, an understanding of the nature and purpose of text and the use of effective process strategies for writing and reading, and the development of spelling skills. The computer is capable of offering a range of highly supportive and responsive teacher-centred and student-centred environments in which these skills and understandings may be developed. In tutorial mode, for instance, the computer is able to assist students in the learning of graphophonic relationships and provide opportunities for students to practice that learning in systematic ways. In so doing students are able to learn at their own pace in a highly structured yet responsive environment. Just as readily, the computer may be used for students to explore possibilities in written expression for themselves. Word processing programs enable them to experiment with the elements and processes of written expression in seeking to convey meaning to themselves and others.

Writing to Read is a program developed in the U.S.A., that uses the computer in both of these ways to teach writing and reading skills and processes. It assumes that an early introduction to writing with word processors together with a phonemically-based invented spelling program, and a language experience reading emphasis will promote effective learning of literacy amongst school beginners. Children write what they can speak with the assistance of a 42 phoneme spelling system to overcome the major initial problem of the irregular sound/symbol system of traditional English orthography. A microcomputer program teaches the 42 phonemes and graphemes which are presented in a carefully sequenced instructional pattern. Children are then assisted to read that which they have written and thus early reading is founded on their own oral language usage.

In the Writing to Read program children progress systematically through a series of learning stations, viz, a computer station, typing/writing station, a work journal station, a listening library station, a make words station, and an optional activities station (e.g. games and puzzles). The prominence which each part is given has to be determined by the teacher's judgement of the learning needs of the child. These needs change as the child progresses in learning to write and read according to his or her own pace. Since these needs change developmentally, heavy demands are made upon the teacher's professional judgement in the effective implementation of the program. There is, however, a core of learning tasks which it is expected all children will work through as is required.

The authors are engaged in an evaluation of the

Writing to Read program which is being trialled in a Sydney primary school. As part of that Evaluation, the children's development and achievements in writing and reading are being monitored by documenting both the products of learning and the processes by which those products were attained. This has been done using specially chosen or prepared tests, the naturalistic observation of reading and writing, and interview and questionnaire to monitor the qualitative reactions of the teachers, the pupils and the parents.

2. METHODOLOGY

The instruments and the timing and frequency of their use with Kindergarten (K), Year 1 (1), Teachers (T), Students (S) and Parents (P) are shown in Table 1.

TABLE 1. DESIGN OF THE STUDY

	Apr	Jun	Aug	Oct	Nov
Metacognition					
Units of Print	K				K
Alphabetic Principle	K,1				K,1
Reading					
Process (1)					
Stage Level		K	K	K	
Scale Score		K	K	K	
Product					
St Lucia	K,1				K,1
CAT Comprehension					1
Word Analysis					1
Writing					
Process (1)					
Stage Level		K	K	K	
Scale Score		K	K	K	
Product					K,1
Teacher Meetings and Interviews		T	T	T	T
Student Interviews (1)		S	S	S	S
Parent Questionnaire					P

Note: (1) = administered to sub-group only

The metacognitive tests seek to show whether the children understand the nature and function of the print and can use that knowledge to assist in reading and writing. The Units of Print Test, a group measure, requires the child to distinguish a number, a letter, a capital letter and a word (Watson [7]). The Alphabetic Principle Test, which was one devised for this evaluation, is administered individually and requires the child to identify the sounds which letters make in words, in nonsense words and singly. Its reliability (alpha) was found to be .93.

Reading was assessed in three different ways; with the St Lucia Graded Word Reading Test (Andrews [8]), with a modified form of the Miscue Analysis (Goodman, and Burke [9]) for oral reading (process) and for Year 1, with the Comprehension and Word Analysis sections of the Californian Achievement Test [10]. Oral reading process was scored according to the strategies used in approach to the book, in determining an unknown word and in general response to the text, e.g., fluency, self correction. These were determined on the basis of the stage levels of reading development proposed by Watson [11]. The Cronbach alpha reliability coefficient for the oral reading analysis was found to be .87.

Writing process was monitored by informal observation of children (one at a time) as they composed their stories in the lab. This was followed immediately by a structured interview based upon the writing observed. Questions were asked to find out what each child thought about the task he/she was performing. These questions were based on the level of progress the child had attained ranging from scribble to punctuated story. A score was determined from this interview data based on children's preliminary metalinguistic knowledge, their understanding of the message and the sources they use to construct the text. The reliability of this writing measure was .87 (alpha). Both reading and writing process observations and interviews were conducted with a sub-group of the sample (n=29) chosen with a random stratified procedure to represent good, average and poor Kindergarten achievers on Single Seriation and Units of Print.

Writing product was assessed from children's final piece of written expression in class. These were scored according to the criteria and levels used in the ETS study of Writing to Read (Murphy and Appel [12]). Two experienced and highly competent infants teachers independently rated each piece of work and the mean was taken as the score. The correlation of the scores of the two raters was .78.

Teacher opinion of the program was obtained through the regular bi-monthly meeting of the evaluation team with the teachers, by informal discussion over coffee or in the corridor and through structured interviews conducted at the end of the year. In addition to this, the Principal, who has taken a close interest in the project, provided written reports at the completion of Term 2 and Term 4.

Pupil opinion of the program was determined by informal observation as children worked in the lab and by small group interviews in Term 3 and at the end of Term 4 conducted with a sub-group of 45 children (22 from Kindergarten, 23 from Year 1) chosen randomly to represent above average, average, and below average pupils. This was corroborated by asking parents in the

Parent Questionnaire how their children felt about the Program.

Parental opinion was obtained by a questionnaire (administered at the end of Term 4) which was a modified form of that used in the ETS study (Murphy and Appel [13]).

3. RESULTS

3.1 Achievement Measures and their Interrelationships

3.1.1 Reading Achievement

Reading scores measured in April and November on the St Lucia test for the Kindergarten and Year 1 pupils are summarised in Table 2. With both Kindergarten and Year 1 classes there was a significant increase in reading score over the six month testing period. The mean reading age of the Kindergarten class increased from 5 years to 5 years 9 months, while the mean reading age of Year 1 pupils increased from 6 years 3 months in April to 7 years 10 months in November.

TABLE 2. MEAN SCORES - ST LUCIA READING TEST

	April	November
Reading raw score		
Kindergarten	00.57	14.74*
Year 1	18.31	32.72*
Reading age (mths)		
Kindergarten	60.23	69.79*
Year 1	75.69	94.61*

* Significance of change <.001

While the average gain in Kindergarten of 9 months reading age over the testing period is encouraging although modest, the 19 month average gain over the same period in Year 1 is quite spectacular. In Table 3, frequencies of reading age increases for the Kindergarten and Year 1 pupils are presented. It will be observed that 26 of the Kindergarten children showed no gains at all over the six month period and a further 6 children showed increases of no more than 6 months. Almost half of the children, however, showed gains of beyond 6 months with 18 of them showing gains of more than 12 months.

This result reveals that, as formal reading instruction is introduced, there are wide differences in initial achievement with some children spurting ahead and some taking longer to cope with the program of instruction. By the second year of instruction, however, readiness is greatly improved and the earlier instruction appears to provide a firm basis for further gains. For the Year 1 class, 75% of children recorded gains of between 12 months and 48 months over the 6 month testing period.

It may be objected that word reading without

TABLE 3. FREQUENCY TABLE OF READING AGE INCREASES OVER A SIX MONTH TESTING PERIOD

Reading age increase	Kinder		Year 1	
(in months)	F	cum%	F	cum%
0	26	43.3	3	5.3
1- 6	6	53.3	4	12.3
7-12	10	70.0	7	24.6
13-18	5	78.3	16	52.6
19-24	3	88.3	12	73.7
25-36	7	95.0	11	93.0
37-48	3	100.0	4	100.0

F = frequency cum% = cumulative%

context is not reading at all and that the St Lucia Test is inappropriate as one index of reading in this study. It has shown itself to be highly reliable in extended use over a five year longitudinal study (M alpha=.95) and it correlates about as strongly with several measures of comprehension (including cloze) as the comprehension tests do with each other (Watson [14]). The Test is an individual one and its difficulty level is adaptable to the performance of the child. Difficulties caused by the wide range of individual differences amongst beginning readers are overcome. Children do not need to complete an extensive number of tasks which are too difficult for them and hence problems of guessing or unnecessary distress amongst Kindergarten and Year 1 children who may not have progressed far in reading, are avoided.

As a further index of the validity of the St Lucia Test, its relationship to a process measure of oral reading and to the comprehension section of the CAT was examined. For the three occasions when Kindergarten oral reading was monitored, June, August and October, the correlations with St Lucia Word Reading given in November were .68, .77 and .59. CAT comprehension given in November to Year 1 pupils correlated .73 with Word Reading. Such strong correlations with a range of other reading measures is consistent with the findings of Watson cited above and cannot be explained if word recognition is not a vital part of early reading progress. The St Lucia Test has sound validity for this study.

3.1.2 Reading and Its Correlates

The alphabetic principle refers to the way the alphabetic symbols of writing represent the sound system of speech. In Table 4, mean scores on the Alphabetic Principle Test in April (AP1) and November (AP2) are found for the Kindergarten and Year 1 children. It will be observed that development is extremely rapid during Kindergarten. During Year 1 development is not as rapid, however the increase recorded is still significant. The rationale for the Writing to Read program indicates that a strong relationship will exist between reading achievement and an understanding of the alphabetic principle.

TABLE 4. MEAN SCORES - THE ALPHABETIC PRINCIPLE TEST

	Apr	Nov	Significance of Change
Kindergarten	3.00	27.25	<.001
Year 1	27.86	34.14	<.001

Correlations between reading achievement in April (R1) and November (R2) and performance on the Alphabetic Principle Test in April (AP1) and November (AP2) may be examined in Table 5. At the beginning of the program in April there is no relationship between reading achievement and performance on the alphabetic principle test (r=.06).

TABLE 5. CORRELATIONS BETWEEN READING AND ALPHABETIC PRINCIPLE

	R1	R2	AP1	AP2
(R1)	--	.56	.06	.29
(R2)	.89	--	.43	.76
(AP1)	.80	.81	--	.46
(AP2)	.62	.70	.78	--

Note: Kindergarten correlations are in the upper segment of the table and Year 1 correlations are in the lower segment.

At the end of the first year of the program in November, however, the relationship is very strong (r=.76). Throughout Year 1 the relationship between reading and the alphabetic principle remains very strong (April testing, r=.80; November testing, r=.70). It is also of interest that while the April measure of the alphabetic principle has no relationship with reading achievement at that time (R1-AP1, r=.06), the April measure of the alphabetic principle is significantly related to the November measure of reading (R2-AP1), r=.43). The relationship between reading and the alphabetic principle, therefore, a strong one. Further data gathering and analysis will, however, need to be undertaken to determine whether it is possible to conclude that grapho-phonemic competence, as embodied in the test of the alphabetic principle, operates to influence reading achievement directly.

There is evidence from the study, as well, of strong development taking place in the learning and understanding of the processes underlying reading and writing. In Table 5 mean scores are summarised on the tests of Units of Print (U of P), Reading Processes (R Process) and Writing Processes (W Process). The first of these measures is available for all the Kindergarten children and was obtained in April and November. The measures of Reading and Writing Processes, however, were obtained only from a subsample of the Kindergarten class, but were obtained from three testing occasions. It may be observed from Table 5 that significant development occurred in each of these measures. This indicates that the program with its strong eclectic emphasis is associated with the development of meaning and understanding about the processes underlying reading and writing as well as with the understanding of the alphabetic principle.

TABLE 6. KINDERGARTEN MEAN SCORES FOR UNITS OF PRINT, READING PROCESSES AND WRITING PROCESSES

	April	June	Aug	Oct	Nov
U of P	20.88				27.28*
R Process		4.70	7.30	8.33*	
W Process		12.57	14.45	19.17*	

* Significance of change <.001

The Units of Print Test measures children's knowledge of some of the basic units of literacy - the word, the letter and the sentence. As instruction progresses children gain a clearer understanding of the nature of print units and how they may be distinguished from other common symbols e.g., numbers.

3.2 Attitudes Towards the Program

The teachers have experienced some problems in accepting and adjusting to the program. Some teachers with a very strong commitment to experiential, whole-word approaches to learning to read found it difficult, at first, to accept the phonic teaching component of the program. An appreciation of the eclectic nature of the total program, however, and the realisation that the phonic emphasis is balanced by an equally strong whole-language emphasis on process writing and on listening to children's literature, helped overcome the initial doubts.

Also initially difficult to accept was the special phonemic spelling system used in the program. Of concern was the belief that the modified alphabet would lead to later problems in the transition to conventional spelling. A discussion about the nature of children's invented spelling and how children progress to use traditional orthography, and the ways in which it was possible for the special phonemic system to exist side by side in the classroom with conventional spelling helped to relieve some of those concerns.

Since Writing to Read took place in a specially prepared lab setting there was also, initially, a tendency for activities and experiences in the lab to be kept quite separate from activities and experiences in the regular classroom. This problem was addressed in a workshop with the teachers after which they were encouraged to consciously plan ways by which the link between the Writing to Read lab and the classroom could be strengthened.

The learning stations approach used in the program was considered to be a very effective one. It introduced variety for the children, enabled self-paced learning to occur, and allowed the teacher to concentrate attention on helping individual children at tasks where that help was most needed. In this way, children received the opportunity to work independently and the teacher was able to 'conference' daily with pupils while other children were profitably occupied, an experience that was most difficult to implement in the regular classroom. Some learning stations, however, were considered to be more effective than others. The journal work station, for instance was found to be tedious and the materials need extensive revision. The listening library station could be improved if a selection of engrossing Australian children's literature and the children's own best stories replaced the American stories. On the other hand, the writing process station was very popular and made good use of the power and capabilities of the computer.

In addition to the teachers, a sample group of 45 children, 22 from kindergarten and 23 from Year 1 were randomly selected from the 120 children involved in the program and interviewed. Generally speaking, the pupils were positive about the program because it helped them make progress in learning to read and write which they considered to be important. The great majority of the pupils enjoyed reading and writing and were able to use the skills learned in a range of out-of-school activities. In many cases, also, the program was considered to be a source of fun as they learnt at the work stations. The word processing activity, in which they developed considerable expertise, was the most strongly favoured activity. The reality of seeing their own stories created and published was a particular source of satisfaction.

In regard to their children's attitudes, parents indicated that 90% of them liked the program or liked it very much, while 5% did not like it (5% of parents did not respond to the item). An overwhelming majority of parents (97%) endorsed the use of computers "as soon as possible" in the education of their children. Similarly, 96% of parents disagreed that children in Kindergarten and Year 1 are too young to learn or familiarise themselves with computers. The parents indicated that their children were making use of their new skills in reading and writing in many different ways. They read signs, labels, books and other materials. They wanted to read autonomously and to write words and stories. Parents also mentioned that they wanted to read and be read to, left notes around the house, showed their school work and read what they had written or been given to read at school. The parents also identified two main concerns about the program. One concern was that Writing to Read was being used to the exclusion of other literacy instruction approaches. This was a simple misunderstanding since other approaches were being used in regular classroom teaching. The other was a concern about the modified teaching alphabet used in the program and the possibility that conventional spelling may be being neglected. Again, a greater understanding of the rationale of the program and its implementation would have alleviated that concern. Finally, the parents indicated that 3 of the 51 children in the present Kindergarten had been able to read on starting school, while 6 of the 40 Year 1 children had been able to do so.

4. DISCUSSION

The Writing to Read program has emerged as an effective alternative to established approaches to teaching reading and writing. The positive results recorded confirm the favourable results of other evaluations (Chrichlow [15]; Cleckner [16]; Collis, Ollila and Muir [17]; Innotech [18]; Levison and Lalor [19]; Murphy and Appel [20]) both in terms of the progress of pupils and the attitudes of teachers, parents and pupils towards the program. While, in the present study, direct comparisons with other literacy programs was not possible, the results indicate that the Writing to Read pupils made gains in reading achievement that were well beyond that which would have been expected given normative data about Kindergarten and Year 1 pupils. At the same time, however, it should also be recognised that in implementing the program, the school received a great deal of assistance from the formative evaluation process used by the two evaluators, one a reading educator and the other an educational psychologist.

A central component of the Writing to Read program, learning the alphabetic principle, has been found to be a very strong predictor of success in learning to read and write. This result confirms the importance given to the alphabetic principle in the construction of the program and, in addition, provides evidence supporting the underlying importance of that meta-cognitive skill in literacy learning. This evidence, together with earlier work (Watson, Sinclair, Cooney and Marsh [21]), suggests a learning continuum along which children gain momentum as their emerging conceptual reasoning interacts with experience (formal and informal) of print to bring about an understanding of the concepts of a word and letter. With further print experience (through instruction) the children start to use the alphabetic principle as an important source of cues in deciphering text. This, then, provides the basis for a dramatic surge in the development of reading and writing skills.

The learning stations approach used in the program has many effective features. As discussed, it introduces variety for the children, enables self-paced learning to occur, and allows the teacher to concentrate attention on helping children at tasks where that help is most needed, e.g., in conference writing. Some learning stations, however, were found to be more effective than others. The work journal and listening library stations, for instance, need extensive revision to suit them to Australian conditions. The writing process station, on the other hand, was very popular and made good use of the power and capabilities of the computer.

One very successful spin-off from the program has been the progress made by the five and six year old pupils in writing with computers. The quality and quantity of their output, the enthusiasm they show for the writing station and their skill with word processing make writing with computers an attractive feature of Writing to Read. It is a major reason that parents are very pleased with the program and wish it to continue. As children are learning literacy, they are also becoming confident and skilled with computers at a very young age.

REFERENCES

[1] Martin, J.H. and Friedberg, A., Writing to Read (Warner Books, NY, 1986).
[2] Read, C., Preschool children's knowledge of English phonology. Harvard Educational Review (1971) 1-34.
[3] Chomsky, C., Write first, read later. Childhood Education (1971) 296-299.
[4] Clay, M., What did I write? (Heinemann, Auckland, 1975).
[5] Turbil, J., No better way to teach writing, (PETA, Rozelle, 1983).
[6] Graves, D., Writing: Teachers and children at work. (N.H. Heinemann, Exeter, 1983).
[7] Watson, A.J., (1984) Cognitive development and units of print in early reading, In J. Downing and R. Valtin, Language Awareness and Learning to Read. (New York, Springer Verlag).
[8] Andrews, R.J., St Lucia Graded Word Reading Test. (Teaching and Testing Resources, Brisbane, 1969).
[9] Goodman, Y.M. and Burke, C.L., Reading Miscue Inventory Manual (MacMillan, NY, 1972).
[10] California Achievement Test, Form E Level II Reading (CTB McGraw Hill, Monterey, 1985).
[11] Watson, A., Reading as a conceptual reasoning task: Towards a cognitive developmental theory of learning to read (PhD thesis, University of Sydney, 1983).
[12] Murphy, R.T. and Appel, L.R., Evaluation of the Writing to Read instructional system: Second year report (ETS, Princeton, NJ, 1984).
[13] Murphy, R.T. and Appel, L.R., ibid.
[14] Watson, A., op. cit.
[15] Chrichlow, R., Report on the Writing to Read Pilot Project 1985-1986 (Bermuda Schools, Bermuda, (mimeo), 1988).
[16] Cleckner, J.E., IBM - "Writing to Read" (Paper presented at the IBM Executive Conference Surfers Paradise, 1988).
[17] Collis, B., Ollila, L. and Muir, W., Interim report on the Victorian installation of Writing to Read (University of Victoria, BC, 1986).
[18] Innotech (1987). Writing to Read program in Pinyohan Elementary School. (Seameo Regional Center for Educational Innovation and Technology, Philippines, 1987).
[19] Levinson, J.L. and Lalor, I., Computer assisted writing/reading instruction of young children: A 2 year evaluation of Writing to Read (Paper presented at the annual meeting of the American Educational Research Association, San Francisco, 1989).
[20] Murphy, R.T. and Appel, L.R., op. cit.
[21] Watson, A., Sinclair, K., Cooney, G. and Marsh, H., The Development of Children's Cognition, Oral Language and Reading. Genetic, Social and General Psychology Monographs, (1988) 511-533.

Computers in Education
A. McDougall and C. Dowling (Editors)
Elsevier Science Publishers B.V. (North-Holland)

PRESCHOOLERS AND MICROCOMPUTERS: PROBLEM SOLVING IN TWO DIMENSIONS

Gillian K. THOMAS and Kwok-Wing LAI

Department of Education, University of Otago, P.O. Box 56, Dunedin, New Zealand.

Conceptualized within a framework of Piagetian theory, this paper documents a study investigating six 4-year-old children solving problems in two and three dimensions. The children were observed and questioned as they used a microcomputer to solve problems involving the attributes of shapes (a two-dimensional activity), and then solved the same problems with "real" attribute blocks (a three-dimensional activity). Their performance on the two activities revealed significant differences in favour of the three-dimensional activity.

1. INTRODUCTION

As microcomputers are becoming increasingly accessible to young children with their rapid introduction into homes and preschools (Chin, 1984), a critical examination is needed to evaluate whether it is appropriate for young children to use microcomputers. There appear to be two opposing viewpoints. The opponents' arguments centre on the belief that the microcomputer is not 'real' in the way that other preschool activities are - such as blocks, paint and water. They contend that using a microcomputer requires abstractions beyond the cognitive capabilities of young children (Barnes & Hill, 1983; Cuffaro, 1984). Within a Piagetian framework children of this age are in the preoperational stage, and are characterised as being inflexible in their thinking. For example they are unable to reason backward as well as forward and therefore cannot deal with "reversibility", they are unable to think flexibly or hold two thoughts at the same time, which is required for "conservation", and their reasoning is dominated by their perceptions of the moment (Hill, 1985). Traditional activity for young children is characterized by manipulating materials in three dimensions.

However the microcomputer limits the parameters of the child's activity to a single viewpoint with a focus on a two-dimensional screen. As well as being unable to handle abstractions, young children are seen by some educators as being too egocentric to understand the need to make themselves understood by the microcomputer, in the commands that they use or keys that they press. Basing their view of the child on Piagetian theory they are challenging the appropriateness of microcomputer use with young children.

Others, however, believe that children younger than 6 are more competent than has been thought and can, under certain conditions, exhibit thinking traditionally considered concrete (Papert, 1980). In response to the concern that microcomputer use demands the ability to work with symbols - words, numbers, graphic representations - is the argument that much of the activity young children naturally engage in is symbolic. They communicate in gestures and language, and they employ symbols in their art and their play. The symbolic nature of the microcomputer per se does not make it incompatible with or inappropriate for use by young children. It seems more likely that the appropriateness of the activity will depend on the nature of the software being used.

In view of the importance of cognitive development and the paucity of previous research in this area, a study was conducted investigating whether preschoolers could use two-dimensional abstractions of real objects (on the microcomputer) to solve problems. The strategies that young children used when solving problems on microcomputers were compared with the strategies they used when solving similar problems with attribute blocks. The attitudes of the participants towards computer use in problem solving were also investigated.

2. METHOD

2.1. Participants

Three girls and three boys participated in this study. Their ages ranged from 4 years to 4 years 9 months. They were all known to the researcher and had volunteered to be participants. Four of the participants had no previous experience with a microcomputer. The rest had only limited experience.

2.2. Setting

An IBM personal computer with a colour monitor was placed in the "play-room" of the researcher's home; a room that was familiar to all the participants. The computer problem-solving activity used was "Gertrude's Secrets" (The Learning Company, 1984). Gertrude is a "puzzle-loving" goose who has a variety of puzzles for the user to solve. The puzzles used in this study were Loops and Trains.

The objective of the Loop puzzle was to discover which three of nine objects Gertrude was collecting. The three objects had one attribute in common, either shape or colour. The objective of the Train puzzle was similar: the user was asked to link together objects that had one attribute in common.

Two board games were developed in this study to replicate Gertrude's train and loop secrets in three dimensions. The loop replication was called Mrs Marbles' shopping basket. The child was presented with a picture of a shopping basket and nine plastic attribute blocks. As with Gertrude, the objective was to discover which three shapes Mrs Marbles wanted to buy. The child picked up the pieces and put them into the basket. If the block was correct it stayed in the basket; if not, the researcher told the child that Mrs Marbles did not want that shape and took the shape out of the basket and put it at the bottom of the board. The train replication was a board in the form of a train, driven by Mrs Marbles, with six carriages. The first carriage had an attribute block in it, and the child had to use five of the remaining eight blocks to fill the carriages.

2.3. Procedures

The children each made two visits to the researcher's home. On the first visit three of the children played Gertrude's loop puzzle followed by the train puzzle on the board. The other three children first played Mrs Marbles' shopping basket game and then played Gertrude's train puzzle. On the second visit the groups were reversed, with the first group playing Mrs Marbles shopping basket and then Gertrude's train puzzle. The second group started with Gertrude's loop and then completed the train puzzle on the board. The purpose behind the structure of the visits was to determine whether the children were able to transfer their problem-solving strategies to a similar problem presented in a different dimension.

The child was required, where possible, to complete five games of each activity. At the end of the second visit the researcher conducted an informal interview with the children to obtain their reactions to the games played.

2.4. Instruments

For the purposes of this study, three instruments were developed:

1. Observation schedule - A schedule was developed to record information on the games played. The researcher used a stop-watch to record the length of each game. A running record of each puzzle piece selected and whether it was correct or incorrect was kept. The researcher also kept a tally of the number of requests for assistance and the number of times the child asked to stop the activity.

2. Encoding Responses - In order to determine whether the children developed strategies for solving the games in this study they were required to complete three items for each game.

The researcher recorded the responses to the three items on the observation schedule. These items were:

1. Request for a shape - Before the participants were able to move a puzzle piece or attribute block

they were required to tell the researcher why they wanted it. By requiring the children to give a reason for their selection the researcher was able to distinguish whether they were guessing at or were using a strategy to select the puzzle piece. Their responses were coded as valid (supported with a valid reason), invalid (supported with an invalid reason), and nil (no reason was given).

2. Statement of the secret - At the conclusion of each game the children were asked to state the rule or secret of the game. Their responses were also coded as valid (correct statement), invalid (incorrect statement), and nil (no statement given).

3. Statement of strategy - At the conclusion of each game the children were asked to state the strategy they had used to discover the secret. The researcher wanted to see if young children could verbalize the methods they had used for solving problems.

3. Interview - To determine any preference for problem solving in three or two dimensions, the children were interviewed at the conclusion of their second visit. A pilot observation was conducted with a four-year-old girl in order to practise with and check the feasibility of the observation and recording techniques. The instruments were modified after the pilot study.

3. RESULTS

The participants were requested to play five games at each activity (computer and board), but the average number of games completed on the computer was only 3.25. However, the average time spent at the computer was considerably longer (24.8 minutes versus 10.2 minutes spent on the board games).

There was a significant difference (F=268.16, p<0.01) between the average length of time taken to complete a problem-solving game on the computer (1486 seconds) and on the board (466 seconds). The computer games took almost four times as long to complete. More errors were made on the computer (4.22) than on the board (1.63) per game, and the difference was significant (F=97.11, p<0.01).

3.1. Problem-Solving Strategy

The children were required to give verbal responses to three items for each game: requests for a shape, the game rule, the strategy used. The observer recorded the responses to the three items on the observation schedule. The responses were tape-recorded. One of the twelve sessions was transcribed and coded by an independent rater who followed the corresponding completed observation schedule. An inter-rater agreement of 0.76 was obtained. The majority of the disagreements (12 of the 17) were in the classification of nil or invalid responses. When the invalid and nil responses are grouped together an inter-rater agreement of 0.94 was obtained.

3.2. Request for a shape

Before the child moved a shape in either activity he/she was required to give the observer a reason for selecting that particular shape. The reasons given were categorized as:

1. Valid - e.g. "It is blue and Gertrude wants blue ones", or "It is a triangle like the others (in the loop)".

2. Invalid - e.g. "I like pink shapes", or "I just want it".

3. No Response - This also includes statement about "not knowing". Example: "I don't know", or "I'm not telling".

There were significantly more valid reasons (F=50.66, p<0.01) given per game in the board activity (3.71) than on the computer (1.02). Correspondingly there were significantly less invalid reasons (F=31.14, p<0.01) given per game in the board activity (1.67) than on the computer (6.22). There was no significant difference in the mean number of no responses between the activities.

3.3. Rule Statement

At the conclusion of each game the child was asked to identify the rule or secret of the game. In the loop activity this involved identifying the common attribute. In the train activity they were required to identify that the carriages were linked by common attributes. The rule statements were categorized as:

1. Valid - e.g. "Gertrude wanted all the yellow shapes", or "Mrs Marbles bought the triangles".

2. Invalid - e.g. "A blue circle, an orange circle, a yellow circle", or "All different shapes."

3. No Response - This included statements about "not knowing". Example: "I don't know", or "I don't want to tell you."

There were significantly more valid rule statements given (F=19.51, p<0.01) in the board activity (0.85) than on the computer (0.38). Correspondingly there were significantly more invalid rule statements (F=, p<0.01) given per game on the computer (0.52) than on the board (0.15). The difference between the number of no responses was not significant.

3.4. Strategy Statement

At the conclusion of each game the children were asked to recall how they had solved the problem. Their strategies were categorized as:

1. Valid - e.g. "I saw a blue triangle in first box, so I put another triangle in the next box. It was yellow so I put a yellow circle next to it. I kept putting things the same together."

2. Invalid - e.g. "I just knew what she (Mrs Marbles) wanted and I got them."

3. No Response - This included statements about "not knowing".

There was no significant difference between the rule statements given for the computer activity and those given for the board activity.

3.5. Transfer of Strategies

In order to determine if there was any transfer of strategy from the computer to board activity or vice versa within a session, the performance on the first activity was compared with the second one. The results, in terms of the time taken, the number of incorrect attempts, the number of valid rule statements are shown in Table 1.

		ACTIVITY			
		Computer		Board	
		1st	2nd	1st	2nd
Time per game(sec).	mean	370	562 *	119	126
Incorrect per game	mean	3.7	4.9	2.1	1.1
Valid requests per game	mean	1.1	.4	3.3	3.7
Valid rules per game	mean	.7	0 *	.9	.7

* indicates a significant F value, p<0.01

Table 1: The transfer of strategy from activities.

A one way analysis of variance was conducted between the first and second presentations of each activity. With the exception of two results the differences between the activities, when presented first or second, were not significant. The time taken to complete a game on the computer was significantly less when it was the first activity presented. The mean number of valid rules per game on the computer was significantly less when the computer activity followed the board activity.

3.6. The Interview

At the conclusion of the computer and board activities on the second visit the participants were interviewed to gain an insight into any qualitative differences between the two activities as perceived by the children. The interviews were tape recorded and later transcribed for analysis. The interview was structured around seven items with the interviewer rephrasing the questions until an answer was given.

All the participants reported that they preferred playing with the board and attribute blocks. When they were asked why they hadn't enjoyed playing with Gertrude on the computer, most of the answers were related to the difficulty they had had with moving the shapes and with solving the problem ("I didn't know what to do [with Gertrude]"). Mrs Marbles was the easiest game to play "because you just pick it up and put it down [with your hands]" [but] "pushing the buttons (on the computer] that's very very hard."

4 DISCUSSION

There was considerable support from the study that preschool children performed better on problems presented in three dimensions as opposed to those presented on the microcomputer. There were differences between the performance of the children on the time taken, the number of attempts to solve a problem and their preference for the three-dimensional problems. Also, the results suggested that preschoolers were unable to verbalize or transfer their problem-solving strategies.

The participants spent more than three times as long solving the problems on the microcomputer. Most of the extra time spent was on moving the shapes. In the computer problem this involved using the arrow keys and spacebar to pick up, move, and drop the shapes. As five of the six subjects were unfamiliar with the use of the keys to move the cursor around the screen, it is possible that with practice they would operate these keys with greater speed and ease. However the one child who was familiar with the use of the keys took a similar amount of time to solve the problems. In the board problem the children were able to physically pick up the attribute blocks and place them on the board. When the children were questioned about the activities, their inability to move the pieces with ease on the computer was a major source of frustration. If this study were to be repeated it would be interesting to see if the use of a joy-stick or touch screen would increase the speed at which they were able to solve the problems.

To complete the train problem the child had to correctly place five shapes. The loop activity was solved with the correct selection of three shapes. The children were not told the "rule" of the game (this was the problem that they were to solve). In the board activity the children made less than half the number of incorrect attempts per game than they did on the computer activity. This suggested that the children were using different problem-solving strategies in the two activities, with their approach to the problems in three dimensions (the board and blocks) resulting in fewer errors. When the pattern of games within each activity was examined it was shown that the first and second board games for each child contained the majority of these incorrect attempts. On the other hand there was a more even distribution of incorrect attempts between the games on the computer.

The children made fewer errors when solving the board problems, suggesting that they were using a strategy other than trial and error. By considering the ratio of valid requests to total requests one can determine whether the children were guessing or whether they were following a strategy in selecting the shapes. If the children were guessing or using a trial-and-error approach this would be reflected in a low proportion of valid requests. If the child was using a valid strategy to select the shapes one would expect the proportion of valid requests to be high. For the board the percentage of requests that were valid was 65%, compared to 13% for the computer.

These results indicated that the children were using different problem-solving strategies for the two activities. Given the number of incorrect attempts and invalid reasons the children were only "guessing" or using a trial-and-error approach in the computer activity. On the board activity the children appeared to use a trial-and-error approach for the first or second game. After that they appeared to use a strategy. For the loop game this involved guessing the first shape and then using its attributes (shape or colour) to select the correct shapes to complete the game. In the train activity the children appeared to use the first game or two to establish the rule which linked the "carriages" together. They then used the attributes of the given shape to select the succeeding shapes.

It would appear that there was no transfer of strategy from either problem-solving activity. As the children did not develop a strategy for solving the computer problems it was expected that there would be no transfer. However it was surprising that the children did not use the strategy they had adopted in solving the board game when they were presented with a similar problem on the computer. When interviewing the children it appeared that the children failed to see the similarities between the two activities and thus did not transfer their strategy. On the basis of the results from this study there was no transfer of strategies between the activities.

The results from the present study suggest that preschool-aged children had difficulty using the microcomputer to solve certain problems. The children were unable to develop a strategy, other than trial-and-error, to solve the problem when they were using abstract objects on the microcomputer. However when using "real" three-dimensional objects they could solve the identical problems with relatively little difficulty. In doing so the children demonstrated their inability to reason with abstract objects, as represented by shapes, on the screen of the microcomputer. When interviewed it became obvious that the children had failed to detect the similarities between the activities. While they identified the board activities as problems involving the attributes (colour and shape) of objects they did not appear to understand that exactly the same was required in the computer activity. As well as having difficulty with the cognitive aspects of the computer activity the children were frustrated with the use of the keys to move the shapes. Although not stated by the children, the author wonders if the children focussed their attention on the movement of the pieces rather than on solving the problem. At this stage it is not possible to identify the relative importance of these two difficulties in the failure of the children to solve the problems, other than by guessing, on the microcomputer. In any future research the possible interference of moving the shapes could be minimized with the use of a touch-sensitive screen.

According to Piagetian theory, children younger than seven do not have a "mental representation" or overall picture of a series of actions (Mussen et al, 1974). The researcher was interested to see whether the children in this study were able to state the series of steps that they used when solving problems on either the microcomputer or with the attribute blocks. At the conclusion of each game the children were required to state the rule of the game and the way that they solved the problem (their strategy). Their replies were classified as valid, invalid or no response. There were no differences between the computer and board activities in these categories. None of the children made a valid strategy statement. Even when it was obvious that the child had established the "rule" of the game and then had selected shapes in accordance with this rule, none of the children were able to express that that is what they had done. The majority of the responses were invalid but 40 of the total 67 in this category were statements of the "I just knew" type, with no further explanation. It would appear that preschoolers are unable to give retrospective reports of their problem-solving strategies. It would be of interest to adopt a "think-aloud" or "talk-aloud" approach in any future research to see if young children can verbalize their strategy as they solve the problem (Ericsson & Simon, 1984). It would appear then that it is inappropriate for preschoolers to use microcomputers to solve problems. Two-dimensional representations are far removed from interactions with real objects in a real environment. A time does come when the learnings derived from interactions in the physical and social world are transformed to a symbolic level. What must be remembered is the variety of experiences and time that is needed before this can happen; a happening not likely to occur in the preschool-aged child. This is consistent with the views held by other researchers in this field and with Piagetian theory (Barnes & Hill, 1983; Block, Simpson, & Reid, 1987; Gebhardt-Seele, 1985; Sanger, 1984; Zagong, 1984).

Two limitations which restrict the generality of this study need to be acknowledged. The first concerns the nature of the software. "Gertrude's Secrets" is an example of just one of the pieces of problem-solving software available for young children. These results may not be replicated with another type of problem. Another limitation is the sample used for this study. Due to the preliminary nature of this study a small number of subjects was chosen and of these only one of the six children had any regular contact with a computer. It is possible that a group with more computer experience may have had different results. They may have had less difficulty in using the keys and consequently less frustration with the mechanics of operating the activity. This may have allowed them a better opportunity of solving the problem.

The use of microcomputers with preschoolers is a relatively new and unexplored area of research.

Decisions concerning the use of microcomputers by preschoolers for problem-solving must be made with caution as there is still some doubt whether they have the understandings necessary to control and think with symbols presented in a two-dimensional format.

REFERENCES

Barnes, B.J. and Hill, S. (1983), Should Young Children Work with Microcomputers - Logo before Lego?, The Computing Teacher, 10 (9), 11-14.

Block, E.B., Simpson, D.L. and Reid, D.K. (1987), Teaching Young Children Programming and Word-processing Skills: The Effects of Three Preparatory Conditions. Journal of Educational Computing Research 3(4), 435-422.

Chin, K. (1984), Personal Computing: Too much, too soon?, Infoworld, 6(8), 26-27.

Cuffaro, H.K. (1984), Microcomputers in education: Why is earlier better?, Teachers College Record, 85, 559-568.

Ericsson, K. and Simon, H. (1984), Protocol Analysis, Cambridge: M.I.T.

Gebhardt-Seele, P.G. (1985), The Computer and the Child - A Montessori Approach, Maryland: Computer Science Press Inc.

Hill, S. (1985). Beware of commercials: Young children may not need microcomputers, Australian Journal of Early Childhood, 10(3), 16-20.

Mussen, P., Conger, J. and Kagan, J. (1974), Child Development & Personality. NY: Harper & Row.

Papert, S. (1980), Mindstorms: Children, Computers and Powerful Ideas. New York: Basic Books.

Sanger, D. (1984), For the record, Teachers College Record, 85(4), 539-547.

The Learning Company (1984), Gertrude's Secrets.

Zagong, A.G. (1984), Computer pedagogy? Questions concerning the new educational technology, Teachers College Record, 85(4), 569-577.

Computers in Education
A. McDougall and C. Dowling (Editors)
Elsevier Science Publishers B.V. (North-Holland)

LANGUAGE DEVELOPMENT AND MICROS WITH PRE-SCHOOL CHILDREN

Barry WAKE

Martineau Education Centre, Barden Road, Harborne, Birmingham B32 2EH, England

There is increasing evidence now accumulating, as in the Birmingham Nursery Computing Project for example, that micros have a powerful role to play in the education of pre-school (3 to 5 year olds) children in many areas of the curriculum but particularly in terms of social skills, early learning skills and, above all, in the area of language development.

> "There is no better play material
> in the world than words."
>
> Lucy Sprague Mitchell
> *Here and Now Story Book*

1. LANGUAGE, LEARNING AND MICROCOMPUTERS

In the arena of education, a common starting point for any discussion on language is the Bullock report (1):

> "It is the role that language plays in generating knowledge and producing new forms of behaviour that typifies human existence..." (para 4.1)

It goes on to say, however, that there exists some confusion in the fact that "knowledge" is commonly seen as something independent from the "knower" (para 4.9). Indeed, the "knower" must be actively involved in forging a new link, normally by means of language between the framework of his or her own experience and the new knowledge:

> "To bring knowledge into being is a formulating process, and language is its ordinary means, whether in speaking or writing or the inner monologue of thought" (ibid).

It is interesting to note that, from some fifteen years of studying the language development of very young children, Wells (2) arrived at similar conclusions to Bullock's in that knowledge cannot be transmitted: "It has to be constructed afresh by each individual knower." Hence education should no longer be concerned with simply imparting knowledge but in the active, shared, indeed negotiated "construction of meaning" to encourage the learners to take increasing, and eventually unaided, control of their own learning.

Control of learning and interaction are two key concepts in the educational use of the micro. Papert (3) talks of his aim of placing the children in control of the computer and not being controlled by it. Stonier and Conlin (4) refer to books of the future not being passive, and fixed sources of information, but " 'smart' encyclopaedias responding to and collaborating with the needs and wishes of the studying partner, all through the medium of language."

Moreover, it is also becoming increasingly evident that very young children possess the capacity to think about their own developing use of language.They are able to tailor their utterances to meet the perceived needs of their audience (5). They are able to understand and make jokes, often involving puns. They can also be made aware of their own inappropriate language usage, e.g.:

> Child: Mommy goed to the store.
> Father: Mommy goed to the store?
> Child: No, Daddy. I say it that way, not *you*! (6)

A further example from a four-year-old reveals his ability to correct his use of language, moving from "I brang it home from school" via "bringed" and "brung" to "brought" without any constructive help from the adult present (7).

Children begin to reflect on certain aspects of language at an early age but usually in quite concrete and context-dependent situations (8). Yet, the development of such metalinguistic and metacognitive skills is precisely the area where the micro can be a powerful influence. With its facility of placing the child in control, it has the potential of offering more active learning, nearer to the speed of thought as well as being a better aid for abstraction (cf Walker in Donohue et al (9)). Furthermore, the language, especially the collaborative talking, discussion and problem-solving engendered by the micro, bridging the gap between the concrete and the abstract (10), encourages children not just to do, but to think about what they are doing.

2. THE USE OF THE MICRO WITH VERY YOUNG CHILDREN

> "Computers are the most important pedagogic invention since grandmothers." (11)

Admittedly, the use of micros with the under-fives is only a fairly recent innovation, and research evidence is minimal, piecemeal and often equivocal. The micro is seen as "neither a panacea nor a menace" (12). For some it neither stimulates creativity nor merely takes the place of traditional activities (13). Not that this has prevented the rapid expansion of micros in early childhood education, especially in America where Chin (14) claims that one quarter of their preschools already had microcomputers by 1984 and, by 1989, they all would.

Against the background of rapid technological change and uncertainty in educational assumptions and priorities, however, one current trend is towards the need for children to experience and understand the process of learning not simply reproduce its content, to move from "an answer-based to a question-based curriculum" (15). The micro is in fact extremely useful in its ability to prompt and cope with a questioning "what if" approach, even for very young children, with its interaction and instant feedback. It is seen as a powerful resource to support teachers on the one hand and to offer children a tool for their own learning on the other. Straker (16) sums it up as using micros "to support, enhance, extend or even change the curriculum".

This concept of the micro being at the same time a powerful agent of change is echoed in many quarters. Papert (17) states that his book Mindstorms is concerned with the micro challenging current beliefs "about who can understand what and at what age". Indeed, Chandler (18) expresses the further hope that computers might not just free teachers from administrative chores but free the children from the teachers!

However, it is becoming more and more apparent that the micro will support basic skill acquisition on the one hand, and the development of learning strategies on the other, as in evaluating alternatives or isolating errors (19). In a similar vein, research into the improvement of thinking skills involving computer-presented problem-solving activities with four-year-olds suggests that such skills may well be transferable to performance in other areas (20).

Stonier and Conlin combine their fourteen "principal advantages" of using a micro as its being capable of making "custom-tailored education for individuals" (21). With very young children in mind, the following points are worth extracting: the micro can be "interactive", (allowing at least the feeling of being in control) and "fun", and have "infinite patience" with "positive reinforcement"; the graphics and animation can make concepts more interesting and intelligible; it offers instant responses and the potential of making and correcting errors easy (a unique concept in educational circles); and, the two sides of the same coin really, it allows some privacy ("the computer won't tell") but at the same time can stimulate social interaction.

The recent development of more powerful hardware and hence more powerful software has led to improvements in screen layout and the increasing use of icons and graphics allowing young children to have more control and greater ease of access. There are also concept keyboards, mouses, trackerballs and lightpens that help obviate the "qwerty" keyboard problem. (Even then, teachers found that the capital letters did not prove such a barrier after all and that, in the event, young fingers discovered the keys they needed quite quickly.) Micros are indeed making the curriculum generally more accessible especially to young children.

3. A NURSERY COMPUTING PROJECT

> "We are amazed. We have totally underestimated the children's capabilities." (22)

Early in 1986, three LEA nursery schools in Birmingham, England, were invited to participate in a project with a very broad brief of "exploring the potential of the micro-computer with nursery age children". After the initial encouraging responses, the equipment was upgraded and extended, and a further five nursery schools were included in 1988. (Another three schools have been able to raise funds to purchase their own equipment.) It was reported early on that these very young children soon became very adept and confident with the hardware as well as gaining noticeable educational benefits (23). On the one hand, areas such as individual hand/eye co-ordination, manipulative skills, attention span, and short-term memory skills, for example, were given an extra boost by using the micro with its capacity for immediate response and motivating power. On the other hand, the social value was also noted, in the interaction and co-operation that took place among the children. One headteacher commented on the pleasure they had in watching the children's "growing self-confidence as they share their experiences, knowledge and understanding" (ibid).

A video of the three original schools taken in in 1988 shows many of these aspects in some detail. The accompanying notes (24) stress the fact that firstly, nursery-age children can manage the "hi-tech" quite competently and confidently (whether with mouse, trackerball, Concept or QWERTY style keyboard); secondly, the micro is treated as a flexible, general educational resource, just as one nursery activity among many; and thirdly, the children find it highly motivating and extremely enjoyable.

It is not that the micro replaces a teacher or a particular activity. It is rather an additional way of supporting and enhancing the quality of learning. What it does provide is an opportunity for very young childen:

1. to look closely and purposefully at what is happening;
2. to talk about it, bearing in mind the important inter-relationship between language and learning;
3. to work together and collaborate on a task;
4. to use one's imagination creatively;
5. to think about what is happening, to ask questions and develop problem-solving skills;
6. to become actively involved and not just passive recipients;
7. to take responsibility for one's own learning, to be in control rather than be controlled.

The early findings from the Project reveal that the micro does not usurp or replace other activities at all but quickly finds its own place, for girls and boys alike, alongside the dressing-up, the water-play, the jigsaws and cutting-out. It is used to support various aspects of the nursery curriculum with programs that reinforce and extend particular skills such as discrimination and sequencing (cf BLOB) to much more open-ended programs for graphics (like PAINTPOT) or story-telling (such as COLLAGE) for language development, as Riding and Tite showed (25). Indeed it has often been noted as an undoubted strength of micro usage that open-ended programs, particularly, can be extremely stimulating and motivating in prompting the use of more oral language in a more purposeful way than expected. The microcomputer can create a stimulating, almost language-independent environment to extend language for discussion and description, and is particularly valuable for non-English speakers and those English speakers with poor language development.

4. MICROCOMPUTERS AND LANGUAGE IN THE EARLY YEARS

The one aspect of micro use with young children that regularly arouses comment by teachers is this unexpected amount and quality of talking that is generated (26). Although some programs will instigate it more than others, the micro generally provides a focal point for task-orientated discussion. Baynes (27) notes that the extension of language arising from computer use with her nursery-age children is the single most important development. The software is usually extremely easy to operate (perhaps involving only the space-bar, or a Concept Keyboard), and largely language-independent. With little text on the screen and often icons or small, simple pictures to avoid large amounts of text, bilingual children are able, and motivated, to join in.

Three main reasons for this increased language activity can be identified. The first, as indicated above, is the central focus that the screen offers. Playing in the sand tray may well give children essential tactile experiences but they do not necessarily talk about their sensory perception of the sand or their feelings towards it, unless guided by an adult. On the other hand, the conversation around the micro is usually much more on-task, and centred on the problem or experience involved.

Secondly, a lot of the software for this age-range is nearly totally visual, with colour, movement and an almost tactile quality. (It is interesting to note how often very young children physically touch the screen when using a program.) The micro, this silent, inert, undemanding arbiter, almost forces verbal activity from the group in terms of discussions, disagreements and decisions. Even with individuals, research in an English nursery setting shows that dynamic computer graphics can have a beneficial effect on children's story-telling, in both the number of words used and the structuring of them (28).

Thirdly, the micro provides a focus for in fact all four modes of language to be brought together in a relevant, meaningful and purposeful context. The inter-relationship between oral language and the written benefits the older children especially. (It will be important to discover if the increased motivation in understanding key computer jargon such as "Clear, Save, Please wait" etc. as well as the program names and messages of "welcome" or reward that appear on the screen will help the awareness of print and earlier reading ability. Shostak (29), using a concept keyboard with preschool children, believes this to be an invaluable area.)

Whether or not children are best left on their own depends to some extent on the software. There are certainly programs where an adult's presence is necessary or at least desireable to draw out and build upon relevant ideas and experiences. The Wellsian concept of reciprocity of shared learning has major implications here.

5. TYPES OF LANGUAGE USAGE

In looking at the types of language used by preschool children around the micro, there seem to be three broad categories. The first might be termed "operational" language, i.e. that closely associated with the operation of the hardware and the software. This includes words such as "'puta' (computer), keyboard, mouse, screen, space bar, disk, clear, menu" etc.

Using the micro encourages exact, precise language, such that a second distinct set of important vocabulary has to do with such labelling aspects of the visual and spatial dimension of the screen itself: "up, down, on the right, at the top, underneath, behind, red, yellow, light blue, round, straight" etc. It may well be purposeful language, too, as when the children control the movements of a turtle. Here the children are often collaborating in small groups, which will encourage other social and often imaginative uses of language, and thus overlap into a different category.

This third area is much more open-ended and concerns the uses to which the language is put. Rather echoing Tough's categories (30), Shostak gives eight uses of language with pre-school children which could be summarised as follows:

- seeking and giving help
- thinking aloud
- factual, and imaginary, naming/labelling/ describing
- discussion
- debate
- solving problems
- make-believe
- reading/written language.

Some schools in the Birmingham Project are currently investigating these varieties of language use and, as yet, it is by no means certain that the nature of the discourse prompted by the micro automatically encompasses such categories. It is also important to examine the different settings: to what extent not only different software but also child/child or child/adult groupings affect the style and the quality of language.

6. CONCLUSION

Shostak (31) notes that the talking generated from using the micro formed an integral part of the pre-school children's play activities: "The many and varied uses of language that occurred dispelled all fears about the unsociable nature of the computer". Baynes (32) also found that staff had underestimated the children's ability in taking turns, helping each other, and sharing experiences and knowledge. Indeed, she goes further:

> "There is no other piece of equipment in school which produces as many physical, intellectual, emotional and social skills at the same time and with such enthusiasm."

The micro may not oust the teacher, but it has already shown that it can certainly offer him or her a powerful and flexible resource to support the quality of language and of learning of the children in their care. Precisely because of the interaction of very young children with the micro, and their control over it, they are not only encouraged to do but to talk and to think about what they are doing. It offers them a context not only for enjoyment and increased self-esteem but also to employ, develop and be aware of a wide range of strategies of learning. Many of these capabilities and attitudes are already evident in today's preschool "computerate" children!

REFERENCES

[1] Department of Education and Science, A Language for Life: the Bullock Report. (London: HMSO 1975)
[2] Wells G W, The Meaning Makers: Children learning language and using language to learn. (London: Hodder and Stoughton 1986) pp208, 101
[3] Papert S, Mindstorms: Children, Computers and Powerful Ideas. (Brighton: Harvester 1980) p5
[4] Stonier T and Conlin C, The Three C's: Children, Computers and Communication. (Chichester: John Wiley and Sons 1985) p147
[5] Menig-Peterson C L, The modification of communicative behaviour in preschool-aged children as a function of the listener's perspective in: Donaldson M, Grieve R and Pratt S (eds) Early Childhood Development and Education: Readings in Psychology. (Oxford: Blackwell 1983) p70
[6] Grieve R, Tunmer W E, and Pratt C, Language Awareness in Children in: Donaldson M, Grieve R and Pratt S (eds) Early Childhood Development and Education: Readings in Psychology. (Oxford: Blackwell 1983) p293
[7] Grieve et al (op cit) p295
[8] Clarke M in: Grieve et al (op cit)p292
[9] Walker T in: Donohue et al [13] p6
[10] Wake B, Micros or Sandtrays. Microscope 22 (1987)
[11] Stonier and Conlin (op cit) p29
[12] Killian J, Nelson J Byrd D (1986) Child's play: computers in early childhood programs, The Computing Teacher August/ September 1986
[13] Donohue W A, Borgh K and Dickson W P (1987) Computers in Early Childhood Education, Journal of Research in Childhood Education 1987, 2 (1)
[14] in: Goodwin L D, Goodwin W L and Garel M B (1986) Use of Microcomputers with Preschoolers: A review of the literature, Early Childhood Research Quarterly 1986 (1)
[15] Longworth N, We're moving into the Information Society: what shall we teach the children? in Gibson D (ed) Wordprocessing and the Electronic Office - MEP Reader 2. (Newcastle upon Tyne: CET 1983) p295
[16] Straker A, Children using Computers. (Oxford: Blackwell 1989)
[17] Papert (op cit) p4
[18] Chandler D, Young Learners and the Microcomputer. (Milton Keynes: Open University Press 1984) p11
[19] Yawkey T, The Computer in nursery school. Prospects 26 1986 (4)
[20] Riding and Powell, "The Improvement of Thinking Skills in Young Children using Computer Activities: a replication and extension" Educational Psychology, 6, 2 (1986)
Riding and Powell, "The Effect on Reasoning, Reading and Number Performance of Com-

puter-presented Critical Thinking Activities in Five-year-old Children" Educational Psychology, 7, 1 (1987)
[21] Stonier and Conlin (op cit) p21
[22] Baynes A, Project Report in: MicroScope 26 Micros and the Under-Fives Special (1989)
[23] Wake B "Micro Tots" The Times Educational Supplement. Computing Extra. 17.6.88
[24] Wake B, Birmingham Nursery Computing Project Video (unpublished accompanying notes) Birmingham Educational Computing Centre (1988)
[25] Riding and Tite, "The Use of Computer Graphics to Facilitate Story Telling in Young Children" Educational Studies, 11, 3 (1985)
[26] Straker (op cit), Wake [23] and Baynes (op cit)
[27] Baynes (op cit)
[28] Riding and Tite (op cit)
[29] Shostak G, Microcomputers and the Early Years in: MicroScope 26 Micros and the Under-Fives Special (1989)
[30] Tough J, Listening to children talking: a guide to the appraisal of children's use of language. (London: Ward Lock Educational for Schools Council 1976)
[31] Shostak (op cit)
[32] Baynes (op cit)

Computers in Education
A. McDougall and C. Dowling (Editors)
Elsevier Science Publishers B.V. (North-Holland)

THE CHARACTERISTICS OF INTRINSICALLY MOTIVATING EARLY CHILDHOOD AND SPECIAL EDUCATION SOFTWARE

Denise L. WOOD

The Crippled Children's Association of South Australia
P.O. Box 209, Kilkenny, South Australia, 5009

This paper reports the findings of a three year investigation conducted at the Regency Park Centre for Young Disabled aimed at identifying the most salient characteristics of intrinsically motivating early childhood software. Findings from three separate studies support the hypothesis that computer programs are highly motivating if they include fantasies, multiple levels of goals and opportunities for decision-making.

1. INTRODUCTION

Activities are said to be intrinsically motivating if they are carried out in the absence of any external reward or punishment [1,2]. In effect, intrinsically motivating activities are activities engaged in because they are "interesting", "captivating", "appealing" or "fun" [3]. Lepper and Chabay also believe that learning should be fun, and describe how learning occurs in young children through normal play activities. They assert, however, that through the process of formal education, learning often becomes a chore; in their own words, "work has replaced play" ([4], p. 217).

The emergence of computers in the classroom has added fuel to the " ... traditionally heated debates between the proponents of direct and didactic versus exploratory and discovery based learning" ([4], p. 222), and made " ... issues concerning motivation more salient" ([5], p. 3). While microcomputers have the potential to motivate, poorly designed programs can undermine intrinsic motivation by leading children to believe that they are incapable of succeeding [5]. This is of particular concern in special education where children have been observed to give up in the face of failure and become amotivated; a motivational state said to arise from feelings of learned helplessness [6,7]. Since motivational factors have been found to exert as much influence on children's achievement as cognitive factors [4], it is imperative that consideration be given to the use of feedback and reinforcement in microcomputer programs designed for use in early childhood and special education.

The findings from research undertaken by Malone [3], and later incorporated into an expanded Taxonomy of Intrinsic Motivations for Learning [2], provide some useful insights into the ways in which feedback functions in microcomputer programs and the effects that different presentations have on feedback. According to this taxonomy, microcomputer programs are more intrinsically motivating if they include emotionally appealing fantasies, elements of surprise, challenging activities and the opportunity for students to play an active role in the learning process.

2. A STUDY OF THE EFFECTS OF DIFFERENT COMPUTER PROGRAM FORMATS ON MOTIVATION IN YOUNG CHILDREN

In 1985, an investigation was undertaken at the Regency Park Centre for Young Disabled in South Australia aimed at identifying the most salient characteristics of intrinsically motivating software designed for young children with disabilities.

Based on the findings of Malone [3] and later, the framework provided by Malone and Lepper's Taxonomy of Intrinsic Motivations for Learning [2], three separate studies were conducted between 1985 and 1988. In each of these studies, features identified by Malone and Malone and Lepper as intrinsically motivating for "non-disabled" children were systematically varied and presented in different computer formats to young children attending the Regency Park Centre Preschool.

It was hypothesised that children would attain highest performance scores in drill and practice and maintain a high level of attention in arcade versions of the software. It was further hypothesised that an optimal level for both performance and attention would be obtained in software which included the following features:

- . adventure fantasies
- . a combination of proximal and distal goals
- . opportunities for decision-making.

3. METHOD

In preparation for the study, 24 early childhood programs were evaluated on Apple II computers to identify key features characterising drill and practice, arcade and educational adventure game formats. A survey of parents and teachers of children participating in the study was also conducted in order to determine what sorts of fantasies the children were interested in. On the basis of the findings from the software evaluation and parent survey, a teddy bear matching program used for training purposes and different versions of a colour and shape matching program were developed (see Wood and Correll, [8]).

3.1. Subjects

The subjects of the study were 24 male and 21 female children with physical disabilities who attended the Regency Park Centre Preschool between 1986 and 1988. All of the children were aged between 3 years and 4 years 11 months at the time they commenced the project.

3.2. Procedure

All of the children were assessed to determine their cognitive functioning level, conceptual status relevant to the task and single switch accessing skills. A computer-based single input control assessment program was used to provide objective measures of the children's ability to respond to a a stimulus and stop scanning at random locations on the video screen. This information was then used to customise software developed for the project according to the needs of individual children.

Following assessment, the children were given the opportunity to familiarise themselves with the computer in a teddy bear matching program. During this training session, baseline data were obtained using performance scores automatically stored on disk and videotaped recordings of the sessions.

The investigation was carried out in three separate studies. In each of these studies, 15 children played with 3 different versions of a colour and shape matching program alternately over 5 experimental days. The order of presentation was randomised to control for possible sequential effects.

In the first study, the software was presented to 15 children in drill and practice, arcade and adventure game formats. In the second study, the adventure game version was modified and presented to another group of 15 children in immediate goal, multiple level goal and long term goal formats. In the third study, three new versions of the software were developed using the multiple level goal format tested during the second study. In one version, no extrinsic reinforcers were presented for correct responses, in the second, the reinforcer and adventure goal of the program was set on the basis of children's expressed interests, and in the third version, children were given the opportunity to choose the reinforcer from a pictographic menu display. These versions were presented to a third group of 15 children using the same alternating treatment design as described for the first two groups.

In each session, the date, time of day, software setup and performance scores were recorded on disk. Attention to the task and the number of verbal and physical prompts made by the trainer were obtained from rating the videotaped sessions using time interval recording procedures.

4. RESULTS

The experimental design used in this study controlled for sequential confounding effects by randomly alternating the presentation of different versions of the software. The lack of any significant relationship between either performance or attention and order of presentation (Tables 2, 4 and 6) suggests that the design adequately controlled for sequential effects. Similarly, time of day effects were minimised by counterbalancing the presentation of different versions of the software across morning and afternoon sessions.

As the alternating treatments design used in this study involved repeated measures for individual subjects, lag correlations were carried out to determine whether data points for the dependent variables were correlated over time. Serial dependence was noted in dependent measures in all three studies. Since serial dependence violates the independence-of-error assumption [9], non-parametric statistics were used for the data analysis.

4.1. Study One

A significant correlation ($p < .001$) between the dependent measures was observed in the drill and practice, arcade and adventure versions of the software. Attention and performance were positively correlated, and both correlated negatively with verbal prompts, physical prompts and number of responses. Verbal prompts, physical prompts and number of responses were positively correlated with each other. Children who attended well, performed better and children who performed and attended less well, elicited fewer prompts from the trainer during sessions.

The mean values and standard deviations for performance, attention, verbal and physical prompts are shown in Table 1. Overall, children both performed and attended to the arcade version of the software marginally better than for the other two versions, and a greater number of verbal prompts was noted in the adventure version.

TABLE 1
Mean (Standard Deviation) Values for Drill and Practice, Arcade and Adventure Versions of the Software

Version	Performance	Attention	Verbal	Physical
Drill	70.95 (25.7)	85.87 (18.1)	16.68 (20.3)	7.45 (12.6)
Arcade	76.01 (22.7)	87.42 (15.5)	18.79 (19.1)	7.29 (11.2)
Adventure	73.63 (24.4)	84.91 (16.7)	23.64 (20.6)	8.35 (11.9)

Comparisons of the dependent variables (performance, attention, verbal and physical prompts) and version, IQ, conceptual status level, day, order, time and sex are summarised in Table 2. Of the dependent variables, a significant effect across versions was found for verbal prompts. A strong effect was noted for all dependent variables across IQ and conceptual status levels, indicating that children with higher IQ and conceptual status scores tended to perform and attend better and required fewer verbal and physical prompts. A small effect was noted for performance scores across days indicating a gradual improvement over the duration of the project. There was also a significant effect for sex noted, with females performing and attending better to the tasks than males, and males receiving more verbal and physical prompts.

TABLE 2
Independent Samples Rank Tests for Study 1

Kruskal-Wallis One-Way Analysis of Variance (X^2)

Variable	Performance	Attention	Verbal	Physical
Version	0.93	1.84	8.61**	1.01
IQ	69.45***	56.39***	98.74***	89.72***
Concept	66.65***	45.85***	54.41***	60.25***
Day	9.19*	4.42	4.89	6.00
Order	0.36	1.54	2.15	1.57
Mann-Whitney U Test (Z scores corrected for ties)				
Time	-1.43	-0.58	-2.27*	-2.36*
Sex	-5.75***	-2.07*	-2.36*	-2.71**

* $p < .05$ ** $p < .01$ *** $p < .001$

4.3. Study Two

In the second study, a significant correlation between performance and attention ($p < .01$) was only evident in the multiple level goal version of the software. A significant negative correlation existed between performance and the number of verbal prompts for all versions ($p < .01$) indicating that children who performed better elicited fewer verbal prompts from the trainer during experimental sessions. Attention was negatively correlated with the number of verbal and physical prompts ($p < .001$) in all versions with the one exception being a lack of any significant correlation between attention and the number of verbal prompts in the immediate goal version of the software.

Table 3 shows mean values and standard deviations for performance, attention, verbal and physical prompts in the second study. While there were no significant differences in either performance or attention scores across versions, there was clearly a tendency for children to perform and attend better to the versions which incorporated proximal goals (immediate and multiple level goals).

TABLE 3
Mean (Standard Deviation) Values for Immediate Goal, Multiple Level Goal and Long Term Goal Versions

Version	Performance	Attention	Verbal	Physical
immediate	76.76 (11.3)	86.66 (10.5)	27.89 (26.5)	4.45 (4.2)
multiple	76.11 (12.1)	85.24 (9.7)	21.27 (14.0)	3.81 (3.7)
long term	73.37 (14.5)	83.91 (14.0)	20.77 (14.5)	2.96 (3.1)

Comparisons of the dependent variables (performance, attention, verbal and physical prompts) and version, IQ, conceptual status level, day, order, time and sex are summarised in Table 4. Strong effects were found for all dependent variables across IQ levels and for attention, verbal and physical prompts across conceptual status levels. Children with higher IQ and conceptual status scores tended to perform and attend better and require fewer verbal and physical prompts. Females performed significantly better than males and elicited fewer verbal prompts from the trainer.

TABLE 4
Independent Samples Rank Tests for Study 2

Kruskal-Wallis One-Way Analysis of Variance (X^2)

Variable	Performance	Attention	Verbal	Physical
Version	1.09	0.44	0.73	5.53
IQ	54.72***	58.39***	92.05***	46.27***
Concept	5.16	14.18***	18.78***	15.91***
Day	2.95	16.27*	4.95	4.50
Order	3.78	0.31	0.30	0.31
Mann-Whitney U Test (Z scores corrected for ties)				
Time	-0.38	-0.83	-0.02*	1.17
Sex	-2.74**	-1.17	-2.37*	-0.85

* $p < .05$ ** $p < .01$ *** $p < .001$

4.4. Study Three

In the no reinforcement and set reinforcement versions of the software, significant correlations occurred between performance and attention ($p < .001$). There was, however, no significant correlation between performance and attention in the learner's choice version. Closer inspection of the data revealed that children who were poor performers maintained a higher level of attention in the learner's choice version than in the other two programs. Significant negative correlations were observed between performance and attention and both verbal and physical prompts in all versions of the software ($p < .01$). This indicates that children who performed and attended well required fewer verbal and physical prompts during experimental sessions.

The mean values and standard deviations for performance, attention, verbal and physical prompts are shown in Table 5. Children both performed and attended better to versions of the software in which they had some control over the choice of reinforcement. Marginally higher scores were obtained in the learner's choice version which allowed children to select the reinforcer on each of the 5 experimental days. Fewer verbal prompts were required by children in the learner's choice version, despite the inclusion of additional decision-making components in the program.

TABLE 5
Mean (Standard Deviation) Values for No Reinforcement (Rf), Set Reinforcement (Rf) and Learner's Choice Versions

Version	Performance	Attention	Verbal	Physical
No Rf	76.97 (13.2)	75.42 (16.8)	28.80 (13.6)	5.05 (3.6)
Set Rf	81.65 (11.9)	83.78 (11.2)	27.51 (16.1)	6.05 (5.2)
Choice	82.24 (10.9)	85.33 (10.4)	26.64 (13.1)	5.54 (4.0)

Comparisons of the dependent variables (performance, attention, verbal and physical prompts) and version, IQ, conceptual status level, day, order, time and sex are summarised in Table 6. Of the dependent variables, a significant effect across versions was found only for attention, this being attributable to a higher level of attention in the set reinforcer and learner's choice versions. A strong effect was noted for performance, verbal and physical prompts across IQ levels, indicating that children with higher IQ scores tended to perform better and require fewer verbal and physical prompts during sessions. There were no significant effects noted for attention across IQ levels, suggesting that children with lower IQ levels still attended well to the programs. Significant effects were also noted for both performance and attention across conceptual status levels, but there were no significant effects for either verbal or physical prompts across conceptual status levels. A strong effect was noted for performance scores across days indicating improvement over the five experimental days. There was also a significant effect for sex noted, with females obtaining higher performance scores than males.

TABLE 6
Independent Samples Rank Tests for Study 3

Kruskal-Wallis One-Way Analysis of Variance (X^2)

Variable	Performance	Attention	Verbal	Physical
Version	3.51	6.77*	0.60	0.08
IQ	9.74**	1.01	11.52**	17.37***
Concept	19.74***	10.80**	5.13	3.49
Day	17.55***	1.83	4.10	2.38
Order	0.23	0.64	0.52	1.60
Mann-Whitney U Test (Z scores corrected for ties)				
Time	-0.26	-1.51	-1.79	-0.23
Sex	-3.05**	-0.28	-1.18	-0.54

* $p < .05$ ** $p < .01$ *** $p < .001$

5. DISCUSSION

5.1. Fantasy

Fantasies are said to derive their emotional appeal from the fact that individuals can identify with them at a personal level. To be effective in the learning situation therefore, fantasies should be personally meaningful and provide images that the learner can identify with.

The findings from the first study demonstrated significant differences in the amount of verbal interaction which occurred between children and the trainer in drill and practice, arcade and adventure versions of the software. While the adventure version did not hold children's attention as well as the arcade version, the increased verbal interaction observed suggests that adventure game formats tend to encourage greater social interaction, while other types of programs tend to encourage solitary behaviour (for example, drill and practice).

The parent survey was conducted to ensure that the fantasy theme presented in the first two studies was of interest to the majority of children. It was clear, however, that some children would have preferred different reinforcers than the ones used. Some children actually requested other forms of reinforcement (such as a teddy bear riding a motorcycle). Evidence from the third study suggests that parents are not necessarily the best judges of what their children are interested in. Moreover, children explored a number of different fantasy themes (without regard for sex stereotyping) in the learner's choice version of the software.

5.2. Curiosity

Intrinsically motivating environments tend to arouse the learner's curiosity. Malone and Lepper [2] distinguish between sensory and cognitive curiosity in their Taxonomy of Intrinsic Motivations for Learning. Sensory curiosity can be evoked by varying environmental stimuli such as visual and sound effects, while cognitive curiosity is aroused by providing an optimal level of informational complexity.

It was hypothesised that children would maintain a higher level of attention in the arcade version of the software, which incorporated a number of additional auditory and visual enhancements. It was further hypothesised, that children would attain highest performance scores in the drill and practice version, which had minimal distracting elements. While the hypothesis that children would attend best to the arcade version was supported, contrary to expectations, highest performance scores were also obtained in the arcade version. While not statistically significant, this finding indicates that the use of auditory and visual embellishments does not have a detrimental effect on performance.

5.3. Challenge

The importance of challenge in activities that are intrinsically motivating has been addressed by Csikszentmihalyi [10] and Malone [3]. Learning environments, it is argued, can be made more challenging by the use of hierarchical goal systems. According to Malone, computer-based activities can be made .ore challenging by including variable difficulty levels, multiple levels of goals and uncertain outcomes. Observations made by Bandura and Schunk [11] suggest proximal goals are superior to distal goals for producing sustained intrinsic motivation and enhanced performance.

There were no significant differences in either performance or attention for immediate goal, multiple level goal or long term goal versions of the software. However, visual inspection of the means revealed a trend suggesting that children perform and attend best to versions incorporating proximal goals (immediate and multiple level goals). The significant correlation observed between performance and attention in the multiple level goal version, suggests that an optimal level for performance and attention is obtained in programs which use a combination of proximal and distal goals.

5.4. Learner Control

Intrinsic motivation has been described as a striving for competence and self-determination [12,13,] and is said to arise from activities which provide the learner with a sense of control [14,15]. Indeed even an illusion of control is said to produce powerful effects [16].

During the first study an attempt was made to create an illusion of control by allowing children to choose the road they wanted to travel down in their search for a surprise birthday party. Contrary to expectations, this decision-making component in the program had no obvious positive effect on student motivation; indeed many children were frustrated by the unnecessary delays and distractions caused by this option. This finding suggests, that, unless students see a direct consequence as a result of their actions, they will be unlikely to perceive themselves as having control of the learning situation.

This issue was investigated further in the third study. When given the opportunity to select their own fantasy themes from a pictographic menu, children chose a variety of different reinforcers. The significant effect noted for attention across software versions supports the hypothesis that children are motivated by the inclusion of options which enable them to be in control. Further support for this hypothesis is provided by the finding that poor performers still maintained a high level of attention in the learner's choice version of the software.

Anecdotal evidence obtained from analysis of interactions between children and trainer during the sessions revealed that children did not make random choices, but rather evaluated and discussed alternatives before making their selections. Moreover, when denied the opportunity to choose their fantasy (for example in the no reinforcement version of the software), significant behaviour problems emerged. This suggests that once children are given the opportunity to take control for their own learning, denial of that control may has significant implications for classroom management.

6. CONCLUSIONS

The aim of this study has been to identify the most salient features of intrinsically motivating software designed for young children with disabilities. The findings from this study support the hypothesis that children perform and attend best to software which include fantasy, multiple levels of goals and provides the opportunity for children to make decisions. The hypothesis that children attend best to software which incorporates auditory and visual embellishments has been supported, but the prediction that this would have a detrimental effect on performance has not been demonstrated.

These findings are consistent with those of other researchers and suggest that many of the features shown to be motivating in computer games for "nondisabled" children are also important determinants of motivation in young children with disabilities.

ACKNOWLEDGEMENTS

The author wishes to acknowledge the assistance of psychologists, Greg Ireland, Michael Correll and Kate Caudrey during the early stages of this project, and the co-operation of the Manager of Early Childhood Services, Pauline Mc Gregor. Acknowledgement is also given to the Apple Computer Education Foundation for providing equipment for the project, and Dataflow Software for providing software for evaluation.

REFERENCES

[1] Cohen, M.W., Intrinsic Motivation in the Special Education Classroom, Journal of Learning Disabilities, 19 (5), May 1986, pp. 258-261.

[2] Malone, T.W. and Lepper, M.R., Making Learning Fun: A Taxonomy of Intrinsic Motivations for Learning, in: Snow, T.E. & Farr, M.J., (eds.), Aptitude Learning and Instruction, Vol. 3, Lawrence Erlbaum Associates, New Jersey, 1987.

[3] Malone, T.W., Toward a Theory of Intrinsically Motivating Instruction, Cognitive Science, 4, 1981, pp. 333-369.

[4] Lepper, M.R. & Chabay, R.W., Intrinsic Motivation and Instruction. Conflicting Views on the role of Motivational Processes in Computer-Based Education, Educational Psychologist, 20 (4), 1985, pp. 217-230.

[5] Lepper, M.R., Microcomputers in Education: Motivational and Social Issues, American Psychologist, 40 (1), 1985, pp. 1-18.

[6] Deci, E.L. and Ryan, R.M., Curiosity and Self-Directed Learning: The Role of Motivation in Educationn in: Katz, L.G. (ed.), Current Topics in Early Childhood Education, Vol. IV., Ablex, New Jersey, 1982.

[7] Dweck, C.S., The Role of Expectations and Attributions in the Alleviation of Learned Helplessness, Journal of Personality and Social Psychology, 31, 1975, pp. 674-685.

[8] Wood, D.L. and Correll, M., Research Implications for the Use of Microcomputers in Early Childhood and Special Education, in: Alp, P. (ed.), Golden Opportunities: Proceedings of the Sixth Australian Computers in Education Conference in Australia, September, 1988, pp. 378-386.

[9] Kazdin, A.E., Single-Case Research Designs, Oxford University Press, New York, 1982.

[10] Csikszentmihalyi, M. Intrinsic Rewards and Emergent Motivation, in: Lepper, M. and Greene, D. (Eds.), The Hidden Costs of Reward: New Perspectives on the Psychology of Human Motivation, Lawrence Erlbaum Associates, New Jersey, 1978.

[11] Bandura, A. and Schunk, D.H., Cultivating Competence, Self-Efficacy, and Intrinsic Interest Through Proximal Self-Motivation, Journal of Personality and Social Psychology, 41 (3), 1981, pp. 586-598.

[12] Deci, E.L., Intrinsic Motivation, Plenum, New York, 1975.

[13] Zuckerman, M. Porac, J., Lathin, D., Smith, R. & Deci, E., On the Importance of Self-Determination for Intrinsically Motivated Behaviour, Personality and Psychology, 4 (3), July 1978, pp. 443-446.

[14] Lepper, M.R. and Milojkovic, J.D., The "Computer Revolution" in Education: A Research Perspective, in: Campbell, P.F. and Fein, G.G., Young Children and Microcomputers, Prentice Hall, New Jersey, 1986.

[15] Lepper, M.R. & Greene, D. (eds.), The Hidden Costs of Reward: New Perspectives on the Psychology of Human Motivation, Lawrence Erlbaum Associates, New Jersey, 1978.

[16] Langer, E.J., The Illusion of Control, Journal of Personality and Social Psychology, 32 (2), 1975, pp. 311-328.

Computers in Education
A. McDougall and C. Dowling (Editors)
Elsevier Science Publishers B.V. (North-Holland)

COMPUTER COACHING FOR BEAUTIFUL HANDWRITING OF JAPANESE CHARACTERS IN ELEMENTARY SCHOOL

Toshinori YAMASAKI*, Masahiro YAMAMOTO**, and Seiji INOKUCHI**

*Faculty of Education, Kagawa University, Takamatsu, Kagawa, 760 Japan.
**Faculty of Engineering Science, Osaka University, Toyonaka, Osaka, 560 Japan.

We have developed an instruction system for correctly writing beautiful characters using a personal computer. The student can learn the handwriting skills with a data-tablet system and a standard database in the knowledge base. After the student writes a character on the writing pad with a pen, the system evaluates the input character and gives instructions for forming a more beautiful character. Through this system, the children can acquire the art of handwriting and become familiar with computers.

1. INTRODUCTION

It is very important to improve the handwriting style of young students. In Japan, handwriting is supposed to reveal not only its literal meaning but also the writer's personality and sensibility. The Japanese language consists of several kinds of characters such as Kanji, Hirakana and Katakana. It is difficult to read and write because its structure is more complicated than that of an alphabetic character. Therefore, a course in penmanship is part of the school curriculum in Japan. It is one of the skill-based subjects. Students can acquire good writing skills through repeated training. Today, since they must teach a very heavy curriculum, Japanese teachers have become too busy to teach each student individually. For the above reasons, there is a need to develop an effective handwriting system, such as the CAI, based on recent technology.

We had formerly developed a training system for good writing characters using OLCR (On-Line Character Recognition) techniques[1],[2],[3]. It enables us to know what each stroke should be and also provides interactive correction. Though we use character recognition techniques, we do not attempt to recognize unknown characters. The purpose of this system is to teach the fundamental skills of properly writing known input-characters.

In this paper, we shall try to introduce a rule-based training system for penmanship. This system is also intended to be used in the elementary school. It can analyze not only the handwritten characters but also a student's skills or knowledge of writing. Thus, the coaching activity becomes more intelligent and effective.

2. CAI SYSTEM FOR BEAUTIFUL HANDWRITING

2.1. System Overview

The student can master techniques for proper handwriting through writing practice. Such systematic training, effected by the skills of writing, is derived from long experience. The skills of writing taught by teachers are as follows.

1) Dynamic features : stroke order, writing pressure and writing speed.
2) Macro-form features : arrangement of character in sentence, letter shape (outline of character) and subpattern.
3) Fine shape features : corner, termination, crossing point and contact point of each stroke.

These skills are arranged in suitable order according to school grade level and degree of difficulty. The students are instructed step by step in the proper skills.

We must take all of these skills into account in order to achieve a beautiful handwriting system. This system stores a handwritten primary Japanese character database. We can obtain the reference features such as stroke order, letter shape and fine features of the model character. This database enables us to evaluate input character, improve the character, display a model form and give guidance for learning. About 2000 characters can be used in this system, including Kanji, Hirakana and Katakana. The input characters are evaluated through comparison with the reference structures in the standard database. The evaluation criteria are stroke order, letter shape, writing speed and so on.

This system identifies the undesirable features in input characters. The student can learn good writing skills with the guidance of this system.

2.2. Instructions for Good Writing Skills

2.2.1. Learning the Stroke Order

In the Japanese language, the stroke order is essential because the number of strokes of a Kanji character is greater than that of an alphabetic character. For writing beautiful letters, we must write characters in the proper stroke order. The stroke order of the input character is evaluated in comparison with the model character in the database. That is, the input character is matched to the model character using an interstroke distance matrix[1]. A sample of stroke order practice is shown in fig.1. In fig.1, the upper and lower part is the input and reference stroke order respectively. The middle part is the instruction from this system. After that, the student can rewrite for practice.

2.2.2. Macro-Form Feature

Here we deal with the overall structure of the character, such as the letter shape, and the subpattern called the macro-form feature.

The similarity of the letter shape between input and model is evaluated based on the Hamming distance d_h. In fig.2, the upper and lower part correspond to the calculated convex hull and the letter shape respectively. The smaller the value of the d_h, the more the letter shape of the input character resembles the shape of the model.

The reference subpattern in the database consists of a stroke set. The input character is improved by fitting the location of the subpattern to the reference character. Fig.3 shows the input (lower part) and the model (upper part) characters. The improved characters, by fitting them with the subpattern (called improved-1), are displayed in the middle part. In order to teach the stroke shape, the distorted strokes are recognized by calculating the distance of each stroke. Fig.3 shows the original, improved-1 and improved-2 characters. The colored line in the improved-1 shows the improved strokes.

2.2.3. Handwriting Pen Speed

Proper writing speed is necessary to develop beautiful handwriting. We introduce the handwriting pen speed into the evaluation of written characters[3]. The handwriting letter form is evaluated by comparing it with the pen speed. The dynamic state of pen speed in a character is displayed by using velocity vectors (fig.4).

3. APPROACH TO THE KNOWLEDGE BASED CAI

3.1. Knowledge of Penmanship

The knowledge of penmanship shown in fig.5 is as follows.
1) Declarative skill knowledge.
2) Procedural skill knowledge.
3) Model character.
4) Part composition.
5) Model script.
6) Prerequisite relationship between each skill knowledge of penmanship.

Here, 1) and 2) are the skill knowledge of

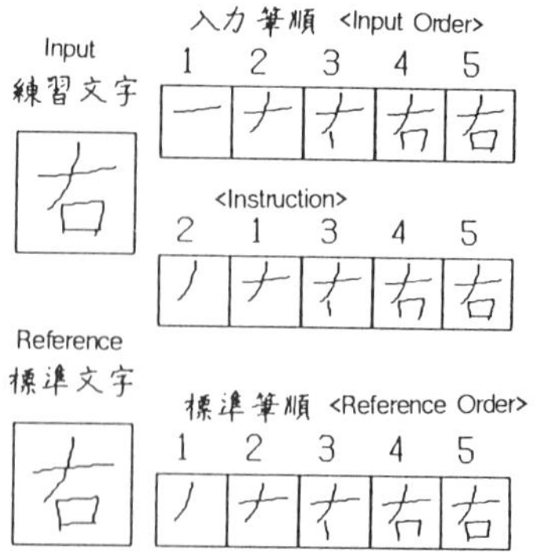

Figure 1 Learning the Stroke Order

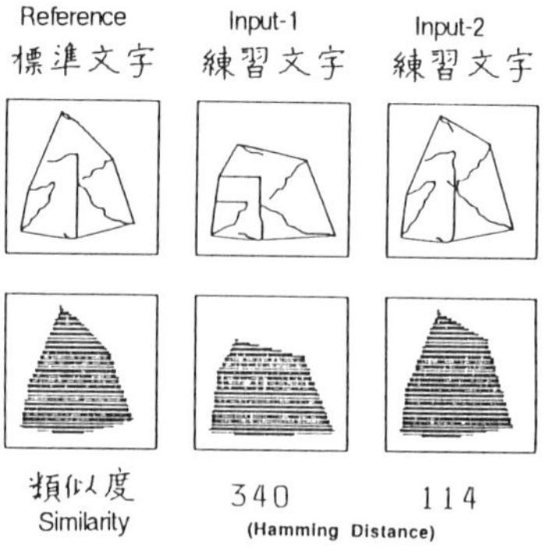

Figure 2 Learning the Letter Shape

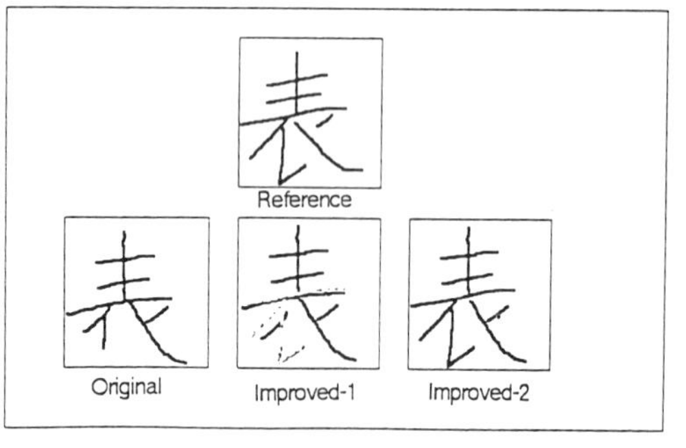

Figure 3 Learning the Letter Form

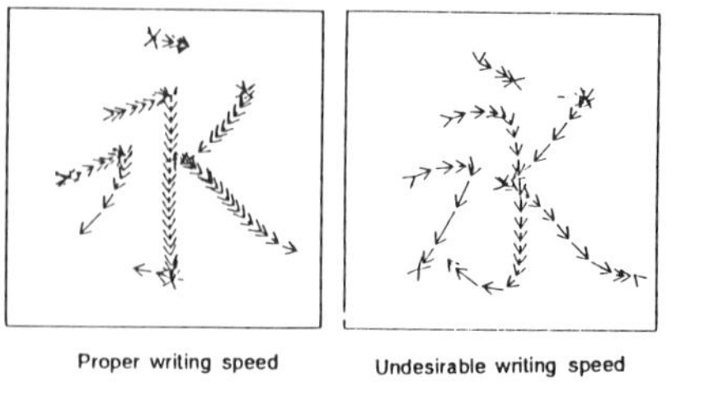

Figure 4 Dynamic Display of Pen Movement

penmanship. Skills 1) to 4) act as the text knowledge in this system. 5) and 6) are the teaching knowledge and are used when the system decides a coaching.

The skill knowledge of penmanship is expressed by the word for remarkable items in beautiful handwriting and the skills to be used. Here, we adopt the skills shown in fig.6 according to the skills of writing described before.

3.2. Representation of the Skill Knowledge of Penmanship

3.2.1. Representation of the Character Structure

We must define the structure of the script when we represent the skill knowledge in this system. The representation needs to correspond to the character pattern data because the skill knowledge is intended to act upon the pattern data. Here, we represent the handwritten script shown in fig.7 as a tree structure. The class of the tree structure consists of the script, character,stroke and stroke segment. The script pattern is classified according to each class of the tree structure. After that, each component of the class is represented by a node coded individually.

We add the subpattern to the tree structure. Some subpatterns like "kunigamae" do not have a continuous stroke sequence. Therefore, in this case, the nature of the subpattern is not a pattern set, but the knowledge of the character structure. For the above reasons, the subpattern is not classified between the character and the stroke. It is described as an attribute element of the structure.

3.2.2. Representation of the Declarative Skill Knowledge of Penmanship

The skill knowledge consists of the name, category, condition and object node ID. In addition to the above, we add the skill type that is error knowledge. We classify the skill knowledge according to the property of the skill. This skill knowledge is expanded on the script tree.

3.2.3. Inspection of the Skill Knowledge in the Character Pattern

The declarative skill knowledge and its applied objects are described in the knowledge base. The skill knowledge is applied to the object of the pattern. The procedure of pattern processing (procedural knowledge) is needed to check whether the skill knowledge is applied to the input character. Thus, we can regard declarative skill knowledge in the knowledge base as the direct "glass box" knowledge, and the procedural knowledge as the indirect "black box" knowledge respectively. Each piece of procedural knowledge in the pattern operations module acts as a predicate of the character(we call it pattern predicate). The system can estimate the degree of skill knowledge learning from the right or wrong of the pattern predicate.

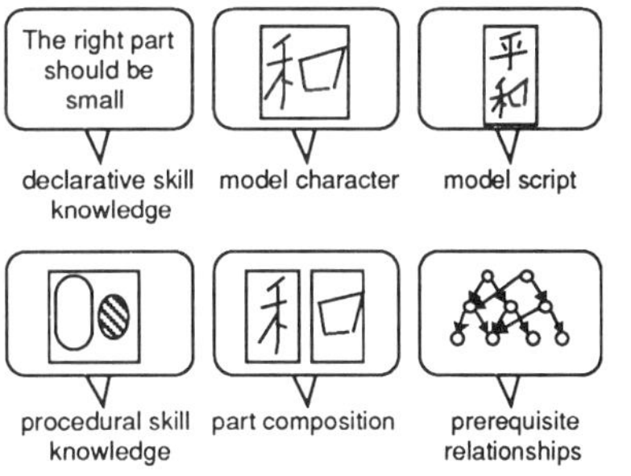

Figure 5 Knowledge of Penmanship

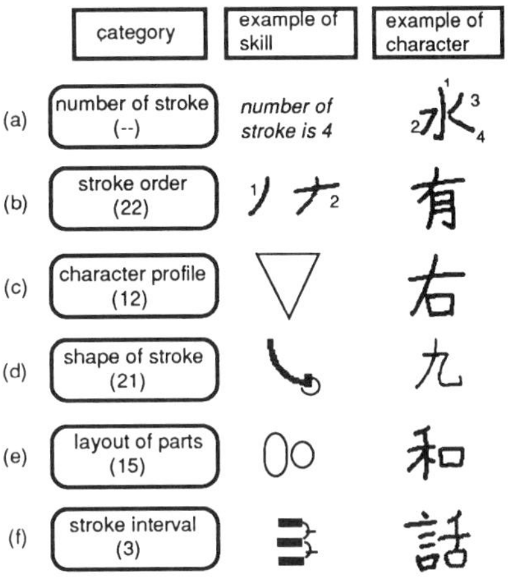

Figure 6 Skills of Writing

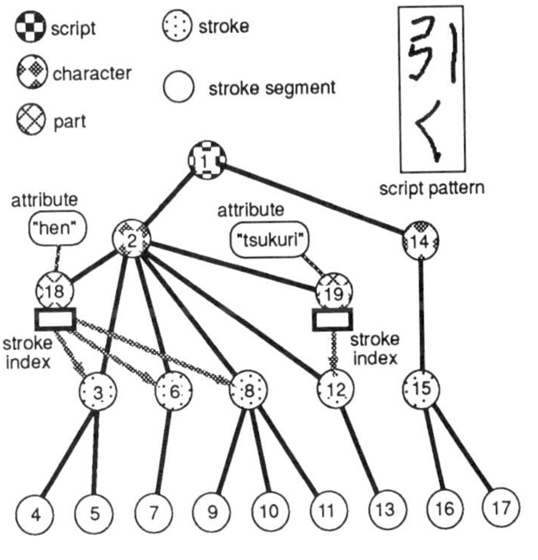

Figure 7 Representation of Handwriting

3.3. Configuration of the Knowledge-Based CAI

The software configuration of the system is shown in fig.8. The upper module of the knowledge and the lower module of the pattern operation are described as a production rule by OPS83 and by the C language respectively. The number of the production rule in the upper module is about 200 including 50 for describing the knowledge, 40 for checking the knowledge and 60 for choosing the strategy of teaching.

The nodes of each class of the input script are checked through comparison with the skill knowledge expressed in each node of the model script. After that, the system knows the learning degree of the skill knowledge of the student. We call these results the student model. In contrast to the ordinary ICAI, the student model used here does not have the ability to solve problems.

The instruction style of this system is mainly the drill and practice mode, and does not use the mixed initiative. The main role of the teaching strategy is to decide how to show the checked mistake and to give adequate guidance by checking the input script of the student. The system selects the appropriate instruction according to all noted mistakes.

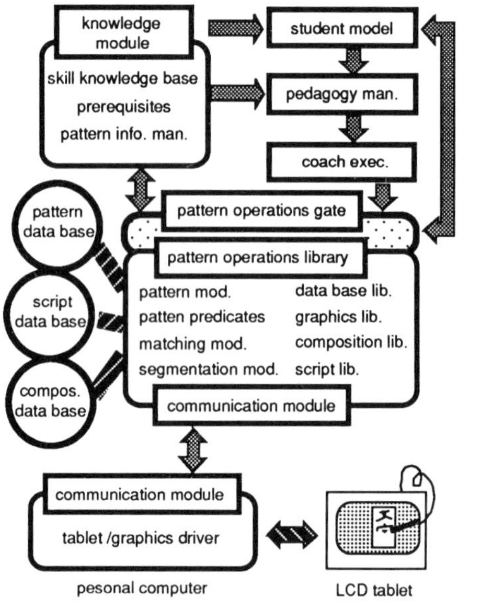

Figure 8 Software Configuration of the System

3.4. Example of Coaching

Instruction derived from the evaluation of the student's script is done with both an explanatory sentences and the suitable display/ practice training. Instruction about the allocations of subpattern is shown in fig.9. In this case, the skill knowledge proper to the character such as "Hen should be written small" is described beforehand. In addition to this, the knowledge becomes active "If the character consists of small hen, its hen should be written at the position of vertical center". The system may decides that the student has not mastered that skill yet, and then would give adequate guidance.

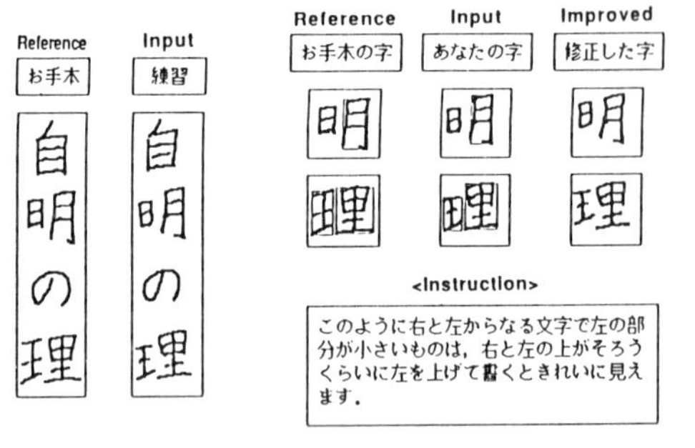

Figure 9 Coaching of Allocation of Subpatterns

4. CONCLUSIONS

We have developed a knowledge based instruction system for correctly writing beautiful Japanese characters in elementary school. This system stores a handwritten primary Japanese character database and knowledge of the skill of writing in the knowledge base. We can obtain the reference features such as stroke order and letter shape of the model characters. Students can learn how to improve their handwriting through the use of this system. Training skills are stroke order, letter shape, subpattern, writing speed and so on.

Through this system, we can detect the undesirable structures in the input character and give adequate guidance for writing a beautiful character. The teacher can observe the handwriting of the students on his CRT screen and instruct each student accordingly. Thus, this computer aided teaching system can improve the ability of teachers to instruct individual students.

REFERENCES

[1] T.Yamasaki, S.Inokuchi and Y.Sakurai: "Training System for Well Writing Based on On-Line Character Recognition", 7th Int. Conf. on Pattern Recognition, pp.1039-1041 (1984).

[2] T.Yamasaki, S.Inokuchi and Y.Sakurai: "Training system for Well Writing of Chinese Characters Based on Their Local Structure", Trans.IECE Japan, J67-D,4,pp.442-449 (1984).

[3] T.Yamasaki, M.Yamamoto and S.Inokuchi: "CAI System for Acquiring Good Writing Skills Based on the Analysis of Pen-Speed", Trans. IECE Japan, J70-D,11,pp.2071-2076(1987).

RAINBOW STREAM

Computers in Education
A. McDougall and C. Dowling (Editors)
Elsevier Science Publishers B.V. (North-Holland)

COMPUTERS IN THE ISRAELI EDUCATIONAL SYSTEM - IMPLEMENTATION ASPECTS (1984 - 1989)

Ben Zion BARTA, Efraim ENGEL, Samuel KAPLAN, Daniel MILLIN

Ministry of Education and Culture, Jerusalem, Israel

The paper deals with the implementation of the national policy on computers in education in Israel. The main categories of computer-based actions and their sub-categories are presented, as they were considered at decision-making stages. The structure of the Israeli educational system and its available computing infrastructure are described . A survey of activities regarding kindergarten, primary schools, junior high-schools, high schools, vocational education, teacher pre-service and in service training, evaluation and licensing of systems and educational management applications follows.

1. INTRODUCTION

This is the third in a series of articles, presented at 4-5 years' intervals [1,2] summarizing approaches, achievements, outcomes, problems, difficulties, trends and prospects for development regarding, first, the penetration and further-on the full integration of computers and informatics technologies into a national (even if small) educational system.

The situation described is the outcome of the developments of almost two decades - it represents not only the deep changes of the approaches of the educational authorities and policy-makers, and the expertise gained, but also the tremendous progress of the information and computer technologies, and their availability.

Section 2 of this paper summarizes some of the main policy decisions made during this period of development.

Section 3 covers in short, the whole field (or most of it), space limitations not allowing to go into more detail.

2. REVIEW OF POLICY DECISIONS

The educational uses of information technologies and of data communication systems, are classified within 3 broad categories:

a. Enhancement of The Educational and of The Teaching/Learning Processes.

As an overall approach, information technology should be applied to assist solving problems of the educational system in those areas where the computer has specific advantages, which may conceivably promote solutions.

Computer based activities should be aimed at the development of learning and thinking: proficiency in methodical thinking, planning, knowledge, calculations and the development of problem- solving and abstraction capabilities.

Using the computer to enrich the teaching of different subject-matter has to be carried out in the whole variety of ways generally known as Computer Aided Learning (tutorials, simulations, modelling, micro-worlds, educational games etc.) (CAL).

Drill and practice is intended to entrench skills, mainly the basic ones. Drill and practice should be well integrated in the regular teaching activity, in order to promote the pupil's accomplishments and to facilitate the teacher's pedagogical work. Its effectiveness is reduced if delivered as an independent activity.

Another powerful way of integrating information technologies in education is the use of "Software tools" as part of the learning activities of different subject matter:

* Using the word processor in its broader sense : skills, creative writing, language, etc.

* Using data bases, electronic spreadsheets and similar packages for processing and displaying by numeric and graphic means.

* Using real data banks, within the teaching process and within the framework of the student's individual work. It may be done by connection to existing data banks, or by extracting parts of existing data banks for educational applications.

* Using software packages as an integral part of technological education, and of the teaching of sciences and other subjects.

* Communications (electronic mail and conferences, networks and similar facilities) among pupils as well as among educational staff, within the framework of formal and informal education.

Different ways should be considered for integrating computers in teaching, in active and individual learning, in laboratory learning, in learning centers, in classrooms, and as an aid for lecture-style teaching. Integration of the computer should be carried out in those very subjects and activities where the computer has a notable relative advantage over conventional learning.

b. Teaching of Informatics, Information Technologies and Computer applications as Subject Matter.

This is a broad and important field, having in view the preparation of the new generation for the informatics-oriented, technological world.

The variety in this category depends on the age group, the general goal of the teaching and the special interests, if any, of the group of pupils:

* First indirect, intuitive knowledge of computers is provided by the computer based learning activities, starting at the earliest grades.

* Formal teaching of "computer literacy": basic concepts in informatics and a structured introduction to computer applications and to information processing concepts.

* Informatics and information technologies taught indepth, similar to other scientific disciplines.

* Vocational training of professionals in software and hardware and related information technologies.

* End-users' training in all professions, at basic and advanced level.

c. Enhancement of Educational Management and Decision Making.

Computers and communication can be used in a variety of ways to help general and educational management and decision-making. Among the steps to reach this goal, the following should be considered for gradual implementation:

* Computerization of the school office, day-to-day management, use of word processors and electronic-mail facilities.

* Management of the attendance and of the teaching systems at different levels within the school (student, classroom, institutional) as well as at the levels of local, regional and national systems.

* Implementing local, regional and national networks for educational-management and decision- making.

* Evaluation and assessment of the achievements of students, adapting the teaching process to individual requirements,individual and group teaching based on feed-back, diagnostics and guidance of individual learning.

* Computer aided preparation of questionnaires for examinations at school and classroom level: preparation of questions banks, classification and evaluation of questions, production of examination forms.

The aspects of implementation described in the following sections reflect the practical outcomes of policy decisions. The actions selected for implementation are always a subset of the whole range of desirable activities. This selection was based, through the years, on social, political and economic factors as well as on educational and technical ones. We should not disregard practical factors of feasibility or the intuitive, subjective way of reasoning of the group of people involved with the decision- making.

The main policy decisions were centered around:

* Selecting the main issues and giving priorities to research development and implementation of the three above mentioned main categories (a., b., c.) and their sub-categories.

* Defining (and giving priorities to) the target population.

* Dealing with the necessary infra-structure.

* Human resources development.

3. SURVEY OF MAIN ACTIVITIES

3.1 The Environment

3.1.1 The Israeli Schooling System.

The organization of the Israeli schooling is similar to what can be found in many countries.

We have about 7000 Kindergartens, 2300 primary schools and 600 high - schools, many of them comprehensive running all paths of secondary education. At the tertiary level of interest for this survey, there are 6 academic schools of education, 30 teacher-training colleges, 20 colleges training technicians and practical engineers in various disciplines.

3.1.2. The Computing Infrastructure.

During the last years one can see a constant progress of quality and quantity of courseware and computer-based learning activities available for schools. This fact, and the interest in the new and esteemed media as well as the continuous decrease of computer prices and increase of their capabilities, caused a fast increase of the number of computers available in schools and of the amount of time that pupils spend with the computer during the schooling hours.

Computers are not any more a scarce and rather strange technology, even if they still are innovative. They are by now a well established media capable to provide effective, innovative and motivating learning activities. They are actually used in a variety of approaches and methodologies within education and the formal teaching/ learning process, and in a range of extra-curricular activities. They are also used for pedagogical and general school management. Individual teachers use computers as a help for their preparatory work.

Computers not only improve teaching and management, but, in more and more instances they cause more profound changes of the school organization, of the ways teaching is delivered and learning is done, of the assessment and follow-up of pupils achievements, of communication channels, etc.

Not only hardware and courseware quality and availability did change but also those of the off-the-shelf software tools like spread-sheets, application generators, word-processors, compilers and related programming-tools, engineering and scientific packages. The prices reached a level low enough to make them affordable and the much improved performance made them attractive for schools too. This fact causes profound changes of contents and methodologies of teaching informatics, information technologies and professional computer applications.

The extent of penetration of computers to the Israeli school system can be summarized by the following data:

Academic schools of Education and Teachers Training Colleges, are all equipped with computers dedicated to educational purposes. Some of them have large amounts of equipment, including advanced technology items. Others may have the minimal equipment needed for providing the compulsory introductory courses.

Most high-schools, the technological ones and the academic ones, about 95%, do have on-site computer equipment. It is mostly used for teaching informatics, information- technologies and computer applications, partly as learning activities of different subject matters.

About 70% of elementary schools and of kindergartens have computers and are using them mainly for the variety of ways to enhance education and improve teaching/learning.

About 65% of the equipment consists of micro-computers most of a few brands, selected according to the national policy, the same brands as in most other countries.

Many of the schools are using a mini-computer configuration assembled in Israel, the "Toam" system. It developed from a dedicated arithmetics drill and practice machine to a powerful general-purpose system, made up of a network of personal computers (AT-type) with a strong central machine and providing many learning activities and general data processing. [3].

Many schools locate the computers in a dedicated room - the computer laboratory, as stand-alone's or in a local network configuration. But more and more schools are moving the computers to the class-rooms, to the various laboratories, libraries and other locations within the school. Networking at the school level is at its beginning, regional educational networks are planned and may be implemented within a short time.

3.2 SURVEY BY AGE GROUPS

The survey is arranged in age sequence, activities with a general nature being at the end.

3.2.1 Kindergartens.

Kindergartens are the last among our educational institutions that had computers integrated into their educational activities. First trials of computer usage with so young children, development of adequate activities and their evaluation started in 1982. Some 3 years later, larger scale introduction of computers to the kindergarten curriculum has been approved and in 1988/89 some 60% of the kindergartens are using computers. The introduction of computers to the kindergartens has been preceded by extensive training of teachers' and supervision staff, and is accompanied by adequate support. The development of this infrastructure has been based on the experience accumulated when computers entered the primary schools.

We can now positively state that, with adequate infrastructure and preparations, the use of computers in kindergartens is feasible and worthwhile. [4].

3.2.2 The Primary Schools.

As stated by the policy outlines, there is no attempt to teach in a formal way concepts of informatics at the primary school level. Activities are intended to educational purposes and to improve the teaching/learning process. However, there is an indirect process of learning of concepts and of habits regarding computer usage. Therefore, attention is to be given to the correctness of this indirect learning - starting from correct presentation of concepts encountered (e.g. files, data, program, etc.), to good examples of professional practice (e.g. well designed man-machine interaction), to ethics of information- systems (e.g. respect of privacy, of copy rights).

As regarding the variety of computer activities - part of them are based on drill and practice, mainly of the basic skills but more and more emphasis is given to other, perhaps more advanced and demanding ways like use of models and simulations, use of open ended teaching application generators, use of word-processors, data bases, electronic spread-sheets, Logo-type activities. These last approaches can be fit to the teaching of almost any discipline - the actual implementation depending mainly upon the preparation of the teaching materials (by the teacher, himself, or by other adequate agencies) definition of methodologies and, perhaps availability and limitation of equipment. Drill and practice has its importance that should not be neglected; here the main effort of the teacher is to correctly integrate it into his/her classroom teaching and to use the individual achievement reports for adequately dealing with each pupil. One of the recent surveys in this area is related to the already mentioned TOAM System [5]. There is only a very limited use of tutorial programs.

As a rule of thumb, schools are recommended to dedicate about half of the "computing time" to drill and practice, the rest to the other type of activities. Teachers or schools first introducing computers are advised to limit, at the beginning, the variety of applications and to diversify them gradually, later on. Many will choose drill and practice for their first application.

There is presently no more controversy whether computers should be used as part of the regular school activities. There are discussions about the priority they should be given among the other needs of the school; about the priority to be given to the various subjects, when the demand for computers is higher than their availability.

Two main issues require intensive activity to support the integration of computers into the teaching/learning and educational activities, requirements that will keep growing for the next years - perhaps for a whole generation:

a. Training and on-going support and updating of all members of the educational staff. Some aspects of these support activities have been published [6].

b. A continuous effort to enrich and improve the range of available computer based activities and the quality of courseware.

It should be pointed out that the very nature of the computer-based activities is in contradiction with the frontal way of teaching still in use in most schools. There are two outcomes of this contradiction: On one hand, it is an additional encouragement (even pressure) for changes of the organization of the teaching to alternative methods based on small group and individual activities. On the other hand, activities apt for frontal classroom activities are developing and gradually getting in use.

The situation is similar with special education using much of the courseware intended for primary education, but courseware and applications specially prepared for the special education are also available. There are, as well, special devices and man-machine interfaces suited to these special needs. Several teams are dedicating their time and talents for developing and evaluating computer based activities in special education. [7]

Some achievements were reported by Margalit [8] in implementation of special courseware. The main issues were identified as individual differences and teachers preparation (training).

3.2.3 The Junior High Schools.

The approach for using computers for Improvement of teaching/learning and education is similar to that described in Sec. 3.2.2. The actual quantity of available courseware is smaller - causing these activities not to be so wide spread as in primary education.

Concerning the teaching of concepts of informatics, a formal course of "Introduction to Computers and Information Processing" is offered for the 7th and 8th grades. It is based on a 2-year's curriculum, 2 hours per week, a total of 120 hours. The first 60 hours can stand alone - making sense to teach the subject for only one year too. The recommended way for teaching is in the computer laboratory in groups of 24-30 pupils, one workstation (micro) for each pair.

The contents cover a variety of computer applications, referring not only to their use but also to an understanding of the processing done to perform the application. Planning of computer-based solutions and an introduction to programming are part of the course but not its main part. The world of computing, its advantages, capabilities and limitations, as well as social aspects of computing are presented at a level adequate to this age.

3.2.4 Secondary Schools.

At the Secondary School (high school) level the main activities are related to teaching of informatics, information technologies and computer applications. Use of software packages, models and simulation and other computer related activities within the teaching of the various disciplines is progressing gradually as adequate methods are developing.

The curricula for teaching informatics, as a general scientific subject are under revision. Procedural languages (like Pascal or Logo [8]) or declarative languages (like Prolog [9] or electronic spread - sheets) are used as means of implementation. The technicalities are considered secondary in importance and no effort is made to have complete coverage of language details, as it should be necessary to train programmers. The main issues are related to clear, systematic, scientific statement of the problems to be solved, analysis of possible solutions, systematic development of the solution (data representation, modular, top-down procedure development), verification, documentation etc. The approaches emphasized by the new curricula, the languages on which they are based are new to most of the present computer-science teachers - accordingly introduction of the new curricula involves again, a major retraining effort.

As for the vocational training - it is undergoing a far-reaching revision in general and especially in all issues related to teaching of information technologies and computer applications. These changes involve the I.T. department (training information technology - data processing - professionals) as well as 10 other departments specializing in different professions. The final product regarding the I.T. department will be the renewal of a major part of the curricula with updated approaches and new means and tools. Among the innovations: new fields of specialization; a new approach to teach software engineering, principles and tools; a new selection of programming languages. The new Curricula covers a total of some 1500 hours of professional training, provided in grades 10- 12, in addition to the general studies of the pupils.

The other large scale development involves most professions in which training is provided within the vocational education. Training for these professions, from the computing point of view, is training of end-users - either at basic level (limited to operational capability) or at advanced level. This operation involves end-user training for more than a dozen of different applications: curricular development, production of training materials and development of methodologies, training of large number of teachers. The main guidelines for running this project and the foreseen difficulties have been recently published [10].

The support to the teaching of informatics is provided by a separate team of advisors (distinct from those dealing with primary education). They provide advice and guidance to teachers and school principals about contents and methods of teaching, curricula, matriculation examinations, equipment purchase and organization of laboratories.

3.2.5 Teachers' Training and Updating.

Human resources development is the main effort related to computers in education, as important or even more important than the development of materials. It is dealing with all people involved in the educational process - from the seniors of the educational administration, supervisory staff, school management, secretarial staff, teachers - even parents. It is involved with new methodologies, new materials, new subject matters, new means for management and decision-making as well as the use of the technology. Also, there are new tasks like the school computing coordinator which requested definition and adequate training. A more detailed overview, reflecting our approaches can be found in [11, 12].

In 1983-84 it seemed to be a "revolutionary" decision to provide to all students at colleges of education a compulsory 60 - hours' course of initiation to computers. Nowadays, such a course is considered as insufficient. The present initiation course is mainly based on a general introduction to computers in education. It is usually followed by specific methodology for the various disciplines. Elective courses on courseware selection, planning, development are also offered. Most of colleges also offer the possibility of specialization in educational computing, at the extent of 4-8 academic hours per week for the 3 or 4 years of college.

Similar courses are offered as in-service training, to acting teachers, principals, supervisors. A few thousands of teachers, representing 5 - 10% of the teaching corp, are taking in-service courses every year. Some will learn rather short courses 40 -80 hours, other may learn up to 300-500 hours in one or two years. The longer courses train school-computing-coordinators or teachers of informatics or, else, vocational teachers of professional computer applications.

Not less important are the short sequences of 4-24 hours, mainly dedicated to updating of staff already active in educational computing.

Two issues have to be mentioned before concluding this short summary of activities:

* The fast change of course contents. Within a time-span of 3-4 years a given course may have almost completely different content.

* The high interest of teachers and their readiness to spend their time for learning and updating.

3.2.6 Evaluation and Licensing of Educational Computing Systems.

A few years ago it was believed that the bureaucracy should not interfere the natural, free process providing to every school the freedom to select the system to be purchased out of any choice offered by any distributor or manufacturer. Nowadays, the accepted approach is that the Ministry of Education has to test and license all components of the system - hardware, basic software systems, application software, courseware. The selection done by the school is from a limited set of licensed suppliers and systems. This approach reduces the diversity of systems, enables to deal with compatibility and transportability of software and courseware, ensures the reliability of the suppliers as concerning distribution of tested and approved computers, reasonable prices, adequate maintenance and training.

Two teams are involved with the process- one deals with hardware and system software the other with courseware and application software. The outcomes of their work are lists of licensed suppliers and of licensed products, with additional descriptive materials providing details of performance. These lists are updated from time to time by adding and removing items (suppliers or/and products).

3.2.7 Educational Management.

By their one initiative, some of our schools started using computers in educational management as far as the late seventieth. As micro's became more powerful, private enterprise produced and marketed educational management software to schools.

It was in 1985/6 that the Ministry of Education decided to set up a national data bank and network for educational management and decision making and to run a pilot project to study the various aspects of it. [13]. The final goal is to build an integrated information system including the central and regional offices of the Ministry of Education, municipalities and other local authorities and all schools.

From the school point of view, the pilot project relates to the standardization of software and data bases, study of communication and networking aspects, study of organizational and human aspects, testing training and support methodology.

It is expected that in a span of a few years, on one hand, most schools will use computers for educational management and, on the other hand, will gradually integrate into the developing national educational management network.

3.2.8 Computer-Communications Networks For Education.

The use of computer-communications in in Education, permits a new step forwards and new application of computers in the educational system. It will enable:

* On-line communication among teachers & students within and outside, schools.

* The use of electronic mail and electronic conferencing for communication, exchange of expertise and consultancies.

* Parents involvement and improved communication with school authorities.

* Broadening of the educational horizons to far-apart populations.

* Regional activities for carrying-out geographically dispersed experiments.

Several projects are active in this field, three of them directly supported by the Ministry of Education, namely "Comptown" [14], "Geshernet" and "The Northern Star". Two stearing committees dealing with infrastructure and educational aspects coordinate the whole activity.

4. SUMMARY

The integration of computers into a national education system is a multi-faced, interdisciplinary, long-range, complex and highly dynamic action having to deal with many aspects: social, human, educational, disciplinary, technical, financial, organizational and perhaps many others. It is the result of the activity of many organizations and individuals, each one having its points of view and interests. It is based on many decisions taken intuitively, with rather broad ranges of uncertainty. It has to be based on a sound estimation of future developments and to consider conclusions and experience gained in the nearby past.

We summarized in this paper many of the aspects of our national activity, have provided information about some of the implementation projects and have been able to refer to a reasonable, but incomplete, group of colleagues working in this field of common interest.

We hope that the information included will be useful to other similar projects - active or under preparation, that it will stimulate cooperation and exchanges of view with other, national groups having similar interests.

REFERENCES

[1] Barta, B.Z., Computers in the Israeli Educational System, in Lewis and Tagg (eds.) Compters in Education, (North Holland, 1981) pp 617-623.

[2] Barta, B.Z., Computers in the Israeli Educational System (1980-84) in Duncan and Harris (eds.), Computers in Education (elsevier, 1985) pp 901-908.

[3] Osin, L., TOAM3 - General Description, Internal report, Centre for Educational Technology, 16 Klauzner Str. Tel Aviv, Israel.

[4] Michaelovitz, R., Levite, A., Computers in Kindergartens - Educational Rationale and its Implementation, Hong-Kong Conference on Computers in Education, July, 1989.

[5] Hativa, N., Shapira, R., Navon, D., Computer Managed Practice - Effects on Instructional Method and on Teacher Adoption - to be published in "Teaching and Teacher Education, 1990.

[6] Barta, B.Z., Millin, D., Youval,A., Feinmesser, A., Considerations about the Logistic Infrastructure for Full Integration of Computers in Education, in Lewis and Tagg (eds.), Computers in Education (Elsevier, 1988) pp 413-420.

[7] Margalit, M., Integration of Technology into Cognitive Behavior Therapy: Social Skills Learning for Special Needs Adolescents, 3th World Congress on Behavior Therapy, (Edinburg, 1988).

[8] Margalit, M., Integration of Technology for Social Skills Training, in Lewis and Tagg (eds.), Computers in Education (Elsevier, 1988) pp 107-111.

[9] Leron, U., Lapidot, T., Communication to Logo Exchange, May, 1989, pp. 20-21.

[10] Shertz, Z., Maler, O., Shapiro, E., Learning with Prolog - a New Approach, J. of Computers in Mathematics and Science Teaching, Fall 1986, pp. 31-37.

[11] Barta, B.Z., End-Users Education at High School Level - A Preliminary Report, Education and Computing, Dec. 1989.

[12] Barta, B.Z., Training of Educational Staff for the Information Technology Age, Prospects, Vol. XVII (No.3), 1987, pp. 397-406.

[13] Millin, D., Barta, B.Z., In-Service and Pre-Service Training of Primary School Teachers in Informatics and Computer Applications in Education. Proceedings of Working Conference on Informatics and Teacher Training, (Elsevier, 1984).

[14] Ministry of Educationa, Department of Management Information Systems, A Pilot Project on Integration Schools into the Education Information System - (in Hebrew), internal report, August 1989, Jerusalem, Israel.

[15] Peled, E., Peled, Z., Alexander, G. Project Comptown: Educational Intervention and Action Research, British Journal of Educational Technology, Vol. XX (No.2) 1989, pp. 94-105.

Computers in Education
A. McDougall and C. Dowling (Editors)
Elsevier Science Publishers B.V. (North-Holland)

NEW INFORMATION TECHNOLOGY AT THE SECONDARY LEVEL - A SURVEY OF THE SITUATION IN THE FEDERAL REPUBLIC OF GERMANY

Dr. Ulrich Bosler

IPN - Institute for Science Education, Olshausenstr. 62
D - 2300 Kiel 1, Federal Republic of Germany

This paper provides an up-to-date survey of various aspects of New Information Technology (NIT) in general education and may be seen as a continuation of the European Conference publication of 1988 (cf. [1]).
Major changes are taking place in lower secondary education. Much is being done to develop syllabi and to produce teaching units for computer literacy valid for *all* pupils at the age of about 13.
The infrastructure for the development of courseware was built up in a nationwide initiative. The programme aimed to qualify a core of authors and to produce a set of exemplar CAL packages.
The reasons for the small amount of NIT in elementary education (age 6 to 10) are also indicated.

1. GENERAL REMARKS

The Federal Republic of Germany including Berlin (West) has a total population of approximately 60 million. The authority for the school system lies with the 10 "Länder" and Berlin (West), the states which comprise the FRG. Authoritative control includes regulations regarding the curriculum, time schedules, professional requirements and recruitment of teachers, school buildings and equipment. The system helps to ensure that irregularities in facilities and teaching personnel are avoided to a large extent.

The educational system in the FRG is primarily chararacterized by its 4-year elementary school ("Grundschule", age 6 to 10), followed by the tripartite system of secondary education, with "Hauptschule" (up to age 15), "Realschule" (up to age 16) and "Gymnasium" (up to age 19). In upper secondary education at the Gymnasium (age 16 to 19), a system of courses providing for various optional subjects has been introduced.
A minority of "Länder", most private schools and the several dozen comprehensive schools spread throughout the FRG, either postpone the decision as to which type of school a pupil should attend, or use a setting system.

Judging from various reports, I should estimate that approximately 60 % of general schools - especially in upper secondary education and excluding the Hauptschule and the primary sector - are well equipped with microcomputers of different makes (with a trend to MS-DOS).

Due to the concentration of work in the highest grades first, computer literacy as a general school discipline and the production of courseware has developed more slowly than in other countries.

2. NEW INFORMATION TECHNOLOGY FOR ALL PUPILS

Some of the "Länder" have now successfully finished 4-year pilot experiments ("Modellversuche") and are introducing computer literacy to *all* pupils at lower secondary level. Indicators for this work are the number of available teaching units e.g. in Nordrhein-Westfalen (cf. [3], [11]), and a lot of In-Service Teacher Training. The articles in the special LOG IN issue "Informationstechnische Grundbildung" ("NIT for all pupils") - produced with the support of the "Länder" Bremen, Berlin (West), Hamburg, Hessen and Nordrhein-Westfalen - describe the situation best (cf. [4]). A lot of work is also going on in Bayern (cf. [5]) and Niedersachsen (cf. [6]).

Comparing the reports of Norfolk in 1985 [2] and of Lausanne in 1988 [1] it is obvious that, after a phase of recommendations from 1983 onwards (cf. [7], [8]), a phase of model syllabi (cf. [9]) and pilot experiments (cf. [10]) many "Länder" spend quite a lot of energy and money in the implementation of their curriculum.

In such an up-to-date survey, only two examples of the dessimination can be described:

(1) <u>Involving a large number of subjects:</u> In Niedersachsen, an integrative concept in the existing subjects and in different grades was being developed. This "integrative approach" proceeds from the assumption that all subjects can be involved (cf. [6]). A lot of mainly subject-related commissions were set up. The work can be compared with the composition of a mosaic, each piece contributing to the whole.
My impression is that such an approach would at present be still difficult to implement in the FRG, but that this pilot experiment could yield a range of ideas for the use of computers and NIT in various subjects.

(2) <u>A 60-period curriculum in grade 8:</u> In Nordrhein-Westfalen (in the "Land" which houses about 1/3 of the West German population) a 60-period curriculum mainly for 13 year old pupils is to be introduced. The approach is to a great extent project-oriented.
Teaching materials and a concept for In-Service Teacher Training were developed in a 4-year pilot experiment finished in summer 1989 (cf. [11]). Hardware was provided: most of the schools in the pilot experiment were supplied with MS-DOS computers. Software tools were improved, e.g. easyBase was developed, the dBASE-software tool with an additional shell for pupils.
One of the central considerations is how to reflect the changes NIT has brought to our work and leisure activities in the three learning areas (1) robotics, (2) word processing and databases and (3) simulation. Several teaching proposals were developed for each learning area. The assumption is that basic instruction will consist of one unit chosen from each of the three categories. In comparison with the above mentioned work in Niedersachsen, the starting points are not mainly the school subjects but areas which should be a mirror of the use of NIT.
About 12 teaching units were developed e.g. CAD/CAM, noise, book or video, media in pupils' leisure time, (school) newsletters and a lake goes out of balance.
Normally two teachers - from Mathematics, Physics, Technology, or of German as a first languagage - teach such a unit in grade 8.
After this pilot experiment the final evaluation report will be presented in spring 1990, and the curriculum will be gradually introduced to all pupils.
It seems to me that this is a realistic strategy to be implemented in larger parts of the FRG.

3. COMPUTER ASSISTED LEARNING (CAL)

This area has changed greatly in the last two years. The infrastructure for the development of courseware was built up in a nationwide initiative. A programme - which was instigated at the IPN and done in collaboration with King's College London (cf. e.g. [12]) - qualified a core of authors and produced a set of exemplar CAL packages. In addition to this, further products were published by German publishers.

Comparing this with the situation described in the Lausanne-report of 1988 [1], it is obvious that the limited use of courseware until 1986 was followed by a phase of documentation and assessment (cf. [13], [14]) and a first phase of the production of some CAL materials, e.g. the materials developed in the context of NIT for all pupils in Hessen, Niedersachsen, Nordrhein-Westfalen, and by the Deutsches Institut für Fernstudien (DIFF) (cf. e.g. [15]).

Despite these promising developments, in 1987 there was no *national* coordination of educational software development in the FRG which would form the basis for future work and encourage the development of high standards.

The national scheme started at the IPN in January 1988 did not aim to establish a *national* centre for the production of educational software as in, for example, the POCO project based in the Netherlands (cf. [16] and also [17]). The essential strategy was to build up an infrastructure of trained authors located throughout the FRG. It seemed to be unrealistic to expect trainee authors to specify, design and implement CAL programs based on completely new ideas. The range of skills and the level of experience required to do this would be too great. Instead the decision was made to base the training programme on the adaptation and re-designing of exemplar foreign CAL packages. As with any other medium, educational software makes implicit cultural assumptions. In the selection and adaptation of packages in such an "import model", this issue was taken account of.
All the 25 selected authors had long established qualifications in writing text-books or teaching materials.
They were produced only for MS-DOS, mainly with Turbo-Pascal 5.0 using an "IPN tool-box" for authors.
About half of the "Länder" and some institutes supported this project.
In a programme of national importance, a number of publishers should have the chance to participate. This was effected through the involvement of a cooperative publishing house called "CoMet Verlag für Unterrichtssoftware", which was formed by three German speaking publishers specifically to publish educational software [18].
This approach had the advantage of being very cost effective, requiring realistic funds to enable it to start, but it depended on the continued enthusiastic involment of the trainees.

By October 1989 about 15 packages were finally published or ready for school based evaluation. Through the experience gained through these activities, about 70% of the authors started to produce new packages by themselves. Because of its success this training programme is being repeated with another 20 authors between October 1989 and September 1990.

Details of this work are described in [19].

4. CONSEQUENCES FOR INFORMATICS IN OPTIONAL COURSES

Projects for the introduction of informatics in the Federal Republic of Germany were focused about 20 years ago on pupils aged 16 to 19, where informatics developed into an independent subject. The application-oriented content of this subject, together with the projects currently in progress, bear witness to a high level of informatics (for more details see [2]).
The introduction of NIT for all pupils will lead to a modification of the contents in the optional courses. Some work for pupils aged 13 to 16 was undertaken, but the modification of the subject informatics (age 16 to 19) has not yet started.

5. TEACHING NIT IN ELEMENTARY EDUCATION

In most "Länder" in the FRG, the elementary school, attended by every child, comprises only four years - in contrast to many other countries (e.g. folkeskole in Denmark). The "Länder" spend quite a lot of money establishing computer literacy in about grade 8 and want first to stabilize that area.
The situation has not really changed in the last years: The educationalists still have great reservations about the extensive introduction of NIT in these first four years.

As reported in Norfolk 1985, the reasons in my opinion are still as follows:

- The FRG has a well established curriculum of good quality, highly interactive in its social, physical and emotive dimensions;

- It is based on the assumption that direct experience with people, nature and technology provides the fundamentals of child development, including cognition;

- The historical experience with the "book school" fosters the apprehension that informatics at too early an age may reduce direct experience, leading to "verbalism" void of understanding;

- International research has barely touched on the question of personality change and child development through extensive computer use. Projects such as Papert's have concentrated on cognition within highly favourable environments uncommon in the normal school setting.

6. FURTHER INFORMATION

The referenced literature gives further hints. Perhaps the best source is the specialist publication "LOG IN - Informatik in Schule und Ausbildung" which provides a regular view of the situation in the FRG.

REFERENCES

[1] Bosler, U.: New Information Technology - A Survey of the Situation in the Federal Republic of Germany, in Lovis, F. and Tagg E. D. (eds.): Computers in Education, Proceedings of the 1st European Conference on Computers in Education ECCE 88 (North Holland, Amsterdam, 1988) pp. 491-495.

[2] Bosler, U.: Teaching Informatics at Various Levels in General Education, in Duncan, K. and Harris, D. (eds.): Proceedings of the 4th World Conference on computers in education (North Holland, Amsterdam, 1985) pp. 959-966.

[3] Landesinstitut für Schule und Weiterbildung (LSW) (ed.): Unterrichtseinheiten zur informations- und kommunikationstechnologischen Grundbildung (Soester Verlagskontor, Soest, 1989).

[4] LOG IN - Sonderheft "Informationstechnische Grundbildung", 1989.

[5] Bayerisches Staatsministerium für Unterricht und Kultus (ed.): Gesamtkonzept für die informationstechnische Bildung in der Schule (Bayerisches Staatsministerium, München, 1987).

[6] Niedersächsisches Kultusministerium (Ed.): Neue Technologien und Schule, in: Schulverwaltungsblatt 8/85, pp. 227-229.

[7] Bund-Länder-Kommission für Bildungsplanung und Forschungsförderung (ed.): Rahmenkonzept für die informationstechnische Bildung in Schule und Ausbildung. Reihe "Materialien zur Bildungsplanung", (B-L-K, Bonn, 1984 and 1987), Polyscript.

[8] van Weert, T. J. (ed.): A model syllabus on literacy in information technology for all teachers (ATEE, B-1050 Brussels, 51, rue de la Concorde). German version in LOG IN 4 1984), issue 4.

[9] Bosler, U., Hampe, W., Wanke, I., van Weert, T.: Grundbildung Informatik (J. B. Metzler, Stuttgart, 1985).

[10] Bosler, U.: Informationstechnische Grundbildung - Übersicht über die Arbeiten in den Bundesländern, LOG IN 6 (1986), issue 5/6.

[11] van Lück, W.: ITG in Nordrhein-Westfalen, LOG IN-Sonderheft Informationstechnische Grundbildung, 1989.

[12] Watson, D.: Developing CAL: Computers in the Curriculum (Harper & Row, London, 1987).

[13] Biehler, R., Rach, W., Winkelmann, B.: Dokumentation und Bewertung von Software für den Mathematikunterricht (available: Landesinstitut für Schule und Weiterbildung, D-4770 Soest, 1987), Polyscript.

[14] LOG IN issue 5/6 of 1986 with the topic "courseware".

[15] Deutsches Institut für Fernstudien (DIFF): Lehren und Lernen mit dem Computer, (3 basic articles and 10 pieces of courseware (available: DIFF, Wöhrdstr. 8, D-7400 Tübingen, 1989).

[16] Educational Computing Consortium (ed.): POCO-brochure. Enschede (available: EEC, Postbus 217, NL-7500 AE Enschede, 1988).

[17] Haugen, H.: Development Tools for Educational Software: Open-Ended Software and Creative Programming Tools. In Tinsley, D., van Weert, T. (eds.): Educational Software at Secondary Level. Proceedings of the IFIP WG 3.1 Working Conference on Educational Software at Secondary Level, Reykjavik, Island, 19-23 June, 1989 (North-Holland, Amsterdam, 1989).

[18] CoMet Verlag für Unterrichtssoftware, Pappenstr. 34, D-4100 Duisburg, Fax: +49 (203) 37 87 225.

[19] Bosler U., Squires, D.: Training Teachers to Design Educational Software: an International Collaboration based in the FRG. In Tinsley, D., van Weert, T. (eds.): Special Issue on Educational Software at Secondary Level. Proceedings of the IFIP TC 3/WG 3.1 Working Conference, Reykjavik, Island, June 18-22, 1989, Education and Computing (Elsevier, Amsterdam, 1989).

Computers in Education
A. McDougall and C. Dowling (Editors)
Elsevier Science Publishers B.V. (North-Holland)

STEP BY STEP: LEGO LEGGED LOCOMOTION

Peter J. Carter

Plympton High School, Plympton, South Australia, 5032

Most mobile machines use wheels, but wheels work best on hard. smooth surfaces. For many environments, legs offer greater mobility, and legged locomotion is an object of research worldwide. This paper includes a brief overview of that research, and describes a number of models in LEGO/Logo that can be used by students to explore many of the issues.

The wheel has been a very useful invention. But wheels have their limitations and work best on hard, smooth surfaces. For rugged terrain or soft surfaces, where wheels could become trapped between rocks or bogged, legged locomotion offers some advantages, and machine walking is an object of research at a number of universities and other institutions worldwide. LEGO/Logo makes aspects of machine walking accessible to students.

We tend to take walking for granted, as something we do naturally, but watch a young child learning to walk and you realise that it is, in fact, a very complex skill, requiring balance and coordination. There are two types of balance involved, static and dynamic. Any animal or machine that moves without becoming unstable has static balance; an insect, for instance, that always has at least three legs on the ground is statically balanced. Such an animal or machine does not have to concern itself with balance, and its control systems can therefore be relatively simple. Walking humans are dynamically balanced; there are stages in our gait where we are, in effect, falling for a short period, and our vestibular apparatus and kinaesthetic sense are busy controlling our movements. Without accelerometers and rate gyros, any models we build will need to be statically balanced, although Pawson (1985) describes a 'walking man' model that relies on what he describes as 'quasi-static' balance. You can best describe that to yourself by walking very slowly and noting how the motions differ from your normal gait as you lean to maintain balance. Jameson (1985) describes a gyroscopic biped, balanced and driven, through precession, by its gyroscope.

Not surprisingly, the walking of animals, including insects, has been studied for any information that may help the design of machines. Observing animals and then modelling their movements with LEGO has been an activity at the Hennigan School in Boston, and proved very fruitful. Alexander (1984) describes the gaits of animals with diagrams such as Figure 1:

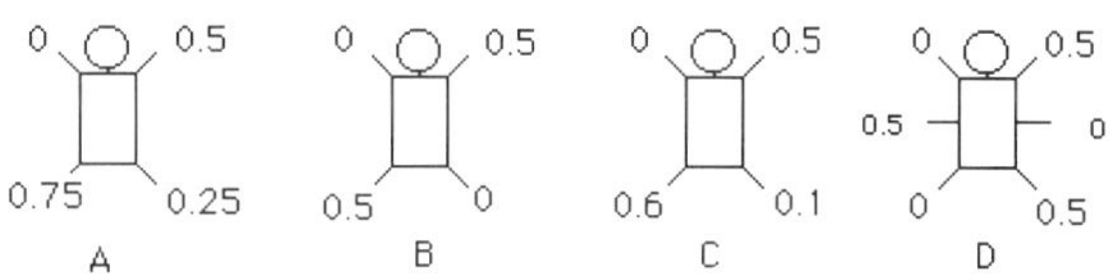

Figure 1 A Amble B Trot
C An efficient Turtle gait
D Alternating tripod gait for hexapods

The numbers by the feet show their relative phase, defined as the stage of the stride at which it is set down, expressed as a fraction of the duration of the stride following the setting down of the reference foot, the left front in our examples. The reference foot is assigned relative phase 0 and the others are in the range 0..1. A foot with relative phase of 0.5 will therefore touch the ground midway between two groundings of the reference foot, as in our own walking. Among the animals studied by Alexander was the turtle (ie. tortoise), and he devotes more than two pages of text and diagrams to discussion of efficient turtle gaits.

There have been quadruped machines, with perhaps the most prominent being the General Electric Walking Truck, photographs of which appear in most robotics books, built during the 1960s. Since every movement was directly controlled by the driver without the aid of a computer it was a very awkward and tiring machine to operate. The problems led later workers to use computer control, with varying degrees of success, with one of the first being the 'Phony Pony', whose legs had hip and knee joints and were controlled by electronic sequencers. A machine built by Petternella in Italy had telescopic legs and resembled a table, which is what it became at the end of the project. Hirose (1984) describes research with four legged machines capable of stair climbing and other feats. Walking robots have been popular in film and literature, witness those of the *Star Wars* series. Interestingly, most of them have been bipeds, with only the occasional quadruped.

Many recent machines have been hexapods, with Sutherland's machine designed to explore the control and use of hydraulics, and being the first to carry a driver, around a car park of Carnegie-Mellon University. Another man carrying hexapod, the Adaptive Suspension Vehicle, is being developed at the Ohio State University, its legs making use of sliding joints. Yet another, with electric drill motors, was in use at the same institution for exploring the use of sensors such as video cameras, for manoeuvering over obstacles, stair climbing and other problems. Perhaps the most spectacular machine has been one legged, the Carnegie-Mellon University hopper, a very interesting study in balance and control, and whose techniques are applicable to bipeds and quadrupeds.

During the 1960s there was interest in legged machines for use on the Moon, although in the event, the only vehicles ever driven or dragged on the Moon (Lunokhod, MET and LRV) have been wheeled. We may see renewed interest in legged vehicles for Mars exploration, with the 'Ambler' from Carnegie-Mellon University already existing in a one legged test version.

LEGO Machines

With the limited computing power available with LEGO and Logo, we will have to confine ourselves to statically stable machines that crawl, rather than walk (but that was how we learned anyway). The simplest mechanism, with variations used in many models, uses two outer legs and a single central one, often the base of the machine. There are three gears on each side, with the two end ones connected to the 'feet', and the mechanism can be used horizontally or vertically. The parallel in nature is the pentapedal gait of kangaroos, and the idea is used in large excavating machines, where the base can rotate, either for swinging the jib or for changing direction as the machine moves. It would be easy to build that into a model with a second motor and suitable gearing. A not very different scheme is used in underwater robots built by Komatsu.

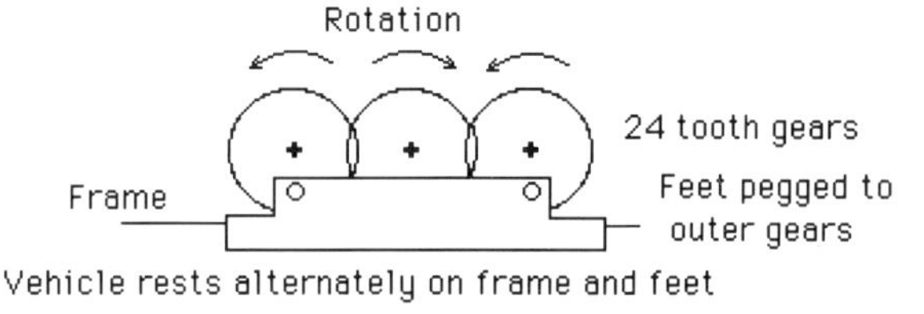

Figure 2 Basic walking mechanism

Hexapods moving their legs in threes as alternating tripods (gait D in Figure 1), are therefore statically balanced, making them potentially the most suitable models. To quote Sutherland and Ullner (1984): 'We tried quite a few algorithms for controlling the sequence of leg recovery, but one of the simplest turned out to be the best. An alternating tripod gait seemed to work consistently well for all directions of travel.' Our first attempt is shown in Figure 3. Only one of the six legs is shown on the diagram, disconnected. Care must be taken when assembling the drive shaft that the legs are properly phased.

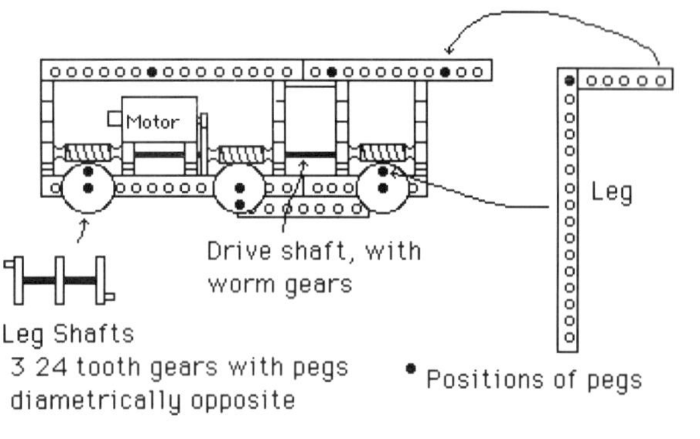

Figure 3 Hexapod 1

The machine is surprisingly stately in its movements, gently rising and falling as it progresses. That is a sign of wasted energy (the problem is known as 'geometric work'), for good leg mechanisms would keep the body height constant. That is an issue in real machines, and animals too, and it has been claimed that women, with shorter legs, and therefore less up and down movement, are more efficient walkers than men. Obvious experiments are with legs of different lengths, and perhaps with 40 tooth gears instead of 24.

Another leg mechanism experimented with briefly was, in effect, the previous one upside down, with a sliding pivot instead of the pivoting link (the 'knee'). It can be used with or without feet, but the steps are short and the system seems to have little promise.

Another hexapod, shown in Figure 4, uses 16 * 1 bricks, pivoted in the middle, as its legs. Efforts to use LEGO parts to connect the legs to the gears were eventually abandoned, and wire used instead, because the connections must pivot in two planes.

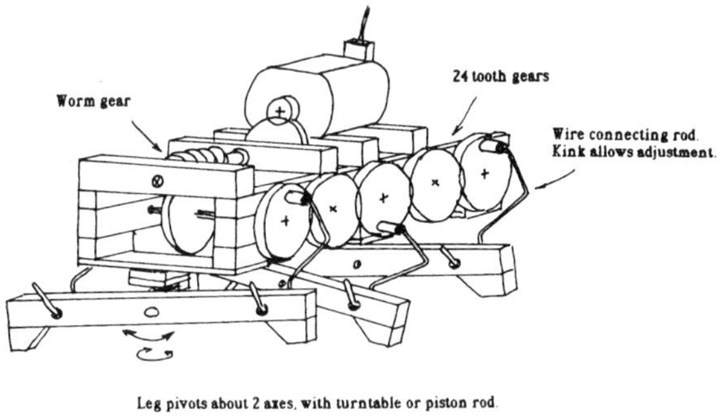

Figure 4 Hexapod 2

These machines can move only in straight lines. To be able to turn, either an extra degree of freedom is needed in each leg, in other words, another hinge and more mechanism, or the machine can be built in three sections, with universals connecting their drive shafts, and steered by 'bending' with a separate motor and linkage.

Legs like those of Hexapod 1 can be used for quadrupeds, and our first example lost two legs and part of its structure to become a quadruped. We tried it with the trot gait, and also with the amble and Alexander's optimal turtle gaits (A, B, and C in Figure 1). The machine did work with all three, but looked decidedly precarious as it pitched and rolled, and was very slow. For a human rider, definitely most uncomfortable. It was improved slightly by fitting wide feet to reduce the rolling. It can obviously be used to explore different gaits provided the frequent toppling can be tolerated. For success with a quadruped, each leg would have to be individually driven so that at least three legs are on the ground at all times. This is a focus of current work, and is proving to be an interesting building and programming task.

A quadruped that keeps all four 'feet' on the surface, remaining statically stable, is a much more feasible proposition, although the resulting shuffling may be considered even less like real walking than the creeping of the other machines. Many years ago there was a toy tortoise, the 'Toytoise', which consisted of a pressed steel shell and two pairs of legs which rotated in opposite directions. The 'feet' were small rubber wheels with a simple one-way ratchet, and the whole thing was operated by squeezing a handle, connected to the mechanism by cable. It would move forwards only, but could turn in either direction by biasing the leg rotations one way or the other.

The only difficulty with a LEGO version is the ratchet wheels, and this is solved with a paper clip, as shown in Figure 5. As the wheel rotates one way the clip rides over the tread in the tyre, the other, it drops in and locks the wheel.

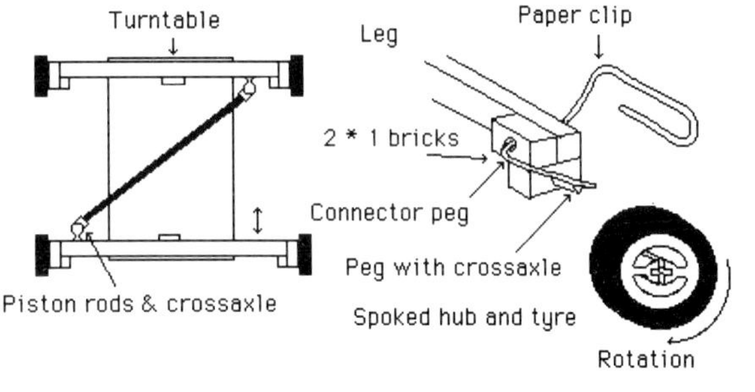

Figure 5 Shuffling vehicle with ratchet wheels

The legs are connected by a push-pull rod, and the whole mechanism driven through reduction gearing and another push-pull rod, not shown on the diagram. It is possible to make machines like this turn, either by having the motor operate such that the crank is biased towards one end of its travel or the other, or by varying the distance between the leg pivots. The second scheme is the easier of the two, and one machine of this type was built with a second motor, gearing, and a pivoting mount for one leg. The first method would require position sensing and programming.

The same ratchet system can be used to make an 'inch worm' machine. The frame vaguely resembles a step ladder, with the motor opening and closing the two halves, and our version was made by rebuilding the toytoise vehicle.

A different ratchet mechanism is used on the leg shown in Figure 6. The geometry is such that the wheel end of the leg moves in a straight line.

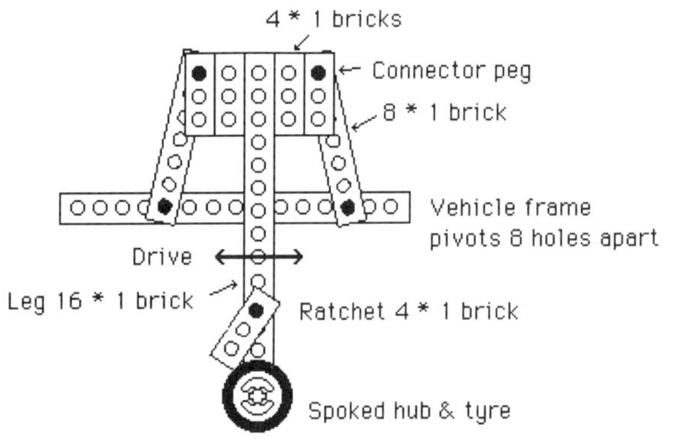

Figure 6 A 'constant length' leg

The prototype machine used the trot gait, although almost any gait would work. It should be possible to make such a machine turn by driving the left and right legs at different speeds with separate motors, or by steering the wheels at one end.

Little has been said about the programming aspects of these machines. Unlike the real machines, these require very little programming unless sensors are used to monitor the positions of parts of the machines, during turning for instance. As the complexity of machines increases, with numbers of motors, so will the complexity of programming. Machines interacting with each other will also require programming.

As with all LEGO and Logo activities, students will devise their own theories: that is, after all, an essential part of the process of Piagetian learning. A group of Year 8 students working with the hexapod and toytoise machines decided that they would both move at the same speed, because they used identical motors. They connected all the available cables, placed tables in line, and proceeded to race the machines. Sure enough, they did move at very nearly the same speed. It was the end of their time with the LEGO materials and they never did falsify their theory. But it was real science in action.

A pair of Year 10 students made some curious choices in building a quadruped. They could offer no real reason for using four rather than six legs, and the structure had a number of redundant parts, as well as some flashing lights. It proved to be very slow and unsteady, and they began to realise that their machine could be greatly simplified and improved. Here again, there is an interesting issue, because both science and engineering, including programming, often progress by developing and refining rather awkward and 'woolly' ideas, and the real value if LEGO/Logo is not the fact that a machine can be made to move, but the development of planning and thinking skills as the project progresses.

Conclusions

With LEGO and Logo we can now explore, in a small way, some of the issues in robotic locomotion, and our aim has been to develop simple, but workable, machines to aid that exploration. The references listed below, particularly Todd's book and the special issue of *The International Journal of Robotics Research*, contain much for those with the interest to pursue the subject to some depth.

References:

Alexander, R. 'The Gaits of Bipedal and Quadrupedal Animals', in *The International Journal of Robotics Research*, Vol 3 No 2, Summer 1984

Hirose, S. 'A Study of Design and Control of a Quadruped Walking Vehicle', in *The International Journal of Robotics Research*, Vol 3 No 2, Summer 1984

Jameson, J. 'The Walking Gyro', in *Robotics Age*, January 1985

Pawson, R. *The Robot Book*, Colporteur Press, 1985

Pearson, K. and Franklin, R. 'Characteristics of Leg Movements and Patterns of Coordination in Locusts Walking on Rough Terrain', in *The International Journal of Robotics Research*, Vol 3 No 2, Summer 1984

Raibert, M. and Sutherland, I. 'Machines That Walk', in *Scientific American*, Vol 248 No 1, January 1983

Sutherland, I. 'Footprints in the Asphalt', in *The International Journal of Robotics Research*, Vol 3 No 2, Summer 1984

Time-Life editors *Robotics*, Time-Life Books 1986

Todd, D. 'A Pneumatic Walking Robot', in *Robotics Age*, January 1985

Todd, D. *Walking Machines: An Introduction to Legged Robots*, Kogan Page, 1985

Waldron, K. *et al* 'Configuration Design of the Adaptive Suspension Vehicle', in *The International Journal of Robotics Research*, Vol 3 No 2, Summer 1984

Computers in Education
A. McDougall and C. Dowling (Editors)
Elsevier Science Publishers B.V. (North-Holland)

EDUCATIONAL COMPUTING IN CHINESE SCHOOLS

Chen Qi Wang Ben-Zhong

National Research Center on Computer Eduacation in Secondary Schools
Beijing Normal University, China*

ABSTRACT An overview of computer education in Chinese schools is depicted in this article. The optional computer course related issues such as its purposes and requirements, its position and functions in school curriculum, its contents and teaching materials are discussed. New trends of computer use in education including the development of hardware, educational software and teachers training have been introduced. Problems are pointed out and the authors' suggestions for further development are given.

I. INTRODUCTION

Computer education as an educational experimental project in Chinese Schools was started in 1982. Before that time, it was known only in the form of extracurricular activities in several secondary schools of Shanghai and Beijing. In 1982, on the suggestion of some computer scientists, the previous Ministry of Education required Beijing Normal University, Tsinghua University, Beijing University, East China Normal University and Fudan University to make an experimental offering of an optional computer courses in each of their affiliated secondary schools. No special funds and personnel were available for these experiments; therefore, those universities had to provide their own facilities and teachers. That requirement commenced the prologue to the planned experimental project of educational computing in China. The formal experimental project started in 1983. A few key schools in six cities were required to offer an optional computer course with special funds and equipments provided by the previous Ministry of Education and the Hua Xia Educational Foundation. From then on, every local educational administration began to take this work seriously. More and more funds--a total of about 100 millions Chinese Yuan--were invested in schools for installing computer laboratories over a period of three years. Even though the "computer craze" caused some problems such as lack of trained teachers, of facilities and appropriate instructional materials, educational computing in Chinese schools developed rapidly and healthily in general.

By the end of June 1989, there were about 52,185 microcomputers (including 21,414 Apple compatible), 12,016 drivers, 4646 printers and 2,620 full-time computer teachers in 4,738 secondary schools and primary schools according to the statistics of 25 provinces, municipalities (directly under the Central Govervment) and autonomous regions.

II. TWO STAGES OF DEVELOPMENT

The Development of educational computing in Chinese schools could be divided into two stages covering the last seven years.

1. First, the stage of experiments in big cities and key schools, from 1982 to 1986.

Since the start of the formal experiment project in 1983, educational administrations in many provinces and cities have begun to raise funds for computer education. The number of experimental schools and the microcomputers these schools owned increased so rapidly that the model and the policy of educational computing had to be explored seriously and clarified thoroughly. After an experimental period of four (actually three) years, the State Education Commission held the 3rd National Conference on Experimental Work in Computer Education in Secondary Schools in May 1986 to discuss and sum up the experiences and reach some conclusions. The following conclusions were drawn:

1.1. The position and function of computer courses in Chinese secondary schools.

*Chen Qi, Associate Professor,
Department of Psychology, Beijing Normal University,
Beijing 100875, China
Wang Ben-Zhong, Principal, Beijing Normal University attached Experimental Middle School,
Beijing 100032, China

On the basis of the conditions in China, it is quite necessary to offer an optional computer course in our secondary schools, but it is not suitable, for the time being, to place the course on the same level with basic courses such as Math, Chinese, Foreign language, etc. The computer course is a rather flexible, but only an auxiliary course. It should be offered as an optional course in senior high schools and as an extracurricular activity in those junior high schools which meet basic conditions (at least one full-time computer teacher, more than 10 microcomputers, a special computer room and a minimum of routine funds).

1.2. The direction of educational computing

With the changing of the concept on computer literacy in the world, the appropriateness of the model of mainly teaching programming language acccepted in Chinese schools should be examined. Since offering an optional computer course was only in the experimental stage and the schools involved in this experiment were but a small proportion of the whole number of secondary schools, no definite direction for educational computing had evolved yet. The State Education Commission argued that both the world trends in educational computing and the Chinese situation should be taken into account. Rather than opening for radical changes the purposes and objectives of educational computing were to be modified only and its contents updated according to world-wide experiences. The 3rd National Conference on Experimental Work in Computer Education in Secondary Schools had considered this issue seriously and decided to arrange Computer Education on the following three levels:

(1) For the regions and schools which have already offered or are going to offer an optional computer course, using the model mainly including BASIC language, the potential of the facilities should be made full use of, the teaching method and instructional materials should be explored and completed, and the quality of instruction ensured. Instead of expanding this model blindly, current achievements must be consolidated and developed gradually.

(2) Create greater computer awareness among the junior high students in regions and schools with the necessary facilities and teachers by means of extra-curricular activities. It is needed to pay more attention to the interests of the kids. The content and the requirements should be limited. The purpose of this activity is to develop interest and to get rid of the "computer phobia", to make the kids understand the new technology and its role in modern society.

(3) Organize special professional groups to develop qualified educational software. Create favourable conditions for computer use in subject matters and computer uses as a tool, as a kind of resource. Of course, those developments need time and will be brought about gradually.

The three level arrangement means that computer education should not be limited to teaching programming language only, we should change the direction gradually and step-by-step.

1.3. The purposes and requirements of the optional computer course

Over three years, the purposes and requirements of the optional computer course were defined on the basis of "programming is the second literacy". The main purposes were the following:

(1) To gain a preliminary understanding of the fundamentals of computing, the systematic structure of microcomputers, and the role of the computer in modern society.

(2) To master the BASIC language and develop programming and debugging skills by using computers.

(3) To develop logical thinking, problem solving ability and creativity.

According to these purposes and based on the first year experiment and on the appraisement by experts, the Ministry of Education developed and issued a teaching syllabus for the optional computer course which prescribed the requirements of the contents and class hours. The course required 45-60 class hours and at least 1/3 of the time for hands-on practice.

The 3rd National Conference decided to add some computer applications such as wordstar, database and spreadsheets to the teaching syllabus, which meant that the objectives of application should be included in the course. However, the schools could select some parts of the application for teaching only according to their own conditions, especially according to the facilities available to them.

1.4. The compilation of teaching materials should follow the principle "one syllabus for a variety of textbooks" to suit the local conditions

Since China is a vast country and the development of her economy is out of balance, the State Education Commission encouraged the teachers to compile instructional materials for their regions and schools under the guidelines of the relatively unified syllabus. More than 20 different editions of teaching materials with distinguishing features of different regions have been compiled and published in those three years. This policy enhances the zeal of every region and school, to promote the development of computer education and to inquire more deeply into the educational computing.

1.5. The teaching of the optional computer course is only one significant component part of computer education

There are also many other important ways to develop computer education, such as to popularize computer education in such places as "Children's Palace", "Science and Technology Station (Center)" or the "Family of Youngsters", to conduct various kinds of computer competition on different levels (for instance, computer manipulation, program design, etc.). National Youngsters Computer Competition organized yearly since 1984 by the Chinese Computer Association plays an important role in promoting the development of computer education and in discovering especially talented youngsters. The number of computers used in after-school activities had been more than 30,000 by 1986, which was almost equal to the number of computers the schools owned at that time.

2. The stage of expanding the area of experiments and developments in a planned way

2.1. Strengthening of research and development

2.1.1. Establish national and local research centers of computer education in secondary schools

The State Education Commission decided to transfer and develop the National Experiment Center on Computer Education in Secondary Schools into a National Research Center on Computer Education in Secondary Schools. This Center functions both in administrative management and research work such as policy making in educational computing, organizing software development, teachers training and workshops for instructional materials and teaching methods, and orgnizing international exchange activities. The establishment of the Center in 1987 has promoted the development of educational computing tremendously. For example, a plan for developing educational software has been worked out; the criteria of educational software evaluation have been formulated and a Committee for software evaluation and management has been established; the staff members of the Center are often sent to different provinces to investigate the situation and to check into problems of educational computing, etc.

Around ten local educational computing associations have been set up in different provinces and regions.

2.1.2. Organize workshops for exchanging teachers' experiences

Following the three-level arrangement, decided by the 3rd National Conference on Experimental Work on Computer Education in Secondary Schools, educational administrators and school teachers have been working very hard. Many teachers who teach the computer course have tried to improve their teaching method and accumulate instructional experiences. There has been accumulated a wealth of integrated instructional experiences in different disciplines in Chinese schools; for instance, how to stress the main point and how to teach the difficult points in each lesson, how to develop thinking skills through the teaching of the lesson itself. Since the optional computer course is so new and most of the teachers are quite young, a new pedagogical domain has to be explored and completed. After several years of teaching, they have discovered some rules in teaching, such as how to teach the concept of variable, of loop, how to teach programming in a structured way, how to develop thinking skills through the teaching of flowcharts, etc.

A series of workshops has been held to exchange those experiences.

2.1.3. Extend experiments in junior high schools

Teaching LOGO programming language in junior high schools. Expanding computer interest groups to get more youngsters involved in educational computing and to create the youngsters' interest in computer-related activities.

2.1.4. To set up a standard examination for the optional computer course

Since the computer course in secondary schools is an optional one, it is hardly advantageous for students to be motivated because it will not be examined in the College Entrance Examination. Some big cities such as Shanghai and Beijing started to set up an examination for this course. If a student passes this standard examination, he or she can get a certification, and it will be recorded in the student's documents. These records play a part in recruiting new students and new workers. Some areas such as Guang-Xi Autonomous Region and the city of Tianjing are considering to introduce this examination where the conditions are being met.

2.2. Develop Chinese made educational computer

A Coordinate Group which includes the related departments from the State Planning Commission, the State Science and Technology Commission, the State Education Commission, the Ministry of Electronic Industry and Chinese

Science and Technology Society has been formed to further the development of Chinese-made Educational Computer(CEC). A group of computer scientists has been invited to design and develop CEC machine with built-in Chinese Characters. Special funds have been invested from the Seventh-Five Year Plan and a special policy for investment and the tax-free import of chips has been drawn up. The CEC-I machine was tried out and put into operation only for a year. About 80,000 sets have been sold which were mainly bought by families and schools. The cost performance has been much better than that of imported machines. For a decade, at least, it will remain the main type of machine for computer use in schools, and it will end the history of using imported machines for educational computing in schools.

2.3. Software development and evaluation

It is becoming more and more manifest that software and courseware development is the Achilles heel, if the teacher wishes to use the computer as a device to assist his or her students' learning in school. Under the leadership of the Coordinate Group, special attention has been paid to educational software. The following actions have been taken:

(1) Special funds have been provided for the development of software and tool software.

(2) A special integrated team has been called for and organized to bit the design and development of educational software.

(3) An organization for software registration and evaluation has been established. A nationwide software evaluation committee has been set up which holds 1-2 meetings every year, then disseminates the software to the schools at low prices.

(4) In addition to the regular software registration on the part of the schools and the teachers, collect through programming and software contests good and qualified software, developed by students and some teachers.

2.4. Bring into play the initiative of both the central leadership and the local administration

Chinese education has been centralized in policy making and in planning. The function of centralized administration which has its advantages should be fully brought into play. However, without the enthusiasm of the local administration, it will be very difficult for the schools to conduct educational computing. The local educational administrations' investment to computer education comprises 2/3 of the total investment in the whole country.

2.5. Train ordinary teachers for different ways of educational computing

Under the support of UNESCO, a computer education workshop for trainers of secondary teachers was convened by the National Research Center of Computer Education in Secondary Schools. It is a fact that in the course of several years we could not change the model of educational computing which is mainly teaching about computer and programming language. Therefore, the main emphasis in teachers' training should be on the training of computer teachers. However, we have to prepare the ordinary teacher for educational computing. Whenever enough software is available for teaching and learning, the ordinary teacher should be ready to use it. A small exemplary group composed of a city (Beijing), a school district, two schools and one university was selected to do pioneer work for the ordinary teachers' training pilot project which includes in-serve and pre-service training. Beijing and the schools in question meet the basic conditions and are willing to train ordinary teachers. The National Research Center tries to accumulate experience in this pilot project, then will expand it gradually.

III. SOME PROBLEMS TO BE FURTHER EXPLORED

1. What's the best model or the ideal direction for educational computing

About thirty years ago, there existed mainly three modes of using computers in education according to R. Taylor's conclusion--Tutor, Tool, Tutee. Different countries focused on different modes in different developmental stages. In some developed countries during the 60's, the Tutor mode was the dominant mode. It means learning from the computer. In the middle of the 70's, the Tutee mode became salient, that is, learning about the computer and computer programming. In the middle of the 80's, people in this area realized that the concept of computer literacy is not necessarily to learn programming language. The Age of Information will require most people to be able to use the computer as a tool instead of programming; only a low percentage of the computer users needs to deal with programming. Therefore, the Tool mode may be more appropriate to most of the students.

China had been greatly influenced by the Tutee mode in starting the experiment of educational computing. However, most of the schools involved in this experiment from the very beginning were key point schools. Those schools aimed mainly at providing the universities with qualified and excellent graduates so that most of the teachers and students were inclined to accept the Tutee mode. With the expansion of computer education, with the increasing number of students taking the optional course, more and more students feel that learning programming is quite a heavy burden. They like to manipulate the computer and its application, but reject learning programming. It has led us to think that the requirements for computer courses should be addressed differently for different types of schools and students. There are different levels in educational computing in the world, also in China. Which is the best model depends on the conditions of the school. These conditions include the type and the goal of the school, the level of the teachers and the facilities the school provides or can provede. Some cities and regions started to travel different roads in educational computing as their conditions improved. It could be assumed that we will have different modes in educational computing not only in the short run but also in the long run, since the development of the economy and of education in different areas is so unbalanced. It's impossible to prescribe a unified mode for all the different regions and schools on different developmental levels.

Therefore, the development of educational computing should be explored continuously within the framework of various structures and various modes, we should learn to formulate and to try out relatively efficient models.

2. The functions of the computer in fundamental education

The functions of computer education or the so called informatics in fundamental education refers to two aspects: on the one hand, to the intellectual development of the youth; on the other hand, to the schooling system. There has been a debate on this issue. Some computer educators predicted that a revolutionary change would be caused by the new information technology. They also predicted that the information technology would strongly influence the children's intellectual development, foster their thinking skills. As a result, it would change the instructional principle and thus the whole traditional education system, etc. Others opposed to this view argued that information technology could play a part in teaching and learning; however, 30-years of evidence show that this function is limited. Microcomputers are very popular now in developed countries, they have become standard equipments in the majority of schools; however, the early predictions do not seem to have come true.

China is a developing country. Microcomputers are becoming common in the schools, especially in some big cities. However, there will be a long way to go for most of the schools in the whole country, especially for these in the rural areas and remote border districts. Without practice and experimentation we should avoid advocating the anecdotical myth of the computer in education; we also should not underestimate the potential impact of information technology on education. Educational media (including information technology) in instruction or intellectual development of children do not function spontaneously. Certain experiments conducted by our center such as On Cognitive Consequences in Programming Learning, CAI in Secondary School Math showed that information technology itself will not have positifve functions automatically. It's necessary to observe the interaction between teachers, students and technology, to consider the best instructional strategies, to explore the positive effects of technology and carefully avoid the negative effects. Only under these conditions, can technology have a positive impact on both instruction and intellectual development. How to take advantage of information technology and tap its potentiality will be a long term issue and an important domain to be explored.

3. Design and development of computer curricula

High quality educational software becomes more and more important for tapping the potential of the computer in education. It will require both the investment of manpower and money. The Government has done a lot for software deveopment, but since we are only at a beginning stage and the starting point is quite low, not enough tools are available for software design and development, the quantity and the quality of the existing educational software are far from meeting the requirements of the schools. Nevertheless, if we appreciate our special reservoir of talented people in software development and make reasonable use of our expertise and try our best to develop serialized and intellectualized software, we may meet the needs of the schools gradually.

UNESCO has proposed to establish an international educational software bank, aiming at exchanging and disseminating qualified software. That is a good way to help developing countries to share resources and save manpower and money invested in software development. If UNESCO would be able to support the organization of an international cooperation project to develop curriculum materials using a high component of technology, it could make full use of highly qualified experts and produce a large amount of curriculum materials. If so, we would be willing to join this project and contribute our talented people for the work.

4. Computers in families

By the middle of 1989, 80,000 of the CEC-I machine had been sold. It was estimated that 70% of them were bought by families. The original idea to open the family computer market was to use the computer as a good family tutor for the students. Because of the shortage of qualified educational software, the computer in families has been more and more misused as a game machine. Therefore, the function of the family computer has become an issue that is still being debated. Concentration on the following points might lead to a solution: first, special attention should be paid to speed up the development of educational software and to shorten the process of software dissemination; second, school education and family education should be combined and integrated to foster the students' learning through computers. It will be a mistake if the function of the computer in family education is neglected and separated from school education. We have to deal with this problem appropriately.

REFERENCES

[1] Chen, Q., Microcomputers in Chinese Secondary Schools, in: Moriguti, S. et al (eds.), Microcomputers in Secondary Education (North-Holland, Amsterdam, 1987) pp. 377-381.

[2] Taylor, R.P., Introduction, in: Taylor, R.P. (eds.), The Computer in the School: Tutor, Tool, Tutee (Teachers College Press, New York, 1980) pp. 1-10.

[3] Chen, Q., Journal of Research in Science Teaching Vol.25, No.6, (1988) pp. 493-500.

Computers in Education
A. McDougall and C. Dowling (Editors)
Elsevier Science Publishers B.V. (North-Holland)

EXPLORING THE UNPREDICTABLE - THE COMPUTER AS A CATALYST FOR CREATIVE THINKING IN THE CLASSROOM

Carolyn DOWLING

Institute of Catholic Education - Mercy Campus, 251 Mt. Alexander Road, Ascot Vale, Victoria 3032 Australia. Phone : (03) 377 8578. Facsimile : (03) 377 8499.

The computer as a tool and the computer as a medium for undirected exploration are two concepts favoured in educational computing circles throughout the world. Are they complementary, or contradictory? Advocacy of the computer as a tool for the achievement of the student's own purposes, while applauded in theory, is often undermined in practice by the requirement that pre-determined ends be achieved in the classroom. Problem solving is frequently more valued than the less easily directed and assessed activity of problem creation.

But not all human beings are problem solvers in the traditional sense. It is neither the preferred nor the most effective cognitive style of every person, nor does it necessarily represent the peak of human intellectual endeavour. The computer can offer special opportunities in the classroom for undirected exploration, for the encouragement of divergent and creative thinking, and for the attainment of such aims as eventually spring from this type of mental activity.

Contrary to popular wisdom, not all children enjoy the types of computing activities offered in the classroom. While on the one hand this might be dismissed simply as a reflection of individual differences, on the other it raises questions as to whether the enormous versatility of the computer as a medium for human activity and expression is being sufficiently exploited.

Two key ideas have done much to shape the directions taken by classroom computing in the 1980's - the computer as a tool [1], and the computer as a medium for the user-directed exploration of ideas and concepts [2]. Are these views of computing complementary or contradictory? In principle it would seem that they should complement one another. The idea of the computer as a means of personal empowerment, as a tool for the achievement of the individual's own purposes, is central to visions of computing such as that of Papert. In practice, however, by far the greatest part of classroom computing is curriculum driven and relates to externally determined goals. The computer is generally used by students to achieve ends carefully defined by the teacher. Even outside the confines of particular subject areas, generalised problem solving activities most often stress the development of particular strategies seen as effective in dealing with certain types of tasks. Students are all too rarely given the opportunity to construct and explore their own problem domains, particularly in the later years of schooling, when more obviously productive activities take precedence. "Getting it right" is generally the name of the game. The computer is a tool for the carpenter rather than the sculptor.

This is not, in itself, such a terrible thing. New technology is quite typically and reasonably put first at the service of existing practice. But if, as is sometimes claimed, the computer is a new type of tool, a tool for the mind, then it surely has the potential to be used in other ways. If indeed it has the capacity to become, as it were, our intellectual partner, then the nature of such a partnership should be questioned. Does empowerment consist only of the acquisition of greater processing capacity in the service of preconceived ends? Certainly this reflects usual practice in computer usage outside the classroom. But is this type of usefulness, that of an obedient, competent servant, eager to assist in the realization of our every aim, necessarily the quality we would seek in an intellectual companion [3]? Seymour Papert in his introduction to Brian Silverman's <u>The Phantom Fishtank</u> writes : "...a whole software industry is committed to the idea that programmers will make computers do what they are told - no more and no less. But there are times when the thrill comes from the computer doing something that one did not anticipate and perhaps could not have imagined even if one has tried. The excitement is not what was specified but in what emerges." [4]

Not all human endeavour is directed towards the achievement of preconceived goals. New ideas and understandings, surely among the most precious forms of intellectual attainment, do not necessarily arise from the application of a series of clearly defined logical steps to a piece of existing knowledge. In many cases original, creative insights spring, in fact, from the disordering of the customary systems of thought and action within which ideas or objects are perceived and utilised. Alone or in groups we "brainstorm", tossing concepts and arguments into the air to fall where they may, hopefully to be picked up in new and unanticipated configurations.

Can the computer then be a tool of a different type, perhaps enhancing our thinking in ways more like those of our human peers who assist in the development of our ideas by contradicting, arguing, misunderstanding our intentions, thereby giving us new perspectives, new impetus and often quite new directions? If this can be done, is it an appropriate activity for the classroom?

Problem solving, both in mathematical and other curriculum areas, is rightly regarded as a critically important cognitive skill. As mentioned above, classroom computer use often takes place within this context. Alternative thinking strategies are debated and explored - top-down versus bottom-up, inside-out versus outside-in. What about problem creating? Life does not consist wholly of applying one's mental capacities to pre-existing problems. A large part of one's conscious (and probably unconscious) existence is spent in mental, physical and emotional "puddling about", that is, in activity which is not oriented towards already articulated aims. The goals of such activity are at worst flexible, and at best have yet to arise. Difficulties in monitoring and assessment presumably have a lot to do with the lack of encouragement for this type of thinking in many classrooms, however common and however productive it might be in the world outside.

There is also a question of equity. Are some students significantly disadvantaged by the restrictions of current fashions in classroom computing? To what extent are particular styles of thinking and learning supported by computer use in schools, indeed by many aspects of educational practice, to the detriment of others [5]? How much of the creative potential of a number of our students is currently unrealised?

Can the computer be used right now in the classroom to better support a more open-ended style of thinking and learning; to contribute more to the disordering of preconceptions and to the generation of unexpected outcomes? Brian Silverman's program The Phantom Fishtank [6] is a rather sophisticated example of the type of computing activity I am advocating. The generation of apparently unpredictable patterns and forms serves as a catalyst for speculation on a number of issues. This software is unlikely to solve many problems in the narrower sense, but is an environment which gives opportunities for questioning and for further exploration. It supports both the creation and the investigation of hypotheses.

On more familiar ground, in Australia as in other parts of the world there is a well documented tradition of the basic Logo language being used in an open-ended way. The essence of this approach is neatly encapsulated in Wills' phrase, "Doodle, Design, Debug" [7]. A similar philosophy permeates Nevile and Dowling's Let's Talk Apple Turtle, where the "hum", a string of Turtle graphics commands typed without initial regard to the outcome, is the starting point for all activities [8]. This is in keeping with the value placed on both debugging and deplanning in much of the Logo literature, and is very different from the use of Logo as a medium for the type of problem solving where a task or problem is set, and a specified outcome must be achieved.

Is it a waste of valuable class time to have students type a series of Turtle graphics commands at random, observe the result, play around with the initial input, see what happens next, fiddle some more... and so on? Education is, for sound reasons, strongly associated with the imposition of order, logic and discipline upon the chaos of the unschooled mind, and upon the irregularities of the world around us. During a recent debate at a school Council meeting concerning whether or not raffles should be a part of school fetes, the point was made that raffles were against what the school was really about. Education was described by the speaker as being about order and structure, while raffles were perceived as being about something else altogether. They were seen to threaten the basic ethos of the school.

In a similar vein, the following week a letter appeared in the local paper deploring the encouragement of choose-your-own adventure books, on the grounds that they appear to "endorse a model of decision making...where decisions are made on the throw of a dice." The letter continues : "In an increasingly complex society, it is surely the role of educators to encourage the young to seek knowledge, acquire understanding, explore options and make decisions based on reason and morality. The model endorsed by (the book in question) represents at best an opting-out of responsible decision-making, at worst a retreat into chaos and unreason. Our young people deserve better." [9]

Is the generation of Logo hums and other forms of unpredictable output indeed a subversive, anti-educational activity? Does it do little but encourage our subjugation to the forces of chaos and entropy? Or does it, on the contrary, afford an opportunity for the development and exercising of valuable skills in experimenting with different possibilities for the imposition of order on experience?

In my own work both with school students and with older learners, I have found there to be a fascination and a delight taken in the production and subsequent manipulation of something which has not been created in the service of a specific intent. It is non-threatening; there is no possibility of error and of subsequent mortification. But does it lead anywhere?

It would be foolish to claim that in every case these unstructured beginnings lead to prolonged purposeful activity culminating in penetrating insights. I can say, however, that a significant number of the most sustained, complex and intellectually rewarding projects that have taken place in my classes have had their roots in just such a sequence of activity.

One such example comes from a group of first year primary education students in 1988. Intrigued by the results of applying the RANDOM command in Logo to choice of colour, numerical variables and words, one group decided to try it with the TOOT command in the production of sound. The result was described as being "like a sigh". This suggested an idea. Could the TOOT command be used to mimic the intonation of the human voice? The group set to work and produced a sequence of sounds which did indeed bear some resemblance to the rises and falls of speech. But there was more. "This couldn't be Italian." "Why not?" "That's not how Italian sounds." One member of the group carried this discussion, and the program on disk, back to her language class, where the question of intonation patterns in different languages was explored further. Another student who had a part-time teaching job in a school were Logo was used, introduced this idea to her pupils, who went on to produce entertaining "dialogues", still using the TOOT command, but in an extremely precise and goal-oriented manner.

I have no hesitation in claiming that the educational benefits of this activity to all who took part, including myself, were many and varied, and certainly not trivial.

A delight in the contemplation of the unforeseen is not peculiar to novice Logo users. It is not just an easy way out. One has only to observe the intensity with which groups of very sophisticated Logo programmers ponder the curious outcomes of certain tricky little pieces of recursion, to recognise the fascination and intellectual involvement that such phenomena can induce.

Curiosity is engaged, hypotheses are formed, the consequences of different possible courses of action are explored. Deplanning is sometimes discussed in terms which suggest that it reflects some inadequacy or immaturity on the part of the Logo user; that this is simply a less demanding alternative to more acceptable forms of debugging. This may of course be so in some instances, but in others one can well argue that the final result is more interesting, more complex, more original, perhaps even more appropriate than the original goal or concept.

There are undoubtedly many ways in which the computer, unconstrained by human expectations of what is usual or potentially useful, might assist us in moving beyond the more predictable pathways of thought. Word processing programs already give flexibility to the goals and the outcomes of writing. Suppose there were an option which allowed the computer to jumble one's existing text in unexpected ways, or a database feature which reorganised data into alternative sets of categories, or a graphics package which doodled interactively in response to one's input? It should not be beyond the capacity of programmers to have computers surprise us even a little with new contexts, perspective and combinations of ideas, in the interest of encouraging the asking of new questions and the formation of new insights. It should not be beyond teachers to welcome such a style of computer use.

Creative or divergent thinking may not be the major goal of education, but it should surely have some role in the classroom, at every level. Computer programs which provide appropriate environments for this type of activity already exist, and others are likely to be developed in the future. It is important that such uses of the computer should be treated seriously. Papert describes the computer as "...the Proetus of machines....Because it can take on a thousand forms and serve a thousand functions, it can appeal to a thousand tastes." [10] If we can only give it the chance to do so!

REFERENCES

[1] Taylor, Robert P., The Computer in the School: Tutor, Tool, Tutee, (Teachers College Press, New York, 1980).

[2] Papert, S., Mindstorms, (Harvester, Brighton, Sussex, 1982; first published 1980).

[3] Dowling, C., Editorial, COM 3, Journal of the Computers in Education Group of Victoria, Volume 12, No. 2. (1986).

[4] Papert, S., Foreword in : Silverman, B. The Phantom Fishtank : An Ecology of Mind, (Logo Computer Systems Inc., Canada, 1987) p.v.

[5] Dowling, C., Participation, equity, access and control, unpublished address, Educational Computing - Ritual or Revelation, Australian Council for Educational Research/Computers in Education Group of Victoria conference, (Melbourne, 1988).

[6] Silverman, B., (1987) The Phantom Fishtank: An Ecology of Mind, Canada: (Logo Computer Systems Inc., Canada, 1987).

[7] Wills, Sandra, Doodle, design, debug, in: Oakley J. (ed) Computers in Education: Issues and Applications, (Computer Education Group of New South Wales, 1985; originally published 1983) pp.219 - 226

[8] Nevile, L. & Dowling, C., Let's Talk Apple Turtle, (Prentice-Hall, Melbourne, Australia, 1983).

[9] Simpson, Jennifer, in : Letters to the Editor, The Age, (Melbourne, 11th August 1989).

[10] Papert, S., Mindstorms, (Harvester, Brighton, Sussex 1982; first published 1980) p.viii.

Computers in Education
A. McDougall and C. Dowling (Editors)
Elsevier Science Publishers B.V. (North-Holland)

UNDERSTANDING CLASSROOM COMPUTERS: STUDENT AND TEACHER PERSPECTIVES

Brian Durell

Faculty of Education, University of Toronto
371 Bloor St. West
Toronto, Ontario, Canada M5S 2R7

There is a tradition in research on computers in education of viewing computers as non-problematic in classrooms. That is, research into classroom computing tends to focus on the effects computers have on such variables as student achievement, with the tacit assumption that all else in the classroom remains as before, with only the introduction of computers and their effects on an otherwise unchanged environment to be investigated. This paper takes a different approach. From a theoretical stance of concerns-based innovation implementation and technology as a non-neutral force, the experience of a large-scale introduction of computers into an elementary school is analyzed. The study employed ethnographic techniques. Evidence concerning how teachers and students made sense of this change in classroom operation is presented.

1. WAYS OF VIEWING COMPUTERS IN CLASSROOMS

Most studies of computers in classrooms proceed from a set of assumptions that Schön (1983) has called "technical rationality" -- a model which expects technology to be applied in an instrumental manner to the solution of problems. This seems to be the basis for the innumerable studies which seek to show that the use of computers for instruction raises achievement scores in various subject areas or produces favourable attitudes in students toward the use of technology. Work in this tradition, while undoubtedly of some value, sees nothing problematic in the introduction of technology into a workplace. An unstated assumption is made that bringing computers (or other technological devices) into a situation changes only one factor. That assumption is being increasingly questioned.

Winner (1977, 1986)has challenged the concept of neutral technology. The common notion is that technology has no inherent valence. It may be used well or badly, but its effects will be determined entirely by the choices made by its user. Winner rejects this view. He argues that technologies have built-in tendencies in certain directions that may have nothing to do with the purposes for which they were originally constructed. An often-overlooked example of this effect is the automobile. Originally designed and produced as a more efficient means of transportation, it has developed into a way of life, a source of mythology, a strangler of communities, a necessity of life, a polluter of the environment, a shaper of landscapes, and a bedrock of the economies of major industrialized nations. Similar views of technology are espoused by Zuboff (1988) and Roszak (1986).

The adoption of innovations has been studied extensively by Hall (1974, 1979, 1985). From his studies, Hall has developed the Concerns-Based Adoption Model (CBAM). In this model, innovation adoption is viewed as a developmental process, not an event. Understanding of the adoption process comes from paying attention to the adopter, not the innovation itself. CBAM asserts that innovation adopters progress through roughly three stages from non-use to full adoption of innovations. The stages are characterized by the concerns that adopters express and show in action about the innovation. Analyses of this type assert that the important aspects of innovation adoption are more psychological than technical. First there is a stage of personal concerns where the adopter attempts to come to terms with the innovation at a personal level. Next is a task-oriented level of concern. At this stage the adopter concentrates on the innovation in itself. This is a time of "getting it right." The final stage of concern deals with the implications of innovation -- how may an innovation be used to improve the lot of the clientele served by the adopter?

Traditionally, innovation adoption is pursued as an essentially instrumental business. A situation exists and a new, and supposedly better, way of handling the situation is proposed. Most attempts at innovation introduction concentrate on the benefits to be realized with the implicit assumption that, once the benefits are seen, adoption is an unproblematic matter of welcoming the innovation with open arms and working to become proficient with it. Hall's research indicates otherwise.

The concepts of CBAM and technology as a non-neutral force have been useful to our research team in examining the adoption of computers in a school setting. We have looked beyond the standard improvement of schooling effects towards an understanding of how teachers and students make sense of the computers in their midst. Our findings support the view that computers in schools are not simple additions to traditional classroom operation. Nor are they mere one-to-one replacements for previous ways of carrying out instruction. In many senses, classroom computers are puzzles for teachers and students to come to terms with on their own levels.

2. THE SCHOOL SETTING

A suburban school board decided to place a minimum of three computers in each of its classrooms (Durell, 1989a). A JK-8 elementary school was chosen as a pilot site for this innovation. Our research team was invited to study the adoption of computers within the school. This arrangement provided an unusual research opportunity. The more common situation is for researchers to decide to study the effects of computers in a school. The researchers then arrange to bring in the hardware, teach the teachers how to use it and closely monitor the project to see that things are done correctly. Thus most researchers have a large stake in the "success" of the instances of computers in schools that they study. Our research team, in contrast, experienced a high degree of freedom to study what happened in the pilot school without concern for the success or lack thereof of the overall project.

Another advantage of this arrangement was that it is more representative of the way that computers typically enter schools. In this sense, we were able to study a more "real" process of innovation adoption than would be found in a more researcher-controlled study.

The suburban school board installed UNISYS ICON educational microcomputers (Durell, 1983; McLean, 1983). The Ontario Ministry of Education has approved UNISYS ICONs as a Grant Eligible Microcomputer System. The ICON computers that students use are actually workstations networked to a fileserver. Each fileserver contains a high-capacity hard disk for storing instructional software. Thus the same material is readily available to all students. Every classroom in the pilot school is equipped with at least three computers and a printer. Some have as many as six ICONs. By the start of the third year of the project, there were 142 ICON-2s in the school, served by 11 fileservers, and 41 printers. The fileservers are networked so that students may log in on any computer in the school and have access to their personal files.

The school board "launched" the teachers into the use of computers by providing some initial training. However, most of the teachers have not had detailed exposure to all of the software available to them and their students. The school administration encouraged the teachers to use the computers, but did not require them to do so. The administration provided no prescription for classroom computer use.

3. METHODOLOGY

We used a qualitative ethnographic approach (Jacobs, 1987; Lincoln & Guba, 1985) to studying the use of computers in the school. We were also influenced by the reconnaissance model described by Schwarz (1985). Five researchers observed within classrooms with each observer visiting two classrooms for a half day per classroom per week. We entered our observation notes into a computerized text base for later analysis. Publications of the school related to the computer project, samples of student work, and out-of-class comments of teachers were other sources of data. Samples of both teachers and students were interviewed and completed questionnaires.

4. FINDINGS

4.1. Findings: Teachers

The way in which the teachers adapted to the computers in their classrooms shows indications of conformity to the CBAM model. Although the stages of CBAM are sequential, they are not necessarily distinct (Hall, 1985). That is, an innovation adopter may not have resolved all problems related to one stage before starting to deal with next level of concerns. The stages of concern evident among many of the teachers we studied can be roughly aligned with the second and third years of the project (Durell, 1989b). The first year was a difficult one for teachers and project staff. Much of the year was consumed with getting the machinery functioning. These problems did not end with the first year, but technical problems declined to a level where the system became usable.

The dimensions on which teachers showed signs of their concerns were: psychological - how they themselves reacted to the machines, physical - where the teachers located the machines within the classroom, curricular - to what extent the computers were used for curricular purposes, temporal - how teachers allocated student time on the computers.

Psychological indicators of concern included statements that the teachers made about the computers. In the first and second years, most of the teachers were quick to protest their ignorance of computers. This seemed to protect them from responsibility for misuse of the machines in an educational sense. It also relieved them of responsibility for mechanical malfunctions. The implicit message was clear: "These things have been placed in my classroom, but I didn't put them there. Ask someone else about them." During the second year, a change occurred. A co-op university computer science student worked in the school as a technician. She reported that over the course of the year the number of calls she got to solve simple problems, such as paper jammed in a printer, decreased dramatically. Apparently teachers were learning to cope with simple problems on their own. The computers didn't frighten them as much.

Mid-way through the third year, one teacher epitomized the change in confidence that had grown among the staff. A university credit course on computers in education was to be offered within the school. The teacher suggested that it might not draw many participants because the teachers have "so much experience and have attended so many seminars" that the course might be seen as redundant. This, while a bit of an overestimate of the average competence level of teachers in the school, is a long way from loud protestations of ignorance that were common in the first year of the project.

During the second project year, a board computer consultant who worked closely with the project offered after-school sessions to help teachers with difficulties they were having with the computers and to discuss the software available. There was very little response to this offer and eventually the sessions were dropped. In the third year, the teachers organized a computer committee which was very active. It provided many of the functions of the after-school sessions of the previous year. The committee also offered special events related to computers and a newsletter which contained short reports on how some teachers were using the software within their classrooms. There was no indication that the teachers just didn't care or that they wouldn't stay after school for computer information. Rather, it seems that as Hall (1979) suggests, they first had to deal with the machines on a personal level before they were willing to consider the task-oriented (technical) issues of their use.

The physical location of computers within the classrooms provided similar evidence of a need to resolve some personal concerns. In the first two years of the project, the computers in most rooms were located in a back corner. One teacher went even further. Not only were the computers placed in the back corner of the room, but they were turned so that their screens were toward the wall. Thus it was impossible to see what was on the video displays from the main part of the classroom. Students, teacher, and researchers had to slide along the wall behind the chairs of the computer users to see what the machines were being used for. Another, primary-level, teacher made an arrangement with a junior-level class to have students from that class come to the primary classroom to work with the primary students at the computers. This seemed to be an extreme example of providing the mandated computer experience while shielding the teacher from any need to interact with the machines. There was a generalized distancing of teachers from the computer users. In our observations, most teachers had no interaction with the students who were using the computers. This likely was because the teachers did not want to have to deal with problems for which they felt they lacked competence. In the third year, a number of teachers moved the machines into a more prominent location in the room taking up an entire wall or out into floor space. While some teachers continued to ignore students while they used the computers, this behaviour was less in evidence in the third year.

In the first two years, most teachers made sure that their students used the computers, but just what programs to use was left up to the students. Since the hard disks contained a significant amount of software, the machines served as electronic smorgasbords. Toward the end of the second year some teachers began to have students produce assignments in curricular areas using word processing and desktop publishing programs. Primary-level teachers encouraged their students to use arithmetic drill programs.

A few teachers continue the electronic smorgasbord tradition, but this is becoming uncommon. In most classrooms, students have definite tasks to complete using the computers. At all grades levels most of the curricular work uses word processing or drawing programs. Primary-level teachers monitored use of arithmetic program more closely. Teachers are less inclined to believe that computer time will be good for students in some unspecified manner. Instead, most feel that time on the computers should be related to the general flow of academic work in the classroom.

From the start of the project, most teachers established schedules for student computer use. Many tried to give every student some computer time each day or on at least four days out of five. The priority of computer use varied among classrooms. Some teachers allocated very little time for computer use. In most classrooms, computers were available to the students for most of each school day, but students might be called away from the machines to attend to lessons that the teacher considers particularly important. In a few classrooms, computer use had the highest priority. Students were responsible for catching up on any topics whose presentation they missed due to using the computers, but no presentation preempted computer time in these classrooms.

By the third year of the project many teachers still used schedules, but there was a growing interaction between curricular use of the computers and the time allocated for their use. The size of the task that a student had to complete was more likely to determine how much time a student was given on the computers. At least two teachers went a step further. They required students to create their own tasks and to provide a rationale for any computer use they requested.

There was not a simple relationship among the various dimensions through which teachers reflected their adaptation to classroom computers. For instance, we saw teachers who expressed great enthusiasm for educational computing who banished computers to the back of the room, gave the students no direction about what to do with their computer time, and never interacted with students while they were using the computers. Conversely, we saw teachers, who were quite apprehensive about the computers, use them for curriculum-related assignments and monitor carefully the work of the students who used the machines. We also saw more predictable patterns, but we learned that teachers do not progress evenly along all the dimensions.

During the summer between the second and third project years, some teachers were able to take computers home. This was undoubtedly a major factor helping many of the teachers to deal with their personal concerns and to start to consider technical matters at the level of task-related concerns.

4.2. Findings: Students

The approach of students to classroom computers is not readily characterized in terms of concerns. However, students also showed that they were engaged in making sense of the machines that had become part of their educational world.

A predictable way for students to make sense was to relate educational software to previous experience with computer and arcade games. Students never "ran" programs -- they "played" them. This is quite a natural interpretation for drill programs, many of which are dressed up in game format. Simulation programs are a bit more removed from games, but students looked for a win/lose interpretation and always managed to find one. Some of the simulations contain actual games as a subcomponent of the total program. This encourages students to think of the simulation as a game.

Even skills within a simulation or other program were commonly viewed as game-like. One simulation of sailing in the days of tall ships emphasized using latitude and longitude to find ports. Once a "day" the student is given the opportunity to determine her position by making a sighting of the sun, usually called "shooting" the sun. To be useful, the sighting must be done when the sun is at its highest point in the sky. This situation is represented pictorially on the computer screen. Most students did not realize the importance of this aspect of the task. It was common to see students get the cross-hairs located on the sun, then press the button and loudly proclaim to friends in the class that they had "shot the sun" in a manner that suggested a target gallery rather than the use of a sextant. Students who made this proclamation almost universally failed to heed, or perhaps even to see, an information screen which explained that they took the sighting at the wrong time.

Perhaps a more extreme example of the tendency to see computer use as game playing showed up when students discussed their use of the tool programs available to them. A variety of simple word processing, desktop publishing, communications, and graphics programs were available on the fileservers. These programs were tools for writing, drawing and sending messages and files to other students. There seemed to be little in them to suggest playing games and yet students commonly spoke of playing them rather than using them.

The game view of educational software, although partially attributable to the style of some programs, stemmed mainly from students' prior experience with a range of home computer and video arcade games. This previous experience with computers or computer-like devices provided students with a way of viewing or making sense of the computer programs that they encountered in the classroom.

Transfer of previous non-computer experience was also seen in students' use of computers. We first noticed this among primary-level children who used simple word processing programs to write stories. The ICON microcomputers are equipped with trackballs for moving pointers about on the screen. We saw students in grade 2 type their words and use the trackball to position the cursor for the typing of the next word. This is a clear analogue of writing with a pencil. After putting the letters for each word on paper it is necessary to move the pencil to the position where the next word is to start. In a parallel manner, the children would use the trackball to position the "electronic pencil" for the next word. The children were aware of the existence and the effect of the spacebar on the keyboard, but the trackball seemed to offer a more natural or "sensible" way of positioning the cursor on the screen.

The trackball was also used to position the cursor for the start of a new line of text. It was very common for students to move the cursor down two lines for a new line of text. Some were even more generous with space and triple- or quadruple-spaced their lines. In the early grades this may be due to simply not realizing that a feature such as word wrap could exist. However, we saw the same thing amongst students in grade 7 who did know about word wrap. In fact some of the upper level students used word wrap in a peculiar manner to produce this effect. These students didn't use the trackball, but rather the spacebar to insert multiple spaces at the end of each line of text until the cursor moved down to the next line.

Another "strange" practice in word processing, which we first noticed at the grade 2 level, was the tendency to erase an incorrectly typed word completely when making corrections rather than just removing and replacing incorrect letters within the word. This suggests a very strong correlation in the minds of the students between the rubout key on a keyboard and an eraser. This, too, was seen at upper elementary grade levels as well as among the primary-level children.

Students also showed consternation when their writing filled the computer screen or when previously written lines were no longer visible on the screen. Here the analogy with writing on paper broke down. Many students worried about where the next words would go or how they could "get back" text that was no longer in sight. Worried calls for the teacher brought demonstrations of what to do in each case, but confidence that disaster would not overtake them in such situations only came with considerable experience. This phenomenon has also been noted among student teachers who are novice computer users. The problem is more one of lack of experience than of immaturity.

5. CONCLUSIONS

Smith, (1975, 1988) emphasized the importance of making sense as a fundamental process in human cognition and learning. Similar views have been expressed by Barnes (1976), Mayer (1987), and Neisser (1976). Both the teachers and students that we studied showed a need to make sense of the computers in their daily school environment. The teachers, being teachers, accepted a responsibility for the use of the computers. This responsibility was seen in their concerns about the innovation. Often the concerns were not verbalized, but were evident in teacher behaviour. During the period of the study, most of the teachers progressed from personal concerns about the classroom computers to the level of task orientation. They were able to confront the machines and strive to become effective users. At the end of the third project year a few of the teachers were starting to become concerned with the impact of the computers upon their students. These teachers were looking for ways of using the machines to provide a classroom climate geared to better learning. They had moved through a stage of "any use of the computers will do" and a stage of not very imaginative "correct" computer use. Finally they were beginning to consider how the technology could be used most effectively.

This progression mirrors a process of changing understanding of the computers. Initially the computers were largely a threat. They undermined the teachers' positions as experts in their classrooms. Olson (1988) has noted a similar phenomenon which he discusses as the effect of computers on the influence of teachers in the classroom. Some of the reaction to that state of affairs was expressed in a sort of denial of the computer presence. The machines were "banished" to back corners and given little attention. Next the computers were approached as devices to be mastered and finally there was a start at understanding them as machines to be exploited, in a positive sense.

Students didn't accept ownership of the computers and so showed no signs of the types of concerns that teachers showed. However, there was evidence of students struggling to make sense of the machines. This came out in computer use which was clearly analogous to non-computer work that the students were familiar with. A few students were proficient users of graphics and word processing programs. However, the majority of students were using the computers in far from optimal ways. Even when shown more efficient ways to use the computers, many students would revert to their old approaches which made sense to them.

This is not a simple matter of lack of training of teachers and students on how to use the computers "properly." Rather, it is a symptom of the need for people to have the time to construct their own meanings for the devices which are thrust upon them. This is not to say that these teachers and students will not become proficient computer users. Indeed, because they have had time to build a sense of what the computers are and what they can be used for, they are likely to become very effective users of the technology.

A major lesson from this project is that time is needed for people to make sense of new technology so that they can construct useful and personally meaningful models of computer use. Intensive training could speed the teachers and students toward superficially efficient computer use, but the kind of deep and personal understanding that the people studied in this project were building is unlikely to disappear when the project ends.

More consideration needs to be given to providing adequate time for teachers to resolve personal concerns and then task-related concerns in preservice and inservice teacher education programs. Students also profit from an environment in which they can explore computer possibilities and build their own sense of what the machines are about. For with computers, as with any other technology, each user must construct a personal understanding of the innovation. The computers change the classroom and what happens within it. Teachers and students who have time to reflect on how they will use the machines are more likely to be creative in their use and to have a firm grasp of what can and what should be done with the technology.

REFERENCES

Barnes, D. (1976). From communication to curriculum. Harmondsworth, England: Penguin.

Durell, B. (1989a). Teacher adaptation to computers in the classroom. Proceedings of the Sixth Canadian Symposium on Instructional Technology, Halifax, Nova Scotia, May, 341-344.

Durell, B. (1989b). Bringing computers into the classroom: A concerns-based analysis. Paper presented at the XVII Annual Conference of the Canadian Society for the Study of Education, Quebec City, June 1989.

Durell, B. (December, 1983). ICONic implications. ECOO Newsletter, 4(4), 33-35.

Hall, G. E. (1974). The concerns-based adoption model: A developmental conceptualization of the adoption process within educational institutions. Austin: University of Texas, Research and Development Center for Teacher Education. (ERIC Document Reproduction Service No. ED 111 791)

Hall, G. E. (1979). The concerns-based approach to facilitating change. Educational Horizons, 54(1), 202-208.

Hall, G. E. (1985). A stages of concern approach to teacher preparation. Paper presented at the Annual Meeting of the American Educational Research Association (Chicago, Illinois).

Jacob, E. (Spring 1987). Qualitative research traditions: A review. Review of Educational Research, 57(1), 1-50.

Lincoln, Y., & Guba, E. (1985). Naturalistic inquiry. Beverly Hills, CA: Sage.

Mayer, R. E. (1987). Educational Psychology: A cognitive approach. Boston: Little, Brown.

McLean, R. S. (1983). The Ontario Ministry of Education specifies its microcomputer. Proceedings of the Fourth Canadian Symposium on Instructional Technology, Winnipeg, October, 435-441.

Neisser, U. (1976). Cognition and reality. San Francisco: W.H. Freeman.

Olson, J. (1988). Schoolworlds/Microworlds: Computers and the culture of the classroom. Oxford: Pergamon.

Roszak, T. (1986). The cult of information: The folklore of computers and the true art of thinking. New York: Pantheon books.

Schön, D. A. (1983). The reflective practitioner: How professionals think in action. New York: Basic Books.

Schwarz, P. A. (1985, August). Evaluation of the Pakistan primary education project: A methodological case study. In B. Searle (Ed.), Education and training. Evaluation in World Bank education projects: Lessons from three case Studies (pp. 73-105). Washington, DC: The World Bank.

Smith, F. (1975). Comprehension and learning: A conceptual framework for teachers. New York: Holt, Rinehart & Winston.

Smith, F. (1988). Insult to intelligence: The bureaucratic invasion of our classrooms. Portsmouth, NH: Heinemann.

Winner, L. (1977). Autonomous technology: Technics-out-of-control as a theme in political thought. Cambridge, MA: MIT Press.

Winner, L. (1986). The whale and the reactor: A search for limits in an age of high technology. Chicago: University of Chicago Press.

Zuboff, S. (1988). In the age of the smart machine: The future of work and power. New York: Basic Books.

Computers in Education
A. McDougall and C. Dowling (Editors)
Elsevier Science Publishers B.V. (North-Holland)

COMPUTERS IN THIRD-WORLD SECONDARY SCHOOLS: THE MINISTRY'S VIEWPOINT

David HAWKRIDGE

Institute of Educational Technology, The Open University, MK6 7AA, U.K.

What should Third-World Ministers of Education and their staff think about computers in their secondary schools? An answer to this question is provided by an international cooperative study funded by the Harold Macmillan Trust. Teachers and officials in several African, Asian and Arabic-speaking countries worked with three British researchers in describing and evaluating how computers arrived in their schools and what the machines are being used for. Drawing on their reports and other sources (covering altogether 23 developing countries), this paper analyses the position facing many Third-World Ministers of Education and their officials.

1. INTRODUCTION

What should Third-World Ministers of Education and their officials think about computers in their secondary schools? With John Jaworski and Harry McMahon, both experienced practitioners, I went in search of an answer to this question and others related to use of computers in schools in developing countries. The Harold Macmillan Trust provided £10,000 for an international cooperative study completed in 1989. This grant was used to pay teachers and officials in several African, Asian and Arabic-speaking countries to describe and evaluate how computers arrived in their schools and what the machines were being used for. Drawing on the teachers' and officials' reports, our own wide experience in the Third World, and many other sources (covering 23 developing countries), we wrote a book, *Computers in Third-World Schools* (Macmillan, 1990). Here we analyse the position facing Ministers of Education and their staff. Where does the Minister stand on computers in the schools? What political factors should he or she take into account, and are there likely short- or medium-term gains and losses? What policy options are likely to be available to choose from? We outline the sort of national strategy Ministry officials might devise, and discuss where the Ministry can probably obtain advice and assistance. Lastly, we comment on evaluation by the Ministry of its own progress in this field.

2. THE ISSUES IN POLITICAL TERMS

In any Third-World country, the Minister for Education has his or her hands full. Education is a political hot potato. It requires a large portion of the national budget often second only to defence. It never meets the demand, particularly at post-primary levels. Indeed, population growth can make even universal primary education an unattainable goal. Teachers often constitute a very powerful trade union or professional pressure group, and expect to be paid salaries well above the average national wage. Expansion of the educational system calls for substantial capital expenditure on buildings and equipment, as well as an increased salaries bill for teacher trainers and teachers, to say nothing of paying for textbook production.

In this context, the Minister may be inclined to treat talk about computers in schools as trivial, intrusive. To provide them requires radical revision of goals and priorities. He or she grew up without microcomputers. Why should today's child- ren learn about these machines? Why should teachers use computers? I suggest there are at least four educational rationales: the Social, Vocational, Pedagogical and Catalytic. Ministers have to decide to adopt one or more of these, or else to reject them all.

The political cost of rejecting computers for schools must surely be seen in terms of diminished Ministerial authority and lack of coordination. In many Third-World countries where the Ministry has not taken a lead computers have entered schools anyway. The situation has become chaotic. A Ministry of Education inactive on this front is likely to be seen by other Ministries, to say nothing of parents, teachers and students, as disorganised, sluggish and old-fashioned. Schools that obtain computers believe their action commands respect elsewhere, even if it does not at the Ministry. This is one sort of serious pressure on Ministries of Education.

But say the Minister proclaims the urgency of other priorities, such as increasing participation in secondary education. Or say the government is obliged to cut education expenditure. Even then, significant numbers of the public, including members of political, economic or other elites, are likely to expect the Ministry to take a lead by declaring a positive and constructive policy on computers in schools. The Minister can ill afford to ignore the votes and other expressions of allegiance of such people, and at very least must indicate the matter has been seriously considered.

2.1. Ideological reasons for adopting the technology

The Minister's ideological reasons for adopting computers in schools vary from country to country. In a socialist country, education policy is couched in terms of modernisation and reconstruction. Policy on computers in schools is based on the greatest benefits going to the greatest possible number of students but in the service of society as a whole. This policy is modified in practice by conditions in different parts of the country. For example, urban schools in China are more likely to benefit than rural.

In developing countries which have adopted more capitalist economic models, the underlying ideology is not as consistent or clear. For instance, Kenya has a meritocratic society, in which some individuals can achieve wealth and status through education. It is not that education guarantees a good income, but possessing it enhances a person's chances of achieving one, whereas this is not so in China, where salary differentials between well-educated and fairly uneducated people are small or non-existent. In a meritocracy, therefore, the Minister is likely to refer to opportunities for individual achievement that computers would bring in the schools, and to students' potential as employees. This policy too is modified by local conditions. The Minister is less likely to allude to disadvantaged groups who are excluded from the policy by reason of their poverty, location, language, gender or tribal, religious or political affiliation.

Policy may be partially obscured by an overlay of nationalism. Ministers announcing a policy on computers in schools may well include a nationalistic reference, even if the computers and their software are being imported. They may even declare that indigenous hardware manufacture and/or educational software development are in the national interest, despite little evidence to support this view. The country will gain from adoption of the new policy, they say.

Whatever the underlying ideology, Ministers in developing countries are forced by financial constraints to adopt a policy that embodies selection. The Minister has to give reasons why computers will go only to certain schools, initially at least, since they cannot go to all. Reasons must be found why other schools may or may not get computers later.

2.2. Short- and medium-term political gains and losses

Short-term political gains from putting computers into schools lie chiefly in the public's awareness of publicity favourable to the government. Computers in Third-World countries are news, and the media quickly take up photo opportunities and stories about children using them. Short-term gains may also lie in the approbation of local manufacturers, assemblers, importers, retailers and repairers of computers and suppliers of software. Ministers may also gain support from members of the industrial and commercial community who anticipate being able to employ workers who have learned about computers at school. Conversely, short-term political losses from adopting computers in education lie in any adverse publicity accompanying their introduction. Public criticism was sparked in India when the CLASS project chose the locally-manufactured Unicorn machine. Some said that such 'cosy' licensing ignored the potential of IBM-PC clones from the Far East, obtainable at competitive prices and commonly used in business. Short-term political loss is also possible if the allocation of funds to computers in schools is perceived as ill-advised, in the light of other priorities, by the press, opposing political parties, teachers' unions or parents.

Medium-term political gains lie in continued satisfaction of parents and those associated with providing and maintaining the computers. They also lie in the satisfaction of employers of school-leavers who have received computer education. These employers look for practical skills as well as theoretical knowledge. Political losses in the medium-term lie in the same quarter as in the short-term. In addition, teachers in post-secondary institutions, particularly those teaching computer science, may declare that resources were wasted in putting computers into selected schools, instead of increasing provision in their own institutions. The worst losses, however, may be those sustained if the public's expectations are raised, then speedily dashed, concerning the impact computers will have on student achievement or as an alternative to teachers.

3. THE ISSUES IN ADMINISTRATIVE TERMS

While the Minister considers political aspects of introducing computers into schools, Ministry officials must consider the issues in broad administrative terms. They must develop, implement and monitor a plan of action, for approval within the policy framework. Throughout, the Minister will expect to be advised. Like the Minister, all today's officials grew up without microcomputers. On the other hand, they are more likely than the Minister to use one, or at least to use a terminal connected to a minicomputer. Officials, like the Minister, may wish that computers for schools would go away. Their workload is already too heavy as they deal with buildings, teachers' pay, curricula, examinations and so on. But assuming that the Minister is calling for development of policy and wants a plan of action, what should officials put forward?

3.2 Difficulties of choosing among policy options

Policy will be determined by the rationales adopted by the Minister. If the *Social Rationale* is dominant, for example, a large number of cheap, low-powered computers, with scarcely any software and minimal teacher training, may seem appropriate. When resources are scarce such choices come closest to resolving problems of social equity and equality of opportunity. Although the total cost is high, it can be spread over several years. If the Minister adopts the *Vocational Rationale*, aimed at preparing selected students to use computers in the economy, more expensive medium-powered machines will be needed, with applications software, and some teachers must be trained properly. At first, if only a few students are taught, the cost will be moderate. The *Pedagogical Rationale* calls for computers to be used to improve teaching and learning across the curriculum. This requires much software and teacher training, plus many medium-priced and medium-powered machines. The cost is high, even if restricted to a minority of schools. The *Catalytic Rationale* is aimed at changing schools and curricula through bringing in computers. Such a revolution requires much software, including locally-prepared programs, a great deal of training, and many medium- and some high-powered machines, at costs beyond Third-World countries except where the revolution is in only a few schools.

4. A NATIONAL STRATEGY FOR INNOVATION

Computers in schools, like other kinds of innovation in education, need a national strategy. Introducing, say, a new secondary school examination is a tricky matter, calling for consultation, foresight and careful planning. The continuing support of political and official opinion-leaders is essential.

4.1. An advisory committee

Many Ministries of Education, as the first step, set up a committee, usually to advise the Minister. Regrettably, some such committees contain not a single person who has used a computer. The members should always include computer users from industry, commerce and government, teachers already using computers, university computer scientists, principals, teacher trainers and Ministry officials, and possibly computer manufacturers or suppliers. Their terms of reference should include advice on the Ministry's plan. Later, they should advise on implementation. They should monitor the innovation.

4.2. Advice from elsewhere

Advice may arrive unbidden. Other Ministries with an interest may exert pressure. The Minister of Industry may want to push computers into schools. The Ministry of Planning may want to be involved because of long-term implications for the national economy. The Minister may be obliged to take advice from the National Computer Board, or its equivalent. The Board's policies may exclude certain actions being considered by the Minister, such as importing a particular brand of microcomputer. Institutions with an interest may offer advice in the hope of securing their position: for example, a hoteliers' and travel agents' association, members of which use computers, may try to ensure that the Ministry's syllabus for computer education helps them to recruit suitable employees from among school-leavers.

Advice may also be available from other countries. In theory, the best sources are countries with similar cultures, and at much the same stage of economic development, where computers have been introduced into schools already. In practice, few such sources exist: even in the South East Asian Ministries of Education Organisation, differences between cultures are considerable, within the same region, and between economies they are vast. Where there is a national computer education project, the project director's perspective is often well worth taking into account. In turning to a particular industrial country for advice, Ministers run the risk of that country obtaining a technological foothold, or even a monopoly. The relevance of the country's experience must be questioned.

International organisations and regional centres may be helpful too. For example, UNESCO's Regional Office for Education in Asia and the Pacific compiled an inventory of training institutions, publications and societies for computers in education in its region (UNESCO, 1986). Such groups have difficulty in maintaining up-to-date documentation, however, and seldom contain specialists in this particular field.

4.3. A national syllabus in computer education

The Ministry can take the lead in promoting computers in schools by establishing a national syllabus in computer education, laying down what should be taught and to which age-group. The course need not necessarily lead to an examination and a certificate, though we saw substantial demand for this kind of recognition, not least from teachers using computers in their teaching. An examination in computer education immediately boosts the subject's importance in the eyes of parents and the general public. Lack of any national syllabus leaves teachers to develop their own, often in isolation or under very limited guidance from Ministry officials.

4.4. A national software and hardware standard

There are good reasons for developing countries to adopt a national software and hardware standard. The Ministry should give preference to software and hardware that meets certain specifications. Some governments agree to exclude all others from financial support. Others allow a degree of variation, usually to avoid being accused of excluding specific suppliers or rejecting gifts. King (1984) notes that in principle, Ministries of Education should be in a strong position to bargain about technology on offer, because so many suppliers are competing. Unfortunately, he says, Third-World countries do not yet have the expertise with which to make sound judgements concerning competing offers, or else do not make good use of the expertise they have.

4.5. A national training plan

Ideally, before computers arrive in schools, the Ministry should plan to train all categories of concerned personnel. At very minimum, one teacher from each receiving school must be trained through short in-service courses. Many developing countries then depend on the specially-trained teachers training others until there are enough. Such in-service courses are supplemented by a developing 'community of users'. For example, teachers who were among the very first to innovate take the lead in helping other teachers, who turn naturally and quite freely to their more knowledgeable and experienced colleagues. Teachers in neighbouring schools can get together and, if possible, promote a newsletter or journal in which teachers can exchange views and experiences.

For the medium-term, the plan should also look to initial teacher training. Student-teachers can only learn about computers if training colleges are suitably equipped and their staff trained appropriately. To expect that all new teachers will have taken a basic computer awareness course is a goal for the next century in most developing countries, like training of technical and other support staff.

4.6. Research required

Few countries have a sound base for policy decisions about an innovation such as computers in schools. For example, the Ministry may not know answers to questions such as: Which educational institutions already have computers? How many do they have? Of what kinds? How many teachers are qualified to teach about computers? What courses for teachers and others have been held and what did they cover? What does computer X cost? Which companies are making or assembling computers? Which are importing them? What sort of after-sales service can they offer? Are they likely to go bankrupt? What does a set of appropriate software cost? How many schools have software? What software? If it is unsuitable software, how can they get better programs? How many businesses are using computers? What for? What do they expect from employees who use the computers? How do they train them? What is the policy on computers in schools in similar or neighbouring countries? What has been their experience to date? Who in the country knows most about the issues behind this policy? What foreign aid might be available? It seems very reasonable to set up a small unit to find out answers.

4.7. A pilot project

The Ministry may decide to mount a pilot project, or at least permit others to mount one. Pilot projects enable experience to be gained, at low cost and minimum risk. Without doubt, they also delay formal acceptance of computers studies as an examination subject, and they scarcely serve the Social Rationale. Even if there is no formal recognition by government of a pilot project, national policy, should it emerge, will clearly be influenced by experience in prominent private schools.

Another view of pilot projects is that they are not evaluative experiments, but marketing devices which demonstrate the wares of sponsoring nations or computer companies and allow time for the market to develop. Decision-makers must want the product before they will allocate funds for it: a pilot project allows the desire to grow and gives time for those supporting the innovation to marshall arguments for acquiring scarce resources. If the opportunity cost is to accepted, political opinion in the country must shift, to see the innovation's relevance. Publicity must be sought. Sometimes a video of a computer pilot project is commissioned and screened, in the vernacular.

4.8. Support services

The Ministry's plan should also take into account the need for support services, provided nationally or regionally, but probably not locally. The need arises because teachers are likely to feel nervous about the new technology. Support services should offer further training and technical advice on hardware and educational software. National policy must include proper arrangements for maintenance, repair and spare parts.

5. EVALUATION

Does the Ministry intend to evaluate the introduction of computers into its schools, and, if so, against what criteria of success? Although lip service is often paid to evaluation, many innovations in schools proceed to apparent success or failure without ever being evaluated formally. Instead, officials privately gather what evidence they can through channels open to them, and decisions about future provision may be made much more on political and financial grounds than on educational ones. In developing countries, where resources are desperately scarce in education, there should be no grounds for thinking that the innovation is untested and worthless. In South East Asia, the Australian-funded survey of six countries (Pak and Punyapinyophol, 1987 and 1988) was a step in the right direction, although it could not answer the fundamental question: Was it right to put computers into schools in the first place? The survey was conducted by supporters of computer education. Problems were discussed, but not in much detail nor with a view to changing Ministry policy. At best, Ministries of some of the six countries were able to confirm where the computers were, who was using them, and what for.

Evaluation of the impact of computers in schools is by no means easy. It requires specialists to design evaluative studies so that the Ministry's essential policy questions are answered. Even identifying and clarifying these questions can be difficult, since within the Ministry there may be opposing views. One department may want to show, in the hope of securing additional funds for computers, that the machines have brought about worthwhile changes in children's learning. Another may seek to demonstrate that shortages of mathematics teachers are the fault of the department which introduced computers, because some of these teachers have shifted over to computer education. A third may wish the evaluators to produce results confirming its view that money spent on computers would be better spent on chairs for rural schools. Yet a fourth may want the studies to prove that the country's experiments with computers in schools have produced vastly better results than those in a neighbouring country. Out in the schools, principals and teachers also tend to hold strong views on what should be the essential policy questions. Since their futures may be affected by evaluation studies of what has happened in their schools, they feel they have a right to be heard, perhaps before evaluation begins. Once the policy questions have been agreed, evaluators must devise methods of answering them validly. Ideally, all concerned in the Ministry and schools will be satisfied afterwards that the answers represent the true situation. Of course, this ideal is never reached. Ideologies and power structures abound in every educational system, and influence evaluators as well as those being evaluated. The outcomes of an evaluation should influence future policy, but often the links are weak. By the time the evaluators' report is published, computers in schools may have moved on, with installation of new models, introduction of new software. The Minister may even have adopted a new rationale! Evaluators' best hope may be to influence practice at the time, rather than to wait for the report to be released.

6. CONCLUSION

We have looked at computer education policy and practice from the point of view of the Minister of Education and Ministry officials. Clearly the policy issues are difficult. Careful planning is essential, in which policy options are weighed against each other, and the views of principals, teachers, parents and employers are taken into account.

Within a broad policy framework, the Ministry needs a national strategy for implementation and evaluation. We have offered suggestions about components of such a strategy. Neither Ministers of Education nor ourselves can stop the clock: policy on computers in Third-World secondary schools is urgently needed, and practice must be further developed as quickly as possible.

REFERENCES

King, Kenneth (1984). Propositions, assumptions and an agenda for research. Notes for a lecture given at a Symposium on New Developments in Science Education, at the Tata Institute for Fundamental Research, Bombay, 24-25 November 1984.

Pak, Leong Yong and Punyapinyophol, Kittiporn (eds.) (1987). Final Report of the Regional Seminar on Computers in Education Project, Penang, 24-27 November 1986. Penang: SEAMEO Regional Centre for Education in Science and Mathematics.

Pak, Leong Yong and Punyapinyophol, Kittiporn (eds.) (1988). Final Report of the Second Seminar on Computers in Education Project, Penang, 5-8 April 1988. Penang: SEAMEO Regional Centre for Education in Science and Mathematics.

UNESCO (1986).*Computers in education: Inventory of training institutions, publications, societies in Asia and the Pacific.* Bangkok: UNESCO Regional Office for Education in Asia and the Pacific.

This paper is abridged from *Computers in Third-World Schools* by David Hawkridge, John Jaworski and Harry McMahon (Macmillan, 1990).

Computers in Education
A. McDougall and C. Dowling (Editors)
Elsevier Science Publishers B.V. (North-Holland)
IFIP, 1990

A DEVELOPMENT PROGRAMME FOR COMPUTING IN SRI LANKAN UNIVERSITIES*

C. HAWKSLEY[1] and A.S. INDURUWA[2]

[1] Department of Computer Science, University of Keele, Staffs ST5 5BG, UK.
[2] Department of Computer Science & Engineering, University of Moratuwa, Sri Lanka.

In 1983 the Sri Lankan government made a request through the UK Council for Computing Development for assistance with setting up a new academic discipline in the universities. The request was acknowledged; an expert sent to assess; and a report produced outlining a philosophy for introducing computing into the nation's eight (now nine) universities. This paper charts the train of events which were sparked off by this request and tries to assess, with hindsight, the success of the programme. The development programme is characterised by its training programme for staff in a wide range of disciplines across all nine universities. Emphasis was placed on teaching of computing as a component in the courses of these many disciplines. The use of overseas 'experts' to teach students was avoided in favour of a series of workshops and curriculum working parties geared towards the local needs of academics in these varied disciplines.

1. INTRODUCTION

Third world countries are aware of the dominant role that Information Technology will play in future society but their lower level of development places them in a disadvantageous position to reap the benefits of the IT revolution [1]. They need computers if they are to prevent further widening of the gap between the developed and the developing. Unlike previous industrial revolutions, development in IT is not bounded by shortage of raw material or industrial infrastructure but is tied very closely to the rate of development of human resources.

Sri Lanka, with a population of 16 million occupying an area of 64,000 sq. kms. has limited natural resources but very high literacy rate. The nation has recognised the potential benefits of IT and has initiated new projects to exploit it. It is potentially well-placed to leapfrog the Western cycle of computer development and to exploit directly the power of cheap modern computer hardware. The universities have an important role to play, both in educating the new generations of software engineers and, perhaps more importantly, in introducing IT into the courses offered in virtually all faculties, in virtually all subjects.

In 1983 a report was commissioned following a UNDP/ILO study the previous year [2]. The brief of the "Reeves Report" as it has since become known almost affectionately [3] was deceptively simple: what is the best way to introduce computer science into degree studies in Sri Lanka? The report was prepared by Professor Colin Reeves, a senior UK academic with considerable experience of course and curriculum design in the UK university context and a long standing member of British Computer Society examining bodies. On the Sri Lankan side, the then Chairman of the University Grants Commission (UGC) Dr F.S.C.P. Kalpage rapidly became an enthusiastic ally who was to play an important part in smoothing the path.

At that time the universities had very little in the way of computing, with two notable exceptions. The Department of Statistics at Colombo had been using mini-computer facilities for some years, funded largely by commercial initiatives and assisted by a long-standing link with the University of Reading, UK. Also two universities with engineering faculties, Moratuwa and Peradeniya, had comparable experience of computing in connection with specific research projects, and in teaching some students to program in FORTRAN. Few university staff had qualifications in computing, though an increasing number returning from

*Programme supported by the Overseas Development Administration and The British Council. Dr. Induruwa held an Association of Commonwealth Universities Fellowship at the University of Keele at the time of writing of this paper.

overseas training had picked up computing skills in their research. Significantly, very few senior academics had computing experience. However, the coincidental arrival of the PC in large quantities from neighbouring South East Asian countries was in the process of fuelling an explosive rise in the number of computers in Sri Lanka just as it was doing elsewhere [4].

2. THE REEVES REPORT RECOMMENDATIONS

The Reeves Report became a milestone in Sri Lankan academic computing and resulted in a number of key developments, particularly in the organisation of computing within the universities and in the training of staff. The three main conclusions of the Report are presented below.

2.1. Type of Course

It was clearly identified in the Report that a balance must be struck between the teaching of Computer Science as a distinctive discipline and the teaching of computing skills as an essential tool within other disciplines spread across all faculties. Not all universities could sensibly aspire in the foreseeable future to specialist teaching of full-blown courses in Computer Science. Initially at least, the needs of the employers of university graduates would be weighted towards the identification, design and implementation of computer applications in diverse fields.

2.2. Equipment

The Report recommended immediate installation of a laboratory of ten microcomputers in each university, with a common programming language (Pascal). This relatively modest provision of microcomputers was implemented rapidly. The Report recommended further levels of equipment support which should be provided when an institution could demonstrate that it was ready for it.

2.3. Staffing and Organisation

Shortage of expertise was clearly recognised as the most serious bottle-neck to progress and the main thrust of any development programme must lie in addressing this problem. The Report drew three main conclusions:

1. A staff training programme is essential.
2. In the absence of a sizeable pool of computing staff the training programme should be targeted at existing staff in other disciplines.
3. With expertise so thinly spread it would be a nonsense for each university to proceed in isolation from the rest.

The approach to training recommended in the Report is interesting in one respect for the action that was not proposed. A classic solution to lack of local expertise is to import a crew of foreign experts to teach one or more cohorts of students and to hope that the material left behind can be taken up subsequently by local staff. The 'expert replacement' approach was strongly discouraged in this programme for a number of reasons, quite apart from the high cost that would be involved. A more dynamic strategy was required; teach the teachers.

A further characteristic is that the individual universities are relatively small and the staff unevenly distributed, with 45% at the two largest. This reinforces the attractiveness of cooperation between universities to pool available expertise. To foster this cooperation the Report recommended establishment of a national forum for university computing, given the title Sri Lanka Inter University Committee on Computing after the UK body of similar name. Unlike the UK body, however, the SLIUCC was established subsequently as a UGC subcommittee chaired, exceptionally, by the Chairman of the UGC. As such, SLIUCC was to adopt a much wider role, embracing administrative and financial aspects as well as providing a forum for matters of common concern.

2.4. Reeves Report Summary

In essence, the Reeves Report recommended a programme to support computing developments across all the universities with the first priority to introduce the subject as widely as possible as components of existing degree courses. With encouragement, the more advanced, or more adventurous universities would ultimately push ahead with single degree courses in Computer Science as resources permit (which they did not, in 1983). The concept of a community of academic colleagues in computing transcending university boundaries to share expertise and teaching resources would play an important part. The universities could further benefit by forging links with overseas institutions for research, exchange of software, and for sabbatical leave, for example.

3. THE COMPUTER SCIENCE WORKSHOPS

A three-week lecturers' workshop in computer science was held in Colombo in the summer of 1984 for approximately three academic staff from each of eight universities. The objective of this pump-priming exercise recommended in the Reeves Report was to present a range of material from which typical computing modules might be selected in particular disciplines [6].

The workshop was relatively intense, with lectures from four UK academics interleaved with practical sessions using a laboratory of BBC Microcomputers running Pascal. Copies of eight textbooks and over 650 pages of notes produced by the lecturers were distributed to each participant, who was also offered a three-day pre-workshop course in Pascal programming. This successful workshop was repeated in a modified form in 1985 [7] to a further group of about 30 staff selected primarily from non-physical science or mathematics disciplines to extend the material of the two workshops to staff in approximately 18 subject areas. Substantial further copies of textbooks were presented to university libraries, the British Council Library and to participants. The UK input to both workshops was funded by the UK Overseas Development Agency (ODA) and organised by the British Council (BC). They involved staff from both the University of Keele and Staffordshire Polytechnic, with local coordinators and demonstrators.

Clearly, a workshop of this length can provide little more than a taste of the broad subject matter, but the general reaction was very favourable. In particular, some of the participants were relatively senior academics who used the workshops to obtain a perspective of Computer Science and how it might be relevant to their discipline. For the junior staff participants the workshops provided a first introduction to computing and an opportunity for them (and others) to assess future commitments to the subject.

4. THE KEELE-RUHUNA LINK

Following the two workshops it became clear that further external support would be most effectively directed at staff training on a number of fronts. A package of several events spread over three years from 1986 to 1989 was proposed under the title of the Keele-Ruhuna Link in Computer Science, and supported once again by the ODA/BC [8]. At the Sri Lankan end one university, at Ruhuna, was invited to host the Link but the programme was to involve all Sri Lankan universities in its activities on an equal basis. Keele and Staffordshire Polytechnic continued to provide the major input and coordination at the UK end, with many other institutions also selected to provide training. Four main types of activity are distinguished in the following sections.

4.1. Curriculum Working Parties

Each of these six working parties spread over the three years of the Link revolved around a group of six to eight Sri Lankan staff from different universities working with a UK convener over a period of six weeks. The residential working parties were based at Ruhuna initially but moved later to a venue close to Colombo. Each working party was assigned to study a particular area of the computing curriculum. Appropriate textbooks were selected by the convener and multiple copies provided for university and BC libraries.

A National Co-ordinator was appointed for the Link and he proved to be invaluable in setting up the working parties, assisting with selection of the participants, and generally liaising with SLIUCC and the UK Link Director (Prof. Reeves).

At the end of each working party the benefits were firstly the increased theoretical knowledge and experience of the participants and secondly a set of lecturer and student notes prepared by the group on word-processors, running typically to 200 pages. The UGC arranged for these to be duplicated and bound for sale at cost (under one pound sterling).

A number of published curricula were found to be particularly useful in the working parties and in selection of earlier workshop material. Sources used included the classic series of ACM Recommendations [9], the ACM Small Colleges Report [10], the UNESCO proposals [11] and a paper prepared by a National Co-ordinator of the Link during sabbatical leave spent at Keele [12]

4.2. Directors' Visits to UK

During the three years of the Link provision was made for the nine Directors of Computer Units or equivalent senior staff to visit UK, in groups of three, for three weeks. Each visit comprised a tour of selected UK universities, polytechnics, computer manufacturers, software houses and professional bodies to compare experiences and to formulate their own policies.

4.3. UK Training Awards

In the four academic years to 1988-89, a total of 32 Sri Lankan staff have been sponsored to attend taught conversion-type MSc courses in the UK. 25 were funded by ODA and 7 by the Sri Lankan UGC. Three further awards will be made in 1989-90.

These training awards were offered to staff across a wide spectrum of disciplines. A small number of further awards were made, on merit, to enable a few staff graduating from these courses to return to UK after a year or two to complete a Ph.D. In addition, a small number of technician training awards were provided by ODA. The UK Link Director adopted a deliberate policy of trying, where possible, to distribute MSc students and technicians to different UK universities.

4.4. Annual Review Visits

Short reviews of the Link programme were undertaken by Prof. Reeves or one of the authors (CH) at the end of each year of the Link [13, 14, 15]. These visits were used by the reviewers to organise short programmes of events to take place during the review. Thus, an Inter-University Conference on Computing in University Education was held after year one of the Link and a series of seminars, one per university, on Computers in Applications the following year. These special events provided valuable feedback on progress and yet further occasions to gather the faithful together.

5. COMPUTER TECHNOLOGY CENTRE

Prior to, and during the second workshop visit one of the authors (CH) undertook a study of computer and science laboratories in the universities and gave a series of seminars and demonstrations on computer control applications [16]. The main purpose of these studies was to assess the support requirements in computer laboratories, particularly for developing low-cost computer-based equipment in teaching and research.

Following this, the two authors submitted a proposal to establish a Computer Technology Centre at the University of Moratuwa (the main engineering-based university in the Colombo region) [17]. The principle objectives of this Centre are to promote the development of fundamental skills in computer hardware technology, to support hardware developments in Moratuwa and other universities, and to provide training facilities in the university and industrial sectors. The Centre was established with SLIUCC support in 1987 within the Department of Computer Science and Engineering. Development of this Centre will take place gradually, given the limited human resources available. A small further link funded by the BC, the Keele-Moratuwa Link, has provided for two short visits to Moratuwa by staff from Keele to assist in establishing the Centre [18]. Also, during the sabbatical leave of one author (ASI) spent at Keele, a project proposal [19] has been prepared regarding the development of LEARN, a Lankan Experimental Academic and Research Network.

6. LOOKING BACK

In July 1983, four months after publication of the Reeves Report, simmering ethnic differences erupted into riots and violent clashes in Sri Lanka. University life has been severely disrupted since that time and achievements in the computing development programme have been very much less than they would otherwise have been.

Fundamentally, the recommendations in the Reeves Report and virtually the whole of the subsequent programme are characterised by a strong reliance on local self-determination and self-help. External assistance has been provided for relatively short, discrete events in which the role of the visiting 'expert' was usually that of a Co-ordinator, or occasionally a lecturer addressing a selected group. Every support and encouragement has been given in these events to the staff involved but it was always believed that ultimately they, and their Heads of Department, must take the initiative in deciding how and where to introduce their selected material to their students, according to local needs.

This combination of local self-determination with a broad discipline base has led inevitably to wide variations in the way computing courses have been adapted to local needs and this diversity is in itself a considerable strength of the approach.

Brief comments on aspects of the programme are presented below.

6.1. A Review of Programme Activities

The workshops and curriculum working parties appear to have been universally well-received by the participants and others. Undoubtedly, the key to their success was the high level of commitment given to them by both participants and overseas visitors and the format of both was very successful from a staff training point of view. Feedback from universities indicates that some of the material produced in the curriculum working parties has already found its way into teaching programmes, especially the early material on programming and program design, computer systems, and data structures. Some have commented that the notes are incomplete, too low-level or not appropriate for their purposes. This is inevitable given that the material was the output from a limited training exercise and serves to further indicate that needs are different in different local situations and courses.

The MSc conversion course training programme has been partially successful. It achieved its objective in the sense that approximately 30 junior members of staff attended courses in the UK and all are believed to have completed the courses successfully. One year MSc courses were chosen deliberately to provide rapid feedback to departments and, indeed, this was achieved, with many of the returned staff being back in post in time to attend Link working parties, for example. Unfortunately, this accelerated programme came into conflict with a rather rigid university promotion policy in a way unforseen by the Link team and this is believed to have deterred some very able staff from taking up places offered.

Despite some difficulties in providing a balanced programme of events, the short Directors' visits to UK proved to be extremely valuable opportunities to establish contacts and to visit a selection of computing organisations in the UK.

6.2. SLIUCC, Computer Units and Computer Science Departments

The establishment of SLIUCC turned out to be one of the most important parts of the programme. SLIUCC provided a direct channel of communication between its members, the Computer Unit Directors (and occasional UK advisers) and the UGC Chairman. SLIUCC was able to make decisions and allocate resources to establish computer laboratories, to purchase PCs, define computing cadres, co-ordinate Link and training activities, for example, in a very short timespan. The importance of this should not be underestimated. Universities world-wide are not renowned for their abilities to adapt to rapid change and Sri Lanka is no exception. Without an equivalent body to SLIUCC, the road to success would have been paved with procedural pitfalls. Much of this success is attributable to a UGC Chairman who had the vision and the will to raise computing to a high priority in UGC affairs and who was prepared to keep a close eye on its development as Chairman of SLIUCC.

The translation of the concept of a Computer Unit into practice has presented difficulties in some universities. The post was conceived as having wide responsibility for academic computing in a university, actively promoting teaching in all disciplines as appropriate as well as maintaining a central laboratory of computers. The Units play such a key role that a full-time senior appointment as Director was very strongly recommended. Any less commitment, it was argued, would inhibit effective guidance on curriculum revision in all faculties, pursuit of university computing policy and, perhaps most importantly, effective leadership of staff.

In practice most universities, with SLIUCC's assent, chose instead to appoint part-time Computer Unit Directors from among the pool of senior academics, who retained firmly an allegiance to their parent department, in some cases as head of that department. Two factors influenced this decision strongly. Firstly, the Sri Lankan university staffing structure is extremely rigid compared, for example, to that in the UK, and weighs against a switch to what is not yet a well-recognised post. Secondly, and importantly, the total pool of senior academic staff in most universities, particularly in Science and Engineering faculties, is so small that a move into computing must deprive some other worthy discipline of a significant proportion of its human resources. Nonetheless, it will be some time before the newly qualified computing staff will be able to fulfil the role of Director effectively and the delay in filling the leadership gap continues to limit progress.

By contrast, some universities have now established Computer Science or equivalent departments and are in the process of mounting degree courses under titles such as Computer Science, Computer Science and Engineering, and Computer Engineering. Most have sought links with foreign institutions to assist in running the courses and these links will certainly need appropriate support by external agencies for some time. Importantly, a balance will need to be struck between the national need for computer scientists and the need for computer-trained graduates of other disciplines.

On the subject of equipment, the original computer laboratories were very successful and the equipment has now been supplemented or replaced by the ubiquitous PCs, which provide increased power and an extensive range of software, all at achievable cost. The growth in usage of higher-level software packages on these PCs is an additional facet of computer development which deserves special consideration in future programmes.

6.3. General Comments and Conclusions

Most examples of external assistance at university level work on a one-to-one institution basis and emphasise technology transfer or cultural exchange. The programme described in this paper involved 11 or more institutions and emphasised inter-university cooperation in computing development. Hence, it was a relatively unusual package and continually broke new ground.

In terms of value for money the approach offered great leverage in the sense that a relatively modest input of assistance had a wide reaching effect across many departments in many universities. The programme was geared towards a programme of staff development with a strong element of self-help and self-determination, avoiding dependence on visiting experts to teach courses directly to students. Essentially it fostered a spirit of cooperation among staff with common interests in computing and involved all concerned in the development process. Overall, it met these objectives extremely well.

With hindsight we should qualify these remarks with a few observations of areas in which the programme was not so effective. The Link programme actually consisted of a series of discrete events linked together only loosely, as far as the overseas visitors were involved, by communal activities during the annual review visits. To push home the advantage it would have been highly desirable to have had many more locally organised activities filling in the gaps between the Link events and maintaining the momentum. Local seminars and workshops, special interest groups, revision groups for updating and extending Link working party material and common software development groups were all ideas suggested by visitors or others at some stage in the programme. Many of these fell by the wayside as no one had the responsibility, or initiative, to take them up. Their organisation certainly fell outside the resources of the Link, and in many ways the initiative for following through these extra activities should come, it was felt, from the Sri Lankan side. SLIUCC in particular provided great continuity of administrative and financial development but was not able to offer substantial help in maintaining this academic momentum. The lack of full-time Computer Unit Directors committed to an evangelical role was undoubtedly a further factor. Looking back, it may have been useful to have had an academic subcommittee of SLIUCC or, possibly, a full-time national Co-ordinator in computing charged with promoting continuity of academic development.

At the time of writing, an independent ODA review of Sri Lankan academic computing is pending and this will determine the future nature of UK-funded support.

In conclusion, the authors would like to thank the many people who have contributed to this programme, both in Sri Lanka and in the UK. There is, alas, insufficient space here to list all who have helped.

A longer version of this paper is available on request from the first named author.

REFERENCES

1. Samaranayake, V.K., 'Computers in Education. A Third World Perspective', Computer and Information Technology Council, Colombo, 1989.
2. UNDP/ILO, 'Toward a National Computer Policy in Sri Lanka', The Report of the UNDP/ILO Team, Colombo, June 1982.
3. Reeves, C.M., 'On the Introduction of Computer Science into Degree Studies in Sri Lanka', Report to the Ministry of Higher Education, Colombo, March 1983.
4. Induruwa, A.S., 'Towards an Information Society in Asia', Bulletin of the Asian Regional Exchange for New Alternatives, Special Issue on Policy and Planning, Vol iii, Nos 2 & 3, pp 49-59, 1984.
5. UGC, 'Corporate Plan for University Education', Sri Lanka University Grants Commission, Colombo, 1988.
6. Reeves, C.M., 'Report on Lecturers' Workshop in Computer Science, Sri Lanka 1984', Report presented to the British Council, 1984.
7. Reeves, C.M., 'Report on the Second Workshop in Computer Science, Sri Lanka 1985', Report presented to the British Council, 1985.
8. Reeves, C.M., 'Proposal to the ODA for a Keele-Ruhuna Link in Computer Science', in [7], 1985.
9. ACM, 'Curriculum '78. Recommendations for the Undergraduate Program in Computer Science', CACM, Vol 22, No. 3, March 1979.
10. ACM, 'A Computer Science Program for Small Colleges', CACM, Vol 16, No. 3, pp 139-147, March 1973.
11. UNESCO, 'A Modular Curriculum in Computer Science', UNESCO Report, 1984.
12. Tillekeratne, K., 'Towards a Unified Curriculum in Computing for Universities in Sri Lanka', Private Communication, 1986.
13. Reeves, C.M., 'The Keele-Ruhuna Link in Computer Science First Annual Review and Visit Report', Report submitted to the British Council, July 1987.
14. Hawksley, C., 'The Keele-Ruhuna Link in Computer Science Second Annual Review and Visit Report', Report submitted to the British Council, Sept 1988.
15. Reeves, C.M., 'Keele-Ruhuna Link in Computer Science Third Annual Review', Report submitted to the British Council, Aug 1989.
16. Hawksley, C., 'Report on Development of University Microcomputer Laboratory Facilities', Report submitted to the British Council, May 1985.
17. Induruwa, A.S., and Hawksley, C., 'Proposal for a Computer Technology Centre at the University of Moratuwa, Sri Lanka', Report submitted to SLIUCC, 1987.
18. White, N.H., 'Report on the First Keele-Moratuwa Link Visit, July/Aug 1988' Report submitted to the British Council, 1988.
19. Induruwa, A.S. and Hawksley, C., 'Keele-Moratuwa Link in Computer Science - A Proposal to set up a Lankan Experimental Academic and Research Network (LEARN)', Tech. Rep. KML/89/02, Department of Computer Science, University of Keele, May 1989.

Computers in Education
A. McDougall and C. Dowling (Editors)
Elsevier Science Publishers B.V. (North-Holland)

COMPUTERS IN EDUCATION: JAPAN VERSUS THE UNITED STATES*

Gerald Knezek†, Keiko Miyashita∆ and Takashi Sakamoto‡

† Department of Computer Education & Cognitive Systems, P.O. Box 5155, University of North Texas, Denton, Texas USA 76203
∆ University of North Texas, 5-3-2 Fukazawa, Setagaya-ku, Tokyo, Japan
‡ Department of Systems Science, Tokyo Institute of Technology, 1259 Nagatsuta, Midori-ku, Yokohama 227, Japan

This paper contains a comparative analysis of the use of computers in primary through secondary education in the United States and Japan. Historical developments and plans for future implementations of informatics in education are discussed. Conjectured reasons for national similarities and differences are also provided, within the framework of traditional educational philosophies and cultural values.

1. INTRODUCTION

Since 1970, Japan has possessed the highest literacy rate of any nation in the world [1]. In 1988, the value of its stock market surpassed that of the United States [2], and, during the same year, Japan began providing more foreign aid than any other nation [3]. The overall excellence of the Japanese educational system is often listed as a major contributor to Japan's economic might [4]. "The average high school graduate in Japan is said to be as well educated as the average college graduate in the United States [5, p.14]."

2. COMPUTER UTILIZATION

However, education in Japan does not place equal emphasis on all fronts. In particular, when compared with the United States, education below the university level in Japan does not appear to have involved extensive exposure to computers and other information technologies [6]. As shown in Figures 1 and 2, the introduction of computers in the elementary and junior high levels of Japanese education has lagged behind the U.S. by 4-5 years throughout the 1980's.

Selected raw data serves to reemphasize the general trends shown in Figures 1 and 2. For example, in 1983, just 148 of 24,692 elementary schools in Japan reported computer usage [9], making it quite likely that a Japanese primary school student would advance to junior high without ever having seen a computer in school. Even in 1987, the total number of computers in K-12 schools for the entire nation of Japan (22 million students) was just 101,540 machines [9;10], considerably fewer than the 115,028 found in the individual state of California (4.5 million students) during the same year [7].

3. EDUCATIONAL COMPUTING PURPOSES

In the United States, K-12 computer usage focused on instructional applications throughout most of the 1980's [11;12], while in Japan the emphasis has been on administrative applications and CMI [6]. This explains why the typical U.S. school installation is 15-20 machines in a computer laboratory used for CAI, computer literacy, and programming [11], while two-thirds of all computers in Japanese education are located in teacher's lounges and used for electronic gradebooks, developing examinations, counseling students, and planning classroom instruction [13]. It is noteworthy that four reports issued by the Japan National Council on Educational Reform since 1985 [14;15;16] have recommended increased instructional utilization of computers in Japan, while recent studies in the U.S. have recommended "a computer on every teacher's desk by 1991" [17] and reported rapid growth in the installation of

* This research was supported by a grant from the Meadows Foundation of Dallas, Texas

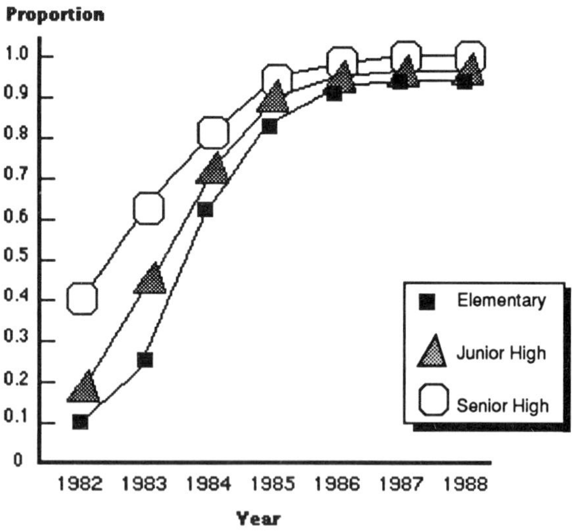

Figure 1
Proportion of American Schools with Computers [7]

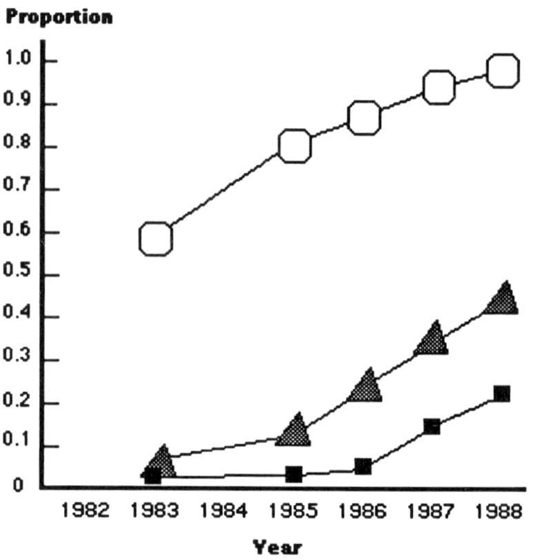

Figure 2
Proportion of Japanese Schools with Computers [8]

Integrated Learning Systems incorporating both CAI and CMI [18]. Apparently, the United States and Japan are evolving toward a common ground regarding ways of using computers in K-12 education.

The two nations are already quite similar in their applications of instructional computing to specific subject areas. Math, Science, Reading & other language arts, and Foreign Language were responsible for roughly 70% of all CAI applications in the United States during 1986 [19], while Math, Science, Foreign Language, and Japanese Language (arts) were responsible for approximately 80% of Japan's CAI applications during 1987 [9;13]. Drill, practice, and tutorials were the dominant types of CAI in both countries during the 1980's, but educators in both countries recognize the need for more software (e.g. simulation) which the student manipulates to aid learning [20;21].

4. INSTRUCTIONAL COMPUTING GOALS

Japan and the United States have two goals in common for instructional computing: (a) aiding instruction in subjects other than computing, and (b) fostering computer literacy [11;14]. Both recognize three distinctive plateaus of computer instruction as appropriate for different curricular goals and/or grade levels: (a) Computer Assisted Instruction (CAI), (b) Applications Tools (word processing, spreadsheet etc.), and (c) Computer Programming [11;13]. Programming was required only in vocational high schools throughout Japan during the 1980's [21;22], and will not be available in junior high schools until 1993 [23]. This can be contrasted with U.S. states such as Texas, where programming has been one component of a required junior high computer literacy course since 1985 [24].

Both nations agree on the use of computers to motivate students, and both recognize the need to teach information processing skills to the current generation of students to prepare them for the society of the 21st century [22;25;26].

Japan far outdistances the United States in its emphasis on the potential dangers of information technology, as evidenced by the following excerpt from the Second Report of the National Council on Educational Reform:

> It should be carefully noted that recent progress in information technology ... carr[ies] both promise and danger. It must be remembered that the spread of information technology may cause problems by robbing us of direct experience, mediating and controlling our experience, or subjecting us to a useless flood of information [14, p.8].

By contrast, in the United States, negative aspects of information technology are typically given much less emphasis. It is common to simply introduce the topic to computer-using teachers and students during one lecture in a course, or through a chapter in a supplemental reading text.

5. COMPUTING VERSUS INFORMATICS

Japan's plans for the utilization of technology in education appear to stress the broader aspects of information automation, transmission, and storage (informatics), rather than the more narrow focus on computers per se that was initially common in the U.S. Both the third and fourth reports on educational reform refer to the use of open data bases, artificial model environments, networks, television, facsimile, as well as traditional computing applications to promote "information literacy" in society [15;16].

The United States has also recently begun to emphasize the broader aspects of information dissemination in education. During 1988-89, 42% of all K-12 schools reported ownership of at least one modem, and 32% reported having microcomputers connected in a network [18]. States such as Texas have upgraded educational master plans to include extensive use of telecommunications [27] and have begun to require computer telecommunications in computer applications courses. Still, at the federal level, U.S. support is biased toward computing rather than informatics. 1989 allocations from the Fund for Innovation in Education (FIE) included $14.7 million for the Computer-Based Instruction Program and just $1 million for Technology in Education. The latter program is charged with supporting education in K-12 classrooms through television, radio, and telecommunications networks [28].

6. TEACHER TRAINING

Inadequate teacher training has often been cited as an obstacle to more rapid implementation of computer education in Japan and the United States [21;25]. In the United States, most teachers have access to retraining through computer courses offered by three-fifths of all colleges of education in the country, while Japanese teachers must generally retake a difficult university entrance examination if they wish to enroll in university courses [25]. As a result, in 1987, almost no Japanese teachers with formal computer training gained it through university coursework. The primary sources for training were Ministry of Education and prefectural board of education inservice programs (53%), and private organizations (27%) [9].

Not surprisingly, the primary teaching fields of half the computer-using teachers in American and Japanese secondary schools are math and science [11;9]. One surprising point brought out by Becker [11] is the relatively large proportion of vocational subject area teachers (business, industrial arts, agriculture) among computer using educators in the United States. Vocational teachers account for roughly 20% of the computer-using secondary school teachers in the U.S. [11], quite similar to their proportional representation (25%) in Japan, where vocational teachers have been given priority for computer training [29].

7. GOVERNMENTAL AND CULTURAL INFLUENCES

7.1. Centralization vs. Decentralization

There is no national policy for computer education in the United States [26]. Each of the fifty states makes its own decisions regarding issues such as whether computer literacy should be a subject, like math or English, with its own course, or whether it should be a thematic component incorporated into every other discipline. Some states, such as Texas, have adopted the course-based philosophy, while others, such as Hawaii, have adopted a totally thematic approach [30].

Japan, on the other hand, has a single Ministry of Education, Science, and Culture (MESC or Monbusho) which determines major policy issues for every public school in the nation [10;25]. As determined by national policy, an information processing course for the Upper Secondary Curriculum (grades 10-12) has been listed as an elective since 1971 [31;32]. However, as previously-reported statistics indicate, few ordinary (non-vocational) high school students were actually offered the course over the past 15 years. Japan now appears to be adopting a dual-pronged approach to K-12 computing, introducing required information literacy courses while it simultaneously incorporates computers into traditional subjects [33].

7.2. Individuality vs. Uniformity

While Americans prize individuality, Japanese culture holds uniformity in high esteem [34]. In Japan, about 40 students typically study in an elementary or junior high classroom, and 45 in a high school classroom. It is unusual for a teacher in the United States to have more than 35 students in a classroom. In the United States, a teacher often divides students into three to five groups according to student levels of understanding, and provides different materials to each group. A Japanese teacher often instructs the whole class from the same textbook, and each student in a class studies the same pages of the textbook every day [35].

7.3. Effects on Computer Laboratory Environments

These philosophical differences may have carried over into existing computer laboratories in the two countries. In the United States, the typical computer laboratory contains 15-20 machines [11], enough for a large class demonstration with two students per computer. Highly varied individual work activities are common during open laboratory times. For Japan, "In many of the schools famous for their CAI, nearly 50 computers are installed in a single classroom and all students ... learn a subject matter passively by only responding to questions given in succession on the computer screen [36]." Compared with Japan, computer laboratory activities in the U.S. appear to be less centralized and less uniform, similar to education practices in general.

8. NEW TECHNOLOGIES

8.1. Standardized Operating Systems

Uniformity is also being sought in the operating system arena in Japan. TRON, the real time operating system nucleus project, was first proposed by Ken Sakamura of Tokyo University, then changed to a joint project of universities and electronic firms in 1984. One of TRON's main goals is to eliminate software incompatibility among different vendors of microcomputers by providing a common operating system for all [37]. During 1988-89, it appeared that an educational version of TRON (ETRON) might be adopted for all computers to be used in education [33;38], but in mid-1989 Japan's Center for Educational Computing announced that ETRON will be just one of many operating systems endorsed for use in education [39].

Many U.S. teachers frustrated by incompatibilities between Apple and MS-DOS based machines supported ETRON, in hopes that it would encourage U.S. manufacturers to consider a single standard for the United States [33]. Ironically, U.S. actions such as the September 8, 1988 letter to Japan's Ministry of International Trade and Industry (MITI) by U.S. Deputy Trade Representative Michael Smith, in which he protested ETRON on the grounds it would "unfairly restrict" U.S. access to Japanese markets [40], may have contributed to Japan's failure to standardize on ETRON.

8.2. Artificial Intelligence Applications

The race between the United States, Japan, and other nations to capture the lead in fifth generation computer technology has been well publicized for several years [41]. Not so well publicized is the fact that Japan plans to finish its quest and begin using this technology in 1991 [29]. One potential area for application is education.

It would appear that Japan has unique prospects for using AI techniques to quickly improve the use of computers in education, since the existence of three different character sets and thousands of kanji hinder traditional Japanese-computer communication through typing [21;42]. This can be contrasted with a single twenty-six letter alphabet in English, which makes a keyboard with approximately ninety-six characters quite acceptable for English-computer communication.

In addition to being more urgently needed, speech input and output systems should also be more readily achievable in Japan than in the United States. This is because the sounds involved in spoken Japanese are more manageable than in English. In Japanese, "...there is nothing comparable to the dread five-pitch tonal system of Chinese. The five vowels in Japanese have one pronunciation each, whereas there are twenty-nine ways to pronounce the five English vowels [43,p.25]." Therefore, Japan should have a double incentive to rapidly develop speech-based human-computer communications. Written communication is more difficult than English, while spoken communication may be easier.

In the United States, developmental activities for applying artificial intelligence to education date back at least as far as the early 1970's [44]. Yet, by 1985, only about 20 functioning Intelligent Computer Assisted Instruction (ICAI) systems were well known to the academic community [45], and just two were commercially available [46]. One major reason for this is that ICAI often requires ten times more development effort than CAI, assuming the author uses high level programming languages and third or fourth generation technology [47]. Nevertheless, the Air Force, Army, and National Aeronautics and Space Administration have all initiated significant ICAI development efforts during the 1980's [48;49].

It seems certain that the development and utilization of ICAI will continue to grow in the U.S. as well as Japan for the forseeable future.

9. SUMMARY

Although Japan and the United States are similar in economic might, technological sophistication, and educational philosophies, the use of computers in education for the two nations is not directly comparable. The principal authority for educational policies in Japan is centralized in the Ministry of Education, Science and Culture (Monbusho), while in the United States, each of the fifty states is responsible for formulating its own educational policies.

Nevertheless, the following general observations regarding the role of computers in K-12 education for Japan and the United States can be made:

1. The rate of Japanese introduction of computers into primary (K-6) and lower secondary (7-9) schools lagged behind the United States by four-to-five years throughout the 1980's.
2. The U.S. has tended to involve its computers in the process of instruction while Japan has allocated its machines to managerial functions including CMI.
3. Both Japan and the U.S. agree on three utilization plateaus for instructional computing: (a) Computer Assisted Instruction (CAI), (b) Applications Tools (word processing, spreadsheet, etc.); and (c) Computer Programming.
4. Japan has a much greater concern than in the U.S. for the "dark side" of information technology.
5. Japan's plans stress informatics more strongly than plans in the U.S.
6. Culture in Japan stresses uniformity while the United States stresses individuality. This affects activities in the classroom and the computer laboratory.
7. Japan appears to have greater prospects for immediate benefit from the application of A.I. techniques to speech synthesis and recognition.

ACKKNOWLEDGEMENTS

The authors wish to thank Jenny Jopling for helpful information gathered on her trip to Japan during the summer of 1989. We also gratefully acknowledge the assistance of Dhanapong Saengrussamee and Greg Jones in desktop publishing.

REFERENCES

[1] De Mente, B., The Whole Japan Book (Phoenix Books, Az, 1983) 81.

[2] Sculley, J., Keynote address to the National Educational Computing Conference, (Dallas, Texas, June 15, 1988).

[3] Greenwald, J., Japan: From superrich to superpower, Time (July 4, 1988) 29.

[4] Yano, I., Nippon: A chartered survey of Japan, (The Kokusei-sha Corporation, Tokyo, 1989) 316.

[5] Ravitch, D., Japan's smart schools. The New Republic, (January 6, 1986) 14.

[6] Ikai, A., Use of the computer in education in Japan, (ERIC Document Reproduction Service No. ED 260 704, 1984).

[7] Hayes, J., Microcomputer and VCR usage in public schools, 1981-82 to 1987-88, ERS Spectrum 6(2) (1988) 1-6.

[8] Ministry of Education in Japan, Annual report of computer education in 1989 (Tokyo, 1989).

[9] Ministry of Education in Japan, Annual report of computer education in 1988. (Tokyo, 1988).

[10] Monbusho (Ministry of Education, Science, and Culture), Education in Japan: A Brief Outline (Tokyo, MESC Doc. 4-8602, 1986).

[11] Becker, H. J., The second national survey of instructional uses of school computers: A preliminary report (World Conference on Computers in Education, Norfolk, VA, 1985).

[12] Chambers, J. A., & Bork, A., Computer assisted learning in U.S. secondary/ elementary schools (ERIC Document Reproduction Service No. ED202461, 1980).

[13] Sakamoto, T., Computers in the Japanese educational system, Business Japan (March 1987) 28-32.

[14] National Council on Educational Reform, Summary of second report on educational reform (Government of Japan, Tokyo, April 23, 1986).

[15] National Council on Educational Reform, Third report on educational reform. (Government of Japan, Tokyo, Apr. 1, 1987).

[16] National Council on Educational Reform, Fourth and Final Report on Educational Reform (Government of Japan, Tokyo, Aug. 7, 1987).
[17] Godspeed, J., The NEA Publishes Two Powerful Reports on Educational Technology, Electronic Learning (Sept. 1989) 21.
[18] Quality Education Data, Inc., Microcomputer usage in schools: A 1989 QED Update (Denver, CO, 1989).
[19] Smith, P. L., CAI in the classroom: What does the research say? Paper presented to the 6th Annual Texas Computer Education Association State Conference (San Antonio, Texas, February 1986).
[20] Sakamoto, T., A SYNOPSIS OF COMPUTER-ASSISTED LEARNING IN JAPAN, Japan Computer Quarterly 77 (1989) 4-25.
[21] Nishinosono, H., Informatics in general education: The Japanese plan, Prospects, 17(4) (1987) 539-546.
[22] Sakamoto, T., Market for educational computing in Japan, Business Japan (March 1988) 28-30.
[23] Sakamoto, T. and Stern, S., Educational Computing in Japan, Educational Technology Resources 11 (1988) 1-9.
[24] Pratscher, S., State computer literacy training, Proceedings of the 5th Annual Texas Computer Education Association State Conference (Austin, 1985) 318-323.
[25] Dorfman, C. H. ed., Japanese education today (OERI Japan Study Team, Washington D.C., Jan. 1987).
[26] Zucker, A., Computers in education: National policy in the USA, European Journal of Education 17(4)(1982) 395-410.
[27] Texas Education Agency, 1988-2000: Long range plan for technology of the Texas State Board of Education (Austin, 1988).
[28] Knauth, K., Scattered federal initiatives add up to big spending on technology, Electronic Learning (Sept. 1989) 20-22.
[29] Tanaka, M., Personal interview through interpreter conducted by Jenny Jopling, University of North Texas graduate student, in Ministry of Education Offices (Tokyo, Japan, Aug. 1989).
[30] Knezek, G. A., Computer literacy inservice training model for the Hawaii exploratory computer literacy curriculum guide, in: Computers in Instruction: Framework for Administrators (Dept. of Education, Honolulu, 1984).
[31] Ministry of Education, Science, and Culture, Revised course of study for upper secondary schools in Japan (Japanese National Commission for UNESCO, Tokyo, 1971).
[32] Ministry of Education, Science, and Culture, Course of study for upper secondary schools in Japan. (Notification No. 163, Tokyo, 1983).
[33] Knauth, K., Japan launches national educational computer project. Electronic Learning (Apr. 1989) 16-17.
[34] Cobb, D., Educators see differences in styles (Denton Record Chronicle, Texas, Dec. 9, 1988).
[35] Duke, B.C., Japanese School [M. Kunihiro & I. Hirano, Trans.] (Kodansha, Japan,1986).
[36] Yamagiwa, T., Computer use in the Japanese educational system, Business Japan (Mar. 1988) 38-39.
[37] Sakamura, K, TRON (Uncited newspaper story provided to K. Miyashita by M. Tanaka of the Ministry of Education during spring 1989).
[38] The CEC Concept Model '87, CEC News (Center for Educational Computing, Tokyo, May 1988) 24-27.
[39] Nikkei Sangyo Newspaper, Is this a dream? B-TRON for educational personal computer (June 14, 1989).
[40] Lachica, E., Japan is pressed on education computers (The Wall Street Journal, Nov. 8, 1988).
[41] Feigenbaum, E., & McCorduck, P., The fifth generation: Japan's computer challenge to the world, Creative Computing (Aug. 1984) 103-111.
[42] Hitotumatu, S., A forecast of the potential quality of education in Japan in the year 2000, T.H.E. Journal 13(5) (Jan. 1986) 105-07.
[43] Seward, J., Japanese in action (John Weatherhill, Tokyo, 1979).
[44] Carbonell, J. R., AI in CAI: An Artificial intelligence approach to computer-aided instruction. IEEE Transactions on Man-Machine Systems, 11 (1970) 190-202.
[45] Ross, P., Intelligent Tutoring Systems, Paper presented to the Fourth International Conference on Technology and Education (Ft. Worth, Texas, Apr. 1987).
[46] Yazdani, M., Intelligent Tutoring Systems Survey, Artificial Intelligence Review, 1 (1986) 43-52.
[47] Knezek, G. A., Intelligent tutoring systems and ICAI, The Computing Teacher, 15(6) (Mar. 1988) 11-13.
[48] Polson, M. C., & Richardson, J. J. eds., Foundations of intelligent tutoring systems (Lawrence Erlbaum, 1988).
[49] Dede, C., Artificial intelligence applications to high technology training, Journal of Educational Communications and Technology (Fall 1987).

Computers in Education
A. McDougall and C. Dowling (Editors)
Elsevier Science Publishers B.V. (North-Holland)

NEW DIRECTIONS FOR EDUCATIONAL BROADCASTING:

A MULTI-MEDIAL PACKAGE INTEGRATING INFORMATICS IN SECONDARY EDCUATION

Jan Lepeltak and Tineke Zeelenberg-Meuleman

National Institute for Curriculum Development
Postbox 2041
7500 CA Enschede, The Netherlands

and

Betty Collis

University of Twente
Postbox 217
7500 AE Enschede, The Netherlands

This paper describes the development and contents of an innovative approach to informatics instruction. The approach involves a variety of media, was developed at the national level, and has as one of its goals the stimulation of cooperation between informatics teachers and teachers of language-related disciplines in the secondary school.

Background:

Informatics Education in The Netherlands

Informatics is seen as an important component of the secondary school experience in The Netherlands. After considerable experimentation, a core course in informatics has been proposed for the national level, and all secondary schools are provided by the government with a network of at least eight computers, a starter kit of software, and access to teacher training. The nature of information, of information sources, and of the uses of information in society are seen as central focuses of informatics instruction (for a fuller description, see Van Weering, in the Proceedings of the IFIP TC 3 First European Conference on Computers in Education, Lausanne, 1988, pp. 421-425.) In particular, the following areas are seen as distinct within the informatics curriculum:

a. The significance of information technology for society
b. Information and data processing
c. Applications of information technology
d. Data-view systems

Integrating informatics into other curricula

In addition to this, national policy in The Netherlands also stresses the integration of information technology (IT) as well as informatics (learning about IT) into other subjects areas in the secondary curriculum. There is a particular interest in promoting this integration within the so-called "mother-tongue" curriculum, writing and composition, grammar. However, this goal has been, as yet, little achieved, as the use of computers still primarily occurs within the separate curriculum of informatics. Less than seven percent of mother tongue (Nederlands) teachers indicate any use of computer-related technology at all, let alone a use which stresses the integration of informatics concepts.

Various efforts have been made to stimulate the integration of IT and informatics into mother-tongue instruction.

For example, there is a national inservice program for the inservice training of Nederlands (mother tongue) teachers with respect to the use of IT in instruction. The aspects of informatics which relate to language processing have been stressed as important aspects of informatics. The increased attractiveness of informatics for female students when informatics is integrated within the language curriculum has also been argued. Nonetheless, this integration still is proving to be a difficult matter.

Motivation for a course integrating informatics and language instruction

In order to better stimulate the integration of informatics within the mother-tongue curriculum areas, the National Institute for Curriculum Development (SLO), the Netherlands School Television Network (NOT), and the Dutch national communications utility (PTT) have combined forces in the development of new curriculum materials (the "Computerjournaal") that has the following pair of general goals:

> *to stimulate language and humanities teachers to integrate IT in their lessons while at the same time emphasizing a new approach to traditional informatics curriculum through an emphasis on applications of information technology to language-related applications in society.*

To meet these general goals, the computerjournaal approach includes a variety of media that can used directly in the language classroom. The course must also include pedagogical advice to teachers -both informatics and mother tongue- as to how they can use its innovative material.

Partners in the "Computerjournaal" course

To meet these goals, the "Computerjournaal" materials have been developed and begun their nationwide dissemination in October 1989. Before the course is further described, the background of three partners in its development should be briefly mentioned.

The National Institute for Curriculum Development (SLO) has extensive experience in curriculum development in The Netherlands. The SLO has already developed a wide range of informatics materials and has already cooperated with the NOT in a successful educational television series aimed at introducing informatics to secondary students.

The NOT (Nederlandse Schooltelevisie) company is an active and well-known educational television network in The Netherlands. It is an independent, non-profit educational broadcasting company which broadcasts during daytime hours on one of the national television networks. The programs of the NOT are especially made for elementary and secondary education. Teachers frequently capture the broadcast materials on videotape for use during subsequent class hours. More than 90% of the schools in The Netherlands have one or more video recorders. All of the NOT television programs are accompanied by written lesson material, produced and delivered by NOT.

The Dutch PTT has particular interest in modern information technologies, particulary telecommunications and the use of "viditel" (now called VIDEOTEX) as an information source available to the Dutch public through ordinary television receivers.

In order to utilize the specific expertise of these three partners, the "Computerjournaal" course has been developed. This is a multi-medial course involving educational broadcasting, computer software, print materials, telecommunications, and videotex. The SLO is responsible for the content and curriculum aspects of the course and develops the learning materials and software. NOT is responsible for the television production. The PTT gives specific advise about modern information technologies and also provides funds to support the course and software development.

Description of the "Computerjournaal"

The "Computerjournaal" package consists of three different physical components:

a. Eight educational television programs, of 25 minutes each, to be broadcast once per month (each with one repeat broadcast) beginning October 1989. Approximately 15 minutes of each broadcast have a documentary character while the other 10 minutes are used for studio interviews about current affairs that are interesting for the students and that have some connection with IT.

b. Eight sets of print materials, one to accompany each of the eight broadcasts. The print materials include teacher guides and student workbooks.

Within these print materials, suggestions are given for activities that make use existing educational software already in the schools (particulary word processing), or software that is relatively easy to obtain (desk-top publishing). In addition, activities involving the use of videotex and an existing telecommunications network available to educators in The Netherlands are also given in the print materials.

c. A software package, SCOOP, accompanied by print materials for both teachers and students. The program SCOOP is a British educational software package described by its authors as "presenting some of the applications of information technology in an interesting and motivating way. The computer program is an adventure game concerned with the efforts of a journalist to secure a 'scoop' about the sudden appearance of a millionaire recluse." The Computerjournaal project has obtained a license from the UK producers of this software to use the package in Dutch schools registered in the Computerjournaal course. A Dutch translation of the software and the accompanying print materials was partly done in the UK in consultation with SLO computerjournaal team members.

These three components are organized around the following eight topics:

Program 1 Computers, Information, and the Journalist

following the stream of data and data processing during the last parliamentary elections (September 1989) in The Netherlands and the way in which a Dutch newspaper uses IT to cover the election and to produce news stories about the election.

Program 2 The Office and the New Writing Environment

showing recent developments in using IT and spelling and grammar checkers for local-area networks in the business office. This segment is filmed at the research laboratory of a multinational company in The Netherlands.

Program 3 Image Processing and Graphical Design

showing examples of the impact of IT in the creative process and also about techniques for desk top publishing.

Program 4 Poetry and Music

showing how some students are using IT tools as they write poetry. The broadcast also shows a poetry generator and ends with a Haiku (a sort Japanese poem) competition.

Program 5 Automatic Language Translation

demonstrating why it is so difficult to translate text with a computer. The program covers recent developments in automated translation in Europe sponsored by the European Community.

Program 6 Public Opinion Polls--Use and Misuse

examining the influence of IT on the development of marketing and interviewing strategies. The program shows this kind of research in practice and discusses the possibilities of manipulating data and information.

Program 7 The Library of the 1990s

showing new trends in storing and retrieving information by using CD-ROM, CD-I (CD-interactive), and relational databases.

Program 8 Telecommunications

showing new ways of using telecommunications, including teleconferencing, E-mail, and telecopiers.

Other Aspects of the Computerjournaal Project

The course is being brought to teachers' attention in a variety of ways.
During September 1989 an extensive mailing occurred, in which a letter explaining the course, a brochure about the course (a copy of which is attached) and a copy of the first student workbook has been sent to every secondary school in The Netherlands, and also to the home address of every informatics teacher and every Nederlands (Dutch language) teacher in the country.

An article has appeared in the national journal for computer-using educators (COS) and descriptions of the course appear in the NOT catalogue of educational broadcasts, which is widely distributed throughout the country. In addition, the course is being offered to teachers for a very low price, appoximately $40US, because of the subsidization of the project by the PTT. The registration procedure is simple-teachers simply return a card attached to the information brochure. Print materials will then be sent on a monthly basis to the registrants and the SCOOP package will be supplied to accompany the first broadcast. Because the television broadcasts will be available freely on the television network, no additional provisions need to be made for receiving the broadcasts. Schools have permission to videotape the broadcasts for reuse.

Another feature of the computerjournaal project is the involvement of a research-evaluation team from Division of Educational Instrumentation at the University of Twente. This team did not participate in the development of the course, but will be actively involved in the investigation of its implementation and impact in schools. This evaluation will focus on suggestions relative to factors that are important to the success of a centrally development multi-media instructional package, and in particular will offer formative evaluation during the period that the course is being used.

Overview of Aspects of the Development Process

The course had developed in a "bottom-up" way. The SLO quickly developed a concrete plan for the series but then ideas have been worked out by the project team presenting the three partners. Two teachers have been centrally involved in the development process, particularly with regard to writing texts for the written materials, trying out materials in classrooms, and providing advice on the concept material.

Producing course materials around fixed broadcasting schedules is a demanding process for the SLO curriculum developers. Time for many tryouts is not available, given an monthly broadcast schedule, and many publicity activities are being carried out at a very brisk tempo. In order to include descriptions of the course in the school television guide published by the NOT, descriptions had to be supplied before the planning of the series had been completed. The impact of this time pressure will be one of the focuses of the evaluation.

Considerable discussion took place about the principle of distributing the materials as a package, or allowing teachers to purchase component parts separately. Because of the limited use of IT by mother tongue teachers which is currently the case in The Netherlands, it was decided that the support of the integrated materials was important and therefore component parts could not be ordered separately.

Difficult decisions had to be made concerning the translation of SCOOP.
An adventure set in London with many references to London place names and institutions had to be translated into Dutch. Should the place names and institutions be renamed? The decision was made to keep the London setting in the software, to avoid extensive reprogramming. It would have been particularly appropriate relative to the computerjournaal situation for the journalist in the software adventure to use VIDEOTEXT instead of PRESTEL, but the impact of that substitution on the sense of realism of the simulation (would a British journalist use a Dutch information service?) had to be considered. In general the decision was to translate concepts into Dutch equivalents, but to maintain British street names and the newspapers names. The translation of the software package into Dutch took almost half a year and two testing periods.

Implications of the Computerjournaal Project

The computerjournaal project has a wide range of implications. For the partners in its development, there are obvious immediate implications relative to the productivity of subsequent collaborative projects of this sort. For educators interested in innovative approaches to both the content and delivery of informatics courses, the experiences of the project can be considerable interest. For developers and theorists interested in the use of multi-media solutions to educational problems, the course offers a valuable observation base. The course has particular implications for those involved with distance education, as all materials are developed and disseminated centrally. The portability of the course materials to other countries is also an interesting consideration. What else, besides language and translations, would have to be done?

In February 1990 about 35% of the schools for secondary education in the Netherlands ordered the Computerjournaal package that consists of teaching manuals, student workbooks an the software package Scoop. Plans are made for a new series of programs focussing on the relation between informatics and geography in secondary education.

Computers in Education
A. McDougall and C. Dowling (Editors)
Elsevier Science Publishers B.V. (North-Holland)
IFIP, 1990

IT IN SCHOOLS: POLICY AND PEDAGOGY

P.S. LEWIS

Department of Education and Science, London

1. The only thing that matters on information technology in schools is what happens when pupils learn with IT and what happens between pupils and teachers. Everything that Governments do has to be directed with that end in mind. It is Government's job to facilitate, stimulate, underpin all that is best on IT in schools and in the classroom. It is right therefore that much of this conference should be about pedagogical matters. But I believe that it is equally important that those of you engaged in this field should have an understanding of the kinds of consideration which go into the formation of Government policy since these also necessarily bear upon the pedagogy.

2. I want today to set up some sort of a model within which we might be able to understand the way that information technology is proceeding in schools in the various countries from which we come and I hope you will forgive me if I do this partly by reference to the United Kingdom although I am hope that you will see that what I have to say has very general application. And I want to talk today about three stages of a development of a programme of this sort. Firstly I want to talk about a *pilot* stage, secondly a *development* stage and thirdly a stage of *institutionalisation*. It is very much part of my theme today that one cannot short-circuit any of these processes and in each country they all have to be followed through although in each country they may require rather different activities.

3. Let me, then, start with the *pilot* stage and first describe briefly to you what we endeavoured to do under our own Microelectronics Education Programme from 1981 to 1986 and how we structured the arrangements for this. The background against which this programme was established is an interesting one. There was very little experience of the use of arrangements for this. The background against which this programme was established is an interesting one. There was very little experience of the use of microcomputers in schools in 1980-81 in the United Kingdom and certainly very few microcomputers around in schools although one or two people had done some interesting experiments. We decided at that time that one would get nowhere by academic experiments on the applicability of IT in schools. Rather we took the view that we had to have a rather wide-ranging pilot to form a view as to what was achievable and what was not. So as many of you will know the Department of Trade and Industry provided for each secondary school a microcomputer at half-price limiting the choice of computers to two companies, Acorn Computer and Research Machines.

4. And at the same time the Department of Education and Science set up its Microelectronics Education Programme. I want to stress that this was very much an experimental programme; there was very little evidence on which to go; the programme was aimed at investigating and exploring uses of what we then used to call microtechnology in the classroom. We set up this programme separate from Government in the belief that if such a programme was to be truly creative it should be in some sense distanced from Government. We gave the Director of that Programme, Richard Fothergill, a very substantial degree of freedom to make proposals on the kinds of activity that should take place.

5. The programme set out to do a number of things. Firstly, it created Regional Information Centres (14 of them) around the country involving every local authority in the country in one of those centres with 4 separate centres for

special education. Second, it set out to produce a substantial amount of software in a number of areas across the curriculum. And thirdly, it set out to train teachers in a number of specialist areas of microcomputing - computer studies, microelectronics, communication of information systems, special education, primary education and computer assisted learning.

6. I think it is right to say that that programme had a great deal of success in a number of particular areas, but also some areas where the achievements were rather smaller. First it was very successful in influencing local education authorities to become interested in the potential for microtechnology - to use the old word - in schools. But it was less successful in schools themselves. Many teachers we found, did not welcome the new technology with open arms. We should not have been surprised but we often were. Second it created a large number of experimental software programs. Many of the programs were on simulation which seemed at that stage to be an important use of information technology. By the time we got to the end of the programme there were some 2,000 software computer programs around. All of them I suspect were being used in small pockets around the country but very few of them on a very wide scale. But some publishers who had come in hope at the beginning of that era found that they had many programs on their shelves which were rather sadly not selling. In other words we knew even at that stage about the problems of finding large enough markets for software production to be worthwhile - a problem that has continued to dog many, perhaps all of us right up to the present time. And third those appointed to do the teacher training in specialist areas found that they were spending far, far more time on helping teachers to learn how to switch on the machine and not be afraid of it rather than getting in depth into the specialist aspects.

7. But I think what was important about that programme was that we created an atmosphere on which subsequent edifices might be built. The pedagogy or perhaps the atmosphere surrounding the pedagogy in this pilot phase was an interesting one. It was I think a happy if difficult time for educationalists. Those involved were enthusiasts wanting to pilot a whole range of applications. If you like one might call this the period when educational technologists were at play - play that is in the best sense - in the sense in which we often use of research scientists investigating, exploring but with no definitive end in view other than to find out what works and what does not work. It was a most enjoyable time.

8. My own belief is that every country has to have that pilot stage. There is no escape from it. A country can draw certain lessons from other countries but it has to have its own pilot stage to create the right atmosphere for itself.

9. But there came a time in the UK when some of us realised that the pilot stage had gone on long enough. There was a danger that those involved would go on piloting more and more applications without seeking to consolidate them across schools as a whole. They found it difficult to make the transition from exploration and investigation into the consolidation phase of integrating what had been learnt across schools and across the curriculum as a whole. So we felt we had to close down the Microelectronics Education Programme in order to set up new programmes aimed specifically at consolidation. The processes involved were not easy. Why should we go on at all, some asked? Where was the experimental evidence? There was none - and there is not very much now. To the administrator it is one of the more curious aspects of this scene that one is expected to take so much on faith.

10. I want now to turn to the phase of consolidation and development. For that development phase we decided that very different structures and different staff were required. What then were the requirements of a development programme? The first essential from our point of view was to make clear to the local education authorities that the responsibility for carrying forward information technology - you note that I move to the new designation - in schools had to be part of their everyday activities. A second requirement was to set up support structures. So we set up the Microelectronics Education Support Unit placed in the middle of the country and gave it some fairly stern instructions that its job was to seek to consolidate what had gone on up to date rather than going on with more exploratory and investigative work.

11. This Unit rapidly saw that one of the things that was not needed was more software. What were needed however were more materials which supported and helped teachers to understand how to use IT constructively in the classroom in fairly

clear and straightforward terms. So first the Unit set out to produce, and has produced, a great range of materials aimed very much at subject teachers helping to understand how to use information technology in the classroom. And second it set up an information service available to all those engaged in the training of teachers. It would have been too massive a task to give teachers direct access to that Centre and in any case this would have undermined the responsibility which we had placed on the local education authorities to carry things forward. And the third aspect of its work was to set up a teacher training service to provide training to the trainers in the LEAs and to the staff in Teacher Training establishments so that they could receive training on aspects relevant to them of the application of IT in the curriculum.

12. And last but by no means least - the Unit set out to carry out work on information technology in special education which had been successfully developed by Microelectronics Education Programme. Because the work was some way behind mainstream education we decided that it was necessary to continue the pilot phase for rather longer than had taken place in mainstream education. Thus we continued with four specialist centres that had been established under the Microelectronic Education Programme - centres that is in the regions along with a specially created centre for software development in special education and perhaps even more importantly an Aids to Communication Education Centre which had been set up at Oxford.

13. If I might digress for a moment, IT in special education is one of the most interesting fields of all. On the communication difficulties side we found under both programmes, the Microelectronic Education Programme and the Microelectronics Education Support Unit that IT had a crucial role to play in helping children with communication difficulties. Often it made more sense to link a child up to a microcomputer through the use of suitable switches rather than giving him speech therapy for we were finding that the child would make faster progress looked at overall if he used IT to help him than if he followed the speech therapy route alone. If you find out this sort of thing what do you do about it? How does one influence health and education professionals? What happens if divisions between them are no longer tenable? Are there implications for the training of some of those professionals? We do not yet know the answers.

14. So much for the diversion. What next in the development phase? Once we had established the Microelectronics Education Support Unit we had a platform on which we could build a very serious development programme. So year by year we began a fairly massive programme to consolidate everything that had been learnt to date; we gave grants - about £10m last year and £10m this year with more next year - to assist local education authorities to put microcomputers into schools. And how successful that has been! The money has generated other money from industry and from parents, and we moved from the position of no microcomputers in schools in 1981 to a position, now 8 years later where we have about 30 microcomputers on average in each secondary school. We have been less successful in primary schools where we have only 3 microcomputers on average in each primary school.

15. But if you were to believe that this hardware provision was the most important part of what we had done to consolidate and develop the use of microcomputers in schools you would be mistaken. Training we believe has been as important. And here I think we have entered on rather a novel experiment. We have funded the local education authorities around the country so that between them they can appoint some 600 advisory teachers from a range of specialist subjects. We made it a condition of appointment that the teachers so appointed should not be IT specialists but rather should have an expertise in their own subjects. We then set about a very substantial training programme to train them in what they needed to know about IT. The purpose of this was to ensure that these teachers had credibility with other subject teachers rather than being IT boffins who might be dismissed as irrelevant to what was going on in the average classroom. I think it is fair to say that these advisory teachers have been a resounding success. They have gone round schools, worked with teachers in the classroom, understood the limitations that there are on the use of IT in the classroom and hence been effective in helping those teachers to use IT constructively and well. They have operated across many subjects, and in primary schools as well as in secondary. Increasingly of course much of their work is focussing and will continue to focus on our new National

curriculum.

16. To complete the picture on our development programme we have also made some £5m or £6m available to local education authorities for training grants again to train teachers in the appropriate uses of IT in schools but this time taking them away for courses. It is this mixture of courses and training on the spot which has proved so conspicuously successful. And we have set up a £750k programme of software development.

17. What then are the characteristics of a development phase? There has to be more structured experimentation and development. It is if you like a more serious business more especially because one has to begin to try and impact upon those who are not enthusiasts as well as those who take to information technology more readily. But still it is a phase where there is a substantial amount of choice - where teachers can choose to engage or not to engage in information technology and from that point of view I feel that it is at a half-way point between the pilot stage and the stage of institutionalisation to which I shall turn in a moment. It is I believe still enormously satisfying and rewarding. One begins to see for the first time teachers who are long stuck with traditional methods beginning to become receptive to entirely new approaches to teaching and learning. Information technology provides the opportunity for all teachers to re-examine pedagogic techniques and make them think afresh about the approaches which they use in the classroom.

18. Finally I want to talk about the stage of institutionalisation. But allow me another digression if you will. It is about the balance between central Government action, local government action and action in the schools. The Government's role is to point the way, to take hard decisions. But if we allow the local authorities too little scope they in turn will give still less scope to their schools. If on the other hand we allow everything to develop in the schools we may not get very far and find that we are going in a number of disparate directions at once. I cannot offer any solutions here but only note that the balance has to be watched carefully if beneficial outcomes are to follow.

19. Back to institutionalisation. This is a stage on which we are now just embarking. Our national curriculum has given us a splendid opportunity to institutionalise a good deal of the pilot and development that has gone on in the earlier stages. And I want to distinguish between three separate aspects of information technology. First we have to make sure that children have clear learning objectives within IT - that they understand what information technology is about and know how to use it. Secondly in particular subjects where there are corresponding uses of IT in the outside world, then they have to use IT within those subjects as the regular part of the educational process. And the third aspect of IT is the use of IT for help with the learning process. I believe that the first two aspects of these need to be established and institutionalised within any national curriculum. I am not sure whether many of you are familiar with our national curriculum. Let me tell you a bit about it. There are 10 core and foundation subjects and in each there are a number of attainment targets. Within each attainment target there are specific statements of attainment running from Level 1 - when the child enters schools - right the way up to Level 10. We have taken care to ensure that we cover what children need to know about IT in two subjects. There is a whole attainment target on the scientific aspects of information technology within the Science curriculum and within Design and Technology (it was placed there as a convenient place to put it) a whole attainment target on the general aspects of information technology. There are a number of components - developing ideas and communicating information, information handling, modelling, measurement and control and applications and effects. Taken together these subjects should ensure that children have a thorough grounding in all aspects of information technology. But I want to stress that we do not necessarily see general IT being taught as part of a single course. Increasingly, as teachers in a range of subjects gain experience in the applications of information technology we hope to see teaching on information technology spread across the curriculum. Of course there are enormous problems of progression there - how for example do you ensure that the child progresses from a simple use of a database in say Geography to a more complicated use in History? And can those same teachers in the various subjects assess not only the child's competence in a particular subject task but also his use of IT within that task?

We do not know the answers to these questions as yet and it may be that for some time to come children will learn about information technology in separate courses and in separate modules. But again I stress that this is not the ideal. As schools become more sophisticated and informed about the use of information technology across the curriculum we hope to see its use spread widely and assessment taking place within that whole range of other subjects.

20. Now let me turn to the second aspect of institutionalising IT - the use of IT in particular subjects. Serious mathematics in the outside world is rarely done without the use of a computer. We therefore have to ensure that children understand something about the uses of IT in mathematics if their maths education is to be complete. So at a number of points within the mathematics curriculum we have specified that children should use a microcomputer for particular mathematical tasks. The range is not as great as we would like. We have been constrained by limitations on resources and limitations on the expertise of teachers. But there is enough there to ensure that all mathematics teachers have to acquire some familiarity with what IT can do in order to teach their children appropriately. Much the same applies in English. English is concerned inter alia with the retrieval of information and the development of meaning and ideas. It would not be right to try to educate children on the retrieval of information without introducing them to modern methods that is to say access to databases and electronic mail. And of course wordprocessing as we all know brings an entirely different dimension to the development of meaning and ideas. It is important here too that children should have some experience of using this tool for that purpose in the classroom. Again we have endeavoured not to make too heavy demands on teachers. But there is quite enough there to lead them in that direction. And then turning to Design and Technology no serious design in the outside world and little technology takes place without the use of computers. It is important therefore that children should understand something about the use of computers in the design process and understand too about how IT is used to control industrial processes. There may be other subjects too where we need to take the same sort of approach.

21. You will notice here that the pedagogy has changed. What we are now saying about IT is that certain aspects must be taught by all teachers and studied by all children. That is a big step forward from the pilot stage and indeed the development stage but it is a necessary stage if we are to provide a satisfactory and complete education for all of our children.

22. But I want to dwell a little longer on the uses of IT for teaching and learning. This is not something which needs to be institutionalised. Spreadsheets, graphics packages and other tools are an invaluable aid to learning. And new technologies offer new opportunities. Here there are new pilot phases, new development phases, to be getting on with. In interactive video we have just begun the pilot phase by commissioning the production of 5 interactive video discs on the topic of number. CD-ROM offers a number of possibilities and we have been considering what role that technology has to play in schools. And we are conscious of Compact Disc-Interactive and DGV around the corner which may again revolutionise our approaches. And we have been developing an electronic database for schools - called the National Educational Resources Information Service so that all the national curriculum information to which teachers need access is on that database and - most importantly - the materials produced by various developers and publishers can be related to the specific attainment targets within the various subjects.

23. Ladies and gentlemen I hope you will not believe that there is a reward awaiting any who have tread this path from a pilot stage through to institutionalisation. Rather one has to begin to review one's national curriculum and to ensure that what is said about the applications of IT within the various subjects is up to date and new technologies are developed to maximise learning opportunities. So there is no end to the process. I think we shall benefit if, in that process, we keep the relationship between policy and pedagogy constantly under review.

Computers in Education
A. McDougall and C. Dowling (Editors)
Elsevier Science Publishers B.V. (North-Holland)

THE OWNERSHIP OF CHANGE: - AN EXPERIMENT IN EXPERIENCE EXCHANGE

Professor R.Lewis

ESRC-InTER Programme, Department of Psychology, University of Lancaster, Lancaster LA1 4YF UK

As the pace of technological innovation increases, very rich opportunities for the use of computers to support learning will become available. However, before that happens it is urgent to prepare educationists for making decisions on the cognitive basis on which such activity should be developed and supported according to particular social, cultural and economic needs. This was a part of the rationale behind a four-week Summer School for teacher educators from developing countries which was held in Kotor, Yugoslavia in 1989. It was made possible by support from the Intergovernmental Informatics Programme of UNESCO following a proposal from ALNeT, a Yugoslav-British association for the Advancement of Learning through New Technologies. This paper reports on the rationale, philosophy, methodology and realisation of the Summer School. It includes reaction to the School from tutors, and from the participants and their respective governments or institutions.

1. INTRODUCTION

It is believed that the way to help developing countries is by technology-transfer. Well-meaning attempts to assist development in such ways have a history of ill-defined success or failure (depending on one's perspective). Often plans for 'development' assume that changes should be stimulated which make some nations more like others. Only rarely is it acknowledged that all nations develop most effectively within their own cultural, social and economic mores.

For many years, and certainly well documented for the last twenty (for example, Schumacher, 1973), there has been an awareness that alternative (appropriate or intermediate) technology should be considered in efforts to support development. It would be very narrow minded to view this approach as only applicable to nations or regions which are labelled as 'developing'. There are many regions in Britain where "alternative" methods are now being implemented; these should have featured more strongly in planning for at least half a century. The simplistic, direct technology-transfer mechanisms belong to an earlier, less understanding era.

Nonetheless, there are still many forces, both within developed countries and within those which are termed developing, which seem to ignore the basic social processes involved in human change. An alternative to technology-transfer is to consider development as a process of exchange of experience and to emphasise the multidirectional nature of that exchange. Nowhere are such processes so critical as in education.

It is becoming recognised that a key factor in inculcating change is the personal ownership of the innovation by those whom it is hoped will become the agents of change. In the context of innovation in education, a recent seminar report (Rhodes, 1989) identified two models for the professional development of teachers. The two models contrast perspectives of teachers as learners.

"In courses based on the *deficit model* of the teacher, the teacher's fear of the innovation is regarded as a primary barrier to be overcome. In IT courses which adopt this model, the emphasis is on giving teachers confidence in using the hardware and software. In such technology-led courses the technology is central whilst the educational issues assume a secondary role.
..... References to the educational goals of the software were minimal. At the end of these courses many teachers said they were unable to implement computer use in the classroom.....
..... one major problem with this type of course is that it 'deskills' teachers by reducing them to the position of novices. Another difficulty is that the training is seen as a self-contained activity which is physically distinct and separate from what is happening in the classroom. On returning to school teachers find that they have no time to reflect upon what they have learned and no time to consider what they need to do to implement the new ideas."
" .... courses based on a *skills model* acknowledge the teachers as experts who possess the knowledge and skills of their profession. Therefore, they rather than the technology, are central to the course. .. In this type of course the emphasis is on encouraging teachers who are expert practitioners, to use the technology in the classroom and then return (to the course) in order to discuss the educational outcomes. .. In such courses the "how to use" emanates from the teacher not the tutor."

A Summer School for change agents in developing countries was planned as an experiment in applying the skills model, particularly in the methodologies it adopted. With support from UNESCO and a number of Yugoslav agencies, the School was held during the summer of 1989 in Kotor, Yugoslavia.

The tutors, drawn from Britain and Yugoslavia, were joined by 15 teacher educators from 8 countries (Mexico, Mauritius, Bulgaria, Hungary, the People's Republic of China, Ethiopia, Burkina Faso and Morocco). A micro-computer laboratory of networked, IBM-compatible stations of British origin (*Research Machines*) provided access to a wide range of educational and utility software.

The underlying philosophy for the Summer School was that all those present, tutors and participants alike, join together to exchange views and share experiences. Part, but only part, of the experience would originate from those 'technologically advanced' nations in which information technology had been used in attempts to support learning and in which much research into the possible benefits had been undertaken. More fundamental to the goals of the Summer School was the understanding of human learning processes and the needs of widely differing cultural and economic contexts of individual countries which all those present represented. It was the belief that there was *no single* 'best' strategy in applying information technology to support learning. The aim of the Summer School was to place all opportunities on the agenda for consideration as of potential benefit and for individuals to decide which, if any, of those potentialities could prove valuable according to local conditions. It must be stressed that *all* participants gained from the views and experiences of the others; the tutors added their experiences to those of the other participants.

2. THE PLAN FOR THE SUMMER SCHOOL

The planning paper for the Summer School expressed these notions in more concrete terms:

"The main objective of the Summer School is to provide opportunities for teacher educators from developing countries to select for themselves, the ways in which new information technologies (IT) may best be applied to meet educational needs within the cultural and socio-economic framework of their own countries. This focus of selection and adaptation to suit local needs is based on the view that it is not profitable for developing countries to adopt directly the innovations which appear to work in more developed nations. Local experience and needs are of paramount importance.

Hence, it is necessary to work in partnership in examining the various applications of IT in education and for local experience to decide the most appropriate form for local use.

There are six stages proposed for this partnership:

- the local context for cultural analysis and curriculum planning;
- an analysis of the human acquisition of cognitive and behavioural skills;
- a matching of styles of IT use to those skills;
- practical experience of a range of IT materials and equipment;
- local selection of most appropriate IT uses;
- course planning and implementation.

The first four of these stages will be covered during the Summer School and tutors will be in a position to support (directly or indirectly) the later stages in particular countries.

This approach contrasts with support for developing countries in which an outside expert delivers lectures or runs workshops. That expert, however good, is unable to:

- cover all aspects of IT potential from a *multi-disciplinary* stand-point;
- relate his/her experience to *local needs* in anything but a superficial way;
- provide a sense of *ownership* of the innovation for local experts.

The team and partnership approach, possible in a Summer School setting, combats all of these major difficulties providing direct benefit of breadth and depth for teacher educators who will become skilled in the critical area of local implementation of in-service courses and projects."

3. REPORT ON THE SUMMER SCHOOL

The main focus for each week of the Summer School remained largely as planned though the latter part of the final week had a more open nature with tutors responding to individual requests from participants.

3.1 The tutorial method

A similar style for the sessions ran throughput the Summer School, though this varied in the last two weeks depending on the topic for the session. The strategy was as follows. A topic would be introduced for a period of up to half an hour. The participants then split into discussion groups of around 4-5 members (sometimes culturally linked, at other times purposely cross-cultural) and responded to a number of questions or issues highlighted in the introductory presentation. The whole group then re-convened for a feedback of views. The tutor offered a short summary and consolidation. For a number of these discussions, participants from one country were encouraged to develop a distinctive response reflecting the circumstances of their own situation. These were word processed and eventually printed for further discussion. Over the course of the Summer School, a dossier of papers developed from each national group and this collection formed part of a report circulated to all participants and to UNESCO.

3.2 Theme 1

The overall objective of Theme 1 was to stimulate participants to conceptualise the educational use of IT within a perspective that sees IT as part of a broader process of cultural development: a process in which 'computer literacy' is seen as complementing and enhancing existing oral, textual and social skills and conventions.

The initial strategy was to engage participants with the practical implications of the underlying concepts and models through discussion of concrete examples (distributed in advance). Each example was (local) 'culture-friendly', showing how the ground-rules of existing skills and conventions could be reinterpreted rather than supplanted by a new technology. Participants were then invited to apply the concepts/model (as educational criteria) to issues of curriculum design and management within their own cultural experience and material circumstances. The topics for discussion were introduced in an outline paper.

"*Analysis of one's professional situation and assumptions*. It is inevitable that anyone's perception of the implications and educational potential of Information Technology (IT) is selective. Anyone's perception is, to some extent, 'ideologically blinkered', in part by professional interests. Therefore there is a need for the interrogation of personal experience and exchange of ideas about the social, economic and cultural context of IT. We need to recognise the full range of cultural trends associated with the spread of IT and to evaluate how this is affecting different societies and educational practices.
Key ideas:
- cross-curriculum planning and the 'hidden curriculum';
- culture, cultural development;
- market forces, the 'information society' and 'post modernity'.

Review of one's pedagogic orientation to IT. While being open to alternative interpretations of current trends, we must also try to get our educational goals and institutional priorities into a clear focus. In particular, there is a need to clarify the criteria by which we recognise 'good' IT software, and which guide our design of students' learning experience. What do we consider to be 'good' statements of learning objectives? What form of educational evaluation is most appropriate for IT in the curriculum?
Key ideas:
- curriculum design, criteria, learning activity;
- competence, understanding, public knowledge/personal knowledge;
- process evaluation.

Using the 'management of change' perspective. When people think about curriculum development or educational innovation, they focus most of their attention of the intended change itself. They usually give inadequate attention to the *process* of change, and to the social relationships affected, to the need for clarification of the change, and to the unintended consequences. Therefore any person who has responsibility for introducing complex changes associated with IT needs models for 'mapping' the process of change and for anticipating problems in its effective implementation.
Key ideas:
- implementation (of innovation), change agent, strategy (for change);
- negotiation, 'ownership' (of innovation), professional learning;
- management of change, mutual adaptation, accommodation of interests."

Participants were invited to crystallise their individual thinking about the problems discussed in the form of a 'situational analysis', plus an outline of *either* their pedagogic orientation to IT *or* a strategy for curriculum develop-ment in relation to IT. A number of key papers from the literature were provided as an additional focus for discussion.

The first week was a critical time for the Summer School as the methodology of interaction was established. By the end of the week, the informal discursive approach had been well established mainly through non-technological issues which each participant shared. The stress was on a critical appraisal of the individual situation of each participant and the most appropriate role for the technology in meeting the needs of their culture. Some seminars during the first week had a greater technology focus included a framework for computer supported learning and teaching, questions of basic cognitive development and criteria for the evaluation of software in achieving specified learning goals.

In addition, all participants had been introduced to the computer network and had begun to consider the opportunities which could be provided for learners. The first requirement was fluency in word processing which even those who had never touched a computer keyboard before used to prepare their analysis reports. The computer network had been set up to allow easy (menu-driven) access to a range of computer-assisted learning and software, general utilities all of which was supported by printed documentation.

3.3 Theme 2

The second theme focussed on developmental psychology and was introduced in the following way.

"Much modern educational practice derives from Piagetian principles, now modified, in providing for the develop-ment of learning and learning skills through concrete experience. There is much emphasis on learning-by-doing in the recent curricula in science, mathematics and other disciplines (such as language development through the stimulus of communication skills and creative writing). More recently, problem solving skills have been enhanced by the use of the new technologies as 'laboratories' for exploring new ideas. The most well known work in this field draws on the ideas of Papert but experience is showing that very careful selection of tasks and level of teacher guidance is required. There is, however, still a place for more directive instruction and reinforcement of a Skinnerian kind. In using either strategy, major consideration must be given to pupil-pupil interaction and to pupil-teacher interaction, both of which may be stimulated by work at a computer. Such experience will be the basis of the course as it underpins the rationale behind current computer use in stimulating learning."

The second week's discussion sessions covered psychological research relating to learning and instruction. This area was considered in special relation to issues arising from the deployment of new technology within educational settings. The material naturally followed on from discussions of structural and political issues arising from IT implementation strategies. These topics led to practical work with educational software that increased in emphasis over the following two weeks.

Topics covered

(a) *Theories of learning* as discussed by Psychologists. Special consideration was given to the Behaviourist tradition of explanation and then to modern Constructivist views. These topics permitted wide-ranging discussion of issues relating to motivation in learning as well as to models of expertise and its transmission to novices. The influence of these theories on educational software was considered and some limits to the more fashionable constructivist perspective were noted.

(b) *Social processes in educational practice*. This topic was introduced through discussion of a widespread concern that information technology would exert a *dehumanising* effect on educational experiences. Two main themes were considered along with their implications for the use of IT:

- Social processes as they arise within peer interactions in classrooms. The positive role of computer-based tasks was stressed, and
- Social processes as they occur within the instructional interactions between experts (say, teachers) and novices (pupils). This theme identified a contemporary theoretical interest in mechanisms of internalising joint activity and the difficulty of embedding such experiences within intelligent (computer) tutoring systems was noted.

(c) *Formal and informal learning*. This topic concerned finding relationships between schooled and informal learning (as in apprenticeship practices for example). The discussion was guided towards recognising the potent nature of informal learning experiences and thence to some reflection on the features that were crucial to their success. This permitted some consideration of the claims for *schooled* intelligence as something distinctive and the potential of IT for realising some of the effectiveness of informal learning situations.

(d) *Cognition as mediated*. The purpose of this topic was to highlight the manner in which human intelligence is mediated by our legacy of cultural artefacts and how such mediation is associated with particular *modes* of thought. The example of literacy was considered and then a parallel drawn with information technology. The particular case of education within a networked computer environment was discussed.

(e) *Discussion of a review paper*. The various themes (and others) discussed above were crystallised by discussion of one fairly critical review (Larsen, 1988) of current practice relating to educational computing on which initial discussion had taken place during the first week.

3.4 Theme 3

Week 3 began with a review of the ground covered to date and all tutors and participants worked together in discussion groups to address two key questions:

- What impressions do you now have of the applications of IT to learning in relation to what you may want to "take back home"?
- What do you now feel you need to know or have more experience of? What are your priorities for the remainder of the time?

The first afternoon was devoted to an experience in collaborative writing, role play and decision-making. This took the form of a "newsroom" scenario in which each of four groups received about 40 "telex" messages at varying intervals over the course of an hour. The telexes were authentic copies of those received by the BBC following a terrorist incident in London. Each group had to prepare a "front page story" for a first edition of their newspaper after 30 minutes and a second edition by the end of an hour. The reports were compiled with word processing software and edited as new telex information arrived. Following the exercise a discussion was held concerning the learning goals and experiences of such an activity.

The following four days each took one specific theme and related software. Each day had a similar format with one tutor (supported formally by a second but informally aided by other tutors) introducing the topic and its learning goals in both cognitive and process terms. This was followed by discussion groups on the goals.

In most cases the remainder of the day was spent in workshop form with participants working collaboratively with the software on problems of the kind used by students in schools. In this way they became familiar with the software and also to the methodologies of its use in schools and colleges. Plenary discussions were held from time to time to share experiences and perspectives.

The themes for these workshops were:
- instructional design and the use of an easy-to-use authoring system, MICROTEXT
- problem solving and microworlds using LOGO;
- model building with DMS and STELLA;
- qualitative tools with PROLOG and MITSI.

3.5 Theme 4

In planning Week 4, it was agreed that as much time as possible should be devoted to meeting participants' specific, at times individual, needs. Within this overall goal, there were three specific workshops planned:
- on electronic networks
- on artificial intelligence and expert systems
- on models of in-service education courses.

The workshop on networks started with a discussion on the variety of communication styles which could be supported: one-to-one, one-to-many, many-to-many, access to professional or collective databases, sharing resources in a local network (such as the Summer School laboratory), research community networks, interaction after the Summer School, and so on. This was followed by descriptions, richly illustrated and supported by detailed notes, on key aspects of a variety of networks used in education and their functional and technical features. The day finished with a "network game" using the laboratory network designed to illustrate both the technical and human communication aspects of this form of interaction.

The workshop on artificial intelligence was illustrated by various pieces of software which led on from earlier work in PROLOG and, in particular, BELART, a medical consultant's expert system. Many of the issues surrounding the claims and achievements of AI were discussed.

The specific theme for one morning was the rationale and design of professional courses for teachers. A range of "typical" courses were outlined by the tutors and participants were given the task of preparing a document for what they believed was a priority course in their own country. The groups presented and discussed plans which had a common (proposed) framework:
- who should be the target audience (taking into account the earlier situational analysis paper and identified local needs)?
- what should one aim to achieve?
- what style of course would be appropriate?
- what are the minimum (human and other) resources necessary?
- what should be criteria of course "success" (long and short term)?
- what would be the next stage in a wider plan?

For the final two days, all tutors offered at least six topics on which they were able to lead workshops or discussion. There was clearly far too much to do and the activities continued right through the final day without respite. A final collective task was the preparation, by various groups, of items for the "ALNeT Recorder", a newspaper which was eventually printed (in a first edition!) at 2000 hours on the final day.

4. CONCLUSIONS

It was felt that the general method of carrying out the sessions was successful. Most of the participants seemed to benefit from the informal discussion arrangements and the most were actively involved in the whole group exchanges. The topics covered seemed appropriate. However, it was hard to judge how critical the participants were prepared to be in providing feedback on the content and style of the sessions. It might have been useful to have built some formal evaluation procedure into the schedule but this was considered to be best achieved after the event when more reflective, locally influenced feedback could be obtained.

One tutor commented as follows: "I think the sessions I was involved in were moderately successful - particularly if other tutors were able to keep the issues alive in the context of discussing their own work in the following weeks. If doing the work again, I would shift the emphases but would cover basically similar material. I would try to make a more direct link between the psychological theory and the practice: this would mean having these sessions more closely linked to hands-on sessions. Finally, I would try to tighten the organisation of the network-based documentation of discussions."

It is still too early to judge the long-term outcomes of this experiment. There is, however, some evidence showing that those present are beginning to collaborate after the Summer School in preparing materials and providing courses for the professional development of teachers in the various countries represented. It is worth noting that this is not only in the form of tutors being invited to work in other countries but in exchange visits between all the participants.

Since the Summer School the report of the UNESCO Congress on Education and Informatics - strengthening international cooperation has been published (UNESCO, 1989). Amongst the recommendations and proposals for future activities are to be found a number of statements indicating that such experiences as took place in Kotor are of particular value.

"It is education's responsibility to change the perspectives of education and industry relationships. The real dialogue has not yet started, it is a daunting task, but it is essential and the returns to education and industry could be substantial." (p.752)

This viewpoint was one held at the Summer School in two forms:

- one form related to the identification of economic and social needs, aspects of which clearly relate to the aspirations of local industrial development;
- the second to the importance of establishing a sound infra-structure in a country prior to an investment in technology in order that indigenous expertise and resources provided the hardware and software support required.

Another UNESCO activity proposed was that: "Support should be encouraged to develop initiatives in teacher training at the *national levels* since the ultimate objective is to strengthen national capacities in teacher training for the effective use of informatics in education." (p.754)

One theme of the Congress was the impact of computer technology on national languages and cultures. A section from one paper from Nigeria (Olutimayin, 1989) reinforces the basic philosophy of our Kotor experiment:

"Ethnocentrism is an aspect of 'growing in culture' and thinking that one's culture is the best there is. This must be avoided in evaluating culture because it could be misleading. Cultural relativism determines the effects some introductions (may) have on the culture of the recipient society. This suggests that culture must be measured in terms of whether or not it satisfies the needs and the expectations of the people. Applying these principles to the Nigerian society, the impact of computer technology on culture should be measured from the standpoints of Nigerians, rather than from the experiences of the Western world. Education, economics and standard of living (in addition to music and language) would probably be good indicators of the present impact of this technology on Nigerian society; in the Western world, politics, family life, religion and art would certainly be added to the above factors as evaluation subjects. Impact of computer technology on cultures should therefore be examined *sui generis*. Indeed, the impact of any technology on a culture should be assessed in the individual terms of the culture concerned. Take the case of the Yir-Yoront people of Australia. For this people, the stone axe was the main technological tool, a tribal totem, as well as a symbol of masculinity. These axes were very scarce and were held in high esteem by the culture because they were mainly owned by very senior men who acquired them through bravery and experience. But the arrival of missionaries in Australia changed the situation: the missionaries provided the people with steel axes (in place of stone axes) in such numbers that even women and children had their own. Thus steel axes eliminated the male/female and adult/adolescent relationship of respect in the culture. Since the steel axe could not be related to the tribal totem, the whole ideological system of the people began to disintegrate - the introduction of steel axes undermined the whole structure of the Yir-Yoront society and no substitute for the older order could be found. Technology is often (if not always) seen as being only of positive value, especially by those who introduce them but the Yir-Yoront story illustrates the fact that technology can have negative values, in particular on the cultures of developing societies."

5. ACKNOWLEDGEMENTS

The Summer School was made possible by a grant from the Inter-governmental Informatics Programme of UNESCO and also by UNESCO support of participants from the least developed countries. Additional finance came from the University of Belgrade, the Montenegian Academy of Sciences and Arts, the Yugoslav Government and GENEX. My colleague, Professor Zvonimir Damjanovic carried a heavy burden in orchestrating the Yugoslav support. Organisational and communications support was provided by the ESRC-InTER Programme in Britain and the Summer School could not have taken place without the personal dedication of its members, Maureen Boots and Mark Bryson, both in Lancaster and in Kotor.

I would like to take this opportunity to thank the Yugoslav and British tutors for their contributions to the Summer School and for their comments on drafts of this paper. Finally, I should thank those partners whom I have termed 'participants'; but for their critical comments and dynamicism in debate, none of us would have benefited from or enjoyed the experience so much.

REFERENCES

Schumaker, E.F. (1973) Small is Beautiful. Blond and Briggs: London

Olutimayin, J. (1989) The impact of computer technology on Nigerian culture. In Education and Informatics. UNESCO, Paris

Rhodes, V. (ed) (1989) Barriers to Innovation - a seminar report. ESRC-InTER Programme, Occasional Paper InTER/11/89, University of Lancaster.

Larsen, S. (1988) How should new technologies be used in education? In World Year Book of Education, 1988: Education for the New Technologies. Duncan Harris (ed). Kogan Page: London

UNESCO (1989) Education and Informatics. Proceedings of an International Congress, April 1989. UNESCO, Paris.

Computers in Education
A. McDougall and C. Dowling (Editors)
Elsevier Science Publishers B.V. (North-Holland)

A "SLICE" OF TOMORROW'S SCHOOL: A SCHOOL RESTRUCTURING PROJECT

Nancy A.S. Miller, Education Consultant

INTEConsulting, 4035 Dayton Road, Lafayette, Indiana, USA 47905
Phone or Facsimile (317) 296-9257

The Indiana Department of Education with the advice of the Indiana Consortium of Computer and High Technology Education sponsored the development of a school restructuring project during 1989. Due to limited funding, but an intense desire to see an implementation in this field, the idea of developing a "Slice" of Tomorrow's School was conceived. A national advisory council with representation from Indiana and other states was commissioned to identify attributes of tomorrow's schools. This resulted in a "Request for Proposal" process that yielded two local school districts committed to developing and implementing their "visions" of tomorrow's schools.

Many barriers – state and local policy, organizational and personal – were broken in this important school restructuring project. Attributes of quality education including Choice, Flexibility, Learner-focused, and Collaborative teaching/learning were key components of each district's implementation. Flexible scheduling, individualized newspapers, home computers, student produced videos, and videoconferencing were all elements of the Summer, 1989 implementation. Without the pervasive and articulated use of computers and other new technologies, many of the program offerings and implementations would not have been possible.

INTRODUCTION

What will the school of tomorrow look like? How will it function in the community? Where will technology fit in? What roles will students, parents, teachers and administrators play in education? The Indiana Consortium for Computer and High Technology Education through the auspices of the Indiana Department of Education approved expenditures of $400,000 for the planning and implementation of A "Slice" of Tomorrow's School in which alternative teaching strategies, styles, technologies and environments are explored. A select group representing teachers, administrators, curriculum experts, technology specialists, policy makers, and publishers from Indiana and across the country formed a national advisory council which provided leadership and guidance in planning and development of the "Slice" project. Members included: Judy Crawford, Darien Public Schools, CT; Kolene F. Granger, Utah State Office of Education; Eugene Hungate, Elkhart Comm. Schools, IN; Ralph Lieber, Bartholomew Consolidated Schools, Columbus, IN; Lawrence Lipsitz, Educational Technology Publications, Englewood Cliffs, NJ; Jane Marshall, Rockville Elementary, IN; Tom Snyder, Tom Snyder Productions, Boston, MA; and John Vanausdall, Children's Museum, Indianapolis, IN.

The council met in October, 1988 to identify characteristics of tomorrow's school as well as to define roles and attributes of tomorrow's students, teachers, and educational systems. Through a selective "Request for Proposal" process, two Indiana school systems were chosen in December, 1988 to host the "Slice" of Tomorrow's School 1989 development and summer implementation project. Lafayette School Corporation in Lafayette, Indiana and North Adams Community School Corporation in Decatur, Indiana were the recipients of the first two grant awards. A fourteen-member working committee with heavy representation from each of the two school districts as well as experts in curriculum, media, management, administration and technology met on a regular basis to help the schools develop fully resourced, quality programs.

Two "lead" teachers from each district were released from classroom duty to manage and coordinate the planning, staff and program development during the Spring semester. Each site team's plan had elements that addressed many of the key attributes identified by the National Advisory Council for tomorrow's schools including: Learner-focused programming and management, Flexibility, Choice, Media-rich Environments, Relevance and Connectivity. As part of their own professional development and planning activities, the teachers visited several schools around the country to gain a better understanding of how innovative ideas transform into successful program performance.

An overview of the "Slice" implementations at each of the two school sites follows:

LEARNINGSPHERE 2008
Lafayette School Corporation

Program Beliefs

Schools must value and respect their clients, and make the learning environment learner-centered. Learners must have time for interaction and to ponder germinating thoughts and interests. Affection, ownership and attention to improvement, enrich and empower teachers and their learners.

Program Goals – Mission

To assist people throughout life to:

➡ be citizens who can and will communicate, gather, understand and use information.

➡ engage in creative, responsible, decision-making.

➡ adapt to challenges of the 21st century.

➡ foster positive physical, emotional, and social development in a changing environment.

Program Objectives

The "slice" of curriculum addressed in the 1989 summer program was an interdisciplinary approach in three selected "spheres" of learning. Each sphere overlapped with the other two spheres allowing for collaborative and cooperative planning, teaching and learning to occur. Core objectives (for all students) were covered to facilitate future learning in all content spheres as well as for synthesis of learning within the program.

Core Objectives – All Students

As appropriate to the student's ability, the learner will

1. find and use the best source of information available.
2. demonstrate ability to work with others.
3. demonstrate ability to utilize technology appropriate to the task.
4. share his/her learning orally, in writing, visually, or artistically with others.

Interest Area Objectives – Students will select one of three spheres.

Communication: Lafayette's Link to the World

The learner will . . .

1. compare the various forms of communication.
2. understand the importance of communication skills.
3. evaluate the changes technology has made in communication.
4. demonstrate improved communication skills as per learning plan.

Lafayette's Culture: Its Link to the World

The learner will. . .

1. compare contributions of two cultures to the Lafayette community.
2. be exposed to beginning French language instruction.
3. evaluate cultural similarities through communication with another culture.
4. explore a culture of his/her own choice.

Lafayette's Environment: Its Link to the World

The learner will . . .

1. compare the advantages and disadvantages of a specified environment.
2. appreciate the environmental diversity of the Lafayette community.
3. evaluate environmental similarities through communication with other communities.
4. create a "mini-environment" of choice.

Learners

The LearningSphere program's philosophy and goals were presented to interested parents in April of 1989. 110 learners were randomly selected from an application pool of 276 students, representing a cross section of the Lafayette School Corporation student body. Learners represented all neighborhoods and schools in the Lafayette school district as well as students from kindergarten through eighth grade at all ability levels. One child, who is completely blind, and just finished first grade at the Indiana Blind School was also enrolled in the program. The learners were divided into two multi-age groups: "5 to 9 year olds," and "9 to 14 year olds."

Learning Guides and Staff Development

Learning Guides for the program were selected by the lead teachers and project director based upon ability, interest and teaching styles. The teachers on the LearningSphere team represent diverse subject area and grade level backgrounds, but most were experienced "master" teachers. It was imperative for successfully meeting project objectives that the teachers could, in fact, work together as a collaborative team within the program. An interdisciplinary approach which utilized "special" resource teachers (French, Fitness, Music, Media, & Art) as consultants to the sphere teachers demanded a lot of cooperation and flexibility among the staff. Art, music, language, and fitness curricula and activities were closely tied to sphere topics. A full time guidance counselor became a liaison between the families and the LearningSphere as well as helped the teachers identify and match learning styles with teaching styles.

As an important issue for making giant leaps into our educational future, Lafayette teachers devoted constant and thoughtful attention to the staff development and curriculum planning needs of the twenty professional staff involved in the project. A two-day retreat to kick off the program was held in March, and periodic planning and development meetings of the whole LearningSphere staff were scheduled. During the summer implementation, each Friday morning was reserved for staff development activities, cooperative planning and program coordination.

Learner Objectives — Individual Educational Objectives

The individual learner objectives were jointly established by the student, parent, and staff at a preprogram series of parent conferences. One objective was universal: the learner will exhibit an increase in self-directed learning. Within the program, learners were required to spend eight hours per week on site and complement that on site work with eight hours of participation per week at home or in outreach explorations of the sphere content. In some cases, the individual learner objectives were based on academic needs and issues; in others, they focused on the social or emotional health of the individual learner.

LearningSphere 2008 — Instructional Strategies

A variety of instructional strategies was employed, but great emphasis was placed upon promoting healthy mind/healthy body and the learner's high self-esteem. Students met in general assemblies and large group sessions for some core skills training, small seminar sessions with learning guides for specific topic exploration as well as worked individually or paired with other learners or learning guides for individual study and questions. Each learner and parent(s) met with a lead teacher at enrollment to discuss specific needs and choices of the learner within the "slice" offered. Lunch and snack programs as well as daycare for the learners before and/ or after learning center use were offered within the facility and program. The media specialist, counselor, and special resource teachers provided holistic care and added interdisciplinary value to the program.

Management Plan: Program Structure

In the LearningSphere "vision" the school would be totally flexible in time and learning opportunities and facilities. Learners could select courses of study, choose appropriate times for attendance according to their personal plans, and work independently at any time day or night. Daycare and meal programs would be available as needed by client learners. In the 1989 "Slice", Lafayette offered a modified flexible schedule which was open for participation Monday through Thursday with evening hours available on Tuesday and Wednesday. The center was closed for the supper hour and reserved for staff development and planning each Friday morning. Students, arriving and leaving at all hours during the day, provided significant challenges to the transportation and student management systems of the district.

At first, more time in the LearningSphere was devoted to "Core Objectives" with several general assemblies and small group training opportunities than to individual study activities to allow learners to gain an understanding of self-directed learning techniques and how to use the technologies made available to them. As the summer progressed, more time was spent on covering the individual learning objectives and development of individual projects. Attention to the "Content Area Objectives" and small group seminars on the topics contained and overlapped in the three spheres remained fairly constant throughout the summer program. Two professional staff were assigned to each sphere. Though intended to be identified as Primary and Intermediate learning guides, the Cultures sphere staff chose to divide responsibilities according to the two cultures to be studied with each taking responsibility for both primary and intermediate learners within that culture topic.

Applied Technologies

Technology was applied in many varieties and aspects to support the operation and goals of the LearningSphere program. Technology was not the focus, but a tool used to achieve project, learning guide and individual learner goals and objectives during the summer implementation. In addition, many special field trip, guest lecturer, and outreach activities were organized and open to student and parent participation. Some of the special projects and features offered in LearningSphere 2008 which, in many cases, incorporated the use of high technology included:

1. Video Conferences — Learners in the Cultures sphere participated in a videoconference with students at an international school in Paris, France. Environment Sphere learners participated in one with naturalists in Hawaii, and the Communications sphere learners videoconferenced with students from the Los Angeles Open School in California. GTE North provided facilities, satellite time and expert assistance to make these "high-tech" experiences possible.

2. A series of five personalized newsletters for each learner were produced by project staff during the program. Each newsletter featured an article common to all in the LearningSphere, an article common to learners in the individual spheres, and at least one article that was particularly created for that individual learner. Information about learner interests was gathered from the students at enrollment time and was used as the starting point for researching and writing individualized articles.

3. Computers at home for everyone! — All learning guides and learners were furnished an Amiga computer for use at home during the program. A software program called *Talking Animator* (JMH Publishing) was the used for student projects, creativity and communication. Other software was available for check out from the LearningSphere media center.

4. Learning Lunches — The lunch program offered was designed to provide a relaxed,

family style atmosphere. Centerpieces at each round table, "real" dishes, and family style serving were some of the details that made a difference. Learning Guides and visiting adults were encouraged to join students (At least one adult at each table) in the "table topic" of the day. A predetermined topic such as "A place I would like to visit," "My most embarrassing moment" was the main item for discussion during lunch. Entertainment was also provided daily including musicians, clowns, storytellers, celebrity presentations, and guest "fun topic" lecturers to round out the "full hour" lunch experience.

5.An Exploration Center including high and low tech items allowed students the opportunity to relax or "play" as the mood strikes them in a supervised but "non-expectation" environment. Centers within the Exploration Center included: Interactive Video experiences in the National Art Gallery or the world of natural sciences, "Touch screen" lessons on earth and space science, Robotics exploration centers, Art center, a Living room complete with couches for reading and dozing, music and storybooks on compact disc, and a Holography center with several gadgets for wonder and exploration.

6.A production center including Macintosh computers networked for writing and desktop publishing activities, and video production equipment including a genlock to marry the Amiga computer to the video medium were available for class and individual learner and learning guide use.

7.Computer labs – An Amiga computer lab for sharing and printing of "homework" activities was right next door to an IBM networked lab with basic skills software for class and individual use on building specific computation, reading, spelling or keyboarding skills.

8.The "Spa" was provided for supervised activity in strengthening the "well-body" concept and reality. Learners could attend individually during the day and the Spa learning guide also worked with the sphere teachers to develop fitness activities for group interaction.

9.A media center program allowed students to access information on online databases and CD-ROM as well as check out software or just a good book. A media professional coordinated sphere learning resources for learner and learning guide use.

10. The daycare center was provided for the convenience and use of LearningSphere staff's children as well as learners who needed to come early, stay late, or hang-out in between scheduled learning sessions. It also featured high tech centers and the daycare "enrollees" were allowed to visit the media, exploration center, spa and art centers as well.

11. Frequent field trip experiences throughout the summer program brought additional community and business involvement with the school experience. LearningSphere 2008 opened its doors to visitors from universities, businesses, and other schools as well as always being open to visits from parents or community patrons.

Evaluation and Outreach

A conference was held at the end of the summer program to help provide closure for staff and students as well as spread the word about what was accomplished in the initiative. Nearly 200 participants at the conference saw the culmination of a dedicated group of teachers' intense efforts to make a difference in the educational program and in the lives of their community's children.

As a result of the multiple successes of the program and enthusiasm of the community for what they feel is an important "choice" in education, Lafayette School Corporation is incorporating many of the aspects of the LearningSphere program into the regular school year. The Learning Lunch program in several buildings, a "writing at home" project in an "at-risk" classroom, a team teaching project at the local high school have all resulted. Two of the learning guides are teaming in a multi-age primary classroom (40 students in grades 1-3) to use and more fully develop the interdisciplinary, student-focused education plan designed as the LearningSphere concept. Once again the school received, within a few days, more than three times the applicants than could be enrolled in the program.

Evaluative information gained from all participants and visitors was collected and summarized. The students' top marks went to the "computer at home," Learning Lunches, the Spa, and the "fact that teachers really listened to what I had to say." Staff members appreciated the flexibility and choice of scheduling and teaching strategies to be employed. They felt "in control" of their own professional activities. The parents and families evaluations of LearningSphere 2008 were overwhelmingly positive. The most visible result of this has been the large number of phone calls asking about how they can enroll their children in future programs.

PROJECT SLICE: A LEARNING COOPERATIVE
North Adams Community Schools

There are only two lasting bequests we can hope to give our children. One of these is roots: the other, wings. ~ Hodding Carter

Program Goals

1.To promote experiences which foster the development of a child who is able to communicate globally, who is technically literate and who strives for life-long learning.

2.To assist persons of all ages in breaking conventional educational mindsets and boundaries which impede learning.

3.To educate the total child -- social, emotional, intellectual, and physical -- through the direct involvement of the child's home and community environments.

1989 Summer Program – Major Areas of Exploration

Social Environments – Explore media and pathways of communication and human interaction. (Oral Expression, Kinesthetic Awareness, Visual and Performing Arts, Sign Language, Visual Representation, Signs and Symbols, Interactive Media, Telecommunications). North American Indian, Japanese, and Australian were among the cultures studied in this area.

Physical Environments – Explore the physical and social dimensions of alternative surroundings. (Space Exploration, Inside the Earth, Population Trends, Developing Resources, Aquatic Living, The Earth [Then, Now, Tomorrow], Family Structures, Multicultural Awareness)

Economic Environments – Explore the internal and external framework of economics. (Impact of Decisions; Multicultural Affinity; Monetary Systems; Business, Government, Community, Individual, and Socioeconomic Realities)

Multi-age groupings of learners participated in individual and group learning applications within their choice of topics. The learning guides and students collaborated and cooperated in units of exploration that overlapped one or more spheres. Communication and Cooperative Learning were the overall themes of the Project Slice: A Learning Cooperative program.

Program Objectives

Learners will show an increase in self-directed learning by:
- formulating appropriate questions
- identifying, finding, and using appropriate sources of information.
- identifying, finding, and using technology appropriate to their needs.

Learners will be able to work effectively in a group by:
- sharing/accepting different veiwpoints.
- demonstrating their ability to collaborate.
- demonstrating their ability to compromise.

Learners will share their explorations by:
- organization and display of their work.
- communicating their experiences to another audience.
- demonstrating self-assessment of learning.

Instructional Learning/Teaching Strategies

Under an umbrella of Cooperative Learning the program components addressed and used the following skills: Research, Group Process, Critical/Creative Thinking, Consensus Building, Interpersonal Relations, Collaboration, Inquiry

The Learning Cooperative Roles

Student –
- responsibility for learning
- choice in what, when and how to learn
- self assessment: reviewing learning results

Parent -
- join in their child's learning, hence embodying the idea of lifelong learning
- actively participating with child in structured learning activities
- assisting child in defining, implementing and assessing his/her course of study

School -
- learning center
- hub around which educational resources are located
- make available to learners the necessary tools and support staff
- bring the world to the student and the student to the world

Teacher -
- facilitate a curiosity and love of learning for students of all ages
- coordinate learning materials and provide avenues to information
- serve as the collaborative hub between the home, the school and the community

Community -
- develop interdependent partnerships with schools
- assist in linking learning to living
- actively promote lifelong learning among members

Learning Guides and Staff Development

The instructional team for the Learning Cooperative was made up of certified, paraprofessional, student interns, consultants and volunteers. A comprehensive staff development plan focusing on curriculum development and cooperative and collaborative teaching strategies was facilitated by working learning guide teams. Individuals involved in the program included primary through high school experience teachers in diverse subject areas. A total of twenty-one staff members were involved in the summer implementation. In each of three Project Slice spheres and in the Mini-Slice Primary a team including a professional teacher, a paraprofessional learning assistant and a high school student intern were selected. In addition, the two lead teachers, project clerical support staff and project director provided administration, guidance and instructional resources for the learning guides.

A series of twelve staff development opportunities and work sessions were scheduled in April and May of 1989 for Project Slice staff. All staff participated in Cooperative Learning training as well as spent several evening sessions in learning to use new technologies and to write curriculum for the summer program. Many of the staff also visited other Indiana schools who were involved the incorporation of technology and vision into educational programs.

Learners

Project Slice was advertised and presented to North Adams families as one of several summer school offerings. All 188 applicants to participate in the program were enrolled in one of the three offerings described below. The philosophy behind the enrollment process at North Adams was not to enroll a true cross-section of the ages and abilities within their community, but to provide the experience for all who wished to participate.

Management Plan: Program Structure

Program Strands. . .(serving 188 students in all)

1. Project Slice: A Learning cooperative (June and July, 8 weeks) – Students in grades 2-8

2. Mini Slice: Primary (June, 4 weeks) – Students Preschool through 1st grade

3. Mini Slice: Intermediate (July, 4 weeks) – Students in grades 2-8

Project Slice learners and guides were grouped in heterogeneous mixed age "family groups" which met for three hours on Tuesday through Thursday mornings. The Mini-Slice Intermediate offered a short session (four-week) version of Project Slice without the long-term individual or group project component to facilitate participation by students involved in other summer school or extracurricular programs. The Mini-Slice Primary program included two-hour morning or afternoon options with group and individual learning experiences planned. A requirement for participation in the Primary Slice program was that a "significant other" attend with each learner. This person could be the child's parent, older sibling, sitter, neighbor, or grandparent.

An intermediate (Grades 2-8) learner's weekly schedule consisted of 12 hours of required, structured activities including whole group sessions, "Family group" meetings, and seminars. SLICE was open an additional 24 hours per week (mornings, afternoons and evenings) to provide opportunities for open computer labs, exploration and production labs, individual learner consultations, extra "family group" sessions, and staff preparation and development. Each learner was required to schedule an additional minimum of four hours per week on site to complete individual projects or learning plans. Primary learners were encouraged to spend additional time in their own customized learning and exploration centers, but were required only to attend the scheduled six hours of activities during morning or afternoon programs each week.

Applied Technologies

New technologies, especially computer use, played major roles in the curriculum design and implementation of Project Slice. It was important to the staff that the learners have ample opportunity to learn and use all technologies possible. Apple IIGS, Macintosh, and IBM computer systems were all used by learners and guides in the program. In addition, midi synthesizers, digitizers, scanners and video equipment were heavily used and experimented with by a majority of the participants. An exploration center for relaxation and a production center for exploration and experimentation were open for learner, parent and learning guide use. Apple IIGS computers were available to be checked out for short term use at home by Project Slice participants.

Program Evaluation and Outreach

Student learning growth was evaluated through self-assessment, conferencing between learning guide and student, culminating experiences review, photo and video documentation and curriculum-based assessment. Program evaluation was gained through student, parent, and staff participation surveys as well as working and advisory committee feedback. Feedback was also sought from visitors to the program. Impact on the community was also studied through interviews with community organizations and businesses and discussion by the school board. A conference was held on the last day of the program which drew the attention and attendance of several educators from other schools around Indiana, many Department of Education consultants and managers, an many of the North Adams Community school educators who were not involved in the implementation.

Significant integration and access to technology use, the "significant other" program in the primary "slice" and the articulated staff development plan gained top praises respectively from the learners, parents and teaching staff. For many observors and participants, it was difficult to identify and separate the key elements of the program. In many cases, the response was that the key element of the program's success was that all components were integral to the whole.

The enthusiasm and multiple successes in the summer program prompted North Adams to incorporate several elements of the program into its regular school year offerings at a variety of grade levels. Experiments continue in flexible scheduling, interdisciplinary curriculum design, and cooperative learning strategies. During the 1989-90 school year staff development and planning activities are preparing for implementation of a total "Project Slice" elementary school in 1990/91.

ADDITIONAL INFORMATION REQUESTS:

For additional information please contact the author or the Indiana Department of Education.

Computers in Education
A. McDougall and C. Dowling (Editors)
Elsevier Science Publishers B.V. (North-Holland)

COMPUTER APPLICATION IN PRIMARY SCHOOLS (AGE 9 - 10 YEARS)
The first German research project about CAL and Word Processing in Primary Instruction with inner differentiation,

by Hartmut Mitzlaff and Karl A. Wiederhold,
University of Dortmund

Introduction

This paper describes research and applied tests on the following questions: Appropriate hardware; effect of computer application on specified learning processes; field of application as an instrument of labour and as a tool; consequences of computer application on social behaviour, working methods and organisational forms in class.

The research was carried out by the working group "Computers in Primary Schools", Department 12; University of Dortmund - Prof. Dr. Karl A. Wiederhold and Dr. Hartmut Mitzlaff.

The following abridged version of this research project, financially supported by the German Ministry of Education and Science (BMBW) and by the Minister of Education of Northrhine-Westphalia, refers to a period of approximately 10 months: 4 months of preparation in which the didactic conception was specified, literature and software were analysed and the teachers involved in the project were trained; just under 4 months for carrying out and another 6 weeks for the completion of the report. More information is given in the February 1989 comprehensive report and the book "Computer im Grundschulunterricht" (McGraw-Hill, Hamburg, New York et. al. 1990).

I. Leading ideas

The investigation is based on the following leading ideas and convictions:

Today's society would be unthinkable without computers. Whether their existence is supported or refused, in the lives of the future adults they will play an important role. A primary school intending to prepare children for life cannot afford to exclude new technologies; it should rather form the first basis for a major use. The final perspective of the major use includes both critical open-mindedness on positive fields of application and the conscious rejection of negative offers, e.g. militant computer games.

Referring to contemporary and future society, some educators elevate so called 'computer literacy' to the fourth culture skill. If this estimation is basically right, then the teaching of the roots of this skill belongs to the area of basac general knowledge taught in primary schools. In as much as there are no other developmental-psychological or learning-psychological barriers there is no reason why this fourth culture skill should not be taught on the same level or even together with the other three skills.

The assumption that working with a computer and teaching culture skills is bound to provoke a conflict is based on mere speculation. Anglo-Saxon experience, especially in Great Britain, the USA and Australia substantiates the assumption all the more that an educationally sound and controlled computer application in primary schools can support the learning of culture skills and also encourage children's writing motivation, numerical skills, self-esteem, self-reliance and creative independent work.

Up to now education knows only little about children's out-of-school use of the new technologies. The number of primary-school-aged children who already have a computer at home is steadily increasing (more than 1/3 of all children involved in the Hagen research = 38%). In view of these data, no primary school which has to deal with children's experience and must clarify them can afford to ignore computers.

In many families computers and the new technologies are being discussed: mothers are forced to acquaint themselves with word-processing in the office; the jobs of some fathers are in danger because of industrial robots; older brothers and sisters want to work in the fields of the new technologies.

Primary school children take over numerous and often diffuse ideas of computers, robots and new technologies from mass media and their different genres (e.g. computer magazines, science-fiction movies). This could develop into a belief in miracles which could possibly form the basis for uncritical consumption later years and therefore could hinder a major use of data technical tools.Science-fiction movies especially can create fear and totally unrealistic estimations in children, which have to be reduced by appropriate educational means.

Primary school children show interest in computers and easily find access to the new technologies. Why should we not use this interest to establish corresponding learning processes which will be of importance in the future?

Numerous computer games address primary-school-aged-children. A lot of primary school children know computer games, a great number find computers interesting. In view of the increasing supply of computer games and the structures of content and method of various products, primary school education should participate in the media-educational discussion.

Meanwhile various teaching-aid suppliers in the FRG offer computer programmes for primary schools. Most of them have been designed for the home-computer market and correspondingly are advertised by tempting promises. As soon as households are supplied with suitable home computers a lot of these programmes are likely to be used by parents for direct learning encouragement. In this situation both parents and pupils will want media-education and primary education to provide them with guidelines.

If the actual discussion of computers remains restricted to the family's privacy, new unequalities of opportunities will impend to emerge because outside school a new 'computer elite'can develop in privileged homes. An effect like this would contradict the basic approach of a democratic primary school. If it is generally agreed that there already is an educationally sound computer application in primary schools, then a new general educational mandate emerges which is to be held by state-run schools, not by parents.

In the future a very high percentage of working women will have to deal with computers. Politicians responsible for education, however, complain about discrimination against girls and women especially in the field of data processing education. The social prejudice of female deficit talents in the fields of technology, arithmetic and data processing affects the actual behaviour of the sexes as a self-fulfilling-prophecy and thus determines the framework of socialization. If such role stereotyping is to be broken, the development of barriers in the field of technology and data processing should be opposed at an early stage. Here again, primary school age is considered to be an important stage in which learning can easily be affected. Probably a girl's expertise and self-esteem in the use of the new technologies could be influenced effectively in this stage by a suitable way of using the computer.

There are numerous research reports from abroad about computer applications in primary schools. The majority of them contains very positive results which should invite primary school education in West Germany to take part in a critical examination. We think that some of the concepts from abroad -especially from Great Britain and Australia- contain interesting and creative approaches.

If computer-assisted learning (CAL) highly effects children's motivation, then good educational software is suitable to support special phases in class and to encourage individual learning processes. This could have a great impact on children with learning difficulties and learning deficits. Computer-assisted learning could provide them with better individual, self-controlled exercises and learning sequences than has ever been possible. The fact that the recent supply of German software for primary school is extremely deficient does not principally oppose computer-assisted learning and practising but asks working groups of educationalists and computer experts to develop new software products.

In recent years primary school education has again discovered learning with working materials and with means of self-instruction. Good computer training programmes, being much more than working papers transmitted onto the monitor, could support this progressive idea. The aspects of independent practice and of self-control of the work's results can be realised by the computer without problems.

The new data processing techno-logies contain numerous didactic possibilities which could enrich teaching in primary schools especially in regard to learning-psychology. Today many of these possibilities are not yet clearly visible. For example, it is now easier for the teacher to present data graphically by using highly developed computers and graphics.

These basic ideas led us to ask for scientific experiments in German primary schools which were to be carried out in order to enlarge our knowledge of educational possibilities and limits to computer application at this schooling level. With respect to today's knowledge the general introduction computers to German primary schools is not the essential point. The increasing spread of new technologies in the next decades, the didactic possibilities offered by today's and future computer technologies and last but not least the access of primary school children to the new technologies: all these are reasons why the introduction will take place sooner or later. Today there is no immediate need for action in this direction. This provides the margin which should immediately be used for scientific projects. The possibility of not using this margin may be attractive because of medium-termed financial reasons, but this possibly forces education and educational planning in some years time to react rashly without preparation.

II. Carrying out the empirical phase

After the teachers, -most of them computer-inexperienced- were introduced to the handling of hardware and software, after a joint concretization of the didactic-methodic conception and after co-operation with the parents, the empirical working phase was started in 5 Hagen primary school classes on September 5, 1988. After the autumn break a sixth primary class was included. The first empirical phase ended on the 22nd of December, 1988 including only 15 weeks of school.

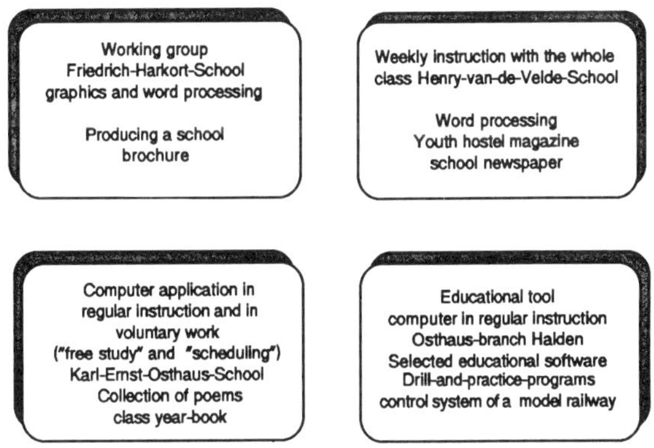

The figure above illustrates the project's emphasis in the four schools involved and also shows the organisational frame in which these projects were realised. In this abridged version it is not possible to illustrate the project's course in all four schools.

The basis for all parts of the project was the integration of work with a computer in primary school instruction which was pupil-orientated, action-orientated and offered a great deal of freedom of action.

III. Trends and first results

The carrying out of the projects in the schools involved and their results are illustrated in the comprehensive book *Mitzlaff/Wiederhold: Computer im Grundschulunterricht (MacGraw-Hill, Hamburg, New York u.a., 1990).* This paper canly give a brief summary of the results and trends of the project. Above all, three different groups involved in the computer application in the school shall be observed more closely: the pupils, the parents and the teachers.

The pupils

The dimension of behaviour which could be observed in all four project schools can be summed up like this:

There was a great and long-lasting interest in nearly all pupils in the work with the computer. The pupils observed were highly motivated and enjoyed their work with the computer and solved difficult and tiring problems (text-correction, text-revision). The experience gained in the discussed period of time seems to indicate that a computer with corresponding software is a medium which produces high motivation and which is suitable to encourage the attitude for learning and working.

These observations were illustrated by two questionnaires used at the beginning and at the end of the project. A majority of the pupils answered the question "How did you like working with a computer?" with "very much", "I liked it" or "It was superb". Only one child said that it "didn't like" the work. The children gave interesting reasons for their positive responses (see Mitzlaff/Wiederhold, 1990).

There was a high/ very high degree of long-lasting concentration during the work at the computer which could even be observed in disadvantageous lessons at the end of the day. This is true for pupils with weaker performances as well.

A long-lasting motivation to write was shown by most of the children in all projects referring to texts. A higher motivation to write went along with an increased readiness to revise and correct texts. According to the childrens' statements this was due to the fact that texts done by computer-assisted word-processing did not have to be completely rewritten .

The children's enlarged understanding of writing in a typographic dimension was developed in the projects centred on the texts through testing of various fonts.

The quick change from the computer as a new and special medium to an every-day tool could be used to carry out different operations in different qualities.

The ability to cope with the available hardware and software and to use it in a sound and direct way was achieved very quickly and without problems. The main difficulty in these three projects was the use of the keyboard. Altogether the introduction into the basic skills took less time than expected. These observations indicate that children in primary schools develop a different approach to new technologies than adults do: the basic skills are gained much faster, most of the children do not fear simply trying new commands and ways of working. The learning of computer terms is a by-product.

The co-operative forms of work which were developed in the project's course were preferred by most of the children. In the final inquiry 52.78% of the pupils said they preferred to work at the computer together with another pupil (individual work = 35.19%).

The skill in using the computer and its creative and imaginative application could be observed with both boys and girls.

Self-confidence in using the new technologies and a sense of achievement was gained by most children.

Changes in attitudes which -without direct discussion- resulted from using hardware and software. While in the opening inquiry still 64% of the children thought a computer was capable of thinking, in the final questionnaire the percentage was reduced to 13.89%. While at the beginning of the project still 54.76% of the children thought a computer was "cleverer than a human being", at the end of the project only 10.19% still shared this point of view.

In both of the project schools which could be compared through similarities in subject matter and hardware technology the children were asked to independently solve the same exercise. All pupils solved this task more than satisfactorily. Besides using the computer they mastered the programme MacWrite to independently give in texts, design and save them. After almost four months of computer experience this is an excellent result showing a sound mastering of the new medium. The girls in this age group did not show any distaste of technology. Their knowledge and skills could well be compared to the results of same-aged male pupils in the class. In the Friedrich-Harkort-School in which the children had mostly worked in groups of mixed sexes the average score of the girls was clearly above the boys' score.

This project could not give an insight into long-term effects. Therefore the question whether or not the above described high level of interest or concentration will still be valid after a longer computer application cannot be answered. As no parallel work was done in control groups not using computers there is no comparable information about increasing learning achievement. These questions will have to be answered in future research projects which should be long-running and well equipped.

The parents

The parents responded to the whole project with great interest and acceptance. We think that the high acceptance of computer application in primary schools is rooted in the knowledge of concrete tasks and of the educational context. All parents agreed that their child should take part in the project. Some of the parents answered to the first question about their reaction on the project's announcement spontaneously: "I thought it was time for the school to respond to these new questions!"

In this paper only some results can be quoted from the written questionnaire of the parents which was carried out at the end of the project where 101 parents were involved:

In the anonymous inquiry 94.1% of the parents rated their child's work with the computer as "very good" or "good".

66% thought their child liked working with the computer "very much", 33% thought that the child "liked it".

After the experience the parents themselves and their children gained in the "Hagen computer project" 89.1% of them supported the general introduction "in using the computer" in the classes 3 and 4.

When asked for suggestions to supplement or change the work, 55 out of 101 parents recommended to offer a "computer course" for them in the future. 36 mothers showed interest in such a course. New perspectives for intergenerational learning may be possible.

The teachers

All teachers took part in the projects with great interest and enthusiasm. The interest in the project was very high in the entire Hagen school dstrict.

More teachers than could actually be involved wanted to take part in the project. Out of the six teachers who were involved in the project only two had had any experience and knowledge of using the computer before the introductory sessions. All four female teachers started their work without previous knowledge. After short basic instruction all of them got acquainted with the new material with enthusiasm and a lot of autodidactic learning. The scepticism some of them showed in the beginning soon vanished with progressing work and after the use of user-friendly systems such as Apple Macintosh and Atari. Even after the end of the project all teachers still supported the project's approach. They were convinced by the pupils' high motivation and concentration and the teachers stressed the aspect of equal opportunity. Most of them suggested an integration of computer-assisted work into the context of primary class teaching with pupil orientation and setting. The teachers shared the opinion that "all pupils" had acquired knowledge of the computer and knowledge of working with the selected software within a very short period of time. All teachers stated that in the future they wanted to continue working with computers in primary because of the project's success. All of them would participate again in a similar research project as well. The previous experience and the work's results made all teachers involved in the project answer the question in the affirmative as to whether "all pupils of primary schools should be introduced to using the computer in the third or fourth class" some time in the future.

Hardware and Software

Our study "Computer im Grundschulunterricht" discusses the characteristics of software and hardware in detail (cf., p. 184ff) and describes the selected learning-software or courseware which was tested. **Especially for primary schools maximum quality is necessary with respect to hardware equipment and in the development of software.** It would be a mistake to think that the weakest and often complicated software could be offered to the youngest pupils just because the material is inexpensive at the moment. **It is just the contrary: The best hardware having the highest technical and ergonomic standard and the simplest usage should be chosen for the primary schools. The same goes for software: The youngest pupils should as a matter of principle be given software products which are best with respect todidactic conception and motivation.** As illustrated in various examples the development of learning-software in the German-speaking area is still far reaching from this high standard.

Computers as a working material and as a tool

Within the closely described didactic context the computer proved to be useful as a new instrument and as a tool especially for word-processing and control systems. The project report illustrates this statement with numerous examples of work and practical results.

Recommendations

In the final chapter of our study 10 recommendations for further activities within the primary schools are given. Here the emphasis lies on the progression of research projects and of model projects within the context of primary-school didactics and education. A second point of emphasis is placed on the extension of media-use research and media-effect research and the development of software on an inter-disciplinary basis. For the realisation of this work specific questions are asked and organisational recommendations are given.

Hagen, 20.11.1989

Computers in Education
A. McDougall and C. Dowling (Editors)
Elsevier Science Publishers B.V. (North-Holland)

DEVELOPING SCIENTIFIC THOUGHT IN A LOGO-BASED ENVIRONMENT

Gary S. STAGER

President of ISTE's Logo Special Interest Group (SIGLogo)
Network for Action in Microcomputer Education - Fallon Education Center -
51 Clifford Drive, Wayne, NJ USA 07470

1. Abstract

For the past several years I have been working to create an intellectual laboratory in which elementary school students learn the scientific method while developing mathematical thinking and problem-solving skills. My goal is for students to approach the acquisition of new scientific knowledge in an environment that inspires the type of intense passion, interest, and purposeful exploration one would observe while watching a student "play" with their chemistry set at home. How unfortunate it is that much of the tinkering, fun, and sense of discovery present in the pursuit of scientific knowledge has been replaced by the artificial, fact-based and passive text-book centered science curriculum present in many schools.

Three Logo-based environments; LogoWriter™, LEGO® TC logo, and the Phantom Fishtank™ create a dynamic environment for learning critical scientific concepts and experiening the process of science. Science is something you *do* as well as *study*.

When used together, these three software environments extend the types of experiences possible with the best simulation software by providing the student scientist with an opportunity to test and observe scientific phenomona in a universe they control. Problem solving is natural in the context of the student confronting real problems while in the pursuit of knowledge. Rarely does the student confront a question the teacher or textbook doesn't have an answer for, and they almost never have a question the world doesn't have an answer for. This paper will attempt to share ideas for activities in which this "real" scientific inquiry may occur.

2. Introduction

Can anybody remember elementary school science? Most educators would agree that one of the greatest areas of deficiency in our schools is science education. While the symptoms of mediocrity may be present at the secondary school level, the prognosis for elementary school science education is presently terminal.

Most elementary school science education (like other curriculum areas) is textbook based. Students are expected to memorize a set of facts about plants, animals, and rocks and abstract formulas which have very little to do with their everyday experiences, or in fact, real science. While this collection of facts may be important to a child's development, school children rarely get the chance to experience what it is to be a scientist and the "magic of science" - to learn the powerful ideas that emerge from the ability to draw upon one's curiosity and experiences to create an experiment, test and refine a hypothesis, and draw conclusions. Elementary school students are hard-pressed to comprehend how the seemingly random facts and formulas being imposed on them may be useful in their lives.

These problems do not end at the elementary school. Despite the fact that secondary and college teachers are normally trained and knowledgeable in their subject matter, students are more often than not deprived of the experience of exploring new scientific ideas and making the knowledge their own. High school and college students are still required to memorize formulas which they don't understand so that they can regurgitate them on an exam. The underlying concepts are often abandoned in a quest for the right answer.

"*In the current era of emphasis on science education, it has become a cliché to call scientific research a great adventure. Well it may be; but the student approaching his first hard science course with this maxim in his mind is in for a rude shock. Rarely does much of the sense of adventure manage to come through the hard work, for the subject matter often seems both difficult and dull. The student headed for a scientific career is usually told that he must face diligent drill before he can understand anything really profound.*" (March, 1980)

LogoWriter and the Phantom Fishtank are trademarks of Logo Computer Systems, Inc.
LEGO TC logo is a registered trademark of LEGO Systems A/G

Education, especially science education, need not be a passive experience. Students should be actively engaged in constructing their own knowledge. This paper will address these issues by focusing on three computer environments, LogoWriter™, LEGO TC logo, and the Phantom Fish Tank™, which enhance the study of science without abandoning the need for manipulatives and the learning of fundamental concepts. Being Logo-based, they require minimal confusion and offer maximum flexibility. With increased access to such powerful intellectual tools, children have the ability to create their own scientific models and solve problems that are intrinsically interesting to them. They extend the type of experiences possible by even the very best of simulation software and manipulatives because now, budding scientists can test and observe real-world (and non-real) phenomena.The microcomputer is used as a transparent open-ended tool for scientific inquiry - a laboratory for studying the great discoveries of scientists and a telescope into a world of infinite questions.

Although LogoWriter, LEGO TC logo, and the Phantom Fishtank contribute differently to the creation of the scientific culture, there are a number of important educational themes common to all three environments:
1) Out of simple beginnings complex structures may emerge.
2) Each environment is child-centered. Students are motivated to think and solve problems because the problems were generated by themselves in the process of creating a project.
3) Debugging is encouraged and strongly parallels important aspects of the scientific method. Experience in debugging encourages a healthier attitude towards learning and provides students with strategies for approaching any problem.
4) Each computing environment has "no threshold and no ceiling." Students are free to explore, create, and learn at their own level. Students are challenged by their imaginations. They will never reach the limits of the software.
5) The three environments support the philosophy of constructivism, embraced by Piaget and Papert. Students learn new concepts by reflecting on previous experience and constructing their own intellectual models.
6) The materials discourage passivity. Learning becomes an active and exciting life-long process.
7) The three computing environments are Logo-based so that the "young scientist" need only learn one environment, set of syntax, and rules of behavior. Fluency with the materials allow for creativity and intellectual discovery.
8) All three environments encourage cooperative learning and collaborative problem solving. Students help each other explore new intellectual frontiers.

3. Enter Logo

In Dr. Seymour Papert's now classic book, Mindstorms, he presents a profound vision of what he calls a "Mathland." Papert is also critical of the way mathematics and science is presented to children as a collection of abstract facts which have very little to do with a child's personal experiences or interests. Papert suggests that this why so many children suffer from "mathphobia." I would extend this feeling of detachment to explain student's "sciencephobia" and perhaps more importantly teacher's "sciencephobia."

In "Mathland" students would be as fluent and able to converse in a mathematical language as a living language. It is like learning French by going to France and being immersed in a culture that speaks French instead of attempting to learn French in an American classroom. I hope to extend Seymour Papert's powerful ideas by conveying a vision of a "Scienceland" in which students (and teachers) will feel comfortable thinking scientifically.

The line between math and science may seem blurred. This ambiguity is desireable and compatible with the Logo philosophy of conveying to students a sense that knowledge is unified. If a person learns to think scientifically or mathematically, they will be able to solve problems in other domains. If students learn scientific concepts in a meaningful context they no longer learn *about* science - they actually *do* science by becoming part of the problem they are attempting to solve.

Logo, a powerful programming language built on an even more powerful educational philosophy based on the ideas of Piaget, Dewey, and Montessori, provides an environment in which students can say "What If?" and solve problems in almost any curriculum area. In fact, working in Logo often blurs the artificial distinctions between disciplines by providing a medium for expressing yourself. In the process of solving a problem the student is free to explore many routes towards a solution; selecting the route or parts of routes that are compatible with their learning style and experiential background. Students are confronted by unanticipated problems while working in Logo. The ability to creatively solve problems in a natural, meaningful manner empowers the student to be a better learner. In the best Logo cultures, the child is the most important aspect of the curriculum. Learning becomes an active experience and the student is empowered by the realization that they are in control of their own learning.

Logo programming is a scientific activity. The programmer begins with a goal or problem he/she wishes to solve (the problem may change several times), then they test and refine their program until their problem is solved satisfactorily. The goal is not to learn to program in Logo, but rather to use Logo as a transparent tool for solving a variety of problems. In this context, students learn to program because programming is necessary in accomplishing their goals.

One of the most educationally beneficial and engaging aspects of programming is the debugging process. The valuable by-product of learning debugging skills is a new attitude about errors. *"Errors benefit us because they lead us to study what happened, to understand what went wrong, and, through understanding, to fix it. Experience with computer programming (especially in Logo) leads children more effectively than any other activity to 'believe in' debugging."* (Papert & Brand, 1987).

In Mindstorms, Dr. Papert adds: *"Many children are held back in their learning because they have a model of learning in which you have either "got it" or "got it wrong." But when you program a computer you almost never get it right the first time. Learning to be a master programmer is learning to become highly skilled at isolating and correcting bugs, the parts that keep the program from working. The question to ask about the program is not whether it is right or wrong, but if it is fixable. If this way of looking at intellectual products were generalized to how the larger culture thinks about knowledge and its acquisition, we all might be less intimidated by our fears about "being wrong."* (Papert 1980)

The following relevant quote is also attributable to Seymour Papert. *"The question the Child Answers, He always answers correctly."* It should be obvious how the acquisition of debugging skills and a healthier intellectual attitude towards debugging has a positive effect on the scientific process. Debugging enhances students ability to understand not only science, but any new piece of knowledge.

Generations of children have spent hours fascinated by their chemistry sets, LEGO, and tinkering with broken radios and mechanisms. My goal is for the Logo-Based activities outlined in this paper to inspire the same type of excitement and scientific inquiry in the classroom that the chemistry set provided in the home.

4.1. LogoWriter

LogoWriter combines all of the power of Logo with programmable wordprocessing, four turtles, thirty customizeable turtle shapes, and a vastly improved/simplified user-interface. LogoWriter is a tool which can be shaped by a culture of users based on their needs. I have identified three broad categories to describe ways in which LogoWriter can be used by students as a tool for developing scientific reasoning and to solve scientific problems. I will illustrate how LogoWriter can be used to 1) Simulate scientific phenomena; 2) Collect and interpret data; and 3) As a catalyst for powerful thought.

4.2. Simulating Scientific Phenomena

One of the best ways in which microcomputers are being used as a tool for learning/teaching science is in simulating phenomena that would be too dangerous, costly, large, or slow in the real world. Computer simulations often provide the learner or scientist with greater control over experimental conditions then in real life. LogoWriter can be used by students, even elementary school students, to create models of scientific phenomena, alter experimental conditions, make observations, and arrive at conclusions. Advanced scientific practices such as comparing experimental and control data can also be done in LogoWriter.

For purposes of this paper, I would like to illustrate one scientific concept which many students have explored in LogoWriter; the concept of motion. Due to LogoWriter's multiple turtles and customizeable shapes, many students enjoy creating their own animations. Animation is something children love and is an outstanding problem solving activity in that it requires many trade-offs between aesthetics and the microcomputer's inability to do more than one thing at a time. Animation causes a conflict between sequential and parallel processes. Children learn elements of physics, geometry, art, time and space, and programming, while designing an animation.

A basic element of animation is motion. Set the shape of the turtle to a car and ask, "How would we make a car drive in LogoWriter?" This question leads to all sorts of implications of vector quantities - the turtle needs to have a direction and a magnitude (velocity), "How would we make the car drive with a constant speed?"

REPEAT 10 [FD 1] What happens if you type:

REPEAT 100[FD 1] "How would we make the car go faster?"

```
REPEAT 100[FD 2]
```

How much faster did the car go? The answer should be twice the speed of the first try because the car went twice the distance in the same amount of time. Try substituting different numbers, then predict and observe the effect.

REPEAT 100[FD 5 WAIT 1] *WAIT causes Logo to pause for a specified number of counts*

How did the car behave now? The WAIT 1 can represent a force resisting the forward momentum of the car. The physics term for this phenomena is friction.

Other concepts have been simulated including: velocity, acceleration, life cycles, chemical reactions, plant growth, orbits, constellations, and volcanoes.

4.3. Collecting and Interpreting Data

LogoWriter may be used create charts, graphs, diagrams, and reports to explain observations or data. The ability to communicate scientific knowledge can be enhanced with graphics, sound, and animation. Junior scientists can use LogoWriter's wordprocessing capabilities to painlessly keep track of hypotheses, procedures, and data. One way in which computers are particularly useful is in collecting data from external microcomputer-based laboratory probes.

A group of imaginative ten year-olds was disappointed by the less than dramatic performance of a burglar alarm activity (from Broderbund's Science Toolkit) using an analog light sensor to detect an intruder. The students decided that their burglar alarm should sound an alarm and flash a message on the screen. They were then faced with interpreting the 0-255 range of numbers reported from the probe, the inverse relationship between the probe reading and the amount of light, and calibrating the probe and software. By writing two simple, one line, LogoWriter procedures, they had *invented* an obnoxious burglar alarm that became the sensation of the school.

4.4. A Catalyst for Scientific Thought

There are many simple LogoWriter activities which encourage students to think scientifically - to make, test, and refine hypotheses, modify the experiment, and possibly draw conclusions. These "experiments" begin with small Logo procedures and can be left for students to explore with for weeks.

4.5. A Microful of Monkees

One experiment explores word construction and probability. This experiment was inspired by Seymour Papert and the legend that if an infinite number of monkeys were sitting at an infinite number of typewriters, they would eventually type the entire works of Shakespeare. We will have less lofty goals. Our objective is to explore randomness and linguistics by creating random words in the hopes that the word CAT will appear. Using simple procedures, students can control variables/randomness, collect sizeable quantities of experimental data, and analyze the data by determining the percentage of English words created in each experiment.

This activity is a nice vehicle connects linguistic issues with combinatorics and probability - an opportunity to reinforce the concept of mathematics being the language of science.

A complete set of activities and Logo procedures based on this theme and others are available from the author.

5. LEGO TC logo

Jean Piaget tells us that children are wonderful learners and that they rediscover a vast amount of knowledge as they grow. However, he was puzzled that despite children's enormous potential to learn they are often incapable of learning even the simplest things in schools. Piaget concluded that children learn best when they have materials from their culture to build with. Even school dropouts are often able to make change or read comic books. But when knowledge is not well represented in a culture, or feared by a culture - as in math, science, and grammar - children fail to learn. Papert applies the term, constructionism, to the process of being actively involved in constructing one's own knowledge.

There are few materials in a child's culture with which they are more comfortable with or passionate about than LEGO construction toys. Building with LEGO is an activity which embodies the philosophy of constructionism and Logo. With LEGO bricks children can build anything their imagination suggests and complex structures can be built out of simple elements - just like programming in Logo. The Logo vision of being an educational environment with "no threshold and no ceiling" is shared by LEGO.

LEGO TC Logo combines the LEGO Technic materials - LEGO bricks, motors, gears, pulleys, lights, sensors - with a special version of LogoWriter called LEGO Logo. Students build machines with the LEGO materials and control them by programming in Logo through a simple, yet powerful, microcomputer interface.

With LEGO TC logo, students learn first-hand, concepts in engineering, mathematics, physics, electronics, robotics, gears, calibration, feedback systems, and computer science. Students wrestle with trade-offs such as power vs. speed. They learn science with unbridled enthusiasm when science is encountered in a meaningful, concrete, and fun manner. With LEGO TC logo students assume a role they rarely get to play, that of an inventor. They are encouraged by the materials to invent their own knowledge and invent their own machines. With LEGO TC logo, students can build new and imaginary machines and models of real-world machines.

As "real inventors" and "real scientists" children, students are much closer in contact with the truly important ideas of science. The emphasis shifts from rote learning of facts and techniques to a new way of thinking that requires systematic, critical, and creative thinking. With LEGO TC logo children truly care about their work. Appropriation is an important aspect of Piagetian learning and constructionism. Children are not inhibited with LEGO TC logo by the threat of failure or of being wrong. They can pursue all sorts of ideas, even seemingly silly ones. Who knows? Someday we may have wind-powered cars, a computer controlled mousetrap, or a xylophone playing robot.

Important concepts such as, Friction, are no longer understood superficially by rubbing two blocks of sandpaper together, but rather more accurately as an opposing force keeping my car from performing the way I want it to. Friction takes on a vastly different level of importance. A framework has been set for more formal understanding.

"With LEGO TC logo, students have an environment in which children can readily develop an understanding of the process of science. Children develop theories to describe the behavior of the things they build, then run experiments (designed by them) to test out the theories." (Ocko & Resnick, 1987)

While developing their LEGO TC logo projects, students use scientific techniques, methods, and terminology based on necessity. Students think anayltically and are often overheard to be discussing units of measure - how fast something traveled, how big their invention was, is a gear transmission more efficient than a belt transmission? These too often abstract concepts are now internalized by students.

LEGO TC logo provides opportunities for academic success for students with strong spatial and mechanical skills who may not perform well in traditional classroom settings which emphasize memorization, verbal skills, and artificial top-down problem solving strategies.

6. The Phantom Fish Tank

The Phantom Fish Tank must be explored to be appreciated. The Fish Tank's author, Brian Silverman, refers to his book and accompanying software as "an ecology of mind" and "mathematical recreation." The Phantom Fish Tank is a laboratory for doing real science in an unreal world. In this world you have complete control over all of the rules, conditions, and variables. Users not only get to make scientific observations, form and test hypotheses, and draw conclusions, but they also experience being the creator of the world they are studying. This experience certainly can not be replicated in a traditional classroom.

The Fish Tank deals with cellular automata, a branch of mathematics and computer science which strives to create a universal computational object and computers, not based on electricity which can reproduce themselves. Cells are placed on the screen's 40 X 40 matrix and then behave - reproduce, die, move - according to simple rules. Brian Silverman's book with the Phantom Fish Tank provides examples of how cellular automata can be used to explain principles of genetics, electricity, evolution, physics, mathematics, biology, and computer science. The most famous cellular automata "game" was created by John Conway and called "The Game of Life." Where the Phantom Fish Tank differs from other "Life Games" is that it is built on a version of Logo which makes it easy for the "scientist" to control his/her laboratory, collect data, and store new life forms. There is a built in rule editor that allows the student to create his/her own new rules of behavior for the world.

The Phantom Fish Tank appeals to different people on many different levels. Dr. Cynthia Solomon suggests that children learn best with materials that are graphically interesting. The Fish Tank's graphics generate enough interest for years of study. The author compares the software to a microscope and some of the "sample slides" (files) included with the software help illustrate logic gates, diodes, circuitry, inverters, organisms, calculators, and other physical objects in a non-physical environment controlled only by simple rules of how a cell should interact with neighboring cells. He goes on to state that no scientist would want a microscope which can only work with prepared slides. The furtherance of science is dependent on the ability to create your own slides and the Phantom Fish Tank's software provides a flexible laboratory environment for exploring millions of possibilities.

7. Putting it All Together: Logo from Another Planet

One open-ended activity with potential for individual and group discovery is creating new life forms in Logo. A new and exciting multidisciplinary area of scientific research is called, artificial life. Artificial life research combines elements of psychology, physics, artificial intelligence, mathematics, biology, and computer science with important intellectual ideas, including: emergence, bottom-up design, and systems-oriented thinking. The intellectual tools sharpened in this activity have relevance far and beyond the field of artificial life research. If it is in fact important for students to develop problem solving skills, I am hard pressed to think of a more fertile pursuit than creating a new universe and it's inhabitants.

"In certain fields, such as high-energy physics and much of current mathematics, it is difficult to make cutting edge ideas accessible and relevant to children. But that is certainly not the case with artificial life. Children all share a strong interest in living things and animal behavior. Moreover, the general approach to artificial life research is one that meshes nicely with children's natural ways of learning. Artificial life researchers often learn by building things. They start with simple, easily understood rules or units, and they study how complexity emerges from interactions among these units." (Resnick, 1987)

The classic Elementary School Science Curriculum's unit on observing mealworm behavior is an excellent introduction to artificial life.

The creatures the students invent can be models of real-life animals or new organisms, never seen before. Issues of locomotion and movement can be modeled in all three Logo environments. Some behaviors and senses can be better simulated in LogoWriter or LEGO TC logo. For example, the sense of touch can be dealt with by a screen creature in LogoWriter who will bump it's way through a screen maze or a LEGO creature programmed to navigate a physical maze. Sight and visual perception may also be modeled in both environments. Smell, hearing, and taste are better simulated in LogoWriter because they are not dependent on the LEGO TC logo light and touch sensors. Issues of reproduction and colonization may be explored with the Phantom Fishtank.

What happens when we combine several senses or the mechanical emotions of psychologist Valentino Braitenberg's vehicles? How does a creature with one eye behave differently than a creature with two eyes? What happens if a predator is added to your world? How could you simulate social behaviors?

8. Conclusion

I have attempted to illustrate how students, beginning in the elementary school grades, can construct their own scientific knowledge and, thereby, learn to think scientifically in more meaningful and effective ways than are commonplace today. My tool of choice for stimulating interest and understanding of scientific concepts is the microcomputer. I use the microcomputer in the way Seymour Papert would like to see the computer used; as a transparent tool always available to the student for solving problems that are intrinsically interesting and important.

The three Logo-Based environments I have discussed place the child in control of his/her own learning. The curriculum is designed to be child-centered and not only teach a collection of discrete facts, but empower the learner by providing challenging opportunities for fun, self-expression, problem solving, and a love of life-long learning.

9. References

Abelson, H. & A. diSessa (1981), Turtle Geometry (Cambridge: MIT Press)

Abelson, H. & E.P. Goldenberg (1977), Teacher's Guide for Computational Models of Animal Behavior - Logo Memo number 46 (Cambridge: MIT A.I. Laboratory).

Bass, Alison (1987) "Computers in the Classroom - An Interview with Seymour Papert," Technology Review.

Braitenberg, V. (1984), Vehicles (Cambridge: MIT Press).

Brand, S. (1987), The Media Lab: Inventing the Future at MIT (New York: Viking).

Caney, S. (1985), Invention Book (New York: Workman Press).

Dawkins, R. (1976), The Selfish Gene (New York: Oxford University Press).

Feynman, Richard P. (1985), Surely You're Joking Mr. Feynman! (New York: Bantam).

Flannagan, D. (1988), Flannagan's Version (New York: Vintage Books).

Franz, S. & S. Papert (1988), "Computer as Material: Messing About with Time," Columbia Teachers College Record.

Gelman, M. (1986), "Methods of Simulating

Robotic Behavior in LogoWriter," Proceedings of the 1987 East Coast Logo Conference (Eugene, OR: ICCE/Meckler).

Goldenberg, E. Paul (1989) "Linguistics, Science, and Mathematics for Pre-College Students: A Computational Modeling Approach," Proceedings of the 1989 National Educational Computing Conference (Eugene, OR: ISTE).

March, Robert H. (1978), Physics for Poets (Chicago: Contemporary Books, Inc.).

Minsky, M. (1985-86), Society of Mind (New York: Simon and Schuster).

Ocko, S., S. Papert, and M. Resnick (1988), "LEGO, Logo, and Science," Technology and Learning. Volume 2, number 1.

Papert, S. (1980), Mindstorms: Children, Computers, and Powerful Ideas (New York: Basic Books).

Peterson, I. (1988), The Mathematical Tourist - Snapshots of Modern Mathematics (New York: W.H. Freeman and Company).

Poundstone, W. (1985), The Recursive Universe... (Chicago: Contemporary Books).

Resnick, M. (1987), "LEGO, Logo, and Life," Paper presented at the First Artificial Life Workshop, Los Alamos, NM.

Silverman, B. (1987), The Phantom Fishtank: An Ecology of Mind (Montreal: Logo Computer Systems, Inc.).

Stager, G. (1988), "A Microful of Monkees," The Logo Exchange. October, 1988 Issue.

Stager, G. (1988), "Physics for Kindergarteners," The Logo Exchange. November, 1988 Issue.

Turkle, S.. (1984), The Second Self: Computers and the Human Spirit (New York: Simon and Schuster).

Computers in Education
A. McDougall and C. Dowling (Editors)
Elsevier Science Publishers B.V. (North-Holland)

THE BULGARIAN STRATEGY OF INTRODUCING NEW INFORMATION TECHNOLOGIES IN EDUCATION

Prof. Ivan Stanchev

International Research Centre for Educational Informatics, CICT
bl 25A, Acad. G.Bonchev Street, 1113 Sofia, Bulgaria

This paper describes the Bulgarian strategies of introducing new information technologies in education and the results achieved under the Long-term Programme. Special attention is paid to the Research Group on Education and the International Research Centre for Educational Informatics' activities in research implementation and teacher training. Stress is laid on the achievement of international collaboration in the field of research and transfer of educational software and courseware.

1. INTRODUCTION

Specific policies and strategies for introducing computers and related information technologies into schools of countries differ, although broad common trends are apparent. In particular, there is a shift from "restricted" policies intended to promote instruction in computer science and computer literacy towards "comprehensive" policies designed mainly to increase the effective use of computer-based teaching and learning across the curriculum (1). The real challenge confronting countries seeking to effectively harness the capacity of the computer for education is now seen as pedagogical, namely how can the technology be used to improve teaching and learning processes. Implementation strategies for these comprehensive policies and specific strategies for the development and use of hardware, software, teacher training, and evaluation must now be considered in the light of this challenge. Countries which have made use of technology in education for many years have followed different strategies, although common trends now appear, and analyses of their successes and failures should be brought to the attention of countries less advanced in this area. Furthermore, in the light of the value of international cooperation in this area, it would be worthwhile to try to identify which parts of these national strategies could be transferred to other countries and which aspects of them could be developed in common. This paper discusses the context of policies, the two broad policy approaches and their convergence, the main strategies of policy implementation, the specific strategies in hardware, software, teacher training, research and evaluation and the possibilities for the transfer of these strategies and approaches between countries.

National, regional, state and local policies for introducing computers into schools have largely responded to pressures from outside education. The pressures exist in every country, they differ only in the degree to which they have influenced policies and strategies:

- Demands from the economy: the restructuring of the economy calls for new, technology-related skills.
- Industrial interests: the introduction of technology in education complements and strengthens the development of the national microelectronics industry.
- Commercial pressures: manufacturers promote the introduction of technology in schools as part of their marketing strategies aimed at increasing sales to business and to families.
- Social pressure: parents often take a lead in bringing computers into the schools, and young pupils bring with them an interest in computers and basic technological expertise acquired at home.
- Cultural dimensions: the media frequently report on social and economic changes that appear to be driven by and are associated with, information technologies.
- Political pressure: political leaders regard programs for introducing computers in school, particularly for the purpose of computer literacy, as a good way to demonstrate a visible and concrete commitment to improvements in education.
- Technological developments: the progress in technology itself increases the range and speed of its applications while reducing its costs.

In response to these pressures, most of the developed countries started ambitious and costly programs in the beginning of the 80's. The programs differ in terms of their specific objectives and strategies of implementation. However, some common trends have emerged in broad policies and in broad strategies for implementation.

During the mid-1980's, countries could be divided into two groups according to broad policy approaches. The first group consisted of countries which could be called "restricted". The first objective of these policies was to introduce the teaching of computer science into vocational and upper secondary education, in order to develop computer-related skills for participation in the labour market. A second objective was to teach computer literacy to all students at all other levels of education in order to provide them with a basic understanding of the way computers work and the impact of computers on society and on the individual.

The second group consisted of countries who developed "comprehensive" policies, intended not only to promote the teaching of computer science or technological literacy, but also and mainly to use information and communications technologies to improve teaching and learning processes. This last objective includes a number of different and complementary aims such as: to improve the quality of the teaching process; to enhance learning and to better understand the related cognitive processes; to review education, especially curricula; to compensate for the decline in the number and quality of teachers; to improve access to education; and to develop communications between schools intra- and internationally.

Countries have moved towards comprehensive policies, either by changing the orientation of programs planned some years ago, as in Italy (1985 Program), Portugal (The Minerva Plan 1985-1988), Norway (Programme of Action 1984-1988) and Spain (The Atenea Plan 1985-1989), or by introducing entirely new programs, such as in the Netherlands (The OPSTAR Project 1989-1992).

If the trend is clear, there are still different views about the role of computers for improving teaching and learning and there are different stages of development across countries. Developments in the United Kingdom, in some states of the United States, or in some provinces of Canada cannot be compared with developments in Austria, the Federal Republic of Germany, Japan or Sweden. Among the reasons accounting for the differences, two stand out: differences in the specific objectives of the educational systems and the way they work, and differences in an array of cultural and sociological factors. But the trend towards comprehensive policies should be understood as a very important one. We know that the teaching of computer science or computer literacy does not modify the traditional methods and organization of schooling. But as an integrated tool for learning, information technologies can have a profound impact on the learning process, on the content of courses and relationships between courses, on the role of the teacher and on school and classroom organization. Educational authorities in many industrialized countries have begun to recognize that information technologies can be used as a lever to modernize or to bring about substantial changes in their educational systems.

2. STRATEGIES FOR INTRODUCING INFORMATICS INTO EDUCATION

Two main strategies for implementation have emerged. The first deals with the equipment - in the broad sense - of selected pilot schools versus all schools and the second with centralization of decisions versus decentralization.

The choice to equip only some pilot schools, or to support experimental project-based or course-based materials, has been based upon two related considerations: cost, as most countries cannot meet the expense of equipping all schools, and evaluations of effectiveness, since focussing the limited resources on some schools could, in some cases, permit them to reach the "critical mass" in terms of access to hardware, integration of quality software within the curriculum, and complementary training of teachers. In the mid 1980's, countries aiming to introduce technology as a tool for learning and teaching started with pilot schools, numbering from less than fifty in Norway to hundreds in the Netherlands, Portugal or Spain. One issue related to this strategy is that in a number of countries, there has been a great deal of "grass-roots" activity leading to the introduction of technology in schools which is not part of the program. In this situation, what should be the relationships between the experimental and the non-experimental schools?

This approach contrasts with that taken by a few countries such as France or the United Kingdom, where all schools have been equipped, even with a small number of computers per pupil. This strategy was chosen for political reasons in order to avoid inequalities between schools and also to stimulate outside individual initiatives taken by teachers, students, headmasters or parents.

It seems that the ideal strategy would be to combine these two approaches and that governments could help by introducing technology in all schools, and at the same time, by taking a major responsibility for experimenting in a very few well equipped schools in order to assess how technology actually improves the quality of the teaching and the learning processes. Countries which have adopted this combined approach include Japan, Sweden or some states of the United States. Florida, for example, has one of the highest average ratio (1:18) of computers per student, and has set up a five-year $10.5 million program for five "Model Technology Schools". Other countries (or states) could, in a more modest way, follow this strategy, particularly if pilot schools are funded by various private and public partners and participate in networks supported by international co-operation.

So, whatever the structure of the educational system - centralized as in France or decentralized as in Norway and in the federal countries - the role of the national authorities appears to be essential, particularly during the initial introduction of information technologies in schools. The government's role extends to five areas: hardware, since software compatibility is facilitated by the use of common operating systems; software, where a viable market should be organized and where good reviews and evaluations should be made available to teachers; teachers, for whom appropriate pre-service and in-service training should be given; research, which should be adequately supported and co-ordinated and evaluation, a central policy issue.

But the introduction of computers in education is an innovation which requires ideas and the possibility to implement them. It is probable that the required creativity develops better in a decentralized context. Furthermore, there is a de facto situation brought about by spontaneous grass-roots developments in a number of countries. The large-scale, uniform and prescriptive quality of such an approach may rigidify the use of technology in schools long before the educational potential of the technology has been developed and researched. In any event, clearly the form of decentralization is intimately bound up with the stage of development. In each country a balance between grass-roots, co-ordinated and centrally-controlled actions must be found.

3. STARTING ACTIVITIES IN BULGARIA

The curriculum prepared for the new Bulgarian 12-grade school, and its implementation in practice necessitates a search for new techniques of instruction, as well as new means for reducing the overload on students. Our search was particularly active in the sphere of new techniques of instruction, such as the application of school television, tape-recorders, programmed instruction with the use of computer technology as well. In the 1970's all these experiments did not produce any substantial results. The reasons for this are varied and generally known. We sought new factors which would make it possible to expand the educational process, to attract both teachers and students, and to encourage the creative process. At that moment, microcomputer technology emerged and began to be widely applied in secondary schools. We analyzed the experience of the USSR, Britain, France, Japan and the USA in introducing this technology, and became aware of the need to start using microcomputers in Bulgarian schools as well. In view of the importance and ever-increasing role of the computer in the Bulgarian society, the Ministry of Education adopted a number of goal-oriented measures related to the computerization of secondary education, to pre-vocational education and to the acquisition of knowledge, skills and other requirements needed to work with computer equipment. In 1985 the Ministry of Education announced that 6000 domestically produced microcomputers would be installed in secondary schools before the end of the year, and that by 1990 about 40,000 microcomputers of the Pravetz type would be in use in secondary schools.

During the three years following the adoption of the Program many results have been achieved (2):

- more than 16,000 school micros have been delivered to schools;
- a 120-hour course in informatics was made compulsory in all secondary schools (10th and 11th grade in the 1986/87 school year);
- two versions of initial textbooks in informatics in two parts (for the 10th and for the 11th grade) have been written and published;
- teachers' handbooks, as supplements to the first and the second parts of the informatics textbooks, have been written and published;
- a large number of study aids and other materials have been published;
- considerable success has been achieved in the training and retraining of the teachers (there are about 1,000 schools in the country). About 17,000 teachers have completed a one-week (36-hour) computer literacy course; 2,300 have finished a one-month course; 650, a three-month course, and 350, a one-year course;
- a teachers' training Chair for Informatics was established in the Department of Mathematics and Informatics at Sofia University in 1986. Similar chairs have been created in teachers' training colleges throughout the country;
- research units in the area of education have been organized in some of the higher educational schools.

The Ministry has been allocated some 12 million leva annually towards the development and transfer of new techniques in secondary education (which is about 1 per cent of the total yearly expenditure for the national educational system, including pre-school education and construction projects).

4. THE LONG-TERM PROGRAMME

There are consequently many prerequisites for the implementation of computer technology within the secondary education system, namely:

- The solution of the problems related to the material structure, to the supply of computers, and to the modification and development of computing equipment, peripheral devices, etc., produced in Bulgaria;
- The possibility of using the experience and results of the practical implementation of computer technology in the higher educational institutions of the country, and the research potential of the higher institutions, the Academy of Sciences, as well as other institutions and organizations.

Both these are prerequisites for the stable functions, self-renovation and constant improvement of the education system. The procedure for introducing computers into the secondary education system, the relevant stages, objectives and tasks, were part of a complex programme for the implementation of computer technology in secondary schools, worked out and approved by the Higher Council for Education at the Ministry of Education in Bulgaria (3).

This programme is on a national and long-term scale - until 1990; it guarantees the implementation of the resolutions concerning the introduction of computers into secondary schools and is linked to various programmes at district and regional levels. The social and political significance of the programme lies in the creation of conditions for the creation of multilaterally developed individuals who are familiar with the modern trends towards automation and the extensive use of computer technology.

The following facts were given particular consideration when the programme was being worked out, namely:
- The wide application of computer technology, particularly microcomputers and microprocessors in education, raised a number of questions related to its study and application as a technical aid for improving the quality of the educational process.
- Computer technology and its study are important for the formation of the students' world outlook, since they create conditions for new trends in thinking, revealing the role of computers in automation and control systems, in changes in the character of labour, and in problems of quality and productivity. The cultivation of algorithmic thinking is particularly important for the students' development.

In view of this, the main trends in the implementation of computer technology in Bulgarian secondary schools may be determined as follows:
- Training in the field of computer technology and the basic principles of programming, as an element of general education;
- Application of computer technology (microcomputers and microprocessors) as technical school aids;
- Application of microprocessor and microcomputer equipment as a means of control in such subjects, as automation of production, introduction of cybernetics, automation and computer technology, etc.

The programme has been elaborated with a view to complying with a number of basic needs, namely:
- The introduction of qualitatively new control systems for different objects and processes and systems of an organizational type raises the problems of training specialists, their pre-vocational education, and the acquisition of knowledge, skills and needs.
- The control of complex technical devices, equipment and apparatus requires the acquisition of new skills and habits, development of the intellect - combinatory and intellectual thinking - a description of the various objects and systems, and the setting up and use of information facilities.
- The application of computers makes it possible to intensify and individualize the educational process, the means of individual control and the change in teaching strategy.
- The introduction of computers in education, particularly in secondary schools, is aimed at creating and pursuing a scientifically substantiated strategy for their implementation, in addition to encouraging research into the educational, psychological, physiological and other problems of computerization.

The main aims of the programme are as follows:
- To provide for both theoretical and practical study of computer technology with the aim of training secondary school graduates in the programming, operation, maintenance and production of computer equipment, i.e. to provide for the particular profession;
- To provide extensive computer education with the aim of imparting a system of knowledge and skills in using computers, i.e. to promote computer literacy;
- To guarantee the effective use of computers as teaching aids, and to create the necessary software for general education;
- To provide the necessary technical facilities and personnel for the introduction of computer technology into secondary schools - training of teachers;
- To provide the necessary hardware and software for the control of the educational process and of the educational institutions.

The complex programme for the introduction of computer technology in the process of instruction and education, as well as in the management of secondary schools, links in with other programmes which are being implemented concerning education in secondary schools, namely:
- Complex programme "Teaching and Technical School Aids, and the Training of Teachers for Subjects Forming the Basis of Vocational Training".
- Complex programme "Higher Education and Professional Qualification of Teachers of Computer Technology and Programming, and the Application of Microcomputers in the Educational Process and Management".

In accordance with the complex programme "Teaching Aids", the disciplines involved in professional training in the 11th and 12th grades of the Unified Secondary Polytechnical School (mechanical and engineering science, automation of production and computer technology, electronics and electro-technology) should be provided with the necessary teaching and technical school aids, methods and equipment, and steps should be taken to improve and update the professional qualifications of the teachers. The functioning and implementation of this complex programme provides for research, development and production of experimental specimens, technical design of study-halls and laboratories, software, teacher training and the introduction of the necessary school aids to consolidate the foundations of the students' vocational training.

5. THE IMPLEMENTATION IN THE CURRICULA

The Ministry of Education took a number of concrete actions aimed at aligning educational goals, curricula and methods with the requirements of techno-scientific progress. The first specific act in this direction was the decision to incorporate into the general curriculum the basic theoretical and practical aspects of computer technologies.

From the 4th to the 7th grade (10 to 13 year-olds) pupils learn to use pocket calculators to solve mathematical problems when appropriate. Elements of informatics are introduced in the instruction of mathematics. This line of education in informatics continues in the 9th grade in which all students complete a 34-hour course on some elements of informatics outside its eventual computer application. The emphasis is put on the algorithmic approach to data processing.

In the 10th and 11th grade informatics is taught as a separate subject. The Ministry of Education suggested that two different textbooks should be published and that the teachers should choose one of them. (We should mention here that as a result of the strong centralization of the Bulgarian educational system all the schools have the same curriculum. Furthermore, until recently, only one textbook existed for each school subject. In 1986, for the first time, the Ministry of Education decided to engage two teams as authors of textbooks in informatics. This was followed by a similar decision in connection with mathematics textbooks.)

Programming in BASIC is the main area covered by the first of the textbooks. The second one also introduces elements of BASIC, but only as a tool for describing some basic structures and algorithms. The emphasis is put on the information structures and the means for their description and processing. Within the framework of the informatics course one third of the time is spent on practice with microcomputers. Special software supporting these courses has been developed and distributed to the schools.

Most of the secondary vocational schools and the technical ones have the same informatics curriculum as the general secondary schools, but with a special emphasis according to the type of training offered. Some of the technical colleges do a great deal in this direction. The electronics colleges, for instance, offer courses in the foundations of programming, mainframe computer peripherals, hardware architecture, etc.

The Ministry of Education considers that informatics has yet to enter into active interdisciplinary relationships with the other subjects. Efforts are now aimed at updating the concept of the place of the new information technologies within the curriculum of general and professional secondary schooling. Among the first steps in this direction are the two new 8th grade mathematics textbooks. The first of these represents an attempt to integrade mathematics and informatics, i.e. not to mix their elements mechanically but to integrade them as far as possible. In such a way mathematics motivates the introduction of elements of informatics and uses them later to clarify some mathematical concepts. The language LOGO is used in this textbook. This method is also continued in the project for textbooks for the next two grades.

6. THE TEACHERS' TRAINING

Considerable attention and financial resources are devoted to the training and retraining of teachers and lecturers. A model system has been worked out for training in periods of different duration, which has already embraced 21,000 secondary school teachers. A specialization in informatics was instituted at the Sofia University in 1985 for training of teachers in this discipline.

The programme for improving the teachers' qualifications in computer technology and programming is an element of the complex programme and covers the 1985-1990 period. It defines all types of activities related to the pre- and in-service training of teachers.

The main aim is to train the teacher to apply computer technology in the educational and the educational-productional process, to provide qualified teachers for theoretical and practical training of students in computer technology and programming, to train educational management staff in the application of computers to the control and management of education, and to provide the material prerequisites for qualification projects.

In the first place, the organization of qualification courses presupposes the existence of a module structure for the courses, which are divided into four levels:

First level - duration of training one week, 36 hours. This course is intended for all teachers and management staff in the education system.

Second level - duration of one month, 140 hours. Intended as general introduction in computer technology for nonspecialist teachers.

Third level - duration three months, 440 hours. Intended for teachers who are to teach computer technology and programming in secondary schools.

Fourth level - duration of one year, 940 hours. Intended for training specialist teachers. After successfully completing this course, they are entitled to teach computer technology and programming.

Teachers trained at the last two levels are appointed deputy head-masters of the schools in which they teach, with the obligation to teach 8 hours per week.

In accordance with the programme, it is necessary to organize laboratories for the training of teachers, to create the necessary technical and teaching aids, and to provide for the writing of textbooks and manuals. These courses are already functioning and it may be said that the training they provide is not always without problems. In spite of selection procedures, the trainees have different background qualifications and this creates certain difficulties.

7. THE HARDWARE AND THE SOFTWARE

Microcomputers are the principal technological instruments applied in education. Two types of Bulgarian-manufactured microcomputers are used in the various stages and forms of education - 8-bit (Apple-compatible) and 16-bit (IBM-compatible). The 8-bit Pravetz microcomputer is used in the field of secondary education. Over 20,000 such microcomputers have been centrally distributed until now in a total of about 1000 schools. The practice at this stage involves organizing computer classes of 18 workplaces in every school. The computers from these classes are being linked to the local network. Instruments for working with graphic information and for the tracking and control of experiments and technological processes are gradually being introduced for the needs of technological and vocational secondary education.

Essentially, a computer is both a subject of study and a tool in the system of education. An experiment is now under way on a national level for the incorporation of informatics as part of the educational content of mathematics throughout the entire course of the secondary school on the basis of the LOGO language. Specialized schools in mathematics and informatics have been set up. Textbooks have been issued for all school disciplines connected with informatics.

As a technological instrument involved in the educational process, computers are being used at all stages and in all forms of education. Examples can be quoted for all school disciplines - humanitarian as well as natural - science and mathematical. The major problem here is the creation and spreading of the educational software. There exists no centralized organization in this respect. The country's higher educational institutions, in which integrated teams are being set up that include secondary school teachers, play a leading part in the development of educational software. The strategy in recent years has been to work out instrumental means and systems that will be made locally available and will help teachers and students in the development of educational software without any need of specialized knowledge in computing technology. The use of computers as a technological instrument in the educational process is accompanied by appropriate ergonomic, psychophysiological, medical and pedagogical investigations and relevant recommendations.

8. THE EXTRA-CURRICULAR ACTIVITIES

A nationwide system of extra-curricular informatics training has been set up. The facilities are run by different schools, local youth organizations, and so-called Computer Clubs, established by the Dimitrov Youth Organization, throughout the country. Every year over 100 pupils pass through the National Informatics Training Camp. Several national competitions in informatics are organized, including: a National Informatics Olympiad for pupils, which is held in three rounds - school, regional and national; a Banner of Peace Winter Mathematical Festival; a Spring Informatics Tournament, which, annually, gathers more than a hundred pupils from all over the country; a programming contest for 10 to 14 year-old pupils in three rounds, etc. Participants in the national olympiads and other contests are invited to training camps in informatics and mathematical linguistics during the vacations.

Bulgaria is the initiator and active participant in a number of international undertakings in the field of computerization of education. The international conference Children in the Information Age which third session was held in May this year, has become very popular. Bulgaria is an active member of UNESCO's International Informatics Programme with acad. Bl.Sendov as the Vice-President. The country is the CODIESEE coordinator on topic IV.1. An UNDP project is being worked out in Bulgaria with UNESCO as executive organization for the Research Centre for Educational Informatics, financed with 200,000 US$ and 4,000,000 leva. Within the framework of this project 12 subprojects embracing all aspects of the use of computers in education are under way. It is expected that conditions will have been created by the end of 1990 for the regular training of educationalists from the developing countries.

REFERENCES

(1) Duguet, Pierre, National Strategies and Their Extension to the International Level, delivered at the IC "Education and Informatics: Strengthening International Co-operation", UNESCO (Paris, 1989)
(2) Vasko, T. and Dicheva,D., Educational Computer Policies: An International Overview (IIASA, A-2361 Laxenburg, 1988)
(3) Pisarev, A., The National Program of the People's Republic of Bulgaria for the Introduction of Computers in Secondary Schools, in Sendov, Bl. and Stanchev, I. (eds.), Children in an Information Age: Tomorrow's Problems Today (Pergamon Press, 1985)

Computers in Education
A. McDougall and C. Dowling (Editors)
Elsevier Science Publishers B.V. (North-Holland)

THE CONTRIBUTION OF EDUCATIONAL COMPUTING TO INTELLECTUAL DEVELOPMENT AMONG ZIMBABWEAN PRIMARY SCHOOL CHILDREN

David WILSON, Alistair MUNDY-CASTLE and Pauline SIBANDA

Department of Psychology, University of Zimbabwe, P.O. Box MP 167, Mount PLeasant, Harare, Zimbabwe

LOGO is premised to promote cognitive growth. Two studies of the cognitive effects of LOGO among primary schoolchildren were conducted in the cross-cultural milieu of Zimbabwe. In Study 1, an experimental group of 52 11-12-year-old children was exposed to LOGO for a year and a control group of 41 11-12-year-old children received no formal exposure to computers or supplementary non-computer instruction. Both groups were approximately equally comprised of black and white pupils and boys and girls. They completed pre-tests on cognitive scales at the outset of the project and post-tests one academic year later. Multivariate analysis of covariance, using pre-test scores as covariates, indicated that experimental condition children achieved greater gains in arithmetical reasoning and black girls made particular gains in spatial reasoning. Cultural explanations for these results are presented. The second study focused on girls and incorporated a control group exposed to another form of computing. An experimental group of 49 8-9-year-old schoolgirls was exposed to LOGO for approximately one year and a control group of 56 girls was exposed to Computer-Aided-Instruction programmes emphasising English, mathematics and problem-solving for a similar period. Pre- and post-tests on cognitive scales were held at an approximately one-year interval. Analysis of covariance, with pre-test scores as covariates, revealed no significant differences in pre-test post-test improvement between the two groups. It is concluded that LOGO may be no more effective than Computer-Aided-Instruction in promoting cognitive growth, but that several methodological concerns temper the confidence of this conclusion.

1. INTRODUCTION

Logo is a graphics-orientated, educational computer language and a philosophy of education that emphasises learning by exploration and discovery. In its graphic mode, which is especially popular among primary school children, Logo uses either a robot on wheels called a "floor turtle", which moves around the floor, or a triangle on the computer screenm called a "screen turtle", which moves around the screen. The turtle contains a pen which leaves a trail. This pen may be used to create shapes and figures. The turtle's movements are controlled by primitives, which may be used to construct procedures, which in turn may be incorporated in more elaborate procedures.

Papert [1], the originator of Logo, presented an exciting vision of education in the computer age. Specifically, he argued that Logo stimulates mathematical attainment by reducing the tedium of traditional numerical curricula and by linking advanced mathematical principles to immediate, clearly observable consequences, and that Logo promotes widely transferable reasoning and problem-solving skills.

Papert and his colleagues offer some support for these claims [2-4]. However, this evidence rests on descriptive data and lacks experimental rigour [5-11].

Recent reviews of the intellectual benefits of Logo have confined themselves to studies employing adequate experimental or quasi-experimental controls. Chang [12] considered 20 journal articles or dissertations on the effects of Logo and opined that "Logo had a positive effect on problem-solving skills, metacognitive skills, reasoning skills and learning of geometry" (p. 220). In contrast, Feldman and Uhlig [13] reviewed 17 doctoral dissertations and concluded that "Logo is usually no more effective in modifying the dependent variable, whatever it may be, than non-Logo computer-based instruction or, in many cases, non-computer instruction" (1987, p. 434). Maddux [14] noted that Logo studies have yielded mixed results. Aspects of Logo may be appropriate among African children and other aspects may be less appropriate. Logo is a socially-mediated educational activity which encourages interaction and co-operation between children. This may be especially fitting in Africa, in view of evidence that the African cultural tradition ascribes greater weight to social than technological facets of intelligence, views child-rearing goals in terms of social skills and regards interactions with people as inherently more important than objects, thus fostering a more socially orientated set of cognitive skills [15-23]. However, while the social character of Logo may be fitting, it is admittedly an unfamiliar and perhaps alien educational approach in Africa. The appropriateness of Logo in Africa is thus uncertain. Zimbabwe, whose population comprises black children raised in the African cultural milieu and white children reared in a Western milieu presents an ideal setting for investigation of this issue. The studies described here examined the cognitive effects of Logo in cross-cultural context.

2. STUDY 1

2.1 MATERIALS AND MEASURES

2.1.1 Subjects

The experimental group comprised 52 Grade 7 (11 to 12 year old) children (27 girls, 25 boys: 30 white, 22 black) from four classes at an urban middle-class primary school in Harare. No pupil in this group had received any formal Logo tuition before the study began. As all Grade 7 children at this school learned Logo, a control group had to be selected from another school. Therefore, the control group comprised 41 Grade 7 (also 11 to 12 year old) children from two classes at an adjacent, urban, middle-class, primary school in Harare. No pupil in this group received any computer instruction in school either before or during this study.

2.1.1 Equipment

BBC microcomputers, each equipped with an EPROM - based, Logo programme by Acornsoft [24] were used.

2.1.3 Measures

The following four subscales of the Wechsler Intelligence Scale for Children - Revised (Wechsler [25]).

2.1.3.1 Arithmetic

Children are required to perform numerical calculations.

2.1.3.2 Vocabulary

Children are asked to define the meaning of words.

2.1.3.3 Block Design

Children are required to produce various designs with patterned blocks, which provides a measure of spatial reasoning.

Picture Arrangement

Children are asked to organize a set of pictures in logical sequence, which provides a measure of problem solving.

2.1.4 Procedure

Experimental condition children received about 45 minutes tuition each week in Logo. There were usually two pupils per microcomputer. Pre-tests were held at the end of the academic year.

2.2 RESULTS

The use of a quasi-experimental, non-equivalent control group design necessitated use of multiviate analysis of covariance, with pre-test scores as the covariate. Performance on the four measures of cognitive ability served as the dependent variable. A 2x2x2 factorial design was employed, with experimental condition (experimental, control), sex (girl, boy) and race (black, white) as the factors. Main effects and all possible interactions between these factors were examined. The MANOVA main effect for experimental condition was significant, $F(4,78) = 3.25$, p .05. Univariate ANOVAs were computed to establish where the differences lay. Experimental group children achieved significantly higher convariate adjusted post-test scores on the arithmetic measure, $F(1,81) = 6.73$, p. 01.

One of all possible higher order interactions was significant. The experimental condition x sex x race MANOVA was significant, $F(4,78) = 3,88$, p .01. Univariate ANOVAs indicated that this significant result was accounted for by the large covariate adjusted gains on the spatial reasoning measure made relative to other groups, by black girls in the experimental condition, $F(1,81) =$ p. .01.

2.3 DISCUSSION

Results suggested that Logo may promote numeracy. Interestingly, black girls exposed to Logo achieved particular gains in spatial reasoning. Technologically orientated cognitive skills may be less emphasized among black girls than among other groups of children. Logo's emphasis on spatial reasoning may thus be of special relevance to black girls.

This suggestion, albeit very tentative, raises interesting questions about the possible contribution of Logo to compensatory education.

An important limitation of this study was the absence of a control group comprising children exposed to another form of educational computing.

The design used does not enable one to differentiate the effects of Logo from those of computer exposure in general. The gains observed may have been due to computer exposure, not to Logo itself. It is even possible that an equal amount of appropriate non-computer instruction or practice in numerical or spatial concepts might have had equal or greater effects. Another major reservation concerns the measure of cognitive ability used, the Wechsler Intelligence Scale for Children-Revised, which like other standardized tests of Intellectual abilities, tends to be culturally-biased and of limited sensitivity.

To redress the absence of a control group exposed to another form of educational computing, another study, including such a control group, was undertaken.

3. STUDY II

3.1 MATERIALS AND METHODS

3.1.1 Subjects

The experimental group comprised 49 (23 black. 26 white) girls from both Grade 4 (8 to 9 years old) classes at a middle-class urban primary school for girls. As all girls in Grade 4 at this school did Logo, the control group, which consisted of 58 (29 black, 29 white) girls, was drawn from both Grade 4 (8 to 9 years old) classes at another urban middle-class, primary school for girls. Neither group had received any exposure to computers at the outset of the project.

3.1.2 Equipment

Both schools were equipped with BBC micro-computers.

3.1.3 Measures

The SRA Primary Mental Abilities test for Grades 2-4 (Thurstone [26]). It is a group test comprising the following subscales:

3.1.3.1 Number Facility

Children are examined on numerical concepts, mechanical arithmetic, arithmetical problems and numerical reasoning.

3.1.3.2 Verbal Meaning

Children are given a noun and must select from four choices the picture depicting the noun and are given a short narrative and must identify from four choices the picture that completes the narrative

3.1.3.3 Spatial Relations

Children are shown an incomplete square and are required to select from four choices the segment that completes the square.

3.1.3.4 Perceptual Speed

Children are given a figure and must select from four choices the figure corresponding to that given.

3.1.4 Procedure

Children in the experimental group received about 40 minutes tuition each week in a Logo programme by Acornsoft [24]. There were generally two chldren per microcomputer. Class teachers taught the children Logo and they had been taught Logo by the authors. Several workshops were held for the teachers and they also received tuition manuals prepared by the authors.

Control group children received roughly 40 minutes exposure to Computer-Aided-Instruction each week. Commercial Computer-Aided-Instruction packages written for the BBC micro-computer were used. Most packages taught English or mathematics. There were usually two children to each computer. Lessons were taken by the class teachers, who were taught to use the microcomputers by the schools' computing master. Post-tests were held approximately 10 months after the pre-tests.

3.2 RESULTS

Data were again analyzed with multivariate analysis of convariance, using pre-test scores as the covariate. The depedent variable was performance on the Primary Mental Abilities scales. A 2x2 factorial design was employed with experimental condition (experimental, control) and race (black, white) as the factors. The school, $F(4,90) = 2.00$, $p \quad .05$, and race, $F(4,90) = 0,88$, $p \quad .05$, MANOVAs were non-significant as was the school x race MANOVA interaction, $F(4,90) = 1.22$, $p \quad .05$.

3.3 DISCUSSION

Conclusions about the effectiveness of Logo must be tempered by several concerns. Although skilled teachers taught Logo, they had no previous exposure to computer education, which may have limited the effectiveness of the Logo treatment. Pea and Kurland [10] emphasize that cognitive benefits are not inherent in Logo, but depend on how it is used. They criticize the Logo literature for failing to specify how educators may use Logo to stimulate intellectual development.

Classroom observation revealed that many children were unfamiliar with the keyboard, which inhibited Logo learning. Pre-Logo keyboard familiarization activities would thus be desirable /¯13¯/.

Kurland, Pea, Clement and Mawby /¯8¯/ emphasize that typical Logo curricula offer too limited an exposure for students to master integral programming concepts and without such mastery, wide transfer of thinking skills is unlikely to occur.

There were difficulties integrating Logo into the curriculum. The pupils had not learned about angles in Logo and this concept had to be introduced during Logo classes.

Concerns about the sensitivity of the dependent measures merit reiteration.

4. CONCLUSIONS

Because Study II did not include comparison groups who received non-computer based Logo instruction or no supplementary instruction, it was not possible to compare the effects of Logo or Computer-Aided-Instruction with non-computer instruction or a standard curriculum. It is therefore uncertain whether both these forms of educational computing are equally effective or equally ineffective. This question is important, for if evidence were to suggest either or both had some benefits, it would be desirable to examine whether their key elements could be simulated without computers, with, for example, tasks involving distance and angles substituting for Logo and programmed instruction manuals replacing Computer-Aided-Instruction. If the educational benefits of computing could be realized without computers, this would be of obvious value in developing countries, where the widespread installation of computers is unaffordable.

The scope of this research must be expanded, both within and beyond the domain of Logo. Concerning the former, LOGO is a highly modular language, which is premised to reduce computer anxiety and foster good programming habits. Research must examine whether Logo does help to reduce computer anxiety and whether students in secondary and tertiary institutions exposed of programming through Logo do indeed demonstrate better programming habits. Concerning the latter, does exposure to programming at primary level produce significant gains in programming ability at secondary, tertiary or vocational levels? Does exposure to computing applications in primary school yield discernable gains later? These questions have important implications for policy, because negative results would suggest it would be more appropriate to focus computer resources at secondary, tertiary or vocational level.

In conclusion, some developing countries are introducing computers into education in haste in the hope that this may provide a shortcut to development. These and other data suggest that the benefits of educational computing may be more modest and that if they are even to have a modest impact, the way in which they are to be introduced must be determined by the accumulating findings of ongoing empirical studies. Above all, educators in developing countries must weigh the benefits of computers against those of funding other, often mundane, educational priorities.

REFERENCES

/¯1¯/ Papert, S. Mindstorms: Children, Computers and Powerful Ideas (Basic Books, New York, 1980).

/¯2¯/ Papert, S.D. Watt, D., Disessa, A. and Weir, S. Final Report of the Brookline Logo Project. Part II : Project Summary and Data Analysis (Massachussets Institute of Technology, Massachussets, 1971).

/¯3¯/ Papert, S. and Weir, S., Information prosthetics for the handicapped. memo 51 (Massachussetts Institute of Technology, Massachussetts, 1978).

/¯4¯/ Weir, S. LOGO as an information prosthetic for the handicapped. Seventh International Joint Conference Artificial Handicap. (Massachussetts Institute of Technology Massachussets, 1979).

/¯5¯/ Clements, D.H., and Gullo, D.F. Effects of computer programming on young children's cognition Journal of Educational Psychology (1984) 76 1051-1058.

/¯6¯/ Hughes, M. Macleod, H. and C. Potts, C., Using LOGO with infant school children. Educational Psychology 5 (1985) 287 - 301.

/¯7¯/ Krasnor, L.R. and Mitterer, J.O. Logo Logo and the development of general problem solving skills. The Alberta Journal of Education Research (1984) 30 133-144.

/¯8¯/ Kurland, D.M., Pea, R.D., Clement, C., and Mawby, R. A study of the development of programming ability and thinking skills in high school students Technical Report, with Appendices. (New York : Centre for Children and Technology, Bank Street College of Education, 1985).

/¯9¯/ Mitteret, J. and Rose-Krasnor, L.R. Logo and the transfer of problem solving: an empirical test.

The Alberta Journal of Educational Research (1985) 32 176 - 194.

[10] Pea, R.D. and Kurland, D.M. On the cognitive effects of learning computer programming. New Ideas in Psychology (1984) 2 137 - 168.

[11] Siann., G and Macleod, H. Computers and children of primary school age: issues and questions. British Journal of Educational Technology (1986) 17 133 - 144.

[12] Chang, M.K. Logo research in general and special education. Proceedings: Second European LOGO conference (Gent, Belgium, 1989) pp 219 - 234.

[13] Robinson, M.A. Feldman, P., and Uhlig, G.E. The effects of LOGO in the elementary classroom: An analysis of selected recent dissertation research. Education (1987) 107 434 - 442.

[14] Maddux, C.D. Logo: scientific dedication or religious foundation in the 1990s? Educational Technology (1989) 29, 18 - 23.

[15] Berry, J.W. Towards a universal psychology of cognitive competence. International Journal of Psychology (1984) 19 335 - 361.

[16] Dasen, P. The cross-cultural study of intelligence. Piaget and the Baoule. International Journal of Psychology (1984) 19 407 - 434.

[17] Irvine, S.H. Contribution of ability and attainment testing in Africa to a general theory of intellect. Journal Biosocial Sciences, (1989) 1 91 - 102.

[18] Irvine, S.H. Affect and construct: a cross-cultural check on theories of intelligence. Journal of Social Psychology (1970) 80, 23 - 30.

[19] Kingsley, P.R. The measurement of intelligence in Africa: some conceptual issues and related research. University of Zambia Human Development Research Reports (Lusaka 1977, 28.)

[20] Mundy-Castle, A.C. The descent of meaning. Social Science Information (1970) 9 125-141.

[21] Serpell, R. Estimates of Intelligence in a rural community of eastern Zambia. University of Zambia Human Development Research Reports (Lusaka 1974 25).

[22] Serpell. R. Strategies for investigating in its cultural context. Institute for Comparative Human Development Quarterly Newsletter (1977) 1 11 - 15.

[23] Wober, M. Culture and the concept of intelligence. Journal of Cross-Cultural Psychology (1972) 3 327 - 328.

[24] Acornsoft LOGO. (Acornsoft, Cambridge, 1984).

[25] Wechsler, D. Wechsler Intelligence Scale for Children - Revised (The Psychological Corporation, New York, 1974)

[26] Thurstone, T.G. Examiners manual for the Primary Mental Abilities for Grades 2 - 4 (Science Research Associates, Chicago, 1963).

Computers in Education
A. McDougall and C. Dowling (Editors)
Elsevier Science Publishers B.V. (North-Holland)

PRE-UNIVERSITY COMPUTER EDUCATION IN THE PEOPLE'S REPUBLIC OF CHINA AND THE SOVIET UNION: AN ANALYSIS OF TWO PROFESSIONAL EXCHANGES

Judith D. WILSON

Computer and Information Sciences, Temple University, Philadelphia, PA 19122, U. S. A.

G. Joy TEAGUE

Department of Computing and Mathematics, Deakin University, VICTORIA, 3217, Australia

In 1987, a delegation of computer professionals with interests in computer science education participated in an information exchange with colleagues in the People's Republic of China. In 1989, a similar delegation visited Bulgaria and the Soviet Union. We report on the delegations' observations of computer education in Chinese and Soviet primary and secondary schools. Our site visits and discussions with Chinese and Soviet educators suggest that the curriculum efforts in both countries face difficult problems but that although many of the problems are similar the approaches to solving them are quite different.

1. INTRODUCTION

During May 1987, at the invitation of the Chinese Computer Federation, a delegation of computer professionals from the United States, Australia and Europe with interests in computer education participated in a three week information exchange with colleagues in the People's Republic of China. The exchange was coordinated through the People to People International Citizen Ambassador program, a non-profit organization that promotes international exchange, and was led by Dr. Robert Aiken. Details of the exchange were arranged in China by the Chinese Computer Federation.

In May and June 1989 a similar delegation visited Bulgaria and the Soviet Union. This delegation was the first to be hosted by the Soviet Academy of Sciences by an invitation arranged through Y. P. Velikhov, a Vice President of the Academy. The exchange was coordinated through the People to People organization and again led by Professor Aiken.

As participants in these delegations, our objectives were to observe the current state and direction of computer education in the host nations and to discover differences between Western and Chinese and Soviet approaches to computer instruction. An important additional objective of the delegation to the Soviet Union was to observe and compare work in computer-based education and the use of Artificial Intelligence models in developing intelligent systems. Our hosts in both countries provided tours of their computing facilities and demonstrations of software products developed for commercial and instructional uses. Delegation members also had an opportunity to visit computer laboratories and to observe class sessions in many of the sites visited.

Members of each delegation visited select institutions in several cities in the host countries. The institutions visited are listed in Table 1 and Table 2. Site visits did not follow a standard protocol, and in many cases the visits were brief. Consequently, the information we gathered from these visits is neither uniform nor complete. Moreover, there was little attempt to structure the two exchanges to enable accurate comparisons between computer education programs and philosophies in the two countries. Nonetheless, accumulated informal observations and written documentation [1] have provided insight into the status of computer education in the two countries and permit some informal comparisons. Our experiences in China and in the Soviet Union are discussed separately in the following two sections.* These experiences are analyzed and compared in the final section.

2. PEOPLE'S REPUBLIC OF CHINA (1987)

2.1 Computer education in the primary and middle schools.

Primary school education comprises the first six years of formal training while secondary education is provided by junior and senior middle schools during the next six years. Students who have completed three years of junior middle school training are recruited by vocational or general senior middle schools. General schools prepare students to compete for admission to universities while vocational schools provide students with specific job skill training. By the time students enter senior middle school, their general vocational or professional direction has been determined [2].

A small percentage of primary and middle schools are designated as "key" by the Ministry of Education based on past excellence in education. Key schools receive a large proportion of governmental resources allocated to education and are generally affiliated with a university or enterprise. These affiliates provide equipment, lecturers, teacher training, and curriculum and pedagogical direction. Over 98 percent of graduates of the best key middle schools are admitted to universities. In contrast, a very small percent of non-key school graduates pursue a university education.

Professional computer studies were instituted in China during the late 1950's. However, due to China's political and economic isolation during the 1960's and 70's, and particularly the repressive Cultural Revolution (1966 - 1976), computer education developed only recently and still suffers from a shortage of trained teachers and equipment [3, 4].

Computer instruction was first introduced into key middle schools in 1982-83 and into key primary schools in 1984 [5]. Since this time, national initiatives in computer education have been largely confined to key schools in larger cities and economically advanced areas where a concentration of scarce computing resources can be found.

National plans to expand computer education throughout China do not propose to have all schools conform to a single standard. In fact, the amount of funding targeted for education at the national level, estimated at about 2.5 percent of the national income [6, 7], probably could not support a thorough-going reform of any aspect of the educational system. Consequently, the Chinese encourage local planning and initiative in developing computer activities and curricula in the primary and middle schools, and this permits regional differences to flourish.

2.2 Curriculum

2.2.1 Primary school curriculum

Chinese primary schools that have computer programs typically offer computer instruction as an extra-curricular activity. Those schools that include computer education in the curriculum have done so recently. In the Experimental Primary School in Xi'an and Nanjing's No. 1 Elementary School, for example, computer instruction became part of the curriculum in 1986 and 1987 respectively. Both schools had about twenty microcomputers each in 1987, a large number for Chinese primary schools.
All primary school children are introduced to the abacus and to calculators that are, we were told, easily available and inexpensive. However, if computers are available, students may be introduced to keyboarding and computer fundamentals in their fourth and sixth years for one or two periods a week. The curriculum generally consists of BASIC language programming, although some teachers we met in Beijing and Shanghai considered Logo a more appropriate introductory language for children. A few schools, such as Beijing Gucheng No. 2 Primary School, have integrated computer-based training systems into the curriculum.

2.2.2 Middle School Curriculum.

Computer education is typically offered only as an extra-curricular activity in middle schools. In the schools where computer education is part of the curriculum, it is usually taught in the first and second years of the senior middle school for 40 to 60 hours a semester. The plan of study normally includes an introduction to the general functions of the computer and its impact on modern society along with an introduction to programming and problem solving using the BASIC language [8]. The only school we visited that deviated from this pattern was Shanghai No. 2 Middle school where students were introduced to computer programming with one semester of Logo.

The Chinese are beginning to integrate computers into other areas of the curriculum at several of the schools we visited. At the Experimental Middle School in Guangzhou, for example, we observed a mathematics class which had both a lecture and a computer laboratory component.

2.3 Computer Centers and Institutes

Computer centers and institutes have been created to foster computer literacy among the youth and to train computer teachers. These centers offer intensive structured extra-curricular programs for motivating and training talented youth. Such centers are often founded with gifts from Chinese and foreign agencies. Enterprises, universities, and the Chinese government then become involved in their organization and continuing support, providing qualified instructional and technical staff as well as equipment. We visited several of these centers, including the Beijing ComputerLand Institute and the Children's Palace Computer Center in Shanghai.

The Beijing ComputerLand Institute was established in May 1985 with a donation of 64 microcomputers and 60 printers from the ComputerLand Company in the United States. The Institute had 112 computers of different types when we visited in 1987 [9]. The

Beijing Science and Technology Association and other Chinese agencies provide teachers and facilities and determine the curriculum to be offered by the Institute.

The Institute provides extra-curricular computer activities for children and young people, fosters information exchange, and functions as a computer training base. During the Institute's first two years, 20,000 students were taught to program in BASIC. The Institute also sponsors computing competitions and lectures for children and youth, and serves as a liaison between outstanding students and universities.

Children's Palaces have been planned by the Chinese government for a number of municipalities throughout China. These Palaces are intended as centers for extra-curricular training and structured activities in various disciplines for talented youth. The objective is to build proficiency in a student's chosen interest.

Members of our Delegation visited the Computer Center associated with the Children's Palace in Shanghai. Enrollment in the Center is based on performance on a citywide examination. In 1986, the top 15 percent of examinees were selected to attend. The center offers four levels of classes with training in data structures, operating systems, fundamental algorithms and structured programming. Students enroled in the fourth level design and develop programs for educational use.

2.4 Resources

2.4.1 Computing Equipment

There are regional differences in the availability of computing equipment in China. Guangzhou, for example, which benefits economically from its proximity to Hong Kong, had 1700 microcomputers in its schools in 1987. This represents about 3.2 percent of the 53,950 microcomputers owned by or available to China's primary and middle schools [8].

Throughout most of China, however, schools that offer computer education programs must make do with minimal computing resources. Commonly, a few microcomputers, or a single machine, are operated for long hours through the week, and shared by many students for short periods of time each.

The schools we visited all had microcomputer laboratories containing a variety of computers. Most of these machines were Apple II, IBM and Apple clones. But there were many other types as well, including Sinclair Spectra, Lessai, Comax, LASER-310, COMX-35, DTS-83A, PZ80, US21, as well as the Chinese made Panda-100.

In the early 1980s, China's microcomputer industry was largely limited to assembly of imported kits [10], and to duplication of foreign software and equipment [11]. China now has its own microcomputer factories and manufactures microcomputers such as the GF20 ("Great Wall") series of microcomputers designed and produced at the Beijing Guangdong Computer Institute in Guangzhou. It was reported in 1986 that China would be able to manufacture 100,000 microcomputers within two years, more than double the quantity produced in 1985 [12].

2.4.2 Teachers

There is a general shortage of qualified teachers in China in all disciplines and at all levels of education. The teacher shortage is attributed to a number of factors including low pay, poor living conditions, generally low public esteem, and poor working conditions [6, 7, 13, 14, 15]. Few teachers have had a university education and some possess no more than a junior middle school education [2]. Teachers trained during the Cultural Revolution must supplement their weak training with additional courses for certification [3, 16].

So far, key schools have been the primary beneficiaries of national reforms intended to attract more teachers and improve the quality of instruction. Nowhere in China has teacher pay and esteem gained the ground lost during the Cultural Revolution [7].

The shortage of qualified teachers is critical in the area of computer instruction. Our Chinese hosts informed us that teachers can get their computer training through programs offered by universities and by regional or local computer centers, or by participating in special computer workshops [See also 14, 17]. Computer teachers in the primary and middle schools are usually former mathematics or physics teachers, and their retraining may last from one month to several years [8, 18].

Members of the Delegation visited a teacher training base in Xi'an, the Shaanxi Province Educational Institute. The Institute was founded in 1978 to provide additional training for middle school teachers, among others. All students at the Institute are provided with a general computer education consisting of two courses: a first course that introduces general hardware and software concepts, and a second course that teaches BASIC Programming. In view of the approaches to computer instruction in middle schools visited by the Delegation, the teacher training program at the Shaanxi Institute is probably typical.

In spite of efforts to train more computer teachers, plans to implement universal computer literacy in some of China's large cities will further tax the already inadequate instructional staff. Chinese educators consider instructional technology to be the most promising way to deal with this inevitability since it can both extend teacher productivity and provide one way to achieve broad-based teacher training [11, 14, 19].

2.5 Computer-Based Education

Development and production of instructional technology in China includes educational television and radio, video and audio tapes of lectures by qualified professionals, and computer-based education technology [14, 19]. The importance attached to computer-based education is indicated by the fact that teachers using computer-assisted instruction (CAI) systems must now be trained and certified at a teacher training base [5].

A 1986 report on CAI technology in China reports that most CAI software is not standardized, hence not portable, and that most CAI packages stress grammar rather than communication skills, drill rather than understanding [12]. Yet it is apparent that CAI technology is an active research area at key universities in China and that Chinese educators are searching for instructional techniques that will foster understanding rather than drill.

Our delegation found that CAI technology is an active research area for computer scientists in several of the universities we visited including Xi'an Jiaotong University. Shortly after our visit to China, Chinese researchers described a variety of research projects on CAI software during an IFIP conference on microcomputers in secondary education held in Japan. A number of projects were described by research teams from China [20]. One team described a courseware-authoring language that provides pattern recognition facilities enabling more appropriate and flexible responses to student input [21]. Another team is working on an intelligent instructional system for algebra that features an "expert analyzing module" for error diagnosis with quick feedback. The system also selects appropriate instructional strategies based on types of error.

2.6 Competition, Innovation and Dedication to National Goals.

The computer curriculum in many schools and institutes is now geared toward discovering and training talented students for programming competitions. Preparation for high-level competitions begins months in advance and may include help from outside computer experts. In some cases, extra-curricular student organizations have been formed to select and train the most gifted competitors. Involvement in computer competitions increases student interest in computer technology and producing competition winners is the most effective way for a computer education program to prove that it is worthy of additional support from governmental and nongovernmental institutions [22, 23].

Programming competitions are held at school, municipal, provincial and national levels with only very few winners from each level allowed to participate at the next highest level. The most prestigious competition is the annual National Teenagers' Computer Programming Competition, founded in 1984 and sponsored by the Chinese Computer Federation and other state organizations. National competition winners may be accepted early at prestigious universities and receive other honors as well.

A new shift in attitude favoring creativity and initiative in Chinese primary and middle school education has been reported [17, 24] and encouraged [25, 26], and was noted in the key schools visited by members of our Delegation. Computer students are encouraged not only to be competitive, but to take the initiative and to be innovative. At the national level, innovativeness is one of the qualities prized in software entries for the National Teenagers' Programming Competition [23]. We also found that educators in key Shanghai middle schools and universities are interested in encouraging greater responsibility and discouraging passive learning among young computer students. Yet independence and initiative are encouraged within a well-understood framework of social responsibility and dedication to national goals.

3. THE SOVIET UNION (1989)

3.1 Computer education in the primary and middle schools

There is no clear distinction between primary and secondary education in the Soviet Union with some schools offering classes from grades 1 to 11 (equivalent to our grades 2 to 12) [27]. Almost all schools, vocational and nonvocational, are affiliated with some enterprise or institute [28]. In 1983-84 over 90 percent of nonvocational schools were general schools. The remaining schools were specialized schools emphasizing one subject, for example mathematics or a foreign language. Entry to most specialized schools is competitive and based on previous academic performance.

Vocational schools train students for a particular occupation and offer continuing education classes in the evening. Two representative schools were visited by our delegation in Moscow, the Electromechanical College which trains engineers and engineering technicians and Vocational School No. 199 for metalworkers, computer operators and secretaries. Students may enter these schools as early as grade eight or as late as grade eleven. The vocational tracks are of one to five years duration and each provides students with skills for a different level of employment in industry or in a research institute. Each student is channelled into a suitable course of study and is employed on graduation since work is guaranteed by Soviet law.

Computer technology and education are significantly less advanced in the Soviet Union than in western countries. Early Soviet computing research and development was in the hands of the military and kept pace with western computing development. The large scale commercial use of computers which began in the 1960s and has been the impetus for much of the computing research and development in Western countries for the past thirty years, ran counter to the Soviet policy of controlling information and Soviet computing technology has not maintained its early promise [29]. In addition, the Soviet government decision to cancel the computer division in the Academy of Sciences in 1962 further hampered development of computing technology [29]. Meanwhile, the Western embargo on the export of any technology with possible military applications (monitored by the Paris-based organization COCOM [30]) has made it impossible for the Soviets to obtain legally state of the art computers.

Computer education also has been affected by these national policies. In the mid-1960s non-compulsory computer science courses were available in secondary schools throughout the Soviet Union [27]. Yet by 1984 the Siberian Division of the Soviet Academy of Sciences in Novosibirsk (which has been a leader in Soviet computer education research) deemed only two Russian schools to be using computers successfully [30]. In that year Mikhail Gorbachev headed a commission which recommended more vocational counseling and training in education [31]. Consistent with this recommendation was the Politburo directive the following year that all secondary students study computing (or "informatics") in grades nine and ten [31, 32, 33].

All schools throughout the Soviet Union follow a standard curriculum for each discipline, including a detailed syllabus, and use the same texts [27]. The goals, methods, tools and texts for the new informatics course sequence, "Basic Information Science and Computer Technology", have been developed by a team of scientists headed by A. P. Ershov of the Academy of Sciences in Novosibirsk and V. M. Monakhov of the Academy of Pedagogical Sciences in Moscow [32]. During the summer of 1985 thousands of mathematics and physics teachers were trained to teach the first course of the sequence which was introduced during the 1985-86 academic year.

Although the content and methods to be used in the new course had been planned in detail, there were insufficient textbooks, equipment and software to ensure that all schools followed the plan when the course was introduced. This gave teachers an opportunity to develop their own curriculum and software and resulted in greater diversification of approaches and supporting materials than in other subjects [28]. This unusual situation may be consistent with a new Soviet policy on education. A representative of the Ministry of Education in Moscow explained to us that this is a time of new concepts and experiments in the Soviet Union and that, accordingly, the new model of education is less rigid than the previous model.

There is no national policy for informatics education in elementary schools yet. The programs we saw at this level were rare and experimental. Most of these programs have introduced computers into education to help teach other subjects such as mathematics or languages, or to foster creativity, or to support pedagogical research.

The Delegation visited a number of schools and scientific institutes with research programs in educational computing. The schools we visited were well-endowed with computing resources and were not representative of typical schools. The scientific institutes we visited either support model schools such as the Baytik Computer Science Center in Troitsk, or administer short term computer camps for children such as those managed by the Program Systems Institute at Pereslavl-Zalessky.

3.2 Curriculum

3.2.1 Primary school curriculum

Computers are not readily available in primary schools. The schools which do own computers have had them provided by some organization which has an interest in the school and has raised or made available funds to purchase one or more computers. In some cases, schools that use computers are associated with scientific or pedagogical research institutes where efforts are made to collect data that bear on the effectiveness of educational software or on the development of cognitive models of learning. Kindergarten No. 1623 in Moscow is the home of the Play and Learn (PAL) Computer Centre for Pre-School Education, developed by Electronica Central Scientific Research Institute and Scientific Research Institute for pre-school education of the USSR Academy of Pedagogical Sciences. The PAL center contains a room with eight Soviet made Electronica BK-0010 computers and Electronica C401M color TV sets. The computers sit on specially designed tables and run educational programs each with its own keyboard cover where the children are required to press a picture on the cover. Data from these machines are collected for analysis by psychologists. Uri Gorvitz, a software expert with the project, admitted that he and his colleagues have found it as challenging as military projects and more enjoyable. Computer scientists at the Program Systems Institute in Pereslavl-Zalessky and at the V. Glushkov Institute of Cybernetics in Kiev made similar remarks about the research challenges offered by the educational use of computers.

Versions of Logo are used throughout the school system [28, 33, 34]. The kindergarten at the Baytik Computer Science Center in Troitsk had about a dozen IBM AT compatible computers (American Research Corporation computers made in Taiwan) which were running games and some graphics software when we visited. At Baitik, children learn LOGO when they begin school. They are taught angles at the age of five and coordinates at the age of seven. Our guide, a teacher at the Centre, spoke with great intensity of the failure of the school system to handle both slow and advanced learners and the benefits these two groups gained from using computers at the Centre.

3.2.2 Secondary school curriculum

The required secondary school informatics curriculum is supported by a text, student workbook and teacher's guide. The program allows for one hour of instruction a week in grades nine and ten [28, 33]. Schools with access to computers offer a computer laboratory component in year ten for an additional hour a week. The year nine course designed in 1984-85 was centred around algorithms, while the year ten course emphasised computer design and operation, programming and the role of computers in society and the economy [35, 36].

The Informatics course has been recently revised to include increased emphasis on data structures, programming strategies and other concepts [27]. Three hundred thousand copies of a revised text have been distributed and are being tested [27, 28, 33]. However, the updated course still places a high priority on algorithms. Word processing, database and spreadsheet packages have little application in the Soviet Union and are not included in these classes. The purpose of the secondary computing syllabus is to train students who will be using them in scientific and technical fields [31]. Informatics will be next introduced at grades seven and eight and eventually at lower grades [27].

The Soviets have traditionally promoted the development of algorithmic thinking and the new informatics course builds on this tradition. The objectives are to develop the ability to express algorithms using flowcharts (graphical notation), algorithmic languages (pseudocode) and programming languages [35]. In the view of the curriculum designers, computer science is concerned not so much with programming computers as it is with algorithmic problem-solving. Within this general focus, however, we noted variations. Comparing the computer camps sponsored by the Program Systems Institute at Pereslavl-Zalessky and the Baytik center, scientists at the Institute considered the Baytik camps to have more of an engineering focus. Yet, at Baytik, where computers are integrated throughout the curriculum, wall posters explaining Ershov's algorithmic methods are displayed prominently on laboratory walls.

Where computing is being taught a school tries to associate with an enterprise or institute which can provide technical support [28]. Those schools which do have their own facilities share them with neighbouring schools [28, 33]. Schools without access to computers use calculators to teach algorithmic skills. Electromechanical devices which can be used to simulate computers are being developed for classroom use [37].

3.3 Resources

3.3.1 Computing equipment

The twelfth five year plan called for one million computers in sixty thousand secondary schools by 1990 [30, 31, 33]. It was envisaged that there would be ten to fifteen personal computers in a laboratory and twenty to twenty-five terminals connected to a more powerful system [31]. The reality is likely to be one hundred thousand computers [28, 33]. A. Semenov, Deputy Director of the school project and member of the Academy of Sciences, estimated that approximately one in twenty Soviet schools has computers. The plan has been hampered by low production and poor quality of local products [29, 37, 38] and the embargo on the importation of state of the art western technology. Like Porteous [28], we saw computers only in laboratories, never in individual classrooms, in all of the schools we visited. The majority of the machines were 8-bit micros running a version of CP/M. The few 16-bit and mainframe computers generally were copies of IBM machines, including ATs and IBM 360s. Versions of the Apple II are common and there are a large number of Yamaha machines imported from Japan. These latter were apparently a bulk purchase from Japan to equip schools for the new program when locally produced computers were not available [28, 31].

Locally produced hardware is unreliable and well behind state of the art western hardware in all areas. Chips, floppy disks and printers are included in the diversity of products which are substandard [28, 29, 33, 37]. Efforts to increase production and improve quality have not been as successful as anticipated [28, 39]. In many of the schools we visited, students used either cassette tape or a file server as secondary storage devices and printers were rare [37].

The Soviet telephone system is notoriously unreliable and is unsuitable for computer communication [29, 31]. We visited two school centres which have facilities for external electronic communication. Both schools communicate with schools in other countries but not with other Soviet schools. For most schools it is likely to be many years before external electronic mail or database searches are feasible.

Computer keyboards ranged from the standard qwerty keyboard through keyboards with both Roman and Cyrillic character sets to wholly Cyrillic keyboards. Roman letters did not necessarily follow the qwerty layout. In some rooms a number of combinations of alphabet and layout were available. The teachers did not consider that students had any difficulty learning and using several different keyboard layouts.

3.3.2 Teachers

The summer of 1985 saw a massive training program to retrain 60,000 mathematics and physics teachers for the introduction of the new informatics course at the beginning of that school year [31, 32]. Teachers were required to gain a detailed knowledge of the new study guide, copies of which were in short supply. Following this came a study of algorithms using scientific calculators. The final stage was hands on experience with computers, although it is doubtful that this could be obtained by all trainees. This training program was conducted by experienced computer users but not necessarily by experienced teachers. The program was not considered to be notably successful [31]. There are currently 60,000 to 80,000 mathematics and physics teachers teaching computing and retraining programs are continuing [27].

Reeves [33] reports that a teacher shortage is expected in the 1990s. In common with their western counterparts, Soviet teachers are experiencing pay and working condition problems. Despite this, we met many exceptionally loving and caring teachers who exhibited intense pride in the achievements of their students.

3.3.3 Computer-Based Education

The applications which we most often saw in schools were programming with third generation languages, most commonly BASIC, computer games and CAI packages. Generally CAI packages are more structured and of lower standard than in the west and include more drill and practice programs [31]. Despite this common problem, we were very impressed with much of the local software, particularly when the hardware and software limitations were taken into account.

A common solution to the scarcity of software is for teachers to make use of whatever resources are available to them. Frequently we were shown programs, both CAI and games, which had been developed by students and were in use in the teaching program. The BASIC language is typically used for this purpose although some schools also have Pascal, LOGO, FORTRAN and C.

Science classes at Baytik use computer-based tutorials and simulations. The practice at Baytik is to give students experience with course content by way of computer instruction and simulation before they use the actual equipment. The philosophy is that students will learn the concepts better and learn to use the equipment properly. These computer-based systems are created by students. We were shown an impressive superconductor simulator that had been written in BASIC by 13 and 14 year old students. The program was demonstrated on a Japanese made Duet 16 computer running under MS DOS with color graphics.

CAI projects provide challenges for Soviet school students and members of extra curricula computer clubs. But, perhaps more significantly, CAI is an active research and development area in scientific institutes and universities. Soviet scientists are using Artificial Intelligence techniques and models to build intelligent instructional software.

Scientists in Moscow, Kiev and Pereslavl-Zalessky described CAI systems that take a more flexible approach to education than simple drill and practice. In many cases, computer scientists, psychologists and educators are cooperating in these efforts. The systems described below are all grounded in psychological models of learning.

Scientists at Pereslavl-Zalessky are working on knowledge representation and knowledge bases for use with expert systems in tutorial software. Institute scientists developed the Robotland project which is designed to assist the teaching of algorithmic thinking to children between the ages of nine and twelve. The project is being tested in several schools in Pereslavl, Moscow and Leningrad and is the basis for the UNESCO sponsored summer camps [40].

The foundations and design of intelligent tutoring systems is an active research area for scientists at the Cybernetics Institute in Kiev. Institute scientists are developing several representative systems [41]. One of these is BETS, an intelligent tutor for an expert system building shell called BESS that uses a Bayesian approach to decision making to help domain experts develop knowledge bases [42].

4. MAKING SENSE OF IMPRESSIONS: A COMPARISON OF APPOACHES

We found computer educators in both the Soviet Union and China struggling with a shortage of computing resources and teachers needed to support ambitious national plans to achieve broad-based computer literacy. In China, the resource shortage is also impacting the development of computer science as a scientific discipline. The shortage of computers in both countries is exacerbated by a very small domestic computer industry and by restrictions on imports from western countries. Both China and the Soviet Union are experiencing shortages of well-qualified computer science and computer technology teachers in the schools, a problem that appears to be easing in western countries. The teacher shortage is far more critical in China due to extremely poor working conditions and a poor public image for intellectuals, including teachers.

Our observations in China in 1987 and in the Soviet Union two years later suggest that the Chinese and the Soviets are attempting in different ways to solve these resource problems and to achieve wide spread literacy and use of computers. The differences between the Soviet and Chinese approaches include differences in curriculum development, in computer education research and in the underlying interpretation of Computer Science.

The development of a pre-university computing curriculum appears to be more centralized in the Soviet Union than in China. The Chinese, perhaps out of necessity, are encouraging local ingenuity and experimentation in the development of computer education programs while the new curriculum developments in the Soviet Union are centrally organized and controlled and are fairly uniform across schools. It should be noted, however, that in spite of the lack of strong central control over computer education in China, we found that schools tended to have very similar curricula and focus. We found the Chinese willing to use computer science curriculum recommendations developed in western countries, particularly the United States, to structure their own programs. In China, most university Computer Science and Engineering programs followed ACM or IEEE curriculum recommendations while pre-university school programs focused on the use of computers and programming. In contrast, the Soviets have their own curriculum committees. Certainly these differences in approach to developing computer education programs must be attributed to differences in history and political structure in the two countries, but they also may be encouraged by a difference in assumptions about the nature of Computer Science.

One reads that Computer Science in the Soviet Union is practised as a fundamentally theoretical discipline, a science of algorithms firmly grounded in mathematics. Our experiences in the USSR were consistent with this understanding of Soviet Computer Science, while we found computer science programs in China heavily focused on engineering issues and problems. It is not likely that the Chinese would consider teaching Computer Science or computer literacy without computers, while the Soviets are doing just that. In China, local initiative allows enterprising and strategically located schools to obtain the scarce equipment required to support computer education. Scarce national and provincial government resources can then be channelled to a small percentage of the most promising programs.

Differences in Computer Science research programs in the USSR and China, including research into educational computing, were consistent with underlying differences in belief about the nature of Computer Science. The Chinese educators and research scientists we met did not appear concerned with algorithmic thinking as a goal distinct from the engineering of software and hardware to solve practical problems. We also noted that research agendas even at the most prestigious universities in China emphasized applications rather than theoretical foundations. In fact, this research focus has been encouraged as a matter of national policy. It is understood that technology based research should have practical economic benefits for China consistent with the goals of China's national five year plans for progress.

These differences in research focus were found also in research into computer assisted instruction. The Soviet scientists are committed to exploring theoretical foundations, to discovering psychological models of learning and development and to designing expert tutoring systems and computer-based learning environments based on these models. CAI research in China, at least in 1987, appeared to be far more results-oriented and less coordinated across research institutes, universities, computer centers and schools. The interest of Chinese researchers in CAI has been closely tied to the need to relieve the severe teacher shortage in China. Yet, while the Soviet scientists appeared to have a more theoretical interest in such research, they also believe that flexible computer-based systems can provide excellent support for teaching children languages, technology, mathematics and the natural sciences.

5. CONCLUSION

Computer educators and computer scientists in the Soviet Union and China are addressing many of the same problems in their attempts to implement national computer literacy agendas for the schools. Our visits to research institutes and schools in both countries suggest that the Chinese and the Soviets are solving these problems in different ways. These differences in approach may provide insights and alternatives useful for developing computer education programs in countries with less critical resource problems.

FOOTNOTE

* The section on China is based on a lengthier discussion in "Computer Education in the Primary and Middle Schools in the People's Republic of China: the Late 1980's" by H. P. Baouendi and J. D. Wilson which is forthcoming in *Education and Computing*.

REFERENCES

[1] *Journal: People to People Computers in Education Delegation to the People's Republic of China, May 12 - June 2, 1987*, Dr. Robert Aiken, Director (People to People Citizen Ambassador Program, January 1988).

[2] S. Thogersen, China's Senior Middle Schools in Social Perspective: A Survey of Yantai District, Shandong Province, *China Quarterly 109* (March 1987) 72-100.

[3] B. O. Szuprowicz, Electronics, in: L.A. Orleans, ed., *Science in Contemporary China* (Stanford University Press, Stanford, California, 1980) 435-461.

[4] Wang Ya-Min (Deputy Chairman & Secretary-General, China Computer Federation Education & Training Society), Computers in Education in China (Address to the Delegation, CAST Headquarters, Beijing, 16 May 1987).

[5] Computers in Education: An Outline of Country Experiences. *Report of the Asian Seminar on Educational Technology: China* (United Nations Educational, Scientific, and Cultural Organization, Bangkok, Thailand, 1985) 20-25.

[6] Ch'ien Chia-Chu, Problems of Economy, Education, Ethics (excerpted from Hong Kong, Wenhui Bao, April 1988), *Inside China Mainland 10* (6 June 1988) 9-12.

[7] The Crisis in Education (excerpted from People's Daily, March 3, 1988), *Inside China Mainland 10* (6 June 1988) 15-17.

[8] Chen Q., Microcomputer in Chinese Secondary Schools, in: S. Moriguti, S. Ohtsuki & T. Furugori, eds., *Microcomputers in Secondary Education* (North Holland, 1987) 377-381.

[9] *A Brief Introduction to Beijing Computerland Institute* (Beijing Computerland Institute, May 1987). Published in [17], Appendix C.

[10] D. Simon, China's Computer Strategy, *The China Business Review 13* (November-December 1986) 44-48.

[11] L. Gubser, China is Hungry for New Technology, *TechTrends For Leaders in Education and Training 31* (2) 15-18.

[12] Zhang C.D., Computer-Based Education in China, *Educational Technology* (July 1986) 41-43.

[13] Central Committee of the Democratic Alliance on the Present Condition of Intellectuals, A Petition on the Plight of Intellectuals (excerpted from Alliance Central Documents, November 1987), *Inside China Mainland 10* (6 June 1988) 13-15.

[14] S. Deng, Sweeping Reforms in Education, *China Reconstructs 34* (11) (1985) 15-17.

[15] Teaching Profession Downgraded (excerpted from Hong Kong, *Ta Kung Pao* 27 November 1987), *Inside China Mainland 10* (2 February 1988) 16.

[16] J. Johnston, A Traveler's Notes, *TechTrends For Leaders in Education and Training 31* (2) 19-22.

[17] Guo Wenxian, My Middle-School Students - A New Breed, *China Reconstructs 35* (2) (1986) 42, 44.

[18] M.-D. Pan, Computer Education of Young People, in: S. Moriguti, S. Ohtsuki & T. Furugori, eds., *Microcomputers in Secondary Education* (North Holland, 1987) 343-345.

[19] S.-K. Chen, C.-C. Hsu & J.-X. Lin, Development of Computer Education in China, in: S. Moriguti, S. Ohtsuki & T. Furugori, eds., *Microcomputers in Secondary Education* (North Holland, 1987) 7-13.

[20] S. Ohtsuki & T. Furugori, eds., *Microcomputers in Secondary Education* (North Holland, 1987).

[21] Lu L.-J., Wang J.-Q. & Wan J.-R., Authoring Language ALC: Design and Implementation, in: S. Moriguti, S. Ohtsuki & T. Furugori, eds., *Microcomputers in Secondary Education* (North Holland, 1987) 241-245.

[22] Chinese Computer Federation, Pamphlet printed in English and Chinese by the Chinese Computer Federation (CCF), Liaison: Chen Shukai, Senior Engineer or Jiang Siliu, Engineer, P.O. Box 2704 Beijing, China (1987).

[23] Zhoa (Guangzhou Municipal Education Bureau Department Director), The Outline of computer education in primary and middle schools in Guangzhou (Presentation to the Delegation on 28 May 1987). Published in [17], Appendix J.

[24] Zhang Ling, Encouraging Creativity: Middle School No. 161, *China Reconstructs 36* (6) (1987) 54-56.

[25] Tan R.-M., Zhuang M.-S. & Wendel, R., Education in the Information Age: The Impact on Teacher Education in China, *Educational Technology* (February 1988) 48-49.

[26] Wang S., How to Develop the Computer Training for School Children: A Pedagogic View, in: S. Moriguti, S. Ohtsuki & T. Furugori, eds., *Microcomputers in Secondary Education* (North Holland, 1987) 49-53.

[27] P. E. Resta, Technology in Soviet Schools: Up Close and Personal, *Electronic Learning* (April 1989) 7-9, 60.

[28] D. Porteous, CAI Russian Style, *T. H. E. Journal* (December/January 1988/1989) 75-78.

[29] Soviet Education, *Business Week* (7 November 1988) 68-78.

[30] R. Owen, Soviets Aim to Put Desk-Top Computers into All of Nation's Schools

and Colleges, *The Chronicle of Higher Education* (6 February 1985).

[31] S.T. Kerr, Soviet Applications of Microcomputers in Education: Developments in Research and Practice During the Gorbachev Era, *Journal of Educational Computing Research 3* (1) (1987) 1-17.

[32] The Introduction of Computer Science into Soviet Secondary Education (Editor's Introduction), *Soviet Education, A Journal of Translations XVIII* (10-11) (1986) 5-10.

[33] T.C. Reeves, East Meets West at Historic Educational Technology Conference in the U.S.S.R., *Electronic Learning* (January/February 1989) 20, 21.

[34] Y.A. Pervin, The Development of a Computer Science Course for Young Schoolchildren, *Proceedings of the Third International Conference on Children in the Information Age* (Preprints), Vol. 1 (Sofia, Bulgaria, May 1989) 373-385.

[35] V.M. Monakhov, The Content of the Basic Information Science and Computer Technology Course, *Soviet Education, A Journal of Translations XVIII* (10-11) (1986) 142-155.

[36] USSR Ministry of Education, On the Road to School Reform, *Soviet Education, A Journal of Translations XVIII* (10-11) (1986) 132-141.

[37] S. Morgenstern, Our Man in Moscow, *Family and Home-Office Computing* (June 1988) 51-53.

[38] Top Officials Discuss Computer Lag Problem, (*Pravda*, 31 January 89. Trans. from Russian) *Foreign Broadcast Information Service* (2 February 1989).

[39] L. Sorin, Ministry Hinders Personal Computer Industry, (*Izvestia*, 16 February 89. Trans. from Russian) National Affairs, *Foreign Broadcast Information Service* (6 March 1989) 95-97.

[40] A. Duvanov, Y.A. Pervin, Y.N. Zaidelman & E.N. Ermakov, Robotland, A.N. Prokhorov, Trans. (Institute of Software Systems of the USSR Academy of Sciences, Pereslavl, USSR).

[41] A. Dovgiallo & V. Gricento, Role of Computerized Teaching Technology in Informatization of Education, *Proceedings of the Third International Conference on Children in the Information Age* (Preprints), Vol. 2 (Sofia, Bulgaria, May 1989) 312-326.

[42] O.V. Ibragimov & V.A. Petrushin, Expert-Tutoring Systems: Concepts and Examples, *Proceedings of the Third International Conference on Children in the Information Age* (Preprints), Vol. 2 (Sofia, Bulgaria, May 1989) 350-361.

TABLE 1

Chinese Institutions Visited

City
  Institution
    Affiliation (if known)

Beijing
  Gucheng No. 2 Primary School
  Experimental Middle School
    Beijing University
  Computerland Institute
    Beijing Science & Technology Assoc.
Xi'an
  No. 1 Middle School
    Far Eastern Machinery Manufacturing Co.
  Middle School
    Shaanxi Normal University
  Experimental Primary School
  Shaanxi Province Educational Institute
Shanghai
  No. 2 Middle School
    East China Normal University
  Children's Palace
Hangzhou
  No. 1 Middle School
  Teenager's Activity Center
Nanjing
  No. 1 Elementary School
    Nanjing Normal University
  No. 4 Middle School
Guangzhou
  Experimental Middle School
  Zhixing Middle School
  Chao Tian Road Primary School

TABLE 2

Soviet Institutions Visited

City
  Institution
    Affiliation (if known)

Moscow
  Electromechanical College
    Moscow Inst. of Physical Engineering
  Vocational School #199
    Inst. of Theoretical & Exper. Physics
  Kindergarten # 1623
    Electronika Scientific Research Inst.
    Soviet Academy of Pedagogical Sciences
  Inst. of Electronic Machine Building
    Moscow
  Center, C.S. Education, Voroshilovshy Region
    Atomic Energy Institute
  Electric Engineering Institute
    Moscow
Troitsk
  Baytik: Interschool C.S. Center
    Atomic Energy Inst., among others
Pereslavl-Zalessky
  Institute of Program Systems
    USSR Academy of Sciences
  International Children's Computer Center
    UNESCO
Kiev
  V.M. Glushkov Inst. of Cybernetics
    Ukranian SSR Academy of Sciences
  Taras Shevchenko Kiev State University
  School # 57
Leningrad
  Leningrad State Pedagogical Institute
  Leningrad State University

WCCE 90 MINI-CONFERENCES

COMPUTERS IN EDUCATION: NATIONAL PERSPECTIVES

Computers in Education
A. McDougall and C. Dowling (Editors)
Elsevier Science Publishers B.V. (North-Holland)

ORGANIZING THE USE OF COMPUTERS IN SPECIAL EDUCATION IN NORWAY

Stig KLINGSTEDT

Director General, Ministry of Education and Research, Postbox 8119 Dep, 0032 Oslo 1, Norway

1. INTRODUCTION

For some years now, Norway has given priority to the development of peripherals, software and methodology for the use of computers in education. Parallel to this, it has been our aim to achieve an education which is adjusted to the individual needs of each pupil. This certainly also involves handicapped pupils, who so far primarily have received their education in special schools. In connection with the current integration of handicapped pupils in regular schools, computer technology is used as one of many tools. We are confident that with the development of relevant aids for the use of computers in schools, we shall be able to obtain results which will benefit both handicapped pupils and other pupils. Thus we hope to achieve a harmonious combination of forces effecting the whole school-system.

2. THE PRESENT SITUATION AS REGARDS THE EDUCATION OF HANDICAPPED PUPILS

As a consequence of compulsory education, all children have the right to schooling from the age of seven to fourteen. Handicapped youth also have a legal right to secondary education, but this is not compulsory. This means that municipal and county school authorities must provide education for all pupils at the primary level, as well as for handicapped youth who wish to continue their education at the secondary level. The laws concerning these matters have been passed during the last 15 years.

Previously, the education of handicapped pupils was the responsibility of state schools. Thus the state owns and administers 40 such schools. The majority of these are for pupils with learning difficulties or behaviour disorders. In addition, seven of the schools are for the partially hearing, two for the visually handicapped, and three for pupils with speech disorders.

The state schools for special education are boarding schools, where the pupils are taught and cared for during the school terms. This, however, means that the pupils must leave their natural surroundings and their homes, and the effect is therefore one of segregation for these pupils. The Norwegian Government and Parliament have decided to alter this by giving the municipalities the responsibility they should have according to law.

3. AIMS FOR THE INTEGRATION OF HANDICAPPED PUPILS IN REGULAR SCHOOLS

Segregation and isolation of specific groups of people is today considered humiliating, and therefore an obsolete "ideology". The aim is to create measures which can secure the right of all people to live a worthy life as full members of society. This thinking is expressed in the formulation of the main aims for special education in Norway.

"Society must establish conditions which guarantee medical, pedagogic and social help for all handicapped people, so that they may make the most of their abilities. An important principle in this thinking is normalization. This means that one must avoid creating unnecessary differences between the handicapped and others as regards medical and social treatment, upbringing, education, employment and behaviour."

It is an important principle that the Norwegian society provides educational opportunities for all, so that children and young people, with or without handicap, and irrespective of place of residence and social class, are ensured equal rights to learning.

Equal educational rights are only possible if the teaching is adjusted to the pupils' individual abilities and needs.

4. PLANNING AND CREATING REMEDIAL ACTIONS FOR SPECIAL EDUCATION

It is important to ensure comprehensive planning for all levels of society as regards the integration of handicapped pupils and the choice of remedial actions. The Ministry of Education and Research is responsible for the national planning, and must also make sure that regional and local planning is carried out.

Development and dissemination of knowledge about special education is also seen as the responsibility of the State. To this end, several competence centres for special education will be established throughout the country. Primarily, these centres are intended for low-frequency groups among the handicapped, such as pupils with visual handicaps or partial hearing, or pupils with substantial speech disorders. Such handicaps are relatively rare, and for many municipalities it would therefore be difficult to gain enough experience in these areas. In addition, it might be necessary to establish a few competence centres for some of the more frequent handicaps, in order to give much-needed assistance to the schools.

These centres must have specific competence on a high level within the various fields. They must be able to supply the necessary services in the pupils' local school environment. The centres will work with all age categories, from pre-school children to adults. The handicapped pupils must be diagnosed properly, and the plan for the tuition must be tailored to the individual needs of each pupil. The centres will handle each pupil individually, and make sure that the pupil is given appropriate education and training according to the plan. In order to manage this, the centres must also be able to supply relevant tuition and guidance to parents, siblings, nursery school personnel, teachers and others.

5. COMPUTER TECHNOLOGY IN THE EDUCATION OF HANDICAPPED PUPILS

In 1984, the Norwegian Government initiated a four-year Programme of Action for experimental activities with the use of computers in schools. One of the main areas of priority was the use of computer technology in special education. The Programme of Action has shown that with the help of new technology, the educational opportunities for the various categories of handicapped pupils can be enhanced. The Programme of Action was terminated in 1988. It has since then been evaluated, and as a consequence, the work in this area will continue for another period of four years. In the new four-year plan, the use of computers in special education has also been given priority. One of the main aims in this connection, as it is for all areas of special education, is that one thus may contribute to the removal of all existing barriers in education, and in addition avoid creating new categories of handicapped people.

6. PUPILS WITH HANDICAPS CAN USE COMPUTERS IN MANY WAYS

Computer technology in special

education may be divided into two main areas:

a) Computer technology may be used as a "prosthesis" to remedy the lack of a sense or a function.

b) Computer technology may be used as a tool for learning.

These two areas are interwoven. Pupils who increase their functional abilities with the aid of computer technology will, apart from tuition in the use of the hardware and software, also need special education through computer-aided learning.

7. CONTINUED DEVELOPMENT OF COMPETENCE AND PRODUCTS

One of our main aims for the use of computer technology in special education, is that handicapped pupils preferably should be able to use the same software and hardware as other pupils. This coincides with the aims for integration, and will force the schools to consider the needs of the handicapped when buying new hardware or software. There is definitely a great need for the development of new products, both software and hardware. By combining the development of products for schools in general with the specific need for products for handicapped pupils, we are trying to reduce costs and increase the possibilities of integrating handicapped pupils in regular education. An important factor in our experimental activity is distance learning through the use of newly-developed communication software. This is of interest for the schools in general, but even more so for handicapped pupils.

8. DEVELOPING METHODOLOGY FOR HANDICAPPED PUPILS

We are at present developing methodology concerning the use of computer technology in special education. In this connection, it is important for us to make sure that the curriculum guidelines and the educational methods of evaluation are subject to continued adjustment and change, so that the technological innovations may benefit all categories of pupils. This is done through cooperation between the national educational authorities and those who use technology in the classroom at a local level.

9. BUILDING AND DISSEMINATING COMPETENCE

In connection with the administration and coordination of the centrally-initiated development projects under the previously-mentioned Programme of Action, a new organization was established. This organization, the Datasecretariat, is part of the Ministry of Education and Research, and is thus under centralized direction. By building up and activating relevant development milieus in various parts of the country, the Ministry has managed to develop both competence and actual products which will benefit the schools through organized dissemination.

It is a national challenge to create up-to-date curriculum guidelines and methodology for the in-service training of teachers. In addition, pedagogic use of new technology must be strengthened as part of the basic preservice teacher training. Finally, in cooperation with the regional school authorities, the national authorities aim to develop plans for the further activities involving the use of computers in schools.

Within the field of special education, there is a specific need for dissemination of experience and competence. This is also the case as regards the use of computer technology. To this end, and as previously mentioned, the Ministry of Education will initiate the establishment of a regional network for the use of computers in special education. Each region will have its own competence centre, with know-how in the fields of both special education and computer technology.

The handicapped pupils must be taught how to use different software. Teachers will need the same training, and other personnel, parents and siblings will need to be trained and updated as regards new products, versions or methods. The peak competence built up under the Programme of Action and afterwards must continuously be made available for pupils and other users.

10. THE COMPETENCE CENTRES MUST DEVELOP AND IMPART KNOWLEDGE

In the competence centres, special educators, psychologists and other experts in the field will cooperate with technological experts to develop individually-adapted plans for each pupil. For this purpose, the centres must cover the following areas:

* diagnostication and counselling
* course-planning and dissemination of information
* technical services
* software adaption, using tools for the development of software applications
* development of systems for diagnosis and the adaption of peripherals
* methodology
* cooperation with various local and regional institutions and authorities

The establishment of the above-mentioned centres will coincide with the reorganization of special education. It is our intention that the regional centres and the local schools cooperate closely in order to offer the necessary help to pupils in need of special pedagogical or technical adaptions. While staying at the centre together with the parents and the teachers, the pupil will be diagnosed and receive a plan based on the diagnosis and the applicable pedagogical and technical solutions. The centre will also give instructions as regards the use of the technical equipment, the methodology and anything else which could benefit the pupil in his or her learning situation. By concentrating on the individual pupil, and constructing a network in the pupil's home environment, both the pupil and the school stand to gain. The pupil will be helped and supported, and the school will increase its competence in the field. The competence centres must also be able to supply or develop the necessary aids adapted to the pupil's specific needs. This would imply that the centres must strive to be updated as regards pedagogical and technological innovations.

11. RESEARCH AND DEVELOPMENT

It is an important element that the competence centres function as a link between education and research. The needs brought to light at the centres, for development of methods and pedagogical or technical solutions, must immediately and effectively be channelled to the responsible research institutions. It is also important that the results of relevant research conducted at universities, colleges and other institutions reach the schools without too much delay. This will be one of the many tasks for the competence centres for special education. The centres will thus function as initiators by challenging the researchers with requirements based on factual needs. In addition, the centres can receive and counsel students and researchers, and thereby contribute to establishing a fruitful climate of cooperation. Among the research institutions involved in this project, the teacher training schools will play an especially important role, as they are responsible for the education of tomorrow's teachers.

12. CONCLUSION

Organizing special measures and services to enable all children and young people to receive individually-adapted education in their own surroundings constitutes a giant step towards a more just and humane society. Through pedagogical methods and modern technology, it will be possible to give the entire younger generation a chance to grow up and learn in their rightful environment. Ultimately, the schools will gain experience and knowledge which can also benefit pupils without disabilities. The integration of handicapped pupils in regular schools will give a new dimension to the classroom. The world in miniature, the classroom, where children learn about themselves and each other, will also include those who started life with a handicap; the handicapped.

Computers in Education
A. McDougall and C. Dowling (Editors)
Elsevier Science Publishers B.V. (North-Holland)

CULTURE AND CONTEXT IN COMPUTER APPLICATIONS IN EDUCATION

Bruce W. MCMILLAN and Kwok-Wing LAI

Department of Education, University of Otago, PO Box 56, Dunedin, New Zealand.

This paper examines the notions of "computer cultures" and "learning environments", and considers the relationship between them with some reference to New Zealand's use of computers in education. We suggest that in New Zealand, curriculum developments have been driven by external pressures, and that consequently, computer applications in education risk being governed by what is economically feasible and productive, rather than by what is necessarily appropriate for children. We also suggest that there is a need for greater theoretical debate about the place and purpose of computer applications in New Zealand education. We also suggest some of the issues requiring serious investigation if the educational outcomes of differing kinds of uses for computers are to be understood in the context of this country's education system.

1. INTRODUCTION

Technology is normally regarded as a-political. But the uses to which technology are put may imply value systems which have different effects on differing cultural systems. In this paper, we examine the notions of "computer culture" and "learning environments", and the relationship between them in terms of New Zealand's use of computers in education. Our major assumption is that recent curriculum developments in New Zealand have been strongly influenced by an increasing emphasis on outcomes, as measured by employment and economic indicators. To Diorio (1987), this is "instrumentalism": the belief "that schools should be instruments for achieving purposes defined outside educational institutions" (p.93). While there are debates about what is considered to be acceptable general purposes for education, there is little theoretical discussion about current computer applications in education. We suggest that such theoretical debates are essential if the uses of computers are in fact to contribute to educational purposes.

2. THE "COMPUTER CULTURE"

This phrase can refer vaguely to computers being widely used in developed societies, either as a part of the workplace, or as a "hidden" part of most people's lives (through bank operations, and so on). But to some writers, the phrase conveys more than the idea that computers are a significant technological achievement for such societies. It implies that there is a set of beliefs about the relationship between computers and people which derive from or have implications for cultural values. These values have an impact on educational processes, and make it essential that educators examine the assumptions about education which can become imbedded in computer applications.

One of the most radical statements about computing with children originated with Papert (1980). He argued that a computer is "an object to think with", rather than an instrument for mechanical learning, and suggests that educators tend not to think of the way either a computing or "real" language shapes and reflects the culture it is based in. The major emphasis in Papert's writings is that children should not be taught by the computer, but should be empowered to teach it: they can thus use computers as tools to achieve their own purposes, and learn "without being taught" (that is, without having received specific instruction).

Instruction may include mathematics, but is not limited to that area.

Papert regrets the lack of critical thinking about computers in education. He considers too much criticism has been stalled at a "technocentric" point: that is, "the tendency to give ... centrality to a technical object" (1987, p.23). He has the continuing use of BASIC in mind, arguing that those who decide that this particular language should be built in to the hardware are making decisions about the most likely ways the hardware will be used (given the structured nature of BASIC). But he suggests there is a greater problem:

> There are other ways in which the attributes of the subculture involved with computers are being projected onto the world of education. For example, the idea of a computer as an instrument for drill and practice that appeals to teachers because it resembles traditional teaching methods also appeals to the engineers who design computer systems: ... The machine designers do not actually decide what will be done in the classrooms. ... But they have no way to measure the ... effects of the biases built into the machines. (1980, pp.35-36)

Papert's view emphasizes children's active construction of meanings, and can be designated as a constructivist perspective (reflecting his involvement with the work of Piaget). It is a more explicit rationale than for most other writers in the field of computer applications in education, and hence has generated substantial literature dealing with the context for teaching Logo (see Forman & Pufall, 1988). It is not the only writing on computer applications with a strong theoretical orientation, but it is a valuable addition to the literature which is otherwise dominated by learning theory (Solomon, 1985).

The major point, however, is that in order to understand the cultural impact of computers on children we need to do more than examine the ways in which computers can reflect or be sensitive to cultural values. We must also consider a theory of education, and attend to issues relating to the social context within which computers are used in schools.

3. THE SOCIAL CONTEXT

Social context is an important variable in all learning. Consequently, there are a number of concerns which can be raised for computer applications in education. If computers are significant items for school-based learning, is it better for classes to have one computer, or to have one for each pupil? What preparation should teachers have for working with computers in their class? Do children's previous experience of them facilitate their current learning? If so, is it preferable for children to become familiar with computers during early childhood education?

Some view these as empirical questions with no theoretical pre-suppositions. But research questions emerge from systematic examination of the phenomena, and are never totally divorced from the assumptions underlying that system or theoretical framework. And as evidence relating to such questions accumulates, the task of discerning trends becomes more complex, and it is thus imperative to have some framework within which an interpretation of the information can be offered.

Take as an example the issue of "earlier is better": that is, the belief that if a thing is shown to be of value in education, then it is likely that some will endeavour to ensure that their children gain that valuable experience at an earlier age. There is a substantial literature on computers in early childhood education (for example Goodwin, Goodwin, Nansel & Helm 1986), including considerable negative comment about the value of computers for this area of education (Cuffaro, 1984).

Despite that, there is subtle pressure placed on early childhood centres to consider purchase: marketing something as "educational" encourages parents to believe they will gain an advantage for their children; and the emphasis on learning while working with a computer makes it readily marketable. In the USA, for example, Hill has commented on television commercials which claim that "unless preschool children have the opportunity to work with microcomputers they will be unsuccessful in college" (1984, p.1).

But even if parents do not buy a computer for their own use, they may expect the preschool to provide one or more. There are signs of this pressure in New Zealand. A recent article in the Playcentre Journal (for parents in a cooperative preschool service), reports a study in which one result was that:

Many parents were in favour of having a computer in both kindergarten and in the home. They reasoned that, as computers are now part of the work place, children and young adults are going to have to come to terms with the new technology - so the sooner the better. (Podmore, Slowley, Agnew & Renwick, 1988, p.36).

Such writing makes it clear that the matter of whether a school or early childhood centre should have a computer is a question requiring serious thought, and a reasonable understanding of the issues involved, for there are significant theoretical assumptions involved in any applications of computers to education (Weizenbaum, 1984). Because they are usually implicit rather than explicit assumptions, they embody "hidden values", the significance of which is not always apparent to teachers. For this reason, Ragsdale (1989) comments that "we cannot afford to be passive observers of technological applications, absorbing their values" (p.11). When people advocate computers being used in early childhood education, for example, they may well reflect a belief that specific learning accomplishments have greater value than does play, physical activity, exploration, or other "traditional" aspects of the early childhood curriculum.

There are many ways in which the relationship between the social context and educational processes can be conceptualized. One of the most significant theories to re-emerge in recent years is that of Vygotsky, the Soviet psychologist who was a contemporary of Piaget's, but who emphasized the powerful inter-relationship between the developing individual and the society in which she lives. Vygotsky was particularly interested in the role of language as a tool which both shapes and reflects human interaction. In this, he was radically different from Piaget, who saw the major aspects of language as being an outcome of cognitive (and internal) organization.

Vygotsky's writings help to explain how computers have found a ready use in one particular area of early childhood education: the Kohanga Reo centres. The most common use for computers in those centres possessing them has been to assist in learning Maori vocabulary. (Tawhiwhirangi, June 1988, personal communication). Software (largely of the "drill and practice" variety, which is not normally regarded as the most appropriate to use in computer applications in education) has been specifically developed for the centres. There has been debate about the use of computers in this way amongst the kohanga whanau, some of whom "argue that such technological resources lack the wairua of the kaumata and kaiako" (Government Review Team, 1988, p.26). But there has never been any doubt that learning the vocabulary is only part of the business of learning the language, and that Maori language mastery is only accomplished when it is used and shared amongst speakers of Maori from all age groups.

Another theoretical framework which enables the context for education to be examined is that of Bronfenbrenner (1979). His framework for the ecology of human development emphasizes the inter-locking of differing systems surrounding the developing person. One of the major implications of Bronfenbrenner's work is that it points to the necessity of going beyond simplistic levels of analysis for the study of environmental effects (McMillan, in press). In the context of the present paper, for example, we suggest that the educational question is not a matter of investigating whether a certain group of children have experience with computers or not: rather, it is a matter of investigating the meaning of that experience for the persons concerned, and of taking account of the differing contexts within which that experience is to be understood. From the perspective of a child within the family system, what happens at school may have greater or lesser relevance. But from the perspective of the parent, what happens to the child at school is going to be understood from within a set of beliefs shared with others in the neighbourhood (the "exosystem") as well as within the value systems of culture and community (the "macrosystem"). This provides us with additional ways to understand the role of computers in Te Kohanga Reo centres.

Thus, when we do have a framework which enables us to consider these inter-relationships, we are in a better position to consider the place of computers as part of a broader context for learning, rather than being the entire learning environment. If we expect learning to occur simply because of children's exposure to a computer, we will be disillusioned. If we see computer experience as necessarily reflecting children's total learning environment (as it is immediately experienced, and as it is influenced by settings and persons beyond that immediate context), we will have a healthy respect for the complexity of human development. We will also recognise the unpredictability of particular experiences: certain experiences may well be "educative" in general terms, but the meaning of the experience is not necessarily identical for all who participate in it.

Such a framework also can enable us to appreciate the positive values which can be associated with computer experience for children. There are some enormous advantages to be gained from the use of computers in education. Perhaps one of the most significant is in terms of the computer as a means by which power can be exercised by those who otherwise are deprived of the opportunity to do so in a conventional manner.

4. THE COMPUTER AS AN EMPOWERING TOOL

The most important aspect of this is in terms of computer usage for persons who do not have access to expensive aspects of education or family experiences. Computers are more likely to be provided in "white" families, or those with higher incomes. For example Sutton (1989) cites studies undertaken in the USA which indicate that schools with majority Black enrolment had about half the computer access of those schools with almost completely White enrolment. She also refers to work demonstrating that computers are used differently in these schools:

For low SES students, 56% of their use was for drill and practice and only 13% of the use was for computer programming. In contrast, for high SES students, 39% of the use was with drill and practice, with 30% of the use for programming.... This means that low SES children, who are disproportionately Black and Hispanic, are gaining most of their experience with a computer when it is in control.... In contrast, the high SES students, who are disproportionately White, are gaining considerable experiences when they are in control. (p.5)

We are well aware that computers can assist in removing barriers to physical action for those with physical disabilities. Common examples are word processing with varying input devices (perhaps making keyboard entry unnecessary), speech synthesizing, visual magnification, and robotics (computer control of everyday devices, operated easily by those with a disability). This form of control enables a person who is limited in ability to function in acceptable ways. One positive outcome is that someone who is "culturally different" (in the sense of having a visible disability) can be socially "normal". By the same token, it is important for children to know that there is a Maori Spelling Checker available for use with the Fulltext Pro 80 word processing programme: teachers should not assume that English is the only language their computer can "write".

But there are other aspects. As people study the ways in which computers can help learning, there has been much literature on artificial intelligence: getting computers to model human thinking processes. But what model of "thinking" (or epistemology) is used ? Freud, and Pavlov, used a mechanistic model, because that was readily available as an "image" to them. Gavriel Salomon has written extensively on this, and argues that the "intelligence" of the computer can be used to help children learn. He designates this as "AI in reverse", and bases his argument on Vygotsky's work:

"the internalization of culturally-evolved symbol systems (eg, language, the number system) and tools (actual objects) turned into internal mediating signs, leads to profound developmental changes.... It is not only human interaction, the language used in particular, that is internalizable. Vygotsky speaks also of the internalization of actual tools which serve as auxiliary means to solving problems.... Most importantly, the use of the tool precedes the development of cognitive signs ... (and) underlies the development of cognitive tools." (1988, p.126)

Salomon has reported a preliminary study to investigate some aspects of this idea, following children's use of a "Reading Aid". Children (N = 74) read 11 text pieces over three sessions. The "tool" was external metacognitive guidance ("self-monitoring concerning the generation of images while reading, identification of key phrases ... making sense out of headings). There were three groups: a metacognitive group; a " questions only" group; and control. The study was interested in both the changes for reading scores, and in generalization to writing. Salomon reports that " the metacognitive group, but not the content-questions or the control groups, made impressive progress in reading comprehension" , and for writing, " the metacognitive group significantly out-performed the other two groups" . These results suggest that the hypothesis concerning the benefit of seeing " artificial intelligence in reverse" is tentatively confirmed.

5. SOME IMPLICATIONS

We have already indicated two major implications of this emerging perspective on computer applications in education. Firstly, children's learning experiences are not confined to computer experience, nor even to classroom activities. The implication is that research into computer-based learning cannot confine itself only to the immediate context within which the computer (or other activity) is used (Bronfenbrenner, 1976). Rather, the whole ecological context needs to be borne in mind, so that conclusions about the effects of (for example) computer-based learning are not attributed only to the single most apparent cause, rather than to other variables.

The second implication is a consequence of the first, and has to do with cultural sensitivity. It is too readily assumed that the way computers have been designed to work is the way they must work, rather than seeing opportunities for variety in their modes of functioning. In particular, the assumption that English is the only way to communicate with computers in New Zealand schools must be balanced by a recognition of the possibility of using Maori (for example, in using word processing). Nor should it be assumed that all computer-based activity is intended to lead to greater proficiency only in terms of that which is valued by the dominant culture. For example, Pongudom and McMillan (1990) show that the process of writing is facilitated with ESL children when they have access to a computer, but that the different language structures and experiences ESL children have, make for differences in the way such process writing can be approached in the classroom.

A number of other issues requiring careful consideration could be mentioned briefly. New Zealand has committed itself to participation in an International Evaluation of Education study dealing with computers in education, which is expected to yield useful information about what is happening to children at Standard 4, Form 3 and Form 7 levels. But there is no indication of what will be done with the results from such a study, nor is it clear (at the time of writing) what structures within the new Ministry of Education are being developed to take responsibility for the issue of computer use across the curriculum.

Yet there has been debate about the nature and desirability of computer studies at the secondary level, with official Ministry policy (expressed by Werry, 1987) being that the introduction of a Bursaries-level examination prescription has a lower priority than "the promotion of educational computing in its broadest sense in the school curriculum as a whole" (p.13).

There is also the matter of the "Exploratory studies" of computers in education (Atmore, 1986), funded by the Department of Education: few have yet yielded a final report. While the projects so funded have clearly been of benefit to the schools who participated, they are unlikely to produce guidelines for policy, partly because the context for computer use has changed markedly in the interim period. For example the only one of the "exploratory" studies so far published to provide information about the ethnicity of the participants

(Podmore & Craig, 1989) provides much useful information on its major area of investigation, but comprises too few Maori to draw any conclusions about bi-cultural aspects of computer usage. All of these items signify relatively piecemeal approaches to the issue of computer applications in education.

The most significant implication of the ideas presented in this paper, therefore, is not in terms of particular policies, research topics or strategies, but that the matter of computer applications in education requires serious theoretical debate. It is a matter affecting the provision of education in this country, not a matter for computer "experts" alone simply to make unilateral decisions about matters affecting general educational policy.

6. CONCLUSION: THE NEED FOR THEORY

Computer applications in education do not represent a single philosophy of education. But there is a clear tendency for the advertising of software to place emphasis on learning as the major factor shaping children's behaviour. The problem is that such an emphasis tends to be interested in specific behaviours: counting sequentially, recognition of objects or words, "appropriate" responses for word meanings, and so on. It implies that learning these items ensures adequate educational experience; that they should be learned at a certain age; and that instruction from a teacher (or computer) is necessary if they are to be learned. Kohlberg describes this as the "psychologist's fallacy": statements about what ought to be valued are derived from psychological statements describing what is (Kohlberg, 1987). Teachers know that "what is" reflects a complex interaction between developmental processes, family and social contexts, and uniquely individual response to experience. To assert that a certain item of software ought to be part of each young child's learning experience, or (even worse) to assert that experiencing that software will produce predictable outcomes, is quite contrary to the variability we meet in education.

Clearly, there are different perspectives on education. Equally clearly, those which assume that learning (defined primarily as the acquisition of knowledge or skill) is the major influence on children, and ignore contextual, developmental, or critical perspectives, result in simplistic educational prescriptions. Perhaps what we need most is not a single theory of education, but a vigorous debate about how various theoretical contributions may clarify the ways in which we may best use computers in education. The ideas presented in this paper are intended to indicate that there is a basis from which such a discussion can take place, and offer a contribution to it.

REFERENCES

Atmore, D.L.(1986, November), Some exploratory studies in educational computing, Paper presented at the Annual Conference of the NZARE, Hamilton, New Zealand.

Bronfenbrenner, U. (1976), The experimental ecology of education, Educational Researcher, 5, 5-15.

Bronfenbrenner, U. (1979), The ecology of human development, Cambridge, MA: Harvard University Press.

Cuffaro, H.K. (1984), Microcomputers in education: Why is earlier better?, Teachers College Record, 85, 559-568.

Diorio, J. (1987), Instrumentalism, instruction and transition education, In W. Korndorffer (Ed.), Transition: Perspectives on school-to-work in New Zealand, Palmerston North: Dunmore Press, pp. 91-116.

Forman, G. and Pufall, P.B. (Eds.) (1988), Constructivism in the computer age, Hillsdale, NJ: Erlbaum.

Goodwin, L.D., Goodwin, W.L., Nansel, A. and Helm, C.P. (1986), Cognitive and affective effects of various types of microcomputer use by preschoolers, American Educational Research Journal, 23, 348-356.

Government Review Team, (1988), Report of the Review of Te Kohanga Reo, Wellington: Government Printer.

Hill, S. (1984, April), Beware of bandwagons: Young children may not need microcomputers, Paper presented at the American Educational research Association Conference, New Orleans.

Kohlberg, L. (1987), Child Psychology and childhood education: A cognitive developmental view. New York, NY: Longman.

McMillan, B.W. (in press), An ecological perspective on individual human development, Early Childhood Education and Care.

Papert, S. (1980), Mindstorms: Children, computers, and powerful ideas, New York, NY: Basic Books.

Papert, S. (1987), Computer criticism vs. technocentric thinking, Educational Researcher, 16 (1), 22-30.

Podmore, V., Slowley, C. Agnew, A. and Renwick, P. (1988), Computers in early childhood, Playcentre Journal, 72 (2), 36.

Podmore, V.N. and Craig, B.H. (1989), Study 9: The impact of microcomputers on teachers and on the observable behaviours of children aged four to seven years, Wellington: New Zealand Council for Educational Research.

Pongudom, W. and McMillan, B.W. (1990), Developing ESL children's writing with computers and responsive feedback, Unpublished paper, Department of Education, University of Otago.

Ragsdale, R. (1989), Surviving the use of technology in education. Computers in New Zealand Schools, 1 (1), 8-11.

Salomon, G. (1988), AI in reverse: Computer tools that turn cognitive, Journal of Educational Computing Research, 4, 2, 123-139.

Solomon, C. (1986), Computer environments for children, Cambridge, MA: MIT Press.

Sutton, R. (1989), Will the use of computers in schools lessen or enlarge inequities in education?, Computers in New Zealand Schools, 1 (2), 5-9.

Vygotsky, L.S. (1978), Mind in society, Cambridge, MA: Harvard University Press.

Weizenbaum, J. (1984), Computer power and human reason, Harmondworth: Penguin.

Werry, B. (1987), Computer studies in the Seventh Form: A Departmental view, Computers in education in New Zealand, 1(2), 9-13.

Computers in Education
A. McDougall and C. Dowling (Editors)
Elsevier Science Publishers B.V. (North-Holland)

INFORMATION LITERACY AND COMPUTER LITERACY - THE 'MIXED' APPROACH IN THE NETHERLANDS

Tjeerd PLOMP

Department of Education, University of Twente, PO Box 217, 7500 AE Enschede, The Netherlands

Bram van WEERING

National Institute for curriculum Development, PO Box 2041, 7500 CA Enschede, The Netherlands

This paper discusses the way in which information technology can best be integrated into the curriculum of secondary education. It describes the international trend: a shift away from teaching computing to teaching applications, information handling and problem solving. It also describes the recent approach in the Netherlands.

The results of the work of the National Development Committee on Information Literacy and Computer Literacy are presented.

1. INTRODUCTION

Around the middle of the 1980s, curricula for computer literacy showed a remarkable overall shift away from teaching computing to teaching applications, information handling and problem solving. This means that computer use is no longer viewed as a goal in itself, but is introduced as a powerful means of fulfilling information needs and the performance of other learning and instructional tasks (Plomp and van de Wolde, 1985).
In this paper we will discuss how this shift of emphasis may have an influence on the place of computer literacy in the curricula of schools.

Parallel to the shift in emphasis away from teaching computing, some other developments have taken place. Computer hardware has become cheaper and at the same time more powerful, leading in many of our countries to an increasing number of schools being equipped with many computers of a more powerful kind, while in many households computers are also available for children, providing them with computer literacy of some kind. Although courseware development remains a major problem in the process of introducing computers in education, an increasing quantity of good educational software in the 'tradional' subject matter domains has been developed, particularly in the Anglo-Saxon countries
In addition, a trend towards open, content-free software (making educational use of word processors, data bases, etc) could be observed, allowing teachers in almost all subject matter areas to adjust computer applications more precisely to their styles and contents of teaching. These parallel developments led to the question of whether separate courses in computer literacy were still needed or whether computer literacy goals could be better attained in other ways. Although separate computer literacy courses still exist, two interesting new lines of thinking can be observed. The first implies the integration of computer literacy goals with 'traditional' educational goals by promoting the abandoning of separate computer literacy courses, in favour of the instrumental use of computers in existing courses (exponents of this approach are Hunter (1984) and Collis (1988)). The second development, now being discussed in the Netherlands, can be characterized as a 'mixed' approach, with part of the computer literacy goals being realized via 'traditional' subject matter courses, while more specific information handling goals being addressed in a short separate course. Both approaches will be discussed shortly.

2. COMPUTER LITERACY SEEN AS INTEGRATION OF THE COMPUTER INTO THE CURRICULUM

Although Hunter (1984) and Collis (1988) have different starting points and rationales, their work results in similar proposals for integrating computer usage in the existing curriculum of the schools.

Hunter (1984) starts from the 'philosophy' that schools have no choice but to adapt to the information age. Learning about computers is only a part of that adaptation. "The more fundamental need is for children to learn to handle information, to solve problems, to communicate with people, and to understand the changes that are taking place in their society. If computers are the powerful intellectual tools they are claimed to be, then they should help in the achievement of these goals" (p. 6). She takes the position that there is no need for a separate computer literacy course or unit, but that computer-related objectives and activities must be integrated in the curricula of mathematics, social studies, science, and language arts. "For students in grades K (=Kindergarten) through 8 computer literacy means the ability to use suitably programmed computers in appropriate ways to assist in learning, handling information, and solving problems; and the ability to make informed judgments about social and ethical issues involving computer and communication systems" (p. 9). By designing computer-related activities to support the regular curriculum, computer literacy is viewed as a means, not as an end; there will moreover be less risk of developing a computer literacy curriculum which is obsolete before it is even used.

Collis (1988) states that much computer use in schools is a result of social pressure, and a response to a sense that computer literacy was a 'survival skill' that even young children must obtain. The most typical response at the elementary-school level was to obtain one of two computers and provide drill and practice in a separate room; at the grade 7-10 level to offer a separate computer literacy class; and at the grade 11 and 12 level to establish computer science courses. According to Collis this is an underutilization of computer resources, resulting from an inappropriate or unproductive view of educational computer usage itself. This situation is reinforced by the difficulties involved in bringing about any real change in the established teaching and learning procedures present in schools: avoidance of change by teachers if there is no personal need to change their instructional practice. Taking the trend that application programs became a major focus for computer literacy experiences she proposes, instead of a single course (or units) in computer literacy, an approach to computer use in schools that begins with educational needs related to the existing school curriculum, as well as with applications that are tuned in to the traditional organizational patterns and instructional styles of teachers by focusing on effective uses of computers in the whole-class setting.

Both Hunter (1984) and Collis (1988) illustrate that current trends in computer literacy are away from teaching computing towards the teaching of applications and information handling. Both believe that the latter type of goals may best be realized when integrated with the 'traditional' curricula of our schools, not just because applications and information handling are empty in itself and need substance for practicing, but because in this way computer literacy can be taught the most effectively, and also because in this way a more effective use of computers in education can be established. The fact that Hunter developed her approach for grades K to 8, while Collis did it for grades K to 12 is not a fundamental difference between their approaches. The question which remains is whether the characteristics of the new information technologies and their uses are not sufficiently complex that it is justifiable to pay attention to these separately in the curricula of our schools, in addition to the approach to computer literacy via computer applications which are instrumental in the context of attaining the goals of other subject matter areas. The approach chosen in the Netherlands is an illustration of an affirmative answer to this question.

3. THE 'MIXED' APPROACH IN THE NETHERLANDS

In the Netherlands since the early 1980s much attention has been given to the question of how information technology should be introduced in Dutch education. From the very beginning one of the considerations for Dutch policy was a balance between the need to prepare the young to function adequately in a society permeated with information technology (IT) by giving them also a basic education in IT, and the starting point of using computers (or more generally new technologies) instrumentally to improve instruction and learning (Plomp & van Muylwijk, 1985). All Dutch policy documents and advisory reports agreed that this basic IT education should be part of junior secondary education (grades 7, 8 and 9) and would encompass basic skills in the domain of information science as well as computer science. This introductory education was called 'information and computer literacy' (ICL). A first operationalization of these skills and understandings clearly illustrates both the information handling orientation and the computer orientation (AEIT, 1984; Plomp & van Muylwijk, 1985):

> The selection, production, collection, storage, processing, retrieval and distribution of data and messages given a certain problem of a defined need for information, with or without the help of a computer;
> The drawing of information from data and messages;
> The assessing of the reliability and the precision of data and messages and of the validity and relevance of the drawn information for a given problem;
> Principles of the architecture of hardware and software;
> The design of algorithms and the principles of programming.

Later developments in the Netherlands also followed the international trend away from the teaching of computing towards the teaching of applications; in the Dutch case, the teaching of information handling and computer applications (van Weering, 1988). With respect to the place of introductory computer education in the curriculum of the junior secondary schools, the present approach in the Dutch policy can be characterized as a 'mixed' approach. When preparing the plans for a reform of the junior secondary education (grades 7, 8 and 9), the government decided to have ICL as a very small, separate course (20 lesson periods) in the curriculum (in addition to 13 other subject matter domains). However, besides this small course, elements of ICL and information technology (IT) will be incorporated in other subject matter areas, such as language arts, mathematics, and technology, (another new subject area in the Dutch Secondary school curriculum).

For each of the subject areas of the reformed secondary education a committee was appointed to develop its new goals and objectives.
The development committee for ICL was not only responsible for generating the goals and objectives for the 20-lesson course in ICL, but also for the elements of ICL and IT that will be included in other subject matter domains. In their proposal to the government, the development committee for ICL chose explicitly that ICL should consist of the teaching of computer applications and of information handling skills. In its report the Development Committee ICL (DCICL , 1989) makes a distinction between the subject matter domain of information and computer literacy (ICL) and the small course on ICL, planned for the new junior secondary curriculum, which may be considered as covering only a part of the subject area. Goals and objectives for the subject area of ICL are very broad and have to be realized not only via the separate ICL course, but also via other subject areas. The operational goals and objectives for the subject matter domain of ICL proposed by the development committee reflect the orientation on information handling and computer applications. They are organized in the following four categories:

<u>Data, data-processing, information</u>:
Students have insight in processes of purposive data collection, processing, and re'trieval, and are able to deal, with comprehension, with data and information;

<u>Data-processing systems</u>:
Students have correct functional images of data-processing systems (such as the computer) and, on the basis of these, can use the systems;

<u>Applications of information technology</u>:
Students know some application possibilities of information technology, and can use some applications;

<u>Social impact of information technology</u>:
Students have an insight into the social impact of information technology.

All categories of goals and objectives for the subject areas of ICL need to be realized in the curriculum of the new junior secondary school, on one hand by having a small separate course in ICL, and on the other hand by having computer applications in as many other subject areas as is functional and feasible. The committee asked for the separate course in ICL consisting of 40 lesson periods (instead of the 20 periods proposed by the government), while the time spent in computer applications in other subject areas should altogether be the equivalent of 80 lesson periods.

The public discussions about the proposal of the committee reflect a general acceptance of the chosen emphasis, and of the 'mixed' approach proposed by the committee; many development committees for other subject areas are now developing goals and objectives reflecting applications of information technology.
If the proposal for the revised junior secondary education is accepted by the Dutch Parliament, then very soon this 'mixed' approach towards introductory computer education with an emphasis on information handling and computer applications will be reality in all Dutch (junior secondary) schools.
In the next section we summarize the rationale the Development Committee ICL used in their report (DCICL, 1989).

<u>Rationale of the Dutch approach</u>

The basic starting point was that the teaching of an basic introduction to new technologies, regardless of if it is taught as a separate course or integrated as applications in other subjects, should have three components: elements from information science, elements from computer science, and computer applications. The central focus of the <u>computer science aspects</u> is the hardware and software, and their operation, but only from operational and instrumental angles (that is, students must be able to operate the computer, as a machine, and students must have a correct functional image of the computer in order to be able to use the computer purposefully).
So, one of the goals of this basic education is the preparation of students for the operation and the application of computers. In this way, ICL, as a basic education, serves as a foundation for more fundamental knowledge and skills. ICL has also information science aspects, because it will deal with knowledge and skills needed for data collection, organization, processing, and retrieving, understandings which usually come up only implicitly in IT-applications in other contexts in the more 'traditional' subject matter areas.

We are dealing with a class of skills for which the computer is an important, versatile aid. The general idea behind emphasizing information handling skills is that data and information are different concepts. Data are codified signs and messages, and therefore controllable and incontestable entities. Information exists by processing and then interpreting data, following certain rules depending on the need for certain information. It is essential that students realize that data and information are not necessarily identical, and that the same data may imply different information for different persons. It is also important that students know that data can be collected, organized, processed and retrieved in many ways and for many purposes.

Important elements from information science are therefore:

There are many kinds of data bases (including electronic) which will be used by everybody; examples are dictionaries, encyclopedias, registers, time tables of buses and trains, videotex systems, research data, examination files, etc.;

Data bases need a structure or organization to make the collected data accessible and usable; examples are alphabetical, or numerical, or chronological structuring;

The processing of data (such as ordering, selecting, and combining of data) takes place within a certain data structure, with the purpose of relating the original data to the desired information, and follows certain rules;

The interpretation of the results of data processing must also follow rules, which depend on the stated goals, and which have to meet criteria such as acceptability, reliability, controllability, and validity.

As data collection and processing (with or without the computer) have to be related to 'contents', the third element of ICL consists of the application of new technologies in other subject matter areas. These applications are referred to in the Dutch policy plans, when there is a reference to elements of ICL and IT in other subject matter domains. Here we have to distinguish two clearly different aspects. First, certain goals and objectives of information and computer literacy can be optimally realized in the context of other subject matter areas, but complementary to this, it is supposed that certain goals and objectives of those other subject matter areas can also better be realized by the instrumental use of the computer. This can be illustrated with the example of word processing. In other subject matter areas outside of ICL (not only language arts), word processing is a 'means' to realize certain goals (often better than before). From the perspective of ICL, using word processing in other courses, such as mother tongue, will contribute to the perfection of the correct mental image that a student must acquire as he increases his skill in using computers (the operational aspect of computer use) and in clarifying the concept of word processing an an important application of information technology (the instrumental aspect of computer use) (Hartsuijker and van Weering, 1987)). Also, societal aspects of the application of new technologies can be discussed when students work with applications (for example, in the context of word processing, changes in the printing and publishing professions (van Weering and Zeelenberg, 1988)).

The Development Committee proposes that in realizing the goals and objectives in the subject matter domain of information and computer literacy (ICL), consistsing of the three above-mentioned components, three phases can be distinguished, (1) a preparation course, (2) IT-applications on other subject areas, and (3) a separate ICL-course concluding. This approach to the subject matter domain of information and computer literacy (ICL) is schematized in the following figure:

```
<---------------------------junior secondary education------------------------------->
<----a preparation course----><----ICL-applications----><----a separate ICL-course---->

operational and              ICL-applications in other    specific knowledge and
instrumental computer use,   subject areas                skills of information
elementary concepts of                                    handling
information science
```

Subject Area of Information Literacy and Computer Literacy (ICL)

Applications of information technology in other domains are only possible if students possess knowledge and skills to operate the computer as an instrument. Therefore a preparation to applications is needed, in which students learn operational and instrumental aspects of computer use, as well as some introductory elements from information science, such as the concepts of data and information, and ways of ordering data. Then, after students have become familiar with a number of applications used in other subject areas, they are prepared to study information handling skills. So, to assure that all the goals and objective of ICL will be attained, a short, separate concluding course, in which specific information handling knowledge and skills (on a general level, transcending other subject matter areas) will be taught. Such a concluding course is desirable, because in the computer applications in courses such as mathematics, science, language arts, social studies, etc., goals and objectives of those courses are the central focus; while it is believed that for the attainment of the goals and objectives of the subject matter domain of ICL it is necessary that students explicitly learn some general principles and skills of information handling, as well as societal aspects of the new technologies, from an information science perspective. By teaching these information handling goals and objectives in the context of a separate course, and not in competition with goals and objectives of other courses, the experiences with computer applications in other courses can be lifted to the level of knowledge and skills with respect to data collection, organization, and processing.

The Development Committee for ICL operationalized the subject matter domain of ICL in such a way that the separate course with an emphasis on information handling (with the help of computers) is the essential closure of a "route", consisting first of a preparation (mainly consisting of an operational and instrumental introduction of computer use) and then of a substantial middle part of computer applications in other subject areas. In the proposal to the Dutch government, the committee recommended that the available 20 hours be reserved for the separate course at the end, and that there are at least 80 hours of computer applications in other subject areas (math, science, language arts, social studies, technology, arts), while the schools have the responsibility to organize the initial operational and instrumental preparation in accordance with the entry level of the students entering secondary school in grade 7.

CONCLUDING REMARKS

The approaches of Hunter (1984), Collis (1988) and in the Netherlands (DCICL, 1989) illustrate that the trend away from the teaching of programming to the teaching of applications and information handling has rekindled interest in the issue of the place of introductory computer education (computer literacy) in the curriculum. Research is needed to answer the question whether for a sufficient acquisition of the knowledge and skills minimally required to be able to handle information, the approach proposed by Hunter and Collis is adequate, or whether the Dutch 'mixed' approach should be adopted.
It is important to realize that this trend in introductory computer education generates a new relationship between programming and applications. In the 'early' days doing 'something' with computers as part of computer literacy education was only possible by teaching student programming: being able to program meant being able to apply the computer (Luehrman, 1981). Nowadays, with the many open-ended and tool-type software packages available, it is not longer necessary to teach programming in order for students to apply the computer. Many student activities with tool-type software (such as using a data base or a spreadsheet program) are of such a type that we can say that principles of programming are being applied. If teachers explicitly emphasize and instruct these principles to students, an important goal of information and computer literacy teaching can be attained without the direct teaching of a computer language.

REFERENCES

Anderson, R.E. & Klassen, D.L. (1981). A conceptual framework for developing computer literacy instruction. AEDS Journal, 14(3), 128-141.

Akker J.J.H. van den, Keursten and Plomp (in press). The integration of computer use in education. International Journal of Educational Research.

ACEIT, Advisory Committee for Education and Information Technology (1984). Informatieleer en computerkunde (Information and computer science). The Hague: Ministery of Education and Sciences.

Collis, B. (1988). Computers, curriculum, and whole-class instruction. Belmont (CA, USA): Wadsworth.

Culbertson, J. (1986). Whither computer literacy? In Culbertson, J.A. & Cunningham, L.L. (Eds): Microcomputers in education. Chicago: National Society for the Study of Education, 85th yearbook; 109-131.

DCICL, Development Committee for Information and Computer literacy (January, 1989). Advies over de voorlopige eindtermen basisvorming in het voortgezet onderwijs: informatiekundė (Advice about the preliminary goals and objectives for the new junior secondary education: information and computer literacy). The Hague: Ministry of Education and Sciences.

Fullan, M.G., Miles, M.B. & Anderson, S.A. (1988). Strategies for implementing microcomputers in schools: The Ontario case. Toronto, Ontario: Ministry of Education.

Hade, D.D. (1982). Literacy in an information society. Educational Technology, 22(8), 7-12.

Hartsuijker, A.P. & IJ.H. van Weering (1987). Curricular aspects of the development of educational software in the national project for computer and information literacy. In: EURIT '86: Development in Educational Software and Courseware, J. Moonen and Tj. Plomp (editors), Pergamon Press, Oxford p. 567-574.

Hunter, B (1984). My students use computers. Reston (VA, USA): Reston Publishing Company.

Lockheed, M.E. & Mandinach, E.B. (May, 1986). Trends in educational computing: decreasing interest and the changing focus of instruction. Educational Researcher, 21-26.

Luehrman, A. (1981). Computer literacy - What should it be? The Mathematics Teacher, 74(9): 682-686.

Marland, M. (Ed). (1981). Information skills in the secondary curriculum: the recommendations of a working group sponsored by the British Library and the Schools Council (Schools Council Curriculum Bulletin 9). London: Methuen Educational.

Plomp, Tj. & Muylwijk, B. van (1985). Information technology in education: plans and policies in the Netherlands. In Duncan, K. & Harris, D (Eds): Computers in education. Amsterdam: Elsevier Science Publishers: 879-886.

Plomp, Tj, & de Wolde, J. van de (1985). New information technologies in education: lessons learned and trends observed. European Journal of Education 20(2-3): 243-256.

Plomp, Tj., Pelgrum, W.J. & Steerneman, A.H.S. (in press). Influence of computer use on schools' curriculum: limited integration. Computers and Education.

Russell, H.H.(1985). Computer literacy: educational programs. In Husen, T. & Postlethwaite, N.T. (Eds): International Encyclopedia of Education. Oxford: Pergamon, 937-8.

Weering, IJ.H. van (1988), A National Curriculum Informatics for Lower Secondary Education. In: Computers in Education, F. Lovis and E.D. Tagg (eds), Elsevier Science Publishers B.V.,IFIP p. 421-425.

Weering, IJ.H. van & T. Zeelenberg, eds. (1988), Informatics accross the curriculum in lower secondary education. SLO, Enschede.

Wolde, J. van de (1984). Burgerinformatica: opties bij de inrichting van een nieuw leergebied (Computer literacy: options in the development of a new subject matter domain). Enschede (Netherlands): University of Twente, Dept. of Education, and SLO, National Institute for Curriculum Development.

CBT 90

Computers in Education
A. McDougall and C. Dowling (Editors)
Elsevier Science Publishers B.V. (North-Holland)

SYSTEMS THAT TRAIN AS THEY WORK

Dr Trevor John BENTLEY

Trevor Bentley Consulting, The Bungalow, Harewood Road, Collingham, Wetherby, West Yorkshire, LS22 5BZ, U.K.

Computer software is usually extremely competent and functional, at least it is for someone who knows how to use it. For people new to the software a user guide or manual is usually provided. This is as equally incomprehensible as the software itself. This paper describes why we should have, and can have, self-explanatory systems.

I find it amazing that, as we enter the last decade of the twentieth century, industry, commerce, and government organisations, both local and central, are still spending millions of pounds to train people to use computer systems. The advances in computer technology, both hardware and software, have made it possible for systems to be built that are completely self-explanatory, and which train as they work.

I have just read about a major computer project at the U.K. Department of Social Security (DSS) which is going to mean the training of 50,000 people in the use of a new system. The training is being treated as a separate project from the systems development project. The approach uses off-line PCs with Computer Assisted Learning modules, and a separate on-line facility to a training computer for practice. This sounds a sensible and effective approach; however, the cost is approximately 2000 pounds per person, or 100M pounds in total. All this, because the system has not been written on a self-explanatory basis. And what support will users get from the system when they have finished training, and how will system changes be handled? The DSS approach is a big advance on instructor-led training, but why is it still necessary to go to these lengths when we know it is possible to build systems that train and support people as they work?

We have known for a long time that the best way for people to learn is by actually doing things. People learn best in environments that are directly related to the learning that is taking place; because of this the working environment is one of the most successful learning environments. In the working environment people learn most about what they do by actually doing it. People learn from their superiors, and from their colleagues. This learning is intentional, in that people ask about the things they need to do, and how to do them, and yet it is not done as a specific learning activity, but is done in the course of doing the job.

This natural learning is the result of people using their inherent learning abilities to enquire, to observe, to copy, to experiment, and to explore the environment in which they work. We have for thousands of years used this natural ability. By placing a learner with a master the learner gradually acquired the master's skills. This happened even if the masters made no real effort to teach their apprentices.

People learn well and naturally in the working environment. All around them there are examples of what to do, how to do it, and how to think about it. The power of the working environment can and often does outweigh any "off the job" training that might take place. It is difficult if not impossible to train people to work in a way that does not fit neatly into their working environment. Because of this it is vital that the working environment supports and encourages the learning process.

What is needed is some means whereby individuals can receive continuous updating and training when they need it, when they ask for it, and delivered to them in their workplace. This can be provided by supervisors, by more experienced colleagues, or via the technology they use in their daily work. It would be nice if everyone could have their own personal coach constantly available to guide and advise as appropriate.

Continuous training is a three-stage process of learning, practising, and reviewing performance. It should not stop. People should not reach a satisfactory level and switch off, because their performance will deteriorate. Continuous training is an investment in performance.

For most people this process only works if they have targets to aim for. These targets must be related to their current level of knowledge and skill and must be based on realistic levels of expectation.

All three stages of the process are vital elements of success, but perhaps the most critical element is the review. This is always difficult for both the reviewer and the person being reviewed. No one responds with pleasure to criticism, yet unless people accept and understand the outcome of the review they cannot improve. Everyone has been conditioned to love praise and to feel bad about criticism, but if criticism is properly and positively delivered people learn from it. People enjoy praise, but they don't learn from it.

The review must tell people three things:

* how they are performing - preferably in relation to some predetermined and measurable standard;

* why they are performing at that level;

* what action they can take to improve.

The review is usually followed with more learning, then by a period of practice at what is hoped is an improved level of performance. This process should never stop. People might change direction, add new skills, and grow both in the level and extent of their performance, but they should never stop the development process. However, for many people the process does stop. WHY? Some of the reasons could be:

* personal desire to stop - give up;

* the process itself stops;

* personal refusal to follow the process;

* motivation is lacking;

* opportunity is not available;

* individuals decide they have reached the peak.

If the organisations can provide the infrastructure to maintain this continuous development process and provide the motivation through self-generated learning, practice, and review, then there should be significant improvements in performance.

When the need for continuous training services is related to the use of high technology in the workplace, it can be seen that a facility is required that is permanently available to the user. This facility must do three main things. It must measure performance; assess what the measurements indicate; and then lead directly on to coaching so that performance can be improved.

Continuous training and support quite simply means providing everyone with the capability and opportunity of constantly assessing their own performance against agreed standards, and then taking action to undertake the learning that they think will help them to improve.

There are, in effect, three components

that need to be built into the system. First is the information and guidance necessary for users to be able to learn to use the system. Second is a comprehensive support facility that provides information and/or prompts users when they ask for it or when the system thinks they might find it useful. Third is a monitoring facility which lets users know how well they are doing in their use of the system, possibly giving examples of more proficient ways of doing things. All these components can be, and I maintain should be, built into all new software. The technical facilities are available to do it, and techniques and skills are becoming available to make it happen.

The majority of people working in the high technology workplace have little, if any, interest in the technology itself. They want to know how to use it, NOT what it is and how it works. If and when they do want to know, then the right time for them to find out is when their curiosity motivates them to do so, by asking the system itself.

Such a system involves the creation of four main elements. These are a comprehensive context sensitive Help system, training information and tutorials, simulations and exercises that make use of the working system, and an activity monitoring system.

To provide such a comprehensive training and support facility the training team has to work closely with the systems development group. The work will involve advice on screen design, the writing of all the messages that will be accessed by users (this will replace the need for user manuals and guides), and the production of initial learning information. The information from the monitoring system will be used to give people an idea of how well they are performing, with suggestions for more training or alternative working methods.

If we add to this the power of expert systems it becomes possible to develop really supportive systems that will enable users to learn and grow continuously.

The potential of expert systems for the trainer lies in the ability to manipulate large amounts of information held in the knowledge base, and to explain (reasoning on the basis of the rule set) why the information leads to the stated conclusions. Learners can be presented with a variety of problems for which information has to be accessed and used to arrive at a solution. The expert system can watch this process and then indicate, with reasons, why certain information led to certain results, and how other information would have led to different, possibly better results.

This could be very powerful when dealing with learning in areas such as diagnosis, evaluation, choice of best approach, and decision-making. This is made even more effective if the expert system has been built specifically for the subject domain in which the learners are working.

Expert system shells exist, which allow the knowledge base to be populated, and the rule set constructed, thus allowing trainers to build their own expert training tools. This does, however, require skills in logic design, and in the programming of the rule sets.

Expert systems can also impact on training when they are used to support people who, in the past, would have needed to learn a great deal of information about the job they are doing. This can now be stored in the knowledge base, and accessed in an expert way. This is done using the inference engine built by 'experts' in the field. The effect is to remove the need for the original learning to take place. In addition expert systems can help the trainer to produce effective training.

An innovative Israeli software company has produced a system that automatically creates a CBT tutorial and exercises, from the minimum of data about the target system. This piece of software is called ACE (Automated Courseware Expert). The ACE system can best be described as a CBT automated production tool. It is an 'Expert' system that manages a series of knowledge bases in accordance with a range of 'rule sets'. There are over 800 in the current version. The system has been developed to receive a set of information about a computer-based system, and from this information to create a computer-based training programme.

The system is aimed specifically at producing training for computer applications. It is not considered by its developers to be appropriate for producing CBT that is of a more generic nature, although with some imagination this seems perfectly feasible.

Expert systems are still in an early stage of development, but there are more and more examples of their being used in an effective and practical way. Trainers should invest some time and effort in looking at the possibilities that expert systems present.

Creating a computer-based training programme that can be managed by an 'intelligent tutor' is another potentially exciting prospect. Instead of the traditional 'page turning' CBT, with so-called interaction with the learner, a really meaningful dialogue could be developed.

What is required is a computer-based tutorial linked to an expert system, which is able to monitor the learning interaction that is taking place. As the 'tutor' picks up information from the learner's responses it is able to direct the tutorial to present more relevant information, or to return and review information. If the learner wants to find out what is happening, the 'tutor' will explain its reasoning.

For this approach to work, every CBT programme will need to have a specific 'tutor' attached. It might be possible to design and build a 'tutor' shell, which will need to be populated with the specific knowledge and rules for the subject being dealt with, together with rules for learning intervention. The biggest problem will be deciding the appropriate points for learning intervention, and this will mean that effective 'intelligent tutors' are only going to be built by people with an extensive knowledge of, and skill in applying, learning psychology.

The development of 'intelligent tutors' is currently an area of research being pursued by a number of universities and companies interested in expert systems and artificial intelligence. The outcomes of this research will need to be carefully examined to determine whether the application of 'intelligent tutors' is going to be practical and to have the effect of improving learning.

The use of expert systems to increase the relevance and interactivity of the responses given to users will lead directly to the design and building of systems that are truly self-explanatory and, therefore, very easy to use.

This will lead to the development of systems that are error-free, and for which training is simply unnecessary.

The benefits from building systems that train as they work are:

* Improved performance, bringing increased profits via improved accuracy, increased productivity, and improved sales and service.
* Reduced training costs, and increased training effectiveness. By reducing the need for training, and by doing the training that is needed in a better way, substantial savings can be made.
* A sharpened competitive edge by improving the performance of people, particularly in the way that they use the technology in which the organisation has usually invested a great deal.

These benefits can be achieved without a significant investment in time, effort, and money. This is possible because what I am talking about is a switch of emphasis; a change in the way people look at things, particularly system developers and trainers. I am not talking about expensive new tools, or the development of new skills, although both may be involved if the need is great enough. In fact the suggested approach is potentially much cheaper in the long run.

There is no reason today why major organisations and software producers should continue to produce systems that need extensive manuals, and which are difficult and complex to use. If they do, then it is a clear signal that the needs of users for simple, easy-to-use systems are being ignored. The result of this is high cost, ineffective training and low user performance; things which cannot, and should not, be tolerated.

Computers in Education
A. McDougall and C. Dowling (Editors)
Elsevier Science Publishers B.V. (North-Holland)

NEW DIRECTIONS IN COMPUTER BASED TRAINING: A U.S. PERSPECTIVE

Greg KEARSLEY

Park Row Inc. 4640 Jewell St., #232, CA 92109, USA

New directions in the field of Computer Based Training are discussed including minimalist theory, online help systems, intelligent advisors and expert systems, hypertext/hypermedia, interactive video, automated instructional development, and electronic networks.

1. INTRODUCTION

One thing can be said for sure about the future of Computer Based Training (CBT): it won't resemble the past very much! Having made that remark, let me describe what I see as the new directions in this field. These perceptions are largely based upon a survey that I recently conducted for the Office of Technology Assessment, U.S. Congress, on the current and future role of instructional technology in the workplace [1]. This survey involved interviews with the managers responsible for CBT activities in many U.S. companies and government agencies.

2. COMPUTER LITERACY

In the CBT context, computer literacy refers to teaching people how to use computers to do their jobs. Thus it refers to teaching people *about* computers rather than teaching people *with* computers. In almost all medium and large sized businesses in the U.S. today, most employees have to use a computer to do some part of their job. This applies to all types of businesses from manufacturing to retail, and all levels of employees from clerks to executives. The number one training concern in these companies is how to train people most effectively to use the computer.

Naturally this provides a wonderful opportunity for CBT. After all, the computers are there so why not use them to conduct the training? And indeed people have tried. The problem is that the classic and most common form of CBT, namely tutorials, does not work well for teaching people computer skills. People approach computers with a strong action orientation that can be described as the "just teach me what I need to know now so I can get on with the job" philosophy. They do not, and will not, sit through lengthy online tutorials.

John Carroll at IBM Labs has studied this phenomenon extensively and has developed a learning theory called "minimalism" that does seem to work [2]. The minimalistic approach involves teaching people (or designing the system) so that people learn only what is absolutely necessary at any given moment to do a particular task and in a very procedural way.

3. ONLINE HELP SYSTEMS

But the minimalist approach is only one way of addressing the computer literacy problem. A second approach is essentially to give up on training altogether. Instead, you provide people with powerful online help and documentation systems that allow them to find out what they need to know when they want. Indeed, most software developed today includes online help and documentation capabilities. You could call this the "failure-based" approach because you let people try to use the system until they get stuck and then (hopefully) provide them with enough information to get going again.

The problem with this approach is that it is *very* difficult to build online help or documentation systems that work well [3]. The key to a successful help system is context sensitivity -- the help information provided or available must be tied into what the user is trying to do in order to be helpful. Developing a context sensitive help or documentation system takes an incredible amount of time and effort. A lot of observation and try out data is needed to discover what kinds of problems people have and how to deal with those problems.

By the way, the online help approach is closely related to two other forms of CBT you might hear about: embedded training and performance support systems. Embedded training refers to any online training that is built into a system or product as an integral function. Performance support systems are any computer based tools provided to employees to help them do their jobs better. In many cases, both embedded training and performance support systems take the form of online helps.

4. INTELLIGENT ADVISORS AND EXPERT SYSTEMS

One way to improve the context sensitivity of online helps and documentation would be to build intelligent advisors that are capable of "understanding" what users are doing and hence what kind of information or advice they need. This means employing artificial intelligence techniques in the design of user assistance programs. While there has been a great deal of research in this arena [4,5], the deployment of such programs in practical settings is not really feasible yet.

What is feasible, however, is a slightly different tack -- building expert systems that people can use in lieu of learning how to do something. We could call this the "intelligent job aid" approach. Instead of teaching a person how to use a program to complete a task, they respond to questions asked by the expert system and it does the task for them (or tells them what to do). The expert system can be provided to the employees or they can build their own. Expert systems can also be used as a training tool to help employees improve their decision-making and judgement skills [6,7].

5. HYPERTEXT/HYPERMEDIA

At the other end of the spectrum is the idea that if we could develop more advanced user interfaces, people would be able to find the information they needed from online help/documentation and database systems on their own. A great deal of attention is being given right now to the concept of hypertext -- ways of accessing and organizing information in non-linear formats [8,9]. In a hypertext system, information is connected by links that let the user jump instantly from one part of the database to another. In a hypermedia system the information linked together is multimedia in nature and can include graphics, photographs, video sequences, or audio.

Hypertext/hypermedia systems make it relatively easy for people to browse through large databases and acquire information about products, procedures, or technical specifications. They are ideal ways to implement online help or documentation systems. Alas, authoring a hypertext database is a considerable amount of work since each link has to be defined and tested.

6. INTERACTIVE VIDEO

Not everyone works at a computer terminal -- there are still lots of people who need to learn how to operate or maintain some kind of equipment. This includes aircraft, trains, tanks, bulldozers, nuclear reactors, radar towers, and so on. Such individuals need to practice hands-on skills on the equipment. The training problem is that much of this equipment is too expensive, too dangerous, or too scarce to use in training.

This is where computer-based simulation comes in. Such simulators can provide cost-effective practice [10]. However, in many cases, there is a need for video sequences in order to provide the necessary realism. Interactive video either from videodisc or computer-generated images has become an important element of computer-based simulators.
A new technology called DVI (Digital Video Interactive) being developed by Intel Corp promises to extend the capabilities of current videodisc systems through the use of digital compression techniques.

Ironically, interactive video simulation is also beginning to make a big contribution to teaching people how to interact with other people as well as machines. There are many types of training such as customer service, supervision, leadership, patient management, or labor relations where people need a lot of practice in "face-to-face" situations. Simulations using interactive video sequences are able to provide realistic practice in a range of interpersonal skills. Furthermore, the U.S. military is developing a system called SIMNET (networked simulators) that allow soldiers to practice team skills during electronic combat exercises. This could represent a major breakthrough in the training domain because team work has always been a difficult skill to teach.

7. AUTOMATED INSTRUCTIONAL DEVELOPMENT

All of these new forms of CBT just mentioned are exciting but there is one serious problem -- the tremendous amount of development time and high level of instructional expertise needed to create such programs. Powerful authoring systems help out somewhat but they don't address the majority of the instructional design and development tasks involved, nor do they help when the training materials are not computer based. So, many organizations are currently working on automated instructional development systems that will speed up the entire CBT creation process.

One very interesting system called ID Expert is being developed by Dave Merrill at the University of Utah [11]. ID Expert is an expert system for instructional design -- it can help novice designers turn out very sophisticated instructional materials in a very short time. Another system called the Expert Media System, marketed by IntelliSys Inc., uses an expert system approach to help instructional designers make cost-effective media selections [12]. Park Row Inc. markets a number of programs for personal computers that provide help in the analysis and design stages of training.

8. ELECTRONIC NETWORKING

Lastly, let me mention a form of CBT that may eventually become the most important way of using computers for training: electronic networking. Many organizations are starting to use electronic mail and conferencing systems as a vital part of their training activities. Networks let employees interact with each other and the instructor during a training course in both formal and informal ways. They make distance learning possible -- students can "attend" class at home or at the office without having to go to a training center. Furthermore, they provide a natural bridge between training and job activities since the same networks can be used for work after the training is completed. Electronic networks also provide access to online databases that can be used for training or job purposes.

Historically, we have conceived of computers as a medium for delivering formal instruction. However, computers are wonderful communication devices. And a lot of training involves people sharing their knowledge and experience with each other. It shouldn't come as too much of a surprise that one of the major forms of computer based training in the future will be the use of networks for informal learning activities. Of course, we have to teach people how to use networks.

9. CONVERGENCE & DIVERGENCE

As you can conclude from my remarks, I see CBT going off in a lot of new directions. However, these directions are not as divergent as they may seem. There are lots of interesting cross-overs on the horizon. For example, I mentioned the idea of teaching team skills using networked simulators. It appears that artificial intelligence techniques are going to be important in the design of effective help systems as well as automated instructional development systems. Hypermedia and interactive video go hand-in-hand. And, as we move more towards digital video, the dividing line between computer-generated graphics and television will blur.

What all these new developments mean to the training field is that CBT will be able to address an increasingly wider range of training needs and situations. CBT is expanding into a variety of different approaches rather than being a single instructional medium. As CBT practitioners, we need to start thinking much more broadly about the application of computers to training.

REFERENCES

[1] G. Kearsley, Instructional Technology and Worker Learning Needs.

in: *Worker Training: Implications for U.S. Competitiveness*. (Office of Technology Assessment, U.S. Congress, Washington, DC,1990).

[2] J.M. Carroll. *The Nurnberg Funnel.* (MIT Press, Cambridge, MA, 1990).

[3] G. Kearsley. *Online Help Systems.* (Ablex Publishers, Norwood, NJ, 1988).

[4] Poulson, M.C. & Richardson, J.J. *Foundations of Intelligent Tutoring Systems*. (Erlbaum Associates, Hillsdale, NJ, 1988).

[5] Psotka, J. Massey, L. & Mutter, S. *Intelligent Tutoring Systems: Lessons Learned*. (Erlbaum Associates, Hillsdale, NJ,1988).

[6] McFarland, D. & Parker, O.R. *Expert Systems in Education and Training*. (Educational Technology Publications, Englewood Cliffs, NY, 1990).

[7] Lippert, R.C. Expert Systems: Tutors, tools, and tutees. *Journal of Computer Based Instruction* (Winter 1989) 16(1).

[8] Shneiderman, B. & Kearsley, G. *Hypertext Hands-On! A New Way of Accessing and Organizing Information.* (Addison-Wesley, Reading, MA, 1989).

[9] Jonassen, D. *Hypertext/Hypermedia.* (Educational Technology Publications, Englewood Cliffs, NY, 1989).

[10] Orlansky, J. The productivity of training. in: J. Zeidner (ed.), *Human Productivity Enhancement*. (Praeger, NY, 1986).

[11] Merrill, M.D., & Li, Z. An instructional design.expert system *Journal of Computer Based Instruction* (Summer 1989) 16(3).

[12] Olson, M.J. The Expert Media System. *Journal of Interactive Instruction Development* (Summer 1989).

Computers in Education
A. McDougall and C. Dowling (Editors)
Elsevier Science Publishers B.V. (North-Holland)

GRAPHICAL AUTHORING OF MULTIMEDIA COURSEWARE

Christian BESSIERE Jacqueline VACHERAND-REVEL
CNRS-IRPEACS 69131 ECULLY -Cédex- FRANCE
TEL.33 72 29 30 12 - FAX : 33 78 33 33 70

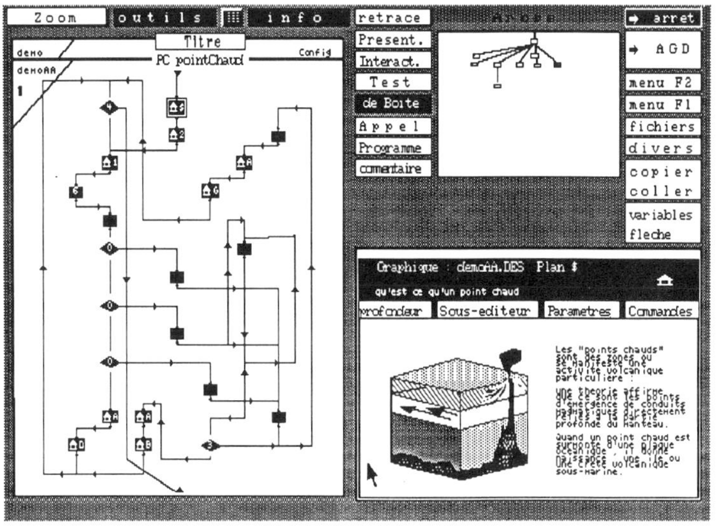

1. INTRODUCTION

The questions addressed in this paper concern Computer Assisted Learning (C.A.L.) in a multimedia context, with respect to a particular application -adult training. The introduction of computers into this sphere of human activity has deeply modified the way human beings relate to knowledge, in introducing new relationships between text, images and sound, and thereby creating in fact a new context for knowledge processing.

The recent evolution of C.A.L towards «Artificial Intelligence» (Intelligent Tutoring System) reinforces multidisciplinary approaches. This orientation is more and more necessary, the problems studied being as complex as the tools and the tasks involved. Within this context, human-computer interaction holds an important place. A system intended for learning which would be unable to interact in a flexible and effective way with a user would fail to meet its objectives.
Human beings learn with all of their senses, so they may learn better with a multimedia system which uses the eye, the ear and gesture, and computers can integrate these media.

AI approaches can improve flexibility and adaptability for authors and users.
These factors facilitate the cognitive activity of users, the creativity of authors, and the training of learners. But for this another condition must be fulfilled, it concerns the quality of the author-machine and learner-machine interaction which is an essential factor in the use of new training technologies.

This paper is focused, from a cognitive perspective, on a particular modality of person-machine interaction: graphical interaction. We will then show, through examples taken from studies and research projects carried out at C.N.R.S. IRPEACS, how this modality applies in the area of authoring tools.

This paper on the theme of the integration of audiovisual and computational media is the result of work carried out within the framework of the European research programme "DELTA", (Developing European Learning through Technological Advance), in the sub-project "AAT" (Advanced Authoring Tools).

2. GRAPHICAL INTERACTION

To analyse graphical interaction from a cognitive point of view we propose a model turning on five axes, based on findings of different disciplinary origins, which we summerise here. Details of this approach can be found in Bessiere Vacherand-Revel.[1]

2.1. The question of meaning in the human-artificial interaction

Within the framework of C.A.L., transmission and construction of knowledge results from the interaction between the human and the artificial. A source of difficulty is the ontological difference between these two components. As one goes from the person to the machine, there arises a frontier: the question of meaning. It is at the very moment of interaction that the question of meaning is raised. There are objects which have significance to the user, which one might refer to as *signifiers*. The user can interpret the signifier and thereby associate it with that which it signifies. This encounter is neither automatic nor natural. The signifier's "form" is decisive. This is where the good characteristics of graphical interaction -representation and manipulation of symbolic «objects»- intervene.

2.2. Mental models.

The system mediates an inter-human relation. In C.A.L., the question of meaning comes up twice : once in the designer-system-author combination, then in the author-courseware-learner combination. At each stage, two mental models of the computer system are present : the "design model" and the "user's model", between which there is a "gulf" Norman [2]. The objective is compatibility, i.e. equating the two models. Graphical interaction helps authors to make the content of their mental models explicit, and facilitates the elaboration of the content of the mental models by enabling the representation and manipulation of symbolic objects in a representational form.

2.3. The virtual representation of reality.

Graphical interaction allows the transposition of human representation of these entities of the real world in artificial representations, compatible with the technology used but in the most "faithful", "transparent" and "coherent" manner possible for the user. These mappings can be conceived and/or evaluated from two points of view: one static -the representation of knowledge itself- the other dynamic - the manner of acting upon it, of accessing it and transforming it. An important concept unites these two dimensions: that of direct manipulation Shneiderman [3], Hutchins, Hollan & Norman [4] O'Malley [5]. From the point of view of meaning, the analysis of the "directness" of the relation is subdivided in several aspects : evaluation of the distance between the user's objectives and what he will really have to to, and what he obtains. "Semantic directness", "Articulatory directness"and "conceptual fidelity" Wenger [6].

2.4. The personnal and sensory experiences of the users.

Many knowledge domains, problems or tasks can be decomposed and modelled in four dimensions. The spatio-temporal model can be transposed to other knowledge and action universes and this transposition is undoubtedly one of the components of the essence of "mapping". A metaphor transposes the representation of the real domain concerned into a virtual representation referred to a mental universe and bodily experience. "I", the subject, exists in a virtual universe, and is at the center of the metaphor. A person can feel psychologically subject in this virtual universe and becomes engaged, rationnally and emotionnally.

2.5. The field of signs.

This spatial modelling can apply to certain situations that would not easily be expressed in a linear and sequential way like written language. As with textual presentations, it is clear that graphics and graphical interaction also have their limits. The strength of graphical interaction is thus to furnish the potentiality of graphically expressing domains that would otherwise be "invisible"- not yet visible in the case of anticipation or not visual by essence like conceptual knowledge - and of also visualising the actions undertaken.

3. GRAPHICAL INTERACTION AND AUTHORING

3.1. Multimedia authoring tools

The initials C.E.T. (Courseware Engineering Tool) aim to underline the essential technical link between C.A.L. and other fields of computing applications. The author's task consists in "teaching the machine" with the aid of a software tool - C.E.T.- to produce courseware which takes into account, through anticipation, the learners to whom it is geared.
The visual dimension made possible by the integration of audiovisual materials and computing gives authors the means to see what the learner will see, but also to foresee future interactions with him. This concrete instantiation of a virtual image allows the formalisation and the simulation of the interactive and incremental learning process. Clarifying the pedagogical alternatives, and trying to model the training process, are tasks at the heart of courseware design. The system must be even more author-focused, that the author is focused on the learner.

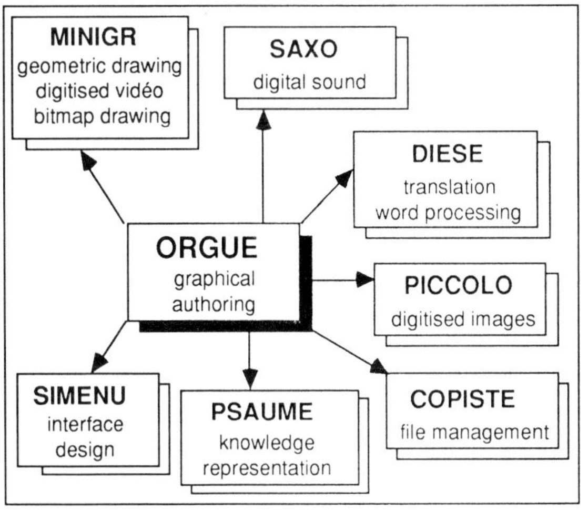

Figure n°1

The C.E.T. is made up of a set of specialized editors according to
- media used ,
- levels of knowledge representation,
- particular functionalities.

An appropriate editor with specific funtionalities, is dedicated for each particular task, but in each editor the very simple functions are available to novices. The basic functions: opening a file, activating a function, creating a simple figure, moving, suppressing it , can be seen as a sort of graphical "Esperanto", resulting from the work done at the Palo Alto Xerox Center and popularized by Macintosh®.
This horizontal link is essential in the team work of authors. In order for the final product to be harmonious in its different dimensions (technical, mediated and semantic) and focussed on the cognitive activity of the learner, all the produced components must be coherent amongst themselves. Author synergy is possible only if each one is aware of the possibilities and limits of the work of the others. Therefore the homogeneity of the graphical dialogue in the different editors helps the whole system adapt to the different types of users and makes possible their necessary cooperation.
Let us begin by examining the presentation editors.

MINIGR is a graphical colour editor. Its vectorial structure allows the production of dynamic visual scenes. It can also : import drawings or bitmap photographs from other editors, do graphical animation, insert and synchronise analogic or "on the fly" digitised video

DIESE allows text retrieval in its graphical context and the need for word processing whilst respecting the visual layout in which it is inserted. Its basic applications are finalising translations of courseware.

PICCOLO is an editor of digitised still photographs. It allows the combination of photography with text and graphics.

For the preceding editors, which produce *visual* objects, a *visual* creation mode is obviously required, and is put into effects by graphical interaction. This modality surpasses the "WYSIWYG" orientation, and facilitates the creation and manipulation of "invisible objects", as illustrated in the more detailed description which follows.

SAXO is a digital sound editor, allowing the recording, modifying and retrieval of natural sound at several levels of quality , in a mode compatible with the Integrated-services digitalized network. (I.S.D.N.).

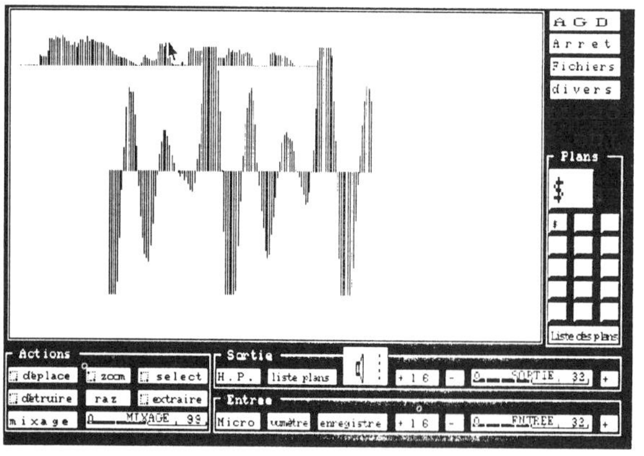

Figure 2

Once natural sound is digitised, words, music, noise can be represented graphically by a chart. The possibility of "seeing sound" allows for visual manipulation. Suppressing, moving, or transferring a sound can be obtained by doing the corresponding action to the drawing. The sound layers can then be assembled with other media according to the conditions of interactivity foreseen by the author. Graphical interaction allows sound editing in a mode homogeneous with that of the other editors. Courseware can also contain sound interactions for the learner who will have to look, hear, and talk.

SIMENU's function is to create or modify the dialogue of all the C.E.T. editors. It can also be used by the authors to produce specific learners' menus such as the control panel of a simulation.

This packaging of person-machine interface proposes "made to measure" ergonomics which adjust to users, authors or learners, and adapts to their tasks, according to a more "user friendly" and complex interactivity.

3.2. Visual authoring.

With ORGUE the author textually or graphically programs interactivity and the progressive sequencing of courseware. A composition function makes it also possible to assemble the information produced by the other audiovisual editors. A source programme is then automatically generated and then compiled. Finally, link editing provides an executable (runnable) program.

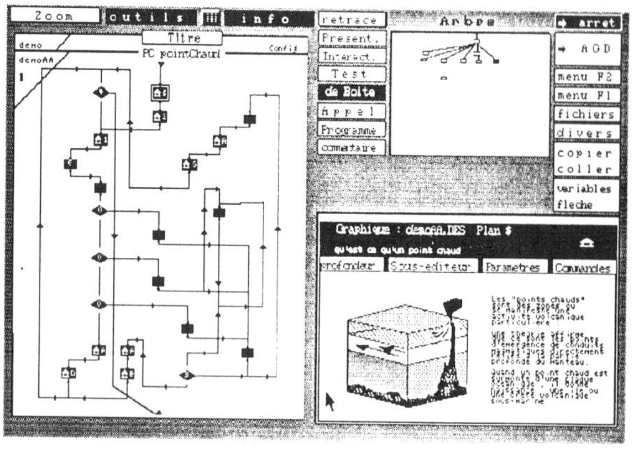

Figure 3

The tree-like representation used in ORGUE (left window) does not result from the historic instruction flowcharts developed by computer scientists in the '60s, but rather from more recent observation of the paper designing methods used by authors. The ubiquity of graphics quite obviously lends itself to the expression by and for the author of the conditionality and visualisation of the possible courses of progression of different types of learners. In this window, the third dimension gives access in depth to the different levels of this progression. The other windows provide the author with a global vision of the courseware (upper right) and, in reduced size, what the learner will see at a specific step of the program according to his answers (lower right). The author must be able to see the different mediated mobilized elements, the structure and the links of his pedagogical steps, the alternatives in the learners choices, and as much as possible, see all of this at the same time (!). This is typically a multi-constraint activity favourable for space-mapping. Writing-reading, talking-listening are powerful but linear and limited modalities compared to multi-factorial situations. Graphical spatiality and the ubiquity of its perception favour simultaneous apprehension of numerous elements and especially of their interrelations. The author's work often implies the analysis of complex situations and the manipulation of the relations between the elements of the pedagogical environment he is creating. In this sense, graphical interaction is a means for reflection and action.
The underlying metaphor is the establishment of a pedagogical map of the knowledge field and the visualising of the significant and foreseeable progression courses of the

learners. In the interactions between the author and the system, as in those he is preparing for the learner, what is again at stake is the question of meaning. As we have already indicated, with C.A.L., the frontier between human and artificial is doubly present. The previously quoted concepts: -'semantic directness', "articulatory directness", "conceptual fidelity"- are largely assumed by graphical interaction.

Another metaphor combined within ORGUE with that of the map and the learning progression within the courseware is that of "boxes". These "boxes" are entities which the author "opens", "fills" with media or logic objects, that he "closes", "places" one after another or one within another like "Chinese boxes", "moves" etc. The boxes are places which are reached through the pedagogical graph, the global homogeneity of ORGUE metaphors is indeed spatial, one circulates and moves about with graphical interaction, the objects are directly manipulated. Graphical interaction facilitates interpretation, and helps reduce the distance the system introduces between the author and the learner. Facilitating the work of the author is all the more important since he must use a complex system but also be the designer of an interactive training system intended for learners. In the pedagogical editor, graphical interaction basically allows visual programming foreseeing the learner's activity through a spatial representation based on the metaphor of possible courses of his cognitive progression.

The complexity involved for authors in conceiving courseware, as well as the rigidity of courseware for learners has generated a need for A.I. in order to overcome existing limitions.

3.3. Towards A.I.

The evolution towards AI is progressive and is being developed in the AAT DELTA project within the context of a collaboration between IRPEACS and the OPEN UNIVERSITY, by the combination of ORGUE and of ECAL Elsom-Cook, [7]. (ECAL : Extended Computer Assisted Learning, advanced CAL) uses simple AI techniques to represent knowledge and model the learner. ECAL is fundamentally based on the pedagogical model of course design of Posner and Rudnitsky [8].

ORGUE produces a set of interactive pedagogical modules or frames, according to the arborescent mode previously indicated.

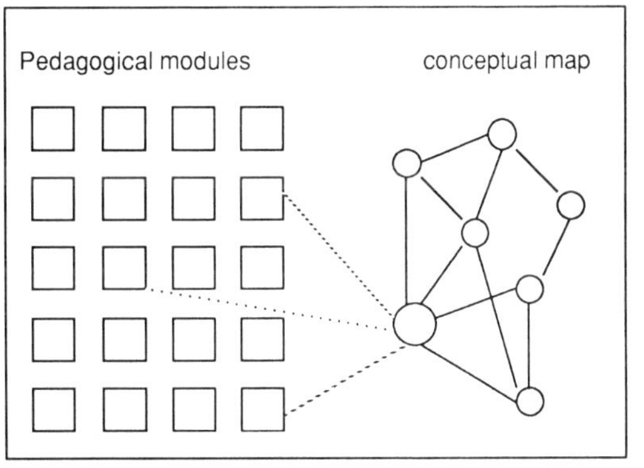

Figure 4

ECAL allows the production of a conceptual map. This new knowledge representation makes it possible to determine the course the learner will follow in the modules according to his activity.
The conceptual map is a particular semantic network linking ILOs (Intended Learning Outcomes) that can be considered as knowledge atoms or molecules which make up the learning material for the student. The semantic link between concepts and modules where the pedagogical content can be found is expressed by the author through key-words describing these modules. On this basis, the system automatically generates the initial semantic network.
At the level of the computer system, these networks, their links, their strength are expressed through instructions, matrices, and equations far removed in their forms from their pedagogical finality. In this new "intelligent" level, graphical interaction, continuing the ORGUE dialogue makes this abstract and modelised representation of knowledge more readable and manageable. The pathways between frames are not orientated, the links between concepts can be of different semantic nature; they do not directly express the fine and predetermined connections, but rather a map of possible intellectual processes. This modelling of content is the activity of the author who thus includes the forecast of the learner's activity. This is also formalised in a learner model of which the actual version in ECAL is simple and of the 'overlay' type, but which nevertheless allows enrichment of the anticipations of the author through the user's activity. The model allows for successive improvement and is not fixed as in classical CAL. The tool helps the author with these formalisations and the graphical

dimension helps with visualising and handling simultaneously words, lines, concepts and their links. For the domain and pedagogical expert, this representation and action modality aims at being conceptually faithful to the idea and the image that one has of the cognitive activity of the learner in the relevant knowledge domain.

4. CONCLUSION : DEPTH OF SURFACE

We share Brown's [9] opinion that the design of complex systems must not aim at being «idiot-proof», but be centred on the management of difficulties and structurally facilitating self-learning and discovery. In the doubly interactive context of CAL, graphical interaction makes an important contribution to the analysis and construction of meaning by making explicit the "invisible" that the other's anticipation constitute, this being a major difficulty in mediated teaching. Graphical interaction is also a socialization factor for CAL for it adapts learning tools to team work, going again here in the direction indicated by Brown [9], in inserting this approach of training within contemporary changes.

Technological evolution is upheaving society and constitutes a challenge for training systems and methods: will we be able to pedagogically and socially master these technologies? Answers can probably be found in all that facilitates and reinforces the users' activities, authors and learners.

The interface allows synergy between the two complementary entities that are the person and the computer. Graphical interaction is but a link but it is important and our research strategy will continue to link it to others.

To link up : -the *base*, in-depth AI, representing knowledge and modelling the learner,

-the *form*, the multimedia dimension the user hears and sees,

-the *interface*, the surface AI and the interaction, what the user does.

What is involved here is research and development in the technical dimensions concerned, especially an anchoring in experimentation to validate and fertilise these areas of research, and link them to their goal : **USE**.

REFERENCES

[1] VACHERAND-REVEL, J, BESSIERE, C «Playing graphics in the design and use of Multimedia courseware» NATO Longman
BESSIERE, C ; VACHERAND-REVEL J : «PLAYING GRAPHICALS... TO DO SOMETHING ELSE» in INTERACTIVE MEDIA, THE HUMAN ISSUES - part 2- eds by TUCKER (R.N) - La Haye (1988) 77.

[2] NORMAN, D.A : «COGNITIVE ENGINEERING» in NORMAN ; DRAPER, J.W éds : «USER CENTERED SYSTEM DESIGN» - éd : LAWRENCE ERLBAUM associates - Hillsdale-New jersey (1986) 31-61.

[3] SHNEIDERMAN, B : «DIRECT MANIPULATION : A STEP BEYOND PROGRAMMING LANGUAGES» in IEEE COMPUTER (1983) 16 , 57-69.

[4] HUTCHINS, E.L, HOLLAN J.D, NORMAN D.A: «DIRECT MANIPULATIONS INTERFACES» in NORMAN ; DRAPER, J.W éds : «USER CENTERED SYSTEM DESIGN» -éd LAWRENCE ERLBAUM (1986) 87-124.

[5] O'MALLEY, C : «ICONIC INTERFACES Some issues for the design of learning environnements» rapport projet Delta - I.E.T. - Open University (1988).

[6] WENGER, E «ARTIFICIAL INTELLIGENCE AND TUTORING SYSTEMS» ed MORGAN KAUFFMAN -Los Altos (1987).

[7] ELSOM-COOK, M : «INTRODUCTION TO THE E.C.A.L SYSTEM» (Extended Computer Assisted Learning), Report ñ 43- I.E.T.- Open University (1989).

[8] POSTNER, G.J. & RUDNITSKY, A.N. COURSE DESIGN. Longman. (1985).

[9] BROWN, JS : «FROM COGNITIVE TO SOCIAL ERGONOMICS» in NORMAN (D;A).

[and] ZEILIGER, R : Principal architecte et maçon de ORGUE - IRPEACS- (1987).

This article is based on works done by the multidisciplinary team of the «Informatics and training» Departement at the C.N.R.S. IRPEACS laboratory.

Computers in Education
A. McDougall and C. Dowling (Editors)
Elsevier Science Publishers B.V. (North-Holland)

SUCCESSFUL LEARNING IN TODAY'S WORLD

A. BORLEY, J. ELLIOTT, L. RENFREE and H.WELLER

InHouse Technologies Pty Ltd Melbourne

This paper explores the requirements for training in industry and the need for a new model to meet these requirements. The new model addresses the need for a new approach, new instructional design and new development tools.

The new model and production techniques developed by InHouse Technologies are examined in terms of the first product in its "Urban Gorilla" range of software.

"Urban Gorilla Environment Watch" embraces the elements of the new model. It is a learner-centred product that encourages the user to explore environmental issues and their relationship to the environment. The learner is supported in making the best decisions to effect change.

This new approach to learning highlighted by the "Watch" is discussed in a business context. Business is in a state of continual change and needs well-trained staff to maintain a competitive edge. Training and education using computer technology must be made available to those who need it, when they need it.

A NEW MODEL REQUIRED?

Until comparatively recently, training in the workplace has been viewed as a "separate issue", removed from the working environment, and based on the trainer imparting knowledge to the trainee in whatever way that trainer thought was most appropriate. The effectiveness of this type of training was rarely questioned and it survived mainly because it was never subjected to the enormous pressure of today's training needs. This philosophy carried through into computer-based training, partly because at the time the technology was difficult to deal with, and partly because most people are loath to discard traditional methods in favour of something new and unfamiliar. The historical tradition is hard to break!

A critical point has now occurred where traditional training, computer-based, or otherwise, is not keeping pace with training needs. As a result the CBT community has taken a long hard look at what training must achieve and how it should achieve it.

Our proposition is to examine some new instructional models which largely ignore traditional theory.

REQUIREMENT OF TRAINING IN INDUSTRY

It needs to support a workforce of people who are continually learning, not simply gaining knowledge, but learning new skills in the context of their job, so that they can then combine and apply them to the job. They must know how to evaluate, analyse and respond to situations appropriately and speedily. As it has been said, "they haven't got time to learn each step, they must simply learn to dance". [1]

Training must also be available to today's workforce when it is needed. It must be satisfying in order to be effective, and it must create confidence and enthusiasm.

We believe to achieve this, training must focus on three key issues:

* Learning should be learner-centred
* Learning should be integrated into the job
* Learning should be context-based and provide a range of learning mechanisms.

We have designed the "Urban Gorilla Environment Watch" to demonstrate the possibilities of a new approach to these issues.

USER-CENTRED LEARNING

Although it is recognised that people learn in a number of different ways, it is often easier to ignore that fact and develop a training programme that suits the trainer and ignores the needs of the learner.

User-centred learning must be responsive to individual needs, there should be a structured learning environment available for those who learn best that way, which does not confine those who do not. It must cater for those who prefer to learn by trial and error, and those who choose to roam freely through information. This type of learning environment is very different from the linear explanation-question-practice model of the past.

While it is all very well being responsive to the many and varied learning styles of the user, unless the learner can recognise that this training is meeting his or her acknowledged need then it is of limited value. The learner, under pressure of time and change, must be able to see the relevance of the training to the job, and have it available immediately it is required.

We live in an era of continuous change. We have to respond more quickly or we fall behind. Business, like society, is geared to immediate results.

The banking and insurance industries provide a useful example. Over the last few years there has been much change. Not only has there been increasing use of technology in administration and processing, but also an ever increasing range of services offered to clients. For example, bank tellers now have to be multi-skilled, in that they not only handle transactions, but also are expected to answer clients' enquiries. It is not possible to find the time or circumstance to be fully prepared in advance. This means that learning for staff must be available when it is needed where it is needed in the workplace.

Not only is it essential for staff to have immediate access to learning, but once there, the learner must have access to all the tools required to tailor the learning experience to their individual learning style. The learner should be able to pose questions, find and apply answers, create hypothetical situations, and test various methods of dealing with them. The learning environment must enable the user to achieve this tailoring.

Having established that learning must be user-based, we need to look at how we will achieve the key factors:

* making learning relevant to the learner's needs
* catering for individual learning styles
* making learning immediate.

This is achieved firstly by ....

INTEGRATION OF LEARNING INTO THE JOB

Training need not be separated from the workplace, it can be integrated into the job. This can be done in a number of ways:

Embedded training: the training is available to the learner while the job is being performed. This can be reactive - the student can call on it when necessary, or proactive - the system is "smart" enough to know when difficulty is occurring and responds with appropriate help.

Simulating the job: not only the individual tasks, but the whole work environment. The simulation can also be supported by a data-base which allows the learner to find the information required to learn how to do the job. He or she can tackle the simulation in a structured fashion, on a trial and error basis or learn the information from the database first then apply the knowledge, it is entirely up to the learner!!

Successful user-centred learning integrated into the job can be achieved by an instructional model which contains the following elements:

The Learning Event
The Information Base
Transition Tools
Validation
Action
Style

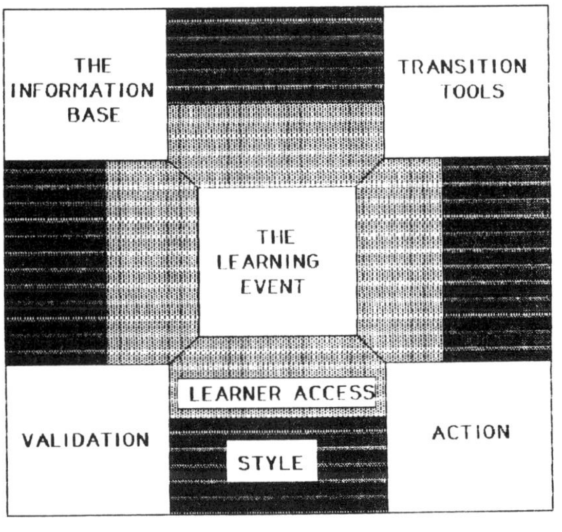

THE LEARNING EVENT

The essential ingredient of any person-centred learning is a well-designed contextual "event", within which the learner operates, and from which comes the impetus, challenge and focus for the student's learning. The event may be a simulator, a model, an experience, or even a real time situation, such as an over-the-counter enquiry from a client.

A properly-designed event will allow for differences in knowledge and experience, levels of competence and approaches to learning. It will provide easy and comprehensible bridges to the other elements of the model which, in providing support and extensions to the event, will make learning a real experience.

Although the specifics of the learning event will vary depending on the topic area, there are a number of common motivators which can be provided for learners. These are challenge, novelty, fantasy, goals and outcomes. If learners can be provoked to become self-motivated in learning and can create and achieve, then they are likely to become motivated to apply that knowledge and skill in their job.

The "Urban Gorilla Environment Watch" provides such motivators. The "Watch" is a game that simulates a real household.

The game is a realm in which environmental issues are brought into everyday life to be interacted with. The learner has to face problems and provide solutions. Solutions that are appropriate are rewarded with "Greenie" points according to the level of difficulty. Solutions that are less than appropriate cause the realm to become more difficult to deal with.

The learner is being pro-active and rehearsing an appropriate response to the real world.

At any stage of the event any other components of the "model" are available. Whilst simulating a shopping trip, the learner may use the Information Base to find alternatives to chlorofluorocarbon based aerosols. An example of this model being applied to a business situation could be in dealing with hazardous chemicals. We can link the learning event to a real chemical database which would then act as it would in the real job.

THE INFORMATION BASE

Samuel Johnson once said: "Knowledge is of two kinds; either I know the subject, or I know where to find information on it". Access to information has never been easier. However making sense of the huge volumes of data, linking and applying it to job situations is becoming difficult. Information is empowering. For this reason we have emphasized the use of databases of information to support the Learning Events.

The best databases for these programs are those which are available on a context-sensitive basis, and which allow the user to explore outwards through the database. A person should be empowered to access and utilise information as required. This is where the linking of a database to a learning event is critical.

Hypermedia is the most visible of these database tools. It provides an organic person-centred approach to obtaining information. "Urban Gorilla Environment Watch" employs a Hypermedia-style database which is context-sensitive. The learner may select "Information" regardless of where he is in the program, and an information card relevant to the subject currently being addressed will be made available.

The learner is also able to browse through any related card or select any other part of the "Watch" as required. For example, a card on aerosols may lead to a card on ozone depletion which may in turn lead to Antarctica. From there the learner may choose to join an "Antarctica Wilderness Park Society", and print the appropriate form letter. In a business application, browsing through a product catalogue may take the learner on a similar journey.

TRANSITION TOOLS

Learning is not an end in itself. There must be a transition to the job. So it is critical that the learner is provided with tools which allow this. These tools provide a means by which the learner can interpret and express the learning that has taken place, and to reinforce and affirm the most useful and meaningful elements. Such tools may also continue where the learning material has left off, supporting future performance whenever the learner perceives the need.

An example is an online journal or notebook which the learner can use whilst in the learning package. It is their personal summary of the key things from the learning material. It will contain affirmation, notes, tentative action plans. This may be printed and carried about with the learner, for reference, fun, scrap paper. The learner has created this, has filtered the most meaningful and relevant aspects of his or her learning experience through to the job. The "Urban Gorilla Environment Watch" incorporates a diary which can be used in this way.

VALIDATION

The validation element is for those learners who need to be convinced, to see results and to be able to prove something. In the old days pre and post tests performed this role. The difference here is that the learner sets the criteria and the scope.

The learner is making decisions about what is relevant to his or her job and performance in it. They are able to refer to this on an ongoing basis. While using the "Urban Gorilla Environment Watch", the learner can use a spreadsheet to validate the actions that have been learned. A pre-defined model can be used or the learner can choose to set his own. The spreadsheet can be used to record expenditure on household expenses such as gas, food, electricity, petrol, detergents etc. The learner can make comparisons and see the impact of making minor lifestyle changes.

The learner is able to validate the "think globally, act locally" concept through the use of a "world spreadsheet". This reflects the data that the learner is recording in his own personal spreadsheet, and extrapolates it to indicate the global effect.

THE ACTION ELEMENT

The gap between knowing and doing is the failure to turn theory into practice. It is often one of the major criticisms of traditional training, whether it is technology-based or not.

To aid the transition to real life the learner has to be empowered to turn learning into action. The other elements of the model have been geared towards the learner achieving this. Here, the best reinforcement of a new behaviour is its immediate and successful exhibition in job performance. The computer can provide immediate tasks or opportunities for this. Some of the current examples are in the embedded tutorial/application situations, or in using the computer in a point of sale context.

In "Urban Gorilla Environment Watch", the learner can choose to join for example the Wilderness Society or the A.C.F. The "Watch" provides numerous form letters with addresses that can be printed out and posted. The point is to provide the learner with the necessary encouragement to take individualised action and hence fulfil his needs.

STYLE

The total experience of the learner is directly influenced by the package interface. The way the learner interacts with the computer is decided by the screen layout and presentation, the use of colour, graphic images, and the use of language and metaphor.

The appropriate use of graphics is always strongly debated. Within the new model the use of graphics is integral to the learning event. We cannot achieve context-based learning by dismissing the power and contribution of visual imagery. (After all we are surrounded continuously by sophisticated and powerful marketing imagery.)

"Urban Gorilla Environment Watch" makes use of such visual imagery. Its information base consists of a set of index cards. A particular example is the "ENDANGERED WILDLIFE" category, which includes an information card on harp seals. The impact of the learner seeing a baby seal being clubbed to death is a most powerful experience. This could not be achieved by mere text alone.

IMPLICATIONS OF ADOPTING THE NEW MODEL

Firstly we have to throw away our old tools and methodologies. This will be difficult for some, for others it will be an exciting new opportunity. Authoring Languages as we know them are a thing of the past, and will be replaced by expert systems, databases, graphics packages appropriate to the particular training need.

Secondly, training will no longer be separated from the work environment. Trainers will be part of the teams which are developing new computer applications. In this way the training can be built into and with the system, so that it is integrated, and available with the product. This implies some organisational restructuring, but we need integrated teams to build integrated products.

An additional benefit of integrated teams is that the data processing element of the team will greatly facilitate the technology required to optimise the training, while the training component will be on hand to ensure that the application system is developed with the user in mind. It will also bridge the communication gap between the two fields, which has to be a bonus!

Because training is part of the job or at least simultaneous with it there is no time lag between learning and performing. Where this lag exists it allows the learner to slip below the required performance level; they then have to either retrain or perform the job at a less competent level.

Of course the greatest implication of all is the improvement in performance of the workforce. An organisation's greatest resource is its people. Surely effective training leads to improved job performance which in turn leads to improved profits.

IMPLICATIONS OF NOT FOLLOWING THE NEW DIRECTIONS

There is mounting evidence to show that traditional training methods are not keeping pace with the increasing rate and complexity of change. This inevitably leads to performance gaps the cost of which is unacceptable. Business can no longer afford to have people constantly making mistakes, missing opportunities, or upsetting customers. The question every business must ask is ...

Can we afford the cost of incompetence?

If the answer is no then effective new model training is essential.

REFERENCES

[1] Quote from Gloria Gery, President U.S.-based consulting firm Gery Associates.

Computers in Education
A. McDougall and C. Dowling (Editors)
Elsevier Science Publishers B.V. (North-Holland)

AN EXPERT SUPPORT ENVIRONMENT FOR LANGUAGE TEACHERS

Christopher CORBEL

Adult Migrant Education Services, 1st Floor, Myer House, 250 Elizabeth Street, Melbourne, Victoria, 3000, Australia.

This paper describes the development of Exrater, a computer program designed to assist in rating the language proficiency of Non English-Speaking Background speakers, using the Australian Second Language Proficiency Ratings (ASLPR). It describes the use and training needs associated with the ASLPR, and the reasons for the development of a computer program to meet them. A shift in thinking away from the expert system paradigm towards the concept of an "expert support environment" [1] which took place during prototyping is described. The functioning of the final program, Exrater, is described, and the issues it raises are considered.

1. BACKGROUND - THE ASLPR

1.1. Purpose

The Australian Second Language Proficiency Ratings describe language performance in the four skills of speaking, listening, reading and writing across a nine point continuum from zero to native-like proficiency. Its purposes are " .. to provide an overview of the path of development of proficiency in a second language as an overarching framework within which a number of integrated programs in English as a Second Language for migrants to Australia could be coherently planned. .. to provide a means of specifying second language proficiency in terms of practical language skills or observable language performance, i.e. in terms of the sorts of language (especially communication) tasks learners can carry out and how they are carried out." [2]

1.2. Use

Since February 1979 the ASLPR has been used throughout Australia, primarily in the Adult Migrant Education Program. Every teacher of the several thousand in the AMEP needs to be familiar with the scale. It is the main way in which learner proficiency and achievement is recorded on the AMEP computerised information system and all teachers will at least once have to provide a rating for each of their learners. These learner ratings may be considered in course and lesson planning by teachers and may also be used diagnostically to identify language problems.

1.3. Problems with the ASLPR

Brindley [3] identifies a number of problems in the use of the ASLPR. There is difficulty in standardizing agreement, partially as a result of its use by inexperienced teachers; there is a tendency for administrative reasons to standardize the rating process in a way inconsistent with the authors' intentions; the ASLPR has not been validated in empirically-based studies; it is open to question on grounds of construct validity, particularly the mixing of various behavioural criteria in one level; and there is a loss of information when users do not refer to it when rating.

Quinn and McNamara [4] are also critical.

"A major weakness ... is its built-in tendency to become a variable instrument ... Although all instruments contain measurement error, it is especially important with the interview based approach to establish the validity of a rater's interview, and the accuracy and consistency of his or her ratings." (p.8)

1.4. Training Needs

Since a degree of ASLPR expertise is called for in all Adult Migrant Education Program teachers there is a continual need for ASLPR training. In the state of Victoria alone there are over four hundred full time and part time teachers. A regular part of the professional development program involves the introduction of new teachers to the ASLPR, and the encouraging of experienced teachers to update their understandings and skills in the use of the ASLPR.

This involves considerable repetitive inservicing of staff, and accounts for a considerable proportion of the time of experienced teachers who have professional development responsibilities.

The Adult Migrant Education Services Curriculum Development Unit was interested in alternatives to such a repetitive, labour-intensive program. It was therefore decided to investigate ways of enhancing ASLPR training and use through the use of computers, and particularly using an expert system.

2. AN ASLPR EXPERT SYSTEM?

2.1. Prototypes

In order to test the idea of an expert system as a device for ASLPR training and for enhancing rater reliability two experimental programs were written using simple public domain shells, Inference Engine and Artie. Each of these offered a slightly different approach, each of which had strengths and weaknesses.

2.1.1. Inference Engine

IE enables the designer to write rules using keywords. It presents the components of each rule one at a time to the user, in the form of questions requiring a Yes/No answer. When all the conditions of a rule are met, IE presents the THEN component of the rule as a conclusion. (see [5] and [6] for a more detailed discussion)

This had some attractions. It required very little keyboard input from the user and it was relatively easy to write rules in the required format with a word processor.

There were significant problems, however. Full data on a person's language may not have been available, but IE could not accept "Don't know". Secondly, it was not clear where to have IE start the search, at the bottom of the scale or the top. In either case, the IE would appear to the user to be behaving very "inexpertly", since human raters use heuristics to immediately narrow the possible range of levels, whereas IE had to plow through some obviously irrelevant questions wherever it started.

2.1.2. Artie

ARTIE accepts input in the form of IF/THEN statements, and also asks the designer for a probability rating for the truth value of the statement and its reverse. By using the THINK option, the designer can create new rules, since the program will identify all implicational relationships not explicitely stated, and work out the probability ratings for them.

The user interrogates the program by typing in statements for which the program produces all related THEN statements and their probabilities or by asking for the probability that a certain IF/THEN statement is true. (see [7] for a fuller description)

This had a number of attractions. The user could enter known data about a person's language behaviour without going through a tedious consultation, and the probability ratings appeared to address the problem of insufficient data.

There were, however, further problems. Artie required much greater keyboarding from the user. It needed exact matches in input for a rule to fire, and it was very easy to miss rules as a result. And it was not at all clear how to assign probability. Furthermore, running the THINK option could generate incorrect rules. (see [8] for a more detailed critique)

2.2. Issues

The work with the prototype programs led to the consideration of the following issues as a prelude to further development.

2.2.1. The nature of the ASLPR levels.

The nature of the ASLPR is such that a person does not have to exhibit all the aspects of a level in order to be considered as being at that level. Likewise a person may have several characteristics from a number of levels. Writing rules for every possible combination of aspects and levels would be a near impossible task. It was therefore decided to seek alternatives to the standard expert system paradigm that would be simpler to prepare and would allow for greater rater involvement if necessary.

2.2.2. How an ASLPR "expert rater" works

At first it was thought that the heuristics of the expert informant would be independent of aspects of the scale. In this expectation we were guided by Neeson [9] who noted that agreement on global ASLPR scores could be reached from different bases, and sought "to see if there are distinctive features in the discourse at different ASLPR levels which may be a contributory, though unconscious, element in these subjective, yet reliable assessments." (p.86)

However, it turned out that this particular user's key indicators of a particular level were actually contained within the ASLPR itself (at least consciously). It was therefore decided to use this information to rewrite the ASLPR in such a way as to more readily reflect the indicators that a person was at a certain level, and so that the differences between levels were clearly identifiable. The rewritten ASLPR would replace the expert system rules that had proved so hard to write.

2.2.3. The appropriacy of the concept

Carr [1] argues that the focus on expert systems is misguided, and that we should be seeking to enhance human work rather than replace it, through the use of Expert Support Environments (ESEs). "An ESE would use expert system and other appropriate software technology, such as hypertext, in a very different way from a typical expert system - to develop and amplify the skills of human experts instead of trying to replace them." (p.80)

"It can operate on any of three levels depending on the expertise of the user. If the user is a neophyte, the ESE operates as mentor. It keeps the initiative, guiding the user to the correct conclusion. The mentor has many characteristics of an expert system, but focuses as much on teaching as on reaching conclusions.

"With more experienced users the ESE operates as coach. Here the initiative passes to the user, with the ESE available to offer whatever level of assistance the user requests. The coach still has the ability to intervene, however, if the user unwittingly gets in over his or her head.

"On the highest level, the ESE can operate as assistant ... taking care of the details and processes the user neither needs nor wants to know." (p.80)

"An ESE is designed to help develop and amplify human expertise. This expertise has a flexibility and an intuitiveness that well may lie beyond the reach of even the most powerful traditional expert system." (p.79)

This concept was in keeping with the needs of the program to be able to offer different kinds of support to users with different levels of experience, and had an appropriate focus on learning.

2.2.4. The appropriacy of the tools

It was clear that we may well have been expecting too much from the prototyping tools. A more flexible and powerful program was needed. Our search for a relatively cheap, PC-based development environment that would enable us to apply the ESE concept led to KnowledgePro, which was chosen on the basis of a comparative analysis of expert system shells [10].

Of particular interest was the fact that KnowledgePro combined an expert system shell with hypertext, a programming technique that enables the "layering" of information rather than a linear presentation, thus enabling the creation of a more flexible program. It also combines windows, colour and mouse control for ease of use.

3. THE FINAL PROGRAM: EXRATER

The central point of Exrater is the Main Menu. It serves as a home base from which the user can go to one of four main options.

3.1. Find Out More

Selection of this option takes the user to a screen offering further information about all aspects of Exrater, including an interactive map of the program.

3.2. The ASLPR

Selection of this option takes the user to a screen which lists all the ASLPR levels in the form of descriptions, examples and summaries. The user can move rapidly around these, looking at the details as required. These are provided via hypertext links. This option can be used to find out details about an ASLPR level, or to do a quick comparison between levels. It is most likely to be used by experienced raters as a quick way to check a rating arrived at by other means, and as such represents Carr's "assistant" mode.

3.3. The Simplified ASLPR

Selecting this option takes the user to another screen which offers a choice of aspects of language performance, such as fluency, production, intelligibility, appropriacy, grammar and vocabulary, definitions of which are provided at a key stroke with hypertext links to a dictionary of applied linguistics. Selecting any one of these aspects takes the user to a screen that presents a summary of language behaviour in this area, from which the user can easily make fine distinctions between levels. The full ASLPR descriptions are available for reference at a key stroke.

This option is used if the user has only partial information about a person's language behaviour, or to get a sense of how development occurs across levels within an aspect of language behaviour. Since it leaves the final decision about the level to the user, while simplifying the task and offering multi-layered support, it most closely resembles Carr's "coach" mode, though without allowing the program to override the user's decision.

3.4. Consult

Selection of this option results in the user being presented with each of the screens in The Simplified ASLPR (3.3. above), and being asked to choose which of the descriptions best matches what is known about the person's language behaviour. The program then suggests the probable ASLPR rating, and invites the user to go to The ASLPR option (3.2. above) to double-check it. This is closest to the "mentor" mode of Carr's model, though without any overt teaching, and still allowing the user to override the program.

4. DISCUSSION

4.1. Exrater and language proficiency assessment

The way in which the Exrater Consult mode generates an ASLPR rating by adding scores for individual skills is somewhat controversial. Although the approach adopted has similarities with that of the Foreign Service Institute test of speaking proficiency, which calls for the rater to provide a ranking on a six point scale for accent, comprehension, fluency, grammar and vocabulary, as well as a global score, the

ASLPR itself does not do this since

"the purpose of the scale is to identify points in a complex stream of development and not to focus predominantly on one component of that stream." [11] (p.25)

Quinn and McNamara [4] comment favourably on this aspect of the ASLPR.

"What is attractive about rating scales like the ASLPR is the courageous move away from measuring the assumed components of proficiency (lexis, phonology, syntax, etc) to observation of global performance" (p.9)

However, Neeson [9] argues that "In one sense the distinction is artificial, as even a global assessment is based on specific factors whether we are aware of it or not. An assessment must be based on something. The question is whether it is desirable to isolate different aspects of performance and if desirable, is it possible?" (p.25). Exrater shows it to be possible, but leaves the question of whether it is necessary open.

In investigating the FSI scale, Clifford [12] found that "although there was a relationship between the relative scores assigned to individual factors, no combination of factor scores was adequate to predict completely the global score." (28). The results of a trial of the Consult mode did find a correlation between Consult mode scores (based on a combination of factors) and global scores provided by teachers ($p = .0005$, $r = .8731$, $n = 16$, $df = 14$, one tailed) However, Exrater is not intended to model expert behaviour in the Consult mode, and the correlations achieved do not imply that raters should use what is in fact a programming convenience as a rating technique.

4.2. Exrater as an ESE

Exrater in its final form does not conform to the standard expert system concept. Although it mimics the consultation paradigm, it does not really use inferencing - it is a case of addition written as rules instead of procedures. Its heuristics are not really rules of thumb but are a variation of the "facts". Likewise, in the presentation of the questions it allows a greater range of human choice then in many expert systems.

At the same time, Exrater is far too undeveloped to be regarded as a fully-fledged Expert Support Environment, or in any sense a definitive test of the concept.

However, the development of Exrater has shown that the ESE concept is useful in planning a program to enhance the work of professionals.

It encourages the program developer to think of support for professionals' work, rather than substitution for it. It encourages a view of the users as continuing learners, however experienced they may be. It is more user-directed, offering choices to the user and allowing the user to self-select the level of support. The use of hypertext enables one version of a text to be accessible to all levels of experience. In other words, it reflects what we know about adults learning. As Carr puts it: "an ESE is much more facilitator than expert." (Carr 88:79)

Exrater is the beginning of a larger hypermedia project for language teachers. It is in this project that the ESE concept will be more fully implemented.

5. REFERENCES

[1] Carr, C. 1988. Brain Waves. AI Expert. November. pp.79-80.

[2] Department of Immigration and Ethnic Affairs. 1984. Report on the formal trialling of the ASLPR. Australian Government Printing Service. Canberra. p.1.

[3] Brindley, G. 1985. The Assessment of Second Language Proficiency: Issues and Approaches. Paper commissioned by the Committee of Review of the AMEP. Canberra. DILGEA.

[4] Quinn, T.J. and T. McNamara. Australian Second Language Proficiency Ratings. In Alderson C et al (eds). 1987. Reviews of English Language Tests. Washington, TESOL.

[5] Hageman, G. 1985. Inference Engine. Softman Enterprises.

[6] Hageman, G. 1987. This Inference Engine includes predicates to invoke stand-alone executables. The C Users' Group Newsletter. Sept/Oct.

[7] Cheatham, D. 1987. Artie: A rule-oriented inference engine for small expert system experiments. The C Users' Group Newsletter. May.

[8] Harris, G. 1987. Can Artie make it on the farm? The C Users' Group Newsletter. Sept/Oct.

[9] Neeson, S. 1985. An Exploratory Study of the Discourse Structure of the ASLPR Test of Oral Proficiency. Unpublished MA thesis.

[10] Freedman, R. 1987. Evaluating Shells. AI Expert. September.

[11] Ingram, D. 1981. The ASLPR: Nature, Development and Trialling. In Read, J.A.S. (ed) 1981. Directions in Language Testing. RELC Publications. Singapore University Press.

[12] Clifford, R.T. 1980. Foreign Service Institute Factors Scores and Global Ratings. In Frith, J.R. (ed) 1980. Measuring Spoken Proficiency. Georgetown University Press.

Computers in Education
A. McDougall and C. Dowling (Editors)
Elsevier Science Publishers B.V. (North-Holland)

SELECTION AND IMPLEMENTATION OF A COMPUTER BASED TRAINING SYSTEM FOR THE SOUTH EAST QUEENSLAND ELECTRICITY BOARD - A CASE STUDY IN INTRODUCING LARGE SCALE COMPUTER BASED TRAINING

Michael CROCK†,
Frank O'MARA††,
Jo SPRING†††

†CAL Unit, University of Queensland, St Lucia, Qld 4067;
††D.E.C., UCSQ. P.O. Darling Heights, Toowoomba, Qld 4350;
†††Div. of Commerce and Admin, Griffith University, Nathan, Qld 4111

In August 1988 the South East Queensland Electricity Board (SEQEB) proposed the idea of introducing an organization wide computer based training (CBT) system which would facilitate the management, delivery and assessment of training activities/programmes. As a result of this proposal, an organizational plan aimed at introducing an integrated CBT system was developed and implemented. The following case study details the procedures developed and results obtained from pursuing the proposed organizational plan. These procedures and results will be detailed from inception through to the current stage of developing complete system specifications and a functional trial implementation.

1. INTRODUCTION

In 1988 the South East Queensland Electricity Board (SEQEB) instigated action resulting in an organizational plan aimed at introducing an integrated CBT system. This plan originally had four steps as outlined below.

Step 1 was to be the establishment of the benchmark criteria for SEQEB's CBT system. These criteria would specifically detail SEQEB's requirements for both the computer management of training programmes and courses, as well as the computer delivery of training material and the assessment of training objectives. In both cases, the criteria would take into account personnel, hardware, and software considerations within the context of SEQEB's available resources (both human and financial) and required implementation timelines.

The end result of this step would be a written report detailing a criteria checklist which delineated essential, highly preferred and preferred capabilities for the CBT system.

Step 2 was to be the identification of commercial products which would be suitable for use in the SEQEB CBT system. An initial screening of these products would be carried out by comparing the functional capabilities of these products against established criteria from step 1.

The end result of step 2 was to be a written report recommending products for extended testing which would include the explicit rationale for the selection or non-selection of products evaluated.

Step 3 was to be the extended product trial for CBT systems successfully passing the screening process of step 2. This trial was to include the complete evaluation of systems as they existed "off-the-shelf", the feasibility of modification and enhancements using the products existing facilities, and the specifications for the development of the product (both user and manufacturer specific) in order to satisfy the CBT system criteria established in step 1.

Again the end result of this step was to be a written report detailing the measure of fit between commercial products as they existed, and the established CBT system criteria. The report was to include the required development specifications for the user and/or the manufacturer to customize the product for SEQEB's specific requirements.

Step 4 was to be the individual analysis and validation of manufacturers' responses to specifications for CBT systems enhancements from step 3. This was to include a comparative analysis of all products from step 3, and take into account the analysis of individual manufacturer's costs and timelines for development work outlined as essential to meet the specifications in step 3.

This last step was to culminate with a final report containing (1) a comparative analysis of the selected products (including the proposed enhancements to each product), (2) the recommendation of a CBT system based on an acceptable level of fit between the product capabilities and the CBT system criteria established in step 1, and (3) a draft implementation plan for the selected product.

The proposed elapsed time for all four steps, dependent on the number of products evaluated, was originally estimated as between 20 and 30 weeks. In reality, the four steps were compressed into two distinct CBT design and development phases with an elapsed time of approximately 34 weeks. The remainder of this case study details the procedures and results which eventuated from these two phases, and provides an insight into the existing technologies and industry specific considerations for the introduction of large scale CBT.

2. ORGANISATIONAL PLAN

2.1 Phase 1: Benchmark Criteria

Step 1 and phase 1 of the project were equivalent, and it was in fact the compression of the last three steps into phase two, which ultimately changed the original organizational plan. Phase 1 required extensive consultation with a variety of management levels and sections. These extended interviews culminated in the presentation, in October 1988, of the working report by Crock and Pfeffer [1]. The report was tabled with senior management and accepted by SEQEB in November, 1988.

In order to adequately detail the benchmark criteria for the critical (distinct) areas of management, delivery and assessment, the report presented a written description of the essential and preferred criteria in each of these three areas. The report concluded with an operational checklist to be used to assess existing CBT systems capabilities against those required. This checklist contained the following evaluation categories:

- Question Types/Answer Judging Capabilities
- Interactive Feedback Specifications and Processing
- Batch Processing
- Systems Management and Delivery Characteristics
- Student Management
- Course/Module/Unit/Lesson Management
- Results Management
- Systems Reports
- Courseware Editors
- Peripheral Support
- Hardware Requirements
- System Costs and Support

2.2 Phase 2: System Specifications

Phase 2 began by evaluating a series of CBT products against the established benchmark criteria, and discussing the possible function each product could fulfil in the ultimate CBT solution for SEQEB.

Following this series of evaluations, the working report by Crock and O'Mara [2] detailed a draft set of ideal SEQEB CBT system specifications. These were used to provide the background and rationale required to determine the appropriate developmental scenario(s) from the four possible CBT solutions which were to be detailed in the report.

In order to determine the appropriate developmental scenario, a structured evaluation of these system specifications was undertaken. This resulted in the delineation of the required and/or preferred functional capabilities of a SEQEB CBT system at three set developmental checkpoints of 1, 3, and 5 years.

All assumptions used in the development of the 1, 3, and 5 year criteria were explicitly detailed to ensure the correct perspective on the systems capabilities were presented. Where appropriate, prototype database structures, report formats, and management structures were included to illustrate the CBT system capabilities at the three developmental checkpoints.

The report concluded with an elaboration of the preferred developmental scenario, and recommendations regarding an appropriate strategy for the selection and implementation of a SEQEB CBT system.

An elaboration of these phase 2 activities will now be discussed.

3. CBT PRODUCT EVALUATION METHODOLOGY

3.1 CBT Product Evaluations

Following discussions with the SEQEB Technical Training Centre(TTC), a range of microcomputer and mainframe based CBT products were selected for investigation. A total of eleven products/systems were ultimately selected for evaluation.

The eleven products were initially assessed against the following five points derived from the original benchmark criteria.

1. The development and use of the CBT management system for SEQEB must be able to be effectively controlled by user defined requirements;

2. The introduction of software, hardware and personnel required by any segment of the ultimate CBT training solution must be consistent and/or cost-justified with current and proposed developmental strategies for SEQEB computing resources/services;

3. The delivery and delivery control capabilities of the CBT system must be flexible, permitting a variety of user defined applications;

4. The ultimate CBT training solution must allow for a variety of assessment scenarios (ie print-based, interactive, batch, subjective assessment);

5. Any product which may be used in the ultimate CBT training solution must have an adequate support structure in place, and have substantiated success in user support.

At the completion of these initial evaluations, six products did not warrant further investigation.

The vendors/distributors of the five remaining CBT products were requested to complete, in writing, answers for the full set of benchmark criteria developed by SEQEB for evaluation of CBT products. The information obtained in confidence from suppliers provided the required input to complete the evaluation, thereby leading to the development of possible solutions.

While the specific responses and results of these five evaluations remain confidential, the methodology and subsequent delineation of possible CBT system scenarios provides a significant insight into the nature and capabilities of systems which were ultimately identified as viable alternatives.

3.2 System Specifications

The following provides a summary of the steps taken in establishing the system specifications, and is subsequently followed by a full elaboration of each step:

1. A basic component model of the complete CBT System was used to quantify the essential requirements. Two approaches to the implementation of this model were proposed.

2. Utilizing the essential requirements, a description of the ideal End-Product was derived, and a number of options/scenarios were considered which broadly delineated the two approaches.

3. From these scenarios, a preferred option was identified and a broad System Specification developed using this scenario as a base.

This specification provided the starting point for a detailed evaluation/ investigation of preferred or feasible options, and the subsequent development of a recommended implementation strategy.

3.2.1 The Model

The model outlined in Figure 1, was used to quantify the essential requirements.

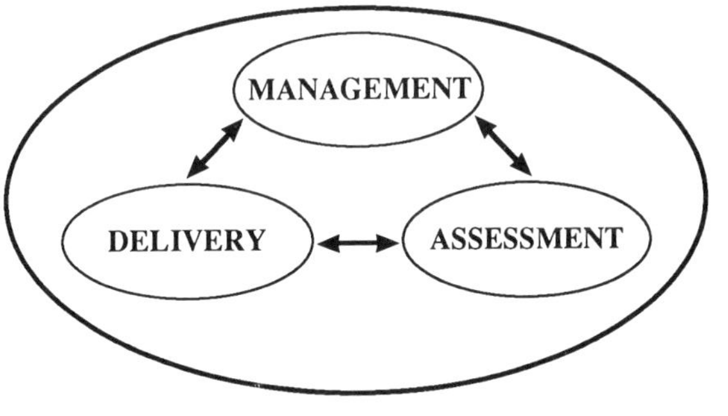

Figure 1: Relational Components of a CBT System

The area of critical concern and highest priority was the management component, and it was the user's view that this component would be a centrally controlled mainframe based system - a view consistent with the majority of SEQEB's major management and control system implementations, eg., Manpower, Personnel.

3.2.2. The Approach

Two basic approaches were considered when investigating proposed systems: (1) a constraints driven approach, and (2) an application driven approach.

A constraints driven approach basically

looks at the current hardware operating environment, and examines ways that the existing resources can be utilised to accommodate a proposed solution ie., The CBT System is integrated into the existing computer environment, and software packages/solutions are sought which have maximal compatibility with this environment. This approach minimizes the capital expenditure required on hardware, and assumes the existence of a variety of suitably compatible and feasible software solutions, and/or software productivity tools in the current environment to economically produce a component(s) of the proposed solution in a timely manner.

An application driven approach has as its basic tenet that the application determines the operating environment. This approach can be considered when a "complete solution" software package exists that ostensibly meets the user's requirements, and has a majority of the essential and/or preferred requirements. Software development costs can be minimised with such an integrated package, and the approach has enhanced merit when such a software package can operate in the existing hardware environment.

3.2.3 The End Product Description

Taking into account the two possible approaches, the user's perceptions of the ideal CBT system were refined. These refined perceptions formed the basis for the following description of a desirable End-Product:

An integrated system comprising three distinct modules:
-Managing training systems/programmes;
-Delivering a wide variety of training material; and,
-Assessing accurately the performance of trainees and training material.

An essential element of this system was to be its ease of use for management, for the authors of CAI material, and, in particular, for the trainees. This was to include both fast navigation for the experienced user, and response prompting for the inexperienced user, incorporating the use of menu driven screens with context sensitive help functions.

Of equal importance was the security/access consideration, which would allow/inhibit access to the system functions according to class of user. The menu system would present only those functions available to the class of user, and restrict supervisor/author access to the particular course or set of modules for which that person is responsible. Access to results and reporting would be likewise controlled by the security system.

Finally, the quality of the outputs from the management module, the management and control reports, was noted as being heavily dependent on the quality and completeness of the data that drives the application.

4. CBT System Options

The following describes four possible scenarios which resulted from work in phase 2. The four options reflect the range of developmental options available based on the two fundamental approaches discussed above.

4.1 Scenario 1

The first scenario involves a user developed mainframe base management component (using fourth generation database management tools), with the assessment and delivery components being provided by a PC based authoring system. The PC based system is to be enhanced to care for print based as well as the supplied interactive assessment and delivery of courseware.

With respect to the model in Figure 1, all three components are clearly identifiable, and the interfaces between them have the demonstrated ability to be modified to suit the user's requirements.

The approach for Scenario 1 is driven more by the constraints of minimizing hardware outlays, and is geared to utilising to the utmost the existing mainframe hardware and software development environment.

In terms of fitting the established requirements, all of the basic criteria outlined earlier can be met, as the system is to be developed from SEQEB's specifications.

4.2 Scenario 2

This scenario involves a user developed mainframe base management component (as per scenario 1), with the assessment and delivery components being provided by PC based systems which can be readily modified to produce print based testing.

With respect to the noted model, all

three components are clearly identifiable. However, due to the alternate software proposal, the interfaces between the components are not as readily able to be modified (compared to Scenario 1) to produce the outputs (results, etc.) to the user's specification.

4.3 Scenario 3

Scenario 3 involves implementation of an existing integrated mainframe/PC CBT solution.

With respect to the model, the three components are uniquely identified in the CBT product, but the extent to which the user is able to modify the format and content of the interfaces is often limited.

The approach for Scenario 3 is an applications approach - the CBT application requirement looks to existing/proposed software solutions to satisfy the need for a CBT system, and in-house software development costs are minimized.

In terms of fitting the established requirements, there is a general understanding that customization of such products could well prove to be an expensive and timely exercise given the unique requirements of SEQEB.

4.4 Scenario 4

Scenario 4 involves a completely user developed CBT system, to cater for print based as well as the interactive assessment and delivery of courseware.

Since, the system capabilities are user defined, all of the existing basic criteria would necessarily be met. However, because no attempt is made to utilise the expertise and functionality of existing products in the CBT sphere, experience shows this type of scenario to be extremely costly and time prohibitive. This therefore was deemed to be the least viable option.

5. THE PREFERRED SCENARIO

5.1 System Specifications Elaborated

Scenario 1 was selected as the option to provide the basis for the elaborated system specification, as it provided SEQEB with the greatest control over the development and content of the System's most important component - the Management component.

This specification outlined the requirements for developing a user defined mainframe management component of the CBT System for SEQEB. It noted the use of prototyping techniques to refine and clarify the user requirements, and utilised the microcomputer based TENCORE Authoring Language, to provide the assessment and delivery modules. The major benefit in adopting this scenario was that it outlined an "open architecture" approach, ie., the user could define the inputs to the management component, and the assessment and delivery components could be modified to produce the necessary outputs to be uploaded to the mainframe management component.

The specification included an introduction to the use of prototyping in the Structured Development Life Cycle (SDLC); an outline of the capabilities of the proposed CBT solution; and the accompanying time-frame over which the implementation could be phased. As and when was necessary, reference was made to the capabilities of the current computing environment at SEQEB to meet these requirements, and how the suggested implementation was likely to fit in with any future directions SEQEB may have considered making.

5.2 Prototyping

Many potential users of computer systems have quite complete mental pictures of the ultimate system they require, often down to many of the minor details. One of the major problems in the development of computer systems in the past has been the lack of an efficient interface between the user and the systems analyst which allows both parties to have a complete understanding of documentation of requirements.

Prototyping has been successfully used to quantify the user's requirement, and has allowed the systems analyst to interatively develop with the user a full specification of scope and functionality of the ultimate system, with the various stages of the working prototype serving as a tangible basis for further development and/or refinement. Software tools now exist that allow the systems analyst to rapidly develop input and enquiry screens to the user's satisfaction, quickly produce a variety of reports, and automate the documentation of the prototype to facilitate the technical specification requirements for the subsequent development of the production system.

From the systems analyst's point of view, prototyping fits into the SDLC in the Requirements Definition phase. In this exercise the use of prototyping was used to completely document the specification of the ultimate system.

The critical factor in the successful use of prototyping is that the computer environment has:

- The appropriate tools to quickly develop a working prototype;
- Such tools can cater for quick response to modifications to the prototype to cater for iterative development; and
- The outputs of the prototype can be directly used in the coding of the eventual system, so that there is a minimal time lag between the working prototype and the operational system. (2-3 months maximum).

A draft prototype of the management component of the CBT system was developed using dBASE III, and was presented as a component of the report ultimately submitted to SEQEB.

This first draft, was intended to serve as the starting point for the subsequent development of the complete management component which would ultimately address the requirements of SEQEB.

6. CONCLUSIONS

The final reported development plans included specifications and expectations of the CBT system at the nominated stages of 1,3, and 5 years from implementation.

The two phases completed to date were to provide SEQEB with a viable starting point for the implementation of a SEQEB CBT System.

Implementation of a trial CBT system based on the recommendations contained in this case history is now proceeding. This reflects a commitment from SEQEB management to the project, and to the accepted developmental scenario.

Such a commitment was, in the end, easily realised when one of SEQEB's major critical success factors, Safety, was readily identified with the proposed CBT system. SEQEB's management will have the capacity to manage trainees through all aspects of professional training necessary to become efficient, safety conscious practitioners in the electrical industry. With such a system, SEQEB would also be able to demonstrate and document that all aspects of training have been satisfactorily completed before a prospective employee/contractor begins and/or continues working for SEQEB.

It was the recommendation that Scenario 1 provides the solution which maximizes SEQEB's input into the management and control aspects of the CBT system, while effectively utilising the TenCORE range of PC Authoring, Delivery and Assessment tools. By combining these two factors, and utilising the existing hardware and personnel structures within SEQEB, Scenario 1 satisfies the specified requirements for a SEQEB CBT system as they currently stand.

6.1 Future Prospects

At the time of going to press, the first prototype solution incorporating both the PC based products and a mainframe based management system has reached a functional stage. Initial reactions of the CBT project team to the working prototype have been positive. Alterations and enhancements to the prototype point positively to providing SEQEB with a fully functional integrated CBT system by the end of 1990, and a fully automated CBT system within the guidelines of the three year plan. Since the initial discussions, TenCORE product developments have provided additional features which SEQEB would have had to develop, thus reducing the total estimated development time.

With the latest prototype system, there are clear facilities in place to enable the CBT system to ultimately link directly with other SEQEB databases, such as their human resource database, thus providing a complete and customized training management system.

REFERENCES

[1] Crock, M. and Pfeffer, A. Selection and Implementation of a SEQEB Computer Based Training System: Benchmark Criteria for the Evaluation of Existing CBT Systems. SEQEB Working Report, October 1988.

[2] Crock, M. and O'Mara, F. Selection and Implementation of a SEQEB Computr Based Training System: System Specifications for SEQEB's CBT System. SEQEB Working Report, March 1989.

Computers in Education
A. McDougall and C. Dowling (Editors)
Elsevier Science Publishers B.V. (North-Holland)

COMPUTER BASED TRAINING IN THE ROYAL NAVY

Cdr A.E. MIZEN, Cdr P.S. MARLEY, Lt Cdr G. MOORE

Directorate of Naval Educational Training Support, Ministry of Defence, Whitehall, London SW1A 2BE and Royal Naval School of Educational Training Technology, HMS Nelson, Portsmouth.

1. BACKGROUND

The impact of new technology on the design of the Navy's equipment has been tremendous. The men and women who are destined to operate and maintain the Navy's weapons, machinery and sensors need comprehensive training of the right quality. It is the task of the Navy trainers to ensure that this training is provided. The Royal Navy makes a major investment in training with some 7,500 personnel under instruction at any one time. The Navy provides over 1,000 different courses in subjects that range from reactor physics to cookery and in length from 3 years to just a few days. The scope of Naval Training is immense both in terms of breadth of subject matter and in the nature of the delivery strategy. In any of our major training establishments we can see a spectrum of strategies ranging from classroom-based "chalk and talk" through equipment related practical instruction to full scale simulation.

It is believed, with some justification, that the Royal Navy has earned an enviable reputation for the quality and relevance of its training methods and this is due, in no small measure, to its willingness to incorporate new training methods whenever appropriate. This most certainly applies to CBT which has a long pedigree stretching back to the 1960s.

Naval interest in programmed instruction took an active form in the Winter of 1961-62 when the Admiralty conducted a small scale trial at HMS ST VINCENT, a training establishment for new entry sailors. This trial was sufficiently successful to allow the planning of a much larger trial at HMS COLLINGWOOD, an establishment responsible for training in electrical engineering. This later trial used Auto Tutors which were based on 35mm film slide. These machines could use branching techniques and the programmes were intended to be fully automated and be completely self-contained. The trainees' reaction to the early programmes was not, however, completely favourable. After the novelty of pushing buttons had worn off, the trainees began to hate the machines and longed to get back to conventional instruction.

All sorts of methods were considered in overcoming this 'Luddite' mentality on the part of the trainees. Not least was the concept of integrated programmed instruction, which advocated a mixture of traditional and programmed instructions, tutorial work, practical work and sporting activities.

Several claims were made for this method:

1. It could significantly reduce the length of course for the average trainee.

2. The quality of the training material and assessment were known.

3. The instructors could devote more time towards the weaker trainees.

Yet the fundamental problem remained .... the trainees disliked it. Resistance to its more widespread introduction grew and grew until the whole method was rejected.

However, the investment in programmed learning was not wasted. It has forced those charged with the task into a critical examination of the courses and syllabuses from which they were to work. Increasingly, trainers were being asked to state their learning objectives in measurable terms and to justify systematically the traditional methods they were using. The search for a more rigorous approach to solving training problems was now on. From this effort the Navy's Systems Approach to Training evolved.

Put simply, a man's job is analysed and the task, knowledge, skills and attitudes are defined and then used to form a model. Next the training design takes place when the operational objectives are set, these define precisely what the man will be able to do when he is operational. The training objectives are derived from these .... and here we look for statements of what the trainers are to achieve within the establishment. The shortfall between these two objectives is made up by On Job Training. The training design team go on to state exactly what subject materials are to be taught in the Instructional Specification and finally they specify, in detail, the assessment that the trainees are to undergo. The next stage is the training execution. The Instructional Specification is put into operation and used to generate lesson plans and practical work. Resources are allocated and as the course runs the performance of trainee and instructor is monitored. Before leaving the training establishment, the trainee is provided with a detailed task book that describes all the material he must cover during his On Job Training. Internal Quality Control is used to monitor performance within the training establishment and is, if you like, a measure of efficiency. External Quality Control is used to assess a man's performance when operational and acts as a measure of the training effectiveness. Both these controls are used to refer back to the Job Analaysis so that necessary improvements can be made to the original model.

The 1970s gave clear indications to the Navy's trainers that not only were computers here to stay, but that they clearly promised much for the training environment. An early example of Navy CBT will serve as an illustration. The Action Data Automated Weapons System or ADAWS requires an operator to memorise a lot of manual injections which are used to input data gathered from a variety of sensors in order to build up and maintain an action information picture. These injections must be both quickly made and accurate. The techniques were taught by traditional means with a normal failure rate of 20%. The introduction of a CBT keyboard trainer using high quality courseware led to a reduction in the failure rate to 3%. However, considerations of cost and capability meant that, for a time this promise was not fully realized.

In 1984 a CBT Pilot Study Project was set up by DNETS. Divided into Procurement and Evaluation phases, the trial was designed to see if the Navy could capitalise on CBT, so it addressed the following questions:

a. Is CBT instructionally effective?

b. How do trainers and trainees respond to it?

c. Are there any clear cost savings?

d. How far can CBT equip trainees for their jobs?

In September 1984 RN Training Establishments were asked to submit suggestions of their own training problems that could possibly be solved by using a CBT strategy. Some 47 separate projects were proposed and already at this stage it was clear that few establishments knew enough about CBT to specify their hardware and software requirements and more importantly, few were able to justify CBT as the optimum solution to their training 'problem'. Despite this early set back, the study progressed with selection based on the need to provide a spread of applications across the training programme as well as a set of 22 criteria including: Fleet's priority, stability of course content, effects on down-stream training and current course failure rate.For each of the 6 projects selected the requirement was to provide a Turn-Key solution of hardware plus a nominal 5 hours of courseware. The courseware was to be delivered on stand-alone, IBM compatible personal computers providing high-resolution colour graphics. The projects were duly implemented at 6 sites spread across the South of England and became operational in November 1986. The evalusation process began immediately, with both quantitative and attitudinal data being collected throught 1987. Several limitations were quickly encountered such as: lack of evaluation manpower and turbulence, technical difficulties with hardware at sea, 'poor' choice of CBT projects, conflict between shore and sea training needs, difficulties in quantifying changes in trainee performance (CBT material only small part of total training package) and lack of control classes. Perhaps these serve as salutary reminders for any would-be evaluators of CBT in the future that it is essential to carry out a comprehensive training needs analysis. It is not enough simply to accept the instructional analysis provided by normal training documentation. Such documentation is basically instructor orientated which means that an experienced instructor can ensure that a training objective has been taught well. Conversely CBT courseware must be seen to relate directly to the requirements of the training objective. The tendency to assume that the good qualities of the CBT medium will emerge automatically whatever the application, must be resisted.

The evaluation of the trial did produce some general answers. Tutorial CBT produced no significant increase in trainee performance, but it was believed that the trainees gained a deeper understanding and their retention was better. The reception to tutorial CBT was good, but only when the courseware was of a high quality (which in turn means high cost) with a strong gaming component, but even then, trainees were wary of over-exposure. High quality courseware can be best described as bespoke software produced by a professional authoring company totally versed in the language used and adopting a minimum branching technique offering at least two chances to the trainee before reverting to an alternative presentation route; the response requirement should be varied and not simply yes/no and/ or multi-choice. Just as with the machines of the 1960s, it was clear that sailors would not accept total replacement of traditional instruction with CBT.

All in all, the case for further investment by the Royal Navy in tutorial CBT was not sufficiently proven. As a result, funding for this mode of CBT has been stopped.

The results for CBT used in the drill and practice mode were much more encouraging. Trainees and trainers responded positively and could identify clear improvements in performance. Equipment savings were considerable and were sufficient to compensate for the fact that Naval training cannot easily capitalise manpower savings. Consequently, the Royal Navy will continue to fund projects of this type. Only a small amount of simulator CBT was tested in the evaluation trial but the evidence gleaned from this showed that this mode of CBT has tremendous promise both in the quality of training and the savings in capital costs. Once again further funding will be made available for appropriate projects.

2. CURRENT APPLICATIONS

Of the many examples of courseware currently in use within the Royal Navy training environment a good example is a package called Rule of the Road. Written in TENCORE it was produced by Rediffusion Simulation Ltd to the Royal Navy's specification. It allows Officers of the Watch to practice their application of the international sea-going Highway Code. The courseware is divided into two components; the Student package and the Tutor package.

With the student package all facilities are presented to the student via a menu which, depending upon his/her expertise, can be partially disabled until proficiency has been demonstrated. The facilities available include:

a. An introduction to the system which includes a small gaming package to improve the student's ability to manipulate the mouse.

b. A "rule book aid" which is available to the student as a reference during certain stages of the course when he needs a reminder. He might ask to see a vessel's light configuration and by pressing the space bar the data is presented from any of four aspects: dead ahead, starboard, port and astern.

c. Access to three scenarios covering:

(1) Guided Demonstration - where the student is taken through a scenario and presented with the "staff answer" to the situation.

(2) Practice Scenario - in which the student may practice the application of the rules given a choice of various weather, light conditions and sea areas. The student has full access to the rule book aid and is given screen prompts when actions or decisions have to be made. For every action taken the student is given feedback which compares his/her choice of action with the staff answer and other alternatives.

(3) Test Scenario - in which all the actions of the student are recorded for subsequent expert debriefing by an instructor. The student has no access to hints, prompts and aids.

The Tutors Package contains a powerful simulation engine which allows the expert instructors to set up scenarios or modify existing scenarios without any authoring or computing expertise. All are generated by means of a series of menus and space exists for up to 999 scenarios. They may all run as guided demonstrations, practice scenarios or tests. The parameters available to the instructor include:

a. Own ship type (eg Frigate, yacht, Aircraft carrier etc)

b. Sea conditions

c. Visibility conditions

d. Own ship course and speed

e. Other ships involved - up to 6
- their course and speed
- their actions

f. Time jump available

g. Time prompts (ie assessment of situation deadlines)

h. Staff answers to - situation assessments
- actions required

There remains one further element of the Rule of the Road package and that is the "hidden" management package which records details of students' performance in the test scenarios. Rather than seek a computer generated intelligent debrief of the students' actions in these situations, for which there are no "absolute" correct answers, it was decided that the best debrief was available from the instructor. Thus the instructor can, at a time suitable to himself, assess the actions of his students and provide an expert debrief.

In sum this application illustrates many of the principles which the Royal Navy is currently seeking in its CBT solutions, in other words:

a. They allow training in skills which are otherwise only capable of being practised and assessed in expensive and not necessarily controllable or predictable situations.

b. They allow scenarios to be generated by subject matter experts without their needing authoring or computing skills.

c. They are readily transportable and can be used at sea.

d. They are very cost effective.

e. They are successful.

3. FUTURE DEVELOPMENTS

The government purse is limited and, consequently, the Royal Navy is always seeking value for money in its various purchases. Little wonder then that all prospective projects are scrutinised very carefully with an investment appraisal, comparing different training methodologies and styles, being the cornerstone to future developments.

The successful use of computers in training requires more than simply a knowledge of computing. Practitioners also need knowledge and skills in training, training technology, educational psychology and graphics design. The cost of computer hardware is falling rapidly but the cost of software development remains high. Commercially produced courseware is of varying quality and requires careful evaluation before acceptance.

In the early days of Naval Computer training there was always a conflict between the Operational Staff, who wanted realism (represent the actual task and its environment), and the Trainer who took the educational theorist attitude that the objective could be satisfied by less sophisticated simulation. More recently there has been a general acceptance that, whilst high fidelity may offer the potential for high positive learning transfer, it may not create an efficient environment in which learning may take place. The requirement to facilitate learning and that to encourage transfer is not necessarily the same. So a device in which skills may be effectively acquired ie against criteria such as speed and accuracy, may not produce high levels of transfer. The aim of training to 80% of the level of skill required in the Operations Room and to obtain 100% transfer, is not the same task as training to 100% of the Operations Room required skill level but accepting only 80% transfer. The former task is likely to be possible with a less sophisticated training device and the training standards will probably be reached more quickly. This is, however, a simplistic view and does not take into account the ability of the operational world to achieve these training tasks or the necessary delicate balancing of cost and training transfer needed to obtain the maximum cost effective training benefits.

The potential of the cheap micro for drill and practice and simulation is acknowledged, but it is all dependent on the ability of the people responsible for training to be able to complete the training analysis necessary to produce a comprehensive specification and assess which delivery media to use. Since not all training managers are adequately qualified or experienced to make the decision of how best and when to apply CBT a checklist has been devised (see Annex A). There is no ideal "score" but each statement which applied to the training in question increases the liklihood that it would benefit from CBT. It is acknowledged, however, that any of the factors might be so important that it outweighs all the others.

For CBT Procurement the Royal Navy has endeavoured to aid the "Non-expert" training manager by steering him through the vagaries of contractural placements. The interface between any contracted commercial company for CBT courseware provision and the training manager is very important. The success of the project is very dependent on the ability of the trainer to be able to specify exactly what instructional outcome is required - ie a functional specification. The lessons learned so far have indicated that the normal teaching documentation is too Instructor orientated to specify completely the learner outcomes necessary for a CBT solution. Consequently it has been RNSETTS task, as experts in the field, to devise a template for writing a functional specification and to act as advisers to both schools and the civilian companies. The favourite watchword is "do not impose a solution on the contactor" instead give him the training objective in precise behavioural terms and allow him the opportunity to satisfy the training needs. Having stated that there is one avenue of approach in which to encourage a tighter specification; the days when the in-house amateur programmer was given time and money to develop, so called, useful and effective material are limited unless some common standard is adopted which is Navy-wide compatible and, thereby, allows an individuals knowledge, flair and enthusiasm. As with the Rule of the Road programme, and there are other examples in the Navy's arsenal, the provision of a "Toolbox" programme has much to merit it and allows the amateur to continue his work. Another feature of the standardisation deal lies in the hardware and the Navy has settled for the IBM 286/386-chip clone, with MS-DOS and VGA colour facility. Specialist peripherals, printers and unusual boards may be added as required but the requirements must be within the original specification. It is acknowledged that some military CBT application will fall outside the standardisation package and manufacturers may respond accordingly.

What of the future? So far CBT in the Royal Navy has, quite rightly, been directed towards training that is delivered to individual trainees at work stations. Whether these work stations are stand alone or part of a classroom network is of no consequence to the trainee, as none of his actions at his terminal will affect any of his fellow trainees. This concentration of effort into areas of training that involve one-to-one instruction means that CBT to date has had little influence on team training. This has remained the province of traditional simulators which frequently employ equipment which is similar to, if not the same as, that fitted at sea.

High Fidelity simulators are excellent for assessing the skills of the trained man or team; they are not so good at teaching those skills. The reason for this is simple, it is very difficult for the trainer to make a traditional simulator, often based on actual equipment, respond intelligently to the differing needs of a trainee during the various stages of his training. In order to improve this, future simulators should make greater use of some of the techniques developed by the CBT industry. Such developments may still be round the corner, so for now we are content that drill and practice and low fidelity simulation applications are proven success stories that the Royal Navy will continue to fund under the value for money banner.

It is also planned that future developments will address that area of Naval training over which there is least control - on-board continuation training. Although there has been little opportunity to trial CBT courseware at sea programmes like the Rule of the Road are about to be launched at the sea-going trainees. The compactness of the new generation PCs will allow it to be used at sea as an onboard trainer, thus enabling maintenance of perishable skills in the operational environment at a very low cost.

Another possibility is the provision of some alongside facilities that could be developed to offer the ships in harbour a more attractive alternative to ship board training, which is often conducted under adverse conditions, but also provide a facility for checking courseware before being taken onboard and instructing ship's staff how best to utilise the material.

In summary, it is fully realised that CBT is not the answer to all the Navy's problems, and is merely another training medium which can be used to advantage in appropriate circumstances. However as the technology of the micro-computer and the video disc become more and more sophisticated, we envisage an expanding programme of low cost CBT applications both ashore and afloat to capitalise on the obvious benefits to be gained from the strategy.

CBT CHECKLIST

ANNEX A

	STATEMENT	YES	NO
1.	The basic content is likely to remain over a long period.		
2.	There is a large throughput of students (hundreds rather than tens).		
3.	Highly standardised instruction is required at a number of different locations.		
4.	There is a long student waiting list for the training.		
5.	There are clear, testable training objectives.		
6.	The training can easily be broken down into short courses or modules.		
7.	There is a high ratio of trainers to students.		
8.	The equipment used in the training is costly, dangerous or simply not available.		
9.	The subject matter of the training is procedural or knowledge based.		
10.	Error free job performance is vital.		
11.	It is desirable to reduce stress in the early stages of skill training.		
12.	There is pressure to reduce the time students are away from work to attend a training course.		
13.	There is a need for the training to be available on demand wherever it is required.		
14.	Qualified instructors are rare or difficult and expensive to train.		
15.	The training is related to the use of a computer application.		
16.	Dynamic graphics are required for the training to be effective.		

Computers in Education
A. McDougall and C. Dowling (Editors)
Elsevier Science Publishers B.V. (North-Holland)

SOME THOUGHTS ABOUT COMPUTERS IN TRAINING AND INSTRUCTIONAL DESIGN

Harry MOUTON

Applied Learning Australasia, 71 Epping Road, North Ryde, NSW 2113, Australia.

Technology-based training systems such as CBT, ICBT, CBIV may not reach their potential unless instructional design theory and practice advances as quickly as the development of such technologies. Bloom's notion of *alterable variables* provides an alternative approach for ensuring mastery of required performances. Merrill's *Component Design Theory* suggests ways in which designers may more effectively use the special abilities of the computer to develop instruction that could not be delivered in another medium. Both these theoretical positions can be of tremendous benefit to designers and developers of CBT.

1. INTRODUCTION

There has been much research into learning and the effect of instruction on the learner. Many researchers seem to be looking for that elusive panacea, the technological marvel that will solve the problems of education and training. Is Computer-Based Training (CBT) that solution?

There seems to be a general consensus that CBT is not fulfilling its potential. Other innovations such as teaching machines, programmed instruction, individually prescribed instruction, the Keller plan, language laboratories and instructional TV have similarly failed to fulfilled their promise. Will Intelligent Computer-Based Training (ICBT) and Computer-Based Interactive Video (CBIV) also prove to be less effective than their apparent potential?

In their book *Understanding Computer-Based Instruction*, Siegle and Davis (1986) examine the computer courseware problem. Whereas they recognize that "computer delivery can increase instructional effectiveness dramatically", they also state that "the most serious problem facing computer-based instruction is the lack of sufficiently excellent courseware packages".

Many who argue that CBT is ineffective choose the worse of drill and practice tutorial instruction to support their case. As Siegle and Davis show, there are effective software packages. However, is it possible that even these effective packages could be more effective?

Merrill (1986a) argues that research which compares CBT with a live teacher is meaningless. The computer allows us to use instructional strategies that would be difficult or impossible to use with live trainers, TV or text? Thus it is the instructional strategy that leads to the improvements in learning not the fact that the instruction was computer delivered.

Merrill argues that it is instructional strategies and not software/hardware that will cause differences in learning outcomes. He believes that more and better instructional strategies and different content representations must be identified if CBT and CBIV are to reach their potential as instructional delivery systems.

Romiszowski (1986) states that instructional design "is intellectually more difficult" than programming. Effective instruction is hard to design. Those involved in designing CBT or CBIV must use the better instructional designs if they are to design effective instruction.

Intelligent tutors and expert systems are often discussed, although there is little evidence that ICBT is more effective than conventional CBT. Instructional design is likely to be more important then technical production and programming in the design of intelligent systems.

Reigeluth (1983, 1987) outlines the contributions of instructional theorists to the present knowledge base. However, the instructional theorists therein are simply describing pre-1977 theories. Apart from Merrill's new theory, there seems to have been no real developments in instructional design theory since 1977.

U.S. and Australian institutions which offer instructional design or CBT courses are producing practitioners who easily find lucrative employment in business and industry. There appears to be no new theorists on the horizon.

If this trend continues, our field will become top heavy with practitioners and nobody will be developing new or improved instructional design methodologies and theories, or doing essential research on instruction. We desperately need more instructional scientists if the abilities and practices of practitioners are to improve.

This paper discusses two areas of research that may help. First, Bloom's (1976) *alterable variables* can be easily altered in CBT, to lead to astounding improvements in learning. Second, Merrill's *Component Design Theory* (1986) may be the first instuctional theory to be developed especially for the computer's characteristics.

The following sentence evaluates the present state of the use of computers in education and training: CBT has not fulfilled its potential as an instructional medium because instructional design theory and (consequentially) practice have not kept pace with advances in hardware development and computer programming.

2. BLOOM'S THEORY OF LEARNING

In his book *Human Characteristics and School Learning* (1976) Benjamin Bloom offered a theory which included the idea of alterable variables. This part of the paper discusses the implications of Bloom's alterable variables for the design and development of CBT, ICBT and CBIV.

2.1 A Brief Review of Bloom's Theory

Bloom suggests that trainees become very similar with regard to achievement, rate of learning and motivation for further training when provided with favourable learning conditions. Such favourable learning conditions can be obtained by the manipulation of three interdependent alterable variables, which are:
1) Cognitive Entry Behaviour (CEB) - the extent to which the trainee has already mastered the prerequisites for the proposed training.
2) Affective Entry Characteristics (AEC.) - the extent to which the trainee is (or can be) motivated to engage in the training.
3) Quality of Instruction (QI) - the extent to which the cues used, practice given, reinforcement given and feedback/correctives used are appropriate to the trainee's needs.

Bloom's learning theory has relevance to trainers and designers involved in developing adaptive computer based instruction. CBT, ICBT and CBIV may be more effective, efficient and appealing if we use strategies which deliberately alter Bloom's alterable variables.

Bloom argues that differences among trainees after CBT have occurred as a direct result of their arriving for training with different preparation. They arrive having mastered different amounts of the prerequisites, with different motivation levels and with different preferences for the type of CBT instruction used.

If CBT designers and developers are able to use instructional strategies where every trainee in the group enters each training task with:
a) all the basic *prerequisites* for the learning involved, and
b) high *motivation* to attempt the learning,
and if the training is so varied that it:
c) caters for differing needs of trainees in:
   * the type and quality of the *cues* received
   * the amount of *practice* required,
   * the type of *reinforcement* required, and
   * the type of *feedback/correctives* needed
then there should be little variation in achievement, motivation and learning speed.

Bloom argues that when the three interdependent variables are manipulated IQ and aptitude are no longer good predictors of success. Amount of prerequisites learned, motivation to train and quality of the CBT are better predictors.

At present, most CBT does not address Bloom's alterable variables. There are differences among trainees in prerequisite knowledge and skills, and in attitudes and motivations, when they start the CBT. There are also differences and in the quality of instruction provided by the computer for each learner.

Developers of CBT, ICBT and CBIV courseware can alter Bloom's variables to improve learning. We can increase the quality of the instruction and can cause better attitudes to learning. We can use better diagnostic/corrective techniques to help students attain mastery of each learning task and thus the prerequisites for the next.

2.2 Altering Cognitive Entry Behaviour

Cognitive entry behaviour is defined as those prerequisite types of knowledge, skills and competencies that are essential if a particular new performance is to be learned. A Trainee's CEB is alterable by appropriate instruction.

Cognitive entry behaviour is by far the most important variable in training. There is a definite predictive relationship between CEB measured before training and achievement measured after training. Entry variation in CEB accounts for approximately 50% of the final variation in achievement (typically $r = +0.70$).

Cognitive entry behaviours are not fixed, they can be altered. Trainers designing CBT can better prepare their trainees for their CBT by developing a system which allows trainees to:
a) gain the prerequisites for the first task before the course or unit begins, and
b) gain mastery of each performance in the sequence before they proceed to the next.
Whether you use system or learner control depends on the maturity of your trainees.

To ascertain whether trainees have the prerequisites for the first performance to be learned diagnostic measures could be included in the CBT, or the computer could consult the record of previous learning of the particular trainee and design appropriate remedial training.

Also, we can use mastery learning strategies to assist each trainee to master each performance and, consequentially, to obtain the prerequisites for the next performance in the sequence.

If trainees do not obtain the objectives during their first interaction with the learning, the computer can advise them to undertake correctives. Such correctives would normally be in alternative CBT lessons - those with different cues, sequencing, participation and practice.

The computer can be used to diagnose whether the reason why a trainee if having difficulty with the present CBT learning task is because of deficiencies in assumed prior learning or problems with the present training/learning.

Once designers realise the importance of the alterability of cognitive entry behaviour then CBT will be more effective. Because a student can, by appropriate remedial instruction, be given the cognitive entry behaviour necessary for him to achieve well, designers should strive to incorporate strategies which attempt to alter a trainee's cognitive entry behaviour.

2.3 Altering Affective Entry Characteristics

Trainees' affective entry characteristics are a complex compound of their interest in the content, motivation, attitude to training, and self concept, all of which are shaped by their history of success in related training.

Trainees' who believe that they are successful learners tend to have a more positive attitude towards training, try harder, and are more likely to achieve than trainees' who lack such positive attitudes. Affect and achievement are closely related with 25% of variation in achievement being attributable to entry variation in affect (typically r = +0.50).

Affect is alterable. The affective entry characteristics of a trainee can be modified by deliberate use of motivational strategies, and are modified by the student's ongoing experience in mastery situations. As always, success in training/learning breeds further success.

We can alter affect by trying to develop CBT which lead trainees through successful learning experiences. Rather than frustrate trainees with unnecessarily complex ideas or problems early in the learning sequence, developers can ensure trainees' encounter learning hurdles in a systematise and sensitive progression.

Using a feedback/corrective system can enhance the affect of trainees and lead to greater achievement levels. Trainees should feel that they are only being assessed to diagnose and overcome weaknesses. Testing if for them.

A criterion referenced system will also enhance the motivation and self concepts of trainees. If trainees are compared with performance criteria rather than with each other they are less likely to feel inadequate and are more likely to attempt to achieve those criteria.

2.4 Altering Quality of Instruction

Bloom's four components of quality of instruction are the appropriateness of the instructional *cues*, the amount of *participation*, the frequency and type of *reinforcement* and the effectiveness of the *feedback and correctives*.

Instructional *cues* include information about the training, text and graphic screens about the procedures, concepts, and principles to be learned, and directions about what to do next or how to do any activities. The quality of the cues and trainee achievement are related.

The *participation* of trainees in training relates to the active involvement of trainees in carrying out the directions and suggestions in the CBT. Trainees differ in the amount of participation and practice they need before they gain proficiency. The extent and type of participation in training is the best indicator of quality and is highly related to achievement.

One major difference between good and poor CBT is the use of *correctives* rather than merely correct/incorrect feedback. Feedback devices diagnose learning deficiencies and correctives provide alternative cues, additional practice and additional time. The relationship between feedback/correctives and achievement is high.

Trainers and designers who develop CBT courseware need to react positively to research about Quality of Instruction. They need to:

* Improve the quality of the instructional cues in text, graphics, animation and sound,
* Increase the frequency of reinforcement and match it to the individuals preferences,
* increase the amount of participation and practice of the trainers in their learning,
* develop trainee/system manageable feedback systems so trainees can assess their learning and make decisions about what to do next, and
* provide alternative corrective instruction so the trainees/system may initiate correctives when learning deficiencies are detected.

Better cues can be provided by use of a greater variety of alternative instruction - text, computer graphics, animation sequences, graphs, diagrams, tables, adjunct readings, texts, video-tapes, additional CBT and computer games.

CBT can be made more interactive by use of simulations, activities and questions. Trainees' receive CBT presentations and attempt questions and activities before receiving feedback about their attempts. The CBT should attempt to raise the level of cognitive processing by trainees.

Feedback about the accuracy of manipulations within a simulation, answers to questions, or the results of activities can be provided by a complete computer analysis of the trainees' attempts compared with expert model practice.

Corrective suggestions can be provided during or following the feedback about what a trainee can do to remedy the situation if they have an incorrect answer to a question or the wrong result for an activity or simulation.

About 25% of the variation in trainee learning can be attributed to the quality of the CBT.

If developers improve the quality of their CBT instruction then the level of achievement of trainees will increase, more trainees will have more of the prerequisites for subsequent learning, and, because they have more successful experiences, trainees will become increasingly motivated to attempt further training.

2.5 Summary

Instructional designers and CBT developers have largely ignored Bloom's (1976) Model. They have used only one part - feedback. Bloom sees mastery learning as the use of any strategies that enhance mastery - not just the use of feedback.

Bloom's alterable variables may be an excellent base for the development of new theory and practice for the design of CBT, ICBT and CBIV.

3. MERRILL'S COMPONENT DESIGN THEORY

Many technological advances have promised great improvements in learning. None have delivered. Presently, ICBT and ICBIV advocates are promising massive improvement in learning and argue that "conventional CBT and CBIV" is ineffective. However, the advocates of such "high tech" instructional methods have not collected any hard data support their claims.

As previously stated, if CBT or ICBT improves learning then it is because better instructional strategies and content representations are more easily implemented with a computer than with other delivery methods. As for ICBT, the use of sophisticated programming techniques will not automatically guarantee more effective instructional strategies, more adequate content representations, or better trainee learning.

Merrill (1986a) argues that the computer's number crunching ability may best be used with "experiential content", where the trainee uses the computer to experience a simulated reality. Does this mean that a computer is not useful for the delivery of tutorial instruction?

3.1 CBT Tutorial - Where does it fit?

A lot of CBT uses a Branching Programmed Model of instruction. This consists of the following:
1) Present a page of text (and graphics?).
2) Ask a question.
3) If the student's answer is correct provide feedback saying "you are correct".
4) If the student's response is incorrect provide feedback saying "you are incorrect" and then provide the right answer.
5) Repeat this cycle for the next page of text.

Note that typical CBT as described above seldom includes corrective instruction when an error is made. Note also that the above instructional model is applicable to a live teacher or programmed texts - a computer was not necessary.

Some tutorial CBT attempts to use a Socratic Model. Such CBT asks questions to draw out of trainees their understanding of the phenomena. A Socratic procedure attempts to correct trainee errors by showing how their reasoning is faulty, where they have misconceptions and where their understanding is incomplete. This model may be used by a computer or live teacher but is hard to develop in text or video.

However, most tutorial CBT fails to follow the rules of inquiry set out by Collins and Stevens (1983) and others. Usually the computer program selects information from a subject matter database and presents it to the trainee via text/graphic frames, or tests the students understanding of the content via question frames.

There are useful CBT tutorial models. In a "mixed initiative dialogue" the trainee is able to control the sequence of content presentations and questions a little. The critical variable remains the presentation of parts of the content and embedding these content fragments with questions for the trainee. Merrill (1986a) calls this type of content "structural" - subject matter as it is represented in text. Trainees may be able to branch from place to place but to where they can go is controlled by the instructional designer/trainer, who also selects what information is presented there.

Is the tutorial the best CBT teaching strategy? Merrill (1986a) argues that it is not. It is difficult, via a tutorial, to teach the procedures for operating a nuclear reactor, for trouble shooting an electrical circuit, for designing a house, for running a power station, or solving chemical corrosion problems. Applied Learning finds the best way to teach such performances is in simulations where trainees exploring the content "experientially".

If the simulation seems to be the best strategy for teaching real life performances are CBT tutorials useful? Yes, in two ways. First, a tutorial dialogue may help trainees focus their attention and see relationships while they are in the simulation. Second, tutorial CBT may help a trainee overcome misconceptions or misunderstandings after exploring the experiential environment. CBT tutorials may have a remedial or clarifying role within the simulation.

Because training develops the competence of the trainee, and competence involves performance not merely knowledge, then computer-based training should be moving away from knowledge orientated tutorial courseware to performance orientated simulation-based courseware.

3.2 Merrill's Experiential Instructional Model

Merrill argues that computers may best teach "experiential content" where the learner interacts with a computer simulation of reality. Such content is responsive and enables the trainee to change parameters and see the consequences. It simulates real events and procedures where input from the trainee results in a change in the content simulated. An example is a flight simulator. Merrill (1986c) argues that for a simulation "the computer can be not only the tutor but also the subject matter".

Almost any phenomena can be simulated and the trainee can be given control over this simulation to "explore, experiment, predict and interact with the subject matter itself". Applied Learning Australasia has simulated computer systems, power stations, electrical circuits, oil refineries and business environments.

Merrill (1986b) argues that the computer can also be "an expert to demonstrate the correct way to perform a procedure or to show the correct way to set up an experiment" or it can be "a coach or adviser to watch over the trainee's shoulder while he performs complex activities, designs systems, and solves problems". When trainees are in trouble the computer can intervene to help them with a problem, provide information or guide them down a different path.

The most effective instruction would enable the trainees to interact directly with the subject matter in a simulation, watch simulated experts perform tasks, discuss their explorations with a "Socratic" tutor, or receive coaching as they attempt to perform the real-life task. Merrill argues that to "limit the trainees interaction with the computer to only one or some subset of these possibilities fails to take advantage of the tremendous flexibility of this tool".

Merrill (1986a, 1986b, 1986c) represents his experiential model of computer instruction in a diagram similar to that shown below.

Figure 1: Merrill's Experiential Model of Instruction.

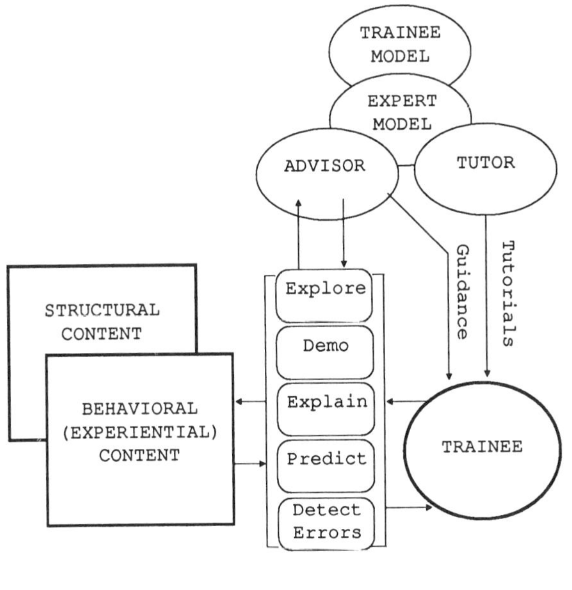

A experiential content representation is one which provides a controllable microworld which the trainee can manipulate and observe. It provides a "simulation of some process or procedure which enables the trainee to interact in such a way that the consequences of the trainees actions are reflected in the reactions of the system (Merrill, 1986a, p6).

Merrill calls trainees' interaction with the computer a "transaction". The most common form of transaction with such a controllable microworld is *explore* where trainees "discover" the relationships involved. An example could be a simulated nuclear reactor (Grabowski, 1987). Here trainees can manipulate the controls to move the rods up and down. As they do this they can watch the temperature gauge readings rise and fall and learn the consequences of excess manipulation. They can even practice controlling dangerous situations such as melt downs.

There are several other types of transaction. A *demonstration* may pose a problem and show trainees the consequence of certain actions, or it may show how the system works or illustrate some specific principles within the system. An *explanation* explains or shows the underlying principles on which the simulation is based. A *prediction* requires the trainee to form/test hypotheses about likely outcomes. *Error detection* introduces inconsistent principles or errors and requires trainees to find and correct those errors. Figure 1 shows such transactions.

In Merrill's model trainees interact with the experiential content through the transactions. Trainees are often able to learn more from some form of structured transactions than from open ended learner controlled exploration. This is similar to guided discovery which has proved more efficient than completely free discovery.

Figure 1 also shows an *adviser* function. An adviser monitors the trainee's explorations and provides guidance about what the trainee could try next. The adviser may also suggest what transaction could be used next and when to change to a different type of transaction.

Also included is a *trainee model* and an *expert model*. The trainee model provides the necessary information about trainee progress so the adviser function can guide trainees' interaction with the simulation in an individualized way. The expert model enables the system to judge trainee performances against an expert performance and enables the system to demonstrate expert performance with the simulation.

Finally, a *tutorial* system is combined with the experiential system. This would enable trainees to focuss attention on critical relationships in the experiential representation and help trainees overcome misconceptions which may have arisen during the interaction.

3.2 Merrill's Component Design Theory

Considerable advances have been made in the development of advanced programming techniques and in hardware development. Developers of ICBT, ICBIV and expert systems now desire information about instruction and learning that they can use. Merrill (1986b) argues that existing instructional theory and practice "needs to be synthesized into a systematically organised body of prescriptions that can then be coded into production rules" appropriate for the development of the various computer based instructional systems.

Merrill's Component Display Theory (1983, 1987) gave prescriptions for tutorial instruction but said little about experiential instruction and instruction intervention strategies. If instructional design theory is to guide the development of CBT, ICBT and CBIV then it must be appropriate for both tutorial instruction and experiential instruction combined with tutorial instruction. Merrill (1986b) is attempting to extend Component Display Theory to enable it to guide the design of experiential computer based instruction. He calls his attempt "Component Design Theory".

Merrill's new theory is an attempt to develop consistency rules for the following:

* Transactions Rules.
* Goal-Transaction Consistency Rules.
* Content Organization Rules.
* Goal-Content Consistency Rules.

Transaction rules advise about how to design each transaction. Goal-Transaction consistency rules match goals with the most appropriate transactions. Content Organization rules advise about hierarchical and elaborative content structures. Goal-Content consistency rules match goals with the most appropriate content.

Merrill also includes four classes of instructional intervention rules which are not an explicit part of Component Design Theory. These rules include guidance rules, strategy rules, sequence rules and control rules.

Transaction Guidance Rules advise on what type of guideance to use for a given type of content structure and transaction. Transaction Strategy Rules advise how to select which transaction should be next._Content Sequence Rules advise on sequencing content. Control Rules help determine when the trainee make decisions and when the system should take over.

3.3 Summary

This part of the paper outlined Merrill's Component Design Theory, a theory which, when it is fully developed, will provide the type of instructional design guidance needed for developers to develop effective and efficient experiential computer based instructional systems. CBT, ICBT and CBIV will be much improved if Merrill and his colleagues are able to develop a workable set of production rules.

Applied Learning Australasia is developing performance-based courseware that uses both experiential and tutorial content. Such courseware is difficult to design and we have found Merrill's Model extremely useful.

4. CONCLUSIONS

The computer allows designers of CBT to use strategies that are unavailable to the live teacher or developers of text or video. Therefore, why use strategies that can be used by other delivery methods with the computer.

Instructional design has a solid knowledge base for delivery media other than the computer. It is time we researched CBT from an instructional point of view and developed solid theory for computer instruction - particularly training.

Bloom's model provides us with a framework for the development of such theory. Because the computer can monitor trainee learning and adapt the instruction as required Blooms's identification of variables that can be altered to improve instruction/learning is very important.

Developers of CBT are not using the computer's number crunching potential fully. Merrill is beginning to develop a theory of simulation CBT that will help us understand how to use the computer to develop better, more functional performance orientated courseware.

REFERENCES

Bloom, B.S. (1986) *Human Characteristics and School Learning*. NewYork: McGraw-Hill

Grabowski, B. (1987) Personal Communication.

Merrill, M.D. (1986a) *ICAI in Military Training:Conceptual Issues*. Unpublished paper, March 23, 1986.

Merrill, M.D. (1986b) *Instructional Design Production Rules for ICAI*. Unpublished proposal, April 25, 1986.

Merrill, M.D. (1986c) *Component Design Theory: Instructional Design for Courseware Authoring*. Unpublished paper, May 5, 1986.

Reigeluth, C.M. (1983) *Instructional Design Theories and Models: An Overview of their Current Status*. Hillsdale, NJ: Lawrence Earlbaum Associates.

Reigeluth, C.M. (1987) *Instructional Design Theories in Action: Lessons Illustrating Selected Theories*. Hillsdale, NJ: Lawrence Earlbaum Associates.

Romiszowski, A.J. (1986) *Developing Auto-Instructional Materials*. London: Kogan Page.

Siegle, M.A. & Davis, D.M. (1986) *Understanding Computer Based Education*. New York: Random House.

Computers in Education
A. McDougall and C. Dowling (Editors)
Elsevier Science Publishers B.V. (North-Holland)

THE IMPACT OF COGNITIVE STYLE DIFFERENCES ON TRAINING PROGRAMS

Jasminka Novak

University Computing Centre, 41000 Zagreb, Engelsova bb, Yugoslavia

The overall goal is training for use of the new information systems. There are five subgoals which have to be achieved if we want to help trainees to be successful members of the computerized society: basic computer knowledge, conceptual model of the system, knowledge of certain hardware and operating system, knowledge of specific software package, confidence in working with computers. The role of representation of the system external to the trainee is outstanding in the training phase. If the trainees are able to understand the system well enough to be able to use it without concentrating all their mental potential on the technical component of the activity it means that they have an accurate mental model of the target system. In such a case they are able to show their other abilities. Realization of such a concept of training demands additional time for training, tailored examples and well chosen conceptual models. The selection of a model heavily depends upon task and audience.

1. INTRODUCTION

Computers and computer-controlled equipment are penetrating every aspect of our lives - homes, factories and offices. Information technology is a catalyst in, and possibly a medium for, great changes in the commercial, scientific and technical domains. Information technology is radically transforming a lot of occupations. It is pretty obvious that the current workforce will have to be retrained for technically sophisticated jobs.

In order to succed in an information-oriented society people are likely to need other kinds of skills than before. People will be increasingly called upon to manipulate symbols and information. The ability to sort, weigh and transmite information will be essential. People will need greater problem-solving skills than are required in most jobs now. There will be pressure to attend to broader and more global aspects of a job. To perform a job well a person will need to be more flexible and adaptive. Reassessment of vocational training programs content and methods is needed in response to broader social changes involved in the new age.

Any discussion on computers in an educational context focuses upon the computer and its use in teaching: sometimes it is observed as the object of teaching, when speaking about computer literacy or teaching about computers; sometimes it is observed as a tool, when we speak about teaching through computers (e.g. training, programmed instructions) and with computers (e.g. simulation, data exploration). First of all the primary concern of education must be preparation for change with the special emphasis on rapid pace of change. Life-long education is going to become a central activity. It focuses either upon preparation and accomodation to change or persuits in place of work (1). With these ideas in mind courses were prepared to help practitioners to shift from finite education to life-long education and involve in changes that computers bring (2,3).

2. THE TRAINING PROGRAMS

It is obvious that direction in automation is to eliminate the type of jobs which have too "poor" job content. The term "job content" represents the conceptual framework (4) and within it the tasks and skills that are needed can be observed. Job content can be defined as:
- a set of operations
- the ability to perform.

If we speak about job content as a set of operations we usually think about a job description for a specific workplace. The ability to perform includes hidden or invisible skills such as technical, interpersonal, cognitive and experiential skills which underlie the manipulation of the task. Technical skills are critical for entry into automated workplace, but interactive and abstract skills are key to maintaining jobs. We recommend the type of training that includes a technical component which emphasizes computer use and a component which focuses on developing and encouraging interactive and abstract skills.

The purpose of the training program that we practice is to improve computer knowledge and to encourage and develop the use of problem-solving, analytic and communication skills that are identified as critical to working at the specific workplace. The purpose of the training program and the method of instruction have to be interrelated. The method of instruction has to be based on the individual engaging in participatory, problem-solving activities whereby the instructor acts as a facilitator too.

The overall goal is training for use of the new information systems. There are five subgoals which have to be achieved if we want to help trainees to be successful memebers of the computerized society:

* Basic computer knowledge

The history of computing and future trends have to be presented briefly to give the trainees an opportunity to feel how fast information technology is growing. The basic concepts of computer architecture and computer operations have to be presented. Practice has already shown that treating the computer as "the black box" is worthless. Nobody can use computer inteligently if she/he doesn't know certain fundamental facts. Besides, this societal component is essential if we want users to accept the system. Many approaches to computer litaracy, and almost all training programs have no societal component. We agree with those (5) who think that this component is needed. Computerization and informatization are not only problems of technical culture.

* Conceptual model of the system

The conceptual model used in the past has been almost exclusively analogical. But no ready analogy exists for computing systems. At some point the analogical models have shown shortcomings in performing more complex tasks. Research findings (6,7) show that an abstract conceptual model proves to be effective in helping users form an accurate mental model, with special advantages for performance in far transfer tasks. The selection of a model heavily depends upon tasks and upon audience.

* Knowledge of certain hardware and operating system

The trainees have to be given the basic knowledge (syntactic and semantic) of specific hardware and operating system and they improve their knowledge in practice.

* Konwledge of specific software package

For those using specific software packages the basic konwledge about them (syntactic and semantic) has to be given and improved in practice too.

* Confidence in working with computers

Computer literacy and improved computer abilities will help trainees to liberate themselves from fear and to gain self-confidence and trust machines. The realization of the concept of trust is specially needed in the individual use of computers - in using computers as a dialogue partner and as a tool. According to Muir (8), the concept of trust between human and machine can be explained as "expectation held by a member of a system of persistence of natural and moral social orders, and of technically component performance and of fiduciary responsibility, from a memeber of the system, and related to, but not necessary isomorphic with, objective measures of these qualities".

3. COGNITIVE COMPATIBILITY

If the trainees are able to understand the system well enough to be able to use it without concentrating all their mental potential on the technical componente of the activity it means that they have accurate mental model of the target system. In such a case they are able to show their other abilities.

In the conceptual framework of mental models Norman (9) points out four entities which have to be considered: target system - the system the user is using or learning, conceptual model of the target system, the user's mental model of the target system and scientists' conceptualization of the user's model of the target system. A conceptual model is invented by designers and teachers (trainers) to provide an appropriate representation of the target system. The mental model facilitates an understanding of how the system works. It aids the user in making inferences about the system and reasoning about it.

There is general agreement on the importance of mental models, but opinions are divided on whether users spontaneously build them. From our experience conceptual models act as the first class aids which help novice users induce mental models and they convey basic concepts of the system. If we accept the framework of the mental model formation process proposed by Bostrom et al. (7) we can see that Streitz's (10) thesis of cognitive compatibility suits, and the term - cognitive compatibility - can be extended to the process of training as well.

Bostrom et al. suggest that the system to be learned is mapping via usage and via training to the trainee's mental model. The role of a representation of the system external to the trainee is outstanding in the design phase and in the training phase.

The thesis of cognitive compatibility emphasizes that only if there is compatibility between the designer's conceptual model and the user's mental model of the functionality will there be compatibility between a system's realization of the functionality and user's mental model of the system's realization of given functionality. The thesis of cognitive compatibility supposes if the first goal is achieved the user has a chance to build up an adequate mental model of the system's realization of the given functionality. The role of trainer becomes prominent in the phase of mapping conceptual model to the trainee's mental model. So we can say that if the first part of the thesis of cognitive compatibility is satisfied, the user has a chance to build up an adequate, accurate mental model of the system or system's realization of the given functionality only if there is compatibility between the trainer's conceptual model and the user's mental model (3). This is important to be recognized because regularly the designers of the system do not train the users to use it.

4. APPROACHING METHODS AND SITUATIONS

If we agree what to teach, the crucial element of training program becomes how to do it. Motivation and quality of education are the critical components that influence the success of any course. The motivation of most of participants is usually high because information technology in our society (Yugoslavia) is not so wide spread in working and everyday life. Many people are excited by "the new". The participants are also forced by demands for greater efficiency at their working place. Last, but not least, motivation factors result from the participants conviction that they must use computers in their work if they want to remain on the same working place.

The quality of education is achived by satisfying the critical attributes of excelent training. Excellent training has to be valid, reliably effective and efficient (11).It means that it meets the needs of people and requirements of their work. It also means that a high percentage of trainees achieve the performance goals. Such training consumes the least possible time and the fewest resources. Our experience supports the decision to ensure excellent training by a systematic approach (2). A systematic approach incorporates established principles of instructional science and proven methods of instructional technology (12). Systematic methods are employed in technical development, but their application to training is not recognized and encouraged enough. Instructional systems have phases that make up their life cycles.

Problem definition
: assess human performance needs, determine trainig and non-training issues

Analysis
: analyze and document training requirements, analyze learner characteristics

Design
: develop learning objectives and strategies, select media

Testing
: perform formal testing, perform production testing

Maintenance
: deliver, adjust and upgrade courseware

The phase of analysis is very important and we'll speak more about it, because in this phase we analyze the learner's characteristics; constraints and available resources are taken into account. One of these constraints is gender-based differences in learning style.

5. GENDER-BASED DIFFERENCES IN LEARNING STYLE

There is a strong general trend in employment structure characterized by the fact that a number of occupations are filled by women and the others mainly by men. In Yugoslavia this phenomenon hasn't been studied yet, but in everyday life we can see that store-assistants, secretaries, typists, chasiers, administrative personnel and educators of every kind are almost always women.

Some studies (13) suggest that gender, cognitive style and preferred learning strategies are of great importance in transmitting a conceptual model of the system. Although research was done taking into account user and computer in direct communication, it seems quite resonable to us that the same concept can be used for acquisition of knowledge in person (trainer) to person (trainee/user) interaction.

There are a number of cognitive style theories, but Witkin's theory of Psychological Differentiation (13) seems the most applicable to human-computer and trainer-computer user interaction. Psychological differentiation is a global theory of a person's social, perceptual and cognitive functioning. It suggests the existence of two different cognitive styles: field-dependent and field-independent. The difference in cognitive styles is concerned with processing and responding to information. The field-independent cognitive style is associated with good analytic and restructuring skills, while the field-dependent cognitive style is associated with more holistic approach. In the learning and problem solving domains, field-dependent individuals usually adopt a spectator approach. The field-independent individuals tend to take more participant approach. The author of the theory found women, on avarage, to be more field-dependent than men.

The theory of psychological differentiation can

be confirmed in practice if one observes a person's style of learning computer skills. One style of learning is rule-based (14). The rules are accepted with no understanding of why they are valid. Understanding is gained through experience. The other style of learning is more holistic. This means that an overall understanding is attained before detailed rules are encountered. This style of learning uses the generalized understanding to provide a framework within which the rules are organized.

Understanding the process by which the various components inter-relate is the necessary prerequisite for learning which key to press. These disparate learning styles and their gender relationship are obvious especially when working with computer novices. A men who has never touched a computer, hits some key and waits to see what happens. He is willing to learn by trial and error trying to discover with experimentation how and why computers work. A woman, generally, needs to understand the holistic sense of reasons behind the rules to feel comfortable working with machines. Working with computers demands linear processing and schemantic representation. Women, culturaly, have little experience with it.

It could be argued that because of their predominantly passive and field-dependent approach to learning, women may prefer firm guiding through training programs. They prefer sequentially organised materials and inflexible dialogue structure which restricts the range of user responses to set questions in specified sequences. They take computers very seriously. On the other hand, men prefer more self-management and more flexible dialogue structure and simultaneous processing to accommodate their field-independence.

Most computer conversation adopt the task-oriented and poor style which is similar to that found between business partners. Such a style may not be acceptable to the more person-oriented individual (field-dependent or female users). Problems in conversing with a computer arise specially in the early phase of the interaction. It is therefore critical for trainers to communicate knowledge in the most appropriate way - perhaps using analogy.

In future we plan to compare effectiveness of analogical and abstract conceptual models conected with field-independent and field-dependent cognitive style. Although, in some cases, analogy was considered harmful in "tertiary education" it is mighty weapon.

The field-independent users are more likely to prefer to develop an effective mental model by themselves, prior to interacting with the system, usually by means of reading manuals beforehand. It is therefore important that manuals or other documentation are in form which can help develop an accurate mental model. More task oriented, rather than function oriented manuals, would be useful.

It could, therefore, be arguet that gender and cognitive style differences could provide some guidance as to the choice of the initial learning strategy.

6. CONCLUSION

We recommend the type of training that includes a technical component which emphasizes computer use as well as the component which focuses on developing and encouraging the interactive and abstract skills, because we are convinced that computerization and effective use of information technology are not only problem of technical culture. Such a concept of training demands additional time for training, tailored examples and well chosen conceptual models. The selection of a model heavily depends upon task and audience. The compatibility between the trainer's conceptual model and the user's mental model is very important especially because the designers of the system regularly do not train users to use the system.

To earn cognitive compatibility we prefer instructional technology as a method of training, and gender and learning style differences should always be taken into account.

REFERENCES:

(1) Novak, J., Human Factors-Designing Systems for Usability, Proc. 9th International symposium "Compute at the University", Cavtat, 1987, pp. 81-85

(2) Novak, J. and Racki, Dj., Instructional technology in Practice, in: De Blasi, M;, Donio, J., Luque, E. and Scerri, E. (eds.), Education and Application of Computer Technology, (Edizioni fratelli Laterza, Bari, 1988) pp. 67-76.

(3) Novak, J., The Implication of the New Skill Requirements for Training Programs, in: Salvendy, G. and Smith, M. (eds.), Designing and Using Human-Computer Interface and Knowledge Based Systems (Elsevier, Amsterdam, 1989) pp. 145-151.

(4) Pullman, C. and Szymanski, S., The Impact of Office Technology on Clerical Worker Skills in the Banking, Insurance and Legal Industries in New York City, IFIP Conference on Women, Work and Computerization, Amsterdam, 1988.

(5) Peterson, J. T., Goals for and Lessons from Computer Literacy Course, SIGCE Bulletin, Vol. 19, No. 1, pp. 504-507.

(6) Halasz, F. and Moran, T. P., Mental Models and Problem Solving in Using Calculators, in: Janda, A. (ed.), Human Factors in Computing Systems (ACM, Boston, 1983) pp. 212-216.

(7) Sein, M. K., Bostrom, R. P. and Olfman, L., Conceptual models in training novice users, in: Bullinger, H. J. and Shackel, B. (eds.) Human-Computer Interaction - INTERACT'87, (Elsevier, Amsterdam, 1987) pp. 75-82.

(8) Muir, B. M., Trust between humans and machines and the design of decision aids, Int. Journal Man-Machine Studies 27, (1987) pp. 527-539.

(9) Norman, D. A., Some observations on mental models, in: Stevens, A. L. and Gentner, D. (eds.), Mental Models, (Lawrence Erlbaum Assoc., Hillsdale, 1983) pp. 7-14.

(10) Streitz, N. A., Cognitive Compatibility as a Central Issue in Human-Computer Interaction: Theoretical Framework and Empirical Findings, in: Salvendy, G. (ed.) Cognitive Engineering in the Design of Human-Computer Interaction and Expert Systems, (Elsevier, Amsterdam, 1987) pp. 75-82.

(11) Medsker, K. L. and Medsker, L. R., Instructional Technology: A Key to Successful Information Systems, Information & Management, Vol. 12, No. 4, (1987) pp. 195-208.

(12) Gagne, R. M., Instructional Technology: Fundations (Lawrence Erlbaum Assoc., Hillsdale, 1987)

(13) Fowler, C. J. H. and Murray, D., Gender and cognitive style differences at human-computer interface, in: Bullinger, H. J. and Scackel, B. (eds.), Human-Computer Interaction - INTERACT'87, (Elsevier, Amsterdam, 1987) pp. 709-714.

(14) Brecher, D., Gender and Learning, Do Women Learn Differently, IFIP Conference on Women, Work and Computerization, Amsterdam, 1988.

Computers in Education
A. McDougall and C. Dowling (Editors)
Elsevier Science Publishers B.V. (North-Holland)

TOWARDS AN INDIVIDUALISED LEARNER-COMPUTER INTERFACE

Rod SIMS

Department of Information Studies, UTS (Kuring-gai Campus)
Lindfield NSW 2070 AUSTRALIA

This paper explores options for the learner-computer interface, specifically in terms of non-verbal cues for student control and the implementation of a processor which permits the student to modify views of the instructional material. This latter approach requires a nodal concept of the lesson, with each node providing an array of options through which the student may study instructional content. This concept incorporates the processing power of the computer as well as elements of intelligent CAL and knowledge-based applications. Aimed at the adult learner, the implementation provides a new approach to addressing individual learner needs.

1. OVERVIEW

In 1980, Alfred Bork predicted that:

> by the year 2000 the major way of learning at all levels and in almost all subject areas will be through the interactive use of computers (Bork, 1980:53)

Prior to this, the use of technology as an educational tool had received significant support, with formal research studies identifying faster and more effective learning through the use of computers (Vinsonhaler & Bass, 1972). More recently, Kulik, Kulik & Cohen (1980) evaluated 59 computer-assisted instruction strategies for a meta-analysis of educational uses of computers. While acknowledging the effects as modest, computer technology was found to reduce the contact time for teaching.

It was in such an environment that Bork (1980) made his prediction - and yet computers have not realised the potential so many had predicted. In the majority of research articles published in the computer-assisted learning (CAL) field, the over-riding factor has been the successful applications of the technology to teaching and instruction, ranging from pre-school to business and industry. And yet the question remains: why have technological resources been so slow to dominate education if their value has been proved through research?

The answer lies in their application rather than their potential. Technology is a tool for people to use - in virtually every profession. However, many advocates of technology have perceived it as a solution and have been too impatient to wait for the users to demand specific resources directed towards their individual needs. Consequently, many educators have implemented the technology without having a real demand. While their intentions have been sound, their choice of tool has often been without justification. Consequently, the very programs used have had the potential to be instructionally unsound. It is the argument of this paper that technology has too long been a reflection of the trainer rather than a tool for the learner. Put in its correct perspective, as an instructional resource, the computer can and will be a viable tool for learning. In this analysis, the developments in CAL through research and technological innovation are considered in terms of determining a general model for the delivery of effective and motivational instructionl technology.

2. INTRODUCTION

Growing from the early applications of behaviourism (programmed learning), computer-assisted learning was based on a simple stimulus-response pattern. Initially on teletypewriter terminals, the computer presented a problem to which the student made a response. Based on the content of the response, feedback was provided as to its accuracy. As the technology grew to provide colour graphics and animated displays, so did the variety of educational software applications. In parallel, as software engineering changed, so did the complexity of the instruction: from the simple stimulus-response examples to sophisticated applications based on Artificial Intelligence and Expert Systems.

In the beginning of widespread implementation of educational technology, however, the major consideration was the effectiveness of CAL in terms of learning (quite often misinterpreted as instructional time). Some advanced work was completed using the PLATO system (Smith & Sherwood, 1976), although the initial effort required to develop the resources reflected the comparatively high-quality. Interestingly, 10 years later, Whiting (1986:281) criticises the PLATO system because it was "too behaviouristic".

The real issue is that it is not the system which is responsible for courseware, but the developers. In fact, there is an increasing tendency for research to focus on the instructional design elements of the courseware (Hagler & Knowlton, 1987; Scandura, 1984; Hobbs, 1983; Hooper & Hannafin, 1988; England, 1984), which supports the contention of instructional design theorists that up-front design is essential for quality instruction (eg. Romiszowski, 1986). While this application of theory to instruction is not new, it is apparent that many CAL programs have been developed to test new technology rather than as an outcome of formal design, and thus their subsequent failure as effective teaching tools (Gery, 1989). An emphasis on successful performance has the potential to reduce the requirements for formalised instructional design methodologies, as alternate sequences may vary from accepted mastery-based structures.

While research is vital to the success of any new resource, there is a move in the training sector from demanding technological innovation to seeking technological solutions for clearly identified performance problems. The actualisation of this phenomena is seen in the increasing interest in a variety of people-oriented aspects of educational technology (Sims, 1989a). Additionally, the difference between learner competencies must be emphasised. Much of computer-based learning practice has been based on the young learner, and the need for guided learning. However, it is also important to consider the adult learner who will have the experience and motivation to determine their own learning preferences, irrespective of accepted instructional design practices. This warrants a reappraisal of the learner-computer interface.

3. LEARNER-COMPUTER INTERFACE

3.1 Learning Styles

One of the considerations concerning individual access to and interface with CAL has been learning style. Martin (1982) determined that feedback helped minimise differences between field-dependent and field-independent students. Tennyson (1982) explored the effect of cognitive style from both the designer's and the student's perspective; the major conclusions recommended that cognitive elements be seen as a significant component of instructional design. Other studies have suggested learning-style may affect preference for CAL (Burger, 1985; Post, 1987). More recent research has focused on the provision of choices for students to select the style most preferred (Clarke, 1989). However, this approach assumes that an individual adopts one style for a particular learning activity.

The premise of this paper is that students should be given the choice of style throughout the lesson, selecting the display most appropriate to their immediate learning requirements. This places focus on learner control, whereby the lesson becomes a tool in which the learner accesses instructional content according to his/her preference. This option is now available through the rapid developments in technology.

3.2 Learner-Computer Interface

There is increasing attention on the link or interface between the human user and the technology (for educational applications, the learner-computer interface). While much of the research has focused on elements of screen design such as colour, text format, locus of display objects (Rambally & Rambally, 1987; Surber & Leeder, 1988; Sawyer, 1985), the emphasis has tended towards the instructor, in terms of their concept of effective instructional presentation.

This approach supports a didactic instructor-controlled instructional resource rather than a learner-centred performance tool. The argument is not that screen design is unimportant, but that too much emphasis can be placed on providing a well-structured display, which is not necessarily based on user preferences. In terms of many courseware packages, the learner may therefore be presented with too many options which can distract from the actual content. To this end, it is important to consider other successful software tools, such as those used in the Apple Macintosh environment, which allow the learner to use non-verbal control cues.

For example, Figure 1(a) displays a traditional control screen with instructor supplied controls. The student has five options, each of which must be interpreted; and which are a potential distraction in the learning processes. Not only is the student required to assess the instructional material (in this example represented by a graphic of a cat), but also the control options associated with the five Function Keys. While it is recognised that learners, over time, may automatically recall the Function Key operations, the screen still displays two unrelated sets of information (content and control). If the control cues could be simplified, or displayed non-verbally, conflict with content could be minimised.

Figure 1(a)

Alternately, Figure 1(b) provides a series of icons (pictures) which the learner may use "intuitively" to move from one display to the next. This is not an original concept in software applications (cf. Apple Hypercard) but is new in terms of learner access to instructional materials. The icons depicted in Figure 1(b) were also incorporated into Xerox's VENTUTOR, CBT for Ventura Publisher.

Figure 1(b)

The idea is that learners will make control choices subconsciously, thereby maintaining a comparatively high level of concentration on the subject matter. This approach emphasises new concepts for learner-control and interface.

The attempts to create a more "friendly" interface have in part resulted from the inability of software to maintain its impact with students. While CAL has the feature of being self-paced and individual, the pacing is often from one screen (or display) to the next without significant interaction. Overall, the individuality of CAL has not been established.

In an attempt to alleviate this, elements of Artificial Intelligence have been incorporated with CAL to generate Intelligent CAL (ICAL) and knowledge-based systems (Kearsley, 1987). This approach has typically involved the development of a learning resource which will interpret or parse a student's response to generate an accurate interpretation and assessment of the student's misconceptions. Interestingly, much of the research has focused on the student's inability to solve problems rather than their success rate. Despite the potential of ICAL to individualise instruction, the design emphasis has frequently remained instructor-based rather than learner-oriented.

An associated difficulty is that developing ICAL resources typically requires some skill in knowledge engineering as well as an advanced programming language such as PROLOG or LISP. While there is some evidence that systems can be built without such tools which, to the student, provide an environment in which responses to theoretical situations are treated intelligently, the promise of truly individualised resources has yet to be kept (Sims & Farrow, 1989).

The answer, therefore, is to assess alternate forms of instructional presentation, especially those which are learner-oriented with effective control options. It is suggested that by using the principles of knowledge-based systems and software engineering, CAL systems can be developed which provide an individualised environment for enhancement of job performance through problem-solving resources.

4. INDIVIDUALISED CAL

One difficulty with developing individualised CAL is that each student will have some unique learning preference or style, and that this would theoretically require a different instructional sequence (i.e. lesson) for each student in the target group. While attempts have been made to address this issue by providing alternate paths through a single lesson, the content is nevertheless constant.

However, rather than considering the development of one lesson for each learner (which is totally impractical), it is suggested that the processing power of the computer be considered to provide each individual learner with as many choices for different screen display and format as possible, such as being portrayed in early multi-media resources (Murray, 1989). In terms of instructional developmental, the lesson can be conceptualised as a set of flexible nodes.

Figure 2 illustrates a lesson-structure with starting (S) and ending (E) nodes, with intermediary nodes linked by possible lesson branches, with the highlighted nodes and links representing one such path through the lesson. Each node can be thought of as a discrete instructional objective or event, where the student is working with a specific task. The concept of the node provides "break-points" within the lesson where students have the opportunity to determine the display characteristics of the current content. For example, the figure identifies a specific node within the lesson (X), which provides the student with five alternative display formats (F1, F2, F3, F4, F4) as depicted in Figure 3.

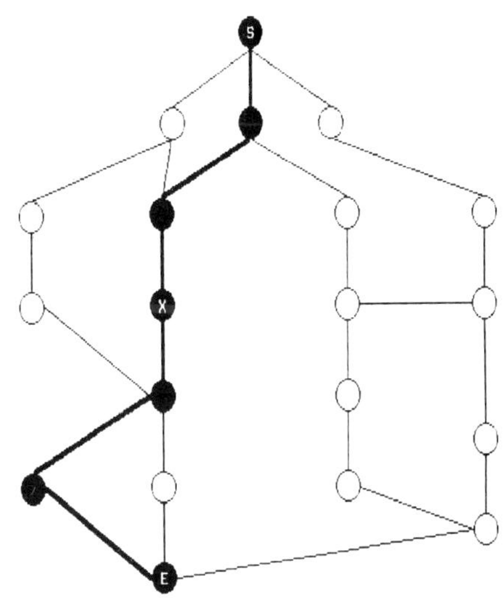

Figure 2

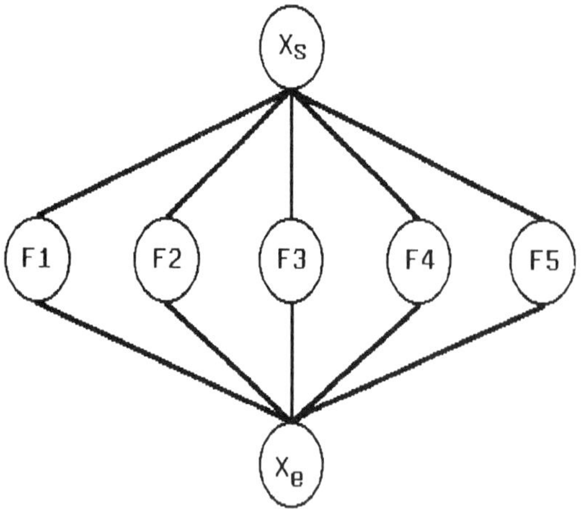

Figure 3

This model represents an instructional resource with design structured on the computer's power. At each node-point, the student can elect to view the content in various ways, with the content display being parameter- based and computer-generated rather than fixed. Thus students may view text according to their preferred format, watch a video rather than read a paragraph, hear the words rather than have them displayed or a review a combination of all available display options.

The introduction of this format will require the use of an integrated and multi-media knowledge-base linked to powerful processing and display software. More importantly, it will provide CAL which caters for the individual needs and learning preferences for students. This structure minimises the need for the lesson to cater for individual learning styles and preferences, allowing the student to select their preference(s) for the current content material.

This concept is not new when business software applications are considered. For example, the Lotus 1-2-3 (Lotus Development Corporation) spreadsheet application allows the user to display graphs of data in various ways. For example, identical data may be depicted as a bar-graph or a pie-chart, as shown in Figures 4(a) and 4(b), depending on the user's display preference.

Similarly, the Boeing 3D graphics package allows data to be depicted on a three dimensional display. Of importance is the options available to the user: a choice of the perspective of the graph as well as how the data is to be represented (bars, lines, planes etc.). The point is that the user has the choice to display information according to their particular preferences.

In terms of Computer-Assisted Learning, especially when applied to adult learners, this concept can be incorporated into the learning routine. Rather than the developer providing the screen-design in fixed format, the choice for display could be provided to the user. This is an accepted option in most PC applications, where the user (not the writer) has the choice of how the screen should appear and is becoming even more important with the emphasis on hyper- card and multi-media applications.

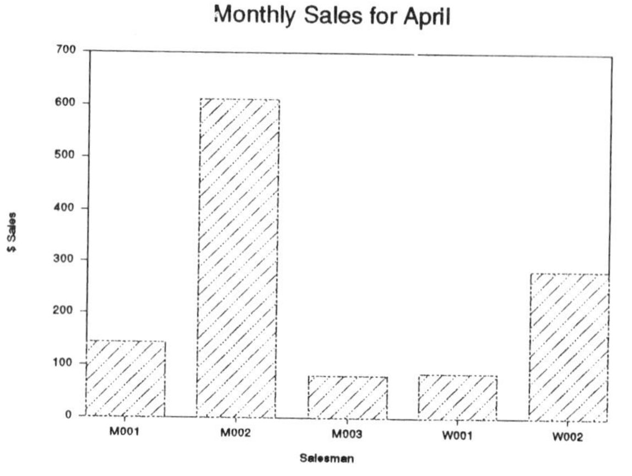

Figure 4(a)

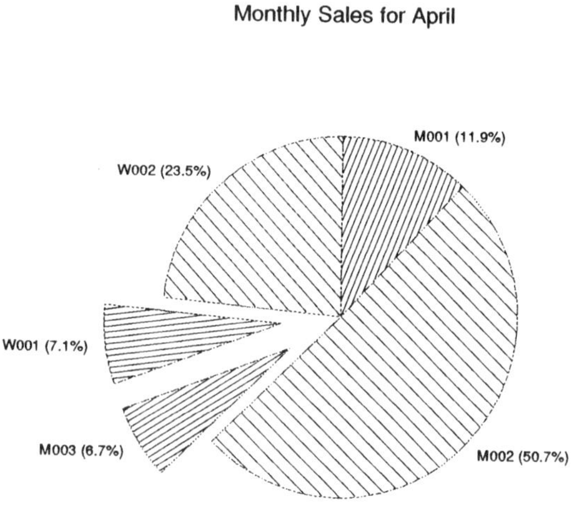

Figure 4(b)

5. CONCLUSIONS

This paper has presented an alternative method for developing instructional software, based on using the computer's processing power to provide the student with as wide a range as possible of display options. The challenge is here for instructors and trainers to assess the effectiveness of current resources and to consider the potential of multi-media resources based on learner preferences rather than fixed instructional sequence.

REFERENCES

Barr, A. & Feigenbaum, E.A. (Eds) (1982). **The Handbook of Artificial Intelligence Volume II.** California: Heuristech Press.

Bork, A. (1980). Interactive Learning, in R.P. Taylor (Ed), **The Computer in the School: Tutor, Tool, Tutee.** New York: Teachers College Press.

Burger, K. (1985). Computer assisted instruction: learning style and academic achievement. **Journal of Computer-Based Instruction, 12**(1), 21-22.

Clarke, J.A. (1989). Cognitive style and CAL: what can you do about it?, in G. Bishop & J. Baker (Eds), **ASCILITE-89.** Proceedings of the 7th Annual ASCILITE Conference. Queensland: Bond University.

England, E. (1984). Design and evaluation issues in CAL materials. **CALICO Journal,** September, 11-13.

Gery, G.J. (1989). Training vs. Performance Support: Inadequate Training is Now Insufficient. **Performance Improvement Quarterly, 2**(3), 51-71.

Hagler, P. & Knowlton, J. (1987). Invalid implicit assumption in CBI comparison research. **Journal of Computer-Based Instruction, 14**(3), 84-88.

Hobbs, D.J. (1983). Effects of content sequencing and presentation mode of teaching material on learning outcomes. **Programmed Learning and Educational Technology, 24**(4), 292-299.

Hooper, S. & Hannafin, M.J. (1988). Learning the ROPES of instructional design: Guidelines for emerging interactive technologies. **Educational Technology, 28**(7), 14-20.

Kearsley, G.P. (Ed) (1986). **Artificial Intelligence and Instruction.** Massachusetts: Addison-Wesley.

Kulik, J.A., Kulik, C.C. & Cohen, P.A. (1980). Effectiveness of computer-based college teaching: A meta-analysis of findings. **Review of Educational Research. 50**(4), 525-544.

Martin, M.A. (1982). **Cognitive Styles and Instructional Variables.** Paper presented to the American Educational Research Association.

Murray, J.H. (1989). MIT's Athena language learning project: videodisc and natural language processing applications for community-based language learning, in G. Bishop & J. Baker (Eds), **ASCILITE-89.** Proceedings of the 7th Annual ASCILITE Conference. Queensland: Bond University.

Post, P.E. (1987). The effect of filed independence/field dependence on computer-assisted instruction achievement. **Journal of Industrial Teacher Education, 25**(1), 60-67.

Rambally, G.K. & Rambally, R.S. (1987). Human factors in CAI design. **Computer Education, 11**(2), 149-153.

Romiszowski, A.B. (1986). **Developing Auto-Instructional Systems.** New York: Kogan Page.

Sawyer, T. (1985). Human factors considerations in computer-assisted instruction. **Journal of Computer-Based Instruction, 12**(1), 17-20.

Scandura, J.M. (1984). Cognitive instructional psychology: System requirements and research methodology. **Journal of Computer-Based Instruction, 11**(2), 32- 41.

Sims, R. (1989a). Bringing it all together: Perspectives on people-oriented information systems, in R.H. Sprague (Ed), **HICSS 89 Proceedings Volume IV.** Washington: IEEE Computer Society Press. @REFERENCE = Sims, R. (1989b). Intelligent Computer Assisted Learning, in T. Dupé (Ed), **ACEC89 - Backup the Future.** Proceedings of the 1989 Australian Computers in Education Conference. Canberra: CEGACT.

Sims, R. & Farrow, M. (1989). Multi-disciplinary Intelligent Computer Assisted Learning. Paper presented at the ADCIS 89 Conference, Washington.

Smith, S.G. & Sherwood, B.A. (1976). Educational uses of the PLATO computer system. **Science. 192,** 344-352.

Surber, J.R & Leeder, J.A. (1988). The effect of graphic feedback on student motivation. **Journal of Computer-Based Instruction, 15**(1), 14-17.

Tennyson, R.D. (1982). Interactive effect of cognitive learning theory with computer attributes in the design of computer-assisted instruction. **Journal of Educational Technology Systems, 10**(2), 175-186.

Vinsonhaler, J.P. & Bass, R.K. (1972). A summary of ten major studies in CAI drill and practice. **Educational Technology, 11**(7), 29-32.

Whiting, J. (1986). Student opinion of tutorial CAL. **Computer Education, 10**(2), 281-292.

Computers in Education
A. McDougall and C. Dowling (Editors)
Elsevier Science Publishers B.V. (North-Holland)

LARGE SCALE CBT DEVELOPMENT AND IMPLEMENTATION AT THE COMMONWEALTH BANK OF AUSTRALIA

Robert SPENCE

Computer Based Training, Personnel Department, Commonwealth Bank of Australia, GPO Box 2719, Sydney, Australia

The introduction of Computer Based Training (CBT) into a large diversely spread organisation represents a significant investment in not only training technology but the opportunity to exploit the media by using it in isolation or in tandem with other media. Requirements for success in business, market share and lean operating expenses rest on many factors and astute decisions, but the need to train and develop an organisation's most important asset, people, outranks all.

This paper tells of the macro level steps taken to introduce CBT into the Commonwealth Bank of Australia. Of CBTs two major components, Computer Managed Instruction (CMI) and Computer Assisted Instruction (CAI), concentration has been on the latter. Many of the decisions taken and opinions put forward reflect an appropriate methodology for the establishment of a centralised development unit and 1000 decentralised delivery points. This occurred at a time when the technology based training industry in Australia was in its infancy and little commercially relevant experience could be drawn from overseas.

The experiences recorded are for the benefit of others, bearing in mind that since the Bank made its initial commitment to CBT in 1985 new philosophies towards the instructional aspects of technology based training have been expounded, methodologies regarding development have been recast and advanced technologies have widened the delivery possibilities.

1. INTRODUCTION

The Commonwealth Bank of Australia is one of almost 40 banks operating in the volatile and deregulated Australian banking industry. With assets of over $60000m and a staff in excess of 35000 spread over 1000 branches throughout Australia, the organisation is large by any standards.

So too is its commitment to Computer Based Training, which also reflects the importance placed on the training and development of its staff and recognition of a continuing quest for improved organisational performance.

In the vicinity of 1200 PCs dedicated to CBT have been installed across the branch network, with a range of courseware levelled mainly at the new entrant and those in their first twelve months of service. The courseware is mainly tutorial, with criterion referenced mastery tests.

A courseware development team of 25 design new and maintain existing courseware which equates to over 100 student contact hours.

The staff complement of a "typical" branch could be as few as four and as many as 150. Training responsibilities rest with the Branch Manager who delegates the performance of in-branch training activities to the line supervisors in the branch. Line supervisors then also fill the role of "Training Supervisor" as an inherent part of their job. Given customer service responsibilities, the challenge these supervisors have is utilising available time for training. CBT is seen as a tool, to assist with the Training Supervisor's role becoming one of facilitating through the monitoring of trainee progress, ensuring consolidation of learning on-the-job and administering the CBT system.

2. JUSTIFICATION

2.1. Some History

For some years heavy emphasis had been placed in on-the-job (in-branch) training methods supplemented with courses in technical skills at centralised classroom based venues. The early 1970s saw the introduction of paper based programmed learning techniques, essentially for basic banking skills and teller training. Although these materials, which were made available to all branches, assisted the in-branch training effort, a great deal of reliance remained on supervisors at the branches and, wherever possible, centralised courses were utilised for added support. Over subsequent years changing procedures, brought about principally by the enhancement of banking products through market pressures and emerging technology generally, began to bite. This concerned not only the currency of the paper based material, but the logistics involved in updating thousands of pieces of paper. As a result of the problems associated with those arrangements, the very real benefits in record keeping, the centralised control features and the evaluation aspects offered by CBT technology, particularly Computer Managed Instruction (CMI), became clear. The watchful eye being kept on CBT, brightened.

In 1983 deregulation of the Australian banking industry saw sixteen additional banking licenses approved by the Australian Government. That spelt competition, a rush for market share and generally a need to operate more leanly and efficiently. A well trained staff was to be essential.

Within months a project team commenced the piloting of systems. This effort culminated in early 1985 with the purchase of McDonnell Douglas' AIS II Authoring System. Selection criteria, which included a "programmerless" authoring system, provision of high resolution colour graphics and software capable of operating across a range of hardware devices, had been met.

2.2. Pilot Study

The Bank accepted the use of CBT as a technology with great potential, but cost benefits and an examination of the extent to which it could be exploited within the Bank would need to be pursued.

Office space was located, workstations delivered (specified through a general perception of what an Author would require) and a production mainframe (Gould 6031 Mini-computer) purchased. Courseware development was to be undertaken centrally (in Sydney) and delivered in branches by stand-alone DOS based PCs.

In keeping with policy pertaining at the time, courseware development staff were sought from within the Bank. With very limited experience and certainly an absence of precedent, the choice of the initial staff was based on little more than impressions gleaned from the available literature and a willingness of people to join a project team which had a lot to learn, and an uncertain future. Author training, which honed a perception of the vital role of instructional design, was completed by McDonnell Douglas consultants and shortly thereafter the first courseware development activity commenced.

1987 saw the completion of a teller training course and the establishment of a pilot study to measure cost benefit variables, assess the reaction of branch staff to the technology, obtain solid confirmation of the instructional effectiveness and provide a framework around which detailed implementation planning could take place.

2.3. Self Installation

It was obvious prior to the pilot study commencing that the installation of up to 1200 PCs across Australia would pose logistical issues. Hardware and software costs, human resources, timeframe and acceptance of the technology, given no other PCs were in the branches at the time, were all important but substantially unknown factors. After careful consideration it was decided to approach implementation of hardware and training in use of the software on a "self install" basis which would hopefully alleviate the foreseen difficulties. Therefore the purpose of the pilot extended to an examination of this factor. Following purchase of hardware and the identification of 29 sites, a series of draft instructions was developed.

These covered the receipt of equipment, its unpacking, step by step instructions on unpacking and installing the PC, and learning how to use the software to enrol students and generally carry out other administrative functions. Once we were satisfied the document had reached the best possible state of presentation and accuracy, it was tested at a usability laboratory.

Naturally, some refinement to the documentation was necessary, but once in place and with a newly formed help desk function at the ready, the equipment was dispatched to the pilot branches. While interested in a number of matters, the reaction of branch staff to the technology and their acceptance was of vital importance to us, particularly as many of the branch supervisors were unfamiliar with PC technology.

The acceptance of CBT technology, the enthusiastic use of PCs and an appreciation of the benefits CBT offers were all demonstrated through a strong sense of system ownership which permeated the pilot branches. Some problems surfaced but these were resolved and overall help desk calls were minimal. The effectiveness of CBT as an instructional tool could not be measured objectively at that time, but evidence strongly suggested trainees had increased enthusiasm and confidence and also a greater level of knowledge than through media previously used.

The successful outcome of the pilot study is best illustrated through the Bank's decision in December 1987 to purchase 1200 PCs for CBT presentation.

3. IMPLEMENTATION PLANNING

News of the decision attracted the attention of PC vendors and subsequently tenders were called. Olivetti and NCR were successful with their 286 based M290 and PC710 respectively, optioned up with 40 Mb hard disks and VGA graphic capability. This decision necessitated two self install documents and further usability testing.

A great deal of investigation was necessary to establish criteria upon which to base an implementation plan. For example: the geographic distribution schedule; workflow and work pressure issues which could affect supervisors' ability to carry out the installation; the available space within some branches to place the equipment; and which branches would require more than one PC to satisfy training requirements.

Concurrently, planning was in progress with the vendors to facilitate a myriad of activities such as hardware configuration, burning in, software loading and hardware packaging to enable the dispatch of 1200 PCs from August 1988 to March 1989.

4. COURSEWARE DEVELOPMENT

Courseware development continued throughout the period of implementation planning but not before an extensive range of procedures and conventions were established.

The need for these became very clear once the initial author training was complete. Efficiencies in courseware production were going to be essential if an acceptable development ratio was to be achieved. Consequently, the importance of quality control measures spanning both quality of instruction and presentation became obvious. The need for the development of an in-house CAI Style Manual embodying these principles was deemed essential.

For the Bank's requirements such a document would need to assume use of a relatively straightforward instructional design model. To this end the Instructional Quality Inventory [1] was chosen as a set of procedures to be considered during instructional development and to supplement Instructional Systems Design (ISD). The recently trained staff participated in identifying the broad content of the CAI Style Manual and through trial and error, patience, frustration but always enthusiasm, conventions regarding screen layout, and step by step procedures for courseware production, were laid down for the typical analysis, design, development and evaluation elements of ISD.

The content of the CAI Style Manual includes specific matters and techniques concerning the arrangement of screens; use of various facilities within the AIS II Authoring System; conventions regarding the layout of particular screens such as question frames; procedures to be followed by authors when requesting development of graphics from the Graphics Section of the group; and conventions regarding general style, for example, punctuation, vocabulary, use of capital letters, tabulation and alternatives to generic masculine pronouns.

The courseware production procedures are housed within the Style Manual. These detail the activities in each stage, the format of supporting documentation, who is responsible and the expected outcome.

5. SYSTEM PROPAGATION

With a large number of PCs ordered, configured to specifications, tested, loaded with a range of courseware and packaged complete with the self install and training documentation, August 8 1988 was an exciting day for the CBT Group at the Commonwealth Bank.

At the height of propagation up to 75 PCs were dispatched each week with the hardware vendors playing a major role in the preparation, packaging and transport of equipment. Figure 1 illustrates the rate at which the equipment was distributed.

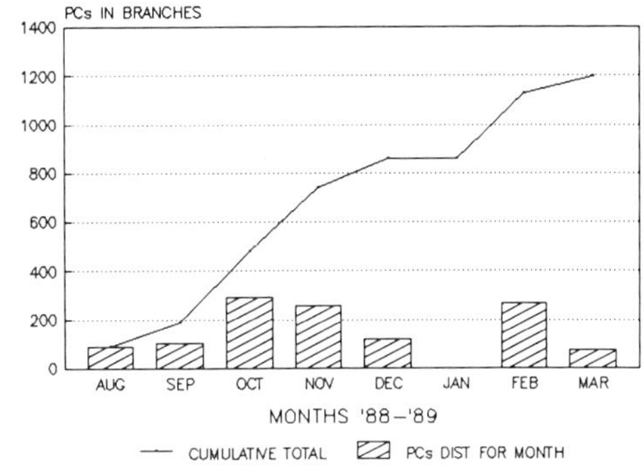

Figure 1

The help desk provided support for the branches who required assistance. As at the end of March 1989, 2145 calls had been received. Figure 2 sets out the details with the exception of calls relating to hardware problems. Interestingly, installation problems encountered by branches with regard to unpacking, assembling and booting up accounted for only 12 of the total calls received (see Category 1). The detailed work put into the self install document had paid off. Savings in monetary terms was and remains subjective, but not insignificant compared with conventional methods and the speed of implementation.

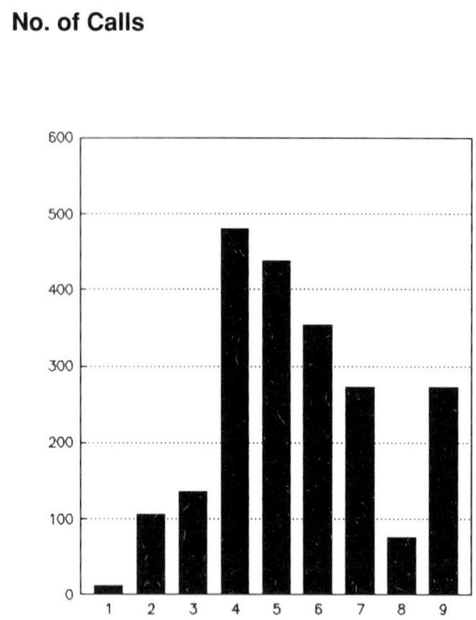

Categories

1. Installation – Set up
2. Installation – Operation
3. Documentation
4. Passwords & System Security
5. PC Administration
6. CBT System Administration
7. Trainee Administration
8. Trainee Access
9. Courseware

Figure 2

6. THE CHALLENGE OF DECENTRALISATION

6.1. Updating Courseware

With 1200 PCs now in place, thousands of trainees and a range of courseware which is highly volatile due to the enhancement of various product and procedures, locating specific areas within lessons affected by change and then updating the courseware held on all the PCs at branches, is an ever increasing challenge.

Although the Bank has an extensive on-line network to service branch transactional terminals and automatic teller machines, CBT lacks at this stage, a facility to distribute new courseware and updates by on-line file transfer. Consequently, diskettes containing courseware amendments or new courseware are duplicated and dispatched to all branches as necessary (usually once each month).

6.2. Collection of Trainee Records

Every two weeks trainee record data is downloaded to diskette at each branch. The data collected also contains a verification that previous updates have been dealt with. Once received at the central point, the data is read and transported into the Computer Managed Instruction (CMI) component of AIS II for processing. Other data bases sort the information into branch/region categories for output on hard copy reports.

For evaluation of courseware purposes, objectives passed/failed data for all lessons attempted is collected with the trainee record data. This is amalgamated and applied against evaluation criteria. For example in excess of a 10% failure rate on any objective would prompt the setting up of software on PCs at a number of "control" branches where further in-depth data is collected for analysis. Unanticipated responses, time to complete individual questions and student comments are examples of data which assist highlighting, say ambiguity within question stems or the instruction itself. Irregularities in branching logic are also identified during the process.

The forthcoming ability to dispense with the duplication and physical distribution of diskettes through the provision of an on-line link to a mass storage device at each branch will alleviate most of the logistical problems encountered. As needs become clearer, data base development to manage the impact of changing procedures on courseware will also emerge.

6.3. Instructional Issues

Although the mechanics of the system are functionally important, it is the instructional efficiencies which can make or break CBT.

We have found Computer Assisted Instruction (CAI) to be effective for having trainees remember steps in procedures (ie. the teaching and testing of instructional objectives with a verb such as "recall" or "list"). Mastery testing can also be relatively straightforward under these conditions. However, on-the-job behaviours require the trainee's application of, say steps in a procedure, by carrying out a task. A higher level behavioural objective would include a verb such as "demonstrate" and as such, in the absence of a computer generated simulation which could be used to confirm mastery, reliance is placed upon performance testing (on-the-job) as a method for trainees to demonstrate mastery.

Simulation training (and testing) is not impossible. The technology is in place, the development expertise available and with time the ingredients will merge with technologies such as the interactive video disk thus providing a solution for the Commonwealth Bank's particular requirements. In the meantime mastery testing is dealt with either by the development of scenarios on screen which imitate the job situation or by relying on branch Training Supervisors to carry out performance tests by observation.

7. THE HUMAN SIDE OF CBT

7.1. Training Facilitators

There are many ways in which people react or associate with CBT. Experience shows some are wary of the technology, some are concerned for the future of classroom teaching while others have reservations about its effectiveness.

Educating and conditioning branch staff at all levels is an important issue in assisting with the acceptance of CBT. To this end a series of video presentations, made available to all branches, was produced and in-house seminars addressed. The concepts were explained and responsibilities outlined. The reaction of staff, particularly Training Supervisors, was positive. However, the changed emphasis in responsibilities to that of a facilitator represents an adjustment which will take time to consolidate.

One of the major difficulties then of operating in a decentralised environment is the obvious lack of a trained facilitator dedicated to monitoring trainees as is the case in a centralised learning centre. To overcome the distance learning problems inherent within a country such as Australia, technology based training has a role to play but it will be appreciated the sheer size of the Bank's CBT operation has made it difficult to come to grips with the present and future role of a training facilitator. The relatively low throughput of trainees at many branches does not warrant dedicated resources. However when supervision of CBT activities are mixed with other day to day responsibilities, it will be appreciated that a varying standard of understanding and commitment to this vital role in the learning process will take time to stabilise.

7.2. Survey of Users

A survey conducted by an independent group showed that following installation 92.2% of Training Supervisors found the CBT system easy to use with 90.6% referring to the reference material provided, rather than the help desk, as a first step. 97.3% of trainees found CBT easy to use and stimulating as a media from which to learn.

7.3. The Courseware Production Team

In contrast to the delivery sites, the on-going need to develop human resources for courseware production is also full of challenge. Dealing with the inevitable turnover of resources, the development of replacements, while at the same time maintaining productivity and quality control, needs to be accepted as part of a commitment to CBT.

The structure of the courseware development group is split into five areas (figure 3). These sub-groups operate separately, but integrate overall. A number of administrative responsibilities are spread through all the staff which provides an opportunity to participate in the overall management process with a break from day to day routines.

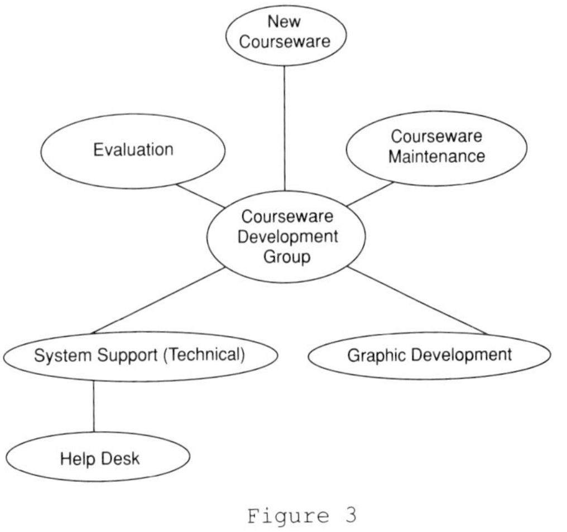

Figure 3

With the need for analysing, specifying, designing, forecasting, scheduling, planning, controlling, monitoring and so forth, interlaced with quality control measures, the development of courseware can be likened to a manufacturing process. Similar skills are required to control it with an exception, the human element, which provides individual courseware developers the opportunity to be creative. Allowing too much creativity can spell disaster for the continuity of lessons in a course, not to mention production deadlines and related costs, but creativity cannot be stifled either. Consequently, a happy medium needs to be met, not by words or written orders, but by moulding a courseware development team that works closely and understands what is expected of individuals and the group at large. In many ways similarities can be drawn with an orchestra performing a piece of music under the conductor's control with the aim of expressing the desire of the composer, but with a great deal of controlled personal skill and creativity on behalf of the individual performers and the conductor, blending and co-ordinating towards a common goal.

Interactivity has been quoted by Gloria Gery [2] as "CBT's raison d'etre" and that is so true from an instructional viewpoint, but interactivity must be present throughout the development process as well in order to achieve it in the finished product. Control and production of mediocre courseware is not that difficult; harnessing creativity to enable the development of interactive, individualised courseware is the challenge.

8. THE CURRENT POSITION

The aim of courseware development at the Commonwealth Bank is to produce instructionally sound, interactive, individualised instruction, with remediation and acceleration built in as appropriate, but overall an enjoyable, non threatening experience during which learning takes place. Data available from our courseware evaluation efforts, feedback via the help desk function, general experience and policy direction is influencing some changes in approach to our development activities. For example we are now endevouring to break courses down into more accessible modules to better cater for remedial and refresher training.

To be useful, courseware must be relevant to training needs but at the same time manageable in terms of the effect changing products and procedures has on the life of courseware and maintenance resources. Consequently a great deal of consideration is currently being given to content and presentation formats.

Methods of exploiting CMI are being researched. Ultimately full utilisation of CMI will assist with the overall control of the training and development function. This is partly envisaged through the provision of profiles of skills for individuals and groups, and prescription learning for the attainment of skill levels. The technology is clearly very powerful.

Technological advances which have enriched the training industry with, as an example, interactive video disk and expert systems are for investigation and use in the 1990s. We have a particular charter to accomodate that. Very recently the installation of a Local Area Network has seen our courseware development move away from a host based (Mini-computer) environment to a PC based solution. This is seen as an early step in streamlining our production procedures and generally taking advantage of new technology.

9. CONCLUSION

CBT is not the answer to all training problems; it is not a panacea. Used wisely it can be very powerful; introduced without commitment its future will be bleak.

Organisations need to look at the experience of others, be sure what is right for them, consider the puristic approach to instruction while accommodating their particular training environment, but always be mindful that only quality CBT results in learning.

To develop courseware systematically and efficiently, conventions, procedures and quality control checkpoints must be established which respect organisational standards.

This paper sets out, very broadly, an approach, one could argue a pioneering approach, appropriate to the Commonwealth Bank given many of the foundations were based on the best principles available at the time. There is no apology in that statement as philosophy, methodology and technology are constantly evolving. New horizons will always appear and it is the responsibility of training technologists to harness, exploit, improve and continue to pioneer into the future.

REFERENCES

[1] Ellis, J.A., Fredericks, P.S., Merrill, D.M., Richards, R.E., Wood, N.D., and Wulfeck II, W.H., The Instructional Quality Inventory I-IV (Navy Personnel Research and Development Centre, San Diego, 1979)

[2] Gery, G., Making CBT Happen (Weingarten Publications, Boston, 1987) p42.

Computers in Education
A. McDougall and C. Dowling (Editors)
Elsevier Science Publishers B.V. (North-Holland)

COMPUTER MANAGED LEARNING AS AN INTEGRAL PART OF EDUCATIONAL TECHNOLOGY

Robert C. Thornborough, Southern Alberta Institute Of Technology,
Calgary, Alberta, Canada T2M OL4

Education in our changing world is of paramount importance to the continued well-being of society. For educational organizations to be effective, we must ensure orderly development of educational technology to support the transportability of courseware, as well as management of education related resources. CML, when used effectively, is an important component of the 'toolkit' necessary for success.

Introduction

The world has changed dramatically during our lifetimes. Whatever our ages, it has changed to a greater degree than for any of those who preceded us. The modern industrial state is a complex held together by information. Indeed, we live in what has come to be known as an "information economy." We can easily identify changes in the way people travel, communicate, work and relax. But these changes will be dwarfed by what lies ahead in the coming decades.

Some of the facts associated with these changes may not be pleasant - but they need to be taken into account when planning for our future. Our institutions should be making major changes to prepare for the society of which we will be a part in 20 years. For us this preparation is more important than most because education will be the most important area affecting our future society. It is imperative that as educators, we assess the directions defined by science and global information and communications resources if we are to compete in an increasingly competitive and global economy.

Preparation requires that we step beyond the very personal concerns we have about technology and our future - concerns which include the following. Will we be able to keep up with the change imposed by technology? Will we remain central to the process of education? Will we be replaced and if so by what - and when? Will we become automatons regurgitating someone else's information? Will we be able to stay home and share our lives to the same degree as in the past with our families? This paper is an attempt to answer those questions and at the same time suggest opportunities we might consider relative to technology and our personal and institutional futures.

Why talk about change as though it is a foregone conclusion? Who is to say we can't continue achieving the same measure of success in the future, using the interpersonal and ancillary resources with which we are familiar?

We may not like some of the things that are happening - but they are happening, and they are happening in the world of which we are a part. The massive change taking place is to a large degree the result of information age technologies used to inform - to educate. When used by the mass media, we take them for granted. When used specifically to support the process of education within a formal secondary or post-secondary organization, most educators rebel.

Let's move from the general to the specific and define what we mean by the term educational technology. Once defined, we can return to the future we will be a part of and assess the role of educational technology in that future.

What Is Educational Technology?

The term educational technology should be defined in relation to the time during which it is used. Textbooks first appeared in numbers about 1700, 250 years after the invention of printing press technology. As an information resource, texts moved from the sole purview of monks and a few learned scholars to libraries, where they were chained to desks, to general use, and the personal possessions of students at all levels. Consider the impact that those sources of information from unknown authors must have had on the educators of the day. For the first time, information was available to students from a source other than the educator. It would be reasonable for educators to fear being replaced by this new educational technology. Sir Clive Sinclair, an inventor of some repute, observed that, "It often seems that each new step in technology brings misery rather than contentment, but this is because it brings change faster than benefits - and change, though often stimulating, is always disturbing."

Current technologies are of themselves probably no more important or potentially damaging, than the introduction of the mass produced written word, but they will have much greater repercussions than previous changes to the patterns of teaching and learning for at least two reasons. First, there are a great many more of us, living in a world comprised not of islands separated one from the other as in the past, but in a world which is a single intertwined society held together by very rapid and efficient information transfer systems. Second, for good or bad, commercial interest plays a major role in the modern world and will play an increasingly larger role in education.

What are the current educational technologies that have replaced the textbook and given rise to concern from administrators regarding cost, and consternation in the minds of instructors?

In the minds of many, the words educational technology describe those things we do by using machines that we don't understand. It is equipment - computers, projectors, television, videodisc, perhaps tied to some sort of control in the form of programmed sequences or software. Some instructors who have a less than enthusiastic outlook when the subject of educational technology arises, consider it to be bells and whistles; fluff; things that are supported with misdirected money. Educational technology is not equipment. Nor is it fluff. It is not a thing. It is a process - a process which uses design, production, delivery, book keeping, and evaluation tools. It is an instructor's toolkit. Perhaps Christopher Dede caught the essence of educational technology when he said it "created empowering environments", a condition that allows a synthesis of the instructor with soft and hard technologies. The information technologies are in large part intellectual tools that empower the user in ways previously inconceivable. Access to these intellectual tools and ability to apply them to real life will ultimately be the factors that to a large degree determine an individual's success or failure.

Perhaps we should move away from the notions of infusion and integration of technology into the curriculum. Education has maintained a specific model for 50 years. The effective application of educational technology is not dependent on this model. Our approach in the past has been to retrofit, with a powerful and complex technology, a structure which has been successful, but at the same time, was defined a considerable time ago, to satisfy yesterday's clients. Entrepreneurial educational organizations are recognizing that curriculum delivery as presently constituted will not always serve well our clients of the future. Modularization initiatives are testament to that fact and a major move toward the required redefinition of transportable offerings. That move also signifies the effective use of educational technologists with their broad conceptual purposes, working in consort with technicians armed with appropriate technology, to implement an effective process.

How Is The Instructional Process Linked To Educational Technology?

The development of the individual and the means by which that development takes place was tied together in the results of 10 years of research at Harvard by Perry. The research resulted in the definition of four stages of learning. The stages may seem only indirectly related to educational technology, however, they are critical to the determination of how we introduce technological change within our formal and informal education organizations.

The four stages of learning followed the student from the dualism stage with memorization paramount to a well rounded individual at the final commitment stage, basing decisions on reason. The student learning stages are paralleled by four approaches to teaching with a teacher dominated environment at the low end through to a true enquiry centered approach at stage four. A parallel series of stages is required for the development of educational technology services. As the student moves from the dualism to commitment stage, educational technology plays an increasingly important part in instruction as we as a society,move further into the information age. Stage four is identified in part by the use of educational technology that is needs-driven, function-oriented, financially effective, and planned for.

The integrated resources comprising the educational technology team must be used to play a significant part in providing information and in assisting the student to gather, organize, interpret, evaluate and use knowledge. A relativistic world demands that we provide these services to our students.

How do we bring about this cohesive approach to using the talent available within our institutions?

Classical approaches to planning usually emphasize the establishment of goals. In a time where technology is growing and changing rapidly, traditional goal setting may be too static and myopic. What may be more fruitful is the development of strategic views of technology in our institutional futures, views that attempt to articulate a philosophy based on missions, that permits seizing opportunities brought about by an effective alliance of people and educational technologies. Some technological advances are clearly predictable; others are not so easily foreseen. Whatever strategic position our institutions assume vis-a-vis the design, presentation, production, communications, data processing, and recording functions, it must be predicated on foreseeable technological advances, and flexible enough to accommodate those that are not so easily discernible.

Connectivity and the merging of technologies are two directions that are established now and will continue to emerge as enabling catalysts for an essential innovation in education. It is important that this be recognized because it impinges directly on the structure of institutions and provides us with the opportunity to develop a single system approach to provide our clients with access to the world of knowledge and ideas, based on their preferred learning style.

Educational Technology And The Instructor

Many instructors have serious concerns that technology imposes itself and assumes a role better served in other ways. In every case that comes to mind, effective application of technology must realize a non-technological transformation for the good. That notwithstanding, technology cannot always be applied successfully without in some way disturbing the system. Long term implementation will change personnel patterns, union relations, and in some cases, even our definition of curricula. Planning, policy, and implementation procedures must be conducted carefully, for they will affect acceptance and thus control outcomes.

We must ask some difficult questions. What is the incentive for the average instructor to learn about and apply new educational technologies? Why should instructors who in most cases consider themselves to be fully employed, take on the additional responsibility of learning about instructional design, computers, CD Rom, videodiscs, information access systems, communications, international database usage, and interactive systems? If they have reached the top of the salary scale, have a permanent position - as describes the majority of instructors - and see satisfaction measured in the success of their current students, what's in it for the instructor to assume more responsibility? Many are asking these questions at a time when they are uncertain that educational technology is not just another fad to hit education, or worse yet, that the application of educational technology might replace them.

Perhaps we will find some of the answers by assessing educational outputs. As things now stand, instructors are paid virtually the same for a unit hourly classroom load - independent of the number of students being taught. If incentives were based on productivity, measured both quantitatively and qualitatively, and technological resources were made abundant, we might expect to find educational technology adopted much more rapidly and readily. Statements like that will not put anyone at the top of a popularity poll. They must be made however, because the economics of teaching has resulted in the acceptance of educational technology by trainers in the private sector. Earlier in this paper mention was made that investment by corporations in education and retraining will double by the year 2000 and that one-half of the funding for formal education will come from business and industry. Either we work with our partners in business and industry to provide educational services or they will do it themselves. Educational technology is not the enemy; it is not going to compete with or attempt to replace our institutional instructors. We live in an increasingly competitive society, for better or worse, and the competition is none other than peer instructors in the private sector.

As mentioned previously, instructors must be central to whatever process an educational organization institutes in the future. An assessment of the concerns relating to specific elements of the process of educational technology may help to provide a better understanding of and less concern about educational technology in general.

The Myth That Computers Will Replace Instructors

Perhaps this myth, more than others, has created subconscious resistance to the use of educational technology in direct support of educational objectives. Because of the capacity of the computer for individualized instruction, information management, and uniform quality control, it may cause both conscious and unconscious reluctance.

This reluctance is well-founded, although the notion of replacement in many cases is more positive than negative. First, it seems inevitable that any tool with the potential to perform so many necessary, but tedious tasks with the speed and accuracy of the computer must eventually be installed on a significant scale. This has already occurred throughout the business sector, and it is increasingly obvious that the role of the computer in education will be expanded as well. The increasing reluctance of the taxpayer to provide ever larger amounts of money to support education, which is largely personnel intensive, and the associated reality that many of the human functions in education can be accomplished less expensively through the computer, is sobering. Second, "burn out," resulting in part from the burden of non-teaching requirements, must be interpreted as a need to free talented individuals to do what they do best - to teach. Certainly, these and several other factors suggest an important role for the computer - a role that must replace some of the lower level functions instructors currently perform.

Let's try and put the computer in perspective by moving back in time, and assess the impact of a major use of the computer at the Southern Alberta Institute of Technology in Alberta, Canada, over the last ten years.

Computer managed learning (CML) was initially defined, developed and instituted at SAIT during the period between 1975 and 1977. It is in use to varying degrees in all academic departments within the institution. Minor use is made to generate examinations in some departments. In others, CML labs are used in association with printed modules, and students progress at their own rate through a course of studies, with the instructor providing one-on-one tutelage as required, and classroom sessions only when necessary to solve problems experienced by a majority of students. This CML computer technology has not been imposed yet the number of users continues to increase year by year with one-third of SAIT students currently receiving exposure in one form or another. Some instructors have no use for it, some use it to their benefit in a limited way, and an increasing number have bought into the system and use it to full potential. It can be said with impunity that no jobs have been lost because of it. It can also be said by many instructors that the jobs they have are more rewarding because of its use.

The use of television is also eyed with suspicion. In the early seventies, experiments were conducted at Scarborough, Ontario in which live lectures were replaced with pre-recorded television broadcasts. The experiment failed. A cartoon of the era depicted a talking face television monitor at the front of the class and a cassette recorder on each of the fifty or so student desks. Since then, we have learned some important lessons. Foremost is that one medium should not be replaced with another unless the replacing medium increases comprehension. Television works best as a teaching medium when demonstrating something which the trainer cannot demonstrate - motion change, information that must be conveyed through animation, or information that for whatever reason cannot be brought into the classroom.

Live television as opposed to canned lectures, offers additional advantage to education, primarily due to the fact it can make affordable and available, international resources that provide leading edge information for both students and trainers. The live format and two-way communications technology allows the student to participate and alter discussion.

Modules/technology

The escalating costs of developing and maintaining curriculum brought about by demands for individualization, transportability, and the ever increasing complexity and density of learning materials, coupled with ever more limiting resources, will dictate that institutions such as ours gravitate towards specializing in the development of the resource materials for fewer and fewer courses. To a substantially greater degree than at present, the component parts of instruction will be developed by institutions with an exceptional range of resources in specific subject areas. Our institutions will become national and to a limited degree, international authorities on basic curriculum support and supply of resource materials in select areas, and will supply pre-produced courseware to similar organizations as a part of our mandates. Similarly, other institutions will also specialize in particular courses of study and we will purchase their base curriculum and resource support products and manipulate these to satisfy local conditions and provide instruction to our students. The supply of course materials to others and manipulation by ourselves of pre-produced course materials requires a logical bite-sized product.

Educational Technology And Academic Support

The boundaries between technologies are breaking down as integration and networking between systems develop. And as those technological boundaries crumble, so too should operational barriers. The expression "the whole is more than the sum of its parts," often holds true. Yet when it comes to educational technology, the conventional approach is to keep one's eyes firmly focused on the pieces and parts, and not on the whole. A unified purpose and direction is the key for dealing with the powerful synergism that results from the synthesis of design, broad information resources, computers, and communications.

It is reasonable to assume that all of the data maintained by our institutions and used to advantage in the form of information, should ultimately support our missions. It is also reasonable to assume that all information and resources of any type, including administration personnel and procedures, and all support programs, ultimately provide the resources necessary to satisfy our clients. The instructor is the conduit by which the institution moves its combined resources in the form of instruction to our clients. The information used by the instructor must be available in a format which is convenient, and malleable, given our needs for efficiency, effectiveness, ever changing curricula, and trans-

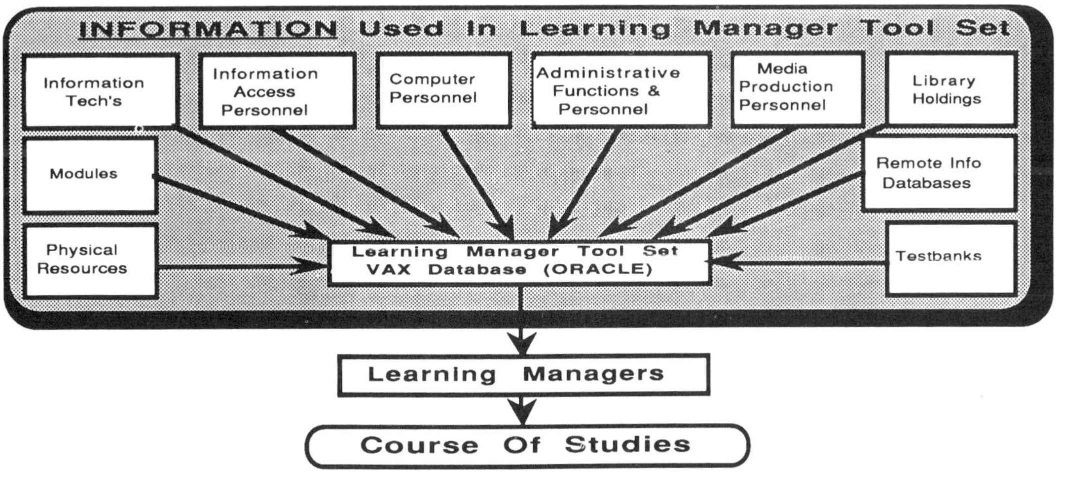

portability. This information, used by instructors, forms a set of tools.

To use the information effectively, we must manage the process of instruction. It is essential that we know how potential students measure up to prerequisites defined to satisfy not only traditional courses but also special courses designed to satisfy the objectives of specific client groups. We must be able to test the same material at varying degrees of difficulty depending on the objectives of the client. We must know what is being offered to whom and when and where. We must know both for local and students operating at a distance, who has and has not successfully completed widely varying courses of study. To support the information tool set we require an effective management system - and the system we find most effective is the CBTS-CML.

Devising the system to move data, to information, to a logical tool set, with effective access, and then to maintain control, is part of the job of the senior education group working with content experts and fulfilling the functions of educational technologists.

The job requires an integrated effort from all sectors of the organization working in consort to provide an integrated system.

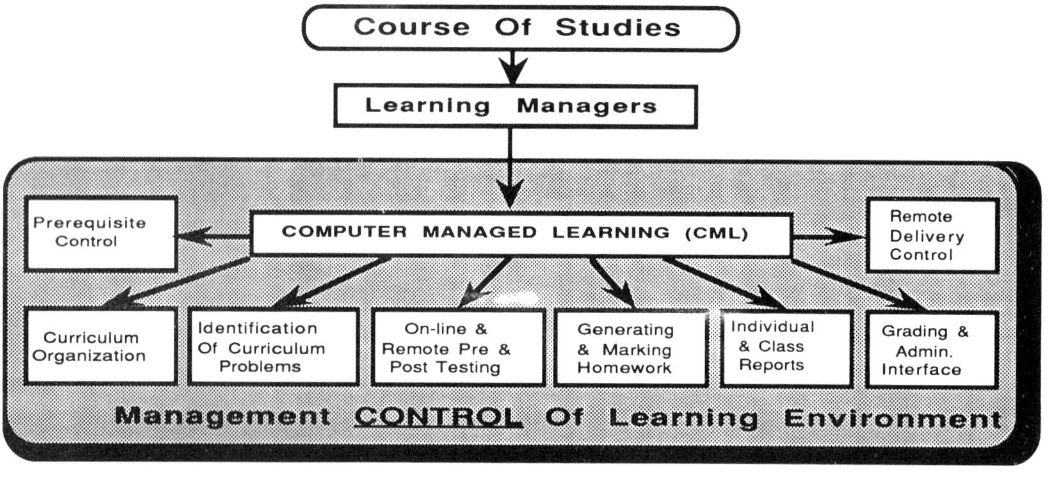

Conclusion

The rapid advance in use of effective technology, coupled with entrepreneurial management, and education staff, together with a leading organizational mission, will allow continued development of an educational communications organization capable of serving formal educational organizations well in the future. This information/production/ communications organization should become the communal "knowledge center" of the organization. It should offer on site and remote access, assistance and instructional support services, and provide a wide range of media. The center should be involved in the design, creation and communication of information.

The goal should be the creation of a single system that provides the ubiquity and simplicity that we associate with the telephone system and will provide to students, access to the world of ideas based on their preferred learning style.

Albert Rosenfeld, the author of "The Second Genisis: The Coming Control Of Life," expressed our education need thus: "In any planning of society, the structure and function of educational organizations will be at the heart of it; and we are less likely to go wrong in our choices if we keep in mind what it is all to be designed for: the whole human being and his fulfillment in a regulated but free society." We here today can help with that lofty fulfillment. Our challenge is to take the good that we have developed and that our eyes can see, and apply that good to what our imaginations know.

TELETEACHING 90

Computers in Education
A. McDougall and C. Dowling (Editors)
Elsevier Science Publishers B.V. (North-Holland)

From Computing to Information Technology to Distance Education - What do we do when teacher isn't there?

Professor Norman Longworth
UNESCO/IBM Chair in Education and Information Technology

Co-Director of Southampton University International I.T.CERES

A Keynote Paper for the IFIP World Conference on Computers in Education, Sydney, July 1990

ABSTRACT

This paper examines current issues in Distance Education in the context of the development of Computer Education. It suggests that use of the computer as a communicating machine creates a more powerful educational tool than its function as a delivery mechanism for didactic software, and this offers exciting possibilities for the future in such areas as distance learning, collaborative global teaching strategies and the creation of a new range of open-ended software based on hypermedia tools. It uses examples from three existing programmes - The European Commission DELTA Programme, the PLUTO International Networking Programme and the EuroPACE Satellite Education Programme. Lastly, it speculates about possible future applications of teleteaching relevant to the problems now facing the planet.

Introduction - the Short March of the Computer Education Revolution

Computer Education is a relatively young religion. Nevertheless, its disciples are among the most convinced and zealous in their application of its rites and sacraments.

And often with good reason. Among the population at large there is a growing band of believers who appreciate, intuitively if with little evidence, that the computer has a mystical significance which is important for future well-being. Among that band there is the inner circle of priestly devotees who have used the machine with wisdom and good effect to improve the measurable performance of their young congregations. This inner circle is small and privileged - not all of it has shewn intelligent devotion.

There is also a heresy among the adherents of other religions, usually those based in humanitarian activities, that perhaps the ikon, the object of devotion, has limitations; worse, that it offers little of relevance to their own rituals and practises. To justify such blasphemies, the unconvinced, who often include the paying members of the same broader Church, point to a lack of research evidence that there is indeed such an idol as improved performance from worshipping the machine; and they resent the vast sums of money needed to make sacrifices to the new religion.

Further, they direct our attention to the schisms within the priesthood - the righteous upholders of Computer Studies against the soothsayers of educational software; the progressives against the traditionalists; the educational mind-closers who insist on the Word of the Computer Gospel as defined in its Bible versus the mind-openers who seek new versions of the Truth through its very diversity.

And of course, as always, the scepticism has a basis in the real world. There *is* little research evidence, true believers *have* oversold their product, and there *is* Doubt in the land. Which is not to say that the doctrine is false - merely that the Medium has not yet become the Message in the Commonwealth of Computer Education. Perhaps it is the marketing of the Word which needs to be repackaged.

Paradigm shifts in the Story of Computer Education

Despite the shortness of its history, there is a detectable, if over-lapping sequence of events in Computer Education, leading up to its recent adoption in the cause of Distance Education.

The first half of the 1970s was the great age of the dabbler, the enthusiast who, through (usually) his consuming passion, managed to kindle the fires of many a youngster in (usually) the remarkable machinery of the machine. Inspired by the pleasures of machine language programming, the delights of logic analysis and the impressive range of peripheral units working at unbelievable speed, the ebullient master and his captivated pupil - usually young, intelligent and creative - managed to give the aura of unfathomable mysticism to the story of the computer.

Then, as time moved into the second half of the decade, there grew a general consciousness that computers were the engines of future careers, and there was a growing demand to make available to a much wider range of youngsters the benefits of a Computer-related Education. And from the forge created by the dabbler there was fashioned a course, based on the precepts and percepts of the computer as a fascination, and adapted downwards for the understanding of the greater masses.

This was the great age of Computer Studies, the BASIC language and the chance of a fortune in 'Working in Computers'. During the five years in which it held sway, changes were made to the syllabus - often with difficulty since examination requirements need new subjects to be set in concrete for at least six years before they become acceptable - and acknowledgements to the wider role of the computer were conceded in the form of education about their applications and implications.

This indeed increased considerably the number of computer literate school pupils and the supply of computer technologists to the Universities. It also, however, raised some pointed questions about the essence, width and relevance of that literacy, often highlighted by the complaints of eager employers that such graduates had to unlearn much of what they had learned before they were employable.

Meanwhile, in the background, other voices had been trying to make themselves heard. The Education Technologists, fresh from the disappointments of the failure of the Programmed Learning movement in the early seventies, and eager to re-establish their reputation, saw in the computer a powerful new tool for delivering education.

And so we moved, in the early 1980s, into the age of 'The Computer as a Tool for Teaching' ; a radically different perception of the use of the computer in the classroom. With the eagerness of the converted, the Education Technologists seized the initiative and seized also the reins of power. National Computer Education Programmes, initiated by politicians heeding the siren cries of their electorates for more Computer Education, were taken over by the new breed. The answers to the malaise of Computer Studies were to be Educational Software, the fostering of fledgling new national micro-computer industries serving the educational marketplace and the opening up of the curriculum across the board to the influence of the computer.

A noble aim, and in some countries a noble failure. The first educational software followed the old Skinnerian Programmed Learning paradigm. It was drill and practice stuff, boring, repetitive, unconvincing to its victims, the children, who resolutely refused to become, or even act like, the pigeons on which the methodology was based.In the words of Seymour Papert, whose software was more generic, more creative and more relevant:

- *The phrase 'Technology and Education' usually means inventing new gadgets to teach the same old stuff in a thinly-disguised version of the same old way... if the gadgets are computers, the same old teaching becomes incredibly more expensive and biased towards its dullest parts - namely the kind of rote learning which is measurable.......*
- *Measurable results can be obtained by treating children like pigeons in a Skinner box. (**1**)*

Not all was gloom - many National Programmes, for example the UK National Micro-electronics in Education Programme (MEP), did try to create new, more open-ended, software, based on the needs of the learner rather than on the predilections of the teacher. Unfortunately they met little coherent response from the publishers or the parents, whose educational attitudes were, not surprisingly perhaps, more rooted in their own generation(s)-old models of learning, experience and disappointments.

But perhaps more importantly, some of these programmes laid the groundwork for new paradigm changes in the Computer Education Story ; changes which, even now, are just beginning to happen.

Interspersed among all of these activities were small and important initiatives. Here a database activity - either provided for classroom use, or built up by the learners themselves - there a scheme to bring the power of the word-processor and the spreadsheet into everyday educational use; here a more dubious attempt to re-automate the turning of pages by presenting screens of didactic information through simple CBT programmes, there a more sophisticated use of CBT which incorporated the strength of multi-media educational tools. All of these, and more, were early grist to the mill of synthesis which is currently taking place.

Nevertheless, at first, the high promise in the early 1980s of a breakthrough in the perception of the computer as a tool which could revolutionise the learning process ended in a period of disillusionment as the lack of good software both to interest children and be of use in a changing world became apparent.

Even toward the end of this period, when better software did become available, the caravan had moved on - publishers were uninterested, having had their fingers burned, and those teachers who had criticised the high cost and doubtful value of computer based education took an 'I-told-you-so' attitude.The resurgence of interest in these new products awaits a different environment which even now is beginning to unfold.

The State of Play in Computer Education

As the technology has improved, as storage has increased, as machines have become faster, as new applications in the commercial world have proliferated, as the cost per working bit has decreased dramatically, so have the resources available to Computer Education opened up new and wider opportunities. Some of the foundations of the next paradigm shift were laid down both in National Programmes and by individuals following up their own lines of research. The activities mentioned in the former section have not ended and will not go away in the future. Rather the situation is one of overlapping waves in which each new advance overtakes and eventually subsumes the old one, making it operate in a slightly modified, but easily identifiable, way.

At the present juncture in Computer Education there are in fact four well-defined pathways to the future, and these are as follows:

- ***1. The first is the advent of what is usually called hypermedia software, as exemplified in the Linkway (IBM) and Hypercard (Apple) products. In a sense this is an extension of the previous paradigm of using the computer as a tool and inventing the software to allow it achieve this role. In fact, the paradigm is changed because of the incredible power and versatility of hypermedia as software generating tools in their own right.***

  They alter the focus of education irrevocably from the teacher to the learner, a movement entirely consistent with the pace of change and the proliferation of information in the modern world, a world in which:

  - *Between 6000 and 7000 Scientific Articles are written each day*
  - *Scientific and Technical Information increases by 13% per year which means it doubles every 5.5 years*
  - *Since this is a self-generating process, by 1990 the volume of information in the world will be 4 to 7 times what it was in 1986 (**2**)*

  Hypermedia tools are relatively easy to work with and require only a little special training. They presage the future when Expert Systems tools will make even more powerful techniques available to the educational programmer. They have another link with the Education Technology movement in that they encourage the use of accompanying education delivery tools such CD-ROM and videodisk. And they represent a potential resuscitator for the flagging Educational Software industry, though it is likely to take some considerable time to convince the publishers, the teachers and the politicians to change their own attitudes to education.

- ***2. The second major paradigm shift is probably the most exciting and motivating of all. It is the use of networks to link teacher trainers, teachers and children in a communicating environment, and explore what these networks***

can do to improve education. Already there are many small examples of projects which have started this process going. To talk to teachers, many of whom had never used a computer and were vociferous in their condemnation of its cost, about the effect which such links have had on them and their children, is to talk to the truly converted.

Perhaps a few examples from the PLUTO (Project to Link Universities and Teaching Organisations) project will give some flavour of the potential and excitement which all levels of education are experiencing.(**3**)

PLUTO is a network of one or two Teacher Training Establishments in Europe, linked by EARN/BITNET, and with a mission in the longer term to create an open network for all Teacher Training Institutions, including some in Industry. Because, in many cases, several schools are also linked into the network through the Teacher Training Organisations, there is potential to create teaching and learning links between Teacher Trainers, Teachers in Training, Teachers in-Service and Children. Industrial training establishments are now being invited to join to add an interesting and valuable new dimension.

The essence of a project like this is to explore the added value which can be given to a simple electronic mail/file transfer connection. The problem in all these things is not the technology - it is the management and the use of the technology. In this respect PLUTO exists to:

- ***develop new educational materials (courseware, software, databases etc) by collaborative work between the network members.*** The PLUTO network has an interesting way of managing such a network by encouraging each node (there are more than twenty such, representing most countries of Europe) to 'own' a development project and to share the development work with other nodes. The resultant 'deliverables' are then made available to all.
- ***test new strategies for teaching about the new information technologies.*** The advantage of course in doing this within a network is that people have to use the technology to communicate
- ***improve language teaching through Europe-wide contacts between teacher trainers, teachers, students and industrial trainees in different countries.*** There is an obvious potential for this which can be built upon and added to as new ISDN and satellite facilities are available.
- ***increase cultural understanding between participants in PLUTO through common exercises.*** For example, Teachers in Training are building databases of eating and travelling habits across borders and are learning a lot about other cultures in the process.
- ***make available databases for teaching and learning from a variety of sources and in a variety of subject areas.*** Again the need to use the technology to create the common database is an invaluable way of learning about its uses and limitations.

The activities carried out under these headlines are too numerous to mention, the motivation given to teachers and pupils who participate with each other across country boundaries is almost too powerful to describe and the limit to the new ideas which can be generated in this sort of environment is a long way away. In her book 'the Aquarian Conspiracy' (**4**) Marilyn quotes many examples of the types of informal electronic network which are proliferating world-wide, and the way in which these are breaking down traditional patterns of behaviour and barriers. This is not just a passing phase in Computer Education - it is perhaps the means whereby it at last fulfils its role as a deliverer of IT right across the curriculum, both in content and methodology.

- ***3. The third major trend in Computer Education is the tendency to respond to the information explosion by using the topic of 'information' itself to provide the 'glue' which holds the curriculum together.***

  To be sure, in these days of national curricula, introduced in the UK for the first time this year, that may be an extraordinary statement to make. And it may be indeed premature to make it. Here however is where industry, which has a real need based on cost-effectiveness, is leading the way, and the increasing number of links between industry and education will begin to allow a gradual cross-fertilisation of ideas. In addition, work on the subject of 'information handling skills' leading to the need for a skills-based, rather than a subject-based, curriculum has been carried out since 1973 and has developed in parallel with developments in Computer Education. (**5**) This resulted in several experiments in the UK under the old MEP in courses in Information Studies and the concept has taken a firmer hold in Australia and several parts of the USA.

  This curriculum response to a real need is one which I believe will grow and perhaps flourish in the later 1990s, as a curriculum response to the increasing use of Information Technology in more standard disciplines.

- ***4. Lastly, the combination of a demand for cost-effectiveness in Education, a wider availability of broadband communications channels, the demographic processes of an ageing population allied to a decline in the number of 18 year-olds coming through university in Europe, the proliferation of information (but not of knowledge), and other factors at local, national and international levels is leading up to an even greater use of Distance Education Techniques in Education, and of course to yet another paradigm twist.***

  In a sense what is happening is a synthesis of much of what has gone before, updated through the increased sophistication of technology. The earlier experiments in Computer-Based Training, the developments in computer-related curricula, the use of database technologies - all are re-emerging through the power of communications technology with greater explicit synergy.

  This movement is taking place first in Industry and Higher Education where the need is more urgent and the motivation is higher. That process has already begun - it will reach the schools, hopefully in a modified form, possibly in five more years. The more sophisticated use of computer technology is the key to a successful implementation of this trend and is a further development of our appreciation of the width and diversity of Computer Education under its new larger umbrella of Distance Education.

  The rest of this paper identifies some of the key issues arising from this, and discusses some of them in the context of existing programmes.

Distance Education - an idea ripe for exploitation?

As many people are aware, the topic of Distance Education is both wide-ranging and immediate. As a mass activity it has neither a long past nor a distinguished pedigree, nor indeed I believe does it have an excellent reputation in the present. Nevertheless it does have a current fashionability and an assured future for a whole variety of reasons connected with rapid change, population growth, economics of scale and, if Arthur C Clarke is to be believed, perhaps even for the survival of the species.

Many years ago he wrote, probably not entirely with tongue in cheek

- *'Everyone will need to be educated to the level of semi-literacy of the average college graduate by the year 2000.*

  *This is the minimum survival level of the human race...' (**6**)*

The words may be apocalyptic but the sense is clear - we need to find new and more effective ways of delivering mass education if we are to avoid destroying our environment and ourselves in the process. And the key to these is the fusion of Information Technology and Distance Education.

The major issues in Distance Education might be categorised under four main headings as follows.

- ***1. Delivering Education over Distance***

  Or how the education gets from the provider to the receiver in traditional and non-traditional classroom situations.

  The enabling technology is a key question here, and it is interesting to note that organisations established to deliver education at distance tend to take root in the technology prevalent at the time of their inception. This is often for logistical reasons, in that the organisation sets up a buildings and people empire around the delivery methodology which is not easily changed even when a less expensive means comes along; sometimes it is as much a function of the inability of large organisations to change at all.

  For example, one of the latest fashions in Higher Education and Industry is to use the power and ubiquitousness of satellite to deliver educational courses. This is not only because it is a la mode and technologically impressive - any educational organisation would soon go bankrupt if those were its major rationales - in some circumstances it is actually more cost-effective to do it this way, despite the high (but falling) cost of satellite transmission.

  An example of this is EuroPACE (**7**), an educational organisation set up by 12 major companies and the European Commission COMETT Programme to deliver advanced level courses from University Centres of Expertise to European Industry. The (still) politically fragmented nature of Europe, in which customs departments wield the power to demand extra charges for the shipment of videos trans-nationally through the post (and the power to hold them up), allied to the rapidly proliferating number of industrial sites which wish to receive EuroPACE courses, and the immediate nature of the educational materials, actually makes satellite delivery a good choice, perhaps the only one. EuroPACE started its full transmission programme in October 1989. The support and feedback structures will be discussed later.

  By contrast, the UK Open University was established in 1969 and uses a sophisticated mixture of postal services, television broadcasts local tutors, summer schools and computer-assisted marking. This is not to denigrate the OU - these structures are entirely appropriate for its operation in the UK, and efforts to update its procedures are often made. In addition, the basic philosophies of EuroPACE and the OU are quite different. In the former the information/education is video-based with text support materials; in the latter the major teaching method is just the opposite. Both would find it difficult to change these philosophies by virtue of the nature of the organisational infrastructures they have set up.

  There are of course many other delivery-related issues including whether the computer is yet a viable medium for delivering education. Past experiments have not been re-assuring in this respect - the delivery of text-based learning materials by computer has not exactly been welcomed by learners, except in very few cases where the motivation was strong and the experiment was short. Perhaps the absence of good graphics support is one reason for this - though of course this deficiency is being addressed through several means. More likely the reasons are based more on the psychology of the individual and the requirements of good course design than the technology itself.

Which raises a second key issue viz:

- ***2. Course Design and Creation***

  Or how and why a course gets from the mind of its creator onto an appropriate medium, how decisions are made and what tools are available to assist in these processes.

Strangely enough, the leaders in the field of Course Design and Creation seem to reside more in Industry than in the standard educational environment. This may be because there is a greater urgency to be more cost-effective and therefore to seek the assistance of technological aid ; or it may be because change and the need to respond to it occurs more frequently there. Because of this there is probably a greater emphasis in Industry on the means of passing the educational message through authoring systems, multi-media systems, and the use of Educational Systems Analysis Techniques than there is on the pedagogical, psychological and philosophical factors in teaching and learning. Here lies the makings of a valuable exchange of experiences and techniques.

Perhaps too it is the model of education which regards the learner as a pot to be filled with information (which he/she will then turn into knowledge and action) which has led to such miserable results so far in the use of computers in Distance Education. One of the more exciting things about the new media and methods such as videodisk, CD-ROM etc is the fact that they can be made interactive and turn the learner from a passive creature receiving the wisdom of superior beings to a participant in the learning process.

It is this new pedagogical and psychological view of the learner who is in charge of his/her own learning which offers hope for the future. Course Designers, wherever they are operating, are in the ascendant in the present Distance Education firmament. But there is also a chronic shortage of courses for these people to give them the empathetic understanding of the needs of the learner which will enable them to use the tools at their disposal in a better way. Where there is a built-in need or motivation to learn, as sometimes (not always) exists in industry, this is not such a serious problem. When it becomes the turn of the schools to benefit from the new methods, the ability to employ well-known techniques now used in television broadcasts in the service of education will be very important.

Even in EuroPACE and its sister institution in the USA, the National Technological University, where motivation is high, the concept of head-and-shoulders TV is unacceptable. The degree of learner participation in a course becomes the key factor in that course's success.

Which gives rise to a third key issue....

- ***3. Feedback/Interaction/Support at Distance***

  Or how the receiver of education gets in touch mentally, electronically and psychologically with the provider of Distance Education in his/her physical absence.

Here there are several models to choose from, some of them more up to date than others. As has been said, the UK Open University, and many of the Distance Education organisations in Europe, offer a mixture of local tutors, assignments which have to be returned and summer schools. Of these, local tutoring is the key, and such a facility is very valuable in any Distance Education Environment.

However, there are situations, particularly in those using the newer delivery technologies, where this is not possible, either because there are very few students on a site, or because there is simply no expertise available at the level of the lecture. Many EuroPACE sites have just such a problem, and figure 1 shows how it goes about trying to resolve this problem.

Euro-PACE
Simplified Euro-PACE Diagram

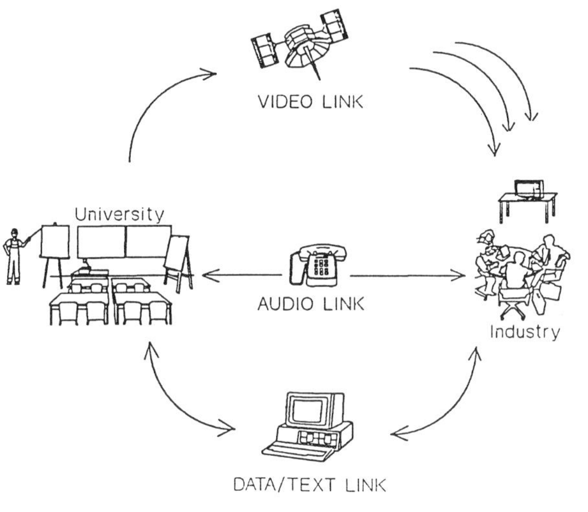

Figure 1 - EuroPACE Concept

One viable means of feedback, especially appropriate when the lecture is received live, is the telephone, and for both conferences and special one-off live events, a telephone link is provided for questions. Because of cost a two-way video link is not normally provided, but in the future increased availability of cheap broad-band channels of communication, satellite or ISDN based, will make this possible.

In some industrial training facilities in the United States, a keypad offering the ability to respond in a limited way to teacher-directed questions is used, but these are not greatly different from what was called a 'feedback classroom' in the 1960's - and that device saw the light of day only for a brief time.

One of the better solutions lies in the area of Computer Conferencing. This has several advantages- in a multi-language, multi-cultural environment, where there may be a reluctance to formulate questions on the telephone or in the classroom, the use of the computer gives the student time to think about how to phrase a question. It also gives the lecturer the opportunity to collect together questions on similar topics in order to give a composite answer. A conferencing system is not time-dependent in another way - questions can be asked and answered at any time during the week of broadcast and then followed up if not clear.

A good conferencing system will allow the easy creation of bulletin boards and forums in which the questions and answers are available to everyone taking a particular course - a sort of electronic seminar - and student to student interaction is achieved through a special 'coffee-shop' facility which simulates the common room. Electronic Staff common rooms and closed conferences for committee work are also a feature of the new electronic university.

Above all, however, the system must be easy to use, and usable by a variety of machine types and people. As always, a system which, however sophisticated, cannot be used by unsophisticated people, is useless - and that is the real challenge to the designers of computer conferencing systems. A particularly good overview of existing systems is given by Torsten Rekkedal and Morten Flate Paulsen in the European Journal of Education.(**8**)

- ***4. Environments in Distance Education***

Or what needs to be created in order to make it easier to provide and receive distance education and to manage its processes.

One of the major concerns of the European Commission DELTA programme is the creation of environments in which the various players in the Distance Education can interact. The tools and needs which the learner requires in order to receive courses are, for example, quite different from the tools and techniques used in the course authoring situation. Similarly Tutoring systems have different capabilities from Production environments. Figure 2 on the next page is reproduced from one of the earlier DELTA documents and shows the interaction of various environments in a Distance Education system.

DELTA is an ambitious programme - it aims to establish a pan-European Education Technology facility using modern delivery and communications techniques, and also to create the connectivities and interoperabilities which enable the system to function as an integrated whole. It is initiating schemes to develop a Portable Electronic Teaching Environment (PETE), which is partly an open-ended Authoring and Expert Systems tool, and to overcome the historic political, economic and cultural barriers which would prevent such a system being installed. One example of the latter has been the setting up of the EuroPACE satellite delivery system - and this is well-expressed in two papers by Peter Zorkoczy of the UK Open University and Jacques Bieber of IBM Belgium in the European Journal of Education. (**9/10**)

There are of course many other issues in Distance Education, and several are key, but there is one insight which, above all else, permeates the pages of the report submitted to DELTA on the establishment of the communications system (   ). This states that **the establishment of a Distance Learning System based on current technology is not primarily a technical problem - to be sure the technology exists and needs to be put together in a particular way - but the major problem is one of management and the organisational infrastructure put into place to make the technology work.** We have seen this in EuroPACE, we see it in the internal structures set up in industry to cope with new learning technologies, and we see it in the management of large national and international development programmes.

Summary - a few last words

I have tried in this paper to establish the links which bind the past history of Computer Education to the present history of Distance Education. A synthesis is taking place in the whole field of using Computers for Education, but there is still far to go. I have also tried to convey some of the exciting possibilities which result from the use of the computer as a communicating tool in addition to its function as a processing tool. The future looks bright indeed. Such initiatives as PLUTO, EuroPACE and DELTA make the prospect of working in this field an attractive one.

At the same time there are major concerns about what man is doing to his environment and how global change will affect the political, economic and ecological affairs which we take for granted on this planet.

Perhaps the use of Information Technology in Education at International, National and Local levels will help present and future generations to understand what must be done to halt environmental degradation and clean up the spaceship. What is certain is that, if we do not create this understanding, little can be done without a great deal of hardship. And so I offer as a final few words some ideas about Information Technology in Education, and particularly Distance Education, can help us in this one, key, area

- *Create access to the major information databases on the environment for Universities, Schools and Teacher Training Colleges - and create courses which turn the data into information, into knowledge, into understanding, into wisdom, into action. The networks and the technology exist already to make it happen....*
- *Pioneer new collaborative teaching strategies by which students, teachers and school pupils learn collectively about their environments by pooling their knowledge into databases. This can also be done nationally, internationally and locally. The networks and technology exist already to make it happen...*
- *Involve, in a controlled way, scientists who are at the forefront of knowledge and experimentation in the teaching process as an additional resource and/or inspiration for the teacher. The networks and the technology exist already to make it happen....*
- *Create new software which simulates the interconnecting aspects of the environmental sciences and make it available nationally and internationally. The networks, expertise and technology exist already to make it happen....*
- *Set up a series of Global Centres networked together to become focal points in the collection, creation, dissemination and facilitation of information, knowledge, understanding and action in the use of IT for Environmental Education. The networks and technology exist already to make it happen....*

The rest is your contribution in adding to this list as an exercise in planetary survival...

References

1. Papert, Seymour, Mindstorms - Children, Computers and Powerful Ideas (Basic 1982)

2. Naisbitt, John, Megatrends - Ten New Directions Transforming our Lives (Warner Books, 1983)

3. Longworth, N and Gwyn, R., The PLUTO International Networking Project (European Journal of Education, Vol 24 No 1, 1989)

4. Ferguson, Marilyn, The Aquarian Conspiracy - Personal and Social Transformation in the 1980s (J.P.Tarcher 1981)

5. Longworth, N., Information in Secondary Schools Curricula (University of Southampton M Phil thesis, 1976)

6. Clarke, Arthur C., Prelude to Space2 (Ballantine, 1976)

7. Longworth, N., and Bieber, J., EuroPACE - a European Education Satellite Delivery Organisation (World Conference on Distance Education, Oslo, August 1989)

8. Rekkedal, T., and Paulsen, M.F., Computer Conferencing in Distance Education (European Journal of Education, Vol 24 No 1, 1989)

9. Zorkoksy, Peter, Using a Pan-European Delivery System for Distance Education (ibid page 55)

10 Bieber, J., Setting up a Satellite Network for Distance Learning (ibid, page 47)

Computers in Education
A. McDougall and C. Dowling (Editors)
Elsevier Science Publishers B.V. (North-Holland)

TECHNOLOGY HANG-UPS AND DISTANCE EDUCATION SYSTEM IN INDIA

Gautam BANERJEE

Head of the Department of English, Government College Serchhip, PO: Serchhip, DT-AIZAWL, Mizoram - 796181, India

This paper investigates the present position of technology in India and the role of the same in the D.L. Programme due to lack of accessibility to the technological media in the field of education. In the name of democratization of higher education in India, so called institutions of DE (Distance Education) only multiply the problems of our country by producing several thousands of graduates and post graduates in general education. As a consequence, the value of education is decreasing day-by-day and the DL system is being relegated to a second class status.

PREAMBLE

The modern age is rightly called the age of Information Revolution. No one could dare to deny the immense implications of modern technology in present day life. But does modernisation mean copying blindly the Western or European models or a peripheral pursuit of certain technology from developed countries?

This paper will investigate the distance learning system in India in the light of D. Broadbent's (1982) remark "If the people won't come to our lectures then our lectures must come to the people" and will attempt to establish that the present distance learning system in India is **severely handicapped** to meet this challenge.

TECHNOLOGY INVOLVED IN DISTANCE EDUCATION

A Distance Education system is basically student oriented. Achieving the main objectives therefore depends mostly on the success of the mass media approach. It is believed that what is lost through the **limited teacher-pupil interaction** will be made up through the use of several media.

A systematic application of communication technology is sought to meet this challenge. The technology on which the distance education system is based can be broadly divided into two categories :- (a) Teacher made and (b) self operated. Teacher made communication technology includes slides, synchronized slides, and tapes, slide commentary work book, transpariencies, audio casette, telephone teaching etc. and self operated technology includes academic and technology expertise besides radio broadcasts, motion pictures, televised broadcasts, video cassettes, electronic books, self-structured programmed materials aided by computers.

Among all the media used in distance education system, television has captured a vital place. It is a very potent and powerful medium of communication which has tremendous potential for improving the quality of education. (It has various limitations as it is not controllable, no drilling is possible, no adjustment is possible for individuals etc.). But in spite of this, TV has an important role to play.

Video tapes or candid class-room video-tapes, audio tapes, paperless electronic books, video discs, micro-processors, computers and telephones are some other popular media through which distance education is transmitted in Western countries.

INDIA'S POSITION IN TECHNOLOGY

There is no dearth of talent in the field of science and technology in India. "We have today in India an excellent infrastructure for understanding complex tasks involving science and technology for resolving the real problems of the nation in the production of food, industrial development, energy resources communication and transportation"., (Vikram A. Sarabhai 1974).

In spite of phenomenal advances in satellite technology, nuclear reactors, nuclear missiles etc. besides having the third largest science community in the world, science and technology have done very little for the common people of our country. Investment of millions of rupees on research projects have found no relevance to actual conditions. Seventy per cent of the people who live in the five hundred thousand odd villages have problems of the past even today. (Lack of proper sanitation, ill-health, high mortality rate, high birth rate, impure drinking water, no proper roads, lack of electricity, no shelter, no proper clothing and so on are some of the more chronic ones). These people are only marginally touched by the increased GNP and as a result **fifty per cent of the total Indian population still live below the poverty line.**

TECHNOLOGY IN THE FIELD OF EDUCATION

The Commission on Instructional Technology (1979) in its report to the U.S. President and Congress defines education technology "as a way of designing, carrying out, and evaluating the total process of learning and communication and employing a combination of human and non-human resources to bring more effective instruction".

In India, technology could not come upto our satisfaction in the field of education too. The same old **`chalk and talk method'** still dominates the Indian classroom including HE (higher education). The condition of DE in India is not an exception. Due to the absence of technology its state is not very encouraging as it cannot keep up to its promise of providing an ideal education system and is therefore relegated to second class status.

(a) Computer in Education

"We are without a doubt, on the threshold of the most revolutionary set of technological innovations that humankind has yet had to deal with. As a nation it behoves us to carefully and thoughtfully consider the future we want for ourselves and for our children". (Goldsworthy 1983).

The most important contribution of bionics science today is perhaps computers which investigate the method of creating a mechanical system. It has influenced a social and economic change and helped to increase the demand of the quality education; education, in particular computer assisted instruction (CAI), permits the pupil to interact on an individual basis with learning materials. In addition to this various other devices like slides, film projectors, tape recorders can also be controlled by computers. As a result computers today have become a common market product in advanced countries.

In India the Electronic Corporation of India (ECIL) has started its production as early as 1965. At present two firms are producing the TDC 332 and ICC 2904 series in the medium range of computers and nearly fifty firms are engaged in the manufacture of microcomputers/ microprocessors. More than a hundred firms are waiting for clearance from the Govt. About sixty firms have been approved for manufacturing computer paraphernalia and out of them thirteen have started fabricating mainly floppy discs and video display terminals.

However, in India hardware is no more a problem. What we need most is trained manpower and software. Our institutions have **neither the required facilities nor the competence to prepare software** And in the field of distance learning our institutions have not developed the organisational effectiveness that distance education requires.

(b) TV in the Field of Education (India Context)

T.V. has started in India in Sept. 1959 with a great hesitancy. At present India has 5,000,000 (6.5 per 1000) T.V. sets, but it still plays a minor role in the Indian Education System. According to the Government of India, there are 362 transmission working at present which claim to cover ninety per cent of the total population. But "in reality ten per cent of our population is within actual reach of a functional TV set" (Mathur 89). He has observed that thousands of village in three large states of India (UP, MP and Rajasthan) have very few TV sets. His findings have further revealed that the voltage of electricity fluctuates between 60 and 300 volts in these villages which is not at all suitable for running any kind of electrical gadget.

Because of its potentiality for mass coverage ETV has been employed in developing countries often at considerable expense to support educational expansion policies for achieving universal education. In India 2400 villages of six states (connected through INSAT 1D) are getting ETV programmes. The duration of the programme is forty five minutes (10.30 AM to 11.15 AM). These programmes are broadcast five days in a week. The important objectives underlying these programmes are to bring about expansion and qualitative improvement of elementary eduction for rural school children. In the words of Arnove (1976) "the main objective of ETV projects is to produce more schooling and better schooling, primarily for children. Teachers are also trained by ETV in many of the projects, but this is a part of the objective of reaching children though ETV. To achieve these objectives because it is believed in the long run, to be cheaper than the traditional teacher". Although the attempt is praiseworthy yet due to the **lack of infrastructural facilities** of the schools these programmes cannot be a real success.

(c) Telephone System in India

Another popular medium of distance education through which teaching/counselling is done in western countries is the telephone system, which provides fast, effective communication links between students and tutors/counsellors. In India out of 570,000 villages, more than 54,000 villages are still without direct access to a telephone network. Out of a population of 800 million our country, has only 4,420,107 (1987) people are connected by the network. This important medium is **completely absent** in the field of distance education in India. However, it is hoped that we will be able to give a telephone to anyone, anywhere in India by 2000 A.D. if we can afford to spend atleast 1.67% of our GNP every year until 2000 A.D.

PRESENT POSITION OF INDIAN HIGHER EDUCATIONAL SYSTEM ANDDISTANCE EDUCATION

In India the system of education has grown lop-sided. On one hand millions of graduate job seekers are on the line while on the other hand the higher education system is taking an elephantine shape day-to-day with 160 Universities, 6000 Colleges, 3,00,000 teachers, four million students with Rs. 62,000 million expenditure. It is awry specially when nearly 65% of the total population is still illiterate amounting to be a total of 400 million and after forty two years of independence universal primary education is still a distant dream.

What we need is skilled manpower and not merely a University degree holder. Further we need to increase our production which means giving stress to the vocationalisation of education. What is required most is to stop the **wastage of human resources** (nearly fifty per cent of the students drop out at the college level) and not access to higher education. What is desired is a better quality of University products and not quantity.

Out system is wrong because a large section of the scheduled casts, and the scheduled tribes which consist of 14.6% and 6.9% respectively are marginally touched by education. And women participation in education is still below our expectations.

The unequal growth of the economy has resulted in inadequate enrolment (five per cent) from the poorer sections of society, whereas the richer sections of society are pre dominant in the field of education too.

At present forty Universities are running distance education programmes in India and more than half a million people are learning through this system. The biggest of these Universities are Indira Gandhi National Open University and Andhra Pradesh Open University. The Growth of these Universities is astonishing. At the undergraduate and post graduate level, it is almost 18% and 23.8% against 3.7% and 5.5% respectively in face-to-face teaching.

It generally follows the same syllabus and the same examination system as that of face-to-face education. It is growing more and more popular mainly because of its unique characteristics like home study facilities, greater capacity and lower cost. Its popularity is more so because of its message of lifelong education which can satisfy the craze of Indians for more and more degrees.

CONSTRAINTS

Constraints can be divided into three groups, namely- (a) on the part of the student, (b) on the part of the teacher and (a) general.

(a) On the part of the student

(i) Because of the **poverty** of the Indian students they cannot afford audio-visual aids. Buying a portable B/W TV and a Tape Recorder will cost them a whole year's savings of their parents.

Even if some students do buy audio-visual gadgets they find it difficult to maintain them oweing to the lack of repairing facilities. Such facilities are available only in the big cities.

(b) On the part of the teacher

(i) The picture is not very different at the institutional level. Video production and computer technology require a lot of financial stability which is a great problem faced by the CC (correspondence) institutions. Geoff Potter's (1981) remark that "mass" communication devices have always been channels of communication for the "elite' is therefore valid.

Another problem which is faced by the teacher is aptly described by Swaminathan (1985) "Beaming educational broadcasts is one thing, creating on impact of these broadcasts on education is another". **Getting rid of stable habits** of the learner is not so easy as they are more or less permanent. This inability on the part of the teachers to take to new methods of communication is also a great problem.

(c) General

(i) Infrastructural facilities like electricity, roads, nutrition and food etc., are **not adequate** specially in rural areas.

(ii) Students of distance education are heterogeneous. They come from different backgrounds and some of them are first generation learners. As a result paying individual attention is required which is not possible in any case in India.

(iii) Distance learning system in India has been basically started for the rural people but to tap them is an herculean task as the problems of the hills are not the same as those of the plains.

(iv) Full fledged libraries which include reading and reference materials, cassettes, video cassettes and other gadgets are rare.

(v) Training of the people - both teacher and student - is a prerequisite element to run a multimedia system of education-the lack of which is acutely felt in India. Preparing video-cassettes is not very expensive but producing quality requires an experienced hand.

(vi) Presentation of complex ideas and giving feedback is a very difficult task in Indian conditions.

(vii) "The diversity of means that the Open University can employ, adequately strengthened by well organised programmes of counselling and guidance provides a new era in our educational endeavour, an endeavour in which education is transformed into voluntary creative learning" (IGNOU 1985). This task is undertaken by 115 study centres and twelve regional centres which has never been possible for other Universities. Absence of counselling service resulted in a great amount of drop-out in distance education system in India.

(viii) Weaker sections today do not have the infrastructure required for availing themselves of the benefit of distance education.

A THOUGHT

It is a general belief that the application of more media will reduce the number of student dropouts. Maltimedia approach is also believed to be effective as it enhances the speed and accuracy of learning and therefore supplementary instruction with electronic media is very essential in distance education system. It is also claimed that media can help to provide individual instruction, and provide variety in programming. But this very hypothesis is not a proven fact. It is agreed that mass media may work as a **psychological boost**to the students but it does not mean that a multi media approach is the only answer to effective distance learning system.

Arnove (1976) says that out of the 421 separate comparisons. Godwin Chu and Schramm have shown that in 308 cases there was no significant difference in examination score gains as a result of the different treatment. Sixty three showed higher gains for those getting ETV and fifty showed higher gains for those getting traditional teaching. "All these summarises show that in the great majority of comparative studies, there is no significant difference between learning from conventional teaching or from DE system and that where there is a noted difference, it is more likely to be slightly in favour of television than of conventional instruction". Hence it is still a doubtful phenomenon. It is also not proved that more expenditure on science and technology will bring considerable growth in national income. It is learnt that Britain i n 1970 had spent nearly three per cent of GNP which amounted to 1000 million pounds but inspite of this, economic growth was very little at the time. Whereas, Japan had achieved a seventeen per cent rise of its economic growth with a minimum spending of percentage of GNP. At present, India is spending 1.1% of GNP on scientific development, but a negligible amount of economic growth is noticed. It is therefore important to see **how we spend rather than what we spend.**

Irrelevant education has already contributed a great deal to the demoralisation of the youth. At present, every year the Indian Universities award more than 600,000 degrees in general and about 15,000 to 20,000 degrees to doctors and engineers. Millions of graduates remain unemployed or underemployed and nearly fifty per cent of the students drop out of the formal education system at the college level. Can distance education solve this monumental problem and provide a competent labour force to achieve the national goal? As the distance education system at present is considered merely a **degree giving machine** it tends to multiply our country's problems rather than to solve them.

Another interesting phenomenon is that out of a hundred graduates of the backward states fifteen per sengi go for a Master's degree whereas only five per cent of the graduates go in for a Master's degree from the forward states. Can distance education stop this unwanted phenomenon? blessly the more degrees they get the less employable they become.

Finally, at present we have only twenty two engineering colleges that run four year Bachelor Degrees in Computer technology, twelve engineering colleges that run M. Tech courses. In addition to this, three year Masters programme in Computer Application (MCA) is run by fourteen institutions and fourteen Universities run diploma programme (1 1/2 year) in Computer Applications after the B. Sc. level. Can they meet the challenge to train millions of teachers of schools and colleges in Computer Technology and create an environment which is necessary for the success of a distance learning system ?

A recent study shows that it is mathematically impossible to teach all existing Higher Secondary School Teachers (of 55,000 Schools) in ten years and as a result the question of teaching primary school teachers is out of the question.

CONCLUSION

The concept of distance education was developed in the context of Western countries and applied in other cultures in the belief that because it worked in the West, it must be equally useful in other countries too. But the condition of third world countries is certainly different from that of the advanced countries of the West in many respects. Here the problems are multiple and complex with conflicting issues and interests interacting with one another.

Each country has to choose and try out its own path, best suited for its resources, its traditions, its culture and its developmental goals. Scientists of the affluent countries did consider it their task to use science and technology for the solution of problem relevant to their areas of the world and succeeded dramatically in increasing the standard of living. But this has not been done by developing countries. As a result in these countries, the poor have remained poor in all senses. The picture is not different in the case of India too. Indira Gandhi in this connection remarked "I am concerned that so much of our scientific work is derivative and imitative. There is too much uncritical acceptance of capital intensive methods. The willingness and ability to explore the possibility of using labour intensive technology are conspicuously lacking. The growth of technology in advanced countries leaves us in a perpetual state of having to catch up and the nearer we are to catching up the further we get from our people and their worries. We should pay greater attention to smaller problems which affect people's day-to-day life; use local materials and power resources; utilise intermediate technology to improve our traditional grind-stone or the wheels of our bullock-cart. There is and there can be no conflict between such technology and modernisation. On the other hand, it will help to make our rural people science-minded and encourage them to participate in the genuine tasks of development". And the Indian National Science Academy (1985) says, "It is clear that since Independence, inspite of the quantitative increase of science and of science graduate quality has been a victim, a large, improved science base has, however, been established. Sometimes under the banner of equality and democracy, circumstances operate powerfully against the development of excellence. Therefore, one of our foremost concerns should be to protect, encourage, and enhance the quality of work and thought which will raise the average level of science and produce leaders of excellence who can contribute to national endeavours".

It is learnt that around sixty per cent of the world's electric power is generated by fossil fuels, twenty two per cent from hydro electricity and eleven per cent from nuclear power. But all these have their own limitations. solar energy on the other hand has immense potential. In India, we have plenty of sunshine. If we could make use of it by the help of solar cells, electrification which has been a major stumbling-block for the development of technology in our country may be solved.

Production of mini computers and microprocessors on a large scale may be helpful for computer assisted instruction imparted for the sake of distance education. Moreover, computer manufacturing firms have to design special computers for distance education system at a cost which could be afforded by the community residing in rural and remote regions.

Moreover, what we need is not a multimedia approach at present, which we cannot afford, but a clear view of our economic development for which we have to give stress on vocational and need-based education (training for Rail, Bank, Postoffice and other Govt. officials may be taken care of). What we need is not to encourage **wholesale distribution of degrees** through distance education indiscrimately but to be selective. If the quality of people is the determiner of our national development then this must be done. Only the institutions which are capable of meeting this challenge must be encouraged.

Finally, we must remember, "Unless education and all those concerned with human resources development stake their claim, communication technology will be developed primarily in the interest of the market and the interest of the Military. It will happen only if the educators seize the opportunities presented by the technologists and make them work" (S. Rampal '89.)

REFERENCE

1. Arnove. Robert F (ed) Educational TV : A Policy critique and Guide for Developing Countries, New York : Praeger Publishers, 1976.
2. Barrie Brennan - Learning components in Developing Activities - Manila Conference Paper 1988.
3. Broadbent Derak - Radio and TV Universities in New South Wales. In D.C.B. Teachers (ed). Towards the community University (1982).
4. Conboy, I and D 'Cruz T.V : - Distance Education and Rural Development, UNICORN, 1988.
5. Faure Edgar etal : Learning To Be, Unesco, Paris - 1972.
6. Golds worthy - Journal Australian Computer Society - 1983.
7. Indira Gandhi National Open University Booklet. 1985.
8. Indian National Science Academy, Issues in Higher Education in Science-1985.
9. Mathur I.S - A TV Signal : What is it ? Who gets it ? Mainstream July 8, 1989. Vol - XXVII No. 41.
10 Potter Geoff : Satellite - based Distance Education 'Problems and Solutions' - paper presented at RSDTA Penang (Malaysia) 1981.
11. Rampal. S : Convocation address - University News Feb. 27, 1989 New Delhi, IGNOU India.
12. Schramm, W : Educational Resources centre report (Ed) Standford : Standford University. 1971.
13. Swaminathan.D : "Utilisation of INSAT Facility for higher education in India" - Paper presented at the Institutional Conference on `New Technologies in higher education' Nov 28-29. 1985. New Delhi.

Computers in Education
A. McDougall and C. Dowling (Editors)
Elsevier Science Publishers B.V. (North-Holland)

COMPUTERS IN EDUCATION: A DISTANCE LEARNING MODEL

S L Berry and D J A Burrows

In this paper Sue Berry, Senior Assistant Registrar at the Open University (UK) and Jim Burrows, Director of the University's Academic Computing Service explore some of the problems which the Open University faced in moving from a fully supported, centralised student computing service to one which is home based and, in the main, financed by the student.

1. INTRODUCTION

The 1988 academic year marked a major transition in the application of computers in the undergraduate curriculum. In that year the Open University made the provision of an industry standard PC by its students a mandatory requirement in a range of its courses. The move away from a University supported terminal network, in 250 local centres up and down the country, was brought about as a result of concerns about the ability of that approach to offer the level of practical experience necessary to maintain the University's academic credibility in the IT area.

Now in its third year the project, known within the University as the Home Computing Programme, is proving extremely popular and successful. The numbers alone are impressive: 13,000 students enrolled in 1990; a £6m capital investment to date by students, Government and the University; £1.5m recurrent investment by the University; 200,000 floppy disks produced and shipped; sufficient courses now to be within one course credit of a B.A. degree. What is even more impressive is that a programme on such a scale has been made to work technically and operationally. Even in US terms it is difficult to find a comparable example. The University's experience in volume course production and presentation has been a significant factor. This project has however taken it into unexplored territory and this paper tells the story.

2. EDUCATIONAL COMPUTING

Computers first came to prominence in education in the early sixties, as research tools. By the mid to late seventies, the teaching of computing (or computer science) was becoming widespread in tertiary education. However, as has always been acknowledged, computing without practical experience is not a practical proposition, and the high cost and centralisation of such facilities as existed proved an inhibiting factor. It was pioneering work on a time sharing computer system at Dartmouth College (New Hampshire), and the development of the BASIC language which eventually made practical computing provision a reality for many educational establishments in the later sixties and early seventies, although such developments were often derided by the purists at the time.

In the sixties those with vision could see the potential of the computer, over and above its role in teaching computing and its application as a research tool. Looking back in 1985, Alfred Bork, who had been an early enthusiast, commented:

> "These are indeed interesting times. The computer is just beginning the long process of changing our educational system. I feel fortunate to have been working in this area at such a time. Since my early experiments in using computers in education while a faculty member at the University of Alaska in 1960, I have been convinced that the computer was eventually going to become the dominant delivery device in education. I see no reason to change that view."
>
> Bork [1]

However, the success of the Dartmouth project lay in combining the development of basic computing skills with the application of the computer as an aid to solving problems. There was no attempt to use the computer as the dominant teaching medium. This has also been very much the tradition at the Open University. Now, of course, the delivery vehicle is the personal workstation rather than a time shared facility. It is an approach which has been successful, and has afforded an opportunity to add value and enrich the teaching material with more innovative computer based activities.

3. COMPUTING AT THE OPEN UNIVERSITY

Founded at a time when computer systems were commonplace in all large and medium size organisations and with a brief to offer education on a national scale, computer based systems were considered essential to the University's operations from the beginning. The Open University was established in 1969 to enable adults to study in their own time for University degrees, by means of correspondence courses linked with regular radio and television broadcasts, a regionally organised tutorial system, an extensive summer school programme and a variety of other educational media, including a country-wide computer terminal network. Over the years the undergraduate programme has been supplemented by post graduate courses and a major continuing education initiative which includes a Business School.

Open University students are adults drawn from a wide variety of educational and occupational backgrounds, and the University has had to adopt a flexible provision of teaching and support services for its students. Through the imaginative use of new teaching techniques, the University has met and continues to meet this challenge.

Computing was identified as a key academic discipline, and a Professor of Computing was amongst the University's first appointments. The teaching of computing was a component of the first mathematics foundation course presented in 1971. Practical facilities for this activity were provided through terminals in local study centres and also at Summer Schools. Initially there were 110 terminals in local centres connected to centrally based computer systems, as well as provision at Summer School sites. By the late 1980's this had increased to 350 in local centres and 120 terminals and workstations at 10 Summer School sites. In parallel with this growth in terminal provision, the University developed its own national data network.

The justification for the provision of practical student computing facilities rested mainly with the requirements of the teaching of computing and the need to apply computers in certain subject areas (e.g. for data analysis). However, there has been an opportunity, particularly at Summer Schools, to integrate the computer more fully into the teaching system through computer assisted learning. A wide range of teaching packages has been developed using high quality graphics workstations, interactive video and compact disc technology.

4. STUDENT COMPUTING - THE NEED FOR CHANGE

As indicated earlier in the paper, the teaching of Computing Science has been a part of the Open University's undergraduate programme from the beginning. The University's first Vice-Chancellor Dr (now Lord) Perry, in his 1972 annual report commenting on the achievement of the university in technical areas in its early years, said:

> "It is estimated that, even in these very early years, we have turned out 2,000 students from the mathematics foundation course who are capable of writing simple but non-trivial programmes. To achieve this in an environment where tutorial support was readily available would not be easy; therefore to do so within the Open University system is extremely creditable". [2]

To offer undergraduates interactive access to computing facilities in the early seventies was indeed an achievement. However the University has had to respond to the pace of technological development and while it has over the intervening period gradually improved its network of computing facilities available to students, it has struggled to keep pace. It has, over the years, expanded student computing from supporting the teaching of Computing Science to using the computer as a general purpose educational tool, although the extent of this use has been limited by the relatively inaccessible nature of the facilities provided in study centres. In general, technical provision has been poor in comparison with that in other institutions, and access being other than home based was inadequate.

In the area of computer applications the University's credibility was therefore being threatened unless:

i) it could provide much more hands on experience in the teaching of Computing and Computing Science than was feasible under the constrained conditions of access via terminals in Study Centres and at Summer Schools;

ii) it was better able to compete with universities in general, with their requirement that their students had easy access to computers.

A fundamental principle of Open University undergraduate study is that the educational process should be largely home based. With the development of the technology, it was envisaged that there were real possibilities for expanding computing applications based on a computing facility that was located in the student's home.

The University therefore developed a strategy for the introduction of home computing in its courses which would open up possibilities within the teaching system, including:

i) improving the level of practical experience in the teaching of Computing and Computing Science;

ii) teaching basic computer literacy which would be transferable to higher level courses and the place of work;

iii) providing students with experience of using the computer as a computational, organisational, modelling and word processing tool;

iv) providing an interactive communications facility for students, staff and tutors;

v) providing another medium for conveying instructional material, especially remedial teaching, material requiring interactive graphics, and material requiring the use of models or mathematically sophisticated computations.

It was acknowledged that home computing could offer the University a real opportunity to make the use of computers an effective and integral part of its teaching system, and also enable the University to provide a means of rapidly improving the computer literacy skills of the adult population, thus meeting a well documented area of national need.

5. A BRIEF HISTORY OF THE DEVELOPMENT OF A HOME COMPUTING PROGRAMME

In developing the home computing programme there were two very significant policy issues that needed to be resolved; one technical, the other concerned with student access.

5.1 Technical strategy

The University's technical strategy assumed the availability of a general purpose machine which would:

i) meet the needs of all planned courses with an essential home computing element;

ii) offer as much of a guarantee as possible of being produced and supported over a significant number of years - (this was a difficult requirement in a rapidly changing technological market place);

iii) not be manufacturer specific, be widely available and have a broad range of commercially available software;

iv) offer a reasonable balance between price and performance, bearing in mind that costs would, by and large, have to be borne by the student and would therefore be a critical factor.

Having attempted to launch a programme some years earlier around the popular Acorn/BBC product, only to see Acorn struggle and eventually be taken over by Olivetti, the University was adamant that, at least in terms of hardware platforms, it would not be dependent on one supplier. The University based its strategy around the de facto industry standard operating system MSDOS (with GEM defining the graphics standard). In taking this decision early in 1986, the University made a basic assumption that reasonably priced MSDOS (IBM compatible) machines would be available in time for the 1988 academic year. Figures available at the time (early 1986) and reproduced in Table 1 suggested the dominance of the IBM PC and compatibles. The University's foresight on price was proved correct when later that year Amstrad entered the PC compatible market.

Table 1: Planning data on PC sales in early 1986

	APPLE MACINTOSH	IBMPC PCs	COMPATIBLES
1981	*	17,5000	*
1982	*	156,000	62,000
1983	*	455,000	404,000
1984	282,000	1,900,000	1,300,000
1985	266,000	1,900,000	2,300,000
1986+	355,000	2,600,000	3,600,000

+ Estimates

Source: Dataquest World Wide Shipments

The principal success in the adoption of the MSDOS standard has been that it has genuinely proved to be hardware manufacturer independent. It has therefore been possible to distribute software which will run on a wide range of manufacturers' systems. Students have been supplied with general purpose, commercially available software and special software produced by the University. There has been a full production system, in operation since 1987, resulting in over 50,000 floppy disks produced in-house and despatched in 1988. This figure has risen to 200,000 by the end of 1989. The in-house software production system is to BS5750 standards, and the University's Academic Computing Service has set up a quality assurance unit which vets all master disks and samples production runs for quality.

The current technical specification will run through to the end of the 1991 academic year and work has already begun in revising the specification. Decisions taken will once again have to anticipate by a couple of years what will be commonly and cheaply available in the market place, this time in 1992.

5.2 Student access

The University assumed that in the long run students would be responsible for ensuring access to a suitable machine in the same way that access to television, radio and audio-cassette players was assumed. The issue of

Table 2: Number of students on home computing courses

Course		Student Numbers 1988	1989	1990 (est)
DT200	An Introduction to Information Technology	1364	1246	1495
M205	Fundamentals of Computing	3023	3185	3535
M371	Computational Mathematics	257	269	180
M353	Programming and Programming Languages	-	1360	1170
M357	Data Models and Data Bases	-	-	978
T102	Living with Technology	-	4955	4423
T202	Analogue and Digital Electronics	-	-	1228
	Total	4644	11015	13009

cost was, however, acknowledged as the major factor affecting student access, and although PCs dropped in price between 1986 and the start of the academic year in 1988, they still represented a significant cost when compared with other components of the University's multi-media teaching system. The University recognised that this was likely to be the case and endeavoured to introduce a range of measures which would minimise the impact on the students. Chief amongst these was securing a DTI grant of £2.25 million for the purchase and operation of a pool of low cost rental machines. Other arrangements included:

i) the offer of fee discounts for courses in the first three years of the programme;

ii) the extension of financial award schemes to unemployed and disadvantaged students studying courses in the programme;

iii) the arrangement of specially discounted purchase schemes for staff and students;

iv) the offer of attractive bank loan arrangements for student purchase;

v) the offer of popular commercial software packages as part of the course material;

vi) DES support in assisting disabled students.

The University also established, as part of its course approval process, a mechanism for vetting carefully all proposals for inclusion in the home computing programme to ensure that students were not put to unnecessary expense and that, where possible, general purpose software was common across a range of courses.

As a result, students have been able to obtain access to an appropriate system (either through rental, purchase, access at work or already having a machine at home). The programme has proved extremely popular as the results reported in the next section attempt to demonstrate.

6. RESULTS ACHIEVED SO FAR

In the second year of its home computing initiative the University added two new courses to the three presented in 1988, and two further courses have been included in 1990.

Table 2 shows the number of students on home computing courses. In the first year (1988), 4644 students participated in the programme. In year two the total number of students rose to 11,015. In general, students on these home computing courses received extensive practical experience in the use of computer based systems in a variety of application areas, while those taking the main line computing courses M205 and M353 were taught, in addition, about the design and development of computer based systems. T102 and M371 also carry CAL packages incorporating use of audio tapes, text and the computer. The programme has been further strengthened in 1990 with the introduction of M357 and T202.

Table 3 shows examination results for 1988 and 1989 students registered on courses in the home computing programme. Given levels of computer literacy in the United Kingdom today, these

Table 3 : 1988 and 1989 student examination results

	1988	1989
Students Registered	4644	11015
Students Examined	3302	7930
Pass rate (as % of students registered)	68.7%	69.2%
Distinctions (as % of students examined)	19.7%	14.5%

figures must be regarded as a significant achievement, particulary since the courses studied are highly relevant to the needs of industry and society today.

Moreover, the ability to make a software standard work across a wide range of machines, given the scale of the operation, is a major technical achievement which has surprised even the technical managers at the University who have been involved in the project from the beginning.

7. IMPLICATIONS OF THE HOME COMPUTING PROGRAMME FOR THE FUTURE

As the University once took a discredited teaching methodology - correspondence tuition - and used it at the core of its multi media approach to distance education, producing the definitive model for many others, so too, we believe, with educational computing.

The University's home computing initiative is an unparallelled development in higher education in the U.K. The scheme has worked and is proving very popular with students. The reasons why can be summarised as follows. The University's achievement has not been educationally innovative, in the sense for example of designing a new educational workstation, but is innovative in its use of existing technology. The decision to adopt MSDOS IBM compatibility as the standard was fundamental to the success of the project. By exploiting what was commercially available, rather than developing hardware and software especially tailored to meet educational needs, the University has not got itself locked into a technical solution that has limited scope within the wider community, as for example happened with the BBC model B strategy adopted in schools.

Just as important to the success of the strategy was the fact that the University recognised that the dominant mode of computing was the single-user machine. The concept of a personal workstation providing easy access was essential if the University was to hasten the time when the computer would become a general purpose educational facility. In industry practising engineers can no longer ignore computer technology. In response the Open University now expects its technology foundation course students to have access to a PC, and they are taught how to use it in their first year of study with the University. That ability can then be exploited in higher level courses.

The programme has worked because it has combined the teaching of IT skills with the use of the computer in the teaching process. While the focus of the programme to date has been those courses which teach computing and its applications, the experience gained will be an essential stepping stone to the integration of the computer workstation into the University's overall teaching and support strategy. The computer offers ways of significantly enhancing the University's ability to teach e.g. through intelligent CAL, and it is now one of the most powerful teaching media at the University's disposal. When networked workstations become commonly available, the way the University offers its student support services will change to take advantage of this technology for enquirers, applicants, admission systems, course registration, results notification, fee payments, and general student to student, student to tutor, student to University communications. When the use of electronic media offers a real alternative to text, the University will be well placed to exploit any opportunity this presents. With its present programme it has demonstrated that it has the technical ability and the administrative and operational systems in place to support a community of 13,000 students with workstations. This system can be built upon and extended to the total student community when home based facilities become generally available.

8. OTHER POINTS OF SIGNIFICANCE TO THE WIDER COMMUNITY

While the University has for many years produced educational software which formed an integral part of particular courses, this software assumed access to one of the University's central computer systems. As a consequence the software could not easily be delivered in a free standing format which would allow it to be marketed as a package. For years some of the University's most popular undergraduate and associate courses have been restricted to solely University use. The move to an industry standard machine and commercially available software now means that courses with practical computing requirements become accessible to anyone or any organisation with an industry standard microcomputer. Even where an investment has to be made, the cost need not be more than £600. The expertise which the University has developed over the years in producing educational software, and integrating practical computing into a wide spread of courses, is now accessible to a much wider audience. We anticipate that the impact which the University has already had on the educational community through text and video material will be extended even further as educational software is added as another standard component of our multi media approach to education.

As far as the business community is concerned, in its report [3] on Information Technology, the DTI Select Committee recorded the scale of IT skills shortages as variously estimated at up to 30,000 and commented that this was a deplorable shortage; the shortages being of the order of one tenth of the number of IT specialists in work. The report went on to suggest that the serious inadequacies in the schools, in higher and further and continuing education, held out little prospect of early remedy. The Committee suggested that the best solution to the IT skills shortage was increased in-service training.

The government, in its response [4] to the Select Committee report, indicated that it considered that all those involved in education and training must play their part in meeting the requirements of industry, commerce and the public sector for a suitably skilled workforce. The government agreed with the Select Committee that demographic trends would increase the need for employers to undertake a massive training effort over the years ahead, directed primarily at people they already employ. To meet this demand, education and training providers need to use open, distance and flexible learning systems. No institution is better placed to assist than the Open University. It is poised to provide thousands of students, each year, with the opportunity to acquire IT skills, and to develop an understanding of the technology and its application.

And if there is to be government support, focused specifically at the training requirements of an existing established workforce, the University's experience in producing packaged, practical IT courses, which use introductory standard systems from a wide range of manufactures, should not be overlooked.

REFERENCES

[1] Bork, A. Personal Computers for Education, Harper Row, (1985).

[2] The Open University, Report of the Vice Chancellor, 1972.

[3] Trade and Industry Committee First Report: Information Technology Volume 1, November 1988, HMSO.

[4] Information Technology: Government's Response to the First Report of the House of Commons Trade and Industry Committee, 1988-89 session, March 1989.

Computers in Education
A. McDougall and C. Dowling (Editors)
Elsevier Science Publishers B.V. (North-Holland)

COMPUTING IN TEACHER EDUCATION AT A DISTANCE: VALUING THE EDUCATIONAL IN EDUCATIONAL COMPUTING

Chris BIGUM

Deakin University
Geelong, Victoria 3217
Australia

Engaging teachers in a beginning of their professional development in educational computing is the purpose of two subjects offered in the School of education at Deakin University. The distinctive nature, principles and practice of the subjects are detailed.

1. QUALIFIERS

When tertiary distance education and educational computing are mentioned in the same sentence, typically images of computers and telecommunications come to mind. On further reflection, contemplating teaching novice computer-using teachers about computing in education at a distance might conjure up images of dementia in those who propose teaching such courses. While there may be some doubt about the latter image in this paper, it is definitely not the former image that characterizes what follows.

This paper is concerned with an account of the teaching of subjects in educational computing for teachers at a distance. At present there are two subjects each offered over a whole year, the first of which is a pre-requisite for the second. The subjects are taught as a part of an offering of subjects for teachers seeking an initial post-graduate qualification in education. This degree, a B.Ed., is comprised of eight units, equivalent to one year's full-time study. Each educational computing subject is worth two units. The B.Ed. is offered by Deakin University, one of a small number of nominated providers of tertiary distance education in Australia.

Offering discrete subjects in educational computing for the professional development of teachers contradicts an important principle of the group of staff who offer these courses. Briefly, we hold that computing is best learned in the context of subjects other than those directly concerned with the new information technologies, i.e. in subjects concerned with the teaching of reading, mathematics, or subjects concerned with curriculum theory or measurement and evaluation. These courses are therefore seen as an interim measure that will eventually disappear when computing is eventually mapped into the teaching of a large proportion of the B.Ed. offerings at Deakin as is the current practice for the education subjects taught on campus (see Bigum [1]).

Apart from meeting the interests of about 150 teachers each year, we see the subjects as providing a window into the prospects for the exploitation of the new information technologies in distance education by teachers who are mainly new to using computers.

Over the five year period in which the subjects have been offered, we have developed a set of principles which have been derived from and continue to inform our practice. As much as anything they reflect a primitive understanding of how best to support the professional development of practising teachers in computing. While principles are important statements for a course team<1> in clarifying its work and in helping students understand the purpose of courses, we are concerned to locate these principles in a broader framework, a theory of the new information technologies in education. Thus the principles we have drawn out of this teaching are one of the bases of a project (See Bigum [2] and Green and Bigum [3]) which currently draws upon postmodern literature as a basis for reframing understandings about the new information technologies in education.

2. IN PRINCIPLE AND IN PRACTICE

This account of the principles and some

of the practice that informs and is informed by them is based upon the text in the current course guides for each subject. No attempt is made in this account to address what might be regarded as some of the mainstream debates in adult learning, mid-career professional development or andragogy, although there is clearly resonance with many of these issues in what follows. Nor does this paper attempt to address issues in distance teaching and learning outside the context of the two subjects that are the focus of this paper.

2.1. Educational rather than computing

Both subjects are based upon the premise that educational computing is essentially an educational enterprise, not a computing enterprise. The significant educational ideas and thinkers that have helped to shape our thinking and practice during the evolution of these subjects are detailed in the discussion that follows.

Placing our emphasis upon the educational of educational computing means that while we are concerned to provide a framework in which teachers can develop particular technical skills in the new information technologies, we understand the development of such skills only as necessary pre-requisites for tackling important educational work that is supported by such skills. For instance, we require all written work to be prepared using a word processor or equivalent software. In the initial course, we have students begin using a word processor very early on in the course. Students with little or no word processing experience are expected to improve their word processing skills as they progress through each subject. We expect that students who are proficient users of word processing software to extend their expertise. We provide scaffolds (discussed below) as one of the means of supporting their improved use of software.

2.2. Human networks and learning

We posit that learning computing skills is something that is best supported by a one to one relationship between individuals, a kind of apprenticeship along the lines described by Collins, Brown & Newman [4] and Brown, Collins and Duguid [5]. This principle was based upon the course team's own experiences of learning computing skills and the observation of the manner in which academic computing professionals employ a large and sophisticated global network as well as local networks to support one another. Students are therefore required to begin the construction of their own personal support network during the course. In particular, a friendly computer person<2> is a requirement of doing the course along with access to hardware and particular kinds of software. Many students find that even during the course that they begin to form part of a personal support network for other novice computing using teachers.

This model of learning computing also draws upon the writing of Freire [6] who regards teaching as learning and speaks of educator-educatee and educatee-educator rather than teacher and student in emphasising the importance of establishing dialogue between individuals as the basis for learning. Following Freire, this view of learning is fundamentally 'anti-expert'. In teaching the two courses we aim to learn from our students and with our students rather than dictating to them facts that they should know. The model emphasises the human side of computing and so students are encouraged to participate in a number of networks of people, not only for technical support but also to support their professional development in educational computing.

Such a perspective of learning is incompatible with a view that knowledge about computing in education can be neatly packaged and delivered in the way that many subjects are taught at a distance. Therefore an important assertion is that knowledge is something that the learner creates and re-creates as she reflects and acts upon the world. Knowledge is something that is man-made. It is a product of individual and collective makings of meaning, of naming things in the world as Freire describes it.

The short history of educational computing is replete with namings of all sorts from the jargon that comes with the technology to the classification schemes invented to 'help' teachers make sense of their classroom practice. To put the practice of classification in some perspective it is useful to recall a quote from the preface of Michel Foucault's The Order of Things:

This book arose out of a passage in Borges, out of the laughter that shattered, as I read the passage, all the familiar landmarks of my thought - our thought, the thought that bears the stamp of our age and our geography - breaking up all the ordered surfaces and all the planes with which we are accustomed to tame the wild profusion of existing things, and continuing long afterwards to disturb and threaten with collapse our age-old distinction between the Same and the Other. This passage quotes a 'certain Chinese encyclopedia' in which it is written that 'animals are divided into: (a) belonging to the emperor, (b) embalmed, (c) tame, (d) sucking pigs, (e) sirens, (f) fabulous, (g) stray dogs, (h) included in the present classification, (i) frenzied, (j) innumerable, (k) drawn with a very fine camel hair brush, (l) et cetera, (m) having just broken the water pitcher, (n) that from a long way off look like flies'. In the wonderment of this taxonomy, the thing we apprehend in one great leap, the other thing that, by means of the fable, is demonstrated as the exotic charm of another system of thought, is the limitation of our own, the stark impossibility of thinking that. (Foucault [7])

Attempting to convey something of the fraility of our understandings of the new information technologies in education is part of a pedagogy that takes into account the importance of the individual in the making of meaning, of making her own understandings. The importance of reflection as a means of creating and re-creating understandings is a practice that is built into the course. Students are required to maintain a personal journal to support their reflection and we use Holly [8] to support this work.

2.4. Space

Much of the work that students do with a computer is done alone. Maintaining a reflective account of this work is an important aspect of such work. The other principle that we espouse to students is one taken from a model of Hodgkin [9] in which he details the importance of play, practice and exploration in learning. A crucial element in this model is the idea of space. Space to play, space to practise and space to explore. Adults we argue, are not very good at the kind of play that younger people engage in when confronted with computing software or hardware. Watching children who, in a non-prescriptive environment, are first time users of something like LOGO illustrates what we mean by play. Playing seems linked to risk taking and even in the safe environment provided by some computing software adults are typically reluctant to play or explore. For this reason, a high value is placed on the notion of giving students space to encourage students to play and explore as well as practise in their computing. In evaluations of our students' work we have found that they spend enormous amounts of time at computer keyboards. We have redesigned the subjects to allow for this time, encouraging them to take on the notion of play and exploration as important as that of practice in working with computing hardware and software.

2.5. Teachers before students

Many teachers who become concerned to add computing to their professional repertoire are keen to take a computer into the classroom and begin working with their students. In these subjects we attach much importance to the development of a teacher's professional development in using a particular piece of software well before such software is used in a classroom. We use the assignments in each subject to provide the necessary structure to our students' practice.

The assignments are not highly prescriptive to allow students to choose tasks that are of use, interest and benefit to the student and to her work. All of the tasks are required to have a primary audience that is not the course team. For example in the initial course, students prepare what we call an issues paper. This paper is addressed to a specific audience. It might be a discussion paper to the School Council. It could be a submission to a departmental group in the school. It might be an address to a parents and friends meeting. The student is required to send a copy for assessment but the primary aim is that the paper is delivered or submitted to the specificed audience.

Because the nature of these subjects is different from that of typical off-campus subjects in education, students have difficulty with this principle of the courses, that all the work they do must be important to them for reasons other than the requirements of the course.

2.6. Scaffolds and other aids

In subjects that are as open-ended as these, it is important to provide support structures that do not get in the way of the principles. Apart from the development of human support networks, acquiring one or more friendly computer people, and locating various professional groups with interests in educational computing,[3] students are encouraged to explore and identify resources of any description that they have found useful. Students are encouraged to share this information in a newsletter that is distributed to students in both subjects. There is no shortage of short technical publications for teachers either available through commercial publishers or through State Education Departments.

Students are also encouraged to read newspapers<4> and popular magazines as a means of identifying some of the contemporary issues the media sees as important in the use of computers in schools.

We discovered that a significant problem of teachers interested in using a particular piece of software for the first time was that often they had only a slight idea of what such software did. For this reason we have prepared what we term 'scaffolds' for some of the common types of software in use in Australian schools, i.e. word processing, database, spreadsheet software and LOGO. Scaffolds, as the name implies are intended to be loose structures in which a student can construct their own understandings of a particular piece of software. They are generic in that they do not describe the features of any particular version of software but attempt to detail a generic set of features and their relatedness for each of the major kinds of software.

2.7. Hubs, spokes and communication

Computing in teacher education at a distance is likely to suggest to some the use of electronic forms of communication as the basis for teaching such subjects. While much could be made of each student having access to a modem and communication software, the reality is that at present, only a small proportion of students that undertake these subjects have the kind of access that would enable them to be regular users of telephone lines for communication between their computer and a remote host.

Importantly, if every student did have such access, it is not hard to imagine what it would be like for a tutor looking after fifty or sixty students<5>: much of the day would be taken in responding to student queries, comments and requests. We have evidence of this in a small course in which all students have modem access. For this reason and the more important principle of valuing student-student interaction in our distance teaching, we encourage and require students to exchange a range of information in small study groups. Because of the low proportion of students who use a modem, we rely upon Australia Post and occasional telephone contact for such communication.

To operationalise such communication we build a number of information sharing tasks into some of the assignments. For instance in the prepartion of issues papers, students are required to share drafts with their study group. Prior to completing a small software study, students collect ten software 'snapshots'<6> and distribute them to their study group. A newsletter is prepared from student contributions and distributed four times a year to both courses. Students send their contributions in as ASCII files on disk. The newsletter is used as a means of sharing three kinds of information: reflections by students on their work in the course; sharing or seeking information concerning the use of computers in schools; and brief accounts of completed student work. The latter are published to allow students to obtain copies of reports or discussion papers from other students. From student journals, it is clear that many students obtain papers and reports from other students.

3. PREPARING POORLY PAID COMPUTER SALES PERSONS

In the current romantic climate that characterises computing in education, it is difficult to find much questioning of the many aspects of the new information technologies that are taken for granted in education. In such an uncritical, accepting climate, it is not difficult to mount a case that the professional development of teachers in educational computing amounts to little more than the preparation of poorly paid computer sales persons. To provide something of a balance for the large number of technical and enthusiastic accounts of using computers in education, the course team has prepared a number of short monographs<7> that are designed to provoke our students into thinking beyond the technical concerns that are usually uppermost in the minds of most teachers who are novice computer users. The development of a critical understanding of the new information technologies in education is developed more strongly in the second of the two subjects. Here the work of Weizenbaum [10], Dreyfus & Dreyfus [11], Hinkson [12], Chesneaux [13], Aronowitz & Giroux [14], Bowers [15] and Cooley [16] among others are drawn upon.

We believe that in a climate shaped and supported by the distributors and manufacturers of hardware and software that are used in schools, that it is important to encourage teachers to engage questions that go beyond the technical 'how do I use a computer to do X or Y? or 'what is the best software for this task?'. Questionning what is taken for granted about computers in schools is not something that novice computer users warm to, nevertheless we regard the development of a critique of the new information technologies in education a fundamental component of any teacher's professional development in educational computing and a necessary part of a teacher becoming an autonomous user of the new information technologies.

4. EVALUATION

Apart form interaction with students over the phone, through assignments and occasionally via electronic mail, we ask students to write a brief and blunt evaluation of the course. Students are also required to furnish a copy of their journal, edited as they see fit, at stages during each subject. We retain all copies of journals and the evaluation reports as one of the bases for further development of the subjects.

NOTES

<1> Deakin uses course teams for the design, preparation and teaching of subjects offered for off-campus study.

<2> An FCP is someone whom the student feels she can turn to easily and obtain technical support for the hardware and software she is using.

<3> Either as the Computer Education Groups in each State or through the professional subject associations.

<4> Every Tuesday one national newspaper has a large computer section, in which there is usually three or four pages devoted to computers in schools.

<5> The metaphor of a bicycle wheel with the tutor as hub and students at the end of each spoke is common enough in most distance teaching.

<6> Brief accounts of a piece of software with sufficent information to convey to another teacher whether the software is worth investigating for themselves.

<7> Sixteen have been published so far. They are available through Deakin University Press.

REFERENCES

[1] Bigum, C., Situated Computing in Pre-Service Teacher Education, this volume.

[2] Bigum, C., Archiving the past in T. Dupé (ed.) ACEC89 Backup the Future, Proceedings of the 11th Australian Computers in Education Conference, Canberra.(1989), pp. 58-64.

[3] Green, B. and Bigum, C., Quantum Curriculum and Chaotic Classrooms: Reframing Educational Computing, this volume.

[4] Collins, A., Brown, J. S. & Newman, S. E., Cognitive apprenticeship: teaching the craft of reading, writing and mathematics in L.B. Resnick (ed.), Knowledge, learning and instruction: Essays in honour of Robert Glaser, (Erlbaum, Hillsdale, NJ, in press)

[5] Brown, J. S., Collins, A. and Duguid, P., Educational Researcher, 18 (1989) 32.

[6] Freire, P., Education: The Practice of Freedom, (Writers and Readers Publishing Co-Operative, London, 1974)

[7] Foucault, M. , The Order of Things (Vintage Books, New York, 1973), p. xv.

[8] Holly, M. L., Keeping a personal-professional journal (Deakin University, Victoria, 1984)

[9] Hodgkin, R. A., Playing and Exploring - Education through the discovery of order (Methuen, London, 1985)

[10] Weizenbaum, J., Computer Power and Human Reason (Penguin, Harmondsworth, Middlesex 1984)

[11] Dreyfus, H.L. & Dreyfus, S.E., Mind Over Machine (The Free Press, New York 1986)

[12] Hinkson, J., Arena 80, (1987) 123.

[13] Chesneaux, J., Arena 81, (1987) 26.

[14] Aronowitz, H. and Giroux, H.A., Education Under Siege (Bergin & Garvey, Boston, Ma. 1985)

[15] Bowers, C.A., The Cultural Dimensions of Educational Computing. Understanding the Non-Neutrality of Technology (Teachers College Press, New York 1988)

[16] Cooley, M., Architect or Bee? The Human Price of Technology (The Hogarth Press, London 1987)

Computers in Education
A. McDougall and C. Dowling (Editors)
Elsevier Science Publishers B.V. (North-Holland)

COOPERATION AND COMMUNICATION IN OPEN LEARNING : THE COCONUT PROJECT

A.DERYCKE, C.VIEVILLE, P.VILERS

Laboratory TRIGONE, Institut CUEEP-Université de Lille I
59655 Villeneuve d'Ascq Cédex - France

In the general framework of the setting up of a regional Open University we are doing some research on new tools and architecture for supported teletutoring. Our general foundation will work as a cooperative and conversational system between actors (learners, tutors). A large project was launched in mid 88 to specify, design and implement a general platform to support various kinds of communication either asynchronous or synchronous.

1. INTRODUCTION

1.1. The CUEEP Institute

The CUEEP is an institute of the University of Lille I in northern France, which has three missions: education of student in the field of foreign languages and written expression, further education and vocational training of adults and scientific research.

Since the late 70's, we have introduced new learning technologies, especially with the help of the computer, on a large basis [2]. An important work has been done in two directions.

- design, working out and experimentation of more than 300 coursewares.

- research and development of new tools e.g. a special classroom computer network : the Nanoreseau [1].

1.2. Development of an open learning strategy based on multimedia tools and networks

The evolution of our action, in both continuing and academic education, has led us to promote an open learning strategy. For two years we have set an ambitious plan to design and work out a complete set of distance learning credit units (in various disciplines).

Our approach is multimedia, i.e based on paper, video, hifi sound cassettes, courseware, and telematics...

Along with this production we are going to develop a global system to support different modes of learning from group learning to distance teaching at home or in firms.
The technical architecture of our interactive and multimedia system is based on :

- 10 learning resource centres which are a sort of smart building with cabling system for LAN of microcomputer, video and sound.

- a Regional Videotex server and courseware database which can be reached from either the learning resource centres or from home or from a firm with a microcomputer or minitel terminal via the packet switching network TRANSPAC.

2. OPEN LEARNING AND NEW COMMUNICATION TECHNOLOGIES

It is obvious that new telecommunications and information technologies will have an important impact on Open Learning, for example the geographical distance will be virtually suppressed. The computer mediated communications can be an important support for the setting of a 3rd generation of Open Learning Systems.

2.1. Some foundations to the introduction of new communication tools

Our main interest is with open learning (not "distance" teaching) and the design of tools for the third generation of systems.

In the second generation of open learning institutions or Universities, emphasis has been put on the design of multimedia documents which can be substituted to teachers. For reasons of pedagogical model/theory of open learning and of technical order, the interactivity was relatively low and this was corrected by the use of human tutors and the participation of learners to some periods of regroupment.

Introduction of new technologies of instruction (N.T.I), especially those based on computers, can drastically improve the interactivity of learners with the media.

For a long time the role of tutor (advisor..) will remain very important in such a process, perhaps greater than now if the tutor has the possibility to adapt, to modify the multimedia documents ("customization") to cope with a particular situation relative to a well identified learner. So it is important to give him all the electronic tools to help him in this function, to make it easier.

So, the next generation will offer not only multimedia packages to the learner and an efficient delivery system but it will offer important communication/conversation facilities, probably mediated by computer. This will enable the learner to have access to the tutor, to the teacher in some case ("Computer Assisted Teaching"), and also to another learner.

This kind of cooperation is, in our view very important, and has several major aspects relevant to :

- society : feeling of a collective entity of learners.

- the efficiency of instruction : group dynamics, emulation, competition...

In fact we want to promote the "cooperative autonomy" concept as a system of education.

- "autonomy" stands for the "open side" of the system (i.e.respect of choices, multiple approaches...).

- "cooperative"stands for the communication side, conversation, conferring system...

2.2. Current state of art

2.2.1. The educational aspects

Many Open Universities have given an important place to the intermediary people like tutors, counsellors or advisers.

In this case the need for a dialogue, or conversations is important . For example, it is claimed that in distant education all the possible means must be used to favour the communications between learners and the course designing team, the tutors, and the local manager.

In fact, the first network used for this task was the telephone either under the face to face model or the more collective audioconference model. In spite of its advantages as accessibility in Europe, and immediate feedback, tutoring by telephone has severe drawbacks : for example, it is almost impossible to discuss around a complex diagram or formula because it is impossible to see and to point some part of such a picture. It is even worse if the learner run a courseware on his workstation during a telephone call in order to remedy to some difficulties in the use of this courseware.

Hiltz [5] has shown the interest of computer teleconferencing systems . She has coined the term "virtual classroom" and she has reported experiments which concluded that the next generation of systems must support multimedia documents. She, also, writes that "new technology based modes of communications can do more than be just a second best emulation of the process of face to face communication in the traditional classroom". And that audioconference might be combined with continuing computerized conference.

For the design of a new generation we must take into account three difficulties/deficiencies of the present system :

- the asynchronous nature of computer teleconferencing which pays on the storage of messages. For learning in the virtual classroom model, or for case studies or group problem solving, asynchronism can give difficulty, cause problems to the users because it allows "multiple thread of the discourse" where the reading of textual messages need not be sequential (depending on the time of their writing).

- the second one is related to the constant danger of information overload. This can be overcome by an intelligent user interface able to filter or to browse messages and to give possibilities to keep a personal track of the previous access.

- the third deficiency is relative to the textual orientation of present computerized conference with two severe drawbacks : no verbal cues as it is expected in traditional teaching and the relative psychological problems ; it is difficult to use in the field of sciences for example because of the lack of pictures, complex drawings...

2.2.2. Technological aspects

These last years, with the emergence of Telematics, videotex network, X400 C.C.I.T.T. standard for Message handling System, there has been a great acceleration for the development of new tools and uses of interpersonal communications systems.

i) Delayed interaction (store message)

Most of the work is done around the multimedia approach. The interest is mainly in the fields of office automation with some "hot" topics like :

- the integration of voices and data,

- the development of well accepted document structuration representation and exchange protocol with a standardisation approach like ODA.

Other works are in connection with the aforementioned deficiencies especially the "information overload" problem. For example, Malone [6] puts forward some intelligent filtering of messages in regards with respect to the interest and activities of the users. Some artificial intelligence techniques have also their place in these communication systems in order to give a more "user's friendly" interface and an appropriate help.

ii) Realtime interaction

The interest has become important over the last few years for the support of cooperation of actors (clerk, "white collar") in the office or in the decision making process. Some new concepts like "collaborative work" have gained a broader acceptance. Roughly there are two approaches of this problem :

* development and experimentation of realtime multimedia conference (voice and data). The system DIAMOND [9], for example, is a multimedia message system built on a distributed architecture and which includes a realtime conferencing system.

However this experimental system was designed for a specialized context and purpose. It was aimed at professional users. We agree with I.Greif [8] that each real time conferencing system will be tailored to a particular organization and to the role of the human user, i.e the tutor and the learner in our case.

* Evolution of hypertext system to cooperative uses. This is particularly true of systems designed for the purpose of multiauthoring of written papers.

3. THE CoCoNUT PROJECT

3.1. Main goals

The acronym CoCoNUT is for **C**ooperation and **C**ommunication **N**etwork **U**tilities for **T**ele**T**utoring. We think that individualization and the so called "intelligent tutors" are the wrong directions if they are not linked to the development of tools to promote communication and cooperation, not only between learners and the teacher, tutor, advisor...; but also between learners themselves.

The field of Computer Supported Cooperative World (CSCW) is a "hot" issue in the office automation domain of research [4]. But we can learn from these experiments that a lot of problems, especially at the cognitive or social levels (usability, impact on organization) still remain.

In order to experiment solutions, to modify, we have launched an ambitious project called CoCoNUT which has as a major goal the design and realization of an experimental platform or laboratory devoted to this approach.

The project is ambitious because :

- it involves not only computer scientists but also psychologists, linguists and researchers in educational sciences.

- it is planned for three years,

- we want to change several fundamental paradigms either in the computer field (introduction of object paradigm) but also in the educational field (hypermedia approach and the conversation paradigm).

After a short analysis, it has appeared to us that these new domains were still relatively non explored. Our main challenge, for the technical side, is then to develop an Open platform able to cope with various situation envisaged in our open learning vision. Open stands for extensible, flexible, and incremental changes in the functionalities or control of the system without enforcing a particular model (role of the actors).

3.2. The technical choices

3.2.1. The hardware platform

The hardware platform is composed of individual workstations linked by an Ethernet Local Area Network. Because we envisaged the use of such tools outside the laboratory we have chosen a distributed computer architecture based on powerful workstation : a mixture of PC/AT 386 and SUN 3/60 with a computing power of more than 2 MIPS each (see figure I). First, We did choose to integrate sound and data in the same physical network (Ie Ethernet for example).

We planned to resolve the multimedia transport problem of integration in a next phase when we will transport our project to a wide area network. We think that ISDN will be a smart solution to these problems in less than five years (see figure II).

3.2.2. The software platform

Our main concern is to make a prototype and not to design a final product. For this purpose we have chosen to use an Object Oriented Programming System for several fundamental reasons :

- the paradigm of object is particularly adapted to distributed systems because objects are entities which contain data, methods to handle data, and attributes (properties) and these objects can communicate by messages.

- the object oriented approach is also the basis of powerful User Interface Management System (Window, Mouse...).

- the object oriented approach (design and programming) is well adapted to multimedia project at the user's level.

- another intrinsic feature of object oriented programming systems is their incremental design ability and reusability of the software components.

From these considerations we have chosen the Smalltalk-80 [3] as the ideal platform.

3.3. Some aspects of the theoretical and pragmatic approaches

We understood at the beginning of the project that cooperation was still an open issue :

- collaborative learning is still at an early stage. There are only a few experiments in this field [7],

- in the office automation domain, fields like computer supported cooperative/collaborative work or decision, "groupware", are open problems which imply the cooperation of scientists of various disciplines from computer sciences to ethnology.

In parallel with the development of tools for educational communications, we must have two approaches :

- A more theoretical one, especially based on linguistic models, to formalize the conversational model. This is the approach used in some projects like COSMOS [10] around the Speech Act theory of Austin.

- but also a pragmatic one based on observation of experimental systems and the contribution from the behavioural and social sciences to analyse the results, the deficiencies...

We think that the interdisciplinary approach is necessary not only in the validation phase but also during the design phase.

4. PRESENT STATE OF THE PROJECT

The first analysis of present system deficiencies and requirements for new systems has led us to develop two subprojects which share the same conceptual methods and tools. The first is relative to the synchronous communication and the second is relative to asynchronous communication.

4.1. Design of a realtime multimedia conference system for teletutoring

Such tools do no exist in our environment so we cannot conduct a first experiment. This is why we have chosen to design a realtime multimedia conference

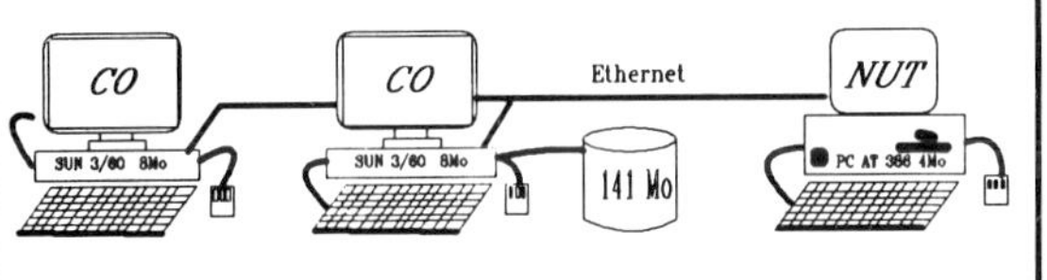

PLATFORM (figure I)

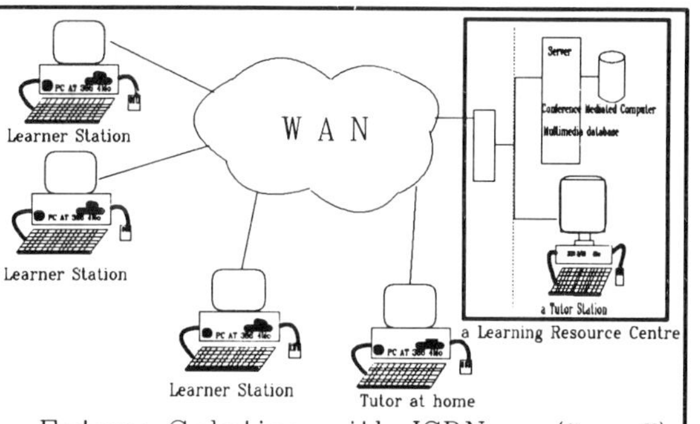

Future Solution with ISDN (figure II)

system for teletutoring. The objective is to give a general framework architecture for such a system. The central concept is "what you see is what I see" or some kind of shared electronic black board between a tutor and a few remote learners (4 to 6).

The first stage has two goals :

- to master the communication on the LAN between Smalltalk system and to give facilities to exchange complex objects.

- to analyse the requirements and write the specification of the user's interface with emphasis on the balance between public window (WYSIWIS), and private window and the mechanism of exchange. Another objective is to give a total view of the conference to the user : identification of the speaker, the writer, the master of conference, messages for the conference management...

The second phase has been under way since June 89 with two major goals :

- to give a distributing architecture of the real time conferencing system and a general control manager of the conference.

- to derive specification of general tools to support cooperation and tutoring. In effect, the system has a general framework architecture not especially devoted to education. It is the application which will be inserted within the framework that will give the specialization.

4.2. Multimedia asynchronous teleconferencing systems

In this case the number of users can be very large. In a first step we have designed a classical, i.e. textual teleconferencing system on our Videotex system.

From this first experiment we have chosen two ways of development :

- a short term and a relatively conservative one : no change is done in the server software to maintain compatibility with Videotex. However for some users who use a microcomputer to emulate a videotext terminal, we have designed, in Smalltalk, an integrated environment to help users in the access to the teleconferencing system. (automatic log-in, private local message handler and manager...). Extensions are underway to remedy the most important deficiencies aforementionned (information overload, disorientation).

- a long term project which plans to use an object database to develop a multimedia teleconferencing system tailored to the educational and tutoring process.

The first step underway is relative to the specification of the requirements for database, investigation of object formalism for multimedia and extension of Smalltalk to support an active object or actor paradigm.

CONCLUSION

We think that communication and cooperation have a central role in the education process especially in the distance learning case.

The emergence of multimedia or hypermedia tools will be of potential interest for education's individualization. However at this stage, hypermedia raise more questions to the educator or course designer than they give answers.

If we follow the major idea of Winograd and Flores [11], there is new foundation for design of computer systems based on a more social view of the world.

In the last decades Computer Assisted Learning has been developed on a buried paradigm that was the automation of the task (of learning).

Besides this approach, there is room for tools to increase the capacity of both learners and tutors. These tools will probably have a foundation based on a communication and cooperation view of the educational process.

REFERENCES

[1] Derycke, A.C., Loosfelt, P., Cornillet, G., Cheap local computer network : an ultimate solution for the classroom, in: J.Moonen, T.Plomp (eds.), EURIT 86, (Pergamon Press, Ensched, 1986), pp. 207-210.

[2] Derycke, A.C., Losfeld, J., Impacts of new learning technologies on an acdemic institution and its environment, in: F.Lovis, Ed Tagg (eds), ECCE 88, (North Holland, Lausanne, 1988), pp. 449-454.

[3] Goldberg, A.,Robson, D., Smalltalk-80 : the langage and its implementation, (Addison Wesley, 1983).

[4] Greif, I., Computer supported cooperative work : a book of reading, (Morgan Kaufman Publishers).

[5] Hiltz, R., The virtual classroom : using computer mediated communications for University, Journal of Communication 36 (2), (1986), pp. 95-104.

[6] Malone, T. et al., Intelligent information sharing system, Communications of the ACM, Vol 30, n° 5 (1987) pp. 390-402.

[7] Newman, D., Sixth graders and shared data : designing a LAN environment to support collaborative work, CSCW 88 ACM Conference, (ACM, Portland, 1988) pp. 291-305.

[8] Sarin, S., Greif, I., Computer based realtime conferencing systems, IEEE Computer (1985), pp. 33-45.

[9] Thomas, R.H., et al., Diamond : a multimedia Message System built on a distributed architecture, IEEE Computer (1985), pp. 65-77.

[10] Wilbur, S., The cosmos project : a multidisciplinary approach to design for computer supported group working, in: R.Speth (eds), research into networks and distributed application EUTECO 88, (North Holland, 1988) pp. 147-155.

[11] Winograd, T., Flores, F., Undestanding computer and cognition : a new foundation for design, (Ablex Publishing corporation)

Computers in Education
A. McDougall and C. Dowling (Editors)
Elsevier Science Publishers B.V. (North-Holland)

PROJECT PEDAGOGY AND COMPUTER MEDIATED COMMUNICATION IN DISTANCE LEARNING

Lone DIRCKINCK-HOLMFELD

PICNIC*, Institute for Communication, Aalborg University Centre, P.O. Box 159, DK-9100 Aalborg, Denmark

This paper will discuss how computer mediated communication can support the learning processes in a special form of distance pedagogy - the "project pedagogy". The paper will stress explanation of the most important principles behind the "project pedagogy". Afterwards follows an assessment of computer-mediated communication based on an empiric "felt-study". The paper argues that computer mediated communication fundamentally offers new potentials in relation to developing a communicative distance pedagogy, but before it could be managed there is an urgent need for pedagogical development work.

1. INTRODUCTION

This paper will focus on how computer mediated communication (CMC) can support distance learning at university level in a special form of distance teaching pedagogy - the "project pedagogy".

As this pedagogic concept may not be very well known in an international context and as an evaluation of computer mediated communication (CMC) presupposes a clear definition of the pedagogic practice in which the medium is used, the present paper will initially explain the most important principles behind the "project pedagogy" and some of the problems attached to this pedagogy when used at a distance.

The evaluations of CMC are based partly on theoretic studies of this way of communication and partly on a qualitative analysis in connection with a - in a Danish context - large field experiment at Jutland Open University, where CMC has been used. [1]

2. PROJECT PEDAGOGY

The project pedagogy is a form of teaching developed in Denmark in connection with the establishment of two new universities, Roskilde University (1972) and Aalborg University (1974), respectively.

As these universities in 1985 and 1982, respectively, began to offer parts of the university studies as "open learning" this teaching was based on the "project pedagogic" foundation.

The "project pedagogy" is based on the idea:

* that the students acquire knowledge "problem-oriented" through communicative and social learning processes, based on group-organised project work supplemented by lectures.
* that the students work action-oriented. Their analyses have to be translated to problem-solving.
* that project work often is related to practice, through problems from the external world.

*PICNIC, Project In Computer Networks In Distance Education Curricula, is an interdisciplinary research project at Aalborg University exploring pedagogical and communicative aspects of computer mediated communication in distance education at university level. PICNIC is founded by the Danish Research Council for the Humanities.

The social- and subject-related aims of the "project pedagogy" are to qualify the students on an interdisciplinary basis and thus strengthen their ability to identify, formulate and solve problems. The project pedagogy emphasizes in particular the acquisition of a methodical-theoretical consciousness and critical-analytical knowledge.

Epistemologically the "project pedagogy" can be explained within the framework of Human-Activity-Theories' interpretation of human learning as a subject-directed, communicative and social process (Leontjew, 1977), as well on Critical Pedagogy's ideas on emancipative learning (Habermas, 1974) and (Negt, 1971) and further developed in Denmark (Olesen, 1985).

According to experience "project pedagogy" is an inspiring and engaging teaching method appealing to most students, which benefits from the group-organized learning, where students to a large extent support and guide each other.

2.1 The Cooperative and Communicative Principle in "Project Pedagogy"

Group-organized project-work is based on the assumption that cooperation and communication are important conditions for developing learning processes. It is based on the idea that cooperation and communication can lead to (Dirckinck-Holmfeld, 1990):

* transgression of the limited capacity of the individual student
* the possibility of specialising and at the same time keeping the overall understanding
* the ability to look at problems from different points of view
* the possibility to verify and develop the individual/the knowledge of the groups in a secure forum.

The basis of learning in group-organized project work is cooperation between students and dialogue with their teacher. In this way, students explore an exemplary problem within the theme of the term.

According to this it is important to recognize that in "project pedagogy" the students do not get a complete package of instruction materials. The students and their teachers choose current relevant material and literature which can support the students' work.

Consequently, in "project pedagogy" there is a built-in, current need for dynamic subject-related communication - between the students and between students and teachers. At the beginning of the work, the communication deals with formulating and identifying the problems. At a later stage the students and the teachers discuss partial aspects and theories related to the object of investigation, i.e. problems of understanding, different interpretations, etc. At the same time, there is a current need for exchanging literature and drafts.

Consequently, there is a current demand for the following types of communication in relation to the learning process:

* subject-related communication as regards both methods and contents.
* planning and coordinating communication, as regards who does what at which times.

Furthermore, the close cooperation in a group is improved through the students gaining an understanding of each other and of the context which leads to the conclusion that it is a condition for the learning processes that the students get the possibility of communicating socially with each other, as well as they get a forum where informal discussions can take place.

In the "project pedagogy", therefore, there is a need for the following types of communication:

Subject-related communication
Planning communication
- - - - - - - - - - - - - - - - - - -
Social communication
Informal communication

Figure 1

In relation to construct knowledge the most important forms are subject-related and planning communication. The social and the informal communications are the bases.

Furthermore, the "project pedagogy" demands different actions of communication - from "information delivering" as the most simple to "dynamic interaction" as the most advanced.

2.2 "Project Pedagogy" and Distance Learning

The "project pedagogy" at a "distance" has so far been conducted in the following way: The students have to participate in four week-end seminars during a year, and they have to practise individual study work between the seminars (15 to 20 hours a week). The four seminars have been used partly for lectures and partly for "project-work".

Experience indicates that it has been very difficult to practise group-based, cooperative and communicative "project-work" after the above-mentioned principles. For the reason the students have either worked alone in geographically local groups or in divided project groups.

The main reason for this has been the absence of communication possibilities during the periods between the seminars - both as regards subject-related - and social communication. It has been very difficult for the students to maintain an intensive level of communication during the periods between the seminars unless they were living close together geographically. In regard to distance learning, the project pedagogy has primarily functioned as individual learning processes. The students have not been able to utilize the cooperative and communicative possibilities which the group based project work ideally offers.

As a consequence, we have in PICNIC found it interesting to analyse in which ways computer mediated communication (CMC) can contribute to qualify the communicative basis of the "distance project pedagogy".

3. AN EVALUATION OF CMC IN RELATION TO "DISTANCE PROJECT PEDAGOGY"

In order to evaluate the possibilities and limitations of CMC in relation to a project pedagogic practice PICNIC has chose a "field-experiment" at Jutland Open University as a starting point. Here CMC has been used as a supplementary means of communication in the teaching at the Foundation Year in the Humanities.

In 1988 48 students started using CMC, 30 female students and 18 male students. One group of 28 students had access to CMC from a number of local study centres geographically spread in Denmark, and a group of 20 students had a PC at home. The computers were placed at their disposal by the university.

In regard to the content there was an equal separation between class teaching and project work. The students were to follow three courses - one course in Humanistic Science Theory and two courses in Humanistic Methods of Analysis. Furthermore, they were to study a problem within the theme: Humanities in modern society.

With the purpose of discussing CMC's potentials in relation to the project pedagogy an impression of how CMC has supported the teaching situation in general is given below, followed by a description and analysis of how CMC has supported the "project pedagogic" practice.

3.1 CMC in Relation to the Teaching Situation in General

In relation to the above problem of lack of communication facilities in distance learning, it is obvious that the computer conference medium offers a new channel of communication in addition to letter, telephone, and "face-to-face" meeting. This has manifested itself in the fact that students and teachers have been able to arrange "on-line" conferences supporting the teaching activities. In regard to the 1988-teaching the following types of conferences have been arranged:

	"Texts"
COURSE conferences, totally	258
INFORMATION conferences, totally	117
"INFORMAL" conferences, totally	1192
TECHNICAL "support" conferences, totally	633
Selected PROJECT Group's Conferences (1)	759

Table 1

(1) It was the selected project group who used most intensively CMC in the project work. There were five students in the group: four female students and one male. The students lived geographically far away from each other. The students explored the topic: "The communication between laymen and experts in the health system".

If we look at the number of "texts" in the different types of conferences some interesting differences should be noticed:

* The conferences with the highest total "score" are the "Informal" conferences with 1192 texts, i.e. the conferences which should be compared with "canteen-like" activities at the on-campus university.
* The selected Project - Groups' conferences follow with 759 texts.
* The third-most used conference is the Technical support conference with 633 texts.
* And first as the fourth-most used conferences the Subject-oriented conferences follow: Course conferences with 258 "texts", and the Information conferences with 117 "texts".

If we look at the distribution between different types of contents in relation to the teaching situation in general, the following can be stated:

* that there is a great demand for "informal" communication.
* that the students have had to spend relatively much time on technical "support" communication which gives an idea of the problems attached to the use of EDP as a tool of communication when the users are unfamiliar with EDP.
* that it should be noticed how low the activity has been in the Subject-related conferences at class-level - the course conferences and the information conferences.
* that there is relatively much activity in the Project-groups' conferences.

This difference in the use of conferences can be interpreted in different ways:

It is evident that in order to get activity in a conference some of the participants should start relevant discussions.

The table indicates that it is easier to discuss subject-related in Project-work conferences than e.g. in Course conferences. The lack of discussion in the Course conferences may be due to the fact that none of the participants have actually taken the initiative to start discussions. It might show us that especially in the course conferences and in the information conferences the teachers ought to be the active contributors providing input, asking questions, and following up on some of the questions asked by the students. Furthermore, the teachers ought to make clear how discussions could be carried on, how different group-dynamic techniques could support discussions, etc. All in all, the teachers do have a very important role especially in Course-conferences if activity should occur.

Another explanation of the low activity in the large subject-related group conferences might be the fact that participating in large conferences demands the "courage/wish" to speak in large gatherings. The table, therefore, might indicate that CMC in large group conferences produces some of the same patterns of communication as we know them from traditional class-room investigations with a very uneven distribution as regards who speaks and who listens.

According to interviews with students, this tendency may have been increased by the fact that at the beginning many of the students feel "alien" to CMC, partly due to the written, screen, and machine mediated code of communication, and partly due to the fact that the medium was experienced as "one-way" because of the delayed conversation and because of the relatively large "unknown" receiver group.

However, the explanation of "courage/wish" in participating in large gatherings is not true as regards the "informal" conference. One explanation might be that some people find it easier to talk "informally" rather than discuss subject-related in a large forum, the reason might be that they feel free of the scientific "judgement" in the informal conference.

From a teaching and learning point of view it is rather disappointing - in particular as regards the courses - what CMC has contributed. However, it is too early to use these results to conclude that CMC cannot be used to support the course work.

In order to understand the table the following has to be reflected:

* that no special efforts were made to teach the teachers how to use the medium in a pedagogically appropriate way.

* that the medium was implemented without changing the work of the teachers.
* that the teachers have only got the standard time-resources.
* that some teachers did not really believe in the system.

As a consequence, the teachers have not been the active contributors to create interesting activities in the conferences between the seminars which I find is the most important explanation of the relative lack of communication.

Before we can conclude about the media as regards the teaching situation in general and the Course-conferences in particular it is therefore necessary to intensify research and development work in order to investigate how the teachers could use the CMC to constructively support class activities, as well as it is necessary to develop the organizing of the teachers' work in relation to the new possibilities, which the media offer.

3.2 Computer Mediated Communication and Project Work

If we focus on the activity of the selected project, the number of texts could prove that there is a demand for much communication in the project work. Same as it might prove that as a matter of fact the medium can be a channel for different types of communication - also subject-related.

The quantitative statement alone does not give any qualitative indications of the conference activity. To judge the quality, it is necessary to analyse the contents: How is "spoken" and who "speaks".

In PICNIC we make such analyses of selected project group's works. As this investigation has not yet been concluded, only partial results are presented below.

The following is a quantitative record of the project group's communication based on a categorization as regards contents (see table 2). The purpose of this table is to show the distribution on what is "talked" about, when is "talked" and how is "talked" in relation to the overall project.

The table shows the following:

The number of "texts" has increased during the whole period, however, most distinctively during the last period, when the number of "texts" were more than five-fold in comparison with the middle periods. On the average there were 12 "texts" per day in the last period.

The table shows, moreover, what the communication is about. Compared to the "class conferences" it should be emphasized that the communication is subject-relevant. Most of the "texts" are related to contents and to the methods and planning of the project work.

The subject-related communication is e.g. about: Identifying and clarifying the problem using scientific research methods. Literature references are exchanged. The students prepare reports of theories which they exchange and comment on. Some students have made interviews with relevant key persons. An interview guide is prepared via the conference system. Reports of the interviews are prepared and distributed via the system and commented on by the other students. On the basis of the theories and the inspiration gained from the interviews a theoretical model of analysis is prepared and analyses are made.

	Periods			
	I	II	III	IV
	01/03 15/05	15/05 02/09	04/09 05/11	07/11 22/12
Social manifestation	16	25	11	51
Social information	8	12	13	36
Social commentation			4	1
Subject-related information	11	35	20	48
Subject-related commentation	18	37	58	171
Technical information	4	24	5	6
Technical commentation	2	8	7	46
Planning information	13	10	15	34
Planning commentation	14	10	19	129
Informal information	3		4	5
Informal commentation	8	4	2	20
Other types of contribution				2
"Text" total	97	165	158	549
"Text" a day in average	1,3	1,4	2,6	11,9

Table 2

The table is constructed on the basis of a study of the contents of the produced "text" and not on the system dependent designations given by the students. This is due to the fact that a "text" often contains more types of communication e.g. both "social manifestation" and a comment. This procedure was chosen to have the most correct "picture" of the study activity via the system.

* Social manifestations refer to greetings and manifestations from which it might appear when you will reply on a "text".
* Information refers to a message or a briefing.
* Commentations refer to discussions where knowledge is exchanged and developed.

This type of activity is what "project pedagogy" is about. To acquire knowledge of a scientific field through an exemplary problem in a close communicative relationship with fellow students.

As appears from the record this form demands a large degree of planning activity - e.g. mutual information as regards who does what, mutual agreements as regards when contributions must be finished, as well as a great number of contributions and discussions as to the most appropriate way of finishing the project report via the computer conference system.

Furthermore, a number of "texts" concerning social information and comments have an explaining function for the study activity. The students are very consequent in saying "thank you for your contribution" and in telling when they intend to reply.

During the first period the students did not do that very much, therefore they felt that the communication "dangled" which some of them found very frustrating.

Although there are technical support class-conferences, this project conference includes communication about technical problems too, and it appears from these contributions that technical problems are the source of much irritation.

Finally, this conference contains a small amount of informal communication. Typically, the students discuss TV broadcasts dealing with subjects of relevance to the project work.

Attention should be drawn to the fact that the communication is very "rational" in relation to the needs of the project work, cf. the above-mentioned variables of communication. It should be noted that in the conference there is no "information-junk" or "information-overload", but only contributions relevant to the project work. The project group has been very disciplined to separate between study-relevant subjects and the more informal ones.

Furthermore, it is worth noticing that there is a high degree of planning communication. My hypothesis is that the group based project work at a distance basis demands a more explicit planning in order to coordinate and decide in respect of the project work. However, the reason may also be that planning communication is more easily produced in CMC than e.g. subject-related communication, as the former does not, in general, demand as much reflection, literature support, etc. A high degree of planning communication may, therefore, also be regarded as a "valve" for "informal" communication.

In relation to the demands of communication outlined in respect of the project work, cf. p. 4, it appears that the conference system has been able to support all these types of communication. However, there has been relatively much planning communication.

One of the explanations of that for instance compared to the class-conferences could be that the "integrated" project work with a common goal demands the students work together. They really have a need for exchanging and discussing their thoughts built into the pedagogical organization.

The next question to be dealt with is: Which types of communication can take place via a computer conference system? How does it influence the students' progress of cognition? Is it primarily informational communication or is there "dynamic" interactive communication, offering the students the possibility of testing and developing their knowledge?

In Table 2 we have separated the informing contributions from the discussing contributions (comments on). It thus appears that the first periods were dominated by informing communication, or by contributions to which there were only few responses. During the third period there is a change resulting in a slowly increasing amount of comments and discussions in connection with the contributions. During the fourth period the number of commenting and discussing contributions are distinctly increased.

The complexity of the communication acts vary much. During the first period there were few "links", and they were not continuous. During the last period they were much more complex. There could easily be 15 to 20 turns in a "dialogue" (cf. L. Dirckinck-Holmfeld, 1990).

On this basis we can conclude that the medium can be used both as a means to procure information and as a medium for discussion. The medium can assist the student in the learning process in obtaining a broader knowledge about the field of subject, as well as the other students' works. Furthermore, the medium provides the students with the possibility through discussion to look at the problem field from different angles, to test their understanding and knowledge, and finally to develop this further.

At the same time it is important to point out, that CMC is a special form of "dynamic interaction", because of the media specific code: written, screen mediated, machine mediated, and asynchronous, demands an explicit and conceptualized communication code (cf. S.F. Larsen, 1984, discussing written language). When used in teaching such code has some potential because it might help the students to be more explicit about the use of concepts. Especially, in project work which beforehand is based on writing drafts, this written communication-code might fit.

The table, however, can also be studied more critically. One could wonder why it takes so long before the project groups get started with their "intense" communication.

The explanation is partly technical, partly pedagogic/organizing. For many of the students it was difficult to master the EDP both technically and communication-wise, cf. Dirckinck-Holmfeld & Lorentsen (1989). Only at a very advanced stage of the process did the EDP became the tool of communication originally intended.

Seen from a pedagogical and organizational angle, the media has contributed to render visible the troubles of the pedagogical working process. In the Project Conferences it has also turned out that the teachers have not participated enough. Their work has primarily been at the week-end seminars. During the periods between the seminars the students have been very much on their own.

Through studies about the use of the medium it has become evident that in particular at the start of a project work at a basic educational level there is a great demand for the teachers to contribute as regards subject-related, methodical, and study-advising input as well as it is important that the teachers help the students to overcome technical and media specific communicative problems in order to ensure that nobody is left out because of the technical problems. In order to meet these demands it is required to change the teachers' working conditions just as it might be necessary to offer the teachers supplementary education in the pedagogical use of CMC.

If the organizational changes are not made at the same time as CMC is implemented, the teachers as well as the students will experience the situation as rather frustrating, because the medium offers new possibilities which cannot be followed up.

4. CONCLUSION

The Computer Mediated Communication opens some exciting perspectives for the possibilities of developing a new pedagogy in distance education which to a high degree more than the existing, mass-media distance teaching concepts (Open University in UK) has a communicative basis.

As may appear above, CMC can be used both for social and subject-related communication, in the same way as the medium can be used for information as well as for discussions.

Our investigations suggest, however, that to draw the full advantage of the medium much more work of development is required. Experiments should be carried out in respect to investigate how CMC can support activities at class level as well as at project level. In particular the course activities at class level need to be watched carefully.

And last it has to be stressed that in order to make CMC a successful tool within the "project pedagogy" it is a must that conferencing systems have to be tailored for teaching purpose, as well as having to have a consistency and transparent user-interface. This is especially important in distance education, where the students have to master the technical problems themselves.

NOTES

1. The Jutland Open University is an administrative "umbrella" for three universities in Denmark: Aalborg University, Arhus University and South-Jutland University which offer "open education" in humanistic subjects. The used conferencing system was Portacom, developed at Stockholm University, Sweden.

2. The figures originate from a more comprehensive report under preparation by Annette Lorentsen offering a general description of the conference activities. For further details see A. Lorentsen (1990).

REFERENCES

[1] Dirckinck-Holmfeld, L. and Lorentsen, A., Vejledning i fjernundervisningskommunikation via datamat (Aalborg University, 1989, Draft).

[2] Dirckinck-Holmfeld, L., Kommunikation pa trods og pa tvoers - et studium af datamatkonferencesystemer og loereprocesser, PICNIC-NYT 9 (Aalborg Universitetscenter, 1990, forthcoming).

[3] Habermas, J., Vitenskap som ideologi (Sv.Norsk, 1974).

[4] Larsen, S.F., Kognitionens logikker I: Psyke og Logos nr. 2 (Argang 5, Dansk Psykologisk Forlag, 1984).

[5] Leontjew, A.N., Problemer i det psykiskes udvikling (Rhodos 1977, Danish edition).

[6] Lorentsen, A., Presentation and Analysis of Project Computer-Aided Distance Teaching (A Research Project at Jutland Open University, Aalborg University 1989, PICNIC-NEWS, No. 4E).

[7] Negt, O., Soziologische Phantasie und exemplarisches Lernen. Zur Theorie und Praxix der Arbeiterbildung, (Europaische Verlagsanstalt, Frankfurt am Main, 1971).

[8] Olesen, H.S., Voksenundervisning - hverdagsliv og erfaring (Unge Paedagoger, 1985).

Computers in Education
A. McDougall and C. Dowling (Editors)
Elsevier Science Publishers B.V. (North-Holland)
IFIP, 1990

TECHNOLOGY IN DISTANCE EDUCATION - Economics, Equity and Change

Colin W Dunnett

Manager, Communications. Education Department of South Australia,
31 Flinders Street, GPO Box 1152, Adelaide South Australia 5001

The provision of distance education is now seen as an adjunct to the actual education process, and it is used to solve problems of disadvantage as well as distance. This intrudes into the organisational models of institutions a their original priorities are now subject to change because new capabilitie are being demonstrated. This paper will provide an overview of the methods, equipment and technologies used in South Australia in many forms of education at a distance and relates their application to the economic situation and their likely influence on the community.

The perceived changes in demand and threat to traditional solutions complicate the issues and makes evaluation extremely difficult. The picture of a blend and mix of provision becomes inevitable, with the overall costs and economics of the present constraining the immediate needs of the disadvantaged, whilst the educator plans for the long term needs of the community.

1. INTRODUCTION

In order to understand the total activity it is essential in the analysis of a distance education procedure for the evaluation to consider those aspect of content and methodology of lesson build up, such as the Seven Levels of Component Resource Analysis (Dunnett 1984 rpt 88), as being quite distinct from the delivery process or technology being employed. This paper deals only with the delivery process.

2. DECLINING ENROLMENT

The major catalyst for change was simply one of numbers. Quite independently from the general economic situation, itself in some decline, the post war bulges were over and schools were experiencing a dramatic fall by more than 20% in the numbers of children, over the past ten years this trend yet has still not bottomed out.

The situation is now being mirrored in the metropolitan areas of Australia where, of course, a similar decline in enrolment is occurring. A solution to the problem is the use of technology and an expansion of the isolated distance education procedures which must now be applied to all schools.

3. THE TECHNOLOGIES BEING USED

In searching for a solution to the distance education problem, it is necessary to be completely realistic in financial terms.

Users of full motion video transmission will inevitably be of high cost in the education children.

Low cost methods must be used and will be based on the use of audio/video media, but limited to audio frequency activity, either in radio, and/or telephone and can include *extravagant* media such as recorded or microwave TV. In brief the following notes outline the equipment and technology we have so far found successful.

3.1. DUCT (Diverse Use of Communications Technologies).

A loud speaking telephone with multiple microphones has been the basis of most of South Australia's activity in distance education when teleconferencing has been used.

This equipment called DUCT was invented by the South Australian Education Department's Educational Technology Centre, and is being used to link up to ten isolated schools at a pre-arranged time, to share lessons.

This whole concept emanated from the successful PEACESAT (Pan-Pacific Education and Communication Experiment by Satellite) using the NASA, ATS-1 Satellite from 1971 onwards. This is well reported by Professor John Bystrom of the University of Hawaii who pioneered the educational use of the Satellite in a Teleconference mode.

3.2. Use of Technologies in South Australia

Without spending time on this issue in this paper I would refer the reader to the papers in the References, which have been selected to cover the development that has occurred.

4. ROLE CHANGE

The origin of the provision of distance education provided for the isolated has now been extended to include the provision of a specific educational need in a situation where all else is provided traditionally.

Whilst the *specialist* distance educator may be an expert, unfortunately that expertise has been acquired in a different environment and will not necessarily be accepted by the regular school.

5. MANAGEMENT OF DISTANCE EDUCATION

In emphasizing the problems I am pointing to the danger of the practice of distance education in the future that could be managed by those who are only aware of the economic problems of declining enrolments and isolated education. Such considerations will offer only traditional and temporary solutions to a problem which is emerging. Closing schools because of reducing enrolments hardly helps a situation which surely must expand and develop new ways of solving delivery problems that can be cost effective and successful without face to face teachers.

Closely following the design of the technological application, the curriculum design, which usually already exists for the face to face teaching, must be rigidly applied to the new media being used. Often is is *only* a matter of training the teacher who has already their own sets of notes and examples, and to convert them to the *distance* mode. I do not believe it is necessary to rewrite a special course, as was the case in the *reactive* correspondence situation where nothing existed on paper as the teachers were there solely to service isolated needs. The continuity in the process became vested in the material of the course instead of the teacher.

6. A DISTANCE EDUCATION AMALGAM WHICH BECOMES ECONOMIC

The *management* problems of distance education should become problems of *management and manipulation* of all the possible ways of providing the solution in a physical sense to a personnel problem.

Regardless of the size of a school, the human teaching resources will tend to be provided by a formula considering the number of children present and be unmindful of the diversity of their needs.

To reduce this to absurdity as an example one could consider a *one teacher school* of 20 students expecting a diversity of 10 high school subjects to be available. A particularly specialised need is always likely to arise and not be able to be satisfied.

As long as the number of hours of instruction available in a school is finite then the possible subject offerings is also finite. Across the whole of a state system the aggregate of those offerings is likely to be greater than the needs if it could be applied in different non face-to-face situations at the same time. Unfortunately if those offerings are constrained to a schools boundaries there becomes an appointing problem for teachers and a cost effectiveness problem with small numbers. However, if the distance education offerings are integrated to the *face-to-face* offerings on a credit-debit basis between all schools then I believe a programme could be developed involving as many teachers as a *State Government* could afford. The number of teachers that are carried, will clearly relate to the teacher skills and abilities that are in the system as a whole and which are therefore available.

Such a scheme would be the topic of a project in its own right but I believe it typifies the management problems that the new technologies can not only create but also solve.

7. TECHNOLOGY DELIVERED RESOURCE

In describing the actual conversions of a *Model* to a real situation, I pause for a moment to again justify *technology*. An added bonus of any technological system is the concept of human resources in terms of expertise or advice, that can be brought into the school from outside for *once off* activities specially planned by the teacher. similarly, debates, meetings, musical occasions, play performances, and other special events can be arranged once the delivery system is operational.

Equally, one must not overlook the advantage of the very use of technology as being of cardinal importance in the curriculum content for a modern society.

8. SUMMARY OF TECHNOLOGIES

One way of amalgamating all of these *user* technologies in distance education, is to classify them as to their need whether they be called Interactive or not.

It is further necessary to define the presence of software to be anything that is prepared in advance. That material used *live* by a teacher with no preparation, other than experience, is intuitively tailored to the needs of the particular class in front of the teacher.

Prepared Material	*Live and Totally or Software Based Interactive Systems
Correspondence	*Face-to-Face teaching*
Broadcast Recordings	*Teleconference (Video or Audio)*
Video Tape Use	*School of the Air*
Computer Use	
Slides and Tape	
Videotex etc	

Material ◄── Spectrum of Course Control ──► Teacher

*Clearly the Live Interactive Methodology can be supplemented and improved with pre-recordings etc or prepared material, but any process of delivery methodology on the other list cannot conduct a programme on its own and as such therefore requires a professional teacher as well at some stage of the process if a response or question is raised that is nor part of the original programme. If the teacher is present it therefore becomes a live lesson with support which falls in the Interactive column.

The need, or otherwise, of a specially prepared curriculum, whether it be because of the content, or the students personal requirements will be the significant factor deciding whether or not a prepared *package* is acceptable.

The cost of a Prepared Package will be able to be balanced against the total costs in the eventual situation to produce a simple cost per student which will reduce as the number of students increase. The focus of control of a course spreads from teacher based to material based.

Unfortunately this is the point at which activity in the USA or Europe is emulated and overseas material purchased as the development is uneconomic in Australia, particularly with the small numbers involved relatively with isolated education.

This approach can be developed and used as a specific measure if we are quite definite in the components being costed.

Typical of such systems to which this applies is the Satellite delivery involvement.

However more broadly let us talk more generally of Delivery Systems:

(NOTE: This Section is designed as stand alone analysis and may be read as such)

9. THE USE OF TECHNOLOGICAL DELIVERY SYSTEMS

This brief overview is aimed at the use of technology in some way for the delivery of education for the benefit of the R-12 schooling years. This particular segment covers the compulsory school years and overlaps into the Tertiary (and TAFE requirements).

Unfortunately many of the cost values quoted in this development will be rated quite differently when viewed from a Tertiary or TAFE view point, and this in itself tends to produce an alternative argument by assuming that in some cases where an educational need cannot quite be justified for the R-12 sector, then with the addition of an extra benefit, such as TAFE, the equation will be conclusive. This is not so unless the use being considered is totally in the overlap (year 11 and 12) area of the two sectors, and weighted accordingly where both are involved, as otherwise the large school sector numbers totally subverts the priorities and does not provide the value where it is needed in the equation.

Generally to understand the costing and analysis one must consider any delivery service to always contain the following sectors.

The result of this comparison is *valued* more highly depending on the quality or the availability of the source. Such cold statistics must at least be carefully assessed if new projects, such as has occurred in many places overseas, are not to stand the risk of economic axing in the future.

If at any stage a new source can be provided which will replace the delivery system and be put *on site* at a lower cost then the delivery system is not cost effective, if the situation is judged in the context of that one activity.

It could be argued that this cost break point is reached in an overall Education Department by traditional methods at a cost of $\frac{\text{(Total Education Cost)}}{\text{(Total No. of Pupils)}}$

ie: in the State of South Australia approximately $4,500.00 per student per year in 1990.

or: less than $6.00 per pupil teaching hour based on a teacher being available 60% of a pupils time, the remaining time being spent in private study or *NON* class time.

If the same calculation is carried out from the other perspective, then a *special* invited teacher at say $50.00 per hour must take 8 or 9 pupils to produce the equivalent cost effectiveness ratio using the same infrastructure. This in distance

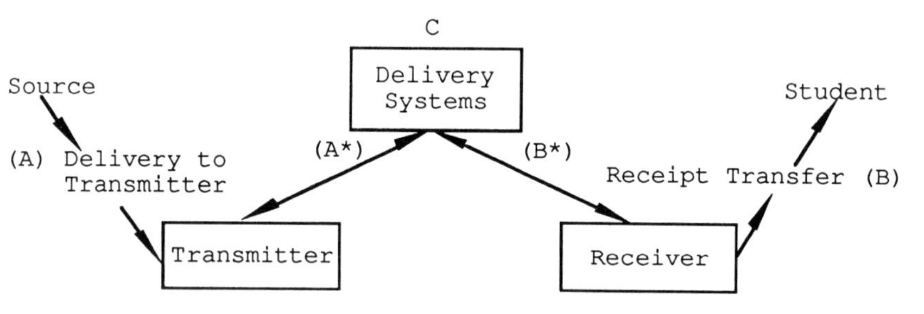

These Sections must be analysed separately

It is quite clear in this analysis that the overall cost effectiveness must be a simple (Total Costs/No. of Students) consideration based on the overall formula:

$$\frac{\text{(Source) (Costs)}+A+(A^*+C+B^*)+B}{\text{Total Students}}=\text{(Cost Per Student)}$$

education terms is a reasonable target *load*, and assumes *no* additional costs for administration over the normal teaching situation.

Such a calculation therefore leads us to the point where a technological delivery system can only be considered cost effective if it leads to an equivalent ratio of approximately $6.00 per student hour. Such a *total* calculation must include the supporting services if it is to be compared in an overall budget. It is noted that the formula A+A*+B+B*+C does not include the cost of material support unless it is specifically included at A+C, or in the source costs.

Therefore if a *face-to-face* class of 15 students has a teacher of their own (this could be considered as typical and equates to the overall cost of a typical class) Cost x No. of pupils in an average class (6 x 15) = $90.00 per hour.

Such an argument can only inhibit distance education but is nevertheless realistic unless the cost of education is to steadily increase by the delivery costs illustrated above by A* + B* + C.

Usually it is made easy to contain the A + B components which approximate to the face-to-face situation.

Such an escalation is avoidable if the places are chosen carefully to maximise the effects. Where the cost per pupil is presently much more than the average, they can be reduced by increasing the number of pupils by using distance delivery methods to add external classes.

It must also be underlined that the *limit* costings of $6.00 per pupil hour really infer that distance education clusters must move towards satisfying clusters of up to 15 children to maintain present costings, unless those places with less than this ratio, (ie in small class, upper secondary groups) move to improve their ratio so as to improve the teacher costing without adding extra points of instruction. The *student hours* saved in this way will pay for the communications involved.

This then summarises the final point that to ensure cost effectiveness distance education classes must *grow* by adding enough extra pupils at a distance to existing groups, so as to equal their own delivery costs at $6.00 per pupil hour. Any dollars saved by improving on this can then be set aside for further development.

10. CONCLUSIONS

10.1. Socio-Economic Issues

Although a project may well be confined to an educational area or a specific community need, just like all roads or highways, other forms of traffic will adapt and easily use them.

In many cases, the justification of a particular media highway may seem a great deal overestimated for a specific purpose, but there could be an immense change if it is valued over an aggregate of other users for different purposes.

This latter point is of great value in a community situation, as if properly surveyed in advance, a project could satisfy many groups beyond those originally voicing the need. This may well involve the survey and investigation component of a project taking, what may seem at first, a majority of the total project time.

A community group may well object to a project, but within a community there will be many sub-interests, ie those sub-interests can each be identified and a specific area of communication use encouraged to service them. A cohesion will emerge and the *highway* being installed will become a success practically, by its very use much more readily than if the groups are integrated after the event.

Finally I believe that the application of Communications Technology to learning is a network evolution of communication itself. Technology will gradually refine, provide and correct all the missing factors and provide, what for Australia has a real meaning, *a removal of the tyranny of distance*.

These methods and systems that we have developed are all in their infancy, and yet already they satisfy the needs of many disadvantaged groups. I feel confident that educators will apply them, use them and continue to develop them for the future benefit of all.

REFERENCES

[1] Books, [2] Journal Articles, [3] Papers.

[1] HOLMBERG, Borje, Recent research into Distance Education I & II Zentrales, Institu fur fern studien fur schung fern Universitat, Hagen, 1982.

[1] UNWIN Derrick, 'Component Resources', C.W. Dunnett, Encyclopaedia of Educational Media.

[2] CHITTOCK, John, Screen Digest 'Background', February 1987, Published London, 1987.

[2] DUNNETT, C.W., The Technologies of Education, Communication and Distance Education, PLET Vol.22, No.4, November 1985.
[2] DUNNETT, C.W., School Community Communication Centres, Education Department of SA, 1985.
[2] EARY John, A plain person's guide to the New Learning Technologies: 'Training and Development', UK, December 1987.
[2] 'Electronics Australia', "Piggy Back" FM broadcasting reaches Australia, (Electronics Australia, August 1987).
[2] HOSIE, P.P., Satellites and Education in Australia - Learning from International Experience, British Journal of Educational Technology, No.1, Vol.18, 1987.
[2] IPPOLITO, L.J., "The ATS I Experience - A Decade of Satellite Telecommunications", Conference, Honolulu, 18 January 1982.
[2] McGUIRE, A.J., The Correspondence School and School of the Air, Education Department of SA, 1987.
[2] PATTON, George, Participants' Perceptives in Effective use of Communication, Educational Media International Journal, Vol.24, No.2, 1987.
[3] BROCKHOUSE, Brenton, Videotex Report. A report of Videotex Committee to the SA Education Department, 1986.
[3] EDUCATION DEPT OF SA, Educational Technology Centre Status Report, 1982/85.
[3] LCSU, Interim report, 'Elizabeth High Schools Network', Education Department of SA, 1987.

Computers in Education
A. McDougall and C. Dowling (Editors)
Elsevier Science Publishers B.V. (North-Holland)
IFIP, 1990

USING THE MICROCOMPUTER TO ASSIST CALCULUS STUDENTS AT A DISTANCE - AN EVALUATION

Phillip Farrands, Mathematics Learning Centre;
Debbie Clayton, Department of Mathematics and Computing;
John Dekkers, Distance Education Centre;

University College of Central Queensland ROCKHAMPTON 4702

In the study of a Calculus subject by distance education, two software tools were incorporated into the study package used by students. An evaluation was undertaken to determine how, when and where students used the software. This paper presents the results of that evaluation. It was found that the software tools did assist the students in deepening their conceptual understanding and it improved their problem solving skills in the subject.

INTRODUCTION

It is generally accepted that the whole range of enhanced communications and computer technologies being introduced to distance education will have substantial impact toward improving the quality of students educational experience. Further, it will enable educators to use a wider range of instructional strategies and techniques.

A consequence of greater availability and lowering costs for acquiring and using enhanced communication and computer technology is resulting in student academic support becoming increasingly multimedia based. This may include the use of audio and video tapes and computer assisted/managed/enhanced learning packages. Communication technologies such as teleconferencing (audio and video) and electronic mail are also being increasingly used for student-staff and student-student interactions.

This paper is concerned with an application of software tools that can be used to enhance the learning of first year undergraduate Calculus. Whilst there has been increasing acceptance in the use of microcomputers for teaching mathematics (Bloom et al, 1986 a & b; Gordon, 1983; Sacharin, 1980; Tall, 1985), Arger and Clayton (1989) have shown that there is a lack of in-depth evaluation to determine their efficacy and utility for distance teaching/learning in Australia.

This paper is an evaluation of student use of two software tools, Capgraph (Clayton et al, 1987) and Microcalc (Flanders, 1987) in a first year, first semester, degree level Calculus subject available by the distance education mode.

EVALUATION METHODOLOGY

Evaluation data was collected using a survey instrument developed by the authors and also through telephone interviews. The survey instrument was administered in June, 1989. In all, 74 questionnaires were sent out. After 8 weeks, another copy of the questionnaire was mailed to the non-respondents. These persons were also telephoned and requested to complete and return the questionnaires. A total of 44 (59%) questionnaire responses were received.

After three weeks, the remaining non-respondents (that could be contacted) were telephoned and simply asked whether or not they had utilised the software for the Calculus subject. This follow-up was necessary to provide more complete information on the use or non-use of the software. Eighteen of the remaining 30 non-respondents were contacted.

The questionnaire data was coded and entered into a microcomputer. A spreadsheet program and a statistics package were used to analyse the data.

Six respondents who had utilised the software packages were telephoned and interviewed about their "typical" use of the software. This aspect obtained case study information on how the software aided the student in understanding the subject material.

AVAILABILITY AND USE OF THE SOFTWARE

All distance education students undertaking the Calculus subject received, by mail, a study package at the beginning of the semester containing a study guide and a series of audiotapes to accompany the text Calculus with Analytic Geometry (Edwards and Penny, 1986). Students had to submit 3 assignments during the semester and take a final formal examination. The study guide provided students with on going guidance and a series of weekly exercises and activities with answers. Students with problems could contact the lecturer and subject tutors (available in study centres) for assistance.

The use of Capgraph and Microcalc software packages was integrated into the course of study. Students were directed in the study guide to use the software packages as follows:

* Iconic & Written Reference: Where appropriate, the study guide makes direct reference and instruction to use of the software.
* Guided Worksheets (Capgraph only): For the topics Limits and Continuity; Differentiation and Interpreting Graphs; Curve Sketching and Derivatives and Exponential Functions; special worksheets can be used in conjunction with the software.

Students were able to access the Capgraph package by: purchasing a student version from the Institute Bookshop for $20; using or copying the software at any one of the Institute's 12 study centres located in regional towns and cities in Queensland or at the Institute's Library.

Copies of Microcalc were placed in study centres and in the library for student use.

The reader should be reminded that the use of software during the semester was voluntary. Students were encouraged to make use of the packages but the use was not mandatory.

RESULTS AND DISCUSSION

The survey results are presented in four sections: demographic details and background; software usage; experiences using software and non-user feedback.

DEMOGRAPHIC DETAILS AND BACKGROUND

The College supports a network of 12 study centres throughout Queensland. Each centre is equipped with an NEC APC III and an IBM AT compatible microcomputer. All software required for distance education courses, including Capgraph and Microcalc, is held at each study centre. At a number of the larger centres part-time tutors are employed to assist distance education students with mathematics, computing and physics subjects.

Students gain access to microcomputers by: attending the study centre; purchasing their own computer; using a machine at work, at a local school or a machine owned by a friend or colleague.

Figure 1 summarises the demographic and background details of all respondents. Eighteen of the 44 respondents indicated that they had used the software during the semester.

In this Figure and in those following, the numbers at the end of each bar represent the number of students.

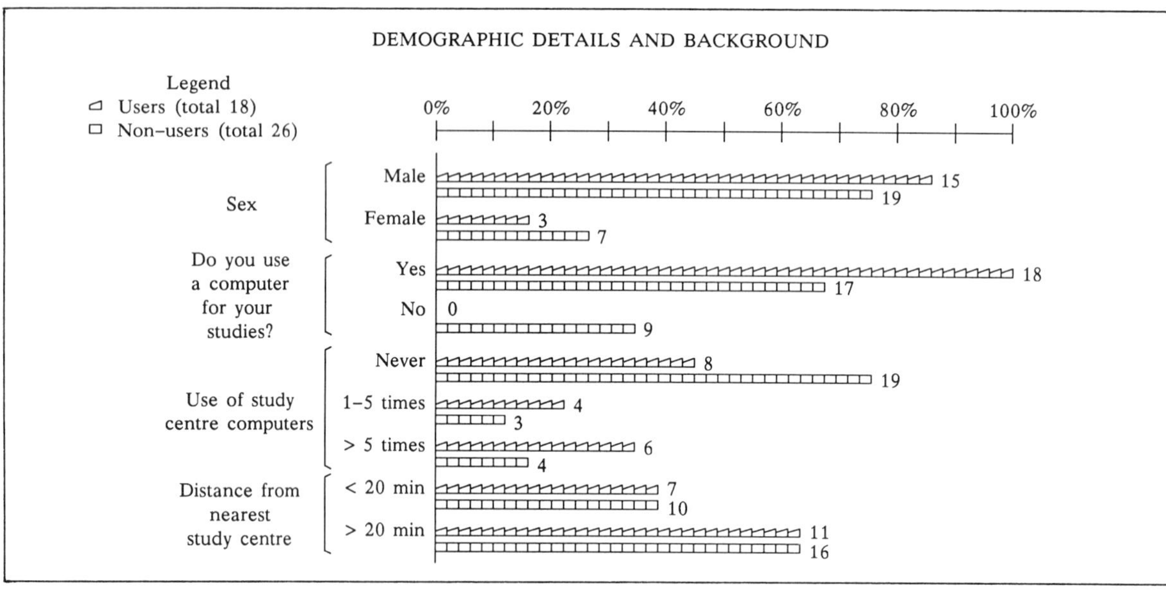

Figure 1

A chi-squared analysis of the users and non-users indicates that use of the software packages is independent of sex (χ^2 = 0.64 p = 0.58). Only a slightly higher proportion of males did use the software.

It is of interest that 17 (65%) of the 26 nonsers of the software stated that that they used a computer for study. This would probably be for completing computing assignments (the language Pascal is often studied in conjunction with Calculus).

Users of the mathematics software do tend to be more frequent uses of study centre computers (χ^2 = 3.68 p = 0.94).

PERFORMANCE IN CALCULUS SUBJECT

Figure 2 compares the end of semester performance in the subject Calculus A with use or non-use of the software packages.

A chi-squared test (ignoring supplementary and deferred results and combining not sat and fail) indicates that achieving a pass grade in the Calculus subject and use of the software are independent events (χ^2~=~2.2~p~=~0.86).

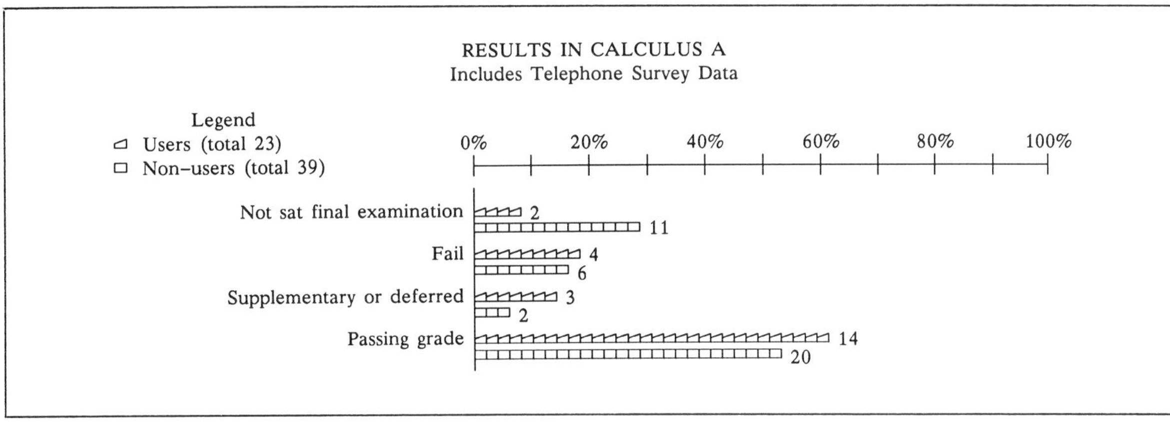

Figure 2

The chart does however highlight some interesting points.

* A much higher proportion of non-users did not sit the final examination (χ^2 = 3.58 p = 0.94). This agrees with an electronic tutorial and distance students trial conducted by Gledhill and Dudley, 1988. These authors found the retention rate of a group using the electronic tutorial system was higher than a group who did not have access to this facility.
* Overall, a higher proportion of students who used the software obtained a clear passing grade.

ASPECTS OF SOFTWARE USAGE

Figure 3 considers the mechanism used by students to obtain access to the software.

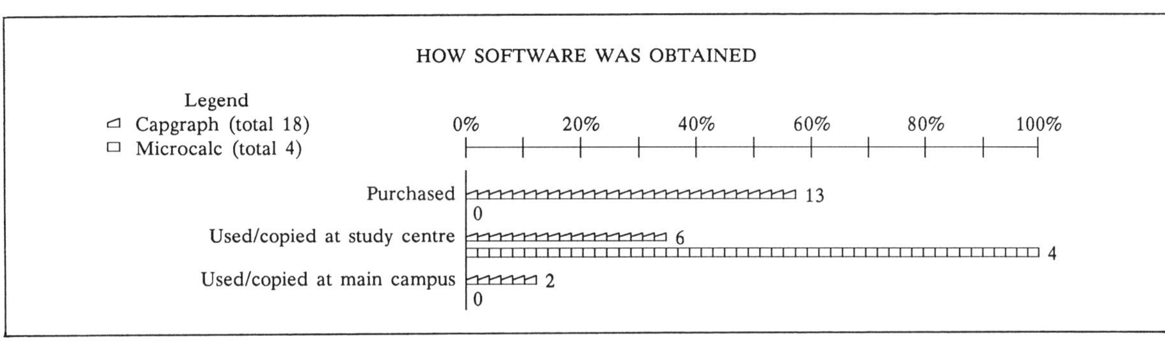

Figure 3

Ten of the 18 Capgraph users indicated they had purchased a copy of the software. All 10 of those students used Capgraph at home.

Microcalc was only available at study centres or at the main campus.

The survey asked students to indicate how often they used a piece of software at a particular location. Options provided were once per semester, once per month, once per week or several times per week. Questionnaire responses have been extrapolated to indicate the total number of times each piece of software was used and are presented in Figure 4.

Six students used Capgraph at a study centre. That use accounted for 18% of all use of Capgraph. Note some students used a software package at more than one location.

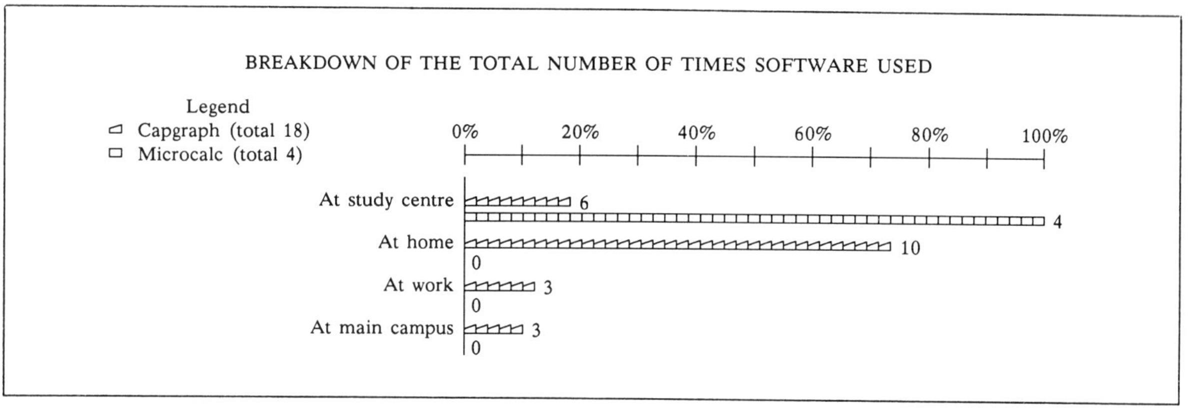

Figure 4

Where a software package and appropriate computer system is available to the student at home, then that system was used much more frequently than systems which require a student to travel to use the system.

Over 50% of students used Capgraph at home and one third of the students accessed the program at a study centre.

Capgraph was used more than Microcalc as shown in Figure 4. The reason for the much higher usage of Capgraph may be due to a wider range of access options for this piece of software.

An examination of how long and how often students spent using the software for a variety of modes of learning indicated that:

* over half the students made use of Capgraph and Microcalc whilst going through the study guide, problem solving and whilst doing assignments:
* the average session times varied for these modes of interaction from 10 minutes to 43 minutes;
* less time was spent by students using the software for completing worksheets and revision.

Regarding the way students used the software, 95% of students mainly interacted with the software when alone, although 6 students studied together or under the guidance of a study centre tutor.

EXPERIENCES USING SOFTWARE

Student experiences on the use of the software are provided in Figure 5.

All Capgraph and three of the four Microcalc users consider the software easy to use and only one student considered more help was needed in using the software packages. This response was encouraging as the user interface of software developed for use by those studying at a distance should not pose problems to the user.

No student considered the software a waste of time. In fact the authors consider that using graphical software instead of drawing complex graphs by hand would provide a considerable time saving to the student. The students were very positive about the tools assisting them with:

* understanding mathematical ideas;
* problem solving exercises;
* experimenting with problems and
* revision work.

Two students responded that the use of the software caused a break in their study routine. One of these students accessed the software at home on weekends and the other student accessed the software at the workplace.

Overall the students found the icons in the study guide provided assistance in indicating appropriate usage areas for the software.

TELEPHONE INTERVIEWS

The survey was then followed up by telephone interviews to six users to obtain more in-depth information on the experience of the software users. Students were asked to describe a typical setting in which they used either Capgraph or Microcalc and to detail a typical interaction.

Students considered that the optimum usage setting was having both software packages available on a home microcomputer. However the fact that students were prepared to drive to study centres to utilise the software does indicate that they considered the study benefits gained was worth this effort.

The interviews with students revealed that the software had the following benefits/purposes:

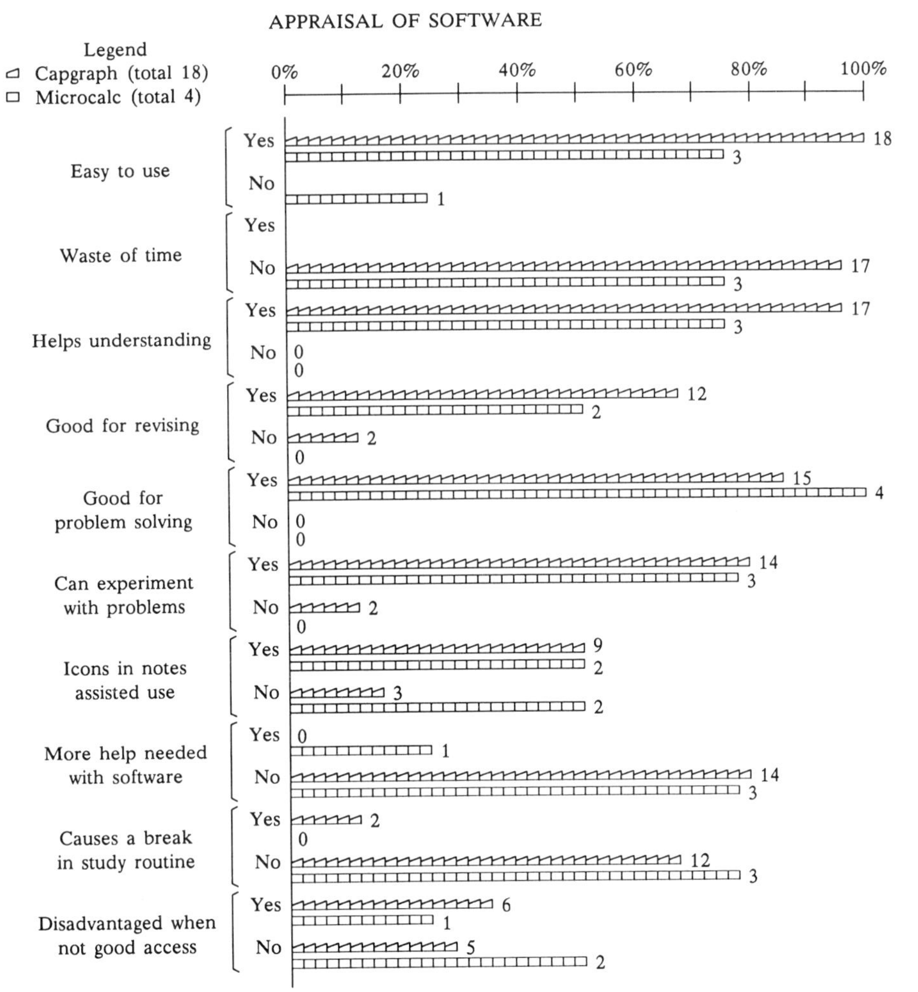

Figure 5

* "time saving" by not having to draw graphs by hand;
* an extra aid to assist and deepen concept understanding;
* a tool that could be used in an experimental fashion and
* a mechanism that provided immediate feedback as a "check" of the correctness of assignment answers and ideas.

NON-USER FEEDBACK

Reasons for non-use of software are presented in Figure 6.

It can be seen from the data that the main reason for non-use did not relate to the software at all, but that 66% of the non-user respondents considered the study materials were adequate and that they did not need extra resources.

Other main reasons for non-use were poor access to a computer and limited time available. The time aspect could refer to the time taken to drive to a study centre to use a microcomputer. Students with limited time perhaps considered that this "driving time" would be more productively spent working with what they perceived as adequate study materials. Significantly 17 of the 26 non-users (65%) do in fact use a computer at home for their studies.

CONCLUSION

The results of this evaluation appear to indicate that the use of software tools do have a number of tangible benefits for the student studying Calculus at a distance. Some observations can be made.

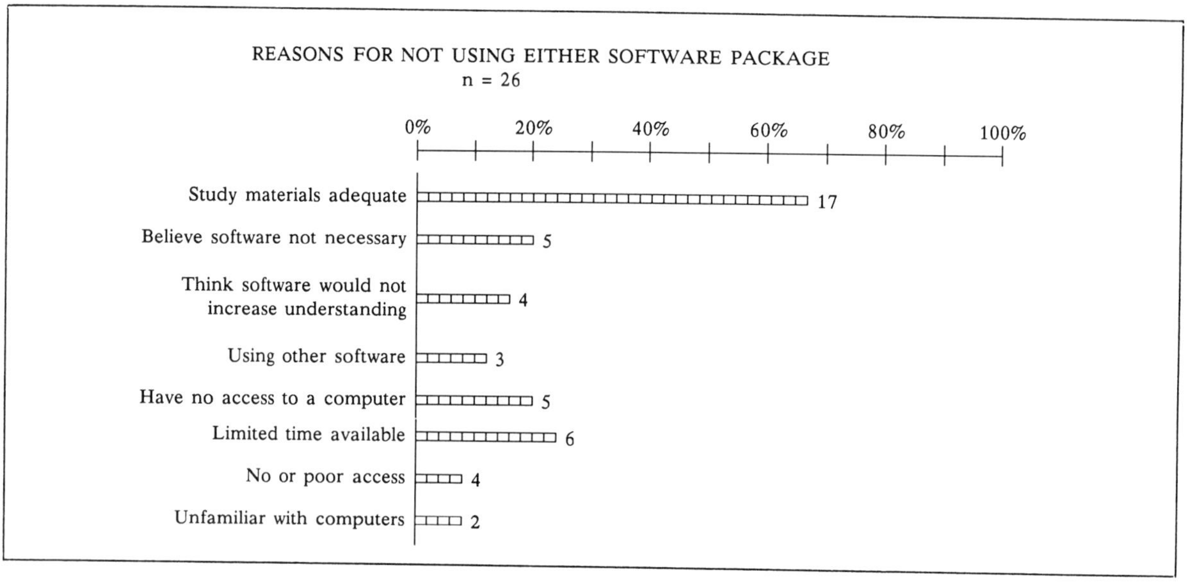

Figure 6

Firstly, the use of such software provides an extra dimension to the learning experience in the areas of:

* experimentation;
* saving time (especially drawing graphs electronically);
* understanding concepts;
* revision and
* problem solving.

Secondly, in this evaluation students preferred to access the software at home. This observation is consistent with the concept of studying at a distance. Thus the use of software for the distance student implies that the software should be provided with the study materials or be inexpensive.

Thirdly, approximately 40% of students used the software package. This result was not unexpected. Higher utilisation would occur if it was compulsory for students to use the software and the software was fully integrated into the study package. This is being explored for future offerings of the subject.

Fourthly, whilst it has been shown that there is no significant relationship between using the software and grades obtained in the subject, the retention rates for students using the software was higher than that of non-users.

Finally, this evaluation raises a number of other issues which warrant further study, namely:

* Have the directions for use of the software tools been appropriately incorporated into the study guide?
* Can mechanisms other than iconic and written references and worksheets provide a better learning experience for the student? If so, what are they?
* Do the results of this survey have implications for on campus teaching, for example making learning more student centred, using electronic blackboards in lectures?

REFERENCES

Arger, G. and Clayton, D. (1989), The Use of Computers in the Instructional Process in Australian Distance Education, Computers and Education, Vol.13, No.4, pp343-354.

Bloom, L.M., Comber, G.A., and Cross, J.M. (1986a), A Microcomputer Approach to Exponential Functions and their Derivatives, Mathematics in School, November 1986, p30-32.

Bloom, L.M., Comber, G.A. and Cross, J.M. (1986b), Using the Microcomputer to Teach the Transformational Approach to Graphing Functions, International Journal of Mathematical Education in Science and Technology, Vol.17, No.1, pp115-123.

Clayton, D., Farrands, P., Kennedy, M. (1987), Capgraph, Capricornia Institute of Advanced Education, Marketed through Australian Association of Mathematics Teachers, ADELAIDE SA.

Clayton, D., Farrands, P., Kennedy, M. (1988), Capgraph - A Tool to Enhance Mathematics Teaching, Australian Senior Mathematics Journal, Vol.2, No.1.

Edwards, C.H. Jr, Penny, D.E. (1986), Calculus and Analytic Geometry, Second Edition, Prentice-Hall International.

Flanders, H. (1987), Microcalc, MathCalcEduc, Ann Arbor USA.

Gledhill, V.X., Dudley, C.P. (1988), Electronic Tutorial System for Distance Education, CTEC Report, Canberra ACT.

Gordon, S.P. (1983), Calculus through the Eye of the Computer, International Journal of Mathematics Education in Science and Technology, Vol.14, No.4, p497-506.

Sacharin, A. (1980), Calculus with a Function Plotter, International Journal of Mathematics Education in Science and Technology, Vol.11, No.1, p15-23.

Tall, D. (1985), Understanding Calculus, Mathematics Teaching, March, p49-53.

Computers in Education
A. McDougall and C. Dowling (Editors)
Elsevier Science Publishers B.V. (North-Holland)

COMMUNICATION FOR THE CURRICULUM

Gordon Jones, Chief Executive,

The Times Network Systems Ltd.(Sales and Marketing Agents for Campus 2000)
214, Gray's Inn Road, London WC1 8EZ, UK

This paper describes some of the innovative ways in which computers and telecommunications have been harnessed to provide a valuable tool to both teachers and students in support of curriculum work.

These projects have all taken place using Campus 2000 - an electronic communications and information service dedicated to the needs of education. It is to be stressed that Campus 2000 is a tool for use with all curriculum subjects and definitely is not JUST for use in conjunction with Computer Science or the other high-tech subjects.

1. BACKGROUND

The advent of the microcomputer in schools, has provided educators with a very powerful tool for use in association with the whole range of curriculum subjects - History to Home Economics, Mathematics to Modern Languages. The use of such technology has enabled the artificial barriers between curriculum subjects to be removed and for much more cross-curricular activity to be evident.

Every curriculum subject involves writing and communication. Every curriculum subject can benefit from the use of Information Technology - computers. Educational standards are rising, students are more highly-motivated and teaching is made easier and more satisfying.

In the UK, various Government-led initiatives during the early-1980s have provided every school with at least one computer - even the smallest rural junior schools. Many larger comprehensive schools, of course, have 50 or more, computers, enabling them to be used more readily in a classroom environment for a wide variety of applications.

It is a vitally important part of the education process for students to be made ready to face the world of work. In any modern office or place of work, the use of personal computers is commonplace. Industry and commerce can reasonably expect for young people to be conversant with such technology and to be comfortable and knowledgeable in its use. This leads on, of course, to many Industry-Education links which - certainly in UK - are now increasing in number and the benefits to both parties are becoming apparent.

As well as the use of computers for word-processing, spreadsheets, simple databases and educational games-playing, it became apparent that great benefit could be obtained by allowing such devices also to be used for communication - between schools, teachers, education authorities, internationally - and for the provision of a wide range of information databases - again, locally, nationally and internationally.

It was with this in mind that, in 1984, The Times - one of the most famous and reputable newspapers in the world - decided to start an electronic communication and information service to schools and colleges. This was termed The Times Network Systems - TTNS for short - and provided a dedicated service to the education community, both in the UK and abroad. In 1988, TTNS joined forces with a smaller service to the education sector operated by British Telecom to form Campus 2000.
Campus 2000 now provides E-mail, information services and conferencing to over 10,000 subscribers - most of which are schools and colleges. At this time, over 60% of all UK Secondary Schools subscribe as well as a wide range of other education establishments and individuals. Campus 2000 also has subscribers in over 20 countries outside the UK, including Sweden, Denmark, Finland, Australia, Japan and many others. This, of course, leads to many interesting international projects and friendships.

It is interesting to note that the Campus 2000 service is supplied to the education sector on a commercial basis by two leading UK companies - British Telecom and News International - thus enhancing industry-education relationships in general.

The use of Information Technology, with fast electronic communications as a key element, has provided many opportunities to education which, hitherto, were just not possible. At a local level, teacher to teacher communication has been made simple and convenient. No longer are there the inevitable, unanswered telephone calls. As a result, there is now a much better 'network' through which teachers can enlist help and exchange good practice and ideas - locally, nationally and internationally. Curriculum issues can be discussed. Self-help is the order of the day! It is easy to find out if anyone else has done work on a specific topic or project idea to avoid 're-inventing the wheel'. Although one cannot pretend that such insular practices have been eliminated, instances have been dramatically reduced.

As far as students are concerned, their uninhibited energy and ideas know no bounds. Maybe because game-playing was the first contact many students had with computers, the 'fun' element persists and acts as a great motivator, even to the more difficult student and the slow-learner.

2. TRAINING TEACHERS TO USE COMPUTERS AND TELECOMMUNICATIONS

The biggest obstacles, of course, to the use of IT across the curriculum lie in the training of experienced teachers and support staff and the level of resource - the availability of computers in the classroom together with associated finance. As we all know, students will happily sit down and play - usually constructively - with a computer, even if they have not seen it before and do not know how to operate it. Eventually, they will find out how to use it effectively by trial and error or, if all else fails, by reading the instruction manual! This behaviour has been observed in very young children- 6 or 7 years old - as well as more senior students.

If you put a teacher into the same situation - particularly someone who has little knowledge of computers or how to use them - a very different result ensues. Some will refuse to have anything to do with such devices, on the grounds that their subject could not possibly benefit! Others profess that they have insufficient time to learn about the technology and how it can be used to support the curriculum. Yet another group believe that if they do something incorrect when using the computer, they may do irreparable damage to it!

In reality, many teachers do not wish to display their lack of knowledge in front of their students or colleagues. This is understandable. Exactly the same attitude is displayed by many middle and senior managers in industry. They also take the view that they are too busy to attend formal training and, anyway, they employ people to do this sort of task for them!

Training of experienced teachers in the use of Information Technology is still a major problem. It must be overcome. It is compounded by the fact that teachers - particularly in the UK - are in very short supply. Taking a teacher out of the classroom to attend external training courses is, therefore, unwelcome and expensive - particularly if a supply teacher has to be employed to cover the shortfall.

A partial solution to this problem, which has already been successfully used in industry, is the use of the training video and associated material. This seeks to provide background training in a way that can be used at the convenience of the individual - during free time or at home. This private and personal form of training also helps to overcome the lack of confidence in the person concerned by not requiring him or her to display their lack of knowledge in front of trainers, colleagues or, worst of all, students. Such a technique may provide just enough knowledge and motivation for a teacher to then seek help from colleagues or to attend formal training sessions with added confidence.

3. CURRICULUM DEVELOPMENT

The advent of a National Curriculum in the UK has thrown some parts of the teaching profession into panic. Not only do their lessons now have to meet various criteria, in terms of content, they also have to carry out pupil assessment, formally, at the ages of 7, 11, 14 and 16 years of age.

One way which is being used to enable teachers to exchange information and to help each other is through the medium of computer conferencing on Campus 2000. The conference, conducted through the computer over a period of weeks or months, enables teachers involved with Geography, for instance, to pose problems - already faced and solved by others - or to contribute ideas and projects which they have already developed.

In this way, not only is 'good practice' being exchanged across the country, teachers actually feel that here is a source of help, not from 'on-high' provided by the Department of Education or Local Education Authority Advisers, but from peer-group teachers who are facing exactly the same problems and strictures actually at the 'chalk-face'.

Although this use of computer conferencing is still in its infancy, the signs are that this valuable new tool will provide a source of help to teachers as well as providing a means of disseminating quality advice and material throughout the UK.

Some examples of project activities which have taken place using a range of Information Technology facilities will now be described.

3.1. English Literature

A very early advocate of the use of Information Technology, starting in 1985, was Derbyshire Local Education Authority, in the centre of England. This was led by a very imaginative IT Advisory team which had the full backing of the Education Authority. They set out to demonstrate how IT could be used in support of every curriculum subject. Teachers were seconded - on a day per week basis - to the Advisory team to develop resource materials for their particular subject. These curriculum resource materials were then made available, through a database hosted on TTNS, to all Derbyshire schools.

For instance, one school had a particularly strong English department. Hence, they were commissioned to provide sets of teacher notes and resources for the teaching of the English Literature set books being studied in schools that year. Another school undertook to provide teachers with up-to-date information on In-Service Training opportunities within the education authority. Yet another coordinated the production of a Gazetteer of all the major towns and villages in Derbyshire. This was produced by students and contained their by-line on the piece of information. This, of course, highlights another reason why communications are popular with students - it gives them the opportunity to display their work to a much wider audience than just their class or school. Arguably, this also helps to raise standards overall. After all, none of us like having work on public display which contain errors or is of a poor standard!

3.2. International Communications

In Devon, in the South West of the UK, some Primary schools set up electronic communication links with schools in Tasmania. This was, originally, started as part of a Government initiative - the Microelectronics in Education Project (MEP) - but was later carried on by TTNS.

At first schools got to know each other personally and collectively. They then undertook a range of curriculum-related activities together. This involved, for instance, both sets of schools carrying out surveys into their respective lifestyles, family environments, housing, employment and general locality. This data was then analysed locally on each side of the world. These analyses were then exchanged, thus allowing those young children to compare and contrast life in Devon and Tasmania.

3.3. Children with special educational needs

Campus 2000 also caters for children with Special Education needs - those with mental or physical handicaps. The Special Educational Needs Database - SEND - has over three thousand pages of information on the ways in which micro-electronics can be used for learners with special needs.

SEND is used by schools, hospitals, occupational therapists, teachers, psychologists, disabled user groups and a host of other people connected with this field of learning.

3.4. Modern Languages

There are many ways in which Campus 2000 can be used effectively at all levels of education - take the case of a Secondary School in Bedfordshire - just north of London. Their Head of Modern languages had already done a year's exchange with a school in Germany. Pupil exchange visits followed and regular postal correspondence between staff and pupils was set up.

On one visit, the Modern Languages teacher helped german pupils to send a message back to the UK via Campus. The message was sent on a Saturday and the pupils downloaded it on a Monday morning. To their surprise, this high-tech German school was using an old Atari computer linked to a borrowed modem.

From then on, all exchanges of correspondence were done using Campus 2000. This led to further exchange visits and a continuing friendship between the two schools.

3.5. Adventure Games

A novel but equally valuable use of the system was pioneered by a Secondary School in Derbyshire - in central England. The third-year pupils sent out this message to a Primary school in the area:

'Anyone picking up this message, please answer so that we know you are there! What we need you to do is to keep looking for these messages. We are going to start as soon as we can and we will be sending them out at regular intervals.

We are using Micky's pocket computer to transmit these messages. Please answer soon if you get this message.

From Chrissie, Steve, Micky and Emma outside the cave in our secret valley.'

Almost immediately, a response came back:

'Dear Chrissie, Steve, Micky and Emma,
We got your message and will look out for more. Where are you? Do you need any help? Hope you enjoy your exploring!'

The Secondary School replied and a computer adventure had begun! More and more students became involved and the adventure took on a life of its own. Some of it was 'live' adventuring with messages coming back immediately, but most of it was time-shifted to convenient lessons in the participating schools' timetables.

The students were learning about communication, using their initiatives, composing storylines as well as becoming experts at word-processing!

4. THE TIMES NEWSPAPER DAY PROJECT

Newspaper Day is now a well-known, international event on Campus 2000. On a designated day, twice a year, schools across the world compete to produce the best newspaper, in real time, on a single school day.

This excellent project resulted from an In-Service Training Course, run by an enterprising Advisory Teacher. The course set out to explore the educational disciplines and benefits arising from producing a newspaper. Teachers were only allowed to take part provided that they brought along at least one pupil! From the outset, it was competitive.

TTNS has now run this project as a competition on six occasions, over a 3-year period. Schools must produce the newspaper on a single school day, thus experiencing the tight deadlines to which every daily newspaper works.

To this original idea, TTNS added many elements relating to electronic communications and, importantly, the Newspaper Industry.

* a News Agency (cf. Reuters, AP, AFP) was set up, staffed by students, to monitor the news of the day - through radio, TV, newspapers, newspaper wire services, etc - and to provide a stream of 'Agency reports' electronically to schools taking part. In addition, interviews are set up with well-known TV and Sports personalities, from which articles are produced and distributed.

* a Panel of Judges was recruited, all of whom are very experienced newspaper professionals. Each entry submitted to the competition, was guaranteed to have a brief, critical appraisal of it returned to the school by the judges.

* the help of a sponsor was enlisted to both finance the prizes - normally PCs, cash and books - to host the prizegiving and to produce a pack of information, badges, etc for the school to use during the competition. In return, the sponsor received considerable publicity both nationally and locally on TV and in the Press.

* the Newspaper Society - the UK organisation to which most local and regional newspapers belong - offered to help by telling its members what was going on and to urge them to advise schools in their locality in the skills of page layout, headlining, team organisation and so on.

The results have been of an extremely high standard. Little guidance is given on what schools should use to produce their finished product. Hence, some use simple word-processing packages, paste-up of pages and a photocopier! Others use sophisticated Desk Top Publishing, digitized photographs and diagrams and colour! One school has pursuaded the local newspaper to print 12,000 copies for distribution in the area. This was a 32-page tabloid newspaper, with colour, financed by advertising sold by members of the newspaper 'staff'. They also made a small profit!

When this competition was run, in March 1989, 170 schools took part, including 30 schools from Europe. Around 5,000 students took part and, in total, produced 45,000 newspapers.

4.1. Newspaper Day - Education Benefits

This project shows Information Technology being used in support of a high-value, cross-curricular activity. Many schools now want all of their students, at the age of 14 or 15, to experience this activity. There are always more schools wishing to take part than can be accommodated on a given day.

Schools see the following benefits for their students:

* working under pressure to very tight deadlines

* working in teams

* leadership, decision-making and delegation

* all students can contribute, regardless of ability

* the satisfaction of producing something to be proud of at the end of an intensive spell of hard work

* bring together a wide range of disciplines - art and design, creative writing relating to every school subject, editing, analysis, use of IT, interpersonal skills, business studies, photography, etc.

Schools also see considerable benefit for the school in becoming involved in such a project. Through the local newspaper, their efforts can be publicised to the local community, links with industry and commerce can be emphasised through advertising. Of course, if the school wins a prize, the local newspaper can headline *'Local School Wins Prize in International Competition'*!

A Public Relations vehicle has been created, inadvertently, for schools to use as they wish. At a time when the UK is undergoing its most radical reforms in the education system, many schools wish to emphasise their excellence in the face of falling rolls, school closures and commercially-minded governing bodies. Newspaper Day is one way in which they can achieve such profile.

5. FUN WITH ELECTRONIC COMMUNICATION

As well as the more formal uses of Campus 2000, there is a fun side as well.

Games and role play exercises have become more and more sophisticated and some, like the Stocks and Shares game, are directly relevant to the current Economics syllabus.

The game introduces students to the concept of Stocks and Shares. The aim is to invest in the shares of a portfolio of companies to maximise profit. As the game progresses, newsflashes appear which can affect the price of the shares. The news reflects typical events in the real world. These may concern the price of raw material used in manufacturing or they may concern a scandal involving the senior memeber of one of the companies.

At the end of the game, the team with the best return on their investment are the winners, although the real winners are the people who learn most from the experience.

Another project, which uses the commercial Travel service on Prestel, requires participants to organise a complete business trip to a remote part of the world using information from this commercial database.

Within a definable time-frame, the student has to prepare a check-list, obtain as much information as possible from the database and prepare a faultless itinerary for the imaginary traveller.

At the end of the exercise, students will have gained valuable experience in problem-solving, information handling, communication and evaluation.

Several adaptations can be made to this game, including limiting the cost of travel, changing the locations which must be avoided due to political unrest, or any other restriction which a teacher may think of.

6. CONCLUSIONS

Over the past five years, the use of Information Technology in schools has taken on a new dimension - it is now accepted as a regular tool in support of all curriculum subjects, for all age ranges from infants to senior students.

In the UK, certainly, the value of Government initiatives made in the mid-1980s is now becoming apparent - MEP and TVEI (Technical and Vocational Educational Initiative) in particular.

In some respects, computers have acted as a catalyst in breaking down traditional barriers between curriculum subjects. 'Cross-curricular' and 'Industry-Education' are the current buzz-words. Such activities will, undoubtedly, help every young person to attain his or her full potential educationally and in later life.

Communications-based projects help young people to understand the points of view and ways of life of students in other countries, perhaps on opposite sides of the world. This can only have a beneficial effect on future generations.

For teachers, computers and telecommunications bring a new dimension to curriculum development activities. The profession now has facilities for proper consultation and sharing of ideas between peer groups which up to now have just not been possible.

Communication for the Curriculum is a new concept. All sectors of education can benefit. Both teachers and students can now prepare for life in the 21st Century.

Give teachers the tools and they will finish the job!

Computers in Education
A. McDougall and C. Dowling (Editors)
Elsevier Science Publishers B.V. (North-Holland)

THE APPLICATIONS TECHNOLOGY SATELLITE NETWORKS: TWENTY YEARS OF DISTANCE EDUCATION IN THE PACIFIC BASIN

Stuart Kingan*, John Flanigan†, Gerald Knezek[Δ], and John Southworth[∂]

* Government of the Cook Islands, Box 66, Rarotonga, Cook Islands.
† Hawaii Loa College, 45-045 Kamehameha Hwy, Kaneohe, Hawaii, USA 96744.
Δ Department of Computer Education and Cognitive Systems, University of North Texas, P.O. Box 5155, Denton, Texas, USA 76203.
∂ Curriculum Research and Development Group, University of Hawaii, 1776 University Avenue, Honolulu, Hawaii, USA 96822.

NASA's Applications Technology Satellites have provided distance education opportunities in the Pacific Basin since 1971. This paper contains descriptions of the audioconferencing networks which have used the ATS series and chronicles how the satellites have aided education.

1. INTRODUCTION

The Applications Technology Satellites (ATS) were a series of six experimental satellites launched by the United States National Aeronautics and Space Administration (NASA) during 1966-75. ATS-2 (1967) reentered the atmosphere after two years of useful life. ATS-4 (1968) had a rocket separation malfunction and lasted just two months. ATS-5 (1969) carried out limited scientific experiments for several years before being ejected from geosynchronous orbit in 1986. ATS-6 (1975) was originally placed over the Atlantic Ocean, but was relocated several times to be used for activities such as the SITE project over India, before leaving orbit in 1979 [1;2].

ATS-1 (1966) and ATS-3 (1967) are nearly identical twins originally placed in geostationary orbit at 149 degrees West Longitude (North of Tahiti) and 75 degrees West Longitude (over the Atlantic), respectively. As ATS-3 began depleting its supply of station-keeping fuel in the early 1970's, it was moved to its present location of 105 degrees West Longitude, south of Baja, California [2]. This placement of ATS-1 and ATS-3 resulted in a combined earth coverage of the majority of the Pacific island nations, plus all of North and South America, plus portions of Antarctica, Australia, Japan and other areas in the Orient (see Figure 1).

In addition to sophisticated equipment which allowed innovations such as the first international television transmission and the first color pictures of clouds, ATS-1 and ATS-3 each contained a simple Very High Frequency (VHF) Transponder suitable for simplex (push-to-talk) voice communications with relatively low-cost, highly maintainable equipment [1]. This made the satellites highly attractive to the people of the Pacific Basin because they could be accessed with affordable ground station equipment readily available in the commercial sector and amateur radio community [3;4].

NASA first permitted educational access to ATS-1 in 1970, and since that time the ATS series has played an essential role in eight major cross-cultural communication networks in the Pacific Basin [5;6]. The remainder of this paper focuses on the activities of networks that have played a role in distance education in the Pacific.

2. THE PIONEERING EFFORTS OF PEACESAT

Pan-Pacific Education and Communication Experiments by Satellite (PEACESAT) was conceived in 1969 by John Bystrom, Communications Professor at the University of Hawaii. Bystrom asked NASA to allow Pacific Islanders free experimental access to ATS-1 when the satellite completed its scheduled NASA activities. His primary goal was the development of an interactive teleconferencing network [7]. PEACESAT was destined to became the first project in the world in which the delivery of instruction by satellite was attempted. It produced the world's first satellite library network, and the first college credit course delivered by satellite [8;4].

2.1. Communication Technology

Each PEACESAT station communicated over the ATS-1 satellite using a single voice channel in a simplex FM mode. Fully operational earth stations could be constructed for under $5000, using easy-to-maintain, off-the-shelf amateur radio equipment to broadcast (149 mHz) and receive (135 mHz) on either side of the amateur 2-meter radio band. A crossed-Yagi antenna with a 100-watt linear amplifier and a standard transceiver could access the transponder. Since no encoding was used, any good FM receiver tuned to 135.6 mHz could pick up the ATS-1 traffic [5]. A

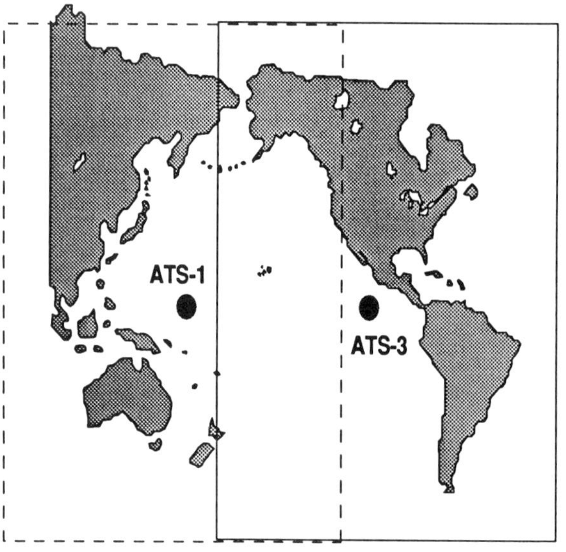

Earth Coverage:
ATS-1 at 195° West Longitude — — — — —
(relocated position as of 1984)
ATS-3 at 105° West Longitude ————

Figure 1: ATS-1 & ATS-3 Footprints

diagram of a typical ATS ground station, which was valid in 1972 and still commonly used today, is shown in Figure 2.

2.2. Developmental Chronology

PEACESAT officially began operations at the University of Hawaii in February, 1971 [9]. It became an international organization in early 1972, initially connecting the University of Hawaii in Honolulu, a remote campus in Hilo, and the community college in Maui, with Wellington Polytechnic in New Zealand, the University of the South Pacific in Suva, Fiji, and the medical center in Pago Pago, American Samoa.

Soon the Kingdom of Tonga was added to the system when a low-power terminal was installed at the teaching center in Nuku'Alofa. Next to become interested in the system was the University of Technology at Lae, New Guinea, where a low-power terminal was added to the system. Soon afterwards PEACESAT was joined by a terminal at Saipan in the Marianas.

The Cook Islands became interested in the PEACESAT network when two of their senior educators visited Honolulu and were given a demonstration in early 1972. As a result, in 1972 the Cook Islands Scientific Research Division set up a receiving facility in order to let people hear PEACESAT activities. Whenever an exchange was of special interest to any particular group, they were invited to come and listen. An application for a transmitting license and membership in PEACESAT quickly followed.

It was at that time in mid-1972, that Rarotonga was able to hear what was the first attempt at direct satellite broadcasting, when the United States rebroadcast a national public radio program via the ATS-1 satellite every afternoon for the benefit of ATS-1 listeners in Alaska. These broadcast programs were received in Rarotonga with excellent quality, rivaling the best reception of overseas shortwave broadcast. By the end of 1973 Rarotonga and a new terminal set up at the headquarters of the South Pacific Commission in Noumea, New Caledonia were cleared for full participation in PEACESAT.

During the remainder of the 1970's and 1980's, several dozen additional PEACESAT ground stations were established at other points in the Pacific islands and throughout the remainder of the Pacific Hemisphere. A representative listing of these is provided in Table 1.

2.3. Non-Credit Seminars

The types and varieties of exchanges conducted during the early days of PEACESAT showed the great potential of such a system in the independent scattered and developing areas of the world. Every week via PEACESAT, four or five exchanges would take place which were really noncredit seminars or conferences conducted on the network. Any terminal on the network was free to suggest a topic. If this was agreed to in a weekly scheduling meeting, a one-hour session was arranged as a pre-planning meeting. Here participants would go to their national terminals in countries which had persons interested in the topic. The procedure for the satellite exchange was discussed, methods were included on the agenda, and subsequent sessions to discuss the content of interest were scheduled. Also resolved at the planning session were issues such as who should chair each subsequent session and how many additional resource persons should be invited in on the discussion. Such seminars have involved subjects as diverse as medicine, agriculture, fisheries and ocean management, Pacific poetry, pottery, turtle farming, use of Landsat satellite images, Girl Guide activities, musicology, geology, soil science, traditional navigation, and many others.

2.4. Credit Courses

Credit courses were offered in PEACESAT's early days as well. These were initiated in mid-1972 with students and teachers at Victoria University in New Zealand, the University of South Pacific in Suva, the University of Hawaii, and the medical center in American Samoa participating. Medical research topics were discussed, particularly between Honolulu and Samoa. Tests using facsimile equipment resulted in very effective transmission of X-rays and EKGs between Honolulu and Wellington.

Other examples serve to illustrate the diversity of curricular topics. A course

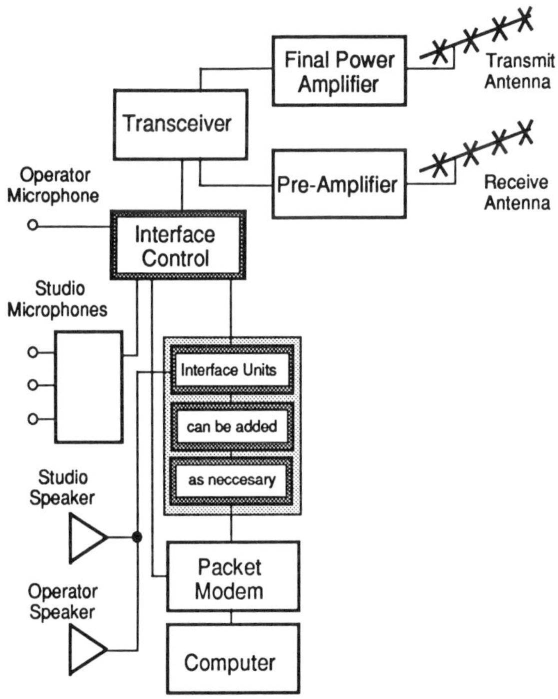

Figure 2
Standard ATS Ground Station

in Comparative Pacific Education was conducted jointly by the University of Hawaii and the University of the South Pacific in Fiji, during 1973. In 1975 the University of Hawaii organized a credit course, Communications in the Future, which occupied about 20 hours of satellite time and was participated in by students from Wellington, Honolulu, Rarotonga, and Suva. A teacher-training course called Politics of the Future was offered from the University of Hawaii to the Northern Marianas during the spring of 1980. This activity was somewhat unique because the instructor conducted lessons from PEACESAT terminals in Hawaii, Micronesia, and California, while at least one student from the Northern Marianas participated, while traveling, from Hawaii, Oregon (via phone patch), and Micronesia.

2.5. Public Sector Education

Public sector general information programs were also initiated during PEACESAT's early days. A weekly one-hour news exchange was initiated by the South Pacific Commission Media Center to keep each territory of the vast South Pacific region informed of activities of interest. Each participating station broadcast up to five minutes of local news which it felt would be of general interest to the region. This then became available to newspapers and radio in each location. This type of session has continued, on a limited basis, to the present day. The Samoan News Exchange continues to be held, in the Samoan language, every Saturday at GMT 2100.

During special events in the Pacific, PEACESAT has also been used for news conferences. These have originated from places such as South Pacific academic conferences and from the South Pacific Forum, an annual meeting of Prime Ministers of the region. For example, on his return from the 1974 Law of the Sea Conference, the Premier of the Cook Islands held a Pacific-wide press conference during which he gave his impressions of the meetings and answered questions from reporters in any country. During his return from Peking in 1975, U.S. President Gerald Ford delivered an important address at the East-West Center in Honolulu. This speech was taped and sent out immediately afterwards on PEACESAT and was rebroadcast by radio stations and published in newspapers throughout the Pacific.

The use of the PEACESAT network by the South Pacific Commission Headquarters in Noumea served a special purpose. It aided research in enabling the SPC headquarters to keep in touch with teams of research and advisory personnel that the Commission provides for the whole South Pacific region. It also gave them direct contact, when required, with senior officials or politicians in most member countries, thereby facilitating various aid projects.

As political changes have taken place in various Pacific territories, political leaders in one country have discussed their plans with leaders in other countries via PEACESAT as well as other networks utilizing the ATS satellites. Some present constitutions have no doubt been influenced in this way.

2.6. Scholarly Collaboration

An extremely important use of PEACESAT over the years has been scholarly international collaboration for the development of works such as this paper. The authors have held roundtable discussions via ATS-3 a half-dozen times during the preparation of this manuscript, in addition to correspondence by letter, point-to-point telephone, facsimile transmission, and electronic mail. PEACESAT has also been used for dissemination of scholarly works, as during the 1981 Pacific Telecommunications Conference, when one of the current authors (Flanigan) gave part of a presentation, via ATS-1, from American Samoa to a sizeable audience in Honolulu, while two others (Southworth and Knezek) delivered their portions of the presentation in person.

2.7. ATS Replacements

During the early 1980's, the amount of positioning fuel on ATS-1 became very low, and it was impossible to keep the satellite at 149 degrees West for more than a few months. In 1982, NASA decided to move it to a gravitationally more stable location at 162 degrees East where a small amount of fuel would keep it on-station for years and still serve the whole Pacific [9]. Unfortunately, there was insufficient fuel to accomplish this, and after running out of momentum when very near its target, ATS-1 started slowly drifting eastward. Finally, in August 1985 it was switched off after already having lost many key stations in the western Pacific. For practical purposes, this ended the Pacific-wide education networks. PEACESAT stations in the eastern Pacific, Samoa, Honolulu, Tonga, and Rarotonga continued on ATS-3.

1988 and 1989 saw a renewal of activity on ATS-1 as it slowly reappeared over the western Pacific, continuing its slow, circumnavigational oscillation around the globe. That its VHF transponder still works well after 23 years is a tribute to what is now regarded as obsolete technology.

The need for a full-scale continuation of Pacific Basin education and communication activities was recognized by the U.S. Congress which allocated money in 1988 to reactivate and improve service to the Pacific. Immediately, and for the next several years, a GOES satellite has been made available. Full Pacific-wide coverage with simultaneous voice and data channels should be aiding Pacific education by 1991.

PEACESAT is currently coordinated through the Social Science Research Institute at the University of Hawaii, under the direction of Dr. Donald Topping.

3. THE USP NETWORK

The University of the South Pacific, headquartered at Suva, Fiji, began its ATS operations as a PEACESAT member in 1972. One year later, USPNet was given its own ATS time-allocation to allow it to communicate with extension centers spread over eleven million square miles of ocean throughout the South Pacific [10]. This university is a regional one for which 10 South Pacific countries are responsible, and so it had a special need for a good communications network. Soon new stations were set up in Niue Island, Honiara, the Solomon Islands, Tarawa and the Gilbert Islands (now Kiribati) and at Port Vila in Vanuatu. Terminals were also installed in Tuvalu and Western Samoa.

The network set up by the University of the South Pacific had a threefold purpose.

Table 1 : Selected ATS Ground Stations and their Networks

Site		PEACESAT			
		ATS-1	ATS-3	USPNet	MicroNet
Honolulu, Hawaii	'71	√	√		
Wellington, New Zealand	'71	√			
Suva, Fiji	'72	√		√	
Nuku Alofa, Kingdom of Tonga	'72	√		√	
Lae, Papua New Guinea	'72	√		√	
Santa Cruz, California	'79	√			
Saipan, Commonwealth of The Nothern Marianas Islands	'72	√			√
Noumea, New Caledonia	'73	√		√	
Rarotonga, Cook Islands	'73	√	√	√	
Niue	'74	√		√	
Honiara, Solomon Islands	'74	√		√	
Tarawa, Kiribati (Gilbert Islands)	'74	√		√	
Vila, Vanuatu (New Hebrides)	'74	√		√	
Apia, Western Samoa	'74	√		√	
Funafuti, Tuvalu	'75	√		√	
Guam, N. Mariana Islands	'75	√			√
Sydney, Australia	'75	√			
La Trobe, Australia	'76	√			
Adelaide, Australia	'77	√			
Perth, Australia	'77	√			
Toowoomba, Australia	'77	√			
Darwin, Australia	'77	√			
Canberra, Australia	'77	√			
Kelvin Grove, Australia	'77	√			
Magill, Australia	'77	√			
Footscray, Australia	'77	√			
Bently, Australia	'77	√			
Launceston, Australia	'77	√			
Alafua, Western Samoa	'78	√	√	√	
Pago Pago, American Samoa	'72	√	√		
Tucson, Arizona	'86		√		
Denton, Texas	'88		√		
Chicago, Illinois	'85		√		
Costa Rica, Central America	'87		√		
Sonora, Mexico	'89		√		
Pitcairn Island	'88		√		
Sonoita, Arizona	'86		√		
Walkerswood, Jamaica	'89		√		
Sweet Home, Oregon	'88		√		
Palau, Republic of Belau	'78	√			√
Majuro, Rep of Marshall Island	'78	√			√
Federated States of Micronesia					
Kosrae	'78	√			√
Pohnepei	'78	√			√
Truk	'78	√			√

Primarily, it was used for administrative communication between the university extension services on the main campus in Suva and each of its extension centers throughout the South Pacific. A second important function was direct instruction to and discussions with extension students. Third, a new university extension teaching method was developed where, in addition to the usual correspondence material and assignments, students were provided with taped lectures by mail each week and these were followed up by one-hour satellite sessions in which the lecturer asked the students questions and introduced further materials.

The success of this method of teaching has often been spectacular. Several years ago in Rarotonga, a fifteen week class which started with twelve students, and in which attendance at satellite sessions was required, ended with no dropouts and all students successfully passing the examination. This contrasted with normal correspondence classes in which the drop out rate was always high, less than one-third normally completing the course. In another example, a degree credit course of 15 weeks was conducted via satellite with students in four territories and simultaneous face-to-face teaching on the Suva campus. A final examination which was conducted externally resulted in a 100% pass rate among satellite students, but only a 66% pass rate was obtained among the on-campus students.

The USP Network is clearly the ATS leader in the category of "traditional tele-teaching." In 1980, 79% of its air time was devoted to external studies. In 1981, the network supported 46 courses, enrolling nearly 2000 students [5].

USPNet ceased to function as an ATS network when ATS-1 began drifting easterly out of the range of many of its ground stations in 1984. USP eventually entered into an agreement to use commercial Intelsat communications to continue its tele-teaching operations.

4. ALASKA EXPERIENCES

In the 1970's the National Education Association (NEA) of the United States organized a monthly series of satellite meetings allowing school teachers in isolated parts of the contiguous U.S., Alaska, and the Pacific to discuss various educational matters. This involved more participants than any satellite discussion yet conducted. The ATS-1 satellite was linked to ATS-3 through a connecting station in Denver, Colorado and the sessions were conducted by NEA personnel operating at the Goddard Space Flight Center terminal in Greenbelt, Maryland. After some initial problems, the quality of the Denver relay signal was quite comparable with those of a single satellite linking. Included as part of this series was a graduate course entitled "Satellite Seminar," which allowed teachers in remote Alaskan villages to earn credit at the University of Alaska.

The Pacific AFS/PEACESAT Educational Communication System (PAFSPECS) held ATS-1 exchanges with American Field Service chapters in Anchorage and Juneau during the early 1970's. The two Alaskan sites participated in the trans-Pacific programming and used PEACESAT to establish the first short-term exchange of American Field Service students between their two otherwise isolated communities.

The National Library of Medicine began an experiment in 1971 to determine whether satellite communication could improve the quality of health care and education provided to native people in remote Alaskan villages. With technical support from the Geophysical Institute of the University of Alaska, simple ground stations were installed in villages in the Tanana region of central Alaska, where communication by HF radio had been unreliable. The doctor at the Public Health Service Hospital was able to contact the village health aides daily via ATS-1 to consult on patient diagnosis and management and to arrange emergency evacuations. A satellite link was also provided to the Alaskan Native Medical Center in Anchorage. A line from the ground stations to the village schools allowed village children and families to participate in educational programs and cultural exchanges [11].

Alaska began the transition to operational satellite service for health communications and public telephone in 1976. Satellite stations purchased by the state and operated by ALASCOM using RCA SATCOM I were located in more than 100 villages by 1981. The Medical Conferencing Network operated by the Public Health Service using this system was modeled on the ATS-1 experimental network [11].

5. PUBLIC HEALTH NETWORK

Another educational/social service network had also developed on ATS-1 by the mid 1970's. That was a medical network involving the National Institute of Health (NIH) in Bethesda, Maryland, the NIH Virus Laboratory in Honolulu, American Samoa, and Rarotonga. Soon the Australian National University in Canberra, Australia joined that network.

Medical research in the Pacific was greatly accelerated and facilitated through the NIH network on ATS-1 and the frequent cooperation of other Pacific terminals in this organization. Two examples will illustrate the value of this network. First, during a number of outbreaks of Denge fever in the Pacific, research workers in Honolulu and Dunedin were kept in frequent contact with doctors and research workers in the field in Fiji, Noumea, Tonga, Niue and Rarotonga, the islands which had outbreaks. These exchanges speeded up virus identification, treatment of victims, and preventative measures against further spread. Secondly, an expedition was made in 1974 and 1975 to the island of Mauke in the Cook Islands from the National Institute of Health in Bethesda, Maryland to study the disease of filariasis. Choice of location and all the arrangements for taking the expedition were made in advance through discussions on the satellite directly between Rarotonga and Washington. Practically no exchange of paperwork was required. Contact was maintained for three months between the Bethesda terminal and the people on the island using the satellite terminal in Rarotonga and a high frequency radio link between the Rarotonga terminal and the island. The result was a very efficient expedition. Instead of being isolated, researchers had all of their excellent resources in the U.S. readily available.

6. WEATHER SERVICE NETWORK

For many years after ATS-1's launch in 1966, its transponder was used for a unique educational broadcasting service, that of WEFAX, a twice daily broadcast on facsimile of the world's weather. The U.S. Weather Service created maps of all parts of the world showing cloud cover and broadcast these together with pages of synoptic reports to whomever wished to receive them. Most major weather stations in the Pacific Ocean were equipped to receive these. Ships and even private yachts could purchase WEFAX receivers and receive these broadcasts from either ATS-1 in the Pacific or ATS-3 in the Atlantic.

7. HIGHER EDUCATION RESEARCH

The ATS-1 transponder was also used by the ALOHA network based at the Engineering School at the University of Hawaii for the sending and receiving of computer data packets between Hawaii, Alaska, and other places. Early work in this field by Dr. Norm Abrahamson and his colleagues later resulted in the creation of Ethernet, now one of the de facto standards for cable-based local area networks worldwide. Early experiments between PEACESAT and ALOHA also showed that voice communications on one channel and data communications on another channel can proceed simultaneously on the main transmitter without either significantly interfering with the other. Similarly, an experiment was carried out in New Guinea where two stations communicated by a portable teletype unit on ATS-1, while Rarotonga and Wellington used the same channel for voice interchange. Very little deterioration to either circuit resulted. Currently, research is underway at the University of North Texas, the University of Guam, and the University of Hawaii to implement computer-based messaging systems via ATS-1 and ATS-3. By utilizing low-cost packet radio technology recently developed in the amateur radio community, it is hoped that operating schedules and seminar agendas can be distributed digitally during off-peak hours, providing more time for discussion during satellite exchanges.

8. THE AUSTRALIAN NETWORK

In 1981, several Australian stations inaugurated an ATS-1 network for experimentation with satellite teleconferencing, in preparation for the Australian Domestic Satellite due to be launched in 1985. It was initiated by Latrobe University to give as many individuals and institutions as possible the opportunity to promote experiments and demonstrations in satellite telecommunications, though not to the exclusion of, or in competition with, established terrestrial systems [5].

By 1984, Kangaroo Net included 15 Australian terminals and occupied 22.5 hours per week on ATS-1. There were eight regular stations active on a daily basis, representing each of the Australian states: The University of Sydney, Latrobe University, the South Australian Education Technology Center, Canberra College of Advanced Education, The University of Western Australia, Darling Downs Institute of Advanced Education, Darwin Community College, the Australian Maritime College and the Australian National University. Occasional stations included portable units owned by Latrobe University and the South Australia Educational Technology Center, and permanent installations at the Western Australian Institute of Technology, the South Australian College of Advanced Education, Mitchell College of Advanced Education, Bruce College of Technical and Further Education, and Footscray Institute. These stations operated on an irregular basis in the Kangaroo Net, and had access to Pacific-wide ATS-1 networks on request [5].

Overall coordination of the Kangaroo Net was provided by Dr. Steve Seumahu of Latrobe University's Department of Electronic and Communication Science and Dr. Peter White of Latrobe's Media Center. Latrobe University was responsible to NASA for the use of the ATS-1 satellite in Australia.

Kangaroo Net as an ATS entity ceased to function when ATS-1 drifted easterly out of Australia's line of sight in 1984.

9. THE MICRONESIAN NETWORK

In 1978, the U.S. Department of the Interior established a network to assist in the administration of the U.S. Trust Territories of the Pacific Islands (Micronesia). This network was used to connect hospitals, schools and administrative centers, as well as to support Peace Corps (the U.S. volunteer service agency) activities in the region. It was used for inter-island communication and for communication to the United States through the Public Service Satellite

Consortium's station in Denver. By the time the ATS-1 satellite was moved out of range of the Denver station in 1982, traffic had dwindled to daily telephone patches between the Ponape (Pohnpei) political status commission and their representatives in Hawaii and Washington. At that time, Mike Caldwell at the University of Guam began an educational and public service network, combining features of the PEACESAT and USP nets, using the time which was left vacant by the earlier Department of the Interior users. These early efforts included audio teleconferencing, slow-scan television, data communication, and even some television experiments via ATS-6. The ATS-1 satellite was used for course delivery and administrative planning within the regional Pacific Post-secondary Education Council, a consortium of schools in the American-flag territories [5].

In 1983, the Pacific Post-secondary Education Council (PPEC) took full control of the former Department of the Interior network to establish Micronet. The Network initially consisted of terminals in the higher education institutions in Saipan, Yap, Guam, Truk, and Ponape (Pohnpei), with users including the Consortium of Pacific Arts Councils, the Secondary Education Curriculum Project, the Headstart (primary school) program, the ATS-1 Computer Project and the Federated States of Micronesia Political Status Commission, in addition to the PPEC members. Each Micronesia station also took part in the PEACESAT network, finding participants for Pacific-wide conferences of local interest [5].

Two examples serve to illustrate the types of distance education credit courses offered in Micronesia. In the spring of 1985, the University of Guam was asked to deliver an American History course to 15 teachers on Kosrae (Kusaie), approximately 1100 miles from the campus [12]. The instructor attended the first and last class meetings in person, mailed videotapes of Alistair Cooke's America series for the major lecture content, and used ATS-1 to conduct follow up discussions with students.

A similarly formatted course concerned with the history and philosophy of science was delivered concurrently to Pohnpei and Kosrae during the spring of 1989 [12]. In this course, single side band (SSB), high frequency radio was the primary discussion medium, while ATS-1, which had once again drifted into sight of the Western Pacific, was the backup medium.

As of December, 1989, the ATS-1 Satellite had again drifted out of sight to the Western Pacific, so the University of Guam began experimenting with HF radio - ATS-3 cross patches, via PEACESAT Honolulu, in hopes of delivering distance education curricula to sites (such as America Samoa) within the remaining satellite's footprint.

10. TRANS-NETWORK ACTIVITIES

Many educational activities spanning more than one ATS network and/or telecommunications medium have taken place over the past twenty years.

10.1. Slow Scan Television Experiments

Some promising experimentation has been done over the years using Slow-Scan Television (SSTV) via satellite and dial-up telephone lines. Participants have been located on the U.S. mainland, in Pacific Basin metropolitan areas such as Sydney, Australia, Wellington, New Zealand, and Suva, Fiji, and at smaller, more remote Pacific locations such as American Samoa (population c. 30,000), Saipan (c. 12,000), Rarotonga (population c. 10,000), and Niue Island (population c. 4,000).

10.2. Multi-Mode Node Teleconferencing

Many ATS sessions have incorporated a technique developed by John Southworth, Multi-Mode Node (MMN) Electronic Conferencing [13]. When using this technique, an MMN moderator typically sat in the ground terminal in Honolulu, listening and transcribing audio satellite discussion for immediate entry into a computer-based infromation system such as the Electronic Information Exchange System (EIES) at the New Jersey Institute of Technology (NJIT). The computer was usually connected to the system from Honolulu, via Telenet, a public data communications network. As feedback from the Mainland U.S. and Canada was received via a service such as EIES in Honolulu, the moderator would read the message to ATS participants. In this way, semi-interactive participation was potentially available from anyone with a computer, a modem, and access to a telephone line. This method also produced a written record of much of a satellite exchange.

10.3. Cross-Cultural Exchanges

Elementary and secondary school students have been introduced to telecommunications through a variety of programs over ATS-1 and later ATS-3. These often involved informal meetings of students at two or more locations to discuss topics of common interest dealing with cross-cultural issues. One of the longer-running projects was coordinated by volunteers of the American Field Service International Scholarship program in Hawaii, New Zealand, Australia, and Alaska. Duplicate sets of colored transparency slides were posted to participating stations prior to a program. The slides were simultaneously projected locally with narration and discussion carried by ATS-1 or ATS-3 [14].

In 1981, Project MENTOR (Marine Educators Network to Organize Resources) involved satellite teleconferencing, computer networking (PLATO and EIES systems), along with an innovative water-quality data gathering experience. Science classes in

American Samoa, New Zealand, Hawaii, and Florida made simultaneous water quality tests from the University of Hawaii College of Education Curriculum Research and Development Group's HMSS (High School Marine Science Studies Program). The data gathered was transmitted via computer from Florida and Hawaii and shared via a PEACESAT teleconference with Samoa and New Zealand [15].

11. LESSONS LEARNED

Twenty years of access to the Applications Technology Satellites have enabled educators in the Pacific Hemisphere to learn valuable distance education lessons. These are briefly summarized for an instructor considering the use of satellite teleconferencing with students.

First, due to varying quality of audio signal strength, the use of good diction, language, voice projection and appropriate volume greatly aids microphone-based communication in a teleconferencing environment. Persons not familiar with audio telecommunication techniques and protocol should first either sit in on sessions as observers or hold practice sessions.

Second, the use of computer communication, facsimile and other multimedia resources can greatly enhance an audio-based teleconferencing presentation. Multimedia resources should be carefully evaluated to determine their most appropriate uses in planning and carrying out teleconferences.

Third, all media-based presentations need a contingency plan. If the particular installation cannot afford a fully redundant complement of equipment, facilities, and support staff, then the individual instructor must plan for alternative methods of carrying on with the business of education, in the event some key component of the preferred system fails.

In the ATS distance education world, contingency plans often include: a) training a second operator, perhaps a student, to provide backup operations in the event the primary operator is unavailable, b) securing permission in advance to use the telephone to make an expensive conference call, in the event of interrupted satellite service, c) planning for more than one medium of presentation (e.g., voice and computer conferencing) so that if one fails, not all is lost, and d) maintaining addresses and phone numbers of class members or seminar participants, so as a last resort, the leader/instructor can contact participants by mail.

REFERENCES

[1] ATS-1 & -3 Experimenter's Guide, Revision 5 (NASA, Mar. 1984).

[2] Eden, P., Personal communications with NASA's ATS-3 Operations Manager during Sept. 1989.

[3] Nose, K., Using the ATS-1 Weather Satellite for Communications QST 55(12) (Dec. 1971) 48-51.

[4] PEACESAT Project Report One: Early Experience (Honolulu: University of Hawaii, 1975).

[5] Lange, J., Casey, R., Dunqua, B., Dunnet, C., Knezek, G., Flanigan, F., Flavel, F., Houlton, E., Livingston, K., Seumahu, S., Scannell, P. and Spooner, P., ATS-1: Social Service Satellite Networks in the Pacific. Proceedings of the Sixth Pacific Telecommunications Conference (PTC) (Honolulu: Pacific Telecommunications Council, 1984) 109-118.

[6] Mukaida, L., Knezek, G., Scannell, P., Jones, G., Avegalio, T., Freese, A. and Haak, J., Pacific Island Interactive Database Network Access: A PEACESAT, PICHTR, University of Hawaii Library Pilot Project. Proceedings of the 11th PTC (Honolulu: Pacific Telecommunications Coucil, 1989) 494-501.

[7] Bystrom, J. and Yuen, P., Report and Request to the National Aeronautics and Space Administration (Honolulu: University of Hawaii, 1971).

[8] Tate, P. J. and Kressel, M. eds., The Expanding Role of Telecommunications in Higher Education (San Francisco: Jossey-Bass, 1983).

[9] Knudsen, G., Marking Time at PEACESAT. Satellite Communications (Nov. 1985) 45-48.

[10] Miller, J. K., The USPNet Outreach Programming: Evaluation and Guidelines for Future Use, Proceedings of the PTC (Honolulu, Jan. 1981) B8-5-B8-12.

[11] Hudson, H. E., Pacific Telecommunications After ATS-1: Reflections on ATS-1's Fifteenth Birthday, Proceedings of PTC 2 (Jan. 1982) 152-154.

[12] Boughton, G. J., Distance Education in the Western Pacific, Pacific Telecommunications 10(2) (May 1989) 21-23.

[13] Southworth, J., Flanigan, J., and Knezek, G., Computers in Education: International Multi-Mode Node Electronic Conferencing., The Printout 3(3) (1981) 8-13.

[14] Southworth, J. H., Use of Multi-Media Technology in Cross-Cultural Education, presentation at the World Educators Conference, (Honolulu, Hawaii, Jul. 1977).

[15] Southworth, J.H. and Klemm, E.B., Increasing Gloval Understanding Through Telecommunications, NASSP Bulletin 69(480) (Apr. 1985) 39-44.

[16] Kingan, S.G., Appropriate Communications for Development. Proceedings of the PTC (Honolulu: Jan. 1980) 2I-1-2I-8.

[17] Kingan, T., The Social Benefits of Good Economical Communications with Isolated Areas,Proceedings of the PTC, (Honolulu: Jan. 1982) 79-80.

[18] Davis, Sir Thomas, KBE, Communication and Developing Countries in the Pacific, Proceedings of the PTC (Honolulu: Jan. 1982) 2-5.

Computers in Education
A. McDougall and C. Dowling (Editors)
Elsevier Science Publishers B.V. (North-Holland)

A NETWORKING EDUCATIONAL SYSTEM WITH NESPAC

Masahiko KURATA,* Yukiko MAEKAWA,* Yutaka NOMURA,* Shigeo MATSUSHITA,*
Koichi INOTSUME,** and Yasuo OHTAKE**

NEC Corporation, C&C Public Systems Div., 7-1, Shiba 5-Chome, Minato-ku, TOKYO 108-01 Japan:* NEC Institute of Management Ltd., 10-3, Shiba 4-Chome, Minato-ku, TOKYO 108, Japan.**

As industrial activities have been spread out throughout all of the country, it becomes important to keep equal education standard throughout the network regardless of region. NESPAC (NEC Satellite Pedagogical Network for Advanced Creative Education) is a bidirectional video distance education system, using a communication satellite, which is produced by NEC Corporation for in-house education. It became operational in May 1987. In NESPAC trainees in all of the classrooms take instructors simultaneously as if they are in the same classroom. In this paper the system configuration and characteristics of NESPAC and a brief evaluation of system utilization after two-and-a-half years experience are described.

1. INTRODUCTION

With the expansion of information usage, the industrial activities will be spread out. Expansion has been increasing in recent years to all of the country. With such dispersion and dissemination of corporate activities, industrial education and in-house education will face new problems as below.

1. How to keep equal education standards through the network regardless of region.

2. How to provide service without regional time lag.

3. How to establish an education structure that can cope with the diversified educational needs.

In order to meet with the above needs, an educational network using the latest media is required to cover not only domestic locations, but overseas locations.

NESPAC (NEC Satellite Pedagogical Network for Advanced Creative Education) is a two-way video distance education system, using a communications satellite, which is produced by NEC Corporation for in-house education. It became operational in May, 1987, linking NEC Technical College in Kawasaki with NEC's Kyushu satellite classroom in Fukuoka. Additional satellite classrooms for NESPAC were built in Sapporo, Sendai, Tokyo, Nagoya, Osaka, Hiroshima, Kanazawa and Takamatsu. NESPAC covers nine major cities in Japan. Figure 1 represents the network map of NESPAC. This system is used to educate all members of the NEC group including engineers, technicians, sales personnel, system engineers and managers.(1)

There are many kinds of teaching/instructional styles in a traditional classroom. It is important to recognize which kinds of teaching/instructional styles are manageable with a two-way video distance education system. The teaching methods for a two-way video distance education system have been investigated using NESPAC.

The system configuration and characteristics of NESPAC has been presented previously (1)(2)(3). In this paper a brief evaluation of system utilization after two and a half years experience is described.

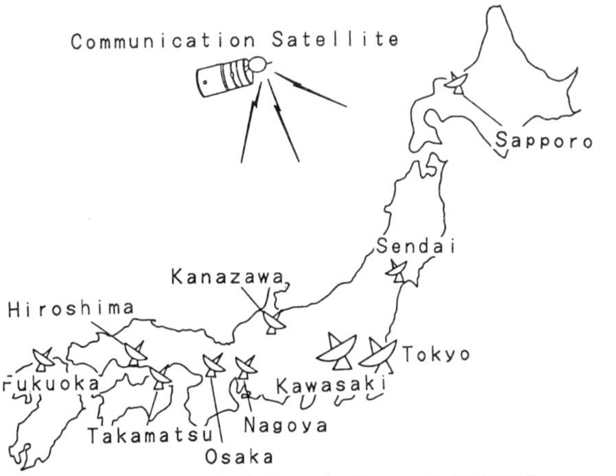

Figure 1. A Network Map of NESPAC

2. SYSTEM CHARACTERISTICS

NESPAC realizes that trainees in all of these classrooms take instructors simultaneously as if they are in the same classroom. It is possible because of two primary characteristics of NESPAC. One of them is real time two way communications by two video frames, audio and data of EB (Electrical Blackboard). The other is 1 to N multi points transmission which represents the one instructor site linking to N trainees' sites.

2.1. Real time two way communication

Trainee action and teacher feedback information are very important in education because they promote trainees' understanding and also increase their motivation. They make the quality of education superior. Therefore exchange of information is essential in education.

NESPAC realizes the importance of the exchange of information by its characteristics, real time two-way communications. It is communication by two video frames, audio and data of EB. Because of this two-way communication feature it is possible with NESPAC for an instructor and trainees to watch and talk to each other simultaneously.

2.2. 1 to N multi points transmission

Information in NESPAC (two video frames, audio and data of EB) is transmitted by satellite communication network. This satellite communication network is made up of two satellite communication circuits which can handle information at 1.5Mbps data bit rate.

Information from a center classroom with an instructor is broadcast to every satellite classroom by one of these communication circuits. Information from any one of the satellite classrooms is transmitted to the center classroom by the other communication circuit. This circuit for information from satellite classroom to center classroom is used by each of the satellite classrooms. This system utilizes the mobile broadcast method.

This method realizes communication between an instructor and trainees in the following manner:

1. Trainees can let their instructor know that they have questions at any time.

2. An instructor can choose a satellite classroom which he/she watches or talks with by himself/herself.

3. Trainees in the classroom that are chosen by an instructor can communicate with the instructor by using two video frames, audio and data of EB. They can watch and talk to each other.

4. Trainees in other satellite classrooms can listen and watch the communication between the instructor and the trainees.

This method is called 1 to N multi points transmission and is presented in Figures 2(a) and 2(b).

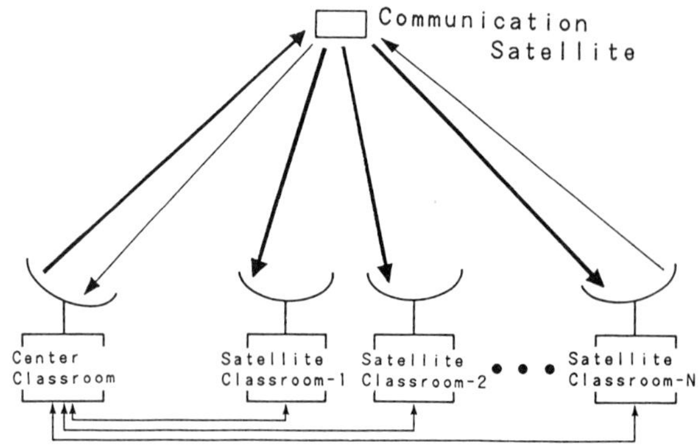

(a) Trainees in every satellite classroom can listen and watch the lecture by an instructor. The instructor can choose a satellite classroom which he/she watches by himself/herself.

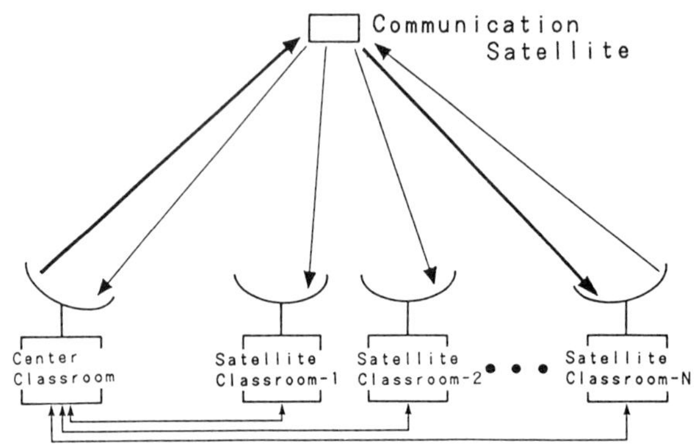

(b) Trainees in the classroom that is chosen by an instructor can communicate with the instructor. They can watch and talk to each other. Trainees in other satellite classrooms can listen and watch the communication between the instructor and trainees.

Figure 2. I to N Multi Points Transmission
According to teaching methods, either of the two transmission systems shown above is selected.

3. THE PRESENT CONDITION OF NESPAC USE

3.1. Usage trend of NESPAC

Usage of NESPAC has been increasing since 1987. The rate of usage versus available time is almost 100%. This means that NESPAC is nearly always used during the available office hour period. Although NESPAC is nearly fully used, requests for use of NESPAC are still increasing. As a result, education courses using NESPAC are recently being held not only during office hours but also after office hours and on holidays.

The sections of NEC which use NESPAC have also been increasing. There are a variety of divisions and subsidiaries now represented as users of NESPAC.

3.2. Education Programs Using NESPAC

A variety of educational programs are currently using NESPAC. They are shown as follows:

* Managerial Skills Development Program,
* Technology Education Program for Engineers,
* Software Education Program,
* New Products Introduction Program for Salesmen,
* Technicians Enrichment Program,
* Language Ability Development Program.

The most frequently held NESPAC program is software education. Over 50% of the courses and trainees are currently registered in the software education program. Other NESPAC programs frequently offered are technology education and sales education programs.

4. HOW TO USE NESPAC SKILLFULLY

Many kinds of teaching methods are tried based on psychological characteristics of two-way video distance education system. This section takes some of the classes using NESPAC and describes techniques for administering distance education effectively.

4.1. Lecture with Discussion

As a typical example of the style of lecture with discussion, one of the classes of software education is presented below. In Fig. 3 and Fig. 4, scenes of this style of education are represented. The purpose of this class is to make the knowledge standard of system engineers equal by giving them the latest knowledge. This class should be given to many system engineers. As a result, this class has a large number of trainees.

The satellite classrooms and the number of trainees in each one are as follows:

Total number of trainees		90
Center classroom (Tokyo)		40
Satellite classroom	(Sapporo)	10
	(Sendai)	10
	(Osaka)	20
	(Fukuoka)	10

The instructor is a software education specialist in our company. The instructor operates the document camera and cameras in the classroom, and selects video frames sent to satellite classrooms and those received from them.

The main part of the class is a lecture by the instructor. She explains topics mainly by using prepared OHP (overhead projector) sheets. Sometimes she writes information on white papers during instructional time and adds explanations to show the new information. This is done by using a document camera.

Figure 3. A Classroom Scene of Software Education

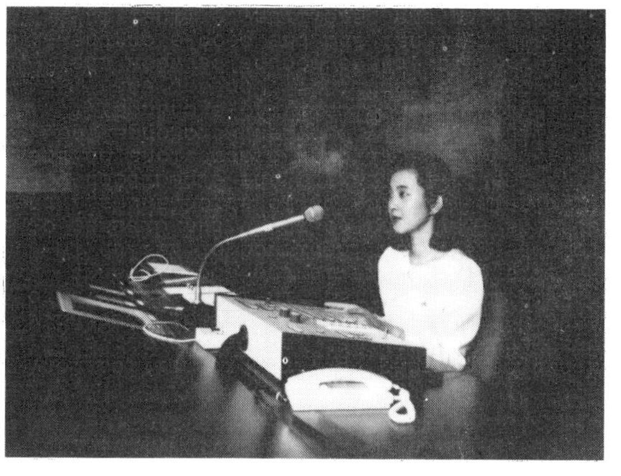

Figure 4. The Instructor and the Control Panel

This method of writing on paper and showing by using the document camera is in place of using a blackboard. It is effective because it avoids the monotony which education with media is apt to create. The monotony of a class is created when teaching materials (e.g., OHP sheets, teaching materials) are too prepared and shown sequentially. The method of writing promotes trainees' concentration on a class even though the content of writing is prepared before.

Videos sent to satellite classrooms during the lecture usually consist of an image of the instructor and an image of the teaching materials. Two images of the teaching materials are also sent to satellite classrooms on occasion. Two video frames are chosen by the instructor according to the progress of the class. These methods make a class interesting with various presentations and also make trainees relaxed with a high concentration level. In education with media, the mental state of trainees should be carefully considered. Therefore the choice of videos according to the class progress or writing becomes an important method of distance education, especially in a class where interactive communications are few.

The instructor asks a satellite classroom to report results from specific prepared questions. At this time, videos from this satellite classroom (including an image of a trainee who is answering) are shown on video projectors of other classrooms. This kind of Q & A format gives communications opportunities to trainees. It promotes them to concentrate on the class and increases their motivation. And it also promotes additional questions. Q & A discussions between an instructor and trainees in satellite classrooms are very effective.

The most important thing in lecture format is to avoid monotony. Another important thing is to send an image of the instructor to satellite classrooms as much as possible. An image of the instructor gives a positive effect especially in the mental state of trainees. This should be considered in distance education more than in traditional local education. Trainees feel neglected if they take a class without an image of the instructor but only with images of the teaching materials. Therefore sending an image of the instructor is also one of the essential methods in distance education.

4.2. Lecture with Problem Solving and Trainees' Presentation

As an example of the style of lecture with problem solving and trainees' presentation, education about software production control is presented as follows. The main part of the class is group practice and presentation about its results. One group is made up of four or five trainees. The process of a class is in order of lecture, 20 minutes of group practice, presentation by a group about the result of practised activity, taking different opinions from other groups, comments by an instructor, and Q & As.

The most important part of this class is presentation about the results of group practice and exchange of opinions about it among all of the class members including an instructor. Therefore the number of trainees is small. The class size is required to be appropriate for making every trainee participate in this exchange of opinions.

The satellite classrooms and the number of trainees in each one are as follows:

Total number of trainees		32 (7 groups)
Center Classroom	(Tokyo)	15 (3 groups)
Satellite classroom	(Sapporo)	8 (2 groups)
	(Sendai)	4 (1 group)
	(Fukuoka)	5 (1 group)

From our experience, the maximum number of trainees in group practice is 48 (four trainees x 12 groups).

The education staff of this class is two. One is an instructor and the other is the operator of center classroom. The instructor is an engineer of our company. He is a specialist of software production control but not in education. The operator is also a specialist of software production control with some experience in teaching the same course.

An operator of the center classroom is necessary in this teaching style. It is more important for an instructor to catch trainees' progress (including their progress of practice, their reactions, etc.) in a class of lecture with problem-solving and trainees' presentation than in a lecture with discussion class. Therefore, communications among members of the class are frequently done.

It is desirable for the operator to know about the content of the class as well. Classes of practice are composed of many different scenes. They have to let all trainees understand what happened in the class. Appropriate operational knowledge about video images becomes more important and also becomes more difficult. Therefore, an operator should be required to know more about the content of the class than system operations.

The design of making teaching materials for presentation (OHP sheets, documents) is very important in distance education. The size of their characters and charts have to be big enough to read.

The quantity of information, the organization of content and expressions have to be suitable to let trainees use their head. They concentrate on the information from an instructor still more by filling their blanks with the instructor's intentions. OHP sheets used in this class are made very well by considering these points in the development of presentation materials.

During twenty minutes of practice, video images of trainees in the center classroom are transmitted to satellite classrooms and those of trainees in a satellite classroom are transmitted to the center classroom. This is effective to promote trainees' feeling that they are all joined in one class.

The most difficult thing for an instructor is how to observe the trainees' progress in working during twenty minutes of practice. In order to observe it, the instructor watches video images of satellite classrooms one by one. Video images of satellite classrooms are made before the class so that the instructor can watch each of the trainees' faces. This is done because there is no operator in satellite classrooms. However it is not possible for the instructor to examine the working progress of each group. Therefore, the instructor asks for a working progress report by every group in satellite classrooms to the center classroom.

Presentations are done by every group. Presentation from a group in the center classroom is done by using the blackboard. Presentation from a group in a satellite classroom is done by writing on white paper and using the document camera. After this, the instructor asks other groups if they have different results or some comments on the presentation of the results. He also provides Q & A time at the end of each lesson.

As this example shows, it is very important to evaluate how well each trainee understands the class in this style of distance education.

4.3. Lecture with Laboratory Activity

As an example of lecture with laboratory activity, one of the classes from a technicians' enrichment program is presented below. In Fig. 5, a scene of this style is represented. It is about a micro-computer circuit. The main part of the class is a 30 minute individual practice session about programming and individual practice with a real machine, a micro-computer training circuit. Each member of the class as well as the instructor has this micro-computer training circuit. The classroom process includes a lecture, 30 minutes of practice or machine training, representations by trainees, different opinions from others, comments by the instructor and Q & As.

In the lecture with laboratory activity class type, an education staff must be composed of an instructor and sub-instructors. Machine training requires face-to-face-type instructions. However, it is almost impossible for the instructor to do this for trainees in a satellite classroom. For example, when a trainee's machine in a satellite classroom doesn't work because of a wrong operation, the instructor can neither fix it nor advise the trainee about this event. Sub-instructors play a vital role in these class types.

The class presented in this paper has a sub-instructor in every satellite classroom. In this type of distance education, it is essential that an instructor and sub-instructors co-operate together. Sub-instructors instruct trainees face-to-face and report their working progress or their comprehension to an instructor. The instructor listens to each of these sub-instructors' reports and administers the class. It is a very important role for an instructor to administer the class so that trainees feel they all join together in the same class.

The satellite classrooms and the number of trainees in each one and the education staff are as follows.

*Total number of trainees	17
Center classroom (Kawasaki)	0
Satellite classrooms (Osaka)	8
(Fukuoka)	9
*Education staff - Instructor	1
Sub-instructors	2

Figure 5. A Satellite Classroom Scene of the Micro-Computer Circuit Course

This class uses only two satellite classrooms. No trainee is in the center classroom. As a result, the instructor frequently exchanges information with sub-instructors and every trainee can get opportunities for presentation. The instructor also can ask each trainee for individual presentations. This is an effective approach in distance education. This is a method to use so that trainees don't feel neglected by the instructor.

5. EVALUATION OF NESPAC

Questionnaires on usage of NESPAC are administered after every course to each of the participants. The questionnaire contains the items on the quality of video/audio, method of instruction, physical conditions and significance of NESPAC. The items on video quality are most severely and seriously evaluated. This is because most information is accepted through the sense of sight. It is said that communication between persons with video is indispensable. However, in our experiences teaching courses could be administered even though video is interrupted as long as printed matters are sufficiently prepared. On the contrary teaching courses could not be administered if audio is interrupted. This fact never means that video is inferior to audio in ordinary teaching courses.

We are familiar with video such as TV and have an ability to evaluate quality of video. Trainees are not satisfied with low-quality video. Low-quality video spoils trainees' motivation. Quality video has two aspects, which include performance of video system and the format of teaching materials. As mentioned above teaching materials should be refined according to system performance.

The evaluation results on the review of teaching method and an atmosphere in a class depends on course topic and instructors. If the instructor does not consider the two-way video distance education characteristics, trainees give a less than positive evaluation. There are two points of view to a less than positive evaluation. One is that "The course is not serious and less attractive because of monotonous lecture ". The other is that "The course is passive for lack of interaction between an instructor and trainees because of the minimal use of the two-way communication function ".

Both instructors and trainees seem to expect higher quality instruction in distance education than traditional courses by the results of the questionaire. The results indicate that instructors are willing to make an effort to improve instruction.

6. CONCLUSION

This paper describes the two-way video distance education system called NESPAC. Based on our experiences it is more important that teaching/instructional methods are developed based on the psychological characteristics of instructors/trainees and distance education system characteristics. These skills or understandings can be accumulated basically through actual usage of the system.

REFERENCES

(1) Sato, T., Shiratori, T., Hashimoto, M., and Matsusita, S., "Education Networking in Satellite Communication Age", Supervision of NEC Institute of Management, Ltd., NEC Culture Center, Tokyo, 1988 (in Japanese).

(2) Shiratori, T., "A Two-way Distance Education System Using Satellite for Advanced Creative Education", NEC Technical Journal, Vol. 41, No. 10, pp.139-146, 1988 (in Japanese).

(3) Ohtake, Y. and Matsushita, S., "NESPAC: A Two-way Satellite Education Network", Proceedings of Pacific Telecommunications Council's 12th Annual Conference, Jan. 1990.

Computers in Education
A. McDougall and C. Dowling (Editors)
Elsevier Science Publishers B.V. (North-Holland)

NEXUS III - TELECOMMUNICATIONS BEYOND THE CLASSROOM

Ralph LEONARD

Education Department of South Australia
Angle Park Computing Centre
Cowan Street, Angle Park
South Australia 5010

The use of telecommunications as a tool for education is becoming increasingly widespread. Many authorities have used public systems onto which have been adapted 'front ends' for specific education applications. In contrast the Nexus system in South Australia has been developed specifically to meet the needs of education users and also to address the issue of student use of such facilities.

Its design has focused on the growing trend for students to access telecommunications facilities on an individual basis and on the need for a system which facilitates the management of access. The solutions used in Nexus and its distinctive features are described.

1. INTRODUCTION

Nexus is an electronic information service provided by the Education Department of South Australia through its Angle Park Computing Centre (APCC). This paper briefly describes the history of Nexus, the features of the latest version of the service and discusses the issues that concerned the designers of the system.

The paper illustrates that throughout its history Nexus has been a service intended for students and teachers, and as a result its features have been designed to suit that clientele. This distinguishes Nexus from many systems which have been created by taking existing public services and adapting front ends to cater for school users.

2. THE HISTORY OF NEXUS

APCC has provided a research and development service within the South Australian Education Department since 1968. In the early 80's the Centre's staff had frequently demonstrated Australian and international services (DIALOG, The Source, BT Gold) during teacher development conferences. It was obviously desirable that teachers should also include data communication activities for students in the various computer awareness courses which were prevalent at that time, and such a service was seen as a logical addition to the services provided by APCC.

In November 1984, Nexus began in a limited form - an Apple II and a telephone line. Yet, from the start it was designed with a consideration for the user which gave the system its distinguishing features.

Becoming a registered user on the first Nexus was particularly easy. At the logon prompt a new user simply entered their chosen ID and, if it did not already exist, the system asked if the user really wanted to create a new ID. If so, it then prompted for a password. From then on the user had full status with ability to send and receive mail, post messages on the bulletin board, et cetera.

Hence teachers and students could assign their own user id and password. *This attitude to simplifying management processes and offering de-centralised management has been a notable and consistent feature of each of the Nexus systems.*

At this stage the role of Nexus was primarily as a demonstration and awareness tool, but with only a single telephone line its availability was limited. Nevertheless it acted as a catalyst in prompting many schools to purchase a modem and so begin gaining familiarity with telecommunications. As the use of the system increased in 1985, so did frustration with the limitation of a single telephone line.

Fortunately, this increasing use of Nexus coincided with the second year of the National Computer Education Program (a three year project funded by the Australian Government). This program provided funds to each State and Territory for computer education activities and a submission was made to the committee responsible for the program in South Australia. It was proposed that funds be allocated for Nexus II, a system offering multi-user access and also that modems be supplied to all non-metropolitan schools with a secondary enrolment.

Most Nexus users had come from metropolitan high schools where only a local call charge applied. More distant schoools appeared to be discouraged by the long distance call charges and had not acquired modems. Including the provision of modems in the proposal was a way of partially overcoming the inequity in the situation.

The committee accepted the proposal for a new system and funding was approved. Within six months of the hardware arriving, Nexus II was online in 1986.

3. THE SECOND NEXUS SYSTEM

Thirteen telephone lines (it never seemed unlucky!) and a host of facilities were included in the second system. The facilities included

◊ Electronic mail

◊ Multiple bulletin boards

◊ Databases

Such facilities are found on many electronic information services, but the distinguishing features of Nexus are its ease of use, de-centralised management and open nature.

Bulletin boards and databases have been popular facilities in Nexus. Each bulletin board develops its own character because it is a forum in which users interested in a particular topic can air their views, exchange ideas or just ask others for help. Its users can either browse through the accumulated information reading each item in historical order, initiate a computer search for items related to a topic of interest or add their own comments to the board. With the passage of time, a board becomes an accumulation of ideas, hints and experiences.

The administration of bulletin boards again reflects the de-centralised management philosophy of Nexus. Boards are managed by a variety users, in many cases the manager is a school student.

The work of a bulletin board manager will vary according to the structure of the board. Most boards are open, i.e. they can be accessed by any user and any user can place a notice on the board. In such boards the manager merely has to keep an eye on the quality of the messages. If required, a board may be configured as a 'closed board', i.e. access is restricted to a group of users. In this case the manager is responsible for maintaining the criteria for access.

Another variable factor in a board's structure is the manner in which messages are placed on the board. Placing a message on the board is similar to sending the message to another user via E-mail. However the manager determines whether such messages are immediately visible to users of the board or whether it is necessary for the message to be vetted, i.e. read and approved, by the manager before it is visible.

Figure 1 indicates the possible variations of board styles. Increasing managerial control is accompanied by additional management work.

In summary, bulletin boards within Nexus;

◊ provide a forum for those users with a particular interest,

◊ enable users to access up-to-date information and/or collected expertise with assistance in searching for items of specific interest,

◊ allow access to and sharing of information in a manner that can have control mechanisms suited to the group of users involved,

◊ ensure that information is available to all members in the organisation or user community without geographic disadvantage.

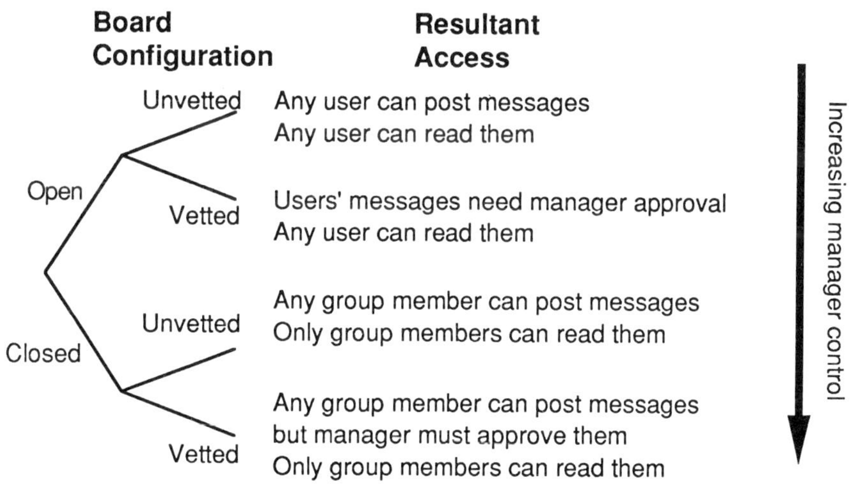

Figure 1

4. DATABASES - ELECTRONIC PUBLISHING

The information in a bulletin board generally comes from the community of users interested in the topic of the board. A database differs from a bulletin board in the sense that the information comes from a particular source and the messages can contain several fields of data.

With E-mail as a messaging service and bulletin boards providing forums, the databases fulfil another information role, namely that of a publishing service. The distinguishing features of the databases are that;

◊ elaborate search facilities can be provided which enable a large amount of information to be 'sifted' in order to find a specific piece of information,

◊ the information can be edited if required to ensure that the user views the latest information available,

◊ management of the database can be performed from any geographic location.

The distinction between bulletin boards and databases lies in the power of the sender. User originated notices on the bulletin boards will appear in the chronological order in which they were sent, and the sender has no control over the appearance of other messages (which may contain competing opinions). Messages on the board can come from a variety of sources.

In a database, the information provider has complete control over the appearance of all the information. The content of messages, their order and the search language used to select them are all determined by the information provider. There is generally one source of the information in the database.

The forms of message delivery within Nexus are illustrated in figure 2.

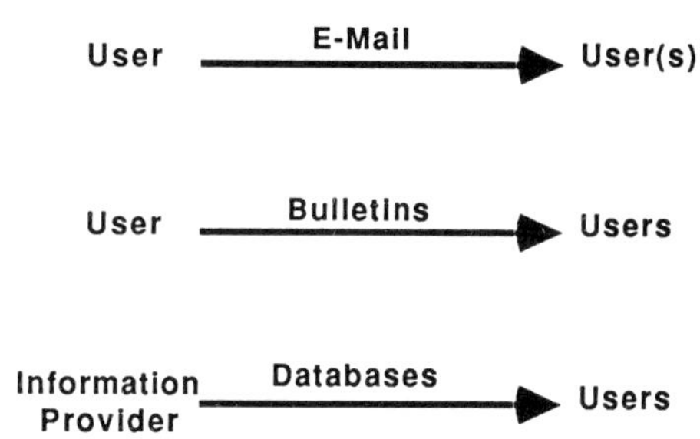

Figure 2

Nexus II, in September 1989, contained 72 bulletin boards and 15 databases. Several databases are worthy of mention to give an idea of the flavour of Nexus.

One of the most used databases is the Australian Associated Press news service (AAP). AAP is a news wire service which provides information to newspapers, radio and television stations. News items are transmitted by AAP as they become available and Nexus receives these 'raw' news items almost continually. An agreement was made with AAP that Nexus could be used to store up to 28 days of AAP news items and that this database could be searched by students and teachers as a source of topical news.

The items are categorised by AAP as 'overseas', 'sport', 'general', 'feature', etc. and with each item is stored the category type, the key word summary and a date/time at which it was recorded. A comprehensive search language can be used to extract the required news items from this database, which has proved to be a valuable research tool for students.

Another database is the Job Guide. The Department of Employment, Education and Training publish a listing of job titles, categorised into interests associated with each job (artistic, physical, scientific, etc.) and the education levels required. Each job description includes comprehensive text, and details of education or training courses that lead to that job.

This data had been compiled for a print publication distributed to schools. The existence of such a data collection made its transfer to Nexus a particularly easy task and the Nexus version allowed the database search language to be used. Hence a student can use Nexus to find, for example, all jobs that have interest characteristics of science and outside work, but require no tertiary training. Such detailed searching was not possible with the original printed version of the data.

A useful database for teachers is the catalogue of video tapes, audio tapes and photographic materials available from the Education Department's unit responsible for such educational materials. This database can be searched to find support material for a given topic.

5. FACTORS IN THE NEXUS DESIGN

Several uniquely South Australian and Australian factors, namely South Australian demography and Telecom Australia's charging policy, have led to extensive student use of Nexus. South Australia is a large State, covering approximately a million square kilometres and it has a population of 1.3 million. However three quarters of the population live within one urban area surrounding Adelaide, the capital city. Hence the great majority of Nexus users can access it with a local telephone call, and in Australia these calls incur a connect fee only with no time charging.

This unique demography and charging system lead to a considerable use of Nexus II by students from their own homes. The free Nexus II service and unlimited time for a local call connect fee made the addition of a modem to a home computer a particularly attractive option for users.

Most student users of Nexus do not use the ID for their school (if indeed it has one) but instead have their own ID. This emphasises the personal nature of the service. In contrast, school use of telecommunications in other States and other countries appears to be based on the concept of a school ID shared by students. This is acceptable if student use is limited to a single computer/phone line within school hours. The access restriction avoids problems that multiple use of a single ID can create.

Student use of telecommunications as a tool in education is enhanced if each student has their own ID and is responsible for it. The Nexus system has generated such an environment. The management of such a large number of individual student/teacher IDs could have been a major nightmare had it not been for a feature designed into the Nexus II system.

Schools have been encouraged to assign to one teacher the responsibility for Nexus use within the school. The teacher's ID is then given access to facilities for managing users. This allows the school to create and delete student IDs on demand. *In this way the management of IDs is devolved to the school with appropriate safeguards.*

6. THE NEED FOR NEXUS III

The Nexus II system represented a well designed service which met the demands of most of its users. However it suffered from several shortcomings.

◊ Users from non-metropolitan regions had to use long distance phone calls which are expensive,

◊ The hardware was limited to thirteen phone lines.

◊ The level of demand was beginning to exceed the system capacity.

To overcome these problems, the development of a replacement system began in June 1989 and Nexus III came online on Australia Day, January 26 1990. The new Nexus III service has considerably more features than Nexus II, but maintains many aspects of the Nexus II philosophy regarding IDs.

However funding for Nexus III depended on introducing fees for usage. This added a further complexity which gave a challenge to the designers - can the previous system of devolved management be kept and yet provide an effective cost control mechanism for schools. (In South Australia schools are responsible for a large proportion of their ongoing costs.)

7. NEXUS III FEATURES

7.1. Profiles

The concept of schools creating their own student or teacher IDs has been maintained but additional features for ID management have been added which permit control over time periods for use of IDs and the concept of a credit limit for an ID has been introduced.

IDs now have profiles associated with them which permit control over the facilities that an ID can access. Profiles will also determine the times at which the ID can be used and will provide a credit limit on ID usage. This offers schools a mechanism for managing the activities which students use on Nexus.

Schools will be able to have several accounts from which IDs can be created. Each student ID may belong to several schools accounts and may have different profiles in each account. The concept of linking across account-ID-profile is illustrated in figure 3.

P1 and P2 are not generic profiles but are sets of features unique to the SchoolA1-SBROWN and SchoolA2-SBROWN combinations. Similarly JSMITH from SchoolB may have a totally different profile P3.

The identification of a profile with a school account-student ID join means that other organisations can also be responsible for some of a student's Nexus use. For example there is a growing trend for students in some sectors to receive part of their education via distance or open learning techniques.

The South Australian Correspondence School (SACS) is providing tuition not only to students traditionally taught by correspondence methods (i.e. remote and/or isolated students) but also to school-based students where the local school cannot offer all the subjects that a student may wish to study. In those circumstances, the Nexus usage for a student such as SBROWN could be determined by a SACS-SBROWN link to yet another profile P4.

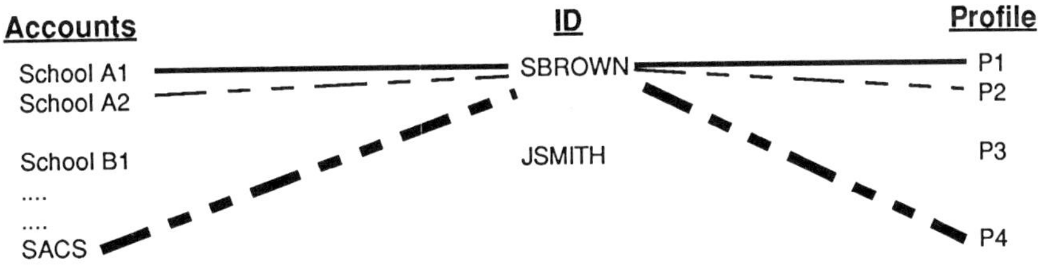

Figure 3

The manager of the associated account controls the credit limit of a profile. The profile accumulates usage, and the user is able to logon provided the usage cost is less than the limit. If the user exceeds the limit, access is barred until the account manager either increases the limit or resets the accumulated usage.

By providing the management system described above, Nexus III enables individual user IDs for teachers and students, offers the ability for a school to create and delete IDs as necessary, but does so within the new environment of charging for usage. The desire to provide such a system came directly from the success of Nexus II as a system used by students who were treated, and regarded themselves, as individuals responsible for their own telecommunications privileges.

7.2 User Customised Menus

Each profile includes a potentially unique menu. Users (or their ID manager) can choose not only which Nexus facilities appear on their menu but also the text of the menu list. This allows facilities most frequently accessed by a user to be presented in the main menu. The user may have direct access to other facilities by command and/or have the ability to permanently alter the menu. Whether such actions are permitted is also determined by the profile.

7.3. Search Assistance

Another concept introduced in the upgrade is the idea of assistance in finding information. In the Nexus III system, all items will be indexed on their full text. It will therefore be possible to request assistance in finding items related to a particular topic. Nexus would then list all databases and bulletin boards containing a reference to the key word sought, with an indication of the number of matching items in each. The list would in effect become a menu from which the user could choose to begin using one of the databases or bulletin boards.

The combination of user customised menus and directory assistance will hopefully avoid either the layer upon layer approach of some systems or the need to memorise explicit commands to reach a desired section of the system.

7.4 Terminal Emulation

Nexus had previously been accessible with any type of TTY communication hardware/software, but a design decision to require terminal emulation was made early in the development of Nexus III. This meant that many aspects of the system could be designed as screen forms rather than the scrolling screen commonly used. This has proved beneficial in the user interface for such facilities as ID creation, profile specification and menu customising.

8.CONCLUSION

The crucial factor in the conversion from Nexus II to Nexus III will be the willingness of schools to pay for a service that was previously free. The use of X25 means that non-metropolitan users will pay far less than the existing long distance rates they currently face and therefore they have expressed support for the new system. However, as noted above, the bulk of existing Nexus users lie within the metropolitan area and will incur considerably increased costs for Nexus use.

Experience has shown that schools are willing to pay for telecommunications service which they perceive to enhance the education of their students. It is hoped that the facilities and in particular the management options provided in Nexus III will provide an environment which allows the full potential of telecommunications for education to be developed.

Increasingly in many developed countries, the computer resources available to students and teachers in their own homes will collectively exceed the computing resources within their schools. A telecommunications system for education should recognise that and provide mechanisms which allow such resources to be used in a manageable fashion. This was a major determinant in the design of Nexus.

Acknowledgement: The success of Nexus is due largely to the programming and design skills of Dean Rosenhain, with whom it has been a pleasure to work.

Computers in Education
A. McDougall and C. Dowling (Editors)
Elsevier Science Publishers B.V. (North-Holland)

HYPERMEDIA IN TELETEACHING

Hermann MAURER, Ivan TOMEK

Institutes for Information Processing (IIG), Graz University of Technology, Grazi Austria; Jodrey School of Computer Science, Acadia University Wolfville, Nova Scotia, Canada

Integration of hypermedia facilities into electronic learning systems is a major contribution to GAI which is particularly beneficial in distance education. Unfortunately, implementation of hypermedia on wide area networks presents a problem in terms of speed and cost of communication. We suggest a simple solution which takes advantage of the special nature of CAI material to preserve those hypermedia features which are most important for education and reduce demands on communication to a minimum. Although the full implication of our argument is that hypermedia principles should be extended from individual applications to complete computer environments, implementation of our proposal does not require such a drastic overhaul of existing systems.

1. INTRODUCTION

The concept of hypermedia is a generalization of the more common term hypertext. It refers to systems that extend hypertext principles from text documents to chunks of information represented in other forms such as graphics, sound, video, and interactive computer programs. While no standard definition of a hypermedia system exists, the term has been applied to computer environments supporting representation of information in nonlinear form instead of the linear style of conventional books [1]. In the final analysis, this means that the mechanisms familiar from the use of books such as turning pages, marking places in the text with bookmarks, use of the table of contents, index, footnotes, and references to other books are mechanized and available via keyboard and mouse functions.

Since the introduction of the concept of hypertext, many systems have been developed and used in a variety of applications. The vast majority of them are capable of handling only text and graphics, but a few extensions to other media have also been described [2, 3]. Examples of hypertext presented in the literature include systems for software development [4], support of documentation [5], argumentation and decision making [6, 7] access of medical information [8] and large dictionaries and encyclopedias [9], computer aided instruction [10, 11, 12, 13, 14], writing [15], nonlinear fiction [16, 17], and others. The introduction of Macintosh HyperCard [18] stimulated the development of a restricted form of hypermedia and led to the popularization of the concept. As a consequence of the wide interest, many experiments have been conducted with both positive and negative results [19, 20, 21, 22, 23, 24, 25]. The general consensus is that, although hypermedia present certain problems, these can be attributed to the novelty of the concept and will be ironed out when more experience is gained.

2. THE BENEFITS OF HYPERMEDIA IN EDUCATION

Workers in CAI have hailed the emergence of hypermedia as a major event in the development of educational environments. The most important among the arguments made to support this position is that hypermedia allow presentation and acquisition of knowledge in multiple perspectives which encourages active exploration of the multiple dimensions of the "knowledge space". This is a great improvement over conventional textbooks whose monolithic structure provides only one perspective and thus fosters the view of knowledge clustered in isolated chunks. Although textbooks abound with references to other material, the access mechanism requires searches of libraries, often fails, and is awkward and time consuming. Independent exploration is thus little used by typical students. The restriction to static text and graphics is another drawback of books in comparison with hypermedia.

Two less direct contributions of hypermedia to education are due to their support for search and annotation. The most obvious benefit of the search facility is that it encourages the student to explore the available information. Its other contribution is that it encourages authors to create widely based teaching environments taking advantage of the potentially unlimited information present in the system. Annotation allows authors to annotate documents extracted from the system for the lesson and makes it possible for students to annotate the course material. Students can use it not only for personal notes but also for communication with the teacher, allowing an individualized dialogue directly linked to the instructional material. This is especially valuable in situations where physical contact between the teacher and the student is impossible, as in distance education.

3. A SCENARIO FOR THE USE OF HYPERMEDIA IN EDUCATION

The life cycle of a CAI course begins with its creation by the teacher. The material is then presented to the student and a multiway communication between the teacher and the students is established. We will now describe how these two phases could be implemented in hypermedia.

3.1 Creating a CAI course

The first step in creating a hypermedia course is to check whether the system already contains a course on the subject. To do this, the teacher will examine the system's database of courses in the area of interest. If a course on the subject exists, the teacher will retrieve it and examine whether it is acceptable or whether it needs editing. If a suitable course is not available, a new course must be created.

An ideal scenario for the creation of a new CAI course could run as follows: To create a CAI course, the author starts from the course outline. The first step is to collect and organize all topics to be covered and gather relevant information available in the system. This will be done by entering the curriculum into the system and associating a collection of keywords with each curriculum item. The system will then search the corpus for all relevant information nodes and attach them to the corresponding topics. With all relevant information collected, the author examines the retrieved items and decides which of them should be kept. Some of these will be used to construct the main line of the course, others will serve as auxiliary supporting material.

Since the chunks selected for the main line of the course are, in general, independent of one another and created by various authors in different contexts, their direct linking would result in a nonhomogeneous unreadable collection. The author must thus produce "glue nodes" to provide transitions and to fill in the missing material. The author may also create or edit relational sidelinks to optional support material. In addition to using existing and glue nodes to build the main line of the lesson and using relational links to attach side nodes, the author can also attach short annotations to the frames.

Because the speed of the computer is much higher than the rate at which the author creates the text, the computer has time to work in the background and provide additional services. One of the possibilities is as follows: While the author creates the lesson examining and editing existing nodes, creating glue nodes, and connecting everything into a linear sequence of lesson frames, the system uses the author's pauses and scans the processed material. It examines the words being displayed or typed and matches them against an index previously created for the course by the author. When it finds a match and if a node with the keyword exists in the corpus, the system highlights the word on the screen and reports the node. If the author wishes to link it, the system performs the internal attachment. Similarly, the system can monitor the author's actions such as word searches and selection of nodes and continuously update the index.

When the author is finished, a structured collection of nodes whose main line corresponds to chapters in a book has been created. The way in which the material was built guarantees that it fully matches the curriculum tree. While the author is working on the course, the material is protected from unauthorized access. When the course begins, the material is made available to students and the part to be covered in the first class marked; this improves orientation and motivation.

Although the scenario that we described is presently only a fiction, a system implementing it would not be difficult to design. In the meantime, a more realistic approach is to customize existing conventional CAI material transported into a hypermedia environment.

Customizing an existing course. When the system contains a suitable course, the teacher may either accept it as is or customize it in one of the following ways:

* Modify course structure by bypassing or adding nodes, linking to other courses, and creating shortcuts for knowledgeable students and detours for those who need more information.

* Edit the existing textual or graphical material.

* Add or delete relational links to supporting material.

* Add pop-up annotations.

Since customization is much easier than creation of a new course, extensive course libraries of future hypermedia systems will make authoring much easier. Although existing systems do not provide large course libraries, much conventional CAI material is available and a good way to start a hyper-media CAI environment is to import existing material and convert it. This is the approach that we are using with COSTOC, a very large set of uniformly structured courses on topics in computer science [11, 12].

3.2 Using the course material

To access the course material, students use methods familiar from their experience with textbooks. Basic operations such as going to the next or the previous frame may be activated by keys or by clicking on icons displayed on the screen. As in books, students can also insert bookmarks, highlight portions of text or graphics, write notes "in the margin", and so on. While a typical student may study the material by simply "turning pages", more motivated students will also explore relational links which can be highlighted on the screen by clicking on an icon.

Selecting a highlighted link by clicking on it displays the name and a short description of the destination node. If the student decides to follow the link, clicking brings the contents of the node on the screen. Since all nodes may have relational links attached to them, the process of exploring auxiliary nodes may be continued any number of levels deep. While the user follows a sequence of relational sidelinks, the system keeps track of the traversed path. By activating another icon, the student can retrace the path by which the current frame was reached.

As students explore the material and find difficult passages or points which require clarification, they can create notes for the teacher and attach them to the material displayed on the screen. These annotations are not restricted to text but may include sketches, pointers to programs, and so on. The collection of notes and questions created by the student is gathered into a special set and transmitted to the teacher in an "off-line" fashion - regardless of whether the teacher is currently available to read it or not. Upon logging in, the teacher is informed that student queries are present, opens the "folder" and examines it. Since annotations are displayed within the material, the teacher can see the context, attach answers, and create links to other nodes to provide further information. The result is then transmitted to the student. After reading the answers, the student may attach further questions requesting additional clarification, send them to the teacher, and so on.

At some point, the teacher may decide that some material requires a global clarification which should be communicated to all students. While this can be handled in the way described above, the principle of the bulletin board used in computer conferencing systems is preferable. Since the bulletin board in our situation is a part of a hypermedia environment, posted messages may be linked to one another and to other nodes. This provides for unlimited group discussion comparable with a discussion in class.

We could continue expanding our scenario and describe handling of tests, homework gathering of statistics, and so on, but we hope that our examples show that hypermedia indeed provide a very desirable foundation for CAI. If the environment includes hypermedia-style mail and bulletin boards, it acquires features comparable with a discussion forum, which is particularly attractive in distance education where direct teacher-student contact is limited. Unfortunately, in distance education, hypermedia as described above pose some serious problems.

4. IMPLEMENTING HYPERMEDIA IN DISTANCE EDUCATION

To illustrate the difficulties involved in the implementation of our scenario in a wide area network, we will now describe our own experience with a videotex CAI system.

The Austrian videotex (called BTX for Bildschirmtext) is available through the Austrian post office to anybody who has a telephone connection and a special purpose microcomputer or a personal computer [26, 27]. Most services are accessible to all users at the cost of the telephone connect time, some are open only to members of special interest groups including lawyers and physicians, and some are available for a fee.

The free services include access to the telephone directory, train schedules, computer lessons, newsletters, a mail capability through which the post office delivers printouts of electronically transmitted mail to any location in Austria, library cat alogs, access to German lexicons (currently being converted to hypertext form [9]), and so on. Services available for a fee include access to the official airline guide for all regularly operating airlines, the Austrian property register, a description of apartments for rent, and so on.

When a user selects a BTX service, the necessary software and data are downloaded from one of about 60 regional centers to the user's computer over a telephone line at 1200 bits per second. This works quite well except for services involving large volumes of data such as COSTOC CAI courses, which normally consist of ten lessons containing between 500k and 1M bytes each. (A typical academic course requires at least three such units.)

The most obvious way to access a COSTOC lesson is to establish the telephone connection for the whole session and transfer chunks of data as they are requested by the user. This, however, would require a very long connect time and the user would have to wait between the individual transfers. A better solution is to parallelize downloading and courseware execution by transmitting blocks of succeeding chunks in the background while the user is examining the lesson [27]. In this way, a whole lesson can usually be downloaded by the time the student has worked through only 10% or 20% of the material, and connection is thus reduced to a fraction of the duration of the session.

From the point of view of connect time, the most efficient solution is to download the whole lesson or course at a time, store it on a disk on the user's computer, and execute it later. With this method, the connection need not be maintained while the user is executing the lesson. Even this approach, however, has its problems: Assuming a 1200 bps rate with 10 bits per character, 120 characters can be transmitted in one second and 432,000 per hour. Downloading a complete COSTOC course thus requires one to two hours of connect time. Since telephone lines are often unreliable, retransmission of blocks of data received in error further increases the required connect time.

The long connect time presents several problems. One of the difficulties is that if many people started using the facility, the telephone network would soon be overloaded. Another problem is cost. In Austria, where one hour of connect time costs about three dollars, transmitting a COSTOC course will cost the user around $5. This appears negligible until one realizes that a student taking a full academic load of five computer science courses may need up to 20 COSTOC courses at a time which would require 30 connect hours at a cost of $150.

In comparison with the difficulties of downloading COSTOC courses, the problems with transmission of hypermedia are much worse because hypermedia software and databases tend to be much larger. Moreover, transmitting the system on the "when needed" basis (a chunk or a block of chunks at a time) is impossible since hypermedia nodes may be linked together and transmitting only a part would make the database useless. The local area model of hypermedia is thus unworkable in a wide area network.

Fortunately, the problem can be easily solved without much damage because the use of a hypermedia-based CAI system consists of access to a very large "static" (relatively stable) hypermedia data base, and a "dynamic" component - student-teacher communication. The solution to the downloading problem is thus to transmit the static component by regular mail on floppy disks along with other course material, and restrict telephone communication to the transmission of the off-line dialogue between the student's and the teacher's computers. Upon receiving the diskettes, the student installs the hypermedia software and database and obtains most of the hypermedia functionality. (Transmitting all information available in our system - presently about 50 Mbytes including, for example, the Information Science Encyclopedia - on diskettes is not feasible.) Hypermedia style communication remains unaffected since it is not performed on line even in the local area network environment.

In comparison with a conventional textbook-based distance course, the only extra expense is the cost of diskettes, perhaps ten dollars. The amount of information transmitted over the telephone line during computer-to-computer communication of annotations, bulletin boards, and other dynamically changing information, is minimal. Assuming that each lesson requires the exchange of several screenfuls of questions and answers, a lesson's worth of communication may amounts to 5k bytes or roughly one minute of connect time. This is probably much less than the time required for personal communication in a regular course.

The question arises as to how the system described above can be implemented. In systems where the corpus of information is rapidly changing, transmission of data linked to the main body might be difficult. CAI environments, fortunately, are relatively stable throughout the duration of the course and the question-answer data can be formatted as chunks consisting of annotation contents and links to fixed stable points within the corpus or within the transmitted code.

To summarize, the inexpensive solution that we described provides both the teacher and the student with a full range of hypermedia facilities. These include text and graphics editing and linking, access to a course containing a large corpus of richly linked nodes, and an annotation facility for personal use and for topical communication between the student and the teacher. Access to a hypermedia-style bulletin board can make student-teacher communication almost as direct as a regular classroom situation.

5. CONCLUSION

We demonstrated that the use of hypermedia in education can bring substantial benefits and improve communication between teachers and students. This is particularly important in long distance education where personal contact between students and teachers is limited. By dividing the hypermedia environment into the static software and corpus on one side, and personal communication on the other, hypermedia can be implemented very efficiently and economically even in wide area network situations.

The implication of the scheme that we described is that hypermedia facilities must be available not only within the CAI framework but much more widely in the system. They must, in particular, be integrated into text and graphics editors, the mail facility, and the bulletin board. Closer examination shows that hypermedia principles should be extended even further and the idea of unlimited linking, structuring, and annotation used as the basis of the whole operating system [25].

While the implementation of our ideas does not depend on such drastic revisions as new operating systems, the collection of facilities that we described is not available on any single hypermedia system. To implement our scenario, a new hypermedia system incorporating all the necessary functions would thus have to be designed. In order to achieve this, CAI and hypermedia designers should formulate a prototype hypermedia standard and cooperate on its implementation. The resulting system would provide a new platform and stimulate CAI designers to develop powerful and transportable new generation CAI products.

REFERENCES

[1] Conklin E. J., Hypertext: An Introduction and a Survey, IEEE Computer, 20 (9), 1937.

[2] Hypertext '87, TR88-013, March 1988, University of North Carolina, Department of Computer Science.

[3] Hypertext II, University of York, England, June 1989.

[4] Bigelow J., Riley V., Manipulating Source Code in Dynamic Design, Hypertext '87, TR88-013, March 1988, University of North Carolina, Department of Computer Science.

[5] Walker J. H., Document Examiner: Delivery Interface for Hypertext Documents, Hypertext '87, TR88-013, March 1988, University of North Carolina, Department of Computer Science.

[6] Conklin E. J., Begeman M. L., IBIS, A Hypertext Tool for Team Design Deliberation. Hypertext '87, TR88-013, March 1988, University of North Carolina, Department of Computer Science.

[7] Smolensky P., et al., Constraint-based Hyper text for Documentation, Hypertext '87, TR88-013, March 1988, University of North Carolina, Department of Computer Science.

[8] Frisse M. E., Searching for Information in a Hypertext Medical Book, Hypertext '87, TR88-013, March 1988, University of North Carolina, Department of Computer Science.

[9] Mulner H., A System of Interactive Encyclopedias, Austrian- Hungarian Computer Conference, Budapest, 1989, pp. 181-190.

[10] Beeman W. O., et al: Hypertext and Pluralism: from Lineal to Non-lineal Thinking, Hypertext '87, TR88-013, March 1988, University of North Carolina, Department of Computer Science.

[11] Huber F., et al., HyperCOSTOC: A Comprehensive Computer- based Teaching Support System. Journal of Microcomputer Applications, (1989) 12, pp. 293-317.

[12] Maurer H., A Report on the COSTOC Project, EATCS Bulletin 35, 1988.

[13] Maurer H., Tomek I., Some Aspects of Hypermedia Systems and Their Treatment in Hyper-G. Submitted for publication.

[14] Yankelovich N., et al., Intermedia: The Concept and Construction of a Seamless Information Environment, Hypertext '87, TR88-013, March 1988, University of North Carolina, Department of Computer Science.

[15] Smith J. B., et al., A Hypertext Writing Environment and Its Cognitive Basis, Hypertext'87, TR88-013, March 1988, University of North Carolina, Department of Computer Science.

[16] Bolter J. D., Joyce M., Hypertext and Creative Writing, Hypertext'87, TR88-013, March 1988, University of North Carolina, Department of Computer Science.

[17] Howell G., Hypertext Meets Interactive Fiction, Hypertext'87, TR88-013, March 1988, University of North Carolina, Department of Computer Science.

[18] Apple Corporation, HyperCard User's Manual. 1987.

[19] Colbourne C. J., Cockerton-Turner T., Using Hypertext for Educational Help Facilities, Hyper text II, University of York, England, June 1989.

[20] McKnight C., et al., A Comparison of Linear and Hypertext Formats in Information Retrieval, Hypertext II, University of York, England, June 1989.

[21] Nielsen J., Lyngbaek U., Two Field Studies of Hypermedia Usability, Hypertext II,

University of York, England, June 1989.

[22] Shneiderman B., User Interface Design for the Hyperties Electronic Encyplopedia, Hypertext '87, TR88-013, March 1988, University of North Carolina, Department of Computer Science.

[23] Simpson A., McKnight C., Navigation in Hypertext: Structural Cues and Mental Maps, Hypertext II, University of York, England, June 1989.

[24] Stark H. A., What do Readers do to Pop-ups, and Pop-ups do to Readers, Hypertext II, University of York, England, June 1989.

[25] Wright P., Lickorish A., An empirical Comparison of Two Navigation Systems for Two Hypertexts, Hypertext II, University of York, England, June 1989.

[26] Maurer H., Report on Videotext Development in Austria, Electronic Publishing Review 4 (1984), pp. 201-214.

[27] Maurer H., Nationwide Teaching through A Network of Microcomputers, Proc. IFIP'86, Dublin, Ireland (1986) pp. 429-432.

[28] Maurer H., Tomek I., Hypermedia and Operating Systems. Submitted for publication.

Computers in Education
A. McDougall and C. Dowling (Editors)
Elsevier Science Publishers B.V. (North-Holland)

TEACHING PASCAL IN A GLOBAL CLASSROOM

William Morgan

Kubasaki High School, Box 881, FPO Seattle, WA 98774, USA

Kent Applegate

Stuttgart American High School, APO New York, NY 09279, USA

Clancy Wolf

School of Education, 610 East University, Ann Arbor, MI 48109, USA

American students in six countries are participating in a course in Pascal programming taught using telecommunications as the medium of correspondence. This approach to distance learning is unique in that the students and teacher are able to create an interactive 'classroom' atmosphere even though they are separated by time and distance. Students learn through the use of videotapes, tutorial disks, worksheets, tests, and programming assignments. All work is transmitted to the teacher through electronic mail. Classroom discussions are held through the use of a communication/conferencing program called Confer II. The entire course is relatively inexpensive to develop and run. This concept in distance learning could easily be adapted to other curriculum areas.

1. Introduction

Is it possible to provide instruction for students located in six countries throughout the world without losing the 'classroom' atmosphere? Can students chat with their neighbors, work on group projects, and argue about grades even when they are separated by ten time zones? All of the above is being accomplished in a unique new course called 'Pascal via Telecommunications.'

This course was created by William Morgan to teach Department of Defense Dependents School (DoDDS) students in remote high schools where upper level programming courses were unavailable. DoDDS schools, serving the children of United States servicemen stationed overseas, are often small and do not have enough students to warrant a full time Pascal instructor. These students are now grouped together via a telecommunications network based at the University of Michigan in an interactive distance learning classroom.

In the spring of 1987, the semester long course began with a class of 18 pupils at 5 high schools in West Germany. It has grown to include more than 100 students in 13 schools from England, Italy, Korea, Japan, Iceland, and Germany. A second, year long course, 'Advanced Placement Pascal via Telecommunications' began during the spring of school year 1989/90.

2. The Communication Infrastructure

The course is designed much like a correspondence course with the added benefit of an interactive classroom environment. The interaction is provided by using a communication/conferencing program called Confer II running on a mainframe computer at the University of Michigan in Ann Arbor. Students access Confer through the use of a microcomputer, a modem, and a commercial packet switching data network. They send all work to the teacher via electronic mail. Classroom discussions are held through 'items' and 'responses.' Items may be uploaded by anyone in the class. Everyone in the course sees the item when they sign on and is able to respond to it at anytime. (See figure 1.)

```
Item 2    09:22 Aug29/89
Mr. Applegate *Stuttgart
Welcome Item

Welcome to ICS:PASCAL

     I am Mr. Applegate, your teacher for
the course.  What you are reading now is an
example of an 'ITEM'.  You can think of an
ITEM as a class discussion.  We will use
ITEMs in the class to post assignments,
conduct discussion on projects, and share
information and help.  Since this is a
'Welcome Item' I would like you to RESPOND
to it by putting in your SCHOOL'S NAME, and
your FAVORITE FOOD so that everyone can
become better acquainted.

Aug31/89 08:27
2:1) Mike Wesley: Iceland High School,
watermelon.
- - - - -
Aug31/89 08:39
2:2) Jennifer Keim: Aviano High School,
cookies and ice cream.
- - - - -
Aug31/89 08:54
2:3) Karl Burge: Bitburg American High
School, pizza!
- - - - -
Sep01/89 03:36
2:4) James Spoo: Alconbury High School, I
like chicken and (don't laugh) spinach!
- - - - -
Sep01/89 01:57
2:5) Jeff Collins: Seoul American High
School, French Fries!!
- - - - -
Sep01/89 05:17
2:6) Mr. Applegate: Quite a bit of variety
here.  My school is Stuttgart High School
and my favorite food is Tiramasu.  Figure
that one out.
- - - - -
```

Figure 1

Lesson 8 Schedule

CHAPTER 8 (72 Points)

1. Read pages 95 - 109 in 'Pascal Primer'.
2. Watch the videotape on chapter 8.
3. (10 pts.) Take the tutorial called TUT8.
4. (10 pts.) Your worksheet assignment is a short programming problem. See the attached sheet.
5. (18 pts.) This is your chance to shine (or go out in a blaze of glory). You get to decide what program to write. You need to show me that you understand the following by incorporating them in your program....
   a. Procedures (use at least two) with value parameters AND variable parameters.
   b. Functions (use at least one).
   c. Intrinsic functions: PRED, ORD, UPCASE, SIZEOF, CHR, ABS, SQRT, etc. (include at least two).
   d. Constants (use at least one) Remember they can also be CHAR or string variables.
6. (34 pts.) Take the test called 'T7-8' and send your answers to me.

Figure 2

3. Course Components

The course is taught through a series of video tapes and interactive tutorial disks which follow a textbook. Students are required to read a chapter in the book, watch the corresponding videotape, run a tutorial disk, complete worksheets, take tests, and write programs. The worksheets, tests, and programs are then sent electronically to the teacher to be graded. (See figure 2.)

4. The Classroom Atmosphere

Pascal via Telecommunications differs from a traditional correspondence course in that students are encouraged to interact with one another through items, responses, and private electronic mail. The discussions are not limited to Pascal and programming techniques. A recent item in one class fueled a discussion of the woman's role in the computer world. A lively debate of why there are fewer women in computer programming followed.

The student's programming, telecommunication, and communications skills are put to the test when the students have to discuss and develop a class project. A discussion on what program to write is usually begun in the 7th week of the course. The students vote and then begin development of the program's algorithm. The class usually chooses to create a game such as Hangman, Trivial Pursuit, or Wheel of Fortune. They are then broken up into groups with each group writing a portion of the code. The projects show the participants the value of communication as well as demonstrate the modularity of Pascal.

5. Advantages of an Interactive Telecommunications Class

Pascal via Telecommunications has all of the elements of a traditional classroom: student discussions, dialogue between teacher and student, or student and student, assigned homework with deadlines, and even a class "yearbook."

Writing skills are developed. Students are encouraged to write all of their responses "off-line". This improves not only their writing ability but also the quality of their discussion. Most students think out carefully what they want to upload to the discussion before sending it.

The course is not self-paced but students are encouraged to work ahead. The materials (videotapes, tutorial disks, and worksheets) are readily available so it is easy for high achievers to work ahead. For those who need a little prodding, a due date is given to each assignment.

A big advantage over a traditional distance learning course is the time zone independence of the course. Students don't have to join in a video teleconference at a particular time of the day. This makes a true "global" classroom possible. Of course for a school system such as DoDDS this is the most efficient way to conduct a telecommunications course. This time zone independence has helped at schools where computer access might be limited due to the large class sizes. Students are given access to the computer during a time when one is available.

Of course a big plus has been the students' reaction to the set up of the course. They enjoy the opportunity to share a "classroom" with others from around the world.

It is difficult to provide immediate feedback in a course which is not conducted in "real-time". However, mentors from the University of Michigan help alleviate this shortcoming by remaining actively involved in the course. University students join in on the discussions and answer student questions. They foster the interaction among the students and provide tutoring assistance for both slower and faster students.

6. Impact at the Local Level

Currently the course is only available to DoDDS schools. Its successful implementation is due, in part, to the dedicated teachers at the local schools. These teachers prod the slow working students to help maintain the pace in the course. They monitor student use of the telecommunications network and the microcomputer, as well as administer tests. The "master" teachers in the course, Mr. Morgan in Okinawa, Japan and Kent Applegate from Stuttgart, West Germany correct all of the student work and recommend a grade to the local teacher.

7. Low Cost Venture

The cost of developing the course is relatively low. An initial investment in hardware such as cameras, special effects generator, editing equipment, microphones and a video/computer combiner of less than US $30,000 was necessary. The actual cost per student (per semester) is estimated to be approximately US $50 for commercial packet switching plus US $50 for the use of the University of Michigan computer. Existing equipment at the individual schools (videotape players, modems, and microcomputers) is used to keep costs down.

8. Future Expansion of Distance Learning

The Department of Defense Dependents School system has seen the potential of courses taught via telecommunications. As mentioned earlier, a pilot course designed to prepare students for the Advanced Placement Examination in Computer Science is currently being developed and implemented. Two "classrooms" of Advanced Placement Pascal should be up and running by the 1990/91 school year.

Courses of this nature need not be limited to computer science. The structure could be easily adapted to teach courses in most curriculum areas. In fact, proposals are being considered in DoDDS to develop courses in Advanced Placement Calculus and German "via telecommunications."

The structure was developed to teach distance learning courses to students in a "global" school system but it could easily be modified to work in any school system. Its highly interactive environment, low cost to produce, and time zone independence make it an interesting alternative to traditional distance learning courses.

Computers in Education
A. McDougall and C. Dowling (Editors)
Elsevier Science Publishers B.V. (North-Holland)

A MODEL FOR INTEGRATING COMPUTER NETWORKING WITH CLASSROOM LEARNING

Margaret Riel

Director, Educational Programs, The AT&T Learning Network, 943 San Dieguito Drive, Encinitas, CA 92024, USA

Abstract. This paper is about what happens when teachers and students put their minds together through electronic networking. It is about the human context of learning. When teachers and students engage in cooperative learning activities mediated by computer networking, the power and speed of human learning is extended by their collective knowledge and rich set of experiences. These human networks--the connections established between people who are distant in time and space--are extending our ability to learn in a social and global world.

1. EDUCATIONAL CHANGE

A debate that has flourished in the last decade concerns the effect of computer technology on education. Recently the *Harvard Educational Review* sponsored three articles on "Visions of the use of computers in classroom instruction." These articles (Schwartz 1989, Weir 1989, LCHC 1989) inspired a vigorous discussion on educational change and the role that educational technology will play in any restructuring of education (Bredo 1989, Cuban 1989, Winn & Coleman 1989, LaFrenz & Friedman 1989).

A factor placed at the center of any educational change by authors and respondents alike was the absolutely crucial role of teachers. As Cuban (1989) pointed out in his response and in his recent book (Cuban 1986), teachers stand at the threshold of classrooms, making decisions about what innovations enter the classroom and how they are used with students. His research on the influence of past technological innovations (radio, television and films) suggests that initial claims are vastly out of proportion with the final patterns of use in classrooms.

For each of these inventions, he documents a cyclic pattern which began with the fervent claims and promises of the reformers, proceeded to academic research validating the changes in a small set of classrooms rich with human and technical support, which was followed by the frustrated adoption of the technology by teachers with little or no resources, leading to the gradual decline in the use of the new technology. He predicts that computers will also follow this exhilaration-scientific-credibility-disappointment-blame cycle.

But there is a flaw in Cuban's analysis; he makes the mistake of casting the technology in the role of a change agent in education. Change lies not with the tool itself, but rather with the teachers and the strategies they use to incorporate it into their educational practices. There are no forces that can revolutionize the classroom and at the same time bypass the teacher. If there is change it will be in the way teachers and students create the context of a classroom and the interaction that takes place among and between the people who make up the life of a classroom.

What Cuban describes in the academic validation of a new technology is a period in which teachers and researchers become a team working to explore new forms of learning. The teamwork among teachers and other intellectuals might well be the critical factor that produces the gains in student learning and the enthusiastic teacher testimonials. There should be no doubt in anyone's mind that teachers working with Seymour Papert and LOGO can create a context for learning that has phenomenal results. The question becomes: What happens to teachers and students using LOGO without the support of extraordinary educators (Pea, et al. 1984)? The next wave of users of the new technology have the tools but not the human resources that were a vital part of the initial success story.

When evaluating the terms of the debate on the impact of computers in education, we need to keep in mind the fact that computers are qualitatively different from the teaching technologies of the past. Unlike the innovations that were designed to be teacher-proof or to perform some technical, mechanical aspect of education more efficiently, the computer can be completely controlled by the teacher and the students. But that control necessitates knowledge and skill. The possibilities of computer use in schools are endless but the reality is a teaching force that is overworked, underpaid and often has to do without the required extensive in-service training.

La Frenz and Freidman (1989), responding to the visions proposed by educational leaders, call for more programs that will affect teacher training and support. Computer networking provides a double edged tool. What makes computer networking unique is that it provides a way for teachers to learn from one another *at the same time* as they are working, within the classroom curriculum, to create learning contexts for their students. The professional development of teachers and the intellectual development of students become flip sides of the same activity. Teaching and learning mediated by computer assisted communication make it possible to extend human resources in new ways.

But how will researchers measure the effect of this new form of interaction among and between teachers and students which takes place over distances and across time? Cuban will not be able to use the same strategy that he used for measuring the use of other forms of technology. Unlike the cases of films, radio or television, the observer cannot see when students are involved in computer networks through a casual visit to the classroom. Students eagerly creating new inventions, canvassing the environment, or completing surveys at their desks may all be involved in learning activities that are linked by computers but which are not dominated by them.

Partnerships between educators and business are creating electronic links among the minds of teachers and students located throughout the world. Teachers and students are working together to learn more about themselves and their environment. This may be a real key to the change that La Frenz and Friedman were seeking. Teachers spontaneously report that they have given up on early retirement, that after a lifetime of teaching they find a rekindling of the "love of learning" that initially drew them to the profession in the first place.

Cuban believes the efforts of the 60's and 70's to uncover the science of teaching by harnessing precision to efficiency failed to recognize the emotional dimension of the teaching and learning process. Emotional, social, and cultural relationships between and among teachers and students are critically important for their intellectual development (Weir 1989, LCHC 1983, 1989, Vygotsky 1978). Teaching moments cannot be artfully programmed. No mechanized system can recognize excitement or disappointment in the face of the learner. Feldman (1988), in his study of the children with prodigious gifts and talents, found that unusual early talent in a child was always coupled with an unusually talented teacher. Learning, even by these children with IQs that are offscale, does not take place without the talent and care of skilled master teachers.

What computer networking offers is a strategy for joining teachers and students in "Learning Circles" where everyone is simultaneously teacher and learner. Education is not spontaneous activity. It must be carefully designed, planned and executed. For computer communication services to offer schools the technology, the promise, and leave the fulfillment up to teachers is to ignore the institutional and social circumstances that keep teachers operating in a professional vacuum. One of the reasons that Dewey's progressive ideas failed to take hold is the high cost in terms of teacher time and energy. How can teachers working alone be expected to recreate year after year an exciting new environment for students' learning? Sarason's response is clear.

> The assumption that teachers can create and maintain the conditions that make school learning and school living stimulating for children without the same conditions for teachers, has no warrant in the history of man (Sarason 1976:123-124).

Computer networking offers the possibility of developing a stimulating cooperative context for teachers and students.

2. THE AT&T LEARNING NETWORK

Recently AT&T has taken a bold step in reaching out to schools. They recognize that educational change takes careful planning and that if computer networking has a place in the classroom it will not be one that is assigned by superintendents or Boards of Education. They are working directly with classroom teachers to create a service that meets the needs of the teacher. Teachers, rather than technology, are at the heart of the program.

The AT&T Learning Network matches teachers and students together in Learning Circles--groups of classrooms from diverse cultural and geographic regions. Computer telecommunications is used to enhance teaching and learning among all of the participants. School students become involved in research on society's problems and global issues, in comparisons of historical, geographic, and environmental concerns, and in sharing local news, events and opinions with their peers.

Curriculum-based educational projects are central in the AT&T Learning Network, with the technology playing an essential but not central role. Electronic mail is sent and received during classroom hours with a single keystroke. Communication software supports most classroom computers and makes it easy to exchange, discuss, and publish student work. The computer takes over the responsibility of calling AT&T Mail, locating personal or shared folder mail, downloading the mail to the classroom computer, and terminating the connection.

Each group of classrooms in a Learning Circle cooperatively publishes a publication at the end of the session which summarizes or collects all the work that was done over the session. These publications demonstrate the quality of learning that takes place when students work with their peers in diverse locations.

2.1 Intellectual Development of Students

The AT&T Learning Network is organized into Learning Circles because this task-oriented grouping provides an effective way to integrate communication technology with classroom instruction. The AT&T Learning Network matches teachers and students who share academic interests but represent different geographic or cultural perspectives.

Research over the past two years on the Learning Network suggests that the ideal size of a Learning Circle is between 6-9 classrooms. This grouping helps to create an intimacy that is often missing in large scale telecommunications projects and provides the important diversity of perspectives that is a critical factor in the learning. Teachers and students work closely together within the Learning Circle sharing plans, ideas and work. Learning Circles have specific timelines and a fixed beginning and ending date.

Teachers and students are matched into Learning Circles and work cooperatively through telecommunications to design and carry out curriculum-based activities which extend the knowledge and skills they acquire in their classrooms. Learning Circles on the Learning Network help older students share written information with distant peers in much the same way "circle time" is used in the primary years to help young students share verbal information.

2.1.1 Learning Circles

When a new group of people comes together to accomplish a task, the first thing that is done is some form of group introductions. Teachers and students work better together when they have some way of conceptualizing their Learning Circle partners. Learning Circles begin with time dedicated to group introductions. They exchange Classroom Surveys with questions organized into sections to help students introduce themselves, their school, their community and their idea for a group project.

Teachers and students also prepare "welcome packs" to send by postal mail to their partners containing graphic and print material difficult or costly to transmit electronically. Some examples of things that students have exchanged are class photos, coins, stamps, flags, pictures of their school, city, and state, descriptions of school colors, mascots, dress codes, homework samples and school rules.

2.1.2 Student Projects

Teaching is creating an environment which enables students to teach themselves (Bredo 1989). All the research on peer tutoring points to the fact that one of the best ways to learn something is to agree to teach it to someone else. The Learning Circle activities capitalize on these educational principles. The teachers and students in the Learning Circle are all teachers and are all learners. As teachers, each class organizes an educational activity for the rest of the learners on the network. As learners, the teachers and students participate in the activities organized by the other classes. No one person or teacher knows exactly what will take place over the semester, yet the activities are well planned and organized by skilled educators. Here are some examples.

Students in one elementary class in Canada sponsored a project on Weather Patterns and the Greenhouse Effect. Their teacher worked with them to integrate weather and pollution data they requested and received from across the United States and in Australia. These students were very proud of their final report which was shared with their peers as part of their Circle publication.

Secondary level students in Germany sponsored a project on Energy and the Environment. They sent a survey asking students to find the answers to questions like: Where is the nearest nuclear power plant to your school? How do you know if it is safe from crashing air crafts, bombs or earthquakes? Do people who live near the plant organize protests? They also included a set of questions about energy conservation. They wanted to know about the packaging of household items and asked how people sort their household garbage.

Community comparison projects have been common and yet what students learn is anything but common. Students in the desert terrain of Coober Pedy, Australia, build their homes underground to escape the heat of the sun. Students in Alaska report on the setting of the sun and schooling in the everyday of night. Skateboards take Californian students to school while snow shoes and skis are more common means of travel reported by students in Canada. All these contrasts help to challenge the unexamined assumptions that we unconsciously hold about the world.

Another school in West Germany located in a farming district sponsored a project on the plight of small farmers. They found that students who lived on small farms in Illinois were facing many of the same extreme conditions that existed in Germany.

Elementary school students have taken over their local bureau of tourism by producing travel brochures for their area. "Welcome to Denmark... the land of the Vikings" or "Come to Israel" begin guides. Another set of guides created by a Circle of secondary students are called "Travel Brochures for Teens" and provide a look at the environment from their perspective. A teacher used this idea to make different time periods more vivid by having students create travel brochures from their area in a different historical period. One brochure reads "journey to the secret places, enjoy the sunny days and cool evenings" of the Aztecs.

High school students begin to appreciate the complexity of society's problems when they work to design studies of the homeless, illiteracy, or substance abuse, or to explore differences in family patterns or causes of suicide across cultures. For example, students discovered that terms like "dependent" and "independent" have very different meanings in different cultural settings when they responded to a survey designed by Japanese students. Traditional Japanese mothers wanted children to be dependent on them for all of their daily needs so that the children will devote maximum time to studies. American parents encouraged early independence of students feeling that taking responsiblity for oneself is part of the education process. Students in Japan related dependence to the cultural value of group conformity in Japan while independence seemed related to the value Americans place on individuality.

Students in a New York school chose to explore drug abuse by teenagers. Student opinions in New York were against serving alcohol at parties. Their Australian peers wanted to know "How do you have fun at a party without alcohol?" They responded by citing the high risks associated with alcohol particularly the number of accidents that involved drinking teenagers. Their own survey of the high school students at each of their Learning Circle schools showed that between 80 and 100% have driven or ridden in cars with drivers under the influence of alcohol.

Students at all levels write at length about themselves, their feelings, their school and their world. They write newspaper articles as well as more expressive pieces. Recipes for success, want ads for teenagers, telephone dramas and outrageous opinions have all been shared in Learning Circles. Stories that are started in one school are sent first to one then to another to be concluded by students drawing on very different perspectives and life experiences.

The philosophy of Learning Circles is to provide teachers with the necessary direction and support to explore creative ways of integrating communication technology with their curriculum. The project approach to exploring and solving real problems that characterizes Learning Circle activities encourages the integration of different subjects helping to place knowledge and skill in the context of their use in the adult community. Knowledge is constructed and owned as a consequence of interaction with the computer, teacher and classmates.

2.1.3 Learning Circle Publications

Many interesting projects in classrooms fail to make a lasting impression on students because little or no time is spent on the important step of reviewing and evaluating the learning experience. Each Learning Circle cooperatively publishes a final report which summarizes or collects all the work that was done over the session. This publication is a way to help students review and evaluate the exchanges they had with students in other locations. The choices they make about what to include in their final report and how to organize the information helps them to mentally organize what they learned.

There were eighteen Learning Circles in Spring 1989. The coordinators of fourteen of the Circles sent copies of their publications back to the Learning Network. The average length of these publications was 33 pages. There was an average of five sections or projects reported in each of the publications. The printing of the publications varied with the resources of the schools. A principal at one school was so impressed with the content that he paid to have the publication professionally printed.

The recognition that students receive from their published work has a lasting effect beyond the knowledge gained in working on a particular topic. Students on the AT&T Learning Network are involved in creating new knowledge, knowledge that is valued by those who read their publication.

2.2 Professional Development of Teachers

The projects and Learning Circle publications document student learning. But what effect does this participation have on teachers? Creative teachers often work in a vacuum. They crave the ability to share good teaching and new ideas, both to demonstrate their skill and to learn from others. When a class sponsors an activity, the classroom activity has a new audience. Teachers and students in other places are not only invited to look into the classroom to see what takes place, but to walk in, sit down and become the learners. The teacher also receives similar invitations from other classes to step out of the role of teacher and join with students from all over the world as a learner.

When teachers involved in Learning Circles were asked to list the most important educational benefit of this type of activity, they placed the professional development of the teachers as more important than the enhancement of student learning. This finding validates what Sarason, Cuban, LaFrenz and Friedman and others assert when they place the education and support of teachers at the source of any educational change.

3. EDUCATIONAL BENEFITS OF COMPUTER NETWORKING

Classrooms work together on the network for a relatively short period of time, but the links made as teachers and students share ideas and feelings often outlast the Learning Circle. As a consequence of this partnership, both students and teachers find their interest in learning renewed. Teachers have reported many lasting benefits from working in Learning Circles.

There can be little doubt that the revolutionary change predicted by the early advocates of computer technology has not been realized in the last decade. But this does not mean that computers can or should be relegated to the heap of innovations that have failed to penetrate the educational community. Revolutions are the actions of people not things. The revolution may still come. As teachers and students find that they can be in the classroom but not constrained by the solid walls, the dimensions of the classroom that have remained intact for so many years may begin to crumble. But if this happens, it will be because teachers and students are changing.

ACKNOWLEDGEMENTS

This paper has been prepared by the author for the World Conference on Computers in Education, Sidney, Australia, July 9-13. I am grateful to Hugh Mehan and Marcia Boruta for their comments. Requests for copies of this paper should be sent to: Margaret Riel, 943 San Dieguito Drive, Encinitas, CA 92024.

REFERENCES

Bredo, E., (1989). Supportive context for learning. *Harvard Educational Review Vol. 59,* No.2: p 206-212.

Cuban, L., (1986). Teachers and Machines: The Classroom Use of Technology Since 1920. New York: Teachers College Press.

Cuban, L., (1989). Neoprogressive visions and organizational realities. *Harvard Educational Review Vol. 59,* No.2: p 217-222.

Feldman, D, (1988). Nature's Gambit. New York: Basic Books.

LaFrenz, D., & Friedman, J., (1989). Computers don't change education, Teachers do! *Harvard Educational Review Vol. 59,* No.2: p 222-225.

Laboratory of Comparative Human Cognition (LCHC), (1983). Culture and cognitive development. In W. Kessen (Ed.) Handbook of child psychology Vol. 1. p 295-356. New York: Wiley.

Laboratory of Comparative Human Cognition (LCHC), (1989). Kids and computers: A positive vision of the future. *Harvard Educational Review Vol. 59,* No.1: p 73-86.

Pea, R., Hawkins,J. Clement, C. A., & Mawby, R., (1984). The development of expertise in Logo by children. New York: Bank Street College of Education, Center for Children and Technology.

Sarason, S. (1976). The creation of settings and future societies. San Francisco: Jossey-Bass.

Schwartz, J. (1989). Intellectual Mirrors: A step in the direction of making schools knowledge-making places. *Harvard Educational Review Vol. 59,* No.1: p 51-61.

Weir, S., (1989). Computers in schools: Machine as humanizer. *Harvard Educational Review Vol. 59,* No.1: p 61-73.

Winn, T ,and Coleman, I.,(1989). Urban and rural: A dialog about computers in schools. *Harvard Educational Review Vol. 59,* No.2: p 212-217.

Vygotsky, L. S., (1978). Mind in Society. Cambridge: Harvard University Press.

Computers in Education
A. McDougall and C. Dowling (Editors)
Elsevier Science Publishers B.V. (North-Holland)

NEW YORK STATE-MOSCOW SCHOOL TELECOMMUNICATION PROJECT: FIRST YEAR OF EXPERIENCE

Alexander Yu. Uvarov and Alexandra A. Prusacova

The Scientific Council of Cybernetics of the USSR Academy of Science

The first stage of a three-year experimental research program devoted to the determination of the possible role and place of telecommunications in the teaching/learning process and its influence on possible changes of the content and methods of education are described. Also discussed is the organization of the experiment whose participants are students, teachers and administrators from more than twenty schools in Moscow and New York State. The experimental method of the project and the targeted evaluation and selection criteria for the development of student-generated projects are enumerated.

1. INTRODUCTION

On the United Nations Day, October 24, 1988, the students of several Moscow schools wrote their first E-mail message to their partners in New York State schools. This was the beginning of the joint Soviet-American project. The realization of this linkup allowed the students and teachers of both countries to communicate with each other using telecommunication networks. This report reviews the goals and objectives of the project and describes experiences of the first year of the work.

2. BACKGROUND

Statements on the necessity of educational system reform and on the need for a new educational content have been made by the majority of the educators. There exists a wide spread opinion that computers and telecommunications can make a significant change in the teaching - learning process. However the center of our attention is still the vital problem of the introduction of new informational technologies into the school, their interaction with rapidly developing processes of the integration of new content and new educational means into traditional approaches. These were the issues that we took into consideration while preparing the NYS-Moscow School Telecommunications Project.

The basic idea was that the use of new technological means of communication and the direct contacts between common people of different countries would become, in the current decade, the global approach to changing the consciousness of the people, and the new communications unity would define the next step of the development of the world culture and the global community. In this context, The NYS-Moscow project can be regarded as one of the attempts to organize a productive dialogue between the representatives of two very different cultures.

The project was founded as a pilot experiment for the evaluation of the potential role of computers and telecommunications in the conditions of the rapidly changing educational content of general education and increasing contacts between the educational establishments, teachers and students of USA and USSR. The results obtained during the experiment can be regarded as a model for reproduction in schools as computers and telecommunications become widespread and cost less and the schools have an easier access to new technologies.

The project was founded by The Copen Family Foundation Inc. and The Council of Cybernetics of the Academy of Science of the USSR with the organizational support of New York State Department of Education, The Putnam/No. Westchester Board of Cooperative Educational Services and the Moscow State Department of Public Education.

3. ORGANIZATION OF COMMUNICATION

The work on the project is planned in three steps, each step targets a new school/year. During the preparatory stage (1988/1989) school year the schools were selected for joint work, the teachers and students got acquainted with each other and the telecommunication equipment was installed in schools.

Twelve public schools in New York State and twelve schools in Moscow were selected for the project. The schools applied for participation in the project and are typical for their regions. The students of these schools study computer science and have access to computer labs. The schools have courses in Russian and English.

In addition to usual school equipment that schools have all of them received Lumaphones donated by the Mitsubishi company and IBM PC's with Concord modems for communications using standard telephone lines. The communications services are provided by VNII PAS /Moscow/ and a business company "San Francisco - Moscow Teleport" (SFMT).

In the summer of 1989, in Moscow, there was a conference for the teachers representing all participating schools. During this conference teachers got the opportunity to make personal contacts, understand each other, discuss the plans for the next stage of joint work, learn about the accumulated experience of using telecommunications in the educational process and methods of organizing joint work on projects. The conference concluded the first step of work on the NYS-Moscow School Telecommunications Project.

The schools' telecommunications project is devoted to the study of the potential of telecommunications as a means for the enrichment of the educational process in schools. The exchange of electronic messages is only one of the possible ways to exchange information. We suppose it will be useful to include other means of communication available for schools. Different means of communications can add a lot to the process of communications according to the requirements of the pedagogical problem being solved by the teacher. That is why, together with the main process of communication-computer-based electronic networking, it is planned to organize telephone conferencing using the lumaphone. Regular mail can also be used. E-mail is comparatively cheap and the costs are covered by the organizers of the project. Students and teachers can use telecommunications on a regular basis and it provides for the greatest proportion of the information exchange. Moscow students use the centralized local network with a channel to SFMT through VN II PAS. The WildCat software package developed by Mustang Inc. is used as the local telecommunications software BBS for this local net. It is user-friendly and has possiblilties for expansion. During the first and second stages the telecommunictions is restricted mainly to E-mail messaging and generally provides the communications between the pairs of sister schools working on joint projects. During the third stage the regular exchange of communications, is supposed to be enriched by the possibilities of telephone conferencing.

Telephone conferences can add to the exchange of E-Mail messages, providing lively dialogue between the participants. All the schools will have the opportunity to try it two or three times a semester. The use of a computer-based electronic network will make it easier for the teachers to prepare for such conferences.

4. EXCHANGES

Mutual visits are quite expensive even in cases when family stays are organized. The organizers of the project can provide enough coverage for travel expenditures for only part of the participants of the project.

According to Katz, Inghiller, McSwiney and Stroud /1/ the social contact of the participants of network do not influence, significantly, the process of telecommunications. It will be elucidated in the course of the Project as to what extent the personal contacts of students influence the results of the research work on the telecommunications project. It is planned that mutual visits can be organized for the participation of students' and teachers' groups in conferences and the visits will take place during the final stages of the work to make conclusions and discuss the results of joint work.

During the first year the participants used regular mail and telephone links very seldom. For the enhancement of introduction of telecommunications into the educational system a Telecommunications Center of the Moscow Telecommunication network (MOSTNET) was organized in Moscow in the summer of 1989. The Telecommunications Center exists to help tutors, learners and their educators to make effective use of the new possibilities of new technologies. Telecommunications Centers runs courses and offers advice on all aspects of hardware, software and educational content for networking activities. It pursues and encourages the development of learning and teaching technologies, new educational methods and original work on telecommunications projects.

5. PROJECT METHOD

The initial interest of Soviet and American teachers to direct dialogue is substantial. This is the result of a global process of the information of a new unity of people on this planet and it demonstrates that, first and foremost, there is a new need to apprehend the new cultural environment. However, to establish a constructive dialogue between the people of different cultures there should be a commonly grounded content besides the initial interest. We envisage that the joint work of our teachers and students devoted to joint problem-solving is personally significant for each of them. Problems important to both communities can serve as a common ground. This focus gets its fullest realization when the solved problem is generated by the participants of the project. That is why the main form of the work of students in the NYS-Moscow Telecommunication Project is the method of student-generated projects. Here, sister-schools' projects are developed on the basis of the ideas generated by the school children with the support and help of the teachers.

The development of the cognitive independence of the students, the formation of the skills to perceive and familiarize the existing reality on the basis of scientific research methodology is one of the main tasks of general education. That is why, among the great number of possible projects, the preference is given to those that can be structured on the basis of generally accepted methods of research work. That is, one can clearly see the following stages: the definition of goals and the formation of hypotheses for the possible results of the future research, the narrowing down of the problem and the description of the procedures of the collection of the necessary data, data collection, data processing and the analysis of the obtained results, compilation of the report or publication and the discussion of the possible ways of the application of the results. Telecommunications projects performed earlier can be regarded as examples and can set prior standards /2/. So the general approach here is the development of student-generated projects on the basis of commonly accepted methods of regular research.

Realization of this method, in practice, leads to the changes in the teacher's role. The teacher is no longer the main source of knowledge. He/she becomes a partner in the research and the organizer of the process of joint work. To meet these requirements the teacher should become familiar with the position of the researcher. The participation in the NYS-Moscow School Telecommunications project supposes that research activities become a part of the daily life of the teacher. The educators engaged in this project form a research team, developing new ways and forms of educational process, together with the students. This teacher's activity is supported in every way by the organizers of the project.

6. CRITERIA FOR SELECTION AND EVALUATION OF STUDENTS GENERATED PROJECTS

One of the main difficulties in organizing joint work seems to be the need to create the coordinated image or pattern in the ways to select and evaluate student generated ideas and projects in the participants' minds. To reduce possible contradictions and misunderstandings we developed a set of criteria considering the uniqueness and specificity of this particular project allowing the selection of the ideas that will most probably be the basis of the most viable educational projects that correspond to the following set of objectives:

1. The project must use the advantages of telecommunications, can be successfully developed within the limits of telecommunications. The project must not be carried out without meaningful E-Mail transmissions.

2. The project must include the joint problem-solving activity of the students of the sister schools. It cannot be done by one side alone.

3. The project must correspond to the conditions of international joint work and should promote mutual understanding. The participants should be culturally sensitive and be ready to cope with possible misunderstandings and show tolerance.

4. The student-generated projects should use, as prototype, the process of research work in the lab. In the course of the instructional process the students should, step by step, reproduce the research approach to solve their problems.

5. The student-generated projects must have clear, well defined, recognizable results. To gain these the aim of the project should be narrowed down, if necessary, to the soluble problem. The result of such work should be significant for the participants of the project and valuable to the community.

6. The project must have educational value. It should be developed according to previously established pedagogical goals. The students are to gain knowledge, skills and improved attitudes.

7. The project must be well-structured. The stages and results are to be defined beforehand. At the same time the structure should be flexible and allow alternative variations.

8. The time-limit for a project or a separate unit must not exceed 4 months.

9. The project must be self-supporting and rely on the materials and equipment available to a school.

10. The project should be open to all those who are available and wish to participate.

For now these criteria seem to be sufficient, but only the expansion of the project will show their usefulness and credibility in the long-term.

7. PROBLEMS FOR FUTURE DISCUSSION

During our work on this project we would like to get a clearer view of the role of this new educational environment in the development of research skills and information processing skills.

Also, it will be extremely interesting to understand the influence of joint problem-solving through telecommunications networking on the critical thinking abilities of the students. We also would like to see if there is any correlation between computer literacy and the development of communication skills in computer-based communications networks. Up to now one of the most difficult problems has been the language barrier. We hope that, in the course of the project, the students will be further motivated to study foreign languages and new opportunities to polish their English and Russian, in particular. In this area there are a great deal of interesting questions such as the relationship between oral and written habits, the possibility of the team studies of foreign languages, the correspondence between communications and the reading skills in foreign languages, the advantages and disadvantages of using authenic texts (e.g., materials commonly used and written by people in their own country in their native language) for foreign language studies.

To define the possibility and usefulness of dissemination of the suggested model of this project, the independent external evaluation of the project is being conducted according to the standard procedures accepted in USA and USSR. The evaluation process is taking place in all Moscow and New York State schools participating in the Project. The project is to be completed in the autumn of 1991 by a concluding conference of educators participating in the project. After that the schools can use the accumulated experience without special support from Copen Family Foundation and the Academy of Science.

ACKNOWLEDGEMENTS

The authors of the projects express their sincere gratitude to Monica Bradsher/ National Geographical Society/, Robert Tinker /TERC/ for sharing their experience on developing KIDSNET.

REFERENCES

1. Katz, M. M., Inghiller, J., McSwiney, E. & Stroud, K.

   Ambiguity And Specificity In Network Discussions: Questions and Implications For Teacher Collegial Exchange Networks, unpublished paper presented at the AERA Meeting, New Orleans, 1988.

2. Waugh, M. L., Levin

   Educational Users of Electronic Networks, Journal of Computers in Mathematics and Sicence Teaching, v.8,N 2, p.29-33, Win 1988-89.

Computers in Education
A. McDougall and C. Dowling (Editors)
Elsevier Science Publishers B.V. (North-Holland)

CURRICULUM USES OF ELECTRONIC BULLETIN BOARDS

John WALTERS

NSW Computer Education Unit, Sydney, Australia

This paper will examine some of the many projects that schools and educators have organised and undertaken using *Keylink*, the electronic mail service that is used by the New South Wales Department of School Education.
In particular, this paper will look at curriculum uses of the *Keylink* bulletin board facility and the many benefits this form of communication can provide for schools with access to a computer and a modem.
The *Keylink* bulletin boards have led to many excellent language and information handling activities for students of all ages in our schools.
Electronic mail curriculum project ideas continue to be developed by innovative teachers and some of these are examined.

1. INTRODUCTION

1.1. Beyond Electronic Pen-Pals

If the use of electronic mail in our schools is to fulfil its enormous educational potential, then its use must go beyond the pen-pal stage. In this paper I wish to look at the educational potential of electronic bulletin boards rather than concentrating on the many pen-pal projects that are under way in this and other countries. An electronic bulletin board is a method of sending a message to an "open" audience where any-one can respond and confer on a range of topics. There are a number of bulletin boards available on *Keylink,* the service used by New South Wales schools. This paper will address the use of the general educational bulletin boards and will look at the many exciting and valuable curriculum opportunities they can provide. I propose to do this by briefly examining a number of case studies involving projects that were undertaken in New South Wales schools during 1989. Bulletin boards can provide the students with many opportunities to write for a relevant reason to a wide audience, explore attitudes and values from a number of perspectives, obtain information from "outside" sources, and provide the obvious personal benefits that this kind of communication can offer. Communication is a vital human need and provides many experiences for personal growth.

1.2. Curriculum Areas

Electronic mail, and in particular the bulletin board facility, provides an opportunity to communicate with distant schools and enables students to use these schools as a resource. This is particularly useful when a wide range of data sources is needed to enrich the students' "local" research and make their datafiles more relevant. As a result of bulletin board projects students are often involved in a wide range of activities both within the classroom and in the wider community as well as in many curriculum areas. These activities often provide experiences in areas such as:

communicating, eg
listening, reading, writing;

investigating, eg
observing, recording, organising, interpreting;

expressing, eg
presenting, reporting;

and thus making the bulletin boards outstanding educational tools.

1.3. Regular Feedback

The successful use of electronic mail, as with any other form of communication, is dependent on feedback. To increase the chances of gaining regular feedback during a telecommunications project, and thus making it a successful one, there are a number of points worth considering.

- You will need to establish:
    - clear aims and objectives;
    - beginning and completion dates;
    - the frequency of contact; and
    - responsibilities of each participating group.
- If you wish to involve other schools in a project then the activity must be just as relevant to them as it is to you.

2. JOINT TELECOMMUNICATIONS PROJECTS OFFERED ON *KEYLINK* IN 1989

Educational bulletin boards are a new and innovative way to communicate and exchange information on a variety of topics. Following is a list of projects that were available on *Keylink's* FORUM bulletin board during 1989. These projects were initiated by Computer Education Consultants from the NSW Department of School Education.

Newsdays - a project offered 4 times throughout the year. This project is outlined in more detail in Case Study Two, later in this paper.

Say It Survey - had students researching how they would say common phrases using their own language. They also surveyed their parents to see how they would say the same phrases. It encouraged students to have a close look at how they use language. Reports were written and "posted" on the bulletin board.

NSW Local Community Data Base - Schools across NSW were asked to collect information about their local town or area and send it to a central collation point where a database was made. This in turn was made available to schools as a downloadable file.

Ask an Author - provided NSW students the opportunity to ask selected authors about one of their favourite books. This was a great way to get classes reading.

Festival Cookbook - Favourite recipes from across the state were "posted" ready for inclusion in each school's recipe book. These recipe books could well reflect the many cultures that exist in NSW.

3. THE CASES STUDIES

At this point in the paper I will look more closely at a number of brief case studies that illustrate the benefits of the use of electronic bulletin boards in our schools. In particular, the case studies highlight the tremendous scope of educational activities that can be stimulated and facilitated by this medium.

3.1. • CASE STUDY ONE •

An Interview With Author, Roald Dahl

In April 1989 the British author, Roald Dahl, visited Australia. It would seem that Australian children are some of his greatest fans. While in NSW he expressed a desire to talk with children who live in isolated areas. To comply with this the NSW Computer Education Unit set up an interview that would take advantage of the *Keylink* bulletin board service. Twelve students from Years 5 and 6 (ages 10-11) at Belmore South Primary School in Sydney formed a lucky group which was given the opportunity to interview the famous author. This group acted as intermediaries between Roald Dahl and other students from schools across the state who used *Keylink* electronic mail to send their questions to Belmore South.
The learning opportunities that sprang from this activity were far wider than just the opportunity to participate in an interview with a famous author. The students undertook numerous valuable learning activities and these are now outlined.

Student activities before the interview.

• The students borrowed numerous Roald Dahl books. Writing characteristics were examined including writing style, vocabulary, invented words, and so on. Some students managed to read all seventeen of his children's books.

• The students composed a clear message to invite interested schools to send in questions for the interview. This message was "posted" on both the FORUM and STUDENTS *Keylink* bulletin boards.
• A great deal of discussion took place before a suitable wording for the invitation was agreed upon.
• The final version was keyed into a word processor and fully edited before it was "posted" on *Keylink*.
• The Belmore students 'logged on' to *Keylink* each day and downloaded the incoming questions that poured in from right across the state.
• Students "posted" messages back to the schools that sent in questions asking them to provide a little background information about themselves.
• The teacher/librarian asked the students to carefully examine and identify questions that - were good; were similar to others questions; and only required yes/no answers.
The students were immersed in reading, analysing, classifying and selecting questions.
• The students constructed a large map of New South Wales for Mr Dahl and marked in the location of each contributing school.
• The teacher/librarian organised an art session where they designed a Dahl information folder. The design incorporated Dahl story titles, photos and book covers.

The Interview

The students handled the interview like professionals.
Thanks to the co-operation and support of Telecom Australia the interview also utilised a telephone link, via the Royal Flying Doctor Service, to allow direct communication with the School of the Air at Broken Hill 900km away. In this way children on isolated properties were able to listen in and "chat" to the author.

Post interview work on answers.

• Soon after the interview the students began work compiling and editing the Dahl answers in preparation for 'posting to individual schools and the *Keylink* bulletin boards. This process saw the students involved in many conferences and informal discussions as they honed the answers into a satisfactory format.

The Roald Dahl project involved the Belmore South students in a multitude of exciting educational activities and had them using many examples of the latest technologies.

The Story Continues ......
A Writers' Camp

As a result of the Belmore students asking for further background information from each of the participating schools, an invitation from Khancoban Public School was received on *Keylink* inviting them to a writers' camp to be held at the old Shelley logging camp, just south of the NSW/Victorian border, some 600km from Sydney. About a month later a group of students and teachers from Belmore South met the Khancoban students at the camp. It seems a little technology can take you a long way.
A group of well known Australian authors and illustrators were in attendance at the camp to run workshops for the students. This provided a rare opportunity for the students to meet these experts and discuss all the processes involved in writing and illustrating a book.

The Belmore South students who conducted the Roald Dahl interview were very fortunate. Rarely does such an opportunity like that arise. These students of course gained far more from the experience than did the schools that contributed questions from afar. This was due more to the involved processes they went through, in particular before the interview, than to their attendance at the actual interview.
Students from the contributing schools, in a more limited but still valuable way, were given the opportunity to be involved and to write, edit and submit questions they believed were relevant and interesting. Most likely they were involved in researching and reading numerous Dahl books which they followed up with group discussions.

Each year students in New South Wales are given the opportunity to participate in a similar project by accessing the *Ask An Author* bulletin board.

3.2. • CASE STUDY TWO •

NEWSDAY a 'real time' simulation

Newsday is a quarterly event where classes or groups of students work as a newspaper team using computers and a modem to produce a newspaper.
Newsday is one of many innovative and valuable uses of the *Keylink* electronic mail service and involvement in this project allows students to research, write, edit, discuss, decide, design, format, publish and gain feedback while participating in a 'real time' simulation of the production of a newspaper.
Schools that participate place articles on the *Newsday* bulletin board, as they would a news service, to enable schools across the state to 'download' and incorporate them in their own school newspaper.
• On the publication day the students are allocated jobs parallel to those in a real newspaper and then briefed on their specific jobs and responsibilities. Generally *Newsday* articles are saved on floppy disk and draft copies are printed on to paper for ease of use.
• The students control the entire publishing process. They make their own decisions about content, layout and style of publication. The role of the supervising teachers on the day is advisory only.
An important rule that each participating school must abide by is that if they use an article "posted" on the *Newsday* bulletin board they must send a copy of their completed newspaper to that author's school. This is a suitable form of recognition for that school and for the author in particular.

Young editors display their newspaper

Participation in a Newsday provides students with the opportunity to develop skills in - article writing, decision making, selecting news items, editing written articles, reporting, discussing, designing, problem solving and of course group cooperation and self direction.

Sub-editors search for suitable graphics

3.3. • CASE STUDY THREE •

National Aboriginal Week Bulletin Board

During National Aboriginal Week a special *Keylink* bulletin board was set up by the NSW Computer Education Unit to make it possible for Aboriginal students across the state to voice their opinions on themselves and their place in society. Messages poured in from all over the state. Schools "posted" a number of acrostic poems and followed these up with letters and Aboriginal stories they had written. Students from as far afield as Wilcannia (far north-west) and Griffith (south-west) sent messages to the bulletin board after attending an exciting camp at the Broken Bay Sport and Fitness Centre. Many people in the Aboriginal community took advantage of this opportunity to "post" messages on the bulletin board.
Judging by the state-wide interest shown, the National Aborigines Week Bulletin Board was a great success. It provided students, both Aboriginal and non-Aboriginal, with the opportunity to use the new technologies to communicate and share ideas while generally raising awareness about the Aboriginal people of Australia.

3.4. • CASE STUDY FOUR •

The Trans-Antarctic Expedition

This bulletin board established late in 1989, is one in which weekly reports from the '1990 International Trans-Antarctic Expedition' are placed so that school children in NSW can join their friends in USA, UK, France, Japan, USSR and China in following the progress of this historic trek as it happens. This immediacy of access to information is one of the main advantages of electronic communications, children no longer need to read reports of events long after they happen but can become involved in the action as it happens.
This bulletin board is called TRANTARCT. It has great potential for encouraging and supporting a broad spectrum of educational processes. Following is part of the initial message posted on the FORUM bulletin board.

"HISTORY IN THE MAKING
Join six explorers from 6 countries as they traverse the Antarctic on dog sleds and cross country skis. The explorers are in contact with a communications ship - the U.A.P. from which their reports are sent to Michigan in the U.S.A. and from there they are accessible electronically.
This is a unique opportunity for you all to participate in important research into weather, the environment, the ozone layer, effects of temperature on diet, etc."

Bulletin boards such as this open up a new "window to the world" where teachers and students can tap into information that was once only attainable through books and journals published well after the 'event'. The students can now access, digest and act on the information almost immediately. Because of the newness of the concept ie. an 'online expedition journal', resourceful and imaginative students and teachers may well come up with hitherto undreamed of activities.

One high school approached their local newspaper and offered to compile and edit a regular Trans-Antarctic Expedition column for inclusion in the paper. These students would have the opportunity to develop research and editing skills while writing for a large audience.

Case studies 1, 2, 3 and 4 are examples of telecommunication projects that have been initiated and organised by central and regional computer education consultants. The following two case studies are examples of school or teacher initiated projects. It is generally the 'school initiated' project that will be the most innovative and educationally relevant and it is this type of project that should be supported and encouraged by computer educators at every stage and level.

3.5. • CASE STUDY FIVE •

A Diet Survey

Late in 1989 a Sydney primary class had been doing an extensive unit of work on food. As part of this unit a diet survey was developed and information from other classes was collected, sorted and analysed using a database program. In an effort to make the file more relevant a request for data for their diet survey was "posted" on the *Keylink* bulletin board FORUM, and also sent to their electronic mail pen-pals in England. The students received valuable data as a result of both transmissions. The students wrote a report after examining the trends that emerged from 'searches' made of their datafile.

Keylink provides a gateway to distant schools and enables students to use these schools as a resource. This is particularly useful when a wide range of data sources is needed to enrich the students' "local" research and make their database more relevant.
Projects like the diet survey that draw information from across the state and overseas provide opportunities for students to reflect on some of the different cultures that are present throughout the world.

3.6. • CASE STUDY SIX •

Key Into Parliament Project

A call for participation in an interview of the leader of the federal opposition by the students of NSW to be coordinated through Hay Public School was posted on the FORUM bulletin board late in 1989. The children of Hay PS (in the far south west) invited questions from schools across the state for Andrew Peacock M.P. (Leader of the Federal Opposition).
The project had many exciting educational possibilities and even attracted commendation from the Prime Minister of Australia. The organising teacher "posted" a series of messages that included a detailed list of project aims, an outline of the planning already undertaken and many practical suggestions for its integration into a unit on Parliamentary studies. This curriculum information went a long way towards insuring the participation of other schools and thus the success of the entire project.
This project was unique for the children of NSW and allowed country schools experiences related to telecommunications within the broader community of Australia, a group who often have little direct contact or access to our National Leaders.

4. CONCLUSION

From simple 'local' pen-pal projects to international correspondence via satellite, communication aided by computer has inspired great interest and enthusiasm among students and teachers. If this interest and enthusiasm is to be maintained then electronic mail must provide opportunities to support relevant curriculum applications.
The 'open' electronic bulletin board offers teachers many ways to enhance the curriculum and widen the learning experiences of their students.

Author, Roald Dahl (seated) and John Walters (standing) are surrounded by the excited Belmore South interview panel.

Computers in Education
A. McDougall and C. Dowling (Editors)
Elsevier Science Publishers B.V. (North-Holland)

COMPUTER NETWORK APPLICATIONS TO DISTANCE EDUCATION

Robert W. Walton

Ontario Institute for Studies in Education
252 Bloor Street West
Toronto, Ontario, Canada M5S 1V6

Computer networks are becoming an increasingly popular means of distance education delivery. They are currently used to gain access to data bases, facilitate student/teacher communications and, at certain institutions, present entire graduate programs on-line. Benefits associated with network education include; the ability to produce transcripts of data, reduced travel time and costs and statistics available for student assessment. As on-line education gains momentum, it is conceivable that a home or office will be the classroom of the future.

1. INTRODUCTION

The majority of modern day universities have computer systems which can be accessed from external communications lines. The evolution of computer networks begins with this ability to 'tap-in' to the computer and the large data banks of information it provides. From the passive utility of withdrawing information, users were provided with an opportunity to interact with the system through the exchange of electronic mail and posting notices on bulletin-board services. Sophistication of computer software added on-line editing facilities and synchronous (and asynchronous) multi-user capabilities, permitting an immediate exchange of information and ideas. This latter characteristic introduced the innovative idea of computer conferencing.

This paper discusses applications of university computer networks to distance education, their success as a delivery medium and issues related to Computer-Mediated Communications (CMC) which require further research. It is important to acknowledge that both similarities and variations in applications exist in many other institutions such as primary and secondary schools and commercial companies.

2. UNIVERSITY COMPUTER NETWORKS

Four institutions with computer networks will be compared in terms of the on-line educational services they provide. These are: The Open University, University of Guelph, The Ontario Institute for Studies in Education and Boise State University. These institutions offer a representative cross-section of many university distance education applications, ranging from simple data access to complete on-line graduate degree programs.

2.1. University of Guelph

The computer conferencing software CoSy has been on-line at the University of Guelph since 1984. It was initially developed and installed as an internal networking system, but was made available to external users when its educational potential was realized.

CoSy offers a variety of educational utilities including its current use in distance education as an information data base and communications medium for degree credit courses. A parallel subsystem used at the University is T-CoSy which faculty members use for communication with students as an adjunct to regular classroom instruction. The system has yet to be developed to the point where courses are offered on-line, similar to The Ontario Institute for Studies in Education and Boise State University.

The future of educational computer networking at the University of Guelph appears very promising. The development of computer conferencing courses, in addition to current communication and data base utilities, will optimize their networking capabilities.

2.2. The Open University

The Open University of Great Britain, offers a computer-mediated communications network which augments a well established multi-media delivery system for distance education. The software package used is a modified version of CoSy. University support to students using computers for course augmentation is very extensive, including: reduced price computer sales, computer rentals, modem and software loans, audio taped instructions and printed user manuals.

Educational applications of the network are quite limited considering the potential of the CoSy system software. Faculty members use the system as a data base to support courses, and tutors are hired by the University to provide on-line assistance, (Kaye, [1]). Computer conferencing as the exclusive method of course delivery in distance education has been relatively unsuccessful to date. Future attempts to involve students on-line will incorporate "cooperative work among students by making practicable the setting of assignments which require cooperative activity", (Thomas, [2]).

2.3. The Ontario Institute for Studies in Education

The Ontario Institute for Studies in Education (OISE) utilizes a computer conferencing software called PARTICIPATE for on-line communications and distance education. PARTICIPATE (PARTI) and CoSy are similar in many respects, varying primarily in user-interface design. PARTI permits users to read and write personal or conference notes, send real time messages, participate in synchronous and asynchronous discussions and 'FIND' notes that they have either sent or received in the past. Communications are also provided for library searches, dialogue between staff and students and student organization information dissemination.

The OISE conferencing system is used to provide graduate degree credit courses in the areas of adult education and computer applications in education. Several courses are offered exclusively through computer-mediated communications, while others utilize conferencing as a supplementary medium. In order to accommodate asynchronous participation, the system is available via modem 24 hours per day, year-round.

2.4. Boise State University

Spitzer [3] indicated that Boise State University commenced one of the most comprehensive computer-mediated communications programs available in distance education, in September 1989. The University offers an on-line Master's Degree program in Instructional Technology to U.S. Military personnel throughout the United States. Topics and assignments required for the degree have been selected specifically to monopolize on the individual and collaborative research opportunities afforded by CMC.

The program requires from two to four years to complete, during which time only two weeks are spent on campus. The off-campus coursework is delivered using a multi-media integration of printed materials, video tapes, computer conferencing, CBI training and teleconferencing.

3. SUCCESS OF COMPUTER CONFERENCING

Successful learning through computer networks depends a great deal on the host network and its supportive organization. It is not difficult for universities to provide one-to-one exchange between students and data bases or students and teachers via electronic mail, consequently these modes of information dissemination and learning have been very successful. Examples of these applications were discussed in relation to services provided by the University of Guelph and the Open University.

The use of networks to provide computer-based instruction (CBI) is the next logical step from the data base concept. There is no reason to doubt the potential of on-line CBI, and its application in the Boise State curriculum should provide interesting research material. There is little doubt that the CMC courses offered at OISE are successful. Admittedly, the courses are difficult to evaluate as to the effect computer conferencing has on learning as compared to the more traditional classroom scenario. Nevertheless, students and staff associated with this aspect of the graduate program agree that this new medium for course delivery provides a challenge and motivation to continue to take an active role in the course.

4. BENEFITS OF COMPUTER CONFERENCING

Benefits derived from the use of computer networks in distance education vary from one individual to another, although there are certain tangible benefits available to all.

4.1. Hard/Soft Copy

Individual learning styles dictate the importance of the ability to save and/or print notes entered into conferences during the course. A significant percentage of students have reported difficulty in following the 'theme' of conferences without a hard copy of transcripts. Under these circumstances, the ability to download and print data from the conference or copy notes from electronic mail system, becomes a decisive factor as to whether the student will successfully complete the course or not.

4.2. Travel

With the exception of an initial class meeting face-to-face (optional), there is little travel involved with on-line education. On occassion, there may exist a requirement to visit the university library for reference material for a course project; however, even library services are now available on-line. This represents a saving in time and cost (in some cases) which may or may not compensate for additional course fees encountered with long distance telephone charges.

The elimination of travel requirements has reportedly had a negative impact on the utility of CMC. For example, a needs assessment conducted by Walton [4] revealed that prospective participants in a computer-mediated professional development network would be less likely to support the program if business travel was curtailed. It is suspected that many professionals consider work-related travel as a bonus (since it is usually paid for) and they can combine business with pleasure at no additional cost.

4.3. Accessibility

The ease of access to university computer networks makes on-line education a very attractive alternative to classroom courses. Students have the benefit of learning without tight schedules and in many instances have access to a computer both in the home and workplace. The availability of a telephone is the only practical constraint for students enrolled in courses, and those required to travel throughout the semester are able to communicate via portable 'laptop' computers equiped with a modem.

4.4. Student Assessment

A variety of statistics are available from computer conferencing software which facilitate student assessment in those instances where the network has been used to deliver or augment an on-line course. For example, one OISE graduate course in adult education offers a percentage of course marks for student participation. Marks are allocated by the number of notes and not their content. The objective of this design is to encourage participation and improve student computer literacy. In this case, the instructor would be provided with statistics on the number, length and time of messages entered into a conference by each student.

4.5. Personal scheduling

The asynchronous nature of CMC permits flexibility in the student's daily routine and class participation, and is considered to be a benefit of the medium. However, time allocation to on-line activity by students can become a considerable problem. Many students enrol in on-line courses with the belief that they will be able to study, participate in conferences, and upload assignments at their convenience. Although this is generally a convenient method of completing a course, it is not always possible to schedule activities at a satisfactory time. Students must 'logon' regularily in order to remain current with conference topics. Delays in reading and responding to notes create problems with relevance, since responses to ideas tend to accumulate quickly and the conference 'flows' from one theme to another, similar to a classroom conversation.

5. RESEARCH ISSUES IN ON-LINE EDUCATION

There are numerous problems and peculiarities encountered when using CMC as a delivery medium for distance education. Research directed toward problem solving in the CMC environment must focus on two areas; the CMC medium itself and activities associated with computer conferencing (CC).

Research into the medium itself must concentrate on how communication takes place and why it differs from other forms of communications media, how and why people use the medium, and the environments most conducive to learning via CMC. Computer conferencing activities must be examined for their potential including activities that utilize CC exclusively for course presentation, and those which incorporate CC into a program as one of several learning 'tools'. The following list of research issues includes issues that have been referred to in the literature most frequently, but are not necessarily the only areas of research required for this relatively new medium for education.

5.1. Ethics

Rice [5] and Johansen [6] agree on the

importance of ethical issues in CMC, particularily as they relate to electronic monitoring of participants. Research is required to determine the effect that this perceived 'surveillance' has on student participation. The fact that written transcripts are readily available (considered a benefit) may reduce the spontaneity normally occuring in face-to-face meetings. On the other hand, there is always the possibility that CMC might lead to greater honesty, in that participants may only make statements that they are ready to defend.

5.2. Analytical Tools

Winklemans [7] suggests that new analytical tools are required to assess the efficiency of CMC. His concerns were primarily that CMC may or may not meet the needs of students or be suitable for tutoring young learners. At present, there is a strong feeling that CMC is a 'novelty medium' in Canadian universities which may make the suitability factor difficult to measure. As mentioned by Johansen, initial uses and observations of CMC are a poor basis for predicting future applications. This is particularily true for networks involving novice users, since use of the medium is governed to a large extent by low-level writing skills and high-level cognitive skills necessary for expressing ideas.

5.3. Communication

Johansen [8] questions how new media such as CMC will affect the way in which people communicate. He suggests that the question of which media should be used, when and with whom, are important issues to be dealt with when considering changes in delivery techniques. Another problem with communication, is the lack of a common language between potential users. A common language, or agreed upon definitions, requires development in order that CMC issues can be discussed and problems resolved. At the moment, the terms computer-mediated communications and computer networks have a variety of meanings, depending on the context of their use.

5.4. Computer Illiteracy

Computer illiteracy is a problem that plagues almost all on-line education courses. New students that are unfamiliar with their hardware and communications software are often delayed in participating with other course members, consequently, the quantity and quality of messages is often affected. Another problem created by illiteracy is the identification of a population that can provide an unbiased value assessment of educational CMC. The identification of such a population is prerequisite to successful data collection and analysis in CMC.

5.5. Learning Styles

Learing styles have an important impact on the way in which students organize their studies to cope with this textual based medium. There is widespread agreement in principle, that CMC differs from face-to-face instruction, although the learning styles developed by students to cope with each environment require further investigation. One approach used to analyze dimensions of learning processes is to investigate the preferred styles of receiving and working with information. Within the field of learning styles, theorists have developed a variety of perspectives of how learning is facilitated or made more difficult under varying conditions.

Learning styles suggested by Torkelson [9] classifies learners into four catagories:

(i) Innovative - students ask WHY? (learn by watching)

(ii) Analytical - students ask WHAT? (learn by thinking)

(iii) Common Sense - students ask HOW? (learn by doing)

(iv) Dynamic - students ask WHERE? (learn by sensing/ feeling, application of concepts)

Investigation is required into the reasons for student failure and dropout from courses incorporating computers for delivery of the material. There could be an element of dissatisfaction on the part of the student resulting from a conflict between learning style and medium presentation. Torkelson states that "the greater the match between the learner experience and the media attributes, the greater the likelihood of the learner's acceptance of the media content".

5.6. Equity

It is difficult to design a system that is equitable to all, and CMC is not exception. As the application of CMC increases throughout the education system, problems of social and economic inequities will arise and require resolution. In some areas of our current educational system, gifted students in enriched programs are already exposed to more on-line experience than regular students. In addition, those students from more economically stable families often have computer systems at home to supplement school experience. Other potential issues facing decision makers in the political and educational arenas are:

(i) Will funds be provided through the education system to subsidize students that cannot afford hardware and software required for CMC?

(ii) Will physically disabled students be afforded the opportunity to take part in CMC courses, when special hardware requirements exist?

(iii) Is a certain learning style or minimum I.Q. required for enrollment in CMC courses?

(iv) Are there groups that have not been able to participate, if so why?

(v) How can anxiety in this medium be overcome? and

(vi) How can groups or individuals be encouraged to use the medium?

6. CONCLUSION

All stages of computer network development have afforded opportunities for educational applications. Computer access to data provided students with a wealth of stored information and services such as on-line library facilities. Networks established within the university complex increased the number of users through the expansion of facilities and extension of their services to distance education students. External access provided distance education with a new medium with which students could interact with course instructors and their peers. This interaction introduced the concept of collaborative learning into a previously solitary learning environment.

This paper has examined the educational applications of university computer networks and characteristics of on-line courses. There are many possibilities for additional computer uses in distance education, such as the introduction of integrated multi-media incorporating sound, graphics, CD ROM and hypertext. The 'newness' of CMC in distance education has introduced a host of new educational problems requiring investigation. It is difficult to assign priorities to many of the issues, since each application of CMC may have unique problems associated with it.

REFERENCES

[1] Kaye, T., Introducing computer-mediated communications into a distance education system, Canadian Journal of Educational Communication, 16(2), p153-166, 1987.

[2] Thomas, R., CoSy Implications for The Open University, in Open U, On-line report, November, OISE, Toronto, 1988.

[3] Spitzer, R., Boise State University M.S. Degree in Instructinal Technology: Remote Delivery Program, Boise State University, Boise, Idaho, 1989.

[4] Walton, R., Training Development Needs Assessment: Computer Networking Requirements, Unpublished Report, Canadian Forces Base Borden, Ontario, September, 1989.

[5] Rice, R., Collection and analysis of data from communication system networks, Communications of the ACM, March, p134-140, 1988.

[6] Johansen, R., Pitfalls in the social evaluation of teleconferencing media, in Second Annual International Communications Conference, University of Wisconsin, May 27-28, 1976.

[7] Winkelmans, T., Educational Computer Conferencing: An Application of Analysis Methodologies to a Structured Small Group Activity, Master's Dissertation, OISE, Toronto, 1988.

[8] Johansen, R., Teleconferencing and and Beyond: Communications in the Office of the Future, McGraw-Hill, New York, pp185, 1984.

[9] Torkelson, G.M., Theoretical basis for research in media, Canadian Journal for Educational Communication, 16(7), p3-10, 1987.

PEG 90

Computers in Education
A. McDougall and C. Dowling (Editors)
Elsevier Science Publishers B.V. (North-Holland)

THINKING, LEARNING AND KNOWLEDGE-BASED TOOLS

Jacqueline DEAN

PEG Exeter, School of Education, Exeter University, Exeter EX12LU, UK

This paper relates human cognitive processing to the learning process and to the effective use of knowledge-based tools in education. It examines how people learn, with particular reference to the importance of the initial mental models formed by learners. PEG's educational philosophy, knowledge bases and knowledge-based tools are described briefly, as are learner's problems with formal logic. The paper identifies the salient features of a teaching methodology, based on PEG experience, which will help students to learn effectively using knowledge-based tools. It closes by proposing that knowledge-based tools have the potential to change the relationship between teachers, learners and knowledge.

1. INTRODUCTION

The development of knowledge-based tools (KBTs) forms an important part of Artificial Intelligence research. AI is concerned to develop conceptual representations which model human thought processes. KBTs are 'intelligent' programs which aim to reflect and support thinking and learning processes. The exciting thing about AI is that, like philosophy, it has tried to develop general theories of mind and thought - it is a "sort of modern-day epistemology." [1]

If AI researchers and cognitive psychologists can produce models of mind which work, we can use them as a basis for improving teaching and learning.

Information processing theory in particular has provided an extremely useful model for explaining how people think and learn. It has provided an explicit language for talking about what happens inside the mind. The brief overview below describes an information processing construct of the learning process.

1.1. What cognitive processes occur when a learner encounters a problem?

First, the learner has to understand the task or problem which is presented. Understanding a task or set of instructions implies an active process of interpretation. This process is very individual because our experiences influence our understanding, so many different kinds of knowledge are called upon for interpretation. This knowledge can only be retrieved quickly and automatically from long-term memory if it is already organised into useful schemata. This ensures that most of the relationships between aspects of a problem have already been established, and most of the inferences have been made. In this case, working memory can overcome its limitations by 'chunking' incoming data.

So, understanding a problem depends on mapping the information presented onto appropriate information structures in long-term memory. These information structures have been variously called schemata, frames [2] and scripts [3]. Appropriate structures comprise all the data which will be relevant to the problem at hand *and* which is rapidly and readily accessible.

At this point learners form an initial representation of the problem or situation in their minds. This initial representation, or mental model, provides a framework for learners as they work through the problem. Thus new data is interpreted in terms of already-existing structures in long-term memory.

As problem-solving progresses, there is a frequent interchange between long-term and working memory. As new states are encountered or formed by the problem-solver, long-term memory is constantly being accessed for more appropriate structures. With new structures being formed, and in turn mapped into long-term memory, the initial mental model is constantly evolving and being modified. During this process new knowledge states are arrived at - learning has taken place. Characteristically, then, learning is the result of some form of problem-solving.

Learning difficulties arise when the learner's representation of the initial problem is inappropriate, for this primary-level understanding is difficult to change - learners find it hard to see the problem in any other way, even when they encounter evidence which conflicts with their model [4,5]. The appropriateness of the initial mental model formed is therefore crucial to effective learning.

2. PEG: THE DEVELOPMENT OF TOOLS FOR THINKING

PEG began as the Prolog Education Group, but now forms a wider collaborative network of teachers and researchers interested in the application of AI and cognitive psychology to education. The PEG research community has used ideas from AI, and an AI research programming language (Prolog), to generate knowledge-based tools for teachers and students. These have developed in many forms, but all are fundamentally concerned with the appropriate representation of knowledge, with clear specification, with logical thinking and with semantic connections. Prolog has been the language primarily used for the development of KBTs because as a declarative, predicate logic-based language it is particularly suitable for knowledge representation.

The work of the PEG-Exeter group has been firmly based in the curriculum [6,7]. During the span of its action research project the PEG-Exeter team taught children aged between nine and fifteen, ranging from secondary school history students to boys with specific learning difficulties.

Its aim has been to provide an environment which reflects and supports students' thinking processes and to develop tools to enable them to represent knowledge appropriately. The group has tried to foster the development of both domain-specific knowledge and metacognitive knowledge and skills, i.e. thinking skills.

To achieve these aims, it has developed:
- *knowledge bases* which enable active investigation by students and which are structured appropriately for the form of knowledge being represented. They provide students with both domain-specific knowledge and models for the organisation of such knowledge;
- effective *knowledge-based tools*, for students to write their own knowledge bases (in order to represent not only what they know, but also how they think about it); and
- *teaching methods* based on what we know about how learning takes place. This has involved the development of tasks structured so that learners can understand and tackle them successfully.

2.1. Knowledge bases

Knowledge bases are collections of information about a particular topic or domain, organised in a form appropriate to the structure of the topic or domain. The first PEG-Exeter knowledge bases were written for history students; they contained documents for students to read, known historical facts and what people in the past were reported to have said. In exploring them, students went through essentially the same processes as professional historians investigating the past. Subsequent knowledge bases have been developed across the curriculum; examples include social studies simulations, historical and mathematical adventures, rock identification and other classification programs, expert systems which will explain to users whether and why they are in a high risk category for AIDS. The potential for learning of content-specific knowledge bases which students can explore is well-documented [6]. Knowledge bases are useful not only as sources of domain-specific knowledge, but also because they can elicit higher order thinking skills.

2.2. The PEG Knowledge-Based Tools

Over the past seven years or so PEG has evolved a set of KBTs which enable learners to structure knowledge within the context of subject learning. These tools and their use in classrooms have been extensively discussed elsewhere [8,9]. The prototypes required users to master Prolog syntax; today's KBTs are menu-driven and appear in pretty windows. It is hard now to remember the time when students writing a prototype DETECT knowledge base had to enter statements in the form:

```
((said doctor (body was Iron Age man)))
```

The removal of Prolog syntax has ensured that learners can concentrate on exploring or representing knowledge without their working memory being taken up with syntactic details - thus the process of forming appropriate mental models and knowledge structures is easier for learners. There is a trade-off, however, in that some of the power and flexibility of the language is sacrificed.

Below is a brief description of PEG KBTs.

- DETECT [10]: a kind of hypertext, analogous to a filing system. Information is organised into categories, and within each category information about different subjects can be investigated through the use of subject keywords. DETECT is ideal for investigations, as the data is hidden until asked for.
- KEYS [10]: also a kind of hypertext, but has menus and the keywords can be highlighted in the text on any screen and investigated further. Excellent for storing large amounts of knowledge about a topic and for developing project ideas.
- THE PLAN [11]: an adventure-writing tool which provides a structure for writing adventures. The adventures generated can then be 'played' by others. Briefly, THE PLAN allows a writer to create a world by specifying and describing locations, objects within any location and actions which the adventure player can take. THE PLAN allows the creation of interactive writing, with particular application to primary work across the curriculum [12].
- LINX [10]: for the creation of any program with a tree structure. Using LINX students can write stories, adventures or simulations; classify things; represent expert knowledge. Indeed, they can construct a program about any topic which involves decision making. LINX allows students writing a story or simulation to carry forward the consequences of previous decisions so that they affect later events.
- KNOWLEDGE PAD [10]: an advice-giving tool which has been created specifically for education as an introduction to the ideas underlying expert systems. Expert systems are rule-based programs which contain expert knowledge. Anyone constructing an expert system must therefore have mastered knowledge of a topic or domain - and its structure. A useful feature of KNOWLEDGE PAD is its ability to explain its reasoning to users of a completed expert system.

2.3. The issue of logical thinking

The PEG community has a common interest in, and enthusiasm for, logical thinking, both *formal* logical thinking and the kind which can probably be more accurately be described as *rational* thinking. Formal logical thinking involves knowing rules of inference, the functions of logical operators, and so on. Most PEG KBTs require the use of formal logic in one form or another. (DETECT and KEYS are the only KBTs that do not require students to write logical conditional rules.) It is the functioning of these rules that causes learners most problems. This is because formal logic is not natural or automatic - it is a discipline requiring the exercise of high-level thinking skills [4,13]. Logical rules can be difficult to understand and apply. They involve learners in constraining and manipulating mental models of problems.

The difficulties that learners have with logic are dependent on many factors, among them:

- knowledge of formal problem domains - having some knowledge of logical rules to draw upon. For example, children frequently do not fully comprehend the functioning of the logical operators 'AND', 'OR' and 'NOT' [14]. A 13-year-old constructing a Prolog database wrote:
  x is best if ....
  and x is second-best if ....
  clearly not realising the logical function of 'and' (in contrast to its conversational use);
- initial representation of the problem - if the problem is couched in natural language, the learner may not be aware that the application of formal logic principles is appropriate;
- whether aids are provided for working memory as it grapples with logical reasoning;
- developmental stage - learners who are not yet able to reason formally often experience difficulty with, for example, conditional rule-writing;
- context - the context in which problems are presented has a great influence on people's ability to solve them. When abstract problems are encountered, many people prove unable to solve them. However, if these problems are placed in a concrete context, like Anno's hats, people can often succeed because the problems make sense in real life terms.

Therefore, because logic is difficult, we need to support learners by a variety of means as they formulate logical rules. It is not so much simple rules (A if B) on which students fall down. Their logical failures occur mainly when there is a complex interrelation between rules, or when more than one condition is involved. These difficulties indicate that the number of elements which have to be manipulated simultaneously overburdens working memory.

2.4. Teaching methods

It is obviously not enough to develop tools which encourage exploratory learning and the logical structuring of knowledge. Students will only learn effectively if the teacher, the learning task and the teaching methodology support such learning. Teachers themselves will choose tasks within the curriculum for their students; the teaching methodology is the final, crucial, part of the learning equation. If we take into account what we know about human cognitive processes, our educational goals and what we have learnt from our experiences with learners and KBTs, we can identify the features of a teaching methodology which will help students to learn effectively.

2.4.1. Representation of the problem so learners can form an appropriate mental model

As discussed earlier, the initial mental model the learner forms of a problem is crucial to the effective solution of that problem. When we asked students to construct their own knowledge bases, we discovered that the manner in which we introduced them to the KBTs was crucial to their ability to express their knowledge effectively (unless previous experiences had furnished them with appropriate schemata in long term memory). So, to help students form appropriate representations of the problem in their minds:

- Use analogies, e.g. DETECT can be represented as a jigsaw of interconnecting pieces, or as a collection of items in a filing drawer.
- Provide, or help children to design, diagrams and tables (see 2.4.2. below).
- Keep initial instructions and explanations simple and few in number. The time to introduce new complexities is when students are ready for them.
- Provide an exemplar, i.e. give the students a knowledge base (with content in the same domain as the task) to explore. Not only will they acquire knowledge within the domain, they will be learning how the KBT functions, and observing how their own finished program will look to a user.

2.4.2. Aids for working memory

Sanford [4] states: "Aids to mental models, such as using notes or diagrams or equations, can be viewed as symbolic physical extensions of mental models, and are of obvious assistance given the limited capacity of human working memory." He reports that learners who spontaneously expressed a spatial problem graphically performed successfully. On another task, not spatial, groups that failed to draw a diagram performed badly; however, groups that were instructed to use a diagrammatic method of problem representation performed as well as the groups in the spatial task.

Diagrams show connections between elements of a topic and allow an overview which would otherwise be difficult to keep in working memory all at once. For example, a 14-year-old boy who knew nothing of LINX was given its *Rock Identification* knowledge base to explore. After about 15 minutes with the program, he started to draw himself a branching diagram. When asked why he chose to express his search in this way, he said that the diagram was the only way to represent his exploration paths. The diagram was a spontaneous way of enabling this student to represent the relationships between items in the knowledge base, and also to provide him with an understanding of the underlying structure of a LINX knowledge base.

A diagram or table provides students with both a map and checklist of the task. Diagrams therefore help to overcome the limitations of working memory - this is especially important with novices who will not yet have developed and consolidated appropriate schemata to enable automatic processing.

2.4.3. Provide support structures

It is essential that this 'scaffolding' [15] be available when learners reach a point where they cannot progress without help. Such support can be provided by:

- peers - children working in pairs or small groups generally learn more than those working alone, as their ideas are refined through discussion [16,17];
- the teacher or other adults. Wimborne [18] discovered that students who had explored a knowledge base written using an early form of LINX

"had developed some way of representing the organisation of the information to their

own satisfaction; however they were unable to explain to anybody else until I suggested that some kind of diagram might help. It did not take very long after this for someone to come up with the idea of using a tree diagram and describing the structure in terms of choices (represented as lines) branching off from events (represented as nodes). It was then quite easy for them to describe the simulation in terms of items of text, choices and links."

- the KBT itself. PEG KBTs are already moving in this direction: DETECT88 knowledge bases can include sophisticated context-driven hints and prompts, based on a model of the lines of enquiry the student is pursuing [19]. Most of the other KBTs also provide templates for students entering data.

2.4.4. Time to consolidate learning

It is crucial to give students adequate time working on the computer, refining and amending their initial mental models through interacting with the KBTs. The example below illustrates how initial mental models which are broadly accurate, but contain incorrect elements, can be modified in this way.

When first constructing interactive adventures using THE PLAN, many of our students made one particular type of error: they described objects in the context of the location where they were initially placed in the adventure world. For example, students would enter a description of an object placed in the great hall of a castle as: "a huge sword, fixed to the south wall". When an adventurer playing the game took the sword and moved to, say, an open field, s/he would be carrying "a huge sword, fixed to the south wall". In the face of such inconsistencies adventure writers modified their mental models of how THE PLAN functioned to accommodate this new insight; i.e. they changed their descriptions of objects so that they were no longer context-dependent.

The initial error can be attributed to two factors:

- the students' previous experience of writing descriptions had been built up in the context of school writing, usually in the form of stories, where the setting tends to be very much part of what is expected in any description; and
- the students had initially conceptualised objects in the same category as locations, i.e. as fixed entities. This misapprehension was strengthened by the fact that descriptive text for both locations and objects is entered in the same way. It was only when they saw how their descriptions were tied to the objects, which were dynamic in nature, that the students' mental models expanded to include a new category for objects.

3. CONCLUDING REMARKS

There has been almost a decade of development work and action research by the PEG research community: we've been through the early evangelical phase of claiming logic programming to be the missing link in our education system; we've worked in the classroom developing tools and interfaces that learners can use; we've run numerous projects using Prolog and knowledge-based tools written in Prolog and embracing subjects across the curriculum.

It seems to be a good time to pause, take stock and ask ourselves: How far have we come? What have we achieved? Have we improved the quality of teaching and learning significantly? Have the findings of cognitive scientists and AI researchers been translated into tools and methodologies which have resulted in better classroom practice, in more effective learning? Designing tools which reflect and support students' cognitive processes is, as we all know, only part of the equation: effective learning cannot take place without the presence of affective factors such as challenge, excitement and motivation (both extrinsic and intrinsic). Without students' interest and willingness very little learning will occur. As it is teachers who structure the learning environment, the ultimate effectiveness of knowledge-based tools is in teachers' hands.

A final question: will the use of KBTs help to alter the traditional relationships between teacher and pupils, where the teacher *transmits* knowledge to the students? [20].

This paper will close by describing a specific incident representing a first step in this direction. It illustrates how the exploration of knowledge bases can challenge and expand children's restricted mental models (and those of their teachers). An historical knowledge base was being field-tested with a class aged 11-12. The knowledge base was about the celebrated engineer, C Y O'Connor. His body was found in shallow surf near Fremantle in 1902. The children were asked to work out what had happened and why (a familiar DETECT scenario). The children conducted their investigations purposefully, following up clues and arguing with each other about their significance and admissibility. During the course of the investigation the students accessed a wide range of archival information in the knowledge base which they would normally never encounter. They were able to assess the raw data of history, organised in a form appropriate to historical enquiry. By the end of the lesson the class had reached a soundly-based conclusion. Then the following interchange occurred, which went something like this:

Class: But what *really* happened?
JD: You know as much as I do - you've looked at all the clues we've got.
Class: But you're the teacher, you *know* what happened.
JD: No, I don't. I have to work it out, as you have done, from the information the past has left behind.

In their years at primary school these children had formed an inaccurate, but firm, mental model of history as *certain known facts* about what happened in the past, all of which were contained in textbooks and the teacher's head.

At this point, the teacher looked somewhat threatened: not only had her students acquired far more, and more accurate, knowledge about the topic than she herself had, but the model of the nature of historical knowledge which she had promulgated had been challenged.

More active, deeper student learning will be possible if, instead of seeing knowledge bases as a threat to their expertise and status with a class, such teachers can recognise them as valuable resources for extending their students', and their own, learning.

REFERENCES

[1] Schank, R C, with Childers, P (1984) The Cognitive Computer: On Language, Learning, and Artificial Intelligence, Addison-Wesley, USA, p. 222.

[2] Minsky, M (1975) *A framework for representing knowledge,* in: P H Winston (Ed) The Psychology of Computer Vision, McGraw-Hill, NY.

[3] Schank, R C and Abelson, R P (1977) Scripts, Plans, Goals and Understanding, Lawrence Erlbaum Associates, New Jersey.

[4] Sanford, A J (1985) Cognition and Cognitive Psychology, Basic Books.

[5] Cleal, D M and Heaton, N O (1988) Knowledge-Based Systems: Implications for Human-Computer Interfaces, Ellis Horwood Ltd, Chichester: UK.

[6] Nichol, J and Dean, J (1984) *Pupils, Computers and History Teaching,* in: M Yazdani (Ed) New Horizons in Educational Computing, Ellis Horwood, Chichester, UK.

[7] Nichol, J, Dean, J and Briggs, J (1986) *Computing, History Teaching and the Curriculum,* in: C Portal (Ed) The History Curriculum for Teachers, The Falmer Press, UK.

[8] PEGBOARD, 1/1 - 3/2, PEG, Exeter,UK.

[9] Nichol, J, Briggs, J and Dean, J (Eds) (1988) PROLOG, Children and Students, Kogan Page, London.

[10] PEG (1985-1989), DETECT, KEYS, LINX, KNOWLEDGE PAD PEG, UK.

[11] Briggs, J H (1985) THE PLAN, Private publication, UK.

[12] Dench, P (1988) *Interactive literature in the school curriculum,* LOGIN, Vols 2/2 & 2/4, ECAWA, WA.

[13] Wood, D (1988) How children think and learn, Basil Blackwell, Oxford.

[14] Flavell, J H (1985) Cognitive Development [2nd edition], Prentice-Hall, New Jersey, p. 97..

[15] Bruner, J S (1978) *Learning how to do things with words,* in: J Bruner and A Garton (Eds) Human Growth and Development, OUP, UK.

[16] Dean, J (1986) Prolog: A New Tool for Learning and Understanding History, M.Ed. dissertation, Exeter University, UK.

[17] Gagne, R M and Smith, E C (1962) *A Study of the Effects of Verbalization on Problem Solving,* Journal of Experimental Psychology, 12/18.

[18] Wimborne, P (1986) *DPSE Project: Hydeburn School: Section 2,* Pegboard, Vol 1/1, Spring 1986, pp 106-112.

[19] Briggs, J H and Brough, D (1989) *Using Prolog in the Design of Knowledge-Based Tools for Education,* Pegboard, Vol, 3/2, Winter/Spring 88/89, pp 55-63.

[20] Barnes, D (1976) From Communication to Curriculum, Penguin Books, UK.

Computers in Education
A. McDougall and C. Dowling (Editors)
Elsevier Science Publishers B.V. (North-Holland)

APPLYING SECOND GENERATION EXPERT SYSTEMS IN EDUCATION - THE CRITIQUING APPROACH

Bent B. ANDRESEN

Institute of Informatics, Royal Danish School of Educational Studies, Emdrupvej 115B, DK-2400 Copenhagen NV, Denmark

This paper explores the premise that critiquing systems can play a central role in the application of expert system technology to the learning of students. Critiquing systems are second generation expert systems used to criticize the student's problem solving. In comparison with the use of mainstream first generation expert systems, the student plays a much more active role as he has to propose a solution of his own before he can get the critique. The paper gives details of the function of critiquing systems in general and classroom experiences with the use of a prototype critiquing system in particular.

1. INTRODUCTION

1.1. Second Generation Expert Systems

The concept of second generation expert systems can be defined in more than one way. In this paper, the concept refers to *task specific systems,* i.e. expert systems tailored to a particular task: diagnosis, designing, planning, scheduling, classification, concept recognition etc. (1).

The subject of the paper is a kind of second generation expert systems called critiquing systems.

1.2. To Solve or not to Solve

According to the mainstream approach to the application of expert systems, expert systems are designed to take the leading role during problem solving activities, i.e. to guide all the activities dictating the observations and actions the user has to take to solve a problem (2). The user's input consists of problem specifications, i.e. goals to be achieved, and case data. The output from the system consists of solutions to the problems. A typical consultative session goes like this: The user initiates the session; the system controls the data gathering; it offers a solution; the user may ask for "explanation" if some capability exists; he receives the machine solution (2).

Expert advice of this kind does have some benefits in education, especially when the main purpose is to solve problems for the students. However, it is a drawback that the student is assigned a somewhat passive role in the process of problem solving. He is not active in the problem solving in the sense that he must propose a solution of his *own*.

With critiquing systems, the situation is different. The role of a critiquing system is to support the student to evaluate and refine his solution - and not simply to tell him what to do. Input, supplied by the student to a critiquing system, consists of problem specifications and case data. It also consists of preliminary solutions to the problem specified. The output, supplied by the critiquing system, consists of a critique of the student's problem solving: e.g., suggestions of corrections, improvements, extensions or a critique of the student's viewpoint with a detailed rationale. To solve a problem, the interaction usually takes place more than once. During several sessions, the student takes the critique into consideration, generates a new proposal, takes the new critique into consideration etc.

2. THE CRITIQUING PROJECT

The following paragraphs deal with a research project called The Critiquing Project. The Critiquing Project, currently in progress, is a three year research project aimed at investigating the use of critiquing systems in education. Three characteristics of the rationale behind the project work are worth emphasizing:

Firstly, since education involves the transfer of knowledge to students, expert systems can have a key role in education in the communication of knowledge (3).

Secondly, the use of expert systems as means of communication should provide an instrumental method that places the responsibility for learning on the student. Since education involves the active participation of the students in the process of learning, students should not be assigned a passive role in the problem solving.

Thirdly, since the human teacher already is in the classroom to deliver learning, the role of the expert systems can be to support and not deliver learning (4). Expert systems can support students who have already been taught a subject matter by their human teacher and then have to practice their skills or concepts (5). The systems can support students when they need feedback to be able to evaluate and refine their problem solving by showing their mistakes, offering suggestions, improvements, alternatives etc.

3. VANDVID - A CRITIQUING SYSTEM

This paragraph deals with the first prototype critiquing system of the Critiquing Project. The name of the system is VANDVID. VANDVID is meant to be used in environmental education. It embodies the knowledge needed to point out areas in a stream with ongoing discharge of polluting matter. It is implemented by the use of an expert system shell called ESU developed by the author. ESU is written in Prolog Professional and currently running on IBM AT and PS/2 and compatible machines (6).

3.1. The Overall Function of VANDVID

A common view on expert systems is centred around the system's overall architecture, i.e. the knowledge base, the inference engine, and the user-interface. Although this perspective might be appropriate for programming personnel, knowledge engineers etc, it is not adequate for research on critiquing systems. The primary design focus in the critiquing generation of expert systems is their *functionality*.

To explain the functionality of VANDVID, let us imagine the following scenario: Some students have investigated a stream and believe that they have found a source of pollution. Their judgement is based on the observation that the absolute number of animals living in the area decreases. They are, however, not quite sure. Therefore, they want someone to examine their results. They use VANDVID. Firstly, they enter their findings into VANDVID. Secondly, they enter their judgement and ask for an evaluation based on knowledge about the level of the pollution of the stream. They experience that the hypothesis can not be confirmed. To their big surprise, the critiquing system does not find a significant amount of pollution in the area where they expected it to be.

They ask for an explanation. The explanation reveals that the quality of the water is almost the same as in other areas. Why? The students consider their findings once again, this time more aware of the variety of species found. Some species are more resistant to pollution than others, i.e. in case of pollution, some species will disappear. Therefore, the presence of the less resistant species indicates that the pollution is nominal. The students notice that several of the less resistant species are present. They experience why their judgement was wrong.

In another area of the stream, the students notice that the less resistant species have disappeared. They believe that there must be a source of severe pollution in that area. This time the critique of VANDVID verifies their hypothesis.

3.2. Details of the Function of VANDVID

A description of the critiquing function of VANDVID in closer details requires a few specialized terms: observed value, expected value, symptom, and hypothesis (a somewhat similar terminology can be found in (7)).

The term *observed value* refers to an estimated value of the quality of the water. It is based on data obtained by students through measurements in a stream. Three characteristics of the students' measurements are worth emphasizing. First, the act of making a measurement is straightforward. The students simply collect samples of the animals living in the stream. Secondly, the students enter their data into VANDVID. Thirdly, based on the data gathered, the biological quality of the water is estimated by the students as well as by VANDVID. The value is estimated on a 10 point scale according to the so called Macro-Index method (cf.(8)).

The term *expected value* refers to propositions about the biological quality of the water. The value of the quality at a particular place in the stream is expected not to decrease outside certain limits, so if the value at the previous place is known, it can easily be calculated. VANDVID uses a simple statistical model assuming that all values are reliable within the limit of plus or minus one unit on the ten point scale.

The term *symptom* refers to a discrepancy detected between an observed value and an expected value. The discrepancy is a symptom of pollution of the stream, i.e. of lack of oxygen in the water.

The term *hypothesis* refers to an abducting inference which goes as follows: given a symptom, then assume that the symptom is caused by a source of pollution. During a consultation of VANDVID, two sets of hypothesis are made. One set is made by the student using VANDVID. Another set is made by the system. When compared, the student's judgement can be evaluated. The student can get feedback to his problem solving. This feedback is assembled dynamically and tailored to the particular judgement of the student. On request, it can be accompanied by an explanation to ensure that the student also learns from his mistakes.

3.3. The Use of VANDVID

In the academic year 1988/89, VANDVID has been used to assist 15 - 16 year old students in judging the quality of the water in a stream

(9). The students used VANDVID to evaluate their hypothesis about the pollution of the water and thereby to find possible sources of pollution in the stream. They managed to find a "real" source of pollution, a factory producing chips (not the kind of "chips" in computers but the kind we eat). They were very proud to tell the local authorities about their findings.

The empirical study on the use of VANDVID indicates that it is successful as a critiquing system. The students acquired skills to recognise, define, and solve problems about environmental issues. The use of the critiquing system fostered this learning process. According to the students, their teacher, and my observations, the critiquing system helped students generate feedback about the quality of their problem solving.

4. FUTURE WORK

The study on the use of VANDVID contributed to the further development of the system. Based on the observation of students using it, the critiquing capabilities have been extended.

The formative evaluation done so far is to be followed by a summative evaluation of the processes of learning with the system. During the academic year 1989/90, the extended version of VANDVID will be used by several hundred students in Danish schools, a high school, and a college of education in a large scale study on students' attitudes towards critiquing systems.

The exploration of the potential and limitations of the use of critiquing systems in education require formative and summative evaluations of the use of critiquing systems within more than one single domain. Therefore, a range of prototype critiquing systems will be designed, developed and evaluated in close co-operation with the school employees. The second prototype system of the Critiquing Project has already been designed. The domain is classification. The prototype critiquing system is meant to be a reasoning assistant in the process of categorisation of sets of objects that can be classified in several ways according to different attributes. The application area will be, among other areas, information retrieval from large databases.

5. RELATION TO PREVIOUS WORK

Several aspects differentiate the research on critiquing systems from previous research on the application of expert systems in education.

Firstly, previous studies most often explore the mainstream approach to computer-based advice in the working life. The attempt is to automate the problem solving process. The research reported in this paper is heading towards another goal. It explores an approach in which the attempt is to support and not to replace the student's problem solving.

Secondly, many previous studies explore an approach which I call "the student as knowledge engineer" approach. The aim is that students themselves construct the knowledge base of the system by formulating the rules of thumb and selecting the information (10). The research on critiquing systems has another goal. Critiquing systems provide an instructional method that does not place the responsibility for system development on the student. The student is assigned the role of user of knowledge based systems made by others than him. The aim is to explore computer-based advice as a means of extending the student's conceptualization power, i.e. the student's ability to conceive the problem to be solved and possible paths to solution.

Thirdly, conceptualization power suggests several kinds of expert systems. One approach is representation aids that use graphic techniques to support the student. It is done to visualize the semantics of the domain of interest, i.e. to make the abstract into concrete, and to restructure the student's view. The specific motivation underlying the research on critiquing systems is along another path. The research is along the path of Miller's critiquing system, ATTENDING (11). The aim is to deploy machine power in the form of an agent which comments and criticizes the student's problem solving.

6. CONCLUSION

I have considered the application of computer programs that display some degree of intelligence. I have reported on research in progress on the application of a new kind of intelligent systems called critiquing systems.

Critiquing systems are second generation expert systems tailored to evaluate the student's solutions, plans, classifications, diagnosis etc. The purpose is not to tell the student what to do but to give him feedback, to help him evaluate and refine his own approach. The critique is assembled dynamically and tailored to the particular case data and the particular approach taken by the student.

The exploration of the potential of the use of critiquing systems in education requires formative and summative evaluations of the use of systems within different domains. A range of prototype critiquing systems have to be designed, developed and evaluated. I have reported on the use of the first prototype, the system VANDVID, to be used in environmental education.

A study on the use of this system demonstrated that a critiquing system can foster learning. It can help students generate feedback about the quality of their problem solving. The conclusion is that critiquing systems can contribute to improvement of instructional methods and educational opportunities.

ACKNOWLEDGEMENTS

My thanks to participants at the four PEG Conferences held in 1986 and 1987 in Exeter, UK, in 1988 in Copenhagen, Denmark, and in 1989 in Uppsala, Sweden. Suggestions made there directly led to this paper.

The work described in this paper is funded by the Royal Danish School of Educational Studies.

REFERENCES

(1) Sticklen, J., Second Generation Approaches to Expert Systems, Ninth International Workshop on Expert Systems and their Applications (Avignon, France, 1989).

(2) Roth, E.M. et al., Human Interaction with an "Intelligent" Machine, Int. J. Man-Machine Studies (1987) 479-525.

(3) Alty, J.L., Relevance of Expert Systems to Computer Based Education, in: Duncan, K. and Harris, D. (eds.), Proceedings of the Fourth World Conference on Computers in Education, (North-Holland, Amsterdam, 1985) 454.

(4) Briggs, J.H., Talk at the Fourth International Annual PEG Conference (Uppsala, Sweden, 1989).

(5) Andresen, B.B., Learning with Knowledge Based Systems, in: Proceedings for the European Conference on Technology and Education, (Herning, Denmark, April, 24-27, 1990), in print.

(6) Andresen, B.B., A Unifying Framework for Application-Specific Expert System Shells, in: Proceedings of the Third International Annual PEG conference (Copenhagen, Denmark, 1988).

(7) Chittaro, L. et al., Diagnosis Based on Co-operation of Multiple Knowledge Sources, in: Proceedings of the Ninth International Workshop on Export Systems and their Applications (Avignon, France, 1989).

(8) Abrahamsen, S.E., Giologiske ferskvandsundersøgelser (Forum, Copenhagen, 1977).

(9) Andresen, B.B. The Use of Knowledge Based Systems, Emphasizing the Critiquing Approach, in: Proceedings of the Fourth International Annual PEG Conference (Uppsala, Sweden, 1989).

(10) Jensen, J.A. and Andresen, B.B., Logic Programming in a Computerized Learning Environment, in: Nichol J. (ed.), Prolog, Children and Students (Kogan Page, London, 1988).

(11) Miller, P.L., A. Critiquing Approach to Expert Computer Advice: ATTENDING (Pitman, London, 1984).

Computers in Education
A. McDougall and C. Dowling (Editors)
Elsevier Science Publishers B.V. (North-Holland)
IFIP, 1990

Building Discovery Environments Using Generic Software

Jacques Bordier, Gilbert Paquette and Serge Carrier

Télé-université, 4835 Christophe Colomb, Montréal, Canada, H2J 4C2
tel: 514 522 3540 fax: 514 522 3608

This article reports on the LOUPE project that led to the construction of ten learning environments from 1987 to 1989. These were built using generic software such as Excel, Supercalc and HyperCard, exploring new ways to use the computer as a learning tool for students. The paper presents the educational philosophy behind the project, the pedagogical characteristics of the learning units and the conclusions stemming from classroom experimentation. In particular, we will underline the characteristics of the methodology and the computer tools used for the construction of the learning environments and the impact of the resulting tools on learning.

1. INTRODUCTION

The LOUPE project presented in this article has its origin in the development and experimentation of a distance learning university course, "Software for Education" [Bordier, Paquette 1986], intended primarily for elementary and high school teachers who wanted to design, implement and validate learning units using generic software tools. Reaching over 1000 teachers, this course has convinced us of the value of educational applications of such tools, while establishing some underlying difficulties in their use by the teachers.

In order to make these generic tools more suitable for educational purposes, we undertook an ambitious research and development project based on the construction, by experts, of specialized application tools. With such specialized tools, henceforth called student templates, the teacher's role becomes centered on the design of learning activities used with the template, a role more compatible with the competence and interest of the majority of teachers.

We first set up a multidisciplinary team formed of field experts, educational software specialists and computer scientists. Since March 1987, the project has been jointly supported by APO-Québec Center, Télé-université and the Montreal Catholic School Board, who helped in the validation of the learning units in the classroom.

2. GENERAL DESCRIPTION OF THE PROJECT

2.1. Basic pedagogical orientations

The basic orientation of the project is to offer environments where the student is engaged in an active learning process. We think that exploratory activities can help the student to identify basic concepts in an area of knowledge, to understand its general trends and, eventually, to feel the need for a formalization of his discoveries. After such a process, the student will be able to undertake an initial formalization and be more receptive to a more complete presentation by the teacher. This presentation could then appear as a synthesis and clarification of a set of personal experiences.

The possibility of an effective use of such an open pedagogy in the classroom is, for us, a sign of an important breakthrough. In the usual chalk-and-blackboard environment of the classroom, it is well known that open approaches give rise to very difficult implementation problems. How can a teacher really assist thirty students involved in an active exploratory process?

At first, in the schools, it was not clear that the computer would bring important changes in teaching methods. Their use were limited to programming courses and computer-assisted teaching with tutorials. Tutorials moved the student through determined paths in a way far from compatible with an active learning process [Heibenstreit 1986].

The construction of new knowledge requires a more open approach favoring multiple representation schemes. With generic software such as text and image processors, spreadsheets or data-base managers, it is possible to build specialized software tools. Coupled with learning activities, these tools can help the acquisition of important knowledge and know-hows such as searching, structuring, representing and transforming information on a given subject. Further more, the student activity in such an environment may help him develop higher cognitive capacities: discovery of general relations between attributes of objects, hypotheses testing, modeling and explanation formulation [Di Sessa 1987; Collins and Brown 1988].

In this same direction, multimedia systems, such as HyperCard, have been made available on micro-computers. These systems favor knowledge organization and presentation in ways far closer to natural thought processes than the traditional datafile systems. These new generic tools can help build learning environments in which students can experience constructive exploration of a field of knowledge [Gaines 1987].

2.2 Summary of the project

Up to now, we have built and tested in schools ten learning environments. Three of them have been developed with Excel on Macintosh, three with HyperCard and three others with Supercalc-3. We have also used the Prolog programming language to develop a knowledge-based system on nutrition.

Each learning environment consist of:

• one or more student templates including data bases and simulations on the knowledge domain and specific tools to process or present the information;

• a set of activity sheets designed to help the student explore the knowledge domain in a more fruitful way;

• a methodological guide for the teacher, proposing ways to integrate the environment in his teaching strategies.

In choosing subjects, we looked for knowledge domains for which suitable didactic materials are particularly lacking. Table 1 summarizes some of the characteristics of the ten environments.

Subject	Student Software	Tool
Lenses	Simulation models	Excel
Chemistry	Simulation models	Excel
Fractions	Graphic models	Excel
Economy	Data manager	Supercalc-3
Meteorology	Data base	Supercalc-3
Demography	Simulator	Supercalc-3
The Forest	Data base/hypermedia	HyperCard
Geography	Data base/hypermedia	HyperCard
Linear measure	Data base/hypermedia	HyperCard
Nutrition	Knowledge-base system	Prolog

Table 1: Characteristics of ten environments

2.3. Description of four learning units

The Forest

The object of this learning unit is to provide a context in which a student can learn about general characteristics of trees, their classification and their use. HyperCard has been used to design an extensible and easy-to-consult data base. The data base holds information on twenty-five trees of the Canadian forest, including a large number of digitalized pictures.

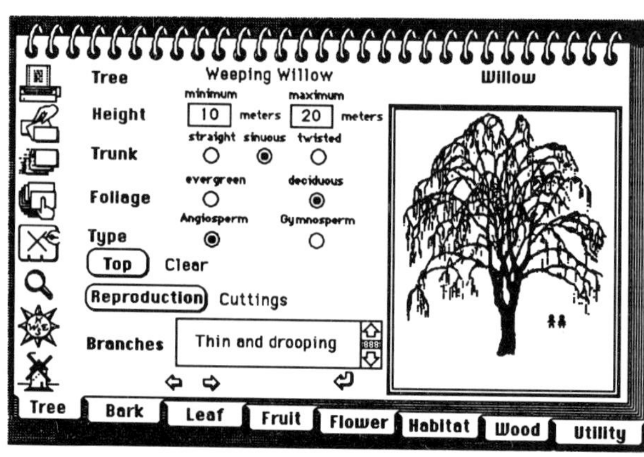

Figure 1: Main card

The environment also provides for searching and sorting tools available through a direct manipulation interface.

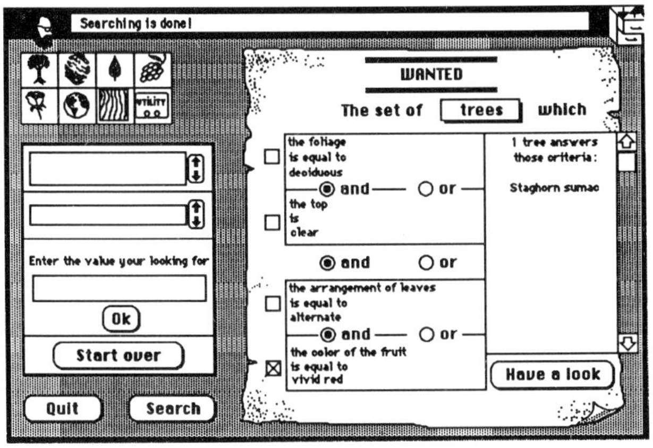

Figure 2: Search tools in the Forest

The student begins by exploring a limited data base containing a handful of trees and an extensive description of general attributes. Then he chooses a tree not defined in the starting environment. With the help of the software he can analyze and determine the characteristics of this tree, gathering pictures, from a specialized scrapbook template, of its main attributes: flower, fruit, wood, leaf, etc. In that way, the student will add to the environment the results of these personal explorations. On the other hand, the teacher can set up many activities using the whole base of twenty-five trees, such as identification games or classification techniques development.

Optical Lenses and Mirrors

The object of this environment is to give the student the possibility to simulate experiments with lenses and mirrors. Using an optical bench, the experiments necessary to the understanding of this subject are often limited by time, cost or impracticability.

Two simulators were built with the graphic spreadsheet Excel. They are used to facilitate the observation of the behavior of light as it strikes lenses or mirrors. With the simulators, the students can construct experiments to test their hypotheses.

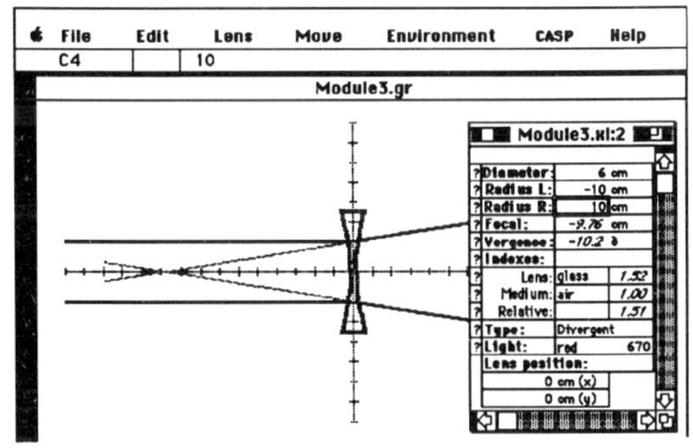

Figure 3: Defining a simulation

The student templates are used:

- to make qualitative observations on the behavior of the image of a triangle through a lens or a curved mirror: the image changes as the triangle is moved;

- to simulate the path of light rays when meeting a lens or a mirror;

- to modify the attributes of a lens or a mirror in order to understand its nature;

- to analyze the relations between the basic variables of a lens or a mirror.

Numbers and Linear Measures

The object of this learning unit is to help the student develop representations and intuitions for very large or very small numbers. The interaction with the environment helps the student make adjustments to his intuitive views on numbers and measures.

The concept of measure is usually clear when the result is a number familiar to the student. But when the result is a very small or a very large number, the student will have no references to interpret the measure correctly.

The HyperCard system has been found useful for the construction of interactive tools enabling the student to solve problems such as the following:

- Find a length that would measure one million with the thickness of a dollar bill as a unit of measure.

- What place would you reach in a hundred years traveling non-stop at the speed of a turtle, a walking man, a bicycle ... ?

• The distance from Montreal to New-York is to the length of a tennis court what this length is to _______________ ?

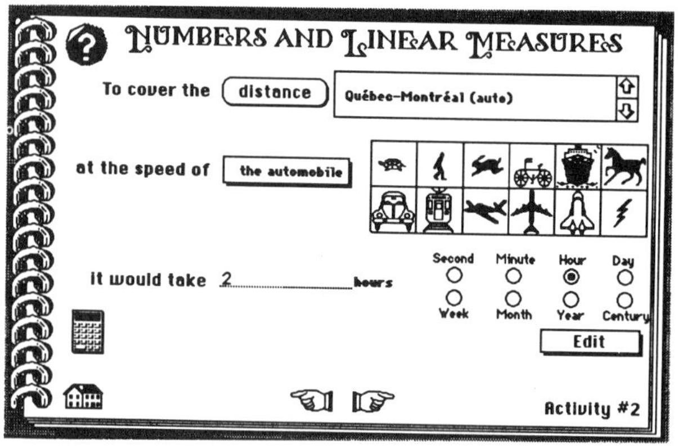

Figure 4: Students estimate the time required to cover a distance using a vehicle of their choice.

The template is extensible in the sense that the student or teacher can, through a simple editor, add or remove information on units, measures and so on. He can also complete a diary on length measurements. This diary is activated by clicking a button.

Demography

The object of this learning unit is to help students explain the numerical growth of the population, formulate theories, verify them or, at least, understand how various factors such as social and cultural circumstances, economic disparity or political conditions relate to each other and what kind of impact they have on the growth of a population. An adequate treatment of the subject entails a lot of data examination, computations and graphic constructions to understand the evolution of the parameters of a population and to make simulations in the style "what would happen if...".

The functionality of the student templates is as follows. A model developed with the spreadsheet Supercalc 3 contains demographic data from 1921 to 1983, which can be displayed graphically, together with extrapolation formulas. With that template the student is able to make projections on the basis of different hypotheses. Starting with a complete set of data, he analyzes different graphical interpretations while trying at the same time to give sense to his observations. By doing so, he studies the phenomena of natural growth and migrations. In the second part of the work the student tries to reach certain goals by making hypotheses and then simulating the phenomena under these hypotheses.

3. RESEARCH RESULTS ON DEVELOPMENT METHODOLOGY AND DIDACTICS

The construction and validation of the ten learning units in the LOUPE project developed over a little more than two years, from April 1987 to June 1989. We have used a development methodology based on verification and revision with students and teachers [Bordeleau 1983]. This approach has enabled us to gather observations both during and after the experimentation and to draw conclusions about the form of pedagogical tools, the apparent impact on learning, and the methodology itself.

3.1. Development methodology

On the basis of a scenario written by a principal designer in cooperation with a teacher, the project team developed a preliminary version of the environment. This version was tested with a small group of students, enabling us to make precise qualitative observations and to improve the template and the written material. On this basis we then constructed a prototype for validation.

The validation was carried out in a normal classroom setting with the help of an observation grid filled by an observer during each experimentation session.

After each session, the observer noted the teacher's remarks. As well, an evaluation questionnaire was filled up by the teacher at the end of the validation. We also held informal discussions with the students. A final revision was made of the pedagogical material leading to a pilot version. This version is now in use in classrooms with no other help than the guide written by the design team after the validation.

3.2. Activity sheets and teacher's guide

With open software tools, some written material is necessary in order to structure the student's work. After experimenting with different formats, we opted for a one-sheet recto-verso task description. All other texts such as situation definitions, concept explanations, non-computer complementary activities or technical reminders are now included in the teacher's methodological guide. This document presents the context of the learning environment: interest and difficulty of the subject, role in the curriculum, learning goals, general pedagogical strategy. Finally, the teacher's guide contains a detailed description of the student activities, with or without the computer, together with advice for their integration and adaptation to the teacher's own pedagogy.

3.3. Pedagogical impact

The project goal was to design, develop and field test a new concept for learning units with the help of a computer. Other studies will be necessary to evaluate their impact on learning. However, some general conclusions can be drawn from the observations gathered during classroom experiments validation.

The students clearly showed a great deal of motivation. For example, during two months at the Jules-Verne elementary school, the students working with the unit "Fractions" became quite involved with the activities we proposed; they showed pride and excitement after solving a problem with the help of the tools provided. Even slow learners wanted to succeed in the activities.

Most of the children did in fact succeed in tasks rated as difficult by their teachers in a first study of the subject. While observing them, one acquires the conviction that the use of the computer as a tool by the student brings something new and important to knowledge acquisition:

• Students manipulate and see in different ways the knowledge in a subject domain;

• The precision and clarity of computerized textual, numerical or graphical representations favor concentration on concepts instead of computations and sketching precision;

• The computer's fast processing allows the treatment of a larger quantity of knowledge in less time, thus increasing cognitive activity;

• The use of the computer as a tool encourages the self-detection of errors and bugs; using the computer tools, students debug their own knowledge;

• This interactive knowledge acquisition should favor the integration of new knowledge to mental schemes and therefore increase the chances of long term retention.

4. EVALUATION OF GENERIC TOOLS FOR THE DEVELOPMENT OF LEARNING ENVIRONMENTS.

Using generic tools makes prototyping faster and facilitates interactive improvement through successive experiments with students. On the other hand, our experience in this project shows up certain flaws limiting their educational possibilities.

4.1. Access to knowledge

Generic-software usually favors specific knowledge representation and access which can be unsuited in certain fields of study. For example, in spreadsheets and data base software, two dimensional matrix or filing-cards are used to present information. As for systems like HyperCard, the screen can display only one card at a time forcing the designer to fit all the information into a limited space. Moreover with most generic software it is difficult to reduce the noise resulting from the complexity of the software; this can hinder the pedagogic impact of the learning activity.

4.2. The type of knowledge

Spreadsheets and data base managers as well as hypermedia systems on micro-computers only allow for factual knowledge processing. When the knowledge to be acquired takes the form of rules, concepts, taxonomies or procedures, those generic tools can offer only indirect support. With some generic software, one can test a rule or an assertion by making a request on the data base, but the tested assertion cannot be integrated into the data base. Consequently, the learner cannot operate on this kind of knowledge, nor use it to generate new knowledge in the domain. For a lasting acquisition of factual knowledge, it is important to integrate facts in a network of concepts using them. This is one of the reason why one must go beyond usual data base systems, in order to be able to operate on more complex forms of knowledge. The construction of systems that can process such kind of knowledge depends on techniques being developed in the field of artificial intelligence [O'Shea 1983].

5. CONCLUSION: TOWARD A NEW GENERATION OF SOFTWARE TOOLS FOR THE STUDENT

Based on our analysis of the strength and flaws of the generic software currently available, we undertook, in March 1988, the development of a student template generator adapted to education. This new generic software, called LOUTI [Bergeron and Paquette (1989)] was constructed using a new language called PRISME [Bergeron, Nadeau, Bouchard (1988)], which integrates the functional, object-oriented and logic paradigms of programming. Even in its current non-completed form we are already able to use LOUTI to build a new generation of student templates. Through the editors in LOUTI, a designer can elaborate student templates that give the student:

• access to knowledge bases and the possibility of extending them through his research activity;

• factual knowledge as well as conceptual or rule-based knowledge presentation and processing tools;

• support at the different phases of cognitive activity, particularly methodological advice for the use of the tools;

• choice between different forms of knowledge presentation which dynamically adjust to changes in the knowledge base;

• interfaces and tools nearer to natural mental operations.

Because the designer can choose the tools that will appear in the student software, he can adapt to the domain, pedagogical strategies and age of the students.

ACKNOWLEDGMENTS

We would like to thank the other members of our research group: Anne Bergeron, Annick Hernandez, Charles Camirand, Martin Longpré and Renaud Nadeau and the educators who participated in the conception of the learning units: Monique Auger, Monique Gascon, Louis Simard and Diane Meilleur.

REFERENCES

Bergeron, A. Bouchard, L. and R. Nadeau. (1988). A Multi-paradigm Development System For Exploratory Environments. The Canadian Society for Computational Studies of Intelligence 1988 conference, Calgary June 1988.

Bergeron, A. and Paquette, G. (1989). Discovery Environments and Intelligent Learning Tools,in ITS: At the Crossroad of AI and Education, Ablex Publishing

Bordeleau, P. (1983). Vérification and révision auprès d'étudiants des documents audio-scripto-visuels éducatifs. Rapport GRERDAVE No 21, Université de Montréal.

Bordier, J. and Paquette, G. (1986). "Software for education" a distance learning course published at Télé-université, Québec, Canada.

Collins, A. and Brown, J,S. (1988). The computer as a Tool for Learning Trough Reflection, in Learning Issues for Intelligent Tutoring Systems, (Eds Mandl and Lesgold), Springer-Verlag.

Di Sessa A.A. (1987). Artificial Worlds and Real Experience in Artificial Intelligence and Education, volume 1 (Eds Lwler and Yazdani) Ablex Publishing, Norwood N.J.

Gaines, B.R. (1987). Knowledge in HyperMedia, Tutorial on the development of knowledge-based systems. University of Calgary, Canada.

Heibeinstreit, J. (1986) Interview of Jacques Heibeinstreit by Bernard Dumont in "Software for education" published at Télé-université, Québec, Canada.

O'Shea, T. and Self, J. (1983). Learning and Teaching with Computers, Artificial Intelligence in Education, Harvester Press.

Computers in Education
A. McDougall and C. Dowling (Editors)
Elsevier Science Publishers B.V. (North-Holland)

PEG: A WAY OF THINKING ABOUT THINGS

Jonathan BRIGGS [†], Jon NICHOL [‡] and Derek BROUGH [§]

[†]School of Information Systems, Kingston Polytechnic, Kingston-Upon-Thames, UK, KT1 2EE
[‡]School of Education, Exeter University, UK, EX1 2LU
[§]Department of Computing, Imperial College, London, UK, SW7

Artificial Intelligence tries both to help us understand the way we think and to assist us in thinking better. Education cannot wait for the 'intelligent tutors' of the distant future but needs to find ways of applying the early results of artificial intelligence research directly to classrooms and learners. PEG was formed to bridge this gap and has focussed on the production of 'knowledge based tools' that allow teachers ready access to these important ideas.

1. INTRODUCTION

At the end of a small-scale project with seven year olds, the teacher remarked when reflecting upon the PEG approach to learning: "It's a way of thinking about things". Enabling children to understand why they know something and upon what that knowledge is based has been at the heart of PEG since its foundation five years ago.

PEG, originally the Prolog Education Group, was established as the direct result of a working relationship between a small group of logic programming researchers from the world of Artificial Intelligence, AI, and practising teachers and curriculum developers.

PEG is a forum which links AI and education in applying AI tools and techniques to children's learning and cognitive development specifically within the everyday classroom context.

2. WHAT IS ARTIFICIAL INTELLIGENCE?

Artificial intelligence research has two main thrusts. One tries to build computer hardware and software that mimic or model the way in which we think or behave. The other is focussed on designing tools and techniques to help us harness our 'mental powers' more effectively. These twin goals are sometimes intentionally or accidentally combined.

Vision research, for example, may help us understand more about how we see and how we process visual images. It may also provide 'eyes' for assembly line robots to make them more accurate tools.

The other commercial product of AI has been expert systems, or knowledge based systems. An expert system is a computer program that mimics the behaviour of a human expert such as a lawyer, accountant, doctor, designer or engineer. The system will contain some representation of a body of human knowledge or expertise, often in the form of rules, and a problem solver, known as an 'inference engine', that will use these rules to answer questions or solve problems.

2.1.What does AI offer education?

In the past AI concentrated on 'mimicking the mind' and this required researchers to study the human mind and the ways in which we solve problems. Some concentrated on simple tasks that were relatively easy for people to solve. These tended to be tasks that children could perform such as simple arithmetic or 'understanding' a short story. It is natural therefore that AI research became involved with education.

2.2.Intelligent Tutoring Systems

Intelligent tutoring systems promise much, as they would automate both the expertise of subject specialists and the guidance provided by experienced teachers, offering advice and routes through a programme of study. They would present material and monitor progress as appropriate.

To teach mathematics,for example, an ITS would combine the skills of both the mathematician and the experienced teacher. It would be able to present suitable parts of a maths curriculum. It would be able to construct appropriate problems to test a child's understanding and be able to evaluate the child's response against model solutions. It would decide when to move the course forward at a faster pace or provide remedial help when difficulties are encountered.

If fully realised, an ITS would provide the learner with a surrogate teacher or tutor. For compulsory education intelligent tutoring is still at the research stage, but provides us with a important insight into future directions for educational software, ie software with an interface which can engage in a plausibly intelligent dialogue with a student.

2.3.'Microworlds'

That LOGO [1] is a product of AI research may come as a surprise, as the language and particularly 'turtle graphics' have already become widely used throughout the world. LOGO was designed to provide children with a computerized environment in which learning was a side-effect of exploration. Instead of the didactic teaching approach adopted by most tutoring systems, the child is in charge (possibly with some help and guidance from their teacher).

'Microworlds' have now been built for other subjects; ARK - the 'Alternate Reality Kit' (Xerox) is a microworld, written in the AI computer language SMALLTALK, to allow a student to explore physics.

Stella (High Performance Systems) provides an environment for dynamic mathematical modelling, useful in economics, medicine and other subjects. Each of these systems provides the child or student with a language with which to communicate with the computer. LOGO provides a set of commands for which there are clear parallels in the child's own language - Forward, Left, Home etc.

ARK and Stella provide graphical languages in which a model is constructed from representations of physical objects. In ARK two graphical objects can be made to behave on the computer screen as if they were two planets with a gravitational field between them. Stella allows models of dynamic mathematical processes, such as the spread of an infection in a population, to be constructed and explored using a graphical 'hydraulic' model based on water, pipes, sinks and valves.

2.4.Knowledge Based Tools for Education

The third type of application involves improving the tools that are available to the teacher and student to assist them in their learning. Although a 'microworld' can be described as a software tool, the range of possible tools is much wider. It stretches from simplified programming languages, through advanced simulations and simulation generators, to expert system shells. These tools can play a diverse set of roles within the classroom or laboratory.

Such tools have formed the backbone of PEG's work [2]. Their development, however, was to be led by another product from AI - a new style of computer programming - using the same tools as chosen by Japan's Fifth Generation Computer Project: Prolog.

3. PROLOG: THE DRIVING FORCE BEHIND PEG

The roots of collaboration between curriculum specialists and those working in AI research that led to the formation of PEG go back more than a decade. In 1979, at Imperial College London, a project was established exploring the use of Prolog as a computer language for children [3].

The emphasis was not on the procedural 'making the computer perform' aspects of the language, but on its clear declarative style. Declarative programming allows the programmer to describe their problem in a high level descriptive language. A Prolog program looks like this:

```
_Person should-take aspirin if
  _Person suffers-from pain and
  not _Person allergic-to aspirin.

John suffers-from pain.
Mary allergic-to aspirin.
```

Instead of a set of instructions or procedures, a Prolog program is a set of descriptive statements or facts and rules.

Educationally, Prolog programming is about constructing models of a subject being studied. The model is tested by asking questions and then modified or extended. These models may be constructed by individual students or whole classes of children. They may be prepared by the teacher in advance - the pupils' job is to extract the 'knowledge' contained in the facts and rules by asking appropriate questions.

Because of the high level descriptive nature of the language the emphasis is on the subject and not on how the computer will process the information it has been given. The project at Imperial College tested out these ideas across the curriculum in a diverse range of subjects from mathematics and science to history and geography.

3.1.From Prolog Programming to Real Classroom Applications

Prolog provides teachers and their students with a powerful way of expressing knowledge about the subjects they are studying. For many teachers, however, the language is too general and their task, of helping their students decide which topics to write programs about, becomes too daunting.

Work with LOGO had demonstrated that with simpler tools children could be powerfully engaged in the learning of mathmatics. LOGO shared with Prolog a paradigm for learning with computers, by exploring a topic through manipulating the topic itself. To be successful across the curriculum, however, Prolog would have to be disguised to provide 'learning environments' that were sufficiently 'transparent' to allow the learner to explore the domain, without being distracted, instead, by the complexity of the language.

The PEG group took the ideas central to Prolog and developed a range of prototypical 'environments'. Each provides a different 'vocabulary' through which a topic can be expressed and explored. LINX [4], for example, allows a story to be represented as a network of decisions and potential outcomes. KEYNOTES [5] provides a hypertext research tool with which information for a project or essay can be collated and sifted. Knowledge Pad [6,7] provides a simplified 'expert system shell' allowing the rules for a domain to be modelled and tested.

These tools share a common philosophy, common in AI programs; a separation of the procedural aspects of the program from the descriptive knowledge about the particular topic. The children can concentrate on describing the topic they are studying knowing that the 'shell' will use their information in a clear predefined manner.

4. MODELLING KNOWLEDGE AND KNOWLEDGE ENGINEERING

Children, students and teachers are being given tools that allow them to 'author' high level computer programs as part of their learning; building and exploring models. The programs they create will sometimes be useful in their own right but it is the process of creation that is being encouraged [8].

It is important to understand that these tools cannot be used without considerable teacher support and they can form only a small part of the learning of any topic. Perhaps they motivate research. Perhaps they help children order and structure the knowledge that they have been presented with in other ways. Certainly they can generate discussion and debate in the classroom.

This process in industry is an important part of 'knowledge engineering'. When commercial expert systems are being designed a team of domain experts is assembled and together with someone who knows about how information may be structured, a 'knowledge engineer', they try and produce a description of the domain for which the system is required.

This may start with a high level overview of the area but soon requires the experts to try and describe the lower levels of the domain. This knowledge is then coded into rules ready to enter into a suitable 'expert system shell'. The prototype is tested and then successively refined until it passes test criteria set by the domain experts. This may take many months of refinement and at each stage the human experts have to re-examine the way in which they have described their 'knowledge'.

It is this description and refinement process that may be a powerful learning experience. Whether this experience can be replicated with 'subject novices' is still open to debate. Before this can be fully tested, further tools will have to be written to help evaluate the educational possibilities.

5. HOW CAN TEACHERS BE INVOLVED WITH AI?

Much AI research in education is lead either by changes in technology or academic research and some of it scarcely involves children at all. While this work may be important in the long term, it is vital that teachers play a major role in the direction taken by a large percentage of the work.

PEG has based all software development on the principle of collaboration between education and AI. We are convinced that without the support of subject specialists the tools that have been created to date would have been ill-conceived and of little use in the classroom.

We have focussed particularly on history as an example domain. This has suggested that there are a number of prototypical ways of using computers in history teaching that lend themselves to a 'knowledge based' approach. We need to consider whether these are appropriate applications across the curriculum or whether new tools are required for other subjects.

The availability of software forms only part of the requirements for effective use of these ideas in the classroom. Increasingly it is the availability of 'courseware' or support materials that will dictate whether a particular program is of use. It is up to subject specialists to help produce these resources.

6. HYPERPEG?: A FUTURE DIRECTION

As computer hardware becomes cheaper and more powerful, the range of AI applications that can be tested in schools and colleges grows. Powerful knowledge engineering tools may soon be within reach of education. In addition, object orientated approaches may soon be commonplace.

One tool, building upon the object oriented paradigm, that has received considerable attention is Apple's Hypercard. Teachers and educational software developers have recognised it as a major breakthrough. Here is a tool with which professional looking software could be designed quickly and easily by people with only limited previous programming experience.

The emphasis here is on presentation. HyperCard's weaknesses lie in its underlying programming language, HyperTalk. This 'scripting' language allows the user to associate sections of program with fields, buttons and cards. HyperTalk has been designed as a compromise between a very natural way of instructing computers and a full programming language. A look at the range of 'stacks' currently available indicates few in which much processesing of knowledge is available.

What is perhaps required is a link between the computing power of a language such as Prolog and the interface provided by a tool like HyperCard producing children as from the proposed marriage between the beautiful actress and Bernard Shaw "with my beauty and your brains". Recently it has become possible to experiment with this link-up using LPA MacProlog. It is too early to examine the classroom implications of such developments.

The strengths of this approach could lie in its ability to further separate components in the program. In addition to the knowledge and the 'shell' the interface also becomes a discrete entity. This will allow considerable experimentation with how the interface 'looks and feels' without altering the other modules. Because of the simplicity with which the interface can be created (using the standard HyperCard features) teachers and students should be able to tailor the interface to their own preferences.

7. CONCLUSIONS

Artificial intelligence programming should be of growing interest to teachers and educators. This need no longer mean learning an obscure computer language. Instead, by using high level knowledge-based authoring and modelling tools, learners can use software that involves them in actively manipulating material they are studying. By using HyperCard and languages like Prolog prototypes for these new ideas will be created and tested quickly and effectively.

The range of computing environments that build on AI research and could be created to help children learn is very large. It is vital that teachers play a significant rôle in the design of these tools so that they are of maximum relevance across the curriculum. There will need to be a continued investment in the development of such high-level software and its creators must be prepared to modify and extend these ideas until they suit the learning for which they are being created.

PEG provides one fertile forum for these collaborations.

ACKNOWLEDGEMENTS

The authors would like to thank Anthony Tomei, The Nuffield Foundation, The University Grants Committee, Göran Nydahl, The Swedish National Board of Education and Logic Programming Associates Ltd for their practical and financial assistance.

REFERENCES

[1] Papert S. Mindstorms: Children, Computers and Powerful Ideas, 1981, Harvester Press.
[2] Nichol J, Briggs J, Dean J, (eds). Prolog, Children and Students, Fifth Generation Computing in Education Series,1988, Kogan Page, London.
[3] Ennals J. Beginning micro-Prolog, 1983, Ellis Horwood/Heinemann.
[4] LINX88, PEG (Exeter, Cheltenham & London), 1988
[5] KEYS88, PEG (Exeter, Cheltenham & London), 1988
[6] Briggs J. Learning with Expert Systems, 1988, The Advisory Unit, Hatfield.
[7] Knowledge Pad, PEG (Exeter, Cheltenham & London), 1989
[8] Nichol J, Briggs, Dean J. Authoring Programs and Toolkits, Logic Programming and Curriculum Development in Computer Assisted Learning in the Humanities and Social Sciences (Kent WA & Lewis R, eds), 1987, Blackwell Scientific Publications, Oxford.

Computers in Education
A. McDougall and C. Dowling (Editors)
Elsevier Science Publishers B.V. (North-Holland)

IS HYPERMEDIA AN EFFECTIVE TOOL FOR EDUCATION?

Wendy HALL, Peter THOROGOOD, Brian SPRUNT, Les CARR and Gerard HUTCHINGS

University of Southampton, Southampton, S09 5NH, U.K., 30 January 1990

Whilst there has been much mention in the literature recently concerning the development of hypermedia systems, there is very little reported work on projects to assess their effectiveness, or otherwise, in education. This paper reports on a project currently underway at the University of Southampton in the UK to develop a hypertext interface for an interactive videodisc application in biology education, and to undertake a thorough evaluation of the resulting system as used by undergraduate students at the University. The system is currently based on Apple's Hypercard and uses existing videodisc material.

1. INTRODUCTION

Until very recently, the costs of both hardware and software made the use of interactive videodisc (IV) systems virtually non-existent in education. Most examples of interactive video material were in the industrial training sector, where it can be very cost-ffective as well as educationally effective to produce videodiscs and related software designed for specific training tasks. Such materials are generally very expensive to make and provide no solution to the most effective way of exploiting interactive video in education (Hall, [1]). However, the combination of scope and power provided by the convergence of computing and video technology has the capability to greatly enhance and enrich the learning process in many subject areas. There are numerous areas of education where the only way to really understand or appreciate a concept is to see a photograph or a moving film. The ability to access from a single workstation any one of thousands of still pictures, or moving film clips, will present new and potentially highly-otivating learning environments for many different types of students. Today this is possible with computer-controlled laser disc technology. A laser videodisc holds up to 55,000 video frames per side, or approximately 30 minutes of linear playing time. Two audio tracks provide the option of sound and can also be used to store digital information. Each of the video frames can be located almost instantaneously giving random access to all the still and moving images stored on the disc. Through software control, the user is no longer a passive watcher of a slide show or a TV programme but is able to interactively determine his or her own learning path through the video information. This information can be integrated with text and graphics stored digitally, either on the same disc or on the computer, making the potential seemingly limitless.

However, it is not easy to provide interactive access to such large amounts of pictorial information. It is far more complicated to index a picture than a text document, and we need to provide environments in which the links between picture and text and picture and picture appear seamless to the user. Hypertext interfaces appear to offer one possible solution to the latter problem. This paper describes the design and implementation of a hypertext interface for an interactive videodisc system to be used in the teaching of cell biology to undergraduate biology students. The system is based on an existing videodisc that is readily available in Europe, and the Apple Hypercard environment. The paper also presents the first results of an evaluation study that has been undertaken with students using the system.

2. DESIGNING THE SYSTEM

By its very nature, biology is a subject that cannot be learnt or understood without access to pictorial information. Biology text books are always extensively illustrated with line drawings, sketches and photographs. Films and, more recently, videotape recordings are used to illustrate concepts and processes that are dynamic in nature and cannot be easily demonstrated in laboratory sessions. It is therefore natural that biologists should be attracted to videodisc technology as a means of disseminating information about their subject. It was the existence of one such disc (in fact now a series of discs), namely "Cell Biology I: Functional Organisation", that provided the motivation for the project discussed in this paper. The disc is produced by the Institut fur den Wissenschlaftlichen Film (IWF) in Gottingen, West Germany, and is distributed by the British Universities Film and Video Council in the U.K. It is the first in a series of three discs on the general theme of Cell Biology and contains nearly one hundred short film sequences, most with alternative commentaries in English and German (Bereiter-Hahn et al. [2]). It provides a video database on the subject it addresses, and can be used in many different ways to explore various aspects of this subject.

The aim of this initial project was to produce software that facilitates access to the information on the disc for first and second year undergraduate biology students, as a complement to various aspects of their cell biology courses. It was necessary that both the software development language and the finished product be easily usable by students and staff unfamiliar with the use of computing technology. It was important that the system was flexible enough to be relatively easily extended and up-dated. After initial familiarisation with the videodisc, the theme of "Cell Motility" was identified as one which would exploit some of the best images and sequences on the disc yet also remain compatible with key aspects of the first year Cell Biology course offered at Southampton.

The overall aim for the software design was to provide a flexible information presentation system that linked text and graphical information to picture sequences on the disc. A number of design strategies were considered, including linear sequencing of the material, hierarchical branching and a network approach. The first two of these were quickly rejected as being too inflexible and directed; it was felt that for use in higher education, the system should encourage the user to determine their own way around the information as much as possible. A network approach, where any one section of the system can be linked to any number of other sections via (generally) bi-directional links, was considered to be the most flexible design strategy, one which would provide the user with a greater degree of interaction with the system.

Of course, this design strategy embodies the concept of non-sequential writing and it is difficult now to disentangle the thought processes that led to the identification of this strategy. At the time of the initial design phase of the project (the autumn term of 1987), the terms hypertext and hypermedia were becoming more and more common in the computer science literature, but were not well-known outside of this. Suffice it to say here that the subject specialists envisaged a network approach for the presentation of information in this integrated and interactive text, graphics and video system, and a hypertext interface seemed to best fit their design criteria.

3. IMPLEMENTATION

Hypertext is the term first used in the early 1960s by Theodore Nelson to describe the idea of non-sequential writing (Nelson [3]). The reader who is unfamiliar with this idea should refer to the new book by Shneiderman and Kearsley [4]. Basically, a hypertext system is one which allows authors and groups of authors to link information together, create paths through related material, annotate existing texts and create notes that point readers to the same or other units of information. The term 'hypermedia' is often used to describe a hypertext system that has been extended to incorporate other media, such as graphics, video or sound, in addition to text. There are a number of such systems under development both in research establishments and the commercial world (Conklin [5]), but there are as yet very few documented reports of their effective, or otherwise, use in education. One example that has been widely reported is the Intermedia system (Yankelovich et al. [6]) at Brown University, which has been successfully used to create educational materials in a number of subject areas including English Literature and Biology. Another is the StrathTutor project (Kibby and Mayes [7]), which is a hypertext system for exploratory learning.

In the early part of 1988, when implementation of the project was due to begin, the availability of commercial hypertext systems in the UK was extremely limited; the availability of 'hypermedia' systems even more so. The only commercially available hypertext system was OWL's Guide (Brown [8]), which exists for both the IBM pc and the Macintosh, but at the time, the software hooks to enable Guide to drive a videodisc player were not readily available. However, when Apple released Hypercard at the end of 1987, they also released a set of video drivers that enable a videodisc player to be controlled easily through Hypertalk (the programming language of Hypercard), and this made Hypercard a natural choice for the project at the time. The way in which the Hypercard stack was set up to incorporate the video commands and to include various other development utilities is documented in Carr [9].

Nielsen [10] describes Hypercard as computationally active hypertext, clicking a button causes a Hypertalk script to run. Thus the links are not necessarily hardwired and the destination may be computed. It is the ability to easily define the action associated with a button via a Hypertalk script that makes Hypercard such an adaptable environment for the development of multimedia applications. Hypertext-like interfaces can be developed using words and icons, within the text and graphics, as buttons that activate links to other cards, or as references to items stored on other media such as video or sound sequences. The limitations of Hypercard for such applications are well-known. For example, current versions do not support multiple windows or multiple fonts within a text field. However, the ease with which it can be used to develop multimedia applications and the fact that it is freely available on any Macintosh computer make it a very practical choice for education.

The final hardware configuration for each workstation in the project was an Apple MacSE computer connected to a Philips 415 videodisc player via the standard RS232 interface. No genlock board is available for the MacSE so overlay of the computer output on the video screen is not possible. Consequently two monitors are used, but this is not a significant disadvantage for the purposes of this project because there are many instances where the students need to see a full-size video picture in conjunction with text or graphics information on the computer screen. In the future we envisage developing applications with multiple video windows and other advanced multimedia concepts. However, we still have much to learn about how students interact with even the simplest type of hypermedia system.

4. THE HYPERTEXT INTERFACE

The network on which the original system was based was designed by the biologists to represent the interconnectivity of the video sequences on the disc identified as being of relevance to the topic of Cell Motility. Details of the biological content of the network can be found in Hall et al. (11]. The nodes of the system are cards in the Hypercard stack; these may contain text or graphics information and some of the graphics cards include simple animated sequences to illustrate particular biological concepts in a dynamic way. A major problem with Hypercard in its current form is the lack of proper scrolling text fields. This forces the author to use continuation cards and to compartmentalize information into card-length packages. This can be very limiting but for educational purposes can be turned to advantage to ensure that the information in the system is not too verbose and is well categorised.

Key-words in the text, or sometimes in a separate icon, are highlighted in bold font to indicate that they are buttons which when clicked will activate a link to another piece of information in the network (text, graphics, animated graphics or video). One major issue that was not addressed in the first implementation of the project is the problem of identifying for the user of a multimedia environment the type of information that they are about to access when they click on a particular button. There are a number of different approaches to the solution of this problem. Some are possible within Hypercard, some are not. The only way such information is available to our users at the moment is on the 'map' of the system (see Figure 1), which represents the network of nodes and links in the system and indicates which nodes are video sequences and which contain animated graphics. During the first evaluation phase, this map was only available as an integrated part of the hypertext system.

Apart from the 'key-word' buttons within the text, the user only has to know about seven specially defined buttons in order to move around the system. There are two 'return' buttons, one returns the user to the last card visited, the other returns the user to the first card in the stack (the initial 'menu' card). Forward and backward arrow buttons are used to indicate further or previous associated information.

Two were introduced to help users navigate around the system: these are the 'index' and 'contents' buttons. Index and contents lists are well-established tools for helping readers find their way around sequential information and are just as effective for jumping quickly to a particular piece of information in a hypertext system. In this case the index was formed out of the words or phrases that appeared as buttons in the stack, that is the items about which some information is given or for which some

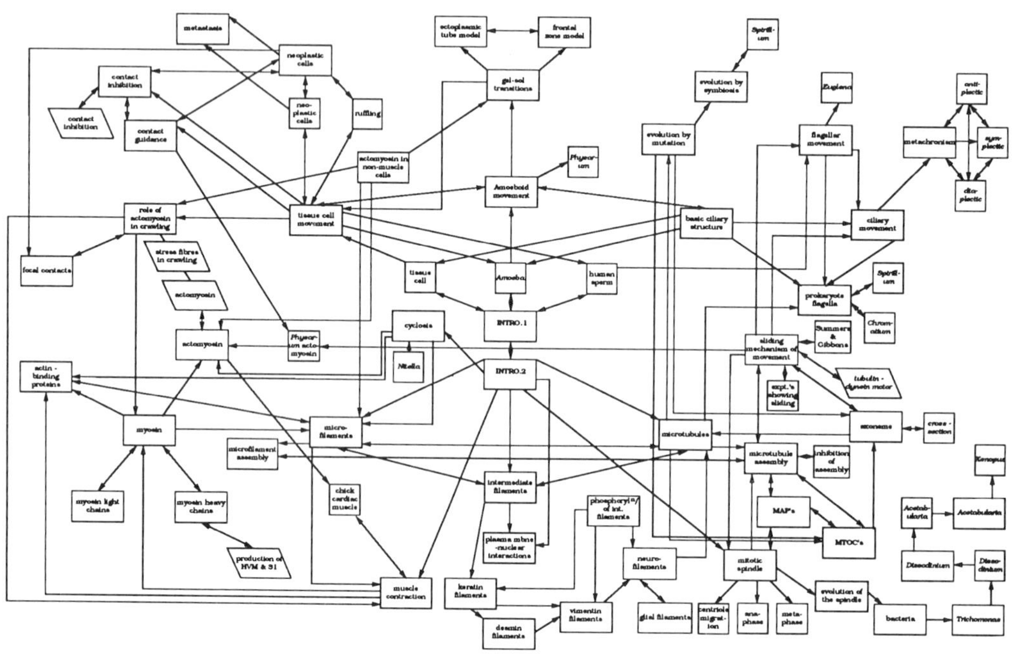

Figure 1: The Cytoskeleton and Cell Motility Map (Reproduced from Hall et al [11], with permission)

cross-reference is made. The contents list was formed out of the titles of all the cards in the stack. Both were generated automatically using software tools written in Hypertalk and both can be used interactively to locate a particular card in the stack. A 'reference' button is also included to link the information on the cards with references to textbooks or papers that the students might normally refer to.

5. EVALUATING THE PROJECT

This paper has described a pilot project that utilises Hypercard to implement a hypertext interface for interactive video, in order to create a learning and reference environment for undergraduate biology students. The project has been a great success on a number of different levels, not least in promoting a very fruitful collaboration between the departments of computer science, biology and teaching media. At the very least, the system provides students with access to some excellent video sequences, at best it will help them to learn more about their subject. But how do we evaluate the levels of success or failure of the system in an educational context?

The current version of the system was used during the spring and summer terms of the academic year 1988/89 to complement the first year Cell Biology course. Students attended their normal lecture course but were asked to attend an extra tutorial where they were given information about the system and how to use it. The lecturer concerned also used the videodisc player in some of the early lectures to demonstrate the type of video material available, and suggested some introductory routes through the hypertext system that particularly complemented these introductory lectures.

Only one IV workstation was available for student use during this period. There were 79 students on the course and they were asked to use the system on a reference basis. Booking sheets were available but since the course took place over a ten-week period and the amount of material in the Hypercard stack was limited to about 250 cards and 50 video sequences, there was sufficient time for all the students to have access to the material if they so wished. Use of the system was not a compulsory element of the course.

Each time the students used the system they were asked to fill out a short questionnaire designed to elicit their reactions to the technology, the software and the content, and to record information about the duration of time they spent using the system. In this way we hoped to be able to monitor not only the students' initial reactions but also their changing views as they became more experienced in using the system. Additionally, observations were made of students using the system and a small sample of students were interviewed in depth.

This evaluation study was designed to provide feedback on how users liked or disliked the program and also to identify particular difficulties that users had in navigating around the stack. No attempt was made to assess the effectiveness of any learning which took place, through pre- and post- testing. Nor was there any direct attempt to compare this mode of learning with others. At the time of writing, the full report of this study is in preparation (Sprunt et al. [12]) but the initial results can be summarised as follows.

A number of lessons were learnt from this initial phase, not least of which was that a voluntary exercise for first year undergraduate students with very full commitments was expecting too much of student enthusiasm and goodwill, no matter how motivating the environment and the software. At the end of the course, a total of 25 questionnaires had been completed and 15 students had been observed and interviewed. Another factor that should be taken into account is that at Southampton there are very few Apple Macintosh computers available on public access and most of the students in this class were unfamiliar with the Macintosh interface.

The overall impression gained from observations and interviews with students was that despite the criticisms they articulated, the irritating bugs in the software and the annoying idiosyncrasies of the hardware, neither the quality of the videodisc material and its related text, nor its overall value as a teaching aid was strongly criticised. On the contrary, in the interviews the students conveyed considerable enthusiasm and interest in the medium being evaluated. The quality of the video sequences far outweighed any inconveniences caused by the technical hitches, although students did comment on the unfamiliarity of the structure of this medium compared to the comfort and familiarity of the book. The majority of the students indicated that they would use the system again and would welcome courseware for a wider range of topics.

The questionnaire presented a mixture of positive and negative statements about the program and prompted the student for responses on a five-point scale. The 15 statements presented related to the program content, the educational aspects of the program as a whole, the characteristics of the delivery system, and the support provided within the software. For those completing the questionnaire, the responses showed a clear consensus of attitude towards most of the statements. An overwhelming majority of the students found the program to be an effective learning resource and an enjoyable form of instruction. Very few found the technology intimidating and only a small percentage found the two screen display distracting. All those who completed a questionnaire found that having reference titles displayed within the text was a great advantage, and most of them considered the contents list and the index vital for navigating through the text.

However, opinion was divided about problems of disorientation within the program. Of the 25 responses on completed questionnaires, 10 agreed or strongly agreed that it was easy to become disoriented within the program. Whilst the remainder disagreed or had no comment, clearly a significant number of the students had some difficulty in navigating around the information in the stack. It is difficult to tell whether this was due to lack fo familiarity with this type of software or whether there are inherent problems in either our hypertext model or hypertext techniques generally.

In order to study the navigation problem and to monitor how the students are using the hypertext interface and the video information, we have developed a software tool that logs each student session on the system. Since any such software tool must contain a model of the system, in order to monitor which nodes are visited in each session and with what frequencies, the same tool can be used to automatically create a map of the system. It has also been extended to enable the author of a tutorial stack to build and display the overall structure map of the field of study showing the topics overed and to link this to the map of cards in the tutorial stack. For followup discussion and evaluation, it can be used to display student paths through the structure maps, and to automatically create a display of the total number of times a card or topic is visited as well as a display of the average time spent on each card or topic. This extremely powerful tool was introduced to monitor student use of the system towards the end of this initial evaluation study and the results are currently being analysed.

In summary, we are extremely encouraged by the very positive response from the students toward their first exposure to a hypermedia system. However, in the next stage of the project we will include material that the students will not have previously seen in lectures and make this a compulsory element of the course. Of course, further evaluation studies are required to assess the novelty effect of both the videodisc technology and the hypertext interface, and to establish how the latter can be used to best effect in the learning process. Nevertheless, the results from this preliminary study indicate that hypermedia can be usefully applied in an educational context and that it is worthwhile to generate further material for this medium.

6. CONCLUSIONS

In this paper we describe the implementation of a hypertext interface in Hypercard to provide access in an educational context to video sequences. We do not claim to have solved the problems of creating and up-dating a generic hypertext/hypermedia system but we are attempting to analyse the advantages and disadvantages of hypertext interfaces for multimedia information systems. Our implementation environment, Hypercard, has its limitations but it does enable quite sophisticated information handling systems to be developed very quickly. The author of the Cell Motility stack was a third year biology student (one of the current authors - GH) with no previous programming experience, who produced a working version of the stack within 10 weeks of first using Hypercard. However, we are not inextricably linked to Hypercard and remain open to changes in the software development environment in the future. Most importantly, all text and graphics produced for the project will be stored in a standard format such as LaTex or SGML, so that it can be readily adapted for whatever hypertext interface is chosen. Our philosophy in this respect is described in Rahtz et al. [13]. This will also enable members of staff to incorporate lecture notes and research papers into the hypertext environment as effortlessly as possible.

Of course, linking this material to video sequences is currently dependent on the availability of suitable videodisc material. This is a serious problem, since making a videodisc is a costly enterprise and with current technology it is not possible to edit the video material created. However, this is no argument for not making the best use of the video material already available and exploring how to use this material to improve teaching and learning. As technology progresses it will become easier to create visual databases, both computer graphics and video-based. It will become possible to network these images to personal workstations and we will be able to manipulate pictorial information with the ease that we can manipulate textual information today. Clearly an international effort is called for to create and share visual databases in many different subject areas and for all levels of education. The development of satellite technology will enable us to readily transmit and up-date such information around the world. There are no language barriers to pictorial information.

Even given this utopia, we have to create the software environments that will allow us and our students to make sense of such vast amounts of information. We have so much to learn about how to design interfaces for the multimedia information systems of the future. Hypermedia techniques may provide us with some of the answers we are looking for.

ACKNOWLEDGEMENTS

The authors of the paper would like to thank Apple Computer U.K. Limited for their donation of equipment to support this project. Also thanks to Sebastian Rahtz for his invaluable help in the typesetting of the paper.

REFERENCES

[1] Hall, W., The Use of Interactive Video in Undergraduate Teaching (Matheias, H. et al (eds.), Aspects of Educational Technology XXI, Kogan Page, London, 1988).

[2] Breiter-Hahn, J., Fischer, A., Hock, B. and Kiermayer, O., Preface to the handbook accompanying the videodisc Cell Biology I: Functional Organisation (IWF, Gottingen, West Germany, 1984).

[3] Nelson, T.H., Getting It Out of Our System (Scheter, G. (ed.), Information Retrieval: A Critical Review, Thompson Books, Washington D.C., 1967).

[4] Shneiderman, B., and Kearsley, G., Hypertext Hands-On: An Introduction to a New Way of Organising and Accessing Information (Addison-Wesley, 1989).

[5] Conklin, J., Hypertext: A Survey and Introduction (IEEE Computer, (20), 1987), pp. 17-41.

[6] Yankelovich, N., Haan, B., Meyrowitz, N., and Drucker, S., Intermedia: The Concept and Construction of a Seamless Information Environment (IEEE Computer, January 1988), pp. 81-96.

Computers in Education
A. McDougall and C. Dowling (Editors)
Elsevier Science Publishers B.V. (North-Holland)

WORKING WITH KNOWLEDGE BASES IN THE PRIMARY SCHOOL

Les Watson,

College of St. Paul and St. Mary, The Park, Cheltenham, England

This paper describes two knowledge based tools, Linx88 and Keys88, and describes some examples of how they have been used by primary school teachers to provide a central focus for their topic work.

1. SOME OBSERVATIONS

'The computer is by all odds the most extraordinary of the technological clothing ever devised by man, since it is an extension of our central nervous system. Beside it the wheel is a mere hula-hoop' [8]

Despite the undeniable truth of this statement many primary schools are failing to harness the power of microcomputers to enhance the learning of their pupils. There are few schools in the UK that use IT for any activity other than drill and practice [4]. This is highlighted by teacher reaction to instructional/ testing type programs on INSET courses, where simple maths and spelling software arouses the most interest! There are some schools using content free IT tools such as word processors, spreadsheets and databases as cross curricular tools and this type of use is likely to increase especially with the requirements of the National Curriculum. However, it is generally true that.....

'The ways in which computers are used at present (in primary schools) suggests that they have not had the impact that many educationalists predicted. Instead of initiating new practices computers have been used to maintain existing ones, supporting a traditional curriculum with new technology.' [3]

The Cheltenham base of PEG has been seeking to address this situation by involving primary school teachers in Gloucestershire and Wiltshire in INSET work involving the use of knowledge based tools in the primary classroom. This programme of work was initiated by the desire to promote the use of microcomputers in education from an educational starting point.

'Thinking about the computer's role in education does not mean thinking about computers, it means thinking about education' [2]

2. THE EDUCATIONAL BASE FOR THE WORK OF PEG CHELTENHAM

This educational base has foundations in sound primary school practice based on exploration and problem solving and using the computer to enhance these activities.

'In developing problem solving skills, teachers have the important task of helping pupils to tackle problems analytically and to adopt logical procedures in solving them. At the same time, pupils must be allowed to make mistakes and to follow false scents in what is essentially an exploratory process; and the teacher has to resist the temptation to give the 'right' answer or to over direct the pupil otherwise the skill is not developed or practised.' [1]

A computer with open ended educational software is never 'tempted' to give the right answer and as a supplier of false scents is hard to beat!

3.THE STARTING POINT

'The curriculum of the primary school should be thought of in terms of activity and experience rather than of knowledge to be acquired and facts to be stored.' [5]

The role of the computer in the schemes of work produced by the PEG Cheltenham group has been to promote a range of activities away from the micro which provide the educational experiences relevant to the curriculum of the primary school. The computer has provided a focus for classroom activity whilst placing the emphasis on investigation using traditional sources of information. The emphasis has been moved from *being told* to *wanting to find out*. The computer has acted as a stimulus for a range of activities such as writing, artwork, drama, and model making. The starting point for the work has always been the curriculum, for example one project school which uses topic work extensively across the whole school decided to use colours as a school theme. The teachers on the PEG Cheltenham INSET were allocated the colour black for their group. This led them to consider space as a project and resulted in the production of a simulation using one of the PEG tools which allowed the class of 64 children to embark on a space journey lasting a whole term.

4. THE TOOLS USED

4.1 Linx88

Linx88 is the latest version of a program originally produced by Jonathan Briggs, Jackie Dean and Jon Nichol. It has undergone extensive trialling in schools and Colleges over the last 5 years and seen many improvements. It is a piece of software which allows the authoring of simulations, adventures and interactive branching stories. The software is menu driven and requires no special programming skills. The authoring screen for Linx88 is shown here in figs.1 and 2.

fig. 1 The Linx88 main menu

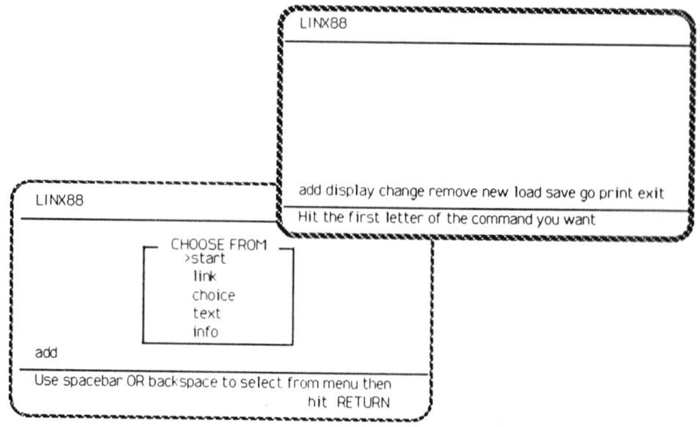

fig. 2 A Linx88 sub menu

Selecting from this menu takes the 'programmer' or 'author' through a series of sub menus until the text entry screen is reached, shown here in fig.3

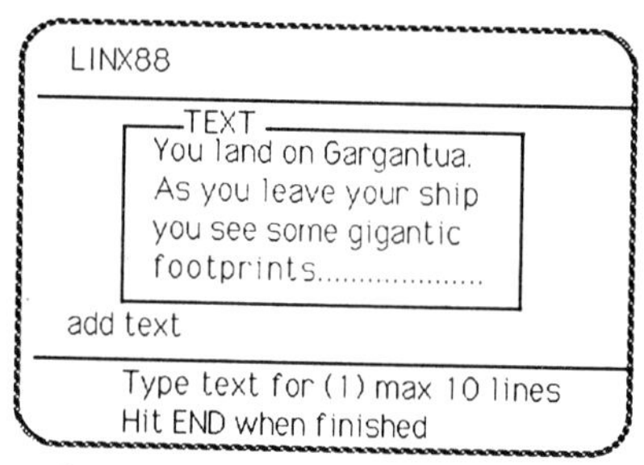

fig. 3 The text entry screen for Linx88

Each text screen can be linked to any other by direct links or choices which are also 'added' by selecting from menus. After construction of such a story the author (or anyone else) can use the story by selecting 'go' from the main menu and will be presented with the screen which has been set as the 'start' screen along with any associated choices. An important feature of the package is the inclusion of a 'look up information' facility. Any word on any text screen can have a link to a screen of explanatory information about it. It is also possible to nest information down to a depth of five levels. Pupils using the adventure or simulation can research topics which the teacher has included information as he/she works through the program. In order to make the best use of Linx88 the author needs to pay special attention to planning the story - in fact this is the essence of using the software successfully as once planned the entry of information is very straightforward.

4.2 Keys88

Keys88 was written and developed by Derek Brough, Jonathan Briggs, Jon Nichol and myself. It was originally conceived as a 'free form' wordprocessor. The user can decide to have one or more categories of information and type text into these categories. Each item of information can contain words which are identified as 'keywords' and which can be used to form links between items. The user interface for Keys88 is very similar to that for Linx88, also being menu driven and having a similar layout. Planning for keys88 is less structured than for Linx88 and a user could use the program for example to take notes on a topic by identifying the keywords and then typing the information concerning each keyword. The way in which the knowledge is structured is very different from Linx88. Instead of the user creating links between the screens of information this is done by the software based on the keywords identified by the user. Consequently a very complicated web of links can be created easily - and unknowingly!

5. THE WORK PRODUCED

Teachers involved in the project have produced a wide range of programs to support topic work with their children some of which are briefly described here.

5.1 Starship Longleaze
(A simulation of a space journey written in Linx88)

This project involved a class of 64 nine and ten year old children in a voyage into space, and lasted for a whole term. The children were allocated to crews, but only after they had applied for particular jobs aboard the spaceship. Once the project was started the computer acted as mission control, being a central focus in the classroom. Each group would take their turn at the machine, making discoveries and being set a range of tasks such as designing games to keep the crew happy on the long voyage, baking moon rock cakes or researching new recipes and menus to feed the crew. Some pupils were involved in designing the spaceship and others charting the planets and producing scale models of them. The reading room which is an annexe to the classroom was decorated with views through the windows of the spaceship produced by the children. The class had not realised how much writing is involved in flying a spaceship, there's the ship's log to complete each day, newspapers to produce to provide the crew with in flight information, and the legends of the planets visited to record for recounting back on Earth. All these tasks were aimed at achieving the objectives set by the teachers such as encouraging the children to work co-operatively, providing opportunities for the use of a range of writing styles, stimulating creative work in art, music and drama, and developing research skills. The project took place as the preliminary guidelines for the National Curriculum in schools were produced. Identifying those areas of work which related to the National Curriculum guidelines and specific attainment targets proved to be a fairly straightforward task see fig.4.

5.2 Longleaze Farm
(A simulation of the day to day running of a farm written in Linx88)

This project provided opportunities for a wide range of tasks although its main focus was on teamwork and discussion skills. The class of nine and ten year old pupils formed management teams each of eight members. Each team had the task of running a farm for one term. The topic was chosen to link with National Food and Farming year. Bank loans were provided for each group to fig. 4 An outline of some of the areas covered by the Starship Longleaze Project

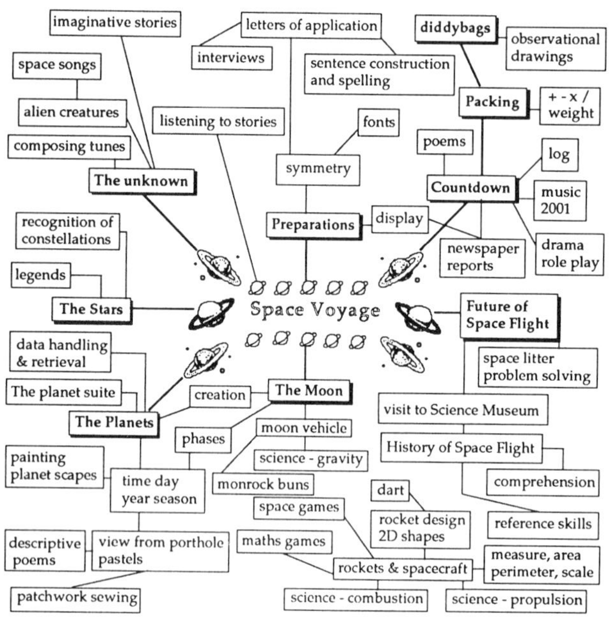

Relating the work to the National Curriculum

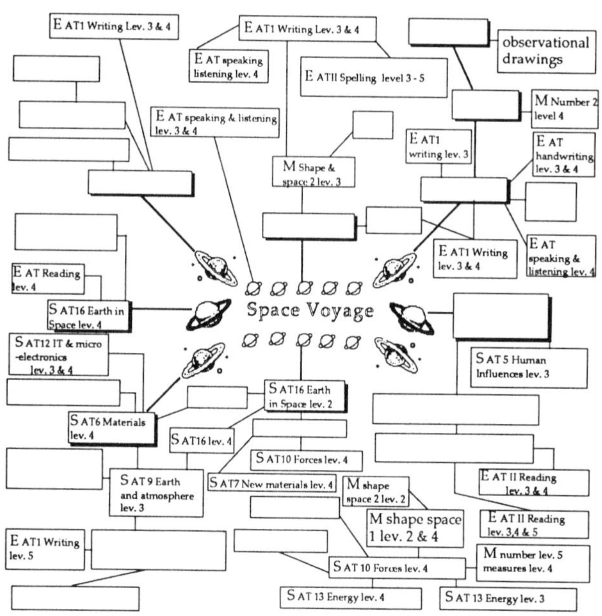

set up their farm based on the quality of their application to the teachers in charge. Information on the daily fluctuations in hay prices and rates on the stock exchange were available within the simulation for the 'management groups' to use when making important decisions regarding their business plan. A key feature of the project was the regular board meetings of each group. I visited the school one Friday afternoon to find these meetings going on. Some important decisions were being made by the children as they had just learned of the crash of the bank by which they were financed. I was impressed not only by the quality of the discussion taking place but by the knowledge the children had concerning farm prices and the consequences of actions such as diversifying their operations or selling certain parts of their enterprise. The strict observance of formal protocol in the meetings was also impressive. The project culminated in each group preparing a prospectus for their business in order to put it up for sale. A local estate agent was called in to comment on the properties and their market value. He was impressed by the children's presentation of their properties and by their realistic valuations.

5.3 Chedworth Roman Villa

(A simulation of the excavation of a Roman villa at Chedworth in Gloucestershire, England)

Another teacher on the INSET course chose to cover the topic of The Romans with her class of seven year olds. After some discussion with me she decided that what she would like to do would be to use the computer to excavate the Roman villa at Chedworth in Gloucestershire. The emphasis in the work was to be on deduction and evidence as she intended to provide the children with clues about what they had found during the excavation rather than actual objects. The starting point for the building of the simulation was a visit by the teacher to the Roman villa. This included a chat with the manager of the site and provided an insight into the problems of archaeological investigation. The ideas she picked up from this visit along with the actual layout of the villa were then used to produce a Linx88 program which the children could use. During their investigation of the site within the computer the children were involved in research of life in Roman times, interpreting data gathered, production of artwork in the form of Roman mosaics, model making - Roman standards, as well as a comprehensive study of the Roman period.

5.4 Creapsville
(A mystery written using Keys88)

There have been some strange goings on in the village of Creapsville and the lady of the manor advertises in the local paper for someone to investigate them. The seven year olds who took part in this work had to 'apply' for the job and were then involved in trying to explain the information contained within a Keys88 database produced by their teacher. The children had to make up a map of the village as they investigated the strange happenings and to not only write reports of their findings but also attempt to explain them. Were they supernatural, extra terrestrial, or criminal? In fact the teacher had made sure that the evidence was inconclusive. Consequently it could be interpreted in a variety of ways and gave the children an opportunity to try to provide evidence for their arguments.

5.5 Human Growth and Development
(A text database written by a group of seven year olds)

This work was linked with a series of TV programmes on sex education. The children gathered information from a number of sources including the TV programmes, books, and a range of school visitors such as the local doctor and a midwife. They then wrote a short piece of text on one aspect of the work and entered it into a keys database, identifying the text by a key word. As explained earlier Keys88 then creates links between these keywords allowing a user to browse the database looking up information on words that they wish to follow up. The building of the Keys88 database was only one of a range of activities which took place in the classroom and served as an additional focus of the knowledge being acquired by the children as well as a reference point containing a summary of the knowledge of the class. As this is a recurring topic in the school it is likely that the database will be used with and extended by other children.

6. THE LESSONS

The above examples are not all the work produced by PEG Cheltenham but are some of the better ones. The range of materials had a realistic variation and this served to identify some key factors in the take up of new ideas by teachers.

6.1 It doesn't suit everyone

As with most innovation the use of materials such as Keys88 and Linx88 is most likely to be taken on board by teachers who are already committed to investigative learning. The bigger the gap between the current practice of the teacher and the innovation the more difficult it is to bring about its introduction.

6.2 Imagination is vital

The teachers who adopt open ended tools such as Linx88 and Keys88 need to be open minded and imaginative. Such teachers are likely to have an integrated topic based approach to their work which is an important asset when using this type of software.

6.3 A gentle introduction is needed

The examples described here and the many others which have been produced by the PEG Cheltenham group were produced over a period of two years. The changes which take place are gradual and cannot be brought about quickly. Time for the assimilation of the ideas embodied in the software and the appreciation of its potential benefits is a vital factor.

6.4 Resources are the key issue

None of the examples above would have been produced without resources. This may seem obvious but what may not be so obvious is that resourcing is a complex issue. A variety of resources are required. The software and hardware resources are vital but can only be of use if provided in conjunction with time - time for training and time for practice. Accessibility of the equipment and ownership of the ideas are also extremely important. Adopting this software means adopting a certain approach to education and to classroom practice. For some this may involve a change in their current ideas and working practices, such changes require time for practice, experiment, reflection, and evaluation.

6.5 Relate it to the National Curriculum

A sure way to attract interest in any aspect of education at the moment is to mention the National Curriculum.

REFERENCES

[1] Curriculum 5 to 16 DES (1985)

[2] Ellis A.B., The use and Misuse of computers in Education (McGraw-Hill 1974

[3] Flux P, Micro-Prolog, microworlds and primary school children Proceedings of the International PEG conference (1989)

[4] Jackson A. et al. A survey of Microcomputer Use and provision in Primary Schools Journal of Computer Assisted Learning (1986) 2,1

[5] Hadow report DES 1931

[6] Linx88 PEG (Cheltenham, Exeter & London) (1989)

[7] Keys88 PEG(Cheltenham, Exeter & London) (1989)

[8] Shushan R. & Wright D., Desktop Publishing by Design Microsoft Press (1989)

[9] Watson L., A Diary of work in school aimed at integrating Prolog software toolkits into the primary curriculum Proceedings of the International PEG conference (1987)

[10] Watson L., Authoring shells - The next generation of content free software RM User Journal (1987)

[11] Watson L., Key Clues, Times Educational Supplement 17/7/88

[12] Watson L., Knowledge Bases in Primary School Proceedings of the International PEG conference (1988)

[13] Watson L., Authoring with Primary Teachers Proceedings of the International PEG conference (1989)

Computers in Education
A. McDougall and C. Dowling (Editors)
Elsevier Science Publishers B.V. (North-Holland)

COMPUTERS AND HIGHER ORDER THINKING SKILLS

Cathie SHERWOOD

Division of Education, Griffith University, Nathan, Queensland 4111, Australia

The development of higher order thinking skills, particularly problem solving, appears to be one of the most enduring issues in curriculum development this decade. The proliferation of computers into classrooms has led educators to consider that higher level thinking will be greatly enhanced by the computer and certain types of software. This paper describes a twelve week study using adventure games in four classrooms. It was designed to explore students' ability to solve problems encountered in adventure games for which they may lack a formal knowledge of efficient solution procedures, but can solve through applying general thinking processes.

1. INTRODUCTION

The last decade has seen increasing pressure placed on education to develop the learners' capacity to adapt to change using decision making, problem solving and other higher order thinking skills which will enable them to think for themselves and to solve novel problems. Schools must now foster these skills, and provide for their effective transfer from one subject area to another. The introduction of the computer into schools, and the influx of 'problem solving software' has led educators to believe that it is the computer which offers the greatest potential for facilitating and enhancing the development of these skills to ensure their automatic transfer to other areas. It is assumed practice on the computer will lead to a 'measurable' performance improvement on tasks off the computer.

2. WHAT ARE HIGHER ORDER THINKING SKILLS?

There are numerous definitions on what constitutes higher order thinking. The term itself can be misleading as it suggests that there is a set of 'lower order' skills requiring little independent thinking or judgement, and which must precede progression to a higher level of thinking [Resnick, 1987:8]. Ausubel [1968] however, considers that higher order thinking is present in any activity in which both the cognitive representation of experience and the components of a current problem situation are reorganised to achieve a designated aim. Patterson and Smith [1986:82] suggest that "higher order thinking occurs when a person is engaged in active and sustained cognitive effort directed at solving a complex problem and when the person makes effective use of prior knowledge and experience in addressing the problem". Presseisen [1985:43] agrees, stating that "... thinking is generally assumed to be a cognitive process, a mental act by which knowledge is acquired". According to Resnick [1987], higher order thinking is complex, nonalgorithimic, and requires considerable mental work. It quite often involves uncertainty, judgement, interpretation, and can yield multiple solutions.

Models for the teaching of thinking are also many and varied. Piaget [1970] advocated relating methods and materials to a student's age and cognitive development. Feuerstein [1980] stressed "autonomous learning", and Heiman [1987] emphasised the importance of 'learning to learn'. The general perception here is that higher order thinking skills programs be taught as a discrete component, separate from the general curriculum, and that they must focus on developing intellectual processes such as problem solving, decision making, critical thinking and creative thinking [Presseisen, 1985].

How then can a child's ability to solve problems, think deductively, synthesise and apply knowledge, and make predictions be assessed and developed? Individuals will continue to use disparate, yet equally efficient strategies in solving a particular type of problem. This may be because of their prior knowledge gained in past experiences, or simply because they hold a different view of the problem. Such strategies may also depend on whether the child is an expert or novice in that particular domain.

3. COMPUTERS AND HIGHER ORDER THINKING SKILLS

Much of the research on computers, thinking skills and problem solving, and the transfer of learning, has been related to *Logo*, other programming languages, or drill and practice software. Findings from this research have been contradictory and less than conclusive, in most instances. The studies did not document significant improvements in students' thinking and transfer [Au and Leung, 1988; Pea and Kurland, 1985]. In fact, the evaluation of the learning outcomes has concentrated on *acquired knowledge,* rather than on whether the *skills* for acquiring knowledge had been developed or enhanced.

Many of these studies have focused on the computer and software as isolated experiences in a classroom. However, other evaluations of computer-based efforts to enhance thinking and problem solving skills suggest that certain elements are essential if 'instruction' is to have lasting effects on children's performance [Segal, Chipman and Glaser, 1985; Stein and Linn, 1985]. These elements – independent inquiry, cooperation, collaboration, and creative expression – appear to be provided sparingly or hardly in classrooms [Goodlad, 1983]. Yet it is these very elements, in particular collaboration, which will enable learners to undertake some responsibility for their own learning. By working collaboratively at adventure games for example, children can verbalise their thought processes. They negotiate, hypothesise, interpret, predict, and make decisions; all of which are complex thinking processes.

Classrooms must be social environments for learning that reflect the kind of epistemology that we want to characterise students' knowledge. Where collaborative work is the main teaching strategy, then this embodies an epistemology of knowing as "socially constructed understanding" [Greeno, 1989:139]. Higher order thinking should not be characterised by correct answers, but by the fact that the combined complex thinking processes of a group of children working together produced that answer or at least increased the probability of a correct response.

Curriculum compatibility can also be a major factor governing the degree to which computer based instruction correlates with classroom performance. Curriculum compatiblility refers to the match between the software's instructional aims and the aims of the curriculum. The software must become an integral component in the learning experiences of the students.

If the computer and appropriate software has been effectively integrated into the curriculum, guided discovery learning may happen as children can work at their own pace through the software, with the teacher supplying a framework within the classroom for related off-computer activities. Papert [1980] uses the term 'microworld' to define a learning environment which promotes active exploration, allowing learners to exercise powerful ideas and intellectual skills. *Logo* may offer one such environment; adventure games another.

4. ADVENTURE GAMES AS TOOLS FOR DEVELOPING THINKING

Patterson and Smith [1986:99] call adventure games "artificial environment simulations (which) generate a make-believe world with a sufficiently rich knowledge base and set of rules so that complex problems can be posed by the programs. Their capacity both to tutor and to pose problems in an integrated fashion allows them to control the influence of prior knowledge; this control enables the computer to provide successively deeper information and more complex problems". They also state that schools do not use adventure games because "they do not fit into the curriculum, they take a long time to run, and they seem frivolous since they are not based on real-life circumstances and are often advertised as games". Yet, Patterson and Smith have little doubt that such games motivate students and engage them in sustained cognitive activity.

Studies which have considered the use of adventure games or simulations in the development of thinking skills have been few [Breuer, 1985; Forsyth, 1987; Okey & Oliver, 1987], and have primarily focused on the interactive fiction role of the adventure game instead of its potential as a tool for the development of thinking skills.

Adventure games on their own make no explicit effort to highlight the metacognitive aspects of the thinking process. Students using adventure games are given clues for solving the problem(s) presented in the software but little feedback on how well they are progressing towards the successful solution of the problem. Children need to use their earlier acquired knowledge, combine it with that acquired by the other group members, and apply it to the situation. Where that knowledge does not exist, then the process of solution may be supplemented by instruction or trial and error [Evans, 1986]. However, there will be children who randomly choose commands, and are pleased when things happen on the screen. Others do not benefit from the feedback gained from previous games, or through discussion with other group members. These students may never progress from using trial and error as a strategy [Linn, 1986].

Therefore, a project was designed to investigate which higher order thinking skills and strategies children used, without teacher assistance, while playing adventure games.

5. THE FRAMEWORK OF THE STUDY

In essence, the basic aims of the study were to determine:

- to what extent children use higher order thinking skills to solve problems and puzzles presented in computer adventure games;
- whether the age of the group, the gender mix, and/or the number of children at the computer facilitated a higher degree of thinking;
- the extent of collaboration between the children at the computer; and
- the implications for curriculum development relating to the integration of the microcomputer.

Since task persistence is also a measure of divergent thinking ability the video tapes were also analysed to compare time on-task between groups and year levels.

5.1 Method

The study took place in two primary schools in suburban communities. A total of ninety children participated in the study. Two groups were in the age range of 7-8 years, with another two groups between 11-12 years of age. The sample represented children in Year Three and Year Seven.

Each class had about twenty-seven students each. Classrooms were chosen by the schools themselves, because the children met the age requirements, and because the teachers expressed interest in participating in the research. Three out of the four classrooms had a female teacher. All classes had experience with using the computer previously, but not in using these particular pieces of software. Three of the teachers were experienced at successfully incorporating the computer into the learning experiences of the classroom while one would be considered to be very experienced.

5.2 A Description Of The Software

The software used for this study was two adventure games - *Detect-A-Pet* (DAP) for the Year Three classroom and *Dinosaur Discovery* (DD) for the Year Seven classroom. These games were chosen for three reasons: (a) They have no gender bias; (b) *Detect-A-Pet* is totally graphics-based, with interaction through five icons, while *Dinosaur Discovery* has a high proportion of graphics screens; and (c) Neither game involves children in making moral judgements, nor do they contain violent elements.

Each of these games is set within a fantasy context with a goal to be reached. In *Detect-A-Pet* the central character in the software is a child who has lost a pet. Players take on this role and search a local neighbourhood for the missing pet. No time limit is set for the search, however, certain conditions must be met before the pet can be taken home. In *Dinosaur Discovery,* children have the task of finding their way about an area that contains several elements essential for the hatching of a dinosaur's egg. The only clues that players have are in a diary left by the scientist who made the original discovery. It is not intended that they should be successful on their first or second attempt. With each attempt, players build up their experiences of the microworld (that is, the adventure game) and by utilising this expanding knowledge base solve the problem.

5.3 Materials

The adventure games selected for each Year level –*Detect-A-Pet* for the Year Three classrooms and *Dinosaur Discovery* for the Year Seven classrooms were run on Apple//e computers equipped with colour monitors.

5.4 Procedure

The classroom teachers, with some input from the researcher, then developed thematic units which incorporated the software – Pets for the Year Three students and Dinosaurs for the Year Seven students. It was felt that the children would be motivated further if the classroom activities were directly related to what they were doing on the computer. These units of work integrated all curriculum areas, and allowed the teachers to provide a wide variety of activities, each having a central theme of pets or dinosaurs.

The children were video and audio taped working at the computer and on some off-computer related activities for a period of twelve weeks. Taping was done on one day at each school. Children were grouped in twos, threes, and fours to determine which size grouping at the computer facilitated the most talk, interaction and thinking. Children were also grouped in single and mixed gender groupings. This was to determine what role, if any, this played in the thinking, discussion, decision making and problem solving that happened. The groups were randomly selected, within the limits of sex and number. On video taping days, each group had approximately thirty minutes on-computer time.

Recordings took place near the classroom, but usually in a withdrawal room. This was to ensure that the audio would be quite clear for analysis. The researcher monitored the videotaping but did not intervene during the session unless the children did not know what key they should press to continue. The camera was in full view of the students. The children used the computer software at various times of the day throughout the duration of the thematic units of work, including the days that the researcher was there to tape.

5.5 Limitations Of The Study

This was an exploratory research study designed to find out generally what higher order thinking skills children use when provided with computer experiences (in this case, adventure games) which have been integrated into the classroom activities. No pre-tests or post-tests were given to determine whether or not there was an improvement in performance on problems. Transfer of higher order thinking skills was not investigated.

6. RESULTS

Finding an appropriate instrument for analysing the data proved to be more difficult than at first thought. Eventually, a checklist was devised which incorporated aspects of Bloom's Taxonomy of Educational Objectives: Cognitive Domain [1974], and John Cradler's Cognitive Skills Task Analysis [1985]. Complete sessions (each of approximately thirty minutes) were then analysed by marking comments or activities (sometimes of a nonverbal nature) that reflected a complex thinking process.

As a detailed analysis of the video tapes is still underway, the results are tentative. However, some patterns are already evident.

1. It had been anticipated that academic ability may not be a major measure of a child's capacity to solve problems. However, what was surprising was the number of children, considered to have learning difficulties, who showed a high incidence of cognitive and social behaviours which were indicative of important thinking and learning activity. All students in this group were boys. They displayed a confidence which had not been evident in off-computer tasks related to the thematic unit.

2. On task time was high throughout each session – almost one hundred percent while students were on the computer. At no point did conversation move away from the problems and puzzles presented. In fact, one of the most impressive parts of the study for the researcher was the intensity and persistence evidenced by some of the children. This was not confined to a particular gender, but it was more apparent in pairs. The off-computer time on-task was much less – approximately sixty percent. Discussions about these tasks were often interspersed with topics of an entirely social nature.

3. Access to the keyboard was dominated by one member of the group to the exclusion of others, particularly in groups of three and four. In general, this dominance was not related to a particular gender.

4. The size of the group, and the gender mix determined the level of interaction between members of the group, particularly in the Year Seven group. Girls were less likely to be distracted by irrelevant conversation, and saw the adventure games as interesting challenges, whereas the boys were more interested in 'getting the answer right', that is, finding a successful solution to the adventure. In the group setting, hypotheses were formulated, predictions made, explanations given, the problem restated by most group members in their own words, and assistance was given to those requiring it. The collaborative setting allowed for social support to be given for even partially successful efforts. This enabled the less confident students to think of themselves as capable of engaging in independent thinking and of exercising control over the learning process.

5. The Year Three children, in the early stages of the study, were less self-critical than the Year Sevens. They were satisfied with their first attempts. Students read the problem, decided to do something and then kept at it to the exclusion of other possibilities. If this tactic failed, they simply moved onto another area instead of trying to implement a plan, or discuss ways of circumventing previously found danger areas. However, as they realised that this 'hit and miss' method was not solving the problem, they formulated a plan and followed the steps, modifying the plan if one approach proved to be unsuccessful. The Year Seven students did this almost from the beginning. Trial and error was not as evident a strategy with the older students.

6. Students working in pairs demonstrated higher levels of cooperation than did the groups of three or four. This was true for both the Year Three and Year Seven children. The Year Seven students discussed available options with their peers, reviewed the situation and gained a consensus.

7. Much of the problem solving was on a trial and error basis. Because of the flexibility of the environment, there were instances when the students tried a variety of hypotheses without giving sufficient thought to the suitability or otherwise of the solution. Motivation, and interest in the game, was consistently high.

In general, the groups demonstrated flexibility, that is, they tried several different approaches, but always within a rigid framework set by themselves. Novel responses to problems were few, nor did they endeavour to create new ideas or rules to fit the available information.

The most obvious benefit from this study was that children developed positive attitudes because they were motivated, and because they could interact with problem situations in a non-threatening environment.

None of these students had had instruction in higher order thinking skills, yet all subjects demonstrated essential thinking processes, with a majority using complex thinking processes. Did these children acquire these capabilities from general instruction in school, or are they a result of their everyday experience or native endowment? When children arrive at a learning situations such as this, do they come with structures of conceptual competence, or do they acquire them within each experience? If they come with these structures then experiences should be provided which allow them to reorganise, manipulate and elaborate so that a new combination of ideas may be developed.

7. CONCLUSION

As yet we do not have a clear vision of what a merger between the computer and appropriate software, and the curriculum can do to develop, extend and transfer into other domains the higher order thinking skills of students. To obtain this blend we may need to radically restructure our curriculum so that the emphasis on content changes to an emphasis on process and collaboration. The fundamental elements of the new curriculum should not include the teaching of higher order thinking skills as a separate component. The emphasis should be on social interaction, cooperative effort, and the provision of linked experiences, perhaps via the computer and adventure games that make use of the thinking capabilities of children. "Teachers do not compare a student's progress with that of other students, but rather select worthwhile experiences appropriate to his or her stage, organize them for meaningful interpretation, and orchestrate them to provoke the student's thinking" [Lowery, 1985:77].

Once students are motivated because teachers are innovative, then all things are possible. Perhaps studies such as this may not provide the significant results we would hope for, but then perhaps we are tending to ask old questions of a new technology.

REFERENCES

Au, W. K. and Leung, J. P. [1988]. "Transfer of Problem Solving in Logo Programming". In Proceedings of the Sixth Australian Computers in Education Conference, ECAWA, Perth.

Ausubel, D. [1968]. *Educational Psychology – a Cognitive View.* Holt, Rinehart and Winston, New York.

Bloom, B. [1974]. *The Taxonomy of Educational Objectives: Cognitive Domain.* McKay, New York.

Breuer, K. [1985]. "Computer Simulations and Cognitive Development". In K. Duncan and D. Harris (Eds). Computers in Education. IFIP, Elsevier, North-Holland.

Cradler, J. [1985]. "CompuTHINK and criteria for selecting software". In A.L. Costa (Ed), *Developing Minds,* Association for Supervision and Curriculum Development, Alexandria, Virginia.

Evans, N. [1986]. *The future of the microcomputer in schools.* Macmillan, London.

Feuerstein, R. [1980]. *Instrumental Enrichment: An Intervention Program for Cognitive Modifiability.* University Park Press, Baltimore.

Forsyth, A. [1987]. "Simulated Travel and Place Location Learning in a Computer Adventure Game". *Journal of Educational Computing Research,* 3 (3), 377-94.

Goodlad, J. [1984]. *A Place Called School.* McGraw Hill, New York.

Greeno, J. [1989]. "A Perspective on Thinking". *American Psychologist,* 44 (2), 134-141.

Heiman, M. [1987]. "Learning to Learn: A Behaviourial Approach to Improving Thinking". In D. Perkins, J. Lochhead, J. Bishop, (Eds), *Thinking The Second International Conference.* Lawrence Erlbaum, Hillsdale, New Jersey.

Linn, M. [1986]. "Science". In R.F. Dillon and R. Sternberg, *Cognition and Instruction,* Academic Press, Orlando.

Lowery, L. [1985]. "The Biological Basis for Thinking". In A.L. Costa (Ed), *Developing Minds,* Association for Supervison and Curriculum Development, Alexandria, Virginia.

Okey, J. and Oliver, R. [1987]. "Learning from Computer Simulations". Paper presented at the Annual Meeting of the National Association for Research in Science Teaching, Washington DC.

Papert, S. [1980]. *Mindstorms.* Harvester Press, New York.

Patterson, J. and Smith, M. [1986]. "The Role of Computers in Higher Order Thinking". In J.A. Culbertson and L. L. Cunningham (Eds), *Microcomputers and Education,* 85th Yearbook of the National Society for the Study of Education, University of Chicago Press, Illinois.

Pea, R. and Kurland, M. [1987]. "On the Cognitive Effects of Learning Computer Programming". In R. Pea and K. Sheingold (Eds), *Mirrors of Mind: Patterns of Experience in Educational Computing,* Ablex, New Jersey.

Piaget, J. [1970]. *The science of education and the psychology of the child.* Orion Press, New York.

Presseisen, B. (1985). "Thinking skills: meanings and models". In A.L. Costa (Ed), *Developing Minds,* Association for Supervison and Curriculum Development, Alexandria, Virginia.

Resnick, L. [1987]. *Education and learning to think.* National Academy Press, Washington DC.

Segal, J.W., Chipman, S.J., & Glaser, R. (Eds) [1985]. *Thinking and learning skills, Relating instruction to research.* Lawrence Erlbaum, Hillsdale, New Jersey.

Stein, J.S. & Linn, M. [1985]. "Capitalizing on computer-based interactive feedback". In M. Chen & W. Paisley (Eds), *Children and microcomputers: research on the newest medium.* Sage Publications, Beverly Hills.

AUTHOR INDEX